Criminal Investigation

Seventh Edition

MICHAEL D. LYMAN
Columbia College of Missouri

PEARSON

Boston   Columbus   Indianapolis   New York   San Francisco   Upper Saddle River
Amsterdam   Cape Town   Dubai   London   Madrid   Milan   Munich   Paris   Montréal   Toronto
Delhi   Mexico City   São Paulo   Sydney   Hong Kong   Seoul   Singapore   Taipei   Tokyo

Editorial Director: Vernon Anthony
Acquisitions Editor: Sara Eilert
Development Editor:
  Elisa Rogers/4development
Editorial Assistant: Lynda Cramer
Director of Marketing: David Gesell
Senior Marketing Manager:
  Mary Salzman
Senior Marketing Assistant: Les Roberts
Senior Managing Editor: JoEllen Gohr
Production Project Manager:
  Jessica H. Sykes
Senior Operations Supervisor:
  Pat Tonneman

Senior Art Director: Diane Ernsberger
Cover Designer: Ali Morhman
Cover Art: Shutterstock
Editor, Digital Projects:
  Nichole Caldwell
Lead Media Project Manager: Karen Bretz
Full-Service Project Management: Abinaya
  Rajendran, Integra Software Services,
  Pvt. Ltd.
Composition: Integra Software Services
Printer/Binder: Courier/Kendallville
Cover Printer: Lehigh-Phoenix Color/
  Hagerstown
Text Font: Minion Pro Regular 9.5/11.5

Library of Congress Cataloging-in-Publication Data

Lyman, Michael D.
    Criminal investigation / Michael D. Lyman.—7th ed.
        p. cm.
    ISBN-13: 978-0-13-300851-7 (alk. paper)
    ISBN-10: 0-13-300851-7 (alk. paper)
    1. Criminal investigation.   2. Forensic sciences.   I. Title.
    HV8073.L94 2014
    363.25—dc23
                                                            2012030774

10 9 8 7 6 5 4 3 2 1

PEARSON

ISBN 10:   0-13-300851-7
ISBN 13: 978-0-13-300851-7

Dedication

This book is the direct result of over 35 years of my involvement with the field of criminal investigation, from my many years as a criminal investigator in the field, my time as a full-time, certified police academy instructor, to my 26 years as a college professor teaching both under graduate and graduate students. Also contributing to this work is my 27-year publishing record and my experience reviewing over 250 cases involving police incidents and investigations throughout the nation where I have provided written analysis and/or sworn testimony as a police procedures expert.

All of these learning experiences have led to the latest edition of this book. Of course, I must mention that without the love and support of my wife Julie and my daughter Kelsey I couldn't have endeavored to complete such a considerable project nor could I have done so without the continued support of the dedicated men and women working within our nation's law enforcement community. I sincerely hope you enjoy this new edition.

Brief Contents

Contents

Preface

Criminal investigation represents a timeless and dynamic field of scientific study. This book, now in its seventh edition, was written with the perception that crime detection is a field that relies heavily on the past experiences of investigators as well as recent practical, forensic, and technological innovations. The investigator's success in crime detection can be influenced by several external variables. For example, increased pressure by public interest groups and courts of law has caused police supervisors to place greater emphasis on case management and officer accountability. In addition, because of increased social problems associated with drug abuse, criminal violence, and the use of cellular and computer technology, the public spotlight has focused more than ever before on methods of crime detection and the successful prosecution of offenders. Finally, due to the ongoing incidence of mass and serial murders, the public is now more insistent that criminal investigations are conducted quickly and with thoroughness.

New to This Edition

The updates in this edition include the following:

New and Updated Information

- New and updated historical information in criminal investigation located in Chapter 1
- Updated graphics of police reports and new material regarding digital photos in Chapter 2
- Updated and enhanced sections and graphics addressing the duties of the first officer as well as a new discussions about aquatic body recovery and the importance of the crime scene "walk through" located in Chapter 3
- New and updated information on DNA evidence, police lineups and eyewitness identifications in Chapter 4
- New and updated information on searches with and without a search warrant, raid planning, expanded sections on investigative detentions and the use of force during arrests in Chapter 5
- Updated information and graphics on the interrogation process in Chapter 6
- New and updated material and graphics addressing surveillance operations as well as satellite-assisted surveillance, tracking technology and the use of GPS in Chapter 7
- Updated material on informant management in Chapter 8
- New and expansive material addressing the forensic autopsy; the forensics of decomposition; gunshot wounds as evidence including estimating the distance of the shooter from the victim, the role of gunshot residue, determining the type of firearm used in shootings, the role of the shotgun as a murder weapon and the investigation of drowning deaths in Chapter 9
- New sections addressing types of robberies and typologies of robbers, contrasting evidence in professional versus amateur robberies in Chapter 10
- New material addressing aggravated assault, domestic violence and investigating assaults in taverns and bars in Chapter 11
- Updated statistics and graphics as well as new material on the legislative history on dealing with missing persons, in Chapter 12
- New material addressing the changing views of child maltreatment; the importance of collaboration with medical and social service personnel in investigations as well as updated case studies found in Chapter 13
- New and improved case studies, graphics and photos and an expanded discussion of identify theft in Chapter 14
- Updated material addressing investigative resources in arson cases and an update in domestic and international terrorism and investigative tactics to destabilize terrorist organizations in Chapter 15
- New and updated information on drugs of abuse, Mexican trafficking organizations, international and domestic drug trafficking gangs in Chapter 16
- Updated statistical crime data and new material on electronic crimes, scams, money laundering, identity theft investigations and computer crimes in Chapter 17
- New material on recent advances in forensic science through out all chapters

- New and improved "Summary Checklist" material at the end of each chapter including thematic questions and chapter summary material designed to assist the student in identifying all key elements of the chapter
- Updated statistics and statistical graphics throughout each chapter
- New and updated case examples as chapter openers throughout the book

Satellite-Assisted Surveillance

In April 2011, an incident involving 21-year-old Richard Anderson and 32-year-old Holli Wrice took place on November 6, 2008, at the Capaha Bank of Tamms, Illinois. Anderson and Wrice entered the Capaha Bank of Tamms, Illinois, each armed with handguns, which they pointed at the tellers and customers. Wrice told the teller, "Give me the money [expletive]," while pointing the gun at the teller, and then handed her a note which stated, "This is a robbery, I have a gun, don't cause a scene, and no one will get hurt. I do have a Gun!!"

Bank video cameras recorded the robbery and showed that Wrice picked up the note shown to the teller and attempted to put it into the bag with the money taken from the bank, but the note fell out as the bag was pulled away from the teller window. Photos taken from the bank surveillance cameras were broadcast to the public on local television stations the same night as the bank robbery and ultimately led to witnesses coming forward to identify Anderson. Those identifications were corroborated when Anderson's fingerprints matched with those found on the demand note. Wrice's fingerprints were also found on the note. Through analysis of surveillance videos, detectives from the Jackson County Sheriff's office were able to positively identify the types of weapons and the make of the getaway vehicle used by the robbers. The Illinois State Police then located the vehicle and through subsequent investigation the FBI was able to track the path used by the robbers both to and from the robbery through cell phone GPS information.[8]

New and Updated Graphics

Figures have been updated throughout the text, and more illustrations have been added to support key information, especially regarding the surveillance of criminal suspects in Chapter 7.

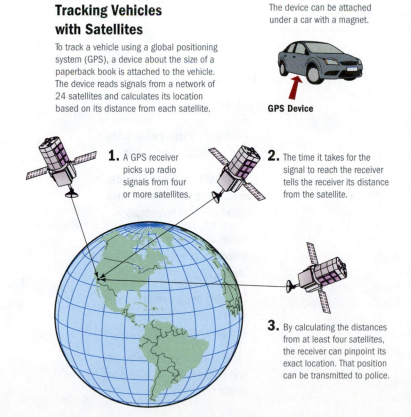

Tracking Vehicles with Satellites

To track a vehicle using a global positioning system (GPS), a device about the size of a paperback book is attached to the vehicle. The device reads signals from a network of 24 satellites and calculates its location based on its distance from each satellite.

The device can be attached under a car with a magnet.

GPS Device

1. A GPS receiver picks up radio signals from four or more satellites.

2. The time it takes for the signal to reach the receiver tells the receiver its distance from the satellite.

3. By calculating the distances from at least four satellites, the receiver can pinpoint its exact location. That position can be transmitted to police.

Updated Case Studies

New case study examples have been added, such as the Annie Le murder case, The 2012 Jerry Sandusky child sex abuse case, The 2011 Yeardley Love murder case, The home invasion and murder case involving the family of William Petit and The abduction case of Jaycee Dugard.

|Fig. 3.1| △

Annie Le was a Yale University doctoral student who was murdered on the Yale campus in 2011.

HANDOUT / MCT / Newscom

Learning Objectives

The learning objectives at the beginning of each chapter ("This chapter will enable you to:") have been rewritten in streamlined language to provide a concise overview of what readers can expect to learn from each chapter.

This chapter will enable you to:

1. Outline the history of policing and criminal investigation.

2. Describe how developments in research and science have aided criminal investigation.

3. Summarize the traits and thought processes of successful investigators.

4. Describe the different types of investigations, investigators, and modes of investigation.

5. Explain the organization, roles, and responsibilities of various police agencies.

This book is intended to meet the needs of students and others interested in criminal justice by presenting information in a logical flow, paralleling the steps and considerations observed in an actual criminal investigation. Additionally, it is designed to fulfill an ongoing need for a book that explains clearly and thoughtfully the fundamentals of criminal investigation as practiced by police investigators on the job in communities across the nation.

The book is written with several observations in mind. First, as its title indicates, it is designed to blend scientific theories of crime detection with a practical approach to criminal investigation. Its underlying assumption is that sound criminal investigations depend on an understanding of the science of crime detection procedures and the art of anticipating human behavior. There is yet another critical observation made in the book: It recognizes that both the uniformed officer and the criminal investigator play important roles in the field of criminal investigation. The duties of each are outlined throughout the book, recognizing that there is a fundamental need for both to work in tandem throughout many aspects of the criminal investigation process.

One underlying theme of the book is that as with all police endeavors, criminal investigation is a law enforcement responsibility that must be conducted within the framework of the U.S. Constitution and the practices of a democratic society. Consequently, court decisions and case studies have been quoted extensively for clarification of issues and general reader information.

Key features of this text include:

Instructor-Friendly Organization

For more efficient use, this book has been designed to follow closely to a standard curriculum format. The 18-chapter organization is designed to make it easier for instructors to align their coverage of the text's material with the class schedule and academic term.

Brief Contents

A Closer Look

In most chapters, this box addresses selected chapter topics in depth, such as technology, careers, tools and techniques, and issues in criminal investigation.

Tracing Firearms

In April 2012, the U.S. Bureau of Alcohol, Tobacco and Firearms (ATF) disclosed that over a five-year period of time, more than 68,000 guns recovered in Mexico were traced back to the United States. More than 30,000 other guns could not be traced. Tracing firearms is often part of the investigative process associated with a shooting.

Firearms tracing provides information on the movement of a firearm from its first sale by a manufacturer or importer through the distribution chain in an attempt to identify the first retail purchaser. This information provides investigative leads for criminal investigations. After the firearm is recovered and the identifiers are forwarded to the ATF's National Tracing Center (NTC), ATF contacts the manufacturer or importer to ascertain the sale or transfer of the firearm. ATF will attempt to contact all federal firearms licensees (wholesale/retail) in the distribution chain until a purchaser is identified or the trace process cannot continue due to a lack of accurate or incomplete information. The success of a trace result, whether domestic or international, relies upon the accuracy of the supplied firearm identifiers. The necessary identifiers for a trace include manufacturer, importer (if applicable), model, caliber, and serial number.

Source: The Alcohol, Tobacco and Firearms. (2012). *ATF Mexico, 2007–2011.* U.S. Department of Justice. Available at http://www.atf.gov/statistics/download/trace-data/international/2007-2011-Mexico-trace-data.pdf

Case in Point

Near the end of most chapters, this box presents case examples of the types of crime discussed in the chapters, and the procedures and techniques that were used to investigate each case. Most boxes conclude with one or more Thematic Questions that ask students to consider the ethical choices, legal implications, and other issues involved in the investigation.

Case in Point

>>Warren Jeffs and the FLDS

Some may describe Warren Jeffs as a tall, gangly, and clean-cut looking man. But according to his followers, Jeffs was distinguished as a "Prophet" of the polygamous sect known as the Fundamentalist Latter Day Saints (FLDS). This group separated itself from mainstream Mormonism in 1890 after polygamy was banned. Estimated at approximately 10,000 followers, the FLDS has communities in Hildale, Utah, and Colorado City, Arizona.

After Jeffs' 92-year-old father died, his legacy was passed on to him. And, in 2002, Jeffs became the leader of the FLDS. While maintaining this position, Jeffs was the only person empowered to perform marriages between minor females and adult males within the FLDS community. Jeffs also assumed the authority to strip male followers of their wives, children, and property without forethought or question.

Jeffs was wanted for two counts of sexual assault on a minor. These alleged offenses took place in March of 2002, and on or between July 1 and December 31, 2002. Jeffs was also being sought for conspiracy to commit sexual conduct with a minor. This incident allegedly happened sometime between January and June of 2002. All of the alleged offenses took place in the vicinity of Colorado City, Arizona.

On June 9, 2005, a Mohave County grand jury charged Jeffs with sexual conduct with a minor and conspiracy to commit sexual conduct with a minor. A state arrest warrant was issued in Arizona on June 10, 2005. Additionally, a federal arrest warrant was issued in Arizona on June 27, 2005. Jeffs was charged with unlawful flight to avoid prosecution. On May 6, 2006, the FBI placed Warren Jeffs, a former accountant and private schoolteacher, on the "Ten Most Wanted Fugitives" list.

Jeffs probably had better days, but August 28, 2006, was not likely one of them. While he was riding in a 2007 red Cadillac Escalade, a Nevada Department of Public Safety trooper pulled over the car for a traffic stop. This occurred after the trooper noticed that valid license plates were not displayed on the vehicle. After questioning one of the occupants in the vehicle, it became apparent to the trooper that this individual resembled Warren Jeffs, an FBI

|Fig. 13.11| △

Warren Jeffs was the president of the Fundamentalist Church of Jesus Christ of Latter Day Saints and before he was arrested for child molestation charges in 2006 he was expanding his compounds in Colorado, Utah, and Texas.

GEORGE FREY / Newscom

"Ten Most Wanted Fugitive." The trooper contacted the FBI and agents responded to the scene. Jeffs was identified by the FBI and taken into custody.

Thematic question

Considering the close-knit nature of FLDS and Jeffs' authority over his followers, what are some investigative challenges that one might encounter in investigating child sexual abuse within the FDLS?

Source: FBI. (2012). *Famous cases.* Available at http://www.fbi.gov/state-services/publications/ten-most-wanted-fugitives-60th-anniversary-1950-2010/famous_cases (retrieved on May 3, 2012).

Summary Checklist

At the end of each chapter, this checklist offers review questions followed by bulleted responses to test students' knowledge of the main chapter concepts and serve as a study tool for review. A list of key terms and Discussion Questions are also included at the end of each chapter.

Summary Checklist

1. **What important points should you remember when conducting a preliminary investigation?**

   Generally, a preliminary investigation is defined as an initial inquiry by officers to establish facts and circumstances of a suspected crime and to preserve any evidence related to that crime.

   The key elements of a preliminary investigation include:

   - Securing the crime scene
   - Considering the possible arrest of a suspect
   - Locating and questioning witnesses and victims
   - Documenting the crime scene
   - Identifying and collecting evidence

   When collecting evidence, it is important to remember the Locard exchange principle, which is also known as the "transfer of evidence theory." Essentially, it says that "Every contact leaves a trace." Locard's principle is applied to crime scenes where the perpetrator(s) of a crime comes into contact with the scene, so he or she both brings something into the scene and leaves with something from the scene. Every contact leaves a trace.

2. **What are the main types of evidence?**

   There are two commonly used classifications:

   - Corpus delicti refers to evidence that establishes that a crime has been committed.
   - Associative evidence links a suspect with a crime.

   Examples of evidence are:

   - Physical evidence
   - Direct or prima facie evidence
   - Indirect or circumstantial evidence
   - Testimonial evidence
   - Trace evidence
   - Demonstrative evidence

In summary, I am hopeful that this will prove to be an engaging textbook that is descriptive of the duties of modern-day crime detection and police professionalism. Accordingly, each chapter contains key terms and discussion questions that also aid in the instructional process. Finally, as a learning aid, this text is accompanied by a companion website that offers videos and test items as well as many other learning tools. I know this book will provide you with what you need to understand the art of criminal investigation as well as the many new forms of scientific innovations that modern investigators now use to catch perpetrators of some of the nation's most heinous crimes. Read and enjoy!

Instructor Supplements

The following supplementary materials are available to support instructors' use of the main text:

- **eBooks.** *Criminal Investigation* is available in two eBook formats, *CourseSmart* and Adobe Reader. *CourseSmart* is an exciting new choice for students looking to save money. As an alternative to purchasing the printed textbook, students can purchase an electronic version of the same content. With a *CourseSmart* eTextbook, students can search the text, make notes online, print out reading assignments that incorporate lecture notes, and bookmark important passages for later review. For more information, or to purchase access to the *CourseSmart* eTextbook, visit **www.coursesmart.com**.

TestGen. The computerized TestGen package allows instructors to customize, save, and generate classroom tests. The test program permits instructors to edit, add, or delete questions from the Test Item Files; analyze test results; and organize a database of tests and student results. This software allows for extensive flexibility and ease of use. It provides many options for organizing and displaying tests, along with search and sort features. The software and the Test Item Files can be downloaded from the Instructor's Resource Center (www.pearsonhighered.com).

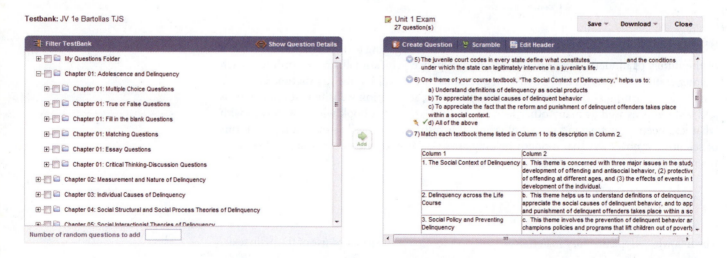

- **Interactive Lecture PowerPoint® Presentation.** This supplement will enhance lectures like never before. Award-winning presentation designers worked with our authors to develop *PowerPoints* that truly engage the student. Much like the text, the *PowerPoints* are full of instructionally sound graphics, tables, charts, and photos that do what presentation software was meant to do: support and enhance your lecture. Data and difficult concepts are presented in a truly interactive way, helping students connect the dots and stay focused on the lecture. The *Interactive Lecture PowerPoints* also include in-depth lecture notes and teaching tips so you have all your lecture material in one place.

• *The Pearson Criminal Justice Online Community.* Available at **www.mycriminaljustice-community.com**, this site is a place for educators to connect, and to exchange ideas and advice on courses, content, *CJ Interactive*, and so much more.

To access these supplementary materials online, instructors need to request an instructor access code at **www.pearsonhighered.com/irc**. Within 48 hours after registering, you will receive a confirmation e-mail that includes an instructor access code. When you receive your code, go to the site and log on for full instructions on downloading materials you wish to use.

Acknowledgments

No book can be written entirely as a solo effort, and this project was no exception. The preparation of this book represents hundreds of painstaking hours maintaining continuous contact with criminal justice agencies, federal information clearinghouses, police practitioners, and colleagues in the field of criminal justice. In addition, to offer the reader the most up-to-date and relevant information, it was important to consult libraries, police journals, periodicals, newspapers, government publications, and other sources of literature germane to the field of crime detection on an ongoing basis.

Many persons were helpful in the preparation of this book, including practitioners in the field as well as experts in academe. Among these, the contributions of certain persons deserve special recognition. Included are the men and women of the Columbia Police Department, the Missouri State Highway Patrol, agents from the Federal Bureau of Investigation and Drug Enforcement Administration, contributors from the Department of Homeland Security, and the International Association of Chiefs of Police.

A special debt of gratitude goes to Detective Michael Himmel of the Columbia Police Department (ret.) and Brian Hoey of the Missouri State Highway Patrol Crime Laboratory, who both provided a number of crime scene and laboratory photos for this new edition. Without the cooperation and guidance of these persons and organizations, this book would not have been possible.

A special thank you is also well deserved for Development Editor Elisa Rogers and Senior Acquisitions Editor Sara Eilert, along with the many other dedicated publishing professionals at Pearson for their hard work and support for the seventh edition of this text. Finally, I would like to extend special thanks to those criminal justice academics and practitioners who painstakingly reviewed the manuscript of this book. These persons include James T. Burnett, Rockland County Community College, Suffern, NY; David Graff, Kent State University—Tuscarawas Campus, New Philadelphia, OH; Harold Frossard, Moraine Valley Community College, Palos Hills, IL; Mark McCoy, University of Central Oklahoma, Edmond, OK; Elvage Murphy, Edinboro University, Erie, PA; and Gary Yoshonis, Grossmont Community College, San Diego, CA.

Thanks also to the following reviewers: Nancy Blanchard, Bristol Community College; John W. Bollinger, MacMurray College; Theodore Darden, College of DuPage; Douglas Evans, Sullivan Community College; Richard M. Hough, Sr., University of West Florida; Freddie W. Komar, Blinn Collge; Thomas R. O'Connor, Austin Peay State University; Carol Schmidt, St. Petersburg College; Michael Sellers, Athens Technical College; and Harry D. Ulferts, Sauk Valley Community College.

Without the support and assistance of all these people and many more, this book would not have become a reality. Thank you all.

Michael D. Lyman

About the author

Michael D. Lyman is Professor of Criminal Justice at Columbia College of Missouri, located in Columbia, MO. In addition to being a teaching faculty member, he serves as the program Coordinator for the Master of Science of Criminal Justice Program and the founder of the college's Bachelor of Science in Forensic Science Program. Before entering the field of college teaching, he was employed as a criminal investigator for state police organizations in Kansas and Oklahoma and has taught literally thousands of law enforcement officers in the proper police techniques and methods of professional criminal investigation. Dr. Lyman has authored numerous textbooks in criminal justice dealing with the areas of criminal investigation, policing, organized crime, drug enforcement, and drug trafficking. He received both his bachelor's and master's degrees from Wichita State University and his Ph.D. from the University of Missouri–Columbia. He has been called upon on an estimated 300 occasions by law enforcement and the legal communities to review criminal investigations and render the results of his evaluations and his opinions in federal court proceedings nationwide.

Textbooks such as this are an ongoing work in progress, and the author welcomes communication and correspondence about his work. Dr. Lyman can be contacted at Columbia College, 1001 Rogers Street, Columbia, MO 65216 or at mlyman@cougarsccis.edu. Thank you for using this textbook.

CHAPTER 1

© ZUMA Press, Inc./Alamy

This chapter will enable you to:

1. Outline the history of policing and criminal investigation.

2. Describe how developments in research and science have aided criminal investigation.

3. Summarize the traits and thought processes of successful investigators.

4. Describe the different types of investigations, investigators, and modes of investigation.

5. Explain the organization, roles, and responsibilities of various police agencies.

Foundations and History of Criminal Investigation

Introduction

 On May 3, 2011, around 2:15 A.M., police were called to the apartment of 24-year-old Yeardley Love in Charlottesville. At the scene, Love was found unresponsive and was pronounced dead. The 911 call from Love's roommate reported that Love suffered an alcohol overdose, but detectives noticed what they termed "obvious physical injuries to her body" upon arrival. The person who soon developed as a suspect was 24-year-old George Huguely, whom Love had dated briefly but had broken up with. Huguely was Love's next-door neighbor. At the Charlottesville Police Department, Huguely waived his Miranda rights and provided investigators a statement containing vivid details of his assaulting Love. Huguely told police that he kicked open Love's locked bedroom door and shook her, and while doing so, her head repeatedly hit the wall.

Police seized evidence from Huguely's apartment that included two laptop computers, a spiral notebook, two white socks, bathroom and entryway rugs, and a Virginia lacrosse shirt with a red stain. Investigators also followed leads of domestic violence between Huguely and Love, including threatening e-mails and text messages that Huguely sent to her before their breakup. A violent incident between the couple was broken up by several lacrosse players visiting from the University of North Carolina at Chapel Hill as well as an incident in which Huguely attacked Love while he was drunk but did not recall striking her.

On May 4, Huguely was charged with murdering Love. In a court appearance on May 6, 2011, Huguely's attorney, Fran Lawrence, stated: "Ms. Love's death was not intended but an accident with a tragic outcome." On February 22, 2012, Huguely was found guilty of second-degree murder and grand larceny.

The murder of Yeardley Love created considerable interest and outrage in the public media. Her murder resulted in conversations about how such a crime could have occurred and what police could have possibly done to prevent it.

Every reader of this text knows that we live in a complicated and often dangerous world. Problems involving crime that is profit motivated, politically motivated, and motivated by other more obscure reasons such as revenge, anger, and personal gratification permeate society at every level. Indeed, the spies, computer hackers, pedophiles, gang leaders, and serial killers located within our communities are all paramount concerns for a free and democratic society.

Accordingly, the study of criminal investigation involves probing several different fields at once, and is therefore a difficult task about which to write. For example, it is important for an investigator to understand basic techniques of collection and preservation of evidence, but to do so, a fundamental understanding of criminalistics or forensic science is often required. In addition to technical competence, modern-day investigators must be well versed in the law. Legal skills include a working knowledge of criminal law, constitutional law, and rules of evidence, all of which are essential for successful prosecution of a criminal case. This chapter is designed to give the reader the underlying essentials of this field of policing, which is both rewarding and challenging.

|Fig. 1.1| ▲

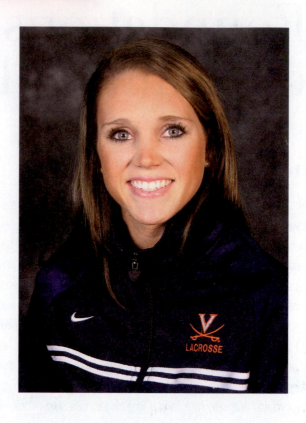

The murder of Yeardley Love occurred in May 2010 in Charlottesville, Virginia. Love, a University of Virginia (UVA) women's lacrosse student-athlete, was found unresponsive in her Charlottesville apartment on May 3, 2010. Later that day, UVA men's lacrosse player George Wesley Huguely V was arrested by Charlottesville Police.

ZUMA Press / Newscom

The Romance and Reality of Crime Solving

Throughout modern history, people have harbored a fascination with cops and criminals—**crime** and crime fighting. Whenever there is a public crime scene, large groups of people gather to watch crime scene investigators in action. For the average citizen, police cars and emergency units with their screaming sirens and flashing lights spark an insatiable curiosity. Fueling people's interest and imagination are newspapers and periodicals that sensationalize criminal investigations, which often involve both heinous and interesting aspects.

Modern-day popular novelists continue the tradition of novels with an investigative twist. These include such novelists as John Grisham, James Patterson, and Patricia Cornwell, to name a few, who provide readers with mysteries, clues, and challenges to figure out the identity of the "bad guy."

Stories such as these become "up close and personal" with television dramas focusing on criminal investigation and the solving of crime through forensic techniques. For example, the time-tested *CSI* (crime scene investigation) series—*CSI: Crime Scene Investigation*, *CSI: Miami*, and *CSI: New York*—is so successful that it is thought to have created the so-called *CSI* effect, whereby jurors have been introduced to forensics through their exposure to television crime shows and expect forensic evidence in jury trials—trials in which no such evidence may even exist (discussed later in this chapter). Other popular television shows showcasing forensics include *Hawaii Five-0*, which follows an elite state police unit set up to fight crime in the state of Hawaii; *Bones*, which focuses on forensic anthropology and forensic archaeology; and *NCIS: Naval Criminal Investigative Service*, which is an American police procedural drama revolving around a team of special agents from the Naval Criminal Investigative Service, which conducts criminal investigations involving the U.S. Navy and Marine Corps. Each of these shows, along with many others, fuels the fires of public interest in solving crimes through forensics, sophisticated technology, and the investigative process.

Adults aren't the only ones who show an interest in crime detection. For example, for the last 85 years the popular book series *Nancy Drew* has featured a fictional young girl who dabbles as an amateur detective in various mysteries. This series was brought to the silver screen in the 2007 movie by the same name featuring Emma Roberts. A companion series for boys is the historically popular *Hardy Boys* featuring Frank and Joe Hardy, fictional teenage brothers and amateur detectives who appear in various mystery series. Children too visualize the clashing forces of good and evil in vividly illustrated children's books, comic books, and early morning television cartoons. Examples are Hollywood movies *Batman: The Dark Knight Rises* (2012) and *The Avengers* (2012), which portray the clash between good and evil. Even television shows watched by young children portray fictional crime fighters such as Kim Possible, Ben 10, and the Power Puff Girls, who, with each episode, confront evil foes. Indeed, American pop culture typically portrays the conflict between the forces of good and evil in movies, novels, and television cartoons.

Notorious outlaw gangs of the Old West have also interested people for decades. Gangs active on the western frontier, such as the Younger brothers and the Dalton gang, represent the colorful heritage of the antihero. Another outlaw, Jesse James, was one of the most famous of the American West. During his time, he acquired a Robin Hood reputation. With brother Frank and several other men, the James gang gained national notoriety by robbing banks, trains, and stagecoaches.

Detective magazines, books, and movies pitting the shrewd criminal against his or her persevering police counterpart have also perpetuated the detective mystique. For generations, fabled yarns featuring sleuths such as Sherlock Holmes and Hercule Poirot have presented readers with a menagerie of far-fetched tales filled with unlikely clues and colorful suspects. In fact, part of the allure of the classic detective novels of the early twentieth century was the introduction of the **private eye.** Mickey Spillane's Mike Hammer, for example, had a remorseless desire to punish wrongdoers who managed to escape an impotent criminal justice system while walking a fine legal line himself.

As with the private eye, the spy of the 1960s enlivened espionage stories featuring such heroes as James Bond, whose popularity rivaled even that of Sherlock Holmes. In reading the material, however, readers would gain little practical insight into the mind of the criminal, the nature of crime, the science of detection, the techniques of law enforcement officers, or courtroom procedures where one is found either guilty or innocent. Although entertaining, such stories bear little resemblance to the real world of criminal investigation.

The Historical Context of Criminal Investigation

The history of criminal investigation is vast, and over the years many writers have attempted to engage the topic. In this section, we focus on the roots of our criminal justice heritage in Great Britain as it pertains to the field of criminal investigation.

Criminal Investigation and Our English Heritage

We begin our story during the era of Europe's Industrial Revolution, which attracted the peasant class from the countryside into the towns and cities. The ensuing crime wave forced law enforcement officials to take drastic measures. As a result, **thief catchers** were recruited from the riffraff of the streets to aid law-enforcement officials in locating criminals. Two classes of thief catchers were identified: (1) hirelings, whose motivations were mercenary in nature; and (2) social climbers, who would implicate their accomplices in order to move up the social ladder.

One hireling, Jonathan Wild, gained fame in eighteenth-century England for operating a London brothel that also served as headquarters for thieves and thugs, with whom he was well acquainted. Coining the phrase

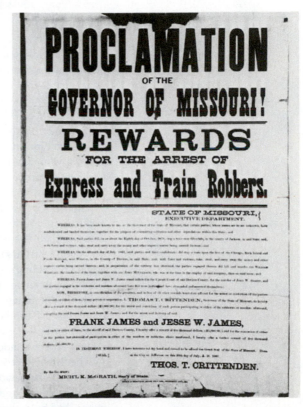

|Fig. 1.2| ▲

During the settlement of the western frontier, "wanted" posters were used to identify persons wanted by law enforcement.

State Historical Society of Missouri

|Fig. 1.3| ▲

Jesse James, the elusive outlaw of the Wild West, helped to establish the mystique of the antihero.

State Historical Society of Missouri

"set a thief to catch a thief," Wild operated simultaneously as an undercover operative for London's authorities and as a criminal in London's underworld. It soon became clear, however, that he could profit more from arranging the return of stolen goods to the police than from selling the goods at outrageous discounts to the local fence. So while he acted as the receiver of stolen goods masquerading as the "recoverer" of lost property, he also served as the middleman, taking his cut for finding stolen goods while hiding and protecting thieves in his employ.

In England, the first police worked only at night and were originally called the Watch of London. They soon developed into the Old Charleys, who were paid by the residents they served. These parish **constables** originated in London in 1253 and lasted until 1829. Soon after the hanging of Jonathan Wild, Henry Fielding was appointed magistrate in Westminster, a city adjacent to central London. Fielding, a writer known for his novel *Tom Jones*, located himself in a house on Bow Street that served as both home and office and soon began what is credited as England's first police force.

THE BOW STREET RUNNERS During the 1750s, crimes such as burglary and street robbery were rampant in England. Fielding took on the challenge of reducing the profits realized by criminals. Working relationships were established with local business owners, in particular pawnbrokers, who were provided with lists of stolen property. Fielding encouraged them to contact him if any stolen property came to their attention. Fielding took seriously his new duty as crime fighter and promptly employed new crime-fighting methods. One such method was the appointment of a handful of parish constables acclimated to night watchman duties. These trackers soon began performing criminal investigation functions and became well known as successful thief takers by using their ties with London's criminal underworld. Originally called "Mr. Fielding's People," they soon became known as the **Bow Street Runners**, the first well-known investigative body in England. Fielding's runners were not paid as police officers but rather, in terms of thief-taker rewards, a percentage of all fines resulting from successful prosecution of thieves. Shortly after his appointment as magistrate, Fielding's health deteriorated, and he started to use a wheelchair. As a result, his half-brother, John Fielding, was appointed to share his magistracy. Because of his blindness, John Fielding was soon dubbed the "blind beak" (*beak* meaning magistrate) to the criminal underworld in London.

The Bow Street Runners were forerunners of a trend in policing for specialization within the police force. In fact, by 1800, the Bow Street Police Office was considered by many to be the leading law enforcement organization in the area. Johnson adds: "Even if the evils of the justice/constable system had been eliminated from Bow Street Office operations, no local jurisdiction could combat the rising crime wave throughout London."[1] Between 1760 and 1800, Fielding was given authority to organize a horse patrol, which was later followed by a permanent foot patrol. The patrol officers, smartly outfitted in red vests and blue jackets and trousers, became the pioneers of England's uniformed police.

THE LONDON METROPOLITAN POLICE The watershed in British police development occurred in 1829 with the establishment of the London Metropolitan Police Department. Officers of the department were dubbed **bobbies** after the department's founder, Home Secretary **Sir Robert Peel**. The "new" police were England's first paid, full-time police force, consisting of about 1,000 uniformed officers. In addition, they replaced the old constables, such as the Bow Street

Runners, who had ultimately gained a reputation of incompetency and inefficiency. Indeed, the bobbies were required to meet rigid standards of professionalism. Minimum standards included minimum weight and height requirements and standards of literacy and character. A detective bureau was created in the police force in 1842 but was not publicly acknowledged until some 35 years, later for fear that the specter of French-style repression would be remembered.

Technology in crime detection began to flourish during the nineteenth century with the creation of a personal identification system by Alphonse Bertillon, the director of the criminal identification section of the Paris Police Department. The **Bertillon system** was based on the idea that certain aspects of the human body, such as skeletal size, ear shaping, and eye color, remained the same after a person had reached full physical maturity. It used a combination of photographs with standardized physical measurements. In the mid-1840s, the study of fingerprint patterns became a popular means to identify suspects in crime. Although the use of fingerprints is a commonplace today, it wasn't until the late nineteenth century that it was learned that a person's fingerprints could act as a unique, unchangeable method of personal identification. Such discoveries have been credited to the Englishmen **William J. Herschel** and Henry Faulds, who were working in Asia at the time. The use of fingerprints was refined by Sir Francis Galton and was adopted by Scotland Yard in 1901.

THE CREATION OF SCOTLAND YARD The name "Scotland Yard" invokes the image of a foggy London street being guarded by a detective in a trench coat puffing smoke from his pipe. But Scotland Yard has an easily confused history, full of misunderstandings and controversy. Neither in Scotland, nor in a yard, it is the name of the headquarters of London's Metropolitan Police and, by association, has become synonymous with the force. The Yard doesn't serve the city either, but instead the Greater London area.

Making the Force The London police force was created in 1829 by an act introduced in parliament by Home Secretary (similar to the U.S. Secretary of the Interior) Sir Robert Peel—hence the nickname "bobbies," for policeman. The new police superseded the old system of watchmen. By 1839 these men had replaced the Bow Street Patrols, who enforced the decisions of magistrates, and the River Police, who worked to prevent crime along the Thames.

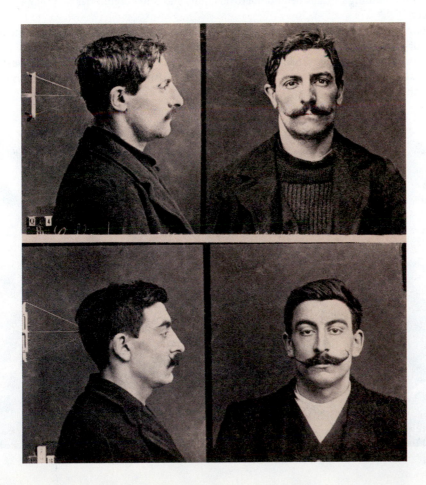

|Fig. 1.4| △

Bertillon System photographs taken of similar-looking men who established their different identities by differences in their ears, noses, and Adam's apples.

Everett Collection / SuperStock

In 1829, the responsibility of organizing the new Metropolitan Police Department was placed on Colonel Charles Rowan and Richard Mayne, who occupied a private house at 4 Whitehall Place, the back of which opened onto a courtyard: the Great Scotland Yard. The Yard's name was inspired by its site, a medieval palace which housed Scottish royalty on their visits to London.

The staff of Scotland Yard was responsible for the protection of important persons, community patrols, public affairs, and recruitment and management of personnel. When the Yard sent out its first plainclothes police agents in 1842, the public felt uncomfortable with these "spies" on the streets. But the force's role in several important cases, and the charisma of many of its detectives, helped it win over the trust of the people.

One such personality, Inspector Charles Frederick Field, joined the force upon its establishment in 1829. He became good friends with Charles Dickens, who occasionally accompanied constables on their nightly rounds. Dickens wrote a short essay about Field, "On Duty With Inspector Field," and used him as a model for the all-knowing, charming Inspector Bucket in his novel *Bleak House.* Field retired as a chief of the detective branch in 1852.

In 1877, four out of the five heads for the detective branch were brought to trial for conspiring with criminals in a betting scheme. In an effort to repair the force's tarnished reputation, Howard Vincent submitted a restructuring proposal to the force. Soon Vincent was appointed director of criminal investigations and he reorganized Scotland Yard, strengthening its central unit. And with that, the Criminal Investigation Department (CID), a respected unit of plainclothes police detectives, was born.

The turn of the century saw many monumental events at Scotland Yard. Britain's "Bloody Sunday" occurred on November 13, 1887, when 2,000 police officers disrupted a meeting in Trafalgar Square organized by the Social Democratic Federation, resulting in more than 100 casualties. A few years later, the force moved to its new building on the Victoria Embankment. The premises became known as New Scotland Yard.

Since its inception, Scotland Yard has always held a place in popular culture. The officers have appeared frequently as characters in the backdrop of mysteries, including Sir Arthur Conan Doyle's Sherlock Holmes stories. On television and in magazines today, Scotland Yard "bobbies" can be found standing stoically behind the royal family and other dignitaries that they are assigned to protect.

In 1967, the force moved once again to its present location, a modern 20-story building near the Houses of Parliament. The CID has become well-known for its investigative methods, primarily its fingerprinting techniques, which have been borrowed by the **Federal Bureau of Investigation (FBI)**. Today, Scotland Yard has roughly 30,000 officers patrolling 620 square miles occupied by 7.2 million citizens.

|Fig. 1.5|

Scotland Yard was one of the first professional police investigative units.

© imagebroker.net / SuperStock

Criminal Investigation in America

As the American frontier moved westward during the nineteenth century, outlaws posed serious problems in newly settled areas. Mining camps and cattle towns seemed to experience more violence than other areas. The movement west had moved men and women far from the institutions that had served them previously. Law enforcement agencies and criminal courts, if present at all, made only minor strides in protecting the vast areas under their jurisdictions. Indeed, it was in these areas that criminals could easily hide and witnesses would often move away, making detection and apprehension of criminals a discouraging task.

Following the lead of London's police force, the first professional police forces were established in the United States at Boston in 1837, New York in 1844, and Philadelphia in 1854. By the 1870s, almost all major U.S. cities had municipal police departments. As in England, criminal investigation by public law enforcement was viewed as politically hazardous because it favored only those who could pay. But the rapid growth of cities produced violence, crime, and **vice** activities that demonstrated a breakdown of social order in small communities. Growing incidents of mob violence between Protestants and Catholics, immigrants and Native Americans, and abolitionists and pro-slavery groups were probably the most crucial catalysts for expanded police functions. During the middle of the nineteenth century, three significant elements emerged that had an impact on criminal investigation:

1. Municipal police were supplemented by the county sheriff in rural areas.
2. Establishment of the **Texas Rangers** (established before Texas became a state).
3. Expansion of police functions with establishment of the U.S. Marshal's Service and the Secret Service, formed during the Civil War to investigate counterfeiters.

In the 1890s, criminal investigators became an important part of the U.S. Post Office and the Bureau of Immigration and Naturalization. Because of the lack of effective law enforcement in rural areas, however, people banded together on their own to investigate crimes and apprehend perpetrators. Vigilantes in the mining camps would conduct trials and even execute some of the most dangerous offenders. Cattle ranchers would often hire range detectives to capture rustlers. As a result, some business firms emerged, such as the famed Pinkerton's Detective Agency, which offered to protect property and pursue offenders for a fee.

THE PINKERTON NATIONAL DETECTIVE AGENCY

Pinkerton's National Detective Agency, founded in 1850 by Scottish immigrant **Allan Pinkerton,** was the first organization of its type in the United States. In fact, its organizational structure was later adopted by the Federal Bureau of Investigation. The Pinkerton Agency was called on by communities to handle cases that local law enforcement officers were unable to investigate due to incompetency or limited resources. Pinkerton offered the field of criminal investigation several innovations in crime detection. For example, he was the first to devise a **rogues' gallery**, which was a compilation of descriptions, methods of operation, hiding places, and names of associates of known criminals.

Pinkerton gained national fame when he uncovered a plot to kill Abraham Lincoln during the 1860s. The plot was designed to kill Lincoln on a train while en route to give his first inaugural speech in Washington. Pinkerton outwitted the assassins by putting Lincoln on an earlier train. Soon after, Pinkerton was placed in charge of the secret service operations during the Civil War. After Pinkerton's death in 1884, agency detectives gained a reputation for the use of

|Fig. 1.6| △

Allan Pinkerton, President Abraham Lincoln, and Major General John A. McClellan at Antietam, Maryland, October 1862 from glass negative, by Alexander Gardner.

|Fig. 1.7| ▲

"We Never Sleep." The famous Pinkerton "private eye" became the logo of Allan Pinkerton's National Detective Agency.

Printed with permission of Pinkerton's, Inc.

|Fig. 1.8| ▲

J. Edgar Hoover (1895–1972), the first director of the FBI.

© Archive Pics / Alamy

violence to undermine unions as well as to frame and convict their leaders. Among the more notable Pinkerton cases were those in which dozens of union spies were used by the infamous Jay Gould to break a strike against the Texas and Pacific Railroads and when Pinkerton detectives were used in 1905 to involve labor leaders in the murder of ex-Governor Frank Steunenberg of Idaho. After Congress declared labor spying unconstitutional in 1937, the industrial division of the Pinkerton agency was officially dissolved.

PROHIBITION **Prohibition** (1920–1933) represented another significant period in which criminal investigation underwent change. Unlike the drug trade of later years, the Volstead Act of the Prohibition period failed to criminalize the purchase or consumption of alcohol—only its manufacture, transportation, and sale. Because liquor was legal in other countries, smuggling (**bootlegging**) was a major criminal enterprise. Prohibition criminals avoided the federal law against alcohol by creating a cottage industry manufacturing beer and wine at home. By 1924, rival gangs organized themselves for control of "speakeasy" operations, prostitution rings, and virtually any other source of illegal income. Police corruption flourished as many law enforcement officers accepted bribes from mobsters. During this time, the FBI had no jurisdiction in enforcing the Volstead Act. Instead, enforcement responsibility was given to the Treasury Department.

THE CREATION OF THE FBI Probably the single most significant development in criminal investigation in the United States was the establishment of the FBI in 1924. Originating as the Justice Department's Bureau of Investigation in 1907, the FBI originally had very few responsibilities. When new federal laws governing interstate transportation of stolen automobiles were passed, however, the bureau gained much notoriety. **John Edgar Hoover,** the bureau's newly named director, announced in 1924 that he would strive to eliminate corruption and get the agency out of politics. In doing so, he raised the qualifications of agent personnel, reduced the number of agents nationwide, and closed some field offices. It was only after Hoover's death in 1972 that many of his abuses of power surfaced. For example, it became widely known that the FBI kept files on certain persons, such as politicians and adversaries of the FBI. Today, the FBI is one of many federal investigative agencies that have made great strides in professionalizing the field of criminal investigation.

The Increase of Research and Science in Crime Detection

The seeds of modern forensic science were sown in the last quarter of the nineteenth century. Progress from that time has been slow but steady. The American Academy of Forensic Sciences (AAFS), a professional organization of forensic scientists in America, was established in 1948. Specific areas of expertise of AAFS members include pathology and biology, toxicology, criminalistics, questioned documents, and forensic odontology and anthropology.

In addition to the development of fingerprinting as an aid to criminal detection, several other forensic advances were either being developed or had already been placed into service by the late nineteenth century. Historic strides in criminal investigation included study in serology, **forensic dentistry,** and ballistics. For example, research into human blood was vastly expanded during the early twentieth century by Paul Uhlenhuth, a German physician. Uhlenhuth's work created serums that enabled one to distinguish one species of animal blood from another. Consequently, **serology** was a procedure that was established to study human blood stains and distinguish them from the blood of most other animals.

A Closer Look

Modern Fields of Forensic Science

Today, a number of fields have surfaced relating to forensics and crime detection. Whether it's peering into the nucleus of a cell to determine guilt or innocence, analyzing the spatter of blood at a crime scene, or linking exploded bomb fragments to terrorists, forensic science techniques are responsible for solving countless crimes throughout society. Some of these techniques are widely accepted, and others have drawn criticism. Modern fields of forensics include:

- *Cryptanalysis*—decrypts manual codes and ciphers found in letters, diaries, ledgers, and other types of written communications, records, and e-mails. Common users of codes and ciphers include national and international terrorists, foreign intelligence agents, members, prison inmates, and violent criminals.

- *Racketeering examinations*—examine and decode records from illicit businesses, such as **loan sharking,** prostitution, sports **bookmaking,** and Internet gambling. Such violations are predicate offenses for RICO charges. Examinations may reveal the type of operation, dates of activity, wagering or loan amounts, types of wagers or loans, number and roles of participants, and accounting methods.

- *Drug records examinations*—examine and decode records pertaining to the type of operation, type of drug, quantity of drugs sold or purchased, unit prices, method of payment, transaction dates, roles of participants, gross and net profits, and operating expenses.

- *Latent print analysis*—scientific examinations in the area of friction ridge analysis, including the development and comparison of latent fingerprints, palm prints, and footprints.

- *Document Examinations*—examine and compare data appearing on paper, including handwriting, hand printing, typewriting, printing, erasures, alterations, indented writing, and obliterations.

- *Trace evidence analysis*—identifies and compares specific types of trace materials that could be transferred during the commission of a violent crime. These trace materials include human hair, animal hair, textile fibers and fabric, rope, feathers, wood, soil, glass, and building materials. The physical contact between a suspect and a victim can result in the transfer of trace materials.

- *Firearms-toolmarks analysis*—the forensic examination of firearms, ammunition components, toolmarks, gunshot residue on victim's clothing, bullet trajectories, and closely related physical evidence. Includes evidence related to firearms, firearm components, ammunition, ammunition components, tools, and toolmarks.

- *Forensic facial imaging*—analysis includes age-progressed imagery, postmortem imagery, and facial reconstruction from skeletal remains.

- *Digital Forensics*—concerns the development of algorithms and software to assist forensic examination. Crimes include computer intrusions, online predators, online piracy, intellectual property rights violations, and identify theft.

- *Forensic anthropology*—the application of physical anthropology in a legal setting, usually for the recovery and identification of skeletonized human remains.

(continued)

A Closer Look... (continued)

- *Forensic archaeology*—the application of a combination of archaeological techniques and forensic science, typically in law enforcement.

- *Forensic DNA analysis*—takes advantage of the uniqueness of an individual's DNA to answer forensic questions such as determining paternity or maternity or placing a suspect at a crime scene.

- *Forensic entomology*—deals with the examination of insects in, on, and around human remains to assist in determination of the time or location of death. It is also possible to determine if the body was moved after death.

- *Forensic interviewing*—a method of communicating designed to elicit information and evidence.

- *Forensic odontology*—the study of the uniqueness of dentition better known as the study of teeth.

- *Forensic pathology*—a field in which the principles of medicine and pathology are applied to determine a cause of death or injury in the context of a legal inquiry.

- *Forensic psychology*—the study of the mind of an individual using forensic methods. Usually, it determines the circumstances behind a criminal's behavior.

- *Forensic toxicology*—the study of the effect of drugs and poisons on or in the human body.

Thematic Question

If you are interested in any of the above-listed career fields, is your interest more in field investigative processes as a criminal investigator or those that take place in a laboratory as a criminalist? To what extent have you given thought to the fields of biology and chemistry to further a career in forensic science?

In what other ways do you foresee the fields of science and crime detection becoming more infused as time goes by?

Sources: FBI website, available at http://www.fbi.gov/about-us/lab (located January 21, 2012); Kind S. and M. Overman. (1972). *Science against crime.* New York: Doubleday, pp. 12–13; McRoberts, F. From the start, a faulty science. *Chicago Tribune*, October 19, 2004. Available at http://www.baltimoresun.com/news/specials/chi-041019forensics,0,4915311.story; Raloff, J. (2008). Judging science. *Science News*, 173(3):42. Available at http://www.sciencenews.org/articles/20080119/bob10.asp.

Today, increases in the demand for scientific techniques by investigators have created special financial burdens on law enforcement agencies. Techniques such as these call for people with a high degree of formal education in areas such as chemistry, forensic science, and physiology.

The "*CSI* Effect"

Sir Robert Peel is credited with creating the first modern police force, the bobbies, in London, in 1829, but the transformation of law enforcement, and especially forensic science, into a professional discipline was, to a great extent, a process of trial and error. Scientists only occasionally took an interest in police work, and courts may or may not have accepted their testimony and conclusions.

As of the writing of this book, things have changed in the forensic sciences. Today, people are fascinated by the idea that science can solve crimes. Moreover, because of television crime dramas, jurors today expect more categorical **proof** than forensic science is capable of delivering. As a result, a new phrase has entered the criminological lexicon: the "*CSI* **effect**," after shows such as *CSI: Crime Scene Investigation*. In 2008 Monica Robbers, an American criminologist, defined it as "the phenomenon in which jurors hold unrealistic expectations of forensic evidence and investigation techniques, and have an increased interest in the discipline of forensic science."[2]

In an article published in *Forensic Science International*, Evan Durnal concluded that the *CSI* effect is indeed real.[3] In his study, Durnal collected evidence from a number of studies to show that exposure to television drama series that focus on forensic science has altered the American legal system in complex and far-reaching ways. The most obvious symptom of the *CSI* effect is that jurors think they have a thorough understanding of science they have seen presented on television, when they do not.

Durnal cites one case of jurors in a murder trial who, having noticed that a bloody coat introduced as evidence had not been tested for DNA, brought this fact to the judge's attention. Since the defendant had admitted being present at the murder scene, such tests would have thrown no light on the identity of the true culprit. The judge observed that, thanks to television, jurors knew what DNA tests could do, but not when it was appropriate to use them.[4]

CSI: Crime Scene Investigation, the CBS television series, and its two spin-offs—*CSI: Miami* and *CSI: New York*—routinely appear near the top of the Nielsen ratings. (An international survey, based on ratings from 2005, concluded that *CSI: Miami* was the most popular program in the world.) In large part because of the series' success, the field of forensic science has acquired an air of glamour, and its practitioners an aura of infallibility.[5]

In the pilot for the *CSI* series, which was broadcast in 2000, Gil Grissom, the star criminalist, who is played by William Petersen, solved a murder by comparing toenail clippings. "If I can match the nail in the sneaker to the suspect's clipping…" Grissom mused, then did just that. In the next episode, the Las Vegas investigators solved a crime by comparing striation marks on bullets. "We got a match," one said. Later in the same show, Nick Stokes (George Eads) informs Grissom, his boss, "I just finished the carpet-swatch comparisons. Got a match."[6]

The fictional criminalists speak with a certainty that their real-life counterparts do not. For example, in their written findings and in courtroom testimony, criminalists avoid the word "match." Instead, the preferred terminology is "consistent with," or "similar," or "is associated with."

Virtually all the forensic-science tests depicted on *CSI*—including analyses of bite marks, blood spatter, handwriting, firearm and tool marks as well as of hair and fibers—rely on the judgments of individual experts and are difficult to verify with statistical analysis. Many of these tests were developed by police departments over a hundred years ago, and for decades they have been admitted as evidence in criminal trials to help bring about convictions. In the mid-1990s, nuclear-DNA analysis—which can link suspects to crime-scene evidence with mathematical certainty—became widely available, prompting some legal scholars to argue that older, less reliable tests, such as hair and fiber analysis, should no longer be allowed in court.

In his research, Durnal does not blame the makers of the television shows for the phenomenon, because they have never claimed their shows are completely accurate. (For example, forensic scientists do not typically carry guns or arrest suspects, and tests that take only minutes on television may take weeks to process in reality.) He argues that the *CSI* effect is born out of a longing to believe that desirable, clever, and morally unimpeachable individuals are fighting to clear the names of the innocent and put the bad guys behind bars. In that respect, unfortunately, the romance of forensic science does not always mirror its reality.[7]

|Fig. 1.9| ▲

The cast of CSI Miami (starring David Caruso and Emily Proctor). Here criminal investigators are depicted working with crime scene technicians at a homicide crime scene.

Criminal Investigation Research

As with other aspects of criminal justice, research plays an important role in helping us to understand how criminal investigations can be more effective. Early studies by both the RAND Corporation and the Police Executive Research Forum challenged long-held opinions about criminal investigation and made some practical recommendations.

The RAND Corporation Study

In the late 1970s, the National Institute of Law Enforcement and Criminal Justice awarded a grant to the RAND Corporation to undertake a nationwide study of criminal investigations by police agencies in major U.S. cities. The goals of the study were to determine how police investigations were organized and managed, as well as to assess various activities as they relate to the effectiveness of overall police functioning. Until this study, police investigators had not been placed under as much scrutiny as those in patrol functions or other areas of policing.

DESIGN OF THE STUDY The focus of the RAND study was the investigation of "index" offenses: serious crimes such as murder, robbery, and rape. Other less serious crimes, such as drug violations, **gambling,** and prostitution, were not considered in the study. A national survey was conducted that assessed investigative practices of all municipal and county police agencies employing more than 150 sworn personnel or serving a jurisdiction with a population over 100,000. Observations and interviews were conducted in more than 25 departments, which were chosen to represent various investigative methods.

The *Uniform Crime Reports* (UCRs), administered by the FBI, were used to determine the outcome of investigations. Data on the allocation of investigative endeavors were obtained from a computerized network operated by the Kansas City Police Department. In addition, information from the National Crime Victimization Survey and the UCRs were linked to identify the effectiveness of arrest and the overall relationships between departments. Finally, the study analyzed case samples to determine how specific cases were solved.

RECOMMENDATIONS OF THE STUDY A number of policy recommendations were made as a result of the study. First, it was recommended that post-arrest activities be coordinated more closely with the prosecutor's office. This could be accomplished by assigning an investigator to the prosecutor's office or by permitting prosecutors discretionary guidance over the practices of investigators, thus increasing the number of prosecutable cases. The second recommendation was that patrol officers be afforded greater responsibilities in conducting preliminary investigations, providing greater case-screening capabilities for investigators while eliminating redundancy. The study suggests that many cases can be closed at the preliminary investigation stage. Therefore, patrol officers should be trained to perform such duties. The third recommendation was to increase forensic resources for processing latent prints and to develop a system to organize and search fingerprint files more effectively. Finally, the study recommended that with regard to investigations of cases that the agency chose to pursue, a distinction should be made between cases that require routine clerical skills and those that require special investigative abilities. Investigations falling into the second category should be handled through a specialized investigation section.

In addition to the RAND Corporation's study, several others have offered support for its findings. Block and Weidman's study of the New York Police Department and Greenberg et al.'s decision-making model for felony investigations both support the idea that patrol officers make the majority of arrests during preliminary investigations and can provide excellent case-screening benefits for investigations.[8]

The PERF Study

In one important study, the Police Executive Research Forum (PERF) considered the roles played by detectives and patrol officers in the course of burglary and robbery investigations. The study examined three areas: DeKalb County, Georgia; St. Petersburg, Florida; and Wichita, Kansas. Of the major findings of the study, several observations were made.[9] For example, PERF concluded that detectives and patrol officers contributed equally to the resolution of burglary and robbery cases.

Recommendations of the RAND Study

☑ Coordinate police investigations more closely with prosecutors.

☑ Expand the investigative role of patrol officers.

☑ Provide additional resources to process, organize, and search for latent prints.

☑ Distinguish between cases that can be handled clerically and those that require specially trained investigators.

However, it was determined that in most cases, a period of four hours (stretched over several days) was sufficient to close cases and that 75 percent of burglary and robbery cases were suspended in less than two days due to a lack of leads. In the remainder of cases, detectives played a major role in follow-up work conducted to identify and arrest suspects. It was determined, however, that both detectives and patrol personnel are too reliant on victim information for identification purposes, as opposed to checking leads from sources such as informants, witnesses, and other information sources in the police department.

The implications of the PERF study suggest that there is not as much waste or mismanagement in investigations as earlier thought as a result of similar studies. The value of follow-up investigations by detectives in identifying and arresting suspects is also thought to be much greater than indicated by earlier studies.

OTHER RECOMMENDATIONS The PERF study also recommended that greater emphasis be placed on the collection and use of physical evidence when applicable. Although physical evidence is seldom used in identifying suspects, it can be effective in corroborating other evidence of suspect identification, indicating that although not all police departments use extensive training of evidence technicians, many have established policies regulating situations in which they should be used. In the past, many departments overused the services of evidence technicians in cases in which physical evidence was minimal, resulting in the collection of more evidence than required. As a result, another recommendation by the PERF study is that police departments develop policies and guidelines regulating the use of evidence technicians in routine cases such as burglary and robbery when there has been no physical injury to victims. This policy should be based on the assumption that if the suspects can be found through other means of identification, physical evidence is not likely to be useful.

Yet another recommendation of the PERF study is that officers dedicate greater effort to locating witnesses through the use of a neighborhood canvass. This was not found to be common practice by patrol officers in the cities studied because initial information was commonly learned via interviews with witnesses and victims. It was suggested that to expand the scope of their investigations, patrol officers seek additional witnesses and victims through a neighborhood canvass. Finally, PERF recommended that patrol officers make more extensive use of department records and informants to develop and identify suspects. Although checking department records would be a relatively easy task, the skills needed to develop and interview informants are not common among patrol officers. Supervisors in the patrol area could make a greater effort to provide such training to street officers to help them develop informants.

The Objectives of Criminal Investigation

Because of the changing nature of criminal activity and the role of the investigator, the objectives of the criminal investigation may be more complex than people imagine. The objectives of criminal investigations are to:

- Detect crime
- Locate and identify suspects in crimes

- Locate, document, and preserve evidence in crimes
- Arrest suspects in crimes
- Recover stolen property
- Prepare sound criminal cases for prosecution

The premise behind the criminal investigation field is that people make mistakes while committing crimes. For example, a burglar may leave behind broken glass or clothing fibers; a rapist may leave fingerprints, skin tissue, semen, or blood. As a result of these oversights, evidence of who they are is also left behind. It is the job of the criminal investigator to know how, when, and where to look for such evidence. In doing so, he or she must be able to draw on various resources, such as:

- Witnesses and informants, for firsthand information about the crime
- Technological advances in evidence collection and preservation
- Their own training and experience in investigative techniques

In summary, almost all crimes require some degree of investigation. The extent to which any particular violation is investigated depends largely on resources available to the department and how the department prioritizes it.

Inductive and Deductive Reasoning

After an initial evaluation of evidence in a case, the criminal investigator draws conclusions through a process of reasoning. This process is typically achieved through inductive or deductive reasoning. The distinctions are as follows:

INDUCTIVE REASONING Induction or **inductive reasoning**, sometimes called inductive logic, is reasoning that takes us beyond what we know (our current evidence or information) to conclusions about what we don't know. Induction is used, for example, in using "specific" propositions such as:

> "All of John Wayne Gacy's victims found to date were male—so Gacy did not kill females."
> Or:
> "This ice is cold. (Or, all ice I have ever touched was cold.) . . . to infer general propositions such as: 'All ice is cold.'"

The calculus of inductive reasoning can also be broken down into conclusions that are strong versus those that are not so strong or even weak. The following are examples of strong and weak induction.

Strong Induction

> "All observed crows are black; therefore, all crows are black."

This exemplifies the nature of induction: inducing the universal from the particular. However, the conclusion is not certain. Unless one can systematically falsify the possibility of crows being another color, the conclusion that all crows are all black may actually be false.

Technically speaking, one could examine a crow's genome and learn whether it's capable of producing a differently colored bird. In doing so, we could discover that, in fact, colored crows are genetically possible. Consequently, a strong induction is an argument in which the truth of the premises would make the truth of the conclusion probable but not necessary.

Weak Induction

> "I always hang pictures on nails; therefore, all pictures hang from nails."

Assuming the first statement to be true, this example is built on the certainty that "I always hang pictures on nails" leading to the generalization that "All pictures hang from nails." However, the link between the premise and the inductive conclusion is weak. In other words, there is no reason to believe that just because one person hangs pictures on nails that there are no other ways for pictures to be hung or that other people cannot do other things with pictures.

Of course, not all pictures are hung from nails, and for that matter, many pictures aren't hung at all. So the conclusion cannot be strongly inductively made from the premise. Using other knowledge, we can easily see that this example of induction would lead us to a clearly false conclusion. Conclusions drawn in this manner are usually overgeneralizations that are in need of further investigation. Consider another example of weak induction:

"Many speeding tickets are given to teenagers; therefore, all teenagers drive fast."

In this example, although the premise is built upon a certainty, it is not one that leads to a reasonable conclusion. Not every teenager observed has been given a speeding ticket. In other words, unlike "The sun rises every morning," there are already plenty of examples of teenagers who have not received speeding tickets. Therefore, the conclusion drawn can easily be true or false, and the inductive logic does not give us a strong conclusion. In both of these examples of weak induction, the logical means of connecting the premise and conclusion (with the word "therefore") are faulty and do not give us a strong inductively reasoned statement.

DEDUCTIVE REASONING Sometimes called deductive logic, **deductive reasoning** is reasoning based on specific pieces of evidence to establish proof that a suspect is guilty of an offense—for example, identifying muddy footprints outside a window where a burglary has occurred. An issue would be whether the footprints belonged to an occupant of the house, to the burglar, or to someone else.

Deductive reasoning is often contrasted with inductive reasoning. For example, by thinking about phenomena such as how apples fall and how the planets move, Isaac Newton induced his theory of gravity. In the nineteenth century, Adams and LeVerrier applied Newton's theory (general principle) to deduce the existence, mass, position, and orbit of Neptune (specific conclusions) from perturbations in the observed orbit of Uranus (specific data).

In the context of criminal investigation, investigators must anticipate all possible scenarios and know what evidence is needed to support prosecution of the case because each issue in dispute must be supported by evidence. The more evidence an investigator collects, the stronger the case and the stronger the proof of guilt. Conversely, the criminal investigator must also consider what evidence is available to exonerate innocent parties.

CHALLENGING INDUCTIVE AND DEDUCTIVE REASONING In 2002, Jon J. Nordby questioned the processes of inductive and deductive reasoning in his book *Dead Reckoning: The Art of Forensic Detection*. Nordby suggested that it's not enough to just collect and analyze evidence; investigators also need a guiding theory that's flexible enough to accommodate new information and sufficiently logical to show a clear pattern of cause and effect.[10]

For example, Nordby states that a homicide investigation could show that the killer did not need to break in to a residence because he had a key. This theory would significantly narrow the possibilities. It is important for investigators to not only have a theory that guides the investigation but also that any theory that is contradicted be discarded. In other words, it is important for investigators to understand how logic and science work together.

Abduction is the process, therefore, of proposing a likely explanation for an event that must then be tested. For example, the killer had a key to the victim's home. Nordby suggests:

Induction is the wrong way of looking at science...because the classic problem of induction is the contrary instance [something that contradicts the claim].

Let us consider the notion that once a crime scene investigator observes a hair or piece of fiber, he or she now has their evidence. The reality is that many if not most crime scenes exist in dirty, debris-filled rooms. Such places are abundant with hair and fibers. So what is the investigator actually looking for? Which of all of those hairs and fibers is actually evidence? Unless the criminal investigator has an idea or theory that will make one object relevant and another irrelevant, the evidence-collection process will be overwhelming. In order to have purpose in what is being done, the investigator must have something in mind. That comes from abduction.

Developing an explanation that can be tested moves the investigation forward and guides the accumulation of knowledge, giving way only when contradicted. Abduction helps to make links among events, and the development of the overall theory of a crime depends on adding new links. Nordby suggests that abduction keeps guessing to a minimum.

Critical Thinking and Scientific Methodology

In addition to the use of deductive and inductive logic in interpreting evidence, the criminal investigator must incorporate skills of critical thinking with known scientific methods in their investigations. Let's look at how these two approaches to criminal investigation compare. In a most basic sense, critical thinking is the use of rational skills, worldviews, and values to get as close as possible to the truth. It is judgment about what to believe or what to do in response to observations or experiences. Fisher and Scriven define critical thinking as: "Skilled, active, interpretation and evaluation of observations, communications, information, and argumentation."[11] Critical thinking can also involve determining the meaning and significance of what is observed to determine whether there is adequate justification to accept whether a conclusion is true.

In contemporary usage, "critical" has the connotation of expressing disapproval, which is not always true of critical thinking. A critical evaluation of an argument, for example, might conclude that it is good.

Whereas thinking is often *casual* or routine, critical thinking deliberately evaluates the *quality* of thinking. In an early study on critical thinking in 1941, Edward Glaser wrote that the ability to think critically involves three things[12]:

1. An attitude of being disposed to consider in a thoughtful way the problems and subjects that come within the range of one's experiences
2. Knowledge of the methods of logical inquiry and reasoning
3. Some skill in applying those methods

Critical thinking calls for a persistent effort to examine any belief or supposed form of knowledge in the light of the evidence that supports it and the further conclusions to which it tends. It also generally requires ability to recognize problems and to find workable means for meeting those problems. Critical thinking may occur whenever one judges, decides, or solves a problem; in general, critical thinking may be used whenever one must figure out what to believe or what to do and do so in a reasonable and reflective way.

Critical thinking is an important element of all professional fields, including criminal investigation. It is important because it enables one to analyze, evaluate, explain, and restructure one's thinking, thereby decreasing the risk of adopting, acting on, or thinking with a false belief.

In contrast with critical thinking, the scientific method refers to techniques for investigating phenomena, acquiring new knowledge, or correcting and integrating previous knowledge. To be termed scientific, a method of inquiry must be based on gathering empirical and measurable evidence.[13] A scientific method consists of the collection of data through observation and experimentation and the formulation and testing of hypotheses. Each element of a scientific method is subject to peer review for possible mistakes.

The processes of critical thinking and scientific method need not be mutually exclusive. Rather, reasonable and informed investigators consider both as tools in their investigative arsenal, allowing for critical thinking in determining the direction of the investigation and scientific methods in evaluating the value of and usefulness of evidence.

The Emergence of the Police Specialist

The process of investigating criminals in the United States is structured very differently from that followed in England. In the United States, typically, a division exists within law enforcement agencies between officers whose responsibility it is to maintain order and those who investigate crimes. In larger departments, specialized squads typically perform the investigative function in law enforcement agencies. In fact, many such departments have several detective divisions within, each dealing with different categories of crime, such as crimes against persons (e.g., rape, assault, robbery), crimes against property (e.g., burglary, larceny, auto theft), and vice (e.g., drug violations, gambling, prostitution). Smaller rural departments often lack financial resources to specialize, so patrol officers often conduct criminal investigations in addition to their patrol duties.

In some types of crime, such as homicide, investigators must develop leads through interviews with friends, family, and associates of the victim as well as witnesses to the crime. In other cases, investigative leads are developed by sifting through files and prior police records and establishing the suspect's mode of operation (MO). In all cases, the investigative process uses traditional and historical methods of detection through the use of official records, photographs, fingerprints, and so on, as opposed to daily face-to-face contacts with the citizenry, such as with the patrol division. The investigative specialist is generally an older person who has had considerable experience in police work. Most detectives are former patrol personnel who have worked up through the ranks due to the common practice of promoting from within.

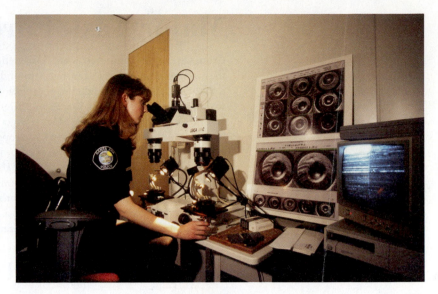

|Fig. 1.10| △

A criminalist in Santa Anna, California using a comparison microscope in the police laboratory

Spencer Grant / Photo Researchers, Inc.

Types of Investigations

The mission of law enforcement is complex and demanding but contains some fundamental components, including the maintenance of peace in our communities and the protection of lives and property. When people choose to violate laws that provide for these essentials, the perpetrators must be identified and brought before a court. It is the task of identifying such offenders that is the quintessence of criminal investigation. Criminal investigators confront investigations in several areas in the regular course of their duties:

- Personal background—to determine a person's suitability for appointment to sensitive public trust positions
- Suspected violations of criminal law
- Infractions of civil law
- Vice (drug and organized crime activity)

Crime Scene Investigators

As discussed earlier, the popular television show *CSI: Crime Scene Investigation* has brought the role of the crime scene investigator to the public, creating widespread interest in the forensic sciences. Of course, crime scene investigators require very specific training with regard to crime scene protection and the identification and preservation of evidence, and not every law enforcement agency is able to support a dedicated CSI unit. Researcher Michael Weisberg (2001) provides a description of the crime scene unit (CSU). He states,

> The CSU provides support services in the form of crime processing, fingerprint identification, and forensic photography. The CSU responds to major crime scenes to detect, preserve, document, impound and collect physical evidence. The unit assists in the identification of unknown subjects, witnesses and victims involved in criminal investigations.... The CSU will work closely in conjunction with the Detective Bureau in providing assistance in follow-up investigations, as well as subject apprehension and arrest. Members of the CSU may be either sworn or non-sworn.[14]

Weisberg's characterization is instructive in that modern crime scene investigation is moving more toward an investigative function performed by civilian rather than sworn personnel. Doing so makes sense from a practical, financial, and operational standpoint. Essentially, today's crime scene investigators need not concern themselves with the field operations of investigations—for example, identification of witnesses, interviews and interrogations, evidence analysis and evaluation, and arrests. Rather, their focus is to control, contain, identify, and collect crime scene evidence.

Major Task Forces

Crimes are often committed across jurisdictional and geographical lines. This can pose restrictions to some law enforcement agencies. A multidisciplinary approach to case investigation is therefore a common, resourceful, and efficient solution. Such units employ specialists in various fields from within a particular jurisdiction. A multi-jurisdictional investigation, in contrast, uses personnel from different police agencies. Many larger municipalities consist of 20 or more municipalities that surround a core city. In many metropolitan areas, multi-jurisdictional **major case squads**, or metro crime teams have organized, drawing the most talented investigative personnel from all jurisdictions. In addition, federal, state, or county police personnel may be used.

In some major cases—for example, homicides involving multi-jurisdictional problems, serial killers and rapists, police officer killings, or multiple sex offenses—it is advisable to form a major case squad from the jurisdictions that has a vested interest in the case. Evidence located from the joint investigation is sent to the same laboratory for continuity and consistency.

Modes of Investigation

Criminal investigations are conducted through the use of three different responses: reactive, proactive, and preventive. The **reactive response** addresses crimes that have already occurred, such as murder, robbery, and burglary. In this case, investigators typically respond to a crime, collect evidence, locate and interview witnesses, and identify and arrest a suspected perpetrator. Investigations are also conducted as a **proactive response** to anticipated criminal activity, as with many vice and organized crime investigations. Proactive investigations differ from reactive ones in two major ways: (1) the investigation is conducted before the crime is committed (rather than after) and (2) the suspect is identified before he or she commits the crime. Finally, investigations are sometimes conducted as a **preventive response**. Prevention through deterrence is sometimes achieved by arresting the criminal and by aggressive prosecution.

The Role of the Criminal Investigator

As indicated earlier, many myths exist regarding the role of criminal investigators. Perhaps these were best summarized by Herman Goldstein, who wrote:

> Part of the mystique of detective operations is the impression that a detective has difficult-to-come-by qualifications and skills; that investigating crime is a real science; that a detective does much more important work than other police officers; that all detective work is exciting; and that a good detective can solve any crime. It borders on heresy to point out that, in fact, much of what detectives do consists of very routine and very elementary chores, including much paper processing; that a good deal of their work is not only not exciting but downright boring; that the situations they confront are often less demanding and challenging than those handled by patrol officers; that it is arguable whether special skills and knowledge are required for detective work; that a considerable amount of detective work is usually undertaken on a hit-or-miss basis; and that the capacity of detectives to solve crimes is greatly exaggerated.[15]

Indeed, some studies have suggested that the role played by investigators is overrated and that their time could probably be spent more productively by focusing on crimes with the best likelihood of clearance.[16] Other researchers suggest that the investigative process is a valid utility in crime detection but should be augmented by the use of **proactive patrol** programs.

Characteristics of the Investigator

What characteristics best define a professional criminal investigator? Certainly, standards vary from one law enforcement agency to the next, but certain commonalities can be identified. To recognize these qualities, many police agencies implement a supervisory performance appraisal system to evaluate suitability for appointment to investigator. Once taken, the police manager can choose from candidates who possess the most sought-after qualities. According to a study by the National Institute of Justice (NIJ), investigative traits most commonly desired include:[17]

- Motivation
- Intuition
- Stability
- Judgment
- Street knowledge
- Teamwork
- Persistence
- Reliability
- Intelligence
- Dedication
- Integrity

Investigators are specialists. They undertake activities related primarily to law enforcement; patrol officers, on the other hand, routinely spend their time in order maintenance and the provision of general services (e.g., emergency aid, finding lost children, traffic control). Despite the diversity of tasks performed by patrol officers, investigators also assume many substantial duties. For example, detectives gather crime information, effect arrests, and prepare cases for prosecution and trial.

Gathering Information

Many criminal investigations are initiated with a call to the police dispatcher during which a crime is reported. Some of the most critical tasks performed by detectives include rapid arrival at crime scenes; searching the area; and identifying, collecting, and preserving evidence. In addition, investigators must be familiar with the department's computer and manual records, which contain such information as mug shots, fingerprints, intelligence, and stolen property files. Depending on the assignment, detectives must be able to follow up on leads through the use of various methods and procedures. These include visits to pawn shops, suspected fencing locations, taverns, and other places thought to be frequented by criminals.

|Fig. 1.11| ▲

Police academy recruits train in crime scene investigation by assisting the search of an actual outdoor crime scene.

Courtesy of Mark Ide

Field Operations

The best investigators have a demonstrated ability to function in **field operations** such as patrol and surveillance functions (stakeouts). At times, an investigator may even be required to perform in an undercover capacity to procure information on illegal activities such as drug trafficking, fencing operations, prostitution, or corruption. In addition, such investigations require the investigator to know how to operate technical and complicated electronic surveillance equipment, such as hidden-body transmitters, night-viewing devices, and photography equipment. Along with these skills, stamina and a willingness to work long hours are prerequisites.

Arrests

One of the basic functions of law enforcement is to arrest violators of the law. Accordingly, making arrests is a significant objective for investigators because they spend so much time collecting and evaluating information on criminal activity. The quality of arrests is also an important variable because an officer who has a reputation for making many poor-quality arrests will probably not be considered for the position of detective. Because a major purpose of an arrest is to secure a conviction, the quality and number of prosecutions and convictions are critical elements in assessing the performance of investigators.

Qualities Involved in Investigative Performance		
Gathering Information	Intelligence	**Prosecutions**
Crime scene management	Perseverance	Quantity
Communication skills	Initiative	Presentation of testimony
Field Operations	Judgment	Percent of convictions
Stakeouts	Teamwork	**Personnel Performance**
Patrol	Involvement	Absenteeism
Crime pattern analysis	Dedication	Complaints
Developing informants	**Arrests**	Awards
Street knowledge	Quantity	Dedication
Personal Traits	Quality	**Qualifications**
Motivation	**Public–Victim Satisfaction**	Education
Stability	Crime reduction	Training
Persistence	Diminution of fear	Previous assignments in department

The Patrol Officer as an Investigator

Traditionally, the responsibility of patrol officers in criminal investigations has been limited. Patrol officers have been required only to collect and record the most basic information by asking simple questions of the victims and witnesses and recording their answers on a report form. While in the past, patrol officers have studied crime scenes for physical evidence, usually the time spent on any one incident has been minimal. As a rule, reports have been reviewed by a supervisor and then sent to the detective division or an investigative unit for follow-up. In many cases, this process has resulted in duplication of efforts by investigators.

Over the past decade, many police departments have expanded the role of the patrol officer to responsibilities which are traditionally assigned to investigators. These new responsibilities include the following:

- The patrol officer provides immediate assistance to victims, locates witnesses, interviews both victims and witnesses, and records information about the crime scene. Depending on the seriousness of the crime or the presence of physical evidence, the patrol officer may call for a more specialized search by evidence technicians. To a great extent, this procedure initiates the case.

- The patrol officer has the authority to initiate and complete investigation of certain classifications of crime, such as all **misdemeanors,** cases that involve property value up to $1,500, and auto larceny cases. Investigations of more serious crimes continue to be referred to specialized investigative units. The practical effect of this "sorting out" of responsibilities for different types of investigations is that patrol officers investigate high-volume crimes that can be investigated as effectively by patrol as by criminal investigators. Conversely, investigations that require more time, specialized skill, and effort are handled by trained criminal investigators.
- In rare cases, the police officer may be given responsibility for the entire investigative process. In these situations, the patrol officer carries out all investigative functions. Investigators, if there are any, perform as consultants to the patrol officers.

For the most part, police administrators agree that these changes in the patrol officers' role have produced a number of benefits, including:

- The cases are handled completely and expeditiously.
- Relationships and communications between patrol officers and investigators have improved.
- The frequency of morale problems among patrol officers has decreased, and the decrease is attributable to the officers' belief that their skills are being better used in the investigative process.
- An increase in investigator productivity has resulted from a light caseload, which produced more time to focus investigative resources on specific high-profile cases.
- There is better management of the entire investigative effort by the police administrator.

Solvability Factors

A police department's reporting system and the investigative role of patrol car are inextricably bound. The redefining of the role of patrol officer is intended to ensure that evidence supporting the continual investigation or case closure is collected at the earliest possible point in the investigative process. This reporting system serves as the foundation for the criminal investigation.

The reporting system is defined by two basic components, which in combination form the basis for an initial investigation. The first is a format that logically guides the identification leads, or **solvability factors**, that experience and research of demonstrated are most likely to result in case solution. The second provides an opportunity for details of the investigation thus far expended so the follow-up plans do not unnecessarily duplicate tasks already completed.

A police department's reporting system should indicate not only that solvability factors are present but it should also identify the investigative effort expended in searching for leads. For example, if witnesses have been sought in a number of locations, the report should indicate where the search was conducted, who was contacted, and what was found. Without this description, the follow-up investigator will not have a clear idea of where the patrol officer has located the existing solvability factors and will end up duplicating his or her efforts.

Unless the patrol officer is able to make an immediate, on-scene arrest, 12 essential questions need direct answers. These solvability factors are logically based on existing police practices. All agencies may have different capabilities and procedures that result in slightly different solvability factors. The primary factors are as follows:

1. Immediate availability of witnesses
2. Name(s) of the suspect
3. Information about the suspect's location
4. Information about the suspect's description
5. Information about the suspect's identification
6. Information about the suspect's vehicle and vehicle movement
7. Information about traceable property
8. Information about significant MO
9. Information about significant physical evidence
10. Discovery of useful physical evidence

|Fig. 1.12| ▲

Patrol officers often conduct their own investigations or assist criminal investigators when requested. Here, a patrol officer is assisting in the investigation of a domestic violence case.

Mark Ide

11. Judgment by the patrol officer that there is sufficient information available to conclude that anyone other than the suspect could not have committed the crime
12. Judgment by the patrol officer on case disposition. If the officer believes there is enough information available and with a reasonable investment of investigative effort the probability of the case solution is high, then the investigation should be continued.

From an investigative standpoint, these 12 structured questions serve to define what the patrol officer should accomplish. By directing his or her activities to areas of inquiry that are the most promising for a successful case solution, the role of the patrol officers is broadened and more effective. Furthermore, utilization of the solvability factors emphasizes the importance of a thorough initial investigation even when it is being turned over for a continuing investigation. The patrol officer has provided the direction of the investigation, up to this point.

In summary, the expanded role of patrol officers in recent years has meant increased efficiency and effectiveness in policing in general and criminal investigation specifically. It has also served to enlighten those who serve the community in the capacity as patrol officers and to make them more aware of their important role as first responders to crime scenes and as the police department's eyes and ears on the street. In their role as first responders to crime scenes, patrol officers have many specific duties. These duties are encompassed in a process known as the preliminary investigation.

The Preliminary Investigation

Although the primary purpose of a patrol force is to prevent crime, patrol officers have assumed many other responsibilities, including the investigation of crimes (discussed earlier). In modern police departments, the patrol force participates fully in the preliminary investigation of crimes.

The preliminary investigation is the responsibility of the first officer at the crime scene. His or her actions at the scene can greatly influence the ultimate success or failure of the investigation. In other words, a job well done during a preliminary investigation should provide the information or evidence needed to build a solid case. Conversely, errors made during the preliminary investigation, especially those that involve a failure to properly safeguard or identify physical evidence, cannot be rectified at a later time.[18]

From the time the officer receives information to when he or she proceeds to a crime scene, his or her preliminary investigation objectives are as follows:

- Determine what has happened
- Locate witnesses and sources of evidence that aid in determining what has occurred
- Locate and preserve physical evidence
- Determine what further investigative steps should be taken
- Obtain and evaluate the accuracy of witnesses' statements
- Determine whether to act on the statements and evidence found at the scene
- Record what has been done, what has been learned, and what is left to be done
- Complete the investigation and make an apprehension if appropriate

One of the primary objectives of the preliminary investigation is to establish whether the necessary **elements of a crime** exist. All information obtainable at the scene of a crime should be gathered and reported at the time of the initial police response. The follow-up investigation by specialists is a second step, when a postponement of the work of investigation will not necessarily jeopardize the successful completion of the investigation.

The preliminary investigation should begin when an officer is assigned to proceed to a crime scene and only terminate when he or she has completed the task to the point at which a delay in further action does not substantially affect successful outcome of the investigation. For the most part, the nature of the crime and the relationship between the time of occurrence and the time of arresting the perpetrator determine whether or not the offense is investigated to conclusion by the patrol officer. When a suspect is arrested at or near the scene of a crime or during or shortly after the crime, the limits of a preliminary investigation need to be extended. If an extensive search of the crime scene for physical evidence is necessary, the preliminary and follow-up investigations overlap into a single operation. An example of this is homicide investigations.

Typically, patrol officers proceed to crime scenes with sketchy information that must first be verified and then expanded to be of investigative use. However, as far as crime scene response only is concerned, the patrol officer usually has two facts that shape his or her preliminary plans: the type of crime and the location of the crime. These facts usually indicate the urgency of a call and thus the degree to which a patrol officer can conduct the culinary investigation.

The Crime Scene Response

While approaching the crime scene, the responding officer must remain observant for potential suspects fleeing the area. The officer should note descriptions of people and vehicles leaving the crime area. A critical decision needs to be made by the responding officer when he or she observes a suspect. The officer must decide whether to stop his or her approach to the crime scene and investigate a suspicious person who may be fleeing or to proceed directly to the crime scene. The decision to stop must be based on the likelihood that the suspicious person is the offender fleeing the crime scene.

If it is necessary to stop a suspicious person, the officer should notify the dispatcher immediately so that other units are aware of the situation. The dispatcher should assign a backup unit to assist the officer and then send another officer to the crime scene.

AID TO THE INJURED The first duties of police officers at the scene of the crime are to administer first aid and obtain medical assistance for injured parties when required. All considerations are secondary to the well-being of injured parties. Even the capture of suspects and the integrity of valuable clues or evidence may need to be sacrificed to aid a victim. Obviously, if other apparently qualified persons are at the crime scene to provide first aid, an officer can then pursue fleeing suspects.

While rendering aid, officers should disturb the scene as little as possible. They should not unnecessarily move furniture, use facilities, or litter the area. For example, first aid supplies should be collected after use. Ambulance personnel should be directed how to enter and work within the crime scene so as not to needlessly disturb it.

EVALUATE THE SITUATION After caring for any injured people, the officer should make an evaluation of the crime scene before proceeding with the preliminary investigation. Evaluation of the scene at this time often prevents false moves and mistakes. By observing the overall crime scene, a police officer can gain a reasonably accurate mental image of how the crime occurred and where it was committed. Of course, if additional assistance is needed at the crime scene, the officer should request it immediately.

After arriving at the scene, the officer must exercise extreme caution. He or she should concentrate on identifying potential evidence and avoid disturbing the likely locations of fingerprints and other evidence. For example, the swinging double doors common to many commercial establishments should be pushed open at a point lower than normally touched by a person. After the doors are identified as possible sources of fingerprints, they can be protected from contamination by locking them or tying them open.

The officer should observe and record the details of the scene. This is done by beginning to take notes as soon as possible. The longer the officer waits, the greater the danger becomes of omitting small but often important facts. The type of small details include whether a door was closed or locked, the lights were all on or off, or the blinds were open or closed.

OBTAIN BASIC INFORMATION   For the most part, the preliminary sources of immediate information at a crime scene are victims and witnesses. From them, the officer can obtain the essential facts of the case. Although a lengthy inquiry cannot be conducted when the officer first arrives, he or she should establish the following points:

* The identities of victims, witnesses, and others present at the scene when the officer arrived
* A brief account from each witness or victim of what occurred, including descriptions of any suspects

After basic information has been obtained, the officer should broadcast a lookout alert or BOLO ("be on the lookout"). Alerting other field units about the nature of the offense and the details about the suspect, mode and direction of travel, description of the vehicle, proceeds of the crime, and type of weapon used may lead to an immediate arrest of a fleeing suspect.

INTERVIEW WITNESSES   The first officer at the scene must detain witnesses. The officer should quickly remove all persons from the crime scene and should not allow them to return until all of the necessary crime scene work is completed. The witnesses should be separated so they cannot discuss the case with each other. Such discussions among witnesses about the crime can adversely influence the witnesses' memories and statements.

The officer must obtain adequate information to identify and locate witnesses. Some witnesses may volunteer and offer to provide information to the officer. However, witnesses are not always easy to find. Many persons are reluctant to accept the role of witness, and they avoid becoming involved with the investigation in any manner.

One technique for identifying witnesses is watching the crowd for persons who are describing what they observed. Also, the officer should ask each witness to point out anyone else who was present at the time of the crime. In major crimes, the license numbers of vehicles parked near the crime scene and in the immediate neighborhood should be documented.

The officer should determine which witnesses have the most helpful information and obtain full details from them. Other witnesses who have not observed a significant part of the crime should be permitted to give a brief statement. When possible, witnesses and others should be interviewed in the following order:

* Victim
* Eyewitnesses
* Persons observing the suspect entering or leaving the crime scene
* Persons having knowledge or events leading up to the crime
* Persons in the neighborhood

When a crime is committed within a residential building, the number of possible witnesses may be few. On the other hand, when a crime is committed in a store or on the street, a large number of persons may typically have witnessed the offense. The officer may need to visit adjoining places of business, apartments, or homes to determine if other persons might have knowledge of the crime.

The officer's inquiries must go beyond simply taking statements. He or she cannot accept without question anything stated by a witness. The officer must be observant and quick to recognize discrepancies or unusual behavior on the part of witnesses. Furthermore, the officer must examine the interrelationships between the accounts of witnesses and other evidence in the case. This involves more than establishing that the witness has personal knowledge of the circumstances of the crime; it also involves an examination of the statements of witnesses in relation to their physical ability, geographic layout of the crime scene, weather, and degree of visibility. Other factors include reasons for the witness being present at the scene.

Summary Checklist

This chapter essentially gives you, the reader, a look at the foundations of modern criminal investigation. See how well you are able to answer the following questions in your checklist.

1. **Why are the lines between the romance and reality of crime solving often blurred?**

   For generations, people have been fascinated with crime and crime fighting.

   - People gather at public crime scenes to watch investigators in action
   - TV dramas focusing on criminal investigation and crime solving through the use of forensic techniques include:
     - *CIS: Crime Scene Investigation*
     - *CSI: Miami*
     - *CSI: New York*
     - *Hawaii Five-0*
     - *Bones*
     - *NCIS*
   - Children's books and TV programs also frequently incorporate mysteries and the clash of good versus evil, such as:
     - Nancy Drew and the Hardy Boys books
     - *Batman: The Dark Knight Rises*
     - *X-Men Origins*
     - *Kim Possible*
     - *Ben 10*
     - *Power Puff Girls*
   - Notorious outlaw gangs of the Old West have fascinated people for decades, including:
     - The Younger brothers
     - The Dalton Gang
     - Jesse James
   - Famous fictional detectives that have perpetuated the detective mystique include:
     - Sherlock Holmes
     - Hercule Poirot
     - Mike Hammer

   However, these popular portrayals frequently misstate or distort the realities of the investigative process and bear little resemblance to the real world of criminal investigation.

2. **How have the roots of our criminal justice heritage impacted our current system of criminal investigation?**

   As with other aspects of American culture, the police criminal investigative process originated in England.

It began with the Bow Street Runners, the London Metropolitan Police, and Scotland Yard.

- The Bow Street Runners
  - Founded by Henry Fielding, the magistrate in Westminster, near central London
  - Forerunners of a trend in policing for specialization within the police force
  - By 1800, they were considered to be the leading law enforcement organization in London.
- London Metropolitan Police
  - Established in 1829 by Sir Robert Peel, the Home Secretary
  - England's first paid, full-time police force
  - Consisted of about 1,000 uniformed officers who were known as "bobbies" after the department's founder
  - Officers were required to meet rigid standards of professionalism, including minimum weight and height requirements and standards of literacy and character
  - Detective bureau created in 1842
  - Scotland Yard was created 10 years after the establishment of the Metropolitan Police Department

Early beginnings of policing in the United States:

- First professional police forces in the United States were established in Boston, New York, and Philadelphia in the mid-1800s
- By the 1870s almost all major cities in the United States had municipal police departments

During the mid-nineteenth century, three significant elements had an impact on criminal investigation:

- Municipal police were supplemented by the county sheriff in rural areas
- The Texas Rangers were established (before Texas became a state)
- Police functions were expanded with the establishment of federal agencies, including the U.S. Marshal's Service and the Secret Service

The early beginnings of criminal investigation in the United States can also be linked to

- The founding of Pinkerton's National Detective Agency, the first organization of its type in the country
- The creation of the Federal Bureau of Investigation (FBI) in 1924

3. **What were some of the early advancements in forensic science in crime detection?**

Advances in research and science have contributed to improvements in criminal investigation. Historic strides in criminal investigation included study in:

- Serology
- Forensic dentistry
- Ballistics

Today, the American Academy of Forensic Sciences has members with a wide range of areas of expertise, including:

- pathology and biology
- toxicology
- criminalistics
- questioned documents
- forensic odontology and anthropology

The practice of considering evidence and drawing conclusions is typically accomplished through the process of inductive and deductive reasoning. These methods allow the investigator to make inferences regarding what is known about the crime and evidence connected to the crime.

4. **Explain the contributions research had offered to criminal investigation research.**

Research plays a role in helping us understand how criminal investigations can be more effective; researchers often challenge long-held opinions about criminal investigation and make practical recommendations for improvement. Research into criminal investigation includes:

- The RAND Corporation study of criminal investigations of index crimes led to a number of important policy recommendations. These included the suggestions that
  - post-arrest activities be coordinated more closely with the prosecutor's office
  - the investigative role of patrol officers be expanded
  - additional resources be established to process, organize, and search for latent prints
  - investigators distinguish between cases that can be handled clerically and those that require specially trained investigators

- The PERF study of the roles played by patrol officers and detectives in burglary and robbery investigations found that
  - detectives and patrol officers contribute equally to the resolution of burglary and robbery cases
  - in most cases, a period of four hours (stretched over several days) is sufficient to close cases
  - 75 percent of burglary and robbery cases are suspended in less than two days due to a lack of leads
  - detectives play a major role in follow-up work conducted to identify and arrest suspects
  - both detectives and patrol personnel are too reliant on victim information for identification purposes

5. **What are the objectives of criminal investigation?**

The primary objectives of criminal investigation are to:

- Detect crime
- Locate and identify suspects
- Locate, document, and preserve evidence
- Arrest suspects
- Recover stolen property
- Prepare sound criminal cases for prosecution

6. **What is the role of the criminal investigator?**

Successful criminal investigators are specialists who focus primarily on activities related to law enforcement. Their duties include

- gathering crime information
- making arrests
- preparing cases for prosecution and trial

7. **What is the patrol officer's role in the investigative process?**

The role of the patrol officer in the investigative process has expanded in recent years. New responsibilities include:

- providing immediate assistance to victims
- locating witnesses
- interviewing victims and witnesses
- recording information about the crime scene

A police officer may be given responsibility for the entire investigative process of a case.

Key Terms

abduction	bookmaking	crime
Allan Pinkerton	bootlegging	*CSI* effect
Bertillon system	Bow Street Runners	deductive reasoning
bobbies	constable	elements of a crime

Federal Bureau of Investigation

field operations

forensic dentistry

gambling

inductive reasoning

John Edgar Hoover

loansharking

London Metropolitan Police

misdemeanor

Pinkerton National Detective Agency

preventive response

private eye

proactive patrol

proactive response

Prohibition

proof

reactive response

rogues' gallery

Scotland Yard

serology

Sir Robert Peel

solvability factors

Texas Rangers

thief catchers

vice

William J. Herschel

Discussion Questions

1. Discuss ways in which the media have affected our perceptions of criminal investigation.

2. Explain how our English heritage affected the beginnings of criminal investigation in America.

3. Describe the "CSI effect" and how it differs from the reality of forensic science.

4. Discuss the ways in which research into criminal investigation has increased our understanding of how criminal investigations can be more effective.

5. Compare and contrast the processes of deductive and inductive reasoning and describe challenges to these processes.

6. Explain the differences between reactive, proactive, and preventive responses to criminal investigations.

7. Discuss the role of the criminal investigator.

8. Explain the ways in which patrol officers may be used to increase the efficiency and effectiveness of criminal investigations.

Notes

1. JOHNSON, H. A. (1988). *History of criminal justice.* Cincinnati, OH: Anderson.

2. THE ECONOMIST. (2010). The *CSI* Effect, 395(8679):77–78

3. IBID.

4. IBID.

5. TOOBIN, J. (2007). The *CSI* Effect. *The New Yorker*, May 7, 83(11):30–35

6. IBID.

7. THE ECONOMIST. (2010). The *CSI* Effect.

8. BLOCK, P., AND D. WEIDMAN. (1975). *Managing criminal investigations: Perspective package.* Washington, DC: U.S. Government Printing Office; GREENBERG, B., C. V. ELLION, L. P. KRAFT, AND H. S. PROCTOR. (1977). *Felony decision model: An analysis of investigative elements of information.* Washington, DC: U.S. Government Printing Office.

9. ECK, J. (1983). *Solving crimes: The investigation of burglary and robbery.* Washington, DC: Police Executive Research Forum.

10. NORDBY, J. J. (2002). *Dead reckoning: The art of forensic detection.* Boca Raton, FL: CRC Press.

11. FISHER, A., AND M. SCRIVEN. (1997). *Critical thinking: Its definition and assessment.* Center for Research in Critical Thinking (UK)/Edgepress (US).

12. GLASER, E. M. (1941). *An experiment in the development of critical thinking.* Teacher's College, Columbia University.

13. NEWTON. (1999). Rules for the study of natural philosophy. From the General Scholium, which follows Book 3, *The system of the world*, 794–796.

14. WEISBERG, M. W. (2001). Recent directions in crime scene investigations. *The Law Enforcement Trainer*, March/April, 44–48.

15. GOLDSTEIN, H. (1977). *Policing a free society.* Cambridge, MA: Ballinger, p. 1.

16. MORE, H. (1988). *Critical issues in law enforcement*, 4th ed. Cincinnati, OH: Anderson.

17. NATIONAL INSTITUTE OF JUSTICE. (1987). *Investigators who perform well.* Washington, DC: U.S. Department of Justice, September.

18. CRIME SCENE INVESTIGATION. (January 2000). *A guide for Law Enforcement: Research report.* National Institute of Justice. United States Government Printing Office.

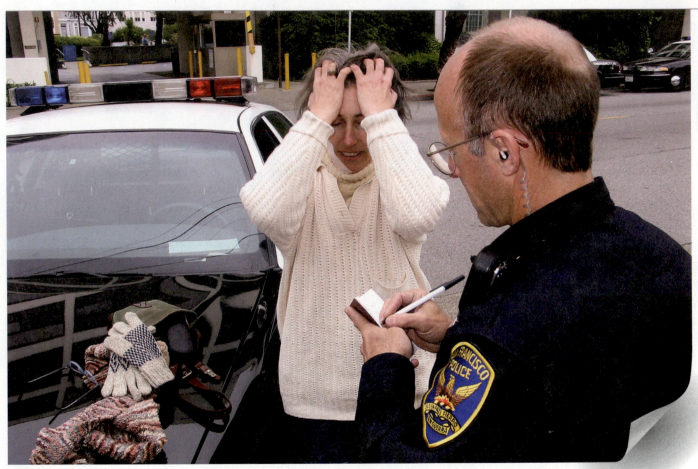

CHAPTER 2

Chuck Burton / ASSOCIATED PRESS

This chapter will enable you to:

1. Outline the proper structure of a police report.

2. Explain the proper methods of crime scene photography and videography.

3. Explain how field notes are taken and used by an investigator.

4. Understand how to properly capture the crime scene on digital video.

5. Explain the proper methods of crime scene sketching.

The Crime Scene: Field Notes, Documenting, and Reporting

Introduction

On July 20, 2012, at Century 16 Movie Theater in Aurora, Colorado, during a midnight screening of the film The Dark Knight Rises, *a mass shooting occurred. Twenty-year-old James Eagan Holmes, dressed in tactical clothing, set off tear gas grenades and shot into the audience with multiple firearms, killing 12 people and injuring 58 others. The shooting was the highest casualty count of any American mass shooting. Holmes was arrested outside the cinema minutes later.*

The investigation into the incident showed that Holmes bought a ticket, entered the theater, and sat in the front row. After about 20 minutes into the film, he left the building through an emergency exit door, which he propped open. He then went to his car, which was parked near the exit door, changed into protective clothing, and retrieved his guns. About half an hour into the film, police say, around 12:38 A.M., he re-entered the theater through the exit door. He was dressed in black and wore a gas mask, a bulletproof vest, a ballistic helmet, bullet-resistant leggings, a throat protector, a groin protector, and tactical gloves. Initially, few in the audience considered the masked figure a threat. He appeared to be wearing a costume, like other audience members who had dressed up for the screening.

Following his arrest, Holmes told the police that he had booby-trapped his apartment with explosives before going to the movie theater. Police then evacuated five buildings surrounding his residence. One day after the shooting, officials disarmed an explosive device wired to the apartment's front entrance, allowing a remotely controlled robot to enter and disable other explosives. The apartment held more than 30 homemade grenades, wired to a control box in the kitchen, and 10 gallons of gasoline.

The Colorado Theater shooting presented a considerable challenge for police and investigators. Not only was there a massive and complicated crime scene present at the theater but a second crime scene was located at Homes' apartment which necessitated the evacuation of the residents of the apartment complex. The shooting and the presence of explosives at Homes' apartment sparked renewed debate about gun control and concerns about the ease in which weaponry and explosives could be obtained through Internet websites.

A fundamental premise of criminal investigation is that investigators have the ability to reconstruct the facts and circumstances surrounding each case. This premise, while seemingly straightforward, requires a considerable amount of thought and preparation on the part of the investigator. For example, crime scenes have different components to consider, such as the entry and exit locations of the perpetrator; possible evidence of forcible entry; the location of the primary criminal act (e.g., the

UNIVERSITY OF COLORADO / Arapahoe County Sheriff's Office / HO / EPA / Newscom

assault, homicide, theft); and the presence of weapons, blood, shell casings, etc. The job of the crime scene investigator is to bring the different aspects of the crime scene together and create a "big picture" of what occurred.

This is generally accomplished through well-written reports, photographs, and crime scene sketches. Accompanying such evidence are the ever-important laboratory testing of objects seized from the scene and supportive testimony by investigators and laboratory technicians. That said, no crime scene investigation should ever be conducted without first considering the legal implications of evidence collection. For example, is a search warrant necessary? Is consent necessary (depending on the nature of the crime at hand)? Should a prosecutor be contacted for consultation? With the exception of unusual circumstances, such as the removal of injured parties or inclement weather at a crime scene, all evidence at the scene is properly recorded before any objects are collected or removed.

Field Notes and Reports

Many law enforcement organizations place a high value on an officer's ability to document information through note taking and report writing. Indeed, good report writing skills are one consideration both in an officer's qualifications for promotion and in his or her ability to present a thoroughly investigated and understandable case to a prosecutor. The practice of taking notes is one that is common in many professions. For example, physicians take notes regarding the physical and psychological condition of their patients; attorneys commonly interview witnesses in criminal and civil cases as well as victims and suspects in crimes; and police officers are certainly in need of accurate notes to document conversations, events, and observations.

A good investigator should develop the ability to write down information as it is learned, not later. Failure to do this could result in information being forgotten or confused. In many cases, it will be difficult or even impossible to locate witnesses or victims of crimes for a second interview because they may relocate or even die. Most departments furnish officers with a notebook in which field notes can be made. It is usually up to the officer what type of notebook he or she carries but it is recommended that notes be taken in a bound notebook in the event defense attorneys later charge that pages were added or notes were deleted by the investigator. Most typically, a small spiral-bound notebook is used. It should be accessible to the officer at all times.

The Role of Field Notes

When one thinks of a police officer taking field notes, the Hollywood portrayal of an officer writing down bits and pieces of information on the inside of a matchbook cover may come to mind. Unfortunately, in some cases, this is a reality, but it is not the prescribed method of note taking. **Field notes** have many benefits for both the officer and the department. Most notes result from interviews, but there are other uses as well. For example, notes may be the most important step in documenting a crime scene initially. An investigator's field notes are his or her most personal and readily available record of the crime scene search. It is difficult, if not impossible, to recommend a particular form of field note taking because most officers usually adopt their own style. However, one objective of this process remains clear: The notes taken at a crime scene must adequately reflect the condition and state of the location at the time of the crime scene search.

When to Take Notes

The investigative process begins as soon as an officer gets a call to the scene of a crime. Accordingly, the note-taking process also begins at this time. Officers should remember that note taking is a continual process that occurs throughout the duration of an officer's involvement in an investigation. Some victims or witnesses may be intimidated by an officer taking down what is said during an interview. If it appears that this is the case, the investigator should take the time to explain the importance of brief notes and how they will benefit the overall investigation. If a subject simply refuses to talk while comments are being recorded, the officer can wait and make the required notes immediately after the interview.

What to Write Down

It would be ideal if investigative notes could begin with the assignment of the officer to the case and follow through in a logical flow of events to the culmination of the investigation. In reality, however, notes most probably are written in the order in which information is learned, resulting in fragmented bits of information being logged. This is not unusual and should not pose a problem for the investigator provided that notes are complete and well organized. Remember to get the specifics.

When first encountering a witness or victim, it is important for the investigator to allow the person to state in his or her own words what occurred. This is best accomplished by asking the simple question, "What happened?" It is likely that much of the desired information will be communicated to the investigator at that point. After the subject provides his or her initial explanation, then more specific questions should be asked to pinpoint exactly what occurred. Most information can be learned with answers to who, what, when, where, why, and how.

For example certain specifics should be included in the note-taking process. The following are examples of some of the essential aspects of information:

- *Dates, times, and locations.* To begin, the date and time of the investigator's assignment to the case should be well recorded in his or her notes. Additionally, officers should include from whom they received the assignment. Supplementary information should include the exact time of arrival at the crime scene, the location of the scene, lighting and

4-16-12

Case # 1122-07

Time of violation: 2015 hours

Burglary – 1210 Watson Place, St. Louis, MO

Victim – Thomas Thompson

Phone – (314) 234-1212

  Mr. Thompson stated that he arrived home at 1930 hours.

He stated that his front door was ajar and a window was broken

and opened.

Mr. Thompson stated the following items were missing from the

residence:

1. Samsung 42" stereo television – serial number not known,

black in color, value $900

2. Gold watch with brown leather band. Wittinauer Longlife

brand, no serial numbers

|Fig. 2.1| △

Sample crime scene field notes.

weather conditions, and the names of other officers contacted and other persons present at the scene.

- *Description of victim.* This information should include all identifiers of the victim, including name, age, Social Security number, height, weight, and the color of hair and eyes. In addition, clothing should be noted as to style (if possible) and color of garment. Special attention should be given to extemporaneous identifiers such as complexion, tattoos, and scars.
- *Wounds on the victim.* Notes regarding the type and location of wounds should be documented carefully. It is important to emphasize descriptions of the wound, and if it is a bruise, its color should be noted. For example, notes of a gunshot wound might read:

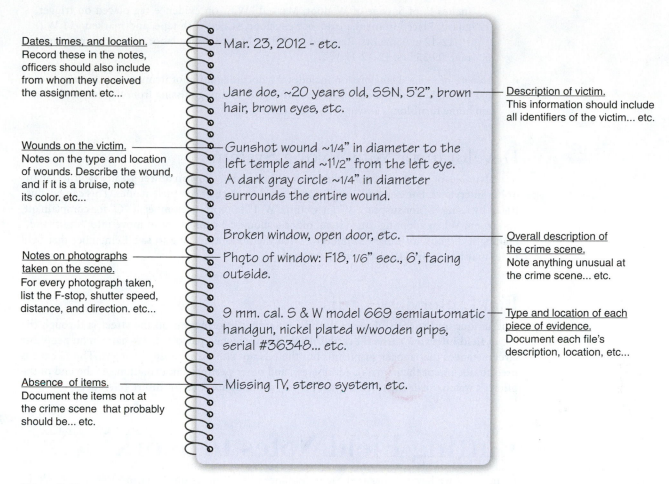

Dates, times, and location. Record these in the notes, officers should also include from whom they received the assignment. etc...

Wounds on the victim. Notes on the type and location of wounds. Describe the wound, and if it is a bruise, note its color. etc...

Notes on photographs taken on the scene. For every photograph taken, list the F-stop, shutter speed, distance, and direction. etc...

Absence of items. Document the items not at the crime scene that probably should be... etc.

Mar. 23, 2012 - etc.

Jane doe, ~20 years old, SSN, 5'2", brown hair, brown eyes, etc.

Gunshot wound ~1/4" in diameter to the left temple and ~1 1/2" from the left eye. A dark gray circle ~1/4" in diameter surrounds the entire wound.

Broken window, open door, etc.

Photo of window: F18, 1/6" sec., 6', facing outside.

9 mm. cal. S & W model 669 semiautomatic handgun, nickel plated w/wooden grips, serial #36348... etc.

Missing TV, stereo system, etc.

Description of victim. This information should include all identifiers of the victim... etc.

Overall description of the crime scene. Note anything unusual at the crime scene... etc.

Type and location of each piece of evidence. Document each file's description, location, etc...

|Fig. 2.2| ▲

Example of field notes and information that is typically documented at the crime scene.

"Gunshot wound approximately 1/4 inch in diameter to the left temple and approximately 1-1/2 inches from the left eye. A dark gray circle about 1/4 inch in diameter surrounds the entire wound."

- *Overall description of the crime scene.* Investigators must note anything unusual at the crime scene. This includes items damaged or in disarray, items that seem misplaced or that don't seem to belong in the scene, and open (or closed) doors or windows.
- *Notes on photographs taken on the scene.* For every photograph taken of the scene (and there should be many), the F-stop, shutter speed, distance, and direction of the photo should be logged in an officer's notes. Also included should be the time and location of each photograph. In the event that a video camera is used to document the scene, an officer's notes should include the type of camera and any special attachments that may have been used.
- *Type and location of each piece of evidence.* An investigator should be careful to document adequately the location of each piece of **evidence** found at the crime scene. This includes its description, location, the time it was discovered and by whom, the type of container in which it was placed, how the container was sealed and marked, and the disposition of the item after it was collected. For example:

9mm cal. S & W model 669 semiautomatic handgun, nickel plated with wooden grips, Serial #36348. 71 inches from the S.W. corner of the master bedroom, 16 inches E. of S. edge of W. door. Marked "WT" on evidence tag placed on trigger guard. Placed in manila evidence envelope, sealed with tape, and marked #11 WT 12-12-12 at 03:25 hrs. Released to Officer Mary Schultz, laboratory firearms examiner, 09:35 hrs. 12-12-12 WT.

- *Absence of items.* This notation includes the documentation of items not at the crime scene that probably should be such as certain articles of clothing missing from the deceased or certain home furnishings absent from the scene.

Developing a Note-Taking System

It is advisable for a system of note taking to be developed to allow an officer greater swiftness in his or her interviews. For example, initials can be used in place of complete names. This can be illustrated by using "S" for suspect, "V" for victim, "W-1" for witness number 1, "C" for complainant, and so on. When adopting this system, officers should be careful not to move into "shorthand," making it difficult for others to interpret what the notes are trying to say. Remember that field notes may be required later as evidence in court.

Field Interview Cards

One unique and successful method of documenting information on the street is through the use of **field interview cards** (FI cards). These are used when patrol officers happen on people or circumstances that appear suspicious but there is not sufficient cause for arrest. The FI card is used to document the name(s), address(es), and other pertinent information. At the end of the officer's watch, he or she turns in the FI cards, and they are filed for future reference.

Putting Field Notes to Work

As much as we have emphasized the importance of field notes on the crime scene, it should be stressed that notes are only a means to aid an investigator's recall at the time that he or she prepares the official detailed investigative report. The officer should be prepared to testify in court as to the findings of the investigation. The notes taken on the crime scene as well as the investigative report will be needed for review by the officer before testifying. The officer must also turn his or her notes over to defense counsel if required to do so.

Storage of Field Notes

After crime scene notes have been compiled, they must be stored in a safe place to avoid loss and tampering. This should remain the rule of thumb even after the suspect is convicted and the case is subsequently closed. This is performed in anticipation of a future appeal of the case, retrial, or possible civil action brought against the department or officer by the defendant.

Using a Digital Recorder

In many cases, investigators choose to use a small digital recorder in lieu of a notebook pad for note taking. Aside from the convenience of using a small recorder, investigators can also make more detailed memos about the scene. A drawback to the use of such a device is the difficulty on the part of the officer to review his or her notes on short notice. In the event that a digital recorder is used, however, transcripts should be made of the information contained on the recorder, and great effort must be made to protect the recording media as evidence and to ensure that it does not become inadvertently erased or damaged during transportation or storage.

Using Field Notes in the Courtroom

As with many other types of evidence, notes are an important item of evidence in the case and can be required by the court. It is acceptable for a person who did not prepare the field notes to testify about their reliability provided that the person was present at the time the notes were written. It is also acceptable for officers to use their notes to refresh their memory before testifying in court. Doing so, however, enables the defense council to take possession of them and examine them if he or she wishes. Typically, the defense will attack the validity of the notes based on the conditions under which they were taken or attack the notes on their face value (e.g., poor weather conditions, poor lighting conditions, spelling errors).

Recalling the matchbook example cited at the beginning of this chapter, at times the type of notebook used by investigators has become an issue in a courtroom. Because the notes taken at a crime scene may be designated as evidence by the court, officers should be careful not to use the same notebook for more than one investigation. This eliminates the embarrassment of disclosure of sensitive information regarding a case different from the one at hand. Therefore, officers should either use a different notebook for every investigation or a loose-leaf notebook so the pages can easily be removed and filed.

As a provision of the **best evidence rule** (*Cheadle* v. *Barwell*, 1933), the original notes must be provided in court whenever possible. In a legal sense, original notes are the archetype from which other documents are copied or duplicated (*Arenson* v. *Jackson*, 1916). In the event that the original notes cannot be located, photocopies may be used pursuant to a reasonable explanation to the court. In any case, however, it is important for the officer to protect his or her original notes by storing or filing them where they can easily be retrieved for court.

Writing the Official Police Report

A criminal investigator's written report represents the final product of his or her investigative efforts. The report informs others of what events have occurred and provides a permanent record useful in numerous ways as evidentiary matter at trial, intelligence information, and crime analysis data. To many readers, the report represents their only opportunity to learn about the background of the investigation. Consequently, it is essential the report be written so it can be understood, and more importantly, so it is not misunderstood.

Many police officers write mediocre reports. A poorly prepared report can easily become evident when one officer tries to read another officer's reports and tries to interpret what is being said. If an official report is difficult to understand, the complaint-issuing process will be bogged down, and it will be difficult for the prosecutor to decipher the facts and circumstances of the case. In addition, a poorly written report gives the defense attorney a tool to use during trial to confuse the officer's testimony and to muddle the issue.

Investigators should remember that the official police report is the backbone of the criminal prosecution process. It is a permanent record of the complaint and of the facts and events leading up to the arrest of the suspect. An important three-pronged rule of thumb to remember is that official reports should be factual, thorough, and to the point because they will be under close scrutiny when the case goes to court.

Factuality

The police report must be prepared carefully so that it accurately reflects all pertinent facts learned by investigators. Special attention should be given to dates, times, and other details of the investigation. In addition, these facts must be written in such a manner that the reader of the report easily understands them. It is important that the police report be factual and not contain hearsay information, speculation, or opinions of the investigator. Facts are generally defined as information learned personally by the investigator and not conclusions presumed by him or her. For example, if an informant tells the investigator that a suspect is a heroin addict, this information should be verified before stating it as fact in the official report.

Steps in Report Writing

1. Collect information about the crime scene, informants, and witnesses.
2. Take complete notes.
3. Organize the information.
4. Prepare the report.
5. Proofread and evaluate the report.

After the information has been verified, the investigator should include in the report how the information was validated. For example, were undercover officers used to converse with the suspect, or were court orders obtained for disclosure of medical records? In the event that verification is not possible, the investigator should mention that the information was "alleged" to be true by the source (e.g., confidential informant, witness, newspaper article).

Thoroughness

All facts learned pertaining to the investigation should be included in the official report. This practice is necessary for completeness of the report and for the credibility of the investigation. For example, if an undercover officer was offered illegal drugs and declined to purchase them, the offer should be documented in the event that the dealer later claims to have sold the drugs to the officer. In addition to the narrative aspect of the report, copies of related documentation should be attached with every report. For example, if investigators are looking at a check-kiting ring, copies of the suspect's checks should be attached to the report. Additionally, if surveillance photos are taken, they become part of the official report.

The report should also reflect the **chain of custody** of all evidence in the case. For example, in a drug case, the report should reflect how the drugs were collected, who handled them after seizure, where and how they were stored, and who now has possession of them (e.g., the crime laboratory).

Getting to the Point

The best investigative report is one that is not only thorough but is concise as well. In preparing such a report, the investigator must be aware that although details and completeness are important, excess information can bog down the report and possibly confuse the reader. For example, if the investigation involves an informant with the assigned number CI-10-28, this should be referred to the first time the informant is mentioned in the report but not every time thereafter. Subsequent references to the informant should simply be "CI," which will result in a more readable document.

Accuracy and Objectivity

An investigator's ability to report accurately is highly dependent on both the ability to conduct an objective and thorough investigation and to express the results of this inquiry and writing. In order to report objectively, the investigator must distinguish between facts and hearsay accounts and be able to relate a factual accounting of the incident.

It is essential that all relevant facts and details be presented in an unbiased manner without any indication of the officer's feelings or

|Fig. 2.3| △

Careful preparation of the police report and related documents is an essential part of documenting the investigation.

Courtesy of Mike Himmel

opinions about the case. Writing the report should be considered as an extension of the investigation in which the officer is basically an inquirer whose purpose is to gather information. Even when conclusions or opinions are called for in the report summary, the officer must make sure that such judgments reflect his/her thinking and not his/her feelings. The officer must be sure to clearly indicate when a statement is his/her opinion.

Word Choice

The narrative portion of the report, in which the reporting officer brings the facts together in a story form, requires the effective use of language. In writing the narrative section of the report, the officer should be concerned with two basic items: presentation and diction (choice and use of words). As a rule, the most effective report presentation is a chronological narrative, in which events are described as they occurred from the officer's perspective. Accordingly, the narrative should unfold from the point when the officer received a service call or otherwise became involved in the case.

One of the most difficult aspects of writing well is the proper choice and use of words. This is especially true with police reports because accuracy and brevity are all important. The following are suggestions in writing effective police reports:

1. Avoid the use of unnecessary words; for example, in "the aforementioned suspect," the word "aforementioned" is not needed. If more than one suspect is involved, they should be identified in some other way.
2. Avoid the use of elaborate or unfamiliar words when a small or commonly used term will do; for example, "the victim is cognizant of" should be written as "the victim knows."
3. Use specific words rather than vague terms; for example, "the victim said she proceeded to the living room" should be written as, "the victim said she (walked, ran, limped, hurried, etc.) to the living room."
4. Try to use the active voice; for example, "The message was received from the dispatcher at 10:40 A.M." can be improved by stating, "I received a message from the dispatcher at 10:40 A.M."
5. Use standard abbreviations; other persons will not necessarily understand individual abbreviations.
6. Write short, simple sentences whose meanings are clear and direct. Do not try to crowd many ideas into one sentence.
7. Avoid the use of double negatives such as, "No evidence could not be found at the crime scene." At the least, such expressions are confusing and, in some cases, the double negative can be misunderstood as a positive statement.
8. Be sure modifiers, adjectives, and adverbs are used sparingly because these words usually do not contribute much to a fact-finding report.
9. Use standard English rather than jargon or slang except when quoting witnesses, victims, and suspects.

The Structure of the Report

The report should be structured so that the reader is able to learn pertinent information quickly and succinctly. To best accomplish this, the effective organization of information on the report is critical.

Documenting Interviews

In forming questions for taking reports, the criminal investigator is much like a newspaper reporter. The investigator needs to know the answers to the questions who, what, when, where, and how. More specifically, the following items are considered as essential information:

- *Preliminary information.* This category of data includes the time and manner in which the complaint was received; identification of the location, time, and nature of the crime; and full identification of the victim.
- *Witnesses.* This grouping refers to information provided by victims, witnesses, or other persons at the crime scene.

Elements of the Report

- ☑ Who the officer was met by at the crime scene
- ☑ What the officer found at the scene
- ☑ What the officer did at the scene (e.g., administered first aid, notified immediate supervisor)
- ☑ Description of injuries to victim or suspect
- ☑ Type of weapon used
- ☑ Description of all evidence
- ☑ Names and identifiers of all suspects arrested
- ☑ Names of all witnesses
- ☑ Copies of written statements given by witnesses

- *Physical evidence.* The search for a discovery of evidentiary items must be included in the officer's records.
- *Modus operandi.* This is an extremely important category because in many cases, the **method of operation** is a clue to determining the suspect.

Obtaining information from victims, witnesses, or bystanders is more demanding than recording conversations at a crime scene. Interviews involve a variety of skills, both communicative and investigative, that require the investigator's full attention.

The use of basic interviewing techniques opens up communication between the investigator and the person being interviewed. However, the investigator must be skilled at forming questions and "digging" for information either temporarily forgotten or considered unimportant by the person being interviewed. At the same time, the investigator should guide the interview so that information flows sequentially and logically. This makes the investigator's job as recorder a much simpler task.

When recording the interview, the investigator must distinguish between items that are known and verified and those that are based on judgment of others or him- or herself. For example, "The suspect was described as 5'6" and 140 pounds by the victim" indicates the source of the information and the fact that it is not verified. In comparison, the phrase, "The suspect is 5'6"and 140 pounds" is an absolute and overly positive. If untrue, such a statement could mislead the investigation.

Conclusions that are unsubstantiated by fact should be presented as opinion. For example, "The witness heard gunfire in the vicinity of its home" should be stated as "The witness heard a loud noise that he believes was gunfire in the vicinity of its home."

As a rule, investigations are documented by the initial complaint (the face sheet) and supplemental reports (describing new findings). Formats for these reports are considered next.

The Initial Complaint

Also called the **face sheet** or **initial page,** the complaint depicts an "at-a-glance" summary of the investigation. This information includes the suspect's name and related identifiers as well as a brief summary of the facts and circumstances surrounding the case (e.g., times, dates, locations, who did what, who saw what, what evidence was collected). The initial complaint is the first report seen by anyone examining the file of the investigation, so it is important to keep it direct and to the point. Although individual departmental policies dictate the precise manner in which the reports are organized, the following sections are usually included:

- *Type of crime.* Depending on the department, crimes are generally designated as crimes against property, crimes against persons, or vice crimes. In addition, they are indexed according to the specific act that is being alleged, such as robbery, burglary, and drug distribution.

COMPLAINT FORM

Note: Hand print names legibly: handwriting satisfactory for remainder.

Subject's name and aliases	Address of subject	Character of case
Baker, Shawn Willis	1234 Cutter Ct. St. Louis, MO 65203	Burglary

Complainant	Complainant's address and telephone number	Complaint received
Officer William O'Shay	City Police Department (555) 456-7899	☒ Personal ☐ Telephonic Date April 14, 2012 Time 7:35 pm

Race W	Sex ☒ Male	Birth date and birthplace	Hair Brn.	Build Avg.	Height 6' 0"
Age 27	☐ Female	9/18/85	Eyes Blu.	Complexion Med.	Weight 190

Scars, marks, or other data

Tattoo on left forearm: "Ride to Live — Live to Ride"

Facts of complaint

Advised by radio at 1930 hours that a prowler was in the vicinity of 309 Watson Place in the city limits. Proceeded to the area and observed a white, older model Ford van parked on Watson Place in front of the residence at 309. Summoned backup and proceeded on foot to inspect the residence and discovered an open window on the north side. Paint chips and pry marks were visible on the window and on the ground.

Standing to the side of the house, suspect Baker exited the dwelling at approx. 1935 hrs. as he was apprehended. In his possession were two bags, one a canvas bag containing a screwdriver, slim jim, and pry bar. In the second bag, which was a brown paper bag, a gold watch and three gold and diamond rings were found.

Suspect was read his rights under *Miranda* in the presence of officers Larry White and Sandra Winslow. Baker then admitted illegally entering the residence and stealing the jewelry. Baker was transported by this officer to the city police department for processing and field notes were turned over to Detective Samuel Ramone for follow-up investigation.

Baker's van, which was registered to him, was towed to the city impound lot.

Action recommended

[signature] (Agent)

|Fig. 2.4| ▲

Sample complaint form.

- *Date.* This is the date of the offense.
- *Case number.* Before any paperwork is filed at the department, it must have a case number assigned by the records division. This number will be used on all subsequent reports in the investigation.
- *Officer's name.* This is the investigator's full legal name (no nicknames), rank, and badge number.

|Fig. 2.5| △

Investigators must carefully document every piece of evidence.

Courtesy of Mike Himmel

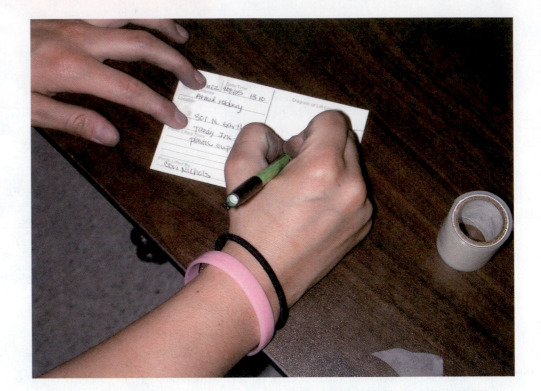

- *Suspect's name and address.* This includes the suspect's full legal name, monikers, addresses, date of birth, Social Security number, and any other pertinent information known about the suspect.
- *Victim.* The name of the victim(s) and address(es). No additional identifiers are required. For vice cases, the victim part of the report will either remain blank or reflect the jurisdiction in which the offense occurred (e.g., the state of Washington).
- *Witnesses.* This includes the names and addresses of witnesses of the crime.
- *Synopsis of crime and investigation.* This section should be no longer than one paragraph and should contain all general details of the case.
- *Details of crime and investigation.* This section is much longer than the synopsis because it encompasses all pertinent details of the investigation in a logical progression.
- *Attachments.* This section includes a list of all evidence relating to the case. Included are drugs, weapons, statements by victims and witnesses, references to video recorders used by investigators, and photos.

Supplemental Reports

As the case progresses, investigators will undoubtedly develop new sources of information, such as new witnesses, physical evidence, and documents. As this information is gathered, a supplemental report is generated to update the case. The supplemental report is considerably longer than the initial complaint because it goes into much greater detail on pertinent aspects of the case. In fact, it is the supplemental report that incorporates the who, what, when, where, how, and (sometimes) why of the case.

The report begins with a brief synopsis of the subject of the report, which gives the reader an overall view of the body of the report. The main portion is the details section. As the investigator formulates this section, events are prepared in paragraphs and in chronological order.

In summary, because reports are the tangible product of an investigator's effort, his or her competency is often linked to the ability to write accurate and complete records of work performed. In other words, a criminal investigator's career is closely associated with his or her success, or failure, to report in writing what has been done.

Capturing the Crime Scene on Digital Video

It is important that investigators both video-record the scene as well as capture details of the scene in digital photography. The video recording process should precede the taking of still photos. This is because it is important to capture the scene in its unchanged state before crime scene technicians enter the scene and begin the process of photography of the scene and evidence contained therein.

In addition to the use of digital photography at crime scenes, the use of digital video of crime scenes is becoming commonplace. There are many benefits to the use of digital video cameras at the crime scene. They are easy to use; relatively inexpensive; faster than photographs; and, in many ways, offer jurors a more complete reproduction of the crime scene.

Several distinct advantages exist in using digital video at crime scenes. For example, officers are able to begin recording at the extreme perimeters of the crime scene (i.e., point of entry) and walk closer and closer to the specific objects in question. Such evidence lends great perspective to photographs, which can depict minute details of the same objects. For example, a panoramic video view of a dead body lying near a handgun can show proportional distance between the two. In conjunction with the video, a close-up photograph can further depict details of bloodstains, possible powder burns, and wounds on the victim.

Another advantage is that digital video can easily be used in the courtroom because many video players can play back such recordings. In addition, because digital media are "developed" instantly, prosecutors can view the evidence moments after recording. Another benefit of digital video recording at the crime scene is the use of the freeze-frame feature in most video systems. This enables the viewer to stop the recording at any critical point for a closer view of the subject being documented. Many photo and video stores also have the capability to make individual photographs directly from digital video, which can be useful in the investigation or prosecution of the case.

Photographing the Crime Scene

As with the use of crime scene sketches (discussed later), the use of photographs in crime scene investigations has been fundamental for decades. It is important to note that both photos and sketches are necessary in criminal investigations because photos may distort distance, color, and so on. Today, the practice of crime scene photography has been extended to digital recorders to depict crime scenes. In this section, the term *photograph* (or *photo*) will allude to either or both forms of audiovisual reproduction.

Although the adage "a picture is worth a thousand words" might seem unrealistic, a visual portrayal of the crime scene clearly adds a dimension to both the investigation and prosecution of the case that no other medium can emulate. In fact, without the benefit of pictures, a witness or juror may be influenced by past experiences, preconceptions, stereotypes, and biases in making decisions about a crime scene. Indeed, photos and video recordings may convey information to the court more accurately than verbal descriptions of the crime.

The New Age of Digital Imaging

A key challenge today in law enforcement is the switch from film to digital imaging technology for criminal investigations. On a global basis, digital technology is becoming state of the art. Not only are many law enforcement agencies going digital, but many camera manufacturers are also abandoning their 35-mm lines in favor of digital technology. Some police administrators are resisting the digital trend, arguing that silver-based film (35 mm) is still the best because it cannot be manipulated and/or changed. However, with today's low-cost computer software, even photos taken with the older 35-mm film are subject to some manipulation.

Although some departments continue to resist the switch, many have gone totally digital. For example, in 2004, the Miami-Dade Police Department adopted digital imaging and had begun to phase out instant-film technology (e.g., Polaroids), initially as a cost-cutting measure.[1] Other departments have been more reluctant to move away from 35-mm film but have adopted some form of digital imaging technology. For example, some departments have almost completely stopped using 35-mm film in capturing latent fingerprint evidence in the laboratory. This is now accomplished through digital imaging. Laboratory technicians are using software packages that enable them to make enhancements to fingerprints. Such enhancements can make identification easier and in some cases make identification possible where it would not have been before.

Making the switch to digital photography is not an easy commitment for a department. Much thought must be given to what must be done before the transition is made. This includes consideration of legal, technical, training, and hardware and software issues, to name only a few. Proper planning helps law enforcement organizations avoid unnecessary expenses and duplication of efforts.

Photographs as Evidence

The principal requirements to admit a photograph into evidence are relevance and authentication. In general, a photograph is admitted into evidence at the discretion of the trial judge. In rare cases, a chain of custody is required, or the best evidence rule may be invoked if the photograph is offered for its truth and is the basis of a controlling issue in the case.

The most important requirement is authentication. Specifically, the party seeking to introduce the photograph into evidence must be prepared to present testimony that the photograph is accurate and correct. In most cases, the testimony need not be from the photographer; a qualified witness who has knowledge of the scene and can testify that the photograph accurately portrays the scene will suffice. Some courts will rule that a photograph is self-authenticating or presumptively authentic. If the authenticity of the photograph is challenged, it is usually a question for the trier of fact (e.g., the jury).[2]

An inquiry into relevancy assures the trial court will at least consider whether a photograph, even if probative, might unduly confuse or deceive the trier of fact. The authentication requirement serves as a check against outright fraud, and a chain of custody requirement applied in particular instances provides additional insurance. Last, although federal laws allow the introduction of a print made from a negative as an original (rather than a duplicate), in the few cases involving the best evidence rule, even this relaxed application provides some protection. At a minimum, it indicates official recognition that there is (or was) a negative—a "super original," which, in accordance with the laws of physics, must bear some logical relationship to any duplicates.

Due to the recent advances in digital imaging technology, it has become necessary for police organizations to develop procedures that support the use of digital images as evidence in criminal investigations.

Preserving Digital Images

From an evidentiary standpoint, digital images must be handled with special care and consideration to preserve their integrity as evidence. As a rule, digital images are stored on removable media such as Secure Digital (SD) cards, flash drives, and Memory Sticks. The original storage media within the digital camera is considered the original evidence and must be protected at all costs. The storage media must be preserved immediately, or as soon as reasonable. Copies of the images contained on the master storage media can (and should) be copied to compact disc (CD) or other protected medium for subsequent reference in the investigation. These copies can also be disseminated if necessary to further the investigation. This way, the original images remain on the master/original media for presentation in court.

The original storage media must be safely maintained until such time as there is an official determination that there will be no future need for the images.[3]

What to Photograph

Extensive expertise in photography and audio electronics is always a clear benefit to a crime scene investigator, but such training is not always required for good pictures of the scene. Any camera is better than no camera at all, and many relatively low-cost cameras come equipped with auto focus and rewind features. In any case, one important point to remember is that when photographing a crime scene, there can never be too many pictures. Depending on the crime scene, 100 to 200 photos may be typical for proper documentation. Note that before taking photographs of the scene, the scene should first be documented using digital video (as discussed above).

Because digital media are relatively inexpensive, most departments can afford to take numerous photographs. In doing so, mistakes or problems encountered with one photo can usually be circumvented through the choice of others depicting the same scene or item. Photographs of the crime scene are usually taken in three stages: from the general view to the medium-range view to the close-up view.[4] This approach enables a picture of all circumstances to be painted for jurors while leading up to the most critical part of the crime scene.

GENERAL VIEWS The general photograph is a sweeping view of the crime scene area (i.e., an overall scene, such as the neighborhood, including angles from all streets leading up to the crime scene). It demonstrates what the scene looks like in its own environment. Examples are:

- Photo of a bank that was robbed
- Photo of a house that was burglarized
- Abandoned "getaway" car in a wooded area

Photos depicting such scenes should be taken at a distance to reveal the natural surroundings of the location. In the case of a bank robbery, the bank should be photographed from across the street and from both sides of the building. This will give jurors a perspective of where the structure was situated and the location of possible escape routes.

MEDIUM-RANGE VIEWS As we move in closer to the subject of the crime scene, additional photos should be taken. These photos should be taken at a distance no greater than 20 feet away from the subject or item being photographed. The intent of the medium-range photo is to depict specific items or objects in the crime scene. Some examples are blood splatters on the walls or an open window that served as the entry point for an intruder. Different lenses can be used to accomplish this phase of photography. For example, a wide-angle digital lens should be considered for a broad panoramic view of the scene. The purpose of the medium-range photography process is to allow jurors to link each print with the general crime scene photos.

CLOSE-UP VIEWS Moving from the broad to the specific, the last phase in photographing the crime scene is the close-up. These photos are taken at a distance of less than 5 feet using the zoom feature on the digital camera, and they should focus on small segments of a larger surface or on specific objects in the scene. Examples are bullet holes in the walls, weapons, blood-splatter stains, latent fingerprints, and so on. As with medium-range photos, these

Crime Scene Photographs

Benefits
- ☑ Provide easy storage and retrieval of data on the crime scene.
- ☑ Remove many inferences by practically placing the judge and jury at the crime scene.
- ☑ Give the investigator a source of reference as to the location of evidence at the scene.

Disadvantages
- ☑ Do not show true or actual distances.
- ☑ Can distort color and perceptions.
- ☑ Can be ruined by mechanical errors in processing.

|Fig. 2.6| △

"Close-up photo of an empty cartridge found on a crime scene with a yellow placard and the victim in the background."

Corepics VOF / Cutcaster Images

photographs should include some identifiable item from the medium-range photos to link object(s) being photographed with the general crime scene. It is also important to note that close-up photos should be taken with and without a small ruler or other item, such as a coin, to provide perspective.[5]

Other Hints

Because many types of evidence undergo significant changes at the crime scene, it is important for investigators to photograph the crime scene in a timely fashion. This should typically precede most other tasks of the crime scene processing because objects cannot be examined adequately until after they are photographed from every angle. Accordingly, it is important that all camera angles and settings be recorded on the crime scene sketch.

Photos of the interior scenes should be conducted to depict the entire area. This is accomplished by overlapping photos from one scene to the next and working in one direction around the room. In the use of video, a slow panorama of the crime scene is necessary. It is usually advisable to either use a tripod or attempt to keep the camera at eye level for all the photos. Fox and Cunningham offer several other considerations that crime scene photographers should consider[6]:

- Approaches to and from the scene
- Surrounding areas (e.g., the yard of a house in which the homicide occurred, the general area surrounding an outdoor crime scene)
- Close-up photographs of the entrance and exit to the scene, or if these are not obvious, those most likely to have been used
- A general scenario shot showing the location of the body and its position in relation to the room or area in which it was found
- At least two photographs of the dead body at 90-degree angles to each other, with the camera placed as high as possible, pointing downward toward the body

As many close-ups of the dead body should be taken as needed to show wounds or injuries, weapons lying near the body, and the immediate surroundings. After the body is removed and after the removal of each item of evidence, the area underneath should be photographed if there is any mark, stain, or other apparent change. All fingerprints that do not need further development or that cannot be lifted should be photographed. Areas in which fingerprints were discovered are photographed to show the locations if these areas were not included in other photographs. Bloodstains should always be photographed, including their locations. Today, color digital images are considered the norm and, almost without exception, are accepted by courts as the best photographic evidence.

PERSPECTIVE It is important that the crime scene photographer show the relationship between one item of evidence and another. This is accomplished by showing the location of the articles in accordance with recognizable backgrounds. In the event that an item to be photographed is smaller than 6 inches, two photos should be taken. The first should be taken at close range, and the second should be taken from at least 6 feet away. This portrays the object in proper perspective.

SUITABLE LIGHTING As a rule, the crime scene photographer will find that natural light at the scene is inadequate for good-quality photos and that artificial lighting is required. Investigators must therefore select the proper equipment for this task. Whether a flash or a more elaborate lighting system is used, it is of utmost importance to avoid unnecessary shadows. Shadows tend to hide details, some of which might be of grave significance to the investigation. In addition, the part of the photo that is closest to the flash may become washed out, and details might be lost. A good solution to this problem is the strategic use of floodlights to ensure consistent illumination.

USE OF MARKERS A generally accepted practice in crime scene photography is the use of measuring or other identifying devices in photos. These include rulers, tapes, and coins. **Markers** such as these are included in the finished photograph and call attention to specific objects or enable the viewer of the photo to get a sense of the size of the object or the distance between objects. Some markings can be made with chalk to show specific locations of objects such as dead bodies, footprints, and weapons. Other markers include ink markings made on the surface of photographs after they have been printed.

Because the use of a marker introduces something foreign into the crime scene, investigators should take a photo of the area before placement of the marker and then take a second photo of the same setting after the marker is in place. Another marking technique is to place over the photo a transparent overlay containing all necessary arrows, circles, and so on to depict relevant information. This technique preserves the original photo and allows for comparison between the two.

Admissibility of Photographic Evidence

Trial courts bear the responsibility of admissibility of photographs as evidence in court. Such determinations have been based on several legal precedents:

1. *Materiality*. The object portrayed in the photo must be material and relevant to the case at hand. All photographs, provided that they serve to prove a particular point in the issue, should be admitted into evidence.
   a. A *material photograph* is one that relates to and makes a substantive contribution to the specific case in question.
   b. A *relevant photograph* also applies to the matter in question and is used to support testimony. It is representative of the evidence that relates it to the matter in question to determine the truth of the circumstances (*Barnett* v. *State*, 1922).
2. *Prejudicial images*. Any photograph or image admitted must not prejudice, or appeal unfairly, to the emotions of the jury. Some judges have suppressed photos depicting unusually gruesome crime scenes. In one recent case, photos were taken of a defendant immediately after his arrest, showing him as dirty and unkempt. The photos were offered as evidence to contrast the defendant's clean and polished image in the courtroom. The judge refused to admit the image into evidence on the basis that it was prejudicial.

|Fig. 2.7| △

A bloody shoeprint is photographed using a marker to show perspective.

Mike Himmel/Missouri State Highway Patrol Crime Laboratory

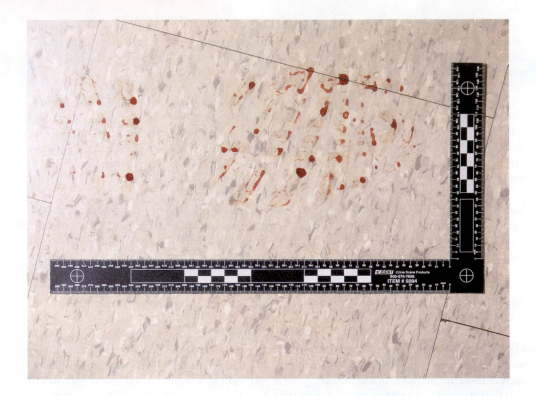

3. *Distorted photos.* Photographs must be kept free of distortion. Three types of distortion have generally been common in crime scene photographs: incorrect point of view, perspective, and misrepresentation of tone or color. These problems commonly occur through improper use of angles of the photo. For example, a handgun lying next to a dead body may be photographed to appear much larger in size than it actually is, thus distorting the perception of the scene. Another example is bruises on a body, which might indicate the extent of the wound or even the time it was inflicted. Therefore, if the tone of a bruise is shown in a photo as greenish in color rather than bluish, a different conclusion may be made as to the extent of the injuries. Because of this, the photographer or laboratory technician may be subjected to rigorous cross-examination regarding his or her expertise in the processing of digital images. Such distortions must be avoided because they will taint the case and will probably cause the images to be excluded as evidence.

Additionally, photos and physical evidence have different requirements regarding the chain of custody. For example, it is not necessary for the person taking the photograph to be the one to testify about it in court. In *State* v. *Fournier* (1963), however, the court held that evidence must be offered to show that the photograph is an accurate representation of the object(s) portrayed (as mentioned above). Such evidence is usually given by an officer who was present on the crime scene and who can vouch for the validity of the photo.

Since the late 1960s, an avalanche of cases have regarded the admissibility of video recordings in criminal trials. Generally, the courts have held that such evidence is admissible on the same basis as **motion** picture films with sound and is subject to the same rules of evidence as motion pictures and photographic evidence. Many courts have even admitted video recordings that had inferior-quality sound but permitted the sound track to be "cleaned up" electronically.

Identification of Photographs

It is of critical importance for investigators to log their photos carefully as to date, time, and sequence number. Also included should be the following:

- Type of case
- Description of subject of photo
- Location

PHOTOGRAPHIC LOG

PAGE __1__ of __1__

LOCATION ___Living Room___

DATE ___4-16-12___

CASE # ___0211-12___

OFFICERS ___Lt. Johnson, Officer Watson, Officer Smith___

CAMERA ___#31___

CAMERA TYPE ___Nikon Coolpix___

___P-1 digital___

COMMENTS ___SD Disk #14___

Photo #	Description of Subject Photographed	Scale	Misc. Comments	Sketch (if required)
1	Long-range shot — living room		Photos from top	
2	Close-up — defense wound			
3	Medium-range shot — knife			
4	Close-up — powder burns			
5	Long-range shot — hallway		From left side	
6	Medium-range shot — handgun		From right side	
7	Close-up — handgun			
8	Close-up — knife			

|Fig. 2.8| △

Sample photographic log.

- Names of persons handling evidence
- Assigned case number
- Any other relevant information

Using this technique will reduce hours of sorting out finished photos and trying to determine what picture goes where.

Surveillance Photographs

Surveillance photography is used covertly in establishing identities or in documenting criminal behavior. Photography of this nature is selective and may have many benefits. For example, it may aid officers in identifying the physical locations of criminal activity or in formulating a raid plan for serving a search warrant. The covert use of **surveillance** is now used commonly in banks and convenience stores as a deterrent for would-be robbers and as an aid in prosecution. Some systems use single-reflex cameras with telephoto lenses, and others use infrared film.

Most investigations using surveillance photography are vice and organized crime operations, and a specially outfitted van or truck is usually used by investigators. In these operations, illegal transactions are made discreetly among criminals, and thorough documentation is necessary to establish proof **beyond a reasonable doubt.** Such photography can be problematic, however, in that proper lighting is sometimes difficult to come by. In response, many police agencies have purchased night-vision devices that affix to surveillance cameras. These devices use natural light emitted by stars or the moon and usually produce identifiable images.

The Crime Scene Sketch

The crime scene sketch complements photographs and videos taken of the scene. With increased use of video and digital cameras at crime scenes, one might argue that preparation of the sketch is no longer needed. In actuality, because videos and photos may tend to distort the dimensions of the crime scene, a properly prepared crime scene sketch is all the more important to a properly documented crime scene. In other words, whereas a photograph represents the scene as it is perceived by the viewer, the diagram represents the scene as it actually is.

In many ways, the crime scene sketch can show certain details better than a photograph. For example, photographs are two-dimensional and may fail to show the distance between objects. Also, a photograph cannot show the entire crime scene, whereas, a sketch can.

A crime scene sketch is a scale drawing that locates evidence in relation to other factors. As a rule, the sketch will not identify such items as the color of a wall, the type of floor, the general condition of the area, and non-evidential matter.

Whereas a sketch that is properly prepared can virtually always be used in court, photographs may not be permitted under certain circumstances. In cases in which photographs may inflame the jury, courts often refuse to admit them into evidence. When this occurs, the diagram is of major importance. Additionally, a crime scene sketch can supplement the verbal description to present spatial relationships of the evidence.

A properly prepared sketch is an important tool for the prosecutor as well. The sketch can become the focus point of courtroom testimony. Witnesses can show on the diagram their relationship to observations of the crime, and each item of evidence can be pinpointed.

Putting It Together

Several methods have been developed over the years to best conduct a detailed sketch of the scene. One should remember that the objective of the crime scene sketch is to portray the scene accurately, not artistically. Too much detail in a crime scene sketch will remove the advantage of a sketch over a photograph. Thus, most officers can be expected to produce a sketch successfully.

In each crime scene sketch, some items are considered essential. As with note taking, however, such items should not be considered the only items needed for complete documentation of the scene. The crime scene sketch should include the following information:

- The investigator's complete name and rank
- The date, time, type of crime, and assigned case number
- The complete names of other officers assisting in the making of the sketch
- The address of the crime scene, its position in a building, landmarks, and so on
- The scale of the drawing (if no scale, indicate by printing "not to scale")
- The primary items of physical evidence and other critical features of the crime scene, located by detailed measurements from at least two fixed points of reference
- A key or legend identifying the symbols or points of reference used in the sketch

Measurement

One general rule of sketching is that the sketch should reflect as accurately as possible the important details of the scene. Such information must be recorded uniformly. For example, if the dimensions of a dead body in a field are recorded accurately but the location of a handgun found near the body is estimated only roughly, the sketch is virtually useless. Accordingly, all measures of distance must be conducted by using the same method. Specifically, one part of the scene should not be paced off and another area of the scene measured with a tape measure.

After the case goes to court and a measurement error is discovered, the explanation of such an error may prove embarrassing and difficult. Use of a tape measure is therefore considered the most effective method of measuring the scene. Other tools for crime scene sketching include:

- Paper for the sketch (preferably graph paper)
- Clipboard
- Colored pencils (if necessary)

- Fifty-foot steel tape
- Thumbtacks to hold down one end of the tape if the investigator is alone
- Straight-edge ruler
- Eight- to 12-foot tape for measuring from the baseline

Rough and Finished Sketches

There are generally two sketches for every crime scene: a rough sketch and a finished sketch. The **rough sketch** is the one drawn by officers on the crime scene. Generally, it is not drawn to scale but should reflect accurate dimensions and distances between objects of importance. At times, it might be necessary to draw more than one rough crime scene sketch. For example, one sketch might portray the overall scene, and a second sketch could show only the body and its immediate surroundings. Alterations to the rough sketch should not be made after the investigator leaves the scene.

The **finished sketch** is simply a completed sketch drawn to scale. This is drawn from information contained on the rough sketch and should accurately reflect all measurements indicated on the rough sketch. With the finished sketch being drawn to scale, however, it is not necessary to include the specific measurements on the sketch itself. If the finished sketch is not drawn to scale, measurements are required. Finished sketches need not be prepared by the crime scene investigator, although in court, the investigator will be required to affirm that the finished sketch is an accurate portrayal of the scene. In many cases, the finished sketch is prepared by a professional draftsperson or is made with the use of specially designed computerized programs.[7]

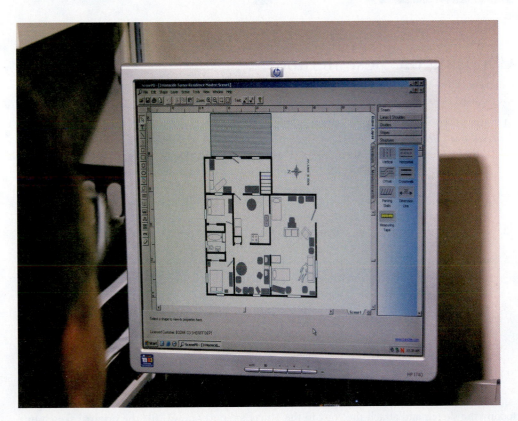

|Fig. 2.9| △

Final sketches much depict precise measurements and can be accomplished using computerized programs such as shown here.

|Fig. 2.10| ▲

In the absence of a computerized program, investigators can rely on a hand-written diagram of the scene. Finalized sketches must be drawn to scale as depicted here.

Michael D. Lyman

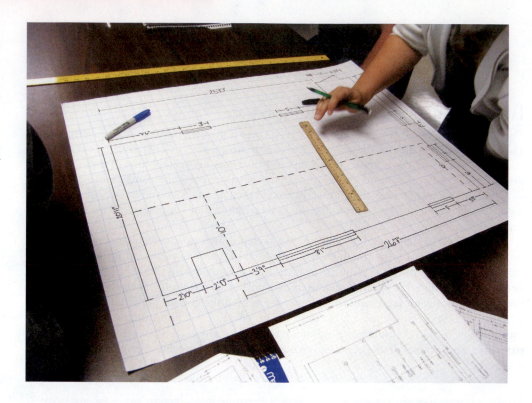

Choosing the Best Method

Different crime scenes present different sketching problems. Let's now consider three of the most widely used sketching methods:

1. *Coordinate method.* The **coordinate method** uses the practice of measuring an object from two fixed points of reference. One such procedure is the **baseline technique,** in which a line is drawn between two known points. The baseline could also be a wall or a mathematically derived point along a designated area where exact measurements can be determined. The measurements of a particular item are then taken from left to right along the baseline to a point at right angles to the object that is to be plotted. This distance is noted in the legend with a circled number after the name of the object.

2. *Triangulation method.* The **triangulation method** is a bird's-eye view of the scene that uses fixed objects from which to measure. This is particularly useful for sketching outdoor crime scenes where there are no easily identifiable points of reference. In this procedure, two or more widely separated points of reference are required. The item of interest is then located by measuring along a straight line from the reference points.

3. *Cross-projection method.* The **cross-projection method** is used in indoor crime scenes. It is basically a top-down view of the crime scene, with the walls of the room "folded" down to reveal locations of bullet holes, blood-spatter evidence, and so on, which would not be apparent otherwise. Measurements are then made from a designated point on the floor to the area on the wall in question.

On completion of the sketch, the investigator should be prepared to do two things: (1) photocopy the sketch and attach the copy to the officer's report and (2) file the original sketch in a secure location so it is ready for presentation in court at a later date. The officer should remember that both the rough and finished sketches are admissible in court if they are prepared or witnessed by the investigator, provided that they both portray the crime scene accurately.

In summary, the crime scene sketch is an integral part of the crime scene investigation because it gives perspective to what happened at the time of the crime. Jurors, typically, can relate to a well-drafted sketch depicting all-important areas of the crime scene location; thus, investigators must take appropriate measures to ensure an accurate and meaningful crime scene sketch.

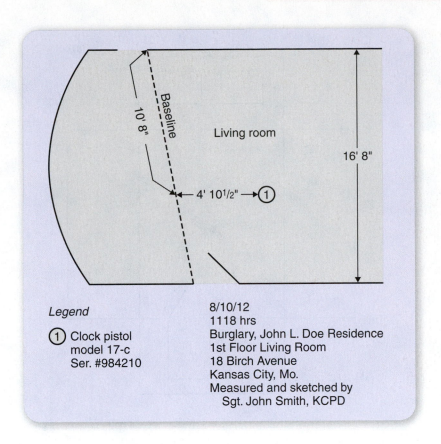

|Fig. 2.11| ◢

Baseline or coordinate
method.

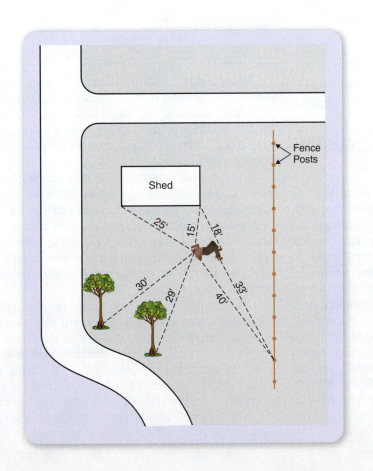

|Fig. 2.12| ◢

Triangulation
sketching method.

|Fig. 2.13| ▲

Cross-projection sketching method. Note that in this type of sketch the walls are drawn as if folded flat.

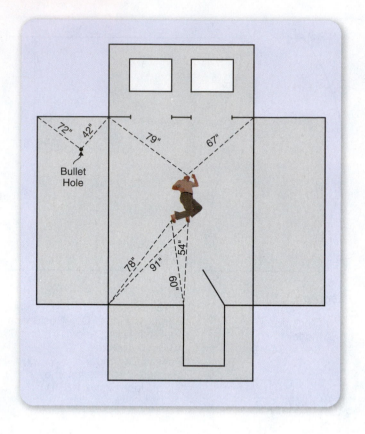

Case in Point

>>Investigative "Tunnel Vision"—The Duke Lacrosse Rape Case

In May 2007, North Carolina Attorney General Roy A. Cooper dismissed rape charges that had been brought against three former members of the Duke University lacrosse team, saying that the players were innocent of all charges. Those charges were brought by Durham County Prosecutor Michael B. Nifong after an exotic dancer who had performed at a house party in 2006 told police she had been raped, sodomized, strangled, and beaten by the partygoers. Contradictions in the accuser's statements, however, along with a lack of DNA and other evidence, convinced Cooper that the attack never occurred. Cooper stated publicly that Nifong should have seen the contradictions himself. Calling Nifong "a rogue prosecutor," Cooper said, "When you have a prosecutor who takes advantage of his enormous power and overreaches like this, then yes, it's offensive."

Nifong, along with the Durham Police Department, relentlessly pursued criminal charges against three Duke University students for the alleged rape of an exotic dancer. The North Carolina attorney general determined that no such crime ever occurred and charges against the students were dismissed.

The case also resulted in public accusations against investigators with the Durham Police Department. Specifically, the methods of the photo identification process were placed into question, and accusations surfaced that police have been known to use intimidation tactics on witnesses and that the police supervisor in the case, Sergeant Mark Gottlieb, has unfairly targeted Duke students in the past.

The majority of criticism came from the police lineup whereby the exotic dancer, Mangum, identified the Duke University students. Lawyers and media reports alike suggested that the photo identification process was severely flawed. For example, during the photo identifications, Mangum was told that she would be viewing Duke University lacrosse players who attended the party, and she was asked if she remembered seeing them at the party and in what capacity. Defense attorneys suggested

|Fig. 2.14| ◢

Former Prosecutor Mike Nifong being scorned by members of the public after evidence was made public that he improperly charged members of the Duke University Lacrosse Team.

Gerry Broome / AP Images

that this was essentially a "multiple-choice test in which there were no wrong answers." U.S. Department of Justice guidelines suggest including at least five non-suspect filler photos for each suspect included.

At least two photo lineups were reported by the media. In the March identification process, Mangum selected at least five different individuals, one of whom was Reade Seligmann (whom she identified with 70 percent certainty). During the April identification process, Mangum identified at least 16 lacrosse players. She identified Seligmann and Finnerty with 100 percent certainty and Dave Evans with 90 percent certainty during the April identification procedure. In the disclosed report, there were only two individuals that she identified during both the March and April lineups—Brad Ross and Reade Seligmann.

Ross (the only player she identified as attending the party with 100 percent certainty during both procedures) provided to police investigators indisputable evidence through cell phone records and a sworn affidavit from a witness that he was with his girlfriend at North Carolina State University before, during, and after the party. Another person Mangum identified in April also provided police with evidence that he did not attend the party at all. In regard to Seligmann's identification, Mangum's confidence increased from 70 percent in March to 100 percent in April.

Gary Wells, an Iowa State University professor and expert on police identification procedures, replied that memory does not get better with time. According to the transcript of the photo identification released on The Abrams Report, Mangum also stated that Dave Evans had a mustache on the night of the attack. Dave Evans' lawyer stated that his client has never had a mustache and that photos as well as eyewitness testimony would reveal that Dave Evans has never had a mustache.

These examples of how investigators conducted their investigation show how police can be blinded and mistakenly led by a prosecutor whose "tunnel vision" blinds them to all available evidence.

One day later, Cooper dismissed the criminal charges. Nifong apologized to the students, saying, "To the extent that I made judgments that ultimately prove to be incorrect, I apologize to the three students that were wrongly accused." He added, "I also understand that when someone has been wrongly accused, the harm caused by the accusations might not be immediately undone by merely dismissing them. . . ." Calls for further action against Nifong led to his being disbarred in 2007 after an ethics hearing by the North Carolina Bar Association. He was later found guilty of criminal contempt of court and spent only one day in jail.

Thematic questions

1. Given what we know about the Duke Lacrosse investigation, in what ways should criminal investigators have changed their tactics to ensure a fair and objective investigation?
2. How does the investigative process in this case contribute to the wrongful prosecution of Duke Lacrosse defendants?

3. Given the discretion of a prosecutor to file criminal charges, to what extent is it proper for a criminal investigator to speak up whenever he or she feels that the prosecutor is abusing their authority?

Sources: David Barstow and Duff Wilson. As Duke rape case unravels, D.A.'s judgment questioned: Defense describes him as willing to skirt law for conviction. *San Francisco Chronicle,* December 24, 2006; Benjamin, N. and A. Blythe.Easley awaiting Nifong resignation. *News and Observer,* June 16, 2007. Available at http://www.sfgate.com/news/article/As-Duke-rape-case-unravels-D-A-s-judgment-2482639.php; http://www.newsobserver.com/news/story/607879.html; Biesecker, M., B. Niolet, and J. Neff. DA on the spot for comments. *The News & Observer,* April 22, 2006; Digital image of 33 page Amended Complaint, as filed; Graham, D. State bar finds Nifong guilty on 27 counts of misconduct. *The Duke Chronicle,* June 16, 2007. Available at http://media.www.dukechronicle.com/media/storage/paper884/news/2007/06/14/News/State.Bar.Finds.Nifong.Guilty.On.27.Counts.Of.Misconduct-2915504.shtml; Neff, J. Quest to convict hid a lack of evidence. *The News and Observer,* March 14, 2007. Available at http://www.sfgate.com/news/article/As-Duke-rape-case-unravels-D-A-s-judgment-2482639.php; Nifong will be disbarred for ethics violations. *Associated Press,* June 18, 2007. Available at http://www.msnbc.msn.com/id/19264396/; Parker, L. Disbarment may not be end for Nifong. *USA Today,* June 19, 2007. Available at http://www.usatoday.com/news/nation/2007-06-17; Pressure on Nifong in Duke case: Misstatements may cost him his career, *The News & Observer,* December 24, 2006; Available at http://news.findlaw.com/hdocs/docs/duke/ncbnifong12407cmp.html.

Summary Checklist

In this chapter, we consider the ways that information about crimes is documented by the criminal investigator. A properly documented case is one that is more likely to succeed in court. See how well you are able to answer the following questions in your checklist.

1. **Describe the usefulness of field notes.**

An investigator's field notes are his or her most personal and readily available record of the crime scene search. They may be the most important steps in initially documenting a crime scene.

- The note-taking process begins as soon as an officer gets a call to the scene of a crime.

- Allow victims and witnesses to state in their own words what occurred. Be sure they answer the who, what, when, where, why, and how of what occurred.

- Key points included in the note-taking process include:

  - Dates, times, and locations

  - Description of victim

  - Wounds on the victim

  - Overall description of the crime scene

  - Notes on photographs taken on the scene

  - Type and location of each piece of evidence

  - Absence of items

- Officers should develop their own systems of note taking but should not move into "shorthand" because field notes may be required later as evidence in court.

Field notes are a means to aid an investigator's recall at the time that he or she prepares the official detailed investigative report.

- Field notes should be stored in a safe place to avoid loss or tampering.

- If a digital recorder is used instead of a notebook, transcripts should be made and the recording media should be protected as evidence.

- Field notes can be required as evidence by the court.

2. **Identify the proper information to be contained in the police report.**

The police report is the formal record of the offense and a record of investigative steps taken to solve the crime. As with field notes, the rule of thumb is to seek answers to the questions who, what, when, why, how, and where. The police report should also be prepared chronologically and factually (i.e., it should contain no personal observations). The police report must also be thorough and to the point. It must be accurate and objective, with facts presented in an unbiased manner.

Key items in a police report include:

- Preliminary information

- Information from victims, witnesses, and others at the crime scene

- Physical evidence

- Modus operandi (method of operation)

3. **How does using digital video to document the crime scene assist investigators?**

The use of digital video at crime scenes has several key advantages:

- Officers can begin recording at the extreme perimeters of the scene and walk closer and closer to the specific objects in question, lending greater perspective to photographs.

- It can be easily used in the courtroom.
- Prosecutors can view the evidence moments after recording.
- The use of the freeze-frame feature allows viewers to stop the recording at a critical point for a closer view of the subject being documented.
- Individual photographs can be made directly from digital video, which may be useful to the investigation or prosecution of the case.

Digital video recordings should be made before still photographs are taken.

4. In what ways do photographs assist in documenting the crime scene?

Photographs are an excellent source of evidence to document the crime scene. They can be either film or digital format, but digital photography is rapidly becoming the standard in crime scene documentation.

The key requirements for admitting a photograph into evidence are:

- Relevance—the photograph will not unduly confuse or deceive the trier of fact
- Authentication—the photograph is accurate and correct

When photographing a crime scene, there can never be too many pictures. Photographs are usually taken in three stages:

- General views—sweeping views of the crime scene area
- Medium-range views—taken from a distance of no greater than 20 feet away from the subject or item being photographed, depicting specific items or objects in the crime scene
- Close-up views—taken at a distance of less than 5 feet, focusing on small segments of a larger surface or on specific items in the scene

Key factors in photographing crime scenes include:

- Perspective
- Suitable lighting
- The use of markers

5. How is the admissibility of photographic evidence in court determined?

The responsibility of determining whether photographs are admissible as evidence is borne by the trial court.

Determinations are based on several legal precedents, including:

- Materiality
- Prejudicial images
- Distorted photos

With regard to video recordings, the courts generally have held that such evidence is admissible on the same basis as motion picture films with sound and is subject to the same rules of evidence as motion pictures and photographic evidence.

6. What benefits are provided by surveillance photographs?

Surveillance photography is used covertly in establishing identities or documenting criminal behavior. It can have many benefits:

- It can aid officers in identifying the physical locations of criminals.
- It can help in formulating a raid plan for serving a search warrant.
- It can record illegal transactions.

Most investigations using surveillance photography are vice and organized crime operations.

7. Why is a crime scene sketch important, especially when investigators can take photographs and videos of the scene?

The crime scene sketch complements photographs and videos and can show certain details better than a photograph. Photographs and videos may distort the dimensions of the crime scene but the crime scene sketch represents the scene as it actually is.

Key issues regarding crime scene sketches include:

- The crime scene sketch is a scale drawing that locates evidence in relation to other factors. Items such as the color of a wall, the type of floor, the general condition of the area, and non-evidential matter are normally not depicted.
- Properly prepared sketches can virtually always be used in court, but photographs that inflame the jury might be excluded from evidence.
- A crime scene sketch can supplement the verbal description to present spatial relationships of the evidence.
- A sketch is an important tool for the prosecutor and can become the central point of courtroom testimony.

Certain items are considered essential in every crime scene sketch, although these are not the only items needed for complete documentation of the scene. The sketch should include:

- The investigator's name and rank
- The date, time, type of crime, and assigned case number
- The complete names of other officers assisting in making the sketch
- The address of the crime scene, its position in a building, landmarks, etc.
- The scale of the drawing
- Primary items of physical evidence and other critical features of the scene
- A key or legend

One general rule is that the sketch should reflect as accurately as possible the important details of the scene. Such information must be recorded uniformly and all measures of distance must be conducted by using the same method.

Two sketches are generally made for every crime scene: a rough sketch and a finished sketch

- The rough sketch is the one drawn by officers on the crime scene and is typically not drawn to scale.
- The finished sketch is a completed sketch drawn to scale from information contained on the rough sketch. It should accurately reflect all measurements indicated on the rough sketch.

Different crime scenes call for the use of different sketching methods:

- The coordinate method uses the practice of measuring an object from two fixed points of reference. One such procedure is the baseline technique, in which a line is drawn between two known points.
- The triangulation method is a bird's-eye view of the scene, utilizing fixed objects from which to measure. This is particularly useful for sketching outdoor crime scenes.
- The cross-projection method is used in indoor crime scenes. It is basically a top-down view of the crime scene, with the walls of the room "folded" down.

Key Terms

baseline technique	digital imaging	initial page
best evidence rule	digital recorder	markers
beyond a reasonable doubt	evidence	method of operation
chain of custody	face sheet	motion
coordinate method	field interview cards	rough sketch
crime scene sketch	field notes	surveillance
cross-projection method	finished sketch	triangulation method

Discussion Questions

1. Discuss the types of information that should be included in an officer's field notes taken at the crime scene.

2. Explain the primary purpose of the official police report and how the three-pronged rule of thumb applies in writing official reports.

3. What are the benefits of using digital video to record a crime scene?

4. Explain the three stages of crime scene photography and why this approach is used.

5. Discuss the key precedents on which determination of admissibility of photographic evidence in court is based.

6. Explain why crime scene sketches are important, even if the scene has been documented using video and photography.

Notes

1. SANFILIPPO, P. J. (2004). Tips on managing the switch from conventional film to digital *Evidence Technology Magazine* 2(5):18–21.

2. TYLER, P. B. (1995). The Kelly-Frye "general acceptance" standard remains the rule for admissibility of novel scientific evidence: *People* v. *Leahy. Pepperdine Law Review.* Malibu, CA: Pepperdine University School of Law.

3. SCIENTIFIC WORKING GROUP IMAGING TECHNOLOGY (SWGIT). (June 8, 1999). *Definitions and guidelines for the use of imaging technologies in the criminal justice system.* Federal Bureau of Investigation; INTERNATIONAL ASSOCIATION OF IDENTIFICATION. (1997). *1997 Resolution and legislative committee, Resolution 97–9.*

4. CRIME SCENE INVESTIGATION. (January 2000). *A guide for Law Enforcement: Research report.* National Institute of Justice. U.S. Government Printing Office.

5. IBID.

6. FOX, R. H. AND C. L. CUNNINGHAM. (1989). *Crime scene search and physical evidence handbook.* Washington, DC: U.S. Department of Justice.

7. CRIME SCENE INVESTIGATION. (2000). *A guide for Law Enforcement.*

CHAPTER 3

ASSOCIATED PRESS

This chapter will enable you to:

1. Describe the preliminary investigation.

2. Describe the different types of evidence and correct methods for collecting and handling evidence.

3. Explain the methods for identifying, locating, and interviewing witnesses.

4. Describe how to properly prepare crime scene reports.

5. Describe the proper ways of conducting a crime scene search.

Processing the Crime Scene

Introduction

On the morning of September 8, 2011, Yale University doctoral student Annie Le left her apartment and took Yale Transit to the Sterling Hall of Medicine on the Yale campus. Around 10:00 A.M., she walked from Sterling Hall to another campus building at 10 Amistad Street, where her research laboratory was located. Le had left her purse, cell phone, credit cards, and cash in her office at Sterling Hall. As documented on footage from the building's security cameras, Le entered the Amistad Street building just after 10:00 A.M. She was never seen leaving the building. On the evening of September 8 at about 9:00 P.M., one of her five housemates called police to report her missing.

Five days later, on September 13, her strangled body was found stuffed inside a wall of a campus lab building. Le had planned to marry Columbia graduate student Jonathan Widawsky on the day her body was found. The investigation into Le's death revealed that she had been placed into the wall upside down, her bra pushed upward toward her head and her panties were pulled down around her ankles. It was also determined that among other injuries, her jaw and one collarbone had been broken at some point before her death. Four days later, on September 17, investigators arrested Raymond J. Clark III, a Yale lab technician who worked in the building. Clark subsequently pleaded guilty to Le's murder and was sentenced to 44 years in prison. In the fall of 2011, both Yale University and the Yale School of Medicine were named as defendants in a civil lawsuit brought by Le's family.

The actions taken by patrol and investigative personnel at a crime scene often determine the success or failure of a criminal investigation. The survival of victims, the apprehension of the perpetrator, and the ultimate outcome of any resulting criminal prosecution may depend entirely upon prompt and proper responses by the officers at the scene. All personnel must understand, and be prepared to carry out correctly, the operational procedures established by the department for the management of crime scenes. Police officers responding to a crime scene have several important responsibilities. They must:

- Be prepared to inform superiors of their findings
- Assist victims
- Secure and protect the crime scene
- Apprehend the perpetrator
- Collect and preserve evidence
- Interview witnesses
- Perform other necessary operational functions

Even though some of these tasks may be the responsibility of departmental specialists, every officer in the department should be able to conduct all of these functions properly if called upon

Discuss:
Is it possible for criminal investigators to identify indicators as to whether a person is a possible target for murder? If so, how?

|Fig. 3.1| ▲

Annie Le was a Yale University doctoral student who was murdered on the Yale campus in 2011.

HANDOUT / MCT / Newscom

to do so. Above all, the patrol officers initially responding to the scene must understand that they have a heavy responsibility to ensure that the appropriate actions are taken to protect life and property, preserve evidence, and make it possible for subsequent investigative work to be successful.

Any officer responding to a crime scene must understand that the proper management of a crime scene has at least three distinct aspects: administrative, operational, and legal. The officer must comply with the administrative requirements of the officer's department as to procedures to be followed en route to the scene, while at the scene, and after departure from the scene (e.g., investigative follow-up and submission of reports). From an operational standpoint, the officer must be aware of all applicable departmental policies (e.g., assisting victims, securing the crime scene, collecting evidence, or preserving it in place for collection by others) and must be able to carry out these functions effectively. Furthermore, the officer must be aware of the legal constraints applicable to the conduct of officers regarding crime scenes (e.g., authority to enter a suspected scene, authority to search the scene, authority to arrest or otherwise detain persons found there). This threefold responsibility can be carried out properly only if the department provides adequate guidance through well-crafted crime scene policies and the necessary training to ensure that all officers understand what is expected of them and what they are and are not permitted to do.

The Preliminary Investigation

Evidence of one type or another exists in all crimes. A logical procedure for identifying, collecting, and preserving evidence is therefore essential. The practice of following prescribed steps in the identification and collection of evidence is critical in making an arrest and in subsequent prosecution of the offender. The evidence collection process begins immediately after the discovery of a crime. In most situations, this precursory investigative phase is known as the **preliminary investigation**. Generally, the term *preliminary investigation* is defined as an initial inquiry by officers to establish facts and circumstances of a suspected crime and to preserve any evidence related to that crime. Preliminary investigation includes:

- Securing the crime scene
- Considering the possible arrest of a suspect
- Locating and questioning witnesses and victims
- Documenting the crime scene
- Identifying and collecting evidence

The function of the preliminary investigation is closely linked with the duties of the first officer to arrive at the crime scene (discussed later), who, in most cases, is a respondent from the patrol division. As with any crime scene, the first officer and investigators should consider the scene itself as evidence. This is because much valuable information can be learned from items left on the scene, provided that it has not been tampered with or altered in any way.

The crime scene represents the ultimate situation that places many responsibilities on the first officer arriving at the scene. These include making an arrest, rendering first aid to injured parties, and protecting evidence at the scene. The latter responsibility includes preservation of trace evidence, firearms, and blood or other bodily fluids.

Investigators must remember that a crime scene is a location where evidence of a crime may be found. It is not necessarily where the crime was committed. Consequently, there are primary, secondary, and sometimes tertiary crime scenes. For example, investigators may use a warrant to search a suspect's home. Even though the suspect did not commit the crime at that location, evidence of the crime may be found there. In another instance, an offender might kidnap someone at one location (primary crime scene), transport the victim (the car being a secondary crime scene), commit another crime at a distant location (murder, for instance), and then dispose of the body at a fourth scene.

Crime Scene Evidence

Crime scene evidence is dynamic. Protection and preservation of the scene are therefore crucial because both avert the possibility of contamination, loss, or unnecessary movement of **physical evidence**. In the evidence-collection process, **contamination of evidence** occurs most commonly when evidence is not properly secured, is wrongfully mixed with other types of evidence, or is altered significantly from its original condition at the **crime scene**. When this occurs, the evidence is usually rendered inadmissible or "incompetent" by the court.

The preliminary investigation involves the identification and preservation of evidence, much of which is minute or "trace" evidence. Trace evidence is any type of material left at or taken from a crime scene or the result of contact between two surfaces. Examples are shoes on a floor covering or soil or fibers from where someone sat on an upholstered chair.

When a crime is committed, fragmentary (or trace) evidence needs to be collected from the scene. A team of specialized police technicians go to the scene of the crime and seal it off. They both record video and take photographs of the crime scene, victim (if there is one), and items of evidence. If applicable, they undertake a firearms and ballistics examination. They also check for shoe and tire mark impressions, examine any vehicles, and check for fingerprints.

Each item found as evidence is put into a sterilized container (contrary to popular belief, this is almost never a plastic bag but is actually a paper bag or envelope, which prevents further decomposition of evidence) and labeled for later analysis at the laboratory.

The **Locard exchange principle**, also known as *Locard's Theory* or the **transfer of evidence theory**, was first put forward by a twentieth-century forensic scientist, Edmond Locard. Locard was the director of the first known crime laboratory, located in Lyon, France. Locard's exchange principle states, "With contact between two items, there will be an exchange."[1]

For the most part, Locard's principle is applied to crime scenes where the perpetrator(s) of a crime comes into contact with the scene, so he or she will both bring something into the scene and leave with something from the scene. Every contact leaves a trace. For example, Locard stated:

> Wherever he steps, whatever he touches, whatever he leaves, even unconsciously, will serve as a silent witness against him. Not only his fingerprints or his footprints, but his hair, the fibers from his clothes, the glass he breaks, the tool mark he leaves, the paint he scratches, the blood or semen he deposits or collects. All of these and more, bear mute witness against him. This is evidence that does not forget. It is not confused by the excitement of the moment. It is not absent because human witnesses are. It is factual evidence. Physical evidence cannot be wrong, it cannot perjure itself, it cannot be wholly absent. Only human failure to find it, study and understand it, can diminish its value (Edmond Locard)

An easier way to remember this is, "Every contact leaves a trace."

Material transferred in this fashion is usually referred to as **trace evidence**, which generally refers to minute or even microscopic bits of matter that are not immediately apparent to the naked eye. Consequently, such evidence is extremely difficult to locate at the crime scene. Because of its microscopic nature, the criminal may be far less likely to eliminate it purposely than with more telltale evidence such as blood splattering or fingerprints. As a reminder of the significance of trace evidence, one should remember that serial killers such as Wayne Williams, John Gacy, and Gary Ridgeway (the "Green River Killer") were apprehended as a result of trace evidence or implements of their crimes being found in their possession.[2] Hence, the first officer at the scene bears the critical responsibility of protecting such evidence from contamination.

In criminal investigations, the utility of physical evidence should be clearly understood. Some types of physical evidence are more obvious in nature than others. For example:

- Physical evidence can prove the elements of a crime or reveal that a crime has been committed. *Case example:* A search warrant served on the residence of a suspected drug dealer revealed a quantity of cocaine, scales, paraphernalia, business records showing drug dealing, and large amounts of cash concealed in shoeboxes.
- Physical evidence may be used to place the suspect at the scene. *Case example:* Shoe impressions found in the mud outside a burglary victim's residence were found to match those of a known burglar in the community.
- Physical evidence can be used to eliminate innocent persons. *Case example:* A murderer was careful not to leave fingerprints at the crime scene. However, blood samples taken from the scene later revealed, through DNA typing, the true identity of the perpetrator.
- Suspects confronted with physical evidence may confess to a crime. *Case example:* Although a convenience store robbery suspect was wearing a ski mask at the time of the robbery, he admitted his role in the crime when a hidden-camera shot of him during the crime revealed a recognizable torn edge on the corner of his jacket.
- Witness testimony can be supported with physical evidence. *Case example:* A neighbor told the police that she heard glass breaking at about 1:30 A.M. Investigators later located a broken pane of glass in a nearby house and, through use of the witness's statement, were able to determine the time of the offense.
- Physical evidence can have a powerful positive impact on juries in criminal cases. *Case example:* As the nickel-plated .38-caliber handgun was handed to the first jury member for inspection, fellow jurists leaned forward and watched while anticipating their chance to touch and hold the weapon that the prosecutor claimed was used in the crime.

Types of Evidence

Evidence can also be classified in several distinct ways. Classifications can be considered either individually or in combination with other classes of evidence. In general, there are two commonly used classifications: corpus delicti and associative evidence. The term **corpus delicti** simply refers to evidence that establishes that a crime has been committed, such as pry marks on a doorjamb. Conversely, **associative evidence** links a suspect with a crime, such as fingerprints, footprints, bloodstains, and fibers. Examples of evidence are:

- *Physical evidence.* As a practical matter, physical evidence could be considered as a classification of its own. Physical evidence is self-explanatory in nature and generally speaks for itself in a court of law. Examples are weapons, fingerprints, blood, and drugs. (See Appendix A for a list of types of physical evidence.)
- *Direct or prima facie evidence.* **Prima facie evidence** is evidence established by law that at face value proves a fact in dispute. For example, states establish the minimum blood alcohol content to show that a person is under the influence.
- *Indirect or circumstantial evidence.* Circumstantial evidence merely tends to incriminate a person without offering conclusive proof. For example, although a person's footprint located outside a burglary victim's residence show that the person who left the print was the burglar, it does suggest that he or she could be.
- *Testimonial evidence.* As the term implies, **testimonial evidence** consists of a verbal statement offered by a witness while under oath or affirmation. It may also be evidence offered by way of a sworn pretrial deposition. Although many people define testimony in the same way as evidence, they are clearly distinct. Simply, testimony is evidence offered in an oral manner and is used most commonly to explain some form of physical evidence (e.g., gunpowder residue, fingerprints).
- *Trace evidence.* Trace evidence consists of extremely small items of evidence, such as hair or clothing fibers. With the aid of modern forensic analysis, trace evidence plays a greater role today than ever before in solving capital cases.
- *Demonstrative evidence.* **Demonstrative evidence** is evidence used to demonstrate or clarify an issue rather than to prove something. An example is the use of anatomical dolls to aid in the testimony of children in a sexual molestation case.

Legal Considerations

Officers collecting evidence, or "evidence custodians," must have a good working knowledge of state and federal laws governing the handling and disposition of evidence under their control. As custodians of evidence, they are often called upon to testify concerning their evidence management practices in general and their control over specific items of evidence in particular. As such, evidence custodians should be familiar with the following general federal restrictions on the gathering, preserving, and disposing of evidence, as well as state law and court rulings that may affect their responsibilities.

SEARCH WARRANTS The Fourth Amendment to the U.S. Constitution is the primary constraint on the seizure of property by government agents. A search warrant designating the specific premises to be searched and the specific items to be seized is the basic requirement for law enforcement officers to seize property. The types of property subject to seizure include stolen property, property unlawfully possessed or contraband, property used or possessed for the purpose of being used to commit or conceal the commission of an offense, and property constituting evidence or tending to demonstrate that an offense was committed.

Under certain circumstances, a warrant to search or seize property need not be obtained. Included are searches conducted incident to arrest and those conducted with consent of the individual having authority over the premises, property in "plain view" of the officer making a lawful search even though the property was not named on the search warrant, property uncovered during the lawful "stop and frisk" of a subject, property seized in hot pursuit of a criminal in order to safeguard the officer, and property seized under exigent circumstances in which there is likelihood that it will be destroyed or removed if time is taken to obtain a search warrant.

CONTINUITY OF EVIDENCE A fundamental rule to remember is that evidence in support of an arrest must be preserved untainted by the passage of time. This requirement mandates that the "chain of custody" of the evidence be documented during custody and storage. Innumerable criminal cases have been lost or their prosecution inhibited by failure to observe commonly accepted procedures for the preservation of evidence and maintenance of records regarding personal custody. Because of the singular importance of this aspect of evidence control, it is examined in depth.

CUSTODY AND DISPOSITION Normally, evidence must be held in custody of the law enforcement agency until a prosecutor or similar authority formally issues a release allowing it to

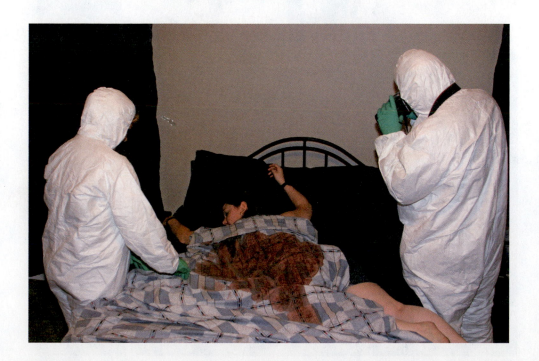

|Fig. 3.2| ▲

When encountering crime scenes such those with biological evidence (homicide scenes) or drug labs (methamphetamine labs) investigators should wear protective gear as shown here to safeguard from blood-borne or airborne contaminants or materials that might be corrosive.

Courtesy of Mike Himmel

be returned to its owner or otherwise disposed of. In certain jurisdictions, release of evidence is guided by statute or case law.

Under other circumstances, however, the custody and release of evidence may be guided by other regulations. Even when no longer needed as evidence in a criminal proceeding, items may be held pursuant to civil forfeiture proceedings under state or federal law. Under the federal Comprehensive Drug Abuse Prevention and Control Act of 1970, Section 511 (a)(6), as amended, 21 U.S.C.A. Section 881 (a)(6), the federal government may seize property for forfeiture as long as there is a substantial connection between the property and illegal drug transactions. Most state forfeiture laws are more restrictive than their federal counterparts.

Evidence in custody may also be subject to other federal or state laws. For example, reacting to public health concerns over the dumping of potentially harmful biological wastes, Congress enacted the 1988 Medical Waste Tracking Act. Although this act addresses the management and tracking of medical wastes in particular, in certain states it also has present and future implications for the disposal of certain biologically contaminated wastes under law enforcement control. This is particularly the case with regard to blood, blood products, and other bodily secretions in vitro; materials contaminated by such fluids; and sharp implements such as knives and IV needles that may also have been contaminated. Law enforcement officers, laboratory technicians, and evidence custodians should be aware of the risks of exposure to HIV and hepatitis B infections through these and related sources and should take the necessary steps to protect themselves and others from exposure. Disposal of these and related waste products should conform to state and federal laws and to procedures set forth by the Centers for Disease Control and Prevention (CDC).[3]

Evidence custodians should also be familiar with federal and any state regulations relating to the handling, storage, transportation, and disposal of chemical wastes. Chemicals seized during drug raids, particularly with regard to clandestine laboratories, can individually or in combination be explosive, toxic, or carcinogenic. At the federal level, the handling of these materials from an employee health and safety standpoint is regulated by provisions of standards CFR 1910.1200 of the Occupational Safety and Health Administration (OSHA). Included in these provisions are requirements that employees be trained in the recognition of chemical health hazards, safe chemical-handling techniques, and first aid. OSHA has also set standards for clothing, equipment, and working conditions in clandestine laboratory-dismantling operations.

|Fig. 3.3| △

Outdoor crime scenes present unique challenges such as the painstaking search for hairs and fibers, which require numerous trained personnel as shown here.

Courtesy of Mike Himmel

The Department of Transportation (DOT), under CFR 49, regulates the carriers of hazardous materials, and the Environmental Protection Agency (EPA), pursuant to CFR Title 40, controls the handling and destruction of hazardous wastes. Law enforcement agencies that are inexperienced with handling these types of chemical wastes should consult their regional office of the **Drug Enforcement Administration (DEA)** or appropriate state or federal agencies for guidance.

RECORDS MAINTENANCE A variety of records are related to the control and management of evidence in custody, many of which vary by state law or local custom. In all cases, however, evidence custodians must take the steps necessary to ensure that these records are properly compiled, organized, and preserved. In so doing, the fulfillment of legally prescribed procedures can be fully documented and referenced as necessary, potential questions concerning the chain of custody and related matters can be readily answered, and cumulative information can be compiled concerning the volume and flow of evidence through the agency's evidence control operation.

The First Officer's Responsibilities

The initial response to a call by the responding officer is a critical phase of any criminal investigation. This response is usually made by patrol officers, who must be prepared to initiate a preliminary investigation and carry out the functions discussed below until they are relieved by superior officers or specialists (e.g., detectives or crime scene specialists) who then assume responsibility for their specific functions at the scene. Unfortunately, improper actions by responding patrol officers can cause a loss of evidence or otherwise so prejudice an investigation that a subsequent successful criminal prosecution becomes impossible. Furthermore, in some instances, improper initial actions may result in aggravation of injuries to victims, endangerment of other officers, and even loss of life. Therefore, the responding officers must be prepared to carry out the following initial actions promptly and correctly.

In certain situations, it may not be possible to perform the actions described below in the order in which they are listed. However, all of the actions discussed below, when appropriate, should be taken as soon as circumstances permit.

1. ***Actions while en route to the crime scene.*** While en route to the location, officers must be alert to the possible presence of perpetrators or perpetrators' vehicles fleeing from the scene. Although actions taken to detain suspicious vehicles or persons must comply with legal requirements for investigative detention and arrest, the information furnished to the responding units by the dispatcher or by other officers normally provides sufficient "reasonable suspicion" to justify detention of persons or vehicles found in or leaving the crime scene area. In addition, the suspects' own conduct (e.g., suspicious appearance or behavior, traffic violations) may provide grounds for an investigatory stop. Although the opportunity to apprehend a perpetrator while en route to the crime scene may not arise in a large percentage of cases, officers while en route to the location of a crime should always be alert for such possibilities.

2. ***Initial actions upon arrival.*** Upon arrival at the location, officers should, if possible, first verify that a crime has been committed. In many instances, it will be obvious that a crime has been committed or that, at the very least, there is sufficient evidence to justify further investigation. However, officers should be aware that, unless the circumstances are sufficient to justify a reasonable belief that a major crime has occurred or is occurring within a dwelling or that some other exigent situation exists, they may not enter that dwelling without a warrant. To do so risks subsequent suppression of evidence and possible civil liability. Even when circumstances do not justify an immediate entry, officers may remain outside to protect the premises

Actions of the First Officer

1 En route to the crime scene, be alert to perpetrators or perpetrators' vehicles fleeing from the scene.

2 Upon arrival, verify that a crime has been committed.

3 Assist victims and protect witnesses and bystanders.

4 Arrest the perpetrator.

5 Follow-up communications with headquarters.

6 Identify witnesses and vehicles.

7 Brief investigators and superiors.

|Fig. 3.4| ◢

Actions of the first officer.

Courtesy of Mike Himmel

while additional information or a warrant is obtained. Reasonable belief that a crime has been or is being committed may be based on such various factors as information from dispatchers, statements provided by neighbors upon arrival, physical aspects of the scene (e.g., broken windows or doors), or sounds from the premises indicating that a crime is in progress within (e.g., screams, gun shots).

Deciding whether or not to enter premises where a crime may have been committed is often difficult. Such entries are considered "searches," and often the police on the scene must make an on-the-spot decision under borderline circumstances. Although each case is different and state or local law may vary, in general it may be said that under "exigent" (i.e., emergency) circumstances, officers are permitted to enter any premises, even using force if necessary, without a warrant and conduct a "protective" search of the premises when the officers have **reasonable grounds** to believe that a person within the premises is in immediate need of assistance or a perpetrator is present.[4]

Officers entering premises under these circumstances are not permitted to search the premises for evidence. The "protective search" is limited by law to a "sweep" of the premises to discover victims or perpetrators. Any search beyond the scope of a protective sweep requires a search warrant. However, if in the course of the protective sweep, evidence is discovered in plain view, it may be seized without a warrant or noted for later removal after a warrant has been obtained.

Whenever possible, verification of a crime at the location, or the responding officers' reasonable suspicion thereof, should be communicated immediately to the dispatcher or superiors so that decisions can be made regarding backup, entry into the structure, dispatch of medical assistance or crime scene specialists to the location, and so on. Failing to communicate promptly may endanger victims, the responding officers, and all subsequent aspects of the investigation.[5]

In many instances, circumstances do not permit transmission of complete information at the time of the initial arrival at the scene. In that event, follow-up communications should be made to provide the necessary additional information. (See "Follow-up communications.")

3. ***Assistance to victims and protection of witnesses and bystanders.*** Administering first aid to and summoning medical assistance for any victims present must be a top priority of responding officers. If the victim(s) is still in danger, either from the perpetrator or from other circumstances (e.g., fire), immediate steps must be taken to ensure the victim's safety. Similar protection must be rendered to witnesses and other bystanders. However, unless the bystanders are in danger or circumstances otherwise make it necessary, the officers should avoid ordering bystanders from the scene until it has been determined which, if any, of the bystanders is also a witness or potential witness to some aspect of the crime.

4. Arrest of the perpetrator. If the perpetrator is at the scene and probable cause for arrest exists or an arrest warrant has been issued, the perpetrator should be arrested in accordance with departmental policy and local law. If officers need to leave the scene to effect the arrest (e.g., the perpetrator is fleeing from the scene and must be pursued by officers), the officers must determine whether it is appropriate to leave the crime scene at that time. Conflicting considerations are often present in such circumstances. For example, the officers must balance the need to remain on the scene to render assistance to victims or to protect others from harm against the risk to the public if the perpetrator escapes. Ideally, sufficient personnel will be available to perform both functions simultaneously; if not, the officers present must decide where the priorities lie. Circumstances will dictate the decision, but in general, protecting the crime scene, any victims present, and the witnesses and bystanders will be the first consideration. Other units may then be alerted to pursue the fleeing perpetrator.

5. ***Follow-up communications.*** As noted above, initial communication at the time of the officers' arrival at the crime scene is essential. However, circumstances may not permit the responding officers to furnish complete information to their headquarters at that point. Further communications should be made to provide, at a minimum, the following information:

Superiors must be informed of the apparent nature of the offense discovered by the officers. When possible, reports should be factual in nature. When it is necessary to state opinions or conclusions in such transmissions, these opinions or conclusions should be supported by the known facts. Approved departmental codes may be used when appropriate.[6] If the exact nature or seriousness of the crime cannot yet be determined, the possibility of the more serious offense should be made clear in the transmission.

If the perpetrator has fled the scene, a full description of the perpetrator, together with any information regarding the perpetrator's mode and direction of flight, should be communicated as soon as possible. If there were accomplices, similar information about them should be included. Likewise, if a vehicle was involved either in the commission of the crime or in the flight of the perpetrators from the scene, this information should also be communicated.

If the perpetrators are known or believed to be armed, it is especially important that this information be transmitted as soon as possible. Any information available regarding the number and nature of the weapons possessed by the perpetrators should be provided. This permits other officers who may encounter the perpetrators to assess the threat level and proceed appropriately.

If not already requested during the initial transmission, support units may be requested during follow-up communications.

6. *Identification of witnesses and vehicles.* The identification and preliminary interviewing of witnesses are extremely important considerations for officers arriving at a crime scene. These functions are discussed in detail below.

License numbers and descriptions of vehicles parked in the area should be noted. In addition, the license number and description of any vehicle moving through the area in a slow, repeated, or otherwise suspicious manner should be recorded.

Officers should also be alert for suspicious persons who, although not present in the immediate vicinity of the crime scene, are observed in the general area. Such persons should be approached; identified; and, if circumstances justify it, detained for further investigation.

7. *Briefing investigators and superiors.* Officers should be prepared to brief investigators and other authorized personnel when they arrive on the scene. All information gathered, together with a summary of the actions taken by the responding officers up to that time, should be provided. Unfortunately, experience shows that in many instances, valuable information known to the officers making the initial response is not communicated to detectives, superiors, or other personnel. Responding officers should therefore make it a point to communicate all known facts accurately and completely to investigators or other authorized persons arriving on the scene.

Broadcasting a Flash Description

Additional preliminary duties may include the broadcasting of a **flash description** of the suspect and the suspect's vehicle (also called a BOLO—"be on the lookout"). If able to determine certain facts about possible suspects, weapons, and vehicles, the responding officer should put out a flash description to other officers in case the suspects are still in the vicinity. Flash descriptions vary in nature, depending on the specific law enforcement agency. Generally, they should be precise and to the point. The flash description consists of the following information:

1. The type of crime, location of crime, and time of occurrence
2. The number of suspects involved in the crime
3. The physical description of those involved:

   - Gender
   - Race
   - Age
   - Height
   - Weight
   - Eye color
   - Hair color
   - Style or type of hair
   - Length of hair
   - Facial hair, if any
   - Clothing description
   - Other outstanding physical characteristics (e.g., tattoos, scars)

4. Weapons used
5. Direction in which the suspect was last observed proceeding and how long ago
6. Means of escape (mention any possible route that suspects may take)
7. If anyone was wounded.

8. Any vehicle used. When broadcasting flash descriptions of vehicles, remember the CYMBL rule:

C: color
Y: year
M: make, model
B: body style
L: license number

Managing Emergency Situations

Unless a life-threatening situation or other exigent circumstances exist, the responding officer must attend to any injured party. Because the preservation of human life is a fundamental premise of public safety, this responsibility should take priority over apprehension of the suspect. If the situation calls for summoning emergency personnel, it should be done immediately. As soon as emergency personnel arrive on the scene, the officer should instruct them carefully on how to enter the scene without causing damage to the evidence at the scene. This must be done in a manner that does not impede the responsibilities of emergency personnel.

Securing the Scene

One of the more important functions of responding officers is to ensure that neither their actions nor the actions of others will disturb the crime scene unnecessarily. Much too often, criminal evidence and many criminal cases have been lost because the crime scene was not adequately secured and protected. Protecting the crime scene has always been essential to good police work, and this is doubly true today because scientific evidence analysis techniques are becoming an increasingly important part of criminal investigations. Unnecessary or improper entry into the crime scene may:

- Destroy or contaminate important evidence.
- Introduce items or substances into the crime scene that may mislead investigators.
- Provide defense attorneys with a basis for discrediting the investigators or the findings of a crime laboratory.

For these reasons, the following principles should be observed. The responding officers should enter the crime scene only for the limited purposes of:

- Determining that a crime has been committed
- Aiding victims
- Apprehending perpetrators
- Securing the area

Unless circumstances or departmental policies dictate otherwise, after these initial functions have been performed, the responding officers should thereafter avoid entering the crime scene and prevent others from doing so until superiors, detectives, or crime scene specialists relieve the responding officers of that responsibility.

Although, as mentioned above, responding officers must often enter the crime scene to perform their essential preliminary functions, every entry into a crime scene area has the potential to destroy evidence and introduce irrelevant substances into the scene. Therefore, even when entering the crime scene to perform necessary actions as described above, responding officers should, to the greatest extent possible, avoid touching or moving objects at the scene or entering areas where entry is unnecessary to accomplish the above-stated purposes. In addition, whenever possible, the crime scene should be entered only by one narrowly defined route to avoid the destruction of evidence, the contamination of possible scent trails, and so on.

In addition to keeping their encroachment upon the crime scene to a minimum, officers should also carefully note the portions of the scene through which they have passed, the routes

|Fig. 3.5| ▲

One of the most important tasks in investigating a crime scene is to keep onlookers away. This preserves evidence for retrieval and protects the scene from contamination.

Corepics VOF / Cutcaster Images

taken, the objects they have touched, and any other actions they have taken that may have altered or tainted the scene. This information will assist investigators in determining the original state of the crime scene and will enable them to disregard matters that are not relevant to the crime itself.

After the responding officers have completed their preliminary examination of the scene, the scene should be secured to protect it from encroachment by unauthorized persons. This is not always a simple task, and circumstances may dictate what can and cannot be done. However, in general, the following actions should be taken:

1. ***The area to be declared a crime scene must be defined.*** This includes any portion of the premises that may reasonably be anticipated to contain useful evidence. Although it is often impossible to cordon off all of the surrounding areas that might conceivably hold such evidence, the area designated as a crime scene should be as large as the circumstances require or permit. Remember that it is always a better practice to secure a larger area and narrow it down than to identify a small scene and attempt to expand it at a later time.

    The seriousness of the crime, the location of the crime, the nature of the surrounding environment, the amount of manpower available to maintain a perimeter, and similar factors determine the definition and extent of the crime scene in a given case. The specific nature of the suspected crime may also dictate the definition of the crime scene. For example, in a homicide case, the place where the body is found is obviously considered the crime scene, even though the actual death may later be determined to have occurred elsewhere; in the case of a suspected kidnapping, the place where the victim was last seen should be regarded as a crime scene and treated accordingly. If the perpetrator has fled or a victim or other significant person is believed to be missing from the scene, the widest possible area should be protected to preserve any evidence present, including any possible scent trails leading away from the immediate scene.

2. ***Backup should be requested to help restrict access to the defined crime scene and to control onlookers.*** Only rarely will one or two responding officers be able to maintain complete control of a crime scene by themselves. Assistance should be obtained quickly before others encroach upon the scene and evidence is lost.

3. ***The interior of the crime scene area should be cleared.*** Persons other than law enforcement officers or other officials actively engaged in crime scene duties should be removed from the

Securing a Crime Scene

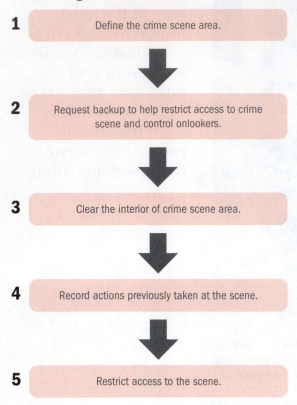

1 Define the crime scene area.

2 Request backup to help restrict access to crime scene and control onlookers.

3 Clear the interior of crime scene area.

4 Record actions previously taken at the scene.

5 Restrict access to the scene.

|Fig. 3.6| ▲

Securing a crime scene.

premises.[7] The crime scene should be secured by the use of tape, rope, barricades, locks, or other appropriate measures. After the crime scene has been secured, access to the scene should be restricted to authorized personnel.

4. ***Record actions previously taken at the scene.*** Responding officers should note and record any alterations that may have occurred to the crime scene due to their own activities or the activities of personnel rendering emergency assistance to victims. In addition, officers should determine if any actions of the persons reporting the crime or of other persons present on the scene before the arrival of the officers may have altered or tainted the crime scene in any way. In particular, actions involving moving or otherwise disturbing the victim's body should be noted. All of this information should be communicated to investigators, superiors, or both at the earliest possible opportunity.

5. ***Restrict access to the scene.*** After the crime scene has been defined, cleared, and secured, access to the scene should be limited to authorized personnel directly involved in the investigation. In the case of major crimes, the identities of all persons entering the perimeter should be recorded, and, if possible, the times at which they entered and left the scene should be noted. Attempts by news media personnel, nonessential city or county officials, and others to gain access to the scene should be referred to the supervisor in charge of the scene or other officer designated to handle requests for entry.[8] When a decision is made to allow any such persons to have access to the scene, they should be escorted by an officer during the period of their entry to prevent their taking any action that might result in the loss of evidence or otherwise endanger the investigation. In this regard, a "contamination log" should also be kept to document all persons entering the scene.[9]

Handling Special Situations at the Scene

Myriad situations may present themselves to officers at a crime scene, so they should be able to adapt to different circumstances. The key in the preliminary investigation is for the responding officer to maintain control. Examples include the following:

Dead Body

In the event that a body is located on the scene, the officer must make a precursory determination of the cause of death or injury. In an obvious cause of death, certain signs may be evident. Such indications may include odor or early stages of decomposition of the body. Other signs include postmortem lividity or rigor mortis. In any case, the body should not be touched, moved, or tampered with until investigators arrive. On discovery of a dead body, supervisors should be notified immediately as to the nature of the scene.

Hanging Victim

In the case of a person found hanging, the body should generally not be moved at all (also see Chapter 9 on wrongful death). Careful attention to protect the knot on the noose is important because many investigative leads may be developed from rope or other materials used as a ligature. If, however, the responding officer finds it necessary to cut down the deceased, the rope should be cut far above the knot so the knot can be preserved for examination. In this case, care should be taken to support the body as best as possible so that there is no additional damage to the body upon impact with the floor or ground. Critical attention should be given to all evidence in hanging cases because the appearance of suicide may actually be a cover-up for a murder.

Firearms

Generally speaking, all objects at the crime scene should remain untouched, particularly firearms, bullets, and shell casings. Additionally, the first officer at the scene must remember that he or she, too, can be a valuable source of physical evidence. For example, ballistics experts commonly testify that shells found at the scene of a homicide match the corresponding markings on a shell test fired from the defendant's revolver.

Accordingly, experts may also testify that an empty shotgun shell casing found at the scene of a homicide was fired from the defendant's shotgun. Such a statement can be made based on breech-face markings on the shell developed through macrophotography. In many cases, however, such evidence is difficult to find and may not be discovered until after the body or other evidence has been removed. Officers searching for firearms should remember that shell casings should be nearby. Both types of evidence are extremely valuable. Fingerprints, for example, may exist on a weapon in the oils present on the weapon. Great care should be exercised in this case to preserve such evidence.

When seizing a handgun as evidence, officers should never attempt to pick up the weapon by inserting a pen or pencil into the barrel. This could damage or destroy valuable evidence such as blood or fibers deposited inside the barrel, which could later be retrieved by specialists. Generally, the prescribed way for officers to move a handgun is to pick it up using two fingers on the textured part of the grip where no fingerprints can be removed.

Other considerations are that officers must never adjust the safety catch, unload, or alter the condition of the weapon in any fashion until a complete examination has been performed. Only after investigators inspect and properly mark the position of the cylinder can the weapon be unloaded. Officers should remember that the weapon and all related objects must remain in exactly the same condition as they were found. Weapons, of course, should always be properly documented through photos and sketching before they are moved.

Discovery of Human Remains

It is common that body parts are discovered by citizens or government workers, or through other sources. When such discoveries are made, investigators must respond immediately and follow all recommended protocols for protecting the scene and keeping curious onlookers, family members, and members of the media away from the scene. Depending on where the remains

|Fig. 3.7| △

The discovery of a skull presents a number of sources of evidence. In addition to the obvious indication that the remains are nearby, the teeth often provide invaluable forensic evidence.

lipowski / Fotolia

are located, they could have been exposed to inclement weather, wild animals, or other sources of contamination. Whatever evidence is still available may still be salvageable and can provide leads for the investigator. In many cases, where bones are discovered, should the law enforcement agency have a forensic anthropologist available, he or she should be requested to come to the scene to assist in identifying bones.

Aquatic Body Recovery

The discovery of a deceased person in a body of water presents unique challenges for the investigator. As with any potential crime scene, great care must be taken to preserve, record, and collect the evidence. A description or record of the crime scene is made and a thorough search is made for evidence. The body itself is wrapped in a body bag and key areas, such as the hands, are wrapped up separately to preserve potential evidence.

Collecting Electronic Evidence

The Internet, computer networks, and automated data systems present many new opportunities for committing criminal activity.[10] Computers and other electronic devices are increasingly used to commit, enable, or support crimes perpetrated against people, organizations, money, and property. Whether the crime involves attacks against computer systems—or the information they contain—or more traditional offenses such as murder, laundering, drug trafficking, or fraud, **electronic evidence** is increasingly important.

It could be said that electronic evidence is information and data of investigative value that is stored in or transmitted by an electronic device. Such evidence is often required when physical items such as computers, removable disks, CDs, DVDs, magnetic tape, flash memory chips, cellular telephones, personal digital assistants, and other electronic devices are collected from a crime scene or are obtained from a suspect.

Electronic evidence has special characteristics: (1) it is latent; (2) it can transcend national and state borders quickly and easily; (3) it is fragile and can easily be altered, damaged, compromised, or destroyed by improper handling or improper examination; and (4) it *may not be* time sensitive. Similar to DNA and fingerprints, electronic surveillance is **latent evidence** because it is not readily visible to the human eye under normal conditions. Special equipment and software are required to "see" and evaluate electronic evidence. In the courtroom, expert testimony may be needed to explain the acquisition of electronic evidence and the examination process used to interpret it.

|Fig. 3.8| △

Police divers recovering a dead body from the seabed. The body is being raised to the surface using buoyancy aids (not seen) that are attached to a stretcher.

James Messerschmidt / Polaris / Newscom

Investigator's Checklist: Crime Scene Equipment

☑ *Surveillance equipment.* Night vision equipment, listening devices.

☑ *Cameras.* The digital camera has surpassed the 35-mm camera as the photographic tool of choice for crime scene documentation. Both cameras and editing software have now become affordable for even the smallest departments. Digital video cameras are another recent innovation in crime scene documentation, offering the best evidence of crimes in progress and fresh crime scene evidence. Camera accessories such as lenses, tripods, and lighting attachments may be required for unusual crime scenes.

☑ *Lights.* Handheld flashlight (e.g., Streamlight), emergency flashing strobes instead of vehicle fog lights, handheld floodlights for crime scenes.

☑ *Notebook.* Sketching material for producing rough sketches while on the scene. Writing aids such as pencils, pens, and markers must be available.

☑ *Other materials.* Tape measures (both cloth and metal), evidence tape, a carpenter-type ruler, eraser, chalk, tweezers, scissors, labels, tongue depressors, a clipboard, and outdoor and indoor templates.

☑ *Containers.* Envelopes, boxes, plastic and paper bags, and glass bottles of all sizes and shapes.

☑ *First aid kit.* To treat injured parties at the scene.

☑ *Casting material.* Plaster or dental stone to make casts (e.g., pry marks, footprints).

In 2002, in recognition of the special challenges posed by electronic evidence, the Computer Crime and Intellectual Property section of the Criminal Division of the U.S. Department of Justice released a how-to manual for law enforcement officers called *Searching and Seizing Computers and Obtaining Electronic Evidence in Criminal Investigations*.

About the same time, the Technical Working Group for Electronic Crime Scene Investigation (TWGECSI) released a detailed guide for law enforcement officers to use in gathering electronic evidence. The manual *Electronic Crime Scene Investigation: A Guide for First Responders* grew out of a partnership formed in 1998 between the National Cybercrime Training Partnership, the Office of Law Enforcement Standards, and the National Institute of Justice. The working group was asked to identify, define, and establish basic criteria to assist federal and state agencies in handling electronic investigations and related prosecutions.

TWGECSI guidelines specify that law enforcement must take special precautions when documenting, collecting, preserving, and examining electronic evidence to maintain its integrity. The guidelines also note that the first law enforcement officer on the scene should take steps to ensure the safety of everyone at the scene and to protect the integrity of all evidence, both traditional and electronic.

Biohazardous Materials

All crime evidence rooms must be equipped to maintain evidence from crimes contaminated by bodily secretions such as blood, semen, urine, and feces. In addition, evidence rooms are generally required to secure laboratory samples and similar items that have been or will be tested. Wherever blood is apparent, there is the potential for infection by HIV (AIDS) and hepatitis B virus as well as other blood-borne diseases. To ensure the highest degree of safety, one should assume that all items contaminated with human or other animal secretions are potential sources of infection and should take steps necessary to protect themselves and others who may come into contact with the items.

Under normal circumstances, evidence custodians should not allow contaminated materials to be brought into the evidence room unless they have been adequately packaged beforehand. Evidence custodians should retain the prerogative of refusing to accept materials that are not properly packaged. Any biohazardous materials should be double bagged in secure plastic bags, taped or secured by adhesives (never stapled), and labeled as a biohazardous material. To avoid reducing its evidentiary value, soaked clothing should be air dried before being bagged. As noted, however, organic matter containing moisture to any degree may be subject to decay if sealed in a nonporous container. Such items should be packaged in porous containers so they can breathe.

In cases in which items must be inventoried at or after intake at the evidence room, "universal precautions"—as prescribed by the CDC for prevention of exposure to HIV and hepatitis B viruses should be closely followed.[11] At a minimum, during inventories, disposable rubber gloves should be worn; cuts or abrasions should be covered by bandages or dressing; hand contact with the mouth, eyes, or nose should be avoided; and smoking, eating, drinking, and applying makeup should not be permitted. The handling of needles and other sharp objects should require the wearing of leather gloves over disposable rubber gloves. Cleanup of any areas, such as counters, tabletops, or equipment that may have come in contact with contaminated items, should be performed using a diluted chlorine bleach solution of one part chlorine to 10 parts water. In all cases after dealing with such materials, one should thoroughly wash any exposed skin surfaces with hot running water and soap for at least 15 seconds before drying. Any contaminated clothing should be carefully removed as soon as practicable, separated from noncontaminated linens, and laundered in water at least 160°F for 25 minutes. Latex gloves should be rinsed before removal, and hands and arms should then be cleansed in the prescribed manner. All sharp instruments, such as knives, razors, scissors, and broken glass, should be encased before being enclosed in the evidence envelope, and the exterior of the envelope should indicate that a sharp object is enclosed. In most cases, contaminated samples that may require laboratory analysis should not be encased directly in plastic because of the possibility of contaminating the evidence. Other packaging material is often required, and laboratory technicians should be consulted for instructions.

Evidence samples that may be subject to DNA testing must be kept in a frozen state to avoid deterioration, and samples destined for blood typing and certain other forensic tests should be refrigerated. A freezer and a refrigerator are required in nearly all evidence rooms for this type of evidence as well as for any perishable products that must be stored for evidentiary purposes.

The handling and packaging of hypodermic needles and syringes have become common tasks for many officers and evidence custodians in the wake of increased narcotics use on the street. Most plastic or paper evidence containers are not puncture-proof, so particular care must be taken to avoid needle sticks. Some agencies use flexible plastic tubes with screw-on or pressure tops for this purpose, although some of these have been subject to leakage. Puncture-resistant containers for used syringes and needles can be purchased from medical supply distributors or local hospitals. A special device has recently been introduced into the market that is a tube constructed of seamless, heavy-gauge transparent polypropylene in two parts with a mechanical seal joining the two halves. It is long enough to accommodate most syringes, even with the plungers extended; comes in a small plastic bag with instructions for use; and is affixed with a label for recording the officer's name, assignment, and case number.

Chemical and Other Hazardous Wastes

Most chemical agents are seized by law enforcement officers in connection with clandestine drug manufacturing operations. Enforcement actions against these operations require specialized training and equipment to avoid the dangers of fire; explosions; and contact with caustic, corrosive, toxic, or carcinogenic substances. As discussed earlier, the occupational and environmental dangers associated with these chemicals have caused federal and state regulatory agencies to impose strict standards for the handling, transportation, storage, and disposal of these substances. The DEA requires that all its agents, chemists, and task force officers who deal with clandestine laboratories be certified by a special safety school. State and local law enforcement officers should not conduct raids on or make arrests within suspected clandestine laboratories without proper training and equipment. Before conducting any such raid, officers without this training and equipment should consult the regional office of the DEA or a properly trained and outfitted enforcement unit of their state or local government.

A chemist or other qualified individual should always be available when conducting enforcement operations on clandestine laboratories. These are the appropriate individuals for making decisions on the packaging, transportation, and storage of all chemical substances. Normally, chemicals should not be housed in evidence storage rooms and require specialized offsite storage facilities. Chemicals seized during the investigation of environmental crimes or under other circumstances should also not be moved or otherwise handled until assistance can be obtained from a hazardous materials (HAZMAT), or similarly qualified, unit. The same precautions should be followed for the handling, transportation, or storage of potentially explosive and other dangerous substances.

Assessing the Crime Scene

To the extent practical, the investigator in charge should develop a plan for processing the crime scene. The plan should include information learned from any responding officers as well as observations and information known to the investigator. Crime scene assessment includes the following steps:

1. Evaluate measures and steps that have been taken to include safety procedures, perimeter security and access control, the adequacy of investigative resources, whether witnesses and suspects have been identified, and the degree to which preliminary documentation of the crime scene has been made.
2. Conduct a crime scene walk-through in cooperation with the first responder and individuals responsible for processing the crime scene to identify any threats to crime scene integrity and begin an initial identification of evidence.
3. Determine the need for a search warrant before collection of evidence.
4. Assess the overall crime scene before evidence collection to develop a plan for working within the crime scene without unnecessarily destroying or contaminating evidence.
5. Identify evidence collection and document team members, including specialists such as odontologists, bomb technicians, arson investigators, entomologists, and fingerprint technicians.
6. Identify protective equipment and clothing that are required to safely process the crime scene.
7. Identify a separate area, if necessary, for equipment and personnel staging and for gathering and sanitizing tools, equipment, and personal protective gear between evidence collections.
8. Assign one officer whose primary responsibility is recording and collecting items of evidence. This will increase efficiency, establish the chain of custody, help prevent loss, and reduce the number of officers who must appear in court.
9. Determine the evidence search method to be used and the point(s) at which the search will begin and establish a working route around the scene to minimize disruption and contamination.
10. Develop, in cooperation with crime scene technician(s) or other trained personnel, a collection plan for identified items of evidence detailing the process and the order of collection.

   - Focus initially on easily accessible areas in open view and work outward.
   - Select a systematic search pattern.
   - Select the best progression of processing and collection so as not to compromise subsequent processing and evidence collection efforts.

Conducting the "walk-through"

The crime scene "walk-through" is a crucial part of the crime scene investigation. It provides an overview of the entire scene, identifies any threats to scene integrity, and ensures protection of physical evidence. Written and photographic documentation provides a permanent record.[12]

The walk-through is conducted by the investigator(s) in charge. They should also be accompanied by CSI personnel who are responsible for processing the scene. During the course of the **crime scene walkthrough**, the investigator(s) in charge should avoid contaminating the scene by using the established path of entry. They should also prepare preliminary documentation of the scene as observed. Additionally, the investigator should identify and protect fragile and/or perishable evidence (e.g., climatic conditions, crowds/hostile environment) and ensure that all evidence that may be compromised is immediately documented, photographed, and collected.

In summary, conducting a scene walk-through provides the investigator(s) in charge with an overview of the entire scene. It provides the first opportunity to identify valuable and/or fragile evidence and determine initial investigative procedures, providing for a systematic examination and documentation of the scene. Written and photographic documentation records the condition of the scene as first observed, providing a permanent record.

Beginning the Search

After an investigator has documented a crime scene, the actual search must begin. Generally speaking, evidence discovered at the crime scene will serve four objectives: (1) to determine the facts of the crime, (2) to identify the lawbreaker, (3) to aid in the arrest of the perpetrator, and (4) to aid in the criminal prosecution of the perpetrator. History has shown that there are many different ways to search a crime scene for evidence. Indeed, methods for crime scene searching vary according to the types of crime scenes and evidence at hand. Varieties of crime scene evidence include firearm evidence, trace material collection, tool mark evidence, collection of bodily fluids, standards of evidence, fire and explosion evidence, outdoor crime scenes, vehicle searches, and interior and victim searches. The search of the crime scene consists of several distinct phases:

- Surveying the crime scene
- Documenting the crime scene through sketches and photographs
- Recording all physical evidence
- Searching for fingerprints

Search Patterns

Regardless of the method used, the search of the scene should be conducted in a systematic way. Of the most often used methods of searching, several have been most commonly used over time. The most common search patterns include the spiral search method, grid search method, strip- or

|Fig. 3.9| ▲

Search patterns.

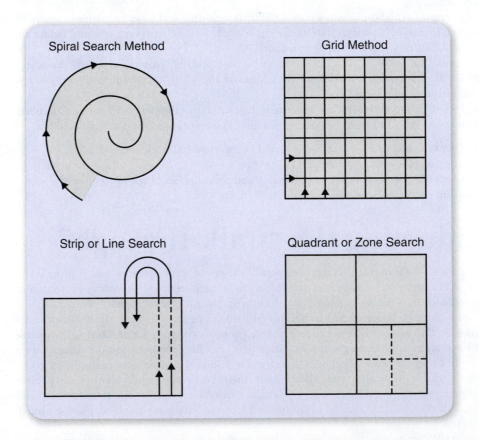

line-search method, and quadrant- or zone-search method. Some methods of searching are best suited for indoor scenes, and others are more applicable to outdoor crime scenes. Other scenes present unique problems and are discussed next. Whichever method is adopted, the rule to remember is that the search must be thorough.

INDOOR CRIME SCENE SEARCHES It is generally recommended that at least two officers search an indoor crime scene. This may best be accomplished by dividing the room in half and having each investigator search half of the room (also known as the quadrant or zone-search method). At the conclusion of the search, the investigators switch halves. In this fashion, each half of the room is searched twice.

OUTDOOR CRIME SCENE SEARCHES In most cases, the outdoor crime scene covers a broader area than those that are indoor. If this is the case, more investigators are required. Accordingly, with the increased size of the scene, a more systematic searching method must be used. One way is to rope off the scene into a grid. Each square, averaging about 6 square feet, represents a specific search area that is a manageable size for each investigator (also known as the grid search method).

NIGHTTIME CRIME SCENE SEARCHES If possible, investigators should wait until daylight to search a crime scene. Obviously, circumstances may require investigators to proceed with the search at night. These may include inclement weather or other emergency circumstances. In the event that such a search is to be conducted, lighting generators should be used to provide sufficient illumination for the search.

VEHICLE SEARCHES The search of a vehicle requires the same degree of attention as indoor and outdoor searches. Obviously, the nature of the crime dictates the area of the vehicle to be searched. For example, whereas a drug smuggling or murder case requires closer examination of the interior of the vehicle, a hit-and-run investigation necessitates examination of the exterior of the vehicle. Similar to an interior search, a vehicle should also be searched for fingerprints. This should be done after other trace evidence has been sought.

The Crime Scene Search

Evidence of crimes is dynamic. That is, it is unique, often fragile, and may constantly be undergoing change. Experience indicates that there is usually only one chance to search a crime scene properly, so for this reason, it is a good idea to survey the scene carefully before embarking on the search process itself.

There are two approaches to crime scene searches. As a first step, the investigator should consider all information provided to him or her by officers who arrived earlier on the scene. Such information includes the officers' perceptions of what occurred and the nature of the evidence. Next, investigators should rationalize which evidence items seem to play the greatest role in the alleged crime. In brief, the principal concern at this point is to observe and document the scene rather than take action.[13]

Of specific importance in the observation phase is the relative distance of any object to the victim. The distance between an object and a victim may play a greater role in the evidence collection phase

|Fig. 3.10| △

An actual crime scene search for hairs, fibers, and small bones. Such searches require sifting through dirt and debris and often takes hours, if not days, to accomplish.

than the item itself. For example, if the crime scene consists of a dead person who has apparently been shot and a 9mm handgun, the locations of spent shell casings could indicate the angle of the weapon or the position of the victim at the time the gun was discharged.

Such a determination could point to either suicide or homicide and may subsequently alter the character of the investigation. As indicated, while observations are being carried out, notes should be taken to organize the sequence of events. Witnesses' statements should be taken as well, regarding the victim(s) or related information. Additionally, videotapes and photographs should be made during this phase to document the scene adequately for future reference. Both of these considerations are discussed in greater detail later in the book.

Collecting Evidence

There is a tendency on the part of many investigators to rush the evidence collection process and focus attention on the obvious. Understandably, the task of observing firsthand the scene of another's misfortune is a difficult one for many, and one might appreciate the desire for

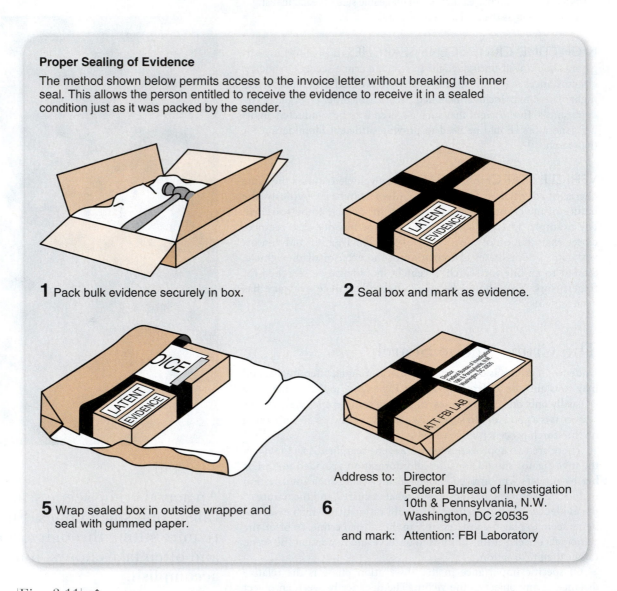

Proper Sealing of Evidence

The method shown below permits access to the invoice letter without breaking the inner seal. This allows the person entitled to receive the evidence to receive it in a sealed condition just as it was packed by the sender.

1 Pack bulk evidence securely in box.

2 Seal box and mark as evidence.

5 Wrap sealed box in outside wrapper and seal with gummed paper.

6 Address to: Director
Federal Bureau of Investigation
10th & Pennsylvania, N.W.
Washington, DC 20535

and mark: Attention: FBI Laboratory

|Fig. 3.11| △

Method for the proper sealing of crime scene evidence.

expeditiousness on the part of the investigator. It is a fact, however, that much critical evidence, often seemingly unimportant, can be located in and around the scene of almost every crime. As discussed in the earlier section on crime scene searches, investigators must choose which method of searching is best suited for the crime in question. Regardless of the method used, evidence must be collected in a comprehensive, nondestructive manner; within a reasonable period; and with a minimum of unnecessary movement about the scene. Although every criminal case is unique and should be evaluated on an individual basis, experience has shown that the following general recommendations are beneficial in organizing the search and preventing errors.

GATHERING AND PRESERVING EVIDENCE After the initial crime scene search has been completed and the sketching and photographing of the scene have been done, evidence should be collected. The manner in which evidence is collected must be consistent with each law enforcement agency's policies and procedures and should be in keeping with accepted rules of evidence. The evidence collected first is usually that which is most fragile. Therefore, fingerprints should be lifted as a priority. Next, other fragile evidence, such as blood and other trace evidence, should be collected. It is important for officers to search the crime scene a second

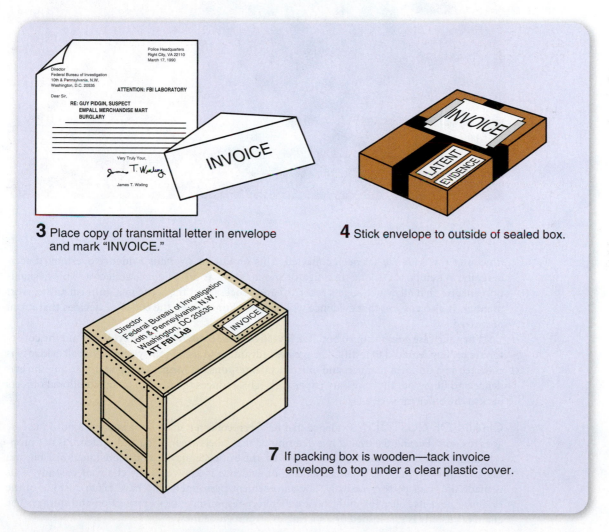

3 Place copy of transmittal letter in envelope and mark "INVOICE."

4 Stick envelope to outside of sealed box.

7 If packing box is wooden—tack invoice envelope to top under a clear plastic cover.

|Fig. 3.11| ▲

(continued)

|Fig. 3.12| ▲

Photo of criminal investigator collecting and bagging a handgun located at the scene of a shooting.

corepics / Shutterstock

time after the evidence has been collected. This should uncover any evidence overlooked accidentally. When possible, one investigator should serve as the evidence collector. This designation ensures that all evidence gets recorded and processed at the scene in a uniform and correct manner. It also ensures that evidence will be moved only when the collector decides that it can be moved.

When the case goes to court, both the investigator who discovered the evidence and the collector are usually required to testify. The greatest advantage to using this system is that all evidence is collected in a uniform manner, and one officer is responsible for packaging and marking the evidence and filling out the necessary paperwork. This reduces the need to tie up additional officers back at the office for such a task.

CHAIN OF CUSTODY Evidence that has been collected must be safeguarded until the case goes to court. During the trial, if it is determined that labels are missing and evidence is not properly initialed or is otherwise missing or altered, the evidence may be considered inadmissible and the case thrown out. The total accounting of evidence is known as the **chain of custody**. This is made up of all persons (usually, law enforcement personnel) who have taken custody of the evidence since its collection and who are therefore responsible for its protection and storage. The chain of custody is established by adhering to certain guidelines:

• The number of persons handling evidence from the time that it is safely stored should be limited. If the evidence leaves the possession of an officer, he or she should record to whom the evidence was given, the date and time, and the reason it was turned over.

- Anyone who handles evidence should affix his or her name and badge number to the package containing evidence.
- A signed receipt should be obtained from the person accepting the evidence. In turn, the investigator should sign a receipt or log when the item is returned.
- When a piece of evidence is turned in, the investigator should check his or her identification mark on it to ensure that it is the same item.
- After an item is returned to the investigator, he or she should determine if the item is in the same condition as when it was discovered. Any change in the physical appearance of the evidence should be called to the attention of the court.

Evidence can be stored in vehicle trunks, strongboxes, property rooms, locked file cabinets, evidence lockers, or vaults. The only stipulation is that it be marked properly and protected from tampering and destruction. Most evidence is turned over to an evidence custodian, who is usually an employee of the crime lab. This person signs off on an evidence form as the recipient of the evidence. The seizing officer then indicates in his or her investigative report the person to whom the evidence was given.

MARKING THE EVIDENCE Another important rule to remember during the evidence collection process is that all evidence must be marked immediately upon seizure to ensure proper identification later because it is common for the officer who seizes evidence to identify it at trial. Such testimony ensures the integrity of the chain of custody. Proper marking of each piece of evidence also ensures organization of all items of evidence for restructuring the events of the crime and the questioning of witnesses. Generally, it does not matter how the officer marks evidence as long as the initials of the seizing officer and the date of the seizure are clearly indicated on the seized item and on any container used to enclose the object, such as an envelope or cardboard box.

In many cases, the officer's department will require additional information. Such information includes the assigned case number; the type of crime; and the victim's name as well as the defendant's name, address, and date of birth. After physical evidence has been marked, sealed, counted, weighed (if necessary), and placed within a sealed container, a label is affixed containing identifying information. The following details should be included on the evidence label:

- Case number
- Exhibit number (when numerous items are seized)
- Date and time of seizure

Details to Include on an Evidence Label

> # EVIDENCE
> Case Number _____
>
> Exhibit Number (when numerous items are seized) _____
>
> Date and time of seizure _____
>
> Name and description of articles _____
>
> _____
>
> _____
>
> Location at time of discovery _____
>
> _____
>
> _____
>
> Signature or initials of officer making the discovery _____
>
> Name or initials of others witnessing the discovery _____

|Fig. 3.13| △

Details to include on an evidence label.

corepics / Shutterstock

|Fig. 3.14| △

A used and potentially dangerous syringe identified by investigators as evidence in a drug investigation.

© alessandrozocc / Fotolia

- Name and description of articles
- Location at time of discovery
- Signature or initials of officer making the discovery
- Name or initials of others witnessing the discovery

Special Cases in Evidence Handling

Just as evidence can be damaged or destroyed in the mishandling of a crime scene, improperly collected and managed evidence can sabotage an otherwise successful investigation. For example, improperly handled evidence, if contaminated, may either result in investigators reaching inaccurate conclusions or wasting time trying to correct the problem. The question commonly arises as to whether or not an object is or is not evidence. The decision is based on the officer's ability to consider the facts and circumstances at the crime scene, as well as his or her good judgment, common sense, and past experience. When any doubt exists, the object should be collected and processed as evidence; the object can be reevaluated later. Let's now examine some ways that certain types of critical evidence should be dealt with at the crime scene.

Infected Evidence

Among the many dangers encountered by law enforcement officers in the performance of their duties is the threat of street violence and even death. The rising specter of AIDS has created a health concern for criminal investigators charged with collection and preservation of crime scene evidence. Problems in collection of suspected infected evidence arise out of the fact that unlike many health care professionals, crime scene investigators are operating in an uncontrolled environment and often under extremely adverse conditions. Even the use of protective devices such as gloves and masks may not provide the investigator with adequate protection from communicable diseases such as HIV, tuberculosis, and hepatitis B.

This is partly due to the fact that such protective measures often fail to protect against cutting or puncturing, allowing the transmission of disease and infection through blood or other bodily fluids. Implements such as weapons, drug paraphernalia, razor blades, and hypodermic needles, which can be secreted in pockets, drawers, and in automobiles, all pose threats to crime scene technicians.

An unfortunate side effect of the AIDS epidemic is that it is likely that officers who either lack adequate protective equipment, who are uneasy about the prospect of contracting certain diseases, or who lack training on how best to deal with such problems might tend to limit their searches, intentionally or inadvertently, for fear of contracting an infectious organism. This could result in the attitude "it's just not worth it," which could have many negative side effects for the overall investigative process, including inadequately seized evidence, resulting in a poorly investigated case, which would, in turn, result in weak prosecution of the defendant. The National Institute of Justice has offered a list of recommendations on how best to deal with the problem of infected evidence.[14]

Firearms

Extreme care should be taken when handling firearms because of the types of trace evidence typically found on such evidence. The guidelines are as follows:

- The firearm should be handled carefully by the grip or the sides of the trigger guard.
- Never stick anything, such as a pencil, into the barrel of a firearm; this could destroy valuable trace evidence.
- No attempt should be made to fire the gun, dismantle it, or interfere with the mechanism in any way.

If the weapon is a revolver, mark empty cases or live cartridges and the rear edge of the cylinder with a code to show the chambers in which each empty case or live cartridge rested at the time of its removal.

Bullets, Cartridges, and Empty Cases

Bullets, cartridges, and empty cases should be handled with particular attention paid to the portions used in identification. Such evidence can be beneficial in determining the type of weapon used by a criminal. A more exact laboratory analysis may also determine the exact caliber of the weapon. Investigations have revealed instances in which criminals have purposely used one gun for the commission of a crime and a second gun to fire rounds into walls or the floor to confuse investigators. Certain areas of cartridges are typically used for identification: (1) the base and (2) the rim or cannelure (just above the base of the case).

The exact location of spent cases should be noted. Bullets must be removed carefully from their points of impact, and the locations they were found must be recorded accurately. In many cases, it is not advisable for a crime scene investigator to attempt to remove spent bullets. If possible, try to remove the material encasing a spent bullet (e.g., part of a door, wall) and transport it to the laboratory to be examined there. A spent bullet can be ruined by attempting to dig it out of an enclosure with a pocketknife. Care must be taken so that a drill, saw, or other cutting instrument does not damage the bullet. Bullets should be handled minimally and packaged to prevent movement and protect the side portions used in ballistic comparison and identification. Rather than attempting to mark a bullet directly, it should be packaged individually and the container marked appropriately.

Stains

Many crimes result in some type of characteristic stain being left at the crime scene. Blood is the stain most commonly found and can provide an investigator with much valuable evidence. Investigators should remember that not all bloodstains found at a crime scene belong to the victim. Indeed, a bloodstain may belong to the perpetrator, who might have been injured while committing the crime. It is usually a good idea in any case to adhere to the following guidelines when considering the collection of blood:

- Good photos and videos should be taken of bloodstains.
- Samples should be taken from all locations where blood is found.
- Blood samples can easily rot, so they should be swabbed and air dried before storage.

Glass

Glass fragments can result from many circumstances. For example, a bullet can shatter glass by passing through it; glass purposely broken will leave behind fragments in the crime scene and on the perpetrator. When collected, glass could be used to:

- Show the direction of travel of a projectile.
- Show the sequence of impact of a projectile.
- Match other broken glass.

Impressions

Many crimes result in the formation of impression marks. Such crimes include burglary and rape, but almost any crime could produce such evidence. In all cases, impression evidence should be regarded as valuable and must be protected. Examples of impression evidence include:

- Tool marks (usually found on metal doors or window frames and on locked metal desks, cabinets, and safes)
- Tire impressions
- Foot impressions
- Teeth impressions (sometimes located on partly eaten food at crime scenes)

Investigators should locate the object that made the impression so a comparison can be made in court.

Drugs

Studies have revealed that drug abuse is the greatest contributor to the commission of crime. Many illicit drugs exist and may appear quite different from one another in form. Therefore, great care must be practiced by evidence collectors to (1) preserve such substances for court, (2) transport the substances, and (3) protect themselves from the possible harmful effects of certain drugs. Most illicit drugs come in one of several forms: plant, powder, liquid, and tablet or capsule. Each requires specific attention from the evidence officer to avoid danger. For example, some drugs, such as liquid PCP and liquid LSD, may be absorbed accidentally through the skin. Others, such as marijuana, are more benign in nature and pose such a notable physical threat from handling. However, certain general considerations apply in any collection process.

Concealed Evidence: Strip Searches

The search for illicit drugs may cause investigators to suspect that contraband is concealed on (or within) a person's body. A strip search must be conducted in a private and controlled environment. This technique requires the suspect to undress completely, and all clothing is searched. In some cases, the suspect's body cavities may need to be searched. Officers are allowed to search the ears, mouth, and nose visually, but the vaginal and rectal areas may be searched only by authorized medical personnel. It is also recommended that investigators communicate with the prosecutor before conducting a strip search of any suspect to safeguard against possible procedural errors.

Concealed Evidence: Body Cavity Searches

In early 2005, officers of the Suffolk County (New York) Police Department arrested 36-year-old Terrance Haynes and charged him with marijuana possession. After placing him in the back of a patrol car, officers noted that Haynes appeared to choke and have difficulty breathing. Soon his breathing stopped, prompting officers to use the Heimlich maneuver, which dislodged a plastic bag from Haynes' windpipe. The bag contained 11 packets of cocaine. Although Haynes survived the ordeal, he now faces up to 25 years in prison.

Although some suspects may literally "cough up" evidence, some are more successful at hiding it in their bodies. Body cavity searches are among the most problematic types of searches for police today. "Strip" searches of convicts in prison, including the search of body cavities, have generally been held to be permissible.

The 1985 Supreme Court case of *U.S.* v. *Montoya de Hernandez* focused on the issue of "alimentary canal smuggling," in which the offender typically swallows condoms filled with cocaine or heroin and waits for nature to take its course to recover the substance.[15] In the *Montoya* case, a woman known to be a "balloon swallower" arrived in the United States on a flight from Colombia. She was detained by customs officials and given a pat-down search by a female agent. The agent reported that the woman's abdomen was firm and suggested that x-rays be taken. The suspect refused and was given a choice of submitting to further tests or taking the next flight back to Colombia. No flight was immediately available, however, and the suspect was placed in a room for 16 hours, where she refused all food and drink. Finally, a court order for an x-ray was obtained. The procedure revealed "balloons," and the woman was detained another four days, during which time she passed numerous cocaine-filled plastic condoms. The court ruled that the woman's confinement was not unreasonable, based as it was on the supportable suspicion that she was **"body-packing"** cocaine (e.g., concealing drugs by taping or otherwise attaching illicit drugs to the body of a person transporting the drugs). Any discomfort she experienced, the court ruled, "resulted solely from the method that she chose to smuggle illicit drugs."

Collecting Evidence

1. *Collection of evidence by responding officers: Limitations.* The collection of evidence at a crime has always involved significant operational and legal considerations. Today, because scientific analysis techniques (e.g., DNA testing) have become such a major part of criminal investigations, it is vital that trained specialists collect, preserve, and transmit evidence. Therefore, officers initially responding to a crime scene should not collect evidence unless

(1) exigent circumstances exist that make it necessary to collect the evidence immediately to prevent its contamination or destruction or (2) authorization has been received from a supervisor to engage in collection activities.

2. Unless one or both of the foregoing circumstances exist, responding officers should limit their activities to securing the scene and preventing unauthorized persons from taking any action that might cause the alteration, loss, or destruction of evidence.

3. ***Collection of evidence by responding officers under exigent circumstances.*** If it appears that evidence will be altered, lost, or destroyed unless the responding officers secure the evidence, the evidence may be collected. However, such emergency actions should be taken in accordance with proper procedures, and even in an emergency, the authorization of a supervisor should be obtained whenever possible. Even when undertaken, emergency collection of evidence should be limited to the least interference needed to preserve the evidence from loss. Supervisory or specialized assistance should be obtained as soon as possible to minimize any adverse effects on the evidence or its admissibility due to the emergency collection.

4. ***Collection of evidence by responding officers under direction of the officer in charge (OIC) of the crime scene.*** When so directed by the crime scene OIC, officers may search the crime scene for the purpose of finding and collecting items that may establish how and by whom the crime was committed. This may include, but is not limited to, the following:

   - Weapons, tools, clothing, stains, blood spatters, fingerprints, footprints, tire or tool marks, broken glass, hair, fibers, soil
   - Any unusual objects or objects found in unexpected or unusual locations
   - Any other object or substance that the police officer believes may be relevant to the investigation

In conducting the search, officers must comply with the directions of the crime scene OIC and all applicable departmental directives. In particular, the officers must comply with the department's policies and procedures regarding evidence control; photographing evidence before and after collection; and preserving, packaging, and labeling criminal evidence. Officers should be aware that failure to follow these procedures may result in the loss of the evidentiary value of the item or substance collected or suppression of the evidence at trial. (For example, the incorrect collection and packaging of a wet blood sample or stain may result in the deterioration of the sample to the point that its unique characteristics can no longer be identified by a crime laboratory, or the failure to mark or label any item of evidence correctly may lead the criminal defense to seek its subsequent suppression at a trial on the grounds that it cannot be adequately identified.)

Officers collecting evidence must preserve the chain of possession or chain of custody of all evidence collected. Departmental directives regarding initial collection, packaging, labeling, transporting, and maintaining custody of such evidence shall be scrupulously observed. Normally, this involves a series of written receipts that document the location of and access to the evidence at all times after its initial discovery by police. Any inability to present written documentation covering any period after this initial discovery of the evidence may result in suppression of the evidence at trial.

Interviewing Witnesses

As noted earlier, persons at the crime scene who are or may be witnesses to the crime or who may have information that may be relevant to the crime should be identified, and preliminary interviews of these persons should be conducted as soon as possible. Promptness is vital in this regard. Often, the arrival of police leads persons who have witnessed the crime or have information about it to leave the scene to avoid becoming involved. Therefore, potential witnesses must be identified before this occurs.

Witnesses' full identities, including addresses and phone numbers, should be obtained immediately. Witnesses who have been identified as such should be requested to remain on the scene until they can be interviewed more fully. Even persons who are present but who deny having witnessed the crime or having any information about it should be identified for further reference. Officers should also attempt to obtain information from those present about other persons who may have been witnesses but who have left the scene.

In addition, those present on the scene should be asked to provide the names of persons who are not present at the scene but who are known to live in the vicinity or who are known to be present in the area on a regular basis.

When circumstances permit, the neighborhood surrounding the crime scene should be canvassed to identify additional witnesses and other persons who may have information bearing upon the crime.[16] Even though detectives or other investigative personnel may conduct the follow-up on the information taken above, the officers who make the initial response must gather as much of this data as possible because crowds may disperse quickly, vehicles may be removed from the area, and so on before investigators arrive. Quick action by responding officers may preserve information that would otherwise be lost.

Contacting the Medical Examiner

The official determination regarding the death of the victim and circumstances surrounding the death is typically made by the **medical examiner** (or, in small jurisdictions, county coroner). The responding law enforcement agency's standard operating procedure (SOP) should set forth the circumstances regarding when these persons are contacted. For example, some police organizations wait to call the medical examiner until after the crime scene technicians have conducted preliminary investigations on the crime scene. Investigators must realize that in almost all jurisdictions, the medical examiner will have jurisdiction over the body, so police may not move it without proper authorization.

In the event that the responding officer must move the body, its position should be documented through the use of both photographs and sketching. Additionally, tape or chalk should be placed on the floor to indicate to crime scene investigators how the head, arms, and legs of the body were positioned. If possible, officers must take care to see that the body remains in exactly the same position in which it was found. Specifically, limbs that are bent should not be straightened; if the body was discovered lying face down, it should be returned to the same position to avoid any shifting of the blood and subsequent altering of lividity.

Conducting a Neighborhood Canvass

A **neighborhood canvass** may also be in order during the early phases of an investigation. Although investigators may perform this function, the first officer on the scene might be directed to conduct a neighborhood or door-to-door canvass of the area to identify witnesses. This could focus not only on residents but also on employees of stores, delivery personnel, utility personnel, bus and taxi drivers, and so on.

The neighborhood canvass is also important because it identifies material witnesses (those who have specific knowledge of the crime or parts of the crime) and general witnesses who can provide important background information about the victim and possible suspects.

Preparing Crime Scene Reports

Both responding officers and those conducting follow-up investigations should prepare reports in accordance with departmental policy. At a minimum, crime scene reports should include the following information:

- The date and time at which the officers arrived on the scene
- Relevant conditions at the time of arrival at the crime scene, including the weather and other observations

|Fig. 3.15| △

Police field interviews, as shown here, can be an important part of the investigative process

© Mikael Karlsson / Alamy

- The manner in which the crime was discovered and reported and the identity of the reporting individuals, if known, including their relationships to the victim or other persons involved
- Identity of any police officers or emergency personnel who were present at the time of arrival of the reporting officer or who arrived thereafter
- Physical evidence collected and the identities of those who collected it (special note should be made of any valuables discovered or collected, such as currency or jewelry)
- Full identification information, including name, address, telephone number, and other identifying data, regarding witnesses to the crime
- The results of interviews with victims and witnesses, including the identities and descriptions of suspects, the methods of operation and other actions of the suspects, and the means and route of escape used by the suspects
- Diagrams, sketches, photographs, videotapes, and other information prepared at the scene or afterward, including the identity of the persons, whether officers or civilians, who recorded or prepared these items
- Recommendations that may be helpful to the follow-up investigation (e.g., the names of witnesses or other persons who may be able to provide additional information)

Performing the Follow-up Investigation

The investigator's duties end at the crime scene. Indeed, they may very well extend into the community to virtually any source of information that may be of value in the investigation. Accordingly, officers should not construe the **follow-up investigation** as a negative reflection on their investigative abilities. Conversely, it demonstrates that officers are conscientious enough to follow up on leads even after the preliminary investigation has long been concluded. The investigator should remember that the follow-up investigation should build on what has been learned in the preliminary investigation. Double-checking addresses, possible escape routes, and other leads may provide the investigator with priceless new information. Tasks required of the follow-up investigator include:

- Analyzing reports of officers conducting the preliminary phases of the investigation
- Reviewing official departmental records and mode of operation (MO) files

- Gathering information on friends and associates of suspects
- Examining the victim's background
- Checking police intelligence files to develop potential suspects
- Organizing police actions, such as neighborhood canvassing, raids, and search warrants

In summary, investigators must possess organizational skills that enable them to sift through detailed and fragmented pieces of information. As with organizational skills, personality traits can aid in communicating with people in the community who may possess valuable information.

Case in Point

>>General Rules of Crime Scene Searching[17]

If there is an indication that evidence is deteriorating significantly with time or by the elements, these have first priority. Crime scene investigators should always wear protective clothing to preserve evidence from contamination and to safeguard themselves as well.

All major items are examined, photographed, recorded, and collected, as appropriate, taking them in the order that is most logical, considering the requirement to conserve movement. Making casts and lifting latent prints from objects to be moved from the scene are done as necessary. Items should not be moved until they have been examined for trace evidence. Fingerprints should be taken, or at least developed and covered with tape, before the object is moved. When an (obviously) deceased person is involved, the evidence items lying between the point of entry to the scene and point of exit from the scene and the body are processed; then the detailed search of the deceased person is conducted. After the search, the body should be removed and the processing of obvious evidence continued as noted earlier.

After processing the obvious evidence, the search for and collection of additional trace material is begun. Trace evidence should be searched for and collected before dusting for fingerprints. After the trace materials have been collected, other latent prints are lifted. When sweeping or vacuuming, surface areas should be segmented, the sweepings from each area packaged separately, and the locations of their point of recovery noted. Normally, elimination fingerprints and physical evidence standards are collected after the preceding actions have been completed.

Case in Point

>>Recommendations for Dealing with Infected Evidence

- *Human bites.* Viral transmission through saliva is unlikely; however, if bitten, after milking the wound, rinse well and seek medical attention.
- *Saliva, urine, and feces.* Viral transmission through saliva is unlikely. In urine, the virus is isolated in very low concentrations and nonexistent in feces. No AIDS cases have been associated with urine or feces.
- *Cuts and puncture wounds.* When searching areas hidden from view, use extreme caution to avoid sharp objects. Cases involving needle sticks are very rare.
- *Cardiopulmonary resuscitation (CPR) and first aid.* Minimal risk is associated with CPR, but it is a good idea to use masks or airways and gloves when in contact with bleeding wounds.
- *Body removal.* As with all crime scenes, when in contact with a dead body, always wear protective gloves.
- *Casual contact.* No AIDS cases or infections have been associated with casual contact.
- *Any contact with bodily fluids or blood.* Wear protective gloves if contact with blood or bodily fluids is likely. If contact is made, wash the area thoroughly with soap and water. Clean up spills with one part water and 10 parts household bleach.
- *Contact with dried blood.* No cases of infection have been traced to exposure to dried blood. The drying process itself seems to deactivate any viruses in blood. However, it is still a good idea to wear protective clothing such as gloves.

Summary Checklist

1. What important points should you remember when conducting a preliminary investigation?

Generally, a preliminary investigation is defined as an initial inquiry by officers to establish facts and circumstances of a suspected crime and to preserve any evidence related to that crime.

The key elements of a preliminary investigation include:

- Securing the crime scene
- Considering the possible arrest of a suspect
- Locating and questioning witnesses and victims
- Documenting the crime scene
- Identifying and collecting evidence

When collecting evidence, it is important to remember the Locard exchange principle, which is also known as the "transfer of evidence theory." Essentially, it says that "Every contact leaves a trace." Locard's principle is applied to crime scenes where the perpetrator(s) of a crime comes into contact with the scene, so he or she both brings something into the scene and leaves with something from the scene. Every contact leaves a trace.

2. What are the main types of evidence?

There are two commonly used classifications:

- Corpus delicti refers to evidence that establishes that a crime has been committed.
- Associative evidence links a suspect with a crime.

Examples of evidence are:

- Physical evidence
- Direct or prima facie evidence
- Indirect or circumstantial evidence
- Testimonial evidence
- Trace evidence
- Demonstrative evidence

3. What are the duties of the first officer on the scene?

The initial response to a call by the responding officer is a critical phase of any criminal investigation. This response is usually made by patrol officers who must be prepared to initiate a preliminary investigation and carry out important and timely functions until they are relieved by supervisors or investigators.

In general, the actions that the responding patrol officers should take include:

- Actions while en route to the crime scene:
  - Officers must be alert to the possible presence of perpetrators or perpetrators' vehicles fleeing from the scene.
- Initial actions upon arrival:
  - If possible, first verify that a crime has been committed.
  - Communicate this verification, or the officers' reasonable suspicion to the dispatcher or supervisor immediately.
- Provide assistance to victims and protect witnesses and bystanders:
  - Take steps to ensure the victim's safety if necessary, as well as the safety of witnesses and other bystanders.
  - Administer first aid to and summon medical assistance for any victims.
- If the perpetrator is at the scene and probable cause for arrest exists or an arrest warrant has been issued, arrest the suspect.
- Follow-up communications:
  - Inform superiors of the apparent nature of the offenses.
  - Provide a full description of any perpetrator who has fled the scene, along with information regarding the perpetrator's mode and direction of flight; similar information should be provided for any accomplices if relevant.
- Identify witnesses and vehicles.
- Brief investigators and supervisors.

4. Why is it important to secure the scene?

One important function of responding officers is to ensure the crime scene is not unnecessarily disturbed as this could result in the loss of vital criminal evidence. Unnecessary or improper entry into a crime scene may:

- Destroy or contaminate evidence
- Introduce items or substances into the crime scene that may mislead investigators
- Provide defense attorneys with a basis for discrediting the investigators or the findings of a crime laboratory

Responding officers should only enter a crime scene for very limited purposes, such as for:

- Determining a crime has been committed
- Aiding victims
- Apprehending perpetrators
- Securing the area

5. **What must an investigator remember when searching a crime scene?**

After an investigator has properly documented a crime scene, the actual search must begin. In general, evidence discovered at the crime scene serves four objectives:

- To determine the facts of the crime
- To identify the lawbreaker
- To aid in the perpetrator's arrest
- To aid in the criminal prosecution of the perpetrator

The search of a crime scene consists of several distinct phases:

- Surveying the scene
- Documenting the scene through sketches and photographs
- Recording physical evidence
- Searching for fingerprints

It is important to remember that the search must be thorough and systematic.

Once evidence has been collected, it must be safeguarded until the case goes to court. The total accounting of evidence is known as the chain of custody. If the chain of custody is not maintained, the evidence may be considered inadmissible at trial.

6. **Describe how to properly prepare crime scene reports.**

The crime scene report is the record of what was done to identify evidence of the crime and reconstruct what occurred at the time of the offense. At the very minimum, the crime scene report must include:

- The date and time at which the officers arrived on the scene
- Relevant conditions at the time of arrival at the crime scene
- The manner in which the crime was discovered and reported and the identity of the reporting individuals (if known)
- The identities of any police officers and emergency personnel who were present at the scene
- Physical evidence collected and the identities of those who collected it
- Identification information regarding any witnesses to the crime
- The results of interviews with victims and witnesses
- Diagrams, sketches, photographs, videotapes, and other information prepared at the scene or afterward
- Recommendations that may be helpful to the follow-up investigation

7. **Explain the importance of the follow-up investigation**

The follow-up investigation builds on what has been learned in the preliminary investigation. Tasks required of the follow-up investigator include:

- Analyzing reports of officers conducting the preliminary phases of the investigation
- Reviewing official departmental records and mode of operation (MO) files
- Gathering information on friends and associates of suspects
- Examining the victim's background
- Checking police intelligence files to develop potential suspects
- Organizing police actions, such as neighborhood canvassing, raids, and search warrants

Key Terms

associative evidence	crime scene walk-through	medical examiner
biohazardous material	demonstrative evidence	neighborhood canvass
body packing	Drug Enforcement Administration (DEA)	physical evidence
chain of custody	electronic evidence	preliminary investigation
contamination of evidence	exigent circumstances	prima facie evidence
corpus delicti	flash description	reasonable grounds
crime scene	follow-up investigation	testimonial evidence
crime scene evidence	latent evidence	trace evidence
crime scene report	Locard exchange principle	transfer of evidence theory

Discussion Questions

1. Define the term *preliminary investigation* and discuss how it applies to a crime scene.

2. What is meant by the term *contamination of evidence* and why is it important to ensure that evidence from a crime scene does not become contaminated?

3. List and discuss the preliminary duties of the responding officer at a crime scene and measures that must be taken to ensure that a crime scene is secured.

4. With the exception of any unusual circumstances, explain why evidence at a crime scene should be recorded before any objects are collected or removed.

5. Discuss some of the special cases that may arise in evidence handling and explain why it is important to properly collect and manage evidence.

6. What is a neighborhood canvass and explain why it may be important to conduct during the early phases of an investigation.

7. Discuss the goals of a follow-up investigation.

Notes

1. THORNTON, J. I. (1997). The general assumptions and rationale of forensic identification. In Faigman D. L., D. H. Kaye, M. J. Saks, and J. Sanders (Eds.), *Modern scientific evidence: The law and science of expert testimony*, vol. 2. Cincinnati, OH: West Publishing Co.

2. KEPPEL, R. D. AND J. G. WEIS. (1993). HITS: Catching criminals in the Northwest. *FBI Law Enforcement Bulletin* 62(April):14–19.

3. HAMMETT THEODORE M. (1989). 1988 update: AIDS in correctional facilities. *Issues and Practices.* Washington, DC: U.S. Department of Justice, National Institute of Justice.

4. The purpose of the entry by the officers affects the courts' views as to whether or not the entry was lawful. Courts have typically upheld an entry and protective sweep if the officers had any substantial reason to believe that there were victims within the premises who might be in need of help. In contrast, courts are much more likely to hold a warrantless entry unlawful when the entry was made primarily or solely for the purpose of apprehending a perpetrator thought to be inside.

5. In emergencies, entry to protect victims may have to take priority over communication with superiors. Even in emergency circumstances, however, whenever possible, communication should be simultaneous with emergency entries or the taking of other emergency measures, or if sufficient personnel is on the scene, one officer should communicate while other officers are performing emergency functions.

6. Note that police frequencies are often monitored by persons other than law enforcement officers and agencies. News media, curious citizens, and even the perpetrators themselves may be listening. This may require the use of discretion as to what is said on the radio. However, even when transmissions are subject to such monitoring, sufficient information must be provided by the responding officers to enable superiors to take appropriate action. The codes used must not be so cryptic that they fail to convey the information necessary to ensure an appropriate response from headquarters or other officers.

7. Persons who are or may be witnesses or have relevant information should not be allowed to leave the scene completely. They should, however, be moved out of areas in which their presence may result in loss or destruction of evidence. If the persons present at the scene include relatives of a victim or other persons who have a legal right to be on the premises, the clearing of the area must be accomplished with tact and, in some cases, may be subject to considerations of the welfare of the persons involved.

8. Local officials may, for various reasons not directly connected with the investigation of the crime, come to the scene of a major crime. Dealing with such persons requires tact. The officer in charge or some other experienced person should be designated to handle such situations.

9. The entry of any nonessential person into the crime scene area threatens the integrity of the case. In any subsequent legal proceeding, the criminal defense may claim that the entry of such persons into the area compromised the scene and cast doubt upon the validity of the prosecution's case.

10. TECHNICAL WORKING GROUP FOR ELECTRONIC CRIME SCENE INVESTIGATION. (2001). *Electronic crime scene investigation: A guide for first responders.* Washington, DC: National Institute of Justice, from which much of the information in this section is taken.

11. HAMMETT. (1989). 1988 update.

12. FEDERAL BUREAU OF INVESTIGATION. (2000). *Crime scene investigation manual: A guide for law enforcement.* United States Department of Justice, U.S. Government Printing Office, January, p. 21

13. HANDBOOK OF FORENSIC SERVICES. (2007). Federal Bureau of Investigation Laboratory Services. Quantico, VA: An FBI Laboratory Publication.

14. NATIONAL INSTITUTE OF JUSTICE. (1987). *Investigators who perform well.* Washington, DC: U.S. Department of Justice, September.

15. *U.S. Montoya de Hernandez,* 473 U.S. 531, 105 S. Ct. 3304 (1985).

16. Some departments prefer that development of this type of information be left to detectives or other investigators.

17. FOX, R. H. AND C. L. CUNNINGHAM. (1985). *Crime scene search and physical evidence handbook.* Washington, DC: U.S. Department of Justice.

PART 2 | Follow-Up Investigative Processes

Chapter **4** | **Identification of Criminal Suspects: Field and Laboratory Services**
Chapter **5** | Legal Issues in Criminal Investigation

CHAPTER **4**

© Marmaduke St. John / Alamy

This chapter will enable you to:

1. Describe the role of the crime laboratory.

2. Understand the fundamentals of fingerprint science.

3. Describe how blood evidence is examined.

4. Identify the different types of fingerprint patterns.

5. Describe science of finger-printing, the different types of fingerprint patterns, and how fingerprints are collected and developed.

6. Learn the legalities of police lineups in suspect identification.

Identification of Criminal Suspects: Field and Laboratory Services

Introduction

Although many investigative techniques used in suspect identification involve forensic procedures, forensics is not the primary focus of this book. Rather, the intent is to provide the reader with a basic understanding of some of the technological advances in suspect identification through brief offerings of some of the most innovative and effective techniques in this area.

Of paramount importance to any criminal investigation is establishment of the identity of the perpetrator or victim. This can be accomplished through numerous investigative techniques. Fact: When criminals are at work, they cannot avoid leaving behind clues as to their true identity. Such clues include fingerprints, bloodstains, and handwriting specimens. Today, such evidence may be a clear indicator of the identity of the criminal and can help expedite criminal prosecutions. In this chapter, we will examine the role of the crime laboratory as well as some of the most critical techniques used in criminal investigation.

The Role of the Crime Laboratory

The crime laboratory plays a pivotal role in criminal investigation. Thus, criminalists are major contributors to the investigative process. The duties and qualifications of criminalists vary greatly from one position to the next. For example, positions in crime labs include specialists in DNA (blood), trace evidence, handwriting analysis, **toxicology**, and ballistics, to name only a few. Students interested in becoming criminalists must be mindful of the very different job requirements and specific college coursework required to successfully compete. Let's now look at a few of the investigative functions performed by the crime laboratory.

Trace Evidence

The Trace Evidence Unit identifies and compares specific types of trace materials that could be transferred during the commission of a violent crime. These trace materials include human hair, animal hair, textile fibers and fabric, ropes, and wood. Physical contact between a suspect and a victim may result in the transfer of trace materials such as hairs and fibers. The identification and comparison of these materials may often link a suspect to a crime scene or to physical contact with another individual. Torn pieces of fabric may be positively associated with a damaged garment, and broken pieces of wood can be fit together. Odontology (forensic dentistry) and physical anthropology (skeletal remains) examinations assist in the identification of human remains.

[Fig. 4.1] △

Criminalist working on DNA results. DNA blood typing in the laboratory is meticulous and all steps must be thoroughly documented.

Courtesy of Mike Himmel

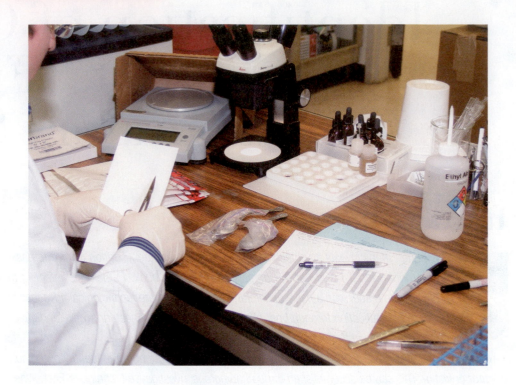

Questioned Documents

The Questioned Documents Unit examines and compares data appearing on paper and other evidentiary materials. These surface data include handwriting, hand printing, typewriting, printing, erasures, alterations, and obliterations. Impressions in the surface of paper, such as those from indented writing or use of a check writer or dry seal, are also routinely evaluated by unit examiners, as are shoeprint and tire tread impressions.

In addition to data contained on the surface of documentary evidence, data *within* paper or other surfaces—watermarks, safety fibers, and other integral features—may be components of document examinations. Unit examiners also match the torn or perforated edges of items such as paper, stamps, or matches.

Other unit examinations include analyses of typewriter ribbons, photocopiers, facsimiles, graphic arts, and plastic bags.

Forensic Chemistry

A crime laboratory's chemistry section is typically divided into three subunits whose analyses and functions include the following:

GENERAL CHEMISTRY SUBUNIT

- Identifies specific dyes and chemicals used in bank security devices; analyzes items such as clothing or currency for the presence of these dyes and chemicals
- Analyzes controlled substances to determine identity and quantity
- Compares stains or markings with suspected sources. Detects the presence of lubricants and compares them with suspected sources
- Compares the formulations of known and questioned ink (e.g., pens, typewriters, stamp pads)
- Conducts chemical analysis of unknown solids or liquids
- Performs pharmaceutical identification of constituent composition, active ingredients, quantity, and weight

TOXICOLOGY SUBUNIT

- Conducts toxicological analyses of biological specimens or food products for drugs, drug metabolites, and poisons
- Investigates claims of product tampering

PAINTS AND POLYMERS SUBUNIT

- Analyzes paint chips for comparison with suspected sources
- Conducts automotive make, model, and year determinations from suspected paint samples
- Compares plastics with suspected sources
- Determines tape composition, construction, and color for comparison to suspected sources; determines manufacturer of suspected duct tape; performs tape identifications with the torn or cut end of the tape and a roll of suspected tape
- Compares caulks, sealants, and adhesives by color and composition with suspected sources.

DNA Analysis

A crime laboratory's DNA Analysis Unit analyzes bodily fluids and bodily fluid stains recovered as evidence in violent crimes. Examinations include the identification and characterization of blood, semen, saliva, and other bodily fluids using traditional serological techniques and related biochemical analysis. After the stain has been identified, it is characterized by DNA analysis using the restriction fragment length polymorphism (RFLP) or **polymerase chain reaction** (PCR) techniques. The results of the analyses are compared with results obtained from known blood or saliva samples submitted from the victims or suspects.

In 1996, a number of DNA crime laboratory analysis units began using mitochondrial DNA (mtDNA) analysis, which is applied to evidence containing small or degraded quantities of DNA from hair, bones, teeth, and bodily fluids. The results of mtDNA analysis are compared with blood, saliva, or both submitted from victims or suspects. The unit examines evidence that may not have been suitable for significant comparison purposes before the development of this technique.

The Mitochondrial DNA Population Database is composed of complete nucleotide sequences of the first and second hypervariable segments of the control region of the human mitochondrial genome and consists of two main data sets. The first data set contains individuals from populations of forensic relevance and is contributed mostly by the Scientific Working Group on DNA Analysis Methods and forensic laboratories. The second data set, based on mtDNA concordance, contains nucleotide sequences from ethnic groups around the world.

|Fig. 4.2| △

Blood evidence such as shown here tells a story as to its origin, point of impact, direction of trajectory, and other points of evidentiary information.

Mike Himmel / Missouri State Highway Patrol
Crime Laboratory

|Fig. 4.3| △

Straw (grass) close-up—dried grass on the roadside had blood on it. The blood trail on the grass led investigators to a body deposited several feet away from the roadside. The DNA matched the body. This evidence helped investigators theorize that the body had been dragged to its location.

Mike Himmel / Missouri State Highway Patrol Crime Laboratory

MITOCHONDRIAL DNA ANALYSIS Both data sets are bundled in MitoSearch, a software package specifically designed for the compilation and analysis of mtDNA databases. MitoSearch estimates the relative frequency of specific sequences for the various populations represented within the database and assesses the relative relatedness of each population with reference to the size of each database.

Ballistics

The Forensic Ballistics Unit receives and examines evidence related to firearms, firearm components, ammunition, ammunition components, tools, and tool marks. Evidence in a typical case may include a number of recovered rifles, pistols, shotguns, silencers and other muzzle attachments, magazines, holsters, and a variety of fired and unfired cartridges. Lead and other metal fragments, shot wads, shot cups, and bullets removed from bodies during an autopsy are also frequently received items in firearms-related casework. Evidence submitted in tool mark cases may include screwdrivers, scissors, knives, pliers, wrenches, crowbars, hammers, saws, wire, sections of sheet metal, chains, safety deposit boxes, human bone or cartilage, plates, locks, doorknobs, bolts, and screens.

Forensic firearms examinations are based on firearms identification, which involves the identification of a bullet, cartridge case, or other ammunition component as having been fired by or in a particular firearm. Firearms examiners microscopically compare bullets and ammunition components with each other as well as to any number of firearms to determine whether an association exists between or among items submitted as evidence and items whose origins are known. Similarly, forensic tool mark identifications involve the identification of a tool mark as having been produced by a particular tool to the exclusion of all others. Examiners compare the micro- and macroscopic features of tool-marked items with known and questioned tools that may have produced them.

Tests and examinations routinely performed by laboratory ballistic criminalists include:

- Trigger-pull tests
- Function tests
- Full-auto conversion tests
- Accidental discharge tests
- Shot pattern examinations
- Gunshot residue examinations
- Ejection pattern testing
- Trajectory analysis examinations
- Silencer (flash suppressor) testing
- Serial number restorations

Latent Prints

The Latent Print Unit conducts all work pertaining to the examination of latent prints on evidence submitted to the FBI laboratory. Latent prints are impressions produced by the ridged skin on human fingers, palms, and soles of the feet. Unit examiners analyze and compare latent prints with known prints of individuals in an effort to make identifications or exclusions. The uniqueness, permanence, and arrangement of the friction ridges allow unit examiners to positively match two prints and determine whether an area of a friction ridge impression originated from one source to the exclusion of all others.

|Fig. 4.4| ▲

Ballistics test. The gun is fired into the tank that is filled with water. The bullet is stopped by the water and can be fished out unharmed and compared to bullets found at a crime scene.

MICHAEL MCMULLAN / AP Images

A variety of techniques, including use of chemicals, powders, lasers, alternate light sources, and other physical means, are used in the detection and development of latent prints. In instances in which a latent print has limited quality and quantity of detail, unit personnel may perform microscopic examinations o effect conclusive comparisons.

One technique for the development of fingerprints is **Amido black protein**. This is an amino acid–staining diazo dye used in biochemical research to stain for total protein on transferred membrane blots. It is used in criminal investigations to detect blood present with latent fingerprints by staining proteins in blood a blue-black color.

In 1999, the FBI developed and implemented a new automated fingerprint system known as the **Automated Fingerprint Identification System (AFIS),** which has since been adopted by most state crime laboratories as well. Although AFIS is primarily a 10-print system for searching an individual's fingerprints to determine whether a prior arrest record exists and then maintaining a criminal arrest record history for each individual, the system also offers significant latent print capabilities. Using AFIS, a latent print specialist can digitally capture latent print and 10-print images and perform several functions with each. These include:

- Enhancement to improve image quality
- Comparison of latent fingerprints against suspect 10-print records retrieved from the criminal fingerprint repository
- Searches of latent fingerprints against the 10-print fingerprint repository when no suspects have been developed
- Automatic searches of new arrest 10-print records against an unsolved latent fingerprint repository
- Creation of special files of 10-print records in support of major criminal investigations

Using the AFIS fingerprint search capability against data from the FBI Criminal Justice Information Services (CJIS) Division, which maintains one of the largest repositories of fingerprint records, identifications are made in cases for which no known suspects have been named for comparison purposes and in cases in which latent prints on crime scene-related evidence were not identified with suspects named in the investigation.

Personnel from a crime laboratory's Latent Print Unit may also form the nucleus of the local or state disaster squad, which renders assistance in identifying victims at disaster scenes.

Forensic Photography

A crime lab's Forensic Photography Unit is responsible for imaging operations. This unit captures, processes, produces, analyzes, archives, and disseminates images using traditional silver-based photographic processes and digital imaging technologies. The unit is typically responsible for the following:

- Crime scene and evidentiary photography
- Forensic photography
- Surveillance photography
- Aerial photography
- Venue photography
- Tactical imaging

|Fig. 4.5| ▲

Pistols commonly encountered in shooting cases. In such cases it is important to locate bullets and/or match spent shell casings to specific handguns in order to identify the weapon used in the crime. Doing so makes it easier to identify the shooter.

(1) 9 mm caliber Smith & Wesson model 5906
(2) 9 mm caliber Taurus model PT 99
(3) .40 caliber Glock model 22
(4) .45 auto caliber Colt model M1911A1
(5) 9 mm caliber Sturm & Ruger model P89DC
(6) .25 auto caliber Beretta model 21A
(7) .22 caliber Beretta model 21A
(8) .380 auto caliber Walther model PPK/S

Michael D. Lyman

|Fig. 4.6| △

DNA analysis—search for bloodstains. Special lighting is often required to cause bloodstains to show up on surfaces that would otherwise hide its presence.

Mike Himmel / Missouri State Highway Patrol Crime Laboratory

- Photographic scanners
- Field photographic equipment
- Regional color photographic processing mini-laboratories
- Silver-based and digital darkrooms
- Digital imaging technologies
- Courtroom presentations and exhibits

Specialized Laboratory Equipment

The use of specialized laboratory equipment is one of the hallmarks of the modern crime lab. For example, the spectrograph is used to identify minute samples of a substance by burning the material and interpreting the light emitted from the burning process. Another device, the spectrophotometer, is used to analyze coloring agents in small samples such as those found in paint and cloth. The gas chromatograph is most commonly used for isolating gases or liquids from complex solutions or mixtures, generally in the analysis of illicit drugs, plastics, and explosives. Another crucial instrument, the mass spectrometer, is used to separate and record ions according to their characteristic masses. It is most commonly used in the detection of trace elements in glass, ashes, and other inorganic material. Throughout the remainder of this chapter, other important instruments used by the crime lab will be featured and discussed according to their particular purposes.

Fingerprints as Evidence

Identifying criminal suspects through the use of fingerprinting has proven to be one of the most effective methods for apprehending persons who might otherwise go undetected and continue their criminal activities. In addition to identifying criminal suspects, the use of fingerprinting also makes it possible to learn accurately the suspect's number (and type) of previous arrests and convictions. This, of course, often results in more appropriate sentences being handed down to repeat or career criminals. Early on, fingerprinting, because of its peculiar adaptability to the field, has been associated in the layperson's mind almost exclusively with criminal identification. Interestingly, the civil fingerprint file of the FBI contains three times as many fingerprints as the criminal file. Such files also provide a humanitarian benefit to society in general by identifying missing persons, amnesia victims, and unknown deceased people.

In the latter case, victims of major disasters can be identified quickly and positively if their fingerprints are on file. The background and history of the science of fingerprints constitute an eloquent drama of human lives of good versus evil. Few developments in crime solving have played a more exciting role than that dramatized by the fascinating loops, whorls, and arches etched on the fingers and palms of a human being. Although faults have been found with earlier identification systems, to date no two fingerprints have been found to be identical.

The History of Fingerprinting

In earlier times, branding, maiming, distinctive clothing, and photography were used to distinguish the criminal for the crime that he or she committed. Thieves, for example, were sometimes deprived of the hand that committed a criminal act. Romans used the tattoo needle for identifying and preventing desertion of military soldiers. In more recent times, law enforcement officers relied heavily on identification of criminals by sight, or what was known as the "camera eye." In using this system, photography lessened the burden on memory but was not the answer to the criminal identification problem because personal appearances change. Throughout history, people have been aware of the friction ridges on the tips of fingers and palms. Although the precise origin of the science of personal identification is somewhat unclear, records show its application extending back to ancient civilizations.

For example, on the face of a cliff in Nova Scotia, a prehistoric Indian picture writing exists of a hand with ridge patterns crudely marked. Other examples include references to fingerprinting in clay tablets of recorded business transactions in ancient Babylon and to ancient Chinese documents identified with the eighth-century A.D. T'ang Dynasty, which refers to fingerprints being impressed on business contracts.

The first official use of fingerprinting was in 1858 by Sir William Herschel, British chief administrative officer for the Hooghly district, Bengal, India. He required natives to affix their fingerprints as well as their signatures to contracts. Although there is no evidence to suggest that Herschel was aware that fingerprints were individualized, he believed that to the native mind, this procedure would be impressive enough to discourage dishonesty.

Herschel continued his study of fingerprinting and in 1877 submitted a report to his superiors asking permission to identify prisoners through fingerprinting. Also around 1870, the French anthropologist Alphonse Bertillon developed a system to measure and record the dimensions of certain bony parts of the body. These measurements were reduced to a formula that, theoretically,

|Fig. 4.7| △

DNA analysis equipment.

Mike Himmel / Missouri State Highway Patrol Crime Laboratory

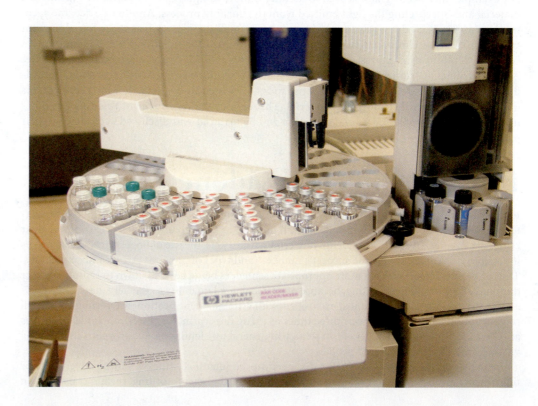

would apply to only one person and would not change during his or her adult life. This system, called the Bertillon system, was generally accepted for more than 30 years but was pronounced as fallible as a result of the Will West case of 1903.

The value of fingerprints as a means of detecting the fallibility of the Bertillon system and establishing the value and reliability of individualized identification for criminal suspects was therefore established.

Between 1875 and the turn of the century, several new developments were documented regarding fingerprinting. For example, an article published in 1880 by Henry Faulds of the Tsukiji Hospital in Tokyo, Japan, discussed future possibilities of fingerprint science. He recommended the use of a thin film of printer's ink as a transfer medium, as is generally used today. He also discussed the potentialities of identification of criminals by their fingerprints left at the scenes of crimes. The first documented use of fingerprinting in the United States was in 1882. Gilbert Thompson of the U.S. Geological Survey, while in charge of a field project in New Mexico, used his own fingerprint on commissary orders to prevent their forgery. Later that year, Sir Francis Galton, a noted British anthropologist, published his book *Fingerprints*. He also contributed to the field by devising the first scientific method of classifying fingerprint patterns.

In 1891, the first files for fingerprint identification were installed as a means of identifying criminals. Juan Vuchetich, an Argentinean police official, based this system on pattern types by Sir Francis Galton. The Vuchetich system is the basis of systems presently used in many Spanish-speaking countries. Between 1890 and 1924, the official use of fingerprinting escalated in the United States. The New York Civil Service Commission implemented the use of fingerprints to prevent applicants from having better qualified persons take their tests for them (1902). The New York State prison system also adopted the first practical use of fingerprints in the United States for the identification of criminals (1903).

As the use of fingerprints became more accepted throughout the United States, the penitentiary in Leavenworth, Kansas, and the St. Louis, Missouri, Police Department both implemented fingerprint bureaus. The St. Louis system was activated through the assistance of a sergeant associated with London's Scotland Yard. As more and more police departments established identification bureaus, many sent copies of their files to the National Bureau of Criminal Identification, established by the International Association of Chiefs of Police. In 1924, the fingerprint records of both the National Bureau of Criminal Identification and the Leavenworth Penitentiary, totaling 810,188, were consolidated to form the nucleus of the FBI Identification Division. Between 1924 and 1954 alone, more than 130 million fingerprint cards had been received by the FBI. It has since become renowned as the world's largest repository of fingerprints.

Types of Prints

Among the most valuable clues for the investigator at the crime scene are fingerprints and palm prints. After such prints have been collected by investigators and evaluated by classification experts, a definitive determination can be made as to the exact identity of the suspect(s). Generally, fingerprints can be divided into three main groups: latent, plastic, and visible.

A **latent fingerprint** (also called a **patent fingerprint**) is one that occurs when the entire pattern of whorls on the finger, which contain small amounts of grease, oil, perspiration, or dirt, for example, is transferred to an object when it is touched. The grease and oil are usually natural and are transferred to the fingers when the person touches other areas of his or her body containing various bodily excretions. Latent prints include those not only visible to the naked eye but also those that can be examined properly only after development. Those are usually found on paper and smooth surfaces.

A **plastic fingerprint** results when a finger presses against plastic material and leaves a negative impression of friction ridges. Typically, these are found on recently painted surfaces; in wax, grease, tar, and putty; in the gum on stamps or envelopes; and on adhesive tape.

A **visible fingerprint** (also called a **dust print**) is a print that has been adulterated with foreign matter. If a finger is placed in a thin layer of dust, for example, the dust may cover the friction ridges. If the finger subsequently touches a clean surface, a visible fingerprint may result. A visible fingerprint may also develop as a result of touching other substances such as blood, flour, ink, or oil.

|Fig. 4.8| ◭

A basic fingerprint showing characteristics such as arches, loops, deltas, and whorls.

Courtesy of Mike Himmel

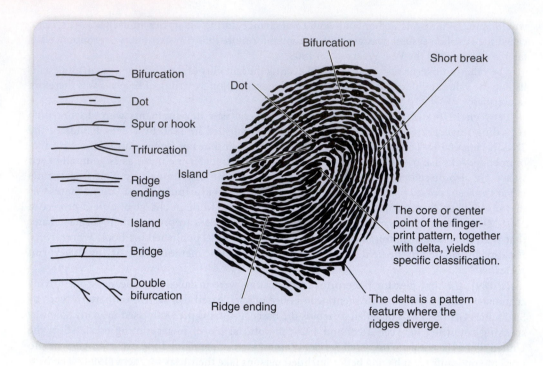

Types of Patterns

The use of fingerprints for identification purposes is based on distinctive ridge outlines that appear on the bulbs on the inside of the end joints of the fingers and thumbs. These ridges have definite contours and appear in several general pattern types. Each type has general and specific variations of the pattern, depending on the shape and relationship of the ridges. The ridge outlines appear most clearly when inked impressions are taken on paper, so that the ridges are black against a white background. This results from the ink adhering to the friction ridges. Impressions can be made by a variety of substances, including blood, dirt, grease, or any other foreign matter present on the ridges or the saline substance emitted by the glands through the ducts or pores that constitute their outlets. The background or medium may be paper, glass, porcelain, wood, cloth, wax, putty, silverware, or any smooth, nonporous material.

Fingerprints may be resolved into three large general groups of patterns: the arch, the loop, and the whorl. Each group bears the same general characteristics. Patterns can be further subdivided by means of the smaller differences existing between patterns in the same general group. Patterns are divided as follows:

- Arch loop
- Whorl
- Plain radial
- Plain tented
- Ulnar
- Accidental double
- Central pocket

Before pattern definition can be understood, it is necessary to understand the meaning of a few technical terms used in fingerprint work. As far as classification is concerned, the pattern area is the only part of the finger impression worth focusing on. It is present in all patterns, of course, but in many arches and tented arches, it is impossible to define. This is not important, however, because the only patterns in which one needs to define pattern areas for classification purposes are loops and whorls. The U.S. Department of Justice defines the pattern area as follows: the part of a loop or whorl in which appear the cores, deltas, and ridges with which we are concerned when classifying.[1] Type lines enclose the pattern areas of loops and whorls. *Type lines* may be defined as the two innermost ridges, which start parallel, diverge, and surround or tend to surround the pattern area. Fingerprint impressions can be made from blood, dirt, grease, or the saline substance emitted by the glands through ducts or pores in the skin.

Searching for Prints

Investigators must be judicious in their search for fingerprints, as such evidence may be located in not-so-obvious places at the crime scene. In a burglary case, for example, the search for prints should begin at the place of entry by the criminal. Investigators should be able, at that point, to determine whether or not the burglar's hands were protected. If a door has been forced open, prints may be located on the lock or its immediate surroundings or in the general area of entry. When entry is gained through windows, broken glass should be searched for and documented. Generally, this method of entry involves the criminal breaking a piece of glass just large enough for a hand to reach through and open the latch.

Broken pieces of glass do not always fall inside a residence. Indeed, they may or may not be in the structure at all, or the burglar might pick up the pieces and throw them outside, out of the way. When attempting to climb through the window, the burglar may leave fingerprints on a window jamb, frame, or sill. The search for fingerprints should begin at the place of entry by the criminal.

Some burglars have been known to eat food or drink something while in a residence. The investigator must anticipate this and take care to preserve any fingerprints left on glassware (including liquor bottles) and even on some types of food (detectable by superglue fuming, discussed later). Electric light switches, circuit breakers, and light bulbs should also be examined closely for prints. If it has been determined that the burglar was wearing gloves, places where gloves would be awkward to wear should be examined because the burglar may have removed the gloves to accomplish a particular task. Experience shows that this is common and that it typically occurs early in the commission of a crime. Many police officers have grown accustomed to wearing gloves during their crime scene search. Today, this has become a recommended practice for the investigator's safety as well as to safeguard against contaminating the evidence.

Another technique used for recognizing fingerprints on a crime scene is shining a flashlight at an oblique angle at the suspected area. Although using this technique on some porous surfaces does not work well, it is effective on surfaces such as tile floors, glass surfaces, and countertops.

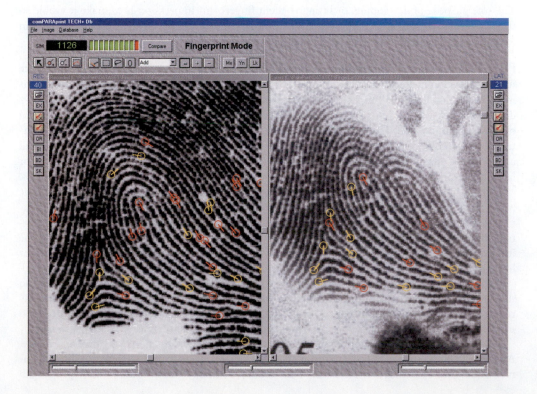

|Fig. 4.9| △

A side-by-side comparison of a latent print found at a crime scene against a file fingerprint

Courtesy of Sirchie Finger Print Laboratories Inc.

|Fig. 4.10| △

Basic fingerprint patterns. Having a general understanding of such patterns gives the investigator knowledge of what to look for once fingerprint evidence has been discovered at a crime scene.

Developing Latent Fingerprints

The sole purpose of developing, or lifting, a latent fingerprint impression is to make it visible so that it can be preserved and compared. Several powders and chemicals are used for this purpose in addition to several techniques designed to develop such evidence.

POWDERS When a latent print is clearly visible, it should be photographed before attempts are made to develop it. Accordingly, wet fingerprints should be allowed to dry before any attempt is made to develop them. Failure to do so will probably result in the print being destroyed. The powder method is used to develop fingerprints by making them show up on a surface where they would otherwise go unnoticed. To develop a latent fingerprint with powder, the powder used should contrast with the color of the surface of the print. The powder is lightly brushed over the print so it will adhere to the oils on the surface of the print pattern. Generally, gray and black powder are best for latent fingerprint development: gray for dark backgrounds and black for light backgrounds.

Usually, a small camel hair, fiberglass, or nylon brush is used in dusting for latent prints. The brush must be kept dry to be effective. A small amount of powder is first placed on the brush for application to the surface being powdered. Some investigators prefer use of the Magna-Brush*, a magnetic brush that is used with magnetic powder. When the particles of the magnetic powder come into contact with the latent surface, the print becomes apparent. The sole purpose of developing, or lifting, a latent fingerprint impression is to make it visible so that it can be preserved and compared.

When brushing, the investigator should try to identify the contour of the ridges of the print so that brush strokes can go the same direction. Powder particles will then affix themselves to the oily ridges of the fingerprint, and the print will become visible. Typically, beginners tend to use too much powder and too little brushing, thus making the print unidentifiable.

Many investigators have adopted the use of fluorescent powders as an investigative alternative. Available in both powder and aerosol form, these are typically used to dust currency or other documents that may be handled by criminals. This technique differs from traditional fingerprinting in that these powders are used "before" the fingerprint is deposited. After the criminal touches the dusted object, the area is examined by the use of an ultraviolet light, which will display any fingerprints clearly. These are then photographed and classified.

Attempting to develop fingerprints on absorbent surfaces such as paper, cardboard, and unpainted wood requires the use of more complicated procedures than the simple use of fingerprint powder, but positive results are worth the effort. Often, because powders cannot be removed from paper surfaces, it is best not to use them because the powder may interfere with writings on the document. In the next few paragraphs, we discuss the use of chemical developers. The first three, iodine, ninhydrin, and silver nitrate, are the most commonly used.

IODINE Iodine is used on the premise that it attacks the object and changes its color. The grease and oils naturally produced by the skin discolor very easily and naturally become good candidates for development with iodine. Iodine prints, generally used on paper and wood, are temporary and begin to fade after the fuming has stopped. It is therefore necessary for the investigator to be prepared to photograph the prints immediately.

Iodine fumes are controlled through the use of an iodine gun for smaller specimens or a fuming cabinet for larger objects. The gun consists essentially of two parts: one tube (through which the breath is blown) containing a drying agent such as calcium chloride to remove moisture from the breath and a second tube containing a small number of iodine crystals that are vaporized by the heat of breath and the warm hand cupped around the tube containing the iodine. The vapor is blown on the specimen.

|Fig. 4.11| △

Great care must go into searching and dusting for fingerprints.

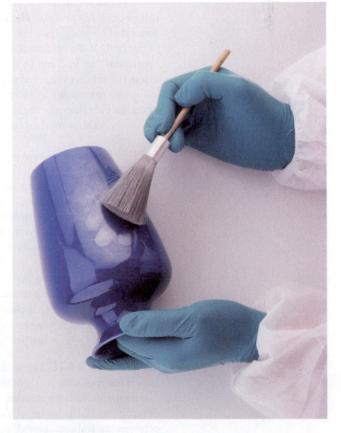

|Fig. 4.12| △

A ceramic vase being "dusted" for fingerprints with a zephyr brush.

|Fig. 4.13| ▲

Latent fingerprints developed
on a doorknob.

Courtesy of Mike Himmel

When an iodine cabinet is used, several pieces can be developed at a time, and the investigator can observe the process. The cabinet is constructed of wood or plastic with glass sides. Fumes are generated by placing a small glass dish containing the iodine crystals in a hole cut in the bottom of the cabinet. As soon as the fumes begin to appear in sufficient amounts, the burner is removed. Specimens can be hung in the cabinet by wooden clothespins fastened to a removable strip. The top of the cabinet is hinged to permit access.

Iodine fumes can be removed by placing the specimen in a current of air from a fan, blow-dryer, or other device. The process should be carried out in a well-ventilated area because fumes can cause respiratory damage if inhaled in large amounts.

NINHYDRIN A second process, involving the development of prints using amino acids present as a result of perspiration, is generally the most common method of fingerprint development for latent prints. Solutions of ninhydrin in powder or aerosol form can be acquired from fingerprint supply companies. Similar to chlorides, amino acids permeate the friction ridges of the fingerprint and remain unchanged for an extremely long time. In some cases, prints have been developed on paper 30 or 40 years after they were deposited. One fundamental requirement is that the paper must have been stored under dry conditions from the time deposited to the time developed.

A ninhydrin solution can be applied to the surface of an object by spraying, dipping, or brushing, with spraying being the method preferred. After treatment, prints should develop within 24 hours but will probably appear within an hour or two. Development can be expedited through the use of heat. Generally, a blow-dryer can accomplish this, but investigators should take care not to scorch the material being printed.

SILVER NITRATE Latent impressions developed by the use of silver nitrate are caused by the reaction of sodium chloride present in perspiration. When a person touches a surface with a sweaty finger, sodium chloride remains (almost indefinitely) while the other chemical compounds decompose. If a solution of silver nitrate is used on the impression, a chemical reaction occurs between the sodium chloride and the silver nitrate, resulting in the appearance of two new chemicals: sodium nitrate and silver chloride. Through the use of ultraviolet radiation or sunlight, the silver chloride is reduced to metallic silver, bringing out a brownish print. One commonly used procedure is to prepare a 5 percent silver nitrate solution in distilled water. The solution is either brushed on the paper or the paper is dipped in the solution. After it dries, the paper is exposed to sunlight or ultraviolet light to bring out the latent prints. Because the entire paper will soon darken, prints must be photographed immediately.

A Closer Look

The FBI's National DNA Database: CODIS

When scientists James Watson and Francis Crick first mapped the structure of the DNA double helix a half century ago, little did they know that they were also unleashing a powerful weapon in the fight against crime and terrorism. DNA can uniquely identify an individual in ways that even fingerprints can't. DNA is found in virtually every human cell. It can be extracted from hair, teeth, bones, and body fluids (blood, saliva, semen, even sweat!). It leaves traces on everything from cigarette butts to postage stamps, from shirt collars to napkins. And it lasts for years—even in harsh conditions, even when there's little left of human remains. For example, after the September 11, 2001, attacks, investigators were able to find traces of DNA in the rubble of the World Trade Center that identified victims and brought some measure of closure and relief to their devastated families.

In 1990, the FBI began a pilot project called the Combined DNA Index System, or CODIS—which became fully operational in 1998. CODIS is a three-hitter:

1. Computer technology (a database program and software)

2. Forensic science (DNA profiles rigorously measured and maintained) and

3. Telecommunications (the ability of local, state, and federal labs to share information and communicate electronically) all rolled into one system

Simply put, CODIS stores DNA profiles from across the country in a series of local, state, and national databases, all linked via computers, enabling crime labs at every level to share and compare DNA profiles electronically. Lightning fast searches using CODIS can link DNA found at one crime to other crime scenes and to convicted criminals whose DNA is already on file.

The overwhelming majority—more than 1.5 million DNA profiles—come from convicted felons. Depending on the state, the felons include those serving time for rape, murder, crimes against children, robbery, burglary, kidnapping, and assault and battery. The National DNA Index System (NDIS) also includes more than 78,000 DNA samples collected from crime scenes, more than 100 from missing persons and another 300 from relatives of missing persons, and some 150 from unidentified human remains. DNA samples from suspected terrorists are also collected today, but they are not uploaded to NDIS. When you add it all up, there are more than 1.6 million DNA profiles in the national system.

CODIS is used by a total of 175 crime labs in all 50 states and Puerto Rico, as well as the FBI Lab and the U.S. Army Crime Lab. And, in a sign of how effective the system is, 31 labs in 18 nations worldwide also use CODIS, but they are not connected to any DNA databases here in the United States. They simply borrow the FBI's technology to help investigations in their own countries, much as we do here.

The success of CODIS is measured primarily by keeping tabs on the number of investigations helped by CODIS through a hit or match that wouldn't have otherwise been developed. In December 2003, that total passed the 10,000 threshold. As of 2005, it stands at 10,770. "Forensic hits" are also measured when two or more DNA samples from a crime scene are linked in local, state, or national databases. "Offender hits" are measured when one or more DNA profiles from a crime scene are linked to a convicted felon. Between 1998 and 2005, there were more than 3,000 forensic hits and more than 7,000 offender hits.

Thematic question

The investigative uses of the CODIS system are apparent, but explain how the system could possibly be misused and how innocent persons could be wrongfully targeted for investigation.

Source: FBI, 2009. Available at http://www.fbi.gov/hq/lab/html/codis1.htm.

|Fig. 4.14| △

DNA fingerprints from a bloodstain left at the scene of a crime and from the blood of seven suspects.

George Preissl / Shutterstock

|Fig. 4.15| ▵

Portable Cyanow and cyanoacrylate ("Superglue") fuming device from Sirchie Finger Print Laboratories inserted in a hole in a cylindrical "superglue fuming chamber" containing a metal stand holding a handgun upright and an alligator clip holding a photo identification card. Superglue fuming is one of the easiest and most effective methods of developing latent fingerprints.

Sirchie Finger Print Laboratories Inc.

SUPERGLUE FUMING Cyanoacrylate resin, or superglue, was developed in the late 1950s as a bonding adhesive for metals and plastics. The substance was first used in fingerprinting, however, by the Japanese national police in 1978. Since then, the process has been refined and accepted as valuable for developing latent fingerprints on various types of surfaces. The use of superglue fuming is a relatively simple procedure and is particularly valuable in developing prints on plastic bags, metal foil, waxed paper, lacquered wood, leather, and almost all hard surfaces. Even fruits, vegetables, and dinner rolls have been processed successfully with this procedure. The process occurs as the fumes adhere to the friction ridges and then harden as ridge detail is built up on the print.

The vapor is controlled through the use of an airtight container such as a tropical fish aquarium or other glass or plastic container. To begin, a small amount of glue is recommended, usually a 1- to 2-inch-diameter pool for approximately 8 cubic feet of container space. The glue can be placed on a disposable receptacle made of aluminum foil. The glue is then heated to emit the fumes. This can be accomplished easily by placing a hot plate or light bulb under the receptacle. Objects to be printed are placed in the container, usually by suspending them with wooden clothespins or spring-loaded clips, allowing maximum exposure to fumes. Exposure time may vary, so periodic inspection of the objects is necessary to check progress. The investigator must remember that because the flashpoint of the glue may vary, great care should be given to maintain a desired temperature level. After the procedure, all prints are photographed, and the specimens should be powdered.

LASERS The detection and development of latent fingerprints left at crime scenes have taken a quantum leap forward with the use of laser technology. Since its development in 1976, this technique has been used to develop prints that could not have been developed through the use of powders, iodine, ninhydrin, silver nitrate, or superglue fuming. The laser procedure is a clean, relatively easy method to develop prints, and pretreatment of the specimen is not required.

As with the ninhydrin method, the age of the print is of no importance. Additionally, there is no alteration of the evidence; therefore, it is generally used before other methods. In this process, an expanded laser beam is used to luminesce certain properties of perspiration, body oils, or other foreign substances found on a latent print. Three types of lasers are currently operational in the development of fingerprints: the argon ion laser, the copper vapor laser, and the neodymium:YAG laser. Because laser light is extremely bright, eye protection must be worn by equipment operators. Special light-filtering goggles can be worn to illuminate latent prints with greater clarity.

Preservation of Fingerprints

Because of the importance of latent fingerprints in any criminal investigation, great care must be taken to preserve them for later examination and use in court. Fingerprints remain on affected areas for varying amounts of time, depending on whether they are plastic, visible, or latent. Generally, plastic and latent prints may remain for years, depending on the type of surface on which they are located. Methods of fingerprint preservation include photography of the print and lifting techniques.

Often, fingerprints are left on a surface that can be transported to the crime laboratory for examination. Undoubtedly, this is the preferred way to facilitate classification of the print. Unfortunately, however, many prints must be processed on the crime scene because they are found on surfaces too large to transport. In general, plastic and latent prints can remain for years, depending on the type of surface on which they are located.

Fingerprint lifters are used to remove the print from surfaces that are curved or otherwise difficult to photograph. For surfaces such as these, rubber lifters are recommended. Rubber lifters are available at fingerprint supply houses and consist of a thin black or white flexible material coated with an adhesive. The adhesive side is guarded by a thin cover that is removed just before it is placed on the print and then replaced just after use. As a general rule, the latent fingerprint is dusted with print powder. The adhesive side of the lifter is then placed against the print and slowly pulled away. The print is preserved by the fingerprint powder being pressed against the lifter. After the print is lifted, the lifter cover is replaced.

Lifting tape is also a commonly used medium for fingerprint preservation. This is a special transparent tape supplied in rolls 1 to 2 inches wide. The procedure is to dust the print with fingerprint powder and then place the tape over the print, thus removing it. The investigator must take care to avoid air pockets in the tape while it is being applied because these will show up as void areas on the print impression. After it has been applied, the tape will adhere to the powder particles and transfer the fingerprint impression.

Prints from Gloves

The notoriety of the success of fingerprinting has resulted in the use of gloves by many criminals as a protective measure. Investigators may discover "smearing" from gloves on a crime scene but may give the matter little consideration. Indeed, such gloves, if located, may produce valuable evidence in locating the perpetrator. The glove itself may have a unique, identifiable pattern, as with a fingerprint.

Leather gloves, for example, may contain fatty material, and fabric gloves are often contaminated with soil or other foreign matter. In both cases, ridge patterns may be left behind. A leather glove may possess certain pattern characteristics that make it distinguishable. This is because animal hide possesses friction ridge skin similar to that of human beings, and its characteristics can readily be identified. Fabric gloves do not offer as identifiable a pattern as that of leather gloves, but certain features may still be identifiable. After wearing gloves for a period, certain wrinkles or cracks in the material may create distinguishable markings. Sometimes a fingerprint can be recovered from a glove, particularly if it is made of latex material.

The Integrated Automated Fingerprint Identification System

The Integrated Automated Fingerprint Identification System, more commonly known as IAFIS, is a national fingerprint and criminal history database maintained by the FBI's CJIS Division. The IAFIS provides automated fingerprint search capabilities, latent searching capability, electronic image storage, and electronic exchange of fingerprints and responses, 24 hours a day, 365 days

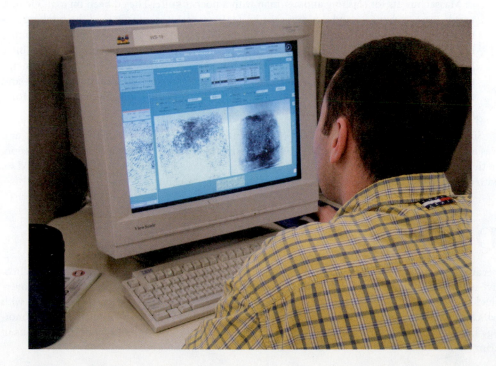

|Fig. 4.16| △

The IAFIS fingerprint identification has revolutionized suspect identification. Here, an analyst examines identifiable points in a suspect print for comparison with the computerized fingerprint database.

Courtesy of Mike Himmel and the Missouri State Highway Patrol.

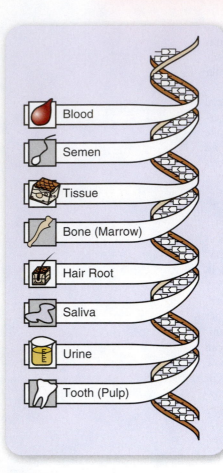

|Fig. 4.17| ▲

Sources of DNA
evidence.

Sirchie Finger Print Laboratories Inc.

a year. It combines with criminal histories, mugshots, scar and tattoo photos, height, weight, hair and eye color, and aliases to help match evidence with identities. As a result of submitting fingerprints electronically, agencies receive electronic responses to criminal 10-print fingerprint submissions within 2 hours and within 24 hours for civil fingerprint submissions.

The IAFIS maintains the largest biometric database in the world, containing the fingerprints and corresponding criminal history information for more than 47 million subjects in the Criminal Master File. The fingerprints and corresponding criminal history information are submitted voluntarily by state, local, and federal law enforcement agencies.

Just a few years ago, substantial delays were a normal part of the fingerprint identification process because fingerprint cards had to be physically transported and processed. A fingerprint check could often take three months to complete. The FBI formed a partnership with the law enforcement community to revitalize the fingerprint identification process, leading to the development of the IAFIS. The IAFIS became operational in July 1999.

Since its implementation, the IAFIS has been responsible for the successful identification of suspects in hundreds of cases. Examples are as follows:

1. *The case of the cocaine murderer.* In April 2004, a man was arrested in Connecticut by a drug task force for possession of cocaine. He was fingerprinted, and his electronic prints were sent to IAFIS. Ten minutes later, there was a match. Turns out he'd been wanted in Miami since September 2002 for fleeing the state to avoid being prosecuted for homicide…and he'd been wanted in Fort Lauderdale since October 2003 on homicide charges. In no time, he was picked up and extradited to Florida for prosecution.

2. *The case of the vicious rapist.* In June 2004, a man was arrested by police in New Jersey for simple assault and endangering the welfare of children. That turned out to be the tip of the iceberg. When officers fingerprinted the man and sent his prints to IAFIS…13 minutes later, a match! Turns out he'd been wanted in Norfolk, Virginia, since October 2000 for rape and sexual abduction…and he'd been wanted in Yorktown, Virginia, since May 2001 for kidnapping and sexual assault. In no time, he was facing charges in New Jersey before being shipped off to Virginia to face charges there.

3. *The case of the Christmas murderer.* In September 2004, a 57-year-old man was arrested in Massachusetts for slashing another man with a pocket knife. They'd been on a public bus, words were exchanged, and out came the knife. Fingerprints were taken at the booking station and sent to IAFIS. Turns out he was the man accused of a horrific crime in Baltimore in 1974. It was Christmas Eve 30 years earlier when police department employee McKinley Johnson was helping to put together food baskets for the poor. Suddenly a young man approached and stole a can of lunch meat from one of the baskets. Johnson ran after him—and the thief shot him point blank. Before dying, Johnson identified his alleged assailant from photographs…and the hunt had been on ever since.

Since that time, the suspect had lived in different places, assumed 10 different identities, and was arrested five times in Boston in the 1980s for charges from shoplifting to weapon possession. In the meantime, though, IAFIS was created, allowing matches of fingerprints nationwide. And so, with the slash of a pocket knife, 30 years on the run came to an end.[2]

DNA: The Genetic Fingerprint

Because of its success in identifying suspects, fingerprinting has proven to be one of the most effective methods in law enforcement. However, a dramatic advance in forensic science may now overshadow the technique of fingerprinting: **DNA technology**. DNA has given scientists the means with which to detect the remarkable variability existing between individuals. The results of this technology hold great promise in aiding the criminal justice system in making positive determinations of criminal identity.

What Is DNA?

In all life forms, from viruses to human beings, the basis for difference lies in the genetic material known as **deoxyribonucleic acid** (DNA). In every living organism, with the exception of certain viruses that possess ribonucleic acid (RNA), DNA represents a genetic facsimile, or "blueprint," of that organism. Additionally, in every cell within each human body, the DNA is identical. This applies whether the cell is a white or a red blood cell, a piece of skin, spermatozoa, or even a follicle of hair.

Although DNA is extremely complex chemically, it consists of only five basic elements: carbon, hydrogen, oxygen, nitrogen, and phosphorus. These five elements combine to form certain molecules known as nucleotides. The four bases that code genetic information in the polynucleotide chain of DNA are thymine, cytosine, adenine, and guanine (T, C, A, and G, respectively). Although just four letters exist in this short alphabet, a variety of different sequences of nucleotides exist. A single strand of DNA can be millions of nucleotides long. For example, 6 billion nucleotides constitute the DNA in one human being.

In human beings, 23 pairs of chromosomes originate from each parent: one of each pair from the mother and one from the father at the time of conception. Therefore, when a person is born, his or her genes are made up of a combination of maternal and paternal genes. Because of this, no two persons are exactly alike except identical twins.

The History of DNA

Since it was introduced in the mid-1980s, DNA fingerprinting has revolutionized forensic science and the ability of law enforcement to match offenders with crime scenes. Literally thousands of cases have been closed and innocent suspects freed with guilty ones punished because of the power of a silent biological witness, DNA, at the crime scene.

DNA "fingerprinting" or DNA typing (profiling) as it is now known, was first described in 1985 by an English geneticist named Alec Jeffreys. Dr. Jeffreys discovered that certain regions of DNA contain DNA sequences that are repeated over and over again next to each other. He also discovered that the number of repeated sections present in a sample could differ from individual to individual. By developing a technique to examine the length variation of these DNA repeat sequences, Dr. Jeffreys created the ability to perform human identity tests.

These DNA repeat regions became known as VNTRs, which stands for variable number of tandem repeats. The technique used by Dr. Jeffreys to examine the VNTRs was called restriction fragment length polymorphism (RFLP) because it involved the use of a restriction enzyme to cut the regions of DNA surrounding the VNTRs. This RFLP method was first used to help in an English immigration case and shortly thereafter to solve a double homicide case. Since that time, human identity testing using DNA typing methods has been widespread.

The past 15 years have seen tremendous growth in the use of DNA evidence in crime scene investigations. Today, more than 150 public forensic laboratories and several dozen private paternity testing laboratories conduct hundreds of thousands of DNA tests annually in the United States.[3] In addition, most countries in Europe and Asia have forensic DNA programs. The number of laboratories around the world conducting DNA testing will continue to grow as the technique gains in popularity within law enforcement.

Let's go back to the early 1980s and review a murder case in England that was the first to use DNA technology in criminal investigation. Since the Narborough murders (discussed later in this chapter), the DNA technique has often been used successfully in the United States, beginning in 1987 in the *Florida* v. *Andrews* case, involving a sexual assault. Although it has been used successfully in many criminal trials, future issues will probably focus on the admissibility of DNA test results.

In the *Florida* v. *Andrews* case, police in Orlando, Florida, suspected that one man was involved in more than 20 cases of prowling, breaking and entering, and attempted sexual assault. In every case, the modus operandi (MO) was similar: The man would stalk his victim for weeks, prowling around her house and peeping through windows. When attacked, the victim had little or no opportunity to make a visual identification. Until Tommie Lee Andrews was arrested, all police had to go on were composite drawings and several calls about a prowler. After his arrest, one rape victim (who had seen her assailant for only about six seconds while being attacked) picked Andrews out of a photo lineup.

When attorney Hal Uhrig was appointed to be the defense attorney for Tommie Lee Andrews, his concern was not about DNA evidence. Instead, he was worried about the amount of time and

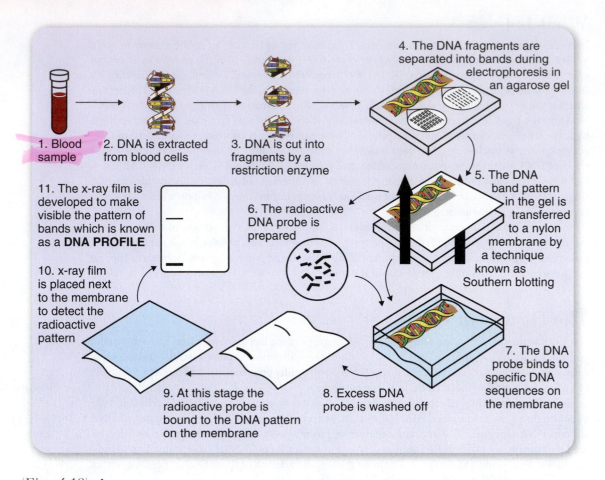

|Fig. 4.18| ▲

The steps typically followed by criminalists in DNA profiling.

effort that would be required for him and his small law firm to defend Andrews against multiple rape charges. It was not until later, after prosecutor Jeffrey Ashton read an advertisement in a legal publication about DNA testing and employed the services of Lifecodes, Inc., that Uhrig discovered he was involved in the first-known DNA criminal case in the United States.

At Andrews's first trial, prosecutors successfully introduced results from the test by Lifecodes. The defense, however, successfully challenged the introduction of any testimony regarding the statistical probabilities resulting from the test. The trial ended in a hung jury. At the retrial, DNA evidence was again admitted. This time, the prosecution was prepared to argue that the statistical probabilities of the test be introduced. Using a relevance standard similar to that in the federal rules of evidence, the court admitted the statistical data. Andrews was subsequently convicted.

Prosecutor Ashton said that he was unaware at the outset that this was the first case to use DNA testing in the United States but that he believed it would be a powerful tool in future cases, especially when the suspect is a serial rapist who is careful not to leave much evidence. Defense attorney Uhrig said that he came away from his experience in defending against DNA evidence most concerned about the use of statistical data, which he believed carries inordinate weight in the minds of the jury. As more population data are collected, the numbers could become much smaller and lose "real-world meaning" to juries.

Hypothetically, said Uhrig, odds of 10 billion to one could be introduced into court. But if the defendant in such a case had an identical twin (and hence identical DNA patterns), the odds of a random match would be 5 billion to one but still a 50 percent probability that the DNA in question would not belong to the defendant. DNA typing, Uhrig said, might well result in more rape defenses that center on consent rather than on alibi or denial defenses.

Analyzing DNA

Genetic patterns found in blood or semen can be just as distinctive as fingerprints. Traditional serology tests on bodily fluids often do not discriminate enough to either exclude or include a suspect in a crime. DNA analysis provides much more conclusive analysis. The unique genetic patterns found in each person's DNA make it possible, with a high degree of accuracy, to associate a suspect with (or exclude a suspect from) a crime. Except in the case of identical twins, every person's DNA and resulting DNA pattern are different. The process of analyzing, or "typing," DNA begins with DNA source material such as blood or semen. After the DNA is removed from the sample chemically, restriction enzymes known as endonucleases are added that cut the DNA into particles or fragments. The particles are then mixed with a sieving gel and sorted out according to size by a process called electrophoresis. In this process, the DNA moves along the gel-coated plate, some faster than others. At the completion of the process, the double-stranded fragments of DNA are treated so that the strands separate from each other.

Next, a transfer method developed by Edward Southern, called Southern blotting, is used. In this process, the DNA is transferred to a nylon membrane in much the same way that ink is transferred to a blotter. The nylon sheet is then treated with radioactively labeled DNA probes, single-stranded pieces of DNA that can bind through complementary base pairing with target DNA. Whereas a single-locus probe "looks" for only one field, a multilocus probe looks for numerous fields simultaneously. The radioactive probe then merges with the specific DNA sequences found on the membrane fragments. The images that result from x-ray film placed in contact with the membrane to detect the probe configuration look like the price bar codes used on supermarket products.

These images are analyzed visually or by computer. Although not yet considered a routine procedure for all police agencies, it is clear that DNA will prove to be one of the most exciting and valuable investigative tools developed in recent decades, possibly even more significant than that of fingerprinting technology. As time goes on, there will undoubtedly be significant legal and scientific challenges to the application of DNA technology in crime solving. Certainly, however, as the "bugs" are worked out, society as a whole will be the beneficiary of this captivating science, which enables virtually positive identification of both criminal suspects and their victims.

Because of the importance of biological evidence, investigators and laboratory personnel should work together to determine which pieces of evidence are more significant. As such, every officer should be aware of important issues involved in the identification, collection, transportation, and storage of DNA evidence. These issues are as important for the first responding patrol officer as they are for the experienced detective and the crime scene specialist. This is because biological material may contain hazardous pathogens such as the human immunodeficiency virus (HIV) and the hepatitis B virus that can cause potentially lethal diseases.

Biohazardous materials should be housed in a segregated area within the evidence room that is clearly marked "Biohazardous Material Only." Care must be taken to package items separately to avoid cross-contamination of other evidence.

Transportation and Storage

When transporting and storing evidence that may contain DNA, it is important to keep the evidence dry and at room temperature. After the evidence has been secured in paper bags or envelopes, it should be sealed, labeled, and transported in a way that ensures proper identification of where it was found and the proper chain of custody. DNA evidence should never be placed in plastic bags because plastic bags retain damaging moisture.[4] Direct sunlight and warmer conditions can also be

|Fig. 4.19| ◢

Crime lab biologist working with blood samples on the analysis of DNA.

Mike Himmel / Missouri State Highway Patrol Crime Laboratory harmful to DNA. Consequently, investigators should avoid keeping evidence in places that may get hot, such as a room or police car without air-conditioning.

Elimination Samples

As with fingerprints, the effective use of DNA may require the collection and analysis of elimination samples.[5] Elimination samples can be used to determine whether the evidence comes from the suspect or from someone else. It is important for the investigator, while still on the crime scene, to think ahead to the time of trial and possible defenses. For example, in the case of a residential burglary in which the suspect may have drunk a glass of water at the crime scene, an officer should identify appropriate people, such as household members, for future elimination sample testing.

These samples may be needed for comparison with the saliva found on the glass to determine whether the saliva is valuable evidence. In homicide cases, be sure to collect the victim's DNA from the medical examiner at the autopsy, even if the body is badly decomposed. This may serve to identify an unknown victim or distinguish between the victim's DNA and other DNA found at the crime scene.

When investigating rape cases, it may be necessary to collect and analyze the DNA of the victim's recent consensual partners, if any, to eliminate them as potential contributors of DNA suspected to be from the perpetrator. If this is necessary, it is important to approach the victim with extreme sensitivity and provide a full explanation of why the request is being made. When possible, the help of a qualified victim advocate should be enlisted for assistance.

All contaminated evidence that is ready for disposal, as well as all disposable equipment or cleaning materials contaminated with bodily fluids, should be bagged in accordance with state and federal laws. The Centers for Disease Control and Prevention recommends that, in general, infective waste be either incinerated or decontaminated before disposal in a sanitary landfill.[6] Bulk blood or other bodily fluids may be carefully poured down a drain connected to a sanitary sewer. Sanitary sewers may also be used to dispose of other infectious wastes capable of being ground and flushed into the sewer. In all cases, departments should be familiar with state and local laws governing such disposal.

Admissibility of DNA as Evidence

For evidence to be accepted into court, it must be offered by one of the parties and be admitted by the court. Questions regarding the admissibility of evidence have generally been handled at a pretrial hearing. Two standards have been used to govern the admission of scientific evidence: the **relevancy test** and the **Frye test**.

The relevancy test, which is based on the federal rules of evidence, permits the admission of **relevant evidence** that is helpful to the trier of fact. The second pretrial hearing, the Frye test, or Frye standard, involves the admission of scientific evidence. This test, named after the defendant in a 1923 murder case, is the oldest test and the one used most often for determining the admissibility of scientific evidence. Under the Frye standard, courts admit evidence based on novel scientific techniques only when the technique has gained general acceptance in the scientific community to which it belongs. General acceptance under the Frye test appears to require a two-step analysis:

1. Identifying the field in which the underlying theory falls (i.e., in determining whether the technique meets the test of acceptance in the scientific community, defining what community is relevant)
2. Determining whether the principle has been accepted by most members of the field identified

The Frye test has several perceived advantages and disadvantages. Its proponents note that the test guarantees a minimal amount of support by experts for a scientific test or procedure in its introduction in a court of law. As noted by one court, the experts "form a kind of technical jury, which must first pass on the scientific status of a procedure before the lay jury utilizes it in making its findings of fact." After the pretrial Frye or evidentiary hearing, a court rules whether DNA testing will be admitted into evidence and, if so, under what conditions. At trial, any party may offer expert testimony. It is the obligation of the party calling expert witnesses to lay the foundation for such testimony. The foundation includes the qualifications and experience of the witness, details on how DNA testing works, what procedures were followed, the results of the test, and facts and opinions that can be drawn from the test results.

The Daubert Standard

The Daubert standard is a legal precedent set in 1993 by the Supreme Court of the United States regarding the admissibility of expert witnesses' testimony during federal legal proceedings. The citation is *Daubert* v. *Merrell Dow Pharmaceuticals*, 509 U.S. 579 (1993). A Daubert motion, raised before or sometimes during trial, attempts to exclude the presentation of unqualified evidence to the jury. This is a special case of "motion in limine," which is typically used to exclude the testimony of an expert witness who has no such expertise or used questionable methods to obtain the information.

In the Daubert case, the Supreme Court held that federal trial judges are the "gatekeepers" of scientific evidence. Under the Daubert standard, therefore, trial judges must evaluate proffered expert witnesses to determine whether their testimony is both "relevant" and "reliable," a two-pronged test of admissibility. For example:

1. *The relevancy prong.* The relevancy of a testimony refers to whether or not the expert's evidence "fits" the facts of the case. For example, you may invite an astronomer to tell the jury if there was a full moon on the night of a crime. However, the astronomer would not be allowed to testify if the fact that the moon was full was not relevant to the issue at hand in the trial.
2. *The reliability prong.* The Supreme Court explained that for expert testimony to be considered reliable, the expert must have derived his or her conclusions from the scientific method. The Court offered "general observations" of whether proffered evidence was based on the scientific method, although the list was not intended to be used as an exhaustive checklist:

   - Empirical testing: the theory or technique must be falsifiable, refutable, and testable
   - Subjected to peer review and publication
   - Known or potential error rate and the existence and maintenance of standards concerning its operation
   - Whether the theory and technique is generally accepted by a relevant scientific community

Although trial judges have always had the authority to exclude inappropriate testimony, before the Daubert trial, courts often preferred to let juries hear evidence proffered by both sides. After certain evidence has been excluded by a Daubert motion because it fails to meet the relevancy and reliability standard, it will likely be challenged when introduced again in another trial. Even though a Daubert motion is not binding to other courts of law, if something was found not trustworthy, other judges may choose to follow that precedent. Of course, a decision by the Court of Appeals that a piece of evidence is inadmissible under Daubert would be binding on district courts within that court's geographic jurisdiction.

Other Uses of DNA

In addition to its utility in criminal investigations, DNA blood typing can be put to use in other ways. For example, with the use of a new process called PCR, cells producing billions of DNA strips can be reproduced rapidly in a test tube, a feat that would take a dividing cancer cell at least a month to perform. The PCR technique has recently been used to perform the following examinations:

- Comparing the DNA of extinct animals with that of their closest living relatives
- Assisting the military in identifying the remains of soldiers who fought in wars such as Operation Desert Storm
- Helping physicians detect small numbers of cancer cells circulating in the bloodstream and to make prenatal diagnosis of genetic diseases such as sickle-cell anemia
- Ensuring better matches between organ donors and transplant recipients

In January 1992, the Defense Department announced that it would establish a repository of genetic information on all U.S. service members as a way of identifying future war casualties. The Armed Forces Institute of Pathology now collects t samples of DNA from blood and oral swabs and adds the information to fingerprint, dental, and other records.

DNA profiling may be the most significant breakthrough in forensic science since the development of fingerprinting. Federal, state, and local crime laboratories are currently working to enhance profiling techniques and to establish a national DNA index. In addition, a uniform approach to DNA testing is being sought to ensure an effective and secure system.

A Closer Look

When Forensic Evidence Lies

Since forensic science results can mean the difference between life and death in many cases, fraud and other types of misconduct in the field are particularly troubling. Falsified testimony, exaggerated or fabricated statistics, and laboratory fraud have led to wrongful conviction in a number of states.

Because forensic evidence is offered by "experts," jurors routinely give it much more weight than other evidence. But when misconduct occurs, the weight is misplaced. In some instances, labs or their personnel have actually aligned themselves with police and prosecutors to target and convict subjects, rather than focusing on the true goal of criminal investigation—to search for the truth. In other cases, criminalists lacking the requisite knowledge have embellished findings and eluded detection because judges and juries themselves lacked background in the relevant sciences.

In some cases, important evidence has been lost, contaminated, or destroyed, so that re-testing to uncover misconduct has proven impossible. Evidence in these cases can never be tested again, preventing misconduct from ever being exposed.

The identification, collection, testing, storage, handling, and reporting of any piece of forensic evidence involve a number of people. Evidence can be deliberately or accidentally mishandled at any stage of this process.

In many cases, the risk of misconduct originates at the crime scene, where evidence can be planted, destroyed, or mishandled. Evidence is later sent to a forensic lab or independent contractor, where it can be contaminated, improperly tested, consumed unnecessarily, or mislabeled. Then, in the reporting of test results, technicians and their superiors sometimes have misrepresented their findings. DNA exonerations have even revealed instances of "drylabbing" evidence—reporting results when no test was actually performed.

Disturbingly, numerous cases of forensic fraud have become known over the past 20 years. One such case was the Joyce Gilchrist case. Gilchrist, a forensic chemist working for the Oklahoma City Police Department, participated in over 3,000 criminal cases in 21 years. She was accused of falsifying evidence. Her evidence led in part to 23 people being sentenced to death, 11 of whom were executed. Gilchrist earned the nickname "Black Magic" for her ability to match DNA evidence that her fellow forensic examiners could not. In 1994, and after only nine years at her current position of forensic chemist, Gilchrist was promoted to supervisor. Her co-workers, however, began to raise concerns about her work. Gilchrist was later dismissed due to "flawed casework analysis" and "laboratory mismanagement."

Concerns about Gilchrist's actions were first raised when a landscaper, Jeffrey Todd Pierce, whose 1986 conviction for rape was based to a great extent on Gilchrist's evidence despite a clean record and good alibi, was exonerated based on additional DNA evidence. Pierce, a husband and the father of two infant children, was misidentified in a police lineup. In spite of voluntarily giving hair and blood samples to the police investigators to clear his name, he was arrested and charged with the rape. Gilchrist claimed his hair samples were "microscopically consistent" with the hairs found at the crime scene. In 2001, after DNA evidence was re-examined Pierce was cleared of the crime; he was released after 15 years in prison. He later filed a civil suit against Oklahoma City and sought 75 million dollars and charging that Gilchrist and former District Attorney Bob Macy conspired to produce false evidence against him. The suit was settled for $4 million in 2007.

Other examples of forensic fraud include:

- A former director of the West Virginia state crime lab, Fred Zain, testified for the prosecution in 12 states over his career, including dozens of cases in West Virginia and Texas. DNA exonerations and new evidence in other cases have shown that Zain fabricated results, lied on the stand about results, and knowingly omitted evidence from his reports.

- Pamela Fish, a Chicago lab technician, testified for the prosecution about false matches and suspicious results in the trials of at least eight defendants who were convicted, then proven innocent years later by DNA testing.

Sources: Luscombe, Belinda. (2001). When the evidence lies. *Time Magazine*, May 31; Scheck, B. and P. Neufeld. (2001). Junk science, Junk evidence. *The New York Times*, May 11; Yardley, Jim. (2001). Inquiry focuses on scientists employed by prosecutors. *The New York Times*, May 2.

Handwriting Analysis

Similar to skills acquired in piloting an aircraft or interpreting a polygraph, accurate handwriting analysis requires many years of study and practice. From our earliest years in elementary school, we are taught how to sculpt letters of the alphabet meticulously to form words and sentences. People often adopt unique styles of their own, frequently characteristic only of that person. Such characteristics are identifiable to handwriting experts, who must be knowledgeable in both photography and microscopy.

Writings may occur in many forms, including that on personal correspondence, desks, walls, and even dead bodies. In all cases, they may offer the investigator valuable evidence in identifying suspects. To understand how best to proceed with the handwriting analysis process, we should first consider that the average handwriting specimen has 500 to 1,000 characters, including elements such as form, movement, connections, alignment, punctuation, slant, spacings, and embellishments. Any object containing handwritten or typewritten markings and whose source or authenticity is in doubt may be referred to as a questioned document.[7]

Collection of Exemplars

Cases involving questioned documents require a comparison between the suspect document and a sample or exemplar (also known as a *standard*). Two types of **exemplars** exist: the requested and the collected. In both cases, its origin must be well documented before analysis to ensure genuineness.

REQUESTED EXEMPLARS A requested handwriting standard is obtained from a suspect at the formal request of a law enforcement officer and is performed solely as a means to acquire a comparison document. It is logical to assume that no two samples of a suspect's handwriting are identical. Therefore, a sufficient number of exemplars must be collected to demonstrate to the examiner the range of natural variations in a suspect's writing peculiarities. In the event that investigators might not be successful in obtaining exemplars of a suspect's handwriting, an exemplar may be obtained directly from the suspect.

In a 1967 case, *Gilbert* v. *California*, the court held that requiring a suspect to give a handwriting sample does not violate a person's Fifth Amendment protection against self-incrimination. Therefore, he or she cannot refuse. Exemplars requested by the police are a means to acquire a comparison document from a suspect.

COLLECTED EXEMPLARS A collected handwriting exemplar is a sample of the suspect's handwriting that was not written for the purpose of examination and is not evidence in the crime under investigation. The obvious reason for this is that the sample document must be one that the suspect has not prepared or altered deliberately to match a suspect document.

The most valuable collected document is one that has been acquired close to the time the suspect document was produced. For example, if the document questioned was produced on a typewriter, an exemplar of the suspected typewriter would be collected. Accordingly, if the suspect's signature is in question, a standard of his or her handwriting must be collected. Typically, collected exemplars can be acquired from such documents as insurance policies, credit card receipts, canceled checks, and personal letters. Collected exemplars are samples of the suspect's handwriting that were not specially written for the purpose of examination that are used as comparison documents.

The Writing Medium

The process of collecting handwriting exemplars includes being sure that the writing instruments (e.g., paper, pencils) used in the sample are the same as those used in the suspect document. Things to look for in selection of paper include its size, thickness, color, and condition. In short, the sample paper should match, as closely as possible, that used by the suspect.

If more than one sample document is being acquired from the suspect, they should not be stacked on top of each other. This is because writing impressions might press through one page to another and hinder the examination of them. Additionally, each handwriting sample should be taken from the suspect's sight as soon as it is obtained. This prevents the suspect from attempting to compare his writing from one exemplar to another.

The same type of instrument used for the document questioned should be furnished to the suspect for the control exemplar. This includes the pencil, pen, felt-tip marker, and so on. Special attention should also be given to matching the lead number of a pencil, the color of an ink pen, and the width of a felt-tip marker to that used on the questioned document.

The Writing Area

The suspect should be afforded a comfortable writing area. The backseat of a police car, for example, will prove to be a waste of time. The investigator must make sure that the suspect is writing in the same general style as in the suspect document: block letters for block letters, cursive writing for cursive writing, and so on. It might also be advisable to obtain a sample of writing in the suspect's opposite hand in the event that the suspect used this technique as a deception. In addition, the investigator will have to observe as the suspect writes the sample document because his or her testimony will be required in court. The investigator must make sure that the suspect is writing in the same general style as in the suspect document.

Facial Composites

One method of developing an idea of the suspect's general description is to have the witness provide information to a police artist so that a *facial composite* can be generated. In previous years, construction of the **composite** was done by a trained artist through drawing sketching or painting in consultation with a witness or crime victim. In the 1960s, techniques were devised for use by those who are less artistic, using interchangeable templates of separate facial features, such as Smith & Wesson's **Identi-Kit**. More recently, computer-generated imaging systems have been developed, such as Smith & Wesson's "Identi-Kit 2000." Today the FBI maintains that hand-drawing is still the correct method for constructing a facial composite. Many police agencies, however, use software because developed artistic talent is often not available. Technologically, the most commonly used software in the United States is FACES, although there are other popular products such as "IQ Biometrix," "CompuSketch," and "SuspectID."[8]

Although the classic use of the facial composite is the citizen recognizing the face as an acquaintance, there are other ways that a facial composite can prove useful. The facial composite can assist law enforcement in a number of ways. These include:

- Identifying the suspect in a wanted poster
- Additional evidence against a suspect
- Assisting investigation in checking leads
- Warning the public against serial offenders[9]

Facial composites have been used successfully to identify suspects in numerous cases. Included are the Oklahoma "Murrah Building" bomber Timothy McVeigh and Baton Rouge serial killer

|Fig. 4.20|

The composite sketch can be an important component to the identification process. Here an investigator discusses a suspect's physical characteristics with a witness.

Derrick Todd Lee.[10] They have also been used extensively in television programs, such as *America's Most Wanted*,[11] that aim to reconstruct major unsolved crimes with a view to gaining information from the members of the public.

Criminal Investigative Analysis

For years, the means of identifying the type of person responsible for a particular crime was known as **personality profiling.** Today, the process, known as **criminal investigative analysis**, is accomplished by identifying psychological and social characteristics surrounding the crime as well as the manner in which it was committed. An example is the Unabomber case, in which mail bombs killed four people in a period spanning 15 years. Forensic investigators subsequently determined that the bomber chose his postage carefully, using Frederick Douglass stamps when he wanted to injure his targets and stamps of playwright Eugene O'Neill when he intended to kill. O'Neill's plays were known for their dark themes.

One of O'Neill's plays, *Dynamo*, was highly critical of America's growing reliance on machinery and industrialization, a theme echoed in the Unabomber's manifesto. The profiling technique can be advantageous in illuminating certain clues at the crime scene that may not be apparent upon first examination. The **psychological profiling** technique recognizes that hate, passion, fear, and confusion may all have certain indicators somewhere at the scene. These can include postmortem slashing or cutting, rapes, lust, and mutilation murders.

The practice of profiling was developed during World War II by government psychologist William Langer to predict Adolph Hitler's future actions. As it relates to criminal investigation, profiling is based on the notion that crime is, directly or indirectly, based on the personality of the person committing it. Profilers typically scrutinize evidence found on the crime scene and attempt to re-create the circumstances surrounding the crime and to predict the offender's frame of mind. The profile is then used to narrow down the list of suspects as it develops. From a practical standpoint, profiling can be helpful in investigating any crime in which the evidence suggests that the suspect is irrational or mentally or emotionally unstable.

|Fig. 4.21| △

Eyewitness viewing a photo array. The important thing for the investigator to remember is to avoid any suggestiveness either through the composition of the photos themselves or the actions or words of the investigator.

Courtesy of Mike Himmel

Profiling gained popularity during the 1980s, when the FBI became heavily involved in the profiling of violent sex offenders and arsonists. More recently, caregivers with a disorder called Munchhausen syndrome by proxy (MSBP) have become the subject of profilers. The disorder involves offenders who injure or cause illnesses in their children to gain attention and sympathy for themselves. Past cases have revealed that most suspects are women who victimize their children so as to become the center of attention by police, doctors, family members, and others. MSBP is thought to be a serial offense usually affecting families with more than one child. Characteristics of offenders include a history of self-inflicted wounds, past psychiatric treatment, past attempted suicides, a middle- to upper-class background, a better-than-average education, and knowledge of the medical field and related procedures.

The field of psychological profiling continues to grow as new areas are developed. Two of the newest areas include hostage negotiation and terrorism.[12] The psychological profiling technique was used successfully by the FBI in the investigation of Theodore (Ted) Bundy, the serial murderer responsible for the murders of 30 young women in the northwestern United States between 1973 and 1978.

According to John Douglas and Robert Ressler of the FBI, most (normal) persons have personality traits that are more or less identifiable. However, an abnormal person tends to become more ritualized and tends to display a "pattern" to his or her behavior. Often, the suspect's personality is reflected in both the crime scene and in the furnishings of his or her home. Because of the nature of such evidence, the profiling procedure has limitations and should be used in conjunction with other investigative techniques. The profiling technique requires the collection of certain types of information:

- *Photographs* focused on the extent and depth of wounds
- *Neighborhood information*, including racial, ethnic, and social data
- *Medical examiner's report*, including photos of damage to body, such as stabs, gunshots, bruises, and lividity, and information regarding toxicology, postmortem wounds, and personal observations of the medical examiner
- *Map of the victim's travel before death*, including residence and employment information, where last seen, and crime scene location
- *Complete investigation report of the incident*, such as date, time, location, type of weapon used, and detailed interviews of witnesses
- *Background of victim*, including age, race, gender, physical description, marital status, lifestyle, sexual preference, medical history (physical and mental), personal habits, use of alcohol or drugs, and friends or enemies

After the information has been collected, the investigator analyzes the information and attempts to reconstruct the event. Techniques used are brainstorming to critique the case, use of intuition to follow hunches, and educated guessing. Profiling factors do not consist of clinical observations solely but rather a collection of investigative data from which to draw inferences about the suspect, victim, and motive of the crime.

Investigative Psychology

Another relative newcomer to the investigative process is investigative psychology. This technique essentially brings together the retrieval of investigative information and draws inferences about that information in as far as the ways that police decision-making can be supported through scientific research. This area is different from investigative analysis or "profiling," which grew out of the experience of police officers offering opinions about the possible characteristics of unknown offenders.

Investigative psychology is grounded in empirical research and logical inference to cover the full range of investigative activities in addition to the preparation of "profiles." The inference processes at the heart of investigative psychology differ from the approach used by the FBI, which emphasizes a subjective process such as "thinking like the criminal." Rather, investigative psychology stresses that the results of scientific psychology can contribute to many aspects of civilian and criminal investigation, including the full range of crimes from burglary to terrorism, not just the extreme crimes of violence that have an obvious psychopathic component.

The contribution to investigations draws on the extent to which an offender displays various tested characteristics[13] as well as procedures for enhancing the processes by which interviews are carried out or information is put before the courts. One goal of investigative psychology research is determining behaviorally important information regarding the consistency of the behavior of many different types of offenders. Although to date most studies have been of violent crimes, there is a growing body of research on burglary and arson. It is also important to establish valid and reliable methods of distinguishing between offenders and between offenses.[14] Holmes and Holmes (2008) identified the three main goals of criminal profiling:

- The first is to provide law enforcement with a social and psychological assessment of the offender;
- The second goal is to provide law enforcement with a "psychological evaluation of belongings found in the possession of the offender:"
- The third goal is to give suggestions and strategies for the interviewing process.[15]

Psychological profiling technique was successfully used in the investigation of serial killer Ted Bundy. Psychologist Richard B. Jarvis, using profiling techniques, was able to predict the age range of Bundy, his sexual psychopathy, and his above-average intellectual traits.[16] It was also used in the investigation of the "Green River Killer"—Gary Ridgway. Former FBI agent John Douglas authored a 12-page profile for Ridgway, which identified the following points about the killer:

- Probably a white male who had a dysfunctional relationship with women
- Organized since he tried to hide the bodies and appeared to spend some time at the river
- Cunning in using rocks to weigh the victims down in the water to conceal them
- Very mobile with a vehicle
- Going to kill again
- Like other serial killers, he would be prone to contacting police wanting to help in the investigations.[17]

It should be noted, however, that the profile created for Ridgway also disclosed characteristics that did not apply to him, such as being an outdoorsman and being incapable of closeness to other people.[18] Ridgway was not an outdoorsman, but frequented the Green River with one of his wives, and also had a very close relationship with his last wife, which contradicted the point in the profile of being incapable of closeness. So while not a foolproof tool, criminal profiling has assisted criminal investigators on numerous occasions and will continue to do so in the future.

Different phases of profiling have been identified. For example, according to former FBI agent Gregg O. McCrary, the basic premise of criminal profiling is that "behavior reflects personality."[19] In a homicide case, for example, FBI profilers try to collect the personality of the offender through questions about his or her behavior. These questions occur at four phases:

1. *Antecedent*: What fantasy or plan, or both, did the murderer have in place before the act? What triggered the murderer to act some days and not others?
2. *Method and manner*: What type of victim or victims did the murderer select? What was the method and manner of murder: shooting, stabbing, strangulation, or something else?
3. *Body disposal*: Did the murder and body disposal take place all at one scene, or multiple scenes?
4. *Post-offense behavior*: Is the murderer trying to inject himself into the investigation by reacting to media reports or contacting investigators?[20]

Crimes of a sexual nature (which are sometimes homicides) are analyzed in much the same way. Researcher and Professor David Canter developed the discipline of investigative psychology as a response to his dissatisfaction with the scientific bases for criminal profiling. Another phase of criminal profiling is **case linkage**. According to Brent E. Turvey, case linkage or linking analysis refers to the process of determining whether or not there are discrete connections between two or more previously unrelated cases through crime scene analysis.[21]

While criminal profiling has gained much public attention, it is still not free from controversy. Investigators may identify a suspect early on who appears to fit a profile but by doing so they ignore other investigative leads. An example is Richard Jewell, who was extensively investigated (and discredited in the media) following the Centennial Olympic Park bombing in Atlanta in 1996. This not only caused considerable grief and embarrassment for Jewell but also delayed identifying the actual perpetrator, Eric Rudolph. The added cost of the "false positive" on Jewell was that FBI and local police gave up the search for other suspects for a significant period of time.

Geographic Profiling

Geographic profiling is a criminal investigative technique that analyzes the locations of a connected series of crimes to determine where the offender most likely resides. The technique is typically used in cases of serial murder or rape (but also arson, bombing, robbery, and other crimes); it also helps police investigators prioritize information in large-scale major crime investigations that can involve hundreds or thousands of suspects and tips.[22]

Although the use of spatial analysis methods in police investigations goes back many years (think of detectives gathered around a large city map with pins stuck in it), the formalized process known today as geographic profiling originated out of research conducted at Simon Fraser University's School of Criminology in British Columbia, Canada, in 1989. The theoretical foundation is in environmental criminology, particularly crime pattern theory, routine activity theory, and rational choice theory.[23] The Vancouver Police Department instituted the world's first geographic profiling capability in 1995, but the technique has now spread to several U.S., Canadian, British, and European law enforcement agencies. Originally designed for violent crime investigations, it is increasingly being used on property crime.

Tools used by geographic profilers include specialized software systems, such as Rigel or CrimeStat. System inputs are crime location addresses or coordinates, often entered through a geographic information system (GIS). The output is a jeopardy surface (three-dimensional probability surface) or color geoprofile, which depicts the most likely areas of the offender's residence or search base.[24]

Geographic profiling is a subtype of offender or criminal profiling (the inference of offender characteristics from offence characteristics). It is therefore related to psychological or behavioral profiling. If psychological profiling is the "who," geographic profiling is the "where."[25] All certified geographic profilers are members of the International Criminal Investigative Analysis Fellowship (ICIAF), a professional profiling organization first begun by investigators trained by the FBI in the mid-1980s.[26]

Eyewitness Identifications

One recurring problem in criminal investigation is the overreliance by criminal investigators on eyewitness accounts of crimes. This is especially a concern when the identification of a criminal suspect relies heavily on the word of eyewitnesses or victims. The problem is pervasive. For example, in 2009 the Innocence Project reported: "Eyewitness misidentification is the single greatest cause of wrongful convictions nationwide, playing a role in more than 75% of convictions overturned through DNA testing."[27] For more than 30 years, research has proven the unreliability of eyewitnesses testimony.[28] For example, (1) criminal suspects have been identified by eyewitnesses seated in the back of a patrol vehicle, a long distance away on a dimly lit street; (2) witnesses have been shown photo arrays in which only one photo is clearly marked with an "R"; (3) witnesses have changed their physical description of a criminal suspect after speaking with police and learning additional information about the suspect; and (4) eyewitnesses and victims have been reluctant in identifying a suspect, but at trial prosecutors inform the jury that witnesses did not waiver in their identification.[29] Many such cases have resulted in innocent persons being wrongfully accused and convicted of crimes they did not commit.

It is common in criminal investigations for investigators to rely on eyewitness identifications. Experience and research have shown that civilian eyewitnesses frequently prove to be unreliable observers, and erroneous identifications are often the result. A number of factors contribute to misidentifications by eyewitnesses. For example, human perception tends to be inaccurate, especially under stress. The average citizen, untrained in observation and subjected to the stress of being a victim of or witness to a crime, is seldom able to describe a perpetrator accurately even in some cases after coming face to face with the individual. Also, a witness, especially one who is unsure what the perpetrator actually looked like, may be easily influenced by suggestions conveyed to him or her during the identification process. This fact was recognized in *United States* v. *Wade*, in which the Supreme Court of the United States stated:

> The influence of improper suggestions upon identifying witnesses probably accounts for more miscarriages of justice than any other single factor. Perhaps it is responsible for more such errors than all other factors combined.[30]

Law enforcement officers can also cause misidentifications by suggestive words or conduct. The average witness, anxious to make an identification and influenced by the police officer's image as an authority figure, tends to be very sensitive to any suggestion made by the police regarding the identity of the perpetrator. Officers may, intentionally or unintentionally, convey to the witness by words or conduct that a particular person being viewed is the perpetrator.

As a result, great care must be taken by officers conducting identification sessions of any type to avoid any action that might lead to an erroneous identification. Carefully adhering to the proper identification procedures will help avoid misidentifications that may lead to unjust accusations or even erroneous convictions of innocent persons and divert the investigation away from the actual offender. In addition, even if the actual offender is caught and brought to trial, using improper identification procedures during the investigation often causes the suppression of identification evidence at trial, resulting in dismissal of the charges or otherwise making it difficult or even impossible to convict the guilty party.

If a court determines that an identification procedure was excessively suggestive, the court may prohibit introduction of the evidence in question. It may rule that any in-court identification of the accused by the victim is inadmissible, suppress other evidence that was obtained as a result of an improper pretrial identification procedure, or both. Of course, any of these actions may result in prosecution being thwarted.

Today, in evaluating proper identification procedure, the courts are generally concerned with whether it was suggestive. If the court finds that the procedure was suggestiveit will then proceed to determine whether, despite the suggestiveness, the identification was reliable considering the "totality of the circumstances."[31] The court will consider the following six factors:

1. The opportunity of the witness to view the criminal at the time of the crime
2. The witness's degree of attention
3. The accuracy of the witness's prior description of the criminal
4. The level of certainty demonstrated by the witness at the confrontation
5. The length of time between the crime and the confrontation
6. Whether the witness was a "casual observer" or the victim of the crime

If in view of these various factors, it appears that the identification was reliable despite the suggestiveness of the procedure, evidence of the identification will be admissible to bolster a subsequent in-court identification.

Identification Procedures

For purposes of this chapter, identification procedures may be categorized as photo identifications, lineups, or show-ups. Photo identification procedures may involve the showing of one or several photographs to a witness for the purpose of obtaining an identification. In a **lineup**, eyewitnesses are presented simultaneously with a number of individuals.

TYPES OF LINEUPS For the most part, the function of a police lineup is to identify a suspect. Lineups are typically shown to victims of crime or eyewitnesses to a crime. From a procedural standpoint, a police lineup involves placing a suspect among people not suspected of committing the crime (fillers) and asking the victim or eyewitness if he or she can identify the perpetrator. This can be done using a live lineup of people or, as more commonly done in the nation's police departments, a lineup of photographs. Live lineups typically use five or six people (a suspect plus four or five fillers) and **photo lineups** six or more photographs.[32] There are two common types of lineups: simultaneous and sequential.

The type of lineup used by most police departments across the nation is the **simultaneous lineup**.[33] In this lineup, the eyewitness views all the people or photos at the same time. In comparison, a **sequential lineup** involves people or photographs that are presented to the witness one at a time.

In either model, the lineup administrator can be blind, meaning he or she does not know the identity of the suspect, or nonblind, meaning the administrator knows the identity of the suspect. Most police departments in the United States use photo lineups.

Historically, the investigator knows who the suspect is.[34] Critics suggest that in these cases, lineup administrators might either knowingly or unintentionally give the witness verbal or non-verbal cues as to the identity of the suspect. For example, if the eyewitness identifies a filler, the investigator might say to the witness, "Take your time....Make sure you look at all the photos."

Such a statement may effectively lead the witness away from the filler.[35] However, in a "double-blind" lineup, neither the officer administering the lineup nor the witness knows the identity of the suspect, so there is no way the officer administering the lineup can influence the witness in any way.[36] In 2008, the National Institute of Justice reported that other variables that can affect the outcome of police lineups include:[37]

- *Pre-lineup instructions given to the witness.* This includes explaining that the suspect may or may not be present in the lineup. Research on pre-lineup instructions by Nancy Steblay, Ph.D., professor of psychology at Augsburg College in Minneapolis, Minnesota, revealed that a "might or might not be present" instruction reduced mistaken identification rates in lineups where the suspect was absent.[38]
- *The physical characteristics of fillers.* Fillers who do not resemble the witness's description of the perpetrator may cause a suspect to stand out.[39]
- *Similarities and differences between witness and suspect's age, race, or ethnicity.* Research suggests that when the offender is present in a lineup, young children and elderly people perform nearly as well as young adults in identifying the perpetrator. When the lineup does not contain the offender, however, young children and elderly people commit mistaken identifications at a rate higher than young adults. Research has also indicated that people are better able to recognize faces of their own race or ethnic group than faces of another race or ethnic group.[40]
- *Incident characteristics, such as the use of force or weapons.* The presence of a weapon during an incident can draw visual attention away from other things, such as the perpetrator's face, and thus affect an eyewitness's ability to identify the holder of the weapon.[41]

In summary, the most common lineup procedure in use by law enforcement is the simultaneous lineup.[42] Researcher Gary Wells argues, however, that during simultaneous lineups, witnesses use **relative judgment**. This means that they compare lineup photographs with each other rather than to their memory of the offender. This is a problem when the perpetrator is not present in the lineup because the witness will often choose the lineup member who most closely resembles the perpetrator.[43]

On the other hand, during sequential lineups, witnesses must make a decision about each photograph or member before moving on to the next, prompting them to use **absolute judgment**. In other words, witnesses compare each photograph or person only with their memory of what the offender looked like.[44]

Research shows that the double-blind sequential method, in which the officer conducting the lineup does not know the identity of the suspect, produces fewer false identifications than the traditional simultaneous method.[45]

Photo Lineups The photo lineup is a commonly used investigative technique to identify suspects. When used improperly, however, innocent persons can be singled out for prosecution. This very thing occurred in the case of Calvin Willis.

One night in 1982, three young girls were sleeping alone in a Shreveport, Louisiana, home when a man in cowboy boots made entry into the house and raped the oldest girl, who was 10 years old. When police started to investigate the rape, the three girls all remembered the attack differently. One police report said the 10-year-old victim did not see her attacker's face. Another report—which was not introduced at trial—said she identified Calvin Willis, who lived in the neighborhood. The girl's mother testified at the trial that neighbors had mentioned Willis' name when discussing who might have committed the crime. The victim testified that she was shown photos and told to pick the man without a full beard. She testified that she did not pick anyone; police said she picked Willis. Willis was convicted by a jury and sentenced to life in prison. In 2003, DNA testing proved Willis's innocence and he was released. He had served 22 years.[46]

Photo identifications may take a number of forms. If a single photo is shown to the witness, the photo identification has all of the shortcomings of the show-up (discussed below) and is generally regarded by the courts as improper and suggestive. Consequently, multiple-photo procedures are preferable. In such procedures, the photos may be shown individually, one at a time, or displayed simultaneously in a book or array. This procedure is similar to a lineup (discussed below), and virtually all of the cautions set forth for lineups in the preceding discussion apply to multiple-photo identification procedures as well.

Specifically, the following recommendations are made regarding photo identifications in whatever fashion they are presented:

1. There should be at least six photographs.
2. The photographs should be of people who are reasonably uniform in age, height, weight, and general appearance and of the same gender and race.

3. The photographs themselves should be similar. For example, color photographs and black-and-white photographs should not be mixed; the photographs should also be of approximately the same size and composition.

4. Mug shots should not be mixed with snapshots because they are generally recognizable as such and have an immediate tendency to "brand" an individual.

5. If mug shots are used or if the photographs otherwise include any identifying information regarding the subject of the photograph, this information should be covered so it cannot be seen by the witness. If only some of the photos have such information, the corresponding portions of photos should be covered so that none of the photos will look different.

6. The array should not include more than one photo of the same suspect.

7. The photo array should be shown to only one witness at a time.

8. As with show-ups and lineups, no suggestive statements should be made. For example, witnesses should not be told that the suspect's photo is in the group or that someone else has already picked out one of the photos as being the criminal. Similarly, nothing should be said or done to direct the witness's attention to any particular photograph. For example, pointing to a particular photo and asking, "Is this the guy?" is improper and may lead to the identification being excluded.

9. If possible, the photo array should be preserved for future reference. In fact, in some states, failure to preserve the array will lead to suppression of the identification process. Additionally, full details about the identification process should be recorded and preserved. Assuming that the photo identification has been properly conducted and that the array itself was not in any way suggestive, preserving this information helps the prosecution refute any claims by the defense to the contrary.

The proper use of photographs to obtain identification of a perpetrator has been approved by the courts.[47] However, the courts appear to prefer that photo identification procedures be used only to develop investigative leads. Some courts have criticized the practice of using photo identifications after the suspect has been arrested, preferring that after the suspect is in custody and therefore readily available, a lineup be used for eyewitness identification.[48]

Physical Lineups The lineup, if properly conducted, is significantly less suggestive than the show-up and hence is generally far preferable. Nevertheless, police officers conducting a lineup must use caution to avoid suggestive influences. Studies of witness psychology reveal that lineup witnesses tend to believe that the guilty party must be one of the individuals in the lineup. Consequently, witnesses tend to pick out the person in the lineup who most closely resembles their perception of the perpetrator, even though the perpetrator is not in fact present.

In addition, it is possible that witnesses, in an effort to please the police officers conducting the lineup, feel obligated to pick out someone from the lineup rather than "disappoint" the officers.[49] Such witnesses are often sensitive to, and strongly influenced by, clever clues conveyed by the officers that may indicate to the witness that the officer believes a particular individual in the lineup is the perpetrator. This makes it even more important that officers conduct the lineup—and their own behavior—in a nonsuggestive manner.

Preparing for a lineup may be as important to the validity of the procedure as actually conducting it. Selecting individuals for the lineup is a particularly important issue. In determining which individuals are to be presented to the witnesses in a lineup, the following principles should be observed:

1. *The lineup should consist of individuals of similar physical characteristics.* Witnesses tend to pick out anyone who stands out from the rest of the group in any significant way. Therefore, the individuals who appear in the lineup should be reasonably similar with respect to age; height; weight; hair color, length and style; facial hair; clothing; and other characteristics such as glasses. Of course, the individuals must be of the same race and gender. Absolute uniformity of the lineup participants is obviously unattainable and is not procedurally necessary.[50]

2. *The lineup should consist of at least five or six persons.* The smaller the lineup, the less objective it is. A lineup with only two or three persons is little better than a show-up, and suggestive factors become excessively influential. As a result, most authorities recommend that at least five, preferably six, persons be in the lineup. In addition, some authorities caution against the use of plainclothes police officers in lineups because they do not naturally look or act like suspects, a factor that causes witnesses to reject them as possibilities.

Preparing a witness for viewing the lineup is another important consideration. Preparation should be limited to nonsuggestive statements, such as explaining the procedure that will be used and making it clear that the individuals in the lineup will be unable to see him or her. Officers

Live Police Lineups: How Do They Work?*

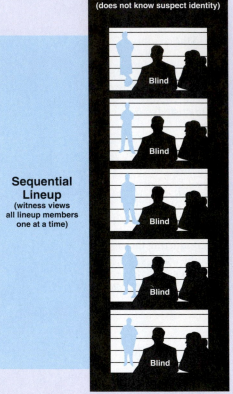

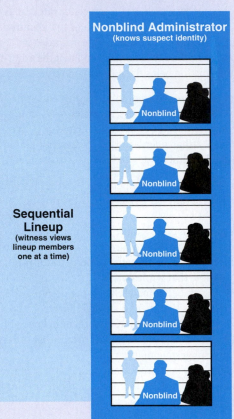

* Most U.S. police departments use photo lineups. The same concepts depicted in this graphic—simultaneous and sequential, blind and nonblind—apply in photo lineups.

|Fig. 4.22| △

Most U.S. police departments use photo lineups. The same concepts depicted in this graphic—simultaneous and sequential, blind and nonblind—apply in photo lineups.

Mike Himmel

should avoid taking any action or making any statement that will adversely affect the validity of the lineup. In particular, before a lineup, officers should avoid:

1. Showing the witness any photos of the suspect[51]
2. Conducting a show-up with the suspect or allowing the witness—accidentally or otherwise—to see the suspect, such as in an office or holding cell, before the lineup
3. Making suggestive statements to the witness, such as telling the witness that the person whom the police suspect will be in the lineup. It is even desirable to tell the witness that the perpetrator may not be among those in the lineup. Other common errors that should be avoided include telling the witness that another witness has identified someone in the same lineup, advising the witness to take special notice of some particular individual in the lineup, or making any other statement or action that may cause the witness to focus on a particular individual or to think that he or she must pick out somebody.

Finally, if more than one witness is to view a lineup, the witnesses should be kept separated before the lineup and should not be permitted to discuss the case with each other, compare descriptions, and so forth.

In conducting the lineup, officers who are not assigned to that case should handle the procedure if possible. This helps to minimize the possibility that the officers who are conducting the investigation will, in their zeal to solve the case, convey (inadvertently or otherwise) clues to the witness as to which person to pick out or put pressure on the witness to pick out somebody. The following should also be observed in conducting lineups:

1. *Statements that put pressure on the witness to make an identification should be avoided.* Witnesses are anxious to please the officers conducting the lineup, so they should not be made to feel that they are expected to pick out someone. For example, telling a witness that the person the police suspect is in the lineup or urging a hesitant witness to make an identification or to "try harder" would be improper.
2. *Statements that may cause the witness to focus on a particular individual should be avoided.* The same sort of statements discussed in regard to witness preparation should be avoided during the actual conduct of the lineup. Officers are often tempted to prompt a witness when someone in the lineup is a prime suspect and the witness is hesitant to make an identification. Statements such as: "What about the second guy from the right?" or "Take another look at the one in the middle" are so suggestive that they will, if challenged by the defense attorney, almost certainly result in any subsequent identification being suppressed by the court.
3. *The lineup should be presented to one witness at a time.* The common practice of having a group of witnesses view a lineup simultaneously should not be permitted. Courts, including the U.S. Supreme Court,[52] have disapproved multiple-witness lineups. If for some reason, more than one witness must be present simultaneously, witnesses should be required to make their identifications silently in writing and should not be permitted to discuss the identification aloud with each other or with the officers present.
4. *If possible, conduct a "blank" lineup.* Conducting two or more lineups, where one lineup includes the suspect and the others do not, assists the prosecution in later refuting any claim by the defense that the lineup was too small or was suggestive.
5. *If multiple lineups are to be conducted for the same witnesses, do not put the suspect in more than one.* Seeing the same face in a second lineup may cause the witness to erroneously "recognize" the person as the perpetrator, merely because the face is familiar from the first lineup. Because of this, the courts have disapproved this practice.[53]

In another context, the U.S. Supreme Court has held that requiring a suspect participating in a lineup to speak, even to the extent of uttering the same words used by the criminal, does not violate the Fifth Amendment because it is not "testimonial self-incrimination." Other actions, such as standing, walking, and gesturing, are similarly not self-incrimination within the meaning of the Fifth Amendment. Similarly, requiring the suspect to wear certain clothing has been held to be outside of the coverage of the Fifth Amendment.

After the lineup, certain precautions should be taken. For example, when more than one witness has viewed a lineup, witnesses should be kept separate after the lineup procedure has been completed. Although discussions between witnesses following a lineup will presumably not render any previously made identification invalid, it may affect the admissibility of a subsequent in-court identification of the defendant by these witnesses during the trial itself.

Additionally, witnesses should not be praised or congratulated for picking out the suspect. This may serve to reinforce a shaky identification, convincing the witness that he or she has picked out the actual perpetrator when the witness is in some doubt. In addition to increasing the chances of a miscarriage of justice, this may lead to suppression of a later in-court identification of the perpetrator by the same witness.

SHOW-UPS   The show-up has been widely condemned by the courts and by experts in law, law enforcement, and law enforcement identification procedures.[54] Whereas the courts have not held show-ups to be categorically improper, they have ruled that the determination of whether a specific show-up was excessively suggestive will be made based on the "totality of the circumstances" attending that particular show-up. In practice, evidence deriving from show-ups is frequently suppressed because the show-up is so inherently suggestive that it is virtually impossible to eliminate suggestion from the procedure.

Consequently, the use of show-ups should be avoided whenever possible. Only when exigent circumstances make it absolutely necessary should this technique be used. When it must be used, certain guidelines should be followed to minimize the suggestiveness of the procedure and the risk of suppression of any resultant identification evidence.

Show-ups conducted in the station house or jail are the most unreliable and hence the most objectionable. When used, station house show-ups should, at a minimum, be subject to the following guidelines:

1. Show-ups should not be conducted when the suspect is in a cell, manacled, or dressed in jail clothing.
2. Show-ups should not be conducted at a late hour.
3. Show-ups should not be conducted with more than one witness present at a time. If show-ups are conducted separately for multiple witnesses, the witnesses should not be permitted to communicate before or after the show-up regarding the identification of the suspect.
4. The same suspect should not be presented to the same witness more than once.
5. Show-up suspects should not be required to put on clothing worn by the perpetrator, to speak words uttered by the perpetrator, or to perform other actions mimicking those performed by the actual perpetrator.[55]
6. Words or conduct by the police that may suggest to the witness that the individual is or may be the perpetrator should be scrupulously avoided. For example, one should never tell the witness that the individual was apprehended near the crime scene, that the evidence points to the individual as the perpetrator, or that other witnesses have identified the individual as the perpetrator. Unfortunately, the mere fact that the individual has been presented to the witness for identification strongly suggests that the officers believe him or her to be the guilty party.

Even when these guidelines are followed, it is entirely possible that a court may suppress the resulting evidence on the grounds that no amount of care can eliminate suggestion, and hence unreliability, from the procedure.

Yet exigent circumstances may justify the use of show-ups in certain instances. For example, in certain instances, a station house show-up may be tolerated by the courts if it can be demonstrated that time or other factors prevented the police from arranging a proper lineup. However, the reasons for not taking the time to prepare and conduct a lineup must be substantial and reasonably explained. Even then, they may not be accepted by the courts.

Exigent circumstances may also justify a show-up in the field. A show-up conducted shortly after the commission of the offense and in reasonable proximity to the crime scene may be tolerated by courts. The court may recognize that the realities of the situation often make it vital that a witness view a suspect immediately at or near the scene. Courts have noted that this procedure has potential advantages both for the suspect and the police. If the identification is negative, it will result in the freeing of the suspect and permit the officers to devote their time and attention to other leads. If the identification is positive, the police can focus their attention on the identified suspect. Consequently, some courts are more willing to tolerate this type of show-up.

The Right to Counsel at Eyewitness Identifications

In 1967, the Supreme Court of the United States held that a suspect has a right to counsel at a postindictment lineup.[56] Subsequently, the Court expanded this ruling to provide for a right to counsel at any lineup conducted after formal adversary proceedings have been initiated against the suspect, whether by way of formal charge, preliminary hearing, indictment, information, or arraignment.[57] There is, however, no right to have counsel present at a lineup conducted before such adversary proceedings have been initiated. These same rules apply to show-ups. However, there is no right to counsel at photo identification sessions.[58] The purpose of having counsel present at the identification is to enable counsel to detect any suggestiveness or other irregularities in the procedure. It should be recognized, however, that the presence-of-counsel requirement may actually help the police in certain instances. First, the department's goal should be to avoid any possibility of an erroneous identification and a resultant miscarriage of justice. Therefore, the presence of counsel may be regarded as a positive step in preventing any such occurrence. In addition, if counsel is present and acquiesces in the procedure being used, this may preclude any subsequent defense contention that suggestiveness or other impropriety occurred. This will strengthen the prosecution's case. Therefore, to the extent that defense counsel is responsible and objective, cooperation with counsel in constructing and conducting a nonsuggestive and otherwise proper identification procedure may benefit all concerned.

Of all investigative procedures used by police in criminal cases, probably none is less reliable than the eyewitness identification. Erroneous identifications create more injustice and cause more suffering to innocent persons than perhaps any other aspect of police work. Proper precautions must be followed by officers if they are to use eyewitness identifications effectively and accurately.

Case in Point

>>The Will West Case

When William (Will) West was received at Leavenworth Penitentiary, he denied previous imprisonment there. The record clerk, however, ran the Bertillon (body measurements) instruments over him anyway because he was aware of the reluctance of many criminals to admit previous crimes. Sure enough, when the clerk referred to the formula derived from West's Bertillon measurements, he located the file of one William West, whose measurements were almost identical and whose photograph appeared to be that of the new prisoner. Indeed, Will West was not being coy about a previous visit to Leavenworth; another William West was already at the prison and serving a life sentence for murder. Subsequently, the fingerprints of both William Wests were compared, and it was found that they bore no resemblance.

Case in Point

>>DNA's First Case: The Narborough Murders

The November 1983 discovery of a murdered 15-year-old girl in the English village of Narborough ultimately had an enormous impact on international criminal investigation. Before the four-year murder investigation was completed, a scientific discovery was applied that not only solved a double criminal homicide but also completely revolutionized forensic identification: the mapping of DNA fragments. At first, the murder of Lynda Mann was barely noticed outside the area known as Leicestershire, but it soon launched one of the biggest homicide investigations in English history. A squad of more than 150 detectives was formed that exhausted every lead in the case. So thorough was the investigation that every male between the ages of 13 and 34 living in the area of the murder was noted and in many cases questioned. Nonetheless, no murder suspect was apprehended.

Then, in July 1986, 15-year-old Dawn Ashworth, also of Leicestershire, was found brutally raped and strangled. The MO indicated the same killer and alerted authorities to the possibility of a serial killer. This time, more than 200 investigators from all across the country were placed on the case. Word of the killings began to be cause for concern in almost all of England, but investigators were still unable to develop significant indicators as to who the killer might be. At last, a case against one suspect was developed. A 17-year-old hospital kitchen porter linked to the murder through circumstantial evidence was arrested. After interrogation, the suspect admitted the second killing but denied the first, despite the belief by the police that both victims were murdered by the same person.

(continued)

Case in Point (continued)

The ultimate solution to the problem was found only a short distance away, at Leicester University. Alec J. Jeffreys, a university scientist working in the field of genetic rese arch since the early 1980s, had recently discovered a process of human identification based on the DNA molecule. Whether the suspect's father or the British police first initiated contact with Jeffreys is still under dispute, but the scientist was well known for his work in a paternity lawsuit in which DNA technology established the identity of the father. In the Narborough murders, Jeffreys analyzed a semen sample from the body of Lynda Mann and then analyzed a sample from the Dawn Ashworth crime scene. The technique yielded a DNA image that was identical for both murders. Then, from the suspect's blood sample, Jeffreys obtained a comparison DNA fingerprint. Alarmingly, the suspect's DNA failed to match up with either murder, including the murder in which the suspect already confessed. The suspect was then released from custody.

Certain of one fact—that the same person had killed both teenagers—investigators decided to single out the perpetrator through genetic fingerprinting.

Accordingly, in January 1987, all males 17 to 40 years of age living in the village were asked to submit blood samples. More than 4,500 samples were examined before the police, in September 1987, arrested a local baker, Colin Pitchfork, and charged him with the murders. Pitchfork had a long history of sexual assault and indecent exposure, and an informant had alerted police that he had cheated on his blood examination by persuading a coworker to submit a blood sample for him. When a legitimate test of the suspect's blood was conducted, an identical match was made with fingerprints found at both murder scenes. Based solely on DNA fingerprinting and the resulting confession, Pitchfork was convicted of both murders.

Thematic question

Absent blood and DNA evidence used to solve the Narborough murders, identify how other investigative methods could have possibly been used to solve this crime.

Sources: Batt, E. (April 1999). DNA fingerprinting: The capture of a murder. Available at http://www.suite101.com/article.cfm/leicestershire/17877; Wambaugh, J. (1990). *The blooding: True story of the Narborough murders*. New York: Bantam Books.

Case in Point

>>DNA Evidence

Evidence suitable for DNA analysis can be found at many crime scenes and is a powerful investigative tool for linking suspects to crimes, eliminating suspects, and identifying victims. All officers must be aware of common sources of DNA evidence, ways to protect against contamination of samples, and basic collection and packaging guidelines, which include the following:

1. Wear a mask to avoid contamination through talking, sneezing, or coughing over evidence.
2. Blood and semen are the two most common sources of DNA evidence. However, other body tissues and fluids can be used for analysis even in microscopic quantities.
3. DNA is particularly sensitive and subject to contamination. Therefore, first responders in particular must be familiar with situations that will degrade, destroy,

or contaminate DNA evidence and must observe the following precautions:

- Wear gloves and change them often.
- Use disposable instruments or clean them thoroughly before and after handling each sample.
- Avoid touching the area where DNA may exist.
- Avoid talking, sneezing, and coughing over evidence.
- Avoid touching your face, nose, and mouth when collecting and packaging evidence.
- Air-dry evidence thoroughly before packaging.
- Put evidence into new paper bags or envelopes, not into plastic bags. Do not use staples.

4. If exigent circumstances dictate immediate action to prevent destruction of evidence, wet bloodstained materials may be rolled or folded in paper or placed in a brown paper bag or box, sealed, and labeled. Avoid folding garments through stains.

(continued)

Case in Point (*continued*)

5. Bloodstained articles and blood samples must be transported as soon as possible and should never be stored in patrol vehicles or otherwise exposed to heat.
6. Use a cotton Q-Tip or swab lightly moistened with saline solution to collect dried bloodstains on fixed objects that are too large to transport or are on porous surfaces. If saline is not available, tap water may be used as long as a control standard of the water is collected for comparison.
7. As in the case of blood samples, clothing and bedding that may retain semen evidence must be air-dried if wet, packaged separately in paper containers, and labeled.

Case in Point

>>DNA Evidence

Advantages

DNA can be used to test any DNA-containing biological trace evidence. The composition of the DNA molecule does not vary essentially from cell to cell; therefore, the DNA in blood is identical to that found in other biological material, such as hair, skin, and bone marrow. Because DNA testing is so sensitive, only a trace amount of biological material is needed for identification purposes. DNA evidence can identify probative physical evidence in some cases. For example, semen left at the scene of a rape is more closely related to the commission of the crime of rape than is the presence of a fingerprint. DNA is especially useful in crimes of violence that yield little useful evidence. Testing is potentially very helpful in identifying perpetrators of sexual assault in cases in which, although biological evidence is found, witnesses are often lacking and identification of the assailant by the victim is unreliable or nonexistent.

Using DNA test results, a crime laboratory can establish data banks that could identify serial criminals. For example, law enforcement agencies could determine that the same rapist is responsible for a series of assaults in several different jurisdictions. As suspects are identified by investigators through DNA data banks, investigators could redirect and narrow their search for the perpetrator. DNA testing provides crime labs and forensic scientists with a new tool that can be used for investigatory purposes (e.g., identifying remains), which in coordination with other types of evidence, could lead to more arrests and convictions.

Criticisms and Limitations

Some critics argue that the development of DNA data banking poses an invasion of civil liberties, particularly due process (the taking of a sample without establishing a foundation of probable cause) and privacy (because DNA can reveal more information than identity alone). Testing may involve the use of expert witnesses from private companies whose primary goal is to get into court first to achieve a judicial imprimatur of acceptability. DNA has been rushed into court without agreement being reached in the scientific community regarding standards that ensure the reliability of the evidence and guidelines for the interpretation of the results. The probability of a sample having come from someone other than the defendant can be so infinitesimal, according to statistical data, as to hold inordinate weight with a jury, thus obscuring other evidence.

Many defendants are not able to afford the cost of rebutting state-induced DNA evidence. Additional costs incurred in cases involving DNA evidence include testing, the cost of expert witnesses, and legal fees. If defendants cannot afford these costs, the difference between defense and prosecutorial resources—already large—could increase further.[59]

Case in Point

>>DNA at Work[60]

- In one amazing success, investigators linked the DNA in the saliva used to lick an envelope to one of the World Trade Center bombers.
- DNA matches have kept families united by allowing immigrants to stay in the United States legally when the genetic study proved they were related to a resident.
- DNA studies have freed persons wrongfully convicted of murder and rape. The Innocence Project at Yeshiva University in New York, founded in 1992 by Barry Scheck, has helped release 144 prisoners (as of July 2, 2004) when DNA tests proved they were innocent.
- Paternity suits are commonly settled by DNA testing. Former mayor Coleman Young of Detroit agreed to child support payments in 1992 after testing resolved a dispute.

Case in Point

>>The Case Against O. J. Simpson

In the early morning on June 13, 1994, two dead bodies were discovered at a West Los Angeles home. Dead were the attractive wife of football great O. J. Simpson, Nicole, and an aspiring young actor and waiter, Ronald Goldman. The murders were discovered at 875 South Bundy Drive in the exclusive Brentwood area of the city. Police discovered sufficient physical evidence along with a history of spousal abuse to charge Simpson with the murders. In a CBS television interview, lead detective Philip Vannatter commented that he had never, in 30 years of investigating crimes, seen so much conclusive evidence in a case.

But this case was unlike others seen by prosecutors and police. Both victims were white, and the defendant, Simpson, was black. In addition, he was a wealthy and famous sports hero with considerable public recognition and a nationwide base of adoring fans. To mount a defense, Simpson quickly hired a team of the best-known trial lawyers in the country. Included on this "dream team" were attorneys F. Lee Bailey, Johnnie Cochran, Alan Dershowitz, and Robert Shapiro. Each attorney brought with him special expertise in different aspects of the case, and all were well known for their considerable success in defending celebrities. The prosecution team was headed by veteran prosecutors Marcia Clark, Christopher Darden, and William Hodgman, and at their disposal were more than 800 deputy district attorneys available to help, including experts on DNA evidence. Long before the trial began, the case was receiving considerable media attention. As the case came to its conclusion, media analysts declared that the Simpson trial received more coverage than any other event in the history of television, with literally thousands of hours of television coverage of the proceedings being offered by network television and cable channels, accompanied by expert commentary from key legal personnel.

Evidence presented at the trial, which lasted nearly a year, was examined closely in detail by defense lawyers, and prosecution witnesses were all rigorously cross-examined. The trial ended in late 1995 with a "not guilty" verdict and cost California taxpayers in excess of $7 million.

Evidence in the Case

- Bloodstains were found on a pair of socks in Simpson's bedroom; one spot of blood matched Simpson's blood, and another matched Nicole Simpson's.

- A total of 11 bloodstains were found in Simpson's Ford Bronco: four were Simpson's blood, one matched Nicole Simpson's, and two were a mixture of Simpson, Nicole Brown Simpson, and Ronald Goldman's blood.

- The glove found on the grounds of Simpson's estate contained a mixture of blood consistent with the mixture of blood of Simpson, Nicole Brown Simpson, and Ronald Goldman. The glove also contained hair matching Nicole Brown Simpson and Ronald Goldman, fibers similar to those found in the Bronco carpeting, and fibers from Goldman's shirt.

- Blood drops were found at the crime scene leading away from the bodies; five drops matched O. J. Simpson's blood.

- The ski cap found at the crime scene contained "unusual" fibers similar to those from the carpet of the Bronco and contained 12 hairs similar to those of O. J. Simpson's.

- Goldman's shirt contained hairs similar to those of O. J. Simpson's.

- Two bloodstains in O. J. Simpson's driveway matched his blood.

- Bloodstains found in O. J. Simpson's house matched his own blood, and these were seen by Kato Kaelin and several police officers while O. J. Simpson was in Chicago before the police had a sample of his blood.

Blood Drops

- *Prosecution:* Argued that DNA tests on blood at the scene and in Simpson's Bronco and estate positively identified Simpson as the killer.
- *Defense:* Attacked DNA tests as unreliable, tried to cast doubt about DNA science, and argued that Simpson's blood at the scene and estate could be old.

Bloody Gloves

- *Prosecution:* Called Detective Mark Furman to testify that he found the bloody glove at Simpson's estate that matched a glove found at the crime scene.
- *Defense:* Attempted to impeach Furman's testimony, arguing that he was a racist who set up Simpson.

Hair Samples

- *Prosecution:* Argued that hair found on Goldman's body and a knit cap at Simpson's estate were those of a black man, and placed Simpson at the scene.
- *Defense:* Argued that hair could belong to any black man, including investigating officers.

(continued)

> ## Case in Point (*continued*)
>
> ### Opportunity
>
> - *Prosecution:* Argued that Simpson had more than enough time between 9:45 and 10:56 P.M. to kill the victims, get rid of the knife, and return to his estate about a mile away.
> - *Defense:* Insisted that Simpson did not have enough time to kill two people and get back home.
>
> ### Motive
>
> - *Prosecution:* Introduced evidence that Simpson abused his ex-wife at least 19 times and argued that escalating violence led to murder.
> - *Defense:* Argued that all of the abuse allegations were isolated incidents and irrelevant to the murder charges.

Summary Checklist

In this chapter, we consider the ways that information about crimes is documented by criminal investigators. A properly documented case is one that is more likely to succeed in court. See how well you are able to answer the following questions in your checklist.

1. **What important points should you remember when considering the role of the crime laboratory?**

   The crime laboratory plays a pivotal role in criminal investigation and criminalists are major contributors to the investigative process. Some of the key investigative functions performed by the crime laboratory include:

   - Trace evidence: The Trace Evidence Unit identifies and compares specific types of trace materials that could be transferred during the commission of a violent crime (human or animal hair, textile fibers, fabric, ropes, wood, etc.).
   - Questioned documents: The Questioned Documents Unit examines and compares data appearing on paper and other evidentiary materials (handwriting, hand printing, typewriting, printing, erasures, alterations, and obliterations) as well as data within paper or other surfaces (watermarks, safety fibers, etc.).
   - Forensic chemistry generally includes three subunits:
     - General chemistry: Identifies chemicals, controlled substances, stains, markings, etc.
     - Toxicology: Analyzes biological specimens or food products
     - Paints and polymers: Analyzes paint chips for comparison with suspected sources, compare plastics, etc.

   - DNA analysis: The DNA Analysis Unit analyzes bodily fluids and bodily fluid stains recovered as evidence in violent crimes.
   - Ballistics: The Forensic Ballistics Unit receives and examines evidence related to firearms, firearm components, ammunition, ammunition components, tools, and tool marks.
   - Latent prints: The Latent Print Unit examines latent prints on evidence. Latent prints are impressions produced by the ridged skin on human fingers, palms, and soles of the feet.
   - Forensic photography: The Forensic Photography Unit is responsible for imaging operations.

2. **In what ways fingerprinting remains an important investigative tool?**

   Identifying persons through the use of fingerprinting is one of the most effective methods for apprehending criminal suspects. The use of fingerprinting also makes it possible to learn accurately the number and type of a suspect's previous arrests and convictions.

   - Fingerprinting has been used for hundreds of years in crime solving.
   - There are three main types or groups of prints:
     - A latent fingerprint (also called a *patent fingerprint*) occurs when the entire pattern of whorls on the finger, which contain small amounts of grease, oil, perspiration, or dirt, is transferred to an object when it is touched.

- A plastic fingerprint results when a finger presses against plastic material and leaves a negative impression of friction ridges.
  - A visible fingerprint (also called a *dust print*) is a print that has been adulterated with foreign matter.
- There are three general groups of fingerprint patterns:
  - Arches
  - Loops
  - Whorls
- Fingerprints can be identified in a number of ways, including the use of powders, iodine, ninhydrin, silver nitrate, superglue fuming, and lasers.
- The Integrated Automated Fingerprint Identification System (IAFIS) is a national fingerprint and criminal history database maintained by the FBI.

3. Explain the uses of DNA evidence and how it is obtained.

DNA is a genetic "blueprint" of an organism. In every cell within each human body, the DNA is identical.

- DNA consists of only five basic elements: carbon, hydrogen, oxygen, nitrogen, and phosphorus.
- DNA fingerprinting was introduced in the mid-1990s and increases the ability of law enforcement to match offenders with crime scenes.
- Genetic patterns found in blood or semen can be just as distinctive as fingerprints.
- Two standards have been used to govern the admissibility of scientific evidence in court:
  - The relevancy test: Permits the admission of relevant evidence that is helpful to the trier of fact.
  - The Frye test: Courts admit evidence based on novel scientific techniques only when the technique has gained general acceptance in the scientific community.
- The Daubert Standard is a legal precedent regarding the admissibility of expert witness testimony during federal legal proceedings—testimony must be both relevant and reliable to meet the standard.

4. Explain how handwriting analysis can be used in criminal investigation.

People often adopt unique styles of their own, frequently characteristic only of that person. Such characteristics are identifiable to the handwriting expert.

- Writings may occur in many forms, including that on personal correspondence, desks, walls, and even dead bodies.

- Cases involving questioned documents require a comparison between the suspect document and a sample or exemplar or standard.
- Exemplars can be acquired by request or collected from numerous sources.

5. What are facial composites and how can they assist law enforcement?

One method of developing an idea of a suspect's general description is to have the witness provide information to a police artist so that a facial composite can be generated. A facial composite can assist law enforcement in a number of ways:

- The citizen recognizing the face as an acquaintance
- Identifying the suspect in a "wanted" poster
- Additional evidence against the suspect
- Assisting investigation in checking leads
- Warning the public against serial offenders

6. Explain the various types of profiling.

- Criminal investigative analysis, or personality profiling, is accomplished by identifying the psychological and social characteristics surrounding the crime as well as the manner in which it was committed.
- Investigative psychology brings together the retrieval of investigative information and draws inferences about that information as far as the ways that police decision making can be supported through scientific research.
- Geographic profiling analyzes the locations of a connected series of crimes to determine where the offender most likely resides.

7. The problem of misidentifications by eyewitnesses has been known for decades. How can an investigator avoid such problems?

One recurring problem in criminal investigation is the overreliance by criminal investigators on eyewitness accounts of crimes. This is especially a concern when the identification of a criminal suspect relies heavily on the word of eyewitnesses or victims.

- For over 30 years, research has proven the unreliability of eyewitness testimony.
- It is common in criminal investigations for investigators to rely on eyewitness identifications.
- A number of factors contribute to misidentification by eyewitnesses.

- Human perception tends to be inaccurate, especially under stress.
- A witness may be easily influenced by suggestions conveyed to him or her during the identification process.
- Police officers may also cause misidentifications by suggestive words or conduct.

- Officers conducting identification sessions must take great care to avoid any action that might lead to an erroneous identification.
- If the court determines that an identification procedure was excessively suggestive, the court may prohibit introduction of the evidence in question.

Key Terms

absolute judgment

Amido black protein

Automated Fingerprint Identification System (AFIS)

ballistics

case linkage

composite

criminal investigative analysis

Daubert standard

Deoxyribonucleic acid

DNA analysis

DNA technology

dust print

elimination samples

exemplars

facial composite

fingerprints

forensic chemistry

forensic photography

Frye test

geographic profiling

Identi-Kit

Integrated Automated Fingerprint Identification System (IAFIS)

investigative psychology

latent fingerprint/latent prints

lineup

patent fingerprint

personality profile

photo lineup

plastic fingerprint

polymerase chain reaction

psychological profiling

questioned documents

relative judgment

relevancy test

relevant evidence

sequential lineup

show-up

simultaneous lineup

toxicology

trace evidence

visible fingerprint

Discussion Questions

1. Discuss the role of the crime laboratory in criminal investigation and identify some of the investigative functions performed by the crime laboratory.

2. Discuss the three types of fingerprints and how they differ.

3. Review the various ways of locating and identifying fingerprints at a crime scene.

4. Discuss the new role that IAFIS fingerprinting technology offers in the field of criminal investigation and identification.

5. To what extent has DNA technology improved methods of criminal identification?

6. Discuss the significance of recent court rulings addressing the admissibility of DNA evidence in the courtroom.

7. Discuss the value of the composite sketch in identifying a criminal suspect.

8. Explain geographic profiling and how it assists criminal investigators.

9. Explain the proper method of conducting a photo lineup.

Notes

1. U.S. Department of Justice Drug Enforcement Administration. (1987). *Intelligence collection and analytical methods. Training manual.* Washington, DC: U.S. Government Printing Office.

2. Source: FBI web site found at http://www.fbi.gov/about-us/cjis/fingerprints_biometrics/iafis/iafis (retrieved on August 27, 2012).

3. FBI web site located at: http://www.fbi.gov/about-us/lab/codis/ (retrieved on August 27, 2012).

4. Ibid.

5. Ibid.

6. Ibid.

7. Saferstein, R. (1990). *Criminalistics: An introduction to forensic science.* Upper Saddle River, NJ: Prentice Hall.

8. Davies, G. M. and T. Valentine. (2006). Facial composites: Forensic utility and psychological research. In Lindsay R. C. L., D. F. Ross, J. D. Read, and M. P. Toglia (Eds.), *Handbook of eyewitness psychology*, Vol. 2, pp. 59–96, Mahwah, NJ: Erlbaum.

9. Brace, N., G. Pike, and R. Kemp. (2000). Investigating E-FIT using famous faces. In Czerederecka A., T. Jaskiewicz-Obydzinska, and J. Wojcikiewicz (Eds.), *Forensic psychology and law*, pp. 272–276. Krakow, Poland: Krakow Institute of Forensic Research Publishers.

10. Bruce, V., H. Hanna, P. J. B. Hancock, C. Newman, and J. Rarirty. (2002). Four heads are better than one: Combining face composites yields improvements in face likeness. *Journal of Applied Psychology* 87(5):894–902.

11. Ibid.

12. Strentz, T. (1988). A terrorist psychological profile: Past and present. *FBI Law Enforcement Bulletin,* April:13–19.

13. Canter, D. (2004). Offender profiling and investigative psychology. *Journal of Investigative Psychology and Offender Profiling* 1(1):1–15.

14. Ibid.

15. Holmes, R. M. and Holmes, S. T. (2008). *Profiling violent crimes: An investigative tool*, 4th ed. Thousand Oaks, CA: Sage Publications, Inc.

16. Rule, A. (2008). *The stranger beside me*. Pocket Books.

17. Guillen, T. (2006). Serial killers issues explored through the Green River murders. Upper Saddle River, NJ: Pearson Prentice Hall.

18. Levi-Minzi, M. and M. Shields. (2007). Serial sexual murderers and prostitutes as their victims: Difficulty profiling perpetrators and victim vulnerability as illustrated by the Green River case. *Brief Treatment and Crisis Intervention* 7:77–89.

19. Douglas, J. et al. (2007). *Crime classification manual: A standard system for investigating and classifying violent crimes.* August.

20. Ibid.

21. Turvey, B. (1999). *Criminal profiling an introduction to behavioral evidence analysis*. San Diego, CA: Academic Press.

22. Brantingham, P. J. and P. L. Brantingham. (1984). *Patterns in crime*. New York: Macmillan.

23. Canter, D. (2003). *Mapping murder: The secrets of geographic profiling*. London: Virgin Publishing.

24. Mackay, R. E. (1999). Geographic profiling: A new tool for law enforcement. *The Police Chief,* December, pp. 51–59.

25. Rossmo, D. K. (2000). *Geographic profiling*. Boca Raton, FL: CRC Press.

26. Ibid.

27. Innocence Project website. (2009). Available at http://www.innocenceproject.org/understand/Eyewitness-Misidentification.php.

28. Ibid.

29. Ibid.

30. *United States* v. *Wade*, 388 U.S. 218, 229 (1967).

31. *Neil* v. *Biggers*, 409 U.S. 188 (1972). See also *Manson* v. *Brathwaite*, 432 U.S. 98 (1977) (*Biggers* test applied to photo identifications).

32. Wells, G. L., A. Memon, and S. D. Penrod. (2006). Eyewitness evidence: Improving its probative value. *Psychological Science in the Public Interest* 7(2):45–75.

33. Wells, G. L. and E. Olson. (2003). Eyewitness testimony. *Annual Review of Psychology* 54:277–295.

34. Wells, Memon, and Penrod. (2006). Eyewitness evidence.

35. Gary L. Wells' comments on the Mecklenburg Report (see note 8) (March 28, 2006). Available at http://www.psychology.iastate.edu/faculty/gwells/Illinois_Project_Wells_comments.pdf.

36. Mecklenburgh, S. H. (March 17, 2006). *Report to the legislature of the state of illinois: The illinois pilot program on sequential double-blind identification procedures*. Available at http://www.chicagopolice.org/IL%20Pilot%20on%20Eyewitness%20ID.pdf.

37. Schuster, B. (2008). Police lineups: Making eyewitness identification more reliable. *NIJ Journal*.

38. Steblay, N. M. (1997). Social influence in eyewitness recall: A meta-analytic review of lineup instruction effects. *Law and Human Behavior* 21:283–297.

39. Wells, G. L., M. Small, S. Penrod, R. Malpass, S. M. Fulero, and C. A. E. Brimacombe. (1998). Eyewitness identification procedures: Recommendations for lineups and photospreads. *Law and Human Behavior* 22(6):603–647.

40. Wells and Olson. (2003). Eyewitness testimony.

41. Ibid.

42. Ibid.

43. Wells, G. L. and E. Seelau. (1995). Eyewitness identification: Psychological research and legal policy on lineups. *Psychology, Public Policy and Law* 1:765–791.

44. Mecklenburgh. *Report to the legislature of the state of illinois.*

45. Ibid.

46. Innocence Project website. (2009). Available at http://www.innocenceproject.org/understand/Eyewitness-Misidentification.php.

47. *Simmons* v. *United States*, 390 U.S. 377 (1968).

48. After a witness has identified a photo, subsequent identifications may be influenced. The contention is that the witness thereafter is really only recognizing the previously seen photograph, not the actual criminal. For this reason, the practice of showing a witness a photograph of the defendant just before trial to "refresh the witness's memory" should be avoided.

49. Although it may surprise many officers to hear it, the average citizen still sees the police officer as a benevolent "father figure" (or perhaps, in the case of a female officer, a "mother

figure"), with the result that the lineup witness is often extremely anxious to please the officer by making an identification—even though the citizen is not at all certain that the person chosen is the guilty party.

50. *U.S.* v. *Lewis*, 547 F.2d 1030, 1035 (8th Cir. 1976).

51. Even a photo array should be avoided. This is especially true if the suspect is the only person in the photo array who is also in the lineup.

52. See *Gilbert* v. *California*, 388 U.S. 263 (1967).

53. See *Foster* v. *California*, 394 U.S. 440 (1969).

54. See *Stovall* v. *Denno*, 388 U.S. 293 (1967).

55. Although such requirements may sometimes be properly imposed during a lineup, the show-up is so inherently suggestive that the same court that would approve its use in a lineup may find it excessively suggestive when used during a show-up.

56. *United States* v. *Wade*, 388 U.S. 218 (1967) and *Gilbert* v. *California*, 388 U.S. 263 (1967).

57. *Kirby* v. *Illinois*, 406 U.S. 682, 688-89 (1972).

58. *U.S.* v. *Ask*, 413 U.S. 300 (1973). At least one state supreme court has held that when simulated lineups are filmed or videotaped for later exhibition, there is no right to have counsel present when the film or videotape is subsequently shown to witnesses, *People* v. *Lawrence*, 481 P.2d 212 (1971). Showing witnesses a film or tape of a previously recorded simulated lineup has become known as a "Lawrence lineup."

59. U.S. Office of Technology Assessment. (1990). *Genetic witness: Forensic use of DNA tests.* Washington, DC: U.S. Congress.

60. Schefter, J. (1994). DNA fingerprints on trial. *Popular Science*, November:64.

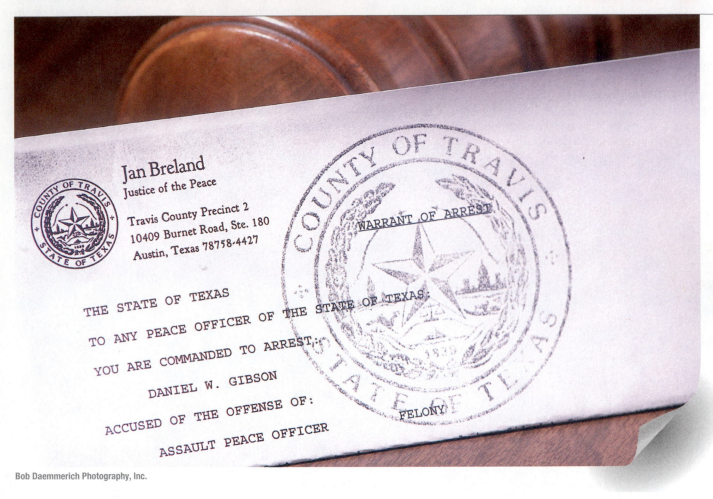

Bob Daemmerich Photography, Inc.

This chapter will enable you to:

1. Summarize the due process rights provided by the Constitution.

2. Summarize the legal guidelines police must follow for searches, seizures, and arrests.

3. Describe the process of obtaining and executing a search warrant.

4. Explain when warrantless searches are authorized.

5. Summarize when the use of force is permitted.

Legal Issues in Criminal Investigation

Introduction

 *The body of constitutional law addressing searches and seizures by police is immense and includes thousands of case decisions from courts in virtually all levels of government. Of paramount importance in criminal investigations is the officer's ability to be aware of and work within constitutional (and departmental) guidelines. Issues such as what to search, when to search, and how to conduct a search play a vital role in determining what is fair in the eyes of the U.S. Supreme Court. In this chapter, we will examine some of the more crucial principles of searches and seizures and how officers must conduct themselves to present a legally sound criminal case.*

The Constitution and Due Process

In addition to affording protection by ensuring a separation of powers within the government, the U.S. Constitution safeguards operations of the criminal justice system. One means of power was granting individual freedoms in what is called the Bill of Rights, which was added to the Constitution in 1791. Initially, the **Bill of Rights** applied only to the manner in which the federal government operated within the justice system. However, in 1868, the Fourteenth Amendment was passed extending **due process** to each of the states as well. Under this amendment, citizens are basically guaranteed three classes of rights:

1. Privileges and immunities of citizens of the United States
2. Due process of law
3. **Equal protection** under the law

For more than 30 years, the U.S. Supreme Court's interpretation of the Constitution has served as the basis for the establishment of legal rights of the accused. The fundamental principles that govern criminal procedure are required by the Bill of Rights. Therefore, it is here that we consider the implications of the Fourth, Fifth, and Sixth Amendments, which limit and control the manner in which government officials operate in our justice system.

1. *Fourth Amendment.* Two clauses of this amendment are significant in the realm of criminal investigation:
   - *Unreasonable searches and seizures clause.* "The right of the people to be secure in their persons, houses, papers, and effects, against unreasonable searches and seizures, shall not be violated."
   - *Warrants clause.* "No warrants shall issue, but upon probable cause, supported by oath or affirmation, and particularly describing the place to be searched and the persons or things to be seized."
2. *Fifth Amendment.* The principal component of this amendment is the self-incrimination clause:
   - *Privilege against self-incrimination clause.* "No person...shall be compelled in any criminal case to be a witness against himself."

3. *Sixth Amendment.* This amendment guarantees people the right to confront their accuser and to have legal representation.

- *Right of confrontation clause.* "In all criminal prosecutions, the accused shall enjoy the right…to be confronted with the witness against him."
- *Right to counsel clause.* "…to have the assistance of counsel for his defense."

Conducting Lawful Searches

Investigators must remember that they not only should have legal grounds to begin a search but that while conducting the search, they must not contaminate any evidence. Doing so will result in the dismissal of such evidence in the courtroom. Additionally, searches must first be justified under law. In the past, officers have not always followed the rules, as the case histories discussed in this chapter show.

The Probable Cause Requirement

For the past three decades, courts have scrutinized virtually every aspect of the Fourth Amendment. The probable cause requirement is one of the most important components of the Fourth Amendment because it lies at the heart of police officers' authority to search, seize, and make arrests. Simply put, **probable cause** is the minimum amount of information necessary to warrant a reasonable person to believe that a crime has been or is being committed by a person who is about to be arrested. Officers generally establish probable cause through their own observations. For example:

- Did the suspect attempt to run away when approached by the officer?
- Did the suspect admit to any part of the alleged crime?
- Did the suspect behave furtively, as if he or she were trying to hide something?

It is unlikely that a single fact or circumstance will establish probable cause, but several such facts put together might. Probable cause is the minimum amount of information necessary to cause a reasonable person to believe that a crime has been or is being committed by a person who is about to be arrested.

It is also common for probable cause to be established through hearsay information provided by third-party sources, typically informants. Here officers must be careful that the information is reliable and verifiable and is not based on rumor or suspicion because such information is not sufficient to establish probable cause.

The Exclusionary Rule

The **exclusionary rule** relates primarily to cases involving issues of **search and seizure**, arrests, interrogations, and stop-and-frisk violations. In addition, it pertains to any evidence obtained illegally even though it may be both relevant and material. The exclusionary rule states that courts will exclude any evidence that was illegally obtained even though it may be relevant and material.

The exclusionary rule originated with the 1914 case of *Weeks* v. *United States* but was geared to apply to federal, not state, governments. Although the *Weeks* case was virtually ignored by the courts, the subsequent *Mapp* decision (*Mapp* v. *Ohio*, 1961) expanded the scope of the exclusionary rule by applying it to both federal and state courts. In 1957, Cleveland police officers went to the residence of Dolree Mapp while acting on information that a fugitive was in hiding there. Mapp refused to admit officers to the residence without a search warrant. The officers left but maintained surveillance on the residence. Three hours later, more officers arrived and forced their way into the Mapp residence. By this time, Mapp's attorney had arrived, but officers ignored him. Mapp then demanded to see a search warrant, at which time one of the officers held up a piece of paper, claiming that it was a search warrant. Mapp grabbed the piece of paper and stashed it in her blouse. A struggle ensued, and the officers retrieved the paper and arrested

Mapp for being "belligerent." The officers then began to search the entire home. Although they never located the fugitive they were looking for, they ran across some obscene material for which Mapp was subsequently arrested and convicted. The U.S. Supreme Court overturned the conviction, stating that the methods used by officers to obtain the evidence were a violation of Mapp's constitutional rights.

The question in the *Mapp* case was whether or not the illegally seized evidence was in violation of the Fourth Amendment's search and seizure provisions, which would render it inadmissible in the state trial, in which Ms. Mapp was found guilty. Although the state supreme court in Ohio upheld the conviction, the U.S. Supreme Court overturned it. In addition to imposing federal constitutional standards on state law enforcement personnel, the Court pointed out that there was a relationship between the Fourth and Fifth Amendments that makes up the legal basis for the exclusionary rule.

Since the early days of the exclusionary rule, other decisions have highlighted the fact that the Fourth Amendment protects people, not places. Stated differently, although the old saying "a person's home is his castle" has a great deal of validity within the context of constitutional law, people have a reasonable expectation to privacy in "homes" of many descriptions, including apartments, duplexes, motel rooms, and even cardboard boxes or otherwise makeshift dwellings of the homeless. Indeed, all of these places can become protected under the Fourth Amendment. For example, in *Minnesota* v. *Olson* (1990), the U.S. Supreme Court extended the protection against warrantless searches to overnight guests residing in the home of another. The deciding factor in one's capacity to claim the protection of the Fourth Amendment depends on whether the person who makes that claim has a legitimate expectation of privacy in the place searched.

Search Incident to Lawful Arrest

The legal considerations of what constitutes an arrest are discussed in Chapter 7, but because this chapter deals with search and seizure, we will now consider a search immediately after an arrest. *Chimel* v. *California* (1969) dealt with areas that are not in plain view that are searched without a warrant. The case also addresses arrest activities by police. Ted Chimel was approached in his home by police officers who possessed a valid arrest warrant for him. The officers then advised Chimel that they wanted to "look around" and proceeded to search the premises without Chimel's permission. After a one-hour search, some coins were located and seized as evidence in a crime. Although initially convicted, Chimel later appealed the case, which was reversed by the U.S. Supreme Court because the coins were not found lawfully. Although the coins were found "incident to a lawful arrest," the evidence was excluded because it was not in plain view and the officers did not have

|Fig. 5.1| △

Photo of the nine members of the United States Supreme Court.

TIM SLOAN / AFP / Getty Images / Newscom

a search warrant to search Chimel's residence, only an arrest warrant. The *Chimel* decision established that a search made incidental to a lawful arrest must be confined to the area around the suspect's immediate control.

The point in the *Chimel* case is that the officers who searched Chimel's house went far beyond any area where he might have either hidden a weapon or been able to destroy any evidence. Therefore, there was no constitutional basis for an extended search of the house. The *Chimel* case is important, as it relates to criminal investigation, because it changed the policy with regard to the **scope of the search** as it relates to an officer's authority to search incident to an arrest. Before the *Chimel* case, officers had more leeway to search the area around an arrested suspect. Since the case, officers can search only the arrested person and the immediate physical surroundings under the defendant's control (i.e., within arm's length of the defendant). Such searches are for weapons or to safeguard against the destruction of evidence. To search further, officers must obtain a search warrant.

In 1990, the U.S. Supreme Court further defined the circumstances under which officers may conduct a limited search in the home of an arrested person. In *Maryland* v. *Buie* (1990), the Court held that a protective sweep during an arrest in a home is allowed if justified. Of course, this case authorized only a "protective" warrantless sweep for additional suspects who might be located in the residence.

In 1989, the U.S. Supreme Court clarified the basis on which law enforcement, lacking probable cause to believe that a crime has occurred, may stop and detain a person for investigative purposes. In *United States* v. *Sokolow* (1989), the Court ruled that the legitimacy of such a stop must be evaluated according to a **"totality of the circumstances"** criterion, in which the defendant's entire behavior is taken collectively to provide the basis for a legitimate stop. In this case, the defendant, Sokolow, appeared to be suspicious to police because while traveling under an alias from Honolulu, he paid $2,100 in $20 bills (taken from a larger sum of money) for a round-trip airline ticket to Miami, where he spent a very short period. Sokolow was noticeably nervous and had checked no luggage. A warrantless airport investigation by Drug Enforcement Administration (DEA) agents revealed more than 1,000 grams of cocaine on the defendant. Upon appeal, the Court ruled that although no single activity was proof of illegal activity, taken together they created circumstances under which suspicion of illegal activity was justified.

Searches of Motor Vehicle Compartments under "Gant"

On April 21, 2009, the U.S. Supreme Court decided *Arizona* v. *Gant* in which the Court announced new, albeit narrow, rules as to when law enforcement officers may properly search the passenger compartment of a motor vehicle incident to the arrest of one of its occupants. For almost 30 years prior to *Gant*, police relied upon the apparent holdings of other U.S. Supreme Court decisions, as well as other state and federal precedents, to provide justification for searches following the lawful arrest of any occupant (or recent occupant) of a motor vehicle.

However, in *Gant*, the Court limited this Fourth Amendment search authority to two circumstances: "police may search a vehicle incident to a recent occupant's arrest only if the arrestee is within reaching distance of the passenger compartment at the time of the search or it is reasonable to believe the vehicle contains evidence of the offense of the arrest."[1]

In *Gant*, Tucson police officers arrested Rodney Gant for driving with a suspended license. After he was handcuffed and locked in the back of a patrol car, officers searched his car and found cocaine in a jacket located on the backseat. Gant moved to suppress the cocaine found on the grounds that the warrantless search of his car violated the Fourth Amendment. The Arizona Supreme Court held that the search-incident-to-arrest exception to the Fourth Amendment's warrant requirement did not justify the search in this case.

The U.S. Supreme Court agreed. Based on the facts of the case, Gant was not within reaching distance of the vehicle at the time of the search (he was handcuffed and locked inside a police car), and there was no reason to believe the car contained evidence of the crime for which he was arrested (driving with a suspended license). Therefore, the search of his car violated the Fourth Amendment, and the contraband discovered during the search was suppressed.

As we have previously discussed, according to the Supreme Court, searches conducted without a warrant are presumed unreasonable. However, the Court has recognized a few specifically established and well-delineated exceptions to the search warrant requirement, to include searches incident to lawful arrest. This exception, as defined by the Court in *Chimel* v. *California*, addresses issues of officer safety and evidence preservation that are typically associated with arrest situations and is limited to areas within the arrested person's "immediate control." In *Gant*, the Supreme Court clarified that *a* two-part rule establishes when such area may be searched (prerequisite). The Gant test is an either/or proposition, meaning that only one prong of the test must be satisfied to be in compliance with the holding of the decision.[2]

The first prong of the holding in *Gant* deals with access and states that "police may search a vehicle incident to a recent occupant's arrest only if the arrestee is within reaching distance of the passenger compartment at the time of the search." The second prong of the *Gant* test permits the search of the passenger compartment of a motor vehicle following the arrest of a recent occupant of that vehicle when "it is reasonable to believe the vehicle contains evidence of the arrest."[3]

While the U.S. Supreme Court has limited the ability of law enforcement to search the passenger compartment of a motor vehicle incident to the arrest of a recent occupant of that vehicle, it certainly has not eliminated this viable search warrant exception. However, officers applying this exception must be familiar with the wording and meaning of the Court's two-part test articulated in *Gant*. It also must be remembered that facts satisfying either prong of the test will result in a reasonable search incident to arrest.

Exceptions to the Exclusionary Rule

Since the *Mapp* and *Chimel* cases, the U.S. Supreme Court has developed several exceptions to the exclusionary rule. These play a considerable role in shaping the manner in which police officers are allowed to behave before, during, and after a search and seizure of evidence.

The Good Faith Exception

In the years since the *Weeks* and *Silverthorne* cases, some people have criticized the U.S. Supreme Court for a "chipping away" of the exclusionary rule. One such case emerged in the summer of 1984 when the laws dealing with search and seizure changed dramatically in *United States* v. *Leon* (1984), when the first good faith exception to the exclusionary rule was decided. During the course of a drug trafficking investigation by the Burbank, California Police Department, officers secured a search warrant for the residence of Alberto Leon. The warrant was reviewed by three prosecutors before its being issued by a state court judge. The subsequent search netted large quantities of drugs, and Leon was arrested and charged with drug trafficking. The defense challenged the validity of the warrant based on the unreliability of the informant and moved to suppress the evidence. The district court and the U.S. Court of Appeals both held that the affidavit was insufficient, but the U.S. Supreme Court supported the prosecution, holding that the exclusionary rule was designed only as a deterrent for the abuse of police authority. The Court specified that evidence might be excluded if (1) police officers were dishonest in preparing the affidavit and (2) the warrant was deficient on its face (e.g., a wrong or missing description of the place to be searched) such that no officer could reasonably serve it or (3) if the magistrate was not found to be neutral.

The practical effect of the *Leon* case is that any evidence seized through a search warrant is immune from suppression even if the judge signing the warrant was wrong and there was not probable cause to believe that contraband or other evidence would be discovered under the warrant. The *Leon* case allows the use of evidence obtained by officers acting in reasonable reliance on a search warrant issued by a neutral magistrate but that is ultimately found invalid.

Another case decided by the U.S. Supreme Court that same year was *Massachusetts* v. *Sheppard* (1984), which reinforced the concept of good faith. In the *Sheppard* case, officers served a search warrant that failed to describe accurately the property to be seized. Although they were aware of the error, they were assured by the magistrate that the warrant was valid. After conviction of the defendant, the Massachusetts Supreme Court reversed the conviction of the trial court. But upon review, the U.S. Supreme Court supported the good faith exception and allowed the original conviction to stand. The scope of the exclusionary rule was diminished further in yet another case, *Illinois* v. *Rodriguez* (1990). In the *Rodriguez* case, Gail Fischer, who was badly beaten, complained that she had been assaulted in a Chicago apartment. She led police to the apartment, which she claimed she was sharing with the defendant, and produced a key and opened the door. The defendant, Edward Rodriguez, was found inside asleep on a bed with cocaine and drug paraphernalia spread around him. Rodriguez was arrested and charged with assault and possession of drug paraphernalia and cocaine.

After his conviction, Rodriguez demonstrated that Fischer had not lived with him for at least one month and argued that she no longer had legal control over the apartment. So the defense claimed that Fischer had no authority to give police warrantless access to the apartment. But the U.S. Supreme Court disagreed by stating that there was no Fourth Amendment violation because the police "reasonably believed" at the time of their entry that Fisher had authority for consent.

The Inevitable Discovery Doctrine

The inevitable discovery exception to the exclusionary rule was developed in the 1984 *Nix* v. *Williams* case. This exception states that evidence that has been seized illegally or evidence stemming from illegally seized evidence (e.g., **fruit of the poisonous tree**) (*Wong Sun* v. *United States*, 1963) is admissible if the police can prove that they would have inevitably discovered it anyway by lawful means. On Christmas Eve, a 10-year-old girl disappeared from the YMCA in Des Moines, Iowa. Shortly thereafter, Williams was seen leaving the YMCA carrying a large bundle wrapped in a blanket. A young boy who had helped Williams carry the bundle reported that he saw skinny white legs in it.

The next day Williams' car was located near Davenport, some 160 miles away. The police assumed that the girl's body would be located somewhere between the YMCA and Williams' car and began conducting a massive search. In the meantime, Williams was located and arrested in the town where the car was located. Williams' lawyer was told that Williams would be transported back to Des Moines without being interrogated. During the trip back, however, the officer had a conversation with Williams in which he suggested that it would be nice if the girl could be located before a predicted snowstorm and have a Christian burial. As Williams and the officer neared the town where the body was hidden, Williams directed the officer to the body, a location about two miles from one of the search teams.

During the trial, the motion to suppress the evidence was denied, and Williams was convicted of first-degree murder. On appeal, the U.S. District Court declared that the evidence was wrongfully admitted at Williams' trial. At his second trial, the prosecution did not offer Williams' statements into evidence and did not attempt to show that Williams led officers to the body. The trial court held that if Williams had not led police to the body, it would have been found by searchers anyway. Williams was convicted of murder a second time.

So, because the *Miranda* warnings were not read to the defendant before he confessed, evidence that was seized was excluded at the first trial. However, because the evidence would have been discovered anyway as a result of the police search, the court admitted the evidence.

The Computer Errors Exception

In the 1995 *Arizona* v. *Evans* case, the Court created a computer errors exception to the exclusionary rule. The exception held that a traffic stop, which led to the seizure of marijuana, was legal even though officers conducted the stop based on an arrest warrant stored improperly in their computer. The case was initiated in 1991 when Issac Evans was stopped in Phoenix, Arizona, for driving the wrong way on a one-way street in front of a police station. A routine computer check revealed an outstanding warrant for Evans, who was taken into custody. Police then found marijuana in Evans' car, and he was later convicted on drug charges. After the arrest, however, police learned that the arrest warrant reported to them by their computer had actually been quashed a few weeks earlier but had not been removed from the computer. The court upheld Evans' conviction by reasoning that officers should not be held responsible for a clerical error made by a court worker and concluded that the arresting officers were acting in good faith based on the information available to them at the time of the arrest.

Searches with a Warrant

Over the years, the **search warrant** has proven to be one of the most valuable tools in criminal investigation. It authorizes the search of homes, businesses, and vehicles of suspects; typically results in the arrest of multiple suspects; and expedites investigation and subsequent case closure.

When Are Search Warrants Necessary?

If the warrant specifies a certain person to be searched, the police can search only that person unless they have independent probable cause to search other persons who happen to be present at the scene of a search. However, if an officer has a reasonable suspicion that an onlooker is engaged in criminal activity, the officer can question the onlooker and, if necessary for the officer's safety, can frisk for weapons.

Technically, a person may require the police to produce a warrant before admitting them into his or her home for a search. However, people sometimes run into trouble when they "stand on their rights" in this way. A warrant is not always legally necessary, and a police officer may have information of which a person is unaware that allows the officer to make a warrantless entry. If an officer announces an intention to enter without a warrant, a person should not risk injury or a separate charge of "interfering with a police officer." Rather, the person should stand aside, let the officer proceed, and allow a court to decide later whether the officer's actions were proper. At the same time, the person should make it clear that he or she does not consent to the search.

When Search Warrants Aren't Required

Most searches occur without warrants being issued. Over the years, the courts have defined a number of situations in which a search warrant is not necessary, either because the search is per se reasonable under the circumstances or because, because of a lack of a reasonable expectation of privacy, the Fourth Amendment doesn't apply at all. Later on in this chapter, we will discuss some circumstances under which a search warrant is not required under law.

|Fig. 5.2| ▲

One of the most important aspects to serving search warrants is the briefing, as shown here. A thorough and properly conducted briefing helps avoid casualties by officers and civilians alike.

Courtesy of Mike Himmel

Advantages of Searching with a Search Warrant

Among the many tools afforded the criminal investigator, the search warrant has proven to be of substantial worth. It represents an authorization by the court for officers to enter a designated location or structure and search for specific items. It can be useful to a criminal investigator in many situations. The search warrant can be used to:

• Recover stolen property
• Seize drugs or other contraband
• Seize any other type of property used in the commission of a crime

The search warrant must contain specifics about the location to be searched, the objects being sought, the probable cause that indicates that there is property to seize, and a signature of the judge authorizing the search. Evidence obtained through the use of a search warrant may also be more readily accepted by courts than the evidence it was seized without a warrant or incident to arrest. In addition, the officer is protected from civil liability when a warrant is obtained. A search warrant also benefits the prosecutor by shifting the legal burden to the defendant. Instead of the prosecutor having to justify a presumably unreasonable search, it becomes the burden of the defendant to show that the evidence was seized illegally. This factor alone has encouraged officers to obtain search warrants when possible.

Structuring the Warrant

A search warrant cannot be issued unless it meets with constitutional guidelines. In addition, for the warrant to be legal, it must meet specific legal requirements. The legal requirements for a search warrant are:

• It must be authorized by the proper official
• It must be issued only for specifically authorized objects
• It must be issued on probable cause

|Fig. 5.3|

Tactical unit being utilized to serve a search warrant while approaching the suspect residence in a tactical "stack."

Courtesy of Mike Himmel

The search warrant **affidavit** presents facts that the officer believes constitute probable cause to justify the issuance of a warrant. Authorization of the warrant is through the judicial branch of government. If a magistrate agrees that probable cause exists, he or she signs the affidavit and issues the warrant. The warrant must contain the following information:

- Reasons to request the search
- Name of the officer requesting the warrant
- Items to be seized
- Specific place to be searched
- Signature of the issuing judge

|Fig. 5.4| ▲

Sample search warrant affidavit.

IN THE DISTRICT COURT OF THE FIFTH JUDICIAL DISTRICT IN AND FOR: JACKSON COUNTY, MISSOURI

Before _____ Judge, District Court of
Jackson County, Missouri

State of Missouri ⎫ ss.
Jackson County ⎭

Affidavit for Search Warrant

On this ____ day of _____, 10, *Agent Brian Johnson* being first sworn, upon oath deposes and says:

That a certain *Residence* within said County and State, located and described as follows, to wit:

2304 N.W. 38th Place, Kansas City, Missouri located in Jackson County being a single family wood frame dwelling facing South, and under the control of Lance T. Anderson, and wife Chelsea. The garage area of the house is to the West end of the South side. The house is on the North side of the street with tan colored brick along the lower third of the front, while being fenced in, with a chain link fence, around the back yard area.

the same being the *residence* of *Lance and Chelsea Anderson* whose more full, true and correct name is unknown to the affiant, there is located certain property particularly described as follows, to-wit:

Controlled substances to include marijuana, Schedule I, LSD, Schedule I, Cocaine, Schedule II, and one fifty dollar bill ($50.00) U.S. currency bearing serial number JO3744496B, and any other records or documents showing illicit business dealings in controlled drugs.

which said property is subject to search and seizure as set out by the laws of Missouri for the following grounds, to-wit:

Violation of the state criminal code controlled substances section RsMo 195.233.

and that the probable cause of the affiant believing such facts exist as follows, to-wit:

1) Your affiant is a sworn police officer with the Kansas City Police Department, who has been a full time narcotics investigator for three years and seven months. 2) On April 30, 2012 at approximately 1630 hours, Officer Johnson purchased one (1) kilo of marijuana for $2500 from Chelsea Anderson which was contained in a black trunk located in the hallway of the residence. 3) On April 30, 2012 at approx. 1945 hours Officer Johnson purchased 100 units of LSD for $4350 from Lance Anderson which he acquired from the freezer area of the kitchen. 4) On April 30, 2012 Lance Anderson also displayed approx. one (1) ounce of white powder claiming it to be cocaine which was also kept in the refrigerator area of the kitchen.

_____
Affiant

Subscribed and sworn before me this ____ day of ____ 2012

_____
Judge, District Court of
Jackson County, Missouri

After a warrant has been issued, it should be executed promptly. During the course of a search, other items of contraband should not be sought unless they are specified in the search warrant. The seizure of items other than those listed in the warrant is not considered "within the scope of the search" and will probably be excluded from the trial as evidence obtained illegally. The search warrant process consists basically of three stages: the affidavit, the search warrant, and the search warrant return.

THE AFFIDAVIT   A search warrant affidavit must be prepared before obtaining a search warrant. The affidavit tells the judge three things:

1. What is being searched for:
   - Contraband
   - Instrumentation of crime
   - Weapons
   - Fruits of crime
2. Where the search is to occur:
   - Residence
   - Business
   - Vehicle
3. Why the search is to be conducted:
   - Probable cause is adequately outlined
   - Facts establishing probable cause

THE SEARCH WARRANT   Basically, the search warrant sets forth the same facts as outlined in the affidavit. Prior to signing the affidavit, the affiant (the officer) must be certain that he or she is first sworn in by a judge. The judge must then sign and date all pages of the affidavit and warrant.

THE SEARCH WARRANT RETURN   The **search warrant return** is an itemized inventory of all property and material seized by officers at the location of the search. A copy is left with the defendant, and the return itself is returned to the issuing judge. In most cases, the officer who executes the warrant is the one to return it, and this must be accomplished within 24 hours after the search. The search warrant return should include the following information:

- The name of the officer serving the warrant
- The date the warrant was served
- An itemized list of all property seized
- The name of the owner of the place searched
- The signature of the officer who served the warrant (usually signed in the presence of the judge)
- The signature of the issuing judge and the date of the return

Execution of the Warrant

After it has been issued, the search warrant is basically an order by the court to execute it. The officer has no choice but to do so. If the warrant is valid on its face, has been authorized by the proper official, and is executed correctly, the officer is protected from both civil liability and criminal prosecution. Certain procedures should be adhered to carefully when executing the search warrant. Search warrant execution guidelines include:

- *A search warrant may authorize a specific officer (the affiant) to execute it.* Typically, however, a class of officers will be authorized to execute the warrant, so that anyone within that class may do so.
- *Time limitations must be adhered to.* Although the word *reasonable* has not been defined by the courts, execution of a warrant must be within what a rational person would consider reasonable. To deal with this issue, many states have outlined a specific period in which the warrant must be issued. Periods may range from 48 to 96 hours. If the warrant cannot be executed within that designated period, it is invalid.
- *Only necessary force can be used in executing a search warrant.* The U.S. Code requires that officers announce their purpose and authority, and if refused admittance, break both outer and inner doors to gain entry. Denial need not be specific or even be inferred, such as the occupants refusing to answer the door.

**IN THE DISTRICT COURT OF THE FIFTH JUDICIAL DISTRICT
IN AND FOR:
JACKSON COUNTY, MISSOURI**

BEFORE _____ JUDGE, DISTRICT COURT OF
JACKSON COUNTY, MISSOURI

State of Missouri } ss. **SEARCH WARRANT**
Jackson County }

In the name of the State of Missouri, to any sheriff, constable, marshal, policeman, or peace officer in the County of Jackson, State of Missouri.

Proof by affidavit having been this day made before me, by _Agent Brian Johnson_ that there is probable cause for believing that in the herein described _residence_ is located the following property particularly described as follows, to-wit:

Controlled substances to include marijuana, Schedule I, LSD, Schedule I, and Cocaine, Schedule II, and one fifty dollar bill U.S. currency bearing serial number: JO3744496B

and that the herein described _residence_ should be searched by reason of the following grounds to-wit:

Possession of the above described controlled dangerous substances and currency is evidence of violation of the state criminal code controlled substances section RsMo 195.233.

YOU ARE THEREFORE COMMANDED at any time of day or night to make immediate search of the _residence_ of _2304 N.W. 38th Place, Kansas City, Missouri_ whose more full, true and correct name is unknown, located and described as follows, to-wit:

a single family wood frame dwelling facing South, and under the control of Lance Thomas Anderson, and wife Chelsea. The garage area of the house is to the West end of the south side. The house is on the north side of the street with tan colored brick along the lower third front, while being fenced in, with a chain link fence, around the back yard area.

for the said property above described, and, if you find the same or any part thereof to bring it forthwith before me at my office in Kansas City, Jackson County, Missouri.

Dated this _1st_ day of _May_, 2012.

_____
Judge, District Court of
Jackson County, Missouri

|Fig. 5.5| △

Sample search warrant.

- **Some states may authorize a "no-knock warrant."** If such a warrant is obtained, specific information must be contained in the affidavit justifying why the no-knock warrant is necessary.

In 2005, the Supreme Court held in _Muehler_ v. _Mena_ that officers executing a search warrant of a residence while seeking weapons and evidence of gang-related activity in the aftermath of a drive-by shooting acted reasonably when detaining the occupants of the residence in handcuffs during the course of the search—especially considering there were only two officers present at the time.

Anticipatory Search Warrants

An anticipatory search warrant is a warrant based on an affidavit showing probable cause to believe that at some future time, particular evidence of a crime will be located at a particular place. Anticipatory warrants may not be executed until some specific event (other than the passage of time) has occurred. The specified events are called **triggering conditions**, and even though the warrant has been issued and is in the hands of the police, until the triggering condition has arisen, the search may not be carried out.

Anticipatory search warrants have been the subject of a great deal of litigation, much of that based on the argument that all anticipatory warrants are unconstitutional because they violate the Fourth Amendment requirement of probable cause. The contention of many defendants has been because, by definition, anticipatory search warrant affidavits show only that there will be probable cause to search the premises at some later time—not that there is at present probable cause to search—the Fourth Amendment requirement is not satisfied. Although this argument has been repeatedly rejected by various federal courts of appeals, the issue has recently come before the Supreme Court of the United States in the case of *United States* v. *Grubbs*, 377 F.3d 1072 (2004). Even though the case involved a warrant obtained by federal officers for a federal crime, the Supreme Court's opinion in that case is of value to all law enforcement officers and agencies in understanding anticipatory search warrants and their use.

In *United States* v. *Grubbs*, respondent Jeffrey Grubbs purchased a videotape containing child pornography from a website operated by an undercover postal inspector. Officers from the postal inspection service arranged a controlled delivery of a package containing a videotape to Grubbs' residence. A postal inspector submitted a search warrant application to a magistrate judge for the

|Fig. 5.6| ▲

Sample search
warrant return.

SEARCH WARRANT RETURN

Received this writ _____ day of _____, 2012

Executed the same on the _____ day of _____, 2012 by going to the within designated place where I found and seized the following property, to-wit:

_____

_____

_____ *(ITEMIZE PROPERTY HERE)* _____

_____

_____

and brought the same before the within named court.

_____
Sheriff - Peace Officer
Marshall - Policeman

Executed the same day on the _____ day of _____, 2012 by searching the within designated place, where I could find none of the above described property.

_____
Sheriff - Peace Officer
Marshall - Policeman

OFFICER'S FEES

Executing writ _____ $ _____

Mileage _____ Miles $ _____

Total: $ _____

_____
Sheriff - Peace Officer
Marshall - Policeman

Eastern District of California, a copy of an affidavit describing the proposed operation in detail. The affidavit stated:

> Execution of the search warrant will not occur unless and until the parcel has been received by a person(s) and has been physically taken into the residence…at that time, and not before, the search warrant will be executed by me and other United States Postal Service inspectors, with appropriate assistance from other law enforcement officers in accordance with this warrant's command.

In addition to describing this triggering condition, the affidavit referred to two attachments, which describe Grubbs' residence and the items officers would seize. These attachments, but not the body of the affidavit, were incorporated into the requested warrant.

The magistrate judge issued the warrant as requested. Two days later, an undercover postal inspector delivered the package. Grubbs' wife signed for it and took the unopened package inside. The inspectors detained Grubbs as he left his home a few minutes later and then entered the house and commenced the search. Approximately 30 minutes into the search, Grubbs was provided with a copy of the warrant, which included both attachments but not the supporting affidavit that explained when the warrant would be executed. Grubbs consented to interrogation by the postal inspectors and admitted ordering the videotape. He was placed under arrest, and various items were seized, including the videotape. Grubbs subsequently pleaded guilty but reserved his right to appeal the denial of his earlier motion to suppress the evidence.

The Triggering Condition

To understand both the *Grubbs* case and the use of anticipatory search warrants in general, it is essential that the concept of the triggering condition be kept clearly in mind. The triggering condition is the anticipated future event that, when it occurs, gives rise to the necessary probable cause to search the premises. Even though the anticipatory search warrant has been issued, if the triggering condition has not yet occurred, the probable cause requirement of the Fourth Amendment has not yet been satisfied and the search is invalid.

The U.S. Supreme Court in *Grubbs* upholds the constitutionality of anticipatory search warrants, provided that the following prerequisites are satisfied:

1. It must be true that if the triggering condition occurs, "there is a fair probability that contraband or evidence of a crime will be found in a particular place."
2. There is probable cause to believe that the triggering condition will occur.
3. The affidavit supporting the warrant provides that the magistrate was given sufficient information to evaluate both aspects of the probable cause determination.

It is apparent in the *Grubbs* decision, however, that it is not essential that the defendant be presented with a copy of the affidavit at the time that the search warrant is instituted nor that the defendant be told at the time of the search what the triggering condition was.

Warrantless Searches

Officers must remember that the rules applying to searches differ from those applying to arrests. An arrest and a search are two completely separate and distinct law enforcement procedures. For example, depending on certain statutory restraints, an officer might be empowered to make an arrest without an arrest warrant, provided that probable cause exists. In addition, arrests are permissible even when there is time for the officer to get a warrant. For searches, the rules are different. The Fourth Amendment says that all searches must be preceded by the officer's obtaining a search warrant. Regardless of how much probable cause an officer may have, if he or she searches without a search warrant, there is a legal presumption that the search is unconstitutional. Several exceptions have been developed in which a warrantless search is authorized under law:

- Consent searches
- Searches under exigent circumstances
- Searches incident to lawful arrest
- Stop-and-frisk searches

- Plain-view searches
- Automobile searches
- Open-field searches

Search by Consent

Police can search without a warrant when a suspect gives them permission to do so. Searches in this instance must, of course, be subsequent to an initial detention that was lawful. As a case in point, *Florida* v. *Royer* (1983) held that evidence obtained as a result of a **consent search** when the detention was made without probable cause is a violation of the defendant's Fourth Amendment rights and will be excluded.

The consent search can be especially useful in cases in which officers have no legal basis for obtaining a search warrant. It is important to remember, however, that a consent search must

|Fig. 5.7| ◮

Sample consent to
search form.

**CITY POLICE DEPARTMENT
CONSENT TO SEARCH**

DATE _____

LOCATION _____

I, _____, having been informed of my constitutional right
not to have a search made of the premises hereinafter described without a search warrant and of my
right to refuse to consent to such a search, hereby authorize _____
_____, officers of the City Police Department, to conduct a complete
search of my:

Premises ____

Curtilage ____

Vehicles ____

These officers are authorized by me to take from my premises any letters, papers, materials, or other
property which they may desire, after receipting me for same. I further state that I am the proper
person to give the consent and authorization referred to herein.

This written permission is being given by me to the above named officers(s) voluntarily and without
threats or promises of any kind.

_____
                                    Signature

WITNESSES:

_____

_____

_____

be authorized voluntarily, with no coercion from officers. This was affirmed in *Bumper* v. *North Carolina* (1968) in a decision in which the U.S. Supreme Court held that a search is not justified on the basis of consent when consent was given only after the officer conducting the search asserted possession of a warrant. Although it is legal for officers to search on the word of the suspect, it is a better idea to have the person sign a consent-to-search waiver authorizing the search in writing. For the consent to be valid, officers must first establish that the person giving consent has legal authority to do so. Just because a suspect is present in a particular residence, he or she may not have legal authority to grant a search. Dominion and control can be verified through the seizing of utility bills, for example, that bear the name of the suspect and the associated address.

One interesting aspect of a consent search is that the suspect does not have to be given the *Miranda* warning or told that he or she has the right to withhold consent for the search to be valid (*Schneckloth* v. *Bustamonte*, 1973). In the event that the suspect changes his or her mind about the search, officers must cease searching or obtain a search warrant to continue.

Another problem with consent searches is that the person giving permission to search can limit the scope of the search. Permission to search can be withdrawn at any time, and any area or container within the search area can be specifically exempted. What if an area or container that might reasonably hold the object of the search isn't specifically exempted? In the case of *Florida* v. *Jimeno* (1991), the Court held that a person's general consent to search the interior of a car includes, unless otherwise specified, all containers in the car that might reasonably hold the object of the search. In this case a Dade County police officer began following a car after overhearing the driver, Enio Jimeno, make arrangements for a drug transaction over a pay phone.

When Jimeno failed to come to a complete stop before turning right at a stoplight, the officer pulled him over. The officer advised Jimeno that he was going to receive a traffic citation for failure to stop at the red light. Next, since he had reason to believe that Jimeno was involved with a drug transaction, the officer asked for permission to search the automobile. Jimeno agreed, claiming that he had nothing to hide. As a result of the search, the officer found 1 kilo of cocaine in a brown paper bag located under the passenger side floorboard. Jimeno was arrested and charged.

The issue here is that because Jimeno had not given specific permission to search the bag, the Florida courts ordered the cocaine suppressed as evidence. The courts claimed that although the officer was proper in asking for permission to search the vehicle, permission was not extended to the bag under the floorboard or any other containers in the car. The U.S. Supreme Court didn't agree. In his delivery of the majority opinion, Chief Justice William Rehnquist stated:

> The scope of a search is generally defined by its expressed object. [The officer] had informed Jimeno that he…would be looking for narcotics in the area. We think that it was…reasonable for the police to conclude that the general consent to search [the] car included consent to search containers within that car which might bear drugs.

Rehnquist further explained that a different degree of privacy should attach to a paper bag than to a locked suitcase and that it is probably unreasonable for an officer to think that a person who gives consent for a search of his vehicle has also given consent to pry open a locked bag inside the car. But it probably isn't unreasonable for the officer to open a paper bag under the same circumstances. Rehnquist went on to say that "a suspect may of course delimit as he chooses the scope of the search to which he consents…but if his consent would reasonably be understood to extend to a particular container, the Fourth Amendment provides no grounds for requiring a more explicit authorization."

In a related case, *Florida* v. *Bostick* (1991), the U.S. Supreme Court permitted warrantless sweeps of inner-city buses. In *Bostick*, the Court ruled that law enforcement officers who approach a seated bus passenger and request consent to search the passenger's luggage do not necessarily "seize" the passenger under the Fourth Amendment. The test applied in such situations is whether or not a reasonable passenger would feel free to decline the request or otherwise terminate the encounter. In the *Bostick* case, the defendant was traveling from Miami, Florida, to Atlanta, Georgia. When the bus stopped in Ft. Lauderdale, two police officers involved in drug interdiction efforts boarded the bus and, lacking reasonable suspicion, approached the defendant. After asking to inspect his ticket and identification, they then requested and were given consent to search the defendant's luggage for drugs. Cocaine was found as a result of the search.

The Florida Supreme Court ruled that the cocaine had been seized in violation of the Fourth Amendment. In doing so, the court noted that the defendant had been illegally seized without reasonable suspicion and that an impermissible seizure necessarily results any time that police board a bus, approach passengers without reasonable suspicion, and request consent to search luggage.

The U.S. Supreme Court reversed the Florida court's decision and held that this type of drug interdiction effort may be permissible as long as officers do not convey the message that compliance with their request is required.

The Court noted that previous cases have permitted the police, without reasonable suspicion, to approach people in an airport for the purpose of asking questions, verifying identification, and requesting consent to search luggage.

Emergency Searches

In the case of an emergency or **exigent circumstances**, a search may also be conducted without a warrant provided that probable cause exists. As a general rule, the police are authorized to make an emergency warrantless search when the time it would take to get a warrant would jeopardize public safety or lead to the loss of important evidence. Here are some situations in which judges would most likely uphold a warrantless search:

- *A threat of the removal or destruction of evidence. Case example:* After a street drug arrest, an officer enters the house after the suspect shouts into the house, "Eddie, quick, flush our stash down the toilet." The officer arrests Eddie and seizes the stash.
- *A danger to life. Case example:* A police officer on routine patrol hears shouts and screams coming from a residence, rushes in, and arrests a suspect for spousal abuse.
- *The threat of a suspect escaping*

Any one of these circumstances may create an exception to the Fourth Amendment's warrant requirement. It is incumbent on investigating officers to demonstrate that a dire situation existed that justified their actions. Failure to do so will result in the evidence seized being deemed illegal. However, if a judge decides that an officer had time to obtain a search warrant without risking injury to people or the loss of evidence, the judge should refuse to allow into evidence whatever was seized in the course of the warrantless search. Judges always have the final word on whether police officers should have obtained warrants.

The need for law enforcement to intervene in the face of a crisis without first obtaining a warrant has long been recognized by the judiciary. As Chief Justice (then Judge) Burger noted in *Wayne* v. *United States*:

> "[A] warrant is not required to break down a door to enter a burning home to rescue occupants or extinguish a fire, to prevent a shooting or to bring emergency aid to an injured person. The need to protect or preserve life or avoid serious injury is justification for what would be otherwise illegal absent an exigency or emergency. Fires or dead bodies are reported to police by cranks where no fires or bodies are to be found. Acting in response to reports of "dead bodies," the police may find the "bodies" to be common drunks, diabetics in shock, or distressed cardiac patients. But the business of policemen and firemen is to act, not to speculate or meditate on whether the report is correct. People could well die in emergencies if police tried to act with the calm deliberation associated with the judicial process. Even the apparently dead often are saved by swift police response. A myriad of circumstances could fall within the terms "exigent circumstances"…e.g., smoke coming out a window or under a door, the sound of gunfire in a house, threats from the inside to shoot through the door at police, reasonable grounds to believe an injured or seriously ill person is being held within."[4]

The need for emergency searches was first recognized by the U.S. Supreme Court in *Ker* v. *California* (1963) and *Cupp* v. *Murphy* (1973) when it decided that police may enter a dwelling unannounced in cases in which a delay in the search would result in the destruction of evidence. In a related decision, the court held that it was lawful for police to enter a residence without a warrant if they were in pursuit of a fleeing robber (*Warden* v. *Hayden*, 1967). In another case, *Mincey* v. *Arizona* (1978), the Supreme Court held that the "Fourth Amendment does not require police officers to delay in the course of an investigation if doing so would gravely endanger their lives or the lives of others." Finally, in the 1995 case of *Wilson* v. *Arkansas*, the Supreme Court ruled that police officers generally must knock and announce their identity before entering a dwelling or other premises with a search warrant. However, in certain emergencies, officers armed with a search warrant need not knock or identify themselves.

In 2006, the U.S. Supreme Court held in *Brigham City* v. *Stuart* that officers can enter a home without a warrant when there is an objectively reasonable basis to believe that an occupant in the residence is seriously injured or is imminently threatened with serious injury.

Searches Incident to Arrest

As we learned earlier, the *Chimel* decision authorized a search of an arrested suspect and the immediate area around him or her. This is justified by an officer's right to search a suspect for weapons before transporting him or her to jail. The area around the suspect is searched because it is considered lunging distance, where a suspect could conceivably acquire a weapon. When the suspect is arrested in a vehicle, the immediate area is defined as the entire passenger compartment of the vehicle, including closed but not locked containers (*New York* v. *Belton*, 1981). In circumstances in which a thorough search is desired pursuant to an arrest, a search warrant should be obtained.

Stop-and-Frisk Searches

In 1968, the Supreme Court of the United States declared in the case of *Terry* v. *Ohio* (1968)[5] that a police officer may stop a person for questioning if the officer reasonably suspects that the person has committed, is committing, or is about to commit a crime. It is not necessary that the officer have probable cause to arrest the individual at the time that the stop is made. All that is required is that the officer has a reasonable suspicion that the individual is involved in criminal activity. However, to be reasonable, this suspicion must be based on articulable facts that would lead a reasonable person to suspect that the individual is involved in criminal activity.

The Supreme Court further declared in *Terry* v. *Ohio* that an officer who has stopped a suspect may "…search for weapons for the protection of the police officer, where he has reason to- believe that he is dealing with an armed and dangerous individual."[6] This case is the landmark legal decision that grants officers the authority to conduct field interviews (also called "investigative detentions" or *Terry* stops) and pat-down searches (an investigative detention is commonly referred to as a "**stop and frisk**"). Numerous federal and state court decisions have interpreted and applied the principles of *Terry*. In addition, many states have enacted statutes dealing with field interviews and pat-down searches.[7]

FIELD INTERVIEWS VERSUS "CONSENSUAL ENCOUNTERS" The principles discussed here apply to field interviews only. They do not apply to so-called consensual or voluntary encounters. As noted earlier, an officer may conduct a field interview as defined in the policy (an investigative detention or *Terry* stop) only when he or she has a reasonable suspicion, based on objective facts, that the individual to be interviewed is engaged in criminal activity. Conversely, an officer who lacks "reasonable suspicion" as defined above may nevertheless approach a suspect and ask questions designed to produce evidence of criminal activity as long as the encounter is voluntary or "consensual."

The distinction is a critical one. Field interviews are "seizures" of the person within the meaning of the Fourth Amendment, and the discovery of any physical evidence during such an interview is valid only if Fourth Amendment considerations are met. On the other hand, consensual encounters are not seizures of the person. If the officer discovers evidence during the consensual encounter, it will normally be admissible in a trial even though there was no basis for "reasonable suspicion" at the time that the officer initiated the encounter. Thus, it is often desirable for the officer to approach a suspect in a manner that will make the initial contact a consensual encounter rather than a field interview.

FACTORS DEFINING A FIELD INTERVIEW The U.S. Supreme Court has held that a police–citizen encounter is consensual (i.e., does not amount to a seizure of the person) as long as the circumstances of the encounter are such that a reasonable person would feel that he or she was "free to leave," that is, to terminate the encounter and depart at any time.[8] The following factors, among others, may be considered by a court in determining whether the contact was a consensual encounter or a field interview (hereafter sometimes referred to as an "investigative stop"):

1. *Interference with the suspect's freedom of movement*. *Case example:* If officers position themselves or their vehicles in such a manner as to block the suspect's path, this indicates that the suspect is not free to leave and may render the encounter an investigative stop.
2. *Number of officers and their behavior*. *Case example:* Confrontation of the suspect by more than one officer may create an atmosphere of intimidation that will cause the courts to consider the contact an investigative stop. Excessive display of weapons, such as drawn or pointed firearms, will have the same effect. Even the prolonged or repeated display of badges or other police identification may be considered intimidating.[9] A threatening or bullying manner may lead to the same result.

The following factors, among others, may be considered by a court in determining whether the contact was a consensual encounter or a field interview.

Interference with the suspect's freedom of movement

Case example: If officers position themselves or their vehicles in such a manner as to block the suspect's path, this indicates that the suspect is not free to leave and may render the encounter an investigative stop.

Number of officers and their behavior

Case example: Confrontation of the suspect by more than one officer may create an atmosphere of intimidation that will cause the courts to consider the contact an investigative stop. Excessive display of weapons, such as drawn or pointed firearms, will have the same effect. Even the prolonged or repeated display of badges or other police identification may be considered intimidating.[i] A threatening or bullying manner may lead to the same result.

Physical contact with the suspect

Case example: Any physical contact with the suspect for purposes of stopping or holding the individual or to search for weapons or evidence will almost certainly cause the contact to be considered a nonconsensual (that is, an investigative) stop or even a full-fledged arrest.

Retaining personal property of the suspect

Case example: If the officer wishes the contact to be regarded as consensual, any personal property taken from the suspect, such as a driver's license or other identification, should be returned promptly to the suspect. Prolonged retention by the officer of such items may lead a court to conclude that the suspect was not free to leave.

[i]Officers must, for reasons of both legality and personal safety, adequately identify themselves as police officers. Proper identification as a police officer does not render an encounter nonconsensual. It is only the excessive, unnecessary, or deliberately intimidating display of authority that affects the consensual nature of the encounter.

|Fig. 5.8| △

The following factors, among others, may be considered by a court in determining whether the contact was a consensual encounter or a field interview.

3. ***Physical contact with the suspect.*** *Case example:* Any physical contact with the suspect for purposes of stopping or holding the individual or to search for weapons or evidence will almost certainly cause the contact to be considered a nonconsensual (i.e., an investigative) stop or even a full-fledged arrest.
4. ***Retaining personal property of the suspect.*** *Case example:* If the officer wishes the contact to be regarded as consensual, any personal property taken from the suspect, such as a driver's license or other identification, should be returned promptly to the suspect. Prolonged retention by the officer of such items may lead a court to conclude that the suspect was not free to leave.

An officer may ask the suspect to move to another area during the encounter without altering the consensual nature of the contact if it is made clear to the suspect that the request to move to another location is just that—a request only—and that the suspect is free to refuse the request.

One method of emphasizing the consensual nature of the encounter is for the officer to advise the suspect that the suspect has the right to refuse to answer questions, the right to refuse to consent to a search, and so forth. Such warnings may not be legally required under the existing circumstances, but if given, they will often persuade a court that any continuation of the encounter beyond that point was still voluntary on the part of the suspect. Even if the contact is not a consensual contact, it is still perfectly lawful if conducted in accordance with the principles applicable to investigative stops.

INITIATION AND CONDUCT OF FIELD INTERVIEWS The initiation of a field interview is justified only when an officer has reasonable suspicion that a suspect is engaged in criminal activity. This suspicion must be based on specific facts known to or observed by the officer that the officer can later articulate in detail to a court. Such facts may include the demeanor of a person (e.g., furtive behavior); the time of day or night; the area in which the encounter occurs; the inappropriateness of the suspect's presence in that area at that time; the fact that the suspect is carrying suspicious objects; objective evidence that the suspect may be armed (bulge in the clothing); and knowledge of the officer that a crime has recently been committed in that area, especially if the suspect matches the description of the perpetrator of the crime.[10]

In addition to the above, on January 12, 2000, the U.S. Supreme Court decided the case of *Illinois v. Wardlow* ([98-1036] 183 Ill. 2nd 306, 701 N.E. 2d 484), which provides officers with an additional criterion for establishing reasonable suspicion to initiate a field interview. *Wardlow* deals with the common scenario in which a person notices police approaching and runs away to avoid them. In the past, it has generally been held by the courts that the act of fleeing from police does not, in and of itself, justify officers to pursue and stop the individual concerned. The *Wardlow* decision does not alter that basic fact, but it does permit officers to include fleeing as one more element that police may consider in determining whether reasonable suspicion exists sufficient to justify a *Terry* stop.

Officers must conduct the field interview in such a manner that the courts will not consider it an unlawful arrest. It must be remembered that in the view of the courts, an arrest may occur even though the actual words "you're under arrest" have not been uttered by the officer. Therefore, unless the stop produces probable cause to arrest the suspect, the officer should still conduct the field interview in a manner that will not convey the impression that the suspect is under arrest. For this reason, the officer should:

- Exercise reasonable courtesy and avoid intimidating or threatening behavior.
- Minimize physical contact, which may induce a court to treat the encounter as an arrest.
- Avoid detaining the suspect any longer than is absolutely necessary. One of the more common bases for judicial rulings that a stop has become an arrest is detention of the suspect for an excessive period of time.

In addition, any movement of the suspect from the point of initial contact, such as to an area where there is more light, should be limited to that which is reasonably necessary for officer safety and the determination of criminal involvement. However, it should be clearly understood here that notwithstanding cautions regarding the legal requirements for a field interview, officer safety should remain a paramount consideration and should be emphasized in all departmental policies.

PAT-DOWN SEARCHES As noted earlier, *Terry* v. *Ohio*, other court decisions, and various state statutes give officers the authority to conduct a pat-down search[11] or "frisk" of a suspect who has been the subject of a valid investigative stop if the officer reasonably believes that the suspect may possess a weapon.

The following points are vital when conducting a valid pat-down search:

- If the stop is invalid, the pat-down search is also invalid. Only a valid investigative stop based on reasonable suspicion of criminal activity justifies a pat-down search.

- The right to stop the suspect for questioning does not automatically give the officer the right to conduct the pat-down search. The erroneous belief that the right to stop automatically gives the officer the right to frisk is one of the more common errors made by police officers. In reality, even if the stop is valid, before a pat-down search may be conducted, there must be a separate basis for believing that the person who has been stopped may possess a weapon and may be a threat to the officer.

- Factors that may justify an officer reaching the conclusion that a suspect who has been validly stopped may possess a weapon include the type of crime suspected[12]; the circumstances of the stop (number of suspects, number of officers present, and time of day and location of the stop); the behavior of the suspect (belligerence); any visual indication that the suspect may be carrying a weapon (e.g., a bulge in the clothing); and any prior knowledge that the officer may have that this particular individual is or may be prone to violence.

- The pat-down search is limited to a "frisk" of the suspect's outer clothing only. It is not a full-scale search such as might be conducted after a valid arrest.[13] An officer may not reach into the suspect's clothing or pockets unless and until the presence of a weapon has been detected by the pat-down.[14]

The officer's belief that the suspect may be armed and dangerous must be both reasonable and actual. For the frisk to be valid, the officer's fear for his or her safety must be objectively reasonable and must actually exist. A federal circuit court has pointed out that an officer "cannot have a reasonable suspicion that a person is armed and dangerous when he in fact has no such suspicion."[15] Therefore, if the officer was not actually concerned for his or her own safety but frisked the suspect anyway, the frisk is illegal. When called on to justify the frisk, the officer must be prepared to make it clear that he or she was both reasonably and actually apprehensive for his or her safety.

Pat-down searches should, if possible, be conducted by officers of the same gender as the suspect. The fact that a male officer pats down a female suspect does not necessarily invalidate the pat-down, but it may lead to contentions of civil rights violations and hence to civil liability.

Frequently, a person who has been stopped for a field interview will have in his or her possession containers such as sacks, briefcases, or bags. Although "frisks" of such containers have sometimes been upheld by the courts, officers should not attempt to open these containers. Rather, the officer is instructed to place such items out of reach of the suspect during the field interview. This ensures the officer's safety while avoiding the risk of an unlawful search.[16]

STATE COURT DECISIONS AND STATUTES As noted earlier, the primary legal basis for field interviews and pat-down searches arises from the U.S. Supreme Court case of *Terry* v. *Ohio*. However, many states, including Illinois, New York, and Virginia, have statutes that govern these activities. These statutes may place restrictions on officers that are more stringent than those imposed by the U.S. Supreme Court. In addition, state constitutions may also place limits on an officer's authority to detain and frisk suspects that are more restrictive than those announced by the U.S. Supreme Court.

Plain-View Searches

Police officers have the opportunity to begin investigations or confiscate evidence without a warrant based on what they find in plain view and open to public inspection. This has become known as the **plain-view doctrine**, a doctrine first stated in the Supreme Court ruling in *Harris* v. *United States* (1968). A police officer found evidence of a robbery while inventorying an impounded vehicle. The court ruled that "objects falling in the plain view of an officer who has a right to be in the position to have that view are subject to seizure and may be used as evidence." This doctrine has been widely used by investigators in such cases as crimes in progress, accidents, and fires. An officer might enter an apartment, for example, while responding to a domestic disturbance and find drugs on a living room table. He or she would be within his or her rights to seize the drugs as evidence without having a search warrant. The criteria for a valid plain-view search were identified in *Coolidge* v. *New Hampshire* (1971). In that decision, the court identified three criteria that must be present:

1. The officer must be present lawfully at the location to be searched.
2. The item seized must have been found inadvertently.
3. The item is contraband or would be useful as evidence of a crime.

Before 1990, the courts required that all items found in plain view be found inadvertently, but in *Horton* v. *California* (1990), the Court ruled that "inadvertent discovery" of evidence is no longer a necessary element of the plain-view doctrine. Other cases supporting the plain-view doctrine include the 1958 *United States* v. *Henry* decision, in which the Court ruled that if an officer discovers evidence of another crime "unexpectedly," that evidence can be seized. In 1978, coinciding cases *Michigan* v. *Tyler* and *Mincey* v. *Arizona* concluded that while officers are present on a person's premises carrying out legitimate emergency responsibilities, any evidence in plain view is seizable. In another case, the Court held that the officer needn't know that the evidence is even contraband, only that it is associated with a crime (*Texas* v. *Brown*, 1983). In this case, the officer's personal knowledge that heroin was transported in balloons was sufficient to seize a balloon without knowing exactly what it contained.

The plain-view doctrine has, however, been restricted by more recent court decisions, such as the case of *United States* v. *Irizarry* (1982), in which the court held that officers cannot move objects to gain a better view of evidence otherwise hidden from view. This view was affirmed in the case *Arizona* v. *Hicks* (1987), which stated that evidence seized must be in plain view without the need for officers to move or dislodge it. In *Hicks*, officers responded to a shooting in a second-floor apartment during which a bullet had been fired through the floor, injuring a man in the apartment below. The premises of James Hicks were in considerable disarray when investigating officers entered.

As the officers looked for the person who might have fired the weapon, they discovered a number of guns and a stocking mask that might have been used in some local robberies. The items were seized. But in one corner, officers noticed two expensive stereo sets. One of the officers approached the equipment, suspecting that it might be stolen, and read a few of the serial numbers from where it sat. But to read the remaining serial numbers, the equipment was moved away from the wall. After calling in the serial number, the officer learned that the equipment had, in fact, been stolen.

Hicks was then arrested and later convicted of armed robbery through use of the seized property. But on appeal, the U.S. Supreme Court decided that the search of Hicks's apartment became illegal when the officer moved the stereo set away from the wall to record the serial numbers. The Court explained that Hicks had a reasonable expectation of privacy, which means that the officers, although invited into the apartment, must act more like guests than inquisitors.

Automobile Searches

The precedent established for warrantless searches of automobiles is the automobile exception, or the **Carroll Doctrine** (*Carroll* v. *United States*, 1925). This decision established that the right to search a vehicle does not depend on the right to arrest the driver but on the premise that the contents of the vehicle contain evidence of a crime. In this case, George Carroll, a bootlegger, was convicted for transporting intoxicating liquor in a vehicle, a violation of the National Prohibition Act. At the trial, Carroll's attorneys contended that the liquor need not be admitted into evidence because the search and seizure of the vehicle were unlawful and violated the Fourth Amendment. Because of the mobility of the automobile, the warrantless search under Carroll is justified. After the *Carroll* decision, there existed some uncertainty about the moving vehicle doctrine. Much of this doubt was laid to rest in 1970, however, when the U.S. Supreme Court reaffirmed the right of officers to search a vehicle that is moving or about to be moved out of their jurisdiction, provided that probable cause exists that the vehicle contains items that officers are entitled to seize.

Since the ruling of the *Carroll* doctrine, related cases have raised the question of whether officers searching under *Carroll* also have the right to search closed containers in a car. In a 1981 decision, the U.S. Supreme Court held that warrantless seizures of evidence in the passenger compartments of a car, after a lawful arrest, are valid (*New York* v. *Belton*, 1981). Before this decision, there was some confusion about the authority of police to search within the vehicle but outside the driver's "wingspan." The Court authorized a search of the entire passenger compartment of the vehicle, including the backseat. It also authorized the opening of containers in the vehicle that might contain the object sought. The following year, the Court held that after a lawful arrest, police may open the trunk of a car and containers found therein without a warrant, even in the absence of exigent circumstances (*United States* v. *Ross*, 1982). This case further defined the scope of police search-and-seizure authority in vehicle searches. The *Ross* case therefore has expanded the scope of warrantless searches only to what is "reasonable." It should be noted, however, that police may not open large containers taken from the car, such as footlockers, without a warrant, provided that there is time to obtain one.

In a high-impact case, *California* v. *Acevedo* (1991), much of the confusion about vehicle searches was eliminated. Federal agents in Hawaii intercepted a package of marijuana being sent via Federal Express to Santa Ana, California. At that time, officers staked out the Santa Ana Federal Express office. The man who claimed the package was then followed to his apartment, where he went inside and came back out a few minutes later with an empty carton, which he pitched into a dumpster. At that time, one officer left the area to obtain a search warrant while the other officers maintained surveillance on the residence.

Before the officer returned with the warrant, Acevedo drove up and entered the apartment. In about 10 minutes, he exited the apartment with an object in a paper bag that was about the same size as a brick of marijuana. Acevedo placed the bag in his vehicle trunk and began to drive away. In an effort to stop Acevedo before he would be lost, the officers stopped him and searched his trunk. The bag was discovered and was found to contain marijuana. Although the trial court found Acevedo guilty, on appeal, the California Court of Appeals ruled that the officer's probable cause was attached to the bag and not the vehicle; therefore, they should have obtained a warrant pursuant to the Chadwick rule. The U.S. Supreme Court didn't agree. Its response included a statement by Justice Harry A. Blackmun, who wrote:

> The [Chadwick] rule not only has failed to protect privacy but it has also confused courts and police officers and impeded effective law enforcement.... We conclude that it is better to adopt one clear-cut rule to govern automobile searches and eliminate the warrant requirement for closed containers. We therefore interpret Carroll as providing one rule to govern all automobile searches—the police may search an automobile and containers within it where they have probable cause to believe contraband or evidence is contained.

Stated simply, the *Acevedo* case holds that if an officer has probable cause to believe that a container in an automobile holds contraband, the officer may open the container and seize the evidence, provided that the evidence is in fact contraband. Two subsequent cases further clarified the authority in which police officers may search vehicles.

The law on vehicle searches has changed dramatically over the past 15 years, enabling police officers more latitude in their search and seizure authority. For example, in *Pennsylvania* v. *Labron* (1993), the Supreme Court ruled that there is no need for a search warrant in vehicle searches if the vehicle is readily mobile, even if there is time to obtain a warrant. In a related case, the Court held that police officers with probable cause to search a car may inspect passengers' belongings found in the car that are capable of concealing the object of the search (*Wyoming* v. *Houghton*, 1999).[17]

VEHICLE INVENTORY SEARCH In 1970, the U.S. Supreme Court reaffirmed the right of officers to search a vehicle that is moving or is about to be moved, provided that there is probable cause to believe that the vehicle contains items that are legally seizeable. In the *Chambers* v. *Maroney* (1970) case, the Court referred to the earlier case of *Carroll* v. *United States* and determined that a search warrant is unnecessary provided that probable cause exists that contraband is contained in the vehicle, that the vehicle is movable, and that a search warrant is not readily obtainable. This doctrine applies even if the vehicle has been driven to the police station by a police officer and there was time to secure a search warrant.

In the *Chambers* case, officers received a report that a service station had been robbed. After receiving a description of the station wagon the robbers were driving and a partial description of the suspects, officers stopped a vehicle matching the vehicle description and arrested the occupants. After the suspects were arrested, the officers took the vehicle down to headquarters to be searched. Although a search warrant could have been obtained, one was not. During the search, officers located two .38-caliber handguns concealed under the dashboard, some small change, and credit cards belonging to a service station attendant who had been robbed previously.

At the trial, the court rejected the search incident to lawful arrest because the search was made at the police station some time after the arrest. On appeal, however, the U.S. Supreme Court stated that there were alternative grounds for the search. When a vehicle is seized, its contents are routinely inventoried to prevent subsequent claims by the defendant that items were taken. The search and the inventory are, however, two separate processes under law but can be conducted simultaneously, as was the case in *Chambers*. Evidence located as a result of the inventory search is admissible in court. It has been recommended, however, that in the case of an automobile that is rendered immobile or one that has been transported to the police station, a search warrant should be obtained as a precautionary matter.

Open-Field Searches

In *Oliver* v. *United States* (1984), the U.S. Supreme Court reaffirmed its position that open fields are not protected by the Fourth Amendment. This differs from constitutional protection over buildings, houses, and the area surrounding them, known as *curtilage*. The curtilage is considered one's yard; thus, both the house and yard are protected and cannot be searched without a warrant or one of the exceptions mentioned. Open fields and pastures outside the curtilage are not protected by the Constitution; thus, searches made by the government of those areas are not considered "unreasonable."

In the *Oliver* case, police officers, acting on reports that marijuana was growing on Oliver's farm, proceeded to investigate, but without a warrant or probable cause. They drove past a locked gate with a sign that read "No Trespassing." However, a path was also observed leading around the side of the property. After following the path around the gate, officers found a field of marijuana located more than a mile from the house. Oliver was subsequently charged and convicted of manufacturing a controlled substance.

This case is significant because the Court essentially stated that a person's "reasonable expectation of privacy" under the Fourth Amendment does not apply when the property involved is an open field.

DEFINING CURTILAGE In a 1987 decision, *United States* v. *Dunn*, the Supreme Court ruled that the warrantless search of a barn that is not part of the curtilage is valid. From this decision came four factors that laid out whether an area is considered a part of the curtilage:

1. The proximity of the area to the home
2. Whether the area is within an enclosure surrounding the home
3. The nature and uses of the area
4. The steps taken to conceal the area from public view

The *Dunn* decision, although still subject to imprecise application, is helpful because it narrows the definition of what buildings should be considered curtilage of the main residence.

Four Factors of Curtilage

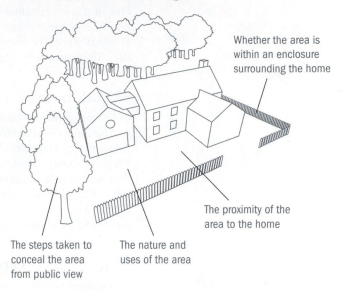

Whether the area is within an enclosure surrounding the home

The proximity of the area to the home

The steps taken to conceal the area from public view

The nature and uses of the area

|Fig. 5.9| △

Four factors of curtilage.

Making an Arrest

The Fourth Amendment reads: "The right of the people to be secure in their persons, houses, papers, and effects, against unreasonable searches and seizures, shall not be violated, and no warrants shall issue, but upon probable cause, supported by Oath or affirmation, and particularly describing the place to be searched, and the persons or things to be seized." It has been said that an estimated 80 percent of a criminal investigator's duties are uneventful, routine, and unglamorous. But the successful completion of an investigation will end in the arrest of a suspect, who will then be prosecuted. This process is far from routine. It is the arrest that is one of the most critical aspects of an investigator's responsibilities. Arrests are always dangerous and often result in injury or even death of the arresting officer. Therefore, certain considerations must be kept in mind by professional investigators before exercising this important police function.

Defining Arrest

One of the fundamental charges of criminal investigation is to identify a suspect in a crime and take him or her into custody. Indeed, when a suspect has been arrested pursuant to the filing of criminal charges or when an officer invokes the criminal process pursuant to the filing of charges, the officer must be familiar with certain critical legal guidelines.

What Is an Arrest?

The term **arrest** may take on many different interpretations. For example, it is the official interaction between a peace officer and a suspected lawbreaker when the suspect is captured and delivered before the court. It may also be construed as the simple restriction of one's freedom by an agent of the government. There may neither be an announcement "You're under arrest" by the arresting officer, nor may *Miranda* warnings be given. In some cases, the suspect may not even consider himself or herself to be under arrest. When a person is arrested, he or she forfeits many constitutional rights. Consequently, because of the severe legal implications, the arresting officer must ensure fair and lawful treatment of the arrestee and the legal process of criminal apprehension.

The Legal Arrest

The general test the courts consider to determine whether probable cause exists for an arrest is whether facts and circumstances within the officer's knowledge are sufficient to warrant a prudent person to believe a suspect has committed, is committing, or is about to commit a crime.[18] Laws of arrest vary from one jurisdiction to another, but peace officers are generally authorized to make an arrest on the authority of an arrest warrant for either a misdemeanor or a **felony** offense. In many cases, the only restriction placed on the officer in these circumstances is the time of day that the arrest is authorized. As a general rule, whereas misdemeanor arrest warrants are authorized only during the daytime hours, felony warrants are typically authorized for daytime or nighttime service. Under the strictest interpretation of the U.S. Constitution, a warrant should be required for all arrests. However, the courts have loosely interpreted this requirement in allowing officers to arrest without a warrant if they personally observe any violation of the law.

Realistically speaking, arrests result after a situation between the officer and suspect develops, whereupon the officer requests information from the suspect. Only when the suspect attempts to leave and tests the limits of the officer's response may the suspect realize that he or she is really under arrest. The "free to leave" test was created in 1994 in *Stansbury* v. *California* in an effort to create a test to determine the point at which an arrest had been made. The *Stansbury* case involved the interrogation of a suspected child molester and murderer, and the court attempted to clarify the issue of arrest. It held that "when determining when a person is in custody, the court must examine all of the circumstances surrounding the interrogation, but the ultimate inquiry is simply whether there [was] a formal arrest or restraint on freedom of movement of the degree associated with a formal arrest."

The most common type of arrest is that which follows the questioning of a suspect. After a decision to arrest is reached, the officer must come to the conclusion that a crime has been committed and that the suspect is probably the one who committed it. The presence of these elements constitutes the probable cause needed for a legal arrest. Under any circumstance, probable cause is the minimum requirement for arrest, and when a suspect is caught in the process of committing a crime, the officer has the immediate probable cause required for arrest. Most jurisdictions permit a felony arrest without a warrant when a crime is not in progress, provided that probable cause has been established. In the case of *Payton* v. *New York* (1980), the U.S. Supreme Court ruled that unless the suspect gives permission or an emergency exists, an arrest warrant is necessary if an arrest requires entry into a suspect's private residence.

In a related Supreme Court ruling, *County of Riverside* v. *McLaughlin* (1991), a person arrested without a warrant must generally be provided with a judicial determination of probable cause within 48 hours after arrest. Arrests are authorized under the following conditions:

- When the officer has probable cause to believe that the person to be arrested has committed a violation of the law "in his or her presence."
- When the officer has probable cause to believe that the person to be arrested has committed a felony but "not in his or her presence."

- When the officer has probable cause to believe that the person to be arrested has committed a felony whether or not a crime has been committed.

The in-presence requirement generally refers to the context of sight, but court rulings have supported prudent use of all five senses to support probable cause for a warrantless arrest. Other cases also have addressed the significance of the probable cause requirement. For example, *Draper* v. *United States* (1959) found that specific information as to the location of a suspect, when provided by a reliable informant, can also constitute probable cause for an arrest. In *Brinegar* v. *United States* (1949), the courts underscored the importance of the probable cause requirement as it relates to arrests by stating that a relaxation of the requirement would leave law-abiding citizens at the mercy of the personal whims of police officers.

Detention versus Arrest

What constitutes an arrest? How does an arrest differ from an investigative **detention**? There are many different types of situations in which it might appear that an officer has arrested someone but has not. Adams states that police intervention may be classified as a contact, a consensual encounter, an investigative detention, or an arrest:[19]

- *Contact.* In this situation, the subject is free to walk away if he or she so desires. It is the sole decision of the subject whether or not to cooperate with an officer.
- *Consensual encounter.* In this situation, the officer may not exert any authority over the subject. Officers can continue to seek the subject's cooperation but cannot demand it.
- *Investigative detention.* This is defined as something less than an arrest but more than a consensual encounter. Generally, this is when a person thinks that he or she cannot just walk away (*Terry* v. *Ohio*).
- *Arrest.* Act of placing a person in custody for a suspected violation of criminal law.

Investigatory Stops

Terry v. *Ohio* (1968) is the seminal case that recognized investigative stops (the investigative detention) as a separate category of seizures allowed on a lower degree of suspicion. Three constitutional requirements exist for a *Terry* **stop** to be lawful:

1. The officer must be able to point to objective facts and circumstances that would warrant a reasonable police officer to link the detainee's conduct with possible criminal activity.
2. The officer must proceed with the investigation as expeditiously as possible to avoid unnecessarily prolonging the period of involuntary detention.
3. The officer must stay within the narrow investigative boundaries allowed for reasonable suspicion in *Terry* stop situations.

To satisfy the reasonable suspicion standard, the officer must possess objective grounds for suspecting that the person detained has committed, is committing, or is about to commit a crime. To satisfy this standard, the officer must be able to point to specific facts that, taken together with irrational inferences that arise from them, provide a rational basis for suspecting the detainees of criminal activity.

Probable Cause

- ☑ An officer has probable cause to make an arrest whenever the totality of facts and circumstances known to the officer creates a fair probability that a particular person is guilty of a crime.
- ☑ Probable cause is analogous to reasonable suspicion in all ways but one: Probable cause requires evidence that establishes a higher probability of guilt.
- ☑ The Fourth Amendment requires probable cause for four different purposes: (1) a warrantless arrest, (2) issuance of an arrest warrant, (3) issuance of a search warrant, and (4) warrantless search and seizure.

|Fig. 5.10| ▲

Examples of how reasonable suspicion may affect criminal investigators.

Examples of how reasonable suspicion may affect criminal investigators

Criminal profiles. Criminal profiles are groupings of behavioral characteristics commonly seen in a particular class of offenders. Although police are allowed to consider criminal profiles in evaluating the evidentiary significance of things they observe, the fact that a suspect exhibits characteristics included in the criminal profile is not a guarantee that a court will find that the officer possessed sufficient reasonable suspicion.

Tips from the public. Police officers may not act on information received from members of the public without independent corroboration unless they have a rational basis for believing this information to be reliable.

Officer-to-officer information. An officer who makes an investigatory stop (or an arrest) at the direction of another police department or officer need not be informed of the evidence that supports the action. However, if the officer making the stop lacks grounds to support the action, the stop will be constitutional only if the department or officer requesting the action had grounds to support it.

Whether the facts known to the officer provided an objective basis for reasonable suspicion is determined from the vantage point of a trained police officer. Courts consider "rational inferences that arise from the facts," as well as the facts themselves, in deciding whether the officer's information was sufficient to satisfy the reasonable suspicion standard. Examples of how reasonable suspicion may affect criminal investigators are:

- *Criminal profiles.* Criminal profiles are groupings of behavioral characteristics commonly seen in a particular class of offenders. Although police are allowed to consider criminal profiles in evaluating the evidentiary significance of things they observe, the fact that a suspect exhibits characteristics included in the criminal profile is not a guarantee that a court will find that the officer possessed sufficient reasonable suspicion.
- *Tips from the public.* Police officers may not act on information received from members of the public without independent corroboration unless they have a rational basis for believing this information to be reliable.
- *Officer-to-officer information.* An officer who makes an investigatory stop (or an arrest) at the direction of another police department or officer need not be informed of the evidence that supports the action. However, if the officer making the stop lacks grounds to support the action, the stop will be constitutional only if the department or officer requesting the action had grounds to support it.

Investigatory stops are allowed on a lower degree of suspicion than arrests because they are designed to be less intrusive than arrests. When the police overstep the lawful boundaries of an investigatory stop, the stop automatically escalates into an arrest, resulting in a violation of the detainee's Fourth Amendment rights unless probable cause for an arrest has already been established.

Some investigatory techniques are too intrusive and too much like an arrest to be validated by reasonable suspicion alone. The police should never do the following unless they have probable cause for an arrest:

- Take a suspect against his or her will to the police station (*Hayes* v. *Florida*, 1985).
- Search a suspect for nondangerous contraband without his or her consent.

Police should also avoid doing the following during a *Terry* stop:

- Give *Miranda* warnings before police have developed grounds for an arrest unless highly intrusive safety measures become necessary during the stop.

- Perform a weapons frisk without a reasonable suspicion that the detainees may be armed or dangerous.
- Transport detainees to a second location unless this action is necessary for officer safety or to further the investigation.
- Display weapons, use handcuffs, place detainees in a patrol car, or perform other acts traditionally associated with an arrest unless these precautions appear reasonably necessary for officer safety or to further the investigation.

When is a Person Under Arrest?

As with uniformed officers, criminal investigators make arrests on a regular basis. In most cases, it is easy to determine when a person is under arrest: (1) a suspect is taken into custody based on a warrant or probable cause; (2) handcuffs are applied, and (3) the suspect is read his or her *Miranda* warning and transported off to jail. However, is a person under arrest simply when an officer displays his or her "authority" to arrest (e.g., turning on the red lights on a police car, calling to a person to stop)? The answer is that such actions may, indeed, not constitute a legal arrest.

The courts have held that a suspect is seized within the meaning of the Fourth Amendment whenever a law enforcement officer restricts their freedom to leave. This occurs when the suspect's liberty is restrained and brought under an officer's control, either through submission to a show of legal authority or physical restraint. For example:

- *Seizure by submission to a show of legal authority.* The test for whether there has been a show of authority is objective—whether a reasonable person in the suspect's place would feel that he or she was not free to ignore an officer's request and walk away.
- *Seizure by physical restraint.* If the suspect does not submit to an officer's show of legal authority, no seizure occurs until the suspect is actually brought under the officer's control. The free-to-leave "test" has been repeatedly adopted by the court as the test for a seizure.[20]

This issue was considered in the *California* v. *Hodari* (1991) case, where the court ruled that a Fourth Amendment seizure does not occur when law enforcement officers are chasing a fleeing suspect unless the officers apply physical force or the suspect submits to the officer's show of authority. A juvenile named Hodari was standing with three other youths on a street corner in downtown Oakland, California. When an unmarked police car was observed approaching, the youths ran in different directions. An officer exited the police car, pursued, and finally caught up with Hodari. Just before being tackled, Hodari tossed away a bag containing crack cocaine that was later used as evidence to convict Hodari of possession of cocaine.

On appeal, the California Court of Appeal held that Hodari had been constructively seized as soon as the chase began; therefore, an arrest had taken place. The officer's display of authority was sufficient to place him under arrest. Consequently, because there was no probable cause for the arrest before the cocaine was discovered, it was inadmissible as evidence. The conviction was overturned.

Upon review by the U.S. Supreme Court, the justices considered the issue of whether or not an arrest had been made. There was no doubt that the officer had displayed his authority, that he wanted Hodari to stop, and that the suspect recognized all of this. However, even though the suspect had not submitted to arrest, was an arrest made? In a majority decision, Justice Antonin Scalia said: "An arrest requires either physical force . . . or, where that is absent, submission to the assertion of authority." He later added: "Neither usage nor common-law tradition makes an attempted seizure a seizure." The conviction was reaffirmed.

When there is no physical contact between an officer and a suspect, the totality of the circumstances must be considered when deciding if an arrest has been made. It must be shown that the officer's words or actions would have led a reasonable person to believe that he or she was not free to leave before the officer attempts seizure of the person. Also, the person must somehow show his or her submission to the officer's authority before the seizure actually occurs. Other factors affecting the legality of an arrest include:

- The officer must have the appropriate legal authority to do so (e.g., jurisdiction).
- Arresting officers must be sure that persons arrested fall under the authority of the law (e.g., being physically placed into custody by the officer or submitting to the assertion of authority).

A *Terry* Stop Must Be

1. Brief (90 minutes maximum)
2. Conducted efficiently so as to avoid unnecessarily prolonging the period of involuntary detention
3. Confined to investigating the suspicion that prompted the stop unless clear grounds for reasonable suspicion of unrelated criminal activity developed during the stop

Related to U.S. Supreme Court decisions include the following:

- *County of Riverside* v. *McLaughlin* (1991). Detention of a suspect for 48 hours is presumptively reasonable. If the time to hearing is longer, the **burden of proof** shifts to the police to prove reasonableness. If the time to hearing is shorter, the burden of proof of unreasonable delay shifts to the suspect.
- *Florida* v. *Bostick* (1991). The test to determine whether a police–citizen encounter on a bus is a seizure is whether, taking into account all the circumstances, a reasonable passenger would feel free to decline the officer's requests or otherwise terminate the encounter.

Use of Force

Police are granted specific legal authority to use force under certain conditions. But the authority of officers to use force is limited. Penalties for abuse of authority can be severe, so police officers must be clear as to what they can and cannot do. The management of force by police officers is a constant challenge facing law enforcement managers. Balancing issues of a violent society with the safety concerns of police personnel creates many obstacles and concerns in developing departmental policies and procedures. The prevailing police perspective is based on a serious concern for the welfare of officers who must cope with the constant threat of a violent society. In contrast, citizens are fearful that police officers may exceed their legal bounds and use force as a means of punishment rather than control.

Public awareness of police brutality was sparked by an unfortunate incident that occurred in Brooklyn, New York, during the summer of 1997. On Saturday, August 9, a fight between two women broke out in a bar, and the police were called. Haitian immigrant Abner Louima, a 30-year-old bank security guard, was taken into custody in connection with the incident. As Louima was being driven to the station house, he was beaten, and upon arrival he was stripped, searched, and sodomized with a wooden stick attached to a toilet plunger. Doctors examining Louima discovered he suffered a ruptured bladder, a punctured lower intestine, and several broken front teeth. Louima claimed that during the assault, the two arresting officers taunted him by saying, "That's yours, nigger," "We're going to teach you niggers to respect police officers," and "This is Giuliani time, not Dinkens time." (The latter comment was an apparent reference to the mayor's zero-tolerance policy, as well as his law-and-order approach to crime control.)

Police officers deal every day with persons who are violent; under the influence of drugs or alcohol; mentally deranged; or just desperate to avoid arrest. To cope, officers are granted specific legal authority to use force under constitutional law and the laws of most states. However, the authority of officers to use force is limited. Those limitations may be enforced through the use of criminal prosecution, civil lawsuits, and disciplinary actions. Our society recognizes three legitimate and responsive forms of force[21]:

1. The right of self-defense, including the valid taking of another person's life to protect oneself
2. The power to control those for whom some responsibility for care and custody has been granted an authority figure, such as a prison guard
3. The institution of a police group that has relatively unrestricted authority to use force as required

Police officers are taught that the penalties for abusing their authority to use force can be severe. To avoid harsh penalties, police officers must be aware of the rules that govern the use of force.

Such rules are included in state law, federal law, and department policy. The federal standard for police use of force was established by the U.S. Supreme Court in *Graham* v. *Connor, 490 U.S. 396 (1989).* This case established the "objectively reasonable" standard under the Fourth Amendment, which means that the reasonableness of an officer's use of force must be reasonable and judged "from the perspective of a reasonable officer at the scene." The literature in professional policing explains the term *objectively reasonable.* For example,

> "This term means that, in determining the necessity for force and the appropriate level of force, officers shall evaluate each situation in light of the known circumstances, including, but not limited to, the seriousness of the crime, the level of threat or resistance presented by the subject, and the danger to the community."[22]

This 1989 landmark case mandated that the determination of objective reasonableness must be judged from the perspective of the *officer on the scene,* allowing for the fact that force situations often call for split-second decisions, and must be reviewed without regard to the officer's underlying intent or motivation. The Court expressly understood and stated that "not every push or shove, even if it may later seem unnecessary in the peace of a judge's chambers," is unreasonable in the final analysis if we are judging it through the eyes of the officer at the scene. Translation? No Monday morning quarterbacking is permissible.

The truth is, people do see Monday morning quarterbacking, particularly in high-profile or video-recorded use of force incidents. To some degree, this is understandable. When the subject addresses inflicting injury or even taking someone's life, individual officers and police agencies need to be willing to submit to scrutiny.[23] However, such scrutiny must be fair, and based upon the "objectively reasonable" standard.

Based on the totality of the circumstances, three key factors can be used to evaluate the extent of an officer's use of force:

1. The severity of the crime committed
2. Whether the suspect poses an immediate threat to the safety of the officer or others
3. Whether the suspect actively resisted arrest or attempted to evade arrest

When police are compelled to use force, a court will use the following standard to determine whether such force was reasonable. First, the officer's conduct will be compared with that of a

Fourth Amendment Requirements for a Constitutional Arrest

There are two types of arrests: formal (i.e., intentional) arrests and detentions that last too long or are too invasive to constitute a *Terry* stop.

☑ The Fourth Amendment requires probable cause for an arrest.

☑ An arrest warrant is mandatory under the Fourth Amendment only when the police make a nonconsensual entry into a private residence to arrest someone inside (*Payton* v. *New York*, 1980).

An arrest warrant has two advantages over an arrest without a warrant:

☑ It ensures that evidence seized during an arrest will be admissible.

☑ It immunizes the officer from a civil suit.

However, both of the advantages above will be lost if the officer:

☑ Deliberately or recklessly includes false information in his or her affidavit, or

☑ Fails to include enough factual information to enable a magistrate to make an independent determination as to whether probable cause exists for the arrest.

A defendant who is arrested without a warrant and not released on bail is entitled to a judicial determination of probable cause without undue delay after the arrest. Absent extraordinary circumstances, this detention must take place within 48 hours after a warrantless arrest.

Use of Force in Making an Arrest or Other Seizure

Making an arrest or serving a search warrant can be extremely dangerous for the investigator. For example, in 2011 a criminal investigator in Utah was killed and five others wounded when they tried to serve a drug-related search warrant in Ogden. The members of a narcotics strike force were met at the door by former soldier Matthew Stewart, who opened fire on the squad, killing 30-year-old Jered Francom.[24] Indeed, the arrest of suspects under any circumstance can be a fatal encounter. Officers must be prepared to respond with appropriate force while avoiding being excessive.

Use of excessive force is regulated by three provisions of the Constitution: the Fourth, Eighth, and Fourteenth Amendments.

☑ The Fourth Amendment standard used to evaluate whether unconstitutional force has been used in making a seizure is whether a reasonable police officer on the scene would have considered this amount of force necessary. This is called the *objective reasonableness standard*.

☑ Physical force may be used for the following three purposes only:

1. To protect the officer or others from danger
2. To overcome resistance
3. To prevent escape

"reasonable officer" confronted by similar circumstances. Second, when the judge and jury evaluate the officer's actions, they must do so from the "standing in your shoes" standard. This means they can only make use of information the officer had at the time that he or she exerted force without the benefit of 20/20 hindsight.

One of the confusing aspects about the use of force is that there are no clear-cut answers regarding how it is applied. Worse yet, there are many severe penalties for police officers who take the wrong course of action on the street. We know that numerous dangerous situations confront police officers every day. From time to time, officers are required to use force—it's inevitable. After a police officer makes a decision to use force, his or her department and the courts will take considerable time scrutinizing the situation to determine if such actions were appropriate.

Remember, modern-day police officers must not only know how to use force techniques, such as the swinging of a baton, but must also know when to apply those techniques. The use of force by police officers stems from the premise that in a modern democratic society, citizens are discouraged by law from using force to solve personal disputes. Instead, they are expected to rely on the justice system to arbitrate and resolve conflicts. With few exceptions, such as cases involving self-defense, this restriction applies to most situations.

Levels of Force

In 1991, the Christopher Commission, which investigated the behavior of the Los Angeles Police Department in the Rodney King beating incident, found that there was a significant number of officers who regularly used force against the public and who often ignored department guidelines for the use of force. Under department guidelines, officers were required to exercise the minimum amount of force necessary to control a suspect. The Commission set forth guidelines that identify levels of force and the permissible use-of-force techniques within each level:

1. Social control (uniformed presence)
2. Verbal control
3. Weaponless control techniques (including pressure or pain holds), starting at "hands-on" with no pain, stunning (diffused impact with soft striking surfaces), and mechanical (skeletal)
4. Electronic control weapons
5. Chemical agents
6. Control instruments (equivalent to weaponless pressure or pain holds)
7. Impact weapons (equivalent to weaponless mechanical modes)
8. Firearms (and other means of force that could cause death or serious bodily damage when used)

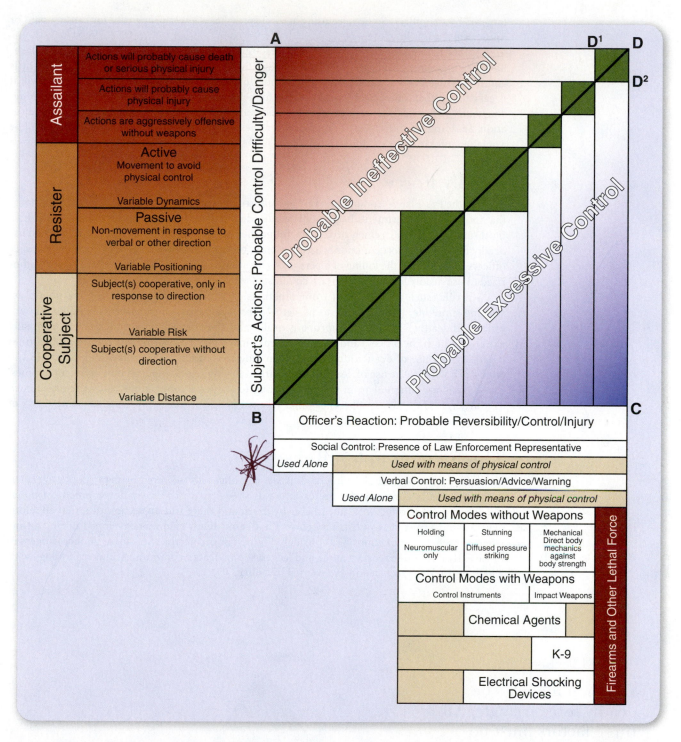

|Fig. 5.11| △

Use of force continuum utilized by many law enforcement organizations across the nation.

Although it is important to consider this continuum in determining the various levels of force, it is also important to consider operational basics that apply to all police officers regarding the use of force. For example, experience tells us that although modern aerosol sprays can cause considerable discomfort, they seldom (if ever) result in bodily injury. In comparison, use of a baton may result in serious tissue damage, depending on the area targeted by the officer. So because using aerosol spray has a lower propensity for causing pain or injury, it has a low level of force.

Another example is the use of impact weapons, such as a baton or a flashlight. The flashlight has a greater propensity to create damage than the baton, and although the flashlight is commonly used as an impact weapon, it is not designed for this use. In comparing the two, it is easy to see that a flashlight would be on a higher level of force than a baton. Officers should constantly consider their options when approaching what they perceive to be a dangerous situation. In doing so, if the need to use force becomes a reality, proper application of force will be available quickly.

Deadly Force

In 1967, the President's Commission on Law Enforcement and the Administration of Justice noted that most police departments had no policy to guide them on the use of **deadly force**. At the time, most state laws were extremely broad in defining the circumstances under which officers could use deadly force. In its most commonly used parlance, the term *deadly force* refers to actions of police officers that result in the killing of a person. As mentioned above, police officers are legally authorized to use deadly force under certain circumstances.

As a rule, such actions result from situations in which persons are fleeing the police, assaulting someone, or attempting to use lethal force against another person (including a police officer). If deadly force is used improperly or illegally, the officers responsible may be criminally liable, and both the officers and the police department may be sued in a civil action. Most rules regarding the use of deadly force come from federal statutes and case law and, as a rule, are concerned with police use of deadly force to arrest fleeing felons engaged in nonviolent felonies. These cases are different from those pertaining to suspects committing violent felonies, such as murder, assault, rape, robbery, or other types of behavior that represent a substantial risk of bodily harm or death.

The Fleeing-Felon Rule

Until the mid-1980s, the shooting of a suspect by police was tolerated by many police agencies. Although this is currently not the case, it was prevalent in the early development of policing, when most felonies were punishable by death and there was an assumption that all felons would avoid arrest at any cost. Therefore, the **fleeing-felon rule** was developed during a time when apprehension of felons was considered more dangerous than it is today. Police officers in those early days often worked alone and lacked sophisticated communications technology with which to track suspects who were wanted by police.

|Fig. 5.12| ▲

Decision model: The deadly force triangle. All three factors must be present to justify deadly force.

Olson, D. T. (1998). Improving deadly force decision making. *FBI Law Enforcement Bulletin,* February:1–8.

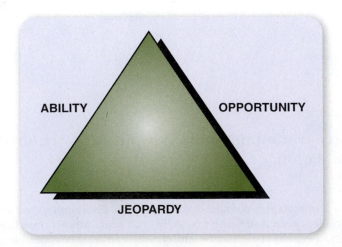

The concern was that felons would escape arrest and retreat to another community, where they could begin a new life of crime. As time went by and more efficient means were developed for apprehension, arrests became easier for law enforcement officials. For a period of time, police still relied on the ability to use deadly force even though some felons were not considered dangerous and posed no particular threat to the officer or the community. Before 1985, police officers were legally authorized by most states to use deadly force in apprehending fleeing felons.

Over the years, many states had modified the fleeing-felon rule, but some still allowed rather broad discretion about when to use deadly force. In a watershed decision by the U.S. Supreme Court in March 1985, it was determined that Tennessee's fleeing-felon law was unconstitutional. *Tennessee* v. *Garner* (1985) involved the police shooting and subsequent killing of an unarmed boy as the youth fled from an unoccupied house. In this case, the officer could see that the suspect was a youth and that he was unarmed. The officer argued, however, that if the youngster were able to leap a fence, he would be able to escape. The state statute in Tennessee at the time permitted officers to shoot fleeing felons to prevent escape. Pursuant to *Garner*, the Court ruled that for the use of deadly force by police to be lawful, it must be "reasonable." **Reasonable deadly force** is authorized under three circumstances:

1. To prevent an escape when the suspect has threatened an officer with a weapon
2. When there is a threat of death or serious physical injury to the officer or others
3. If there is probable cause to believe that the suspect has committed a crime involving the infliction or threatened infliction of serious physical injury and, when practical, some warning has been given by the officer

Summary Checklist

In this chapter, we consider the ways that information about crimes is documented by the criminal investigator. A properly documented case is one that is more likely to succeed in court. See how well you are able to answer the following questions in your checklist.

1. **What ways does the U.S. Constitution guide investigators during the process of a search?**

   Of paramount importance in criminal investigations is the officer's ability to be aware of and work within constitutional (and departmental) guidelines.

   Under the Bill of Rights, citizens are basically guaranteed three classes of rights:

   - Privileges and immunities of citizens of the United States
   - Due process of law
   - Equal protection under the law

   Investigators must remember that they not only must have legal grounds to begin a search but that while conducting the search, they must not contaminate any evidence.

   - Probable cause is the minimum amount of information necessary to warrant a reasonable person to believe that a crime has been or is being committed by a person who is about to be arrested.

   - This is one of the most important components of the Fourth Amendment because it lies at the heart of an officer's authority to search, seize, and make arrests.

   - Officers generally establish probable cause through their own observations.

   - It may also be established through hearsay information provided by third-party sources, typically informants.

2. **Explain the significance of the exclusionary rule and how it relates to the responsibilities of a criminal investigator.**

   The exclusionary rule states that courts will exclude any evidence that was illegally obtained even though it may be relevant and material.

   - The exclusionary rule originated with the 1914 case of *Weeks* v. *United States* and was geared to apply to federal, not state, governments.

   - The 1961 case of *Mapp* v. *Ohio* expanded the scope of the exclusionary rule by applying it to both federal and state courts.

   - The U.S. Supreme Court has developed several exceptions to the exclusionary rule, which play a major role in shaping the manner in which officers are allowed to behave before, during, and after a search and seizure of evidence:

- The good faith exception
- The inevitable discovery doctrine
- The computer errors exception

3. Explain the utility of the search warrant in criminal investigations.

The search warrant is one of the most valuable tools in criminal investigation.

- A search warrant authorizes the search of homes, businesses, and vehicles of suspects; typically results in the arrest of multiple suspects; and expedites investigation and subsequent case closure.
- Most searches occur without warrants being issued—the courts have defined a number of situations in which a search warrant is not necessary.

There are several advantages to having a search warrant:

- It represents an authorization by the court for officers to enter a designated location or structure and search for specific items.
- It can be used to:
  - Recover stolen property.
  - Seize drugs or other contraband.
  - Seize any other type of property used in the commission of a crime.
- Evidence obtained through the use of a search warrant may be more readily accepted by courts than if seized without a warrant or incident to arrest.
- The officer is protected from civil liability when a warrant is obtained.
- It benefits the prosecutor by shifting the legal burden to the defendant—instead of the prosecutor having to justify a presumably unreasonable search, the burden is on the defendant to show the evidence was seized illegally.

For a warrant to be legal, it must meet specific legal requirements:

- It must be authorized by the proper official.
- It must be issued only for specifically authorized objects.
- It must be issued on probable cause.

4. Under what conditions can officers search without a warrant?

The Fourth Amendment says that all searches must be preceded by the officer's obtaining a search warrant.

Regardless of how much probable cause an officer may have, if he or she searches without a search warrant, there is a legal presumption that the search is unconstitutional. However, the courts have identified a number of exceptions, situations in which a warrantless search is authorized under the law:

- Consent searches
- Searches under exigent circumstances
- Searches incident to lawful arrest
- Stop-and-frisk searches
- Plain-view searches
- Automobile searches
- Open-field searches

5. What are the legal requirements for making an arrest?

An officer has probable cause to make an arrest when facts and circumstances within the officer's knowledge are sufficient to warrant a prudent person to believe that a suspect has committed, is committing, or is about to commit a crime. Warrantless arrests are authorized under the following conditions:

- When the officer has probable cause to believe that the person to be arrested has committed a violation of the law "in his or her presence."
- When the officer has probable cause to believe that the person to be arrested has committed a felony but "not in his or her presence."
- When the officer has probable cause to believe that the person to be arrested has committed a felony whether or not a crime has been committed.

In most cases, it is easy to determine when a person is under arrest:

- A suspect is taken into custody based on a warrant or probable cause.
- Handcuffs are applied.
- The suspect is read his or her *Miranda* warning and transported off to jail.

6. Under what circumstances is an officer authorized to use force against a suspect?

Police are granted specific legal authority to use force under certain conditions. But the authority of officers to use force is limited and the penalties for abusing their authority to use force can be severe.

- The federal standard for police use of force was established by the U.S. Supreme Court in *Graham* v. *Connor* (1989), which laid out the "objectively reasonable" standard. The reasonableness of an officer's use of force must be reasonable and judged "from the perspective of a reasonable officer at the scene."

- Based on the totality of the circumstances, three key factors can be used to evaluate the extent of an officer's use of force:
  - The severity of the crime committed
  - Whether the suspect poses an immediate threat to the safety of the officer or others
  - Whether the suspect actively resisted arrest or attempted to evade arrest
- Physical force may be used for the following three purposes only:
  - To protect the officer or others from danger
  - To overcome resistance
  - To prevent escape

Important Cases to Remember

Arizona v. *Gant*	*Illinois* v. *Rodriguez*
Arizona v. *Evans*	*Mapp* v. *Ohio*
California v. *Acevedo*	*Massachusetts* v. *Sheppard*
California v. *Hodari*	*Nix* v. *Williams*
Carroll v. *United States*	*Oliver* v. *United States*
Chambers v. *Maroney*	*Tennessee* v. *Garner*
Chimel v. *California*	*Terry* v. *Ohio*
Coolidge v. *New Hampshire*	*United States* v. *Dunn*
Florida v. *Bostick*	*United States* v. *Grubbs*
Florida v. *Jimeno*	*United States* v. *Leon*
Graham v. *Connor*	*United States* v. *Sokolow*
Harris v. *United States*	*Weeks* v. *United States*

Key Terms

affidavit	due process	plain-view doctrine
anticipatory search warrant	exclusionary rule	probable cause
arrest	exigent circumstances	reasonable deadly force
Bill of Rights	felony	scope of the search
burden of proof	field interview	search and seizure
Carroll doctrine	fleeing-felon rule	search warrant
computer errors exception	fruit of the poisonous tree	search warrant return
consent search	good faith exception	stop and frisk
curtilage	inevitable discovery doctrine	*Terry* stop
deadly force	open-field search	totality of the circumstances
detention	pat-down search	triggering condition

Discussion Questions

1. Explain the roles played by the Fourth, Fifth, and Sixth Amendments in searches and seizures and how they relate to the investigative process.

2. Explain the major exceptions to the exclusionary rule that have been developed by the U.S. Supreme Court.

3. Discuss the advantages of searching with a search warrant.

4. Identify conditions under which a search may be conducted without a search warrant.

5. Define arrest and discuss the legal requirements of a legal arrest.

6. Discuss the ways that an investigative detention differs from arrest.

7. Explain investigatory stops and the constitutional requirements that exist for a *Terry* stop to be lawful.

8. Explain the three legitimate and responsive forms of force recognized by our society and discuss the constitutional standards under which police use of force is identified.

9. Define deadly force and explain when reasonable deadly force is authorized.

Notes

1. MYERS, K. A. (2011). Searches of motor vehicles in a post-gant World. *FBI Law Enforcement Bulletin*, April.

2. IBID.

3. IBID.

4. PETTRY, M. T. (2011). The emergency first aid exception to the fourth amendment's warrant requirement. *FBI Law Enforcement Bulletin*, March.; See also *Wayne* v. *United States* 318 F.2d 205, 212; 115 U.S. App. D.C. 234, 241 (D.C. Cir. 1963).

5. *Terry* v. *Ohio*, 392 U.S. 1 (1968).

6. IBID.

7. State courts' decisions and statutes may place restrictions on officers not imposed by the Supreme Court of the United States.

8. See, for example *United States* v. *Mendenhall*, 446 U.S. 544 (1980); *Michigan* v. *Chesternut*, 486 U.S. 567 (1988).

9. Officers must, for reasons of both legality and personal safety, adequately identify themselves as police officers. Proper identification as a police officer does not render an encounter nonconsensual. It is only the excessive, unnecessary, or deliberately intimidating display of authority that affects the consensual nature of the encounter.

10. Knowledge by the officer that this particular individual has a criminal history or has been involved in criminal activity may also be considered. However, knowledge of a suspect's record shouldn't be the sole basis for the stop.

11. It should be noted that the term *pat-down* does not necessarily describe the proper technique for searching a suspect for weapons. It is a legal term, not a descriptive one. It refers to the fact that the search must be confined to contact with the suspect's outer clothing unless and until the presence of a weapon is detected.

12. Crimes involving violence or the use of weapons (e.g., murder or armed robbery) or crimes whose perpetrators often carry weapons (e.g., distribution of narcotics) may alone be sufficient to justify a pat-down search of any individual reasonably suspected of involvement in the crime. See, for example, *Landsdown* v. *Commonwealth*, 226 Va. 204, 308 S.E.2d 106 (1983).

13. A search is a full-scale attempt to locate evidence—that is, contraband or fruits, instrumentalities, or other evidence of a crime. It may include a complete examination of the suspect's clothing, including interior clothing, pockets, and the like. By contrast, a pat-down is a limited frisk of a suspect's outer clothing or a brief inspection of an object, vehicle, or area for the sole purpose of detecting weapons that may be used to harm the officer.

14. After the officer has detected the presence of a weapon or what the officer reasonably believes to be a weapon, the officer may reach into the clothing to remove the object. If the object proves to be a weapon, contraband, or other evidence that would justify an arrest, the officer may then place the individual under arrest and conduct a full-scale search of the person.

15. *U.S.* v. *Lott*, 870 F.2d 778 (1st Cir. 1989).

16. If the officer detects the presence of a weapon in the container, seizure of the weapon would be justified.

17. DEL CARMEN R. V. AND J. T. WALKER. (2000). *Briefs of leading cases.* Cincinnati, OH: Anderson.

18. *U.S.* v. *Puerta*, 982 F.2d 1297, 1300 (9th Cir. 1992).

19. ADAMS, T. (1990). *Police field operations*, 2nd ed. Upper Saddle River, NJ: Prentice Hall.

20. *Stansbury* v. *California*, 114 S. Ct. 1526, 1529 128 L.Ed2d 293 (1994); *Yarborough* v. *Alvarado*, U.S. Supreme Court No. 02-1684 (decided June 1, 2004).

21. PEAK, K. J. (1993). *Policing America: Methods, issues and challenges.* Upper Saddle River, NJ: Prentice Hall.

22. Found in *Graham* v. *Connor,* 490 U.S. 396 (1989)

23. JOHNSON, J. (2007). Use of force and the hollywood factor. *AELE Law Journal*. Park Ridge, IL, (4) AELE MO. L. J. 501

24. JOHNSON, K. (2012). Cop deaths trigge a training review. *USA Today*, January 11, p. 3A.

PART 3 **Obtaining Information**

CHAPTER 6

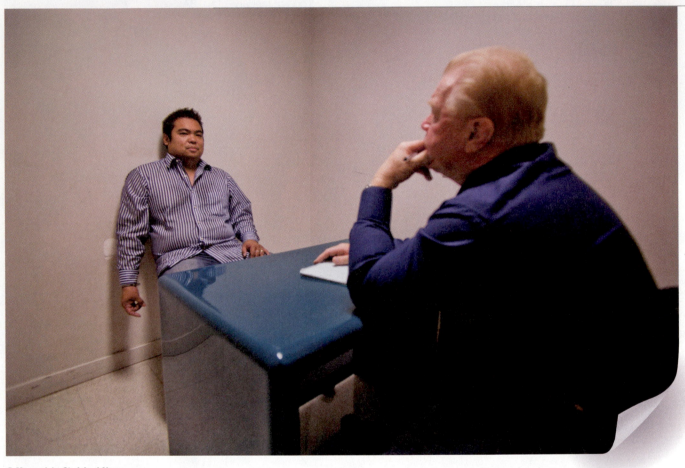

© Marmaduke St. John / Alamy

This chapter will enable you to:

1. Differentiate between interviews and interrogations.

2. Describe effective interviewing and interrogation techniques.

3. Summarize the legal requirements of interviewing and interrogation, including *Miranda* rights.

4. Identify how lying and deception are detected.

5. Explain why people confess and how confessions are documented.

6. Summarize how to take written and recorded statements.

Interviews and Interrogations

Introduction

 In their authoritative book Criminal Interrogation and Confessions, *Inbau and his associates illustrate the importance of gleaning information through interviews and interrogations. They state: "...the art and science of criminal investigation have not developed to a point where the search for and the examination of physical evidence will always...reveal a clue to the identity of the perpetrator....".[1] In fact, experience has shown that in many cases, physical evidence is completely absent, and the only remaining approach is the interview of witnesses or the interrogation of the suspect him- or herself.*

In cases in which physical evidence is identified and implicates a suspect, the investigator's job is still not finished. The matter of proof and prosecution remains. It is the duty of each investigator to attempt to secure a confession from suspects they have arrested. Again, legal considerations must always be kept in mind to ensure that all statements are admissible in court.

Interviews and interrogations are another fascinating aspect of criminal investigation. This is the phase of the investigation in which the investigator wears a different hat, so to speak. Putting the officer's psychological talents to work may come into play to enhance the chances of a suspect admitting his or her role in a crime.

Interview versus Interrogation

Investigators must make a clear distinction between the two processes of interviewing and interrogating suspects. An interview should precede every interrogation. Through an interview, investigators learn about the subjects and their needs, fears, concerns, and attitudes. They can then use this information to prepare themes or arguments to use during interrogations.[2]

To be a good interviewer or interrogator, the investigator must apply certain physical and psychological techniques to the person being interviewed to persuade him or her to divulge information. In the case of the interview, it is the investigator's job to create an atmosphere in which the subject can be relaxed enough to recall and explain details of a suspected crime. Conversely, when a criminal suspect is being interrogated, the investigator must gently and skillfully break down the suspect's defenses to gain an admission or confession and do so while staying within the constraints of constitutional law.[3] In some countries, physical and mental stress is used as ways to coerce information from both witnesses and suspects. It is generally accepted that a person will confess to anything if enough pressure or intimidation is applied. But is a "confession" really a truthful statement under these circumstances? Certainly not!

During the course of an investigation, an investigator will probably conduct many interviews and several interrogations. The distinction between an interview and an interrogation is often blurred, but it can be expressed in terms of the purpose of the contact. Inbau and his associates state that an **interview** is **nonaccusatory**.[4] It is a relatively formal conversation conducted for the purpose of obtaining information. Notes are taken, and major points are reviewed. Interviews, however, may involve virtually anyone, including informants, witnesses, victims, cooperating citizens, and even the suspect him- or herself. In brief, the interview process occurs either before the case focuses on a particular person or in a place where the suspect can clearly terminate the interview at any time.

By comparison, an **interrogation** is **accusatory**.[5] It is the systematic questioning of a person suspected of involvement in a crime for the purpose of obtaining a confession. Legal guidelines affecting the two activities differ considerably as the probability increases that the person being questioned may incriminate him- or herself.

The Interview Process

The interview is a form of communication used extensively by law enforcement. It is used in many ways to glean information from the subject being interviewed. For example, interviewing is used to screen job applicants, extract information from witnesses or victims of a crime, and obtain a confession from a criminal suspect. Interviews of cooperating citizens and witnesses are often conducted outside the office. More often than not, however, the investigator will have a more productive interview if it can be conducted at a location where the subject is mentally relaxed, such as his or her own home or place of business. Regardless of where the interviews are conducted, investigators should follow certain guidelines due to legal and technical considerations.

Investigators should take the time to prepare properly for the interview. Occasionally, this preparation must be done quickly and may consist of no more than a mental review of the details of the case, but some type of preparation should precede actual contact with the subject being interviewed. Generally, the most common interviews that investigators will conduct are with witnesses, cooperating citizens, victims, informants, and suspects. Let's look at the fundamentals of each of these.

Interviewing Witnesses, Citizens, and Victims

Investigators must remember that although the interview process is geared toward those believed simply to have information about a crime, witnesses often turn out to be suspects. Sources for interviews include the victim, witnesses, and the complainant. These subjects should be separated before questioning begins. The following considerations should be observed during the interview process.

- *Develop a plan of action.* To begin, the investigator should be familiar with pertinent data about the incident in question before initiating the interview. He or she should take care to develop questions designed to elicit the particular task at hand. For example, questions directed to a witness should be tailored to obtain specific facts for the police report. Questions that are prepared in advance will tend to add to the flow of conversation and give direction to the interview.
- *Conduct the interview in private.* It is sometimes easier to fulfill this requirement than others, depending on the circumstances. In all cases, it is important to provide interviewees with the greatest amount of privacy possible, both to encourage clarity of thought and to protect the confidentiality of the interview.
- *Place the interviewee at ease.* Most interviews involve a great amount of stress and emotional discord for the interviewee. This is usually created by a sense of uncertainty about the expectations of the investigator and the uniqueness of the situation. If a degree of fear develops in the person being interviewed, he or she may withhold information. Indeed, it is during the preliminary phase of the interview that the investigator's personality will be tested rigorously. The investigator should therefore take great care to make the person being interviewed as comfortable as possible and to build rapport. In addition, the investigator should attempt to uncover any reasons for the interviewee's reluctance to cooperate. It is also important to relax the person being interviewed because comments made by a calm person are easier to evaluate than those made by someone who is nervous. This can be accomplished by beginning the interview casually with friendly conversation. Certainly, a strained or awkward initial contact with the subject might convey the message that the investigator doesn't like something about the interviewee. A friendly approach will help defuse any negative feelings in the subject and reinforce positive ones.

- **Be a good listener.** After the communication barrier is lifted, the investigator must learn to let the interviewee speak freely. Indeed, this is a great shortcoming of many investigators because many feel the need to interrupt or share their personal opinions with interview subjects. It is the job of the interviewer to listen closely and evaluate not just *what* is being said but *how* it is being said. In short, it is the responsibility of the investigator to control the interview but not to dominate it.

- **Ask the right questions.** Not only is it important to know what questions to ask the subject but also how those questions should be asked. During the conversation, the investigator's emotions should be in check at all times, along with an attempt to make the questions easy to comprehend. In addition, the phrasing of questions is critical to the success of the interview. For example, close-ended questions, requiring a simple yes or no response, should be used sparingly. This type of question doesn't elicit personal information from the subject; it simply permits the person to confirm or deny information being offered. A preferable technique is to ask open-ended questions, which force the interviewee to relate in his or her own words what was observed. Hypothetical questions should also be avoided because they tend to make the interviewee guess at a certain response or to tell the interviewer what he or she wants to hear. Finally, the interviewer should avoid asking loaded, or leading, questions that contain the answer and require the person being interviewed to choose between the lesser of two evils.

- **Don't dispute the subject's answers.** The emotional reactions of the investigator must be kept under control at all times. After the subject gives his or her interpretation of what happened, the investigator can later go back and document any discrepancies.

- **Maintain control of the interview.** Frequently during an interview, the subject might try to steer the conversation away from the subject at hand. Again, proper preparation is the key to having a good plan and to staying on track.

- **Take brief notes.** After the interviewee begins to talk freely, the investigator should avoid interruptions. An attempt to take complete notes while a citizen is narrating a story will probably disrupt the flow of information. This generally occurs because the witness sees the investigator writing profusely and will slow down just to accommodate him or her. In doing so, the witness may become distracted and forget important details. Furthermore, some people are just naturally nervous speaking in the presence of someone recording everything they say. Brief notes are therefore the prescribed method of recording the conversation. These generally consist of names, addresses, and certain phrases that will outline the narrative for review. Most important, however, the investigator should listen carefully and not lose eye contact with the witness.

- **Adjourn the interview properly.** Just as the interview process begins with a proper introduction, it should also end appropriately. Generally, a concluding remark is appropriate, such as, "OK, you may leave—thank you for your time." It might also be advisable to summarize the interview briefly with the witness before dismissal. Such expressions of courtesy during and after the interview create a favorable impression and encourage further cooperation.

The Process of Suspect Interrogation

Law enforcement officers investigating criminal activity have increasing amounts of technology to assist them in identifying persons responsible for criminal conduct. Advances in DNA collection and testing, automated fingerprint identification, and a host of forensic techniques are only a few examples of the scientific tools available to the modern criminal investigator. However, despite all of the physical evidence collected in a particular case and all of the scientific analysis used to tie an individual to the commission of a crime, one nonscientific technique continues to play an important role in the investigation and prosecution of criminal activity: the confession.

Confessions made to investigators continue to hold substantial importance within the criminal justice process. Investigators seek to obtain confessions from persons suspected of criminal activity even when the physical, scientific, or other evidence against them is overwhelming. Criminal defendants, faced with the possibility that their confessions may be used against them at trial, attempt to keep their confessions out of court through legal challenges. Both sides recognize the continued influence of the words uttered by criminal defendants on a judge or a jury. There is something powerful in the words that describe the particular events, as well as the thoughts, actions, emotions, or motives, that would otherwise remain hidden and undiscovered from any scientific or forensic test.[6]

During any case, it is important for information to be obtained by means of a direct interview with a suspect. As indicated earlier, it is not at all uncommon during the progress of a case for a person who was interviewed as a witness or victim to become a primary suspect at a later date. In that event, as the case progresses, the investigator can use information learned in the earlier interview.

Goals of the Interrogation

The interrogation is designed to match new information with a particular suspect to secure a confession. The goals of the interrogation process are as follows[7]:

- To learn the truth of the crime and how it happened
- To obtain an admission of guilt from the suspect
- To obtain all facts to determine the method of operation and the circumstances of the crime
- To gather information that enables investigators to arrive at logical conclusions
- To provide information for use by prosecutors in possible court action

Legal Requirements of the Interrogation

According to early English Common Law, the confession of a suspect was by far the most important type of evidence against an accused person. In many cases, failure to produce such evidence was equivalent to not having any evidence at all. Therefore, investigators vigorously pursued confessions at all costs, with little regard for the rights of those accused or the fairness of their methods. Techniques for obtaining the confession included submersion in water, stretching, branding, and other types of physical and psychological torture. Today, such tactics have been replaced with legal guarantees of fairness, such as the Bill of Rights, the Constitution, and statutes prohibiting the use of coercion or duress in the interrogation process. Still, the confession reigns as one of the most influential types of evidence in a court proceeding.

Safeguarding Against Police Misconduct

Several types of behavior have been identified as improper (even illegal) for police investigators and will result in any confession obtained from the suspect being deemed inadmissible by the courts. These behaviors include coercion or duress, physical constraint, unreasonable delay in arraignment, and refusing legal counsel during interrogation.

COERCION AND DURESS Coercion and duress are similar in that they both create an environment of intimidation during the interrogation process. **Coercion** is defined as the use, or threat of use, of illegal physical methods to induce a suspect to make an admission or confession. **Duress** is the imposition of restrictions on physical behavior, such as prolonged interrogation and deprivation of water, food, or sleep. In *Brown* v. *Mississippi* (1936), the U.S. Supreme Court ruled that physical coercion used to obtain a confession was a violation of the Fourteenth Amendment. Following this ruling, the Court focused its attention on cases in which "psychological" rather than physical coercion was used to prompt a confession.

Methods of Coercive Interrogations

Confessions are extremely influential evidence that can often make or break a criminal case. After a confession is given, it is difficult to retract. Consequently, an admission of guilt can ultimately lead to substantial fines, imprisonment, and even execution depending on the nature of the case. It is difficult for most people to imagine why someone would risk such consequences and confess to committing a crime they know for certain they didn't commit. However, it happens more frequently than many realize. Methods used by inexperienced or unscrupulous police interrogators, such as deception, fear tactics, unreasonably long interviews, sleep or food deprivation, and either exaggerating or minimizing the crime. These methods are blamed for a large number of all documented false confessions.[8]

Fear tactics that include direct threats, intimidation, or actual physical abuse have been known to coerce suspects into falsely admitting guilt to a crime. According to Richard Conti, such confessions are referred to as **coerced-compliant confessions**.[9]

An example of a coerced-compliant confession occurred in March 1983 after the murder of a woman from Pulaski County, Arkansas. Not long after the woman's murder, the police took into custody Barry Lee Fairchild, a young, mentally handicapped black man. Fairchild's lawyers said that while in custody, police interrogators forced their client to confess to the crime after they allegedly placed telephone books on his head and hit the books with blackjacks. It has been speculated that this method was likely used because it leaves no marks but causes considerable pain.[10] Fairchild was found guilty and executed for the murder in 1995, even though he continued to profess his innocence to the end.

Of the many coercive police tactics that have been identified over the years, physical abuse is one of the most brutal methods used to obtain a confession and is unconstitutional. But other less obvious techniques, such as the use of deception, trickery, and other psychological tactics, have also been discovered with greater frequency.[11] For example, in their authoritative book *Criminal Interrogation and Confessions*, Inbau and associates state, "The use of such tactics is not only helpful but frequently indispensable in order to secure incriminating information from the guilty, or to obtain investigative leads from otherwise uncooperative witnesses or informants."[12]

Wakefield and Underwager state that another technique referred to as **maximization** is the exaggeration of evidence available, telling the person that the interrogator knows he or she is guilty or stressing the consequences of the crime.[13] The maximization method includes falsely telling suspects they have fingerprints linking them to the crime, that they failed a lie detector test, or that an acquaintance of the suspect witnessed him or her committing the crime. This technique can lead to false confessions. This occurs mostly in highly suggestible and confused suspects who actually begin to believe they are guilty of the crime they didn't commit. This is called **coerced internalization**.[14]

During the interrogation process, interviewers can also use minimization, whereby the seriousness of the crime is downplayed and the suspect believes he or she is less likely to get in trouble. This method can prompt a false confession, especially if it is coupled with other coercive techniques. For example, the interviewing detective might say, "You know, I think you're a really good person. I don't think you intended to do the harm that occurred in this case. Maybe it was an accident or maybe you were provoked or under the influence of some drug." The suspect may feel psychological pressure to satisfy the interrogator, especially if he or she admires or fears the interrogator, or the suspect may even believe what he or she is being told and thus falsely confess to the crime.

Another method used to get suspects to confess is to make them sit through long-drawn-out interrogations, which sometimes last more than hours. The suspect often goes without sleep, food, or both and gets so worn down emotionally and physically that he or she is more likely to give false statements in an attempt to escape from the torture. During such confessions, the police may feed suspects bits of information, which are incorporated into a confession. Similar to physical torture, extended interrogations that are accompanied by sleep and food deprivation are also unacceptable. A number of these techniques were documented as being used in the case of Stephanie Crowe.

Unreasonable Delay in Arraignments

Confessions obtained without coercion or duress may still be deemed unconstitutional and inadmissible if the suspect confessed before being allowed to see a magistrate within a reasonable period after arrest. The case of *McNabb* v. *United States* (1943) first illustrated this vital principle. In this case, McNabb, along with several members of his family, was involved in bootlegging. After the murder of several federal officers in Tennessee, McNabb was arrested for the crime. After his arrest, he was held in custody and was not taken before a magistrate for a considerable period. Subsequently, he confessed and was convicted. The court held that the government's failure to take McNabb before a committing officer was a violation of his constitutional rights; therefore, the confession was inadmissible. What made this case particularly significant is that for the first time, a confession, obtained voluntarily and freely, was still considered illegal because officers failed to comply with other constitutional procedures.

A subsequent ruling in *Mallory* v. *United States* (1957) reaffirmed that an officer making an arrest must take the accused, without necessary delay, before the nearest available magistrate and that an official complaint must be filed without delay. These decisions are based on the due process clause of the Fourteenth Amendment of the U.S. Constitution. The U.S. Supreme Court considers whether or not the case in its entirety represents a good picture of the civilized standards expected in this country.

The Suspect's Right to Legal Counsel

The legal guidelines to protect the rights of the accused were defined further by the U.S. Supreme Court in such cases as *Escobedo* v. *Illinois* (1964) and *Miranda* v. *Arizona* (1966). Surprisingly, before 1964, there were no legal rules requiring the presence of an attorney during the interrogation of a criminal suspect. In a ruling in May 1964, the U.S. Supreme Court reversed the conviction of a lower court because prosecutors had used incriminating statements made by the defendant to a friend that were overheard by a federal agent. The remarks were made after the defendant was indicted and while he was out on bail. The Court held that the statement was made by the defendant without the advice of his attorney, who he had already retained. So, according to the Court, the defendant was deprived of his Sixth Amendment right to an attorney.

In *Escobedo* v. *Illinois* (1964), Escobedo was arrested without a warrant and interrogated in connection with a murder. On the way to the police station, officers told Escobedo that he had been implicated as the murderer and that he should admit to the crime. He then requested to speak to an attorney. After arriving at the police station, his retained lawyer arrived and asked several times to speak with his client. His request was denied on several occasions. In addition, Escobedo requested to speak with his attorney on several occasions and was told that his attorney did not want to speak to him. Subsequently, the defendant made an admission to the crime and was later found guilty.

The legal question here is: Does a suspect have a right to an attorney if he or she requests one during a police station interrogation? The answer is yes. Following this decision, states were directed to require police to advise every person arrested for a felony that they have a constitutional right to counsel and silence. Despite this, the guidelines for police in interrogation settings were still unclear.

THE *MIRANDA* WARNING Two years after the *Escobedo* decision, the U.S. Supreme Court reversed an Arizona court's conviction in a kidnapping and rape case that further defined the *Escobedo* decision and the rights of the accused. In the *Miranda* v. *Arizona* (1966) case, a 23-year-old, Miranda, was arrested and transported from his home to the police station for questioning in connection with a kidnapping and rape. He was poor and uneducated. After two hours of questioning, officers obtained a written confession that was used against him in court. He was found guilty of the kidnapping and rape.

The legal question in this case is: Do the police have a responsibility to inform a subject of an interrogation of his or her constitutional rights involving self-incrimination and a right to counsel before questioning? Again, the answer is yes.

In addition to being informed of these rights, the suspect must also agree, freely and voluntarily, to waive them before police can begin questioning. Accordingly, the suspect may invoke his or her right to stop answering questions any time during the interrogation. Several court cases have arisen over the years that relate to *Miranda* and custodial interrogations. For example, *Rhode Island* v. *Innis* (1980) interpreted the meaning of interrogation by stating that in addition to direct questioning, interrogation also refers to any actions or remarks made by police that are designed to elicit an incriminating response.

In another case, *California* v. *Prysock* (1981), the U.S. Supreme Court found that **Miranda warnings** do not have to be given in any specific order or with precise wording. Furthermore, in *Edwards* v. *Arizona* (1981), the Court established a "bright line" rule for investigators. The Court found that "all" police questioning must be discontinued after a suspect who is in custody has requested an attorney, even if the *Miranda* warning was given a second time. However, in yet another related decision, *Oregon* v. *Bradshaw* (1983), the Court found that the *Edwards* decision doesn't apply if the suspect simply inquires, "What is going to happen to me now?" In this case, police were allowed to continue questioning the suspect. However, in *Minnick* v. *Mississippi* (1990), the Court ruled that after a custodial suspect requests counsel in response to *Miranda* warnings, law enforcement officers may not attempt to reinterrogate the suspect unless the suspect's counsel is present or the suspect initiates the contact with officers.

In related cases, it has been determined that probation officers need not read the *Miranda* warning to clients (*Minnesota* v. *Murphy*, 1984) and that the *Miranda* warning is not required during the issuance of traffic citations (*Berkemer* v. *McCarty*, 1984). The following year, in *Oregon* v. *Elstad* (1985), the Court decided that even though a confession was obtained before the *Miranda* warning was given, confessions obtained after it are admissible. In 1994, however, in the case of *Davis* v. *United States*, the Court put the burden on custodial suspects to make unequivocal invocations of the right to counsel. In the *Davis* case, a man being interrogated in the death of a sailor waived his *Miranda* rights but later said, "Maybe I should talk to a lawyer." Investigators asked the defendant clarifying questions, and he responded, "No, I don't want a lawyer." Upon conviction he

|Fig. 6.1| ▲

Sample waiver of rights form.

STATEMENT OF RIGHTS AND WAIVER	CITY POLICE DEPARTMENT	DATE

PLACE

NAME _____ **CASE NO.** *(If applicable)*

Before we ask you any questions, you must understand your rights. You have the right to remain silent. Anything you say can be used against you in court or other proceedings. You have the right to talk to a lawyer for advice before we ask you questions, and to have him with you during questioning. You have this right to the advice and presence of a lawyer even if you cannot afford to hire one. In such a case you have a right to have a court-appointed attorney present at the interrogation. If you wish to answer questions now without a lawyer present, you have the right to stop answering questions at any time. You also have the right to stop answering at any time until you talk to a lawyer.

You may waive the right to advice of counsel and your right to remain silent and answer questions or make a statement without consulting a lawyer if you so desire.

WAIVER

I ☐ have read ☐ had read to me   the statement of my rights shown above. I understand what my rights are and I elect to waive them. I am willing to answer questions and make a statement. I do not want a lawyer. I understand and know what I am doing. No promises or threats have been made to me and no pressure of any kind has been used against me. I was taken into custody at *(time)* _____ ☐ A.M. ☐ P.M., on *(date)* _____, and have signed this document at *(time)* _____ ☐ A.M. ☐ P.M., on *(date)* _____.

WITNESS _____	SIGNATURE OF PERSON WAIVING RIGHTS
WITNESS _____	

Miranda Warning

A person being interrogated has the right to remain silent; any statement may be used in a court of law. The person also has the right to have an attorney present during questioning. If the suspect can't afford an attorney, one will be appointed for him or her before questioning.

appealed, claiming that interrogation should have ceased when he mentioned a lawyer. The Court, in affirming the conviction, stated, "It will often be a good police practice for the interviewing officers to clarify whether or not [the defendant] actually wants an attorney."

THE PUBLIC SAFETY EXCEPTION TO *MIRANDA*   The public safety exception to *Miranda* was ruled on in *New York* v. *Quarles* (1984). This decision found that police officers who are reasonably concerned for public safety may question persons who are in custody and who have not been read the *Miranda* warning. The U.S. Supreme Court also found that subsequent statements are admissible in court. In this case, a woman complained to two officers that an armed man had just raped her. After giving the officers a description of the man, they proceeded to a nearby supermarket, where Benjamin Quarles was located. After a brief chase, the officers frisked Quarles and discovered an empty shoulder holster. After the suspect was in handcuffs, the officer asked Quarles where the gun was, and he nodded in the direction of some empty cartons and said, "It's over there." The gun was retrieved, and Quarles was arrested and read the *Miranda* warning.

When the case went to trial, the court ruled that under the requirements of *Miranda*, the statement "It's over there" and subsequent seizing of the weapon were inadmissible at the defendant's trial. On review, the U.S. Supreme Court acknowledged that Quarles should have been given the *Miranda* warnings. However, the Court recognized that the need to have the suspect talk was more important than the reading of the *Miranda* warning. The Court also ruled that if *Miranda* warnings had deterred the suspect from giving such information, the cost to society would have been much greater than the simple loss of evidence: As long as the gun remained in the pile of cartons, it posed a public safety hazard.

DEFINING CUSTODY   *Miranda* applies only when testimonial evidence is being sought. In addition, it applies only to **custodial interrogations**, not to circumstances in which the suspect is free to leave. The custodial interrogation rule applies not only when the suspect has been arrested before questioning but also when his or her liberty has been restricted to a degree that is associated with arrest. Therefore, an interview itself can also be considered custodial even though no arrest has been made. It depends on the circumstances. For example, if the suspect is being

|Fig. 6.2| ▲

Sample *Miranda* warning card carried routinely by officers and used after placing a subject in custody and before questioning.

MIRANDA WARNING

1. **You have the right to remain silent.**
2. **Anything you say can and will be used against you in a court of law.**
3. **You have the right to talk to a lawyer and have him present with you while you are being questioned.**
4. **If you cannot afford to hire a lawyer, one will be appointed to represent you before any questioning, if you wish.**
5. **You can decide at any time to exercise these rights and not answer any questions or make any statements.**

questioned in a relaxed atmosphere at his or her own residence, the *Miranda* warning need not be given. Conversely, if the suspect is approached in his or her own home by officers possessing an arrest warrant, the *Miranda* warning must be given before questioning. In brief, the test is whether the interview is custodial, not whether the investigation has focused on a particular person being interviewed.

Preparation for the Interrogation

In preparation for an interrogation, the investigator should review all important details in the case and be prepared to seek answers to basic questions such as what, when, why, where, and how of the incident. In addition, the investigator should give some thought as to what information would be of the most value to the investigation. A series of questions can be drawn up and referred to unobtrusively during the interrogation.

The Interrogation Setting

In addition to the manner in which the interrogator treats the suspect, it is also important to consider the physical surroundings where the questioning occurs. Because of pressure from peers and family members who might be present at the scene, it is important to remove the suspect from familiar surroundings and take him or her to a location with a more sterile and less threatening atmosphere. A key psychological factor contributing to successful interrogations is privacy. This encourages the suspect to feel comfortable in unloading the burden of guilt. The structure of the interrogation setting should also be conducive to the obtaining of confessions. Its surroundings should reduce fear and therefore encourage the suspect to discuss his or her role in the crime. Consequently, the interrogation room should reflect a more businesslike atmosphere than a policelike environment.

The interrogation should be conducted in a room specifically designed for that purpose only. It should be isolated from the bustling activity of the rest of the office, the sound of police radios, overhead intercoms, and other interruptions. Ideally, a soundproof room best serves this purpose. The interrogation room should be well lit but not to the extent that its lights are glaring. In addition, it should be protected from interruptions and equipped with some means of communicating with the outside, such as a buzzer or office intercom. Furnishings should be minimal, consisting of chairs, preferably without a desk, and containing pencil and paper but otherwise nondescript, with no distracting decorations.

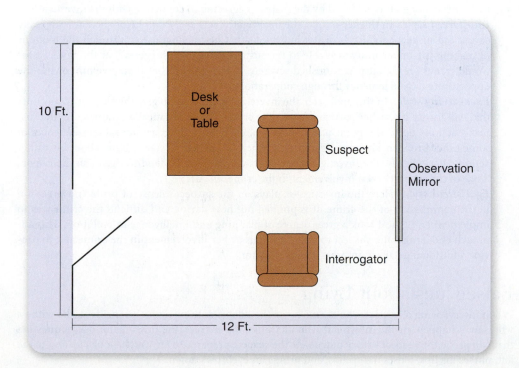

|Fig. 6.3|

Physical layout of a police interrogation room.

Ideally, no obstacles such as tables or desks should block the interviewer's full view of the subject's body. A large portion of nonverbal behavior emanates from the lower body, not just from the hands and face. Feet that fidget or point to the door communicate discomfort. If subjects sit behind a desk or table, the investigator should instruct them to relocate. Deceivers often use soda cans, computer screens, and other objects, both large and small, to form barriers between themselves—behaviors consistent with dishonesty.[15]

The Interrogation Procedure

As a rule, two investigators handle the interrogation: One actually conducts the questioning, and the second acts as a witness to statements made by the suspect. Obviously, the two investigators should meet before the interrogation to discuss their "roles." Frequently, one investigator will assume one approach to the suspect, and the other will assume a different and sometimes contrasting style. The suspect may be more receptive to one approach than the other.

Interrogation Styles

Investigators have developed a variety of interrogation styles and techniques over the years. The decision to choose one style over the other may depend on many factors, including the personality of the suspect, the personality of the interrogator, and the nature of the case. Some of the most common styles of interrogation are described below.

- *Logical style.* In a case in which the evidence seems to be overwhelming, such as a drug trafficking case involving a drug purchase from an undercover agent, the investigator may try to appeal to the suspect's sense of logic. In doing so, the investigator, it is hoped, will persuade the suspect that cooperation is the only way the charges against him or her can be lessened. It is important to note here that promises of leniency to the suspect should not be made without direct authorization from the prosecuting attorney. The only promise that can be made is that his or her cooperation will be brought to the attention of the prosecutor for consideration of some kind of leniency.
- *Sympathetic style.* If the investigator thinks that the suspect is easily affected by an emotional appeal, the sympathetic approach might be a good technique. The interrogation is approached by speaking in low tones and will include expressions of concern and understanding for the suspect, his or her spouse, children, business, and so on. The investigator stimulates feelings of self-pity in the suspect when he or she blames others for his or her plight. Ideally, further relief of guilt is achieved by the suspect's agreeing to cooperate with the investigator.
- *Indifferent style.* In this technique, the investigator acts as though he or she does not really care if the suspect cooperates or not but thinks that he or she must go through the motions of making the opportunity available to the suspect. This style suggests that the investigator would rather see the suspect punished severely by the court rather than give him or her the opportunity to gain leniency through cooperation.
- *Face-saving style.* In this approach, the investigator attempts to give the suspect a "way out" that will justify his or her participation in the crime. By systematically rationalizing the suspect's actions up to the point of the violation, describing them as natural consequences of some other problem, the investigator tries to get the suspect to start talking about his or her actions. Periodically, the investigator interjects comments that tend to diminish the importance of the suspect's own involvement in the crime.
- *Egotistical style.* Here the investigator plays on the suspect's sense of pride and precision in the commission of the crime. It is pointed out how daring and difficult the crime was to implement and that it took a great degree of planning and intelligence to pull it off. This approach encourages the suspect to brag about his or her involvement in the crime and to provide additional details to impress the investigator.

False Cues about Lying

When interviewing a suspect who claims he or she knows nothing about an incident, the witness who saw it happen, or the informant who identified the suspect, the investigator asks a question that will prove the suspect's story untrue. As the suspect prepares to answer, he looks up and to the left, purses his lips, tenses his eyelids, and brings his eyebrows down.

The investigator believes that that when a suspect displays shifty eyes and looks up and to the left when answering uncomfortable questions must be lying. The suspect, while not totally disinterested, is reluctant to partake in the interview. Because the suspect's behavior suggests dishonesty, the investigator prepares to persist in the questioning.

Research has shown, however, that under these circumstances, the investigator would probably be wrong. For example, 23 out of 24 peer-reviewed studies published in scientific journals reporting experiments on eye behavior as an indicator of lying have rejected this hypothesis.[16] No scientific evidence exists to suggest that eye behavior or "gaze aversion" can gauge truthfulness reliably.

Some people say that gaze aversion is the sure sign of lying; others point out that fidgety feet or hands are the key indicators. Still others believe that analysis of voice stress or body posture provides benchmarks. Research has tested all of these indicators and found them only faintly associated with deception.[17]

Relying on false clues, or signs, about lying can result in serious consequences. Specifically, it can lead to the investigator inaccurately concluding that witnesses, suspects, or informants are lying when they are not or that they are telling the truth when additional information might be available. Reliance on false clues leads to misplaced confidence about the strengths and weaknesses of cases and can lead an investigator down dead-end paths. Moreover, a false conclusion can result in wrongful targeting of persons for crime as well as wrongful arrests, prosecutions, and possible convictions.

Behavioral Indicators

In August 2006, Nevada Highway Patrolman Eddie Dutchover pulled over a wanted polygamist, Warren Steed Jeffs. The officer immediately noticed a furiously pumping carotid artery in Jeffs' neck. To the trooper, this was a clue that Jeffs was nervous and he turned out to be right. Jeffs was on the FBI's 10 Most Wanted Fugitives list. Officers who pay attention to subtle clues can often gain insight into a subject's attempts to hide the truth or otherwise be held responsible for a crime. In Jeffs' case, he knew he was about to be arrested and his worries were physically apparent. In other cases, however, suspects often will lie to fool the investigator and avoid responsibility for the crimes they commit.

Years of research have led researchers to focus on the most verifiable behavioral cues to lying. Numerous studies have involved a randomly selected sample of people assigned by chance to lie or tell the truth. However, these studies include participants with no personal, financial, or emotional investment in the lie or any fear of punishment if they are caught. No stakes are involved—no punishment for getting caught and no reward for fooling the investigator.

In one such study, Matsumoto and his colleagues concluded that when motivated people lie and face consequences upon detection, clues to deception emerge and appear as "leakage" across multiple channels. Four of these are nonverbal (facial expressions, gestures and body language, voice, and verbal style). A fifth channel of leakage is in the actual words spoken—verbal statements.[18]

Research has shown that facial expressions of emotion, including subtle expressions, are universal and independent of race, culture, ethnicity, nationality, gender, age, religion, or any other demographic variable. All people express emotions on their faces in exactly the same ways. Moreover, they are immediate, automatic, and unconscious reactions. These are incredible characteristics of facial expressions because learning to read them means that someone can have a bigger window into the soul of almost anyone. It is powerful tools for investigators because facial expressions of emotion are the closest thing humans have to a universal language.[19]

The findings from studies about liars also have clearly indicated that no one indicator of lying exists. Because liars facing stakes betray their untruth by leakage that comes across as a complicated mass of signals, investigators make adequately processing this stream of information more difficult when focusing on inconsistencies in the story, rather than how it is told. The problem is that the liar also focuses on presenting a consistent, albeit false, story.[20] Liars also wrestle with their emotions and thoughts, actively trying to manage facial and body expressions, voice tone, verbal style, and words—all while monitoring the investigator's reaction. This allows reliable indicators of lies to pop out in the verbal and nonverbal leakage, which investigators often overlook because of their intense focus on the story.[21]

|Fig. 6.4| △

Sample voluntary
statement form.

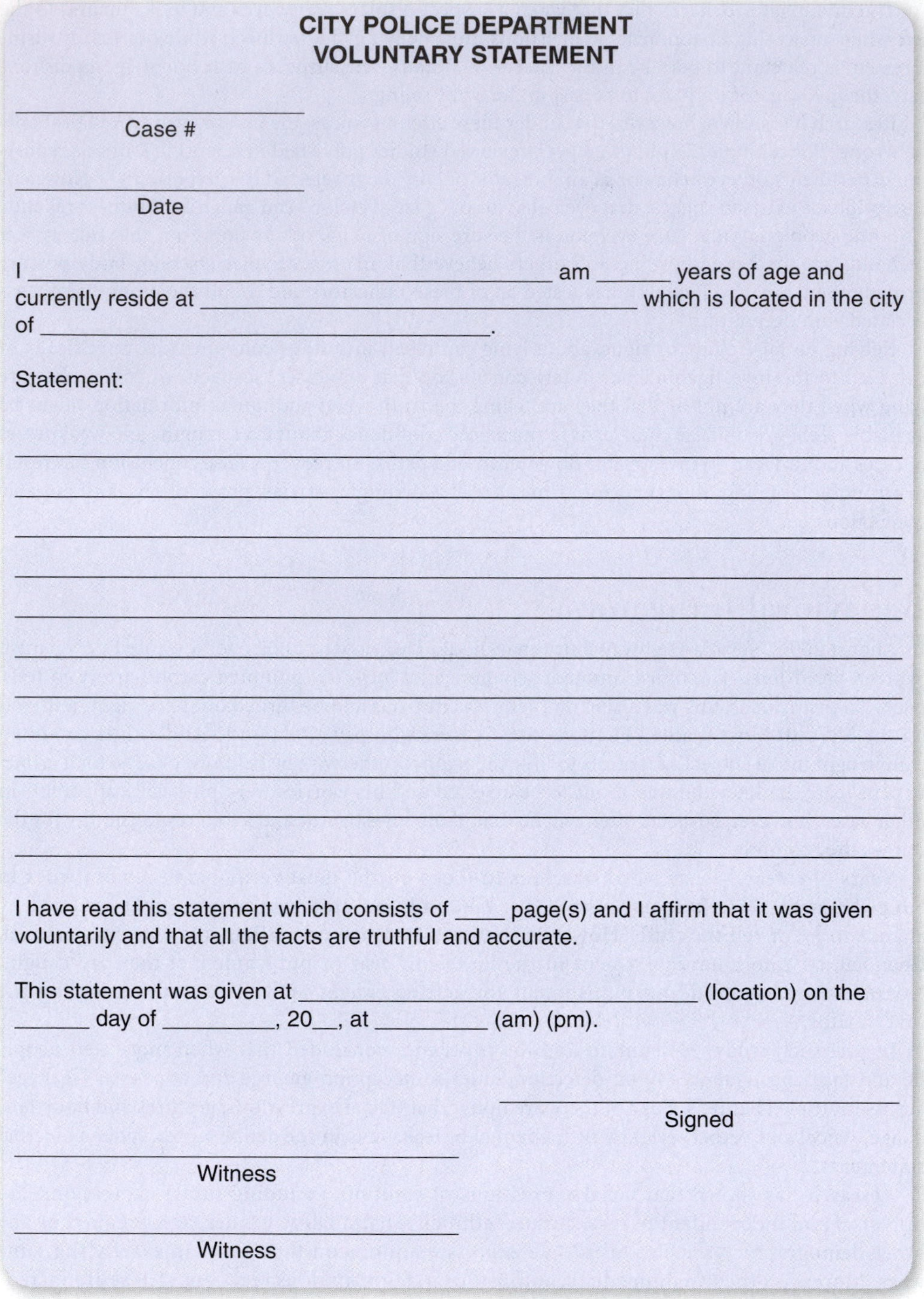

CITY POLICE DEPARTMENT
VOLUNTARY STATEMENT

_____
Case #

_____
Date

I _____ am _____ years of age and
currently reside at _____ which is located in the city
of _____.

Statement:

_____
_____
_____
_____
_____
_____
_____
_____
_____
_____
_____
_____

I have read this statement which consists of _____ page(s) and I affirm that it was given
voluntarily and that all the facts are truthful and accurate.

This statement was given at _____ (location) on the
_____ day of _____, 20__, at _____ (am) (pm).

_____
Signed

_____
Witness

_____
Witness

Verbal Cues

Because of certain psychological and cultural differences, a perceptive investigator can sometimes readily identify the manner in which people lie. For example, a trained listener can observe a pattern of evasiveness in the suspect and after a period is able to identify these statements as lies or efforts to deceive.

LIARS AND LYING Lying requires the deceiver to keep the facts straight, make the story believable, and withstand scrutiny. When individuals tell the truth, they often make every effort to ensure that other people understand. In contrast, liars attempt to manage others' perceptions.

Physical Characteristics of Lying

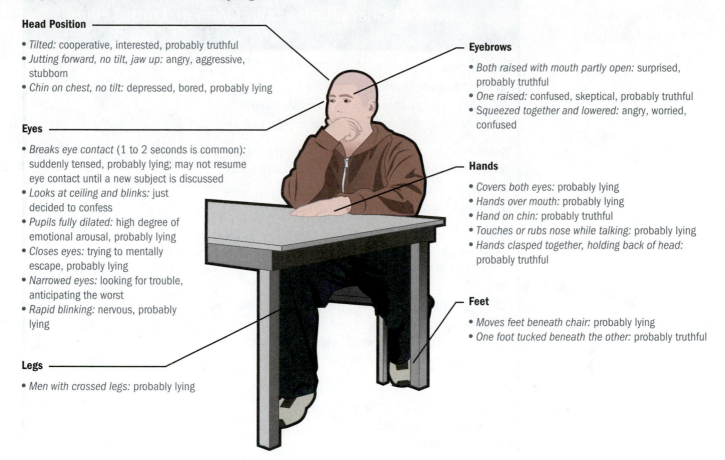

Head Position

- *Tilted:* cooperative, interested, probably truthful
- *Jutting forward, no tilt, jaw up:* angry, aggressive, stubborn
- *Chin on chest, no tilt:* depressed, bored, probably lying

Eyes

- *Breaks eye contact (1 to 2 seconds is common):* suddenly tensed, probably lying; may not resume eye contact until a new subject is discussed
- *Looks at ceiling and blinks:* just decided to confess
- *Pupils fully dilated:* high degree of emotional arousal, probably lying
- *Closes eyes:* trying to mentally escape, probably lying
- *Narrowed eyes:* looking for trouble, anticipating the worst
- *Rapid blinking:* nervous, probably lying

Legs

- *Men with crossed legs:* probably lying

Eyebrows

- *Both raised with mouth partly open:* surprised, probably truthful
- *One raised:* confused, skeptical, probably truthful
- *Squeezed together and lowered:* angry, worried, confused

Hands

- *Covers both eyes:* probably lying
- *Hands over mouth:* probably lying
- *Hand on chin:* probably truthful
- *Touches or rubs nose while talking:* probably lying
- *Hands clasped together, holding back of head:* probably truthful

Feet

- *Moves feet beneath chair:* probably lying
- *One foot tucked beneath the other:* probably truthful

|Fig. 6.5| ◬

Typical characteristics of lying.

Consequently, people unwittingly signal deception via nonverbal and verbal cues. Unfortunately, no particular nonverbal or verbal cue demonstrates deception.[22] The ability of an investigator to detect deceptive behavior depends largely on his or her ability to observe, catalog, and differentiate human behavior. The more observations investigators make, the greater the probability of detecting deception. Here are some indicators of deceptive behavior:

> Research has shown that vocal changes occur 95 percent of the time when a person lies. A liar's speech rate and voice pitch will also increase 95 percent of the time.[23] In addition, liars will usually stall before giving an answer, to give them time to decide if they should lie or tell the truth, or to decide just how big a lie to tell. Liars will always attempt to con the investigator. They may choose to tell a big lie, a misleading statement, or the complete truth. In most cases, they will attempt to dodge the truth. For example, they may restate the question or ask to have it repeated. They might say "I can't remember" or that they don't understand the question. If the subject stammers, stutters, or has a mental block before answering the question, most of the time he or she is lying.[24]

LYING TECHNIQUES Liars often lie by using *specifics*. For example, the suspect may say, "I don't even own a gun!" Although this could be a true statement at face value, he or she might have borrowed a gun to commit the crime but is relying on the fact that the statement is a true one, and the investigator will, it is hoped, infer that the suspect didn't commit the crime. Liars tend to admit only what the investigator can prove and deny what can't be proved. In addition,

Nonverbal Characteristics of Lying or Truth Telling

Head Position

☑ *Tilted:* cooperative, interested, probably truthful

☑ *Jutting forward, no tilt, jaw up:* angry, aggressive, stubborn

☑ *Chin on chest, no tilt:* depressed, bored, probably lying

Eyebrows

☑ *Both raised with mouth partly open:* surprised, probably truthful

☑ *One raised:* confused, skeptical, probably truthful

☑ *Squeezed together and lowered:* angry, worried, confused

Eyes

☑ *Breaks eye contact* (1 to 2 seconds is common): suddenly tensed, probably lying; may not resume eye contact until a new subject is discussed

☑ *Looks at ceiling and blinks:* just decided to confess

☑ *Pupils fully dilated:* high degree of emotional arousal, probably lying

☑ *Closes eyes:* trying to mentally escape, probably lying

☑ *Narrowed eyes:* looking for trouble, anticipating the worst

☑ *Rapid blinking:* nervous, probably lying

Hands

☑ *Covers both eyes:* probably lying

☑ *Hands over mouth:* probably lying

☑ *Hand on chin:* probably truthful

☑ *Touches or rubs nose while talking:* probably lying

☑ *Hands clasped together, holding back of head:* probably truthful

Legs

☑ *Men with crossed legs:* probably lying

Feet

☑ *Moves feet beneath chair:* probably lying

☑ *One foot tucked beneath the other:* probably truthful

---

they sometimes make an issue out of trivial things. For example, if a suspect complains about the manner in which the government has treated him in the past, he is probably attempting to sway away from the real issue.

Other lying techniques commonly used include the following:

- The suspect tries to confuse the interviewer by arguing about trivial points rather than addressing the real issues.

- A debating tactic is used in which the suspect tries to discount the investigator's argument in advance. For example, if the investigator makes a statement regarding a piece of evidence, the suspect replies, "You don't really expect anyone to believe that, do you?" The big lie or repeated assertion is based on the assumption that if you say something over and over, people will start to believe it. Repeated denial of the violation only reinforces the suspect's ability to lie.

- The "you don't understand" tactic is used by experienced liars to block an in-depth interrogation. This is attempted by saying, "You wouldn't understand," "You don't know how these things work," or "How would someone like you be expected to know?"
- The "loophole" liar is a dodger who is unsure just how much the investigator knows about the crime. Loophole liars typically respond by saying, "I can't remember" or "to the best of my recollection." This technique gives the person a way out in case he or she is later confronted with contradictory evidence.[25]

Why Suspects Cooperate and Confess

When we consider that self-destruction and self-condemnation are not normal human behavioral characteristics, it is perplexing why someone would openly confess to a crime. In addition, one could conclude that when a person is arrested and taken to a police station for questioning, he or she will not readily admit (and even choose to lie about) his or her part in a crime. Many criminals, particularly career criminals, have developed a keen sense of observation over the years. It is likely that this sense has aided them in the past in avoiding detection by police. Such criminals can easily see the direction in which an interrogation is going. Logically, then, one would think that the dialogue between the suspect and investigator would be brief. Strangely, because of complex psychological factors, this is not always the case.

Why do innocent people confess? A variety of factors may contribute to a false confession during a police interrogation. Many cases have included a combination of several of these causes. They include:

- Duress
- Coercion
- Intoxication
- Diminished capacity
- Mental impairment
- Ignorance of the law
- Fear of violence
- The actual infliction of harm
- The threat of a harsh sentence
- Misunderstanding the situation

Searching for Information

Depending on the crime in question and the particular suspect, it is logical to assume that many criminals follow the progress of the police through media accounts of the investigation. Still, they really don't have a good sense of exactly what the investigator knows and doesn't know about the suspect. It is the desire of the criminal to want to know exactly what the investigator knows about the crime. This "paranoia" frequently drives the suspect to accompany the investigator willingly to the police station for an interview. Once at the station, however, the suspect not only tries to learn what the investigator knows about the investigation but also attempts to lead him or her away from the focus of the investigation.

Closing the Communication Gap

Research indicates that most guilty persons who confess are, from the outset, looking for the proper opening during the interrogation to communicate their guilt to investigators.[26] Suspects also make confessions when they believe that cooperation is the best course of action. Before they talk, they need to be convinced that investigators are willing to listen to all the circumstances surrounding the crimes. Finally, suspects confess when interrogators are able to speculate correctly on why the crimes were committed. They want to know ahead of time that interrogators will believe what they have to say and will understand what motivated them to commit the crime.

Admission versus Confession

Although seemingly alike, there is a notable difference between the admission of a criminal act and the confession of one's complicity in a crime. An **admission** is a self-incriminating statement made by the suspect that falls short of an acknowledgment of guilt. It is, however, an acknowledgment of a certain fact or circumstance from which his or her guilt can be inferred. Conversely, a **confession** is direct acknowledgment by the suspect of his or her guilt in the commission of a specific crime or as being an integral part of a specific crime. For the confession to be lawful, the investigator must be mindful of the constitutional checks governing its admissibility.

False Confessions

For a number of reasons, innocent people sometimes confess to crimes they did not commit. These reasons include mental health issues and law enforcement tactics that place undue pressure on suspects to "cooperate."

Although it can be hard to understand why someone would falsely confess to a crime, psychological research has provided some answers. Moreover, in 2009, the Innocence Project reported that through DNA exonerations, the problem of false confessions is more widespread than many people think. For example, in approximately 25 percent of the wrongful convictions overturned with DNA evidence, defendants made false confessions, admissions, or statements to law enforcement officials.[27]

The problem of false confessions can be illustrated by the case of Eddie Joe Lloyd. Lloyd was convicted of the 1984 murder of a 16-year-old girl in Detroit after he wrote to police with suggestions on how to solve various recent crimes. During several interviews, police fed details of the crime to Lloyd, who was mentally ill, and convinced him that by confessing he was helping them "smoke out" the real killer. Lloyd eventually signed a confession and gave a tape-recorded statement. The jury deliberated less than an hour before convicting him, and the judge said at sentencing that execution, which had been outlawed in Michigan, would have been the "only justifiable sentence" if it were available. In 2002, DNA testing proved that Lloyd was innocent, and he was exonerated. As mandated in a settlement with Lloyd's family, Detroit Police officials said in 2006 they would start videotaping all interrogations in crimes that could carry a sentence of life.[28]

A number of investigative practices can be identified that help safeguard against false confessions. One of these is recording the interrogation process (discussed earlier). For the recording of interrogations to be effective, the entire custodial interrogation must be recorded. Doing so will improve the credibility and reliability of authentic confessions, will better prepare the investigator's case for trial, and will help protect the rights of innocent suspects.

In some false confession cases, details of the crime are inadvertently communicated to a suspect by investigators during the questioning process. Later, when a suspect knows these details, the police take the knowledge as evidence of guilt. Often, threats or promises are made to the suspect off camera and then the camera is turned on for a false confession. Without an objective record of the custodial interrogation, it is difficult to gauge the reliability of the confession.

For law enforcement agencies, recording interrogations can prevent disputes about how a suspect was treated, create a clear record of a suspect's statements, and increase public confidence in the criminal justice system. Recording interrogations can also deter officers from using illegal tactics to secure a confession.

The Cognitive Interview

Another widely accepted interviewing technique is the cognitive interview technique. As a rule, the cognitive interview technique is used for eliciting information from victims and witnesses, opposed to obtaining confessions from suspects. Two main forces were behind the development of the cognitive interview. The first was the need to improve the effectiveness of police interviews when questioning witnesses. The second was to apply the results of psychological research to this area, particularly the work of Elizabeth Loftus, whose research had already dispelled the myth that an eyewitness's memory operates like a video camera.[29] As a result, Ronald P. Fisher of Florida

International University and Edward Geiselman of UCLA developed the technique of cognitive interviewing.

A number of differences can be identified between traditional interviewing techniques and the cognitive approach. For example, traditional interviewers attempt to bring out information by asking specific questions; they target a question for each content area that they need to address. For example, if an investigator needs to find out how tall the perpetrator was, then he or she asks the question, "How tall was the perpetrator?" And if the investigator wants to find out what was the angle of the plane that was approaching the airport, he or she would ask a direct question such as, "What was the angle of the plane as it approached the airport?"

The traditional interviewer asks many questions, each of which elicits a very brief response. The cognitive interview, on the other hand, is less directive and is in some ways a questionless interview. The goal is to ask as few questions as possible so that witnesses give you long narrative responses that each contains that much more information than a traditional interview. The objective is to try to elicit information, not extract information. The good interviewer tries to create a social environment so the witness generates information without having to wait for questions to be asked.

The two major subtypes of cognitive interviewing methods are think-aloud interviewing and verbal probing techniques.[30]

"Think-Aloud" Interviewing

The think-aloud interview derives from psychological procedures described by Ericsson and Simon (1980).[31] The term *think-aloud* is used to describe a specific type of activity in which subjects are explicitly instructed to "think-aloud" as they answer the survey questions. The interviewer reads each question to the subject and then records or otherwise notes the processes that the subject uses in arriving at an answer to the question. The interviewer interjects little else, except to say, "Tell me what you're thinking" when the subject pauses.[32]

The advantages of the "think-aloud" interview technique is that it elicits responses from the subject that are free from interviewer bias and that little formal training is required to prepare the interviewer for the use of the technique. The disadvantages are that it is easy for the subject to loose focus and stray from the task.[33]

Verbal Probing Techniques

As an alternative to the think-aloud, the use of verbal probing is the basic technique that has increasingly come into favor by cognitive researchers.[34] After the interviewer asks the survey question, and the subject answers, the interviewer then asks for other, specific information relevant to the question or to the specific answer given. In general, the interviewer "probes" further into the basis for the response. Examples of the probing technique include the following:

> "You stated that you saw the man entering her apartment. What means did he use to gain entry?
>
> "When you say you saw the men drive away, describe the manner that they were operating the car."

The advantages of the probing technique are that the investigator can control the interview with relative ease, and the subject of the interview can easily adjust to the method used by the investigator.[35]

Written Statements

Because the interrogation will generally produce much more information than is needed for the written statement, the investigator will have to decide what information he or she needs for preparation of the statement. A confession from the suspect should substantiate the elements of the charge or at least contain information related to the investigation. In addition, the statement of the confession should contain any details of extenuating circumstances or explanations offered by the suspect that might be grounds for additional inquiry. Several variables determine what methods are used to take the statement.

These include the intelligence level of the suspect, the amount and nature of information to be recorded, and the availability of stenographic services. In many cases, the suspect will be willing to give a verbal statement about his or her involvement in a crime but might be unwilling to have it written down at the time. If this occurs, the investigator should not interrupt the remarks being made by the suspect just to ask for a signed statement. Instead, after the suspect is finished giving his or her account of what happened, the investigator should ask if the suspect would be willing to sign (or write) a statement to that effect. The suspect should be assured that only the information given to the investigator will be included in the statement and that he or she will have the prerogative of not signing it if it is not accurate. The following techniques can be used if the suspect decides to sign the written statement:

- The suspect may respond orally to the investigator or a stenographer in response to questions. Responses are then written verbatim.
- The suspect may give a statement orally without direction from the investigator. This technique is the most desirable, provided that the end result is a clear and concise statement.
- The investigator could give the suspect a list of the important points to cover during the statement and suggest that he or she include these and other important points.
- The investigator may choose to write the statement according to the information given by the suspect in his or her oral statement.

If these techniques are adopted, the investigator must use the same phrases that were used by the suspect. The completed statement should then be shown to the suspect so that any changes can be made. Once corrections are in order, the statement is signed. The investigator should be careful to make the written statement reflect only one crime because in a criminal trial, the court will ordinarily not permit the introduction of evidence of additional crimes. Exceptions to this are when additional crimes tend to show intent, the identity of the defendant, or the scheme used in the commission of the crime in question. Therefore, the best policy is to obtain a separate written statement for each crime committed.

Structuring the Written Statement

The statement should begin with the place, date, and identification of the maker and the name of the person who is giving the statement. It is acceptable for the body of the statement to be in narrative or expository form. In addition, it should include all the elements of the crime as well as any facts that connect the suspect with the crime. If the investigator or stenographer prepares the statement, the suspect should be asked to read and sign each page at the bottom. To ensure that the suspect actually reads the statement, he or she should be asked to correct any typographical errors and to initial any corrections in ink. Finally, each page should be labeled "page _____ of _____ pages." The concluding paragraph should state that the suspect has read the statement consisting of so many pages and that the statement is "true and correct." After the suspect signs the statement in the space provided, two witnesses should sign it under the suspect's signature. Normally, the witnesses are the interrogators. Any more than two witnesses could leave the impression with the court that the suspect was intimidated by a large number of police at the time of the statement.

Recorded Statements

Frequently, the investigator will choose to record a statement made by a suspect. This can be especially advantageous when the suspect cannot read or write or when he or she is only fluent in a foreign language. One important point to remember is that when the investigator chooses to record the statement, the interrogation should still be conducted first. When it is time to record the statement, the investigator uses his or her notes from the first interrogation to develop the recorded statement. When the recording is complete, the recorded statement is then played back for the suspect to hear so he or she can verify that it is a true and accurate representation of what was said during the interrogation.

The Recording Procedure

The recording should begin with the investigator identifying him- or herself, the suspect, and any other investigators in the room (people entering and leaving the room during the interrogation should also be identified with corresponding times, but at the end of the recording). In addition, the opening remarks should include the location of the statement or interrogation, the time and date of the statement, and a statement by the investigator to the suspect as to why the statement is being recorded. After the important points of the statement are given, the investigator should ask the suspect if there are any additional comments that he or she would like to make.

Afterward, the investigator should state that the recorder is now going to be shut off and that the suspect can listen and verify its contents. After the suspect listens and verifies the recording, it is then turned back on, and he or she should verbally acknowledge that the contents accurately represent the statement and the recorder was not turned off or stopped at any time during the interrogation except for the time when the suspect reviewed the tape. Finally, the investigator states that the session is concluded and repeats the names of the persons in the room and the time and date of the statement. The recording should then be entered into evidence and processed appropriately.

Videotaped Confessions

On the basis of a national survey, it is estimated that one-third of all large police and sheriff's departments in the United States videotape at least some interrogations, a practice that is most common in cases of homicide, rape, and aggravated assault.[36] Proponents claim that videotaping has a number of benefits, such as deterring coercive behavior on the part of investigators and providing a more complete and accurate record of the confession for the judge and jury to evaluate the voluntariness and veracity of the defendant's statement.[37]

For evidentiary purposes, videotaped interrogations should provide a complete and objective record of police–suspect interaction. But the question is still raised—what is a complete and accurate record? For example, in an actual police confession in New York, police were convinced that they recorded a confession from a "neutral" camera angle. The camera was positioned behind the investigator and focused directly on the suspect. Although this may seem innocent enough, research suggests that it is not. On the basis of studies showing that people make causal attributions to factors that are visually salient, Lassiter and his colleagues taped mock interrogations from three different camera angles so that the suspect, the interrogator, or both were visible to mock jurors. The result was that those who saw only the suspect judged the situation as less coercive than those focused on the investigator. By directing visual attention on the suspect, the camera can lead jurors to underestimate the amount of pressure actually exerted by the "hidden" investigator.[38]

Recap Bias

An important related issue concerns whether jurors are shown a tape of the entire interrogation or merely a recap consisting of only the suspect's final confession. Recaps are common and take an average of 15 to 45 minutes.[39] On the question of whether they should be admitted into evidence, there are two possible bases for concern. First, the jury sees a final self-incriminating statement but not the circumstances that led up to it, perhaps increasing perceptions of voluntariness. Second, after recounting a story over and over again, a suspect is likely to show less emotion and appear unusually callous. In light of the fact that people are more forgiving of others who express remorse and apologize for their wrongdoings, recaps may bias the jury against the defendant.[40] At this point, empirical research is needed to examine these possible effects.

Framing the Tapes

A suspect often provides the police with a statement that is not a confession but is instead ambiguous (i.e., denying the charges but telling an implausible story). So what is the persuasive impact of an interrogation tape when the suspect maintains his or her innocence and goes to trial? One possibility is for the state to introduce the tape into evidence to highlight inconsistencies in the defendant's story. But another possibility is for the defense to show the tape and focus the jury's attention on the defendant's denials in the face of pressure.

To examine this question, in a 1990 study, Kassin, Reddy, and Tulloch had mock jurors watch a 45-minute "confession" of an actual murder suspect who asserted her innocence but told an implausible story. For some participants, the tape was introduced by the prosecution, who harped on the inconsistencies of the story; for others, it was shown by the defense lawyer, who noted that the defendant maintained her innocence despite pressure to confess (the tape was always followed by the lawyer's argument). Results showed that among participants, those who saw the tape being introduced by the prosecution rather than the defense were more likely to vote guilty.[41] With statements that are ambiguous enough to accommodate opposing interpretations, the adversarial advantage goes to the party that introduces the tape and frames it for the jury.

Use of the Polygraph

Of the mechanical devices that have been designed to aid investigators in obtaining information, the **polygraph**, or "lie detector," has proven to be of extreme value. Proper use of this tool can help an investigator determine a suspect's guilt or innocence. However, because of recent court rulings restricting the use of the polygraph in certain settings, the investigator should view this device as an aid only, not as a last resort or panacea.

The polygraph is designed simply to measure whether or not the person being tested is being deceptive. As the subject is asked different questions, the graphs observed by the operator will, it is hoped, indicate a truthful or a deceptive response. Indeed, the device does not actually do what its moniker indicates—it does not detect lies. What it does do is measure the physiological responses from the subject, including fear, anxiety, excitation, and other emotions. So the critical consideration in the use of a polygraph is not the machine itself but the operator's ability to interpret its results accurately.

Accuracy of the Polygraph

The criminal justice field is divided as to its acceptance of polygraph results. In fact, most courts do not accept the findings of a polygraph exam as absolute evidence except when stipulated to by all parties. Problems with the use of the polygraph have been in its application. Specifically, the machine should be used to identify statements as being false, not for the purpose of actually detecting lies.

The value of an examination can be looked at in two regards: reliability and validity. *Reliability* refers to the consistency of the examination's results. This can be shown through reproducing the examination repeatedly and obtaining the same results. Indeed, when properly administered, the polygraph can produce very reliable results. *Validity* refers to the accuracy of the examination. Validity can be affected by two considerations. First is the ability of the polygraph examiner to interpret the results of the examination accurately. Second, if the measurements that are recorded by the instrument fail to indicate lying directly, it lacks validity.

Administration of the Polygraph Exam

Before the exam occurs, the examiner will request certain information from the investigator. Such information includes the specific offense in question, a copy of the case file, a list of the different types of evidence, specific personal information about the subject, and any physical or psychological data about the subject, if known.

A polygraph examiner then attaches a probe to a person's chest and fingers to record his or her heart rate, respiration, and sweat gland activity during the course of questioning. Responses to questions are charted automatically, and from responses to both innocuous and relevant questions, the examiner can generally determine if the person is being deceptive.

Next, specific questions are structured, usually in a "yes" or "no" format. These questions are reviewed with the subject before he or she takes the test. This is to relax the person taking the test and, it is hoped, to elicit an admission of additional details of the alleged crime. When the test is completed, the subject is generally advised of the results in writing. If deception was detected, the subject might be interviewed about the weak points of the test. Frequently, this part of the process results in the subject's admitting to additional complicity in the crime.

Although the polygraph should not be considered a last-resort effort to obtain a suspect's confession, it can save money for the investigating agency. For example, it can weed out suspects in an investigation and let the focus of the investigation fall on specific persons.

A Closer Look

Is the Polygraph Junk Science?

Although the courts still call it "junk science," the lie detector or polygraph has never been so widely used by criminal justice agencies as a tool for determining the truth. In 1998, the U.S. Supreme Court ruled against the use of polygraph evidence in criminal court, but police agencies still rely on the polygraph exam to make critical personnel decisions from hiring to firing. Over the years, the percentage of police agencies using polygraphs to screen new employees increased from 16 percent in 1962, for example, to 62 percent in 1999, according to a study conducted by Michigan State's School of Criminal Justice. The same survey shows that police are confident of exam results—more than three-fourths believe that polygraphs are 86 to 100 percent reliable.

At the FBI, which employs over 11,000 agents, senior officials have requested permission to administer up to 225 polygraphs per year in investigations of suspected employee misconduct. That figure is in addition to the 3,000 tests given each year to new agents and witnesses and informants in major criminal investigations. The CIA, National Security Agency, Defense Department, Treasury Department, and many large police departments across the nation also depend on the polygraph. Failing a polygraph, as in the case of scientist Wen Ho Lee at Los Alamos National Laboratory in New Mexico, can end a career just as quickly as a guilty verdict. Lee was fired after he failed an FBI-administered polygraph in March 1999 and refused to cooperate with the government's investigation of Chinese espionage at the facility, which is the nation's premier weapons facility.

Fearing unwarranted invasions of individual privacy, Congress passed the *Employee Polygraph Protection Act* of 1988 to curb what had been a growing use of polygraph tests in private business. In 1998, the U.S. Supreme Court expressed concerns about the reliability of polygraphs when it upheld the military's ban on use of them in criminal trials. Yet government agencies still consider polygraphs a valuable personnel tool.

Thematic question

Given concerns about the accuracy of the polygraph and it admissibility in court, how can this investigative tool be used in the course of an investigation? Is it more prudent for a law enforcement organization to rely on cognitive interviewing techniques than the use of the polygraph to elicit admissions and confessions? Explain your response.

Sources: Johnson, K. (1999). Government agencies see truth in polygraphs. *USA Today*, April 6, p. A11; McCarthy, S. (2000). The truth about the polygraph. *Health & Body website*. Available at http://archive.salon.com/health/feature/2000/03/02/polygraph/index.html.

|Fig. 6.6| ▲

The polygraph has been used for decades to screen applicants for law enforcement positions as well as to determine whether a person is being "deceptive" during the course of a criminal or internal affairs investigation.

Michael L. Abramson

Admissibility of Polygraph Results

Over the years, the courts have addressed various aspects of the issue of polygraph results and their admissibility in court. Clearly, the machine can only detect certain changes in the human body, and estimates are that such changes can be detected up to 95 percent of the time. Despite arguments in favor of the use of the polygraph, its results are not currently admissible as absolute evidence in court. One early court case upheld a ruling of a trial court that refused acceptance of the results of the polygraph (*Frye* v. *United States*, 1923). Later that same year, the court in *People* v. *Forts* considered the results of the polygraph inadmissible based on doubts about the instrument's reliability. The *State* v. *Bohner* (1933) case also failed to accept the results of the polygraph but acknowledged its usefulness. Exceptions occur, however, when all parties stipulate to the acceptance of the results before administration of the exam.

The Voice Stress Analyzer

An investigative tool gaining considerable popularity with law enforcement agencies is the voice stress analyzer (VSA). Unlike the computer polygraph, the VSA requires no wires be attached to the subject being tested. The VSA uses only a microphone plugged into the computer to analyze the subject's responses. As the subject speaks, the computer displays each voice pattern, numbers it, then saves each chart to file. Unlike the polygraph, drugs do not affect the results of the exam, and there are no known countermeasures that will cause the ubiquitous "inconclusive" results associated with the polygraph.

Rapidly supplanting the polygraph, the VSA has been used in many investigative situations such as homicide, sex crimes, robbery, white-collar crimes, and internal affairs investigations, as well as pre-employment examinations for background investigators. The system has been used as an investigative tool for verifying statements of witnesses and denials of suspects and for determining the validity of allegations made against police officers.

Microtremors are tiny frequency modulations in the human voice. When a test subject is lying, the autonomic, or involuntary, nervous system causes an inaudible increase in the microtremor's frequency. The VSA detects, measures, and displays changes in the voice print frequency.

A laptop computer processes these voice frequencies and graphically displays a picture of the voice patterns. Furthermore, the VSA is not restricted to "yes" and "no" answers and is able to accurately analyze tape recordings of unstructured conversations.

|Fig. 6.7| ◬

For many police organizations, the voice stress analyzer test, as shown here, has replaced the use of a polygraph because it is portable, more accurate, and training is only a fraction of that required by polygraph training programs.

Courtesy of Mike Himmel

Case in Point

>>The Stephanie Crowe Murder Investigation

Interviews and interrogations can result in the incorrect implication of a suspect. This is illustrated in the case of 12-year-old Stephanie Crowe, who was found dead in her bedroom in Escondido, California, on January 20, 1998.

On that date at 6:30 A.M., the noise from Stephanie's alarm clock radio caused her grandmother, Judith Kennedy, to go to the girl's room to see why Stephanie hadn't shut it off. Kennedy found her granddaughter wet with blood. Stabbed nine times through her bed covers, the petite brunette was dead. The six-year investigation, however, had more than its share of challenges and illustrates the consequences when officers are too quick to react to a confession that turns out to be false.

Police learned that six hours before Stephanie's body was discovered, witnesses saw Richard Raymond Tuite, a 28-year-old transient, standing in the Crowes' driveway looking up at their house. Another witness claimed she saw Tuite screaming and spinning around with his hands in the air in the proximity of the Crowes' house that night. Tuite's bizarre behavior that night, which also included his peering into windows of neighborhood houses, led to his being picked up by police the next morning as a possible suspect. The next day, Tuite was detained. The police questioned him about the murder. They took fingernail scrapings and clippings and photographs of him, confiscated his clothing and gave him a sweat suit, and released him. One detective later testified that Tuite was too "bumbling" to have killed the child so stealthily as to not wake her family. The police investigation quickly turned toward the family.

After Stephanie's body was discovered, the police separately interviewed each member of the entire Crowe family. They specifically focused their attention on Stephanie's 14-year-old brother, Michael, who was questioned for 27 hours over a 3-day period. They also extensively interviewed two of his closest friends. By the time the interrogations ended, the police had obtained a confession from Michael and one of his friends and enough incriminating evidence from the third boy to file murder charges against them all.

Although the boys allegedly confessed, there was a great deal of doubt concerning the accuracy of their statements and the method used to get them. The police allegedly used lies, false promises, isolation from parents and attorneys, and even threats of adult prison and predatory older inmates as persuasive techniques to get a confession.

The manner in which the boys claimed to have been interviewed prompted an investigation to determine whether they were coerced into confession. False confession expert Richard Leo analyzed the videotaped interrogations and came to a shocking conclusion. He determined that the interrogations were textbook examples of how not to question suspects, finding that it amounted to a form of psychological torture so coercive that the boys would have said almost anything to make it stop.

Investigators heard about sibling rivalry, about fantasy stories Michael Crowe had penned in which a brother and sister battle, and about a plot the trio of high school freshmen supposedly dreamed up to kill the seventh grader. In the interrogation, Michael Crowe wailed as he said he didn't remember killing his sister, but if the police had evidence pointing to him, then he must have done it. The boys quickly recanted. After much legal wrangling, most of their damning statements were excluded. One of the boys later testified he made up the story, stating, "[I would have] chewed off my own leg" to make the questioning stop. Before the murder trial even began, all charges against the boys were dropped because it became evident they had nothing to do with Stephanie's murder. The boys' exoneration rested on some key evidence—specks of Stephanie's blood that were found on two items of Tuite's clothing.

DNA testing of those items eventually linked Tuite to Stephanie's blood. After Tuite's arrest, many wondered why the DNA tests weren't conducted earlier and why Tuite wasn't held longer. Critics believed that the police were in such a hurry to solve the crime that they failed to conduct a proper investigation or even an ethical interrogation of suspects. In May 2004, Tuite was found guilty of voluntary manslaughter and sentenced to 13 years in a state prison. Resulting from the case were at least two books, a made-for-TV movie about the investigation, and some national media attention. In the meantime, the Crowe family sued the police department and prosecutors for violating Michael's civil rights during his interrogation.

Not only does this case illustrate the importance of conducting a proper and professional interrogation, but it also shows how when a suspect is incorrectly identified, the real perpetrator goes free. It is no small miracle that Tuite did not claim another victim after being released from his initial detention with police.

Thematic question

From a proactive investigative standpoint, in what ways can crimes such as this be prevented? Consider investigative efforts by both patrol officers and investigators.

Sources: Chacon, D. J. Verdict brings mixed reaction in Escondido. *Union-Tribunes SignonSanDiego.com*, May 26, 2004; Sauer, M. and J. Wilkens. Haunting questions: The Stephanie Crowe murder case. *Union-Tribunes SignonSanDiego.com*, May 11, 1999; Witt, A. and P. Schwartzman. Prince Georges prosecutor targets questioning; police must provide interrogation notes. *Washington Post*, June 7, 2001.

Summary Checklist

In this chapter, we consider the ways that information about crimes is documented by the criminal investigator. A properly documented case is one that is more likely to succeed in court. See how well you are able to answer the following questions in your checklist.

1. **Explain the difference between the investigative interview and an interrogation.**

   Investigators must make a clear distinction between the two processes of interviewing and interrogating suspects. An interview should precede every interrogation.

   - An interview is a relatively formal conversation conducted for the purpose of obtaining information. It is nonaccusatory.
   - An interrogation is the systematic questioning of a person suspected of involvement in a crime for the purpose of obtaining a confession. It is accusatory.
   - Legal guidelines affecting the two activities differ considerably as the probability increases that the person being questioned may incriminate him- or herself.

2. **What is the process for conducting an investigative interview?**

   The investigator will have a more productive interview if it can be conducted at a location where the subject is mentally relaxed, such as his or her own home or place of business.

   Key considerations that should be observed during the interview process include:

   - Develop a plan of attack—be familiar with pertinent data before initiating the interview and prepare questions in advance.
   - Conduct the interview in private.
   - Place the interviewee at ease.
   - Be a good listener—evaluate not just *what* is being said but also *how* it is being said.
   - Ask the right questions.
   - Don't dispute the subject's answers.
   - Maintain control of the interview—keep the interview on track.
   - Take brief notes—avoid interruptions after the interviewee begins to talk freely.
   - Adjourn the interview properly.

3. **Explain the process of conducting a suspect interrogation.**

   The interrogation is designed to match new information with a particular suspect to secure a confession. The main goals of the interrogation process are:

   - To learn the truth of the crime and how it happened
   - To obtain an admission of guilt from the suspect
   - To obtain all the facts to determine the method of operation and the circumstances of the crime
   - To gather information that enables investigators to arrive at logical conclusions
   - To provide information for use by prosecutors in possible court action

   Although there are legal guarantees of fairness that govern interrogations, the confession is still one of the most influential types of evidence in a court proceeding. Several types of behavior have been identified as improper and/or illegal for police investigators and will result in any confession being inadmissible in court.

   - Coercion—the use or threat of use of illegal physical methods to induce a suspect to make an admission or confession
   - Duress—the imposition of restrictions on physical behavior

4. **Identify the procedures for conducting an interrogation.**

   In preparation for an interrogation, the investigator should review all important details in the case and be prepared to seek answers to basic questions such as what, when, why, where, and how of the incident.

   - The interrogation should be conducted in a room specifically designed for that purpose only. It should be isolated from the bustling activity of the rest of the office, the sound of police radios, overhead intercoms, and other interruptions.
   - The selection of an interrogation style may depend on many factors, including the personality of the suspect, the personality of the interrogator, and the nature of the case. Interrogation style is of various types:
     - Logical style
     - Sympathetic style
     - Indifferent style
     - Face-saving style
     - Egotistical style

- The investigator should be aware of signs that suggest a suspect is lying but should not rely on false clues about lying.
  - No one indicator of lying exists.
  - When individuals tell the truth, they often make every effort to ensure that other people understand. In contrast, liars attempt to manage others' perceptions.
  - Liars often lie by using specifics.
- Interrogators should seek an admission or confession from the suspect.
  - Admission—a self-incriminating statement made by the suspect that falls short of an acknowledgment of guilt.
  - Confession—a direct acknowledgment by the suspect of his or her guilt in the commission of a specific crime or as being an integral part of a specific crime.

5. **Identify the known methods of improperly conducting an interrogation of a criminal suspect.**

Methods used by inexperienced or unscrupulous police interrogators include deception, fear tactics, unreasonably long interviews, sleep or food deprivation, and either exaggerating or minimizing the crime. These are blamed for a large number of all documented false confessions. These methods include:

- Fear tactics that include direct threats, intimidation, or actual physical abuse that have been known to coerce suspects into falsely admitting guilt (a coerced-compliant confession).
- Maximization:
  - The exaggeration of evidence available, telling the person that the interrogator knows he is guilty or stressing the consequences of the crime.
  - This can lead to coerced internalization, where highly suggestible and confused suspects begin to believe they are guilty of a crime they did not commit and make a false confession.
- Minimization:
  - The seriousness of the crime is downplayed and the suspect believes he or she is less likely to get into trouble.
  - This can prompt a false confession, especially if coupled with other coercive techniques.
- Making suspects sit through long-drawn-out interrogations, depriving them of food and sleep—suspects may become so emotionally and physically worn down that they are more likely to give a false statement in an attempt to escape from the torture.

6. **How should a suspect statement be properly documented?**

A confession from the suspect should substantiate the elements of the charge or at least contain information related to the investigation. In addition, the statement of the confession should contain any details of extenuating circumstances or explanations offered by the suspect that might be grounds for additional inquiry.

- Suspects may be willing to give a verbal statement about their involvement in the crime but might be unwilling to have it written down at the time.
- In this situation, the investigator should wait until the suspect is finished giving his or her account of what happened and then ask if the suspect would be willing to sign (or write) a statement to that effect.
- If the suspect decides to sign the written statement:
  - The suspect may respond orally to questions and responses are written by the investigator verbatim.
  - The suspect may give a statement orally without direction from the investigator.
  - The investigator may give the suspect a list of important points to cover during the statement and suggest he or she include these and other important points.
  - The investigator may choose to write the statement according to the information given by the suspect in the oral statement.
  - The completed statement should be shown to the suspect so that any changes can be made.
  - After corrections are in order, the statement is signed.

7. **Compare and contrast the polygraph and the voice stress analyzer as investigative tools.**

The polygraph, or "lie detector," has proved to be of extreme value. However, because of court rulings restricting its use in certain settings, investigators should view the polygraph as an aid only.

- The polygraph is designed simply to measure whether or not the person being tested is being deceptive.
- It does not detect lies—it measures the physiological responses from the subject.
- Most courts do not accept the findings of a polygraph exam as absolute evidence except when stipulated to by all parties.

The voice stress analyzer (VSA) does not require wires to be attached to the subject being tested.

- The VSA uses a microphone plugged into a computer to analyze the subject's responses.
- Unlike the polygraph, drugs do not affect the results of the exam.
- Unlike the polygraph, the VSA is not restricted to "yes/no" answers and is able to accurately analyze tape recordings of unstructured conversations.

Key Terms

accusatory	custodial interrogation	*Miranda* warning
admission	duress	nonaccusatory
coerced-compliant confessions	false confession	polygraph
coerced internalization	interrogation	public safety exception
coercion	interview	think-aloud interviewing
cognitive interview	maximization	voice stress analyzer (VSA)
confession	microtremors	

Discussion Questions

1. Discuss the practical differences between the terms *interview* and *interrogation*.

2. Define *coercion* and *duress* and discuss how they taint the interrogation process.

3. Discuss how the *Escobedo* and *Miranda* cases affect the interrogation process.

4. Explain why innocent people may confess to crimes they did not commit.

5. Describe the procedure for recording a suspect's statement.

6. Explain the uses of the polygraph in the interrogation setting.

Notes

1. INBAU, F., J. REID, J. BUCKLEY, AND B. JAYNE. (2001). *Criminal interrogation and confessions*, 4th ed. Gaithersburg, MD: Aspen Publishing.

2. VESSEL, D. (1998). Conducting successful interrogations. *FBI Law Enforcement Bulletin* October; p. 24:1–6.

3. BOETIG, B. P. AND A. BELLMEMER. (2008). Understanding interrogation. *FBI Law Enforcement Bulletin* 77(10).

4. INBAU, REID, BUCKLEY, AND JAYNE. (2001). *Criminal interrogation and confessions*.

5. IBID.

6. BENOIT, C. A. (2010). Confessions and the constitution. *FBI Law Enforcement Bulletin*, April.

7. TOUSIGNANT, D. D. (1991). Why suspects confess. *FBI Law Enforcement Bulletin,* March:14–18.

8. LACAYO, R. (1991). Confessions that were taboo are now just a technicality. *Time*, April 8; LAPETER, L. Torture allegations dog ex-police officer. St. Petersburg *Times*, August 29, 2004; LIPTAK, A. Study suspects thousands of false convictions. *The New York Times*, April 19, 2004.

9. CONTI, R. P. (1999). The psychology of false confessions. *The Journal of Credibility Assessment and Witness Psychology* 2(1):13–26.

10. CHACON, D. J. Verdict brings mixed reaction in Escondido. *Union-Tribunes SignOnSanDiego.com*, May 26, 2004.

11. HUMES, E. Experts say false confessions come from leading questions, young suspects, high-pressure interrogations. *Knight Ridder/Tribune News Service*, October 28, 2004.

12. INBAU, REID, BUCKLEY, AND JAYNE. (2001). *Criminal interrogation and confessions*.

13. WAKEFIELD, H. AND R. UNDERWAGER. (1998). Coerced or nonvoluntary confessions. *Behavioral Sciences and the Law,* Autum:423–440.

14. IBID.

15. NAVARRO, J. AND J. SCHAFER. (2001). Detecting deception. *FBI Law Enforcement Bulletin,* July.

16. BOND, C. F., A. OMAR, A. MAHMOUD, AND R. N. BONSER. (1990). Lie detection across cultures. *Journal of Nonverbal Behavior* 14:189–204. Also see, MATSUMOTO, D., H. S. HWANG, L.

SKINNER, AND M. FRANK. (2011). Evaluating truthfulness and detecting deception. *FBI Law Enforcement Bulletin*, June.

17. DEPAULO, B. M., J. J. LINDSAY, B. E. MALONE, L. MUHLENBRUCK, K. CHARLTON, AND H. COOPER. (2003). Cues to deception. *Psychological Bulletin* 129(1):74–118

18. MATSUMOTO, HWANG, SKINNER, AND FRANK. (2011). Evaluating truthfulness and detecting deception.

19. IBID.

20. IBID.

21. DEPAULO, LINDSAY, MALONE, MUHLENBRUCK, CHARLTON, AND COOPER. Cues to deception.

22. IBID.

23. U.S. DEPARTMENT OF JUSTICE, DRUG ENFORCEMENT ADMINISTRATION. (1988). *Drug enforcement handbook*. Washington, DC: U.S. Government Printing Office.

24. IBID.

25. EVANS, D. D. (1990). 10 ways to sharpen your interviewing skills. *Law and Order* August:90–95.

26. COLEMAN, R. (1984). Interrogation: The process. *FBI Law Enforcement Bulletin,* April:27.

27. INNOCENCE PROJECT WEBSITE. (2009). Available at http://www.innocenceproject.org/understand/False-Confessions.php.

28. IBID.

29. LOFTUS, E. F. AND M. J. GUYER. (2002). Who abused Jane Doe? The hazards of the single case history. *Skeptical Inquirer.* Available at http://www.csicop.org/si/2002-05/jane-doe.html.

30. FORSYTH, B. AND J. T. LESSLER. (1991). Cognitive laboratory methods: A taxonomy. In P. Biemer, R. Groves, L. Lyberg, N. Mathiowetz, and S. Sudman (Eds.), *Measurement errors in surveys*. New York: Wiley.

31. ERICSSON, K. A. AND SIMON, H. A. (1980). Verbal reports as data. *Psychological Review* 87(3):215–251.

32. WILLIS, G. B. (1999). *Cognitive interviewing: A "how to" guide.* Short course presented at the 1999 Meeting of the American Statistical Association: Research Triangle.

33. IBID.

34. IBID.

35. IBID.

36. GELLER, W. A. (1983). Videotaping interrogations and confessions. Washington, DC: Department of Justice, National Institute of Justice. *Research in Brief,* March.

37. KASSIN, S. A. (1997). The psychology of confession evidence. *American Psychologist* 52(3):221–233.

38. LASSITER, G. D. AND A. A. IRVINE. (1986). Videotaped confessions: The impact of camera point-of-view on judgments of coercion. *Journal of Applied Social Psychology* 16:268–276; LASSITER, G. D., R. D. SLAW, M. A. BRIGGS, AND C. R. SCANLAN. (1992). The potential for bias in videotaped confessions. *Journal of Applied Social Psychology* 22:1838–1851.

39. GELLER. (1983). Videotaping interrogations and confessions.

40. ROBINSON, D. T., L. SMITH-LOVIN, AND O. TSOUDIS. (1994). Heinous crime or unfortunate accident? The effects of remorse on responses to mock criminal confessions. *Social Forces* 73:175–190.

41. KASSIN, S. M., M. E. REDDY, AND W. F. TULLOCH. (1990). Juror interpretations of ambiguous evidence: The need for recognition, presentation order and persuasion. *Law and Human Behavior* 14:43–55.

Andy Crawford

This chapter will enable you to:

1. Describe the different types of leads and how they are used.

2. Describe the roles and types of criminal intelligence.

3. Outline the process of intelligence collection.

4. Explain how intelligence information is analyzed and shared.

5. Identify the procedures of intelligence collection.

Criminal Intelligence and Surveillance Operations

Introduction

Information gathering, whether done consciously or unconsciously, is a regular part of a police officer's daily responsibilities.[1] The collection of criminal intelligence is another important function of the criminal investigative process and is one that has resulted in significant identification and arrest of major crime figures. Illustrating the importance of the intelligence function, leading expert in the field of terrorism and counterterrorist tactics Brian Jenkins made an argument regarding the need for developing criminal intelligence when he notes that:

> *[P]hysical measures don't reduce terrorism—they only move the threat along. Society cannot invest enough resources to protect everything, everywhere, all the time. Someone wanting to set off a bomb in Manhattan to kill scores of people can do it. And reducing terrorism has nothing to do with access control or how thick you make the concrete wall. It requires going after the terrorists and taking their groups apart.[2]*

Unfortunately, from a national level, the United States apparently lacks the intelligence capabilities necessary to adequately combat terrorism according to a major interagency study of federal capabilities and defenses. The 73-page report, commissioned by the U.S. Justice Department, pinpoints a lack of intelligence sharing on domestic terrorists as a significant problem and added that "the single most significant deficiency in the nation's ability to combat terrorism is a lack of information, particularly regarding domestic terrorism."[3]

Although the above deals specifically with domestic and international terrorism, the same observations hold true with regard to the prevention and interdiction of many other serious crimes. An effort to identify criminal groups and the persons who participate in and control them requires a systematic approach to information collection and analysis. Intelligence within the law enforcement context, whether of a tactical or strategic nature, refers to the collection, collation, evaluation, analysis, and dissemination for use of information relating to criminal or suspected criminal activities of a wide variety. Development of a systematic approach to this function within police agencies is essential to put what may otherwise be scattered—or even unrecorded—information and data to use in a constructive and concerted manner.

The History of Intelligence Collection

The collection of information for intelligence purposes has a long history. For hundreds of years, governments and their military forces have engaged in various activities to obtain intelligence about individuals and groups viewed as threatening. Although the origins of intelligence gathering by the police in the United States are difficult to determine, it appears that the intelligence function was first carried out by large-city police departments when immigrants first concentrated in urban centers of this country. Nationality groups thought to be threatening by virtue of their suspected involvement in vice, narcotics, racketeering, and organized criminal activities were singled out as the primary targets of police intelligence efforts.

The intelligence operations of federal, state, and local police agencies shifted focus over the decades based on perceived needs and threats. For example, during Prohibition, intelligence operations concentrated on crimes directly and indirectly related to alcohol smuggling and sales and its connections to organized crime. In the post–World War II era, intelligence was used to gather information on suspected Communist organizations, and during the Vietnam War period, it shifted more toward information gathering on political activists and dissidents, civil rights demonstrators, and antiwar protesters. Intelligence operations have long been used to aid in monitoring and building information on organized crime operations and are still widely used in this manner, although their focus has expanded to include the involvement of international conspiracies involved in drug trafficking. Most recently, intelligence operations have been directed at countering the threat of domestic and international terrorism. Considering the bombings of the World Trade Center (2001) and the federal building in Oklahoma City (1995) and the continued threat of terrorist attacks, the need for law enforcement intelligence operations has become even more apparent.

Pitfalls of Intelligence Gathering

Although intelligence plays a key role in law enforcement operations, history tells us that it can also be the instrument of abuse if such operations are not properly organized, focused, and directed. Aggressive intelligence gathering operations that resemble fishing expeditions have been used improperly in the past to garner sensitive or confidential information on individuals for whom there is no reasonable suspicion of criminal activity. After it has been documented, such information can develop a life of its own if sufficient safeguards are not built into screening, reviewing, and managing intelligence files. If passed on to other law enforcement agencies as intelligence, it can form the basis for abuse of civil liberties and potential civil liability.

In the same manner, intelligence operations are misguided if they directly or indirectly gather information on persons based solely on their dissident political activities or views because they espouse positions or philosophies that are perceived to threaten conventional social or political doctrines, traditionally accepted social mores, or similar societal values or institutions. Use of law enforcement intelligence resources to intimidate, inhibit, or suppress such activities under the pretext of legitimate police concern for maintaining social order is at best misguided and, in the worst-case scenario, constitutes a threat to the principles of law enforcement in a democratic society.

The Usefulness of Intelligence

It is important to have an understanding and appreciation of potential abuses of criminal intelligence operations so intelligence gathering can be properly directed and information thus collected properly controlled and managed. That said, it is also important to reemphasize the indispensable role that criminal intelligence plays in support of law enforcement and the ultimate protection of society. Even though the Justice Department report is no doubt accurate in its assessment that this nation's intelligence resources are lacking in many regards, particularly with respect to the new threats of chemical, biological, and nuclear terrorism, it tends to overlook many of their successes.

This is probably nowhere better illustrated than in the efforts of local, state, and federal agencies in thwarting international and domestic terrorism in the United States. This concern came to the forefront after the September 11, 2001, attack on the World Trade Center and the Pentagon. It is worth noting that as devastating as these were, we often miss the fact that many attacks of a similar or even a potentially more devastating nature have been thwarted largely through the development and use of criminal intelligence.

Since the September 11, 2001, terrorist attacks, the United States has been fortunate to avoid subsequent terrorist attacks within its borders. But much of that is attributable to the efforts of enhanced intelligence resources. The vast majority of such incidents against the United States continues to be focused against U.S. targets abroad. The largest percentage of terrorist attacks in this country are bombings by special interest groups perpetrated against commercial establishments located in urban areas, such as the Animal Liberation Front, Up the IRS, and the Earth Night

Action Group. Organizations such as these and right-wing groups such as the Aryan Nation, the Order, and Posse Comitatus are among the more threatening. At the same time, left-wing terrorist groups, such as the Marxist-oriented United Freedom Front, have been generally inactive since the 1980s due in part to a large number of arrests of group leaders during the past decade, largely serving as a credit to good intelligence operations.

Organized crime that has traditionally occupied a great deal of the focus of intelligence operations, while still a prominent threat, has experienced serious setbacks over recent years due largely to effective intelligence gathering operations and aggressive prosecution.

But domestic and international terrorism and organized crime are certainly not the only focus of criminal intelligence operations for state and local law enforcement agencies. State and local law enforcement share in the responsibility to counter these threats. Their input into regional and national intelligence databases is essential to this effort.

But state and local law enforcement agencies also are concerned with more provincial criminal matters. Defining these local criminal enforcement objectives and priorities forms the basis for needed information required to drive the intelligence function of individual agencies. Information gathering by individual officers is at the heart of any intelligence operation. Without the input of the officer on the beat, the generation of intelligence that can be returned to these officers for strategic and tactical purposes is not possible. Support of the agency's intelligence function is, therefore, the responsibility of every law enforcement officer who provides necessary information to fuel the process. And if raw information provides the indispensable material to fuel the intelligence function, a professionally organized system of information evaluation, collation, analysis, and dissemination is the refinement process that turns this raw information into useful products in support of law enforcement operations.

Intelligence, even the best of intelligence, does not produce decisions. Decisions on the use of law enforcement manpower and resources are made by command personnel who use intelligence constructively within the context of their professional experience. But without good intelligence to point the way and weigh the options, law enforcement executives are at a serious disadvantage.

Overt and Covert Intelligence Collection

Overt information collection includes personal interaction with people, many of whom are witnesses to crimes, victims of crimes, or the suspects themselves. To best facilitate the overt collection process, agency administrators should require officers from all divisions to document any information on suspected criminal activity and to pass on such information to intelligence officers. The patrol division can be especially instrumental in the overt intelligence collection process by noting any activity around residences or businesses operated by major criminals in the area. Findings should be reported on a special intelligence report form and forwarded to the proper investigators.

Covert information collection is the most common and includes a process known as **intelligence gathering**. This is a process of data collection on criminal acts that have not yet occurred but for which the investigator must prepare. Covert intelligence collection methods use physical surveillance, electronic surveillance, informants, and undercover officers. In this chapter, we discuss both the intelligence collection functions of criminal investigation and techniques for obtaining information through interviews and interrogation.

Criminal Intelligence versus Criminal Investigation

The process of intelligence gathering originated as a function of the military but has now expanded to include "criminal" intelligence as it applies to domestic law enforcement. Despite its technological and scientific advancements, criminal intelligence gathering is one of the least understood aspects of criminal investigation. Additionally, it is probably one of the most valuable (yet underused) resources of the police function.

Defining Criminal Intelligence

To set the pace for this chapter, we should first attempt to define the term *criminal intelligence*. According to the federally funded RISS (Regional Information Sharing Systems) projects (discussed later in this chapter), criminal intelligence is defined as knowledge of past, present, or future criminal activity that results from the collection of information that, when evaluated, provides the user with a basis for rational decision making.[4] Many law enforcement agencies assign sworn personnel to the criminal intelligence division. However, many departments have difficulty adequately defining the mission of the intelligence unit or the tasks of officers working within it, so officers often conduct multiple duties within the unit. Some of these duties are not relevant to the intelligence collection objective. In a practical sense, because it serves the department by delivering information to line personnel, the role of intelligence personnel is more of a staff than a line function. Officers may therefore experience difficulty adjusting to their staff-related duties.

Technically, the role of intelligence personnel is to deliver information to line personnel. To resolve any confusion about the differences between the criminal intelligence function and the criminal investigation function, the four fundamental differences between the two are discussed below.

1. Criminal investigations are usually reactive in nature. Intelligence gathering, conversely, is a proactive function.
2. Criminal investigators generally work with deductive logic. This works by a logical progression through a sequence of events—the general to the specific. An example is collecting evidence from the crime scene, interviewing any witnesses, checking a suspect's criminal records, and so on.

   Intelligence unit personnel, conversely, exercise inductive logic. This affords them the luxury of beginning with the specific and expanding to the general.
3. Investigation case files are generally considered **open files**. They contain information developed for the purpose of eventually making an arrest and gaining a conviction in a court of law.

   In comparison, intelligence files are **closed files**. They contain information regarding ongoing criminal activity, but much of this information has not been verified as factual.
4. Intelligence files must therefore be maintained apart from criminal investigation files to prevent unauthorized inspection of data. The successful culmination of a criminal investigation is the arrest or conviction of a suspect in a crime. Successful intelligence operations are gauged by the cataloging of an intelligence product.

Types of Intelligence

The distinction between the different types of intelligence is often unclear because various methods are commonly used by different departments. To best understand the most common types of intelligence—strategic and tactical—the following definitions will be considered:

1. **Strategic intelligence** plays a role in the investigation of crimes by providing the investigator with a tool for long-range planning. Simply stated, it provides the investigator with information as to the capabilities and intentions of target subjects. Strategic intelligence has proved most useful in organizing long-range plans for interdiction in areas of criminal activity over extended periods.
2. **Tactical intelligence** targets criminal activity considered to be of immediate importance to the investigator. Specifically, tactical intelligence furnishes the police agency with specifics about individuals, organizations, and different types of criminal activity.

It is important to note that many police organizations have established criminal intelligence units that work with criminal investigators. These units are excellent resources of information for investigators who are following leads such as the identification of suspects, suspect associates, where suspects bank or hang out, what vehicles they drive, and other relevant information. On the national level, for example, the FBI is the lead agency for preventing and investigating intelligence activities on U.S. soil. In fact, it is the second highest priority for the FBI because foreign espionage poses a threat to the nation's national security.[5]

The FBI's counterintelligence investigations have resulted in numerous arrests of suspects on American soil who have, in one way or another, compromised the safety and security of the nation. An example is the case of FBI Special Agent Robert Hanssen.

|Fig. 7.1| △

Intelligence report.

CITY POLICE DEPARTMENT	File:
INTELLIGENCE REPORT	Date:

SUBJECT: (Name and any identifying numbers)

SOURCE IDENTIFICATION:
Private Citizen ☐   (Name or Number) _____
Criminal Source ☐
Govt. Agency ☐   Personal Knowledge☐ Documents☐ Hearsay/Rumor☐ Hypothesis☐
Law Officer ☐   Other _____

EVALUATION OF SOURCE:
Highly Reliable ☐   Usually Reliable ☐   Reliability Questionable ☐   Unevaluated ☐

BY:

INFORMATION CONTENT: INFORMATION FILES CHECKED:
Partially Verified ☐   State Criminal Record ☐   Similar Info.
Unverified ☐   State Driver's License ☐   In File No. _____
Verified ☐   NCIC ☐
Other _____

RECOMMENDED FOLLOW-UP:
Investigator to Verify ☐   Source to Verify ☐   Analyst to Research ☐   File Only ☐

DISSEMINATION:

Hanssen was 56-year-old at the time of his arrest at a park in Vienna, Virginia, in February 2001. At the time, he was secretly placing a package containing classified information at a prearranged, or "dead drop," site for pickup by his Russian handlers. On an estimated 20 occasions, Hanssen had received substantial sums of money from the Russians after clandestinely leaving packages for the KGB and its successor agency, the SVR, at dead drop sites in the Washington, DC, area. He also provided more than two dozen computer diskettes containing additional disclosures of information. Overall, Hanssen gave the KGB and SVR more than 6,000 pages of valuable documentary material. During the time of his illegal activities, Hanssen was assigned to New York and Washington, DC, where he held key counterintelligence positions. As a result of his assignments, Hanssen had direct and legitimate access to voluminous information about sensitive programs and operations. Hanssen used his training, expertise, and experience as a counterintelligence agent to avoid detection to include keeping his identity and place of employment from his Russian handlers and avoiding all the customary "tradecraft" and travel usually associated with espionage. The turning point in this investigation came when the FBI was able to secure original Russian documentation of an American spy who appeared to the FBI to be Hanssen, which the investigation into his activities later confirmed.[6]

Procedures for Intelligence Gathering

The intelligence collection process should be thought of as a process of connecting a series of inter-related components of information. Failure on the part of the investigator to adequately connect any of these components could jeopardize the success of the investigation. Therefore, everyone associated with the collection process must have a keen understanding of the entire intelligence function and its various components. The intelligence function includes target selection, data collection, data collation and analysis, and dissemination.

Phase 1: Target Selection

Target selection is the first phase of the process. To obtain the greatest success, intelligence targets must be selected in a systematic manner. They may be based entirely on the utility, or size, of the target or available resources of the department. Factors for investigators to consider in selection of a suitable target include the following:

- Does this target conform to the unit's goals and objectives?
- Does the department (unit) have sufficient resources for the operation?
- What is the expected value of the target?

|Fig. 7.2| ▲

Intelligence target selection.

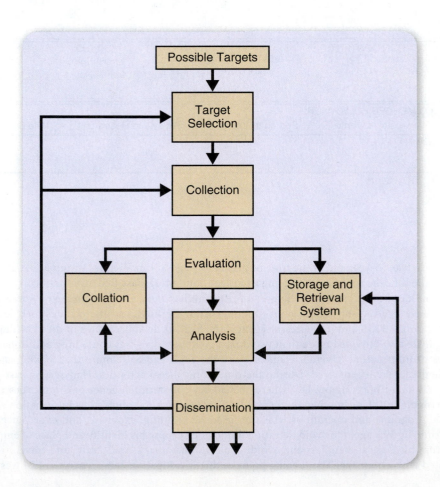

Additional factors to consider in selection of suitable intelligence targets include:

1. *Utility.* This is the worth of the successful result. If the desired information is collected, how valuable is the result? In determining target utility, consider the following:

    - Type of criminal activity
    - Amount and frequency of criminal activity
    - Impact of criminal activity

2. *Probability of success.* What are the chances of success with this target? In determining probability of success, consider:

    - Amount of effort to be expended
    - Experience and expertise of the intelligence unit personnel
    - Past success rate in similar operations
    - Availability of sources of information

3. *Required resources.* What resources are required to collect the desired information? When determining resources, consider the following:

    - Personnel hours—the primary required resource
    - Equipment
    - Confidential funds
    - Travel expenses
    - Amount of time required

4. *Objective.* The primary objective of selecting a target is to guarantee that intelligence efforts are focused toward targets that are an acceptable balance to merit or value, probability of a successful result, and resources used.

Phase 2: Data Collection

Collection of criminal information is the hallmark of the intelligence function and may be done overtly, covertly, or as a combination of both. Written policy should dictate exactly what types of information may or may not be gathered. Because the collection of both personal and sensitive information on individuals could be a high-liability issue for some communities, great care is warranted by the police agency. Generally, intelligence information regarding any suspected criminal activity can be gathered, such as the following:

- Drug trafficking
- Extortion
- Pornography
- Fraud
- Bribery
- Robbery
- Murder
- Gambling
- Prostitution
- Labor racketeering
- Fencing
- Burglary
- Forgery

In addition:

- Organizations that advocate the use of violence or other unlawful means to affect any unit of government
- Organizations that possess or attempt to control shipments of arms, explosives, or controlled chemicals or biological weapons for unlawful purposes
- Organizations that finance violent or unlawful activity
- Organizations whose actions constitute unlawful activity targeted toward other organizations or individuals
- Leaders of organizations such as those above

Information should not be gathered merely because of a person's membership in organizations unless such organizations meet the criteria set forth previously and are found to present a clear and present danger to society. Under no circumstances should information be gathered solely on the basis of race, creed, color, national origin, sexual preference, or political or religious beliefs. After the information is obtained, intelligence units are faced with the problem of maintaining a storage and retrieval system so that the information can become available when needed. Generally, this is done with a computer, but many departments prefer to rely on index cards as a simplified and more secure system. Information to be cataloged may originate from many different sources:

1. Information from investigators assigned to the intelligence unit
2. Information from nonintelligence departments of the agency, for example:

- Offense reports
- Arrest records
- Field interrogation reports
- Identification photographs

- Fingerprint files
- Warrant files
- Traffic records

3. Information from other federal, state, and local jurisdictions
4. Information from sources other than law enforcement organizations, for example:

- Newspapers
- Trial records
- Telephone companies
- Public utilities

- Credit agencies
- Banks
- Professional associations
- Insurance companies

Phase 3: Data Collation and Analysis

The third phase in the procedure is the information collation process. *Webster's Dictionary* defines **collation** as "the process of comparing texts carefully" to clarify or give meaning to information. One example of collation is taking a deck of playing cards and arranging them into four piles, one pile for each suit, and in numerical order. Many different techniques are used by intelligence analysts to accomplish this function. These include linked data charts, different types of flowcharts, frequency distribution charts, and so on. Many of these are discussed later in the chapter. Following the collation of raw information is the analysis chase. This is the heart of any intelligence system, the procedure in which meaning is given to all of the otherwise-fragmented parts of data collected. The analytical process involves data integration and clarification, inference development, inference testing, and finalizing inferences that are relevant and meaningful to the user (the intelligence product).

Phase 4: Dissemination

The **dissemination** stage of the intelligence process is the final stage, in which the process most commonly breaks down. As one intelligence analyst once remarked, "Possessing good intelligence information is like possessing gold nuggets because everybody wants as much as they can get but nobody wants to share what they have." Unless intelligence is shared through the law enforcement community in an interagency fashion, all of the effort and expense of collecting it could become meaningless. Most law enforcement agencies have strict guidelines, however, as to the release of information (e.g., who gets what information).

Analyzing the Information

The purpose of **analysis** is to make fragmented information flow in a logical sequence to make it purposeful to the user, such as taking a group of surveillance reports and arranging them in the order in which they occurred to determine primary suspects, locations most frequented, vehicles driven, and so on. Intelligence gathering can be problematic in and of itself. For example, when officers are working with large amounts of information regarding individuals and organizations, the sources of that information may be varied and unorganized and may include confidential informants, surveillance reports, police reports, and investigative reports.

Link Analysis

To make sense out of the multitudes of information, a process known as *data description and integration* is used. Accordingly, one of the most common methods of data description and

CAREERS | DEA Intelligence Research Specialist Job Description

As a DEA Intelligence Research Specialist, you will have the opportunity to be a part of the nation's leading drug law enforcement agency. You will be recognized worldwide for your skills, commitment, and achievements in working closely with DEA Special Agents to conduct the most significant drug investigations and counter-drug operations within the United States and abroad. Need an exciting place to live? Our Intelligence Research Specialists positions are located in most major U.S. cities, other domestic areas, and foreign countries that need DEA's support in combating drug trafficking, violent crime, and terrorism. Come and use your intelligence skills at DEA to contribute to our nation's war on drugs and terrorism.

Qualifications:

DEA's Intelligence Division seeks candidates who have experience that demonstrates the ability to:

■ Analyze information, identify significant factors, gather pertinent data, and develop solutions;

■ Plan and organize work; and

■ Communicate effectively orally and in writing.

Such experience may have been gained in administrative, professional, or technical positions.

Employment requirements:

Intelligence Research Specialists are subject to reassignment to any location in the United States depending on the needs of the DEA. All applicants must be available for relocation throughout their career with DEA and will be required to sign a statement to this effect when accepting an offer of employment.

Newly hired Intelligence Research Specialists must complete the Basic Intelligence Research Specialist Training Course. All applicants interested in applying for jobs at DEA must also be able to meet all DEA Employment Requirements and comply with DEA's Drug policy.

All applicants must meet the certain conditions of employment to be eligible for employment at DEA. These conditions include:

■ U.S. Citizenship

■ Successfully pass a DEA-administered drug test for illegal drugs

■ Complete a DEA Drug Questionnaire to show compliance with the DEA Drug Policy (see DEA Drug policy for more information)

■ Successfully pass a background investigation

■ Register with the Selective Service System, if male and born after December 31, 1959

You will not be eligible for employment at DEA if you do not meet these requirements. All of theses requirements are thoroughly reviewed during the entire employment process. Please make sure you can meet all of these requirements before applying for a position with DEA.

Background Investigations

DEA, in its unique capacity as the world's eminent drug law enforcement agency, identifies, investigates, and targets for prosecution, organizations and individuals responsible for the production and distribution of illegal drugs. In many cases, our work is sensitive in nature. Therefore, all employees are required to go through an extensive background investigation. Once you have received and accepted a conditional offer of employment, DEA will initiate a background investigation. This investigation includes a credit and criminal records check; interviews of you, co-workers, employers, personal friends, educators, neighbors; and for some occupations a polygraph examination. Additionally, there are certain employment requirements employees must meet to be eligible for employment at DEA. Please use the following links to see if you meet the employment conditions.

DEA Drug Policy

Drug testing is required and continues throughout a career at DEA. Applicants who are found, through investigation or personal admission, to have experimented with or used narcotics or dangerous drugs, except those medically prescribed, will not be considered for employment with DEA. Exceptions to this policy may be made for applicants who admit to limited youthful and experimental use of marijuana. Such applicants may be considered for employment if there is no evidence of regular, confirmed usage and the full background investigation and results of the other steps in the process are otherwise favorable. Compliance with this policy is an essential requirement of all DEA positions.

Source: Drug Enforcement Administration. 2009. Available at http://www.justice.gov/dea/resources/careers/opportunity/intel-research-spec.html

---

integration is link analysis. **Link analysis** charting is a technique designed to show relationships between individuals and organizations using a graphical visual design. It is used to show graphically transactions or relationships that are too large and confusing for one to assimilate through the reading of reports. Typically, decisions made using this method are accomplished through deductive reasoning.

There are several ways to illustrate this type of collation technique suitably. In all cases, the investigator must follow certain mechanical rules for the structure of the diagram. These include:

- Assembly of raw data (usually from a report)
- Selection of certain data points, such as names of individuals or organizations
- Construction of a collation matrix showing the data points
- Entry of the association points on the matrix
- Tabulation of the number of association points on the matrix
- Designation of the types of relationships by drawing different types of lines from one association point to another (usually accomplished by drawing dotted lines, solid lines, and so on)
- Relationship of individuals to organizations by constructing circles for individuals and boxes for businesses
- Examination of final diagram and recommendation(s) regarding a course of action

To illustrate the process of link analysis, consider the following scenario as if it were information from a surveillance report. The objective should be to determine the most appropriate target. Johnson and Taylor are long-time close associates and were cell mates in the Missouri State Prison in 1996. Every Tuesday during the month of October, Johnson met with Stephens at the Playboy Lounge for lunch. Public records reveal that Johnson is the sole owner of Equity Auto Sales. Taylor and Mullen are both employed at Tiger Beverage Company and have been observed on numerous occasions riding to work together.

On November 3, Johnson met Washington in the South Park Shopping Center parking lot at 3:00 P.M., and both sat in Washington's car for approximately 1.5 hours. After Johnson left, Washington drove to Anderson's residence. There, Anderson entered Washington's vehicle, and they drove away. The surveillance team lost them approximately two miles from Anderson's residence, due to heavy traffic. Two hours later, Washington and Anderson returned to Anderson's residence, and both went inside. On three separate occasions, Taylor has been seen with an unidentified man believed to be Stephens. "Pen register" records from Mullen's telephone reveal that several calls were made each day to Equity Auto Sales. The relationships in which each of the suspects is involved may reveal who is the most appropriate

|Fig. 7.3| ▲

Hypothetical link analysis chart.

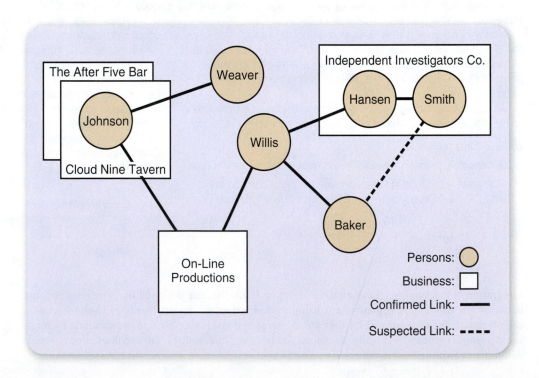

The Role of the Intelligence Analyst

- ☑ To guide data collection
- ☑ To suggest operational recommendations
- ☑ To provide information to decision makers
- ☑ To assume a position of noninvolvement in policy formation

---

target. One can see how the method of link analysis can aid in an understanding of complex raw criminal information.

Flowcharting

Flowcharting is another common technique used in the data description and integration phase. Unlike the "frozen" nature of the link analysis diagram, the flowchart demonstrates a chain of events or activities over a period. Although use of flowcharts is not as common as link analysis, two types of flowcharts have emerged as the most useful in criminal intelligence collection: *event flow analysis* and *commodity flow analysis*. Both types of analysis give investigators a graphic display of a series of events that might be too complex if read in a report. There are no hard-and-fast rules regarding the construction of flowcharts; therefore, the analyst should try to maintain a degree of consistency throughout the chart regarding the symbols used.

EVENT FLOW ANALYSIS Event flow analysis is usually conducted early in an investigation. Examples of flow analysis include charting a brief description of an event enclosed in a symbolic area such as a circle or rectangle. As different events are documented, they are connected by arrows to indicate the direction of the sequence. Consider the following scenario and observe how the information from a reliable informant can best be portrayed by using the event flowchart.

Kevin Johnson is a local businessman in town and owns three small businesses. On August 12, Johnson's Deli burned to the ground, and another of his stores, the Barbecue Shack, was vandalized. Later that night, Johnson's convenience store was bombed. Although Johnson couldn't say for sure who the perpetrator might be, he noted that he had recently fired a 34-year-old part-time

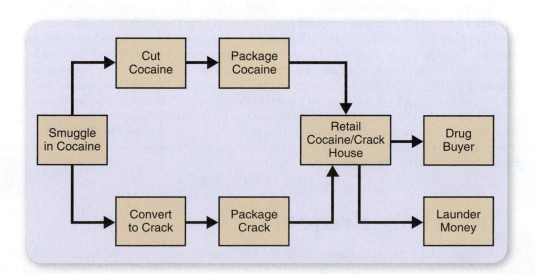

|Fig. 7.4| △

Hypothetical event flow analysis chart.

|Fig. 7.5| △

Hypothetical commodity flowchart.

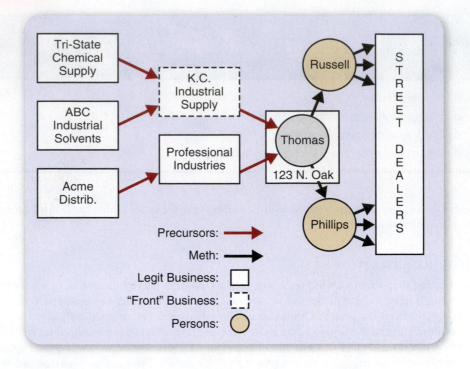

employee who had threatened Johnson as he left the property. This firing took place one week before the problems with the stores.

COMMODITY FLOW ANALYSIS Commodity flow analysis may greatly simplify the investigative process by charting the logical flow of such commodities as drugs, money, and illegal arms shipments. For example, in a drug distribution network, if money can be traced from its origin to certain key individuals, an investigation will probably result in an arrest and conviction. This is particularly useful when the main drug kingpins don't typically possess the drugs themselves.

The structure of a commodity flowchart is generally the same as that of the event flowchart except that rather than descriptions of events being placed in circles or rectangles, persons or businesses are used. A scenario follows in which commodity flowcharting might best be used. Study this information from an investigation report and observe how the resulting flowchart illustrates and clarifies the facts and circumstances of the case.

Eddie Jaso purchased cocaine weekly from Sharon Martin. Jaso paid Martin about $20,000 per week on average. Undercover narcotics agents observed Jaso, along with Mario Barbisca and Timothy Freisen, selling cocaine to several known drug users at a local mall video arcade on several occasions over a period of one month. Records seized during a search of room 32 of the Bradford Hotel showed this location to be a trafficking site for drugs. The hotel's catering department served as a cover for the cocaine distribution network. Seized records also showed payments of about $40,000 per week each from Barbisca and Freisen to the catering department. Records revealed a monthly average of $300,000 in payments to Leonard Smith for various "supplies." Smith, a close associate of Freisen for the past two years, makes monthly deposits of about $500,000 to his accounts at Central Savings and Loan. He also makes large withdrawals on occasion. Both Smith and Freisen have records for drug trafficking.

The RISS Projects

The RISS program began with funding from the Law Enforcement Assistance Administration (LEAA) discretionary grant program. Since 1980, **RISS projects** have been placed under the Justice Department and have been funded on a yearly basis by the U.S. Congress.

RISS is a nationwide program consisting of six regional centers and a technology support center that provide flexible and locally based services to local, state, federal, and tribal law enforcement and criminal justice agencies in all 50 states, the District of Columbia, U.S. territories, Australia, Canada, England, and New Zealand. RISS links thousands of criminal justice agencies through secure communications and provides information sharing resources and investigative support to combat multijurisdictional crimes, including violent crime, gang activity, terrorism, drug activity, cybercrime, human trafficking, identity theft, and other regional priorities. RISS enhances the ability of criminal justice agencies to identify and target criminal conspiracies and activities.

In addition to offering access to intelligence databases and connecting disparate systems, RISS provides essential investigative services, including information sharing, analytical support, investigative support and research, equipment loans, confidential funds, training and publications, field staff support, and technical assistance. RISS provides officer safety through RISSafe program and extensive gang resources through its RISSGang program.[7] In many cases, these are services and resources that agencies would not otherwise receive.

Specifically, the services offered member law enforcement agencies are:

- A centralized database
- Analysis of intelligence and investigative data
- Specialized equipment on loan
- Confidential funds
- Technical assistance
- Specialized training
- Access to telecommunications systems

Regional Information Sharing Systems (RISS) Programs			
	Established	**Executive Director**	**States**
WSIN (Western States Information Network)	1980	Karen L. Aumond	Alaska, California, Hawaii, Oregon, Washington
RMIN (Rocky Mountain Information Network)	1977	John E. Vinson	Arizone, Colorado, Idaho, Montana, Nevada, New Mexico, Utah, Wyoming
MOCIC (Mid-State Organized Crime Information Center)	1980	Michael W. Snavely	Illinois, Iow, Kansas, Minnesota, Missouri, Nebraska, North Dakota, South Dakota, Wisconsin
ROCIC (Regional Organized Crime Information Center)	1973	Donna K. Williams	Alabama, Arkansas, Florida, Georgia, Kentucky, Louisiana, Mississippi, North Carolina, Oklahoma, South Carolina, Tennessee, Texas, Virginia, West Virginia
MAGLOCLEN (Middle Atlantic-Great Lakes Crime Law Enforcement Network)	1981	Patricia A. Borrelli	Delaware, District of Columbia, Indiana, Maryland, Michigan, New Jersey, New York, Ohio, Pennsylvania
NESPIN (New England State Police Information Network)	1979	Donald F. Kennedy	Connecticut, Maine, Massachusetts, New Hampshire, Rhode Island, Vermont

|Fig. 7.6| △

RISS Projects organizational map showing division of regions in the United States.

All states throughout the country are placed in one of the six RISS regions:

1. *Western States Information Network:* Alaska, California, Hawaii, Oregon, Washington
2. *Rocky Mountain Information Network:* Arizona, Colorado, Idaho, Montana, Nevada, New Mexico, Utah, Wyoming
3. *Mid-State Organized Crime Information Center:* Illinois, Iowa, Kansas, Minnesota, Missouri, Nebraska, North Dakota, South Dakota, Wisconsin
4. *Regional Organized Crime Information Center:* Alabama, Arkansas, Florida, Georgia, Kentucky, Louisiana, Mississippi, North Carolina, Oklahoma, South Carolina, Tennessee, Texas, Virginia, West Virginia
5. *Middle Atlantic-Great Lakes Organized Crime Law Enforcement Network:* Delaware, District of Columbia, Indiana, Maryland, Michigan, New Jersey, New York, Ohio, Pennsylvania
6. *New England State Police Information Network:* Connecticut, Maine, Massachusetts, New Hampshire, Rhode Island, Vermont

The goal of the RISS projects is to aid state and local law enforcement agencies in the organizing and sharing of criminal intelligence. The very existence of the massive project illustrates the importance of criminal intelligence information in the field of criminal investigation.

|Fig. 7.7| △

Photo of a crack cocaine transaction taken via stationary surveillance one-half block away.

Michael D. Lyman

Auditing and Purging Files

Intelligence files that are no longer accurate, or are not relevant to the mission of the unit, do not pertain to investigative interests and activities, or contain insufficient supporting documentation are among those that should be purged. When files are deficient in one or more of these areas, consideration may be given to updating or improving them through validation and other means. However, when the basic information contained in these files is of such an age or of such poor quality as to make investigative efforts either too costly or unproductive, a decision should be made to purge the file. A record of any purged files should be maintained by the department.

Use of a qualified outside auditor is typically the best approach to purging intelligence files. This is because independent third parties remove much of the bias or the appearance of bias that may be evident when using in-house intelligence personnel. Although a yearly review of the files for purposes of purging useless materials is recommended, this does not preclude the destruction of files on an ad hoc basis when appropriate and with the approval of the intelligence or investigative unit.

Surveillance and Tracking Operations

On September 6, 2006, 14-year-old Elizabeth Shoaf exited her school bus and was approached by Vinson Filyaw—a 37-year-old construction worker. Filyaw quickly gained Elizabeth's trust by posing as a police officer. He walked Elizabeth around in the woods until she became disoriented and then directed her to a hand-dug 15-foot bunker near his trailer home. The bunker was located within a mile of her home. There he stripped her naked, restrained her with chains, and raped her several times a day. Police initially interpreted her disappearance as a runaway and did not launch an Amber Alert.

In spite of her traumatic experience, Elizabeth did a number of things that ultimately improved her chances of survival. For example, while being led into the woods, she dropped her shoes in the hope that it would provide a clue for someone who was searching for her. In spite of receiving repeated death threats and having explosives hung around her neck, Elizabeth would talk with Filyaw about things that interested him—which made her more of a person, not just a captive. She used this technique to gain his trust. Once this was accomplished, she was permitted to leave the bunker, and would pull out strands of her hair and place them on branches hoping search dogs might pick up her scent.

After 10 days in captivity, Elizabeth convinced Filyaw to let her borrow his cellular phone to play games, but she had an altogether different intent. Once he fell asleep, she text-messaged her mother and friends. They then contacted the police.

Investigators then began to "triangulate" the bunker's position through the cell phone towers accessed by Filyaw's cellular phone. Filyaw saw that he was under pursuit by watching the news on a battery-powered television in the bunker. He asked Elizabeth for advice, and she told him to run away. He did so, allowing her to leave the bunker and yell for help until a rescue team soon found her.

The kidnapping and sexual assault of Elizabeth Shoaf is instructive from an investigative perspective in that it illustrates the usefulness of twenty-first century technology and how it can assist investigators in locating persons, objects, and places. Not only has technology assisted in rescue operations, such as Elizabeth's rescue, but it is also useful in tracking victims and locating criminals.

This chapter section will focus on not only the use of technology in surveillance and tracking operations but will also discuss the time-tested techniques of physical surveillance as it relates to foot, vehicle, and stationary methods to watch the activities of persons involved in criminal conduct.

Satellite-Assisted Surveillance

In April 2011, an incident involving 21-year-old Richard Anderson and 32-year-old Holli Wrice took place on November 6, 2008, at the Capaha Bank of Tamms, Illinois. Anderson and Wrice entered the Capaha Bank of Tamms, Illinois, each armed with handguns, which they pointed at the tellers and customers. Wrice told the teller, "Give me the money [expletive]," while pointing the gun at the teller, and then handed her a note which stated, "This is a robbery, I have a gun, don't cause a scene, and no one will get hurt. I do have a Gun!!"

Bank video cameras recorded the robbery and showed that Wrice picked up the note shown to the teller and attempted to put it into the bag with the money taken from the bank, but the note fell out as the bag was pulled away from the teller window. Photos taken from the bank surveillance cameras were broadcast to the public on local television stations the same night as the bank robbery and ultimately led to witnesses coming forward to identify Anderson. Those identifications were corroborated when Anderson's fingerprints matched with those found on the demand note. Wrice's fingerprints were also found on the note. Through analysis of surveillance videos, detectives from the Jackson County Sheriff's office were able to positively identify the types of weapons and the make of the getaway vehicle used by the robbers. The Illinois State Police then located the vehicle and through subsequent investigation the FBI was able to track the path used by the robbers both to and from the robbery through cell phone GPS information.[8]

The use of **Global Positioning System (GPS)** in the Wrice bank robbery reflects how police across the nation are turning to such devices for surveillance, eavesdropping, and other tasks that traditionally have been performed by uniformed officers and detectives.[9] Recent improvements in cell phone technology and in the quality of satellite signals allow investigators to track and record a vehicle's movements in real time and display the information on a map displayed on a laptop computer.

The Global Positioning System was originally developed for the military and relies on satellites that transmit to receivers that calculate the latitude and longitude of a location. A GPS device installed by police can be used to follow a person 24 hours a day. Data can be analyzed more efficiently and economically than if a surveillance team followed a suspect.[10] A typical GPS tracking device is about the size of a small paperback book and can be affixed to a car's undercarriage with a magnet. The cost for such a device is minimal, at about $1,000.

The simplest form of installation consists of a GPS receiver, an antenna, power supply, and a logging device that records where the vehicle has moved. Depending on the equipment, officers can remotely obtain data electronically or by physically retrieving the logging device from the vehicle. The apparatus could be in single or multiple units. Live-tracking applications will require all of these items plus a transmitter and its separate antenna.[11]

Wiretaps and property searches ordinarily must be authorized by a state or federal judge, who determines whether such tactics are needed to investigate a crime. The surveillance on public roads ordinarily does not require such court orders. Because GPS devices are a substitute for ordinary visual surveillance, for years many police departments believed they can be used without a court order. This changed, however, in January 2012 with the U.S. Supreme Court ruling in *United States* v. *Jones*. In the *Jones* case, the Supreme Court reversed the 2005 cocaine trafficking conviction of Antoine Jones. In that case, a joint FBI/DC police team attached a GPS device to a Jeep owned by Jones, the co-owner of Washington, DC, nightclub, *Levels*, while it was parked in a public parking lot.

A warrant had been granted, but a judge authorized the installation of the GPS device only within 10 days and only in the District of Columbia. Investigators waited until the 11th day to secretly place it on the vehicle, and they did so in neighboring Maryland. Jones was then monitored for 28 days as he drove around the area. He was eventually tracked to a house where law enforcement officers discovered nearly 100 kilograms of the illegal narcotic, along with about $850,000 in cash. Jones was sentenced to life in prison.[12] In its decision, the Court held that a warrant should be obtained for prolonged surveillance through smart phones or other devices with GPS capabilities.

As of the preparation of this text, there are no records of how often GPS is being used nationally in criminal investigations. However, an examination of recent criminal investigations has revealed that its use is somewhat common. For example:

1. In May 2004, a Honolulu police unit that locates stolen automobiles parked a car with a GPS tracker in a high-crime area. The "bait" car was stolen and located quickly. Police arrested the driver.
2. In 2002, criminal investigators in Nassau County, New York, used two GPS devices to track a car driven by burglary suspect Richard Lacey. Prosecutors used GPS records to show that the car was in the vicinity of several homes at the time they were burglarized.
3. In 2000, the FBI in Las Vegas used two GPS devices that had been built into a car to eavesdrop on the targets of an investigation into organized crime. The device, offered as a safety accessory by some car makers, allows lost or endangered drivers to be located quickly if they are calling for help.
4. In 1999, in Spokane, Washington, GPS devices on the Ford pickup and the Honda Accord driven by murder suspect William Bradley Jackson led police to the grave of his missing nine-year-old daughter, Valiree. The GPS data indicated that Jackson made two trips to the site in the three weeks after he reported the girl missing. He was convicted of murder and sentenced to 56 years in prison.

A Closer Look

How Tracking Technology Works

Tracking technology or "location tracking" is not one single technology; rather, it's the merging of several technologies that can be combined to create systems that track inventory, livestock, or vehicle fleets. In criminal investigation, it is typically used to track the movements of a suspect's vehicle or contraband. Similar systems can be created to deliver location-based services to wireless devices. Current technologies being used to create location-tracking and location-based systems include:

Geographic Information Systems (GIS)—For large-scale location-tracking systems, it is necessary to capture and store geographic information. Geographic Information Systems can capture, store, analyze, and report geographic information.

Global Positioning System—A constellation of 27 Earth-orbiting satellites (24 in operation and three extras in case one fails). A GPS receiver, like the one in almost every mobile phone, can locate four or more of these satellites, compute the distance to each, and determine a subject's location through "trilateration." For trilateration to work, it must have a clear line of sight to these four or more satellites. GPS is ideal for outdoor positioning, such as moving surveillance, transportation, or military use (for which it was originally designed).

Radio Frequency Identification (RFID)—Small, battery-less microchips that can be attached to consumer goods—vehicles, money (such as bait money used in bank robberies), laboratory hardware or chemical precursors (such as those being purchased for illicit drug labs), and other objects to track their movements. RFID tags are passive and only transmit data if prompted by a reader. The reader transmits radio waves that activate the RFID tag. The tag then transmits information via a predetermined radio frequency. This information is captured and transmitted to a central database. Among possible uses for RFID tags are a replacement for traditional UPC bar codes.

Wireless Local Area Network (WLAN)—Network of devices that connect via radio frequency, such as 802.11b. WLAN devices pass data over radio waves and provide users with a network with a range of 70 to 300 feet.

Any location-tracking or location-based service system will use one or a combination of these technologies. The system requires that a tag be placed on the object, vehicle, or even person being tracked. For example, the GPS receiver in a cell phone or an RFID tag on a DVD can be used to track those devices with a detection system such as GPS satellites or RFID receivers.

Sources: Clark, M. (2006). Cell phone technology and physical surveillance. *FBI Law Enforcement Bulletin*, May:25–32; Roberts, M. (2005). GPS tracks journey. *Security Management* 49 (February):22–24; Harne, J. and F. Scott. (2009). NIJ testing new technologies. *Corrections Today* 71(4):88–89.

Tracking Vehicles with Satellites

To track a vehicle using a global positioning system (GPS), a device about the size of a paperback book is attached to the vehicle. The device reads signals from a network of 24 satellites and calculates its location based on its distance from each satellite.

The device can be attached under a car with a magnet.

GPS Device

|Fig. 7.9| △

To track a vehicle, a small electronic GPS device is placed on the suspect vehicle and then tracked using any of the available satellites.

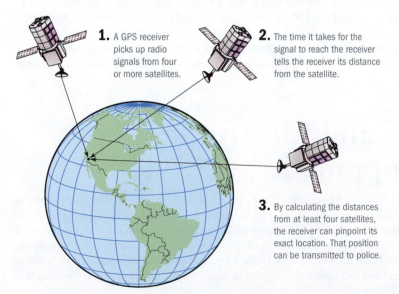

1. A GPS receiver picks up radio signals from four or more satellites.

2. The time it takes for the signal to reach the receiver tells the receiver its distance from the satellite.

3. By calculating the distances from at least four satellites, the receiver can pinpoint its exact location. That position can be transmitted to police.

Tracking Cellular Phones

As we saw in the case of Elizabeth Shoaf, cell phone tracking can be used by law enforcement to locate the current position of a cell phone. To do so, an active call is not required to track the current position of the cell phone, but the cell phone must be turned on for the tracking to be successful.

Many cellular phones incorporate GSM (Global System for Mobile Communications) technology. GSM localization uses "**multilateration**" to establish the position of GSM cell phones, generally with the objective to trace the user. GSM localization is then done by triangulation to locate the user/cell phone, on the basis of the strength of the signals. "**Triangulation**" is the process of finding one's position on a given plane when two visual landmarks are known.[13] While routing a call to the cell phone, the cell towers analyze the signals sent from the phone and then decide which tower is best placed to carry out the communication with the phone. The cell towers monitor these signals, and the location of the cell phone can be determined by comparing the strength of these signals.[14]

Localization-Based Systems can be generally grouped into three categories: Network based, Handset based, and Hybrid.

Network-based models make use of the service provider's network to recognize the position of the cell phone. One of the key challenges of network-based techniques is the requirement to work closely with the service provider, as it entails the installation of hardware and software within the operator's infrastructure. Often, applicable laws need to be in place to force the co-operation of the service provider as well as to safeguard the privacy of the information.

Handset-based identification model needs the installation of client software program on the cell phone to identify its position.

Hybrid-based model uses a mixture of network-based and handset-based models for position identification.

Today, however, new cell phones are equipped with GPS. GPS tracking is done to determine the location of the cell phone. This technique gives accurate results and has assisted investigators in countless investigations.

Global Positioning Tracking uses the concept of triangulation to calculate the location of the cell phone. Satellites and the cell phone are used as the landmarks for this purpose. A GPS tracking system can be used to give both real-time and historical navigation data as it uses the **Global Navigation Satellite System (GNSS)** network.[15]

The GNSS network utilizes a range of satellites that use microwave signals, and these signals are then analyzed to determine the location of the cell phone. A GPS device receives signals from the GPS satellites, and if it can receive strong signals from three or more satellites, then the location is calculated accurately. However, if the signals are weak, it could be difficult to accurately locate the cell phone. An important aspect of GPS tracking is that a GPS device cannot send signals; it can only receive them. So, satellites and the GPS system within the cell phone are two basic necessities for successful GPS tracking.[16]

Of course, locating cell phones are criticized by individual rights advocates because the process enables law enforcement (and individuals, in some cases) to check a person's position without the person's permission.

Wiretaps and Electronic Eavesdropping

With the growing use of high technology to investigate crime and uncover violations of criminal law, courts throughout the nation are evaluating the applicability of constitutional guarantees with regard to high-tech surveillance. Recent technology makes possible increasingly complex forms of communication. One of the first Supreme Court decisions involving electronic communications was the 1928 case of *Olmstead* v. *United States*. In the *Olmstead* case, bootleggers used their home telephones to discuss and transact business.[17] Agents tapped the lines and based their investigation and ensuing arrests on conversations they overheard. The defendants were convicted and eventually appealed to the high court, arguing that the agents had, in effect, seized information illegally without a search warrant in violation of the defendant's Fourth Amendment right to be secure in their homes. The Court ruled, however, that telephone lines are not an extension of the defendant's home and therefore are not protected by the constitutional guarantee of security. However, subsequent federal statutes have substantially modified the significance of the *Olmstead* decision.

Recording devices carried on the body of an undercover agent or informant were ruled to produce admissible evidence in *On Lee* v. *U.S.* (1952) and *Lopez* v. *U.S.* (1963).[18] The 1967 case of *Berger* v. *New York* permitted wiretaps and "bugs" in instances in which state law provided for the use of such devices and officers had obtained a warrant based on probable cause.[19]

The Court appeared to undertake a significant change of direction in the area of electronic eavesdropping when it decided the case of *Katz* v. *U.S.* (1967). Federal agents had monitored a number of Katz's telephone calls from a public phone using a device separate from the phone lines and attached to the glass of a phone booth. The Court, in this case, stated that a warrant is required to unveil what a person makes an effort to keep private, even in a public place. In the words of the Court, "the government's activities in electronically listening to and recording the petitioner's words violated the privacy upon which he justifiably relied while using a telephone booth and thus constituted a search and seizure within the meaning of the Fourth Amendment."

In *Lee* v. *Florida* (1968), the Court applied the Federal Communications Act to telephone conversations that might be the object of police investigation and held that evidence obtained without a warrant could not be used in state proceedings if it resulted from a wiretap.[20] The only person who has the authority to permit eavesdropping, according to that act, is the sender of the message.

The Federal Communications Act, originally passed in 1934, does not specifically mention the potential interest of law enforcement agencies in monitoring communications. Title III of the Omnibus Crime Control and Safe Streets Act of 1968, however, mostly prohibits wiretaps but does allow officers to listen to electronic communications when (1) an officer is one of the parties involved in the communication, (2) one of the parties is not the officer but willingly decides to share the communication with the officer, or (3) officers obtain a warrant based on probable cause. In the 1971 case of *U.S.* v. *White*, the Court held that law enforcement officers may intercept electronic information when one of the parties involved in the communication gives his or her consent, even without a warrant.[21]

In 1984, the Supreme Court decided the case of *U.S.* v. *Karo*, in which Drug Enforcement Administration (DEA) agents had arrested James Karo for cocaine importation.[22] Officers placed a radio transmitter inside a 50-gallon drum of ether purchased by Karo for use in processing the cocaine. The device was placed inside the drum with the consent of the seller of the ether but without a search warrant. The shipment of ether was followed to the Karo house, and Karo was arrested and convicted of cocaine trafficking charges. Karo appealed to the U.S. Supreme Court, claiming that the radio beeper had violated his reasonable expectation of privacy inside his premises and that, without a warrant, the evidence it produced was tainted. The Court agreed and overturned his conviction.

Minimization Requirements for Electronic Surveillance

The Supreme Court established a minimization requirement pertinent to electronic surveillance in the 1978 case of *U.S.* v. *Scott*.[23] **Minimization** refers to the requirement that officers take every reasonable effort to monitor only those conversations, through the use of phone taps, body bugs, and the like, that are specifically related to the criminal activity under investigation. As soon as it becomes obvious that a conversation is innocent, the monitoring personnel are required to cease listening. Problems arise if the conversation occurs in a foreign language, if it is "coded," or if it is ambiguous. For example, in one wiretap operation, heroin traffickers referred to a pound quantity of product as an "elbow" or "LB." Investigators were aware of this street term and were able to continue monitoring the conversation. It has been suggested that investigators involved in electronic surveillance maintain logbooks of their activities that specifically show monitoring of conversations as well as efforts made to minimize noncriminal conversations.

The Electronic Communications Privacy Act of 1986

In 1986, Congress passed the Electronic Communications Privacy Act (ECPA), which brought major changes in the requirements law enforcement officers must meet to intercept wire communications (involving the human voice). The ECPA deals specifically with three areas of communication: (1) wiretaps and bugs, which enable officers to listen to criminal conversations; (2) pen registers, which record numbers dialed from a telephone; and (3) tracing devices, which determine the number from which a call emanates. The act also addresses the procedures to be followed by officers in obtaining records relating to communication services, and it establishes requirements for gaining access to stored electronic communications and records of those communications. The ECPA basically requires that investigating officers obtain wiretap-type court orders to eavesdrop on ongoing communications. The use of pen registers and recording devices, however, is specifically excluded by law from court order requirements.[24]

A related measure, the Communications Assistance for Law Enforcement Act (CALEA) of 1994, appropriated $500 million to modify the U.S. phone system to allow for continued wiretapping by law enforcement agencies. The law also specifies a standard-setting process for the redesign of existing equipment that would permit effective wiretapping in the face of coming technological advances. The law essentially requires telecommunication carriers, as defined by the act, to ensure law enforcement's ability, pursuant to a lawful court order, to intercept communications notwithstanding advanced telecommunications technologies. In 2003, federal and state judges approved 1,442 wiretap requests, and approximately 4.3 million conversations were intercepted by law enforcement agencies throughout the country. Approximately one-third of all intercepted conversations were classified as "incriminating."[25]

The Telecommunications Act of 1996

Title V of the Telecommunications Act of 1996 made it a federal offense for anyone engaged in interstate or international communications to knowingly use a telecommunications device "to create, solicit, or initiate the transmission of any comment, request, suggestion, proposal, image, or other communication which is at the scene lewd, mischievous, filthy, or indecent, with intent to annoy, abuse, threaten, or harass another person." The law also provides special penalties for anyone who "makes a telephone call...without disclosing his identity and with intent to annoy, abuse, threaten, or harass any person at the called number who receives the communication" or who "makes or causes the telephone of another repeatedly or continuously to ring, with the intent to harass any person at the called number; or makes repeated phone calls" for the purpose of harassing a person at the called number.[26]

A section of the law, known as the Communications Decency Act (CDA), criminalizes the transmission to minors of "patently offensive" obscene materials over the Internet and other computer communications devices. Portions of the CDA, however, were invalidated by the U.S. Supreme Court in the case of *Reno* v. *ACLU* (1997).[27]

Thermal Imaging

In 1996, the California appellate court decision in *People* v. *Deutsch* identified the kinds of issues that are likely to be encountered as the United States and law enforcement expand their use of high technology.[28] In this case, judges faced the question of whether a warrantless scan of a private dwelling using a thermal imaging device constitutes an unreasonable search within the meaning of the Fourth Amendment. These devices, also known as **forward-looking infrared (FLIR) systems**, measure radiant heat energy and display their readings as thermographs. Images that a thermal imager produces can be used (as in the case of Dorian Deutsch) to reveal unusually warm areas or rooms that might be associated with the cultivation of drug-bearing plants, such as marijuana. Two hundred cannabis plants, which were being grown hydroponically under high-wattage lights in walled-off portions of Deutsch's home, were seized after an exterior thermal scan of the home by a police officer who drove by the residence at 1:30 A.M.

A Closer Look

The Mechanics of Thermal Imaging

In its simplest terms, thermal imagers operate like the human eye, but are much more powerful. Energy from the environment passes through a lens and is registered on a detector. In the case of the thermal imager, that energy is in the form of heat. By measuring very small relative temperature differences, invisible heat patterns are converted by the thermal imager into clear, visible images that can be viewed by the operator through a viewfinder or monitor. Thermal imagers are usually very sensitive and can detect temperature variations smaller than 0.1°C.

Thermal imagers "see" nothing more than the heat emitted by all objects in the camera's field of view. They do not see visible light, nor do they see rays or beams of energy. Thermal imagers are completely passive and nonintrusive. Because these devices see heat and not light, they can be used for both daytime and nighttime operations.

Thermal imagers can be compared with image intensifiers, which are another type of night vision technology and one that has been used by law enforcement and the military for years. In contrast to image intensifiers, thermal imagers are unaffected by the amount of light in a scene and will "bloom" or shut down indirect light. Unlike image intensifiers, thermal imagers can see through dust, smoke, light fog, clouds, haze, and light rain because infrared wavelengths are longer than visible wavelengths of light.

In the *Deutsch*, because the officer had not anticipated entering the house, he proceeded without a search warrant. A California court ruled that the scan was an illegal search because "society accepts reasonable expectation of privacy" surrounding "non-disclosed activities within the home."

In a similar case, *Kryllo* v. *U.S.* (2001), the U.S. Supreme Court reached much the same conclusion. Based on the results of a warrantless search conducted by the officers using a forward imaging device, investigators applied for a search warrant of Kryllo's home.[29] The subsequent search uncovered more than 100 marijuana plants that were being grown under bright lights. The Court held, "where, as here, the government uses a device that is not in general public use, to explore details of a private home that would previously have been unknowable without physical intrusion, the surveillance is a Fourth Amendment search, and is presumptively unreasonable without a warrant."

Thematic question

The *Kryllo* case and the use of thermal imaging had raised many important questions regarding the right of the people to be safe from criminality and their concurrent right to be free from intrusive police surveillance. If you had to make concessions in either regard, which would you choose: your right to privacy against government intrusion or the ability of the police to conduct surveillance into suspected criminal's homes to identify criminal activity? Explain your response.

|Fig. 7.10| △

A thermal imaging device, shown here, shows how warm objects stand out well against cooler backgrounds; humans and other warm-blooded animals become easily visible against the environment, day or night. As a result, thermography is particularly useful to law enforcement.

Ingo Bartussek / Fotolia

Physical Surveillance Operations

The considerable resources required for physical surveillance draw personnel away from other investigative functions but much can be learned through such operations. If not done properly, the potential also exists for alerting the subject of the investigation to law enforcement's interest, which conceivably could compromise the covertness of not only the surveillance but the entire investigation as well. Proper preparation at the onset can make the difference between a productive surveillance and expending considerable resources without any results.[30] Perhaps the most challenging task in criminal investigation is to keep a suspect under surveillance without arousing his or her suspicions. Surveillance is a process that may take place under a variety of conditions for which the officer must be prepared. The teamwork concept is usually necessary because most surveillance operations involve more than one officer, one mode of travel, and one location.

A surveillance operation may be directed toward a person, a vehicle, or a location for the purpose of bringing an investigation into sharp focus. By identifying individuals in obtaining detailed information about their activities, the criminal investigator can accomplish the following:

- Obtain evidence of a crime
- Prevent the commission of an act or apprehend a suspect in the commission of an act
- Locate persons or watch their hangouts and associates
- Obtain probable cause for obtaining search warrants
- Obtain information for later use in an interrogation
- Develop leads and information received from other sources
- Obtain admissible legal evidence for use in court
- Protect undercover officers or corroborate their testimony

Preparing for the Surveillance

Before initiation of the surveillance, a study should be made of all files relating to the suspects, their activities in crimes, their working and neighborhood environments, and the vehicles involved in the case. In studying information relating to the suspects, the officer should focus on names and aliases used by suspects and detailed physical descriptions, including photographs when available. When possible, the suspect should be pointed out to the surveillance officers.

Identifying characteristics and mannerisms of the suspect should also be studied by the officers. The habits and normal routines of the suspects should be examined, as well as their probable suspicion of, and ability to elude, the surveillance operation. The identities and descriptions of known or suspected contacts or associates should be known, and the officer should be knowledgeable about the scope and extent of crimes and activities in which the suspects are involved.

The officers must also familiarize themselves with the type of neighborhood in which the operation will take place, concentrating on such aspects as the type of inhabitants, their dress, and their use of language. This information will assist the officers in blending in with the neighborhood.

The types of equipment used by surveillance officers are limited only by the improvisational ability of the officers themselves. For example, on a short-term surveillance of a building, the surveillance officers may use utility belts with tools and hard hats to adopt the appearance of public utility employees or may use some other type of "cover" equipment.

A physical reconnaissance should study the areas where the surveillance will take place and identify vantage points suitable for the officers. Similarly, traffic conditions should be observed, and the officers should become familiar with the names and locations of streets in the area, including locations of dead-end streets that may be used by the suspect to spot surveillance officers. The reconnaissance will also yield information on the neighborhood and its inhabitants that would not be in the police files.

The officer must mentally and physically prepare him- or herself for surveillance operations. The officer needs to realize that he or she must be patient and possess endurance. Perseverance is needed while waiting for the suspect to appear or to doggedly follow a suspect through the same routine day after day.

The officer must be alert and resourceful because regardless of careful planning, there are always many unanticipated occurrences in surveillance work. The officer must develop keen powers of observation and memory because often he or she is unable to write down all events, descriptions of contacts, or times as they occur. Furthermore, the officer must prepare a logical explanation for

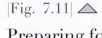

|Fig. 7.11|

Preparing for surveillance.

Preparing for Surveillance

Mannerisms: Identifying characteristics and mannerisms of the suspect should also be studied by the officers. The habits and normal routines of the suspects should be examined, as well as their probable suspicion of, and ability to elude, the surveillance operation. The identities and descriptions of known or suspected contacts or associates should be known, and the officer should be knowledgeable about the scope and extent of crimes and activities in which the suspects are involved.

Area: The officers must also familiarize themselves with the type of neighborhood in which the operation will take place, concentrating on such aspects as the type of inhabitants, their dress, and their use of language. This information will assist the officers in blending in with the neighborhood.

Equipment: The types of equipment used by surveillance officers are limited only by the improvisational ability of the officers themselves. For example, on a short-term surveillance of a building, the surveillance officers may use utility belts with tools and hard hats to adopt the appearance of public utility employees or may use some other type of "cover" equipment.

Recon: A physical reconnaissance should study the areas where the surveillance will take place and identify vantage points suitable for the officers. Similarly, traffic conditions should be observed, and the officers should become familiar with the names and locations of streets in the area, including locations of dead-end streets that may be used by the suspect to spot surveillance officers. The reconnaissance will also yield information on the neighborhood and its inhabitants that would not be in the police files.

Endurance: The officer must mentally and physically prepare him- or herself for surveillance operations. The officer needs to realize that he or she must be patient and possess endurance. Perseverance is needed while waiting for the suspect to appear or to doggedly follow a suspect through the same routine day after day.

Resourcefulness: The officer must be alert and resourceful because regardless of careful planning, there are always many unanticipated occurrences in surveillance work. The officer must develop keen powers of observation and memory because often he or she is unable to write down all events, descriptions of contacts, or times as they occur. Furthermore, the officer must prepare a logical explanation for being in a particular place at a particular time in the eventuality that he or she is approached by the subject and accused of following him or her.

Blend in: The officer must address and adopt the demeanor of local inhabitants to blend into the setting. The type of clothing to be worn will determine whether concealment of weapons or use of personal radios jeopardizes the operation. Ideally, the officer should have an ordinary appearance to avoid attracting the suspect's attention. Doing so will better ensure that the officer is able to blend in to the target's environment. The officer must have the ability to act naturally under all circumstances as if he or she belongs at that scene.

Clothing: Officers should also have such items as caps, jackets, and glasses available to quickly change appearance if needed. Flexibility and versatility are the keys to any surveillance. A change of clothing may suffice for one individual, but another may use clothing to suggest a trade or service. The clothing and behavior should be coordinated to communicate some cover or excuse for being in a neighborhood.

being in a particular place at a particular time in the eventuality that he or she is approached by the subject and accused of following him or her.

The officer must address and adopt the demeanor of local inhabitants to blend into the setting. The type of clothing to be worn will determine whether concealment of weapons or use of personal radios jeopardizes the operation. Ideally, the officer should have an ordinary appearance to avoid attracting the suspect's attention. Doing so will better ensure that the officer is able to blend in to the target's environment. The officer must have the ability to act naturally under all circumstances as if he or she belongs at that scene.

Officers should also have such items as caps, jackets, and glasses available to quickly change appearance if needed. Flexibility and versatility are the keys to any surveillance. A change of clothing may suffice for one individual, but another may use clothing to suggest a trade or service. The clothing and behavior should be coordinated to communicate some cover or excuse for being in a neighborhood.

Foot Surveillance

Generally, the foot surveillance technique is used only during relatively short distances or to maintain contact with a suspect after he or she has left a vehicle. There are four principal methods for conducting a moving surveillance on foot: one-officer surveillance; two-officer surveillance; ABC method; and the progressive, or leapfrog, method.

ONE-OFFICER SURVEILLANCE The single-officer technique is extremely difficult to conduct because the suspect must be kept in view at all times and close contact is required to enable the officer to immediately observe the suspect if he or she enters a building, turns a corner, or makes other sudden moves.

TWO-OFFICER SURVEILLANCE This method affords greater security against detection and reduces the risk of losing the suspect. On streets that are crowded with pedestrian or vehicular traffic, both officers should normally remain on the same side of the street as the suspect. The first officer trails the suspect fairly closely. The second officer remains some distance behind the first. On a less crowded street, one officer should walk on the opposite side of the street nearly abreast of the suspect. To avoid detection, the two officers should make periodic changes in their positions relative to the suspect.

ABC METHOD By using a three-officer surveillance team in this technique, the risk of losing the suspect is further reduced. Under most conditions, this method provides greater security against detection. The ABC method also permits a greater variation in the position of the officers and allows an officer who suspects he has been spotted by the suspect to drop out of close contact. Under normal traffic conditions, officer "A" keeps a reasonable distance behind the suspect. Officer "B" follows "A" and concentrates on keeping "A" in view. Officer "B" also checks if an associate of the subject is being used to detect the surveillance (countersurveillance). Officer "C" walks on the opposite side of the street slightly behind the suspect. On streets with little or no traffic, officers "B" and "C" may be on the opposite side of the street, or officer "C" may be in front of the suspect. On crowded streets, however, all three officers should generally be on the same side of the street. The lead officer should follow closely to observe the suspect at intersections or if he or she enters a building. As with the two-officer method, the officers should frequently alter their positions relative to the suspect to avoid detection.

Surveillance Kit Checklist

- ☑ Department two-way radio
- ☑ Handheld portable radio with spare battery
- ☑ Cellular phone
- ☑ Digital camera with telephoto lens (if available) with extra storage media and spare battery
- ☑ Digital video camera
- ☑ Stabilizing device such as a tripod
- ☑ Binoculars or thermal imaging device
- ☑ Detailed road maps, compass, or GPS navigation device
- ☑ Flashlight with extra batteries
- ☑ Change of clothing, including hat and toiletries
- ☑ Food and water
- ☑ Cash, including coins for toll lanes
- ☑ Extra set of car keys
- ☑ Towels and glass cleaner
- ☑ Equipment bag to contain above items

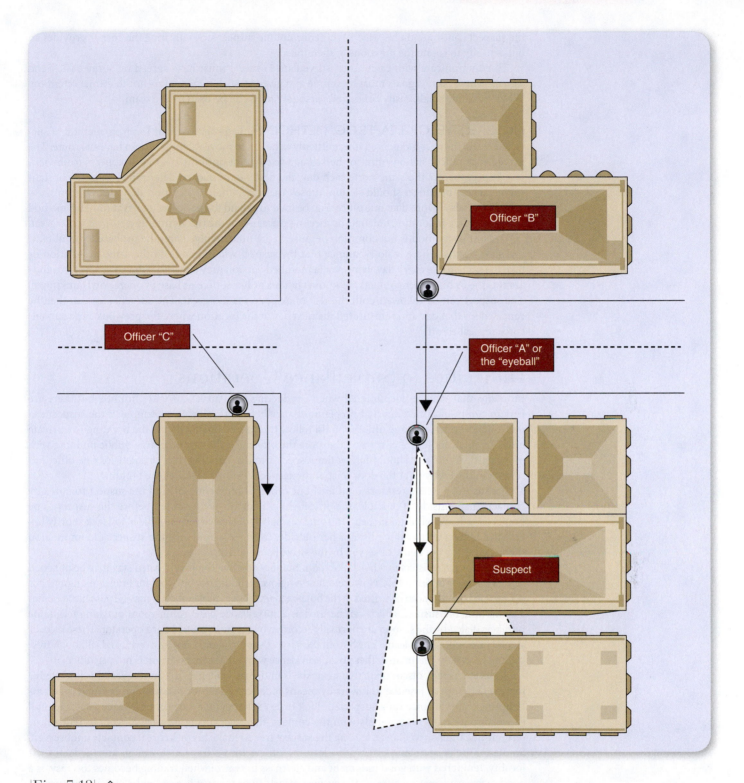

Officer "B"

Officer "C"

Officer "A" or
the "eyeball"

Suspect

|Fig. 7.12| △

Three-officer or "ABC" foot surveillance.

When the suspect approaches an intersection and there is a probability that he or she might turn, officer "C" across the street should reach the intersection first. By pausing at the corner, officer "C" can watch the suspect and signal his or her actions to officers "A" and "B." If "C" signals that the suspect has turned the corner and stopped, both "A" and "B" may have to cross the intersection and proceed to a point out of the suspect's view and rely on "C" to signal them when the suspect continues on his way. Whether or not the suspect stops, turning the corner provides an opportunity to rotate the positions of the officers.

To communicate with each other, surveillance officers must have agreed on some basic hand signals. These hand signals must be simple and given in such a manner as not to attract attention. When possible, small, easily concealed personal radios can be used by the team.

PROGRESSIVE, OR LEAPFROG, METHOD In the progressive, or leapfrog, method of surveillance, the suspect is observed intermittently as he or she moves along a certain habitual route. The surveillance officer stations him- or herself at a fixed point until the suspect disappears from view. If a suspect follows the same route each day, the destination may be determined without constant surveillance. The officer should station himself each day where the suspect disappeared from view the previous day. More than one officer can be used to extend the period of observation. This method may be of value in locating hideouts or meeting places when the risk of trailing a suspect is too great.

Use of this method is not common because of the time involved and the probability of obtaining poor results. There is no assurance that the suspect will either go to the same destination or take the same route every day. However, a modified version may be useful when a suspect's rounds are routine or his or her contacts are known but his or her source or base of operation is unknown. The suspect can be followed until the risk of detection is too great. The surveillance can then be canceled for that day and reinstituted the next day at the location where the previous day's surveillance was called off.

Difficulties in Surveillance Operations

Problems that may be encountered when conducting foot surveillance are infinite, but there are certain common difficulties that preplanning may help to resolve. For example, if the suspect enters a building, at least one officer should follow the suspect inside unless the building is a private home or small shop or if entry would expose the officer. In the case of a large public building with many exits, all officers should follow the suspect into the building. It is prudent for one officer to remain in the lobby or at the door to spot the suspect if he or she leaves the building.

If a suspect enters a restaurant, at least one officer should enter behind the suspect to note any contacts made inside. If possible, the officer should pay his or her check before the suspect to be prepared to leave with the suspect. In some cases, it is desirable for the officer to leave shortly before the suspect and wait for him or her outside. Doing so could give the suspect the impression that he or she is not being observed by the surveillance officer.

If the suspect registers in a hotel, the room number and length of anticipated stay may be obtained from a manager or desk clerk. However, these employees should not be asked for information until it is determined that they can be trusted. If the hotel management is cooperative, it may be possible to obtain a room near the suspect, which can be used as a surveillance base. All in-room outgoing telephone numbers dialed by the suspect are normally recorded by the hotel switchboard operator. These records should be examined for leads. Trash from the suspect's room should not be overlooked, although trespassing to retrieve this or any other possible evidence without a search warrant is not permitted.

A clever suspect, discovering that he or she is under surveillance, may not reveal this knowledge but may attempt to lose the followers by means of false contacts or decoys. For example, when attempting a surveillance on a suspected illicit drug exchange, the suspect may leave a package full of worthless papers or materials with the contact, thereby causing unwary officers to redirect or discontinue their surveillance, leaving the suspect free to make his or her real contacts unobserved. Similarly, the suspect may attempt to lead the officer into a trap. A thorough knowledge of the locality, tempered with good judgment and alertness to realize when trailing becomes too easy, is a good defense against such traps. If a suspect resorts to trickery, it is good policy to change surveillance officers. Some common methods that a suspect may use to detect foot surveillance are:

- Stopping to tie a shoelace while looking for followers
- Stopping abruptly and looking at people to the rear or reversing course and retracing his or her steps
- Stopping abruptly after turning a corner or alternately walking slowly and rapidly
- Arranging with a friend in a shop or other place to watch for surveillants behind him or her
- Riding short distances on buses and taxis or circling the block in a taxi
- Entering a building and leaving immediately via another exit

- Watching in lobby and restaurant mirrors to see who is coming and going
- Starting to leave a location quickly and then suddenly turning around to see if anyone else also suddenly rises
- Opening and closing the hotel door to indicate that he or she has left the room and then waiting inside the room with the door slightly ajar to see if anyone leaves an adjacent room

Vehicle Surveillance

As is the case with foot surveillance, there are four types of vehicular surveillance, or **mobile surveillance**: the one-, two-, and three-car surveillance and the leapfrog method. If only one car is available for surveillance, its position should be behind the suspect car, the distance varying with the amount of traffic in the area. In city traffic, no more than two vehicles should be permitted between the suspect's car and the surveillance vehicle. In rural areas, it is advisable to give the suspect a good lead. If intersections and road forks are far between, the lead can be extended to a point where the suspect car may be even temporarily lost from view over hills or around curves. When possible, there should be another car between the surveillance vehicle and the suspect car. At night, the surveillance vehicle should not have its headlights on high beam unless absolutely necessary to maintain contact. Similarly, all other unnecessary lights on the car should be off.

Whenever possible, the surveillant's car should be occupied by two officers—one driver and one observer to take notes. The second officer can also take over surveillance on foot if necessary. Seating arrangements and appearance of these two officers should be changed periodically to avoid recognition by suspects. The officers should prepare for emergencies by carrying food, raincoats, tire chains, and any other items appropriate for the circumstances of the surveillance. Many agencies install switches (kill switches) on surveillance cars to enable the officers to darken lights, shut off running lights, or shut off individual lights needed to change the vehicle's appearance.

When conducting a two-car surveillance in city areas during daylight hours, both cars should be behind the suspect's car. Occasionally, one car may operate on a parallel route, timing itself to arrive at intersections just before the suspect to observe his route at the intersection. This method is also highly suitable for use at night in suburban areas.

In a three-car surveillance, parallel routes can be more readily used, and the positions of the cars can be changed frequently enough to prevent discovery of the surveillance. One car may be used to lead the suspect vehicle while observing it through the rearview mirror.

The leapfrog surveillance with cars is very similar to leapfrog surveillance on foot. In this type of surveillance, for example, the suspect's vehicle may be observed intermittently as it proceeds along its suspected route. From a fixed position, the officers watch the suspect vehicle disappear from view. After a number of such surveillances, the suspect's final destination is finally determined. This particular approach of the leapfrog surveillance is often impractical due to the greater distances that can be covered by car. For this reason, it would be more beneficial if the surveillance officers followed the suspect's car until the risk of detection is too great, whereupon the surveillance is called off for that day. The next time the suspect makes his or her scheduled trip, the officers can initiate their surveillance at the geographical point the previous surveillance was ended.

As with foot surveillance, the suspect who believes he or she may be being followed can resort to various techniques to detect the surveillance automobile. Some of the most common techniques include:

- Alternating fast and slow driving or parking frequently
- Stopping suddenly around curves or corners or speeding up a hill and then coasting slowly downhill
- Driving into dead-end streets or pulling into driveways

Once a suspect has confirmed his or her suspicion, he or she can use a variety of techniques to elude automobile surveillance. Some examples are:

- Committing flagrant traffic violations such as making U-turns, driving against traffic on one-way streets, and running through red lights
- Using double entrances to driveways—in one entrance and out the other
- Cutting through parking lots
- Driving through congested areas
- Deserting the vehicle beyond the blind curve or corner

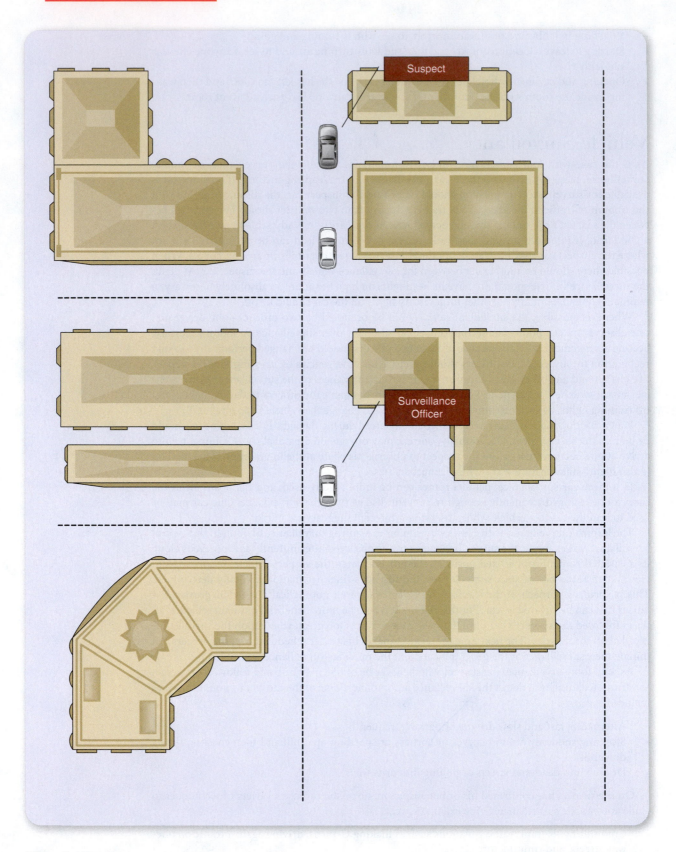

|Fig. 7.13| △

Standard one-car surveillance.

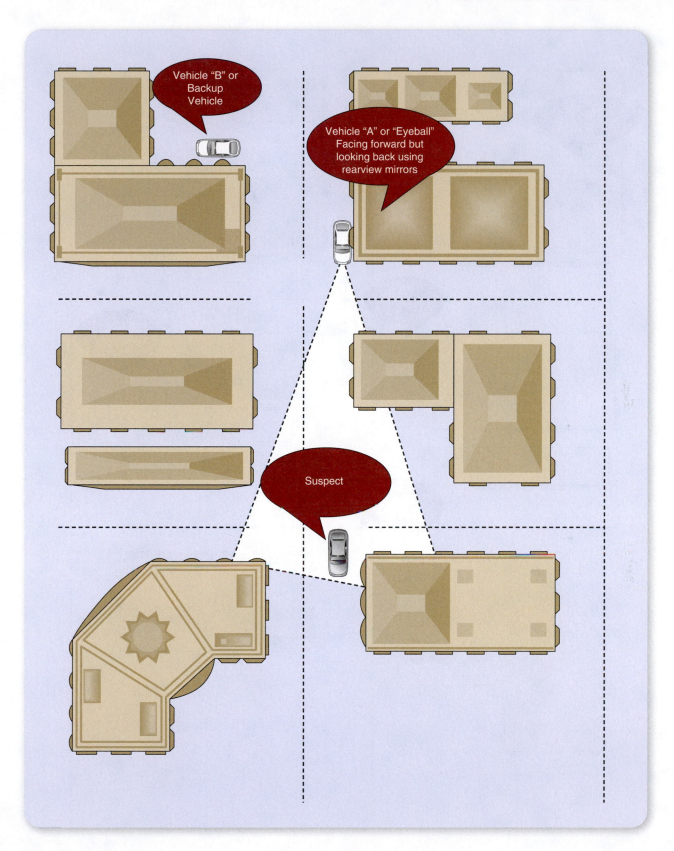

|Fig. 7.14| ▲

Standard two-car surveillance.

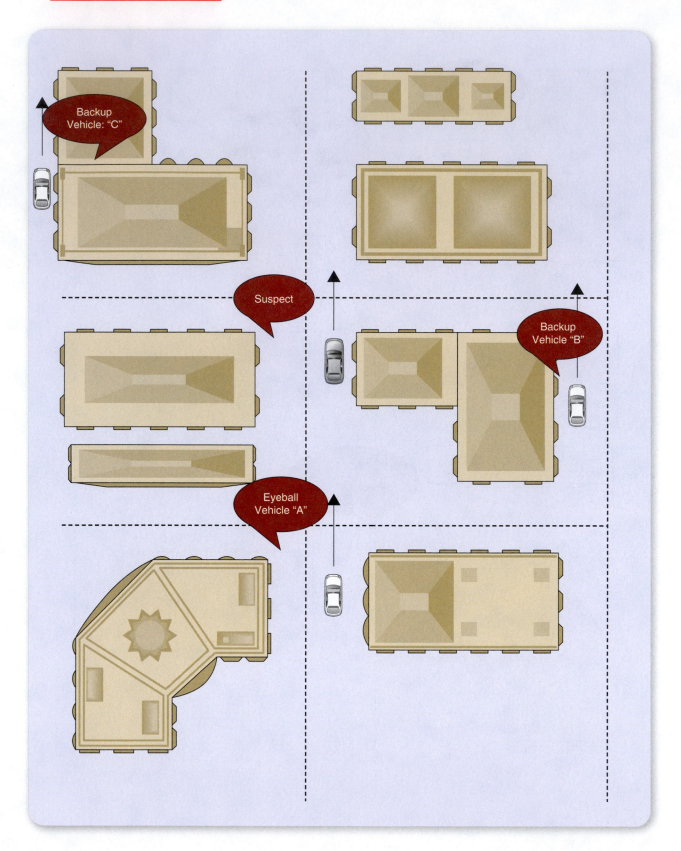

|Fig. 7.15|

Three-car or "ABC" surveillance.

|Fig. 7.16| △

Detective conducting a "moving" or vehicle surveillance. A properly conducted moving surveillance requires the investigator in the lead vehicle (known as the "eyeball") maintain constant communication with other surveillance units to alert them as to the actions of the target vehicle.

Courtesy of Mike Himmel

Stakeouts, or "Stationary Surveillance"

When a **stakeout** is used, officers watch from a **stationary surveillance** vantage point such as a room, house, or camouflaged outdoor fixture located near the premises being observed. A stakeout is the tactical deployment of police officers in anticipation of the commission of a crime at a specific location. The anticipated perpetrators may be known individuals or may be suspects known only by their mode of operation (MO). The purpose of the stakeout is to arrest the suspect(s) during the attempted or actual commission of a crime.

Stakeouts almost always involve enforcement actions against armed criminal suspects. Therefore, the safety of officers and bystanders should always be of primary concern. The objectives of criminal arrest should never supersede the need to protect officers and civilians against unreasonable risks.

Briefings

The briefings preceding deployment of a stakeout should be of two types:

1. The first type is the dissemination of information by detective personnel. The detectives in charge of the case should provide the assigned officers with all information concerning the suspect(s) and his or her MO. This should include, when available, photos or composites, suspect armament, and the suspect's potential for violence based on previous crimes. Is the suspect armed? Has the suspect used his weapon? Has the suspect taken hostages? Does the suspect appear to be in control or is the suspect he under the influence of alcohol or drugs? Does the suspect run after committing the crime or calmly exit the location? Is there a getaway car with a driver? What is the possibility of outside accomplices? Does there appear to be inside help? Are the suspects "counter jumpers," or do they position or station themselves in a particular area or manner? As these and related issues are discussed, one can begin to formulate the tactical actions that officers must take.

2. The second type of briefing is provided by those officers who surveyed, or "advanced," the assigned location. An *advance* consists of assessing a potential stakeout location and developing an initial tactical plan. The advance should be the responsibility of the stakeout supervisor or senior officer(s) with stakeout experience. Organization, manpower deployment, and related concerns should be the responsibility of supervisors with tactical knowledge.

|Fig. 7.17| △

Detective conducting a "stakeout" or fixed surveillance. Such operations are tedious and time consuming but often net valuable information regarding the actions and routines of suspects.

Courtesy of Mike Himmel

Investigative Procedures

Generally, a stakeout consists of an inside team and an outside team of two officers each. The **outside team** is normally designated as the arrest team. Enforcement action should not be taken by the inside team unless a life-threatening situation develops. After the subjects have exited the stakeout location, the inside team is also responsible for securing the location to ensure that the suspects do not reenter and possibly create a barricade or hostage situation.

Although the outside team is normally the arrest team, assignment of this responsibility is ultimately based on factors associated with the specific stakeout location. For example, normally crowded public stores are not generally the best location for an arrest confrontation. But less trafficked locations, such as exclusive jewelry stores that use controlled public access, would be preferable over a busy public street. These and related factors concerning the stakeout location should be addressed during the stakeout advance, and a decision should be made on team responsibilities by the detail supervisor.

The **inside team** is responsible for briefing officers concerning their actions if a crime occurs. They should ensure that employees do not initiate any independent action and should remove any privately owned weapons. All employees must understand that they should not inform anyone that police are present, nor should they seek assistance from the stakeout team for crimes such as shoplifting. If necessary, uniformed officers may respond as usual to handle these offenses. Such incidents should be handled as quickly as possible, and uniformed officers should exit the area after the call for service has been handled. The investigators must conduct themselves in a normal and inconspicuous manner at all times. They should also be cautioned to lie prone on the floor if gunfire develops.

If the inside team is not going to observe from a concealed position, employees must be inconspicuous in their particular setting. If employees wear distinctive attire, then so must the inside team. There is always a possibility that the suspects may inspect a location before committing the crime, so stakeout officers must appear to be part of the local operation. All police equipment must be concealed, and radios must be turned off. Any private security should be dismissed and should leave the area. If the absence of private security would be obvious, security personnel may be permitted to stay, but they should not be armed and should be thoroughly briefed as to their role.

The investigators should be informed that no police action will be taken inside, with the exception of actions necessary to save lives, so as to relieve any unnecessary anxiety on the part of employees. Employees must also ensure that there is nothing on the premises, such as a scanner, that would reveal the stakeout operation. If any employee displays obvious signs of stress, serious consideration should be given to removing that employee with the cooperation of the location's management personnel.

If there is any suspicion that an officer may be involved with the suspects, an inside team should not be deployed, and no one outside of the police agency should be notified of the stakeout operation. In such instances, assigned officers should conduct the stakeout from a covert observation post outside the location.

Concealment of the outside team is a concern that officers sometimes overlook. Just as suspects survey prospective target locations from inside, they also frequently survey the surrounding area. Stakeouts that do not adhere to good concealment practices risk detection. There is simply no way, for example, that two officers can sit in a vehicle or use the same disguise for an extended period of time without being conspicuous.

A sedan is frequently used but may not be the best available option for the outside team. If a sedan is preferred, however, one officer should sit in the front seat and one in the right rear seat. The officer in the rear seat should position himself so he or she has a clear view of activities to the rear of the vehicle. This positioning is necessary because there have been cases in which officers have been fatally wounded while seated together in the front of their vehicle and unable to see suspects approaching from the rear.

Underground parking, carports, and residential driveways also provide concealment and allow officers some freedom of movement. Vans and other businesses or residences are also frequently used. Whatever the location, the observation post should be selected with the understanding that it could be in place for an extended period of time.

The response of the outside team to the stakeout location should be tested, taking into account changing traffic patterns at different times of the day. Experience has shown that 30 seconds should be considered the maximum allowable response time for the outside team to get to the stakeout. To reduce response time, outside teams should not situate themselves on the opposite side of major thoroughfares and should either minimize the number of intersections that must be crossed or eliminate them altogether.

Entry and exit of the inside team to the stakeout location are extremely important. All equipment, particularly weapons, must be concealed, and officers should not arrive at the location at the same time. After they are inside, the first officer should contact the designated manager or person in charge. Officers should seek a private area to brief the manager on stakeout procedures and then reevaluate the situation for safety. If circumstances that could affect safety have sufficiently changed since the advance was conducted, the officers should contact a supervisor immediately and, if necessary, redeploy until the problem(s) can be resolved.

The physical environment of a stakeout is one of the most problematic issues should the use of firearms be needed. Regardless of whether an officer is stationed inside or outside the location, all officers must visually inspect the entire location with background in mind. For example, plateglass windows from floor to ceiling or plasterboard walls are unacceptable background materials if the use of firearms becomes necessary by the inside team.

Officers should be positioned to minimize interior backgrounds. A standard procedure in this regard is to station one officer undercover, at a point in the facility well above eye level. This positioning provides several advantages. If the use of firearms is required, this officer will be firing downward, thus minimizing or eliminating background problems. It also provides for greater visibility and strategic advantage. With one officer in this position providing cover, the second inside officer can be used to collect the suspect's weapons and frisk and handcuff the subject if an arrest must be made inside the stakeout location.

The inside team should alert the arrest team as soon as anything unusual is suspected. Radio contact with the arrest team should be maintained as long as possible to describe the suspects and the types of weapons being carried, anticipated exit route, and other pertinent information that would assist the arrest team and promote their safety.

Weapon readiness is also an important consideration. When shotguns are used, a round should be chambered with the safety on. Shotguns should never be leaned against a wall, table, or other object but should be laid flat when not being held. Semiautomatic handguns should also be in a ready condition with the safety on. There is no time to chamber a round when needed instantly in a tactical situation. In addition, when disengaging the safety in such instances, it should be done as quietly as possible. Placing a finger on each side of the safety release when disengaging is a good way to ensure silence.

Exiting a location is as critical as entering. Officers should exercise the same caution in leaving the location as they did when entering. As a stakeout continues, fatigue may become a factor. Officers and supervisors should be alert to signs of fatigue, and personnel should be rotated as necessary. This is particularly the case with inside team officers, whose level of preparedness and stress is greatest. Rotation can help to alleviate this constant tension as well as allow other officers to become knowledgeable about other duties of the stakeout operation.

Post-Stakeout Procedures

The potential for the use of deadly force is a part of nearly all stakeouts. However, this potentiality does not constitute grounds for an exception to existing policies and procedures that govern the use of deadly force in individual agencies. The safety of officers and citizens alike and overall reverence for human life remain important issues. As in other circumstances, officers should use deadly force only as a last resort after all other reasonable alternatives are exhausted.

If a suspect is shot, he or she should be disarmed and handcuffed immediately. Officers should not diagnose the condition of the suspect to determine whether handcuffs are required. Instances exist in which presumably dead or incapacitated suspects have inflicted serious injuries on unsuspecting officers. The suspect's weapon should also be secured. If the officer is not familiar with the weapon, he or she should handle it only to the degree necessary until it can be rendered safe.

After the arrest, the surrounding area should be checked for accomplices and getaway cars and the immediate area secured as a crime scene as soon as possible. In addition to ambulances, a call should be made for assistance from uniformed support personnel. These calls should be made by telephone because police radio communications are frequently monitored by the news media and the public.

All plainclothes officers should display proper ID and be easily identified as police officers because responding officers may not be aware that the location was a stakeout. Raid jackets are relatively inexpensive, easily obtainable, and easily recognized.

After the location is secured, standard procedures for handling a crime scene should be used. The area should be roped off or isolated, evidence should be preserved, and witnesses should be located and identified. Information to be released should be channeled only to assigned press relations officers. Officers involved in the incident should not be subjected to press interviews and should not make public statements.

Summary Checklist

In this chapter, we consider the ways information about crimes is documented by criminal investigators. A properly documented case is one that is more likely to succeed in court. See how well you are able to answer the following questions in your checklist.

1. **Explain the function of intelligence gathering and its uses.**

   The collection of criminal intelligence is an important function of the criminal investigative process, and one that has resulted in significant identification and arrest of major crime figures.

   - Efforts to identify criminal groups and the persons who participate in and control them require a systematic approach to information collection and analysis.
   - Intelligence operations shift focus based on perceived needs and threats.
   - Criminal intelligence plays an indispensable role in the support of law enforcement and the ultimate protection of society.

2. **Distinguish between overt and covert intelligence collection.**

   - Overt information collection includes personal interaction with people, many of whom are witnesses to crimes, victims of crimes, or the suspects themselves.
   - Covert information collection is the most common and includes a process known as intelligence gathering.

3. **Distinguish between criminal intelligence and criminal investigation functions?**

   Criminal intelligence is defined as knowledge of past, present, or future criminal activity that results from the collection of information that, when evaluated, provides the user with a basis for rational decision making.

   There are four fundamental differences between criminal intelligence and criminal investigation.

   - Criminal investigations are usually reactive in nature. Intelligence gathering, conversely, is a proactive function.
   - Criminal investigators generally work with deductive logic, while intelligence unit personnel exercise inductive logic.
   - Investigation case files are generally considered open files and contain information developed for the purpose of eventually making an arrest and gaining a conviction in a court of law. In comparison, intelligence files are closed files.
   - Intelligence files must be maintained apart from criminal investigation files to prevent unauthorized inspection of data.

4. **Identify the procedures for intelligence gathering.**

   The intelligence collection process should be thought of as a process of connecting a series of interrelated components of information. There are four main phases:

   - Target selection
   - Data collection
   - Data collation and analysis
   - Dissemination

5. **In what ways can surveillance operations be useful in criminal investigation?**

   Surveillance operations can be directed toward a person, vehicle, or location for the purpose of bringing

an investigation into sharp focus. By identifying individuals and obtaining detailed information about their activities, the criminal investigator can accomplish the following:

- Obtain evidence of a crime
- Prevent the commission of an act or apprehend a suspect in the commission of an act
- Locate persons or watch their hangouts and associates
- Obtain probable cause for obtaining search warrants
- Obtain information for later use in an interrogation
- Develop leads and information received from other sources
- Obtain admissible legal evidence for use in court
- Protect undercover officers or corroborate their testimony

6. **Identify the various techniques for conducting surveillance of suspects.**

   - Foot surveillance is generally used only during relatively short distances or to maintain contact with a suspect after he or she has left a vehicle. There are four principal methods for conducting a moving surveillance on foot.
     - One-officer surveillance
     - Two-officer surveillance
     - ABC method
     - Progressive or leapfrog method
   - Vehicle surveillance—there are four types of vehicle or mobile surveillance.
     - One-car surveillance
     - Two-car surveillance
     - Three-car surveillance
     - Leapfrog method
   - Stakeouts or "stationary surveillance"—officers watch from a stationary surveillance vantage point such as a room, house, or camouflaged outdoor fixture located near the premises being observed.
     - A stakeout is the tactical deployment of police officers in anticipation of the commission of a crime at a specific location.
     - The purpose of the stakeout is to arrest the suspect(s) during the attempted or actual commission of a crime.

Key Terms

analysis

closed files

collation

commodity flow analysis

covert information collection

criminal intelligence

dissemination

electronic surveillance

event flow analysis

flowcharting

forward-looking infrared (FLIR)
  systems

Global Navigation Satellite
  System (GNSS)

Global Positioning System
  (GPS)

information gathering

inside team

link analysis

minimization

mobile surveillance

multilateration

open files

outside team

overt information
  collection

physical surveillance

RISS projects

stakeout

stationary surveillance

strategic intelligence

surveillance

tactical intelligence

thermal imaging

triangulation

Discussion Questions

1. Define the usefulness of the intelligence function as it pertains to the collection of criminal information.

2. List and discuss the four fundamental differences between criminal investigation and criminal intelligence gathering.

3. List and discuss the four phases of the intelligence process.

4. Explain flowcharting and discuss the basic differences between event and commodity flow analysis.

5. Explain the two types of teams used in a stakeout and the relationship between them.

6. Explain the role and function of surveillance operations.

7. Compare and contrast the different types of surveillance methods.

Notes

1. Botsch, R. B. (2008). Developing street sources: Tips for patrol officers. *FBI Law Enforcement Bulletin* 77(9):24–27.

2. Interview with Brian Michael Jenkins. (1994). *Omni* 17(2):77.

3. Suro, R. (1998). U.S. lacking in terrorism defenses: Study cites a need to share intelligence. *The Washington Post*, April 24, p. A-18.

4. U.S. Department of Justice. (1988). *Intelligence collection and analytical methods training manual*. Washington, DC: Drug Enforcement Administration.

5. FBI Website. Counterintelligence. (September 5, 2012). Available at http://www.fbi.gov/hq/ci/cointell.htm.

6. FBI Website. Famous cases: Robert Philip Hanssen espionage case. September 12, 2012. Available at http://www.fbi.gov/libref/historic/famcases/hanssen/hanssen.htm.

7. Found in http://www.riss.net/Default/Overview.

8. Located in FBI.gov. Available at http://www.fbi.gov/springfield/press-releases/2011/si040811a.htm (retrieved on January 23, 2012).

9. Gluckman, G. (2006). The eye in the sky. *Law Enforcement Technology* 33.2 (February): 70–75.

10. Harne, J. and F. Scott. (2009). NIJ testing new technologies. *Corrections Today* 71(4):88–89.

11. Hodges, K. (2007). Tracking "Bad Guys," legal considerations in using GPS. *FBI Law Enforcement Bulletin*, July:25.

12. Mears, B. (2012). Justices rule against police say GPS surveillance requires a search warrant. *CNN Justice*. Available at http://www.cnn.com/2012/01/23/justice/scotus-gps-tracking/?hpt=hp_t3 (retrieved on January 23, 2012); Biskupic, J. (2012). Supreme court rules GPS tracking requires warrant. *USA Today*, January 24, p. 2A.

13. CLARK, M. (2006). Cell phone technology and physical surveillance. *FBI Law Enforcement Bulletin*, May:25–32.

14. IBID.

15. ROBERTS, M. (2005). GPS tracks journey. *Security Management* 49. 2 (February):22–24.

16. AKIN, L. (2009). Activity monitors: AKA cell phone and computer eavesdroppers. *Forensic Examiner* 18(2):46–50.

17. *Olmstead* v. *U.S.*, 277 U.S. 438 (1928).

18. *On Lee* v. *U.S.*, 343 U.S. 747 (1952); *Lopez* v. *U.S.*, 373 U.S. 427 (1963).

19. *Berger* v. *New York*, 388 U.S. 41 (1967).

20. *Lee* v. *Florida*, 392 U.S. 378 (1968).

21. *U.S.* v. *White*, 401 U.S. 745 (1971).

22. *U.S.* v. *Karo*, 468 U.S. 705 (1984).

23. *U.S.* v. *Scott*, 436 U.S. 128 (1978).

24. For more information on the ECPA, see FIATAL, R. A. (1988) The electronic communications privacy act: Addressing today's technology. *FBI Law Enforcement Bulletin*, April: 24–30.

25. THE ADMINISTATIVE OFFICE FOR THE UNITED STATES COURTS. (2003). *Wiretap Report*. Available at uscourts.com.

26. Telecommunications Act of 1996, Public Law 104, 110 Statute 56.

27. *Reno* v. *ACLU*, 117 S. Ct. 2329 (1997).

28. *People* v. *Deutsch*, 96 C.D.O.S. 2827 (1996).

29. *Kyllo* v. *U.S.*, 533 U.S. 27 (2001).

30. NASON, J. (2004). Conducting surveillance operations: how to get the most out of them. *FBI Law Enforcement Bulletin*, May:1–7.

G.D.T. / Getty Images

This chapter will enable you to:

1. Describe how surveillance and undercover operations are conducted.

2. Understand the various motivations of informants.

3. Document and process an informant properly.

4. Maintain control of an informant during an investigation.

5. Understand the problems most commonly associated with the use of informants.

Management of Informants and Undercover Operations

Introduction

 Over a 10-month period beginning in 2003, motorists in Ohio were terrorized by a sniper firing random shots at vehicles along Interstate 270 that killed at least two persons. The two dozen shootings had struck a variety of targets such as cars, trucks, buses, schools, and homes in the Columbus area. Initially, investigators had little to go on in their investigation and publicly expressed their frustration in not having developed a suspect in the shootings. But finally in early 2004, ballistic tests on a 9 mm handgun connected Charles McCoy, Jr., to the Ohio Interstate shootings as well as at least eight other shootings.

In March 2004, McCoy checked into the Budget Suites Hotel in Las Vegas, Nevada, at 3:00 A.M. under his own name. That evening, Conrad Malsom, a 60-year-old unemployed car salesman who lived in Las Vegas, spotted McCoy reading a USA Today article about himself in the sports betting parlor of the Stardust Casino. The two even shared a pizza as Malsom got a closer look. As they talked, Malsom learned where McCoy was staying and even took a sheet of paper containing some notes that McCoy was writing down. Malsom called the Las Vegas police, who arrested McCoy outside his hotel at 2:45 A.M. the following day.

The concept of confidential informants (also called "CIs") in society is nothing new. In fact, both police and civilians attempt from time to time to encourage public participation in solving crimes. One well-known program is **Crimestoppers**, which encourages citizens to engage in "anonymous" informing to assist police in developing suspects in crimes or to catch criminals in the act of committing

|Fig. 8.1| △

Suspected sniper Charles McCoy Jr. was turned in by informer Conrad Malsom in Las Vegas, Nevada, in March 2004.

Franklin County Sheriff's Department / AP Wide World Photos

245

them. Although some people complain that Crimestoppers makes "snitches" out of law-abiding citizens, others argue that it is simply a system of public responsibility similar to the old days of the "hue and cry," when all citizens assumed responsibility for public order.

In addition to allowing tipsters to call the police anonymously, many informants receive cash rewards for their cooperation. The amount of the reward depends on the "quality of information" provided by the citizen—that is, information that results in an arrest. All communication between the police and the citizen is accomplished by the assignment of a number to the caller. That number is used in lieu of a name for the remainder of the citizen–police relationship, negating the need for the police ever to know the true name of the tipster.

Along lines similar to Crimestoppers are efforts by victims of crimes to convince the community to become more involved with identifying known criminals and reporting violators to police. One example of this is the well-known television show *America's Most Wanted*. The show has helped track down more than 800 fugitives.[1] Other shows, including *Unsolved Mysteries* and *U.S. Customs*, have had similar success.

Another public forum for locating criminals, which has been around longer than the television shows discussed above, is the FBI's Top Ten Most Wanted list. The FBI has maintained its Most Wanted list since 1950, and although it was once a mainstay in crime fighting, it has all but lost its appeal in today's high-tech age of television, computers, and the Internet. Still, it is designed to encourage citizen participation in sharing information with the police about crime and criminals who are wanted. The Most Wanted list was invented by a wire service reporter and later adopted by the publicity-driven director of the FBI, J. Edgar Hoover. As of 1997, 422 of the 449 fugitives who appeared on the list have been captured, a 94 percent success rate.[2]

In its earliest stages, when few Americans owned television sets, the Most Wanted list contained bank robbers, burglars, and car thieves, criminals who dominated the crime scene. Today's Most Wanted list includes cop killers, drug dealers, and international terrorists who aren't even in the country.[3] Skeptics argue that the list has outlived its usefulness because of the age of modern technology (the Internet, electronic billboards, and television). In 1992, the U.S. Post Office discontinued

|Fig. 8.2|

Tipster Conrad Malsom notified police of the whereabouts of Charles McCoy, the Ohio Interstate sniper.

Joe Cavaretta / AP Wide World Photos

putting Top 10 posters on its walls. Perhaps it could be argued that the FBI's "list" has become ineffective, especially with the advent of so many different high-tech media showcasing the nation's fugitives. Of late, some victims have taken the initiative to seek help from the public by using their own money and resources.

During August 1997, the parents of murder victim JonBenet Ramsey ran their fourth advertisement in a local newspaper appealing for help from the public. The ad included samples of handwriting from the ransom note and commented that "the killer appears to be obsessed with technocrime movies and phrases from them."[4] In addition, the ad included quotes from the movies *Dirty Harry* and *Speed* that the family claimed were similar to the ones used in the ransom note.

In any case, whether it is a paid police informant or an anonymous tip, police rely heavily on information from the public to solve crimes. Experience has shown that a primary component of crime control is proactive law enforcement. Proactive investigations include vice cases such as drug trafficking, prostitution, and gambling, in which investigators actually seek out potential crimes and intervene "before" the crimes occur. Accordingly, the use of *informants* as a source of criminal information in such crimes has proved to be invaluable. Consequently, law enforcement officers are insistent in protecting the identities of their sources so that the well-being of the informants will not be jeopardized and so they will continue to be of use to the officer in future criminal investigations. (Note: Informants are also commonly called *informers, confidential informers*, or *cooperating individuals*, but in this book, they are referred to as *informants*.)

One of the most exceptional examples of informant use was the 1963 testimony of Joseph Valachi, a former Mafia soldier. Valachi's highly publicized role as an informant with the FBI resulted in the convictions of several management figures in the American Mafia. This case raised questions and public concern about the appropriateness of law enforcement officers using "criminals to catch criminals." Another high-visibility case involved Tommaso Buscetta, a crime family boss in Palermo, Sicily, who testified against numerous other Mafia bosses during the mid-1980s. His testimony was instrumental in the arrest and subsequent prosecutions of an estimated 450 fellow Mafiosos. Nevertheless, many misconceptions still exist about the value and utility of the criminal informant. For example, some think that police officers who are using an informant will be tolerant of that person's criminal lifestyle and might be less willing to report criminal wrongdoing on the part of the informant. Although through the years some improprieties have been documented regarding the use of informants, the value of such persons has proved immense in the prosecution of many high-level crime figures and in aiding law enforcement in understanding the inner workings of sophisticated criminal organizations.

In addition, some people believe that in dealing closely with informants, police officers may themselves become tainted and their positions compromised. In this chapter, we consider the role of informants in criminal investigations and how best to manage the information provided by them.

Who Are Informants?

Although the word **informant** has many negative synonyms, such as "snitch" and "stoolie," the term could best be defined as "anyone who provides information of an investigative nature to law enforcement."[5] More specifically, Black's Law Dictionary defines "informer" as "A person who informs or prefers an accusation against another whom he suspects of the violation of some penal statute."[6] Exclusions to this definition, of course, are victims of crime who have reported specific criminal activity to law enforcement. This makes their role more that of a complainant.

The FBI, on the other hand, refers to its sources of information as either informants or cooperative witnesses. The distinction between these two categories depends on the information they provide. For example, according to the FBI's *Manual of Investigative Operations and Guidelines* (MIOG) an informant is any person who provides information on a confidential basis. A **cooperating witness**, on the other hand, is a person whose relationship with the government is concealed until testimony at trial is required and who contributes substantial operational assistance to the resolution of a case through active participation in an investigation.[7]

Indeed, the informant is most typically used in cases in which there is no complainant. These typically include vice and **victimless crimes** such as drug violations, gambling, and prostitution. Because informants can be virtually anyone in a community, a good investigator should consider anybody with whom he or she comes in contact as a potential source of criminal information. That is, the premise of locating a knowledgeable informant is to realize that someone somewhere is aware of various crimes committed. It is therefore the investigator's responsibility to locate and develop relationships with such people.

Generally, people who become informants can be classified into four general groups:

1. *Average citizens.* Although not necessarily a criminal source, people falling into this group may still be an excellent source of information. Most good investigators have several informants of this type who are contacted periodically for leads. Examples of these informants are waitresses, bartenders, dancers, and private investigators.
2. *Fellow law enforcement officers.* On an average day, investigators exchange valuable information with other investigators many times. Although much of this information is between "friends" who are investigators, a considerable amount is also exchanged by officers working in other units within the department. In addition, investigators who befriend officers with other local, state, or federal agencies can also benefit from useful information about criminals and criminal activity.
3. *Mentally ill persons.* It is unfortunate, but a percentage of informants fall into the category of mentally ill or deranged. An experienced investigator can detect when such persons are simply fabricating information or passing on news stories or gossip. One should also consider, however, that although an informant is mentally ill, his or her information might still have some validity.
4. *Criminals or their associates.* Without question, criminal informants have proven to be most valued in many police investigations. These are people who are currently, or have been, associated with a particular criminal element and are therefore in an excellent position to supply firsthand information about criminal activity. Informants are a dynamic group of people who come from diverse backgrounds and frequently view their role in different ways. For example, one informant may give information with no reservations about his or her identity becoming known. Conversely, others may have valuable information to render but may do so only with the understanding that their identities remain concealed. Those falling into the latter category typically want their identities to be kept secret for their own protection and because if their true identities become known, their function as informants would be ended.

Using Informants

On August 8, 2008, Shelby County Sheriff's Office narcotics investigator Eric Curtis identified an individual known as "informant A" as a potentially valuable informant. "Informant A" was on supervised release with the federal district court; therefore, Curtis appeared as a witness before the court and requested permission to allow "informant A" to work as a confidential informant.

At a later time, the district court sentenced "informant A" on his supervised release violation. During the sentencing hearing, Curtis again appeared in court and vouched for the value of information provided by "informant A" as a confidential informant. Curtis told the court that "informant A" had provided information that resulted in the arrest of numerous individuals and the recovery of a litany of narcotics.[8]

On November 19, 2009, the defendant met with agents from the FBI. During this meeting, Curtis repeated to agents that "informant A" had in fact worked as a confidential informant. Curtis then detailed the items recovered as a result of information provided by "informant A." Curtis said that "informant A" was responsible for 7 felony arrests, the seizure of 1,504 dose units of Oxycontin, 4,536 grams of marijuana, 5 kilograms of cocaine, and $35,296 in cash.[9]

Subsequently, agents from the FBI discovered that the number of arrests and items seized attributed to "informant A" by the defendant in federal court and to agents in the November 19 meeting were in fact a result of information provided by a number of different informants and not by "informant A." Curtis had used his position as a Shelby County Sheriff's Deputy to deceive and lie to a U.S. district court judge and law enforcement officers alike. As a result, Curtis was prosecuted and sentenced to 28 months in federal prison.[10]

In contrast to the opening case study involving tipster Conrad Malsom, this case illustrates how informants and the officers that control them can fall victim to a number of operational pitfalls. Many such problems can result in the wrongful targeting, investigation, arrest, and prosecution of innocent persons.

Although a frequent source of valuable information, the use of an informant in a criminal investigation can be problematic. Therefore, the use of an informant should not be considered if similar results could be achieved through other means. Problems that stem from the use of informants are due to three variables. First, informants are often difficult to control. Many of them have been criminals for long periods and are very independent by nature. This independence sometimes results in the informant's attempting to manipulate the investigator and manage the investigation.

Second, an informant can become a source of public embarrassment for the law enforcement agency. For example, an informant might be arrested for a high-visibility crime during the time that he or she is working with the police. The local media could then make headlines that could jeopardize the investigation in which the informant was involved. Such situations are sometimes unavoidable but can usually be minimized with proper management techniques.

|Fig. 8.3| △

Undercover investigator in vehicle meeting with informant who is a gang member. Investigators must often meet their informants secretly to receive important investigative leads.

Monkey Business Images / Shutterstock

A third area of concern is the informant's questionable **credibility** in court. Depending on the role of the informant in the investigation, he or she might have to testify in court proceedings. A good defense council can expose the criminal background of such people and show that their testimony is not to be believed. If this is accomplished, juries will have difficulty finding the defendant guilty "beyond a reasonable doubt." After the decision has been made to use the services of an informant, he or she can be used in a number of ways:

- Make observations in areas where strangers would be suspect
- Furnish information from a source not readily available to the investigator
- Conduct "controlled" undercover transactions or introduce undercover agents to criminal suspects
- Collect intelligence information (e.g., determine street prices of drugs and identify suspects, their associates, and their residences)

The criminal investigator has the responsibility to evaluate every informant used. This saves time and effort if it is determined that the informant's information is unreliable or that the informant harbors a hidden agenda. Thus, the motive is extremely important to identify with each informant candidate because it may directly affect the credibility of the case.

Informant Motivations

The utilization of informants is not without its problems. Because informants are typically criminals themselves, a number of practical, operational, ethical, and even moral problems may present themselves. This is why it is crucial for the criminal investigator to identify the motivations of the informant early on in the investigative process. Researcher Gary Marx, in his authoritative book *Undercover: Police Surveillance in America*, speaks to this concern. He states, "Working with informers can be an excruciatingly difficult and delicate task. They [informers] often have strong incentives to break the law. Because of charges they are seeking to avoid, a desire to punish competitors of enemies, or the promise of drugs or money, they may have little concern with equitable and principled law enforcement."[11]

Successful recruitment and management of informants pivots on the investigator's ability to recognize the **motivation** of the informant. Because the negative stigma of being an informant is so great in the United States, it is sometimes difficult to develop such people successfully. Police occasionally consider average citizens as informants provided that they are willing to offer relevant information in an investigation. The motivation of such people is a sense of civic duty.

As one might guess, mentally ill informants (depending on their illness) are motivated by very different reasons. These reasons are usually very complicated and difficult to determine, and frequently, information furnished by these persons is worthless to the investigator. When a mentally ill informant gives valuable information, however, the person may be motivated by the same reasons as those that motivate criminal informants. Indeed, the criminal informant is the most valuable of all informant categories. As indicated, these people pose many legal, moral, and ethical considerations not generally associated with the other three categories. Motivations for a criminal informant fall into a number of categories:

- *The fearful informant.* Many persons agree to cooperate with law enforcement when fear is the chief motivator. Fear comes in many forms, such as fear of detection and punishment by law enforcement or retribution from criminal associates. "Working off a charge" is a matter of survival for criminal informants.[12] Typically, this incentive arises when a person is arrested for an offense and fears being convicted and imprisoned. Given the opportunity, the arrestee may choose to provide information to investigators in exchange for leniency. Investigators must be careful not to make any promises to persons arrested without the consent of the prosecutor, who is generally vested with such authority. The investigator may, however, advise the informant that such a recommendation may be made pending any cooperation.
- *The financially motivated informant.* Money is probably the easiest motivation to understand. "Mercenary" informants give information in exchange for a fee. In Christianity, Judas was the first recorded paid informant, receiving 30 pieces of silver for betraying Jesus. Often, the financially motivated informant will prove to be a valuable contributor to the investigation. Such persons may, however, attempt to manipulate the investigation to prolong payments to them. This is typically done by extending the investigation through providing

CITY POLICE DEPARTMENT
COOPERATING INDIVIDUAL AGREEMENT

I, _____, the undersigned, state that it is my intent to associate myself, of my own free will and without any coercion or duress, with the City Police Department as a cooperating individual.

As a cooperating individual, I understand and agree that I have no police powers under the laws of the state of (____) and have no authority to carry a weapon while performing my activity as a cooperating individual. Further, I understand and agree that my only association with the city of (____) is as a cooperating individual on a case-by-case or time-to-time basis as an independent contractor, and not as an employee of the police department. Any payment I receive from the City Police Department will not be subject to federal or state income tax withholding or social security. I understand that it is my responsibility to report any income and also that I am not entitled to either workmen's compensation or unemployment insurance payments for anything I do as a cooperating individual.

In consideration for being allowed to associate with the City Police Department as a cooperating individual, and in consideration for any payment I may receive, I agree to be bound by the following terms and conditions and procedures while so associated.

1. I agree that under no circumstances will I purchase or possess any controlled substances or suspected controlled substances without the direction and control of a police officer and then will make a purchase only with monies supplied by him.

2. I agree not to use or sell, dispense, or transfer any controlled substance except that I may use any controlled substance prescribed to me by a licensed physician.

3. I agree to maintain a strict accounting of all funds provided to me by the City Police Department and I understand that misuse of city funds could be grounds for criminal prosecution against me.

4. I agree not to divulge to any person, except the officer with whom I am associated, my status as a cooperating individual for the City Police Department unless required to do so in court, and shall not represent myself to others as an employee or representative of the City Police Department nor use the department or any of its officers as personal references or as credit or employment references.

5. I understand that any violation of the above listed provisions may be grounds for my immediate removal as a cooperating individual and that any violation of law may result in my arrest and prosecution.

    I understand that association with the City Police Department as a cooperating individual may involve strenuous physical activity and may become hazardous to my physical well-being and safety. Nevertheless, it is my desire to associate myself with the department, on an independent contractor basis, as a cooperating individual. I am associating myself with the department in this status freely and without any coercion or duress. In consideration for being accepted as a cooperating individual, I release and discharge the City of (____), the City Police Department and its elected officials, officers, employees, and agents from all claims, demands, actions, judgments, and executions which I may have or acquire and subsequently claim to have against the City for personal injuries and property damage I may sustain which arises out of or in connection with my association with the city. I make this release for myself, my heirs, executors, and administrators. Also, I agree not to maintain any action against the City of (____), the City Police Department, or its elected officials, officers, employees, or agents for personal injuries and property damage I sustain which arise out of or in connection with my association with the City Police Department.

_____
Cooperating Individual

_____
Date

WITNESSES:

_____
Officer

_____
Officer

Fig. 8.4 △

Sample informant agreement form.

misleading information or by "setting up" suspects in criminal violations that they are not predisposed to commit (i.e., entrapment).

- **The revengeful informant.** Revenge is not uncommon to the criminal underworld, and wrongs committed by one criminal against another are commonly settled outside the law. Frequently, however, informants motivated by revenge can produce favorable investigative results. Although those motivated by revenge are seldom concerned about revealing their identity in court, investigators must be careful to recognize an exaggerated or embellished story. In addition, such persons frequently have drifting allegiances and may reconcile with their former adversaries midway through the investigation, thus ruining credibility and jeopardizing the well-being of investigators.

- *The egotistical informant.* Many people take great delight in passing on information to others. Informants falling into this category may also be of great value to an investigator. This motivation is sometimes dubbed the *police complex* because of a person's desire to associate with law enforcement. It is typically characterized by a small-time criminal alleging to have inside information on high-level crime figures.
- *The perversely motivated informant.* People who display a perverse motivation are those who inform with a hidden benefit or advantage to themselves. Sometimes informants with this motivation are trying to eliminate their competition, learning investigative techniques, determining if any of their criminal associates are under investigation by police, or learning the identity of undercover officers. In all cases, the investigator must be aware of such motivations to avoid "setups" and compromising situations.
- *The reformed informant.* Informants characterized by this motivation act out of a sense of guilt from wrongdoing. Such informants are rare but when encountered may provide reliable information to the investigator.

Documenting Your "Source"

Proper management of informants is essential in avoiding unethical, immoral, or unprofessional allegations later in an investigation. The investigator must remember that informants belong to the agency and are not the "personal" resource of the investigator. This understanding will ensure that a system of checks and balances through records and verification of information can be officially maintained.

All candidates for informants should be well documented. They should, therefore, be fingerprinted, photographed, and carefully interviewed by investigators before being used as an informant. Interviews should reflect the informant's true name and any aliases, address, employment history, and so on. In addition, criminal records, if any, should be verified through the National Crime Information Center as well as through local and state law enforcement agencies. All such procedures should be contained in an official informant file established specifically for that person. The file should then be indexed by number, not by name, and that number should be used in all subsequent reports referring to the informant.

During the informant interview, the interviewer must be careful to solicit certain information. Some typical questions asked potential informants include:

- What is his or her motivation?
- Has the informer been reliable in the past?
- What is the intelligence of the informant?
- How does he or she know about the violation?
- Does he or she have a personal interest, and if so, what?
- Does he or she have direct knowledge?
- Does he or she have access to additional knowledge?
- Does he or she harbor any vengeance toward the suspect?
- Is he or she withholding some kind of information?
- Has he or she lied about information in the past?
- Is he or she willing to testify in court?

After the informant responds to the preceding questions, the investigator should have adequate information to proceed with a final evaluation of the person's potential worth. If the informant poses more of a liability than a benefit, he or she should be eliminated from further consideration.

Maintaining Control

In May 2010, five men were arrested after they kidnapped a confidential informant working for U.S. Immigration and Customs Enforcement (ICE) during an attempted drug deal rip-off in Tucson. The incident unfolded as ICE agents, working on an undercover operation, negotiated a deal with a suspected drug dealer, Guillermo Leon-Rivera, for 600 pounds of marijuana. On April 12 agents provided Leon-Rivera and his associates with a pickup truck, which was to be loaded with the marijuana, agreeing to pay for it once it was returned. The truck was eventually returned to the buyer (the informant) empty.

Nonetheless, Leon-Rivera and four other suspects demanded payment from the informant in an act known as a "drug-rip." They kidnapped the informant that same evening at gunpoint and then drove him to a house once owned by one of the suspects. They then bound him, beat him, and repeatedly threatened to kill him.

During the course of the evening and early morning hours of April 13, the five suspects continued to hold the informant hostage, making demands of the informant's contacts for either full payment or return of the 600 pounds of marijuana. Unbeknownst to the five defendants, however, the person that the suspects thought to be a drug buyer was a confidential informant and the people the hostage takers had been communicating with all along were ICE agents. In addition, the ransom calls were audio-recorded and the earlier "load" pickup truck had been under continuous surveillance the entire day, confirming that no marijuana had ever been delivered to ICE or their undercover informant. An ICE Special Response Team raided the house at dawn, freeing the informant and arresting the defendants.

Customarily, the investigator who develops an informer is the one who is assigned to him or her. A cardinal rule in working with informants is for the investigator to command control of the investigation, not the informant. This is sometimes difficult to accomplish because many informants possess strong, manipulative personalities. Although informants should be asked frequently for their opinions, each suggestion should be considered carefully. Additionally, investigators must be careful not to promise anything they cannot deliver (e.g., money, a reduced charge, relocation of their family, police protection).

Control of informants is best achieved through frequent personal contacts with them. These interactions are the best method for debriefing informers and maintaining rapport with them. The officer assigned should make most, if not all, contacts with informants. Doing so reduces additional demands of the informant and ensures the person's allegiance to the control officer. Another critical area of instruction for the informant is **entrapment**. Criminal suspects must be given an "opportunity" for the commission of a crime and not the "motivation" for doing so. If the entrapment issue is not remembered during the course of an investigation, the case may result in the dismissal of charges against the suspect and a soiled reputation for the department.

Protecting the Informant's Identity

Experience has shown that defendants may attempt to injure, intimidate, or even murder people working with the police. Accordingly, investigators bear an ethical and professional responsibility to safeguard the identities of informants and their families to the best of their ability. During initial interviews, investigators should advise potential informants that it is impossible to guarantee the confidentiality of their identities absolutely but that all efforts will be made to do so. In fact, the U.S. Supreme Court has ruled that the identities of informants may be kept secret if sources have been explicitly assured of confidentiality by investigating officers or if a reasonably implied assurance of confidentiality has been made. Measures that can be taken by the investigator to protect an informant's identity include:

- Limiting direct contact with the informant to one investigator or the "control" agent (unless the informant is of the opposite sex, in which case, two investigators should be present); meetings should be brief and held where neither party will be recognized
- Minimizing telephone conversations between control agents and informants in the event that someone is listening in on the line
- Selecting different locations to meet
- Warning informants about discussing their associations with the police to anyone, including their friends and spouses

The U.S. Supreme Court addressed the issue of protection of the informant's identity in court. In *U.S. Department of Justice* v. *Landano* (1993), the Court required that an informant's identity be revealed through a request made under the federal Freedom of Information Act. In that case, the FBI had not specifically assured the informant of confidentiality, and the Court ruled that "the government is not entitled to a presumption that all sources supplying information to the FBI in the course of a criminal investigation are confidential sources."

Legal Considerations

Information gathering is a complex process that raises many ethical and legal questions regarding the techniques used by investigators. For example, when police pay informants for information, critics argue that the informant might be tempted to entrap persons into committing crimes so that the informant can realize some income. Another common use of informants is **flipping**. This is a procedure in which an arrested person is given the choice of providing information to police in exchange for dropping their charges. Flipping is a widely used procedure requiring approval of the local prosecutor, but it still raises questions about the ethical appropriateness of the procedure. Simply put, the informer's primary role is to provide probable cause to police for arrests and search warrants.

Investigators frequently ground their investigation upon information provided to them by informants. For many years the courts used what has become known as the "Aguilar-Spinelli two-prong test" for evaluating whether information provided by an informant properly established probable cause for an arrest or search.

The first prong of that test assesses the credibility of the informant or the "source." In other words, can the informant be believed? Law enforcement officers, prominent citizens, and crime victims all are presumed credible but criminal informants are presumed unreliable. The credibility of criminal informants is a crucial issue in criminal investigation. Credibility must be established through a documented track record of reliability—having made a statement against their penal interests, corroboration of the supplied information, or establishing that the informants have a strong motive to tell the truth.[13]

The second prong of the Aguilar-Spinelli test is an evaluation of the informant's basis of knowledge. Stated differently, how does the informant know what he or she knows? In explaining an informant's basis of knowledge, an investigator is essentially trying to establish that the informant knows what he is talking about. One way to establish a basis of knowledge is if the informant states that he saw the criminal activity; another way is if the information from the informant is so detailed that a reasonable officer could infer that the informant was an eyewitness or received the information from a reliable source who was himself an eyewitness.[14]

The legal playing field regarding informants changed, however, in 1985. In *Illinois* v. *Gates*, the U.S. Supreme Court ruled that probable cause is a practical, nontechnical concept and that it should not be weighed in terms of library analysis by scholars using tests such as the Aguilar-Spinelli two-prong test.[15] Rather, the Court stated that the test for probable cause under the Fourth Amendment should be a **totality of the circumstances** test. The Court reasoned that probable cause is a fluid concept that turns on the evaluation of probabilities in a set of specific facts by those known in the field of law enforcement. The *Gates* totality of the circumstances test gives investigators and courts more flexibility when deciding if there is probable cause in a particular case. Although the Aguilar-Spinelli two-prong test is not a legal requirement in federal and most state courts, the test often is used as a guide by courts in determining probable cause based upon an informant's tip.

Concerned Citizens as Informants

Concerned citizens who have information regarding suspected criminal activity sometimes contact criminal investigators. Typically, concerned citizen informants give police information out of a sense of civic duty. To be considered a concerned citizen informant by the courts, an informant must not be involved in the criminal activity for which they are providing information. Accordingly, a concerned citizen does not usually have a track record for reliability with the police. However, a track record for reliability is not necessary to establish the credibility of a concerned citizen. As a general rule, if a concerned citizen's identity is known to the police, he is presumed credible.

Assuming an identified concerned citizen has a reliable basis of knowledge, an officer could have probable cause to arrest a suspect on only the slightest corroboration of the information. For example, in *State* v. *Lindquist*, the concerned citizen informant identified herself to the police and stated that a suspect had shown her marijuana in his car and told her that in a few minutes he would be driving to a specified geographical area with the drugs.

The informant provided investigators specific details about the suspect's vehicle and license plate number. The officers found the vehicle described by the informant traveling in the foreseen direction. They pulled over the suspect's car and arrested him. The officers found five pounds of marijuana in the vehicle. The Supreme Court of Minnesota characterized the police finding the car as corroboration of many of the details given in the tip and ruled that the officers had probable cause to arrest the suspect.

Anonymous Tips

In the *Lindquist* case, the informant identified herself to the police. On the other hand, if a concerned citizen wishes to remain anonymous to the police, he would not be presumed credible, and the need for corroboration to establish his credibility would be more rigorous. In *Illinois* v. *Gates* (discussed earlier in this chapter), the U.S. Supreme Court reviewed the sufficiency of the corroboration of an anonymous tip. In the *Gates* decision, the Court stated that it was important that the anonymous tip contained details regarding unusual future travel plans of the suspects. The anonymous tipster, in a letter to the police, stated that Sue Gates ordinarily drove her car to Florida, where she would leave it to be loaded with drugs. Lance Gates would fly down later and drive the car back to Illinois, and Sue would fly back to Illinois. The letter indicated that they planned to make a trip to pick up over $100,000 worth of drugs on May 3, 1978.

A police detective assigned to the case determined that Lance Gates made a reservation on a flight to West Palm Beach, Florida, scheduled to depart from Chicago on May 5, 1978, at 4:15 P.M. The detective made arrangements with an agent from DEA for surveillance of the May 5 flight. DEA agents observed Lance Gates boarding the flight, and other agents in Florida observed him arriving in West Palm Beach, Florida. The Florida agents then observed Gates take a taxi to a nearby motel and go to a room registered to Susan Gates. Early the next morning, the agents observed Gates and an unidentified woman, presumably Susan Gates, leave the motel in an automobile bearing Illinois license plates registered to another vehicle owned by Gates. Gates drove northbound on an interstate highway frequently used to travel to the Chicago area. The Court in the *Gates* case ruled that such uncommon conduct was suggestive of a prearranged drug run. Once the police corroborated the major details of the travel of the suspects, which were predicted by the anonymous tipster, it was reasonable to conclude that the information about the future conduct of the suspects likely was obtained directly from one of the criminal participants or from someone they trusted who was familiar with their criminal plans. The Court ruled that the corroboration of the anonymous tip was sufficient to establish probable cause for a search warrant to search the suspects' home and car upon their return to Illinois.

While it is preferable to corroborate suspicious criminal conduct before arresting a suspect based upon an anonymous tip, some courts are satisfied with corroboration of innocent details from an anonymous tip to establish probable cause.[16]

Jailhouse Informants

As discussed, the majority of informants utilized by criminal investigators are criminals. This is not to say that information provided by them is not factual, but it is to say that based on their motivation, information provided may be tainted with "spin" or truth mixed with lies. This is especially critical when considering the use of informants that are incarcerated or **jailhouse snitch**. Jailhouse informants are notorious liars and by virtue of having little to nothing to lose by lying, they might tell the investigator almost anything in exchange for some form of leniency. John Madinger in his book *Confidential Informants* states, "Jailhouse informants are highly motivated. They want out—at least out sooner. It is probably not surprising that quite a few will lie, cheat, steal to get what they want."[17]

In spite of the inherent problems working with informants, they have proven useful on occasion. For example, many cold cases, those that have gone unsolved for many years, are solved by jail cell confessions given by the perpetrator to a fellow inmate.[18] The informant will generally channel their information through a corrections officer or via telephone to detectives. Problems present themselves when investigators subsequently direct the informant to obtain confessions or admissions from the incarcerated target suspect. In some cases unscrupulous investigators have provided informants who then fabricate a defendant's confession. Such actions present the risk of serious Fifth and Sixth Amendment violations and should be apparent to investigators and prosecutors alike.[19]

Other Problems with Informants

As indicated earlier, working with informants can be challenging and, at times, outright problematic. In addition to concerns of entrapment and ethical, moral, and criminal activity on the part of the informant, there are several other areas of concern:

- *Lying.* CIs may exaggerate or fabricate the criminal acts of targets. Some may report truthfully, but may lie about having used illegal methods to obtain the information. Their motives may range from wanting to receive high marks from officers to fancying themselves "super sleuths."[20]

- *Double-dealing.* CIs can make deals with targets as easily as they can with the police, and use both sides to their advantage. They may be faithful to neither side, yet remain trusted by both. CIs may provide criminal associates with information about the identity of undercover agents, cars they drive, hours they work, their tactics, and agency procedures. Further, they may be individuals who are purposely planted and who continue their criminal activities and monitor police operations while eliminating competitors. Money may be the motive for addicts, gamblers, and alcoholics to get involved in double-dealing. Other CIs may do so to help cover their informant activities or ingratiate themselves with criminal associates.[21]

- *Rip-offs.* The CI is in a position to arrange rip-offs of large flash rolls. They have been known to sell government property used in investigations or to pledge it as collateral for loans. They may sell the same information to two different agencies, causing them to unwittingly conduct simultaneous investigations. A major violator arrested by one agency may sell information to another agency about a relatively minor operation, and receive a lenient sentence for doing so.[22]

- *Blackmail.* Officers who get too close to informers may begin to sympathize with their problems and bend the rules. Eventually, the CI may "get something" on the officer, who loses control and, in effect, ends up being "controlled" by the CI.[23]

- *Investigators becoming too friendly with informants.* Because investigators and their informers work together closely, it is possible that an officer can become caught up in an informant's personal problems. Certainly, the investigator should lend a sympathetic ear when possible, but investigators should be cautioned that becoming too close to an informant could jeopardize the investigator's level of control over the person.

- *Informants of the opposite sex.* Over the years, many investigators have fallen victim to allegations of sexual misconduct with informants of the opposite sex. Although some have proved truthful, many have had no basis but resulted in disciplinary action against the officer and a termination of the investigation.[24] To avoid such allegations, a second officer should always accompany the investigator. The location of meeting spots with informants should also be considered very carefully, particularly if a second officer is not present.

- *Crimes committed by the informant.* During initial meetings between the investigator and potential informants, officers should stress that any criminal activity on the part of the informant will not be tolerated. History has shown that after being arrested for a crime, informants will sometimes mention the name of their control officer in hopes of being released or of receiving special treatment.

At times, information provided by informants is of such value that informants are paid for the information they supply. The investigator should be careful not to pay for information that has not been verified or that is not considered useful in the investigation. Accordingly, informant payments should be sufficiently modest as to avoid defense accusations of entrapment. When this occurs, the defense will maintain that the investigator's payment to the informant was so high that the informant was enticed into "setting up" the suspect solely for the monetary reward.

Federal Protection of the Informant

If the case in which the informant testifies involves organized crime, the informant is eligible to enter the federal **Witness Security (WITSEC) program**. The WITSEC program, developed in 1971 and operated under the U.S. Marshal's Service, is designed to relocate government informants, providing them with new names, Social Security numbers, and other identification. Although a controversial program, it enjoys a 92 percent success rate in convictions of organized crime members by persons entering the program.

There are two tiers to the WITSEC program. Tier one involves the relocation of non-incarcerated persons from one area of the United States to another. The second tier provides for the hiding of a prisoner within the nation's federal prison system. These are persons who have testified or who have agreed to testify but who must serve sentences themselves. As of 2007, fifty percent of new witnesses authorized into the program go into each of these two components.[25] To meet the needs of the WITSEC witnesses, the U.S. Bureau of Prisons has constructed Protective Custody Units, which are basically prisons within prisons so witnesses can be housed with other witnesses. The BOP reports that as of 2000, they protected 475 witnesses.[26]

Undercover Operations

Undercover operations are an important part of the criminal investigation function but one that is highly specialized and not practiced by all law enforcement agencies. Investigators require specialized training to successfully perform this function.

Being undercover is the process of using an assumed identity for the purposes of gaining the trust of an individual or organization to learn information or to gain the trust of targeted individuals in order to gain information (intelligence) or evidence (criminal investigations). Traditionally it is a technique employed by law enforcement agencies around the world and a person who works in such a role is commonly referred to as an undercover agent.

Stories abound regarding both investigative successes and failures in this area. From a practical standpoint, undercover work and surveillance are viable options for police investigators because they provide considerable information that is not otherwise available through traditional investigative methods.

For example, in February 2009, the U.S. Drug Enforcement Administration arrested 52 persons in California, Minnesota, and Maryland as part of *Operation Xcellerator*. This investigation targeted the Sinaloa Cartel, a major Mexican drug trafficking organization.

In recent years, the Sinaloa Cartel has been responsible for bringing multiton quantities of narcotics, including cocaine and marijuana, from Mexico into the United States through distribution cells in the United States and Canada. They are also believed to be responsible for laundering millions of dollars in drug money. Suspects in this investigation were charged with engaging in a continuing criminal enterprise by violating various felony provisions of the Controlled Substances Act, **conspiracy** to import controlled substances, money laundering, and possession of unregistered firearms.[27]

The subjects of undercover operations and surveillance are discussed in this chapter because of their close relationship with each other and because of their importance to the investigative function. Typically, undercover work has been associated with drug enforcement, but it is a tool that can be useful in the investigation of a number of criminal activities.

Overview

Motto and June (2000) state that undercover work is best described as a *drama* involving three main participants: (1) the informant, (2) the suspect, and (3) the undercover agent. No matter what kind of operation, sting or undercover, the *drama* will always involve the interaction among these three main players.[28] Working undercover is not for everyone. Not everyone likes working undercover but many of those who do remain in the specialization for as long as they are needed or until they burn out. Experienced officers who have handled many informants and who have extensive experience in undercover work are soon recognized as experts in their fields.[29]

Undercover operations have been used by police agencies for decades. However, they present many problems and concerns for the department because of the delicate nature of undercover work and the officer's role in determining whether someone is committing criminal violations.[30] Undercover work forces the officer to assume a different identity and, sometimes, a lifestyle that thrusts him or her into the criminal subculture, where he or she can be tempted to do things that would otherwise be immoral or even illegal (e.g., using illegal drugs). This has the potential to exact a heavy price on individual officers because, depending on the nature of the assignment, they may be separated from family, friends, and other department members for extended periods of time.

Undercover work is street-level work at its best (or worst, however you wish to view it). Officers are required to participate in undesirable activities, and those who remain in undercover positions for too long a period may begin to adopt the very behaviors of the criminals they are investigating, including undesirable mannerisms and foul language at the least. Even worse, the department can become involved in illegal activities during the course of an investigation. For example, New York City undercover officers ran a pornographic bookstore as part of an undercover sting operation. Officers, as part of their undercover investigation, purchased 1,200 pornographic films and resold them for considerable profit. After eight months, the officers finally arrested several film distributors.

Langworthy observes that some undercover operations result in additional criminal activities.[31] As a result of his analysis of a Birmingham undercover anti-fencing operation, he concluded that the operation caused a substantial amount of crime by creating a market for stolen goods. If the police operation had not existed, no market would have existed, and criminals would have stolen less.

Any undercover operation is subject to claims of entrapment. Officers are permitted to do things that provide the opportunity for a suspect to commit a crime, but they may not induce someone to commit a crime. Because undercover operations generally may be initiated without prior judicial authorization, the results are subject to strict scrutiny by the courts. Allowing police to make the decision to initiate an undercover operation based on mere suspicion has been the subject of much criticism.[32] Recognizing the magnitude of the problem, the FBI now requires that large-scale undercover operations first be reviewed by their Criminal Undercover Operations Review Committee.

Informants are particularly useful and often necessary in the investigation of vice crimes. They can be problematic, however, because police sometimes overlook illegal acts committed by informers to pursue their investigations. For example, narcotics users or lower-level dealers may be allowed to continue violating the law to make cases against their suppliers. Consequently, to move up the distribution network, undercover officers may find it necessary to cooperate with dealers who are selling a significant amount of drugs.

A 1989 informant management case in Cleveland resulted in disastrous consequences for the department.[33] Officers of the narcotics unit enlisted the help of Arthur Feckner, one of the city's major wholesalers, to arrest his supplier. The investigation, which resulted in the seizure of more than 100 pounds of cocaine, caused enormous problems for the department. Allegations surfaced that the police allowed Feckner to continue to sell drugs in a housing project to finance their drug investigation. Detectives maintained that they believed the money came from the sale of his assets and collection of debts from past drug sales. However, Feckner says he sold $20 million worth of drugs with the knowledge of the police.

Undercover operations require a number of decisions. Administrative discretion is exercised in determining what activities will be pursued, and operational discretion is exercised in determining who will be targeted for investigation. Because police do not have the resources to investigate every crime, they engage in selective enforcement, enforcing only particular types of violations or targeting specific types of offenders. The decision-making process for vice crimes is subject to the factors previously discussed. The most important criterion for officers is the seriousness of the offense.[34] Most forms of vice, when considered alone, could be viewed as relatively minor crimes. However, in the current political climate, which emphasizes "zero tolerance," possession of even small amounts of drugs is viewed as serious. Officers are therefore much less likely to use size discretion in their decision to arrest in drug cases.

Understanding Undercover Work

The use of undercover agents is not recommended for every police organization because of resources required for a successful undercover operation. These resources include manpower, training, funding, and specialized equipment.

Police administrators must be careful in the selection of the proper candidate(s) for undercover work. Not every police officer can function properly and professionally in an undercover capacity. Typically, an undercover officer works with minimal direct supervision.[35] As such, officers can be exposed to a number of enticements, which could result in the compromising of the officer's integrity or the investigation. Because of this, the undercover officer must have considerable personal integrity.

One of the greatest challenges to undercover officers is the development of skills that maximize their efforts to match wits with some of the most intelligent and artful criminals on the street.

Undercover assignments are either performed in the short term or long term (or "deep cover"). Short-term undercover operations are normally considerably safer for the officer than those that are **deep cover**. Short-term operations permit the help of surveillance officers and protection that undercover agents working in a deep-cover capacity do not have. However, the benefits of working a deep-cover undercover operation allow an undercover agent time to gain total trust of the criminal suspect to the point of openly discussing criminal operations. This is a great advantage to an undercover agent because as a rule, criminals are very suspicious about meeting new "clients" who could be (and sometimes are) police informers or undercover officers.

While no two cases are exactly the same, Motto and June point out that there are certain elements common to each undercover operation: the introduction, the acceptance, the buy, the arrest, covering the informant, and the "after action."[36]

The informant typically makes the "introduction" of the undercover operative to the suspect. This is the initiation of the case. From this point on, the "acceptance" phase takes over when the undercover agent is either accepted or not. In the event the suspect does not accept the officer, it might be necessary for the informant to meet the suspect at a later time without the undercover officer to determine why the suspect was suspicious. In the event the officer is not accepted, the informant can bring in a second officer with a different cover story. This time, both the officer and informant will try to overcome the difficulties experienced during the first contact.

After the introduction, there is a short period of "bobbing, weaving, and circling": The suspect gets to know or feel if he or she can trust the undercover officer. If a feeling of trust is established, the conversation will quickly turn to the criminal activities in which the suspect is involved.

In the case of an undercover drug operation, for example, this conversation generally results in the undercover agent asking for or obtaining samples, and the suspect will quote the purchase price. After the samples have been delivered and the undercover agent has had an opportunity to examine them, the purchase price is discussed.

This purchase, or the "buy," may or may not go through. In other words, a decision must be made whether or not to arrest a suspect when he or she delivers the contraband (also known as a **buy-bust**) or to take that action after subsequent deliveries (known as a **buy-walk**). If it is determined that the investigation should continue, no arrests should be made and nothing should be done to arouse the suspect's suspicion or to identify accidentally the true role of the undercover operative. This is known as *covering the informant*.

In drug investigations, the first buy is usually a small one whereby the agency doesn't mind losing its **seed money** so that the undercover officer can make a bigger purchase at a later time. Subsequent purchases of contraband are known as the "after action." As a rule, the second purchase or, if necessary, several subsequent purchases should be large enough to warrant not only the appearance of a suspect but also some of the people connected with him or her. These individuals could be present in several capacities, including countersurveillance, protection, main participants, or equal partners, and perhaps even higher-ups. Sometimes it is necessary because of the development of circumstances surrounding the case to arrest a suspect when an initial delivery is made.

Preparing for Undercover Assignments

Undercover work can be defined as assuming a fictitious identity and associating with known or suspected criminals for the purpose of collecting information or evidence on criminal activity. All undercover work has the potential for considerable danger. It requires that officers establish a cover story (which may or may not be blown at any time during the investigation) and that they associate closely with individuals who may be armed, unpredictable, under the influence of drugs, or mentally unstable.

A number of misconceptions exist regarding undercover agents. This is because undercover work is so highly specialized and secretive that even most plainclothes detectives and uniformed officers have little understanding of undercover operations. One fallacy of undercover work is that undercover agents break the law and/or use illicit drugs to protect their cover. The challenge of the professional undercover officer is to act like a criminal without violating the law. Another fallacy is that an undercover agent must be a good actor. This is untrue because being undercover is not acting. Rather, it is acting normally based on how the agent's personality is best suited. Yet another misconception is that the undercover agent must be a big spender. This is also not necessarily the case because experience has shown that many criminals are tight with their money even though they acquire it illegally.[37]

PERSONNEL CONSIDERATIONS The selection, management, and retention of effective undercover employees (UCEs) pose significant challenges to local, state, federal, and international law enforcement agencies. UCEs face unique experiences and stressors that set them apart from their overt counterparts and place them at increased risk for psychological injury, disciplinary action, and other adverse personal and professional consequences.[38]

Given the inherent dangers of undercover work, the selection and training of personnel must be meticulous. Consideration must be given to the particular goals and resources of the unit, the officers' personalities, their professional backgrounds, and their physical and mental conditions. In addition, an officer's proficiency with firearms, good reporting skills, and the ability to keep a cool head and use common sense under stressful conditions must be carefully weighed by police supervisors. Because of concern for officer safety and the increasing potential for agency liability, the days of undercover officers working the streets in deep cover and under minimal supervision are becoming less common.

Those being considered for undercover assignments should be disabused of any myths created by television and popular media stereotypes. Undercover work is not a glamorous job providing the agent with expensive meals, luxurious sports cars, and unheard-of electronic gadgetry. Conversely, it is also not a duty that requires an officer to isolate him- or herself from family and friends and become a drug-using martyr.

Most undercover work consists of a brief meeting between the agent and a suspect, an exchange of dialogue, and a transaction—usually a purchase of contraband such as a quantity of illegal drugs, stolen property, or illegal weapons. Deep-cover assignments, that is, assignments that require agents to operate with minimal protection over extended periods of time, are not as widely used and require specialized training.

Although required to work one on one with a suspected drug dealer, undercover officers must also realize that both their safety and the overall success of the investigation require equal participation by all unit members. Each officer's role (undercover contact, surveillance officer, radar officer, and officers assisting in arrest) is of equal importance. Even though every officer within the unit must maintain his or her caseload, each should regard the overall mission of the unit as an effort of a team rather than of one individual.

FUNCTIONS OF UNDERCOVER OFFICERS There are two general functions for officers within the undercover unit. The **undercover (UC) officer** contacts individuals or infiltrates establishments or organizations suspected of being involved in criminal activity. Usually, such contacts are possible because the officer's appearance, mannerisms, dress, and overall demeanor are similar to those of the suspect. Considerable time and money are spent in carefully cultivating the officer's ability to function effectively in this capacity, so the true identity of the undercover officer should be protected at all times.

The **support officer** (sometimes called an intelligence, cover, or tactical officer) is a plainclothes officer who works with the undercover unit but not in an undercover capacity. Support officers assist undercover officers by observing the illicit transactions (e.g., an illegal drug transaction) in which they, or their informers, are involved. Support officers also participate in drug raids at the culmination of an investigation, interview arrestees, and perform other functions within the unit that would otherwise jeopardize or expose the identity of the undercover agent.

Because criminal enterprises differ in their resources, methods, procedures, and philosophies, the operational distinctions between undercover and support officers may not be feasible in some agencies. In such circumstances, officers may be required at different times to perform both functions.

EQUIPMENT To approach any covert investigation effectively, one of the first orders of business is to determine what equipment is necessary. The choice of equipment will, of course, vary according to the agency's financial resources, the size of the unit, the mission, and the type of assignment at hand. However, when considering an equipment purchase, careful thought should be given to its purpose and user, its usefulness, and its durability.

Undercover investigators require equipment that is different from that given to support officers. In addition, equipment assigned to a criminal investigator might be regularly carried with him or her in an assigned vehicle. Therefore, it may experience much wear and tear from moving around in the trunk of a car or the back of the van, or it may suffer from drastic changes in weather conditions due to changing humidity, temperature, or dust particles, for example.

VEHICLES As a rule, each vehicle owned by the agency should be assigned a separate number, and a maintenance and repair file should be kept on each vehicle. The kinds of vehicles the agency should own and the equipment the vehicles should contain depend on how they will be used. Following are some examples.

Support Officer Vehicles Vehicles for a support officer should generally be nondescript such as two-door sedans or commonly observed SUVs in plain colors such as white, tan, gray, or dark blue. Exotic or expensive sports cars might be advantageous in short-term undercover assignments, but they will also be easily remembered or identified (**burned**) as police vehicles by nervous or attentive suspects during any moving surveillance.

Vehicles should also be assigned to match the driver. For example, a more expensive car should be assigned to an appropriately dressed agent; a sports car should be assigned to an investigator who fits the role of someone who would typically drive one. If local laws permit, seized vehicles, if in good condition, are good assets and can provide a constant source of plausible vehicles for the undercover unit. Undercover personnel should not use vehicles assigned to support officers. Support officers' vehicles need to be outfitted differently from those assigned to undercover officers. These vehicles should have more standard "police-type" electronics that benefit them but would identify, or "burn," an undercover investigator. Support officer vehicles are sometimes equipped with "kill switches." These are standard toggle switches, usually concealed in the glove box and wired so that a single headlight, the tail lights, or brake lights can be turned off. This is beneficial in nighttime surveillance to change the appearance of the vehicle when a suspect is looking for surveillance through his or her rearview mirror.

Undercover Officer Vehicles Vehicles used by undercover investigators should not be equipped like support officer vehicles. Undercover vehicles must be kept "clean." Criminal suspects will often be inside the undercover vehicle, and it is common for them to examine the vehicle for a possible police radio or hidden wires to microphones or even to check the vehicle registration. Consequently, anything the suspect discovers in the vehicle should be placed there purposely to support the officer's cover story.

The Undercover Working Environment

Although undercover operations have unique benefits, they also have a serious downside. On one hand, undercover is an investigative method by which officers can see firsthand the inner workings of criminal organizations. Officers can converse and strategize with their criminal targets and learn the ways criminal minds work. Conversely, this close interaction may place officers in jeopardy because they might inadvertently reveal something inconsistent with their cover story. Furthermore, exposure to criminal elements in a close, undercover capacity for extended periods of time might result in the undercover officer's acting and speaking in a manner other than he or she is accustomed, even when off duty, reflecting poorly on the officer's credibility.

To minimize problems associated with undercover operations, a certain degree of preparation is imperative. This includes establishing a sound cover story and understanding specialized infiltration techniques.

The Cover Story

A prerequisite for assuming an undercover role is to establish a **cover story**. Simply defined, the cover story is a fictitious story that the agent will convey to suspects concerning his or her background, including his or her name, address, hometown (or area), and employment, if applicable. Other details may be included, but it is a good idea to keep the cover story simple in case an agent must deal with inquisitive criminal suspects.

The cover story should fit with the area and people involved with the investigation. When an officer chooses to associate him- or herself with a particular town or area, it should be one with which the officer is already familiar, in case he or she later meets someone from that area. Officers should remember that mixing a partial truth with the cover story makes an officer more believable to the suspect.

When claiming a place of employment, the officer should choose one that cannot be easily checked out by suspects. This is more of a problem in rural areas because people are more likely to know each other. It may be desirable to choose an out-of-town place of employment that requires a lot of travel or to present a fictitious job in which the officer is self-employed, thus making it harder for criminal suspects to verify. Whatever story is chosen, the officer should be provided with business cards, customized stationery, credit cards, checking and savings account books, and other supporting credentials to corroborate the cover story. Moreover, the officer should be familiar with the profession chosen for the cover story for the same reasons he or she should be familiar with the purported hometown.

The officer's appearance and mannerisms should also fit the cover story. If the officer claims to be an oil field worker, for example, it might be out of character for the officer to be seen by the suspect in an expensive business suit. On the other hand, if the officer's cover story is that of financier for a big money deal, then expensive clothing might be more appropriate. It might also be necessary for an undercover officer to wear expensive jewelry to help convince sellers of his or her cover story. Depending on the nature of the investigation, expensive jewelry can sometimes be borrowed from local stores for short periods; however, the safety and security of the jewelry are the responsibility of the undercover officer.

Protecting the Undercover Officer's Cover

After the cover story has been established, the undercover officer is committed to it. Certainly the basics—name, hometown, and location—cannot easily be changed without jeopardizing the officer's safety and the integrity of the investigation. Even if changes are not necessary, however, the undercover officer must be able to detect and withstand attempts by suspects and their associates to test and invalidate the officer's cover story.

Typically, suspects will barrage the officer with questions in an attempt to catch any inconsistency in the cover story. If they are successful, or believe they are, suspects usually attempt to frighten or intimidate the officer into admitting he or she is a law enforcement agent or into abandoning the investigation out of fear for their personal safety.

Panic is the undercover officer's worst enemy. Officers must realize two important things: paranoia is common among drug dealers and no matter what suspects say they know about the agent, many times they're just attempting to lock the officer into an admission for which they have no proof. If the officer keeps the cover story general, most questioning and suspicion should be easily overcome. Moreover, if the officer has been properly trained and responds to the suspects according to his or her training, a bond of trust may develop between the officer and suspects, which can pave the way to a successful investigation.

Different criminals use different methods to expose undercover police agents. Even though good field training should prepare undercover personnel for most of these obstacles, not every confrontation can be anticipated. Undercover personnel should remember that most questions about their cover story are bluffs, and they should remain calm and confident, discounting the challenges presented without appearing scared, intimidated, or paranoid.

An investigator should also be aware that criminals can be quite tricky and cunning when trying to expose possible police infiltration. For example, they may:

- Attempt to intoxicate the officer in the hope that he or she will say something inconsistent with the cover story while under the influence of alcohol.
- Use prostitutes, girlfriends or boyfriends, or associates to attempt to seduce the officer; in doing so, the upper torso will be felt for body mikes, the waist area for weapons, and pockets for police credentials or anything else indicating an association with police work.
- Ask the officer questions about his or her cover story when the suspects already know the answer; the suspects hope to observe nervousness on the part of the officer.
- Ask the officer to furnish drugs to a friend or an associate knowing that it is against regulations for a law enforcement officer to do so.
- Ask the officer to consume drugs furnished by the suspect.
- Attempt to learn information about the officer's family (spouse, children, other relatives, or friends) so that an officer's story can be more easily verified.
- Ask the officer to perform various illegal acts.
- Attempt to rummage through the officer's car or personal belongings to locate police-related material or information showing that the officer was lying about his or her cover story.
- Ask the undercover officer excessive questions to see how many he or she is willing to answer before becoming suspicious or angry.

Infiltration

After a cover story is established, a methodical process of infiltration must take place to uncover criminal wrongdoing and its associated evidence. During infiltration, a relationship is established between the officer and a suspect. Frequently, an officer finds it difficult to meet or establish any rapport with the suspect without the help of an informant. In some cases, however, informants may cause more trouble for the officer and the investigation than they are worth; therefore, their use should be carefully considered. Infiltration requires inventiveness and originality on the officer's part because he or she might have to create his or her own opportunity to speak with the suspect.

After contact has been made between the officer and the suspect, the suspect's confidence must be gained as soon as possible. An officer can best accomplish this by learning the interests of the suspects (e.g., jobs, the opposite sex, local bars, motorcycles, cars, drugs), which the officer can then discuss. Context must be regularly attempted throughout the investigation to maintain rapport with the suspect.

When working without an informant, it might be necessary to canvass a target area. The undercover officer can expedite the investigation by revealing intelligence on target suspects and locations, concentrating on areas with high levels of crime that might provide investigative leads. Typical starting places might be bars, nightclubs, or taverns, which can be excellent sources of intelligence for undercover officers. Much can be learned just by being present at these locations; generally people do not have a reasonable expectation of privacy when "openly" conversing in public in such places as a bar. The undercover agent can simply overhear otherwise private or guarded information about their suspects' names, types of criminal activities, places of employment, and vehicles they drive. After the officer learns such information and it appears that the information might be useful in showing criminal activity, it should be properly documented in intelligence reports. The lack of such properly generated intelligence reports accounts for the loss of much valuable criminal information to the unit.

A Closer Look

Becoming a DEA Special Agent

DEA Special Agents are a select group of men and women from diverse backgrounds whose experience and commitment make them the premier federal drug law enforcement agents in the world. Applicants must be at least 21 years of age and no older than 36 at the time of their appointment.

Education.   The most competitive candidates possess a bachelor's or master's degree, along with a grade point average (GPA) of 2.95 or higher. Special consideration is given to candidates with degrees in criminal justice/police science or related disciplines; finance, accounting, or economics; foreign languages (with fluency verified) in Spanish, Russian, Hebrew, Arabic, dialects of Nigerian languages, Chinese, Japanese; computer science/information systems; and telecommunications, electrical engineering, and mechanical engineering.

Depending on scheduling and candidate availability, the DEA's hiring process may take 12 months or longer. Hiring involves a multistep process that includes the following phases:

- Qualifications review
- Written and oral assessment and panel interview
- Urinalysis drug test
- Medical examination
- Physical task test
- Polygraph examination
- Psychological assessment
- Background investigation
- Final hiring decision

Training. All applicants must successfully complete all phases of the hiring process and remain most competitive to receive a final offer of employment. For more information, contact your nearest DEA field division recruitment office. Scheduling times and locations are handled by the local recruitment coordinators. Special Agent candidates

(continued)

A Closer Look... (continued)

are required to successfully complete a 16-week Basic Agent Training (BAT) program at the DEA Training Academy in Quantico, Virginia.

Through this program, instruction and hands-on training are provided in undercover, surveillance, and arrest techniques; defensive tactics and firearms training; and the basics of report writing, law, and drug identification and recognition. In addition, applicants participate in a rigorous physical fitness program.

Duty Station.   Between the 8th and 12th weeks of the training, applicants are provided with final duty station assignments. Mobility is a condition of employment. Assignments are made based upon DEA's current operational needs.

Mobility.   Mobility is a condition of employment. Special Agents are subject to transfer throughout their career based on the needs of the agency.

Salary.   DEA Special Agents are generally hired at the GS-7 or GS-9 level, depending on education and experience. The salary includes federal Law Enforcement Officer base pay plus a locality payment, depending on the duty station. Upon successful graduation from the DEA Training Academy, 25 percent availability pay will be added to the base and locality pay. After graduation, the starting salaries are approximately $49,746 for a GS-7 and $55,483 for a GS-9. After four years of service, Special Agents are eligible to progress to the GS-13 level and can earn approximately $92,592 or more per year.

Drug Use Policy.   The DEA is charged with enforcement of the Federal Controlled Substances Act; therefore, all applicants must fully disclose any drug use history during the application process. Applicants whose drug use history is outside of acceptable parameters will not be considered for employment. All DEA employees are subject to random urinalysis drug testing throughout their careers.

The Physical Task (PT) Test.   The PT test determines if potential candidates can withstand the rigors of Special Agent training. Candidates must be in excellent physical condition to pass this test.

If a candidate fails the first PT test, administered in the field, a second test must be successfully taken within 30 days. A second failure will cause the candidate's application process to be discontinued. Candidates are encouraged to train to ensure that they are prepared to successfully complete this test.

Background investigation.   A background investigation (BI) is one of the final steps in the application process that seeks to discern a comprehensive snapshot of applicants. The investigation provides information on applicants' personal history, education and work experience, personal and professional references, as well as other necessary checks. The time it takes to complete the BI is dependent on the type and scope of investigation being conducted.

Thematic question

Considering drug enforcement agents often work in a proactive undercover capacity, to what extent do you think that doing so unfairly targets persons for investigation who have not yet committed a crime? Explain your response.

Source: U.S. Drug Enforcement Administration: DEA Special Agents. September 5, 1012. Available at http://www.justice.gov/dea/careers/agent/index.html.

It should be noted that although bars, nightclubs, and taverns can be lucrative sources of information, officer safety is greatly reduced in these settings. If two undercover officers are available, it is a good idea to assign both of them to a particular tavern, working independently of each other. This accomplishes two goals: It gives both officers additional backup, and it provides each officer the chance to identify different suspects in criminal groups operating within the tavern.

If a tavern is to be infiltrated, the undercover officer has several potentially good targets to consider. The first people contacted may not be offenders but might know those who are. Without being too aggressive, the undercover officer might consider befriending one of the following people in the bar:

- **Bartender.** Bartenders may or may not be involved in criminal activity, but they will most likely know of any criminal activity occurring and who is responsible.
- **Waitresses.** Waitresses are also frequently aware of an array of criminal activity taking place within the bar.
- **Bar customers** (regulars). Regular customers in a tavern might also be good players to befriend; they, too, often know who might be involved in criminal activity.

Sometimes an informant will arrange a transaction for the purchase of contraband and a first-time meeting between a contraband dealer and the undercover officer. In this case, the seller will have some degree of suspicion about the officer, and some initial questioning should be anticipated. At this point in the investigation, the officer should remember a few guidelines:

1. The officer should not let the suspect question him or her any more than if the roles were reversed. Some questioning is understandable and justifiable, but it can become excessive. If this

occurs, the officer should deal with it the best way possible, perhaps by acting angry, advising the seller that he's too inquisitive and that the deal is either on or it is not. This should help convince the seller that the officer is aware of what the suspect is attempting to do and that he or she is being manipulated. Undercover officers will find that subsequent transactions are usually much easier because the dealer feels confident because he or she has not been arrested as a result of dealing with the officer.

2. While working in a bar, an officer might purchase drinks or pay for pool or video games to start a conversation with a suspect. However, officers must be careful to abide by established police policy regarding the consumption of alcoholic beverages while on duty. Most law enforcement agencies permit officers to consume liquor while working undercover, but because an officer's judgment may be impaired and because he or she might become less likely to remember necessary facts, this must be done with considerable discretion. Furthermore, in case it becomes an issue in court later, the officer should drink as little as possible in order to avoid attacks on the officer's credibility by defense attorneys after the case goes to trial.

3. If the undercover assignment takes the officer to the suspect's house, in addition to taking additional safety precautions, the officer must recognize that this is a good opportunity to learn new information about the suspect. The officer should mentally map out all entrances, exits, and windows that the suspect may use for escape during a possible future raid. The officer should mentally note the number on the telephone, which might furnish a lead to the name of a new associate later. Discreetly observing mail lying out in the open may also reveal the names of associates or roommates. Finally, noting the presence of controlled substances and their hiding places, in addition to any weapons, may be useful later when obtaining a search warrant or conducting a raid.

4. Officers should remember that the practice of lying and deceiving is common for drug dealers. If the officer gets caught in a lie, he or she should never become prematurely paranoid and fear that his or her cover has been blown. The officer should react with disinterest or perhaps even laugh it off for the suspect's benefit. It is best to try to justify the line by claiming that he or she doesn't "want too many people knowing too much about my personal business." The suspect will most likely identify with and respect such an explanation.

Risks in Undercover Assignments

For investigators assigned to undercover roles, two principal problems can be identified that may pose problems for both the investigator and his or her agency. The first is the problem of maintaining the "criminal" identity, and the second area is the process of reintegration back into normal investigative duties. The maintenance of identity problems are those that are associated with adopting of and living a made-up life in a new environment.

STRESS IN RELATIONSHIPS Undercover work is one of the most stressful jobs that a police officer can undertake.[39] The largest cause of stress for investigators working undercover is the requirement that they distance themselves from friends, family, and their normal environment. This simple isolation can result in the onset of depression and anxiety. There are no data on the divorce rates of undercover agents, but considerable tension in relationships has been known to develop. This can result from a need for secrecy and an inability to share work problems, the unpredictable work schedule, personality and lifestyle changes, and the length of separation. These factors can all result in problems for relationships.[40]

STRESS FROM UNCERTAINTY Stress can also result from an apparent lack of direction of the investigation or not knowing when it will end. The amount of elaborate planning, risk, and expenditure can also place pressure on an agent to succeed, which can cause considerable stress.[41] The stress that an undercover agent faces is considerably different from that faced by investigators who are not assigned to undercover assignments and whose main source of stress results from pressures by the administration and the general bureaucracy of police work.[42] Because the undercover agent is removed from the bureaucracy, it may result in another problem. Because they do not have the usual controls of a uniform, badge, constant supervision, a fixed place of work, or (often) a set assignment, combined with their continual contact with the criminal underworld (members of the opposite sex, pressure and manipulation from criminal suspects, alcohol, availability of illicit drugs, and opportunities to earn or seize large amounts of illicit money), increase the likelihood for corruption.[43]

DEVELOPMENT OF ALCOHOL OR DRUG ABUSE Research shows that undercover agents are more prone to the development of an addiction because they undergo greater stress than other police officers.[44] This is because they are isolated, and drugs are often very accessible. In general, police have very high alcoholism rate compared to most other occupational groups. Stress is cited as a likely factor. The environment that agents work in often involves a liberal exposure to the consumption of alcohol, which in combination with the stress and isolation can result in alcoholism.[45]

This is supported by research conducted by Gary Marx, who also states that undercover agents are more prone to the development of an addiction because they experience greater stress than other police, they are isolated, and drugs are often very accessible.[46] Police, in general, have very high alcoholism rates compared with people in most occupational groups, and stress is cited as a likely factor.[47] The environment that agents work in, including taverns, bars and private residences of criminal suspects, often involves considerable exposure to the consumption of alcohol, which in conjunction with the stress and isolation may result in alcoholism.[48]

FEELINGS OF PERSONAL GUILT There can also be some guilt associated with working undercover because of the need to essentially betray the trust of those (criminal suspects) who have come to trust you. According to Marx, this can cause anxiety or even, in very rare cases, sympathy with those being targeted.[49] This is especially true with the infiltration of political groups because often the agent shares similar characteristics, such as class, age, ethnicity, or religion, with those they are infiltrating. This could even result in the conversion of some agents.[50]

PROBLEMS OF REINTEGRATION The lifestyle led by undercover agents is very different than that for other areas in law enforcement, and it can be quite difficult to reintegrate back into normal duties. Agents work their own hours, they are removed from direct supervisory monitoring, and they can ignore the dress and etiquette rules.[51] So the resettling back into the normal police role requires the shredding of old habits, language, and dress. After working such free lifestyles, agents may have discipline problems or exhibit neurotic responses. They may feel uncomfortable and take a cynical, suspicious, or even paranoid worldview and feel continually on guard.[52]

Case in Point

>>The Anti-Snitch Movement

It was strange enough for prosecutors and police to see the T-shirt with a traffic-sign message: "STOP SNITCHING," but one of those T-shirts was about to show up in court with a matching baseball cap. Worse yet, the wearer was a prosecution witness for Pittsburgh's Prosecutor Lisa Pellegrini.

In March of 2006, Rayco "War" Saunders—ex-con, pro boxer, and walking billboard for an anti-snitch movement—sparked a coast-to-coast debate involving everyone from academics to police to rappers. Pellegrini, while thinking

"witness intimidation," told Saunders to lose the hat and reverse the shirt. Saunders, claiming "First Amendment" rights, refused. He left the courthouse, shirt in place. Case dismissed.

The attitude of "don't be a snitch" is common throughout many communities and, in some cases, even condoned. While the Mafia's traditional blood oath of silence, "Omerta," has been broken by turncoat after turncoat, in some inner-city neighborhoods, the call to stop snitching is galvanizing. Some say it's an attempt by drug dealers and gangsters to intimidate witnesses, but others say it's a legitimate protest against law enforcement's overreliance on criminal informers.

(continued)

Case in Point (continued)

Take the case of Busta Rhymes, the hip-hop star who refused to cooperate with police investigating the slaying of his bodyguard, Israel Ramirez, on February 5, 2006, outside a Brooklyn studio where Rhymes was recording a video with other rap performers. Police claimed that although Rhymes and as many as 50 others may have witnessed the shooting, no one came forward—reminiscent of the echo of silence that followed the unsolved murders of rappers Tupac Shakur, The Notorious B.I.G., and Run-DMC's Jam Master Jay.

Although some argue that it's logical for a witness to a crime to want to talk to the police, others say that because of growing animosities between the police and the public, *not* being an informer is the honorable thing to do.

Informers have always been a key investigative tool but at the same time have been viewed as a necessary evil. In some cases, if a drug dealer needs to make a deal, he or she will tell on friends or family alike if necessary. It may not be right, but it's the only answer for some people. In some cases, criminal informers who are allowed to remain free commit more crimes, return to crime after serving a short prison sentence, frame other people for crimes they didn't commit, or tell prosecutors anything they want to hear.

According to a study by the Northwestern University Law School's Center on Wrongful Convictions, 51 of the 111 wrongful death penalty convictions since the 1970s were based in whole or in part on the testimony of witnesses who had incentives to lie. Based on federal statistics, one of every four black men from 20 to 29 years of age is incarcerated, on probation, or on parole and under pressure to snitch. Estimates are that one in 12 of all black men in the highest crime neighborhoods throughout the nation is a criminal informant.

Hence the backlash—"stop snitching." The slogan appeared in Baltimore in 2004 as the title of an underground DVD featuring threatening gun-wielding drug dealers and a brief appearance by NBA star and Baltimore native Carmelo Anthony. Whatever its intent, the "stop snitching" movement concerns officials who are already enraged about witness reluctance and witness intimidation. State and local governments spend a fraction of what the federal government devotes to witness protection and informant management, although in March 2006, Pennsylvania restored $1,000,000 for that purpose. This move came as more than half a dozen witnesses recanted earlier testimony in the trial of men accused in the Philadelphia street shooting death of a third-grade boy.

The movement has created problems for law enforcement across the country because without informers, many cases cannot be properly investigated. "Stop Snitching" T-shirts have been banned from a number of courthouses across the nation. In Boston, Mayor Thomas Menino sent police officers into the stores to remove "Stop Snitching" T-shirts from the shelves. In Maryland, the crime of witness intimidation was elevated from misdemeanor to felony, and in Baltimore, police made a DVD of their own called "Keep Talking."

Sources: Hampson, R. (2006). Anti-snitch campaign riles police, prosecutors. *USA Today*, March 29, pp.1A–2A; Scolville, D. (2007). How to develop informants. September 5, 2010. Available at http://www.policemag.com/channel/patrol/articles/2007/08/how-to-develop-informants.aspx.

Summary Checklist

In this chapter, we consider the ways information about crimes is documented by criminal investigators. A properly documented case is one that is more likely to succeed in court. See how well you are able to answer the following questions in your checklist.

1. **Do you know the type of citizen who typically becomes an informant for the police and what the various motivations of informants are?**

The term *informant* could best be defined as "anyone who provides information of an investigative nature to law enforcement." People who become informants can generally be classified into four general groups:

- Average citizens
- Fellow law enforcement officers
- Mentally ill persons
- Criminals or their associates

Motivations for criminal informants fall into a number of categories:

- Fear
- Financial motivation—informants who give information for a fee
- Revenge
- Egotism—informants who take pleasure in passing on information to others
- Perverse motivation— a hidden benefit or advantage for the informant
- Reformed individuals acting out of a sense of guilt

2. **Describe the methods and procedures for using an informant.**

The use of an informant in a criminal investigation can be problematic and an informant's use should not be considered if similar results could be achieved through other means. Problems stemming from the use of informants are due to three variables:

- They are often difficult to control
- They can become a source of public embarrassment for the law enforcement agency
- Their credibility in court is questionable

If the decision to use an informant is made, the informant may be used in a number of ways:

- Make observations in areas where strangers would be suspect
- Furnish information from sources not readily available to the investigator
- Conduct "controlled" undercover transactions or introduce undercover agents to criminal suspects
- Collect intelligence information

3. **Explain the ways that an informant should be documented and controlled.**

Proper management of informants is essential in avoiding unethical, immoral, or unprofessional allegations later in an investigation. All candidates for informants should be well documented:

- They should be fingerprinted, photographed, and carefully interviewed by investigators before being used as informants.
- Criminal records, if any, should be verified.
- An official informant file should be established.

It is essential that the investigator, not the informant, command control of the investigation:

- Typically, the investigator who develops an informant is the one assigned to him or her.
- Control of informants is best achieved through frequent personal contacts with them:

  - These interactions are the best method for debriefing informers and maintaining rapport with them.
  - The officer assigned should make most, if not all, contacts with the informant.
  - Informants must be given instruction on entrapment.

4. **What are some of the problems inherent in working with informants?**

Working with informants can be challenging and at times outright problematic. In addition to concerns of entrapment and ethical, moral, and criminal activity on the part of the informant, there are several other areas of concern:

- Lying—informants may exaggerate or fabricate the criminal acts of targets, or may lie about having used illegal methods to obtain information.
- Double-dealing—informants can make deals with targets as easily as they can with the police.
- Rip-offs—informants are in a position to rip off the agency.
- Blackmail—informants may "get something" on the controlling officer, who then loses control and ends up being controlled by the informant.
- Investigators becoming too friendly with informants
- Informants of the opposite sex—may lead to allegations of officer misconduct with informants of the opposite sex
- Crimes committed by the informant

5. **Describe the usefulness of undercover operations in criminal investigation and the problems they can pose for the department.**

Undercover operations are an important part of the criminal investigation function but one that is highly specialized and not practiced by all law enforcement agencies.

- Investigators require specialized training to successfully perform this function.

- Being undercover is the process of using an assumed identity for the purposes of gaining the trust of an individual or organization to learn information or to gain the trust of targeted individuals to gain information or evidence.

Undercover work is best described as a drama involving three main participants:

- The informant
- The suspect
- The undercover agent

Undercover operations present many problems and concerns for the department, such as:

- Undercover officers may be thrust into the criminal subculture and can be tempted to do things that would otherwise be immoral or illegal.
- Undercover officers may be separated from family, friends, and other members of the department for extend periods of time.
- Officers remaining undercover for too long may begin to adopt the behaviors of the criminals they are investigating.
- The department can become involved in illegal activities during the course of an investigation.
- Undercover operations can result in additional criminal activities.
- Undercover operations are subject to claims of entrapment.

6. **Identify the steps that investigators must prepare for undercover assignments.**

All undercover work has the potential for considerable danger. The investigator must establish a cover story (which could be blown at any time during the investigation) and must associate closely with individuals who may be armed, unpredictable, under the influence of drugs, or mentally unstable.

- Officers being considered for undercover assignments should be disabused of any myths created by television and popular media stereotypes.
- Most undercover work consists of a brief meeting between the agent and a suspect, an exchange of dialogue, and a transaction—usually a purchase of contraband such as a quantity of illegal drugs, stolen property, or illegal weapons.
- Undercover officers must realize that their safety and the overall success of the investigation require equal participation by all unit members.

There are two general functions for officers within the undercover unit.

- The undercover officer—contacts individuals or infiltrates establishments or organizations suspected of being involved in criminal activity.
- The support officer (sometimes called an intelligence, cover, or tactical officer)—a plainclothes officer who works with the undercover unit but not in an undercover capacity.

To minimize the problems associated with undercover operations, preparation is imperative.

- A sound cover story must be established that fits the area and people involved with the investigation.
- The officer's appearance and mannerisms should fit the cover story.

Key Terms

burned	deep cover	seed money
buy-bust	entrapment	support officer
buy-walk	flipping	totality of the circumstances
cooperating witness	infiltration	undercover (UC) officer
cover story	informant	undercover operations
credibility	jailhouse snitch	victimless crime
crimestoppers	motivation	Witness Security (WITSEC) program

Discussion Questions

1. List and describe the four groups of people that most commonly become informants for law enforcement.

2. List and discuss the advantages and benefits of using informants in criminal investigations.

3. What are the various motivations for becoming involved with law enforcement as an informant?

4. List and discuss some of the problems that arise in the management of informants.

5. Compare and contrast the ways an undercover operation can benefit and hinder a criminal investigation.

6. List the considerations in preparing for an undercover operation.

7. List and discuss some of the risks that exist in undercover assignments.

Notes

1. ANON. (1996). Police upset by cancellation of *America's Most Wanted. USA Today*, May, p. 16.

2. PUENTE, M. (1997). A no longer most wanted list. *USA Today*, July 29, p. 3A.

3. IBID.

4. GRAY, P. (1997). A heart in her hand. *Time*, August 23, p. 43.

5. U.S. DEPARTMENT OF JUSTICE, DRUG ENFORCEMENT ADMINISTRATION. (1988). *Drug enforcement handbook*. Washington, DC: U.S. Government Printing Office.

6. HENRY CAMPBELL BLACK. (1979). *Black's law dictionary*, 5th ed. West Publishing. p. 701.

7. FBI's Manual of Investigative Operations and Guidelines, Part I—270-2 (1998)

8. FEDERAL BUREAU OF INVESTIGATION. (December 12, 2011). Former Shelby County Sentenced to 28 Months in Federal Prison. United States Attorney's Office, FBI Memphis Division found in http://www.fbi.gov/memphis/press-releases/2011/former-shelby-county-deputy-sentenced-to-28-months-in-federal-prison (retrieved on March 10, 2012).

9. IBID.

10. IBID.

11. MARX, G. (1988). *Undercover: Police surveillance in America*. Berkley: University of California, p. 152.

12. FITZGERALD, D. (2007). *Informants and undercover investigations*. Boca Raton, FL: Taylor & Francis Publisher, p. 23

13. HENDRIE, E. M. (2003). When an informant's tip gives officers probable cause to arrest drug traffickers. *FBI Law Enforcement Bulletin* 72.12 (December):10.

14. IBID.

15. IBID.

16. HENDRIE. (2003). When an informant's tip gives officers probable cause to arrest drug traffickers, p. 13.

17. MADINGER, J. (2000). *Confidential informant: Law enforcement's most valuable tool*. Boca Raton, FL: CRC Press, p. 29.

18. FITZGERALD. (2007). *Informants and undercover investigations*, p. 30.

19. IBID.

20. INTERNATIONAL ASSOCIATION OF CHIEF'S OF POLICE. (June 1990). Confidential informants. Concepts and issues paper. Alexandria, VA: IACP National Law Enforcement Center.

21. IBID.

22. IBID.

23. IBID.

24. MOTTO, C. AND D. JUNE. (2000). *Undercover*, 2nd ed. Boca Raton, FL: CRC Press, p. 6.

25. FITZGERALD. (2007). *Informants and undercover investigations*, p. 263.

26. IBID.

27. DRUG ENFORCEMENT AGENCY. (2009). Hundreds of alleged Sinaloa cartel members and associates arrested in nationwide takedown of Mexican drug traffickers. Available at http://www.usdoj.gov/dea/pubs/states/newsrel/2009/la022509.html.

28. MOTTO AND JUNE. (2000). *Undercover*.

29. IBID., p. 7

30. ADAMS, T. (2001). *Police field operations*, 5th ed. Upper Saddle River, NJ: Prentice Hall.

31. LANGWORTHY, R. (1989). Do stings control crime? An evaluation of a police fencing operation. *Justice Quarterly* 6:28–45.

32. SCHOEMAN, F. (1986). Undercover operations: Some moral questions. *Criminal Justice Ethics* 5(2):16–22.

33. TURQUE, B. AND J. STOFFEL. (1989). Fury over an unholy alliance: How cleveland cops teamed up with a drug dealer. *Newsweek*, May 8, p. 26.

34. BLACK, D. (1971). The social organization of arrest. *Stanford Law Review* 23:1087–1111; LAFAVE, W. (1965). *The decision to take a suspect into custody*. Boston, MA: Little, Brown and Company; SMITH, D. A. AND C. VISHER. (1981). Street-level justice: Situational determinants of police arrest decisions. *Social Problems* 29:167–178.

35. LYMAN, M. D. (2007). *Practical drug enforcement*, 3rd ed. Boca Raton, FL: CRC Press.

36. MOTTO AND JUNE. (2000). *Undercover*.

37. IBID., p. 86

38. KRAUSE, M. (2008). Safeguarding undercover employees: A strategy for success. *FBI Law Enforcement Bulletin* 77(8):1–8.

39. GIRODO, M. (1991). Symptomatic reactions to undercover work. *The Journal of Nervous and Mental Disease* 179(10):626–630.

40. MARX. (1988). *Undercover*.

41. IBID.

42. BROWN, J. (1990). Sources of occupational stress in the police. *Work & Stress* 4(4):305–318. Available at http://www.informaworld.com/smpp/content~content=a782548838~db=all.

43. MARX. (1988). *Undercover*.

44. GIRODO. (1991). Symptomatic reactions to undercover work.

45. IBID.

46. MARX. (1988). *Undercover*.

47. IBID.

48. GIRODO, M. (1991). Drug corruptions in undercover agents: Measuring the risks. *Behavioural Science and the Law* 9:361–370.

49. MARX. (1988). *Undercover*.

50. IBID.

51. GIRODO, M. (1991). Personality, job stress, and mental health in undercover agents. *Journal of Social Behaviour and Personality* 6(7):375–390.

52. MARX. (1988). *Undercover*.

CHAPTER 9

David Zalubowski / Associated Press

This chapter will enable you to:

1. Differentiate between the types of homicide, murder, and wrongful death.

2. Describe how a homicide investigation is conducted.

3. Summarize how time of death is estimated.

4. Explain the use of evidence in death investigations.

5. Summarize efforts to coordinate homicide investigations and share homicide information.

6. Describe other types of death investigations.

Death Investigations

Introduction

 The brutal murder of six-year-old JonBenet Ramsey on Christmas night in 1996 shocked America. Just as the Lindbergh baby kidnapping and murder seven decades earlier had seared the nation's consciousness, this murder—of a beautiful and talented child in a wealthy Boulder, Colorado, home—renewed every parent's worst nightmare: No child was truly safe, not even tucked in at home on Christmas night.

JonBenet's murder—particularly as the days went by and no arrests were forthcoming—quickly became a national obsession, featured day after day on network news, television tabloid programs, talk radio, newspapers, and magazines. Her image displayed across television screens countless times, often showing her in a fancy red cowgirl outfit, singing "I want to be a cowboy sweetheart," or dancing across the stage in a glittering Las Vegas showgirl outfit, complete with heavy makeup. Her unusual first name became so well known that like Cher and Madonna, she no longer had need of a last name.

The public's shock at the murder soon spread to dismay at the Boulder Police Department's investigation—a dismay fed by a steady flow of leaks from the Boulder County District Attorney's office about the inept police investigation being conducted. Specifically, it became known that the police had badly botched the initial investigation by failing to seal off the crime scene. It also appeared as though the police were treating the primary suspects—JonBenet's parents—with kid gloves by not only acquiescing to their refusal to be interviewed at police headquarters but also to being interviewed separately. Fueled with such information, the media, especially tabloid television and talk radio shows, were quick to blame JonBenet's parents, John and Patsy Ramsey. Some in the media began to point the finger directly at her father. Others implied it was her mother who had garroted the girl. Some speculated the crime had to have been committed by both parents. The tabloids even raised the possibility that her brother, Burke, who was just shy of 10 years old at the time, murdered JonBenet.

As of the preparation of this book, JonBenet's killer has not been identified. A grand jury met for over a year, only to disband in October of 1999 without handing down an indictment or even issuing a report, an option that was open to it. Boulder Police Chief Mark Beckner admitted that the case files have been put in storage, although he said some more "forensic testing" was going on. The then newly elected Boulder district attorney, Mary Keenan, promised to look into the case. Nothing seemed to come of it. In April of 2003, she issued a statement saying she concurred with a federal court in Georgia's contemporaneous finding that JonBenet was most likely murdered by an intruder. Two months later, Keenan shifted responsibility for the case away from the Boulder Police Department to the district attorney's office, and she hired Tom Bennett as lead investigator of the case, directing him to focus his probe on the premise that an intruder killed JonBenet.

During the intervening three years, the case all but dropped from public view. The death of Patsy Ramsey on June 24, 2006—of ovarian cancer at age 49—briefly brought the case back into the spotlight. And then on August 16, 2006, the long-dormant case appeared back in the headlines across the world when a 41-year-old child-sex offender by the name of John Mark Karr was arrested in Bangkok, Thailand, at the request of the Boulder District Attorney's Office. Karr was extradited back to Boulder at which time DNA results from the JonBenet crime scene failed to link Karr to the crime. As the Boulder district attorney faced considerable criticism for Karr's premature extradition, his candidacy as JonBenet's killer was dismissed.

While police investigators in Colorado initially suspected JonBenét's parents and her brother, the family was partially exonerated in 2003 when DNA taken from the victim's clothes suggested they were not involved. In July 2008 her parents were completely cleared. In February 2009, the Boulder Police Department took the case back from the district attorney to reopen the investigation.

In all societies, instances of homicide and wrongful death have endured as top concerns for law enforcement officials. These crimes are considered as one of the gravest social problems, and law enforcement plays an important role in investigating the facts and circumstances surrounding each such case. An estimated 15,500 people are murdered every year, and most of these (an estimated 85 percent) involve people who knew each other (e.g., friends, neighbors, family members).

Homicide investigators must do their best to find answers for families who have lost loved ones. Death investigation requires strict adherence to guidelines. Investigators must search for clues that identify a death as natural, suicide, or homicide. In the case of homicide, investigators must carefully collect evidence to help identify suspects and convict murderers.

Murder and nonnegligent manslaughter, as defined in the Uniform Crime Reporting (UCR) program, is the willful (nonnegligent) killing of one human being by another. The classification of this offense, as for all other offenses that make up the Crime Index, is based solely on police investigation as opposed to the determination of a court, medical examiner, coroner, jury, or other judicial body. The program does not include deaths caused by negligence, suicide, or accident; justifiable **homicide**; and attempts to murder or assaults to murder, which are scored as aggravated assaults.

The extent of homicide (identified as "murder" by FBI statistics) in the United States is reflected in the *Uniform Crime Report* published by the FBI. For example, statistics show that nationwide in 2007, an estimated 16,929 persons were murdered, a 0.6 percent decline from the 2006 estimate. The 2007 figure was, however, 2.4 percent higher than the 2003 level. Statistics also show that murder accounted for 1.2 percent of the overall estimated number of violent crimes. In 2007, there were an estimated 5.6 murders per 100,000 inhabitants.[1]

Types of Wrongful Death

Murders may occur in sprees, which involve killings at two or more locations with almost no time break between murders. John Allen Muhammad, 41, part of the "sniper team" that terrorized the Washington, DC., area in 2002, was arrested along with 17-year-old Jamaican immigrant Lee Boyd Malvo in the random shootings of 13 people in Maryland, Virginia, and Washington over a three-week period. Ten of the victims died. In 2003, Muhammad and Malvo were convicted of capital murder; Muhammad was sentenced to die. Malvo was given a second sentence of life without the possibility of parole in 2004, after he struck a deal with prosecutors in an effort to avoid the death penalty.

Murder Trend: Comparative Rates		
Year	Murder and Nonnegligent Manslaughter Rates	Rate per 100,000 Inhabitants
2009	15,399	5.0
2010	14,748	4.8
Percent Change		−4.8

Source: Federal Bureau of Investigation. (2011). *Crime in the Untied States—2010*. Washington, DC: U.S. Government Printing Office.

In contrast to spree killing, mass murder entails "the killing of four or more victims at one location, within one event." Recent mass murderers have included Timothy McVeigh (the antigovernment Oklahoma City bomber) and Mohammed Atta and the terrorists he led in the September 11, 2001, attacks against American targets.

Yet another kind of murder, serial murder, happens over time and officially "involves the killing of several victims in three or more separate events." In cases of serial murder, days, months, or even years may lapse between killings. Some of the more infamous confessed serial killers of recent years are Wichita BTK murderer Dennis Rader; Jeffrey Dahmer, who received 936 years in prison for the murders of 15 young men (and who was himself later murdered in prison); Ted Bundy, who killed numerous college-age women; Henry Lee Lucas, now in a Texas prison, who confessed to 600 murders but later recanted (yet was convicted of 11 murders and linked to at least 140 others); Otis Toole, Lucas's partner in crime; cult leader Charles Manson, who is still serving time for ordering followers to kill seven Californians, including the famed actress Sharon Tate; Andrei Chikatilo, the Russian "Hannibal Lecter," who killed 52 people, mostly schoolchildren; David Berkowitz, also known as the "Son of Sam," who killed six people on lovers' lanes around New York City; Theodore Kaczynski, the Unabomber, who perpetrated a series of bomb attacks on "establishment" figures; Seattle's Green River killer Gary Leon Ridgway, a 54-year-old painter who confessed in 2003 to killing 48 women in the 1980s; and the infamous "railroad killer," Angel Maturino Resendiz.

Modes of Death

It is of primary importance that the investigator learn the manner in which the victim died as soon as possible after discovery of the body. Although much of this information is learned from the autopsy, much can also be discovered through careful examination of both the deceased and the crime scene. Modes of death can be divided into four general categories:

1. *Accidental death*. Many types of death are associated with this category, including drowning, falling, automobile wrecks, and accidental drug overdose. Often, murders are disguised to appear to be accidental in nature.
2. *Natural death*. Deaths from natural causes include heart attack, stroke, disease, and old age. In many circumstances, the deceased will have been under a doctor's care, but often people are found, and their mode of death is questionable. For example, a person might have been forced to consume certain drugs that can cause death, but the symptoms indicate death from "natural" causes (e.g., heart attack).
3. *Suicide*. Methods of committing suicide are numerous and include stabbing, shooting, drug overdose, and carbon monoxide poisoning. As with other modes of death, investigators should be sure that the cause of death was actually suicide and not murder designed to look like suicide.

4. *Murder*. Murder is one person intentionally causing another person to die. Many different situations can result in a person's death. These include:

- Wounds from handguns and shotguns
- Cutting and stabbing wounds
- Blunt-force injuries
- Extraordinary modes of death such as poisoning and death by asphyxia (strangulation)

The Extent of Homicide

Statistics regarding the extent of murder in the United States are instructive. For example, according to the FBI, in 2010 an estimated 14,748 persons were murdered in the United States. This figure represents a 4.2 percent decrease from 2009 and a 14.8 percent decrease from 2006 (17,309 murders). In 2010, there were 4.8 murders per 100,000 inhabitants. Geographically, nearly 44 percent (43.8) of the nation's murders were reported in the South. In comparison, in western states the rate of murder was 20.6 percent with 19.9 percent reported inthe Midwest and 15.6 percent reported in the Northeast.[2]

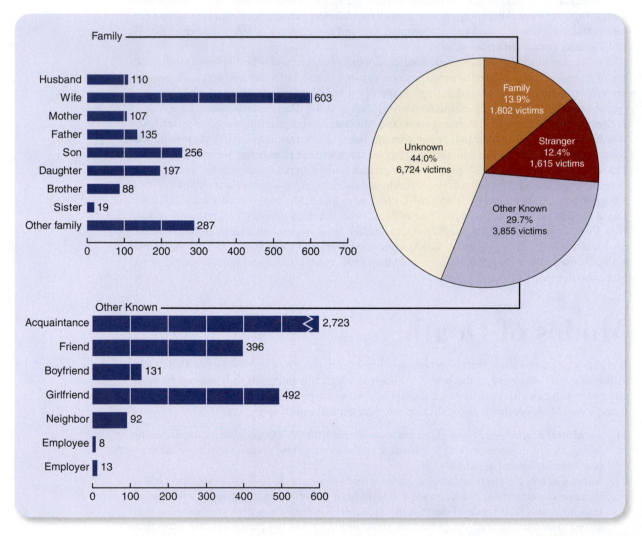

|Fig. 9.1| △

Expanded homicide data—murder by relationship.

FBI, Crime in the United States, 2010.

Legal Characteristics of Homicide

Criminal investigators encounter wrongful death in many ways. Some victims are killed by accident, others in the heat of passion, and still others for profit. Therefore, it is incumbent on the professional investigator to be clear as to what laws best describe the alleged crime. Under law, categories of homicide are generally divided into two distinct classifications: murder and manslaughter. Murder is considered the most serious of all statutory crimes and is defined as the purposeful, premeditated, and unlawful taking of the life of a human being by another person. Persons found guilty of murder receive the harshest of sentences, which may include life imprisonment or the death penalty. Many states classify murder in different degrees, typically first and second. For example, first-degree murder is considered the most serious and includes, as one of the elements, premeditation and preplanning. Second-degree murder is a lesser offense but requires that the person "attempted" to kill his or her intended victim (e.g., a domestic argument that erupts into a physical altercation resulting in the death of one of the parties).

Manslaughter is the deliberate killing of another person and is typically classified into two subcategories: voluntary and involuntary. **Voluntary manslaughter** generally refers to the killing of another person out of an act of passion but lacks premeditation. For example, a man arrives at his home to find his wife with another man. The husband then loses his temper and immediately shoots the man. The key element here is that the scene must erupt into passion and must be followed immediately by the act of murder without premeditation or "cool reflection" about the incident.

Involuntary manslaughter usually refers to the accidental or nonintentional death of another human being, with severe negligence. Examples of involuntary manslaughter include a motorist who is exceeding the speed limit by 30 miles per hour and hits a child playing in the street. If the driver were traveling at the speed limit, he or she would have been able to stop in time to miss the child. Other examples of involuntary manslaughter include the reckless handling of a firearm, resulting in someone's death, and leaving dangerous poisons or drugs in reach of children.

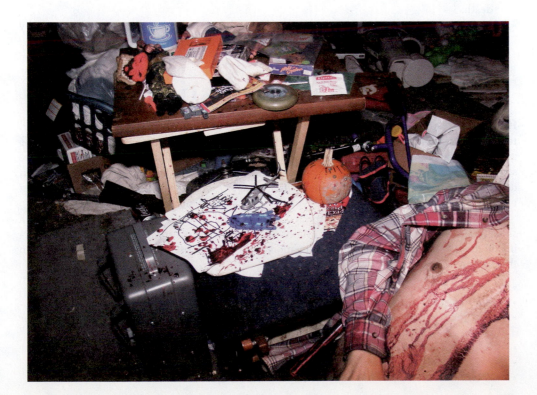

|Fig. 9.2| △

The actual scene of a violent crime resulting in a homicide. Imagine you are the crime scene investigator. What evidence do you see here that must be carefully preserved and documented?

Courtesy of Mike Himmel

|Fig. 9.3|

License plate—blood on back matched victim. Victim beat up on the trunk of a vehicle and subsequently raped and killed. The investigator noticed a small crescent-shaped cut under the victim's eye and theorized that the corner of a license plate could have imparted the cut. When a suspect was developed, investigators took the license plate off his vehicle and found this stain. The DNA matched the victim.

Missouri State Highway Patrol Crime Laboratory

Elements of Homicide

Legal elements of the crime of homicide vary from one state to another but do exhibit some commonalties.

MURDER

- *First degree*. A person commits the crime if he or she knowingly causes the death of another person after deliberation on the matter.
- *Second degree*. A person commits the crime if he or she knowingly causes the death of another person while committing a criminal act and not acting under the influence of sudden passion.

MANSLAUGHTER

- *Involuntary*. A person commits the crime if he or she recklessly causes another person's death.
- *Voluntary*. A person commits the crime if he or she causes the death of another person by being certain of taking the victim's life and acting in the heat of passion.

The Preliminary Investigation

Homicide investigations are usually reactive in nature and are typically initiated by a telephone call to a local law enforcement agency notifying them of some aspect of the offense. Such calls may be a simple request for assistance by an injured person, a call stating "shots were fired," or a report of some form of violence that was observed (e.g., a man or woman being beaten). Rarely, however, does this initial call contain enough information to determine exactly what is occurring or what has occurred. Investigators on the scene typically learn such details.

The first officer to respond to a suspected homicide call is generally a patrol officer arriving a short time after the call is received. The actions taken at the time of arrival may have a critical bearing on the subsequent course of the investigation. Some of the most critical of these are featured in this section. Responding officers might encounter:

- A man who directs the officer to the crime scene
- A crime scene that might be in an isolated place that is untouched and easily safeguarded
- A crime scene that might be filled with people milling around, acting confused, shouting, or crying
- A killer who might either still be on the scene or may have just exited
- A victim who may be dead or may still be alive but in need of medical attention
- A crime scene in a public place that may be difficult to secure

In all situations, the first officer on the scene has several principal concerns:

- Determine if the victim is dead or alive
- Contact medical help for the victim if needed
- Apprehend the perpetrator if still present on the scene
- Make the appropriate notifications if the perpetrator has left the scene
- Safeguard the crime scene
- Detain any witnesses

After these fundamental steps are dealt with, the officer must become what could be termed **scene-conscious**. That is, he or she must become aware of the crime scene situation and be prepared to take certain immediate actions, the focus being identifying any aspects of the scene that might be subject to chemical change, change by dissipation, or change because something was moved.

Protecting the Crime Scene

After the preliminary duties have been performed, the responding officer must protect the crime scene from unauthorized persons who may move, destroy, or otherwise contaminate evidence. It is important for civilians and unauthorized police personnel alike to be denied entrance to the scene. Experience has shown that probably no aspect of the homicide investigation is more open to error than the preservation and protection of the crime scene.[3] Death scenes can be expected to produce an abundance of evidence. All such evidence will enable the investigators to determine the manner of death, weapons used, time of death, and other pertinent information.

ESTABLISHING AND MAINTAINING A "CHAIN OF CUSTODY" **Chain of custody** refers to the sequential documentation of evidence that shows the seizure, custody, control, transfer, analysis, and disposition of evidence. Evidence is used in court to convict persons of crimes and therefore it must be handled in a thoroughly careful manner to avoid possible allegations of tampering, contamination, or misconduct, which can compromise the case. The idea behind recording the chain of custody is to establish that the evidence identified is in fact related to the crime under investigation, opposed to it being, for example, planted to make a person appear guilty.

A specific person must always have the physical custody of a piece of evidence. This means that a police officer or detective will take control of a piece of evidence, document its collection, and turn it over to an evidence clerk for storage in a secure place—typically a crime laboratory. These transactions, and every subsequent transaction between the collection of the evidence and its appearance in court, must be completely documented chronologically in order to withstand legal challenges to its authenticity.

Documentation should include the conditions under which the evidence is collected, the identity of all persons handling the evidence, the duration of evidence custody, the conditions under which the evidence has been secured, and the manner in which evidence is transferred to designated evidence custodians each time a transfer occurs. Typically, signatures of persons involved at each step are required for proof of their role in the "chain."

An example of *chain of custody* would be the recovery of a firearm at a murder scene:

1. Detective Rigby collects the knife and places it into a container, then gives it to forensics technician Stacy.
2. Forensics technician Stacy takes the firearm to the crime lab and collects fingerprints and other evidence from the firearm. Stacy then gives the firearm and all evidence gathered from it to evidence clerk Randall.
3. Randall then stores the evidence until it is needed, documenting everyone who has accessed the original evidence (the firearm, and original copies of the lifted fingerprints).

The chain of custody requires that from the moment the evidence is collected, every transfer of evidence from one person to another be documented *and* that it be provable that nobody else could have accessed that evidence. It is best to keep the number of transfers as low as possible.

Once the case goes to court and if the defendant questions the chain of custody of the evidence, it can be proven that the firearm in the evidence room is the same firearm discovered at the crime scene. However, if there are discrepancies and it cannot be proven who had the firearm at a particular point in time, then the chain of custody is broken and the defendant can ask to have the firearm and all resulting evidence excluded.

Taking Notes at the Scene

Complete notes are critical during the early stages of the homicide crime scene investigation. Because details are of such vital importance, both the investigating and responding officers should take notes. In fact, these notes could later become decisive evidence in the prosecution of the suspect(s). Crime scene notes in a homicide investigation should include the following:

- Names of officers on the scene
- Names and addresses of witnesses at the scene
- Name and address of the person notifying the police
- Manner of entry/exit of the perpetrator to the crime
- Description of weather conditions

As indicated earlier, investigators should also be prepared to draft a sketch of the scene. The sketch should show all critical aspects of the homicide crime scene, such as the location and position of the body; location of any weapons; and positions of furniture, clothing, and other types of evidence. The sketch will prove to be of value later in the investigation when reports are being finalized and in preparing for court.

Identifying the Victim

Homicide crime scenes can vary greatly from one case to the next. For example, in one case, the body might be charred as a result of a fire designed to cover up evidence. In another, the body might have been chopped up and parts distributed over a broad geographical area. In other cases, bodies have been recovered in lakes and rivers and offer little or no immediate clues as to their identity. In all circumstances, the body must be identified.

The Deceased Victim

If the victim is obviously deceased, the officer should not attempt to authorize the removal of the body until after the crime scene has been processed. This will allow valuable time for the identification process. Efforts in identifying the victim may begin with a cursory inspection of the victim's personal effects and clothing. Papers in the possession of the victim may make the identification process easy, particularly if certain items are present (e.g., a driver's license, personal letters).

Witnesses can also provide useful identification information of the victim if known to them. Other people might be able to offer positive identification, such as parents, friends, neighbors, or spouses. A good practice for investigators is to have more than one person identify the remains to avoid a case of mistaken identity. In addition, it is also a sound policy to corroborate positive identifications by additional evidence.

Other identifiers that investigators should look for include:

- *Wounds and blood*. Investigators can also tell if the body has been moved by inspecting wounds and blood around the body. If wounds indicate severe bleeding and little blood is on the scene, the body may have been moved. Blood type and DNA evidence are also options that might be considered by investigators.
- *Fingernail scrapings*. Technicians at the morgue will also look for fingernail scrapings. This evidence might turn up hair, skin, blood, or fibers that might be useful in developing a suspect.
- *Fingerprints of the deceased*. The deceased's fingerprints can be taken by using an ink roller on each finger. Next, while strips of fingerprint paper are placed in a curved holder such as a spoon, each finger is placed against the strip and an impression is taken. Rigid joints can be loosened by working the finger back and forth several times.

The Victim Who Is Still Alive

In cases in which the victim is still alive or conscious, he or she might be willing to give information such as the name of his or her assailant, a description of the assailant's clothing, and the type of automobile the assailant was driving. After this information is learned, it should be passed on to the communication center for broadcast to other officers and departments.

Dying Declaration

If the victim is badly wounded and believes that he or she is dying, the officer should treat his or her statement as a **dying declaration**. Under the Federal Rules of Evidence, a dying declaration is admissible if the proponent of the statement can establish:

- Unavailability of the declarant
- The declarant's statement is being offered in a criminal prosecution for murder or in a civil action
- The declarant's statement was made while under the belief that his or her death was imminent
- The declarant's statement must relate to the cause or circumstances of what the declarant believed to be his or her impending death[4]

Consider this example: Suppose Rachel stabs Steve and then runs away, and a police officer happens upon Steve as he lies in the street, bleeding to death. If Steve manages to sputter out with his last words, "I'm dying—Rachel stabbed me" (or even just "Rachel did it"), the officer can testify to that in court.

The declarant (here, Steve) does not actually have to die for the statement to be admissible, but he or she needs to have had a genuine belief that he or she was going to die, and the declarant must be unavailable to testify in court. In the above scenario, if Steve were to recover instead of dying and were able to testify in court, the officer would no longer be able to testify to the statement. It would then constitute hearsay and not fall into the exception. Furthermore, the statement must relate to the circumstances or the cause of the declarant's own death. If Steve's last words are, "Rachel killed Kayla," that statement will not fall within the exception and will be inadmissible (unless Rachel killed Steve and Kayla in the same act).

Furthermore, as with all testimony, the dying declaration will be inadmissible unless it is based on the declarant's actual knowledge. Suppose, for example, Steve bought a cup of coffee at the coffee shop and was stricken with food poisoning. If his dying last words were, "The supplier who sold them the coffee mix must have used a contaminated packing machine," that statement would be inadmissible despite the hearsay exception because Steve had no way of knowing anything about the conditions in which the coffee was packed.

In U.S. federal courts, the dying declaration exception is limited to civil cases and criminal homicide prosecutions, although many states copy the Federal Rules of Evidence in their statutes and some permit the admission of dying declarations in all situations.

The Forensic Autopsy

A forensic autopsy is frequently used to determine the cause of death. This is especially so in the case of violent or suspicious deaths. Typically, deaths are placed in one of five categories:

1. Natural
2. Accidental
3. Homicide
4. Suicide
5. Undetermined

The role of the medical examiner is to determine the time of death, the exact cause of death, and what, if anything, preceded the death, such as an altercation. A forensic autopsy can include obtaining biological samples from the deceased for toxicological testing, including stomach contents. Toxicology tests may reveal the presence of one or more chemical "poisons," and the quantity of those chemicals. Because postmortem deterioration of the body, together with the gravitational pooling of bodily fluids, will necessarily alter the bodily environment, toxicology tests may overestimate, rather than underestimate, the quantity of the suspected chemical.

In most states, the medical examiner is required to complete an autopsy report and many mandate that the autopsy be videotaped. Following an in-depth examination of all the evidence, a medical examiner or coroner will assign a manner of death as one of the five categories listed above, and identify evidence to that effect.

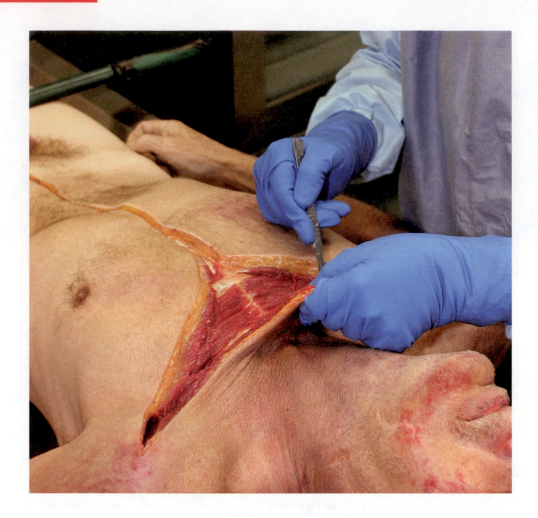

|Fig. 9.4| ▲

The forensic autopsy is conducted by the corner or medical examiner and often provides the criminal investigator invaluable evidence as to the time and cause of death.

Courtesy of Mike Himmel

Estimating the Time of Death

If the wrongful death appears to have been a homicide, all areas around the body become important in determining the time of death. The time of death in a homicide case, particularly when there are no witnesses, is one of the most critical variables in its investigation. It may convict a murderer, break an alibi, or even eliminate a suspect. Time may come into play if the deceased had an appointment with someone around the time of his or her death. In addition, in cases of exclusive opportunity, in which only certain persons are present with the victim, husbands or wives, boyfriends or girlfriends, and so on, may become likely suspects.

Changes in the Body: Decomposition

Simply stated, death occurs when vital functions of the body are halted. These include functions of breathing and circulation. In addition, investigators should observe other changes.

After death occurs, human decomposition takes place in five stages. The process of tissue breakdown may take from several days up to years. At all stages of decomposition, insect activity occurs on the body, as detailed below.

STAGE 1: THE FRESH STAGE The fresh stage of decomposition occurs during the first few days after the death. There are no physical signs of decomposition during this time. However, homeostasis of the body has ceased, allowing cellular and soft tissue changes to occur because of the process of autolysis, the destruction of cells and organs due to an aseptic chemical process. At this point, the body enters *algor mortis*, the cooling of the body's temperature to that of its surroundings.

When the body's cells reach the final stage of autolysis, an anaerobic environment is created, that is, an environment in which oxygen is not present. This allows the body's normal bacteria to break down the remaining carbohydrates, proteins, and lipids. The products from the breakdown create acids, gases, and other products that cause production of volatile organic compounds (VOCs) and putrefactive effects. VOCs are produced during the early stages of human decomposition.[5]

Substances produced during the fresh stage of decomposition attract a variety of insects. *Diptera* insects begin to lay their eggs on the body during this stage, especially member of the Calliphoridae family of insects.[6] If the body is on the ground or buried in soil, there is also considerable insect activity by the insects that live in the soil around the body. The reasoning for this is simple: A dead human body serves as an excellent source of decaying matter to feed on and as such, a hospitable environment.

STAGE 2: THE PUTREFACTION STAGE Odor, color changes, and bloating of the body during decomposition are the results of putrefaction. The lower part of the abdomen turns green due to bacteria activity in the cecum. Bacteria break down hemoglobin into sulfhemoglobin, which causes the green color change. A formation of gases enters the abdomen, which forces liquids and feces out of the body. The gases also enter the neck and face, causing swelling of the mouth, lips, and tongue. Due to this swelling and misconfiguration of the face, identification of the body can be difficult.

Bacteria also enter the venous system, causing blood to *hemolyze*. This leads to the formation of red streaks along the veins. This color soon changes to green through a process known as *marbelization*. It can be seen on the shoulders, chest and shoulder area, and thighs. The skin can develop blisters containing fluid. The skin also becomes fragile, leading to skin slippage, making it difficult to move a body. While in this condition, body hair comes off easily. The color change of the discoloration from green to brown marks the transition of the early stage of putrefaction to the advanced decompositional stages.

During the putrefaction stage of decomposition, the majority of insect activity again comes from members of the Calliphoridae family (included are Formicidae, Muscidae, Sphaeroceridae, Silphidae, Lepidoptera, Hymenoptera, Sarcophagidae, Histeridae, Staphylinidae, Phalangida, Piophilidae, Araneae, Sepsidae, and Phoridae). As with the fresh stage of decomposition, if the body is on the ground or buried in soil, there is also considerable insect activity by soil-inhabiting arthropods.[7]

STAGE 3: THE BLACK PUTREFACTION STAGE After the body goes through the bloating stage, it begins the black putrefaction stage. At this point, the body cavity ruptures, the abdominal gases escape, and the body darkens from its greenish color. These activities allow for a greater invasion of scavengers, and insect activity increases greatly. This stage ends as the bones become apparent, which can take anywhere from 10 to 20 days after death depending on region and temperature. This period is also dependent on the degree to which the body is exposed.

During the black putrefaction stage of decomposition, insects that can be found living in the body are *Calliphoridae* larvae, *Staphylinidae*, *Histeridae*, *Gamasid* mites, *Ptomaphila*, *Trichopterygidae*, *Piophilid* larvae, parasitic wasps, *Staphylinid* larvae, *Trichopterygid* larvae, *Histerid* larvae, *Ptomaphila* larvae, *Dermestes*, *Tyroglyphid* mites, *Tineid* larvae, and the *Dermestes* larvae.[8] Some insects can also be found living in the soil around the body such as *Isopoda*, *Collembola*, *Dermaptera*, *Formicidae*, *Pseudoscorpiones*, *Araneae*, *Plectochetos*, *Acari*, *Pauropoda*, *Symphyla*, *Geophilidae*, and *Protura*. The types of insects differ based on where the body is, although *Diptera* larvae can be found feeding on the body in almost all cases.[9]

It is important to note that the identification of insects has proven to be one way that the time of death can be determined. Examining the larvae of insects found on the body accomplishes this. Investigators should consider contacting an entomologist (insect expert) for advice at this stage of the investigation. This technique studies the various stages of growth of each larva before it develops into an adult insect. Houseflies, for example, deposit eggs on the remains of the corpse, usually in the area of the eyes, mouth, nostrils, and wounds. The eggs then become maggots and feed on the body. Typically, the time span for the hatching of the maggot is 24 hours.

The developmental stage depends on the type of insect in question. An entomologist can identify the specific insect and determine an estimated time span for its development as well as the season in which the death occurred. The recommended procedure is for all insects to be placed into alcohol for preservation.

STAGE 4: THE BUTYRIC FERMENTATION STAGE After the early putrefaction and black putrefaction phases have taken place, the body begins mummification, in which the body begins to dry out. The human carcass is first mummified and then goes through adipocere formation. Adipocere (grave wax) formation is the loss of body odor and the formation of a cheesy appearance on the cadaver. Mummification is considered a post-active stage because there is less definite distinction between changes, and they are indicated by reduced skin, cartilage, and bone. Mummification is also indicated when all of the internal organs are lost due to insect activity.[10]

STAGE 5: THE DRY DECAY STAGE When the last of the soft tissue has been removed from the body, the final stage of decomposition, skeletonization, occurs. This stage encompasses the deterioration of skeletal remains and is the longest of the decomposition processes. Skeletonization differs markedly from the previous stages, not only in length but also in the deterioration process itself.

The strength and durability of bone stems from the unique protein–mineral bond present in skeletal formation. Consequently, changes to skeletal remains, known as *bone diagenesis*, occur at a substantially slower rate than stages of soft tissue breakdown. As the protein–mineral bond weakens after death, however, the organic protein begins to leach away, leaving behind only the mineral composition. Unlike soft tissue decomposition, which is influenced mainly by temperature and oxygen levels, the process of bone breakdown is more highly dependent on soil type and pH, along with the presence of groundwater. However, temperature can be a contributing factor: Higher temperature leads the protein in bones to break down more rapidly. If buried, remains decay faster in acidic-based soils than in alkaline soils. Bones left in areas of high moisture content also decay at a faster rate. The water leaches out skeletal minerals, which corrode the bone, leading to bone disintegration.[11]

The Forensics of Decomposition

Various sciences study the decomposition of bodies. These sciences fall under the general topic of forensics because the usual motive for study of the decomposition of human bodies is to determine the time and cause of death for legal purposes:

- **Forensic pathology** studies the clues to the cause of death found in the corpse as a medical phenomenon.
- **Forensic entomology** studies the insects and other vermin found in corpses; the sequence in which they appear, the kinds of insects, and where they are found in their life cycle are clues that can shed light on the time of death, the length of a corpse's exposure, and whether the corpse was moved.[12]
- **Forensic anthropology** is the branch of physical anthropology that studies skeletons and human remains, usually to seek clues as to the identity, race, and sex of their former owner.[13]

The University of Tennessee Anthropological Research Facility (better known as the "Body Farm") in Knoxville, Tennessee, has a number of bodies laid out in various situations in a fenced-in plot near the medical center. Scientists at the Body Farm study how the human body decays in various circumstances to gain a better understanding of decomposition.[14]

Factors Affecting Decomposition

The rate and manner of decomposition in an animal body are strongly affected by a number of factors. In roughly descending degrees of importance, they are:

- Temperature
- The availability of oxygen
- Prior embalming
- Cause of death
- Burial and depth of burial
- Access by scavengers
- Trauma, including wounds and crushing blows
- Humidity or wetness
- Rainfall

The Body Farm

The "Body Farm" refers to a forensic research facility housed at the University of Tennessee Anthropological Research Facility, located a few miles from downtown on Alcoa Highway in Knoxville, Tennessee, behind the University of Tennessee Medical Center. It was first started in late 1981 by anthropologist Dr. William M. Bass as a facility for study of the decomposition of human remains. Dr. Bass became Chairman of the University's Anthropology Department in 1971, and as official state forensic anthropologist for Tennessee he was frequently consulted in police cases involving decomposed human remains. Since no facilities existed that specifically studied decomposition, in 1981 he opened the department's first body farm.

The Body Farm consists of a 2.5-acrewooded plot, surrounded by a razor wire fence. At any given time there will be a number of bodies placed in different settings throughout the facility and left to decompose. The bodies are exposed in a number of ways in order to provide insights into decomposition under varying conditions. Detailed observations and records of the decomposition process are kept, including the sequence and speed of decomposition and the effects of insect activity.

Each year, over 100 bodies are donated to the facility. Some persons preregister before their death, and others are donated by their families or by a medical examiner. Sixty percent of donations are made by family members of individuals who were not preregistered with the facility. Over 1,300 people have chosen to preregister themselves. The University of Tennessee Body Farm is also used in the training of criminal investigators and crime scene technicians in scene-of-crime skills and techniques.

In addition to the University of Tennessee, other "body farms" have been established to further the knowledge of human decomposition. These include Western Carolina University, Texas State University, California University of Pennsylvania, and Sam Houston University.

- Body size and weight
- Clothing
- The surface on which the body rests
- Foods and objects inside the specimen's digestive tract (bacon opposed to lettuce)

The speed at which decomposition occurs varies greatly. Factors such as temperature, humidity, and the season of death all determine how fast a fresh body will skeletonize or mummify. A basic guide for the effect of environment on decomposition is given as Casper's law (or ratio): If all other factors are equal, then when there is free access of air, a body decomposes twice as fast than if immersed in water and eight times faster than if buried in earth.

The most important variable is a body's accessibility to insects, particularly flies. On the surface in tropical areas, invertebrates alone can easily reduce a fully fleshed corpse to clean bones in less than two weeks. The skeleton itself is not permanent; acids in soils can reduce it to unrecognizable components. This is one reason given for the lack of human remains found in the wreckage of the *Titanic*, even in parts of the ship considered inaccessible to scavengers. Freshly skeletonized bone is often called "green" bone and has a characteristic greasy feel. Under certain conditions (normally cool, damp soil), bodies may undergo saponification and develop a waxy substance called adipocere caused by the action of soil chemicals on the body's proteins and fats. The formation of adipocere slows decomposition by inhibiting the bacteria that cause putrefaction.

In extremely dry or cold conditions, the normal process of decomposition is halted—by either lack of moisture or temperature controls on bacterial and enzymatic action—causing the body to be preserved as a mummy. Whereas frozen mummies commonly restart the decomposition process when thawed, heat-desiccated mummies remain so unless exposed to moisture.

Other Visual Evidence of Decomposition

BODY COLOR After the victim dies, circulation of blood through the arteries and veins ceases. As the body settles, color in the lips and nails disappears as the blood settles into the lower capillaries of the body. The blood then changes from red to a dark purplish color as it loses its oxygen. This is the beginning of lividity, which we discuss later.

CHANGES IN EYES The eyes are the most sensitive part of the human body and, in death, do not react to light, touching, or pressure. In addition, the eyelids may remain open; the pupils may become irregular in size and shape and typically become milky and cloudy in color within 8 to 10 hours of death.

TEMPERATURE OF THE BODY In life, a person's body maintains a body temperature of 98.6°F. Even after death, there may not be a loss of body heat because the body will tend to adapt to the temperature of its environment. The rate of cooling can, however, be a primary determinant as to the time of death. For example, a corpse will feel cool to the touch from 8 to 12 hours after death and will remain the same temperature as its surroundings for about 24 hours after death. Several factors can contribute to the rate in which a body loses heat. The greater the difference between the body and the environment, the faster the body will cool down.

Water and air temperature are the most important contributing factors. The temperature of the body before death can influence its temperature after death occurs. Predeath conditions such as stroke, sun stroke, and strangulation generally result in a higher body temperature at the time of death. One reliable method for determining body temperature is to insert a thermometer into the rectum of the deceased (do not insert a thermometer into the wound). The medical examiner will usually place a thermometer in the victim's liver. Body temperature can also be raised by the victim's excessive body fat or heavy clothing.

The International Association of Chiefs of Police (IACP) offers a working formula to determine the estimated time of death when it is thought to be less than 24 hours:

$$\frac{98.6 \text{ (normal temp.)} \ 2 \text{ (rectal temp.)} \ \text{no. of hours since death}}{1.5 \text{ (average rate of heat loss)}}$$

RIGOR MORTIS **Rigor mortis**, the process of stiffening, or contraction of body muscles after vital functions cease, is generally considered a poor indicator of time of death. As a rule, rigor mortis sets in two to four hours after death, but many variables may contribute to "rigor." Contrary to popular belief, rigor mortis starts at the same time throughout the entire body. However, it is first observed in the jaws and neck.[15] It then tends to progress in the head-to-foot direction. At the time of completion, typically 8 to 12 hours after death, the torso, jaws, neck, and upper and lower extremities are "stiff as a board." Once in this state, the body resists any change in position.

POSTMORTEM LIVIDITY As indicated earlier, when a body's vital functions cease, blood settles to the bottom side of the body because of gravity. A purplish **lividity** stain forms on the skin of the body closest to the surface on which it is lying. So if a body is lying on its stomach and

|Fig. 9.5|

Postmortem lividity located on the back of a murder victim shows where blood has pooled after death.

Mike Himmel / Missouri State Highway Patrol Crime Laboratory

the lividity stain is on its back, the body has probably been turned over. Postmortem lividity may appear anywhere between one-half hour to four hours after death. It is sometimes valuable in determining whether or not a body has been moved, depending on the state of the lividity. If it is determined that the body has been moved, the officer must ask why—perhaps another police officer turned over the body. Generally speaking, however, after lividity has set in for 12 hours, the body will not diminish in color and will remain unchanged.

ANIMALS A body discovered outdoors (and in some cases indoors) will sometimes be mutilated by wild animals. Bodies that have been mutilated will give the appearance of having been grossly injured, but that will not necessarily be evidence of a postmortem attack. Investigators must be careful not to draw false conclusions.

BODIES FOUND IN WATER As described in the preceding section, marine life can also damage and distort dead bodies found in water (floaters). Generally, a forensic pathologist will have to be consulted to distinguish postmortem injuries from those that occurred in life. Experience has shown that bodies found in air will have decomposed twice as fast as those found submerged in water.

Gunshot Wounds as Evidence

Several factors can affect the type of wound inflicted by a firearm. Such wounds may resemble a stab wound at first, but certain physical characteristics may vary, depending on the type of caliber weapon used, the distance between the shooter and victim, and whether the lethal bullet had ricocheted off another object. To understand the firearm wound best, let's discuss the effect that a firearm has on the human body. Vernon Geberth states that when a firearm is discharged, several things can occur:[16]

- Fire or flames are emitted from the barrel
- Smoke follows the flame
- The bullet emerges from the barrel
- Additional smoke and grains of both burned and unburned gunpowder follow the bullet out of the barrel
- The material spreads outward from the barrel as it is emitted
- If the firearm is close to the targeted surface, much of this material will be deposited on it

In addition, if the surface is farther away, less of the material will be deposited. Depending on the material or clothing present on the body, it is sometimes possible to predict the distance between the firearm and the victim.

In the case of a contact wound, where the muzzle of the weapon was held against the body when discharged, certain residue will be present. Soot is always present in such wounds, with powder particles identified in at least half of cases.[17] These particles are often difficult to readily identify, however, and may require expert analysis.

Assessing the Severity of Gunshot Wounds

Gunshot wounds can be penetrating or perforating. In the case of a penetrating wound, the bullet enters an object and remains inside. In contrast, a perforating wound is one whereby the bullet passes completely through the object. In some cases, the wound can be both penetrating and perforating in that it penetrates some part of the body, such as the head, but perforates certain parts, such as the brain.

In the case of a perforating wound, the bullet creates an exit wound as it passes through the body. An exit wound is notably different from an entrance wound. For example, a reddish-brown area of roughened skin, known as the abrasion ring, surrounds an entrance wound and small amounts of blood escape through. On the other hand, an exit wound is larger and more irregular with protruding tissue and no abrasion ring. With an exit wound, far more blood escapes from the body.[18]

After the bullet enters through the skin, the skin retracts due to its elasticity. This will make the wound appear smaller than the bullet that has passed through. A bullet typically travels in a straight line but if it hits a bone, as is often the case, its direction is unpredictable. When this occurs, the bone may be shattered or the bullet might glance off and be redirected to another location in the body.

Estimating the Distance of the Shooter from the Victim

Examining the gunshot wound can provide considerable information about the shooting, including the distance of the shooter from the victim. Gunshot wounds can be classified based on the range from the muzzle of the gun to the target. These classifications include contact, near-contact, intermediate, and distant wounds.[19]

Contact wound: A contact wound results when the muzzle of the firearm is held against the body at the time of discharge. This can be further divided into hard, loose, angled, and incomplete contact wounds.

Hard contact wound: In a "hard contact wound" the muzzle is held tightly against the skin. There is little external evidence that it is a contact wound, although if the entrance is inspected usually searing and powder blackening of the immediate edge of the wound is seen. An autopsy will reveal particles of soot and unburnt powder in the wound track.

Loose contact wound: In loose-contact wounds, the muzzle is held lightly against the skin, and the soot that is carried by the gas is deposited in a zone around the entrance, which can be wiped away.

Angled wound: In an angled-contact wound, the barrel is held at an acute angle to the skin, and gas and soot radiate outward from where the gun does not touch the skin. In an incomplete-contact wound, the barrel is held against the skin, but in a place where the skin is not completely flat. In this case, hot sooty gases escape the gap, leaving a long blackened and seared section of the skin, with scattered grains of powder.

Near-contact wound: In near-contact wounds, the muzzle is close to the skin but is not in direct contact. In this case, the powder grains do not have a chance to disperse and leave a powder tattooing. A wide zone of powder soot and seared, blackened skin surround the entrance wound.

Intermediate wound: In intermediate-range wounds, the muzzle is held away from the skin but close enough that it still produces powder tattooing. Numerous reddish-brown or possibly orange lesions around the entrance to the wound also characterize this type of wound.

Distant wound: Lastly, distant gunshot wounds leave no marks other than those produced by the bullet perforating the skin.

|Fig. 9.6|

Close-up photo showing blood drops and how pooling of blood can occur at crime scenes.

Courtesy of Mike Himmel

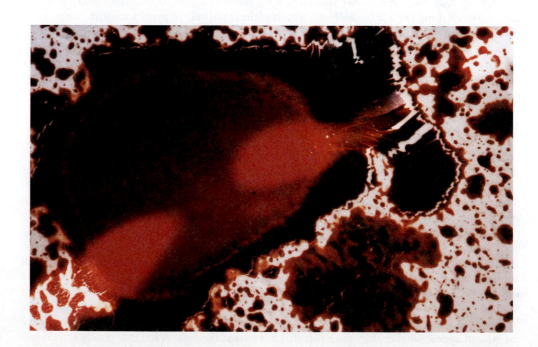

|Fig. 9.7| ▲

Blood drops and spatter are common on violent crime scenes and when properly documented can tell the investigator the distance from its origin/point of impact and direction of travel (trajectory).

Courtesy of Mike Himmel

Determining Whether or Not the Victim Was Alive Before the Shooting

An examination of the wound can also indicate whether or not the victim was alive when he was shot. If a reddish-brown to orange-red powder tattooing exists, that indicates that the individual was in fact alive when the wound was inflicted. However, if the powder has produced gray or yellow marks instead, the individual was deceased before the shooting.[20]

Establishing the Type of Gun Used in the Shooting

The type of gun used in the shooting can often be determined by examining the gunshot wound. The shotgun, particularly the 12-gauge, is one of the most common and most deadly weapons. Fired at close range, the shotgun is the most destructive of all small arms. Shotgun wounds are characterized by massive tissue destruction and embedded wadding—if the shot was within ten feet. By examining the wadding, one can determine the type of shot and gauge of gun, and possibly identify the gun.

The handgun and .22 caliber rim fire weapons produce wound variations based on whether the gunshot was contact, near-contact, intermediate, or distant (discussed earlier). For the most part, handguns produce larger and more obvious tattoo patterns than rim fire weapons because of the use of flake powder. Rim fire weapons instead use "ball powder," which produces extremely fine / faint tattooing. The extent of the injuries that both handguns and .22 caliber rim fire weapons inflict is usually confined to the tissues and organs directly in the bullet's path.

Wounds inflicted by center fire rifles differ from those of the other weapons in that they can damage organs, bones, and tissue without even coming into contact with them. This type of gun has higher velocities and higher kinetic energies than the others, and therefore possesses the potential to produce extremely severe wounds. The organs that are directly hit by the bullets of these guns may partially or completely disintegrate, and the pressure is powerful enough to fracture bones and rupture vessels close to the wound. A gunshot wound from a center fire rifle can result in tissue being ejected not only from the exit wound but also from the entrance wound. As a result, it is not uncommon to find expelled tissue on both sides of the wounded body.

A Closer Look

Tracing Firearms

In April 2012, the U.S. Bureau of Alcohol, Tobacco and Firearms (ATF) disclosed that over a five-year period of time, more than 68,000 guns recovered in Mexico were traced back to the United States. More than 30,000 other guns could not be traced. Tracing firearms is often part of the investigative process associated with a shooting.

Firearms tracing provides information on the movement of a firearm from its first sale by a manufacturer or importer through the distribution chain in an attempt to identify the first retail purchaser. This information provides investigative leads for criminal investigations. After the firearm is recovered and the identifiers are forwarded to the ATF's National Tracing Center (NTC), ATF contacts the manufacturer or importer to ascertain the sale or transfer of the firearm. ATF will attempt to contact all federal firearms licensees (wholesale/retail) in the distribution chain until a purchaser is identified or the trace process cannot continue due to a lack of accurate or incomplete information. The success of a trace result, whether domestic or international, relies upon the accuracy of the supplied firearm identifiers. The necessary identifiers for a trace include manufacturer, importer (if applicable), model, caliber, and serial number.

Source: The Alcohol, Tobacco and Firearms. (2012). *ATF Mexico, 2007–2011*. U.S. Department of Justice. Available at http://www.atf.gov/statistics/download/trace-data/international/2007-2011-Mexico-trace-data.pdf

Identifying a Suspect Bullet

Bullets are also potentially important evidence in shooting cases. They can be analyzed in an attempt to determine the weapon that was used in the shooting. Ballistic experts examine the appearance of grooves, the number of grooves, the diameter of the lands and grooves, the width of the lands and grooves, the depth of the grooves, the direction of the rifling twist, and the degree of the twist. Imperfections of the bullets can also be unique to only one weapon, identifying that weapon as distinctly as fingerprints. For example, if there are no grooves on the bullet, it was likely fired from a large weapon, such as a rifle. If there are elongated grooves with deep incisions, it was likely fired from a weapon smaller in size.

Skid marks are another characteristic that one might notice when examining a bullet. If skid marks exist, the bullet was likely fired from a revolver. Skid marks occur when the grooves are wider at the nose of the bullet than at the base.

One may also find the presence of powder marks on the bullet itself. Powder marks typically occur on lead bullets or full-metal jacketed bullets that have lead exposed at the base. These marks are a result of the powder grains being propelled against the base of the bullet with such a force that they leave a marking. Different types of powder can also leave different marks on the bullet.

THE MAKE OF GUN Recovered bullets can be compared to other bullets to determine the make of the gun. When a bullet is recovered and there is also a suspect weapon in custody, an examiner uses the weapon to fire a bullet into a test box or water tank. The two bullets are then examined under a microscope to see if the markings are the same. However, it is unlikely that the two are similar, even if shot from the same firearm.

While the analysis of a bullet can potentially give the examiner a lot of information, it is not always possible. For instance, a bullet that has been removed from a body can be too mutilated to be useful. If the bullet was fired from a gun for which it was not chambered, it can be corrupted, as in the case of an automatic producing skid marks. Finally, bullets recovered from decomposed bodies are unlikely to be of any value in making determinations about the nature of the weapon.[21]

Smudging

Smudging is usually a ring that results from gunpowder being deposited around the wound. It has a dirty appearance and can usually be wiped off. The significance of smudging is that it indicates that the victim was close to his or her assailant, although the firearm was not actually touching the skin.

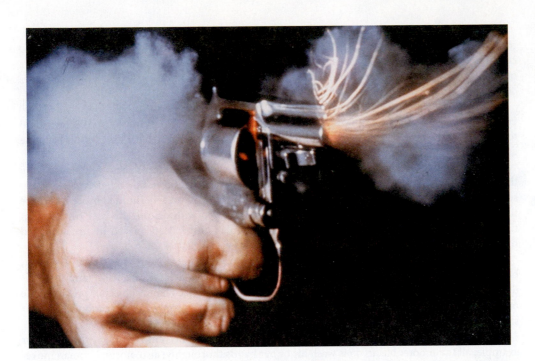

|Fig. 9.8| △

When a handgun is fired, gunpowder and primer residues emit from the barrel. If fired from close range, these residues (called stippling) can possibly be found on the skin of both the shooter and the victim.

Forensic Technology WAI Inc.

Tattooing

Tiny pinpoint hemorrhages may result from the discharge of unburned powder being deposited into the skin. Called *tattooing*, these marks cannot be wiped away. One issue of critical importance in investigating gunshot wounds is the determination of whether or not the victim was murdered or died from suicide. The presence (or absence) of powder burns not only helps in making this determination but also helps the investigator decide the distance between the victim and the firearm.

Understanding Gunshot Residue

Another potentially important source of evidence in gunshot cases is gunshot residue.

Gunshot residue is created in the process of discharging the firearm. According to an article written by Hamilton County, Ohio, Evidence Examiner Michael Trimpe, it results when the firing pin of a gun hits the back of the cartridge, activating the shock-sensitive primer, which ignites the gunpowder, forcing the bullet down the barrel of the gun and on its path. The heat and pressure within the cartridge vaporize the metals from the primer. Vapors escape from any area of the weapon...like the breach area and muzzle. The heat of this explosive reaction and subsequent cooling results in the condensation and formation of tiny metal-containing particles. These particles fall on anything in the vicinity of the fired weapon, including the hands of the shooter.[22]

For decades, gunshot residue (GSR) has been considered evidence that a specific person fired a handgun. But in recent years, GSR has been somewhat discredited and its usefulness limited, if not disregarded. To best understand the role of GSR in death and shooting investigations, it is imperative to understand the operation of a handgun.

If one inspects the back of a bullet larger than a .22, a small circle in the center (known as "centerfire") can be seen. This is a short, sealed cylinder containing primer. When the trigger is pulled, the hammer of the gun strikes this cylinder, and the shock of that blow causes the primer to explode. This explosion blows out into the large chamber of the casing, where the gunpowder is, causing the gunpowder to catch fire. The burning of the gunpowder is what expels the bullet away from the casing, down the barrel of the gun, and out the open end.[23]

Tiny particles of this primer material (GSR) are also expelled from the front of the gun. They can also "leak" from the breechblock area when the gun is fired, either from the open back of the chamber in revolvers or when chamber opens and the cartridge is ejected in automatics. As a result, GSR can settle on the hand of the shooter.

Primer is generally made up of barium nitrate and antimony sulfide; however, most .22 ammunition does not have antimony, and rare brands have neither antimony nor barium.[24] It also contains lead styphnate, but because lead is commonly found in the environment, the presence of it on a person's hands is not considered significant. Therefore, most GSR detection techniques concentrate on barium and antimony.[25]

Most gunpowder used today is "double base," which means it is a combination of nitroglycerin and cellulose nitrate (commonly and incorrectly known as nitrocellulose).[26] GSR tests used to range from the now-discredited "paraffin test," which essentially tested for the nitrates from the gunpowder to "atomic absorption."

Atomic absorption involves swabbing the suspect's hands with cotton swabs and then soaking them in an acid solution. The solution is exposed to high temperatures, and a light reads the absorption rate of the atomized solution. This is a time-consuming and time-limited process because the swabs have to first be "digested," then spun, then diluted with deionized water (in different concentrations for barium and antimony) in tiny sample cups that are placed in an automated machine, a spectrometer.[27]

Atomic absorption only shows that the element is present but not in what form. Moreover, barium and antimony can also be found in other sources such as firecrackers, paint, and some industrial settings. Accordingly, locating these elements on a suspect's hands does not prove that he or she fired a gun or even that he or she handled a gun. Rather, it is only an "indication" that he or she was in the general area of a fired gun.[28]

GSR is composed of extremely tiny particles that can be easily removed from the skin. For example, all the shooter has to do is wash his or her hands thoroughly; also, normal human movement and activity can remove the particles as well. To a great extent, this is the reason why deceased

|Fig. 9.9| △

A close-up of gunshot residue created by a .45-caliber bullet shot at a range of 1 inch.

Courtesy of Mike Himmel

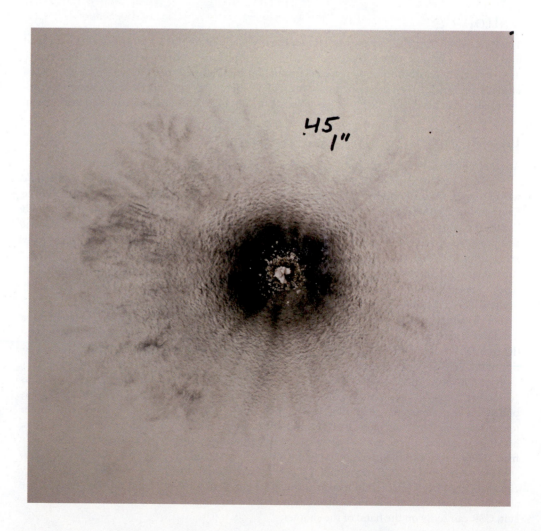

victims' hands are bagged in paper (not plastic as is often depicted in television shows)—to pre-serve the GSR particles. Most labs will not test samples collected from living persons more than six hours after the shooting. This doesn't apply to deceased persons because they're not moving around or using their hands after death.[29]

From this comes the determination that although the presence of GSR doesn't prove someone did fire a gun, the absence of GSR doesn't prove they didn't. As such, attorneys and forensic sci-entists disagree on the usefulness of GSR evidence. For example, prosecutors often say that GSR on the defendant's hands proves that he or she is the killer. On the other hand, defense attorneys argue that the absence of GSR on the defendant's hands proves that he or she is not the killer. Consequently, in recent years, the legal community has become increasingly disenchanted with circumstantial evidence and more interested in evidence that provides a higher degree of scientific certainty, such as DNA. For this reason, a number of crime laboratories across the nation have discontinued GSR analysis.[30]

Why analyze for GSR?

In spite of criticisms about the usefulness of GSR in gunshot investigations, recent evidence still supports it usefulness. For example, according to Michael Trimpe, "...the technology behind the analysis of gunshot residue is unquestionably scientifically sound as methods for analyzing it has existed since the 1970s. Also, studies have shown that average people do not have gunshot residue on their hands, but someone who fires a gun most likely will for a period of time."[31]

Despite efforts by forensic scientists to disprove the usefulness of GSR in gunshot investiga-tions, research has strengthened the fact that clearly identifiable GSR particles come from a fired weapon. The reason for analyzing for GSR lies in the fact that most trace evidence is not conclusive but supportive and circumstantial. Glass, hair, fiber, paint, soil, and, sometimes, shoeprint analyses cannot conclusively identify a common source between a known and an unknown sample. The fact, however, that authorities located evidence with a possible common source is worth noting for the court. Accordingly, GSR found on the hands of a suspected shooter is significant and worthy of consideration by the jury.[32]

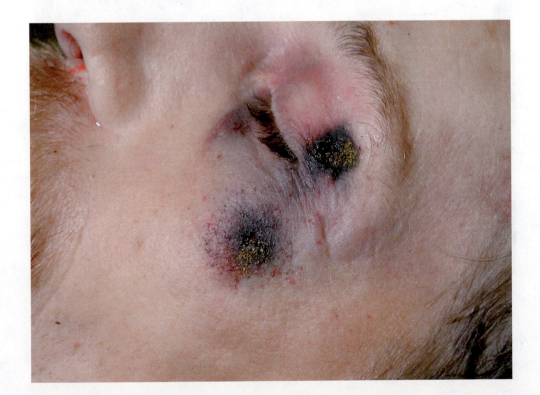

|Fig. 9.10| △

Duel gunshot wounds to the head with stippling.

Mike Himmel / Missouri State Highway Patrol Crime Laboratory

Entry/Exit Wounds and Distance of Fire

Often when a deceased victim has been shot, there will be more than one wound on the body. It is important for the investigation to reveal whether wounds are entrance or exit wound. In other words, where did the bullet enter the body and where did it come out? While the official determination of whether a wound is an entrance or exit wound is typically made by the medical examiner, this finding will assist the criminal investigator considerably in his or her investigation of the shooting.

As discussed in the previous section, contact wounds typically have soot on the outside of the skin, and muzzle imprint, or laceration of the skin from effects of gases.[33] Intermediate, or close-range, wounds may show a wide zone of powder stippling, but lack a muzzle imprint and laceration. The area of powder stippling will depend upon the distance from the muzzle.[34] Distant range wounds are lacking powder stippling and usually exhibit a hole roughly the caliber of the projectile fired.

The most difficult problem is distinguishing a distant from a contact wound. As we learned in the previous section, the factors that can affect the amount and distribution of gunshot residue

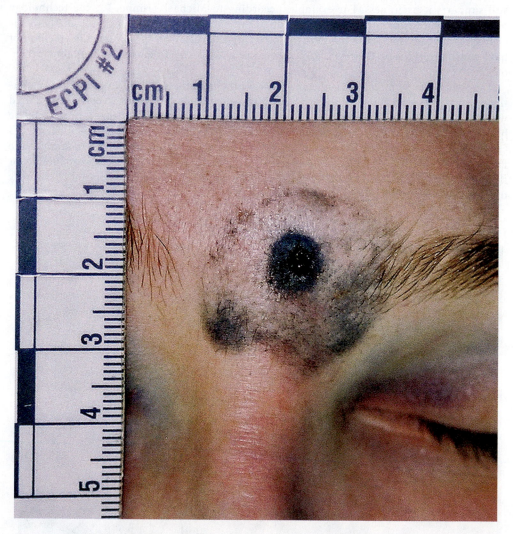

|Fig. 9.11| ▲

Gunshot wound to the center of the eyebrows; also demonstrates the deposit of gunshot residue and stippling.

Courtesy of Mike Himmel

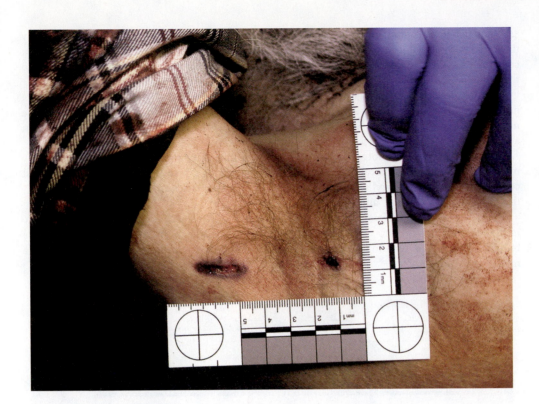

|Fig. 9.12| △

In this case, the entry point of the gunshot is located at the area of the underarm (toward the apex of the ruler) and the exit wound is shown to the left, creating a larger wound as the bullet exited.

Courtesy of Mike Himmel

(GSR) on skin and clothing include: (1) firing distance, (2) length and diameter of the firearm barrel, (3) characteristics of the gunpowder, (4) angle between the firearm barrel and target, (5) characteristics of the cartridge, (6) the environment (moisture, wind, heat), (7) type of clothing, (8) intermediate targets, and (9) characteristics of the target (tissue type, putrefaction, blood marks).[35]

Examination for GSR may aid in distinguishing entrance from exit wounds, for the entrance wound will have more than the exit, or the exit will have none. Most bullets are designed to hit the target without exiting, for this imparts all the bullet's kinetic energy to the target and does the most damage. However, in many situations an exit wound will be present. This may be due to the use of a projectile more powerful than necessary, or the projectile may strike an area (such as an extremity) with minimal tissue.

Exit wounds are generally larger than entrance wounds because the bullet has expanded or tumbled on its axis. Exit wounds either do not exhibit gunshot residues or far less residues than associated entrance wounds. In bone, typical "bevelling" may be present that is oriented away from the entrance wound.[36]

Fragmentation of the bullet may produce secondary missiles, one or more of which may have exit wounds. The bullet path may be altered by striking bone or other firm tissues, such that the bullet track may not be linear, and exit wounds may not appear directly opposite entrance wounds.

It is important to remember that the orientation of the bullet track may be positional. The victim may have been shot while standing or sitting, but when the body is typically examined at autopsy, it is lying down, so that soft tissues may shift position. This must be remembered when rendering opinions as to the angle, or direction, of fire.

The Shotgun as a Weapon of Murder

Many homicides are committed using a shotgun. A shotgun is a notably different weapon than the pistol and presents a number of considerably different investigative challenges in homicide cases. When a shotgun is fired using a multiple pellet shotshell, the pellets exit the barrel of the shotgun and begin to spread out into a pattern that increases in diameter as the distance increases between the pellets and the shotgun. A victim shot with a shotgun generally suffers considerably more tissue damage than if shot with a handgun.

Shotguns are firearms typically fired from the shoulder that are designed to fire shotshells containing anywhere from one large projectile to as many as several hundred small pellets. Shotguns aren't classified by caliber but come in different gauges. The gauge of a shotgun is determined by the number of round lead balls of bore diameter that it takes to equal one pound. Shotguns can come in 10, 12, 16, 20, 28, and .410 gauge. The .410 is actually an exception with .410 referring to the caliber of the shotgun's bore. It would actually be about a 67 gauge in "lead ball" terms.[37]

Although some newer shotgun barrels are produced with rifling, shotguns have traditionally had smooth bored barrels. Except in some rare cases the projectiles fired from them cannot be matched back to the shotgun. Shotguns come in a number of different styles and actions—from auto-loading shotguns to "customized" versions.

In understanding the shotgun, it is also important to understand that shotguns are typically manufactured with what is called a choke in their barrels. A choke is a constriction in the last couple of inches in the barrel and can vary in the degree of constriction. Common choke designations are "full," "modified," and "improved cylinder."

The whole point to understanding the shotgun choke is that the choke plays an important role in the rate at which the shot pellets spread as they travel away from the shotgun. For example, a full-choke barrel will tend to shoot smaller shot patterns at a given distance than a barrel with a modified-choke.

|Fig. 9.13-A| ▲

A test firing pattern of a shotgun showing how considerably more damage is experienced with a shotgun blast opposed to a handgun.

Courtesy of Mike Himmel

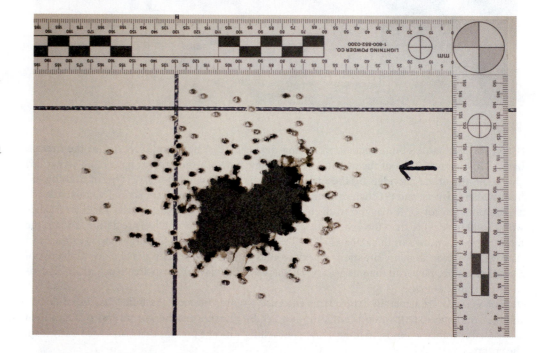

|Fig. 9.13-B| ▲

How the pellets of a shotgun blast spread out the further away the shooter is from the victim.

Courtesy of Mike Himmel.

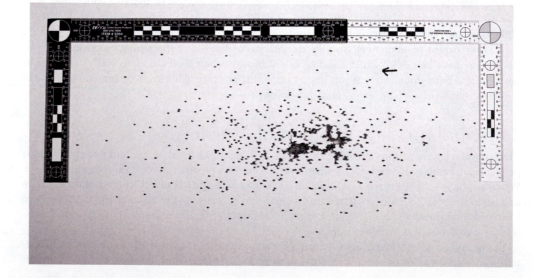

Shotshells are cartridges designed to be fired in shotguns and can contain a single large projectile—a slug—or as many as several hundred small spherical pellets called shot. Shot used in shotshells has traditionally been made of lead but because of its toxicity, other materials are being used as a substitute, with the most common alternative being steel. The size of the shot can vary as can the total weight of the shot loaded into a shotshell.[38] Shot comes in two basic varieties, small pellets commonly referred to as birdshot and larger pellets called buckshot.

All of these variables are important in determining a given shot pattern distance.

When a shotgun is fired, the shot (and wadding) travels down the barrel and exits the muzzle in a concentrated mass. As a result, a contact entrance hole will produce a large hole with significant damage to the margins of the hole. This can vary greatly depending on the material being fired into. The same thing also applies to gunshot residue deposits. Most contact entrance holes will have a significant deposit of gunshot residues like the one seen below, but this is not always the case. Some may display very little visible gunshot residue.

At ranges of around 5 to 10 feet the shot and wadding mass will produce a single large hole in a target. If the target happens to be a person, the wadding material will be blown into the wound tract with the pellets. The close-range entrance (less than 5 feet*) hole is almost square, and is a common shape for this range. You might notice a pinkish color (lead residue) to the material around the hole.[39]

At distances greater than 5 to 10 feet the shot mass starts to break up. Fliers (individual pellet holes) will start to appear around the edge of an entrance hole and the wadding may or may not enter the victim.

As the pellets get further and further away from the shotgun, the pattern will eventually become dispersed to the point that only individual pellet holes are present in a target. Firearm examiners try to reproduce the pattern by firing into witness panels at known distances. Shot patterns can be affected by the load, pellet size, wad type, and choke of the shotgun. This is why it is essential that the shotgun is recovered and the type of shotshells used is known. Hopefully some shotshells will be recovered at the scene that can later be used in firing the distance standards. Also, patterns produced by a shotgun at any given distance can vary slightly (see Figure 9.13 A and B showing test shotgun patterns and varying distances). Multiple tests patterns can be fired at known distances and compared directly to the pattern in question. Based on this comparison a minimum and maximum firing distance can be estimated.

Defense Wounds

Defense wounds are characteristic of a struggle between a victim and an assailant. Such wounds may appear on the body of the victim and may take many forms. For example, in a fatal stabbing, slashing wounds on the hands of the victim may indicate that the victim grabbed the knife during a

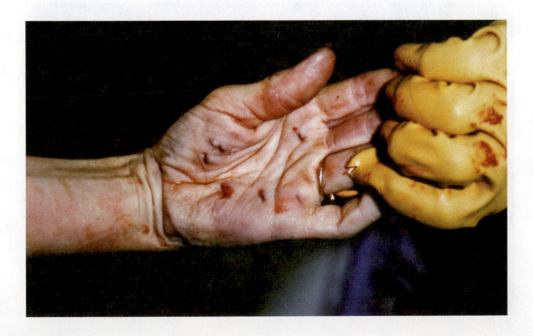

|Fig. 9.14| △

Defense wounds such these suggest that the victim was fighting her attacker at the time of her death. In this case, the victim's attacker was using a knife as a weapon.

Courtesy of Mike Himmel

struggle, only to have it pulled back by the killer. These wounds are usually deep and concentrated on the palms and the undersurface of the fingers. Other indicators of a struggle are bruises on the forearms of the victim of a beating, indicating that the victim was attempting to defend him- or herself from attack by the assailant. In addition, a victim of a shotgun killing might have shot from the shotgun blast embedded in his or her hands or forearms.

Drowning Deaths

Drowning occurs when liquid enters the breathing passages, preventing air from getting to the lungs. Drowning can take place in deep water, such as a river, swimming pool or ocean. It can also take place in water as shallow as six inches. Although drowning is sometimes used as method of homicide, it is very difficult to determine the manner of death when a victim is found in the water.

How Drowning Occurs

When a person is submerged under water, he will obviously hold his breath. Carbon dioxide increases, and oxygen decreases, until a breaking point is reached. The person involuntarily inhales, and takes in water. Some is swallowed, and the person may vomit. The involuntary gasping for air continues for several minutes. A process known as cerebral hypoxia begins until it becomes irreversible, and death occurs.

The irreversibility begins after 3 to 10 minutes in warm water. However, research show that children and infants who are in cold water can be resuscitated after as long as 66 minutes. Whatever the temperature of the water, all humans usually lose consciousness within three minutes. Hyperventilating causes a decrease in carbon dioxide, which leads to cerebral hypoxia. Therefore, the person may lose consciousness before reaching the breaking point. A person is considered a victim of "near drowning" if, after being rescued from, he survives for 24 hours after being submerged in water, even if he dies shortly after or suffers brain damage.

Research shows that 10 to 15 percent of all drownings are considered "dry drownings." This takes place when a small amount of water enters the larynx or trachea and causes a spasm of the larynx. The larynx becomes clogged by mucous, foam, and froth, and water never even enters the lungs. The concept of dry drownings is only a hypothesis, however, and cannot be seen through an autopsy.

After death occurs the body will sink. It will not move far unless strong currents carry it. As the body decomposes, gas forms causing it to rise to the surface, where it is usually found. In very cold water, decomposition is delayed, and the body may stay submerged for months.

|Fig. 9.15|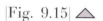

The victim of a drowning following an automobile accident where the body was not discovered for a number of days.

Courtesy of Mike Himmel

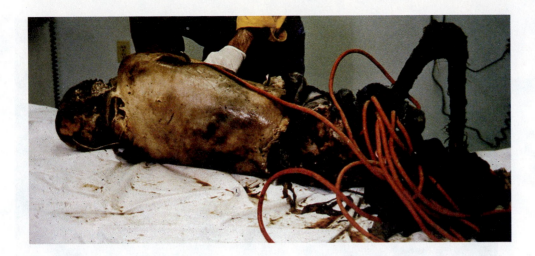

|Fig. 9.16| △

This person was murdered and her body was dumped in a river where it was recovered weeks later.

Courtesy of Mike Himmel

Determining a Drowning

The diagnosis of drowning is based more on the circumstances of the death than on tests. A complete autopsy is done, and if the person is found in water and no other causes of death are discovered, the examiner presumes the victim has drowned.

Chemical tests are nonspecific and unreliable. A test that traditionally was used is the *Gettler Chloride Test*, where the amounts of chloride on each side of the heart were compared to determine if the person drowned in fresh or salt water. Another test uses the gravity of blood on the right and left atrias to determine if the person drowned. The reliability of both tests is highly questionable.

Problems Diagnosing a Drowning

Aside from the unreliability of tests, it is hard to diagnose a drowning based on the circumstances of the death alone. People sometimes die of other causes, such as a drug overdose, heart attack, or epileptic seizure, then fall into water. Also, people can dispose of already dead bodies in water, making it difficult to know how the person actually died. Occasionally, there are also suicides by drowning as well.

Best Practices: Keys to a Successful Homicide Unit

☑ No more than five cases per year as a primary for each detective

☑ Minimum of two two-person units responding initially to the crime scene

☑ Case review by all involved personnel within the first 24 to 72 hours

☑ Computerized case management system with relational capacity

☑ Standardized and computerized car-stop and neighborhood-canvass forms

☑ Compstat-style format

☑ Effective working relationships with medical examiners and prosecutors

☑ No rotation policy for homicide detectives

☑ Accessibility to work overtime when needed

☑ Cold case squads

☑ Investigative tools, such as polygraph, bloodstain pattern analysis, criminal investigative analysis, and statement analysis

☑ Homicide unit and other personnel work as a team

Source: Keel, T. (2008). Evaluating best practices for homicide units. *FBI Law Enforcement Bulletin* 77(2).

|Fig. 9.17| ▲

X-ray of a shooting victim showing locations of bullets in skull.

Courtesy of Mike Himmel

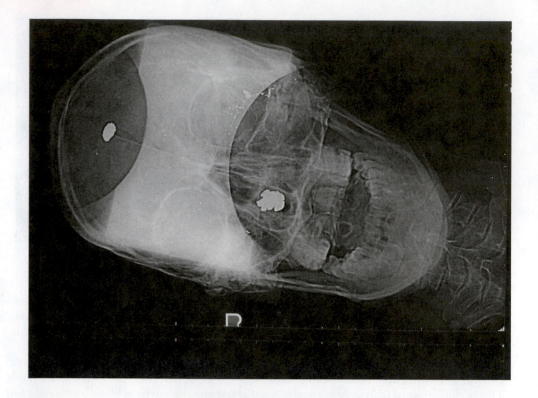

|Fig. 9.18| ▲

One of two bullets recovered from the skull of a shooting victim.

Mike Himmel / Missouri State Highway Patrol Crime Laboratory

Symptoms such as hemorrhages, pulmonary edema, "washerwoman" appearance of the hands and feet, and goose flesh may indicate a drowning. However, heart attacks, drug overdoses, and other causes of death can also cause the same symptoms. Wounds that do not bleed also do not help distinguish the manner of death because they could have been inflicted post- or antemortem.

A good indicator that the person was alive while submerged is the presence of vegetation and stones from the bottom of the water in the hands of the victim. So difficult is it to determine the cause of death, an innocent person could be prosecuted for murder for an accidental drowning or a suicide.

Pitfalls in Homicide Investigations

A recurring theme throughout this book is that the loss of crucial evidence in any criminal case can result in either the guilty party going unpunished or innocent parties being wrongfully incarcerated. This premise certainly applies to wrongful death investigations. In addition, carelessness in the processing of the crime scene can result in undue anguish to families. A study conducted by pathologist Alan Moritz concluded that there are several pitfalls that have been most commonly identified by veteran death investigators in the United States:[40]

System Errors

- Assumption that the case is not provable
- Inadequate staffing of the investigative unit
- Lack of awareness about the objective of the investigation
- Insufficient training
- Alteration of the scene before the investigator's arrival
- Inadequate photographic documentation at the scene
- Inadequate sketches
- Inadequate attention to detail
- Poor documentation
- Failure to follow up leads on a timely basis
- Overlooking evidence

Body Mistakes

- Failure to record body information thoroughly at the scene
- Assumption of identification based on circumstantial evidence
- Mishandling and mislabeling of bodies
- Failure to recognize, record, and safeguard personal property
- Failure to notify next of kin in a timely, humane manner
- Trace evidence
- Follow-up errors
- Failure to report critical facts that determine what examinations need to be performed
- Failure to complete a timely and accurate death investigation report
- Failure to develop the victim's family and social history
- Failure to prepare for courtroom testimony

Personal Pitfalls

- Fallacy that length of service ensures competence
- Jumping to conclusions
- Failure to verify information received from other sources
- Talking too much and too soon to the wrong people
- Cutting corners

Recognizing these (and other) pitfalls will, it is hoped, alert investigators to the possibility that the investigation may be in jeopardy. As soon as problems are identified, the investigator can plan to avoid these pitfalls and discover solutions to problems rather than create more complications.

Serial, Mass, Sensational, and Spree Murders

As mentioned in the beginning of this chapter, serial, mass, and sensational homicide add to the complexity of murder investigations. Such crimes generally have a psychodynamic component that can be very difficult to detect and understand. Because of this component, it is usually a logical decision to incorporate the expertise of psychology professionals in the investigation. For simplicity, let's now define the terms *serial*, *mass*, and *sensational murder*.[41]

|Fig. 9.19| ▲

A shotgun used in a homicide is being tagged as evidence. All firearms associated with crimes must be carefully documented.

Courtesy of Mike Himmel

Serial murder is the murder of separate victims with time breaks as short as two days to as much as weeks or even months between victims. Examples of serial murderers are the Hillside Strangler in California and Ted Bundy, who traveled across the United States leaving a trail of victims. In 1991, serial killer-cannibal Jeffrey Dahmer was arrested in connection with 17 murders in Milwaukee. A search of his apartment revealed 15 dismembered bodies, including a head found in the refrigerator, a heart discovered in the freezer, and a vat of acid for disposing of leftover body parts.

Mass murder consists of four or more murders in a single incident within a short span of time. A recent example of a mass murder is the March 29, 2009, Carthage nursing home incident. In this case, a gunman opened fire at the Pinelake Health and Rehab Nursing Home in Carthage, North Carolina, killing eight people, including one employee of the facility, a nurse, before being shot and apprehended by a responding police officer.[42] The shooter was Robert Stewart, who was charged with eight counts of first-degree murder on the day of the shooting. Stewart's estranged wife was a nurse at the nursing home.

Sensational murder is murder that arouses intense public interest. For example, on August 1, 1966, in Austin, Texas, Charles Witman killed his wife and mother. He then went to the University of Texas tower and, with a rifle, shot and killed 14 people. *Lust murders* (also a subclass of serial murder) also commonly attract public interest because of the instances of torture and violence that are typically associated with this type of crime. These types of crimes often involve some type of psychotic motivation, as in the Tylenol poisonings in Chicago, the Atlanta child killings, the California Night Stalker case, and the Son of Sam case in New York.

Spree murder is killing in a rampage fashion. It is defined as that which is committed when someone embarks on a murderous assault on his or her victims (two or more) in a short time in multiple locations. The U.S. Bureau of Justice Statistics defines a spree killing as "killings at two or more locations with almost no time break between murders."[43] According to the FBI, the general definition of spree murder is two or more murders committed by an offender or offenders, without a cooling-off period; the lack of a cooling-off period marks the difference between a spree murder and a serial murder. The category has, however, been found to be of no real value to law enforcement because of definitional problems relating to the concept of a "cooling-off period."[44]

An example of a spree murder is the Chardon High School shooting on February 27, 2012, which was the deadliest school shooting since 2005. The shooting took place at about 7:30 A.M. in the school cafeteria when students were eating breakfast. Surveillance video of the incident showed a male student, 17-year-old Thomas "TJ" Lane, shooting four male students in the cafeteria using a .22 caliber handgun. While escaping, he shot a female student and was then chased out of the school by the school's football coach. The shooter was arrested outside of the school near his car on a nearby road. The shooting resulted in the deaths of three students: Daniel Parmertor (16 years old), Russell King, Jr. (17 years old), and Demetrius Hewlin (16 years old). Lane told investigators that he did not know the victims and that they were chosen randomly.

National Center for the Analysis of Violent Crime

Renowned FBI agent Robert K. Ressler conceived the National Center for the Analysis of Violent Crime (NCAVC) in 1981 during a conversation with the then Quantico Director Jim McKenzie. Jim McKenzie supported the idea.

The mission of the NCAVC is to coordinate investigative and operational support functions, criminological research, and training in order to provide assistance to federal, state, local, and foreign law enforcement agencies investigating unusual or repetitive violent crimes (serial crimes). The NCAVC also provides investigative support through expertise and consultation in nonviolent matters such as national security, corruption, and white-collar crime investigations. Former President Ronald Reagan gave it the primary mission of "identifying and tracking repeat killers."

The NCAVC uses the latest advances in computer and investigative strategies to combat serial and violent crime. **Violent Criminal Apprehension Program** (ViCAP), PROFILER (a robot, rule-based **expert system** programmed to profile serial criminals), and Criminal Investigative Analysis Program (CIAP) are other programs designed to investigate serial crime.

ViCAP specifically works by identifying and linking the signature aspects in violent serial crimes. The signature of a crime is the intrinsic part of the crime that the criminal must include in order for him or her to be satisfied and thus is present in every crime committed by the same person (although the signature does evolve over time).[45]

Today, every division in the FBI is mandated to have an NCAVC coordinator also known as a "profiling coordinator." The NCAVC or profiling coordinator acts as a liaison to the local law enforcement agencies. Typical cases for which NCAVC services are requested include child abduction or mysterious disappearance of children, serial murders, single homicides, serial rapes, extortions, threats, kidnappings, product tampering, arsons and bombings, weapons of mass destruction, public corruption, and domestic and international terrorism. Research and training programs support the operational services of the NCAVC. Requests for NCAVC services are typically facilitated through NCAVC coordinators assigned to each FBI field office.

The NCAVC is further organized into three components: Behavioral Analysis Unit (BAU), East and West Regions; Child Abduction Serial Murder Investigative Resources Center (CASMIRC); and ViCAP.[46]

Homicide Investigation Tracking System

Another example of a successful information sharing system is the Washington State Homicide Investigation Tracking System (HITS). The HITS system developed out of a research project funded by the National Institute of Justice (NIJ). Initially, it was designed to record information on homicides in Washington State between 1981 and 1986. As part of the project, HITS operators contacted each of the state's 273 police and sheriff's departments, as well as each of the 39 county medical examiner or coroner's offices, county prosecuting attorney's offices, the Department of Vital Statistics, and the Uniform Crime Report (UCR) Unit of the Washington Association of Sheriffs and Police Chiefs, to determine the number of murders in the state during this period.[47]

Working with law enforcement agencies in the state, researchers eventually entered more than 1,300 murder files into the HITS system. All known cases were identified by name, case number, and the jurisdiction responsible for the investigation.

The HITS, housed in the Criminal Justice Division of the Attorney General's Office, was originally funded as part of the Community Protection Act of 1990. The Community Protection Act funding for the HITS unit came on the heels of several high-profile cases, including the following serial killers:

- Ted Bundy
- Gary Ridgway, aka the "Green River killer"
- Wesley Allen Dodd
- Child molester and mutilator Earl Shriner

The Dodd case, in particular, demonstrated the need for statewide information sharing on violent offenders. Before killing three young boys in Clark County, Dodd had been implicated in child luring and molestation in the Tri-Cities and King County areas.

By the time Dodd moved to Clark County, however, he was just another transient offender able to evade law enforcement's statewide view of his propensity for harming young children. He did so by simply moving to another county and another jurisdiction each time he came under the scrutiny of local law enforcement.

At the time, an offender's crossing into another jurisdiction crippled the sharing of information by law enforcement. It is interesting to note that after his conviction, Dodd outlined some of the "holes" in the state's criminal justice system in a handwritten letter to Washington Attorney General Ken Eikenberry. Dodd described himself as a sexual predator, who was basically "ignored" by law enforcement authorities as he moved from community to community.

At the time of its origination, the HITS Unit gathered data related solely to homicide. Over time, the need to capture sex-related and other crime data became apparent. The HITS Unit recognized that gathering more than just homicide data was critical to realizing the full potential of the system. As a result, the HITS Unit currently collects, codes, maintains, and, most importantly, shares data about nearly 65,000 cases.

The HITS database now collects other crimes and incidents that do not rise to the level of rape or homicide. As with rape and homicide, this number continues to grow every day. The data captured in this file typically involve other crimes that have occurred and are historically predatory in nature, such as:

- Nonrape sexual assaults (e.g., molestation, fondling, incest)
- Sex offender registration and changes of address forms
- Child luring
- Stalking
- Child pornography (Internet and non-Internet related)
- Identity theft
- Suspicious circumstances (e.g., children approached on the way to school, bloody clothing found, abandoned vehicles, missing persons)[48]

The HITS system has proven to be a beneficial system in sharing information between law enforcement agencies in the Northwest. As with ViCAP, such information sharing systems allow investigators to quickly learn what is occurring in other jurisdictions so a rapid investigative response can be made.

Autoerotic Death

An **autoerotic death** represents one of the most bizarre and complex crime scenes of all. In this type of wrongful death, a body (typically, male) is discovered in a partially suspended position, nude, or clad only in feminine attire. The actual cause of death in this type of case would probably be asphyxia, but until properly investigated, the mode of death could be diagnosed as suicide or homicide when actually it is an "accidental" death.

Vernon Geberth states that most of the literature of autoeroticism focuses on young boys and older men who gain sexual gratification through a predetermined ritualistic exercise.[49] Over the years, bodies have been discovered in many different conditions, including being completely nude, partially nude, or dressed in women's attire. Use of a ligature is also common and is designed to restrict the flow of oxygen (hypoxia) to the victim during sexual orgasm. Basically, the sensation of choking is believed to heighten the sexual stimulation of the participant. Rob Hazelwood and his associates have identified three ways that autoeroticism may result in death:[50]

1. Failure with the physiological mechanism
2. Failure in the self-rescue device
3. Failure on the part of the victim's judgment and ability to control a self-endangering fantasy scenario

When a possible autoerotic death is under investigation, the investigator should ask him- or herself the following:

- Is the victim nude or sexually exposed?
- If male, is he dressed in women's attire?
- Is there evidence of masturbation?
- Is a ligature present?

In the article "Death During Dangerous Autoerotic Practice," Hazelwood suggests several criteria that can be used by the criminal investigator to determine an autoerotic death:[51]

- Evidence of a physiological mechanism for obtaining or enhancing sexual arousal that depends on either a self-rescue mechanism or victim's judgment to discontinue its effect
- Evidence of solo sexual activity
- Evidence of sexual fantasy aids (e.g., pornography, vibrators, mirrors)
- Evidence of prior erotic practice (e.g., photographs)
- No apparent suicidal intent

As indicated, most autoerotic cases involve men, but it is important to realize that women are sometimes involved. For example, what might appear to be a sexual slaying with bondage and suffocation of the victim may actually be an **accidental death** of a woman who was practicing autoeroticism. One such case involved a 35-year-old woman who was discovered dead by her nine-year-old daughter. The woman was nude and lying on a small-shelved area in the rear of her bedroom closet. She was on her stomach, and an electric vibrator with a hard rubber massaging head was between her thighs and in contact with her vulva. The vibrator was still operating when she was discovered. Attached to the nipple of her right breast was a clothespin, which was compressing the nipple. Around the victim's neck was a nylon stocking that was positioned in loop fashion and fastened to a shelf bracket above the victim's head.

The lower portion of her body was supported by the shelf, and her upper body rested on her arms, which were extended downward in a "push-up" fashion. The victim placed clothespins on her nipples to cause discomfort and used the ligature around her neck to reduce the oxygen flow. She obviously intended to support her upper-body weight with her arms, but she lost consciousness, and the weight of her body, hanging from the nylon stocking, caused her to strangle. Investigators should consider any hanging or suffocation crime scene as a possible autoerotic death, especially if the clues described are present. In addition, the investigator may face problems convincing family members that the victim died accidentally (as a result of autoeroticism) rather than as a result of suicide or murder. Therefore, a sympathetic approach when dealing with family members is highly recommended.

Suicide

In March 2012, a Florida man who had been fired from the Episcopal School of Jacksonville in Florida returned to the school on Tuesday March 6 carrying a guitar case containing a firearm. He then shot and killed Dale Regan, the school's headmistress, and then shot and killed himself. This case illustrates that homicides and suicides may occur together. In such cases, it may be important for investigators to learn the motivation of the shooter/victim to be able to better predict future incidents by persons with similar motivations.

Suicide can be defined as the deliberate taking of one's own life. It has been said that as soon as an apparent suicide has been discovered, the responding officer should question his or her first impression at the scene. Statistics showing the instance of suicide is alarming. For example, in 2009, the American Foundation for Suicide Prevention showed that 33,000 people in the United States die by suicide every year. Statistics also show:

- A person dies by suicide about every 16 minutes in the United States.
- 90 percent of all people who die by suicide have a diagnosable psychiatric disorder at the time of their death. (More than 60 percent of all people who die by suicide suffer from major depression. If one includes alcoholics who are depressed, this figure rises to more than 75 percent.)
- 83 percent of gun-related deaths are the result of a suicide, often by someone other than the gun owner.
- Firearms are used in more suicides than homicides.[52]

Homicide and suicide appear to have many similarities, and the two are often difficult to distinguish. For example, if the case is actually a suicide but appears to be a murder, the responding officer may waste valuable time processing the scene as though it were a homicide. Conversely, if the scene is processed as a suicide when it is actually a homicide, valuable evidence will be damaged or lost.

Reasons for Concern about Suicides

- ☑ The cause of death is an index to society's health.
- ☑ Suicides are the largest group of potentially preventable deaths.
- ☑ Insurance companies are usually liable for double indemnity in accidental deaths.

Certain questions should present themselves to the officer at a wrongful death crime scene. For example, did there appear to be a struggle? Are defense wounds present on the victim? This situation will call on the investigator's powers of observation and common sense.

Evidence of Suicide

Of primary importance to the investigator is to secure the crime scene to protect evidence of the crime. At least until a complete search of the area has been conducted, individuals should not be allowed to move about the crime scene. This includes police officers and family members of the deceased. From an evidentiary standpoint, most wrongful death crime scenes will produce an abundance of physical evidence. The scene should therefore not be disturbed until the search is complete. All objects left at the scene should be left in their original condition. Such objects include shell casings, weapons, notes, and other items.

The Suicide Note

A suicide note or death note is a message left by someone who later attempts or commits suicide. It is estimated that 12 to 20 percent of suicides are accompanied by a note.[53] Although the suicide note has traditionally been the manner in which the victim expresses his or her feelings about his or her death, this should not always be taken as absolute proof of a suicide. The suicide note should be viewed with some suspicion, and elements of it must be scrutinized. For example, if handwritten, an attempt should be made to compare the handwriting on the note with the deceased to see if it is authentic. Investigators should also try to locate the supply of paper from which the note was taken. After it has been located, impressions might be identified on the pad to verify that the note was prepared at a certain location. The content of the note might also indicate a motive for the suicide. It may be a confession to a crime, an appeal for understanding, or even a method of placing guilt on those left behind. Because paper is such an excellent preserver of fingerprints, the note should be handled very carefully and protected as valuable evidence. After it has been collected, it should be delivered to the crime laboratory for handwriting analysis.

Reconstructing the Death

The investigator should attempt to reconstruct the circumstances surrounding the death of a suicide victim. In doing so, the question should be asked: Could the victim logically have killed him- or herself this way? The reconstruction process uses objects found at the crime scene and attempts to make inferences that can, it is hoped, be translated into theories about the commission of the crime. In this process, assumptions should not be made unless supported by some type of evidence. One misconception, for example, is that a gunshot entry wound is always smaller than its exit wound. Another misconception is that suicides by hanging are always accomplished by the total suspension of the victim's body. Again, this assumption is incorrect.

Materials Used

Years of experience have shown that certain self-inflicted wounds happen in a somewhat predictable fashion. Therefore, certain conclusions can be drawn by studying the locations and characteristics of specific injuries. Such conclusions may support certain probabilities about the commission of the act. Persons choosing suicide generally select a method that is as painless as possible. Exceptions to this are cases in which a mentally ill person purposely inflicts immense pain on him- or herself during the suicide. When completing the act, victims will often "personalize" their actions. For example, they might push aside clothing that tends to get in the way of a knife or gun barrel, enabling the weapon to come in direct contact with the skin. In addition, female victims will typically commit the crime while being careful not to disfigure their face. Persons choosing to hang themselves will be careful to place the rope or ligature directly against their skin and not around their shirt collar.

Motives for Suicide

One's behavior can be a good indicator as to why or whether he or she chooses suicide. Indeed, if there is no apparent reason for the victim to consider suicide, homicide should be considered to be the manner of death. Impulses displayed by people who commit suicide are complex and difficult to understand. Therefore, investigators will find difficulty in totally understanding this radical course of action and should be satisfied with explanations that might, at least on the surface, appear sketchy. For example, reasons for suicide have included old age, bad health, a failing love affair, marital problems, financial problems, and fear of arrest or imprisonment. When such indicators exist, the investigator should interview friends, family, neighbors, co-workers, and anyone else who might be able to furnish answers to investigators. Other information can be verified through traditional means. For instance, if the apparent reason for suicide is financial problems, such information can be verified through a check of the victim's financial affairs.

During interviews, the investigator should look for comments made by the victim to his or her associates about suicide. For example, the victim might once have remarked to a close friend, "If that ever happened, I'd kill myself." Or the victim may have stated, "she/he would be better off without me." In all cases, however, such remarks should be verified if at all possible because a false suicide threat might be used to cover up a murder.

Cold Case Investigations

A **cold case** refers to a crime or an accident that has not yet been solved, and is not the subject of a recent criminal investigation but for which new information could possibly materialize from new witness testimony, reexamined documents, or new activities of the suspect. New forensic and technical methods developed after the case can be used on the remaining evidence to reanalyze the case.

Typically, cold cases are violent or other major felony crimes, such as homicide or rape, which, unlike unsolved minor crimes, may not be subject to a statute of limitations. In some cases, disappearances can also be considered cold cases if the victim has not been seen or heard from for some time. A recent example is the case of Natalee Holloway.

A case is considered unsolved until a suspect has been identified, arrested, and prosecuted for the crime. A case that goes to trial and does not result in a conviction can also be kept "active" pending new evidence that may present itself. In some cases, a case cannot be solved but forensic evidence determines that the crimes are serial in nature such as the BTK case in the late 1970s. Another example is the case of Lizbeth Wilson.

In 2003 John Henry Horton, 56, was arrested for the July 1974 murder of 13-year-old Lizbeth Wilson in Prairie Village, Kansas. She had been last seen running across the field of the Shawnee Mission East High School by her brother John who was racing ahead of her about 7 P.M. Her remains were found in an empty field some six months later.

Horton became a suspect when it became evident that she was last known to be alive at the school. He was the only known adult working on the school grounds that night. This was bolstered when other girls reported that he had tried to lure them into the school. Moreover, police investigators found that he took an extended break from 8:30 P.M. until nearly midnight that night. They also searched his car and found a duffel bag and a bottle of chloroform. He explained it by saying he used the chloroform to "get high."

However, the evidence was deemed circumstantial and he went free until 2002 when investigators interviewed a witness overlooked in 1974. She, then 15, had been given chloroform by Horton and while unconscious had been sexually molested by him. This led to his arrest and conviction in 2003. However, the story did not end there. The Kansas State Supreme Court in 2005 overturned the conviction on the basis that the "prior bad act" had not been placed on public record so the witness' testimony should not have been allowed. However, the court did grant leave to retry and refile the case. This time the evidence, which was purely circumstantial, as well as the testimony of two of Horton's fellow inmates, was enough for a second jury to declare him guilty.[54]

Case in Point

>>The Investigation of the "BTK" Killer

Dennis Lynn Rader (born March 9, 1945) is a serial killer who murdered at least ten people in Sedgwick County (in and around Wichita), Kansas, between 1974 and 1991. He was known as the BTK killer (or the BTK strangler), which stands for bind, torture, and kill, an apt description of his modus operandi (MO).

The BTK's Modus Operandi

Using personal jargon for his killing equipment, Rader casually described his victims as his "projects" and at one point likened the murders of his victims to killing animals by saying he "put them down."

Rader created what he called a "hit kit," a briefcase or bowling bag containing the items he would use during murders: guns, tape, rope, and handcuffs. He also packed what he called "hit clothes" that he would wear for the crimes and then dispose of.

Rader developed a pattern for his murders. He would wander the city until he found a potential victim. At that point, he would stalk the person until he knew the pattern of the person's life and when would be the best time to strike. He would also get acquainted with his potential victims if they were his coworkers, making them easier to track down and identify. Rader often would stalk multiple victims at a time, so he could continue the hunt if one victim didn't work out. At the time of the murder, Rader would break into the house, cut the phone lines, and hide until his victim came home.

Rader would often calm his victims by pretending to be a rapist who needed to work out some sexual fantasies on them. This caused many of his victims to be more cooperative and even help him, thinking that once the rape was over, he would leave them alone. Instead, Rader would kill them.

The name BTK, chosen by Rader for himself, also dictated his methods. Rader bound, tortured, and killed his victims. Rader would strangle his victims until they lost consciousness, then let them revive, then strangle them again. He would repeat the pattern over and over again, forcing them to experience near-death, becoming sexually aroused at the sight of their struggles. Finally, Rader would strangle them to death.

Rader's victims included:

- 1974: Four members of one family (Joseph Otero; his wife, Julie Otero; and two of their five children, Joseph Otero II and Josephine Otero) and another separate victim, Kathryn Bright
- 1977: Shirley Vian
- 1977: Nancy Fox
- 1985: Marine Hedge
- 1986: Vicki Wegerle
- 1991: Delores Davis

Police officials say there is no reason to believe Rader was responsible for any other murders. He collected items from the scenes of the murders he committed and reportedly had no items that were related to any other killings.

Evidence in the BTK Investigation: Letters

Rader was particularly known for sending taunting letters to police and newspapers. There were several communications from BTK during 1974 to 1979. The first was a letter that had been stashed in an engineering book in the Wichita Public Library in October 1974 that described in detail the killing of the Otero family in January of that year.

In early 1978, he sent another letter to television station KAKE in Wichita claiming responsibility for the murders of the Oteros, Shirley Vian, Nancy Fox, and another unidentified victim assumed to be Kathryn Bright. He suggested a number of possible names for himself, including the one that stuck: BTK. He demanded media attention in this second letter, and it was finally announced that Wichita did indeed have a serial killer at large.

In his 1978 letter, Rader wrote the following (written verbatim):

I find the newspaper not writing about the poem on Vain unamusing. A little paragraph would have enough. I know it not the media fault. The Police Chief he keep things quiet, and doesn't let the public know there a psycho running around lose strangling mostly women, there 7 in the ground; who will be next?

How many do I have to Kill before I get a name in the paper or some national attention. Do the cop think that all those deaths are not related? Golly -gee, yes the M.O. is different in each, but look a pattern is developing. The victims are tie up-most have been women-phone cut-bring some bondage mater sadist tendencies-no struggle, outside the death spot—no wintness except the Vain's Kids. They were very lucky; a phone call save them. I was going to tape the boys and put plastic bags over there head like I did Joseph, and Shirley. And then hang the girl. God-oh God what a beautiful sexual relief that would been. Josephine, when I hung her really turn me on; her pleading for mercy then the rope took whole, she helpless; staring at me with wide terror fill eyes the rope getting tighter-tighter. You don't understand these things because your not under the influence of factor x. The same thing that made Son of Sam, Jack the Ripper, Havery Glatman, Boston Strangler, Dr. H.H. Holmes Panty Hose Strangler OF Florida, Hillside Strangler, Ted of the West Coast and many more infamous character kill. Which seems senseless, but we cannot help it. There is no help, no cure, except death or being caught

(continued)

Case in Point (continued)

and put away. It a terrible nightmare but, you see I don't lose any sleep over it. After a thing like Fox I come home and go about life like anyone else. And I will be like that until the urge hit me again. It not continuous and I don't have a lot of time. It take time to set a kill, one mistake and it all over. Since I about blew it on the phone—handwriting is out—letter guide is to long and typewriter can be traced too. My short poem of death and maybe a drawing; later on real picture and maybe a tape of the sound will come your way. How will you know me. Before a murder or murders you will receive a copy of the initials B.T.K., you keep that copy the original will show up some day on guess who?

May you not be the unluck one!

P.S.

How about some name for me, its time: 7 down and many more to go. I like the following How about you?

'THE B.T.K. STRANGLER', 'WICHITA STRANGLER', 'POETIC STRANGLER', 'THE BOND AGE STRANGLER' OR PSYCHO' THE WICHITA HANGMAN THE WICHITA EXECUTIONER, 'THE GAROTE PHATHOM', 'THE ASPHIXIATER'.

B.T.K

A poem was enclosed titled, "Oh Death to Nancy." In 1979, he sent two identical packages, one to an intended victim who was not at home when he broke into her house and the other to KAKE. These featured another poem, "Oh Anna Why Didn't You Appear," a drawing of what he had intended to do to his victim, as well as some small items he had pilfered from Anna's home. Apparently, Rader had waited for several hours inside the home of Anna Williams on the 600 block of South Pinecrest. Not realizing that she had gone to her sister's house for the evening, he eventually got tired of the long wait and left.

All of Rader's communications were poorly written, with many misspellings and incorrect grammar usage. It was theorized at times that the writing style was a ruse to conceal his intelligence, but it turns out Rader really does write that way in his everyday life even though he earned a college degree in 1979.

In 1988, after the murders of three members of the Fager family in Wichita, a letter was received from someone claiming to be the BTK killer, in which he denied being the perpetrator of this crime. He did credit the killer with having done admirable work. It was not proven until 2005 that this letter was in fact written by the genuine BTK killer, Rader, although he is not considered by police to have committed this crime.

In March 2004, he began a series of 11 communications from BTK that led directly to his arrest in February 2005. The Wichita Eagle newspaper received a letter from someone using the return address Bill Thomas Killman. The writer claimed that he murdered Vicki Wegerle on September 16, 1986, and enclosed photographs of the crime scene and a photocopy of her driver's license, which had been stolen at the time of the crime.

In May 2004, a word puzzle was received by KAKE. In June, a package was found taped to a stop sign in Wichita containing graphic descriptions of the Otero murders. In July, a package was dropped into the return slot at the downtown public library containing more bizarre material, including the claim that he, BTK, was responsible for the death of 19-year-old Jake Allen in Argonia, Kansas, earlier that same month. This claim was found to be false, and the death remains ruled as a suicide.

In October 2004, a manila envelope was dropped into a UPS box in Wichita containing a series of cards with images of terror and bondage of children pasted on them. Also included was a poem threatening the life of lead investigator Lt. Ken Landwehr and a false autobiography giving many details about his life. These details were later released to the public as though possibly factual, but the police were mostly trying to encourage the killer to continue to communicate until making a major mistake.

In December 2004, Wichita police received another package from the BTK killer. This time the package was found in Wichita's Murdock Park. It contained the driver's license of Nancy Fox, which was noted as stolen at the scene of the crime, as well as a doll that was symbolically bound at the hands and feet with a plastic bag tied over its head.

In January 2005, Rader attempted to leave a cereal box in the bed of a pickup truck at a Home Depot in Wichita, but the box was at first discarded by the owner. It was later retrieved from the trash after Rader himself asked what had become of it in a later message.

A surveillance tape of the parking lot from that date revealed a distant figure driving a black Jeep Cherokee leaving the box in the pickup. In February, there were postcards to KAKE and another cereal box left at a rural location that contained another bound doll symbolizing the murder of 11-year-old Josephine Otero. Rader asked the police whether, if he put his writings onto a floppy disk, the disk could be traced or not. He received his answer in a newspaper ad posted in the Wichita Eagle saying it would be OK.

On February 16, 2005, he sent a floppy disk to Fox TV station KSAS in Wichita. Forensic analysis quickly determined that the disk had been used by the Christ Lutheran Church in Wichita, plus the name Dennis. An Internet search determined that Rader was president of this church. He was arrested on February 25.

After his arrest, Rader stated he chose to resurface in 2004 for various reasons, including the release of the book Nightmare in Wichita—the Hunt for the BTK Strangler by Robert Beattie. He wanted the opportunity to tell his story his own way. He also said he was bored because his children had grown up and he had more time on his hands.

(continued)

Case in Point (continued)

Rader's Arrest

The BTK killer's last known communication with the media and police was a padded envelope that arrived at FOX affiliate KSAS-TV in Wichita on February 16, 2005.

- A purple 1.44-MB Memorex floppy disk was enclosed in the package.
- Also enclosed were a letter and a photocopy of the cover of a 1989 novel about a serial killer (*Rules of Prey*).
- A gold-colored necklace with a large medallion was also in the envelope.
- Police found meta-data embedded in a Microsoft Word document on the disk that pointed to Christ Lutheran Church, and the document was marked as last modified by "Dennis."
- A search of the church Web site turned up Dennis Rader as president of the congregation council. Police immediately began surveillance of Rader.

Sometime during this period, police obtained a warrant for the medical records of Rader's daughter, Kerri. A tissue sample seized at this time was tested for DNA and provided a familial match with semen at an earlier BTK crime scene. This, along with other evidence gathered before and during the surveillance, gave police probable cause for an arrest.

Rader was stopped while driving near his home and taken into custody shortly after noon on February 25, 2005. Immediately after, law enforcement officials—including a Wichita Police bomb unit truck, two SWAT trucks, and FBI and ATF agents—converged on Rader's residence near the intersection of I-135 and 61st Street North.

Once in custody, Rader talked to investigators for hours, confessing right away. Twelve DVDs were filled with Rader's confession.

Observations

The BTK investigation illustrates the complexity of criminal investigation, evidence, and prosecution. Such cases also show how difficult it is for those who sit as jurors to decipher the truth in a criminal trial.

Case in Point

>>The Investigation of the Green River Killer

For 20 years, the bodies of a number of murdered young prostitutes and runaway girls periodically washed up in the Green River, approximately 45 miles from Seattle. By 2004, the total number of victims came to 48, and in addition to the Green River, their remains had shown up in ravines, airports, and freeways, with two of them discovered in Oregon. The victims were strangled. In time, the killer became known as the Green River Killer.

Over the years, the investigation into the murders produced a considerable amount of evidence but nothing sufficiently conclusive to justify the arrest of a suspect. Finally, in early 2004, 54-year-old Gary Leon Ridgway, a slight man with thick glasses, married three times and the father of one child, was charged with all 48 murders. Ridgway was a longtime painter at Kenworth Truck Co.

Ridgway had been a suspect since 1984, when one of the victim's boyfriends reported that he last saw her getting into a pickup identified as Ridgway's. But Ridgway said he did not know the victim, Marie Malvar. A police investigator in Des Moines cleared him as a suspect. Later that year, Ridgway contacted the King County Green River Task Force ostensibly to offer information about the case—and passed a polygraph test.

Investigators continued to suspect him, however, and in 1987 searched his house and took a saliva sample. It was 13 years before technology caught up to their suspicions and they could link that saliva sample to DNA taken from the bodies of three of the earliest victims. Ridgway was arrested on November 30, 2001, and later pleaded guilty to seven killings. But facing DNA evidence and the prospect of the death penalty, he began cooperating and trading information for his life.

He confessed to 42 of the 48 listed killings, as well as six not listed. Furthermore, he led investigators to four sets of previously undiscovered human remains. It turned out that the killings had continued long after investigators thought they had stopped. The last victim on the list disappeared in 1984, but one of the cases Ridgway plead to involved a woman killed in 1990 and another in 1998. Ridgway's pleas to the 48 murders gave him the dubious distinction of having more convictions than any other serial killer in the nation's history.

For example, John Wayne Gacy, who preyed on men and boys in Chicago in the 1970s, was convicted of 33 murders; Ted Bundy, whose killing spree began in Washington State, confessed to killing more than 30 women and girls but was convicted of killing only three before he was executed in Florida.

(continued)

Case in Point (continued)

Ridgway's Motives and Method of Operation

Ridgway stated that his motive for the killings was "to kill as many women as I thought were prostitutes as I possibly could." Ridgway continued:

> I picked prostitutes as victims because I hate prostitutes and did not want to pay them for sex. I also picked prostitutes because they were easy to pick up without being noticed. I also knew they would not be reported missing right away, and might never be reported missing. I picked prostitutes because I thought I could kill as many of them as I could without getting caught.
>
> In most cases, when I murdered these women, I did not know their names. Most of them I liked....I killed them the first time I met them and do not have a good memory of their faces. I killed so many women that I have a hard time keeping them straight....I killed most of them in my house on Military Road, and I killed a lot of them in my truck, not far from where I picked them up....I killed some of them outside....I remember leaving each woman's body in the place where she was found.

Another part of my plan was where I put the bodies of these women. Most of the time I took the women's jewelry and their clothes to get rid of any evidence and make them harder to identify. I placed most of the bodies in groups, which I call clusters. I did this because I wanted to keep track of all the women I killed. I liked to drive by the clusters around the country and think about the women I placed there.

Here are Ridgway's accounts of only a few of his murders:

- Wendy Lee Coffield: "I picked her up, planning to kill her. After killing her, I placed her body in the Green River."
- Debra Bonner: "I picked her up planning to kill her. After strangling her to death, I placed her body in the Green River."
- "I strangled Debra Estes to death. I picked her up, planning to kill her. After killing her, I buried her body near the Fox Run Apartments in Federal Way."
- "I strangled Carol Christensen to death. I picked her up, planning to kill her. After killing her, I placed her body in a wooded area in Maple Valley."
- "I strangled Denise D. Bush to death. I picked her up planning to kill her. After killing her, I left her body just off a dirt road in the neighborhood of Riverton. I later transported some of her remains to a place just off the Bull Mountain Road, near Tigard, Oregon. I left the remains there with the remains of Shirley Sherrill. I did this to throw off police investigators so I could continue killing prostitutes."

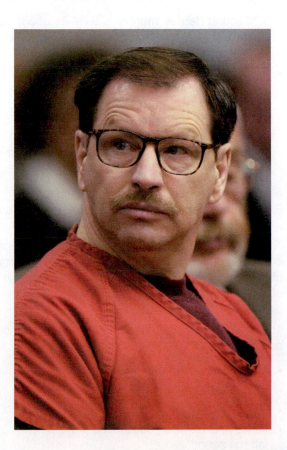

|Fig. 9.20| △

Gary Ridgway, seated to the left side of his attorney, Mark Prothero, was dubbed the "Green River Killer" almost 20 years ago after the bodies of some of his 48 victims showed up in Washington State's Green River, about 45 miles from Seattle.

Elaine Thompson / AP Wide World Photos

Case in Point

>>Checklist: Suicide Shootings and Stabbings

Shootings

- Firearm suicides are common.
- Handguns are used more commonly than rifles.
- An aid such as a string or stick is commonly used.
- A weapon tightly clenched by the victim indicates suicide.
- Gunpowder residue should be located on the "gun hand" of the victim using a firearm. Location of the wound can be used in determining if shooting was self-inflicted. A forensic examination to determine the distance between the gun muzzle and the wound can often distinguish between homicide and suicide.

Stabbings

- Self-inflicted stab wounds are commonly seen in the chest area.
- When there are a large number of stab wounds in the victim, investigators should be suspicious.
- Generally, the body will be located at the point of the act, indicating no struggle with an assailant.
- The depth of a wound does not necessarily indicate the length of the weapon.
- The instrument, when located, must be well preserved in its original condition.
- Generally, there will be no "defense wounds" located on the victim of a suicide, but hesitation wounds might be mistaken for defense wounds.

Summary Checklist

In this chapter, we consider the ways information about crimes is documented by criminal investigators. In all societies, the instances of homicide and wrongful death have endured as top concerns for law enforcement officials. Considered as one of the gravest social problems, law enforcement plays an important role in investigating the facts and circumstances surrounding each such case. A properly documented case is one that is more likely to succeed in court.

See how well you are able to answer the following questions in your checklist.

1. **What are the various modes of wrongful death?**

   Modes of death can be divided into four general categories:

   - Accidental death
   - Natural death
   - Suicide
   - Murder

2. **Identify the legal characteristics of homicide.**

   Homicide is generally divided into two distinct classifications:

   - Murder is defined as the purposeful, premeditated, and unlawful taking of the life of a human being by another person. It is considered the most serious of all statutory crimes and may be divided into different degrees:
     - **First degree murder** includes premeditation and preplanning.

   - **Second degree murder** is a lesser offense but requires that the person attempted to kill the intended victim.
   - Manslaughter is the deliberate killing of another person and is typically classified into two subcategories:
     - **Voluntary manslaughter** is killing another person in an act of passion and lacks premeditation.
     - **Involuntary manslaughter** usually refers to the accidental or nonintentional death of another person due to severe negligence.

3. **Explain the steps of the preliminary investigation of a wrongful death case**.

   The first officer to respond to a suspected homicide call is generally a patrol officer arriving a short time after the call is received. The actions taken at the time of arrival may have a critical bearing on the subsequent course of the investigation.

   The first officer on the scene has several principal concerns:

   - Determine if the victim is alive or dead
   - Obtain medical help for the victim if needed
   - Apprehend the perpetrator if still on the scene
   - Make appropriate notifications if the perpetrator has left the scene
   - Safeguard the crime scene
   - Detain any witnesses

After the preliminary duties have been performed, the responding officer must protect the crime scene and establish and maintain a chain of custody.

4. **Describe the means by which the time of a person's death can be estimated**.

The time of death in a homicide case, particularly when there are no witnesses, is one of the most critical variables in its investigation.

After death occurs, human decomposition takes place in five stages:

- Stage 1: The fresh stage
- Stage 2: The putrefaction stage (bloating)
- Stage 3: The black putrefaction stage
- Stage 4: The butyric fermentation stage (mummification)
- Stage 5: The dry decay stage (skeletonization)

The speed at which decomposition occurs varies greatly, depending on a wide variety of factors, such as temperature, humidity, and the season of death.

Visual evidence of decomposition includes:

- Body color
- Changes in the eyes
- Body temperature
- Rigor mortis
- Postmortem lividity

5. **What are the characteristics of a gunshot wound?**

The type of wound inflicted by a firearm can be affected by a number of factors:

- The type of caliber weapon used
- The distance between the shooter and victim

- Whether the lethal bullet had ricocheted off another object.

In the case of a contact wound, where the muzzle of the weapon was held against the body when discharged, certain residue will be present

6. **Distinguish between serial, mass, and sensational murders**.

Serial, mass, and sensational homicide add to the complexity of murder investigations.

- Serial murder involves killing several victims in three or more separate events, with time breaks as short as two days to as much as weeks or even months between victims.
- Mass murder involves the killing of at least four victims in a single incident within a short span of time.
- Sensational murder is murder that arouses intense public interest.
- Spree murder is killing in a rampage fashion and involves killing two or more victims in a short time at multiple locations (without a cooling-off period).

7. **Explain what a cold case is**.

A cold case is a crime or accident that:

- Has not yet been solved
- Is not the subject of a recent criminal investigation
- One for which new information could possibly materialize from new witness testimony, reexamined documents, or new activities of the suspect

Cold cases are typically violent or other major felony crimes that may not be subject to a statute of limitations.

A case is considered unsolved until a suspect has been identified, arrested, and prosecuted for the crime.

Key Terms

accidental death
autoerotic death
chain of custody
cold case
contact wound
decomposition
drowning
dying declaration
expert system
first degree murder
forensic anthropology
forensic autopsy

forensic entomology
forensic pathology
gunshot residue (GSR)
homicide
Homicide Investigation Tracking System (HITS)
involuntary manslaughter
lividity
manslaughter
mass murder
murder
National Center for the Analysis of Violent Crime (NCAVC)

natural death
postmortem lividity
rigor mortis
scene-conscious
second degree murder
sensational murder
serial murder
spree murder
suicide
tattooing
Violent Criminal Apprehension (ViCAP)
voluntary manslaughter

Discussion Questions

1. List and define the four general modes of death.

2. Explain the legal categories of homicide.

3. List and discuss the duties of the responding officer in a homicide case.

4. Define "chain of custody" and explain why it is so important that it be maintained.

5. What notes should be taken at a wrongful death crime scene?

6. Discuss the importance of determining the time of death at a homicide crime scene.

7. What do the terms *rigor mortis* and *postmortem lividity* mean? How is an understanding of these terms important to the investigation of a wrongful death?

8. To what extent do wounds play a role in understanding the facts and circumstances surrounding a shooting death?

9. Explain some of the problems involved in diagnosing a death as drowning.

10. What are the distinctions among serial, mass, spree, and sensational murders?

11. Explain the problems encountered by investigators in a wrongful death that is believed to be autoerotic.

12. Discuss what evidence should be traced in the investigation of a suspected suicide.

Notes

1. FEDERAL BUREAU OF INVESTIGATION. (2008). *Crime in America, 2007. Uniform crime reports*. Washington, DC: U.S. Government Printing Office.

2. FEDERAL BUREAU OF INVESTIGATION. (2011). *Crime in the United States, 2010*. Uniform Crime Reports. U.S. Department of Justice.

3. GEBERTH, V. (1990). *Practical homicide investigation*, 2nd ed. New York: Elsevier.

4. SEE Rule 403. Available at http://federalevidence.com/rules-of-evidence.

5. STATHEROPOULOS, M. AND A. AGAPIOU, ET AL. (2007). Environmental aspects of VOCs evolved in the early stages of human decomposition. *Sci Total Environ* 385(1–3):221–227.

6. EBERHARDT, T.L. AND D. A. ELLIOT. (2008). A preliminary investigation of insect colonisation and succession on remains in New Zealand. *Forensic Science International* 176(2–3):217–223.

7. IBID.

8. SMITH, K. G. V. (1987). *A manual of forensic entomology*. Ithaca, NY: Cornell University Press, p. 464.

9. IBID.

10. IBID.

11. BUCKBERRY, J. (2000). Missing, presumed buried? Bone diagenesis and the under-representation of Anglo-Saxon children. Available at http://www.assemblage.group.shef.ac.uk/5/buckberr.html.

12. SMITH. (1987). *A manual of forensic entomology*; KULSHRESTHA, P. AND D. K. SATPATHY. (2001). Use of beetles in forensic entomology. *Forensic Science International* 120(1–2):15–17.

13. SCHMITT, A., E. CUNHA, AND J. PINHEIRO. (2006). *Forensic anthropology and medicine: Complementary sciences from recovery to cause of death*. New York: Humana Press, p. 464; HAGLUND, W. D., AND M. H. SORG. (1996). *Forensic taphonomy:* *The postmortem fate of human remains*. Boca Raton, FL: CRC Press, p.636.

14. IBID.

15. GEBERTH. (1990). *Practical homicide investigation*.

16. IBID.

17. DI MAIO, V. J. M. (1985). *Gunshot wounds: Practical aspects of firearms, ballistics, and forensic techniques*. New York: Elsevier.

18. MAHONEY, P. F., J. RYAN, A. J. BROOKS, AND C. W. SCHWAB. (2004) *Ballistic trauma—A practical guide*, 2nd ed. Springer: Leonard Cheshire.

19. IBID.

20. IBID.

21. KRUG, E. E. (ed.). (2002). *World report on violence and health*. Geneva: World Health Organization.

22. TRIMPE, M. (2011). The current status of GSR examinations. *FBI Law Enforcement Bulletin*, May.

23. Note that some small caliber bullets, such as .22s, may have the primer crimped into the rim of the bullet instead of in a center cylinder, and the hammer can strike the bullet anywhere on the rim to fire the slug. This is known as "rimfire."

24. CENTERS FOR DISEASE CONTROL AND PREVENTION. (2007). Agency for toxic substances and disease registry.*Toxicological profile for barium and barium compounds*. U.S. Department of Health and Human Services, Public Health Service; Agency for Toxic Substances and Disease Registry.

25. DAVID, R. (2000). Magnetic susceptibility of the elements and inorganic compounds.*Handbook of chemistry and physics*, 81st ed. Boca Raton, FL: CRC Press; JAMES F. CARLIN, JR. (2009). *Antimony statistics and information*. United States Geological Survey: U.S. Department of the Interior. Available

at http://minerals.usgs.gov/minerals/pubs/commodity/antimony/. Accessed on September 9, 2012.

26. BROWN, G. I. (1998).*The big bang: A history of explosives*. Sutton Publishing: UK.

27. FIREARMS ID.com. Gunshot residue test results. Available at http://www.firearmsid.com/A_distanceResults.htm. Accessed on September 9, 2012.

28. IBID.

29. BYKOWICZ, J. (2005). Convictions tied to controversial gun-residue test: Prosecutor's office counts several cases over 5 years; Defenders seek further review. *BaltimoreSun*, March 27.

30. GUZMAN, D. (2007). Judge rules out gunshot residue evidence in murder trial. *Houston News*, October 29.

31. TRIMPE. (2011). The current status of GSR examinations. *FBI Law Enforcement Bulletin* (May). Available at: http://www.fbi.gov/stats-services/publications/law-enforcement-bulletin/may_2011/The%20Current%20Status%20of%20GSR%20Examinations. Accessed on September 9, 2012.

32. IBID.

33. COHLE, S. D., PICKELMAN, J., CONNOLLY, J. T. AND BAUSERMAN, S. C. (1987). Suicide by air rifle and shotgun. *Journal of Forensic Science* 32:1113–1117.

34. DENTON, J. S., SEGOVIA, A. AND FILKINS, J. A. (2006). Practical pathology of gunshot wounds. *Arch Pathology Lab Medicine* 130(9):1283–1289.

35. TUGCU, H., YORULMAZ, C., KARSLIOGLU, Y., UNER, H.B., KOC, S., OZDEMIR, C., OZASLAN, A. AND CELASUN, B. (2006). Image analysis as an adjunct to sodium rhodizonate test in the evaluation of gunshot residues: an experimental study. *American Journal of Forensic Medical Pathology* 27:296–299.

36. DENTON, SEGOVIA, AND FILKINS. (2006). Practical pathology of gunshot wounds.

37. *Federal Bureau of Investigation web site* 6(2). (April 2004). Available at http://www.fbi.gov/about-us/lab/forensic-science-communications/fsc/april2004/research/2004_02_research02.htm

38. IBID.

39. IBID.

40. MORTIZ, A. R. (1981). Classical mistakes in forensic pathology. *American Journal of Forensic Medicine and Pathology* 2(4):299–308.

41. GEBERTH, V. (1986). Mass, serial and sensational homicides. *Law and Order*, October:20–22.

42. BBC NEWS. (2009). Man kills eight at US care home. Available at http://news.bbc.co.uk/2/hi/americas/7971065.stm.

43. CHARALAMBOUS, N. AND M. DILLMAN. (2006). No evidence of spree killer yet, police say. *Anderson Independent-Mail News*, December 17.

44. FEDERAL BUREAU OF INVESTIGATION. *Serial murder: Multi-disciplinary perspectives for investigators*. Available at http://www.fbi.gov/stats-services/publications/serial-murder. Accessed on September 9, 2012.

45. FEDERAL BUREAU OF INVESTIGATION. *National Center for the Analysis of Violent Crime*. Available at http://www.fbi.gov/hq/isd/cirg/ncavc.htm. Accessed on September 9, 2012.

46. IBID.

47. WASHINGTON STATE OFFICE OF THE ATTORNEY GENERAL. *Homicide Investigation Tracking System*. Available at http://www.atg.wa.gov/page.aspx?ID=2352

48. IBID.

49. IBID.

50. HAZELWOOD, R. R., A. W. BURGESS, AND N. GROTH. (1985). Death during dangerous autoerotic practice. *Social Science and Medicine* 15(suppl E):129–133.

51. IBID.

52. AMERICAN FOUNDATION FOR SUICIDE PREVENTION. (2009). *National statistics*. Available at http://www.afsp.org/index.cfm?fuseaction=home.viewpage&page_id=050FEA9F-B064-4092-B1135C3A70DE1FDA.

53. SHIOIRI T., A. NISHIMURA, K. AKAZAWA, ET AL. (2005). Incidence of note-leaving remains constant despite increasing suicide rates. *Psychiatry and Clinical Neurosciences* 59(2):226–228.

54. WALTON, R. (2006). Cold case homicides. *Taylor and Francis*. Boca Raton, FL:CRC Press.

CHAPTER 10

AP Photo / via FBI

This chapter will enable you to:

1. Summarize the trends and elements of robbery.

2. Differentiate between the types of robbery.

3. Identify robber types and characteristics.

4. Explain how a robbery investigation is conducted.

5. Describe the use of evidence and witnesses in robbery investigations.

Robbery

Introduction

As a police officer responded to the home of the Petit family in Cheshire, Connecticut, on the morning of July 23, 2007, two men were seen running from the scene as flames poured out of the house. The men were 26-year-old Joshua Komisarjevsky and 44-year-old Steven J. Hayes. They were both quickly apprehended.

When officers returned to the house, they found 50-year-old Dr. William A. Petit Jr., who had been severely beaten, and the bodies of his wife, Jennifer Hawke-Petit, 48, and their daughters, Hayley, 17, and Michaela, 11. The victims had been tied up in separate rooms, and that Ms. Hawke-Petit and one of the daughters were sexually assaulted before the house was set on fire.

Investigation of the incident showed that Komisarjevsky was the one who spotted Ms. Hawke-Petit and her youngest daughter at a grocery store on July 22, 2007. He followed them back to the house and returned later with Hayes. Komisarjevsky and Hayes entered the Petit house in the middle of the night, beat and restrained the father, Dr. Petit, and forced Ms. Hawke-Petit to come with them to a local bank and withdraw $15,000. She was able to alert bank employees, who called the police. The two then wreaked havoc, including the rape and strangulation of Ms. Hawke-Petit and setting the house ablaze. William Petit was the sole survivor of the home invasion. The shock the killings caused in the bucolic community was amplified by the prominence of the victims: Dr. Petit was a well-known endocrinologist and Ms. Hawke-Petit had been active in fundraising for local causes.

More than three years later, during more than two weeks of testimony, prosecutors played an audiotaped confession in which Komisarjevsky spoke matter-of-factly and laughed occasionally. He admitted beating Dr. Petit and molesting his younger daughter and taking photos of her, but insisted that it was Hayes who wanted to kill the family because he was worried about his DNA at the scene.

|Fig. 10.1| △

Steven Hayes, left, and Joshua Komisarjevsky. Both were separately convicted for killing the wife and two daughters of Dr. William Petit Jr. during a home invasion in Cheshire, Connecticut, on July 23, 2007.

On October 5, 2010, Hayes was convicted for his role in the brutal home invasion. The jury deliberated less than one full day before reaching a verdict, afterhearing weeks of gruesome testimony, and with more than 200 pieces of trial exhibits to sift through. On November 8, the jury voted to impose the death penalty on Hayes.

On October 13, 2011, a second jury convicted the other suspect, Komisarjevsky, who was a serial burglar and drug abuser and once described by a judge as a "calculated, cold-blooded predator." He was convicted of all 17 charges he faced, including capital felony killing, kidnapping, arson, and sexual assault.

On December 9, 2011, a jury voted to impose the death penalty on Komisarjevsky. On January 27, 2012, a judge in New Haven Superior Court ordered Komisarjevsky to be executed in the summer of 2012, calling the murders a crime of "unimaginable horror."

This home invasion of the Petit family illustrates the violence and horror that can be experienced by victims of robbery. This is why robbery remains one of the most violent crimes known and one which police and prosecutors consider a top priority.

Robbery Offenses

Robbery, often confused with the crime of burglary, is a personal crime and involves face-to-face contact between the victim and the offender. Weapons may be used or strong-arm robbery may occur through intimidation, especially where gangs threaten victims by their sheer numbers. Purse snatching and pick pocketing are not classified as robbery under the Uniform Crime Reporting Program but are included under the category of larceny theft.

Understanding Robbery

The primary motivation for robbery is to obtain money, although some juvenile robbers are also motivated by peer influence and the quest for "thrills." Drug and alcohol use is also common among street criminals and may influence their decisions to choose a particular criminal technique. Indeed, statistics reveal that robbers who use drugs are twice as active as those who do not.[1] Clearly, the distinct advantage of robbery over some other type of crime is that it is quick, easy, and requires little planning or preparation.

Most of what we have learned about robbery is descriptive information about trends and patterns. Statistics show that many robberies do not result in physical harm to the victim or extensive loss, but one in three does involve actual injury. These injuries range from bruises and black eyes to life-threatening gunshot or knife wounds. The statistics, as cited above, are staggering regarding the instance of robbery in the United States.

Defining Robbery

Robbery is defined as the theft or attempted theft, in a direct confrontation with the victim, by force or the threat of force or violence. The range of events commonly associated with robbery is reflected in the vernacular expressions for the crime, including such terms as *holdups*, *muggings*, and **stickups**. A child "rolled" for his lunch money and a bank teller confronted by a gun-toting gang are also both robbery victims.

Victims of burglary often claim that they were "robbed." Such incidents are not actually robbery unless the burglar encounters someone in the structure and uses force or threatens them as a means of completing the theft. For example, pocket picking and purse snatching are not really robberies unless the victim resists and is overpowered.

The Uniform Crime Reporting Program defines *robbery* as the taking or attempting to take anything of value from the care, custody, or control of a person or persons by force or threat of force or violence or by putting the victim in fear.[2]

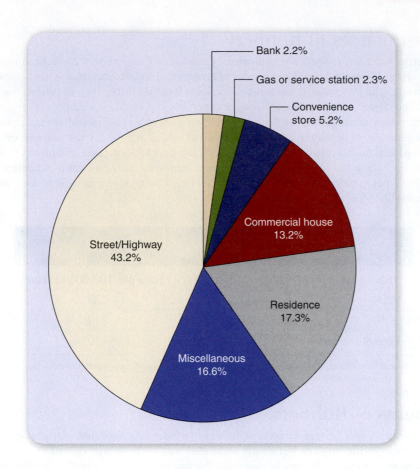

|Fig. 10.2| △

Robbery Location:
Percent Distribution.

Federal Bureau of Investigation. (2008). *Crime in America, 2007.* Uniform crime reports. Washington, DC: U.S. Government Printing Office.

Trends

Statistical data on robberies gives us a perspective about the extent of the problem. For example, according to the FBI, in 2010, there were an estimated 367,832 robberies in the United States. Statistics show a decline in the instances of robbery. For example, the number of robberies in 2010 decreased 10 percent from 2009 and 18 percent from 2006. Furthermore, an estimated $456 million in losses were attributed to robberies in 2010, with the average dollar value of property stolen per reported robbery being $1,239. The highest average dollar loss was for banks, which lost $4,410 per offense.[3]

The FBI also reported that in 2010 firearms were used in an estimated 41 percent of the robberies. In a nearly equal percentage of robberies, 42 percent were **strong-arm robberies** followed by knives and cutting instruments used in almost 8 percent. Other dangerous weapons were used in an estimated 9 percent of robberies in 2010.[4]

Bank Robberies in the
United States, 1985–2004
(Uniform Crime Reports:
1986–2005)

Consequences of Robbery

In the sense that most robbers are motivated by economic gain, robbery could be considered a property crime. However, judged by the value of property taken in robberies, it is not a particularly serious crime. The loss sustained in most robberies is less than $100. It is, of course, the violent nature of the crime that makes it a crime against persons and a serious violation of criminal law. Among the other consequences of the crime, robbery creates a sense of widespread anxiety and defensive behavior. For example, an elderly couple was robbed at gunpoint one summer evening in the parking lot of their favorite restaurant. Although less than $75 was taken and no one was physically hurt, they chose not to return to the restaurant for fear of falling victim to robbers a second time. Other types of defensive behavior include carrying a weapon and moving to the suburbs to avoid the likelihood of becoming a victim of a robbery.

Robbery Trends		
Year	Number of Offenses	Rate per 100,000 Persons
2009	408,742	133.1
2010	367,832	119.1
Percent change		−10.5

Source: Federal Bureau of Investigation. (2011). *Crime in America, 2010. Uniform crime reports.* Washington, DC: U.S. Government Printing Office.

Elements of Robbery

State laws are very specific regarding the definition of robbery. As indicated, many people confuse the term *robbery* with *burglary*, but clearly some elements of the crimes differ considerably. For example, an apartment dweller might claim that his apartment was "robbed" when in actuality it was burglarized. Accordingly, a person might claim she was the victim of robbery when, in fact, she was the victim of a larceny. The distinction between these offenses is evident in the elements of the crime.

The elements of robbery vary depending on certain attributes of the crime. These attributes may include inflicting serious physical injury on the victim or being accompanied by an accomplice during commission of the crime. Because of these differences, many states have chosen to divide robbery into first, second, and third degrees, depending on the seriousness of the act.

Types of Robbery

Attempts have been made to classify and explain the character and dynamics of robbery. In a study conducted in London, McClintock and Gibson found that robbery follows one of five patterns:[5]

1. *Robbery of persons employed in positions placing them in charge of money or goods.* Examples are robberies of banks, stores, offices, jewelry stores, or other sites where money changes hands. The instance of these types of robberies has decreased in recent years.
2. *Robbery in open areas.* This includes **muggings**, street robberies, and purse snatchings. Crimes of this nature constituted an estimated 30 percent of violent crimes in 2007.
3. *Robbery on private premises.* This represents crimes in which robbers break into homes and rob residents.
4. *Robbery after preliminary association of short duration.* These types of robberies typically occur as a consequence of a chance meeting in a nightspot or party or after a sexual encounter.
5. *Robbery after previous association of some duration between victim and offender.* These are considerably less common than stranger-to-stranger robberies, which account for an estimated 75 percent of robberies.[6]

In accordance with the preceding typologies, the following examples of common robberies should be considered. Notice the addition of crimes such as school and vehicle robberies.

|Fig. 10.3| △

A "snatch-and-grab" robbery (mugging). Such crimes often take place in isolated areas where there are few, if any, witnesses.

Martin Lee / Alamy

Commercial Robberies

The **commercial robbery** typically occurs at the end of a workweek and during the evening and very early morning hours. Typical targets of the commercial robber are stores and businesses located close to major thoroughfares, such as main streets, highways, and interstates. Such locations offer the offender a quick and easy means of escape. In addition, stores employing only one or two employees make prime targets for a bandit.

Because many robberies are committed by persons with criminal records, their methods of operation (MOs) can sometimes be established easily. After it has been identified, the MO can be compared with other robberies with similar MOs to identify a suspect. Convenience stores represent a growing target for robbers. Convenience stores are the target for an estimated 6 percent of all commercial robberies. The growing numbers of such businesses have contributed to their victimization by robbers. Many stores have a policy of keeping only a minimal amount of cash on the premises to deter would-be robbers. Others use video cameras to record business transactions and customers in the store.

BANK ROBBERY A *bank* is a specific type of financial institution but the term is widely used to refer to all financial institutions, including banks, savings and loans, and credit unions. In the United States, the term *primarily* refers to financial institutions with deposits that are federally insured and that fall under the Bank Protection Act. For the purposes of our discussion, this book will focus on individual retail bank branches at different locations. Most bank robberies are robberies of bank branches.

The history of bank robberies is rich with stories of brazen robbers with blazing guns escaping in getaway cars with thousands, if not millions, of dollars. Probably one of the nation's best known

Legal Elements of Robbery

☑ Forcibly steal property
☑ Using force or threatening the immediate use of physical force against another person

and infamous bank robberies occurred on Friday, February 28, 1997. On that day, two Los Angeles patrol officers were driving by a bank at 9:30 A.M. when one of the officers glanced into a bank window and saw a customer being shoved by someone holding what appeared to be a shotgun. The officers summoned help and one of the biggest shoot-outs in the city's history ensued. The bank was in fact being robbed and the two gunmen, clad in bulletproof body armor, exited the bank and began unloading hundreds of rounds from fully automatic AK-47 rifles.

The shoot-out was broadcast live via a news helicopter, and all of America watched in horror as the two robbers, showing little emotion, calmly walked down the street as they emptied and reloaded their weapons over and over again. In a matter of minutes, buildings, police cars, and parked vehicles were permeated with bullet holes. The shoot-out, which drew almost 300 Los Angeles police officers, lasted about 30 minutes and ultimately ended with the death of both robbers. Sixteen bystanders and police officers were wounded in the shoot-out, but miraculously, no one other than the robbers was killed.

Robbery ranks among the most serious and feared criminal offenses because it involves both threatened or actual violence and a loss of property to the victim. It is also a particularly significant crime because of the psychological trauma suffered by its victims.

Bank robberies are relatively uncommon: only about two of every 100 robberies are of a bank. Although violence is rare, employees and customers are at some risk of injury or even death. At the very least, being victimized by a bank robbery can be terrifying. Furthermore, bank robberies can invoke fear in the community at large, as most are well covered by the media. In fact, a distinctive bank robbery such as the fatal 1998 shoot-out between Los Angeles police and two bank robbers armed with assault weapons can influence public images of crime for many years.

Because of the risk of potential violence, police always respond quickly to a bank robbery in progress. The likelihood of catching a bank robber on or near the scene is higher than for other crimes. This is because most bank robberies are reported very quickly, most occur during daylight hours, many have multiple witnesses, and some produce photographic images that can be used to canvass the surrounding area for suspects. Consequently, many robbers are caught the same day. In fact, the clearance rate for bank robbery is among the highest of all crimes—nearly 60 percent.[7] While the FBI has jurisdiction over most bank robberies in the United States, local police departments typically respond first.

The most common method of bank robbery is a threat with a visible firearm, most typically a handgun. Most of the remaining robberies are perpetrated with the use of a demand note passed to the teller. In this case, the note can be a valuable piece of evidence if the robber fails to ask for its return. In addition, in the majority of bank robberies, the perpetrator acts alone in the facility, but accomplices may be waiting in an escape vehicle outside. At times, lookouts are also used to spot police cruisers.

Although arrest is a primary risk to a bank robber, most do not believe they will be caught. Indeed, most bank robbers are successful, at least initially—about 10 percent of all bank robberies

A Closer Look

Factors Contributing to Bank Robbery

Understanding the factors that contribute to bank robbery helps investigators determine which measures are effective in which investigative

responses work best. Increases in bank robberies can largely be explained by three factors:

- More bank outlets and extended hours increase opportunities for robberies.

- Banks remain the most lucrative of all robbery targets; moreover, each percent of stolen money is never recovered.

- Bank robberies are usually fast, low-risk crimes, because employees are trained to comply with a robber's demands. Furthermore, although the risk of arrest is high, much of this risk is shortterm, and the risk, as reflected by clearance rates, has declined over time.

Source: Weisel, D. (2007). *Bank Robbery: Problem oriented guides for police problem specific guide series*, No. 48. Washington, DC: United States Department of Justice; office of community oriented policing services, p. 6

fail and as such the robberies are not completed. The failures no doubt contribute to the 15 percent of bank robberies in which robbers are arrested at the scene and the one-third of bank robberies that are solved the same day.[8]

Bank robbers are predictable, as they continue to rob, often on the same day, and employing the same modus operandi in successive robberies. It is often this repetition—the use of particular signature or trademark, such as a distinctively worded note or a similar disguise—that leads to their apprehension. As a result, a single arrest may clear numerous bank robberies.[9]

When robbers are arrested, multiple witnesses, surveillance images, and physical evidence contribute to high prosecution and conviction rates. In the United States, where most bank robberies are federal offenses, 93 percent of bank robbers tried in U.S. district courts are convicted and sentenced. Federal sentencing guidelines result in a 20-year sentence; sentences can be increased by five years if a weapon is present during a robbery.[10]

The types of bank robbers vary. Ever since the air of Bonnie and Clyde in the 1930s, violence—or the potential lease reality suggested by the use of weapons in bank robbery—has shaped some crime prevention efforts. Many security strategies, such as bandit barriers and weapon detection devices, have been developed to thwart armed robberies.

These strategies focus on the risk of bank robberies committed by professional armed robbers. However, most bank robberies do not appear to be well-planned offenses committed by professional criminals; instead, increasing evidence suggests that many bank robberies are spontaneous and opportunistic crimes that are often acts of desperation.[11]

Because most bank robberies are committed by a solitary, unarmed, and undisguised offenders, they can be considered the work of amateurs rather than professionals. In comparison, it is the less common armed bank robberies that more often involve multiple offenders and the use of disguises. Distinguishing bank robberies as the work of amateurs or **professional robbers** provides important insight about the risks of robbery and provides guidance in the most logical investigative strategy. For example, targets that attract amateur robbers may discourage professional robbers, while targets that are attractive to amateurs will often hold little appeal for professionals. Moreover, although discouraging an amateur robber is much easier than thwarting a committed team of professionals, the measures that might deter an amateur may well increase the likelihood of violence by professional robbers.

For the most part, robbers can be classified as amateur or professional based on known characteristics of the robbery—the number of offenders, use of weapons and disguises, efforts to defeat security, timing of the robbery, target selection, and means of getaway.

|Fig. 10.4| △

Quad-plex images made by a surveillance camera and released by the Dewitt County, Illinois, Sheriff's Department show William Ginglen robbing the Bank of Kenney in Kenney, Illinois, on July 12, 2004. Ginglen pleaded guilty in July to seven counts of armed bank robbery on December 29, 2005.

Case in Point

>>Brazen Bank Robbers

In 1995, a pair of **holdup** men who were thought to have robbed at least 18 Midwestern banks were also playing a kind of cat-and-mouse game with the FBI. They wore FBI logos during their holdups, used agents' names when they rented their getaway cars, and wrote letters to the newspapers making fun of the FBI. The "Midwestern Bank Bandits," as they called themselves, concentrated on banks in Kansas, Iowa, Wisconsin, Nebraska, Ohio, and Kentucky. The pair adopted a clear method of operation:

- They spent no more than five minutes in a bank.
- They prohibited tellers from touching cash so the tellers couldn't rig a moneybag with a dye bomb. Instead, they leaned over the counter and grabbed the cash themselves.

- They purchased old used cars before each robbery and signed FBI office chiefs' names on the titles.
- They sometimes wore clothing bearing the logos of the FBI and the ATF.
- They sometimes slowed their pursuers by leaving behind such items as a package they said contained explosives or a grenade pin or taut string tied to the glove compartment door of their getaway car, giving the appearance of a booby trap.

Thematic Question

Research bank robberies in your area and see (1) the locations most commonly robbed, (2) the physical makeup of the suspected robbers, and (3) what techniques were used to commit the crime. To what extent have these factors assisted the police or hindered the successful apprehension of the robbers?

Bank robberies by amateurs are less successful: nearly one-third of all robberies by unarmed solitary offenders fail.[12] Takeover robberies—those involving multiple armed offenders—are less common but more lucrative: losses in takeover robberies are 10 times greater than average.[13]

One of the best tracing clues in a robbery is the vehicle used in the escape. Such clues vary from one offense to another. For example, the professional robber's getaway vehicle may be rented or stolen and may have stolen license plates. This enables the suspects to ditch the vehicle or the plates after they have left the area of the robbery. Conversely, an amateur robber often uses his or her own vehicle. The complexion of bank robbery has changed in recent years due to an increase in the number of branch banks, which tend to be located in such a way as to be highly vulnerable to robbers.

Convenience Stores

The robbery of a convenience store represents one aspect of a larger set of problems related to the crime of robbery of commercial establishments. While all robbery types share some common features, convenience store robbery warrants special attention because convenience stores have special characteristics.

Distinguishing Professional and Amateur Bank Robbers

	Professional	Amateur
Offenders	• Multiple offenders with division of labor • Shows evidence of planning • May be older • Prior bank robbery convictions • Travels further to rob banks	• Solitary offender • Drug or alcohol use likely • No prior bank crime • Lives near bank target
Violence	• Aggressive takeover, with loud verbal demands • Visible weapons, especially guns • Intimidation, physical or verbal threats	• Note passed to teller or simple verbal demand • Waits in line • No weapon
Defeat Security	• Uses a disguise • Disables or obscures surveillance cameras • Demands that dye packs be left out, alarms not be activated, or police not be called	

(continued)

Distinguishing Professional and Amateur Bank Robbers   *(continued)*

	Professional	Amateur
Robbery Success	• Hits multiple teller windows • Larger amounts stolen • Lower percentage of money recovered • More successful robberies • Fewer cases directly cleared • Longer time from offense to caseclearance	• Single teller window victimized • Lower amounts stolen • Higher percentage of money recovered • More failed robberies • Shorter time from offense to case clearance, including more same-day arrests • Direct case clearance more likely
Robbery Timing	• Targets banks when few customers are present, such as at opening time • Targets banks early in the week	• Targets banks when numerous customers are present, such as around midday • Targets banks near closing or on Friday
Target Selection	• Previous robbery • Busy road near intersection • Multidirectional traffic • Corner locations, multiple vehicle exits	• Previous robbery • Heavy pedestrian traffic or adjacent to dense multifamily residences • Parcels without barriers • Parcels with egress obscured
Getaway	• Via car	• On foot or bicycle

Source: Weisel, D. (2007). *Bank Robbery*. Community Oriented Policing Services. Washington, DC: U.S. Department of Justice, March, p. 15

For example, convenience stores are retail businesses with primary emphasis placed on providing the public a convenient location to quickly purchase from a wide array of products (predominantly food and gasoline) and services. There are over 135,000 convenience stores operating in the United States and this number continues to grow. An estimated 100 million Americans visit a convenience store on any given day; each convenience store might serve hundreds, even thousands, of customers daily. Research shows that over 80 percent of all Americans, because of their busy schedules, prefer convenience stores to supermarkets.[14]

Convenience store robberies account for approximately 6 percent of all robberies known to the police. While this makes up a relatively small percentage of total robberies, the problem is persistent and ongoing.[15] For example, over the last 30 years, there has been little change in the proportion of convenience store robberies. Nevertheless, convenience stores in particular locations can be vulnerable to repeat victimization, especially those types of realtors that have large amounts of cash, low security, and few staff and customers likely to resist.[16]

Some convenience stores are repeatedly victimized; you can buy the same offender or different offenders. Reasons for repeat victimization vary. For example, a successful robber might return to rob the same store again or might tell other robbers about the store. Alternatively, a wide range of robbers might see the store as a particularly attractive or vulnerable location. Media accounts may actually play up the vulnerability of the store by reporting successful robberies and may glamorize the crime, giving would-be offenders the notion that those that "Rob with style" do not get caught.

Interviews with convicted robbers reveal that they often select easy targets assuming that "victims [businesses] will not install preventive measures to stop them." In one study of convenience store robbery victims, more than one-half of the respondents reported subsequent changes in store policy or practice following the robbery. It was also found that the store was most vulnerable to re-victimization within the first few weeks after the first robbery.

Convenience store robberies have been classified according to the offender's method of operation. For example:

- ***Straight***: demanding money immediately upon entering a store.
- ***Customer***: demanding money sometime after entering a store and engaging in the act of making a purchase.[17]

Another perhaps less common type is **merchandise robbery**, which involves the forcible taking of goods from a store. A higher number of employee injuries are reported in merchandise robberies, as active resistance and confrontation are more prevalent in these situations.

Robberies at ATM Machines

ATM's were first introduced during the late 1960s in the United States. The number of ATMs has increased dramatically since. ATM users now annually conduct billions of financial transactions, mostly cash withdrawals. Where once one would find ATMs only on bank premises, today one finds them almost everywhere—along sidewalks and in airports, grocery stores, shopping malls, nightclubs, and casinos. There are even mobile ATMs that can be set up at disaster sites or temporary entertainment venues like fairgrounds. Bank customers have come to expect that they can access their funds virtually any time and at any place. To some extent, they have traded safety for convenience.

ATM services are highly profitable for banks, and banks aggressively market the use of ATM cards; ATMs that are off bank premises are usually more profitable for banks because they attract a higher volume of nonbank customers, who must pay service fees. Unfortunately, customers using off-premise ATMs are more vulnerable to robbery.

As yet, there are no routinely collected national figures on the incidence of U.S. ATM robberies. Estimates are derived from periodic surveys of banks conducted by banking associations. According to those surveys, there was an estimated one ATM crime (including robbery) per 3.5 million transactions.[18]

The best one can conclude is that the overall rate of ATM-related crime is somewhere between one per 1 million and one per 3.5 million transactions, suggesting that such crime is relatively rare. But the figures, without further analysis and some comparative context, do not tell us much about the risks of ATM robbery.[19]

A few studies, although they are becoming dated, have provided some data on common ATM robbery patterns. The general conclusions are as follows:

- Most robberies are committed by a lone offender—using some type of weapon—against a lone victim.
- Most occur at night, with the highest risk between midnight and 4 A.M.
- Most involve robbing people of cash after they have made a withdrawal.
- Robberies are somewhat more likely to occur at walk-up ATMs than at drive-through ones.
- About 15 percent of victims are injured.[20]

The average loss resulting from ATM robberies is between $100 and $200. High rates of all types of street robbery, including ATM robbery, are likely to coincide with crack cocaine markets, as street robbery is a quick way for addicts to get the cash they need to buy crack, and it does not require a lot of planning or skill. ATM robbery attracts a lot of media attention and public concern, most likely because the general public perceives that it can happen to almost anyone. Legislation regarding ATM customer safety has been introduced immediately after a prominent person, a legislator or someone close to a legislator, has been robbed at an ATM.[21] There are several additional and distinct ATM robbery patterns, each of which presents unique challenges in responding. As noted above, the most common pattern is for the offender to rob the ATM user immediately after the victim makes a withdrawal. Other patterns include the following:

- The offender forces the victim to go to an ATM to withdraw cash
- The offender robs the victim of his or her ATM card, forces the victim to reveal the PIN, and then uses the card
- The offender robs a victim standing at an ATM of other valuables (wallet, watch, jewelry)
- The offender follows someone who has just withdrawn cash from an ATM and robs him or her away from the ATM.[22]

There is some evidence that offenders who commit street robbery (including ATM robbery) are different from those who commit commercial robbery. We do not know the extent to which ATM robbers commit other types of street robberies, like purse snatchings and muggings.

Street Robberies

The most common type of robbery is the one committed on public streets and alleyways. Street robberies constitute a considerable portion of all robberies. For example, in 2006, 44 percent of robberies reported to U.S. police were street robberies.[23] Nevertheless, U.S. robbery rates have declined since the mid-1990s. In 1994, the robbery rate was 6.3 per 1,000 people, compared with a rate of 2.6 in 2005.[24] These recent declines in street robbery, however, do not hold across all countries. For instance, robbery rates have increased in England and Wales over the last decade, particularly from 2000 to 2002.[25] National robbery rates are informative, but it is sometimes unclear whether they fluctuate with nationwide economic changes, drug trends, or some other pattern.

Most street robberies (also called *muggings*) are committed with a weapon, typically a handgun and usually take place at night, and both the robber and victim are usually on foot. Research has provided a demographic sketch of typical street robbers. First, street robbery appears to be a young person's crime. Offenders tend to be in their late teens and early 20s.[26] In the United States, almost half of offenders arrested for robbery were under 21, and nearly two-thirds were under 25.[27] Second, the overwhelming majority of arrested street robbers are male. Finally, regarding race, more blacks than whites are arrested for street robbery in the United States. Specifically, over half of the robbery arrestees in 2007 were black (56 percent), while 42 percent of the arrestees were white.[28]

Overall, street robbery patterns appear to cluster by times, days, and locations—for instance, street robberies often occur on weekends, when entertainment districts are busier and associated businesses are open later. With that in mind, below we have summarized how street robberies cluster by times, days, and locations.

TIMES Overall, most street robberies occur at night. For some groups, however, peak robbery times vary with their routine activity patterns. For instance, most elderly people run errands early in the day. Accordingly, offenders usually rob older people (65 and above) in the morning and early afternoons.[29] By contrast, offenders are more likely to rob youths (age 17 and below) between 3 P.M. and 6 P.M.[30] This timeframe aligns with school dismissal, when students routinely go home or elsewhere. Yet offenders usually rob young adults during the evening.[31] This group is often in public later at night in pursuit of entertainment. Drunken bar patrons or migrant workers returning home after work on paydays might also be at high risk during late-night hours due to the absence of effective guardians and the remote locations of some entertainment venues.

DAYS In general, most street robberies occur on weekends. For example, according to one study conducted in Cincinnati, most street robberies occur late on Saturday evenings and early on Sunday mornings.[32] In many cities street robberies increase on weekends—a pattern linked to social functions that attract many targets in a single area.

The unarmed **street robbery** is also common in many cities. In this case, the victim is approached by two or more attackers who, through their numbers, intimidate the victim, reducing their willingness to resist. Those who are most likely to become victims of street muggers are elderly individuals and people who are drunk in public. Both categories of victims pose no immediate threat to robbers, are slow to react, and will probably not offer resistance. The unarmed robber relies on opportunity rather than a strategic plan in selecting a victim. The most likely victim is one who walks alone on a secluded street after dark.

Vehicle Robberies

On October 5, 1997, an armored car with $17 million in cash was stolen from its Loomis Wells Fargo and Company warehouse. After a five-month police search, a 28-year-old former Loomis employee, David Scott Ghantt, was arrested in Cozumel, Mexico, together with six others. At the time of Ghantt's arrest, about $14 million was still missing. The police were tipped off because someone noticed that one of the suspects had moved from a trailer park to a $650,000 home, purchased a BMW automobile, and paid for breast implants for his wife—all with cash.

One year earlier, the largest armored car heist in U.S. history occurred in Jacksonville, Florida, where an employee pulled a gun on two coworkers and stole $18.8 million in cash. The robber, Philip Noel Johnson, was arrested five months later as he was attempting to cross the Mexican border. In that theft, all but about $186,000 was recovered from a mountain home in North Carolina.

The victim of the vehicle robbery is often the driver of the vehicle, as illustrated in the example above. Such vehicles often include delivery vehicles, taxicabs, and buses, while the people involved make easy targets for the robber because they frequently work alone and in sparsely populated areas of town. A delivery vehicle, for example, is most vulnerable when it is arriving for a delivery or after a delivery has been made. Sometimes the robbers opt for the cash given the driver after delivery has been made.

Taxi drivers are vulnerable because they are required to work alone and cruise all areas of town. The most common MO for a taxi robbery is for the driver to be asked to drive to an address in a secluded part of town, where the robber makes his or her move. A preventive measure taken by some taxi companies is the placement of a protective shield between the driver and passenger seats. Robberies of buses generally occur during layoff points where there are few passengers. A new trend in vehicle robberies emerged in Miami, Florida, in 1991—the **smash-and-grab robbery**. The robbers stake out streets and exit ramps from airports, and when automobile drivers come to a stop at a streetlight, the robbers approach the car, break the window, and hold up the driver at gunpoint.

ROBBERIES OF TAXI DRIVERS In larger cities in particular, robberies of taxi drivers present a considerable problem. To understand taxi robberies it is necessary to understand the industry in which cab drivers work. The compensation that drivers receive is directly related to the number of fares they have in a given shift, the distance they travel, the amount of tips they receive, and the costs of the vehicle (and any fees paid for access to fares via radio dispatch, if this service is used). Robbery depletes driver revenue and has the potential for extreme physical violence. Therefore, drivers must continually balance the competing concerns of increasing revenue through accepting fares and of risking potential revenue loss (and potential physical harm).[33] Knowing how the taxi industry is organized in a particular locality is an important first step in developing a taxi driver robbery problem-solving strategy related to that place. In general, there are two different types of taxi services:

- "Pay for hire cabs" are cabs that pick up fares off the street or from taxi stands. (This type of service includes "Medallion" cabs such as those found in New York City or some other term related to the color of the vehicles, such as "yellow cabs.")
- "Car services" are cabs that must be booked through a central dispatching office. (This service is also known under a variety of local names, such as "mini-cabs" or "car services" such as those found in the New York metropolitan area.)[34]

While robbery is the primary motive for many attacks and resulting injuries across all occupations, this finding may be location-specific for taxi drivers. Some research has found that alcohol plays a role in driver assaults but it is not clear that these assaults are primarily a subset of robbery-related assaults nor how prevalent they are compared to robbery-motivated assaults. Some cab drivers have suggested that driver behavior, such as overcharging, taking the long way around, and aggression or rudeness, may lead to aggression by passengers.[35] It is unclear whether, or how often, this aggression escalates into a later robbery event or whether other types of verbal harassment or hate speech are related to taxi driver robbery. There is some evidence, however, that driver pursuit of fare evaders can result in robbery.[36] Policing agencies may, therefore, find it useful to look carefully at a variety of incidents involving taxi drivers in order to understand the taxi robbery problems in their area.

Understanding the factors that contribute to your problem will help the investigator frame his or her own intervention points, and select appropriate police responses.

Taxi drivers are at risk of robbery due to a combination of factors related to the nature of their job:

- They have contact with a large number of strangers or people they do not know well.
- They often work in high-crime areas.
- They usually carry cash with them in an unsecured manner and handle money as payment.
- They usually work alone.
- They often go to, or through, isolated locations.
- They often work late at night or early in the morning.[37]

These risk factors, among others, have been mentioned in a number of studies of workplace homicide and violence in general.

Home Invasions

Home invasions represent a growing problem in communities across the nation. For the purposes of illustration, imagine this scenario: After a long week at work, you are finally able to relax at home with your spouse and two teen-age daughters. You're in your living room watching TV with your spouse. Your children are in their own rooms doing…whatever. Because both of you have worked hard for many years, you are now able to live more comfortably in what you thought to be a safe community.

At about 9:30 P.M. you hear a knock on the door and your spouse gets up to answer the door. After the door is unlocked you hear a sudden outburst as two strange men burst through the door and into your living room. As the door crashes open, you see your spouse being punched and beaten to the floor. Before you have time to react you are overcome by physical force and threats of harm to you and your family. The two men are brandishing guns and are shouting obscene threats and comments simultaneously as they push you onto the couch. One of the men quickly searches the house for other occupants while the other stands guard over you.

One of the more frightening and potentially dangerous crimes that can occur to a family is a **home invasion**. As illustrated above and discussed in the opening case study of this chapter, a home invasion occurs when robbers force their way into an occupied home, apartment, or hotel room for the purpose of committing a robbery or other crimes. It is particularly frightening because it violates our private space and the one place that we think of as our sanctuary. According to the FBI, the incidence of home invasions (also called residential robberies) was about 17 percent in 2010.[38] The extent that this figure represents a growing trend is difficult to determine but some statistics show that one out of five homes in the United States will experience a break-in or some type of "home invasion." That constitutes an excess of 8,000 each day.[39] While more homes are being equipped with alarms and video surveillance, the rate of break-ins are only escalating.

Home invasion is like the residential form of an automobile carjacking and it's on the rise. Like the crime of carjacking, most police agencies do not track home invasions as a separate crime. Most police agencies and the FBI will statistically record the crime as a residential burglary or a robbery. Without the ability to track the specific crime of home invasion, little can be done to alert the public as to the frequency of occurrence in their community or devise a law enforcement plan of action to control it.

The home invasion is one of the most terrifying types of robberies because an armed intruder breaks into a home and holds residents at gun or knifepoint. Often, these crimes begin as burglaries but "convert" to robberies after the intruder discovers that there is someone home and chooses to use violence as a means of completing the theft. One common type of **residential robbery** is when someone who has a right to be in the house, such as an invited guest, commits the crime. Indeed, according to the National Institute of Justice (NIJ), 54 percent of all residential robberies are committed by acquaintances.[40]

In most home invasions the most common point of attack is through the front door or garage. Sometimes the home invader will simply kick open the door and confront everyone inside. More common is when the home invaders knock on the door first or ring the bell. The home invader hopes that the occupant will simply open the door, without question, in response to their knock. Unfortunately, many people do just that.

Home invaders will sometimes use a ruse or impersonation to get you to open the door. They have been known to pretend to be delivering a package or flowers or lie about an accident like hitting your parked car. Once the door is opened for them, the home invaders will use an explosive amount of force and threats to gain control of the home and produce fear in the victims. Once the occupants are under control, the robbers will begin to collect your valuables.

Some home robbers have been known to spend hours ransacking a residence while the homeowners are bound nearby watching in terror. Some robbers have been known to eat meals, watch TV, or even take a nap. A major fear is that the robbers might commit more violence like sexual assault or even murder. Some robbers have kidnapped and forced a victim to withdraw cash from their ATM machine or take them to their small business to rob it as well.

Robberies in Schools

According to the National Institute of Justice, an estimated 3.2 percent of noncommercial robberies occur in schools every year. This averages out to be an estimated 1 million school-related robberies annually. Accordingly, the victimization rate for youths ages 12 to 19 is about 1 percent per year. A **school robbery** fails to meet the stereotypic type of robbery in that it is not stickups or mugging but, for the most part, is an instance of petty extortion or a "shakedown" of students or teachers. Ironically, few of these robberies have resulted in property loss. The average dollar loss is typically less than $1.[41]

Characteristics of Robbery

- ☑ About one in 12 victims experiences serious injuries such as rape, knife or gunshot wounds, broken bones, or being knocked unconscious.
- ☑ Most robberies are committed by two or more people.
- ☑ About half of all completed robberies involve losses of $82 or less; 10 percent involve losses of $800 or more. Most theft losses are never recovered.
- ☑ Offenders display weapons in almost half of all robberies.
- ☑ Robbers use guns in about 40 percent of robberies.
- ☑ Offenders using weapons are more likely to threaten than actually attack their victims.
- ☑ In almost 9 of 10 robbery victimizations, the robbers are male.
- ☑ More than half of all robbery victims are attacked. Female robbery victims are more likely to be attacked than are male victims.
- ☑ Victims age 65 and older are more likely to be attacked than younger victims.

Types of Robbers

Conklin developed a well-known typology of robbers.[42] Rather than focusing on the nature of robbery incidents, Conklin organized robbers into the following types:

- *Professional robber.* The professional robber is characterized as having a long-term commitment to crime as a source of livelihood, planning and organizing crimes before committing them, and pursuing money to support a particular lifestyle. Professionals may be robbers exclusively or may be involved in other types of crime as well. The professional robber recognizes robbery as a type of crime that is quick, direct, and profitable. The "pro" might typically effect three or four "big scores" a year to support him- or herself, all well planned, and sometimes while working in groups with specifically assigned tasks for all group members.
- *Opportunistic robber.* The opportunist will steal to obtain small amounts of money when he or she identifies what seems to be a vulnerable target. Examples of opportunist targets are cab drivers, drunks, and elderly people. The opportunist is typically a younger perpetrator who does not plan the crime well (e.g., use of weapons, getaway car). Typically, he or she operates in the environment of a juvenile gang.
- *Drug addict robber.* The drug addict robber robs to support his or her drug habit. Unlike the professional, he or she has a low commitment to robbery because of its danger but a high commitment to theft because it supplies much-needed funds. Although the addict is less likely to use a weapon, he or she is more cautious than the opportunist. When desperate for funds, however, he or she will be less careful in selecting victims and carrying out the crime.
- *Intoxicated robber.* Excessive consumption of alcohol may cause some persons to enter into robbery as a criminal alternative. Alcoholic robbers plan their crimes randomly and give little consideration to victim selection, escape, or circumstances under which the crime will be committed.

Careers in Robbery

The careers of armed robbers can be seen on a progressive scale, with particular characteristics varying as more robbery offenses are committed over time. Beginning as amateurs, robbers tend to be younger and less experienced (i.e., they do not have lengthy prior records) and tend to rob

Typical MO Information for Robbery

- ☑ Type of location robbed
- ☑ Time and day of week
- ☑ Type of weapon used
- ☑ Use or threatened use of force
- ☑ Verbal statements made
- ☑ Vehicle used
- ☑ Object(s) stolen
- ☑ Number of suspects
- ☑ Use of disguises
- ☑ Other peculiarities

individuals opposed to places of business.[43] A large proportion of amateur armed robbers are not likely to go on to become regular robbery offenders. Those who do continue committing robbery offences will become more professional as their career continues. They will be older, become more likely to rob commercial establishments, and have more extensive prior criminal records. Committing more offenses as their career continues, offenders become more likely to commit more robberies, engage in better planning, and be motivated by life's needs, rather than drugs.[44] The common characteristic among all types of armed robbers (and violent property offenders in general), however, is that the offender is a stranger to the victim in the great majority of cases, in contrast to most violent crimes against persons.[45]

Motivations for Robbery

For the majority of armed robbers, the crime is primarily about supporting a particular lifestyle, particularly one fuelled by illicit drugs. For a small group of entrenched armed robbery offenders, the motivation to commit armed robbery appears to be more about earning a regular (illicit) income, a means to pay bills and support a family (i.e., more like a regular job).

DRUG AND ALCOHOL USE Matthews (2002) found that the use of drugs by armed robbers during a robbery takes two major forms. The first is that the person takes drugs or consumes alcohol and then decides to carry out a robbery. The second is that they decide to do a robbery and then take drugs or consume a quantity of alcohol to help them deal with it.[46]

Planning an armed robbery

The amount of time and effort put into planning an armed robbery varies greatly. There are two extremes: at one extreme is the robber who spends little or no time planning and so does not research the target, does not wear a disguise, and makes no plans for escape; this type of robber does not usually choose their target in a calm, deliberate manner, but rather in a state of desperation. The other extreme is the robber who spends a number of weeks planning for the robbery, thoroughly researches the target, considers in detail any security measures that may be present and, where possible, takes action to overcome them, and spends considerable time and effort organizing disguises and escape plans.[47] These two extremes reflect the amateur/opportunistic and professional types of armed robbery offenders, respectively.

Research by Erickson (1996) shows that the amount of time spent planning an armed robbery also varies by the type of target, and there is a close relationship between the amount of money available at these targets and the consideration given to robbing them.[48] Planning the escape appears to be the most critical factor for offenders. Other things that armed robbers appear to consider in their escape plans include security measures (guard/police presence), the type of escape vehicle (e.g., stolen or privately owned vehicle), and the escape route.[49]

The First Officer on the Scene

After receiving a radio call, the first officer's initial responsibility is to arrive at the scene as quickly and safely as possible—safety should be emphasized more so than swiftness. The decision to use equipment such as emergency lights and siren is left to the officer's judgment and may depend on several considerations. Factors influencing the decision to use emergency equipment include:

- Distance to be traveled to the crime scene
- Amount of traffic
- Time of day of the call
- Inability to clear traffic
- Need to halt assault of a victim

Next, the officer should summon assistance and be prepared to wait for backup before attempting to enter the robbery location. When approaching the scene, he or she should be on the lookout for fleeing subjects and persons sitting in parked cars. These might be accomplices or lookouts working with the robber. Police vehicles should be parked a reasonable distance from the robbery location. After removing the keys from the patrol car, the officer should take a shotgun and approach the location cautiously on foot.

The first officer on the scene should cover the most likely exit from the robbery location. After assessing the situation, it is his or her job to direct other responding officers to cover other escape routes. If possible, a determination should be made as to whether or not the robbery is still in progress before officers enter the building.

If the robbery is still in progress, entry into the structure should not be authorized. It is likely that robbers might exit the structure on their own, especially if they are unaware that the police are at the location. If the suspect sees the police, the officer should make every attempt to convince him or her to surrender. If it cannot be determined whether or not a crime is still in progress, officers covering the front should enter together. Under no circumstances should the first-arriving officer enter the location without assistance. Once on the scene, the officer should apprehend the suspect if possible. First aid should then be rendered if victims have been injured. Finally, witnesses should be located and questioned.

The Preliminary Investigation

When responding to calls in which the robbers have already left the scene, officers must prioritize the care of any injured parties. In addition, they must keep in mind that the robbery scene is a crime scene, where valuable evidence may be present. Therefore, possible locations of fingerprints and other evidence should be protected. Next, witnesses should be located and statements taken regarding descriptions of the suspects and their vehicles so that a **flash description** can be broadcast.

When obtaining description information from witnesses, officers should first separate them to minimize discussion about the robbery and provide officers with separate suspect description sheets. It is important during this stage of the investigation to get descriptions while the witnesses' recollection of the crime is still fresh. Officers should remember that although speed is crucial at this stage of the preliminary investigation, so is accuracy. A second broadcast is required after further questioning of the witnesses is conducted. The purpose is to correct any errors broadcast in the original transmission and to provide district officers with additional details. The correct form of broadcast is typified by the following example:

> *Robbery.* Seventh Heaven Convenience Store, 308 Granada, at 2330 hours by two suspects.
> *Suspect 1.* Male, white, 18 to 25 years of age, 6 feet 2 inches, 210 pounds, long brown hair, full beard, sunglasses, wearing black "Poison" T-shirt and faded blue jeans and white tennis shoes. Suspect in possession of proceeds from robbery: brown paper bag containing approximately $350 cash.

Suspect 2.   Female, white, 20 to 22 years of age, 5 feet 4 inches, 120 pounds, wearing red tank top and blue jean shorts, dirty white tennis shoes. Suspect has long brown hair pulled back and is armed with a small semiautomatic handgun, possibly .32 caliber.

Escape.   Both suspects were last seen driving east on Broadway in an older model light tan Ford Mustang, Texas license, with the first two digits believed to be "RW." The paint on the car is faded, and its top is rusted.

The supplemental broadcast should contain as much important information as possible, and when significant information is unavailable, its omission should be so stated. For example, in the preceding scenario, it is not mentioned whether either suspect had a coat. Stating that details are not available at the time of the broadcast will let officers know that there is a possibility that the suspects might, in fact, be wearing coats. The intent here is to eliminate unnecessary inquiries from the field regarding such items.

The Neighborhood Canvass

Typically, a robbery investigation takes weeks or even months to complete. A logical starting place, however, is a canvass of the area surrounding the location of the robbery. Specifically, investigators should consider the suspect's most likely escape route and question residents and business owners in the area. In addition, while the canvass is in progress, officers should look for evidence discarded by the suspect during his or her escape. Because many citizens are apprehensive about the presence of officers at their residence, investigators should immediately state their intended purpose is to place the citizen at ease. It is also important for the officer to stress the significance of all information, regardless of how meaningless it appears to the citizen. Specific questions include whether the citizen observed anyone meeting the description of the suspect or the getaway vehicle. Additionally, it should be determined if anyone heard anything of interest to the officer, such as a car door slamming, gunshots, or tires screeching.

A Closer Look

The "Typical" Robbery

The most common type of robbery is of the individual. And the most common place for it is on your way to and from your car. Nearly half of all robberies occur on the streets and in parking lots. Another 14 percent happen in locations like subway and train stations, indoor ATMs, and other locations. It is always important to recognize when you are entering a "fringe area," where the likelihood of being robbed increases.

There is more than a 60 percent chance that you will face a weapon when robbed. That is, however, a statistical norm across all types of robberies. The odds of facing a weapon go up significantly if you are being robbed by only one person. Strong-arm tactics tend to be the domain of the pack; the individual mugger tends to prefer weapons—and guns are the most common.

Weapons

Although all robberies are felonies, the use of a weapon tends to bring about stiffer penalties. Although all robberies are considered violent crimes, it is common for states to upgrade the class of felony if a weapon is used in the commission of a robbery. That means the person who is robbing you is risking a much greater prison sentence if he or she is caught and convicted. And this doesn't bother the robber.

The weapon of choice is a gun. It is fast and easy to get, and because most robberies happen at point-blank range, requires very little training to hit the target. All the robber has to do is point in the general direction and pull the trigger until either he or she runs out of bullets or you are on the ground screaming in pain. Guns are used in up to 40 percent of all robberies, and knives and other weapons are used in another 20 percent. Again, these numbers are a national average that incorporates every kind of robbery.

(continued)

A Closer Look... (continued)

Needless to say, guns, knives, and other weapons make up 100 percent of all *armed* robberies. And weapons are the norm for robberies of establishments.

Strong Arm

Many people do not realize that 40 percent of all robberies are committed by strong-arm tactics. That doesn't sound too bad until you realize that this means you are being mugged by a wolf pack. A varying number of individuals surround you and then either threaten or proceed to pilfer your possessions. That means 10 or so people proceed to pummel you, and often after you are on the ground, they continue to kick and stomp you.

Furthermore, most states recognize both an extreme disparity of force and the shod human foot on a downed individual as legal justification for the victim to use lethal force to protect him- or herself from immediate death or serious bodily injury—both of which can, and often do, occur during a strong-arm robbery. It doesn't matter if they don't have weapons, ten people stomping a person can kill or hospitalize him or her for months just as well as one person with a weapon.

Packs of young criminals roaming or loitering in an area are a serious danger sign, one that should be avoided at all costs. People should not walk into their midst. Doing so would be literally walking into the lions' jaws.

What makes these kinds of robberies even more difficult is how often they will be explained away as "we were just messin' witcha." And because no weapons have been displayed, it is difficult for prosecutors to prove intent in such cases. Until the robbery has actually occurred, there is no clear-cut crime even if the group is displaying or menacing with a weapon.

The **neighborhood canvass** is also critical in the event that the robber is hiding somewhere close to the robbery location. Therefore, investigators should look in parked cars, dumpsters, and alleyways for the hidden suspect. In addition, local motels or hotels in surrounding towns and car rental companies should also be checked. When speaking to residents in the area of the robbery, it is advantageous to have a sketch of what the suspect looks like. The sketch could also be circulated throughout the community along with the establishment of a "tip line" for anonymous information.

The Robber's Method of Operation

Studies have shown that many people who commit a robbery are often repeat offenders, or recidivists. Therefore, it is important to document the techniques and **method of operation (MO)** used by the suspect. An MO focuses on the behavior of the criminal during the commission of a crime. For example, the location of the robbery, such as a bank or convenience store, may identify certain groups of suspects. Other factors include the type of weapon used; the dress of the robber(s); and the amount of money, merchandise, drugs, and so on, taken.

In addition to the age, gender, height, and race of a suspect, it is important to document specific behavior during a crime. Such behavior might indicate nervousness (or calmness) or could indicate that a person was under the influence of drugs at the time.

The treatment of the victim(s) could also have a bearing on the investigation. For example, was violence used? If so, what were the injuries? Was the victim kicked, beaten, shot, or struck with the weapon? Other actions might also be significant, such as:

- Did the suspect cut the telephone wires?
- Were the victims locked up?
- Were the victims tied up or gagged?

Investigators should remember that because of a lack of abundant physical evidence, robbery scenes may suggest other types of evidence. MOs in connection with any available physical evidence may help identify the perpetrator and ultimately prove a case.

Physical Evidence

The crime scene should be processed as soon as possible after physical evidence has been identified. Evidence in robberies may take several forms, including fingerprints, **binding material**, and fired cartridges. The value of fingerprints at a robbery crime scene is immense, so it is essential to

Physical Evidence in Robberies

- ☑ Blood (if applicable)
- ☑ Fingerprints
- ☑ Notes from the robber
- ☑ Binding material
- ☑ Fired cartridge

conduct a thorough search of all surfaces in or near the scene that the robbers might have touched. These surfaces include countertops, doors and door handles, cash registers and computers, and any furniture encountered by the suspects. In particular, if the robbers handled any paper products (e.g., notes to bank tellers), such surfaces are particularly good for preserving latent prints and should be protected and processed.

Binding material, if located, may include strips of tape, such as duct or masking tape, cloth strips, wire, rope, or any material used to incapacitate the victim. In the event that rope is used as a restraining device, care should be taken not to destroy any knots. These can be used to link the suspect with any specialized technique of tying knots. Such items can be used as comparison items in the event that similar material is later found in the possession of suspects.

Shell casings or cartridges may also provide important evidence of a robbery. Such items may bear latent prints of perpetrators or identify the type of weapon used for the crime. In fact, rifling (impressions) on the sides of casings may be used in linking a specific gun with a crime.

In the case of bank robberies, some banks may use bait money to aid in capturing the robbery suspect. When used, bait money is placed in a specially designated bin in a teller's cash drawer. This cash has had its serial numbers prerecorded in the event that it is later found in a suspect's possession. In other cases, when bait money is removed from a drawer, a silent alarm will be set off, notifying local police that a robbery is in progress.

The Role of Witnesses

Because of the violent nature of the crime of robbery and the imminent threat of injury, witnesses are not likely to remember many specific details of a robbery. It is important, however, that officers attempt to gather as much information as possible from any witnesses. It is vital that witnesses be separated so that their individual perceptions of what happened won't influence other witnesses. Experience has shown that an exchange of dialogue between witnesses might unconsciously alter the way in which some witnesses "recall" an event. After the witnesses have been separated, interviews should be conducted regarding both the event and details about the robber(s).

People at the scene of a robbery will be afraid, confused, and even angry. Because of the emotionally charged environment, officers should expect to receive somewhat different interpretations of what occurred from the witnesses because no two people will perceive a situation in exactly the same way. In fact, if the stories are too similar, the investigator should question the truthfulness of the witnesses' stories. The details regarding perpetrators should be as specific as possible. Information should be sought regarding specifics, such as scars, tattoos, jewelry worn, and other particulars about the suspects. Leading questions asked by the investigator might help draw out these details. These questions include:

- What did you notice most about the robber's appearance?
- What were the most noticeable features about the robber's face?
- Was there anything unique or unusual about the robber's manner of speech?

Such questions encourage witnesses to stop and think about specific details regarding a crime.

Summary Checklist

In this chapter, we consider the ways information about crimes is documented by the criminal investigator. A properly documented case is one that is more likely to succeed in court. See how well you are able to answer the following questions in your checklist.

1. **Explain the definition of robbery**.

   Robbery, which is often confused with the crime of burglary, is a personal crime and involves face-to-face contact between the victim and the offender.

   - Robbery is defined as the theft or attempted theft, in a direct confrontation with the victim, by force or the threat of force or violence.
   - Other terms for robbery include *holdups*, *muggings*, and *stickups*.
   - The Uniform Crime Reporting Program defines robbery as the taking or attempting to take anything of value from the care, custody, or control of a person or persons by force or threat of force or violence or by putting the victim in fear.

2. **Discuss the different types of robbery**.

   McClintock and Gibson have found that robbery follows one of five patterns:

   - Robbery of persons employed in positions placing them in charge of money or goods
   - Robbery in open areas (muggings, street robberies, purse snatchings, etc.)
   - Robbery on private premises
   - Robbery after preliminary association of short duration
   - Robbery after previous association of some duration between victim and offender

   There are several common types of robberies.

   - Commercial robberies typically involve targets such as stores and businesses located close to major thoroughfares.
   - Bank robberies usually involve robberies of individual retail bank branches.
   - Convenience store robberies target retail businesses that emphasize providing the public a convenient location to quickly purchase products and services.
   - Robberies at ATMs
   - Street robberies are committed on public streets and alleyways and are the most common type of robberies
   - Vehicle robberies usually target the driver of the vehicle
   - Robberies of taxi drivers
   - Home invasions involve an armed intruder breaking into a home and holding residents at gun- or knifepoint.
   - Robberies in schools

3. **Identify the different types of robbers**.

   Conklin developed a well-known typology of robbers.

   - Professional robber—has a long-term commitment to crime as a source of livelihood, planning and organizing crimes before committing them, and pursuing money to support a particular lifestyle
   - Opportunistic robbery—steals to obtain small amounts of money when a vulnerable target is identified
   - Drug addict robbery—steals to support a drug habit, has a low commitment to robbery but a high commitment to theft
   - Alcoholic robbery—excessive alcohol consumption may cause some persons to enter into robbery as a criminal alternative

4. **What are the duties of the first officer on the scene of a robbery?**

   After receiving a radio call, the first officer's initial responsibility is to arrive at the scene as quickly and safely as possible—safety should be emphasized more so than swiftness.

   - The officer should summon assistance and be prepared to wait for backup before attempting to enter the robbery location.
   - The first officer on the scene should cover the most likely exit from the robbery location.

- If the robbery is still in progress, entry into the structure should not be authorized.
- Once on the scene, the officer should apprehend the suspect if possible.
- First aid should then be rendered if victims have been injured.
- Finally, witnesses should be located and questioned.

5. What are the various methods of operation of robbers?

Because many robbers are recidivists, it is important to document the techniques and method of operation (MO) used by the suspect.

- An MO focuses on the criminal's behavior during the commission of the crime.
- The location of the robbery may identify certain groups of suspects. Other factors include the type of weapon used; the dress of the offender(s); and the amount of money, merchandise, drugs, etc., taken.
- Specific behavior during a crime should be documented as it may indicate nervousness or calmness, or could indicate that the offender was under the influence of drugs at the time.
- Treatment of the victim(s) should also be documented—was violence used, what injuries were inflicted, etc.

Key Terms

alcoholic robber	home invasion	robbery
bank robbery	merchandise robbery	school robbery
binding material	method of operation (MO)	smash-and-grab robbery
commercial robbery	muggings	stickup
convenience store robbery	neighborhood canvass	street robbery
drug addict robber	opportunistic robber	strong-arm robbery
flash description	professional robber	vehicle robbery
holdup		

Discussion Questions

1. Define robbery and discuss the distinction between someone who has been robbed and someone who has been burglarized.
2. What are the main consequences of robbery?
3. List and discuss the elements of the crime of robbery.
4. What are the most common motivations for the commission of the crime of robbery?
5. Describe the responsibilities of the first officer responding to the scene of a robbery.
6. Discuss the importance of the flash description during the preliminary investigation phase of a robbery.
7. What is a neighborhood canvass, and how does it relate to a robbery investigation?
8. How is an understanding of the robber's MO valuable in investigating a robbery?
9. Explain the different types of physical evidence that should be sought in a robbery investigation.

Notes

1. NATIONAL INSTITUTE OF JUSTICE. (1987). *Investigators who perform well*. Washington, DC: U.S. Department of Justice.
2. FEDERAL BUREAU OF INVESTIGATION. (2011). *Crime in America, 2010.Uniform Crime Reports*. Washington, DC: U.S. Government Printing Office.
3. IBID.
4. IBID.
5. McCLINTOCKI, F. H. AND E. GIBSSON. (1961). *Robbery in London*. London: Macmillan, p. 15.
6. IBID.
7. WEISEL, D. (2007). *Bank Robbery: Problem oriented guides for police problem specific guide series*, No. 48. Washington, DC: United States Department of Justice; office of community oriented policing services, p. 3.
8. IBID., p. 10.
9. REHDER, W. AND G. DILLOW. (2003). *Where the money is: Tales from the bank robbery capital of the world*. New York: Norton publishing.
10. ADMINISTRATIVE OFFICE OF COURTS. (1991). *Federal offenders in the United States courts: 1986–1990*. Washington, DC: U.S. Administrative Office of the Courts.
11. GIL, M. AND R. MATTHEWS. (1994). Robbers on robbery: Offender perspectives. In M. Gil (ed.), *Crime at Work: Studies in Security and Crime Prevention*, Vol. 1.Liecester, UK: Perpetuity Press.
12. BORZYCKI, M. (2003). Bank robbery in Australia. *Trends and issues in crime and criminal Justice*, No. 253 Australian Institute of Criminology.
13. AREND, M. (1994). Drugs and gangs fuel robbery fames. *ABA Banking Journal* 86(4): 40–41, 44.
14. NATIONAL ASSOCIATION OF CONVENIENCE STORES. (2006). What is a convenience store? Available at http://www.nacsonline.com/MACS/Resource/IndustryResearch/what is a cstore.htm (retrieved on April 3, 2012).
15. HUNTER, R. AND C. JEFFREY. (1999). Convenience store robbery revisited: A review of prevention results. *Journal of Security Administration* 22(1–2):1–13.
16. IBID.
17. FAULKNER, K., D. LANDSITTEL, AND S. HENDRICKS. (2001). Robbery characteristics and employee injuries in convenience stores. *American Journal of Industrial Medicine* 40(6):703–709.
18. *ABA Banking Journal* (1987). How safe are ATMs?79:44–45.
19. COURTER, E. (2000). ATM trends: Networking and security. *Credit Union Management* 23(5):42–44.
20. DEITCH, G. (1994). ATM liability: Fast cash, fast crime, uncertainlaw. *Trial* 30(10):34–39.
21. WRIGHT, R. AND S. DECKER. (1997). *Armed Robbers in Action: Stickups and Street Culture*. Boston: Northeastern University Press.
22. IBID.
23. FEDERAL BUREAU OF INVESTIGATION. (2006). *Crime in the United States, 2006*. Available at http://www.fbi.gov/ucr/cius2006/index.html (retrieved January 15, 2008).
24. IBID.
25. U.S. DEPARTMENT OF JUSTICE. (2007). Statistical tables: National crime victimization survey. *Criminal victimization inthe United States, 2007*. Washington, DC: U.S. Department of Justice, Office of Justice Program.
26. IBID.
27. IBID.
28. IBID.
29. KLAUS, P. (2000). *Crimes against persons age 65 or older, 1992–1997*. No. NCJ 176352. Washington, DC: Bureau of Justice Statistics, Office of Justice Programs.
30. IBID.
31. CLARKE, R. AND D. WEISBURD. (1994). Diffusion of crime control benefits: Observations on the reverse of displacement. In R. Clarke (ed.), *Crime Prevention Studies*, Vol. 2. Monsey, NY: Criminal Justice Press.
32. ERICKSON, R. (2003). *Teenage Robbers: How and Why They Rob*. San Diego, CA: Athena Research Corp.
33. BLOCK, R., M. FELSON, AND C. BLOCK. (1984). Crime victimization rates for incumbents of 246 occupations. *Sociology and Social Research* 69(3):442–451.
34. CORNISH, D. (1994). The procedural analysis of offending and its relevance for situational crime prevention. In R.V. Clarke (ed.), *Crime Prevention Studies*, Vol. 3. Monsey, NY: Criminal Justice Press.
35. ELZINGA, A. (1996). Security of taxi drivers in the Netherlands: Fear of crime, actual victimization and recommended security measures. *Security Journal* 7(3):205–210.
36. HAINES, F. (1998).Technology and taxis: The challenge of uncoupling risk from reward. *Security Journal* 10(2): 65–78.
37. MAROSI, R. (n.d.). *One of the most dangerous jobs in New York: Gypsy cab driver*. New York: Columbia University News Service. Available at http://www.taxi-l.org/marosi.htm; KOVALESKI, S. (2003). Taking astand against discrimination: D.C. Taxi company settles suit over refusal to pick up black passenger. *The Washington Post*, October 16.
38. FEDERAL BUREAU OF INVESTIGATION. (2011). *Crime in the United States, 2010*. Uniform Crime Reports.U.S. Department of Justice.
39. HOME OWNERS INSURANCE. Available at http://www.homeownersinsurance.org/home-invasion-statistics-across-the-us/ (accessed on April 14, 2012).
40. NATIONAL INSTITUTE OF JUSTICE. (1990). *Computer crime: The new crime scene*. Washington, DC: U.S. Department of Justice.
41. NATIONAL INSTITUTE OF JUSTICE. (1983). *Robbery in the United States: An analysis of recent trends and patterns*. Washington, DC: U.S. Government Printing Office.
42. CONKLIN, J. (1972). *Robbery and the criminal justice system*. New York: J.B. Lippincott, pp. 1–80.
43. MOUZOS, J. AND M. BORZYCKI 2003. *An exploratory analysis of armed robbery in Australia. Technical and background paper series*, No. 7. Canberra: ACT. Available at http://www.aic.gov.au/publications/tbp/tbp007.html

44. GILL, M. (2001). The craft of robbers of cash-in-transit vans: Crime facilitators and the entrepreneurial approach. *International journal of the sociology of law* 29(3): 277–291; MATTHEWS R (2002). *Armed robbery: Two police responses. Grime detection and prevention paperseries*, No. 78. London: Home Office Police Research Group.

45. INDERMAUR, D. (1996). Reducing the opportunities for violence in robbery and property crime: The perspectives of offenders and victims. In Homel, R (ed.). *The politics and practice of situational crime prevention. Crime prevention studies*, Vol. 5. Monsey NY: Criminal Justice Press, pp. 133–157.

46. MATTHEWS, R. (2002). Armed robbery: Two police responses. Crime detection and prevention series paper no. 78. London: Home Office Police Research Group.

47. WRIGHT, R. AND S. DECKER. (1997). *Armed Robbers in Action: Stickups and Street Culture*. Boston: Northeastern University Press.

48. ERICKSON, R. (1996). *Armed robbers and their crimes*. Seattle, WA: Athena Research Corporation.

49. INDERMAUR. (1996). Reducing the opportunities for violence in robbery and property crime: the perspectives of offenders and victims; ERICKSON. (1996). Armed robbers and their crimes.

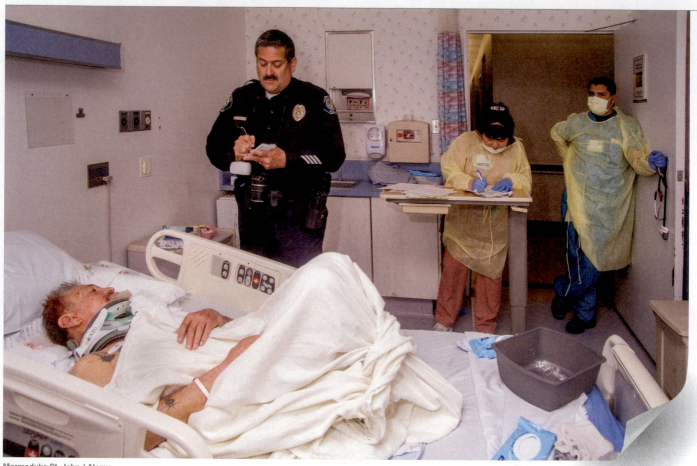

CHAPTER 11

Marmaduke St. John / Alamy

This chapter will enable you to:

1. Summarize assault trends and the types of assault.

2. Describe how an assault investigation is conducted.

3. Describe domestic violence and stalking offenses.

4. Summarize the trends and types of sexual assault offenses.

5. Describe how sexual assault investigations are conducted.

Assault and Related Offenses

Introduction

On March 7, 2012, an estimated 30 students became involved in a brawl at Carson High School, Los Angeles, during recess. The fight was apparently between black and Latino groups and, according to witnesses, was racially motivated. After police and sheriff deputies arrived and restored order, four students were transported to a nearby hospital. Two students were arrested on suspicion of assault and three others were arrested for fighting and seven more were issued citations for fighting.[1]

This story illustrates the commonality of the crime of assault. Whether the scene is a schoolyard, a bar, a sporting event, or elsewhere, the crime of assault is one of the most common crimes of violence encountered. The pattern of assault is similar to that of homicide. One might say that the difference between the two is that the victim survived. Assaults can occur many ways: For example, a rock is thrown by one teen at another, a wife breaks a bottle over her husband's head during a domestic squabble, a drug dealer beats up a customer who steals his drugs. These are all forms of assault. Many "traditional" crimes are also accompanied by assaults against victims. For example, robbery, drug dealing, sexual assault (rape), and loan sharking all frequently contain some aspect of the crime of assault.

Studies of assault cases have revealed that most victims of assault (two-thirds to three-fourths of cases) are acquainted with their attacker. In addition, it is common for such victims to choose not to file charges against their attackers. If charges are filed, many victims later choose not to follow through with prosecution, particularly if the parties are related or are close friends. Such realities can make investigation of these types of crime difficult and frustrating.

Trends

Statistical data provided by the FBI is instructive regarding the extent of assault. For example, in 2010 there were an estimated 778,901 aggravated assaults in the nation. The number represents a decline of about 4 percent from 2009 and 14 percent from 2001.[2] According to the FBI, in 2010, the estimated rate of aggravated assaults was 252.3 offenses per 100,000 inhabitants.[3]

Of the aggravated assaults in 2010, an estimated 27 percent were committed with personal weaponssuch as hands, fists, or feet. Slightly more than 20 percent (20.6) were committed with

Aggravated Assault Trend	
Year	**Number of Offenses**
2009	812,514
2010	778,901
Percent change	−4.1

Source: Federal Bureau of Investigation. (2011). *Crime in the United States—2010. Uniform Crime Reports.* Washington, DC: U.S. Government Printing Office.

|Fig. 11.1| ▲

Violent crime offense figure 2010

Federal Bureau of Investigation. (2011). *Crime in the United States—2010. Uniform Crime Reports.* U.S. Department of Justice.

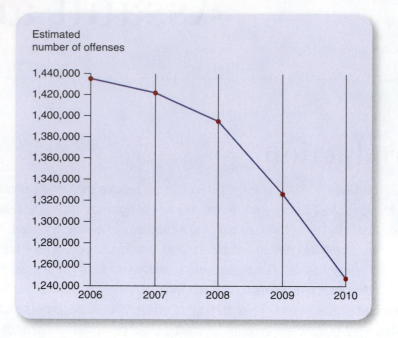

firearms, and 19 percent were committed withknives or other cutting instruments. The remaining 33 percent were committed with other weapons.[4]

Legal Classifications of Assault

Although states often define *assault* differently, some general definitions will be considered. The terms *assault* and *battery* were formerly used to distinguish between threats and actual contact between the suspect and the victim. Today, many revised state statutes categorize threats and actual physical contact as **simple assault** and **aggravated assault**. These are defined as follows.

Simple Assault

- ***Threats by one person to cause bodily harm or death to another.*** Investigators must identify evidence to show specific intent to commit bodily injury; an injury received as a result of an accident is not an assault. A suspect's words and actions or any injuries to the victim may

|Fig. 11.2| ▲

Bruising on the thigh from assault by a blunt instrument.

Courtesy of Mike Himmel

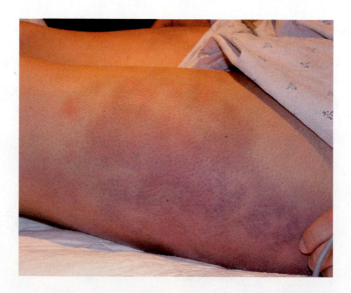

demonstrate intent. The injury must be to another party; injury to property or self-inflicted injury, regardless of its seriousness, is not assault.

- *Purposely inflicting bodily harm on another.* Bodily harm or injury and simple assault need not cause severe physical pain or disability. The degree of force necessary in simple assault may range from a push or a slap to slightly less than that required for the great bodily harm that is characteristic of aggravated assault.

Aggravated Assault, Types of Weapons Used, 2010			
Firearm	Knife or Cutting Instrument	Other Weapon	Hands, Fists, Feet, etc.
137,857	127,509	221,620	183,457

Source: Federal Bureau of Investigation. (2011). *Crime in the United States—2010. Uniform Crime Reports.* Washington, DC: U.S. Government Printing Office.

Aggravated Assault

Aggravated assault includes the elements of simple assault plus an element relating to the severity of the attack. Aggravated assault is usually committed with a weapon or by some means likely to produce great bodily harm or death.

- *High probability of death.* The assault is considered aggravated if it is committed by any means so severe that any reasonable person would think it would result in a high probability of death. For example, a strike to the head sufficient to cause unconsciousness or coma, a gunshot or knife wound that causes heavy bleeding, or burns inflicted over a large area of a person's body would be considered aggravated assault.
- *Serious, permanent disfigurement.* Permanent disfigurement includes such things as loss of an ear or part of the nose or permanent scarring of the face or other parts of the body that are normally visible. It cannot be a temporary injury that will eventually heal and not be evident.
- *Loss or impairment of body members or organs.* Regardless of the part of the body affected, a charge of aggravated assault is supported by the loss or permanent impairment of body members or organs or by maiming.

Only one of these additional elements is needed to show aggravated assault, although two or all three are sometimes present. Some states do not require that there be permanent or protracted injury or loss if the weapon used in the assault is a dangerous weapon that causes fear of immediate harm or death. As with simple assault, the act must be intentional, not accidental.

|Fig. 11.3| △

Depiction of the severity of aggravated assault and shows facial bruises and ecchymoses (bleeding into the skin) around the eyes sustained by an assault.

© JJM Stock Photography / Alamy

Legal Elements of Simple Assault

☑ Threats by one person to cause bodily harm or death to another
☑ Purposely inflicting bodily harm on another

Legal Elements of Aggravated Assault

☑ High probability of death
☑ Serious, permanent disfigurement
☑ Permanent or protracted loss or impairment of the function of any body member or organ or other severe bodily harm

Self-Defense

Under criminal law, persons may defend themselves and their property, and it is not necessary for the victim to wait until he or she has been physically assaulted before acting in **self-defense**. To do so, however, the elements of a threat should at least be present. It is on this point that the law makes a distinction in the interpretation of the word *threat*. For example, derogatory gestures or name calling between two persons does not give one the right to use violence or force against the other (*Naler* v. *State*, 1933). There are many cases, however, in which legal force is permitted under the law. For example, the law recognizes that persons are under no legal obligation to retreat from an attack. However, if escape from the attacker is possible without killing him or her, the victim must do so.

Conversely, if in trying to escape, the victim risks further peril, lethal force to defend one's self is allowed. Accordingly, if a situation erupts to the point where force is used by the victim to defend him- or herself, the degree of force should be no more than a reasonable person, under the same circumstances, would be justified in using. Therefore, the type of force used must be only enough to rebuff the attack, and no more. Any display of excessive force used to "punish" the attacker can be interpreted by the courts as an assault in and of itself.

The Preliminary Investigation

In the event that an assault has been committed and the suspect is not on the scene, the call turns into an investigation. Experience has shown that most victims of assault know their attackers. After arriving on the scene, first aid should be administered to the victim, or, if necessary, the victim should be transported to the hospital. If this is necessary, an officer should accompany the victim in the event that he or she tries to discard any evidence. If the victim is taken to the hospital, the accompanying officer should question the attending physician to determine if an assault has actually been committed. A brief examination by the physician should disclose whether or not the victim is being truthful about the origin of his or her injuries.

Officers arriving on the scene of an assault should do the following:

- Control and disarm those involved in the altercation.
- Provide medical aid to injured people.
- Separate suspects.
- Protect the crime scene.

- Give the *Miranda* warning if applicable.
- Obtain preliminary statements.
- Photograph any evidence observed.
- Collect and preserve evidence.
- Reconstruct the crime.

Documenting the Elements of Assault

An assault that does not involve a dangerous weapon and results in no serious injury is a relatively minor crime. In comparison, aggravated assault is an extremely serious crime. Investigators can establish intent by determining the events that led up to the assault. The suspect's exact words and actions should be documented, and statements should be taken from the victim and any witnesses.

Responding officers should also establish the severity of the assault by taking photographs and describing all injuries in their notes. The size, location, number, color, depth, and amount of bleeding of any injuries must also be carefully described. Some bruises do not become visible for several hours or even days, so assault victims should also be advised that additional photographs will need to be taken later. An oral or written statement should be obtained from qualified medical personnel regarding the severity and permanence of the injuries and any impairment of bodily functioning. Next, the means of the attack and the exact weapon used must be determined (e.g., gun, knife, fists).

Protecting the Crime Scene

The crime scene must be protected to preserve evidence, and photographs should be taken. This is done to document that an altercation actually occurred. It is also advisable for the investigator to photograph the victim's injuries as soon as possible. If this is not done, medical personnel might bandage the wounds without adequately documenting or describing them beforehand, making a description difficult to obtain.

Initial Questioning

Stating the obvious, the simple task of inquiring about "what happened" is one of the criminal investigator's most important duties. Although many people are reluctant to talk with police officials, others cooperate out of a sense of civic duty, and such statements can make the difference between the success and failure of an investigation.

QUESTIONING THE VICTIM The victim and any witnesses should be questioned next. When interviewing the victim, the investigator should ask the victim the facts surrounding the incident to determine that an assault actually did occur. Next, investigators should have the victim describe how the weapon was used (if there was one) and if there was any motive for the attack.

QUESTIONING THE WITNESSES It is also important to locate and question any impartial witnesses who can verify or corroborate the victim's story. Such people might be difficult to locate, however, because they may be friends of the attacker or might be afraid of retribution by the suspect. If possible, statements should be taken from anyone who witnessed the assault. Additionally, it might be advisable to canvass the neighborhood to locate residents who might have heard or observed something relevant to the case. The questioning of witnesses might also reveal threats made by either the attacker or the victim that might have fueled the altercation.

Searching the Crime Scene

As with all crime scenes, a thorough search for evidence should be conducted as soon as possible. In many cases, a brief search can even be made while the victim is still on the scene. When searching, the investigator should look for weapons (this may include broken bottles, ashtrays, or other objects), footprints or fingerprints, and trace evidence (e.g., pieces of torn clothing, lost buttons, hair). In the event that the victim cannot accompany the investigator during the search, it would be a good idea to return to the scene at a later time with the victim and have him or her recount the occurrence. The victim might be able to point out evidence that might have been missed during the initial search.

Domestic Violence

Domestic disputes are some of the most common emergency calls for police service. Domestic violence calls typically involve disputes between males and females but can include altercations between same-sex partners as well. Many domestic disputes do not involve violence; this chapter discusses those that do, as well as the measures that can be used to reduce them. In the United States, domestic violence accounts for about 20 percent of the nonfatal violent crime women experience and 3 percent of that which men experience. Harm levels vary from simple assault to homicide, with secondary harms to child witnesses. Domestic violence calls can be quite challenging for police as they are likely to observe repetitive abuse against the same victims, who may not be able to or may not want to part from their abusers. Police typically view these calls as dangerous, partly because old research exaggerated the risks to police.[5]

Domestic violence involves a current or former intimate (and in many states, a current or former dating partner). Domestic violence tends to be underreported: women report only one-quarter to one-half of their assaults to police, men perhaps less.[6] The vast majority of physical assaults are not life threatening; rather, they involve pushing, slapping, and hitting. Most women victims of domestic violence do not seek medical treatment, even for injuries deserving of it.

The response by police to domestic violence has changed drastically over the last 30 years. For example, in the 1970s, if a woman telephoned police to complain about being assaulted by her husband, she had little hope of getting him arrested. By the 1980s, a revolution was well under way in the manner that police responded to domestic violence. As of 1984, few arrests were made in domestic violence cases that had no visible injury. In fact, at the time, 22 states barred police from making warrantless arrests in cases they had not personally witnessed. By 1988, many police departments had started treating domestic violence as a crime against the state, as though it had been committed by a stranger.

A growing fear of liability put pressure on police to adopt new policies. For example, in 1984, a jury in Torrington, Connecticut, awarded a $2.3 million judgment against the police department for failing to protect a woman and her son from repeated violence by her husband. One year earlier, he had stabbed her 13 times and broken her neck while the police were at her house responding to her 9-1-1 call.

By 1980, all but six states had adopted some form of domestic violence legislation. The new laws provided for funding for shelters, established more effective procedures, and created "protection orders" to prohibit men from abusing their wives. By 1987, more than half the nation's major police departments had adopted "pro-arrest" policies, which require officers to make an arrest unless they could document a good reason not to do so.

|Fig. 11.4| △

Black eye of a victim of domestic violence.

Courtesy of Mike Himmel

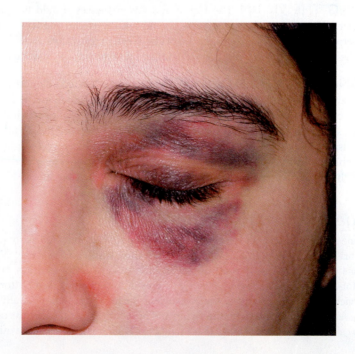

A 1984 study in Minneapolis found that an arrest plus a night in jail cut in half the risk of repeat violence against the victim in the following six months compared with the other two standard approaches: advising the couple to calm down and ordering the suspect to leave his home for six hours. Critics have argued that the mandatory arrest policy may do more to incite violence against women than to cure it.

The Investigative Response to Domestic Violence

Responding to domestic violence calls is one of the most unpleasant duties for police officers. In some cases, officers not trained properly for this type of duty may have preconceptions or biases that it is simply a "family matter" and not a real policing issue. However, domestic assault calls are often dangerous for the police. This is because the highly emotional atmosphere accompanying domestic abuse situations, the raw violence often displayed, the family lives destroyed, and the victim's frequent hesitancy to prosecute or seek shelter all place a heavy burden on the officers sent to deal with such disturbances. Still, an appropriate and effective police response to all domestic calls is warranted.

Response to such calls may be initiated by the dispatcher, who can save hours of legwork by exploring with the victim her frame of mind and that of the potential attacker. From that point on, responding officers' actions are critical. What responding officers do upon arrival often determines what happens in court, whether an effective arrest will be conducted, and whether or not proper evidence will be collected. Domestic violence calls are complicated in that they may unfold simple battery, assault, kidnapping, trespassing, murder, stalking, terroristic threats, spousal rape, or many other types of criminal violations. Police investigators should never assume that the parties involved in a domestic dispute are merely involved in a minor squabble.

Typically, patrol officers respond to domestic violence calls. When that occurs, officers should not park their patrol car within view of the location to which they are responding. Doing so may allow the suspect to see the officers coming and to become even more enraged at the thought of going to jail. This could result in the infliction of additional injuries on the victim or provide the suspect with time to gather weapons with which officers could be assaulted.

After officers have entered the location of the domestic violence call and have secured the area, the investigation begins. The first rule is to interview the suspect and victim separately. Upon first contact with the suspect, the *Miranda* warning should not be read to the suspect. At this point, until a determination has been made as to the nature of the dispute and the relationship between the suspect and the victim, the suspect is not under arrest for domestic violence. The parties are simply under detention for investigation because police officers have reasonable suspicion to detain them. This is a critical point in the investigation. Because of their agitated emotional state, many domestic violence suspects make spontaneous admissible statements that can be used against them later in

A Closer Look

Profiling the Batterer[7]

The profiles of abusive men have been fairly consistent. They tend to be manipulative, persuasive actors. They believe women should be subordinate, although they are often quite dependent on their spouses or girlfriends. They are cons: smart, charming, and cunning. Once they spot vulnerable women, they put on their best behavior and treat women with great respect, but the real anger they feel for women is just below the surface. Many batterers don't beat women out of a fit of rage but rather after some premeditation. In some cases, men have ripped out the telephone wires just before beating their spouses, which prevents the victims from calling 9-1-1 for help. Economic considerations are also a reason why battered women stay with their abusive partners. The cruel choice for battered women is often whether to be beaten or to be poor.

Psychologists have likened battering relationships to the Stockholm syndrome, in which hostages, over time, identify with their captors. Entangled in an intimate relationship that often begins as romance, many women come to agree with their partner's view of them as worthless. Often, a batterer goes into a "honeymoon" period just after a beating, persuading his partner that he will reform.

court. The officers should reduce the level of tension at the scene by separating and talking to the participants. The officers must also consider the safety of the participants and any children present.

Any evidence that would lead an officer to make an arrest in any other situation also applies to spousal abuse situations. Most states allow arrests based on probable cause. In line with the probable cause standard, police officers should arrest all abusers who are not acting in self-defense and issue an arrest warrant even if the offender is absent. Finally, officers should be careful not to detain a potential abuser any longer than other offenders.

Twenty states now mandate police to make an arrest in domestic violence incidents if there is a protective or **restraining order** against the attacker. A number of states make it mandatory for an officer to make an arrest if there is probable cause, even without an assigned complaint by the victim. In Nevada, for example, if the police have sufficient reason to believe that a person, within the preceding four hours, committed an act of domestic violence or spousal battery, they are required to arrest the person if there are no mitigating circumstances.

Officers should not base their decisions regarding arrest on their perception of the willingness of the victim or witness to testify. The victim need not sign a complaint. If the assault was a **mutual assault**, that is, both people involved committed assault, officers must try to determine the **primary physical aggressor** and arrest that person. Some factors to consider in making this determination include:

- Prior domestic violence involving either person
- The relative seriousness of the injuries inflicted upon each person involved
- The potential for future injury
- Whether one of the alleged assaults was committed in self-defense
- Any other factor that helps the officer decide which person was the primary physical aggressor

As with any criminal investigation, evidence must be collected. In domestic violence cases, evidence includes photographs of injuries, victims' statements, prior police reports, doctor or hospital reports, weapons used, damaged clothing or other property, and statements from neighbors and other witnesses. It should be made clear to the victim that an "order of protection" may be obtained from the court to help prevent further assaults.

Legal Approaches to Domestic Violence

In many cities, a high percentage of female victims request that battery charges be dropped or refuse to testify against the abuser after he has been arrested. In response to this, prosecutors in many cities with vigorous prosecution philosophies are increasingly adopting a controversial policy of "no drop." For example, in San Diego, if the victim won't testify, prosecutors use tapes from the woman's 9-1-1 calls and testimony from neighbors and police to build a case.

PROTECTION ORDERS Restraining orders (also known as "stay away" or protective orders) are intended to prevent offenders from further harassing, threatening, or contacting the victims. Courts have made restraining orders widely available to domestic violence victims, whether or not they file a police report. Courts may issue a temporary (time-limited) restraining order even when the "party being restrained" is not present or represented. Protective relief may be temporary or permanent. Violation of these orders is now a criminal offense in all U.S. states.[8]

Domestic violence restraining orders are frequently violated although some offenders may be deterred by them. Some research findings suggest that a victim is more likely to seek a protective order if the partner had a criminal history of violent offending, which may be why so many orders are violated; those with robust abuse histories may be the least likely to be deterred by such orders.[9]

A temporary protection order can be issued the same day the woman requests it and can be put in effect for a year or longer. In comparison, a woman can wait for months for a criminal prosecution to come to trial or years for a property settlement from a divorce decree. On the other hand, in some states, protection orders amount to nothing more than a cruel hoax on victims. Homicides have occurred by husbands and boyfriends against their female partners as well as by members of same-sex relationships while protection orders were in effect against one of the parties.

ARRESTING BOTH PARTIES IN A DOMESTIC VIOLENCE CALL Research and experience show that arresting both participants in a domestic violence incident (so-called "dual arrest") under the principle of "mutual combat" is ineffective toward interrupting the pattern of

A Closer Look

What Is an Order of Protection?

Basic Elements of a Valid Order of Protection

Any court order of protection should be presumed valid if all of the following are found:

- The order gives the names of the parties.
- The order contains the date it was issued, which is prior to the date when enforcement is sought.
- If the order has an expiration date, the date of expiration in the order has not occurred.

- The order contains the name of the issuing court.
- The order is signed by or on behalf of a judicial officer.
- The order specifies terms and conditions against the abuser.

Verifying the Terms and Conditions of an Order of Protection

Verification is not required under federal law and may be necessary only if the order does not appear valid on its face. In some cases, the enforcing jurisdiction's law may require verification if the protected party cannot furnish a copy of the order.

Verification can be accomplished by any of the following methods:

- Confirm the elements of an order in the NCIC Protection Order File.
- Review the elements of an order in state or local registries of protection orders in the issuing jurisdiction.
- Confirm the elements of an order if previously filed with designated authorities in the enforcing jurisdiction.
- Draw upon personal knowledge of the officer or information obtained through an interview.

---

violence between the two. In the context of the longer history of the relationship—as opposed to the one incident—there is nearly always one primary aggressor.[10] When police respond to a domestic violence call, self-defense may look like "mutual combat" and only detailed interviews of the parties (their prior abuse history) and witnesses may reveal the primary aggressor. In addition, at the scene of domestic abuse, "a victim may feel safe to express anger against the batterer in the presence of the police…giving the impression that they are the perpetrators." As a result, more than 20 states have enacted primary aggressor or "predominant aggressor" laws. Even these might not be enough to discourage dual arrest practices unless the law recognizes the importance of ascertaining the pattern/history and not just the aggression within a single incident. To complicate matters, there are couples in which both partners are violent.[11]

These "predominant aggressor" laws are more likely to entail "recurrent acts of minor violence initiated by either party, but the type of violence generally seen by police (and in shelter and clinical samples) is more likely to involve serious and frequent beatings, as well as the terrorizing of women".

Stalking

Stalking creates uncertainty, instills fear, and can completely disrupt lives. It can involve severe—even lethal—violence. Stalking involves a pattern of overtly criminal and/or apparently innocent behavior that makes victims fear for themselves or others.

Stalking is distinguishable from many other types of crime in two important ways. First, it entails repeat victimization of a person the offender targets—it is, by its very nature, a series of acts, rather than a single incident. Second, it is partly defined by its impact on the victim. While legal definitions of stalking vary from state to state, the following is a useful general definition:

> A course of conduct directed at a specific person that would cause a reasonable person fear.[12]

Stalking is widespread. Nearly one in 12 women and one in 45 men are stalked at least once in their lifetime. It is estimated that more than a million women and nearly half a million men are stalked in the United States each year. The overwhelming majority (78 percent) of victims are women, and the majority of offenders (87 percent) are men.[13]

Most victims know their stalkers. Even though we often hear reports of fans stalking celebrities, survey evidence indicates that fewer than a quarter of female victims and a third of male victims are stalked by strangers. Nearly 60 percent of female victims and 30 percent of male victims are stalked by current or former intimate partners. In intimate-partner cases, fewer than half of stalking incidents occur after the relationship ends. Most of the time, the stalking occurs during the relationship.[14]

Stalking and domestic violence intersect in a varietyof ways. Research indicates that 81 percent of women stalked by an intimate have been physically assaulted by that person. Thirty-one percent of women stalked by an intimate have been sexually assaulted by that person. Offenders who stalk former intimate partners are more likely to have physically or sexually assaulted them before the relationship ended.

Stalking is often a feature of relationships involving domestic violence. Like domestic violence, it is a crime of power and control. In one study about stalking and prestalking relationships, over 50 percent of the women were psychologically abused, 65 percent reported physical abuse, and 8.6 percent experienced sexual abuse during their relationship. If stalking is defined as a course of conduct that intimidates or frightens the victim, then relationships involving domestic violence also involve stalking.[15]

Both domestic violence and stalking are linked to lethal violence. Research has revealed that one-third of women killed each year in the United States die at the hands of a current or former intimate. It is estimated that 25 to 35 percent of stalking cases involve violence. And when stalking leads to violence, it is often a precursor to lethal violence. Studies show that stalking precedes an exceedingly high proportion of homicides by intimates. In over 75 percent of completed and attempted female homicides by intimates, the offenders stalked the victims in the year before the offense.[16]

Victims report only about half of stalking incidents to the police. Generally, those who do not report do not think the matter is criminal, do not think the police can help them, or fear that reporting will make the stalker even more dangerous. Twenty percent of victims who reported stalking stated that the police did not act regarding their complaints. Other victims may not report incidents because they may minimize the risk a stalker poses or blame themselves for the stalker's behavior.

Who Stalks Whom?

Although stalking is a gender-neutral crime, women are the primary victims of stalking and men the primary perpetrators. Seventy-eight percent of stalking victims identified by the NVAW survey were women, and 22 percent were men. Thus, four out of five stalking victims are women. Overall, 87 percent of the stalkers as defined by victims were male.[17]

Although the stereotypical stalking incident has been portrayed in books and movies, such as the movie *Fatal Attraction,* as a male victim pursued by a jealous, obsessive woman, many stalking cases involve men stalking men. In 1997, a male stalking case achieved high notoriety, as film producer and director Steven Spielberg was stalked by a 31-year-old bodybuilder and would-be screenwriter, Jonathan Norman. Norman was convicted in a Los Angeles court in March 1997. Spielberg, whose studio had turned down an unsolicited script from Norman, could have been targeted both as a celebrity and as an authority figure.

Experts say that the motive can also be romantic jealousy—gay men are the most likely victims of male-on-male stalking. But male stalking is often linked to the high-profile positions that the targets hold in society. For example, students stalk professors, attractive celebrities are pursued by lonely men looking for famous buddies, and business and political leaders can become objects of hate when consumer complaints turn ugly. Researchers say that men stalk other men for primarily the same reasons that they stalk women: a complex mix of mental and personality disorders that can include schizophrenia, drug dependency, narcissism, and antisocial behavior. Some of the problems with male stalking are that men are more reluctant than women to report being stalked and can have trouble getting police to take them seriously. Furthermore, public services for stalking victims, such as spouse-abuse shelters, are still oriented to the most frequent targets—women.

Although only a small percentage of stalking victims are actually physically attacked, psychological and social consequences are also common. About one-third of women and one-fifth of men who have been stalked sought psychological counseling as a result of their victimization. More than one-fourth of stalking victims said their victimization caused them to lose time from work.

This included attending court hearings, meeting with psychologists or other mental health professionals, meeting with attorneys, and avoidance of contact with the assailants. For those victims who are stalked, the behavior lasts only a relatively short period of time—about two-thirds of all stalking cases last a year or less.

The crime of stalking generally refers to some form of repeated harassing or threatening behavior. A stalker is someone who intentionally and repeatedly follows and tries to contact, harass, or intimidate another person. The Violence Against Women Grants Office adds: "Legal definitions of stalking vary widely from state to state. Though most states define stalking as the willful, malicious, and repeated following and harassing of another person, some states include in their definitions such activities as lying in wait, surveillance, nonconsensual communication, telephone harassment, and vandalism."[18] Other experts have asserted that although statutes vary from one state to another, most define stalking as a course of conduct that would place a reasonable person in fear for his or her safety and that the stalker attempted and did, in fact, place the victim in fear.

Forms of Stalking

Three broad categories of stalking have been identified, based on the relationship between the stalker and the victim:

1. In **intimate or former intimate stalking**, the stalker and victim may be married or divorced, current or former dating partners, serious or casual sexual partners, or former sexual partners. An estimated 70 to 80 percent of stalking cases fall into this category.
2. In **acquaintance stalking**, the stalker and victim know each other casually. They may be neighbors or coworkers. They may have even dated once or twice but were not sexual partners.
3. In **stranger stalking**, the stalker and victim do not know each other at all. This behavior is characterized by the stalker developing a love obsession or fixation of another person with whom he or she has no personal relationship. Cases involving public figures and celebrities fall into this category.

Brody notes that the growth in popularity of e-mail, along with the use of the Internet, has spawned **cyberstalking**.[19] This informal term refers to preying on a victim through his or her computer. Some people say that cyberstalking is the crime of the twenty-first century. Using the Internet to harass, intimidate, and terrorize takes an old problem and adds a diabolically futuristic twist. The types of victims vary: from politicians who get death threats via e-mail to women whose nude photographs, real or doctored, are posted on the Web. Although the average stalking case is serious enough, add the Internet component, and it becomes even more frightening because the stalker could be anyone, anywhere in the world.

Online, stalkers often hide behind false addresses and names and even impersonate their victims. Such a case happened in Los Angeles when a relationship soured and a 51-year-old security guard took to the Internet for revenge. Using his ex-girlfriend's real name, address, and telephone number, the guard went into electronic chat rooms and solicited rough sex during the summer of 1998. He engaged in sexually explicit conversations posing as his ex-girlfriend and introducing the idea of rape. In one instance, he said: "I want you to break down my door and rape me." Six men did, in fact, show up, and it was simply good fortune that the woman was unharmed. During the summer of 1999, the security guard was sentenced to six years in prison.[20]

The State of California has reacted aggressively to cyberstalking by updating statutes that once applied only to physical or telephonic harassment. Today, it is also illegal to harass or terrorize anyone using devices such as pagers, fax machines, or computers.

The range of sentencing for cyberstalking follows the range for physical stalking, which can be anywhere from no jail time at all to a maximum of four years. Prosecutors are often able to enhance the sentences by adding other charges. However, the U.S. Department of Justice estimates that only about one-third of states have followed California's lead. The department recommends that all states review their statutes to make them technologically neutral. The fact that cybercrime crosses jurisdictional lines is a problem for prosecutors. For example, suppose that a threatening message is sent from a computer in Michigan to a computer in California. Who investigates? Who gets the search warrant? And if evidence is turned up in Michigan, can it be used in California?

The first multijurisdictional computer forensic laboratory in the country was established in 1999 in San Diego, California. It aims to identify cyberstalkers, who often operate with little fear of getting caught. Participants include the FBI and the San Diego police, sheriff, and district attorney's office. In 1998, the unit prosecuted Dwayne Comfort, a student at the University of San Diego, who terrorized five female classmates by sending them sexually explicit e-mail that made it clear that he was watching their every move.[21]

The Justice Department released a report in September 1999 that said that based on the number of people who have access to the Internet, there might already have been tens of thousands of victims of cyberstalking.[22] The phenomenon is so new, the report says, that no hard statistics have been compiled. However, experts do know from their experience with ordinary stalking that women are far more likely to be stalked than men.

Some experts predict that the problem is likely to grow because using the Internet to stalk is relatively easy. Technically sophisticated stalkers can generate multiple messages throughout the day without even being present to push the send button. The anonymity they enjoy encourages some who would never have physically stalked a victim to do so with abandon on the Internet. The bad news for victims is that many law enforcement agencies do not have the sophisticated equipment or training that is often needed to track electronic stalkers.

The U.S. Justice Department has noted that all 50 states and the District of Columbia have general stalking laws, some of which can be applied to Internet stalking offenses, and that a number of states have added laws specifically targeting cyberstalking.[23]

Occurrence of Stalking

Research suggests that women are the primary victims of stalking and men the primary perpetrators. Furthermore, stalking is more prevalent than previously thought: 8 percent of women and 2 percent of men surveyed said that they had been stalked at some point of time in their lives. In addition, 1 million women and 371,000 men are stalked annually in the United States. According to the Department of Justice, "60 percent of women are stalked by spouses, former spouses, live-in partners, or dates, while 70 percent of men are stalked by acquaintances or strangers."[24]

The Investigative Response to Stalking

Typically, the police response to stalkers has been to issue restraining orders. Unfortunately, such orders are often ineffective: 69 percent of women and 81 percent of men have reported that stalkers violate such orders. Because of the proven ineffectiveness of restraining orders, the perceived inability of the criminal justice system to handle stalkers effectively, and victims' fear of antagonizing stalkers, many stalking incidents go unreported. An estimated 50 percent of all stalking victims report their stalking cases to the police, and about 12 percent of all stalking cases result in criminal prosecution. Of those offenders convicted for stalking, most were sentenced "for violations of protection orders that had been issued by the court in domestic violence cases."[25]

In dealing with stalkers, an investigator should encourage a victim to make a police report of the incidents and document the harassment. These records can serve as the basis for legal action against the stalker. In many cases, the crime of stalking requires that the victim actually suffer substantial emotional distress because of the stalker's conduct. Consequently, investigators may demonstrate such victim distress through documentation of the victim's response to the harassment. Such documentation may include answers to the following questions. Has the victim:

- Moved to a new location?
- Obtained a new phone number?
- Put a tap on the phone?
- Told friends, coworkers, or family members of the harassment?
- Given photos of the defendant to security?
- Asked to be escorted to the parking lot and work site?
- Changed work schedule or route to work?
- Stopped visiting places previously frequented?
- Taken a self-defense course?
- Purchased pepper spray?
- Bought a gun?
- Installed an alarm system?

Responses to these questions can indicate the victim's state of mind to help prove that element of the crime. In 1996, a federal law prohibiting interstate stalking was also enacted. Such legislation makes stalking a specific crime and empowers law enforcement to combat the stalking problem. Antistalking laws describe specific threatening conduct and hold the suspect responsible for proving that his or her actions were not intended to frighten or intimidate the victim.

Assaults in Taverns and Bars

The growth of the number of bars in many communities has led to increased assaults in and around the bars. While many, if not most, of these are alcohol related, assaults also occur when neither the aggressors nor the victims have been drinking. Most assaults occur on weekend nights. The majority of assaults occur at a relatively small number of places. Not all assaults involve a simple fistfight with a clear beginning and ending; instead, the incidents are often more ambiguous and complicated.[26]

For example, some are intermittent conflicts that flareup over time, some evolve into different incidents, and many involve participants who alternate between the roles of aggressor and peacemaker, often drawing additional people into the incident. Some involve lower levels of aggression (pushing, shoving), others involve moresevere violence (kicking, punching), and still others involve the use of weapons. Many of the injuries treated at hospitals, especially facial injuries, are related to assaults in and around bars.

Those who fight in bars are not deterred by negative consequences (such as minor injuries, tension among friends, or trouble with the police all of which tend to be delayed). The perceived rewards are more immediate and include feeling righteous about fighting for a worthy cause, increasing group cohesion among friends, getting attention, feeling powerful, and having entertaining stories to tell.[27] Although some assault victims do something to precipitate the assault, many do not. Most are smaller than their attackers, are either alone or in a small group, and are often more drunk than their attackers. Attackers target victims who appear drunker than themselves.

Many assaults are not reported to the police by either bar staff or the victim. Bar owners have mixed incentives for reporting assaults to the police. On the one hand, they need police assistance to maintain orderly establishments, but on the other hand, they do not want official records to reflect negatively on their liquor licenses. Many fights and disputes that start inside a bar are forced outside by the staff so they do not appear to be connected with the bar. Victims often are drunk, are ashamed, and see themselves as partly responsible, and so do not report assaults. Other victims

|Fig. 11.5| △

Bar scenes such as this are often the beginning of dispute that can result in violence.

Tonis Valing / Shutterstock

believe the incidents are too trivial to involve the police. Thus police records do not reflect the total amount of violence in and around bars. However, we underestimate the seriousness of the problem if we believe these assaults are just excessive exuberance by young men or "just desserts" for drunken troublemakers.

Consumption of alcohol is the most obvious factor contributing to aggression and violence in bars, but the relationship is not as simple as it might seem. Alcohol contributes to violence by limiting drinkers' perceived options during a conflict, heightening their emotionality, increasing their willingness to take risks, reducing their fear of sanctions, and impairing their ability to talk their way out of trouble. Many of the alcohol problems police deal with can be attributed to ordinary drinkers who go on binges, drink more than they usually do, or drink on an empty stomach.[28] In general, those who drink excessively are more aggressive and also get injured more seriously than those who drink moderately or not at all. Moderate drinkers do not appear to be at significantly higher risk of injury than nondrinkers.

Patrons can use bottles, glasses, pool cues, heavy ashtrays, and bar furniture as weapons. The more available and dangerous these items are, the more likely they will cause serious injury during fights and assaults. Oftentimes, such weapons are not available by the time law enforcement arrives at the scene.

Sexual Assault

On August 5, 1996, recently released serial rapist Reginald Muldrew struck again, this time breaking into the apartment of a Gary, Indiana, woman, putting a pillow over her face, and then raping and threatening to kill her. But this time things went a little awry. As he was leaving his victim's residence, the 48-year-old rapist was chased by and critically beaten by a group of teenagers. The police soon arrived and arrested him. Suspected of more than 200 sexual assaults in the Los Angeles area, Muldrew earned himself the nickname of the "pillowcase rapist."

Sadly, cases such as this are not all that atypical. One does not have to look far to read in the newspapers of yet another incident involving criminal sexual misconduct. Because of intense media (and public) interest, such cases tend to raise the consciousness of society regarding the plight of both victims and their perpetrators. Generally speaking, most sex crimes, rape in particular, are thought to be grossly underreported by victims. In fact, an estimated 50 percent of all sexual assaults are believed to go unreported to authorities. Perhaps this could be attributed to the intense personal nature of such offenses and because victims are too embarrassed or humiliated to report the incident. Indeed, studies have revealed that many victims would rather just forget such crimes than go through the agony of reliving them through police interviews and courtroom testimony. In addition, many perpetrators have turned out to be the friends, relatives, and acquaintances of the victims, creating an even greater disincentive for bringing about formal charges.

Although many different types of sex-related crimes exist, this chapter focuses on the crime of rape. Let's take a broader look at some of the most common types of rape that one might consider as an investigative priority. These include forcible rape and acquaintance rape.

The Role of the Sex Crime Investigator

Historically, the police investigator of sexual crimes has faced a somewhat different professional hurdle than that of most investigators. Many officers, including others in his or her own department, may view this job as a sort of "garbage collector" of the street. In fact, those who commit such crimes are also viewed by many as garbage that must be removed immediately.

Conversational topics involving sex are probably the most socially guarded in our society. Accordingly, many sexual disorders are among the most misunderstood in our culture, and those vested with investigating sex offenders are sometimes viewed as being tainted somehow by the very caliber of criminal whom they investigate.

The professional investigator of sexual crimes seeks out opportunities to become more proficient in investigations through reading, attendance at seminars, or job-related courses.[29] This includes staying abreast of recent research on offender typologies and underlying motivations for the various types of offenses encountered and the emotional impact (short and long term) of sexual crimes on victims. Without doubt, he or she must remain current in the field.

Forcible Rape

In a very broad sense, the term **rape** has been applied to a wide range of sexual attacks and, in popular terminology, may include same-sex rape and the rape of a male by a female. The use of the term *forcible rape* for statistical reporting purposes by law enforcement agencies, however, has a specific and somewhat different meaning. The Uniform Crime Reports (UCR) defines a forcible rape as "the **carnal knowledge** of a female forcibly and against her will." By definition, rapes reported under the UCR program are always of females. In contrast to what may be an emerging social convention, in which male rape is a recognized form of sexual assault, the latest edition of the *Uniform Crime Reporting Handbook*, which serves as a statistical reporting guide for law enforcement agencies, says, "Sex attacks on males are excluded [from the crime of forcible rape] and should be classified as assaults or 'other sex offenses,' depending on the nature of the crime and the extent of the injury." Although not part of the UCR terminology, some jurisdictions refer to same-sex rape as sexual battery. **Sexual battery**, which is not included in the UCR tally of reported rapes, is intentional and wrongful physical contact with a person without his or her consent that entails a sexual component or purpose. **Statutory rape**, in which no force is involved with a girl below the age of consent, is not included in rape statistics, but attempts to commit rape by force or the threat of force are included.

Forcible rape is the least reported of all violent offenses. The FBI estimates that only one of every four forcible rapes is reported to the police. An even lower figure was reported by a 1992 government-sponsored study, which found that only 16 percent of rapes were reported. The victim's fear of embarrassment has been cited as the reason most often given for nonreports. Previously, reports of rape were usually taken by seemingly hardened desk sergeants or male detectives who may not have been sensitive to the needs of female victims. In addition, the physical examination that victims had to endure was often a traumatizing experience in itself. Finally, many states routinely permitted the women's sexual history to be revealed in detail in the courtroom if a trial ensued. All of these practices contributed to considerable hesitancy on the part of rape victims to report victimizations.

Over the past few decades a number of changes have taken place that are designed to facilitate accurate reporting of rape and other sex offenses. Trained female detectives often act as victim interviewers, physicians have been better educated in handling the psychological needs of victims, and sexual histories are no longer regarded as relevant in most trials.

Rape is frequently committed by a man known to the victim, as in the case of date rape. Victims may be held captive and subjected to repeated assaults. In the crime of heterosexual rape, any female—regardless of age, appearance, or occupation—is a potential victim. Through personal

|Fig. 11.6| ▲

Detectives must be quick in their response to a rape. They must attempt to communicate with the victim as soon as possible to receive an initial statement. Here a detective interviews a victim while she is in the hospital.

© Mark Burnett / Alamy

violation, humiliation, and physical battering, rapists seek a sense of personal fulfillment and dominance. In contrast, victims of rape often experience a diminished sense of personal worth; increased feelings of despair, helplessness, and vulnerability; a misplaced sense of guilt; and a lack of control over their personal lives.

Contemporary research holds that forcible rape is often a planned violent crime, which serves the offender's need for power rather than sexual gratification. Statistically speaking, however, most rapes are committed by acquaintances of the victims and often betray a trust or friendship. Date rape, which falls into this category, appears to be far more common than believed previously. Recently, the growing number of rapes perpetrated with the use of the "date rape drug" Rohypnol has alarmed law enforcement personnel. Rohypnol is an illegal pharmaceutical substance that is virtually tasteless. Available on the black market, it dissolves easily in drinks and can lead anyone who unknowingly consumes it to be unconscious for hours, making the person vulnerable to sexual assault. Because Rohypnol is typically added to a drink when the victim is not present, it is advisable for persons to not walk away from their drinks while at bars and taverns.

Trends

The numbers and instances of forcible rape tell a disturbing story about the frequency of the crime. For example, in 2011, the FBI reported that there were an estimated 84,767 forcible rapes reported to law enforcement in 2010.[30] This estimate was 5 percent lower than the 2009 estimate and 10 percent and 7 percent lower than the 2006 and 2001 estimates, respectively.[31] The rate of forcible rapes in 2010 was estimated at 54.2 per 100,000 female inhabitants. Finally, rapes by force made up 93 percent of reported rape offenses in 2010, and attempts to commit rape accounted for 7 percent of reported rapes.[32]

Legal Aspects of Rape

According to common law, there are three elements to the crime of rape when the female is over the age of consent:

1. Carnal knowledge (penetration).
2. Forcible submission.
3. Lack of consent.

Penetration, as an essential element of rape, means generally that the sexual organ of the male entered the sexual organ of the female. Court opinions have held that penetration, however slight, is sufficient to sustain a charge of rape. There need not be an entering of the vagina or rupturing of the hymen; entering of the vulva or labia is usually all that is required. It is important during the victim interview that investigators clearly establish that penetration occurred with the penis. Penetration of a finger is not rape, although it is, of course, another form of assault.

Forcible Rape Trend		
Year	Number of Offenses	Rate per 100,000 Inhabitants
2009	89,241	29.1
2010	84,767	27.5
Percent change		−5.5

Source: Federal Bureau of Investigation. (2011). *Crime in the United States—2010. Uniform Crime Reports.* Washington, DC: U.S. Government Printing Office.

In many states, the victim must have resisted the assault and her **resistance** must have been overcome by force. The amount of resistance that the victim is expected to have displayed depends on the specific circumstances of the case. The power and strength of the aggressor and the physical and mental ability of the victim to resist vary in each case. The amount of resistance expected in one case will not necessarily be expected in another situation. It can be expected that one woman would be paralyzed by fear and rendered mute and helpless by circumstances that would

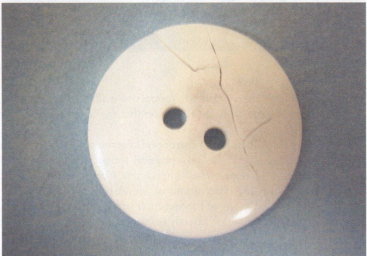

|Fig. 11.7| ▵

Part of the victim's broken button was located at the scene of the sexual assault and part was discovered on the clothing of the suspect. Ballistics comparison made a positive match (photos A & B).

Missouri State Highway Patrol Crime Laboratory

inspire another to fierce resistance or that a woman may be rendered incapacitated by drugs such as Rohypnol or GHB.[33] For the most part, there must be resistance on the part of the woman before there can be a foundation for a rape charge.

The kind of fear, however, that would render resistance by a woman unnecessary to support a case of rape includes a fear of death or serious bodily harm, a fear so extreme as to preclude resistance, or a fear that would render her incapable of continuing to resist. On the other hand, consent prior to penetration may remove the criminal character of rape from the subsequent intercourse. Of course, it is problematic in some cases whether the consent was voluntary or coerced or whether resistance was possible or even prudent on the part of the victim. As one state ruled, "There is no definite standard fixed for the amount of resistance required in rape cases. Resistance is not necessary where it would endanger the complainant's safety or when she is overcome by superior strength or paralyzed with fear."[34] This ruling may reflect the position of some state courts, although other states require more demonstrable evidence of resistance to rape. In any event, most recognize that there is a wide difference between consent and submission by force or threat of force: Consent may involve submission, but submission does not necessarily imply consent.

Corroboration

In the absence of a statute requiring corroboration, common law has traditionally held that the unsupported testimony of the victim, if not contradictory, is sufficient to sustain a conviction of rape. Some states, to provide safeguards against unfounded accusations of rape, have laws that

|Fig. 11.8| △

Crime laboratory criminalists such as this one search for semen stains with a UV light, and work hand-in-hand with criminal investigators in trying to identify a suspect.

© Jochen Tack / Alamy

require corroborative evidence. Corroboration is supportive evidence that tends to prove that a crime was committed. It lends credence to the allegation that the crime occurred and need not be proved beyond doubt.

Investigators should pay close attention to corroborative evidence even if it is not required by statute. Corroboration of a rape offense can take physical forms such as semen stains on clothing, bruises, cuts, and medical evidence of sexual intercourse. Corroborating evidence can also be circumstantial, such as statements and observations of witnesses. Although in some jurisdictions, rape can be proved by the sole testimony of the victim, it is not common. Medical and scientific evidence are of prime importance and often directly influence the successful prosecution of a case.

Date Rape

Typically, people believe that most rapists and victims were strangers to one another. But a disturbing trend in rapes indicates that many victims and offenders were acquainted before the crime was committed. For example, **date rape** is becoming more frequent on college campuses. It has been estimated that 20 percent of all college women have been victims of rape or attempted rape. One self-report survey conducted on a Midwestern campus found that 100 percent of all rapists knew their victims beforehand.[35]

Another troubling phenomenon is campus **gang rape**, in which a group of men attacks a defenseless or intoxicated woman. Well-publicized rapes have taken place at the University of New Hampshire, Florida State University, Duke University, and Pennsylvania State University.

As the interview progresses, the investigator should encourage the victim to recollect any additional identifying characteristics of the assailant. Such inquiries should be phrased so as not to appear to be probing. If the victim's memory is not jogged through these inquiries, the investigator should proceed with the interview.

Evidence in Rape Cases

As with all investigations, the identification, collection, and preservation of evidence are the primary responsibility of the investigator. Rape cases are somewhat unique in that evidence may present itself in three general areas:

1. On the crime scene
2. On the victim
3. On the suspect (or at locations occupied by the suspect)

Victim Interview Checklist

☑ Interviewers should be sensitive to the needs and concerns of the victim.

☑ The victim needs to feel safe.

☑ All victims react differently to incidents of sexual assault.

☑ Police officers react differently to sexual assault victims.

☑ The interviewer must display a genuine interest in the welfare of the victim.

☑ Victim interviews demand patience and perseverance.

☑ Interviewers should ask brief open-ended questions.

☑ It should be established whether the victim knows the suspect.

☑ Descriptions of the suspect and his vehicle must be acquired if available.

☑ Leading questions should not be asked.

☑ Official police jargon should not be used.

☑ Victims should be walked through the crime scene to indicate what the suspect may have touched.

☑ The victim needs to feel that she has regained control of her life.

☑ Investigators must anticipate what information the victim might want to know.

☑ Investigative procedures should be explained carefully if the investigator is asked to do so.

☑ The interview should never be rushed.

Additionally, evidence in rape cases may take many forms. Therefore, after the responding officer has given the rape victim aid, a determination of the circumstances surrounding the attack must be made. When immediate medical attention is required, the officer on the scene may make initial inquiries about the assault while waiting for the ambulance to arrive. The victim should be asked to:

- Describe what happened.
- Describe the assailant.
- Describe the attacker's vehicle.
- Describe the location where the crime occurred.

If the incident was fairly recent, a flash description of the suspect or his vehicle should be given to the dispatcher for possible broadcast. After the crime scene investigation is under way, the investigator should determine if there is any physical evidence to be collected. Typically, the rape victim will scratch the skin or tear the hair of her attacker, and evidence may be present under her fingernails. For example, a single strand of hair may reveal the gender, race, and age of the attacker. Such evidence is seizable by investigators and extremely valuable in court.[36]

The clothing of the victim can also provide valuable information (e.g., stains, blood, soil, grass stains, trace evidence). As early as possible, clothing should be collected from the victim and preserved for laboratory analysis. Other types of evidence that should be considered are bedsheets, mattress, towels and washrags, discarded facial tissues, robes, and sofa or chair cushions. The investigator is limited only by his or her imagination when considering the types and locations of such articles.

If a suspect is in custody, the necessary legal instrument (i.e., court order) should be secured to obtain hair and blood standards to compare with those found on the victim.

THE RAPE EVIDENCE KIT Preassembled kits for rape evidence collection can be found in many different configurations and can be quite useful to the investigator. Typically included are directions for proper use to avoid confusion and error. Hazelwood and Burgess note that commonly included are forms covering (1) medical examination and interview of the victim, (2) consent or release concerning authority to disseminate victim-related information, (3) consent or release regarding evidence obtained from the victim, and (4) chain of custody documentation.[37]

Rape Evidence Checklist

☑ Photograph all physical injuries of the victim.

☑ Note the clothing of the victim (e.g., torn, dirty, missing buttons).

☑ Examine the hair (both victim and suspect) for foreign fiber, debris, and blood.

☑ Obtain fingernail scrapings for clothing fibers, skin, blood, hair, and so on.

☑ Obtain blood samples from the victim.

☑ Obtain pubic hairs from both the victim and the suspect (this includes standards for comparison).

☑ Obtain vaginal swabs from the victim (the attending physician should acquire at least two).

☑ Obtain anal and oral swabs from the victim.

☑ Allow wet articles to air dry using fresh air, not heated air.

☑ Ensure that the victim has a cervical exam by a physician of her choosing.

☑ Obtain a written report from the examining physician.

|Fig. 11.9| △

Sexual assault evidence collection kits such as this one includes all of the necessary evidence collection tools for responding to allegations of rape.

© Scott Camazine / Alamy

These documents are best constructed as a cooperative effort between local law enforcement and medical professionals who treat sexual assault victims. Many evidence recovery procedures can be incorporated into a rape evidence collection kit. The following is a general list of some essential elements of the kit:

• Head hair brushing comb
• Pubic hair brushing comb
• Packages for head and pubic hairs collected (both known and suspected samples)
• Vaginal swabbings
• Oral swabbings
• Anal swabbings
• Fingernail scrapings
• Miscellaneous debris collection

The acquisition of known biological samples is basically the same for both the victim and the suspect. Accordingly, trace evidence can be collected in a similar fashion. In fact, the components of the victim-oriented assault kit serve as a good guide for kits used on a suspect.

INVESTIGATIVE PROCEDURES: THE CRIME SCENE INVESTIGATION An officer's first duty at the scene of a rape is to aid the victim and obtain medical attention immediately if required. If the attack was brutal and the victim is suffering from wounds, briefly question the victim about the attack if she is able to speak. Questions relating to what happened, where the attack took place, and a description of or information about the assailant are pertinent basic facts. This initial attempt to secure information should be made whenever possible while awaiting the arrival of an ambulance or during transport to medical facilities. In turn, the dispatcher should be contacted immediately with this information.

Usually upon arriving at a rape scene, officers will find the victim of a sexual assault under severe emotional stress ranging from hysteria to deep depression. She may be sobbing uncontrollably, excited to the point of incoherence, or in a state of shock. In cases in which the victim was drugged, she may be confused and unsure of what happened to her. When encountering any of these situations, officers must comfort the victim and reassure her that she will be all right and that she has nothing more to fear. A victim in this mental state may best be comforted by another woman such as a female officer, a family member, a friend, or a victim advocate. Such individuals should be summoned as quickly as possible if not objectionable to the victim.

The crime scene should be secured and a search for physical evidence begun as soon as possible. Quite often, the victim will pull hair or tear the assailant's clothes or scratch his face and accumulate skin tissue or bloodstains under her fingernails. The victim's clothing can also provide valuable information. This should be collected and forwarded to the crime laboratory with other trace evidence for analysis.

Clothing When a rape occurs in the home, the victim should be requested by the responding officer not to change her clothing, shower, or touch anything in the area until officers arrive at the scene to give her instructions. Responding officers should assume custody of all the clothing worn at the time of the attack so they may be examined for blood or seminal stains, hair fibers, and other physical trace evidence that may lead to the identification, apprehension, and conviction of a suspect. If the location of the crime makes the immediate recovery of the clothing impractical, the victim should be informed that an officer will collect her garments at the hospital for transfer to the crime laboratory. In these situations, arrangements should be made with a friend or a relative to bring a change of clothing for the victim to the hospital. The number of persons handling the victim's clothing must be restricted. Concerted efforts to protect the integrity of the specimens and to guard the chain of possession also require that evidence be properly marked, packaged, and labeled to facilitate future identification.

The clothing of a rape victim, especially the undergarments, as well as the clothes of a suspect, should be analyzed by crime laboratory technicians for semen stains, bloodstains, hair, and other physical traces, such as soil and grass stains. Scientific analysis of the evidence may link a suspect to the crime, or it may indicate that a suspect is not the person who should be sought.

Recovered clothing should be carefully handled to protect the evidentiary value of the stains it may contain. Seminal traces and bloodstains are highly brittle when dry and may be brushed off the clothing. Clothing should be covered with paper before folding and each item individually placed in an evidence bag.

Semen Seminal traces may be located by ultraviolet radiation because of their fluorescent qualities. Semen is highly proteinaceous serum normally containing a great number of spermatozoa. These traces are usually found on underclothing of the victim, the suspect, or both and may also be located on bedding, mattresses, towels, automobile cushions, and similar types of materials found at or near the crime scene or in the possession of a suspect. Ultraviolet light or an acid phosphatase color test is helpful in identifying semen on these and other surfaces. Vaginal secretions and some other material will react to the latter test but not at the same speed as semen. A positive test requires that the material be subjected to microscopic examination for confirmation.

Bloodstains may also be found in similar locations. Both semen and blood samples can be subjected to DNA analysis.

Hair It is fairly common to find a reciprocal transfer of evidence in crimes involving bodily contact. As such, it is not unusual to find hair of the offender transferred to the body or clothing of the victim and, in turn, to discover some of the victim's hair on the suspect.

Recovered hair is usually subjected to microanalysis at the crime laboratory. The results of this examination can generally narrow the search for a suspect. A single strand of hair may identify the race, sex, approximate age, and the true color of the hair of its host. The analysis can also determine the portion of the body that the hair is from such as the scalp, chest, arm, leg, or pubic region.

Although the crime laboratory examination leads to general identification characteristics of a suspect, a positive finding may suggest the implication of an individual, whereas a negative finding may disprove an erroneous theory. By the same token, hair found on a suspect's clothes can be examined and identified as being similar to that of the victim.

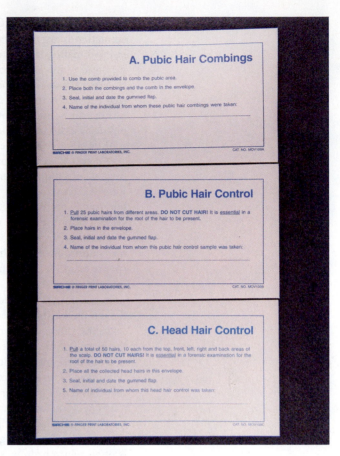

|Fig. 11.10| ◬

Sexual assault evidence collection kit contents: hair samples and pubic hair samples (shown), as well as vaginal, oral, and rectal swabs.

Courtesy of Mike Himmel

INVESTIGATIVE PROCEDURES: THE FORENSIC EXAMINATION The forensic examination is arguably the most critical component in the aftermath of a sexual assault. The exam has two main goals: to treat the assault survivor for medical injuries and to collect evidence that may lead to the arrest, prosecution, and conviction of the offender. Exams are usually conducted by a sexual assault forensic examiner, or SAFE—a medical professional who has received specialized education and has fulfilled clinical requirements to perform medical forensic examinations. SAFEs can be nurses (often called sexual assault nurse examiners, or SANEs), doctors, or even physician assistants. Rape victims should receive medical attention and undergo an examination as soon as possible after the incident.

All sexual assault survivors have the right to a properly conducted exam in which they are treated with dignity, compassion, and respect. In September 2004, former U.S. Attorney General John Ashcroft released the Attorney General's National Protocol for Sexual Assault Medical Forensic Examinations (SAFE Protocol), which offers guidance for communities that want to develop a response that is sensitive to sexual assault victims and promotes offender accountability. Produced by the Office on Violence Against Women and based upon "best practices" from around the country, the SAFE Protocol also examines the roles of other members of the sexual assault response team (SART), which include law enforcement officers, prosecutors, victim advocates, and forensic scientists.

A recent study funded by NIJ examined the efficacy of SANE or SART interventions as tools in the criminal justice system. The study findings indicate that in communities with these programs, sexual assault cases are reported more quickly. In cases involving SANE or SART interventions, the average time between the assault and the report is 5.6 days compared with 33 days in cases without these interventions.[38] According to the researchers, cases with SANE or SART interventions have more evidence available and are more likely to have victim participation. Furthermore, they found that this intervention is a significant factor in the identification and arrest of suspects, is a strong predictor that charges will be filed, and increases the likelihood of conviction.[39]

The victim has the right to be examined by a physician of her choice. However, for practical reasons, this should be generally discouraged. A private practitioner or a hospital staff physician is often reluctant to be specific in officially reporting findings or to take time from a busy work schedule to testify in court. Gentle persuasion and tact will usually influence an unwilling victim or her parents to allow a physician or sexual assault nurse examiner from a public institution to conduct the examination. A written statement or report should be obtained from the attending physician or nurse after the victim has been examined. This record is extremely important at the trial to sustain the victim's allegation that she was raped.

The medical examination usually consists of a visual examination of the vaginal area to determine if there is evidence of tissue damage (lacerations, abrasions, contusions) or other indication of physical trauma that is logically connected with the assault. Smears should be obtained from the vaginal passage to determine the presence or the absence of sperm. However, the presence of sperm merely corroborates that the victim had sexual intercourse, not necessarily that she had been raped. In cases in which a drug-facilitated rape is probable, urine and blood samples should be taken.

If the crime of rape occurs, the victim should be checked out by a medical doctor with training in conducting SAFE exams or a specially trained nurse. If possible, a female law enforcement agent should be present to maintain the chain of custody.

If the victim dies before the physical examination, she should not be examined by the attending physician. Instead, the body should be examined by the posting physician or the medical examiner. This procedure is followed to reduce the number of persons examining the body. Also, an examination before the posting process may destroy or remove important evidence.

The medical examination of a deceased victim should include other body cavities such as the anus, mouth, and ears. Scrapings should also be taken from under the fingernails. A thorough examination is necessary to determine the kind of sexual assault suffered by the victim and to obtain specimens of blood that could possibly be the assailant's. In some instances, assailants insert foreign objects into body cavities before or after the death of the victim. In instances of death, officers should provide the medical examiner with all information surrounding the assault and death of the victim.

INVESTIGATIVE PROCEDURES: THE INTERVIEW Although the victim interview is one of the key components of a rape investigation, it can also be one of the more difficult functions for

Nationally Recognized Sexual Assault Forensic Examination Checklist

Check all items as provided during the sexual assault forensic exam.

- ☑ Utilized appropriate evidence collection kit (city, county, or state forensic lab)
- ☑ Completed screening exam for Emergency Medical Condition
- ☑ Activated bedside advocacy
- ☑ Activated interpreter
- ☑ Interventions for disabilities
- ☑ Obtained history of assault (including narrative)
- ☑ Obtained history of drug-facilitated sexual assault (if indicated)
- ☑ Obtained consent for evaluation and treatment
- ☑ Obtained consent for evidentiary SAFE exam
- ☑ Obtained consent for photography
- ☑ Obtained consent for drug screening (if drug-facilitated assault indicated)
- ☑ Obtained consent for release of information to all appropriate agencies
- ☑ Obtained consent for law enforcement activation (per patient request)
- ☑ Collected urine for drug-facilitated sexual assault
- ☑ Collected underwear worn during or immediately after the assault
- ☑ Collected clothing, as forensically indicated, in brown paper bags, sealed and labeled
- ☑ Obtained swabs and smears from all areas that victim states were bitten or licked
- ☑ Obtained swabs and smears from appropriate areas as identified using an alternative light source
- ☑ Collected blood standard (if forensically indicated)
- ☑ Utilized crime scene investigators for bite mark impressions (if forensically indicated)

- ☑ Collected oral swab for DNA Standard (if forensically indicated)
- ☑ Collected oral swabs and smear (if orally assaulted)
- ☑ Collected anal swabs and smear (if forensically indicated)
- ☑ Collected vaginal swabs and smear (if forensically indicated)
- ☑ Collected cervical swabs and smear (if forensically indicated)
- ☑ Collected penile swabs and smear (if forensically indicated)
- ☑ Collected head hair standard (if forensically indicated)
- ☑ Collected pubic hair standard (if forensically indicated)
- ☑ Completed toluidine dye exam (if forensically indicated)
- ☑ Completed x-rays (if indicated)
- ☑ Completed CTs (if indicated)
- ☑ Collected unknown sample(s) (if forensically indicated)
- ☑ Collected fingernail scrapings (if forensically indicated)
- ☑ Photography (with colposcope or digital)
- ☑ Genital photography by forensic examiner
- ☑ Nongenital photography by forensic examiner
- ☑ Less than 10 photos
- ☑ More than 10 photos
- ☑ Forensic evidence storage/log (as indicated)
- ☑ Completion of DHSS Adult Female, Adult Male, or Child Sexual Assault Exam Form
- ☑ Confidential forensic patient file separate from general hospital medical records
- ☑ Forensic exam conducted by forensically trained physician or healthcare provider such as Sexual Assault Nurse Examiner (SANE)

Source: U.S. Department of Justice. (Septermber 2004). *National Protocol for Sexual Assault Medical Forensic Examinations.*

a criminal investigator. The difficult and, in many ways, specialized nature of these interviews has been a major reason for the introduction and use of rape crisis specialists to assist in these cases. Most agencies do not have such specialized personnel resources, but many agencies have found it helpful to utilize female officers individually or in conjunction with a male officer for such interviews. Female officers, even without specialized training, are generally effective in mitigating some of the anxiety and apprehension that rape victims have concerning the interview process and related investigatory activities. Significant additional benefits can be realized for both the victim and the criminal investigation if the same female officer can be assigned to assist the victim throughout the investigation and prosecution of the case.

Most rape investigations should incorporate a preliminary and subsequent in-depth interview with the victim. The initial interview conducted at the crime scene should be limited to gathering basic facts about the crime sufficient to identify the victim and to describe and locate the offender on a timely basis. The ability of the responding officer or investigator to gather this information will depend greatly on the emotional and physical condition of the victim and the professional and interpersonal skills of the interviewer. However, it is ill advised to attempt to fully explore the events and circumstances surrounding the crime at the scene of the incident. The emotional condition of rape victims generally precludes their ability to clearly focus and to articulate accurate and complete details of the incident. Even in cases in which a victim appears to be under control, officers should be aware that the victim's emotional state may cause her to cloud certain facts, and in cases in which the victim was drugged, she may have blacked out during the assault. Officers should be sure to clarify such information at a later time during an in-depth interview session.

By gathering complete information during the in-depth interview, officers avoid the need to repeatedly question the victim at later dates. Repeated interviews require the victim to relive the experience again and again. A structured interview that will cover all pertinent areas is one of the better means of avoiding such repetitive questioning.

The investigative goal of the police officer in interviewing a rape victim is to determine if and how the crime occurred. It is from the statements made by the victim to the officer that the essential elements of the offense and the direction of the investigation are established. The prosecutor and eventually the court must be given a well-balanced account of the offense describing the actions of the offender, any accomplices, and the victim. It is the investigator's responsibility to provide the court with the explanation and clarification it seeks. Part of the story may be obtained from the analysis of physical evidence, but the eyewitness account of the victim or other persons fills in the missing portions of the picture presented to the court.

Because the interview process may be considered as a routine operation, the police officer may, if not careful, project a feeling of lack of concern for the victim as a person. The danger is that the victim may be left with the impression that she is being treated as an object of physical evidence rather than as a human being. This eventuality must be avoided for its own sake as well as for the good of the investigation. It is by the personal and sensitive communication of the interview that the victim's cooperation is gained and her emotional well-being maintained. If the officer treats the victim impersonally, her confidence will be shattered, the interview will be unsuccessful, and the victim may suffer further emotional stress. The following points should be kept in mind when conducting the in-depth interview.

Officer Attitude   When interviewing a rape victim, the officer must realize that, from the victim's viewpoint, what has occurred is a violent and perverted invasion of her "self." Furthermore, the officer must be constantly aware of personal sexual attitudes and prejudices as well as the subtle and not-so-subtle ways in which they emerge. Special care should be exercised so that the rape victim is not placed in the position of perceiving herself as being guilty because of the personal nature of the crime and the social stigma attached to it. Maintaining professionalism throughout the interview will help the officer obtain an accurate report of the crime without causing the victim to experience unnecessary anxiety.

The interviewer's approach should be informal and natural in order to put the victim at ease. Words should be used that are appropriate to the victim's age, intelligence, and social class. Slang or colloquialisms may be appropriate in alluding to matters indirectly related to the offense, but medical terms should be used to refer to the various sexual organs and parts of the body (e.g., penis, vagina, vulva). In some instances, an officer may have to define terms to the victim before the interview. This adds a degree of dignity to the confidential relationship one should establish, indicates respect for the private parts of the body, and helps allay doubt or misgiving about the officer's sincerity and interest.

Physical Setting   It is unreasonable to expect a rape victim to respond to detailed questioning while she is uncomfortable or in physical pain. The victim may have been beaten as well as raped. If the rape has occurred outdoors, the victim and her clothing will probably be soiled. Sometimes the victim has been urinated on or has been forced to commit oral sodomy. Under conditions such as these, the preliminary interview should be brief, and the in-depth follow-up interview should be conducted after the victim has been medically examined and treated and her personal needs, such as washing and changing clothes, have been met.

Officers often interview a rape victim at the hospital or other medical facility where the victim is being treated. Most hospitals meet the basic requirements of appropriate physical setting for an interview. The physical surroundings of most hospitals provide desired privacy and a professional care environment that can restore confidence in the victim.

Outside the hospital, the interview should take place in a comfortable setting where there is privacy and freedom from distraction. A crowded office or similar location where the interview is subject to interruption is inappropriate. The reluctance of a rape victim to discuss intimate details of the crime will generally increase if there are other people present. This may include persons who would be close to the victim under otherwise normal conditions, such as a husband or boyfriend.

Opening Remarks   The opening remarks represent a critical point at which an officer must gain the victim's confidence and let her know that a major part of the officer's function is to help and to protect her. The officer should make clear his or her sympathy for and interest in the victim. By doing this, the officer contributes to the immediate and long-term emotional health of the victim and lays the foundation of mutual cooperation and respect on which an effective interview is built.

Ventilation Period   After the opening remarks, the officer should allow the victim to direct the conversation into any area of concern to her. This "ventilation" period gives the victim an opportunity to relieve emotional tension. During this time, the officer should listen carefully to the victim and provide answers to questions as appropriate and reassurance when necessary.

Investigative Questioning   After a ventilation period, the victim should be allowed to describe what occurred in her own words and without interruption. As the victim provides details about the rape, she will also relate a great deal about herself. Her mood and general reaction, her choice of words, and her comments on unrelated matters can be useful in evaluating the facts of the case. It is important in such an interview that the police officer be humane, sympathetic, and patient. He or she should also be alert to inconsistencies in the victim's statements. If the victim's story differs from the originally reported facts, the officer should point out the discrepancies and ask her to explain them in greater detail. The officer should phrase questions in simple language, making sure that she understands the question. It is best if the questions are presented in a manner that encourages conversation rather than implies interrogation. Often a rape victim will omit embarrassing details from her description of the crime. Officers should expect a certain amount of reluctance on the part of the victim to describe unpleasant facts. The officer should explain that certain information must be discussed to satisfy the legal aspects of rape and pursue the investigation. He or she may add that the same questions will be asked in court if the case results in a trial. In a majority of cases, the attack is premeditated, and in about 80 percent of the cases,[40] the rapist has known or has seen the victim before the assault. Because of this, certain types of questions should be asked.

The victim should be asked if, and how long, she has been acquainted with the offender. The circumstances of their meeting and the extent of any previous relationship, including any prior sexual relations, should be explored. Although previous sexual acts with the accused will not absolve the offender at this point in the investigation, knowledge of them helps to establish the nature of the relationship with the offender, as well as prepare for possible prosecutorial problems. If it is determined that the victim had known the rapist before the incident, he should be identified and interviewed. If the offender is unknown, the officer must get a detailed description of him, including his clothing, speech mannerisms, and related identifying characteristics. The officer should determine whether the offender revealed any personal facts such as area of residence or places he frequented. Questions should be asked related to the presence of any accomplices, use of weapons, and make and model of any vehicle involved, among other pertinent factors.

With the increasing prevalence of **date rape drugs** such as Rohypnol and GHB, there are new problems that arise during investigations. The victim may have little or no memory of the assault and may not be sure whether or not an assault took place. The questioning should focus on the events leading up to the incident, the beverages ingested, and who provided them. The officer should question the victim as to any unusual side effects she experienced, as well as typical effects on the victim from alcohol and drugs.[41]

Concluding the Interview   As a result of having been raped, many victims suffer long-term emotional problems. Because of this, it is appropriate for the officer conducting the interview to determine whether the victim has sought assistance for any such problems. It is generally advisable to inform the victim that emotional reactions to rape are common and that counseling is advisable. Victims who are not familiar with available community resources to assist in these matters should be provided with information on referral agencies.

Actual versus False Complaints

There have been many misconceptions regarding rape, one of which is the prevalence of false reports. Approximately 1 to 6 percent of rape reports are fictitious, no greater than the incidence of false reports for other crimes.[42] A victim's reactions and appearance may lead an officer to question the validity of the complaint, but a victim's reactions can be quite varied. Even a jovial attitude displayed by a rape victim is not abnormal. Another reason officers question the validity of rape reports is the prior sexual involvement a victim may have had with an offender. But this is not conclusive. Even prostitutes are subjected to sexual assault, which includes the humiliation and trauma of the crime.

Profiling the Rapist

As with the investigation of many other types of crimes, one of the best methods for solving rape and sexual assault cases is to understand the offender's motivations. The use of the rapist **profile** can aid the criminal investigator in understanding the behavioral patterns of the suspect. Profiling will not solve rape cases but will assist in the investigation by focusing on confirming certain events at a crime scene or by eliminating suspects.

Profiles have been of value to law enforcement agencies when investigators review their investigative files and attempt to apply the information to the case. Similarly, profiles can be used to "match" profile characteristics to newly developed suspects who come into only minimal contact with the investigators.

Research by such experts in the field as A. Nicholas Groth, Ann Burgess, and Robert Hazelwood has led to an improved understanding of rapists and their victims. Groth, a leading expert on sex crimes, describes the role of both the "power" and the "anger" rapist. Groth has developed the main premise behind the rapist profile in his typologies.[43] The power rapist has been subdivided into two personality types: the power-reassurance rapist and power-assertive rapist. The **anger rapist** has also been subdivided into two categories: the anger-retaliatory rapist and the anger-excitation rapist. Note that not all traits discussed below are necessarily seen in every case.

THE POWER-REASSURANCE (MANHOOD) RAPIST The power-reassurance rapist has the primary motivation of power over his victim. Accounting for an estimated 81 percent of rapes that are reported, the term *power* does not imply that he desires to harm his victim physically in any way; he does not. Indeed, his psychological disorder focuses on how he perceives his manhood or lack of it. The preoffense behavior of the power-reassurance rapist includes fantasies about having a sexual affair with a member of the opposite sex. Because of his obsession with proving his manhood, his fantasies revolve around "successful" sexual relations with his partner. It is thought that these fantasies center around a relationship that most of the "normal" population enjoys regularly.

Criminal investigations of this type of rapist show that he will usually deploy a particular "plan of attack." If the rapist persists in his attacks, his plan will become more and more refined but also more easily predicted by investigators. In particular, this class of rapist will usually select victims through prior observation or **stalking**. This may be accomplished through prowling, voyeurism, and so on, typically conducted in residential areas. Statistically, attacks occur in the victim's residence after dark and close to the rapist's own neighborhood. Additionally, he will use weapons of opportunity and verbal threats in his attack.

Ironically, studies have shown that after the attack, the offender is likely to apologize to the victim—hence the nickname "gentleman rapist." He may actually view his actions as nonthreatening to the victim and serving only to satisfy his personal needs. Investigations have also revealed that the attacker will sometimes take a personal article from the victim as a souvenir.

Profile of the Power-Reassurance Rapist[44]

- ☑ Rapes between midnight and 5 A.M. every 7 to 20 days.
- ☑ Selects victims by watching and window-peeping.
- ☑ Seeks women about his own age who are living alone and attacks in their home.
- ☑ Uses a weapon of opportunity.
- ☑ Covers the victim's face or wears a ski mask to prevent identification.
- ☑ Asks the victim to remove her clothing.
- ☑ Performs vaginal sex; may experience premature ejaculation or impotence.
- ☑ Asks the victim to say that she likes his sexual performance.
- ☑ Is socially inadequate, a loner, lives alone or with parents, has a menial job, frequents porno theaters and shops, has been arrested for window-peeping or burglary.
- ☑ Has no vehicle; first rapes within walking distance of his home.

Victim Characteristics of the Power Rapist[45]

☑ The victim is usually of the same race as the attacker.

☑ The victim will probably be alone at the time of initial contact.

☑ The victim will have been evaluated by the attacker as one who probably won't resist attack.

☑ The attacker considers her to be meek, nonaggressive, or easily dominated.

☑ Physical size is commonly used in the rapist's consideration of victims.

☑ The victim is typically attacked through a "surprise" method.

☑ The rapist hopes that she will yield to his "initial" advance.

☑ If the rapist does not get the desired initial response from the victim, he will probably flee the scene.

Profile of the Power-Assertive Rapist[46]

☑ Rapes between 7 P.M. and 1 A.M., every 20 to 25 days.

☑ Selects a victim of opportunity; may meet her in a bar or date two or three times.

☑ Selects a woman about his own age, uses an overpowering or con approach, dominates victim, rapes indoors or outdoors.

☑ Uses a weapon of choice.

☑ Uses no mask, may attempt to hide his face, won't let victim look at him.

☑ Is a macho type, body conscious, athletic; frequents singles bars; has a hard-hat job or is a truck driver.

☑ Is married or divorced, has been arrested for domestic disturbance or crimes against property.

☑ Has a flashy vehicle: sports car or four-wheel-drive pickup.

THE POWER-ASSERTIVE RAPIST The second profile occurs in an estimated 12 percent of rape attacks and involves the assertive personality of the rapist. It is the desire of this person to demonstrate his manhood to the victim through sexual assault. Research has shown that this type of rapist seldom plans his attacks and is an opportunist by nature. His victims are, however, typically of the same race and age group as the assailant. Many such offenders have chosen the bar scene as their hunting ground and may typically choose a bar close to the place where they live or work.

The power-assertive rapist will probably use the con approach with his victim, and after he gets her in a location where he can make his attack, he will use a moderate degree of force. After the assault, he will probably threaten his victim with retaliation if she reports him. As with the previous type of offender, he will also desire an object from the victim as a souvenir, such as an article of clothing. The power-assertive rapist is also thought to be a repeat offender whose future targets are difficult to predict.

THE ANGER-RETALIATORY RAPIST The anger-retaliatory rapist profile is that of a person who vents his anger and frustration toward the opposite sex by punishing them. The punishment is based on either real or imagined wrongs that they have perpetrated against him (or the male population in general). Sexual assault is the means by which he chooses to humiliate them.

This category of rapist, which accounts for an estimated 5 percent of all rapes, typically includes preoffense behavior that involves a significant stressor that typically relates to women. Studies show that this can usually be traced back to the offender's family or work relationships. For example, a rapist's stressor may be a woman who continually demeaned him in his early home life, resulting in stress buildup inside. After storming out of his residence, he comes across an

Profile of Anger-Retaliatory Rapist[47]

- ☑ Rapes any hour of day or night, at irregular 6 to 12-month intervals, after fight with wife or "put-down" by a woman.
- ☑ Selects a victim of opportunity, in his own neighborhood or near work.
- ☑ Selects a woman his same age or older, uses a "blitz" attack.
- ☑ Uses a weapon of opportunity: fists, feet, club; beats victim before, during, and after sexual assault.
- ☑ Performs anal and then oral sex and vaginal sex; has possible retarded ejaculation.
- ☑ Uses much profanity and degrading language.
- ☑ May have arrests for domestic disturbance, speeding, or fighting on the night of the rape.
- ☑ Is a loner, drinker, troublemaker; has an explosive temper; is a sports fan, laborer, construction worker.
- ☑ Is a married man; abuses wife and children; has been arrested for fighting, family disputes, drinking.
- ☑ May have any type of vehicle.

Profile of the Anger-Excitation Rapist[48]

- ☑ Assaults are extremely well planned.
- ☑ His violent fantasies are acted out during the assault.
- ☑ Gloves and mask are included in the **rape kit**.
- ☑ The victim's resistance fuels the attacker's rage.
- ☑ Victim selection is day or night at irregular intervals.
- ☑ Brutal force is used to control his victim.
- ☑ While inflicting pain on the victim, the attacker is usually calm.
- ☑ The victim's clothes are usually cut off her.
- ☑ Video recordings are usually made of the assault.
- ☑ The sadistic rapist has no remorse.
- ☑ He may attempt to hide his face by wearing a hood or mask.

unsuspecting woman who he designates as the target of his rage and frustration. Such an assault is usually spontaneous and results from improper management of that stressor.

Victim selection is usually somewhere near the attacker's residence, and she may possess physical characteristics similar to those of the female stressor in his life (e.g., the same age, the same hairstyle). His characterization of the attack on the victim may sound something like: "She was just in the wrong place at the wrong time." This rapist will typically use a blitz-type attack, with the use of force before, during, and after the attack. Although the actual assault is fairly brief, it is typically violent, and the rapist uses any resistance on the part of the victim to fuel his own anger.

THE ANGER-EXCITATION RAPIST Of all of the rapist profiles discussed, the anger-excitation rapist is the most dangerous. The anger-excitation rapist has a strong propensity toward sadism and is prone to severely injure or even murder his victim. In addition, he enjoys the victim's response to the infliction of pain, usually resulting from torture. The planning stage of the attack is done meticulously by this type of rapist, who harbors images and fantasies about sadistic sexual acts with his victims. Typically, every stage of the attack is carefully thought through.

Victims may have certain traits exhibited by women in the rapist's life with whom he has experienced conflict. Research has shown that this type of rapist will usually use a weapon to gain control of the victim while exposing himself to minimum risk of harm or detection. After the victim is in his control, he will use excessive and brutal force to maintain both psychological and physiological control of her.

The Rapist's Approach

For a more complete profile of the perpetrator, it is important that the investigator document the method of approach used by the attacker. Three such forms of behavior exhibited by rapists are offered by Hazelwood and Burgess:[49]

1. *Con approach.* The victim is approached openly with a subterfuge or "cover." Typically, the attacker is friendly and offers some type of assistance or requests directions.
2. *Blitz approach.* Immediate physical assault is used to subdue the victim. This approach leaves no opportunity to cope verbally or physically and frequently involves the use of a gag or blindfold.
3. *Surprise approach.* The attacker waits for the victim in a secluded area where he won't be discovered and then approaches on his own volition (e.g., hiding in the backseat of an automobile or stepping out from behind a wall).

Methods of Control

Through the careful interview of the victim, investigators should attempt to determine the method of control used by the attacker. This is a significant component to the profiling process in which similar characteristics might be identified in the examination of other rape offenses. According to Hazelwood and Burgess, the use of force may include four levels of severity:[50]

1. *Minimal force.* Little or no force is used, but minimal slapping may be used to intimidate.
2. *Moderate force.* The repeated hitting or slapping of the victim in a painful manner is accompanied by the use of profanity.
3. *Excessive force.* The victim is beaten on all or most parts of her body.
4. *Brutal force.* Sadistic torture and intentional infliction of physical and emotional pain are used.

Studies have revealed that rapists reveal a great deal about themselves during the course of the attack through verbal remarks and comments. This makes it extremely important for the investigator to elicit specific information from the victim as to what the attacker said during the assault, specifically comments regarding demands made of the victim as well as compliments made to the victim during the attack.

Another important step in the investigation is to determine whether or not the attacker stole any items from the victim that might serve as a token or "prize" by which to remember the victim. Such items can be valuable evidence if recovered by police and used as evidence in court.

Summary Checklist

In this chapter, we consider the crime of assault and related offenses such as domestic violence and rape. Investigators must keep basic evidentiary considerations in mind when conducting investigation of assault. These include properly following preliminary investigation protocols, interviewing the victims and witnesses, and identifying evidence.

The pattern of assault is similar to that of homicide. One might say that the difference between the two is that the victim survived. Assaults can occur in many ways.

Studies of assault cases have revealed that most victims of assault (two-thirds to three-fourths of cases) are acquainted with their attacker.

1. **Explain the legal classifications of assault.**

In the past, the terms *assault* and *battery* were used to distinguish between threats and actual contact between suspect and victim. Today, many revised state statutes categorize threats and actual physical contact as simple assault and aggravated assault.

- Simple assault:
  - Threats by one person to cause bodily harm or death to another
  - Purposefully inflicting bodily harm on another
- Aggravated assault:
  - Includes the elements of simple assault plus an element relating to the severity of the attack
  - Is usually committed with a weapon or by some means likely to produce great bodily harm or death
  - Generally at least one additional element is needed to show aggravated assault:
    - High probability of death
    - Serious and/or permanent disfigurement
    - Loss or impairment of body members or organs

2. **Describe the preliminary investigation stages of assault investigations**.

When an officer arrives on the scene of an assault, he or she should:

- Control and disarm those involved in the altercation
- Provide medical aid to injured people
- Separate suspects
- Protect the crime scene
- Give the *Miranda* warning if applicable
- Obtain preliminary statements
- Photograph any evidence observed
- Collect and preserve evidence
- Reconstruct the crime

Responding officers should also establish the severity of the assault by taking photographs and describing all injuries in their notes.

3. **What should be the investigative response to domestic violence?**

Responding to domestic violence calls is one of the most unpleasant duties for police officers. However, an appropriate and effective police response is warranted.

- Responding officers should not park their patrol car within view of the location to which they are responding.
- After the officers have entered the location and secured the area, the investigation begins.
- The first rule is to interview the suspect and victim separately.

- Any evidence that would lead an officer to make an arrest in any other situation also applies to spousal abuse situations.
- The arrest decision should not be based on the officer's perception of the willingness of the victim or witness to testify.
- If it was a mutual assault, officers must try to determine the primary physical aggressor and arrest that person.

4. **What is stalking, who is involved in stalking, and what are the main forms of stalking?**

Stalking involves a pattern of overtly criminal and/or apparently innocent behavior that makes victims fear for themselves or others. It is distinguishable from many other types of crime in two important ways:

- It entails repeat victimization of the person the offender targets.
- It is partly defined by its impact on the victim.

A useful general definition of stalking is: "A course of conduct directed at a specific person that would cause a reasonable person fear."

Stalking is widespread:

- The majority of victims are women and the majority of offenders are men.
- Most victims know their stalkers—many victims are stalked by current or former intimate partners.
- Stalking is often a feature of relationships involving domestic violence.

There are three broad categories of stalking, based on the relationship between the stalker and the victim:

- Intimate or former intimate stalking
- Acquaintance stalking
- Stranger stalking

5. **Identify the investigative and legal aspects of rape and evidence in rape cases**.

The term *rape* has been broadly applied to a wide range of sexual attacks and, in popular terminology, may include same-sex rape and the rape of a male by a female.

- The UCR defines forcible rape as "the carnal knowledge of a female forcibly and against her will."
- By definition, rapes reported under the UCR Program are always of females—sex attacks on males are excluded.

- Some jurisdictions refer to same-sex rape as sexual battery, which involves intentional and wrongful physical contact with a person without his or her consent that entails a sexual component or purpose.
- Statutory rape is the nonforcible rape of a female who is below the age of consent.

According to the common law, the crime of rape of a female over the age of consent involves three elements:

- Carnal knowledge (penetration)
- Forcible submission
- Lack of consent

Rape cases are somewhat unique in that evidence may present itself in three general areas:

- On the crime scene
- On the victim
- On the suspect (or at locations occupied by the suspect)

The crime scene should be secured and a search for physical evidence begun as soon as possible.

- The victim's clothing may provide valuable information and should be collected and preserved for laboratory analysis.
- Rape victims should receive medical attention and undergo an examination as soon as possible after the incident.

6. **Describe the different rapist profiles.**

The use of rapist profiles can aid criminal investigators in understanding the behavioral patterns of suspects.

Profiles can be used to "match" profile characteristics to newly developed suspects who come into only minimal contact with the investigators.

Groth suggests that rapists are either "power" or "anger" rapists and has identified two types of each:

- The power-reassurance (manhood) rapist—primary motivation is power over his victim.
- The power-assertive rapist—the rapist's primary desire is to demonstrate his manhood to the victim through sexual assault.
- The anger-retaliatory rapist—the offender vents his anger and frustration toward the opposite sex by punishing them.
- The anger-excitation rapist—this offender has a strong propensity toward sadism, is prone to severely injure or murder his victim, and enjoys the victim's response to the infliction of pain and torture.

7. **What are the primary methods of approach used by rapists?**

Hazelwood and Burgess have identified three methods of approach that are exhibited by rapists:

- The con approach—the victim is approached openly with a subterfuge or "cover."
- The blitz approach—immediate physical assault is used to subdue the victim.
- Surprise approach—the attacker waits for the victim in a secluded area and then approaches of his own volition.

Key Terms

acquaintance stalking	domestic violence	rape kit
aggravated assault	forcible rape	resistance
anger rapist	gang rape	restraining order
anger-excitation rapist	intimate or former intimate stalking	self-defense
anger-retaliatory rapist	mutual assault	sexual assault
assault	power-assertive rapist	sexual battery
carnal knowledge	power-reassurance rapist	simple assault
corroboration	primary physical aggressor	stalking
cyberstalking	profile	statutory rape
date rape	protection orders	stranger stalking
date rape drug	rape	

Discussion Questions

1. List and describe various types of assault.
2. Describe the stages of investigation for the crime of assault.
3. Discuss recent models of legislation in which police deal with domestic abuse.
4. Explain the problem of stalking and the investigative response to it.
5. Define cyberstalking and explain the legal responses to cyberstalking.
6. Explain why assaults in bars and taverns are a serious issue.
7. What are the legal elements of a rape?
8. Discuss the problem of date rape and why it is such a difficult crime to investigate.
9. Discuss the major points to remember when interviewing a rape victim.
10. What types of evidence should be sought in a rape case?
11. What are some of the evidentiary concerns that investigators must face when investigating a rape case?

Notes

1. USA Today Nationline. *Four injured, 2 arrested in school brawl.* March 8, 2012.
2. Federal Bureau of Investigation. (2011). *Crime in the United States, 2010.*
3. Ibid.
4. Federal Bureau of Investigation. (2011). *Crime in the United States, 2010.*
5. Sampson, R. (2007). *Domestic violence. Problem oriented guides for police.* Washington, DC: U.S. Department of Justice, January, p. 1
6. Ibid.
7. Heise, L. and J. Roberts. (1990). Reflections on a movement: The U.S. battle against women abuse. In M. Schuler (Ed.), *Freedom from violence: Women's strategies round the world.* Line Village, NV: Copperhouse Publishing, pp. 5–12.
8. Buzawa, E. and C. Buzawa. (2003). *Domestic violence: The criminal justice response,* 3rd ed. Thousand Oaks, London, and New Delhi: SAGE Publications.
9. Ibid.
10. Healey, K., C. Smith, and C. O'Sullivan. (1998). *Batterer intervention: Program approaches and criminal justice strategies.* Washington, DC: U.S. Department of Justice, National Institute of Justice. Available at http://www.ncjrs.gov/pdffiles/168638.pdf.
11. Ibid.
12. Tjaden, P. and N. Thoennes. (2000). Stalking in America: Prevalence, characteristics, and police response. In C. Brito and E. Gratto (Eds.), *Problem-oriented policing: Crime-specific problems, critical issues, and making POP work.* Washington, DC: Police Executive Research Forum.
13. Ibid.
14. U.S. Department of Justice. (2001). *Stalking and domestic violence: Report to congress.* Washington, DC: U.S. Department of Justice.
15. Ibid.
16. Ibid.
17. Heise and J. Roberts. (1990). *Reflections on a movement.*
18. Violence Against Women Grants Office. (1998). *Stalking and domestic violence: The third annual report to congress under the violence against women act.* Washington, DC: U.S. Department of Justice (NCJ-172204).
19. Brody, J. (1998). Deep disorders drive stalkers, experts say. *Star Tribune,* August 30, p. E5.
20. Alvord, V. (1999). Cyberstalkers must beware of the law. *USA Today,* November 8, p. 22A; National Institute of Justice. (1997). The crime of stalking: How big is the problem? *Research Preview* 10–11; National Institute of Justice. (1998). Centers for disease control and prevention. *Stalking in America: Findings from the national violence against women survey.* Washington, DC: U.S. Department of Justice, Office of Justice Programs; Willing, R. (1998). Men stalking men: Stalkers often gravitate toward positions of power. *USA Today,* June 17, p. 1A.
21. National Institute of Justice. (1998). *Stalking in America.*
22. Alvord, V. (1999). Cyberstalkers must beware of the law. *USA Today,* November 8, p. 22A.
23. Ibid.
24. Tjaden, P. and N. Thoennes. (1998). *Prevalence, incidence, and consequences of violence against women: Findings from the National Violence against women survey.* National Institute of Justice. *Research in Brief.* Washington, DC: U.S. Department of Justice.
25. Ibid.
26. Graham, K., P. West, and S. Wells. (2000). Evaluating theories of alcohol-related aggression using observations of young adults in bars. *Addiction* 95(6):847–863.
27. Graham, K. and R. Homel. (1997). Creating safer bars. In M. Plan, E. Single, and T. Stockwell (Eds.), *Alcohol: Minimizing the harm. What Works?* London and New York: Free Association Books.
28. Graham, K., G. Schmidt, and K. Gillis. (1996). Circumstances when drinking leads to aggression: An overview of research findings. *Contemporary drug problems* 23(3):493–557.

29. LANNING, K. W. AND R. R. HAZELWOOD. (1988). The maligned investigator of criminal sexuality. *FBI Law Enforcement Bulletin,* September:1–10.

30. FEDERAL BUREAU OF INVESTIGATION. (2011). *Crime in the United States, 2010.*

31. IBID.

32. IBID.

33. See for example, THE AMERICAN PROSECUTORS RESEARCH INSTITUTE. (1999). *The prosecution of rohypnol and GHB related sexual assaults.*

34. Peoplev. Mccann, 76 Ill. App. 3rd 184, 186, 394 N.E.2d 1055, 1056 (2d Dist. 1979).

35. MEYER, T. (1984). Date rape: A serious campus problem that few talk about. *Chronicle of Higher Education,* December 5.

36. GRIFFITHS, G. L. (1985). The overlooked evidence in rape investigations. *FBI Law Enforcement Bulletin,* April:8–15.

37. HAZELWOOD, R. AND A. BURGESS. (1987). *Practical aspects of rape investigation.* Boca Raton, FL: CRC Press.

38. ROSE, K. (2007). Sexual assault virtual training takes responders from exam room to courtroom. *National Institute of Justice Journal* (258), October:11–15.

39. IBID.

40. HEISE, L. L. (1993). Reproductive freedom and violence against women: Where are the intersections? *Journal of Law, Medicine & Ethics* 21(2):206–216.

41. See, for example, *Drug facilitated sexual assault: Rohypnol and GHB. Training key,* No.509. Alexandria, VA: International Association of Chiefs of Police, 1999.

42. LEDRAY, L. E. (1994). *Recovering from rape.* New York: Henry Holt and Company, p. 227.

43. GROTH, A. N., ET AL. (1977). Rape: Power, anger and sexuality. *American Journal of Psychiatry* 134(11):1239–1243.

44. IBID.

45. IBID.

46. IBID.

47. IBID.

48. IBID.

49. HAZELWOOD AND BURGESS. (1987). *Practical aspects of rape investigation.*

50. IBID.

CHAPTER 12

This chapter will enable you to:

1. Summarize trends regarding missing and abducted persons.

2. Identify the different types of missing children cases.

3. Describe how a missing person investigation is conducted.

4. Summarize efforts to protect children, including Amber Alerts and the Code Adam program.

5. Summarize the trends and types of crimes against children.

6. Describe how investigations of crimes against children are conducted.

7. Explain the challenges of interviewing children and using children as witnesses.

© ZUMA Wire Service / Alamy

Missing and Abducted Persons

Introduction

 On June 10, 1991, 11-year-old Jaycee Lee Dugard was abducted from a school bus stop within sight of her stepfather, Carl Probyn, who was standing in their home in South Lake Tahoe, California. Probyn saw two people in a gray sedan (possibly a Mercury Monarch or Mercury Zephyr) make a U-turn at the school bus stop where Dugard was waiting, and forced her into the car despite her struggles. He then gave chase on a bicycle but he was unable to overtake their vehicle. For almost 20 years, Probyn remained a suspect in Jaycee's disappearance. Eighteen years later, on August 26, 2009, Jaycee appeared in the office of her alleged kidnapper's parole officer in California, and her identity was confirmed the following day.[1]

Arrested for Jaycee's kidnapping were 58-year-old Phillip Craig Garrido along with his wife, 55-year-old Nancy Garrido, of Antioch, California. The investigation into the kidnapping revealed that Jaycee was kept in a concealed area behind Garrido's house in Antioch, California, for 18 years. Jaycee gave birth to two daughters, now aged 15 and 11, during this time. Jaycee's abductor, Garrido, fathered the children. While Jaycee and her daughters never went to school or saw a doctor, they remained physically healthy.

The details of Jaycee's abduction are disturbing. After the abduction, the Garridos took Dugard to their home in a low-rent, unincorporated area within northeast Antioch. They later built a privacy fence around the property, which already had several large trees in the yard. Phillip Garrido was found to have violated his parole and was returned to federal prison from April to August of 1993.[2]

While she was captive, Dugard had access to the business phone and had an e-mail account. One customer of the printing business indicated that she never hinted to him about her childhood abduction or true identity. Her two daughters told others she was their older sister.

In 2006, one of Garrido's neighbors called 9-1-1 to inform them that there were tents in the backyard with children living there and that Garrido was a "psychotic" with sexual addictions. A deputy sheriff spoke with Garrido at the front of the house for about 30 minutes and left after telling him there would be a code violation if people were living outside the property. After Dugard was found in August 2009 the local police issued an apology.

On August 24, 2009, Garrido went to a University of California, Berkeley, police office seeking permission to hold a special Christian event on campus referred to as a part of his "God's Desire" program. He spoke with UC Berkeley special events manager Lisa Campbell. Campbell found his behavior odd and asked him to make an appointment for the next day. She notified campus police officer Ally Jacobs, who ran a background check on Garrido and learned he was on parole for rape.

Garrido arrived the next day with two girls, aged 11 and 15, whom he introduced as his daughters. At the meeting Jacobs noticed that the girls' behavior displayed some of the same detachment and religious fervor as their father, along with their drab dresses. When asked about a bump near her eye, the younger girl suggested that it was congenital and untreatable, which, because of the way *she said it, seemed to Jacobs to be rehearsed. Jacobs later stated about the meeting that the girls "had this weird look in their eyes like brainwashed zombies." After the meeting, Jacobs attempted to contact Garrido's parole officer to express her concern about the welfare of the two girls.[3]*

The next day, the parole office talked to Jacobs and was shocked to learn that Garrido had children. He called Garrido and asked him to come in for a parole meeting. Later that day Garrido arrived at the meeting with his wife, the two girls, and Jaycee Dugard, whom they all referred by the name "Allissa." After being separated from Garrido for a further interview, the three were discovered to be Dugard and two children she had borne. Garrido and his wife were then arrested by local police. An FBI agent put Dugard on the telephone with her mother, Terry Probyn, who at first thought the call was a prank. Dugard retained custody of her children and was soon reunited with her mother.

The Jaycee Dugard case is an example of the tragedy of missing person cases and how difficult such cases are to investigate. In the Jaycee Dugard case, she was missing for 18 years and gave birth to two daughters fathered by her abductor. Jaycee's case demonstrates the need for a swift investigative response to child abductions to identify and capture those involved in abductions and return victims safely to their homes.

A Look at the "Big Picture"

To begin out discussion of missing and abducted persons we should first consider the extent this presents a problem in American society. Indeed, the statistics show that missing and abducted persons are a serious and ongoing problem. For example, in 2010 the FBI reported that there were 85,820 "active" missing person files. Looking closer, juveniles under the age of 18 account for 38,505 (44.9 percent) of the records and 10,248 (11.9 percent) were for juveniles between the ages of 18 and 20.[4]

Ncic Missing Person File Report For 2010	
Missing Person	
Active Entries as of December 31, 2010	85,820
Total File Transactions	1,927,722
Entries	692,944
Removed	703,316
Locates	46,397
Modified	290,418
Modified Supplemental	159,784
Canceled Supplemental	3,418
Queried Missing Person File Only	31,445
Queried NCIC System-Wide by Name	1,870,669,249

Source: FBI National Crime Information Center. (2011). Available at http://www.fas.org/irp/agency/doj/fbi/is/ncic.htm

According to the FBI, during the course of the year 2010, 692,944 missing person records were entered into the **National Crime Information Center (NCIC)**.[5] This represents a decrease of 3.7 percent from the 719,558 records entered in 2009. Missing person records cleared or canceled during the same period totaled 703,316. Reasons for these removals included a law enforcement

|Fig. 12.1| △

The prevalence of missing persons can be seen in print and electronic media. Here, Yvonne Parker, the mother of 33-year-old Michelle Parker, shows a missing persons poster following her 2011 disappearance in Pine Castle, Florida.

Red Huber / MCT / Newscom

agency located the subject; the individual returned home; or the record had to be removed by the entering agency due to a determination that the record was invalid. Of the 692,944 figure, 312,710 (96.9 percent) were indexed as Runaway, 2,577 (0.8 percent) as Abducted by Non-Custodial Parent, 367 (0.1 percent) as Abducted by Stranger, and 6,944 (2.2 percent) as Adult.[6]

Although this chapter addresses missing and abducted persons in general, it focuses primarily on the thousands of children who are discovered missing each year. The magnitude of the missing and abducted problem is complex, multifaceted, and disturbing. For example, there are different types of missing children cases, including family abductions; endangered runaways; nonfamily abductions; and lost, injured, or otherwise missing children. National estimates for the number of missing children are from incidence studies conducted by the U.S. Department of Justice's Office of Juvenile Justice and Delinquency Prevention.

Child abduction cases, such as the Jaycee Dugard case, occur all too often. According to the National Center for Missing and Exploited Children (NCMEC), every year, more than 200,000 children are abducted by family members. An additional 58,000 are taken by nonrelatives with primarily sexual motives. However, only 115 reported abductions represent cases in which strangers abduct and kill children, hold them for ransom, or take them with the intention to keep, as with Jaycee Dugard.[7]

Child abductions are one of society's greatest concerns. Investigators know that they must move quickly to capture perpetrators because, according to the FBI, 74 percent of children abducted and murdered were killed within the first 3 hours of their disappearance.[8]

Electronic and print media often report that abductors primarily consist of strangers or registered sex offenders. Research has proven this to be untrue at least between 2009 and 2011. When

---

In 2009, the National Center for Missing and Exploited Children Reported the Following Instances of Missing and Abducted Children

☑ 797,500 children (younger than age 18 years) were reported missing in a one-year period of time studied resulting in an average of 2,185 children being reported missing each day.

☑ 203,900 children were the victims of family abductions.

☑ 58,200 children were the victims of nonfamily abductions.

☑ 115 children were the victims of "stereotypical" kidnapping. (These crimes involve someone the child does not know or someone of slight acquaintance who holds the child overnight, transports the child 50 miles or more, kills the child, demands ransom, or intends to keep the child permanently.)

Source: National Center for Missing and Exploited Children, 2011

a child is reported missing, members of the media advise parents to check sex offender registries to prevent their child from possible abduction or sexual victimization. However, according to the FBI, registered sex offenders are only a small percentage of the problem. For example, in 2009, a registered sex offender was the abductor in only 2 percent of child abduction cases. The following year, in 2010, this figure dropped to 1 percent.[9]

Statistics show that there are an estimated 100 cases per year in the United States in which a child is abducted and murdered. The victims of these cases are "average" children leading normal lives and living with normal families, typical low-risk victims. The vast majority of them are girls (76 percent), with the average age being slightly older than 11 years of age. In 80 percent of cases, the initial contact between the victim and killer is within 1/4 mile of the victim's residence.[10]

Profiling the Abductor

A kidnapping is the type of abduction that is most harmful to the child, both psychologically and physically. Many child abductions also involve some type of sexual abuse. An earlier study funded by the Justice Department's Office of Juvenile Justice and Delinquency Prevention (OJJDP) provided additional insight on the child abduction problem. This 1997 survey examined 600 abduction cases across the nation. The findings were very similar to those of the **National Incidence Studies of Missing, Abducted, Runaway and Throwaway Children (NISMART)** project.[11]

More than half (57 percent) of child abduction murders are committed by a killer who is a stranger to the victim. Family involvement in this type of case is infrequent (9 percent). However, the relationship between the victim and the killer varies with the gender and age of the victim. Whereas the youngest girls, one to five years old, tend to be killed by friends or acquaintances (64 percent), the oldest young women, 16 to 17 years old, tend to be killed by strangers (also 64 percent). The relationship between the killer and victim is different for the male victims. The youngest male victims (one to five years old) are most likely to be killed by strangers (also 64 percent), as are teenage boys (13 to 15 years old, and 16 to 17 years old, 58 percent).[12]

The average age of killers of abducted children is around 27 years. They are predominantly unmarried (85 percent) and half of them (51 percent) either live alone (17 percent) or with their parents (34 percent). Half of them are unemployed, and those that are employed work in unskilled or semiskilled labor occupations. Therefore, the killers can generally be characterized as "social marginals."[13]

Almost two-thirds of the killers (61 percent) had prior arrests for violent crimes, with slightly more than half of the killers' prior crimes (53 percent) committed against children. The most frequent prior crimes against children were rape (31 percent of killers) and other sexual assault (45 percent of killers). Sixty-seven percent of the child abduction murderers' prior crimes were similar in method of operation (MO) to the murder that was committed by the same killer.[14]

Commonly, the killers are at the initial victim–killer contact site for a legitimate reason (66 percent). They either lived in the area (29 percent) or were engaging in some normal activity. Most of the victims of child abduction murder are victims of opportunity (57 percent). Only in 14 percent of cases did the killer choose his victim because of some physical characteristic of the victim. The primary motivation for the child abduction murder is sexual assault. After the victim has been killed, 52 percent of the bodies are concealed to prevent discovery.[15] In only 9 percent of cases is the body openly placed to ensure its discovery.

A unique pattern of distance relationships exists in child abduction murders. The initial contact site is within 1/4 mile of the victim's last known location in 80 percent of cases. Conversely, the distance between the initial contact site and the murder site increases to distances greater than 1/4 mile (54 percent). The distance from the murder site to the body recovery site again decreases to less than 200 feet in 72 percent of cases. It was discovered that once the murder investigation has begun, the name of the killer is known to the police within the first week in 74 percent of cases.[16]

The Elizabeth Smart kidnapping emphasizes several characteristics that child abductors seem to have in common. First, they most often have a prior visual sighting of the victim, and the initial contact is frequently made at or near the home. Secondly, the motivation for the crime is often sexual in nature. The victim is usually a girl younger than age 14 years, and the suspect is an unemployed white male with a criminal record. Although the alleged kidnapper, Brian Mitchell, was 20 years older than the NISMART average, he fit the profile reasonably well. Elizabeth Smart could be considered a very lucky victim. That's because girls her age who are abducted under similar circumstances stand a very good chance of being killed.

The duration of a kidnapping episode was usually less than 24 hours (90 percent). Only fewer than 10 percent last longer than one day. Nonfamily abductions show the same patterns, although 30 percent of them last less than even three hours. The most dramatic difference between non-family abductions and kidnappings is in the treatment of the victim. In 99 percent of nonfamily abductions, the child is returned alive. In kidnappings, a safe return occurs only 57 percent of the time. Ominously, the child suffers a sexual or physical assault in an astounding 86 percent of the stereotypical kidnappings. These findings strongly emphasize the extreme danger of these events and the urgency of police intervention as soon as possible.

Stereotypical kidnapping, in which a child is abducted and either assaulted or held for ransom, is a crime that first appeared in the United States in the late nineteenth century. During the 1920s, it became entrenched in the public consciousness when a series of child abduction cases terrified parents across the country.

Case in Point

>>Investigating the Disappearance of Stacy Peterson

On October 18, 2003, Bolingbrook, Illinois, Police Officer Drew Peterson married Stacy Ann Peterson (Cales). Stacy, Peterson's fourth wife, went missing on October 28, 2007, and was officially reported missing in the early hours of October 29, 2007, after her sister, Cassandra Cales, failed to hear from her when expected. Drew Peterson claimed that Stacy called him at 9 P.M. on Sunday to tell him that she had left him for another man and that she had left her car at Bolingbrook's Clow International Airport.

Peterson had a 29-year career as a police officer. He began working with the Bolingbrook Police Department in 1977. A year later, he was assigned to Metropolitan Area Narcotics Squad, and in 1979, he was awarded "Police Officer of the Year" from the department. In 1985, he was fired from the Bolingbrook Police Department after the village board of police and fire commissioners found him guilty of disobedience, conducting a self-assigned investigation, failure to report a bribe immediately, and official misconduct. He had been indicted two months earlier on charges of official misconduct and failure to report a bribe.

Indictments alleged that Peterson solicited drugs in exchange for information about his agency. The charges were later dropped. Special prosecutor Raymond Bolden said at the time that the charges were not provable. Peterson won reinstatement with the department in March 1986. Judge Edwin Grabiec ruled that police and fire commissioners lacked sufficient evidence to find Peterson guilty of the charges. Peterson was also accused of using excessive force for allegedly breaking the thumb of an arrestee in May 2007. The charges were later dismissed on the grounds that Peterson was neither present during the arrest nor was on duty that day.

After Stacy's (his fourth wife) disappearance on October 28, 2007, Peterson retired as a Bolingbrook police sergeant on December 2007. On November 15, 2007, the Bolingbrook Police Pension Board voted to allow Peterson to collect his pension of $6,067.71 per month, stating current law gave them no option because Peterson had not been convicted of a crime.

Peterson's wives: Peterson's first wife was Carol (Hamilton) Brown. The two were married from 1974 to 1980 and divorced after she learned about his infidelity. Peterson's second wife was Victoria Connolly, who he married in 1982. Connolly has alleged a history of abuse during her 10-year marriage to Peterson, as has her daughter, who lived in the household during this time, from the age of 8 to 17 years. In 2007, Connolly stated that Peterson "was a legend in his own mind." The couple divorced after Peterson started dating Kathleen Savio, who later became his third wife. Peterson's divorce from Carol Brown was finalized on February 18, 1992. He married Savio two months later.

Peterson and Savio were married until their divorce on October 10, 2003. Reportedly, between 2002 and 2004, police were called out to the Peterson house 18 times on domestic disturbance calls. On March 1, 2004, Kathleen Savio's body was found in a waterless bathtub. Her death was initially ruled an accidental drowning by a coroner's jury that included a police officer who personally knew Peterson and assured the other jurors that Peterson was "a good man who would never hurt his wife."

However, after Stacy Peterson's disappearance, Savio's body was exhumed and underwent forensic examination on November 16, 2007. Dr. Michael Baden, a former New York City chief medical examiner who conducted the examination at the request of Savio's relatives and Fox News, concluded that she died of drowning following a struggle when her body was placed in the bathtub. Illinois State Attorney James Glasgow told the press that after examining evidence in the case, he believed that the death was a "homicide staged to look like an accident." On

(continued)

Case in Point (continued)

February 21, 2008, Glasgow announced that a pathologist determined that Savio's death was a homicide, adding that the death had been investigated as such reopening the case after the exhumation.

The investigation: The Illinois State Police, along with agents from the FBI, investigated a number of leads in Stacy's disappearance and the death of Kathleen Savio. Four search warrants were executed on Drew Peterson's property after Stacy's disappearance, including seizure of his vehicle and Stacy's vehicle and of Drew's 11 firearms.

A longtime friend of Peterson, Rick Mims, admitted that he and Peterson bought three blue containers from a cable company where they both worked part time in 2003. Mims also provided photos of the containers to police and has sold his story to the tabloids for an undisclosed sum of money. Peterson's stepbrother, Thomas Morphey, who has a history of drug and alcohol addiction, attempted suicide two days after allegedly helping Drew carry a large blue plastic container from Peterson's Bolingbrook home to his sport utility vehicle, fearing he may have helped dispose of the body of Stacy Peterson.

Neighbors reported seeing Peterson and another man hauling a 55-gallon barrel, large enough to hold a person, out of the house shortly after Stacy's disappearance. There were also reports of truckers referring to the containers, but their stories were treated as not credible after it was found they were not in the Bolingbrook area at the times they claimed.

One theory was that Stacy Peterson was romantically involved with Scott Anthony Rossetto or his brother Keith Rossetto, both of Shorewood, Illinois. Both Rossetto brothers denied this allegation. Investigators have speculated that Peterson's body may have been dumped near Rossetto's home in an effort to frame him as the killer.

On May 7, 2009, Peterson was indicted by the Will County Grand Jury and arrested for the murder of his third wife, Kathleen Savio. Bail was set at $20 million. While being arrested, Peterson joked, "I guess I should have returned those library books." As of the writing of this text, Drew Peterson has not been convicted of the death of Stacy Peterson but on September 6, 2012, he was convicted of killing Savio.

|Fig. 12.2| △

Stacy Peterson

|Fig. 12.3| △

Drew Peterson

(continued)

Case in Point (continued)

Thematic Question

Considering Drew Peterson was convicted of Kathleen Savio's murder in 2012, do you believe that he is also responsible for the death of Stacey Peterson? To what extent does the evidence support your conclusion, and what additional evidence should be identified to support bringing criminal charges against him for the killing of Stacy Peterson?

Sources: Walberg, M. and J. Napolitano. Expert: 3rd wife was slain. *Chicago Tribune.* November 17, 2007; Hosey, J. and J. Lundquist. The man Stacy turned to. *The Bolingbrook Sun.* November 18, 2007; Slife, E., EXCLUSIVE: Peterson's second wife tells her story. *Chicago Tribune.* November 16, 2007; Peterson case: Did cops protect one of their own? November 30; Fox Chicago. *Drew Peterson is now accused of police brutality.* Available at http://www.myfoxchicago.com, December 17, 2007; FoxNews.com. *Missing mom Stacy Peterson's family wants husband, Drew, to take lie detector test,* November 30, 2007; NBC5.com Chicago. Peterson's family demands Drew take lie detector test, November 27, 2007; FoxNews.com. *Drew Peterson charged with murdering third wife, held on $20M bond.* Available at http://www.foxnews.com/story/0,2933,519392,00.html, May 7, 2009; Savio V. (2007). *Peterson complaint.* Available at http://www.scribd.com/doc/14542696/Savio-v-Peterson-Complaint; Tarm, M. Relatives try to confront Ill. officer. Available at ABC News.com, November 17, 2007.

Types of Missing Children Cases

In general, missing children cases fall into three basic categories: nonfamily abduction, family abduction, and runaway (or lost).

The **nonfamily abduction** case, in which a child is removed without authorization from his or her family by force or trickery, is the most complex and dangerous type of missing child case. In this situation, time is of the essence because the child is considered to be in great danger. Many experts believe that the first few hours after an abduction are the most dangerous for children.[17]

Also included in this category are abductions of newborns and infants from health care facilities, malls, grocery stores, and public transportation facilities, as well as other public places where the mother's or child care provider's attention may be diverted. Although the snatching of newborns is not a crime of epidemic proportions, naturally, it causes tremendous trauma for the parents or guardians. The offender almost always is a woman and generally does not harm the baby because she usually abducts the child in order to have a baby of her own.

The second type of case is the **family abduction**, which generally occurs in conjunction with divorce and separation. In this type of case, the noncustodial parent removes the child from the care of the **custodial parent** and may flee to another state or even another country with the child. The child may be at risk with the noncustodial parent. There have been recent cases across the nation in which the child of a family abduction was murdered by the noncustodial parent, who then committed suicide. Family abductions are often very complex cases involving court orders, child protection services, and hidden agendas, as well as raw emotions and sometimes extreme possessiveness toward the children on the part of one or both parents.

The third type of missing child case involves the **runaway or lost child**, who is defined as runaway child, often a teenager, who leaves home voluntarily or for a variety of reasons.[18] This category of missing person could be in great danger depending on such factors as age, maturity, and intelligence. The voluntary runaway child is the most common missing child case encountered by law enforcement officers.

Abductions via the Internet

Some child abductions have been connected to the Internet as a result of the easy access both the child and predator have to this worldwide communications network. Susceptible preteens and teens are sometimes lured into false friendships in Internet "chat rooms" and then kidnapped from a prearranged meeting place. In other cases, the abductor may send the child money and a bus ticket to meet in another state. Children and teens who get involved in chat room conversations on the Internet have no way to know exactly who they're talking to. One of the many attractions of chat rooms is the anonymity they provide. People can be anyone they choose to be online, where real identities are hidden and fictitious names and personalities emerge.

In one case, a preteen boy was lured to San Francisco by an adult male pedophile with a large collection of child pornography. The youth told his friends at school and showed them the bus ticket and money he was sent. His friends revealed this information to the police only after the boy was reported missing. A nationwide search was initiated, and they were questioned.

How do investigators determine if a missing child case involves an Internet lure? A computer in a child's room or home with an Internet connection can steer the investigation in this direction, especially if the parents or guardians reveal that the child spent a lot of time "online" and talked about new friends made via "chat rooms." Another clue is the sudden disappearance of the child for no apparent reason (e.g., there was no recent fight between the child and parents, yet the child was gone one day when the parents returned from work). In a case like this, the investigator should check to see whether the child took any favorite possessions, a suitcase, duffle bag or backpack, clothes, or money. Missing possessions indicate a runaway, but runaways are not always what they appear to be.

Other clues to the child's disappearance can be found on the computer itself. The computer may yield electronic mail (e-mail) saved on the hard drive, a disk, or a printout. The child may have left notes in schoolbooks that would provide clues, such as the online friend's address, phone number, or e-mail address. Before searching computers for data and evidence, the investigator should consult with the department attorney as well as agency computer specialists because complex investigations involving computer systems and online access services present unique technical, operational, and legal problems.

Because of the threat Internet predators pose, there have been efforts to use the Internet as a resource to prevent child abduction or to help the families of those who have been abducted. Many organizations have set up websites where users can go to gain knowledge or contribute help to stopping child abduction. Among these are the organizations Enough is Enough and National Center for Missing and Exploited Children, which have partnered with the online community MySpace to help keep the Internet a safe place for children. MySpace also features pages and groups dedicated to helping find missing children.[19]

Legislative History of Child Abduction

In today's increasingly technological world, many people's views concerning police and criminal investigation have become distorted by what they see on television. Those unfamiliar with investigations of missing persons often have watched television shows wherein FBI agents respond and take over all manner of missing person cases, which they then successfully resolve within the one-hour time frame. Many of the general public believe, based on such shows, that the FBI automatically responds to any case involving a missing person. In reality, the local "cop on the beat" usually arrives as the first law enforcement officer on the scene and begins the investigation.[20] At one time, no federal agency had responsibility or jurisdiction to investigate these cases. Kidnapped, lost, or missing people were considered a problem best dealt with by local law enforcement. This changed dramatically, however, with the 1932 kidnapping of Charles Lindbergh's infant son.

As the first person to fly solo across the Atlantic Ocean, Charles Lindbergh became one of America's most notable heroes. This was an incredibly courageous undertaking. In 1927, planes were not reliable; navigation over water was dangerous because there were no landmarks; and choosing additional fuel over the weight of a radio, Lindbergh had no way to communicate if problems arose. After his successful flight, the young hero faced all of the positive and negative aspects of becoming immensely famous. Without a doubt, the most heartbreaking result of this notoriety occurred in 1932, when kidnappers abducted the Lindbergh's baby son from a bedroom in their Hopewell, New Jersey, home and left a ransom note. Several days later, the child was found dead. Local authorities in Hopewell and the New Jersey State Police shared jurisdiction for the investigation, which made national headlines. Although both kidnappers were caught, convicted, and executed, the public was appalled that the vast resources of the federal government could not be immediately focused on a case of this magnitude. Congress responded later that year with the passage of the **Federal Kidnapping Act**,[21] which allowed the use of federal agencies in kidnapping cases.

Few changes occurred in the investigation of missing children from 1932 until 1968. As society changed and divorce became more prevalent, child custody issues took on increasing importance.[22] During a divorce proceeding, one parent normally was awarded custody of the child or children.

To change this, all the other parent had to do was go to another state, find a judge to issue a conflicting order that granted that parent custody, and simply not return to the state where the first order was issued. Although the second ruling could be challenged, it was a long, expensive process that often proved unsuccessful. In 1968, the U.S. Congress addressed this with the passage of the **Uniform Child Custody Jurisdiction Act (UCCJA)**,[23] which made the practice of moving to another state for the purpose of changing custody illegal. Unfortunately, conflicting court orders still were issued, causing confusion for law enforcement officers when parents reported their children as missing. Which court order to enforce had to be decided on a case-by-case basis.

The problem of missing children continued to grow. During the 1980s, the federal government enacted several measures that provided law enforcement with tools necessary to investigate these cases. In 1980, Congress passed the **Parental Kidnapping Prevention Act** to strengthen the UCCJA and allowed states to use the Federal Parent Locator Service to obtain address information on noncustodial parents who abducted their children. This act also authorized the use of the **Fugitive Felon Act**[24] against these same individuals. In 1982, Congress changed National Crime Information Center (NCIC) rules to allow the entry of missing children into the system. Before this, police had to obtain a warrant for the noncustodial parent's arrest. At the time, most jurisdictions considered these cases strictly as civil matters and would not issue warrants, which meant that the vast majority of children taken by a noncustodial parent were not eligible for entry into NCIC. The **Missing Children Act of 1982**[25] allowed the entry of these missing children even though the noncustodial parent would not be charged with a crime. Two years later, Congress revisited this issue yet again and passed the **Missing Children's Assistance Act (MCAA)**,[26] creating a national clearinghouse for missing children and authorizing research to determine the extent of the problem within this country.

Globalization also has played a role in this field. Congress recognized this and, in 1988, ratified the Hague Convention treaty on missing children with the passage of the **International Child Abduction Remedies Act**,[27] whereby the U.S. Department of State would become involved in noncustodial parental abductions in which the abducting parent takes the victim outside the boundaries of the United States.

As the research ordered by the MCAA of 1984 started to come in, society began to recognize the extent of the problem with missing and exploited children. In 1990, Congress again stepped up and passed the National Child Search Assistance Act (NCSAA),[28] mandating law enforcement agencies to enter each reported missing child (younger than 18 years of age) into NCIC, including all reported runaways. NCSAA also increased the involvement of the **National Center for Missing and Exploited Children (NCMEC)** with law enforcement throughout the country. In 1993, those in law enforcement involved in combating international kidnapping received additional support from Congress with the passage of the International Parental Kidnapping Crime Act,[29] making it a felony for a person to remove a child from the United States in an attempt to interfere with lawful court orders granted in custody matters.

Finally, in 1994, Congress passed the **Jacob Wetterling Crimes Against Children and Sexually Violent Offender Registration Act**,[30] designed to determine the number of sex offenders and provide law enforcement with a readily accessible database with possible suspect information should a child go missing. Later modification under Megan's law permits law enforcement to provide information on registered sex offenders to the general public, resulting in numerous publicly accessible websites. Congress made this act stronger in 2006 with federal penalties for failure to register. In 2007, a national database will begin operating.

The discussion thus far and the changing legislation in this area show that the focus and extent of this problem has changed dramatically, especially since 1980. However, the law enforcement community still does not know its true extent because the NCMEC receives fewer than 200 stranger-abduction reports annually.[31] What the profession has learned from the growing statistics compiled by the NCMEC, coupled with supporting legislation passed over the years, is that an ongoing problem exists with noncustodial parental abductions. These crimes—most states consider them felonies—normally are committed against children because the abductors refuse to accept the lawful issuance of a court order.[32]

Amber Alerts

In 2003, Congress took a monumental step in fighting child abductions with the passage of the Prosecutorial Remedies and Other Tools to End the Exploitation of Children Today Act, or, more commonly, the PROTECT Act.[33] Considered by many to be the most comprehensive legislation designed to ensure the safety of children ever passed, the PROTECT Act also created the AMBER (America's Missing: Broadcast Emergency Response) Alert system. The Amber Alert is a partnership involving law enforcement, other government agencies, and the news media to produce public service announcements about certain abducted children whose cases meet identified criteria.[34]

Critics and those unfamiliar with the system ask why some children appear more important than others; all children are equally important. In a perfect world, every case would be handled the same, but not all cases lend themselves to the same investigative tools. Sheer

A Closer Look

Megan's Law and Jessica's Law

Megan's Law

Megan's law is an informal name for laws in the United States requiring law enforcement authorities to make information available to the public regarding registered sex offenders. Individual states decide what information will be made available and how it should be disseminated. Commonly included information includes the offender's name, picture, address, incarceration date, and nature of crime. The information is often displayed on free public websites but can also be published in newspapers, distributed in pamphlets, or distributed through various other means.

At the federal level, Megan's law is known as the Sexual Offender (Jacob Wetterling) Act of 1994 and requires persons convicted of sex crimes against children to notify local law enforcement of any change of address or employment after release from custody (prison or psychiatric facility). The notification requirement may be imposed for a fixed period of time—usually at least 10 years—or permanently. Some states may legislate registration for all sex crimes, even if no minors were involved. It is a felony in most jurisdictions to fail to register or fail to update information.

Megan's law provides two major information services to the public: sex offender registration and community notification. The details of what is provided as part of sex offender registration and how community notification is handled vary from state to state, and in some states, the required registration information and community notification protocols have changed many times since Megan's law was passed. The Adam Walsh Child Protection and Safety Act supplements Megan's law with new registration requirements and a "three-tier" system for classifying sex offenders according to their risk to the community.

Jessica's Law

Jessica's law is the informal name given to a 2005 Florida law, as well as laws in several other states, designed to punish sex offenders and reduce their ability to reoffend. A version of Jessica's law has been introduced on the federal level, known as the Jessica Lunsford Act.

Jessica's law is the name commonly used by the media to designate all legislation and potential legislation in other states modeled after the Florida law. Forty-two states have introduced such legislation since Florida's law was passed.

The law is named after Jessica Lunsford, a young Florida girl who was raped and murdered in February 2005 by John Couey, a previously convicted sex offender. Public outrage over this incident spurred Florida officials to introduce this legislation. Among the key provisions of the (Florida) law are a mandatory minimum sentence of 25 years in prison and lifetime electronic monitoring of adults convicted of lewd or lascivious acts against a victim less than 12 years old. In Florida, sexual battery or rape of a child younger than 12 years old is punishable only by life imprisonment with no chance of parole.

Sources: Levenson, J. S. and L. P. Cotter. (2005). The effect of Megan's law on sex offender reintegration. *Journal of Contemporary Criminal Justice* 21(1):49–66. doi:10.1177/1043986204271676; Levenson, J. S., D. A D'Amora, and A. L. Hern. (2007). Megan's law and its impact on community re-entry for sex offenders. *Behavioral Sciences & the Law* 25(4):587–602. doi:10.1002/bsl.770; Welchans, S. (2005). Megan's law: Evaluations of sexual offender registries. *Criminal Justice Policy Review* 16(2):123–140. doi:10.1177/0887403404265630; Wilson, D. (2009). Appleton attorney fights "Jessica's law" on mandatory sex offender sentencing. *Post-Crescent*, March 21, Florida Statute 800.04; Florida Statute 947.1405; Florida Statute

|Fig. 12.4|

Jessica Lunsford's family and Jessica in a press release after her abduction in 2005. Jessica's abduction and murder resulted in the passing of Jessica's law.

STEVE CANNON / AP Images

volume dictates that the news media cannot become involved in the investigation of all missing children.[35] Moreover, to maintain the intense impact of the alerts, authorities must use them judiciously. Recognizing these realities, those who designed AMBER Alert targeted the stranger abductor. Further evaluation, however, revealed that children often were in more danger from noncustodial parental abductors and other family members than from unknown "bogeymen." Therefore, the system was modified to include the issuance of alerts involving family members.[36]

Dallas, Texas, was the first community to create and use a system involving the media in an attempt to locate missing children. In 1996, a man grabbed nine-year-old Amber Hagerman from her bicycle, threw the screaming child into the pickup truck he was driving, and left the area. Amber was found murdered four days later, and her homicide remains unsolved. A concerned citizen contacted a local radio station and suggested that it broadcast missing children alerts similar to those concerning inclement weather. Within five years, this commonsense approach to a difficult problem achieved national acceptance.

With the goal of effectively recovering endangered children, how do authorities decide if a missing child fits the criteria specified for broadcast? The U.S. Department of Justice, the organizing agency nationwide, recommends that law enforcement agencies:

- Reasonably believe that an abduction has occurred.
- Believe that the child is in imminent danger of serious bodily injury or death.
- Have enough descriptive information about the victim and the abduction to issue an AMBER Alert to assist in the recovery of the child.
- Know that the abducted child is 17 years of age or younger.
- Have entered the child's name and other critical data elements, including flagging it as a child abduction, into NCIC.

Although not specified within this list, other issues are implied. For example, the request for the alert must come from a law enforcement agency. A police report must be on file (a requirement for entry into NCIC). A recent picture of the child and an adequate description of the clothing worn when he or she was abducted are helpful but not required. Additionally, the abduction must have occurred recently, preferably within five hours but possibly as long as 24 hours. Of importance, agencies should remember that no required waiting period exists for entering a missing person into NCIC. As soon as they receive the report, they can enter the information.

Finally, AMBER Alert is only one tool in a criminal investigator's toolbox. After all, child abductors, including noncustodial parents, are dangerous criminals, and officers can use the same tools to apprehend them as they do any other type of potentially violent offender.

Some critiques of the Amber Alert program have argued that it is not appropriate in every missing child case. Instead, sometimes what is needed is a broader, coordinated effort to locate a missing child. Accordingly, the **Child Abduction Response Teams** (CART) teams were developed. CART teams complement the AMBER program by providing a way for a community response to all missing children's cases, even those that don't meet the criteria for an AMBER Alert. CART teams are organized regionally and are designed to meet the demographic and geographic needs of the community. CART can also be used to recover runaway children if they are younger than age 18 years and in danger.

Training typically includes an actual child abduction case study, components on response planning, and first responder protocol, to name a few of the subjects that are addressed in each regional training session. CART includes law enforcement investigators, forensic experts, AMBER Alert coordinators, search and rescue professionals, policymakers, crime intelligence analysts, victim service providers, and other interagency resources.[37]

Code Adam

Code Adam is an internationally recognized "missing child" safety program in the United States (and Canada), originally created by Wal-Mart retail stores in 1994. It is named in memory of Adam Walsh, the six-year-old son of John Walsh (the host of Fox Network's *America's Most Wanted*). Adam was abducted from a Sears department store in Florida in 1981 and was later found murdered. Today, many department stores, retail shops, shopping malls, supermarkets, amusement parks, and museums participate in the Code Adam program. Legislation enacted by Congress in 2003 now mandates that all federal office buildings use the program.[38]

|Fig. 12.5| ▲

John Walsh is the creator of *America's Most Wanted*. Walsh is famous for his anti-crime activism, which he became involved with following the murder of his son, Adam, in 1981. In 2008, the now-dead serial killer Ottis Toole was named as the killer of Walsh's son. By the late 1980s, many malls, department stores, supermarkets, and other such retailers have adopted what is known as a "Code Adam," a movement first made by Wal-Mart stores in the southeastern United States. A "Code Adam" is announced when a child is missing in a store or if a child is found by a store employee or patron.

Wal-Mart, along with the NCMEC and the departments of several state attorneys general, has offered to assist in training workshops for other companies to implement the program. Social scientists point out that the fear of child abduction is out of all proportion to its incidence. In particular, they point to the long-term persistence of retail kidnapping narratives in urban legends to highlight how parents have been sensitized to this issue for generations before the Adam Walsh case.[39]

Companies that do implement the program generally place a Code Adam decal at the front of the business. Employees at these businesses are trained to do the following six steps, according to the National Center for Missing & Exploited Children:

1. If a visitor reports a child is missing, a detailed description of the child and what he or she is wearing is obtained. Additionally, all exterior access to the building is locked and monitored; anyone approaching a door is turned away.
2. The employee goes to the nearest in-house telephone and pages Code Adam, describing the child's physical features and clothing. As designated employees monitor front entrances, other employees begin looking for the child.
3. If the child is not found within 10 minutes, law enforcement is called.
4. If the child is found and appears to have been lost and unharmed, the child is reunited with the searching family member.
5. If the child is found accompanied by someone other than a parent or legal guardian, reasonable efforts to delay their departure will be used without putting the child, staff, or visitors at risk. Law enforcement will be notified and given details about the person accompanying the child.
6. The Code Adam page will be canceled after the child is found or law enforcement arrives.

The Investigative Response

From an investigative standpoint, child kidnapping is one of the most emotionally charged and difficult criminal cases for law enforcement officers. Time is the merciless enemy. In 1997, the U.S. Office of Juvenile Justice Delinquency and Prevention (OJJDP) reported that most children (74 percent) who are murdered during stranger kidnappings are killed within the first few hours of the event. Therefore, it is imperative that investigators use every tool available to them, including the awesome power of the media.

By its very nature, abduction must take priority over many types of cases. Research has indicated that strangers who commit the offense with the intention of fulfilling a sexual desire often murder their victims within three hours.[40] In contrast, noncustodial parents may take the child to use as a weapon against their former significant other. So, in either situation, time may be very short. The person responsible for the investigation must be called immediately to the scene. No agency would assign a homicide investigator a case the next morning and then reconstruct the incident from police reports.

Abductions can be even more complex than some murders. As with all violent suspects, law enforcement officers use proven methods to locate them. All of these and more also come into play during the investigation of an abduction.

As with any other investigations, however, the best efforts by police may not lead to a quick resolution of a case. If the incident is a stranger abduction, law enforcement administrators must be prepared for the anger of the family to be redirected toward their agency. These family members are hurt and, especially if the victim is not recovered, need closure. When this is lacking, they react like any other human being and find somewhere to refocus their anger. Departmental procedures prepared in advance can help investigators cope with such difficulties and reassure the family that authorities are doing all they can.[41]

Noncustodial parental abductions can prove equally dangerous to a child. Often, the suspect takes the child and starts another life outside the investigating agency's jurisdiction. Again, investigators need to recognize and use the methods they would in any other criminal investigation. In most states, a noncustodial parental abduction is a felony. Even before charges are filed, however, the law enforcement agency can enter the child, the suspect, and the suspect's vehicle into NCIC. If the department cross-references all of the information, it will alert officers in other jurisdictions, who may stop the suspect on a traffic violation and possibly recover the child. The custodial parent then can make arrangements to retrieve the child. After the felony warrant is on file and if investigators believe the suspect has fled their jurisdiction, the FBI can help obtain a warrant for unlawful flight to avoid prosecution. This enables a wide variety of federal resources to come into play, including the Federal Parent Locator Service, which coordinates with such agencies as the Internal Revenue Service, the U.S. Social Security Administration, and the U.S. Department of Agriculture to monitor the issuance of checks and notifies law enforcement if the suspect registers for or receives any type of public assistance.

Early in the investigation, agencies may want to request an off-line search from NCIC. Usually, abductions are planned, and within minutes of the act, the suspect may have left the jurisdiction with the child. Often, the abductor may drive too fast, leading to a stop on a traffic violation. The custodial parent may not even know that an abduction has occurred before the suspect has fled the state. An off-line search can show the location of the stop, thereby giving investigators an indication of the abductor's possible destination.

In 2005, this tactic worked for an investigator in Indianapolis, Indiana. A mother was allowed to make an unsupervised visitation with her child, a ward of the state because of the woman's history of drug abuse and neglect. When the mother did not return as scheduled, a child protective services worker made a police report. Officers had no idea which direction the woman would go. An off-line search revealed that an officer in Missouri had stopped her for a traffic violation only a few hours after she had picked up the child for the visit before the Indianapolis police received the report of the missing child. Through a variety of tools, including federal assistance agencies, the Indianapolis investigator tracked the woman to Long Beach, California, where detectives located the suspect and her children living in a van under a bridge. Extradited to Indianapolis, she was prosecuted and convicted on the felony charge. The judge in the case felt that she would continue to be a danger to her children and sentenced her to a prison term.[42]

The Initial Call for Assistance

The initial response to a missing child call is perhaps the most crucial component of the investigation. The manner in which patrol officers respond to the initial call often determines whether the child is found quickly and returned home safely, remains missing for months or years, or is never found.

In most law enforcement agencies, the patrol officer is the first responder to missing child calls. Therefore, all patrol officers need to be trained to respond to such calls efficiently, compassionately, and professionally—paying particular attention to safeguarding evidence, quickly obtaining as much information as possible about the child and the circumstances, interviewing witnesses, and at the same time calming and reassuring the parents or guardians of the missing child. But before the patrol officer even arrives on the scene, information about the missing child should be relayed from the dispatcher to the responding officers. Dispatch operators, working with a standard list of predetermined questions, should gather pertinent information from the caller and relay it to the responding officers. After the dispatch operator has calmed the caller, basic facts and information can be gathered to help the responding officers, including a brief description of the missing child and information about a possible abductor(s).

Dispatch personnel should, to the degree possible, also provide responding officers with an overview of any agency records concerning the child and family, such as (1) history of violence or child abuse calls, (2) criminal activities of family members or other persons living at the address (e.g., arrests, narcotics), (3) runaway reports on the child or siblings, and (4) juvenile delinquency reports on the child or siblings. In addition, dispatch personnel should check to determine if there have been recent problems regarding children in the neighborhood. Such information could disclose many things such as complaints about prowlers, indecent exposure incidents, attempted abductions, convicted child molesters living in the neighborhood, and the like.

Department policy should provide for an immediate city- or countywide radio alert to all other patrol units and all neighboring law enforcement agencies. Even though such an alert may not contain precise factual information about the missing child or circumstances in this early stage, these immediate radio broadcasts often result in prompt, safe recoveries, particularly when a small child has simply wandered away from home and become lost.

A judgment must be made as to when a person is to be declared as "missing" and the corresponding issue of when a missing persons report should be filed. The responsibility for these determinations lies primarily with knowledgeable reporting parties: persons who are in a position to know the behavioral patterns and character of the individual involved—such as parents, guardians, or close personal friends—and who are also often the best judges of what is highly unusual, irregular, or suspicious behavior with regard to the individual's whereabouts. As such, there should be no mandatory waiting period for filing a missing persons report, and such reports should be allowed to be filed either personally or by telephone. The response by law enforcement includes steps to be taken by the responding officer, the supervisor at the scene, and the case investigator.

Responding Officer Responsibilities

The patrol officer initially establishes the seriousness of the complaint about a missing child, safeguards the scene, gathers crucial facts, and conducts preliminary interviews of witnesses. For this reason, patrol officers must learn to become as thorough as they can in responding to missing child reports. Assumptions about such cases must be avoided or officers may overlook crucial information and evidence.

To initiate a successful missing persons investigation, the first responder must focus on quickly gathering factual information and safeguarding potential evidence. This is particularly the case with regard to missing children, whether they may be abducted, runaway, or lost. This may also be true of some elderly persons or others who, because of physical or mental disability or reduced functioning, are not fully capable of taking care of themselves. The elderly, especially those suffering from Alzheimer's disease or similar problems, present specific concerns as the subjects of missing person reports. Open terrain searches for missing persons in general also require adherence to professionally recognized search management principles. Some of the most widely accepted principles of searching for missing persons are discussed later in this chapter.

The patrol officer who responds to the call is best suited to obtain the details of the initial account, particularly because the officer patrols the area or neighborhood and is likely to notice any unusual activities or suspicious persons. The officer should respond to the call promptly, since the time factor is often crucial, especially in cases involving abductions by strangers.

In 1994, the NCMEC developed a checklist for first responders in missing children cases, listing tasks an officer should complete to ensure a successful investigation.[43] These steps are general, but they do provide a framework for the officer's actions.

The Sixteen Steps of Investigation

Sixteen tasks commonly associated with the responsibilities of the first responder are identified in this chapter. However, it is recognized that in the real world, many tasks of first responders, supervisors, and investigators are not distinctly or conveniently divided between these respective agency personnel. The following 16 steps are those that should nominally be taken by officers. It should be understood that not every step may pertain to all situations nor do the steps need to be addressed in the exact order in which they are presented in this book.

Step 1: Interview parents or the person who made the initial report to the emergency operations center (EOC) This interview should be conducted in an area where interruptions are minimal and preferably in private. The purpose of the interview is to obtain a complete description of the missing child, circumstances of how the child came to be missing, and information necessary to make an initial definition and assessment of the type of case.

Case example: The complainant may be the operator of a preschool who reports that the child was approached by a man whom the child called "Daddy." The man then put the child in a car and left without speaking to any of the adults at the school. One of the teachers, however, obtained the license tag number of the car. Further questioning of the complainant reveals that the child's parents are divorced and engaged in a bitter custody dispute, although the court has awarded custody to the mother. The officer can make a preliminary assessment that this is a family abduction that may not warrant calling in additional personnel. *Consider another case example:* The mother of a five-year-old girl calls from the mall reporting her daughter missing; the line of questioning and initial actions of the responding officer should be very different from the above because all initial signs point to a possible abduction by a stranger.

Step 2: Verify that the child is in fact missing Here the officer needs to make certain that the child cannot be located on the premises or nearby. In the preschool case above, three teachers and 40 children (ranging in age from two through five) saw the missing boy (age three) run and greet his father and then leave in the car. At the mall, a search of the grounds by security officers failed to turn up the missing five-year-old girl. However, when the patrol officer asked the mother if she had checked her vehicle in the parking lot, the mother said no. The officer went with the mother to the parking lot and found the girl asleep on the back floor of the family van, which had been left unlocked. The little girl said she was tired and went to take a nap without telling her mother because "Mommy was talking to the lady about the furniture, and Mommy told me not to interrupt when grown-ups are talking to each other. So I just came to the van to take a nap." Case closed.

Before beginning an area search, ask those at the scene if a search has already been conducted, and if so, what areas were covered. Officers should never assume that searches conducted, often by distraught parents or others, have been performed in a thorough manner. However, under exigent circumstances, prior search efforts may help officers focus on other alternatives even if their intention is to research those same areas as time permits. The officers should make a quick check of the house and grounds for small children, looking in such places as closets, refrigerators, large boxes and vehicles in garages, storage sheds, under shrubbery, in doghouses, under beds, and behind furniture. The child may have been playing hide-and-seek with an imaginary playmate and fallen asleep. In the case of teenagers overdue home by several hours, the officer should ask the parents if they've checked their answering machine for messages. Perhaps the teenager left a note in the kitchen explaining the absence, and the parents did not find the note. A variety of possible explanations are possible in apparent missing persons cases depending on the circumstances involved, and concerned parents sometimes overlook the obvious.

Step 3: Verify the child's custody status With divorce so prevalent in the United States and custody battles a common denominator in the lives of many children, the patrol officer should ask the parent if there has been a divorce or separation and, if so, which parent has primary legal custody. If there has been a marital breakup, the officer should raise the issue of a possible abduction of the child by the **noncustodial parent**. Another area of inquiry involves possible emotional problems affecting the child; if the child is taking the parental breakup badly and falsely assuming blame, the child may have run away. All of these issues must be explored, no matter how insensitive the questions may seem under the circumstances.

Step 4: Identify the circumstances of the disappearance Did the child disappear from home or from the residence of a relative or friend? Is the child missing after a visit with a noncustodial parent? Is the child missing from a public place, such as a shopping mall, park, amusement center, or school playground? Was the child seen talking to a stranger? Did the child disappear while the parent or guardian's attention was focused elsewhere, such as paying for a purchase or loading groceries into a vehicle? The NCMEC lists several unusual circumstances that alert the first responding patrol officer to "pull out all the stops" by requesting additional personnel, supervisory and investigative assistance, and any special support units that may be needed, such as K-9 and helicopters. The need for other resources, such as assistance from other law enforcement agencies, fire department search and rescue teams, and **neighborhood watch** teams, can be determined by a field supervisor. Unusual circumstances that may require such additional resources include the following:

- The missing child is 13 years old or younger.
- The missing child is believed to be out of the zone of safety for his or her age and developmental stage.
- The missing child is mentally incapacitated, has attempted or threatened suicide, or has a history of self-destructive behavior.
- The missing child is drug dependent, including prescribed medication or illegal substances, and the dependency is potentially life threatening.
- The missing child has been absent from home for more than 24 hours before being reported to the police.
- Based on available information, it is believed that the missing child is in the company of adults who could endanger his or her welfare.
- Based on available information, it is determined that the missing child is in a life-threatening situation.
- The absence is inconsistent with the child's established patterns of behavior, and the deviation cannot be readily explained.
- Other circumstances are involved in the disappearance that would cause a reasonable person to conclude that the child should be considered "at risk."

When one or more of these circumstances is present, the patrol officer should take immediate action and call for mobilization of additional resources. It is always better to overreact when a child's life may be in danger. Resources can be demobilized quickly if it is determined later that they are not needed.

Step 5: Determine when, where, and by whom the missing child was last seen For example, if the child disappeared while the parent or guardian was paying for groceries, did any of the cashiers, store employees, or other shoppers see the child leave the store with anyone? If the child disappeared while walking to school, did any residents or delivery persons on the child's route witness the child getting into a vehicle? Interview everyone who may have been in a position to see the child.

Step 6: Interview the individuals who last had contact with the child It is especially important to interview the child's friends if the child is a preteen or teenager. Friends of older children often know more about the child's attitudes, emotions, and plans than the parents or guardians. Perhaps friends will reveal that the child is having trouble with his father and is staying with another friend. A teacher may reveal that the child's noncustodial parent came to the school to get permission to remove the child from school because the child was being taken to a dental appointment. In the case of a child missing from a public place, it is important to interview those persons operating stores, concessions, or amusements that may have attracted the child's attention, leading the child to wander away from parents or guardians. For example, if a small boy wandered into a video arcade, was given quarters by an adult man to play games, and then left the arcade with the man, the operator of the arcade should be able to provide a description of the circumstances and the suspect, along with time frames.

Step 7: Identify the child's zone of safety for his or her age and developmental stage Try to determine how far the child could travel from the spot where last seen before he or she would most likely be at risk of being injured or exploited. This perimeter should define the first immediate search zone under many circumstances.

Step 8: Make an initial determination of the type of incident Based on the available information, determine whether the incident appears to be a nonfamily abduction; family abduction; endangered runaway; or lost, injured, or otherwise missing person. This initial classification will help the officer begin investigative actions. To make the initial classification, the officer should analyze the information already gathered. However, officers must be extremely cautious in **labeling**, or classifying, a missing child case, because the classification process will affect the way initial evidence or information is gathered. As the NCMEC advises, even if the initial information suggests a classification into a category considered to be "less urgent," officers should run "parallel investigations" that take all possibilities into account until the case category is clearly determined.

Step 9: Obtain a detailed description of the missing child, suspected abductor(s), vehicles, and the like If several people are at the scene, each person should be interviewed separately by the officer to obtain descriptions of a possible suspect and vehicle. Witnesses should not be interviewed in the presence of other witnesses because there is a tendency on the part of some to "go along"—either consciously or unconsciously—with a description given by another witness. As most officers know, the perception and recall of witnesses can be faulty, and when they use each other to fill in missing details in their memory, important details may be lost.

Step 10: Relay detailed descriptive information to the EOC for relay to other law enforcement agencies and information referral sources Supervisors, in consultation with the public information officer or agency chief executive, may decide at this time to provide descriptive information to the news media to generate assistance from the public in locating the missing child or encouraging any witnesses to come forward.

Step 11: Ensure that any remaining persons at the scene are identified and interviewed and information is properly recorded To aid in this process, take pictures or videotape everyone present, if possible. Note the name, address, and home or business telephone numbers of each person. Determine each person's relationship to the missing child, if any. Note information that each person may have about the child's disappearance. Determine when or where each person last saw the child. Ask each one: "What do you think happened to the child?" Obtain the names, addresses, and telephone numbers of the child's friends and other relatives and friends of the family. Friends, relatives, and neighbors may reveal that there are problems in the home, the child is frequently abused (either verbally or physically), the father or "live-in" boyfriend has a "hot temper," or the mother drinks during the day and screams at the kids. This type of sensitive information may be elicited by the officer; the person being interviewed can be assured of privacy and told that the information provided will not be given to family members. Such information can provide important clues to investigators as to the type of case: a homicide by parents or guardians with lies told to police to cover up the crime, a stranger abduction, or a "runaway" or abused child.

Step 12: Continue to update the emergency dispatcher and other appropriate department personnel Periodically update the public information officer or department spokesperson. If there is no media relations officer or supervisor on the scene handling these duties, the senior officer at the scene may be asked to provide periodic updates to media personnel. Under such circumstances, the officer must follow the agency's media relations policies and procedures, being careful not to release information that could jeopardize an investigation, falsely accuse individuals, or inadvertently implicate anyone in a crime.

Step 13: Obtain and record permission to search houses or buildings This includes any locations where the incident took place or where entry is required to conduct the investigation. To search a house or apartment, obtain the permission of the owner or renter. In the case of a building, such as a shopping mall or store, obtain the manager's permission or the permission of any private security firm working on the premises. Be sure to search any surrounding areas, including vehicles, parking lots, storage sheds, garbage containers, truck trailers at loading docks, warehouse areas behind stores, construction sites, shrubbery, culverts, and other places of concealment.

Even if the child was reported missing from a public place, such as a shopping mall, it is highly advisable to seek permission for a thorough search of the child's home. In some recent cases, the child was murdered in the home, leaving bloodstain evidence, and after disposing the body, the parents or guardians drove to a public place (e.g., mall, gas station), called the police, and reported that the child had been abducted from that location. By not searching the home, vital evidence of a crime can be lost.

Step 14: Secure and safeguard the crime scene   This includes securing the area where the incident took place or the location at which the child was last seen as a crime scene in order to safeguard vital evidence. The patrol officer must take control of the immediate area where the incident occurred and establish an appropriate perimeter to avoid destruction of vital evidence.

It is not uncommon for even well-intentioned citizens at a public site to overrun a crime scene, inadvertently destroying or otherwise carrying off such evidence as fibers, hair, cigarette butts, dropped credit card slips and driver's licenses, a weapon, or other possessions with fingerprints. Pedestrian and vehicular traffic at such locations can also destroy any scent trails that may be used by canine teams to track the missing child. Under exigent circumstances and until backup arrives, the patrol officer may obtain assistance from store managers, private security officers, school principals, and other trusted authority figures to block off crime scenes. As soon as possible, backup should be requested to help safeguard a potential crime scene.

At the child's home or crime scene, items of evidential value and other personal effects that may assist in locating the child should be protected and, if appropriate, collected. These include, but are not limited to, the child's personal articles such as a hairbrush; diary; photographs; and items with the child's fingerprints, footprints, or teeth impressions. The contents and appearance of the child's room and residence should be noted. If possible, photographs or videotapes of these areas should be taken.

The child's current bedsheets can be collected, if appropriate, for use by search dog teams and, under some circumstances, may be necessary for later crime laboratory analysis. Recent photos and family videos may also be useful for release to the media if this option becomes necessary. In many cases, widespread use of a child's photo in the media has precipitated telephone tips that have successfully concluded investigations.

The officer should also obtain a set of the child's fingerprints if the parents have had a set prepared as a crime prevention measure. If a fingerprint card is not available, items should be secured from the child's room that are likely to contain prints, such as a smooth plastic or metal toy, drinking glass, TV remote control, comic books, and game boxes.

Officers should adhere to established department policies and procedures for crime scene processing. However, in addition, when investigating cases of missing children, officers are advised to treat the crime scene processing assignment with a "worst-case scenario" in mind.

Step 15: Obtain photos, videotapes, and any other identifying information on suspects   In particular, any photos of the suspect should be relayed to the shift commander as soon as possible. In some cases, the first responder may be able to secure photos or videos. For example, store security cameras may provide valuable videotape. In other cases, such as an abduction by a noncustodial parent, the custodial parent or child's school may be able to provide a current photograph, address, place of employment, and other identifying information. When a license tag number can help identify a suspect, the state department of motor vehicles can generally quickly provide a photo. If the suspect has an arrest record, photos may be available in local, state, or federal law enforcement records systems.

Step 16: Prepare reports and make all required notifications   Ensure that information about the missing child is entered into the FBI's NCIC Missing Persons File and that any information on a suspected abductor is entered into the NCIC Wanted Persons File.

The NCMEC recommends that a law enforcement agency take several other steps to publicize the incident, to receive tips from the public, and obtain help with a widespread search. These measures, which are usually carried out by administrative personnel rather than the first responder or patrol officer, include:

1. Ensure that the details of the case have been reported to the NCMEC.
2. Prepare and update bulletins for local law enforcement agencies, state missing children's clearinghouses, FBI, and other appropriate agencies.
3. Prepare a flyer or bulletin with the child's and suspected abductor's photographs and descriptive information. Distribute it in appropriate geographical regions.
4. Secure the child's latest medical and dental records. These may be necessary to positively identify the child.
5. Establish a telephone hotline to receive tips and leads from the public.
6. Establish a leads management system to prioritize leads and ensure that each one undergoes a review and follow-up.

The Investigator's Role

Many of the duties of the investigator in a missing or abducted child case are the same as those in conducting almost any type of investigation. Indeed, some have been referenced in foregoing chapters related to the first responding officer and supervisory responsibilities. However, investigative officers can take eight basic steps to help ensure a successful outcome in a missing or abducted child case. These procedures are geared more toward nonfamily abduction cases and situations in which a child disappears and could be in danger. Family abduction and runaway (or lost) child investigative procedures are covered in depth in the NCMEC's manual.

Step 1: Obtain a detailed briefing from the first responding officer and other on-scene personnel The investigator should debrief the first responding officer before conducting any interviews with family members of the missing child or witnesses who may have been identified in the early stages of the case. A thorough debriefing of the first responder will help the investigator analyze the information in order to formulate an approach to upcoming interviews of family members and witnesses.

Step 2: Verify the accuracy of all descriptive information The verification process should include all other details developed during the preliminary investigation. At this point the investigator should begin interviewing the missing child's family members and possible witnesses to determine the facts and sort out any conflicting information obtained by the first responder and other officers on the scene.

Step 3: Obtain a brief recent history of family dynamics This process will help the investigator hypothesize about various possibilities involving the disappearance of the child. Was the family the truly loving, close-knit family the mother tearfully described to the first responder? Or were there previous police calls to the residence for domestic disturbances? Has the child's school reported the family to social service agencies for possible abuse of the child? Is there a large life insurance policy on a four-year-old child? If so, why? Is the missing little girl an "ugly duckling" with a learning disability, while the mother is the glamorous "prom queen" type with a live-in boyfriend who spends all his money on drugs and alcohol? Answers to such questions, often obtained from neighbors, friends of the child, and other family members, can offer invaluable insights to what may have happened to the child and where the child may now be located.

Step 4: Explore the basis for conflicting information Information offered by witnesses and other individuals may not coincide. As such, the investigator needs to conduct in-depth fact-finding interviews with all witnesses, friends, and relatives of the child and the child's parents or guardians necessary to resolve those conflicts. It is at this point that the investigator may consider asking the parents or guardians to submit to a polygraph examination.

After the investigator has interviewed all relevant persons, it is necessary to again meet with the first responder, fellow investigators, and the supervising officer to "compare notes" and work through any conflicting information gathered in the course of the investigation. This collaborative process should provide the investigative staff with a solid foundation upon which to structure the future direction of the case.

Step 5: Review and evaluate all available information and evidence At this point, an information management system becomes a critical tool in the investigative process. The investigator should designate another investigator, a crime analyst, or a patrol officer to serve as the case information manager, centralizing all data as they are gathered, making comparisons, and keeping track of leads and tips. Appointing one person to be in charge of all information pertaining to the case helps ensure that valuable data will not become misdirected and possibly lost.

Depending on the resources available to the agency, data may be computerized or incorporated into a simple card system, in which facts are indexed for cross-reference and easily available for prompt review. The method of filing does not matter as long as the system works for the investigator in charge of solving the case.

After the incoming data and evidence have been organized, reviewed, and evaluated, the investigator can develop and execute an investigative follow-up plan and secure necessary additional resources, personnel, and specialized services.

Step 6: Develop an investigative plan for follow-up By evaluating evidence and the information gathered from interviews of police officers, witnesses, the child's parents or guardians, and others, the investigator can prepare a follow-up plan, which may include the following tasks:

1. Conduct more in-depth interviews with specific people who have been questioned previously.
2. Set up lead-tracking policies and procedures.
3. Gather more complete background information on the missing child, parents or guardians, and possible suspects.
4. Reevaluate the scene and conduct a more detailed search.
5. Canvass the neighborhood to locate potential witnesses and information.
6. Search the child's home even if the child is missing from another location.
7. Obtain search warrants when consent for a search is denied.
8. Administer polygraph examinations to the parents or guardians if officers and investigators suspect they are not telling the truth or something seems awry.
9. Contact social service agencies and the child's school to determine whether the child's family was the subject of abuse investigations or had other problems that may be significant to the progress of the investigation.

Step 7: Determine what additional resources and specialized services are required At this point, the investigator's assessment of the type of incident (e.g., abducted child, possible abduction, family abduction, lost child, or runaway) should help determine what additional assistance may be needed both from within the department and from outside agencies. For example, the investigator may have been told by a relative of the child that the child's parents appeared in family court to answer child neglect charges. The investigator can save time by asking the police juvenile officer to follow up this lead with the family court and social service agency assigned to the family's case. The juvenile officer could also contact teachers where the missing child attends school and might even interview parents of the child's playmates.

If an abduction is suspected and it can be assumed that the child may be transported to another jurisdiction, the investigator may want to contact the FBI for help, along with the NCMEC, state police, state missing children clearinghouses, and other law enforcement agencies in the region. An excellent checklist for investigating Internet-related missing children's cases is provided in the NCMEC manual.

Step 8: Execute an investigative follow-up plan The procedures initiated by the investigator depend on the type of case—runaway, family kidnapping, suspected abduction by a stranger, or lost child. Although the procedures are similar to those involved in investigating other major cases, investigators should be aware that the missing or abducted child case may bring the added factor of emotional stress and that the degree of stress will vary depending on the circumstances of the case.

The 2003 Child Protection Act (Amber Alerts)

In September 2006, Vinson Filyaw, a 26-year-old unemployed construction worker, approached 14-year-old Elizabeth Shoaf as she stepped off her school bus in Lugoff, South Carolina. Posing as a police officer, Filyaw used handcuffs to restrain Elizabeth and dragged her back to a bunker located near his rural trailer home. Filyaw told Elizabeth that the entrance to the bunker was booby-trapped and warned her that if she tried to escape or if anyone tried to rescue her, a bomb would detonate. While Filyaw had Elizabeth in his custody, he sexually assaulted her.

For 10 days, family members, police, and volunteers conducted a sweeping search for Elizabeth but found few clues. Elizabeth engineered her own remarkable rescue by snatching Filyaw's cell phone as he slept and sending a text message to her mother describing the location where she was being held. Investigators using cell phone tracking technology traced the call to Filyaw's cell phone. Investigators deduced Elizabeth's kidnapper was, in all likelihood, a known sex offender who was suspected of a sexual assault against a 12-year-old relative.

Using the signal from a nearby cell tower to triangulate her location, authorities began scouring the area and were able to rescue her. Police also seized a cache of pornography, canned goods, cheap generic cigarettes, homemade hand-grenades, and incendiary devices fashioned out of black powder from fireworks. They did not, however, find Filyaw.

After a failed attempt to hijack a car to make his escape, Filyaw was found walking along the side of Interstate 20. He was charged with kidnapping, first-degree sexual assault, impersonating a police officer, and possession of incendiary devices.

This case illustrates the seriousness and reality of child abductions and points to the need for community and police cooperation in the investigative phase. It also shows the importance of Amber Alerts and how they provide much-needed and timely information regarding child abductions.

In April 2003, President George W. Bush signed into law the so-called Child Protection Bill, which encourages states to establish **Amber Alert** systems to quickly post information about child abductions. The measure was hailed as an important milestone in the protection of America's children because when a child is reported missing, the case becomes a matter of the most intense and focused effort by law enforcement.

The law also enhanced penalties for youth abductions and child sex crimes, boosted funding for missing and exploited children programs, and increased penalties on those convicted of child pornography, including images created digitally.

The Amber Alert system makes use of radio, television, roadside electronic billboards, and emergency broadcast systems to disseminate information about kidnapping suspects and victims soon after the abduction of a child younger than age 18 years is reported. In such cases, authorities say, the child could be killed or seriously injured a short time after being kidnapped.

The alerts, named after a nine-year-old Texas girl, Amber Hagerman, who was kidnapped and killed in 1996, are in effect in 41 states at the time of this writing. Amber's mother, Donna Norris,

|Fig. 12.6| △

Amber Alert signs such as this one in Austin, Texas, are one way to inform large numbers of citizens to lookout for children who have been recently abducted.

David R. Frazier / Photo Researchers, Inc.

attended the bill-signing ceremony along with the survivors of two high-profile kidnapping cases, Jacqueline Marris and Tamara Brooks, two California teenagers rescued in the first use of the system in that state, and Utah teen Elizabeth Smart, whose father, Ed Smart, called for a national Amber Alert system after her recovery in March 2003.

One of the primary purposes of the new law is to encourage states to develop Amber Alert systems of their own. Attorney General John Ashcroft stated the bills aim to create a "seamless" system across the country. After the signing of the bill, an Amber Alert coordinator was appointed at the Justice Department to assist states and was designated $10 million for the establishment of the initiative.

Interviewing Suspects in Abductions

After a suspect has been identified, the investigator must carefully plan an interview to gain as much information as possible without violating the suspect's constitutional rights. A checklist of sample questions to ask a suspect may include:

- What do you think should happen to someone who would do this?
- Have you ever done this before?
- Have you ever thought of doing this before?
- Did you do it?
- Do you know who could have done this?
- Explain to me why…
- Do you keep a diary, calendar, notebook, or computer? Can I look at it?
- Have you ever been arrested for this type of crime before?
- Have you ever been questioned about this type of crime before?
- Do you own, possess, or have access to (items described by witnesses)?
- Do you know this child? His or her family? The family's business?
- Is there any reason why someone would accuse you of this?
- If it becomes necessary, would you…(submit to a polygraph, give fingerprints, stand in a lineup)?
- Would you let me search your…(car, house, storage locker, other places)?
- How do you react to stress?
- What is your general mode of transportation?
- Do you drive around a lot? Go places unannounced?
- What are your sleeping habits?
- Do you ever lie? If so, how frequently, under what circumstances, and why?

During the interview, treat the subject with consideration but be firm. As soon as the interview begins, size up the subject—is he or she intelligent, emotional, or very self-assured? Be prepared for the interview by gathering as many facts as possible about the incident before confronting the subject.

As the interview progresses, the effective investigator may obtain more answers by being a good listener—letting the subject talk, not trying to manipulate what the subject is saying. Concentrate on how the subject answers questions as much as what he or she says. Also watch the subject's body language and facial expressions. Encourage the subject to tell it in his or her own words, emphasizing that the subject should tell you all the facts. At the same time, do not be visibly shocked by anything the subject says—if an investigator shows shock by facial expressions or a look of disgust, the subject could begin to gain the upper hand in the interview. If necessary, the investigator should be empathetic. Be patient and do not expect to obtain answers to all questions quickly. Ask questions that require more than a yes or no answer. Some examples are:

- Tell me what happened then…
- I'd like to hear more about…
- And what happened then…?

Case in Point

>>The FBI "Card" Team

In 2011, the FBI reported that 74 percent of children abducted and murdered were killed within the first three hours of their disappearance. To aid local law enforcement and FBI investigators in child abduction investigations, in 2006 the FBI created the Child Abduction Rapid Deployment (CARD) team. Since its inception, CARD has provided FBI field offices with the resource of additional investigators with specialized experience in child abduction matters. As of September 2011, the CARD team has assisted in the investigation of 69 child abduction cases involving 77 children. Of the 77 children, 31 were recovered alive; 11 remain missing. CARD statistics also indicated that in 70 percent of these cases, the child was abducted by a person with a known relationship to the child. In contrast, 10 percent of abductors were registered sex offenders.

A total of 60 CARD team members are divided into 10 separate groups, 2 within each region of the United States. Regionally, CARD provides a quick, on-site response, including investigative, technical, and resource assistance, during the most critical time period following a child abduction.

CARD has the unique experience of having investigated many child abduction cases, whereas a majority of seasoned investigators have not had the opportunity to do so. This institutional knowledge enables CARD team members to bring valuable insight and expertise to these time-sensitive investigations. When the life of a child is in possible danger, people want highly qualified investigators as every minute counts when a child is reported missing.

Case Examples

- In 2011, CARD assisted in a child abduction investigation in Colorado City, Texas, by providing several investigative strategies, including the establishment of the Missing/Abducted Child Excel (MACE) application. MACE helped track the completion of the neighborhood canvass; identify suspects; run multiple timelines on the victim, witnesses, and suspects to identify discrepancies and any window of opportunity; and monitor evidence collected during the investigation.[1]

- In 2010, the CARD team responded to a child abduction investigation in Greeley, Colorado. CARD employed strategies throughout the investigation, including a neighborhood canvass, interviews of registered sex offenders, and victimology.

- In 2009, the CARD team provided assistance in a child abduction case in South Carolina. CARD helped to structure the command post, refine lead tracking, coordinate with the Behavioral Analysis Unit 3 (BAU-3) regarding possible abductors, formulate a strategy to locate the abductor, and guide the search and recovery teams. As a result, the child was recovered.

- During an abduction in Nashville, Tennessee, in 2009, the CARD team and BAU-3 advised the execution of basic missing child techniques, such as conducting a neighborhood canvass, reviewing surveillance videos, and focusing media strategies. As a result, the suspect and victim were located. The victim was recovered alive, and the suspect was arrested.[2]

- A child abduction case in Dickinson, Texas, involved an eight-year-old victim who was brutally abducted and raped, had her throat slit by the subject, and was left for dead. In 2008, 18 years later, an FBI agent presented this case at a CARD conference where team members recommended that agents use new technologies and reanalyze the DNA evidence. As a result, agents identified and arrested the subject.[3]

- During a 2007 child abduction case in North Carolina, the CARD team advised the case agent that the victim likely was deceased and hidden somewhere in the individual's residence. The following day, the victim—dead for several weeks— was found in the attic.

Source: FBI, 2011. Available at http://www.fbi.gov/stats-services/publications/law-enforcement-bulletin/november-2011/crimes-against-children-spotlight

---

Don't rush the subject; set aside sufficient time for a thorough interview. Be direct and professional—do not make the subject guess what information is needed. Allow the subject to "save face" if embarrassing questions are asked. If the subject feels humiliated, the interview may come to an abrupt halt. Avoid using technical terms or police slang.

As the interview is drawing to a close, try to get the subject to help time-orient the facts, putting them in chronological order. Be aware of what the subject did not say during the interview.

One of the most important procedures to follow throughout the interview is to observe the subject's due process rights (Fourth and Fifth Amendments). Throughout the missing or abducted child investigation, be certain to take all precautions to observe the legal rights of any potential suspects so that a successfully investigated case will not be lost in court.

Summary Checklist

The magnitude of the missing and abducted problem is complex, multifaceted, and disturbing. For example, there are different types of missing children, including family abductions; endangered runaways; nonfamily abductions; and lost, injured, or otherwise missing children. See how well you are able to answer the following questions in your checklist.

1. **To what extent are missing and abducted persons a problem in American society?**

   The statistics show that missing and abducted persons are a serious and ongoing problem.

   - In 2010, the FBI reported 85, 820 active missing persons files, of which 45 percent were juveniles under the age of 18.
   - During 2010, 692, 944 missing person records were entered into the NCIC, a decrease of 3.7 percent from 2009.

   Child abductions are one of society's greatest concerns.

   - Registered sex offenders are the abductors in only a very small number of cases (1 percent in 2010).
   - In 2009, an average of 2, 185 children were reported missing each day, with the majority being the victims of family abductions.
   - There are approximately 100 cases per year in the United States in which a child is abducted and murdered.
   - The majority of child abduction murder victims are girls with an average age of slightly older than 11 years. In 80 percent of the cases, the initial contact between the victim and killer occurs within ¼ mile of the victim's residence.

2. **Describe the profile of abductors.**

   In child abduction murder cases, the offenders have some common characteristics.

   - 57 percent of child abduction murders are committed by killers who are strangers to the victims—family involvement is rare.
   - The relationship between victim and killer varies with the victim's gender and age:
     - Girls one to five years old tend to be killed by friends or acquaintances.
     - Girls 16 to 17 tend to be killed by strangers.
     - Boys one to five years old and older boys (13 to 15 and 1 to 67 years old) tend to be killed by strangers.

   - Killers of abducted children have an average age of 27 years, are predominantly unmarried (87 percent), and either live alone (17 percent) or with their parents (34 percent).
   - Half are unemployed and those that are employed work in unskilled or semiskilled labor occupations.
   - The majority (61 percent) had prior arrests for violent crimes, with more than half of these prior crimes being committed against children.
   - Killers are generally at the initial contact site for a legitimate reason and most victims are victims of opportunity.
   - The primary motivation for the child abduction murder is sexual assault.

   Child abductors (nonmurder) have several characteristics in common.

   - Most often have a prior visual sighting of the victim and the initial contact is frequently made at or near the home.
   - The motivation for the crime is often sexual in nature.
   - The victim is usually a girl under 14 and the suspect is an unemployed white male with a criminal record.
   - Most kidnapping episodes last less than 24 hours in both family and nonfamily abductions.
   - The biggest difference between family and nonfamily abductions lies in the treatment of the victim.

3. **Identify the different types of abductions.**

   In general, missing children cases fall into three basic categories:

   - The **nonfamily abduction case**, in which a child is removed without authorization from his or her family by force or trickery, is the most complex and dangerous type of missing child case. This category also includes abductions of newborns and infants from health care facilities or public places.
   - The **family abduction** generally occurs in conjunction with divorce and separation. The noncustodial parent removes the child from the care of the custodial parent and may flee the state or country with the child.
   - The **runaway or lost child** involves a child (often a teenager) who leaves home voluntarily for a variety of reasons. This is the most common case encountered by law enforcement officers.

Some child abductions have been connected to the Internet as a result of the easy access both child and predator have to this worldwide communications network.

4. **Outline the federal legislative history of dealing with missing and abducted children.**

At one time, no federal agency had responsibility or jurisdiction to investigate these cases. Kidnapped, lost, and missing people were considered a problem best dealt with by local law enforcement. This changed dramatically as a result of the 1932 kidnapping of Charles Lindbergh's infant son.

- The Federal Kidnapping Act (1932), which allowed the use of federal agencies in kidnapping cases, was passed in response to the Lindbergh baby kidnapping.
- The Uniform Child Custody Jurisdiction Act (1968) made the practice of moving to another state for the purpose of changing custody illegal.
- The Parental Kidnapping Prevention Act (1980) was passed to strengthen the Uniform Child Custody Jurisdiction Act. It allowed states to use the Federal Parent Locator Service to obtain address information on noncustodial parents who abducted their children and authorized the use of the Fugitive Felon Act against these individuals.
- In 1982, Congress changed NCIC rules to allow the entry of missing children into the system.
- The Missing Children Act (1982) allowed the entry of missing children into NCIC even though the noncustodial parent would not be charged with a crime.
- The Missing Children's Assistance Act (1984) created a national clearinghouse for missing children and authorized research to determine the extent of the problem within the United States.
- The International Child Abduction Remedies Act (1988) ratified the Hague Convention Treaty on missing children. As a result of this Act, the U.S. Department of State would become involved in noncustodial parental abductions in which the abducting parent takes the victim outside the United States.
- The National Child Search Assistance Act (1990) mandated law enforcement agencies to enter all reported missing children under the age of 18 into NCIC, including all reported runaways.
- The International Parental Kidnapping Crime Act (1993) made it a felony for a person to remove a child from the United States in an attempt to interfere with lawful court orders granted in custody matters.
- The Jacob Wetterling Crimes Against Children and Sexually Violent Offender Registration Act (994) was designed to determine the number of sex offenders and provide law enforcement with a readily accessible database with possible suspect information if a child goes missing.
- This act was strengthened in 2006 with federal penalties for failure to register.
- Prosecutorial Remedies and Other Tools to End the Exploitation of Children Today Act (2003) created the AMBER Alert system.

5. **Identify the steps in the investigative process for child kidnapping.**

Because most abducted children who are murdered during stranger kidnappings are killed within the first few hours of the event, abduction must take priority over many types of cases.

- The person responsible for the investigation must be called immediately to the scene.
- Early in the investigation, the agency may want to request an off-line search from NCIC.
- The initial response to a missing child call is perhaps the most crucial component of the investigation.

  - Patrol officers must be trained to respond to such calls efficiently, compassionately, and professionally.
  - Before the patrol officer even arrives on the scene, information about the missing child should be relayed from the dispatcher to the responding officers, including:
    - History of violence or child abuse calls
    - Criminal activities of family members or other persons living at the address (e.g., arrests, narcotics)
    - Runaway reports on the child or siblings
    - Juvenile delinquency reports on the child or siblings

6. **Describe the investigator's role in dealing with child abductions.**

Many of the duties of the investigator in a missing or abducted child case are the same as those in conducting almost any type of investigation.

There are eight basic steps that investigative officers can take to help ensure a successful outcome in a missing or abducted child case. These procedures are geared more toward nonfamily abduction cases and situations in which a child disappears and could be in danger.

- Obtain a detailed briefing from the first responding officer and other on-scene personnel.
- Verify the accuracy of all descriptive information.

- Obtain a brief recent history of family dynamics.
- Explore the basis for conflicting information.
- Review and evaluate all available information and evidence.

- Develop an investigative plan for follow-up.
- Determine what additional resources and specialized services are required.
- Execute an investigative follow-up plan.

Key Terms

abduction

Amber Alert

child abduction

Child Abduction Response Teams (CART)

Child Protection Act of 2003

Code Adam

custodial parent

family abduction

Federal Kidnapping Act

Fugitive Felon Act

International Child Abduction Remedies Act

Jacob Wetterling Crimes Against Children and Sexually Violent Offender Registration Act

labeling

Megan's Law

Missing Children Act of 1982

Missing Children's Assistance Act (MCAA)

National Center for Missing and Exploited Children (NCMEC)

National Crime Information Center (NCIC)

National Incidence Studies of Missing, Abducted, Runaway and Throwaway Children (NISMART) project

neighborhood watch

noncustodial parent

nonfamily abduction

Parental Kidnapping Prevention Act

runaway or lost child

Uniform Child Custody Jurisdiction Act (UCCJA)

Discussion Questions

1. List and discuss the three types of missing persons cases discussed in this chapter.

2. Explain how the Internet is being used to facilitate child abductions today.

3. What is Code Adam and what are the six basic steps in the program?

4. List and discuss the duties of the responding officer to a missing persons call.

5. List and discuss the steps that a criminal investigator should follow in the investigation of a missing person.

6. Discuss the origin, function, and utility of Amber Alerts.

7. What are the types of questions that should be asked of a suspect in a child abduction case?

Notes

1. See: http://www.amberalert.gov/wireless.htm

2. See: http://www.telegraph.co.uk/news/worldnews/northamerica/usa/6101545/Jaycee-Lee-Dugard-walks-into-police-station-18-years-after-disappearance.html

3. Moore, M. (August 27, 2009). Jaycee Lee Dugard walks into police station 18 years after disappearance. *The Register*. Available at http://www.telegraph.co.uk/news/worldnews/northamerica/usa/6101545/Jaycee-Lee-Dugard-walks-into-police-station-18-years-after-disappearance.html.

4. Federal Bureau of Investigation National Crime Information Center. (2012). Available at http://www.fbi.gov/about-us/cjis/ncic/ncic-missing-person-and-unidentified-person-statistics-for-2010.

5. Federal Bureau of Investigation National Crime Information Center. (2012).

6. Ibid.

7. National Center for Missing and Exploited Children. (May, 2009). Available at http://www.missingkids.com/

missingkids/servlet/NewsEventServlet?LanguageCountry =en_US&PageId=4046 (retrieved on December 5, 2011). Also see Douglas, A. (2011). Crimes against children spotlight: Child abductions—Known relationships are the greater danger. *FBI Law Enforcement Bulletin*, August.

8. Douglas. (2011). Crimes against children spotlight, November. Available at http://www.fbi.gov/stats-services/publications/law-enforcement-bulletin/november-   2011/crimes-against-children-spotlight

9. Ibid.

10. Flores, J. R. (October 2002). *National Incidence Studies of Missing, Abducted, Runaway and Throwaway Children (NISMART)*. Washington, DC: U.S. Department of Justice.

11. Flores, J. R. (1999). *Non-family abducted children: National estimates and characteristics*. Washington, DC: Administrator of Office of Juvenile Justice and Delinquency Prevention.

12. Flores. (2002). *National Incidence Studies of Missing, Abducted, Runaway and Throwaway Children (NISMART)*. This study commissioned by the U.S. Department of Justice, Office of Juvenile Justice and Delinquency Prevention found that there were only approximately 115 stereotypical stranger abductions in 1999.

13. Ibid.

14. Ibid.

15. Center for Missing and Exploited Children. (March 2011). Missing and abducted children: A guide to case investigation and program management. Washington, DC: Office of Juvenile Justice and Delinquency Prevention.

16. Flores. (2002). *National Incidence Studies of Missing, Abducted, Runaway and Throwaway Children (NISMART)*, October.

17. Center for Missing and Exploited Children. (2011). *Missing and abducted children*.

18. Ibid.

19. Ibid.

20. Allender, D. (2007). Child abductions: Nightmares in progress. *FBI Law Enforcement Bulletin* 76(7).

21. 18 U.S.C. § 1201(a)(1)

22. Ibid.

23. 19 U.S.C, Chapter 16.

24. 18 U.S.C. § 1073.

25. 28 U.S.C. § 534.

26. 42 U.S.C. § 5771.

27. 42 U.S.C. §§ 11601-11610.

28. 42 U.S.C. § 5779.

29. 18 U.S.C. § 1204.

30. 42 U.S.C. § 14071.

31. The FBI's Uniform Crime Reporting Program has no category for abductions per se. It has a listing in Part II offenses for those against family and children, but because Part I offenses take precedence, a child abducted and raped will be counted as a forcible rape in most agencies.

32. Allender. (2007). Child abductions.

33. 18 U.S.C. § 2252.

34. For additional information, access U.S. Department of Justice Office of Justice Programs. *Amber Alert*. Available at http://www.amberalert.gov (retrieved on September 18, 2012).

35. National Center for Missing and Exploited Children. (1994). *Missing and abducted children*. Available at http://www.missingkids.com.

36. Allender. (2007). Child abductions.

37. Ibid.

38. Croft, R. (2006). Folklore, families and fear: Understanding consumption decisions through the oral tradition. *Journal of Marketing Management* 22(9–10):1053–1076.

39. Ibid.

40. Ibid.

41. The NCMEC can be contacted as a source for both model policies and excellent training, which it provides at no cost to a wide variety of agencies working with children.

42. Allender. (2007). Child abductions.

43. National Center for Missing and Exploited Children. (1994). *Missing and abducted children*.

CHAPTER 13

This chapter will enable you to:

1. Summarize the trends and types of crimes against children.

2. Describe how investigations of crimes against children are conducted.

3. Explain the challenges of interviewing children and using children as witnesses.

4. Describe the roles and distinctions between the pedophile and the child molester.

5. Discuss the role of the medical profession in cases involving sexual misconduct with children.

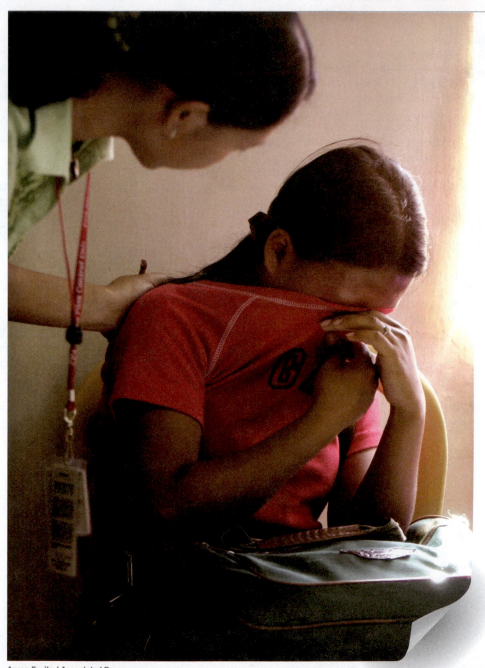

Aaron Favila / Associated Press

Crimes Against Children: Child Abuse, Child Fatalities, and Exploitation

Introduction

 In March 2004, emergency crews in Crystal Lake, Illinois, responded to a call for assistance at the home of 44-year-old Kathy Leonard. When they arrived they found Leonard's son, 15-year-old Seamus M. Leonard, who had cerebral palsy, lying dead amid piles of trash. Emergency personnel commented to local media that the condition of this victim was worse than any victim they had ever seen. McHenry County State's attorney Gary Pack told The Crystal Lake Northwest Herald, *"It would bring anyone to tears."*

A subsequent autopsy revealed the boy died of pneumonia; malnutrition was listed as a contributing cause. Six other children, ages three to 17 years, who also lived in the home, were placed in protective custody under the State Department of Children and Family Services.

After the discovery, the home was deemed uninhabitable by the city's building department and county health department. Case workers from the Illinois Division of Children and Family Services had actually visited the home in January 2003, one year earlier, after a domestic violence complaint. They claimed that there were no indicators of child neglect during their visit. Leonard was arrested and charged with involuntary manslaughter in the death of her son.

The Abuse of Children

The Leonard case illustrates the complexity of **child abuse** cases. The numbers of child abuse cases, of course, reflect only those cases that come to the attention of the police. Statistics show that many more cases exist. In fact, every year in the United States, tens of thousands of children die from a variety of causes, including illness, diseases, accidents, suicides, and homicides.

Child abuse and neglect in the home is but one aspect of the larger set of problems related to child maltreatment that occurs in a variety of places and by people with varied relationships to the victim. This chapter is limited to addressing the particular harms created by child abuse and neglect that occurs in the home, typically by the child's caretaker or someone close to the caretaker (e.g., the mother's boyfriend). Related problems not directly addressed in this chapter, each of which requires separate analysis, include:

- Child physical and sexual abuse in institutions (e.g., correctional facilities, churches, youth organizations, foster care)
- Commercial sexual exploitation of children and organized child sex rings
- Child pornography on the Internet (discussed later in this chapter)
- Child fatalities (including shakenbaby deaths and Munchausen syndrome by proxy—discussed later in this chapter)

- Child abuse among immigrant populations (e.g., excessive discipline of children or other instances in which cultural norms conflict with child welfare laws)
- Exposure of children to hazardous materials (such as being physically present at an illegal methamphetamine lab site)
- Abandoned children
- Juvenile runaways.

Child abuse is a leading cause of childhood serious injuries and fatalities. As the most widely available helping professionals in communities, police have a natural role in preventing and responding to child abuse and neglect. Not only are police legally required to enforce the law and protect residents' safety, but also they are generally committed to children's welfare.

Child abuse and neglect are very difficult problems. The injuries sustained often resemble those caused by unintentional or accidental situations, and police must carefully evaluate all reasonable explanations. The stakes are high—if police misdiagnose the cause of injuries, the potential for future victimization exists. Further, the victim is always a child, and some are very young. Police need to understand children's developmental capacities—their language and cognitive abilities—to be able to communicate with the victims of these crimes. Finally, unlike many other crimes that occur in public places, child abuse and neglect usually occurs in private places, and the victims may try to hide evidence of the abuse or deny that it took place. As a result, collecting sufficient evidence to determine whether a crime occurred and to identify effective responses to the problem is very difficult.

Types of Child Abuse and Neglect

No single, universally accepted definition of child maltreatment exists. Each state constructs its own definition, which can be found using a combination of mandatory child-abuse reporting laws, criminal statutes, and juvenile court statutes. There are three main types of child maltreatment, which often co-occur:

PHYSICAL ABUSE This may range in severity from minor bruising to death. The risk of physical abuse decreases as the child gets older, although adolescents are also victims of it. Boys and girls are equally at risk of minor physical abuse, although boys are slightly more likely to sustain serious injuries. Physical abuse occurs disproportionately among economically disadvantaged families. Income also affects the severity of abuse.

SEXUAL ABUSE This abuse involves varying degrees of coercion and violence. Statistics show that children are at highest risk of sexual abuse from ages 7 to 12, although sexual abuse among very young children does occur and is often undetected because of their inability to communicate

|Fig. 13.1| △

This young boy's black eye may be evidence of physical abuse and should be properly reported by mandatory reporters as well as thoroughly investigated.

Varina and Jay Patel / Shutterstock

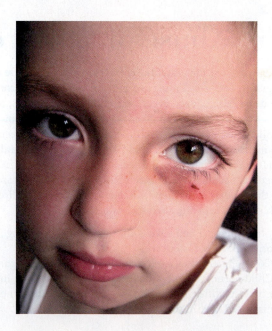

what is happening to them.[1] Sexual abuse victims tend to be selected because they are vulnerable in some way (e.g., very young, passive, quiet, needy). Research also shows that girls are significantly more likely to be sexually abused than boys, although it is possible that boys are simply less likely to report their victimization.[2]

NEGLECT   Neglect ranges from the failure to provide food, clothing, or shelter to the failure to provide medical care, supervision, or schooling. Exposing a child to dangerous conditions or hazards, including crime, may also be considered neglect. The risk of neglect generally declines with age. The mean age of victims of neglect is six years old. Boys and girls are equally at risk of neglect.[3]

Changing Views of Child Abuse and Maltreatment

The abuse of children represents a complex problem whereby numerous behaviors by both the victim and the perpetrator are loosely defined and punishments for such behavior are identified under sometimes complicated laws. It is important to understand the proper context of child abuse before attempting to understand its causes. Child abuse expert Kenneth Lanning in his analysis of child molesters for the Center for Missing and Abducted Children attempts to identify stereotypes and preconceived notions of the problem.

According to Lanning, during the 1950s and 1960s, the limited literature of the sexual victimization of children was on "stranger danger"—the dirty old man and the wrinkled raincoat approaching an innocent child at play. If one was unable to totally deny the existence of child sexual victimization, one could describe the victimization in simplistic terms of good and evil. Hence, the prevention of this "stranger danger" is more clear-cut. We immediately know who the good and bad guys are, what they look like, and whether the danger is external.[4]

The myth of the typical child molester as the dirty old man and the wrinkled raincoat has been reevaluated in recent decades based on research about the kinds of persons who sexually victimize children. The reality is child molesters can look like anyone else and even be someone we know and like.[5] The other part of this myth, however, is still with us and it is far less likely to be discussed. It is the myth of the typical child victim as a completely innocent young girl participating in wholesome all-American activities. It may be more important to confront this part of the myth than the part about the "evil" offender especially when addressing the sexual exploitation of children and acquaintance child molesters (also see the section later in this chapter on child exploitation and Internet pornography). Child victims can be boys as well as girls, and older as well as younger. Not all child victims are "little angels."[6] They are, however, human beings afforded special protection by our laws.

Society today seems to have a problem addressing any sexual victimization case in which the adult offender is not completely "bad" or the child victim is not completely "good." The idea that child victims could simply behave like human beings and respond to the attention and affection of offenders by voluntarily and repeatedly returning to an offender's home is a troubling one.

Child prostitution, for example, is one of the problem areas in **child sexual abuse** and is not discussed as readily in the professional literature as other forms of sexual abuse. It is the form of sexual victimization of children most unlike the stereotype of the innocent child victim. Child prostitutes, by definition, participate in and sometimes initiate their victimization but often do so rather than face subsequent consequences such as abusive home, homelessness, and violence at the hands of those manipulating them to participate in this illegal activity.[7] Child prostitutes and the participants in exploitation cases involving multiple victims are frequently boys.

Therefore, the data about **child molestation** were "misleading" because many of the child victims in question were "prostitutes." This seems to imply children involved in prostitution are not "real" child victims. Whether or not it seems fair, when adults and children have nonforced sex, the child is *always* the victim.

While it is no longer the primary focus of sexual victimization of children literature and training, "stranger danger" still maintains a disproportionate concern for society and is regularly perpetuated in the media.[8]

During the 1970s and 1980s, society became more aware of the sexual victimization of children. Society began to increasingly realize someone they know who is often a relative—a father, stepfather, uncle, grandfather, older brother, or even a female family member—sexually molest most children. Moreover, some lessen the difficulty of accepting this by adopting the view that only family members of socioeconomic groups other than their own commonly engage in such behavior.[9]

It quickly became apparent that warnings about not taking gifts or rides from strangers were not good enough to realistically try to prevent most child sexual abuse. Consequently, prevention programs were developed based on more complex concepts such as "good touching" and "bad touching," the "yucky" feeling, and the child's right to say no. These are not the kinds of things easily and effectively communicated in 50 minutes to hundreds of kids of varying ages packed into a school auditorium.[10]

By the 1980s, many professionals viewed child sexual abuse as being synonymous with **incest**; therefore, the focus of child sexual abuse intervention and investigation turned to one-on-one, father–daughter incest. Even today, a large portion of training materials, articles, and books about this topic refer to child sexual abuse only in terms of intrafamilial, father–daughter incest.[11]

Incest is, in fact, sexual relations between individuals of any age too closely related to marry. It need not, however, necessarily involve an adult and a child, and it goes beyond child sexual abuse. More importantly, child sexual abuse goes beyond father–daughter incest. The familial incest between an adult and a child may be the most common form of child sexual victimization, but it is not the only form.[12]

The progress of the 1970s and 1980s in recognizing the child's sexual victimization not simply as a result of "stranger danger" was an important breakthrough in addressing society's denial. Today, for many child advocates and professionals in the field, the sexual victimization of children is still perceived primarily as one-on-one, intrafamilial sexual abuse. Although they are certainly aware of other forms of sexual victimization of children, when discussing the problem in general their "default setting" seems to always go back to children molested by family members. For the public, the "default setting" seems to be stranger abduction. To them, child molesters are sick perverts or "predators" who physically overpower children and violently force them into sexual activity.

The Problem of Acquaintance Molestation

The often forgotten piece of the puzzle of the sexual victimization of children is **acquaintance molestation**. A few insightful professionals have recognized the problem of acquaintance child molesters for a long time. For example, the *Boys Club Handbook* published in 1939 discusses the behavior patterns of such men trying to gain access to boys through youth serving organizations. Between 1975 and 1985, law enforcement in the United States began to increasingly become aware of these offenders in the investigative challenges they present.

In March 1977, the Illinois legislative investigating commission submitted a report about the sexual exploitation of children to the Illinois General Assembly. The report states, "…most of the child molesters whom we encounter during our investigation follows certain patterns. Frequently, these individuals will look for children involved in legitimate groups—Boy Scouts, summer camps, the big Brothers—and the molester's involvement in these groups provides them open access to a wider range of children." Examples of this type of offender are seen in the Case in Point case studies involving Warren Jeffs and Jerry Sandusky discussed in this chapter.

Acquaintance molesters are still, however, one of the most challenging manifestations of sexual victimization of children for society and professionals to face. People seem more willing to accept a sinister, unknown individual or "stranger" from a different location or father-stepfather from a different socioeconomic background as a child molester than a clergy member, next-door neighbor, law enforcement officer, pediatrician, teacher, coach, or volunteer. Acquaintance molesters often gain access to children through youth serving organizations. The acquaintance molester by definition is one of us. He is not simply an anonymous, external threat. He cannot be identified by physical description and often, not even by "bad" character traits. Absence specialized training or experience and an objective perspective, he cannot easily be distinguished from others.

These kinds of molesters have always existed but society, organizations, and the criminal justice system have been reluctant to accept the reality of these cases. When such an offender is discovered in our midst, a common response has been to just move him out of our midst, perform damage control, and then try to forget about it or demonize him as "evil" deceivers. Sadly, one of the main reasons the criminal justice system, institutions, and the public have been forced to confront the problem of acquaintance molestation has been the proliferation of lawsuits arising from the negligence of many prominent faith-based and youth serving organizations.

The Scope of the Problem

The National Child Abuse and Neglect Data System is maintained by the U.S. Department of Health and Human Services. It is a voluntary, national database that provides information on the incidence of child abuse and neglect. Each state's child protective agency provides data.

In 2010, the U.S. Department of Health and Human Services estimated that there were 3.3 million referrals involving the alleged maltreatment of approximately 5.9 million children. Of the nearly 2 million reports that were screened and received a **Child Protective Services (CPS)** response, over 90 percent received an investigation response and almost 10 percent received an alternative response. Of the 1,793,724 reports that received an investigation, 436,321 were substantiated.[13]

Of the many victims of child abuse, the greatest percentage of children were neglected. CPS investigations or assessments determined the following:

- More than 75 percent (78.3 percent) suffered neglect
- More than 15 percent (17.6 percent) suffered physical abuse
- Less than 10 percent (9.2 percent) suffered sexual abuse

Child fatalities are the most tragic outcomes of abuse. When a child's death is sudden and unexpected, the tragedy is compounded if law enforcement is unable to conduct a proper investigation. If the investigation is flawed, two outcomes—neither acceptable—are very real possibilities. First is that an innocent person will be suspected or accused of either a crime that did not occur or a crime for which the person has no responsibility. Secondly a real crime will remain undetected or unsolved and the person responsible for the fatal maltreatment of the child will never be identified or brought to justice.

Although the vast majority of child deaths are related to natural causes or accidents, all sudden and unexpected child deaths must be properly investigated. Every day, at least four children in the United States die from maltreatment. Only by thoroughly investigating all sudden and unexpected child deaths can society be certain that maltreatment is not involved. Professionally conducted investigations of child fatalities ensure that innocent people are not falsely accused of wrongdoing and guilty people are not allowed to escape arrest and prosecution and possibly harm another child.

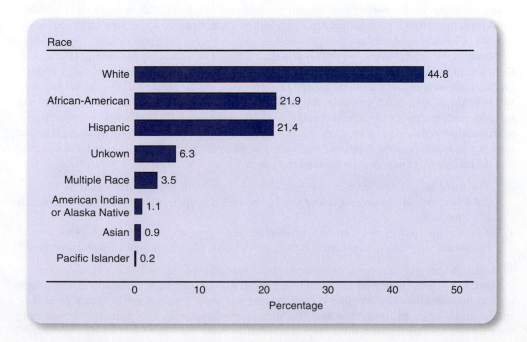

|Fig. 13.2| △

Bar graph showing child victims by race for 2010.

Child Maltreatment 2010. Department of Health and Human Services.

|Fig. 13.3| ▲

Bar graph showing reported child maltreatment types for 2010.

Child Maltreatment 2010. Department of Health and Human Services.

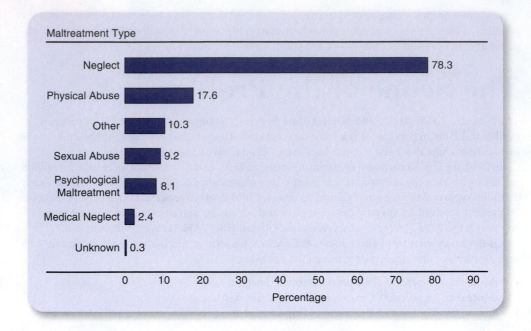

Of the approximately 1,500 children who died from abuse or neglect in 2006, over three-fourths were under four years old.[14] Compounding the problem of the high incidence of child abuse and neglect, many families who come to the attention of child protective services have subsequent referrals for suspected abuse. Thus, it is essential for police and child protective services to identify the situations in which child abuse and neglect are likely to occur so that they can implement appropriate responses.

Reporting Mechanisms

Child abuse is revealed in a variety of ways. For example, the child may reveal the abuse intentionally or accidentally. Family members who observe caregivers interacting with children may suspect or witness abuse. Professionals involved with the child may also suspect abuse based on behavioral, emotional, or verbal clues. Additionally, neighbors may see, hear, or suspect maltreatment based on their observations of the family.

Statistics for child abuse reporting are instructive. For example, according to the U.S. Department of Health and Human Services, three-fifths of reports of alleged child abuse and neglect in 2010 were made by professionals.[15] The term *professional* means that the person had contact with the alleged child maltreatment victim as part of the reporting person's job. This term includes teachers, police officers, lawyers, and social services staff. "Other" and unknown report sources submitted 13.7 percent of reports. An "other" report source includes any state code that does not fit into one of the standardized codes. The remaining reports were made by nonprofessionals, including friends, neighbors, and relatives:

- The three largest percentages of report sources were from such professionals as teachers (16.4 percent), lawenforcement and legal personnel (16.7 percent), and social services staff (11.5 percent).
- Anonymous sources (9.0 percent), other relatives (7.0 percent), parents (6.8 percent), and friends and neighbors (4.4 percent), accounted for nearly all of the nonprofessional reporters.[16]

Although they may suspect or be aware of abuse, many people are often hesitant about reporting their suspicions. They may not want to get involved, may believe that parents have the right to treat their children however they choose, or may not want to accept the implications of their suspicions about people they know and like. Some professionals may worry about compromising their rapport with their clients if they report suspected abuse.

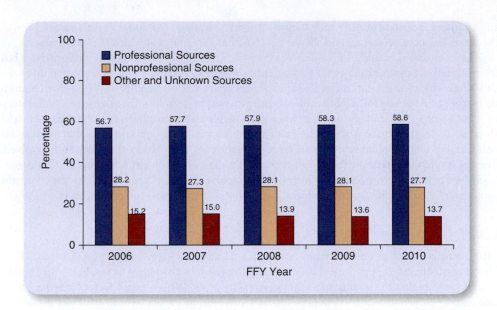

|Fig. 13.4| △

Bar graph showing reporting sources for child maltreatment between 2006 and 2010.

Child Maltreatment 2010. Department of Health and Human Services.

Beginning in the 1960s, all states established mandatory child abuse reporting laws that were designed to ensure that the agencies tasked with protecting children's welfare (i.e., police and child protective services agencies) were made aware of situations in which child maltreatment is suspected.[17] While laws vary across states, most specify the following:

- Categories of people required to report suspected abuse or neglect. These commonly include medical personnel, teachers, mental health professionals, social workers, law enforcement officers, and other professionals who routinely contact children. Some states require *any* person to report suspected abuse.
- Conditions under which a professional must make a report. Most often, professionals must make a report when they suspect maltreatment has occurred. Certainty is not required.
- Immunity from legal liability for reporters, and penalties for the failure to report suspected abuse.
- Timelines within which people must make a report, often within 24 hours of the event that triggered the suspicion.
- Agencies responsible for receiving and investigating reports. Some states require all reports to be made to child protective services, other states require certain reports to be made to the local law enforcement agency, and still other states give the reporter discretion whether to report to child protective services or to law enforcement. Very few states require all reports to be made to a law enforcement agency.[18]

Most child protective services maintain a 24-hour, toll-free hotline to receive reports of suspected child abuse. Reports to law enforcement agencies are usually made to emergency 911 dispatchers. Many states' reporting laws mandate child protective services to relay at least a subset of reports to police (e.g., in the case of serious injury or death of the victim). Whether legally required to do so or not, most police relay reports of suspected abuse to child protective services.

Child abuse, in all its varied forms, is a symptom of a pathologic social environment in general and a signal of a family in distress in particular. The greater availability of highly addictive and generally more affordable drugs, such as crack cocaine, has added more impact on families with children who are already at risk as well as created additional cases of drug dependency and family crises. The debilitating and all-consuming nature of these drugs directly fuels the environment that fosters child abuse and neglect.[19]

One of the traditional problems in dealing effectively with child abuse has been the inability of the two lead investigative authorities—social welfare and law enforcement agencies—to work together in a strategic manner. These agencies often work along parallel lines with one another, each addressing its respective component of the same individual or family problem. Obvious reasons for this are based on differences in philosophy and training of personnel as well as the administrative and statutory demands under which they must work. Although the duties and responsibilities of these two components cannot and should not join, there are points at which they do intersect.

After a situation of abuse or neglect has been reported to law enforcement authorities, it has often already reached a point where permanent or irreparable damage has been enacted upon the child. Law enforcement and social welfare agencies share a responsibility in seeing that children do not become the targets of adult violence and parental neglect. Routine sharing of information by these agencies in a strategic manner, when permissible and appropriate, can often prevent child abuse or neglect from taking place. The point at which social welfare problems start to become law enforcement matters often represents a critical juncture for the welfare of the children involved. The key is often to determine the appropriate point for law enforcement intervention. This is generally best performed by pooling the interests and capabilities of welfare officers, law enforcement prosecutors, and relevant others in a team approach to meet the needs of specific cases.

Child Abuser Profiles

Child abuse occurs in all cultural, ethnic, occupational, and socioeconomic groups. A parent's likelihood of mistreating his or her children is rarely the result of any single factor, but rather results from a combination of circumstances and personality types. While certain factors may be prevalent among perpetrators, the mere presence of a situation or particular trait does not mean that abuse will always occur.

PHYSICAL ABUSE Caretakers who physically abuse their children tend to experience high stress (e.g., from single parenting, health problems, unemployment, poverty) and may have poorly developed coping skills. They may also struggle with personality factors such as low self-esteem, poor impulse control, depression, anxiety, and low frustration **tolerance.** Their expectations for their child may exceed the child's developmental capacity. As a result, they may not interactwell with their child and tend to use more punitive discipline. Perhaps because mothers spend more time with their children, perpetrators are slightly more likely to be female than male.[20] Further, normal adolescent defiance and rebellion increases family tension and may frustrate parents, who respond with excessive punishment. When confronted, physically abusive caretakers tend to offer illogical, unconvincing, or contradictory explanations for the child's injury.[21]

SEXUAL ABUSE Sexual abusers are usually in a position of authority or trust over their victims. They are usually male and typically in their early 1930s, although a significant proportion are adolescents (e.g., siblings or babysitters).[22] Offenders who victimize family members tend to have only one or two victims (usually female), while nonrelative offenders tend to have a much larger number of victims (usually male). Their feelings of inadequacy, depression, isolation, rigid values, and deviant arousal patterns contribute to their offending. Once they have selected a vulnerable victim, perpetrators generally "groom" the victim by progressing from nonsexual touching to sexual activity.[23] They may use their authority to force their victims to participate, or may use various forms of enticements and coercion. Using bribes, threats, isolation, or physical aggression, perpetrators

|Fig. 13.5| △

The laceration seen on this child's leg is evidence of non-accidental injuries which are consistent with child abuse.

© Medical-on-Line / Alamy

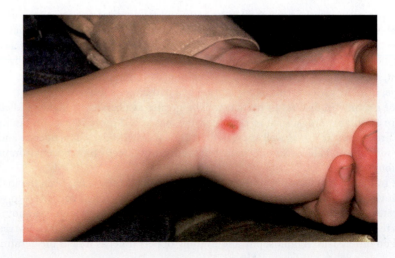

also persuade their victims to remain silent about the abuse so that other adults cannot intervene. Sexual abusers tend to rationalize and minimize their behavior, deny the sexual intent, or project blame onto the victim. That said, most sexual abusers are not attracted exclusively to children (i.e., they are also sexually attracted to adults), and they have relatively low recidivism rates, particularly as they get older.[24]

NEGLECT Single female caretakers are mostly likely to be reported for neglecting their children. Younger mothers, those with large families, and those who experienced neglect themselves are also more likely to neglect their children's needs. Economic hardship and isolation from social activities and peers are also contributing factors. They may also have a substance abuse problem that limits their ability to care for themselves and creates a chaotic lifestyle that compromises their parenting abilities.

The Role of the Investigator

The criminal investigator plays a variety of roles in the identification of and response to child abuse and neglect. Their contact with children in schools, homes, and the community places them in an ideal position to identify situations in which maltreatment may be occurring. Police will also receive reports of suspected abuse, either through calls to the police agency or through their routine contacts with community members. Incidents of child abuse may also lurk behind the scenes of domestic violence calls; thus police should ask about and interview any children at the scene. Police may also be the first responders to the scene of suspected abuse or neglect. While child protective services may be the intended recipient of a suspected child abuse report, an agency representative may not be available when an immediate response is needed. When police arrive on the scene, typical investigatory protocols (e.g., completing reports, taking photographs, conducting interviews) apply. Police are also involved in securing needed medical treatment for the child's injuries or in obtaining forensic medical examinations to determine the presence of injuries. Police may also need to brief medical staff on the facts, allegations, and types of evidence to be collected.

In some cases, police may need to protect child protective services staff. Staff members often need to visit homes in isolated or dangerous areas and deal with unstable or violent people. Accused caretakers may refuse entry to the home or access to the possible victim, both of which are essential to determining whether abuse occurred and whether the child is still at risk of harm. Most people more widely accept police authority than they do that of child protective services. If immediate danger exists, police need to temporarily remove the child from the home. Police are needed both for their authority to remove children at risk of immediate harm and to defuse the tensions removals may cause. Police presence can often have a stabilizing effect.

Child abuse is a crime and therefore police have an obvious role in investigating allegations, arresting suspects, and preparing cases for prosecution, if warranted. Whether a case will be prosecuted or not, police are obligated to coordinate with other professionals (child protective services workers, prosecutors, medical professionals, social service providers, victim advocates, etc.) involved with the case.

|Fig. 13.6| ▲

The investigator's role in investigating child abuse often involves countless hours reviewing available information on social networks as well as pornography sites on the Internet.

Jochen Tack / AGE Fotostock America, Inc.

Child Fatalities

Awareness of some basic dynamics in issues is critical to effective investigations of child fatalities. Research and experience have shown that children are most at risk of dying of maltreatment during the first four years of life. In fact, 40 percent of children who are victims of fatal maltreatment are infants (younger than one year old), and 75 percent are younger than five years old.[25] The Centers for Disease Control and Prevention have reported that the chances of being murdered are greater on the day of birth than at any other point in a person's life. Caring for children during their preschool years can be very stressful for parents and other caretakers. Faced with a young child's persistent problems with sleeping, feeding, and toilet training, a caretaker may lose control and assault the child in anger or may cause injury while punishing the child. Some inexperienced caretakers have unrealistic expectations about what is appropriate child behavior and what children are even capable of doing in the early stages of their development. In these cases, caretakers can become angry because they view a child's crying or bedwetting as an act of defiance rather than being normal behavior for a young child. The deadly combination of an angry adult and a physically vulnerable child can result in fatal or life-threatening injuries to the child.

For the most part, child fatalities can be categorized as either acute or chronic maltreatment. These are discussed next.

ACUTE MALTREATMENT **Acute maltreatment** means that the child's death is directly related to injuries suffered as a result of a specific incident or abuse or act of negligence. In such cases, the child has not been previously abused or neglected.[26]

In cases involving acute physical abuse, the caretaker may have fatally assaulted the child in either an inappropriate response to the child's behavior or a conscious act to hurt the child. Offenders of cases of **shaken baby syndrome (SBS)**, in which a child's brain is injured from violent shaking, often cite the child's crying as the "triggering event."[27]

In cases of **acute neglect**, a caretaker's one-time failure to properly supervise the child may result in a fatal injury. A common example is a fatal drowning that occurs when an infant is briefly unsupervised in a bathtub. Children have also sustained fatal gunshot wounds when caretakers fail to properly secure loaded firearms. Some states have statues that specifically assign criminal responsibility to an individual who makes a firearm accessible to a child, either intentionally or through failure to properly secure the weapon. The penalty for this crime may be increased if the child's possession of a firearm results in either injury or death to the child or another person.[28]

CHRONIC MALTREATMENT In **chronic maltreatment** cases, the child's death is directly related to injuries caused by neglect occurring over an extended period of time. Battered child syndrome is an example of chronic physical abuse (discussed later in this chapter). Although the direct cause of death in a battering case is usually a specific injury (often brain trauma), numerous indications of former maltreatment—old and new injuries and possible signs of neglect—are also typically present. Depriving a child of food for a significant period of time is a common form of chronic physical neglect. In cases of chronic abuse or neglect, a history of the child's previous maltreatment often will appear in either Child Protective Services or medical records. In fact, in 2000, 38 percent of all children who died of abuse or neglect had prior current contact with a CPS agency.[29]

How Child Fatalities Differ from Other Types of Homicide

All persons involved in the investigation of a child fatality must understand that these cases differ from typical homicides in many regards, including the causes of death, the offender's motivations and legal culpability for the crime, the methods used to inflict the fatal injuries, the types of injuries that the victim sustained, the forensic and physical evidence involved, and the investigative techniques used. In the following discussion, some of the unique issues criminal investigators may encounter are discussed.

DELAYED DEATH Many maltreatment deaths involve a delay between the time the child sustains the fatal injury and the subsequent death of the child. Although this may also be true with any serious injury, it often happens in cases of abuse of head trauma and in cases involving internal injuries to the chest and abdomen. Note that abusive head trauma (AHT) is the most common type of fatal injury and maltreatment death and includes brain trauma resulting from SBS and other types of direct blunt trauma to the brain. Experiences show that the investigator will be called to the hospital about a severely injured child being treated or surviving on life support and will learn that the prognosis for survival is slim. Depending on the injuries sustained, the child may survive anywhere from hours to days.

This delayed death scenario can also occur when a child is severely scalded from an immersion burn, suffers an infection or other medical complications arising from the injuries, and then dies weeks or months after the incident occurred. That child may also suffer brain trauma and lapse into a coma for months, only to die eventually from pneumonia or some other medical complication. Even though the abuse was not the immediate cause of death in these situations, the manner of death would still be most likely ruled a homicide because the original abuse was the basis for the medical complication that resulted in the child's death.

WITNESSES AND ACCOMPLICES Another common factor in maltreatment cases is the absence of a witness to the actual incident of abuse or neglect that caused the child's life threatening or fatal injury. Similar to other homicides in which a person may be killed in a public place, maltreatment murders almost always occur in a private location, such as the family's home.

Accomplices are also rare in maltreatment cases. It is unusual for two or more persons to participate in the child's fatal maltreatment. Far more common is the situation in which one person is aware that another (e.g., a spouse, girlfriend, or boyfriend) is abusing or neglecting a child but fails to report the maltreatment or take steps to protect the child. In some cases, the person who is aware of the abuse may actually interfere with the investigation by lying or purposely misleading investigators or even tampering with physical evidence. In such cases, these persons will be held legally responsible for their role in the child's death.

Although an investigation may not present an opportunity to turn accomplices against each other (as is often the case in adult homicide cases), it may be possible to convince the person not actually involved in the abuse or neglect to testify about how the suspect treated the child. More and more states are limiting spousal immunity in child abuse cases and other circumstances. To obtain cooperation, it is often possible to charge a reluctant witness with failure to report suspected child abuse or failure to protect the child. In some cases, these persons may actually have been involved in fatal maltreatment and can be charged as accomplices in the child's death.

WEAPONS Maltreatment murders of children rarely involve traditional weapons such as firearms, knives, or blunt objects. Typical weapons include hands, feet, household items, and scalding water. Often, death results and injuries are caused by shaking, slamming, blunt-force trauma, scalding, starvation, neglectful supervision, and various other forms of physical abuse and neglect. Investigation is unlikely to turn up a weapon that will directly link the offender to the crime in the way that ballistic evidence links a suspect's gun to a victim's death. The exception may be a human bite mark or an instrument such as an electrical extension cord that leaves a distinct pattern injury.

TRACE EVIDENCE In most cases of fatal child maltreatment, trace evidence such as fingerprints and DNA will be of far less value than it might be in other crimes. For example, if a child who lives with both parents is beaten to death at the home, the mere presence of the parents' fingerprints at the scene links neither of them to the crime. Exceptions are cases in which the offender sexually assaulted or bit the child and DNA evidence is involved.

CIRCUMSTANTIAL EVIDENCE Because most fatal child maltreatment cases lack witnesses or any **direct evidence** tying a specific individual to the crime, these cases may often rely on circumstantial evidence. Specifically, the investigator must prove that only the suspect could have committed the crime. Two critically important steps are to establish that the suspect was the only person with the child at the time of the fatal injury and to prove that the injury was not accidental.[30]

INTERNAL INJURIES In many child fatalities, the victim's injuries may not be visible at first. The symptoms or signs of some injuries may begin to appear hours or even days after the child sustained the injuries. Most fatal injuries of children involve trauma to the brain and the internal organs of the abdomen and chest. These injuries can only be detected with medical procedures such as radiographs (x-rays), computed tomography (CT) and magnetic resonance imaging (MRI) scans, and the forensic autopsy. Unless the child's injuries are visible externally, the death may appear natural at first. The investigator must not jump to conclusions based solely on an external examination of the child's body. This is especially true for an infant whose death may appear to be from natural causes such as sudden infant death syndrome (SIDS).

MOTIVES Child maltreatment murderers are, by definition, committed by persons responsible for the care and supervision of the victim. For example, in 2001, an estimated 83 percent of these fatalities involved a parent, and 17 percent involving nonparent caretakers.[31] The motives in these cases differ from those typically found in homicide cases. Caretakers generally do not kill their children for revenge or greed during the commission of a violent crime such as a robbery or sexual assault. This is not to suggest that on occasion children will not be murdered by sadistic or violent caretakers. In many child fatalities, the victim is subjected to violent assault because of crying, bedwetting, or feeding problems or because the caretaker has feelings of resentment, frustration, or hatred for the child.

The Role of Child Protective Services and the Police

As with other types of criminal investigations such as arson, an unusual aspect of child fatality cases is the involvement of an agency other than law enforcement in the investigation. Typically, CPS has legal authority to be involved in the investigation of a child's death if a parent or other member of the household is suspected. It should be noted, however, that the CPS role is very different from the law enforcement role.[32]

The role of CPS is to determine whether maltreatment was involved in the child's death, identify the responsible party, and then take appropriate action to protect any surviving siblings. CPS does not determine whether anyone committed a crime nor are CPS personnel trained as criminal investigators or trained to collect evidence or interrogates suspect offenders. It is therefore important that law enforcement and CPS communicate and coordinate their efforts during the course of the investigation. One coordinated investigation is always preferable to two separate investigations. In fact, at least 30 states have either mandated or authorized implementation of multidisciplinary teams to investigate child maltreatment.[33]

The role of the criminal investigator is to determine whether a crime has been committed and who is responsible. Accomplishing this involves analyzing old and new injuries revealed by an autopsy and by a review of the child's medical history, thoroughly investigating the death scene, collecting and examining evidence, interviewing witnesses, and interrogating suspects.

Although it is important that law enforcement and CPS coordinate their efforts, it is imperative that the police assume the leadership role in the investigation. This is necessary because of the legal and practical issues involved in obtaining evidence and confessions. Only a police investigator has the training, expertise, and legal mandate to execute search warrants, collect and evaluate evidence, interrogate suspects, and file criminal charges.

If the CPS investigator prematurely confronts a parent of a suspected fatal child abuse, the police investigator will find it more difficult, if not impossible, to successfully interrogate that same individual at a later time. It must be remembered that both police and CPS investigators are acting under statutory requirements. Only if these two social actors coordinate their efforts and use their respective resources will the investigation succeed.[34]

Responsibilities of the First Responder

Police officers dispatched to the location of a seriously injured or deceased child—the "first responders" on the scene—have a number of important responsibilities to carry out before investigators arrive. This assumes that paramedics have already reached the scene and are in the process of attending to the child.

The officer's first priority is to identify and secure the potential crime scene or location where the child was injured or discovered. It is important to remember that the scene may involve more than one room in a house and may also involve the outdoors. Officers should then assess the situation and request additional support as necessary, including additional officers to help secure the scene, crisis counselors, paramedics, personnel from the corners or medical examiner's office, and the detectives or investigators who will conduct the investigation. The first responder should clear

Situations in Which Police Presence at Initial Contact Is Strongly Recommended

- ☑ The case is serious enough to warrant arrest.
- ☑ Police cannot reach child protective services and they need an immediate response.
- ☑ A child is endangered and the child protective services worker is not permitted to enter the home.
- ☑ A child must be placed in protective custody against the parents' wishes.
- ☑ The suspect may flee.
- ☑ Evidence must be preserved.
- ☑ The child protective services worker needs protection or order must otherwise be maintained.

Source: Dedel, K. (2010). Responses to child abuse and neglect in the home. U.S. Department of Justice: Office of Community Oriented Policing Services.

all individuals from the scene and make sure that nobody enters the area where they could trample or otherwise contaminate or remove evidence.[35] This can be very difficult to achieve because family members may be very emotional and may not want to leave the deceased child. Patience and diplomacy will encourage cooperation in most cases.

While securing the scene, first responders should be observant. They should look at what is happening and listen to what people are saying. Until the officers have time to write down their observations, they must make mental notes of anything that may be relevant. Without attempting to conduct thorough interviews of the parents or caretakers, the first responder should identify who discovered the child and then find out whether anyone attempted first aid or moved, dressed, or bathed the child. This information should be given to the investigators as soon as they arrive.

As soon as the scene is secure, one officer should be charged with maintaining the log of all personnel who enter the scene. The first responders should also ensure that nobody opens or closes the windows; uses the commode; or disposes of anything, including trash, the child's clothing, medicine, or anything else until the scene has been processed and photographed. Furthermore, until the investigator arrives, the first responder should obtain the names of those present and their relationships to the child. The officers should allow no one to leave the location until this information is obtained.

Collecting Evidence

If the investigator suspects that a child's life-threatening injuries or death may be the result of maltreatment, immediate action is needed to preserve the crime scene and to collect any evidence. Evidence collection includes photographing the victim and searching the location where the investigator believes the injuries occurred. Before searching any possible crime scene, the investigator must determine whether a search warrant or consent to search is necessary. If there are any doubts, the investigator should consult the legal adviser. In most cases of child deaths, there is no exception to the Fourth Amendment requirement for a search warrant for valid consent to search.

The search of the scene should include the following:

- Ensure that scale diagrams are made of the layout and that photographs, a video, or both are taken. Photographs should show the general location and progress to specific items of interest.
- Consider as evidence prescription or over-the-counter medicine the child was taking and other medicine or substances the child may have ingested. If it is not practical to remove such medicine from the scene because someone else in the household needs it, document the information on the label.
- It appears that the child may have died of malnourishment, the investigator may want to take an inventory of the amount of baby food or formula that is present. Whatever is found should be documented and photographed.

- If evidence is located that the caretaker has been abusing alcohol or other substances, this evidence should also be carefully documented.
- Trash cans inside and outside the residence should also be searched for possible evidence such as bloodstained clothing; items used to clean up blood, vomit, urine, or feces; and implements used to injure the child, such as wooden spoons, belts, and electrical extension cords.[36]

Interviewing Witnesses

Conducting timely, thorough interviews of witnesses contributes greatly to the success of a child fatality investigation. The list of potential witnesses varies from case to case but typically includes the deceased child's siblings and parents, the child's caretakers immediately before the death or during the time the child appeared to be in medical distress, neighbors, law enforcement first responders, paramedics, medical providers, and anyone else who may have relevant information about the child or the events leading to the injury or death.

As stated in Chapter 6, an interview differs significantly from an interrogation. It is important to understand the difference between these two police functions. An interview is a nonconfrontational conversation between two people in which information is exchanged. In comparison, an interrogation is an attempt to obtain a confession from a suspect who is believed to have committed a crime. In an interview, the person being questioned may have knowledge the investigator needs. Because the person is not under arrest and formal charges have not been filed, it is usually not necessary to give "*Miranda* warnings" at this point. The *Miranda* requirement in this regard, however, may be governed by state law in the respective jurisdiction of the crime. The following considerations should be kept in mind during the course of interviewing witnesses:[37]

- The interview should be conducted as early in the investigation as practical.
- Witnesses should be interviewed separately.
- It should be determined what a witness actually observed and knows firsthand and what someone else may have told him or her. For example, if a witness states that a child fell from the couch, it is important for the investigator to determine whether the person actually saw the child fall or is just repeating something someone else told him or her. If the investigator later determines that the child did not fall from the couch, the person who told the witness that this occurred may actually have caused the child's injury, as demonstrated by giving false information to conceal his or her actions.
- After witnesses provide a verbal account, a formal statement should be taken. This applies to caretakers, neighbors, first responders, paramedics, medical professionals, and anyone else who has information about the event. It is preferable to record the statement electronically (audio or videotape) or ask the witness to write or type it in affidavit format and then have the witness sign it. The value of the formal statement is that it documents the witness' version of the events and locks the witness into that story. The investigator then can verify or disprove that account during the course of the investigation. A person originally identified as a witness may later be identified as a suspect. Having properly documented the formal statement prevents that person from changing his or her story as additional facts emerge.
- Other children residing in the home of the deceased child can also be important witnesses. They may have observed or heard something directly related to the death and may have knowledge of the child's prior maltreatment. They might even know who is responsible. It is important that someone who has specific training on how to interview children conduct all interviews with child witnesses. If the criminal investigator does not have this training, someone should be located who does to conduct the interview. These interviews are often conducted at child advocacy centers (CACs), CPS, or victim or witness programs available in the community.
- Witnesses should be provided the opportunity to give a narrative account of what they actually know about the event under investigation. For example, in a case in which child was brought to the hospital after having a seizure, the parent should be asked to tell everything that happened to the child in the previous 72 hours. It is important that the investigator does not interrupt with questions or requests to repeat part of the account.[38] It is far better to hear the entire story and then ask about things that were not mentioned or that need clarification.
- In some cases, it may be appropriate to request that a witness or a possible suspect take a polygraph or voice stress analyzer test. Although the results of these tests are not admissible in court, they can be useful in subsequent interviews and interrogations.[39]

Evidence from the Autopsy

The autopsy will determine the official cause of death (e.g., blunt-force trauma, drowning) and manner of death (e.g., natural, accidental, homicide, suicide, undetermined). The criminal investigator should observe the autopsy if at all possible. The information learned from the autopsy will better prepare the investigator for subsequent interviews and interrogations.

The pathologist can provide information about the child's injuries, including those related to the death and those previously inflicted, and about the child's general state of health before death. It is important to ask for details to explain whether a single event or multiple factors caused or contributed to the death.[40]

In turn, the investigator can tell the pathologist what he or she has learned from interviews and record checks. In many cases, the pathologist's knowledge can offer an opinion regarding the possibility that the child's injuries occurred in the manner described by witnesses. The pathologist may also be able to estimate the time of death based on the child's stomach contents and investigative notes about the child's last meal.[41]

Documentation of the Case

The official case file must document the entire investigation from the time law enforcement received the initial call to the time criminal charges are filed. It must include all copies of official police reports, investigators' notes, medical records, the autopsy report and pictures, crime scene pictures, the 911 recordings, witness statements, search warrants, newspaper articles, background investigation on the suspect, and any other relevant information or records obtained during the investigation.

Because most of the information in the official file will be subject to the discovery process by defense attorneys, investigators need to be thoroughly familiar with the file's contents. A defense attorney may attempt to impeach the investigator's testimony on the witness stand by obtaining statements from the investigator that contradict the evidence in the case file.[42]

When entering notes in the case file, investigators should refrain from including personal opinions and ideas outside the scope of their professional knowledge. These include things such as time of death, body temperature, and cause of death. Finally, a check should be made of the CPS investigator's case file for additional items that should be contained in the police case file.[43]

Interrogating Suspects

Proper interrogation of a suspect may be instrumental in identifying the person responsible for the child's injuries. Absent any direct evidence showing who is responsible (which is almost never the case), the suspect's voluntary confession of guilt is probably the most powerful evidence that can be presented at trial. However, a suspect's written or electronically recorded voluntary statement is of little value unless it is admitted into evidence. The defense attorney will almost always challenge a suspect's confession by claiming coercion or some other violation of the client's rights under the Fourth, Fifth, Sixth, or Fourteenth Amendments. Accordingly, the investigator must be thoroughly familiar with the case law in his or her state as it relates to obtaining confessions and the admissibility of confessions as evidence.

Investigators must carefully document that the suspect's constitutional rights are protected and that all applicable departmental procedures and state laws have been followed. At a bare minimum, the case file should contain the following documentation:

- Whether the suspect was under arrest at the time of the interrogation or was just brought in for questioning
- When the interrogations started and how long they lasted
- How long and at what time the suspect was allowed to use the restroom or to have something to eat or drink
- The names of any individuals who participated in the interrogation or observed it
- Whether the suspect had any physical impairments or medical problems that could interfere with the ability to speak, hear, or understand what was being said
- The suspect's level of formal education and whether the suspect can read and write[44]

Suspects should be interrogated as early in the investigation as possible. Investigators can usually begin as soon as the cause and manner of death are known (even if the official autopsy report has not been written) and the evidence indicates who the suspect is. In some cases, it may be best to interrogate the suspect before the autopsy is conducted. The following guidelines will assist in conducting a proper interrogation:

- Dress in business or casual clothes, not a uniform.
- If the suspect does not speak English and an interpreter is needed, make sure the interpreter is an expert in the suspect's language.
- Have another investigator observe the interrogation. If the investigator's agency does not videotape interrogations, then the observer can at least rebut any allegations that the suspect was mistreated or coerced into a confession.

If the confession cannot be obtained, everything the suspect says should be documented. This is helpful because a suspect who is not confessing to causing the child's fatal injuries may offer an explanation of the injuries and surrounding events that is implausible or can be refuted by evidence.

Even if the suspect confesses, the confession may be suppressed at trial for a variety of procedural and legal reasons. This is one reason why the investigator must not stop working on the case even when a confession has been obtained. Rather, the investigator should continue to investigate any new leads and interview anyone he or she thinks might have relevant information.

Child Physical Abuse

In addition to child fatalities, child physical abuse remains a serious problem. As with the investigation of child fatalities, the investigative response to child physical abuse must be timely and thorough. *Child abuse* is a generic term that incorporates a variety of purposeful acts resulting in injuries to a child. Probably the most dramatic of these and the most often reported to the police is physical child abuse that results in death or serious injury. However, child abuse is far more pervasive and often more subtle. For example, as stated earlier, physical battering may be the result of a parent's momentary fit of anger, or it may be part of an ongoing abusive situation. In the case of sexual abuse situations within families, offenses are more frequently calculated and may form a long-term pattern of sexual abuse. Physical neglect of a child's needs for nourishment or medical care, reckless disregard for his or her safety, and failure to provide food or medical care are all elements of the child abuse and neglect problem.

The physical effects of child abuse are only part of a child's injuries. The psychological and emotional impacts of abuse frequently have long-term consequences for the child. Many children blame themselves for the abuse, adopting the feeling that they are bad and deserve the abusive treatment. Others may adopt the long-lasting perception that violence is a natural, even acceptable, component of family life and interpersonal relationships. As a consequence, many abused children carry to the next generation the same type of treatment that they endured. Other children translate physical abuse into later criminal violence. The fact that so many violent offenders have histories of child abuse and neglect is testimony to the fact that child abuse is often an intergenerational phenomenon. As such, it is important not only for the current victim but also for future generations to identify child abuse whenever possible and to bring appropriate enforcement and treatment to bear on the problem.

Investigative Resources

The point at which an investigation of child abuse begins depends largely on the reporting party or agency and the degree to which a case of abuse, neglect, or abandonment can be legally established. For example, abused children who require immediate medical attention suggest a point of investigative departure through interviews with medical staff. In most cases, investigation of child abuse requires contact with one or more sources of information depending on the nature of the complaint and the perceived scope of the abuse. Basic types of questions can be identified for conducting interviews with individuals who report child abuse. Such inquiries are generally warranted before direct contact is made with the family and the child.

Other basic types of information available through the police department should also be collected early in the investigation. This includes such information as the existence of criminal records or charges against any members of the family or court protection orders that may have been filed against any family members. Other general sources of investigative information can be gathered from a variety of resources in the community. These are reviewed in the following sections.

Emergency Room Personnel and Medical Examiners

In the worst-case scenario—the death of a child—a medical examiner may be the primary source of contact for investigative purposes. Police departments in general and investigative personnel in particular must develop a good working relationship with the medical examiner's office. In these and related circumstances, a collaborative relationship generally proves to be far more productive than either the police or medical personnel working independently. The investigative officer should be present at the autopsy or at the initial examination of the body and should brief the examining physician on the circumstances of the alleged accident if information is available. This also holds true for emergency room physicians who treat a child after a presumed serious but nonfatal accident. In both cases, physical examinations may reveal certain types of injuries that confirm or suggest abuse. These include the following:

1. **External signs.** Some injuries have identifiable patterns that can be linked to specific objects used in an attack. For example, one may be able to identify bite or scratch marks; coat hanger or hot iron impressions; fingertip marks caused by tight gripping; straight, curved, curvilinear, or jagged lesions that may indicate whipping by specifically shaped objects; and scald or peculiar burn marks.

   The location of some injuries is also indicative of abuse. These include injuries to the genitals, buttocks, and rectal areas, as well as trauma to the torso, upper arms, and thighs. These and related injuries are particularly incriminating if they are not accompanied by other relatively common injuries suffered by children, such as skinned knees and bruises to the elbows, shins, and forehead, or by other injuries that would have probably been received as part of the accident. For example, most often children who are involved in accidents also display these signs of typical childhood play. On the other hand, children who are abused may show few or none of these signs and, except for the abusive injuries, may even appear well groomed and dressed.

   There may also be signs of old injuries to various parts of the body that are in different stages of healing. Some children seem to be accident prone and may accumulate a variety of injuries over time. However, injuries that are not common to childhood and that appear to have been received over a period of time can be signs of a steadily escalating cycle of abuse.

   In all cases of suspected abuse, injuries should be photographed in color to assist in establishing the extent of damage and the age of injuries at later trial presentation.

2. **Internal signs.** As noted, some injuries are not characteristic of childhood activities and common accidents. For example, it is very unlikely that pre-toddlers would be able to break a major bone, such as a thigh or upper arm bone, or other smaller bones given their lack of mobility. Some fractures will be apparent externally. Others, particularly older fractures, require radiologic examination to be identified. The nature of some fractures provides almost indisputable evidence of abuse. These include spiral fractures, indicating vigorous handling, shaking, or twisting, and fractures to the rear and upper part—occipital and varietal bones, respectively—of the skull, suggesting that the child was swung by the feet into a solid object or suffered a blow to the head. Subdural hematomas, without evidence of contusions on the scalp, or skull fractures may suggest violent shaking of an infant, causing whiplash of the child's head and subsequent internal injuries.

Like the emergency room physician, the medical examiner may be confronted by a child whose history, pattern, or extent of injuries does not correlate with the alleged cause of death. Also typical of the abused child is an inordinate parental delay in seeking medical attention, evidence of administration of home remedies for a serious injury, a history of prior visits to different emergency rooms, frequent changes of physicians, any prior diagnosis of "failure to thrive," even multiple emergency room visits with a well child. If any of these situations are encountered, one should consider child abuse as likely.

Based on the judgment of a physician, the diagnosis of one or more of these suspicious injuries may be sufficient evidence to conclude that the child suffered from abuse. These injuries are particularly incriminating when they do not correlate with parental explanations of how they were incurred. This underscores the importance of a close and ongoing communication between police investigating officers and physicians. Examining physicians must be kept informed about the course of the investigation and the types of questions that should be answered as the result of their examination. A child who suffers from physical abuse is termed a **battered child**. Battered children suffer from a wide array of abuses, including minor assaults to severe beatings, which in some cases cost them their lives. Because of the privacy and nature of the crime, such victims often have nowhere to turn. Child abuse is aggravated by high levels of unemployment, poor parenting skills, stress, marital conflict, and a general lack of information about child development.

As with any assault case, evidence is a primary objective. Bruises, bloody clothes, dramatic changes in a child's behavior, and statements from possible witnesses are all important. Special care must be afforded the interview of a child victim because children are imaginative and highly susceptible to suggestion. Because of this, the use of specially trained child interviewers is recommended to secure a competent statement from the child victim.

Battered Child Syndrome

Battered child syndrome is a tragic and disturbing phenomenon. Unfortunately, it is a crime that is often successfully hidden by its perpetrators. Law enforcement has an important role to play in uncovering cases of battered child syndrome and gathering evidence for successful prosecution. Investigators must have a working knowledge of battered child syndrome and what it means to an investigation. *Battered child syndrome* is defined as the collection of injuries sustained by a child as a result of repeated mistreatment or beating. If the child's injuries indicate intentional trauma or appear to be more severe than could reasonably be expected from an accident, battered child syndrome should be suspected. In such cases, an investigator must do more than collect information about the currently reported injury. A full investigation requires interviewing possible witnesses about other injuries that the child may have suffered, obtaining the caretaker's explanation for those injuries, and assessing the conclusions of medical personnel who may have seen the victim before.[45]

The issue of whether information on the victim's prior injuries or medical condition will be admissible at trial should be left up to the prosecutor. However, an investigator's failure to collect such information leaves the prosecutor without one of the most important pieces of corroborative evidence for proving an intentional act of child abuse. Evidence of past inflicted injuries may also be the only information available to help the prosecutor distinguish between two or more possible perpetrators in the current case and may help refute claims by the child's parents or caretakers that injuries suggestive of physical abuse were caused by an accident.

Recognizing Abuse

There are several signs of abuse that officers can identify while assessing the situation. For example, if the child has an injury that is inconsistent with the explanation given by the parents, abuse might have occurred. If the officer is told that a child's hand was severely scalded in water by "accident," the officer should question why the child didn't take the obvious action of withdrawing his hand. It would be logical to suspect that someone forcibly held the child's hand in the water.

Other injuries can also be good indicators of child abuse (e.g., cigarette burns, bruises, cuts that appear to be nonaccidental in origin). In addition, abused children sometimes have bite marks appearing on the abdomen, scrotum, and buttocks.[46] Most typically, however, abuse takes the form of severe and numerous beatings going far beyond normal disciplinary measures. Such evidence includes injuries in different stages of healing or complications stemming from old injuries that are not explained sufficiently by the parents.

Taking the Initial Report

State laws generally require certain persons to report instances of child abuse, neglect, and sexual abuse. These persons include school officials, medical personnel, attorneys, and social workers. Such reports can be made verbally or in writing to the state department of family or child services, the welfare department, the juvenile court, or a local law enforcement agency. Typically, special forms are used for child abuse and molestation cases, and laws require immediate action. Initial

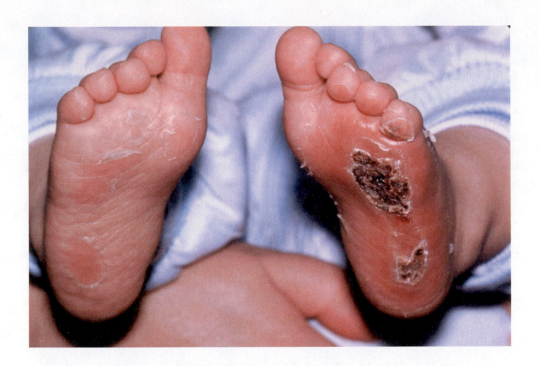

|Fig. 13.7| △

An extreme case of child physical abuse where the feet of this child were severely burnt by being forcibly held against a heater by a parent.

Science Photo Library / Photo Researchers Inc.

Justifications for Officers Making an Arrest

- ☑ Injury to the child is severe.
- ☑ Evidence of a serious crime exists.
- ☑ It seems likely that the suspect will flee the scene.
- ☑ There is a disturbance of the peace.
- ☑ The suspect seems to pose a danger to others.

child abuse reports are confidential in nature and contain the child's name, address, and age as well as information on the child's parents or legal guardians.

In addition, the name and address of the person suspected of abusing the child are documented as well as the nature of the alleged offense. In the case of an emergency circumstance or one that appears to be life threatening for the child, the police can remove the child from the home provided that the welfare or juvenile justice official taking the report deems it necessary. All allegations will be investigated by local law enforcement.

The Initial Police Response to Child Abuse

The time factor is crucial in the law enforcement response to suspected child abuse. Complaints are sometimes logged during or shortly after a battering incident; therefore, the safety of the child is the utmost priority for the responding officer. Consequently, the responding officer's first task is to get medical attention for the child. In the absence of any immediate danger to the child, most state laws require that officers at least attempt to resolve any problems before physically removing the child from the home. In the event that the child is facing imminent danger, of course, removal from the home is appropriate.

The second responsibility of the responding officer is to determine if a crime has, in fact, been committed. If such determination is made, the officer should conduct a criminal investigation accordingly, such as identifying evidence. Subsequent to the investigation, it may be necessary to take a suspect into physical custody.

Steps in Investigating Battered Child Syndrome

Investigators confronted with the case of possible child abuse or child homicide must overcome the unfortunately frequent societal attitude that babies are less important than adult victims of homicide and that natural parents would never intentionally harm their own children. When battered child syndrome is suspected, the investigator should always:

- Collect information about the "acute" injury that led the person or agency to make the report.
- Conduct interviews with medical personnel who are attending the child.
- Review medical records from a doctor, clinic, or hospital.
- Interview all persons who had access to, or custody of, the child during a time in which the injury or injuries allegedly occurred. Caretakers should always be interviewed separately; joint interviews can only hurt the investigation.
- Consider any statements the caretakers made to anyone concerning what happened to the child to require medical attention.
- Conduct a thorough investigation of the scene where the child was allegedly hurt.

Interviews with Medical Personnel

It is important for the investigator to contact all medical personnel who had contact with the family, such as doctors, nurses, admitting personnel, emergency medical technicians (EMTs), ambulance drivers, and emergency room personnel.

- Talk with those who provided treatment for the child about the diagnosis and what treatments were used. The attending physician will often be able to express at least an opinion that the caretaker's explanation did not "fit" the severity of the injury. However, failure to obtain an opinion from the attending physician should not end the investigation.
- Speak with any specialists who assisted the attending physician.
- Have someone knowledgeable about medical terms translate them into layperson terms so that the exact nature of the injuries is clear.
- Obtain available medical records concerning the injured child's treatment, including records of any prior treatment. (Note: If only one caretaker is suspected of abuse, the nonabusive caretaker may need to sign a release of the records. If both are suspected, most states have provisions that override normal confidentiality rules in the search for evidence of child abuse. Procedures for obtaining these records must be confirmed in each state.)
- Interview the child's pediatrician about the child's general health since birth and look for a pattern of suspected abusive injuries.

It is absolutely vital that photographs of the child be taken as soon as possible after a child has been brought to the treatment facility. Most clinics and hospitals have established procedures for photographing injuries in obvious cases of abuse, but when the injuries are more subtle, they may overlook the need for photographs. The investigator should make sure that medical personnel take and preserve photographs or that the investigating team takes them.

Other Important Sources of Information

Interview siblings, other relatives, neighbors, family friends, teachers, church associates, and others who may know about a child's health and history. People who surround the child and are part of his or her life are sometimes overlooked as sources of background information for a child abuse or homicide prosecution.

Review emergency medical (EMT) records or 911 dispatch tapes. These records are frequently overlooked but can be valuable sources of information. Families with one or more emergencies may in fact be abusing their children and not just being hit by a long streak of "bad luck."

After the family history has been obtained, request any police reports that may be held by law enforcement agencies in the jurisdiction where the family lives. Also check the child welfare agencies' files on the family. Collect additional family history concerning connections between domestic violence and child abuse; substance abuse and child abuse; and other connections, even apparently unrelated arrests or charges. These records may be helpful in piecing together the complicated picture of what happened to the child this time and who was responsible.

Consultation with Experts

Identifying experts is important to the child abuse investigator. If the investigator does not have a basic knowledge of the causes of young children's injuries, experts should be consulted. Attending training conferences can provide the investigator with a great deal of basic knowledge and help establish a network of experts.

Interviews with Caretakers

A major trait of abuse by caretakers is either complete lack of an explanation for critical injuries or explanations that do not account for the severity of the injuries. The investigation must not be dictated solely by caretakers' early explanations because after they learn that their excuses do not match the medical evidence, they will come up with new ones.

In child homicide cases, for example, investigators will learn quickly about "killer couches," "killer stairs," and "killer cribs." Abusers freely use these terms in their explanations of the child's death. However, studies show that children do not die from falls from simple household heights; they usually do not even suffer severe head injuries from such falls.

In nearly every case of actual abuse, caretakers will not be consistent in their explanations of the injuries over time. Sometimes the changes are apparent from statements that abusers have made to others. Additional interviews may be needed to document the changes in explanations and to follow up on additional information that the investigation uncovers.

The Crime Scene Investigation

Caretakers' changes in explanations often mean that investigators must visit the home or the scene of the injury more than once. The ideal time to obtain such evidence is immediately after the child's injury is reported before the caretakers have an opportunity to tamper with the scene. If the caretakers do not consent to a search of the scene, a search warrant may be necessary. The strongest evidence of the need for a search warrant is the medical evidence supporting what probably happened to the child and the caretakers' inconsistent or absent accounts of the events.

Whatever explanation caretakers offer for a child's injury or injuries, it is vital that the investigator secure physical evidence. He or she must be thorough in obtaining photographic evidence of the location where the injury took place because physical evidence and records must be preserved; for example:

- The crib from which the child allegedly fell.
- The child's "environment," including bedding on the bed or in the crib and on other beds in the home.
- Any toys or objects on which the child allegedly landed.
- In cases in which the child was apparently burned, a record of any sinks, bathtubs, and pots or pans containing water. In addition to testing the temperature of the standing water, the temperature of water from the water heater and from each tap should be tested. The temperature setting of the water heater should also be checked. This may help disprove an allegation that the child accidentally turned on the hot water. Other sources of heat in the home should be documented, regardless of the caretakers' initial explanation of what burned the child.
- A complete photographic or videotape record of the home or other location in which the injuries allegedly occurred, focusing on areas that the caretakers have already identified as the site of the particular trauma (e.g., stairs, bed or crib, or bathtub).

The investigator should be trained by his or her local crime laboratory personnel on the types of evidence that can and should be processed in preserving these cases:

- If the child suffered apparent cigarette burns, collecting cigarette butts found in the home may facilitate analysis of the burn patterns.

- If the case involves a combination of sexual and physical abuse, collecting the child's clothing and bedding may allow identification of what happened and who was involved.
- If the child shows evidence of bite marks, saliva swabbing should be done to allow positive identification of the biter.
- If the child has suffered a depressed skull fracture, any objects the approximate size of the fracture should be seized for appropriate analysis.

Shaken Baby Syndrome

SBS is a form of child abuse that occurs when an abuser violently shakes an infant or small child, creating a whiplash-type motion that causes acceleration–deceleration injuries. The injury is estimated to affect between 1,200 and 1,600 children every year in the United States.[47] In shaken baby cases, it is common for there to be no external evidence of trauma.[48] Injuries from impacts with hard objects may accompany SBS; this combination of shaking with striking against a hard object is sometimes termed the *shaken impact syndrome* or *shaken/slam syndrome*.

Victims of SBS are age three years and younger. Typically, most child victims are younger than 18 months. The motion required to injure a child often results in bleeding inside the head and may cause irreversible brain damage, blindness, cerebral palsy, hearing loss, spinal cord injuries, seizures, learning disabilities, and even death. It can be traced historically from the mid-1500s and was officially named and defined in 1974. The classic medical symptoms associated with infant shaking include:

- Retinal hemorrhaging (bleeding in the back of the eyeball), often bilaterally (in both eyes)
- Subdural or subarachnoid hematomas (intracranial bleeding, most often in the upper hemispheres of the brain, caused by the shearing of the blood vessels between the brain and the dura mater of the arachnoid membrane)
- Absence of other external signs of abuse (e.g., bruises), although not always. Symptoms include breathing difficulties, seizures, dilated pupils, lethargy, and unconsciousness

According to all credible studies in the past several years, retinal hemorrhaging in infants is, for all practical purposes, conclusive evidence of SBS in the absence of a good explanation. Good explanations for retinal hemorrhaging include:

- A severe auto accident in which the baby's head either struck something with severe force or was thrown about wildly without restraint during the crash
- A fall from several stories onto a hard surface, in which case there are usually other signs of trauma, such as skull fractures, swelling, and intracranial collection of blood

Simple household falls, cardiopulmonary resuscitation (CPR), and tossing a baby in the air in play are not good explanations for retinal hemorrhaging. There simply is not enough force involved in minor falls in play activities to cause retinal hemorrhage or the type of severe life-threatening injuries seen in infants who have been shaken.

In most cases of SBS, there is no skull fracture and no external sign of trauma. The typical explanation given by caretakers is that the baby was "fine" and then suddenly went into respiratory arrest or began having seizures. Both of these conditions are common symptoms of SBS.

The shaking necessary to cause death or severe intracranial injuries is never an unintentional or nonabusive action. Rather, such injuries are caused by a violent, sustained action in which the infant's head, which lacks muscular control, is violently swept forward and backward, hitting the chest and shoulders. The action occurs right in front of the shaker's eyes. Experts say that an observer watching the shaking would describe it as "as hard as the shaker was humanly capable of shaking the baby" or "hard enough that it appeared the baby's head would come off." In almost every case, the baby begins to show symptoms such as seizures or unconsciousness within minutes of the injury. The baby may have difficulty breathing, or his or her breathing may stop completely.

SBS occurs primarily in children 18 months of age or younger. It is most often associated with infants younger than one year old because their necks lack muscle control and their heads are heavier than the rest of their bodies. An infant cannot resist the shaking, but a toddler can, to some extent. Although the collection of injuries associated with SBS is sometimes seen in toddlers, it is rare and is always a sign of extremely violent and severe action against the child.

Munchausen Syndrome by Proxy

Munchausen syndrome is a psychological disorder in which a patient fabricates symptoms of disease or injury in order to undergo medical tests, hospitalization, or even medical or surgical treatment. To command medical attention, patients with Munchausen syndrome may intentionally injure themselves or induce illness in themselves. In cases of **Munchausen syndrome by proxy**, parents or caretakers with Munchausen syndrome attempt to bring medical attention to themselves by inducing illness in their children. The parent then may try to resuscitate or have paramedics or hospital personnel save the child. The following scenarios are common occurrences in these cases:

- A child's caretaker repeatedly brings the child in for medical care or calls paramedics for alleged problems that cannot be documented medically.
- The child experiences "seizures" or "respiratory arrest" only when the caretaker is there, never in the presence of neutral third parties or in the hospital.
- When the child is hospitalized, the caretaker turns off the life support equipment, causing the child to stop breathing, and then turns everything back on and summons help.
- The caretaker induces illness by introducing a mild irritant or poison into the child's body.

Indications of Munchausen Syndrome

Caution is required in the diagnosis of fabricated or induced illness (FII). Many of the items below are also indications of a child with organic but undiagnosed illness. An ethical diagnosis of Munchausen syndrome must include an evaluation of the child, the parents, and the family dynamics. Diagnoses based only on a review of the child's medical chart can be rejected in court. An adult care provider who is abusing the child often seems comfortable and not upset over the child's hospitalization. Medical professionals need to monitor that adult's visits to the child while in the hospital in case that adult does things to make the child sicker. In addition, in most states, medical professionals have a duty to report such abuse to legal authorities.[49]

- A child who has one or more medical problems that do not respond to treatment or that follow an unusual course that is persistent, puzzling, and unexplained
- Physical or laboratory findings that are highly unusual, discrepant with history, or physically or clinically impossible
- A parent who appears to be medically knowledgeable or fascinated with medical details and hospital gossip, appears to enjoy the hospital environment, and expresses interest in the details of other patients' problems
- A highly attentive parent who is reluctant to leave the child's side and who him- or herself seems to require constant attention
- A parent who appears to be unusually calm in the face of serious difficulties in the child's medical course while being highly supportive and encouraging of the physician, or a parent who is angry; devalues staff; and demands further intervention, more procedures, second opinions, and transfers to other, more sophisticated, facilities
- The suspected parent may work in the health care field him- or herself or profess interest in a health-related job
- The signs and symptoms of a child's illness do not occur in the parent's absence (hospitalization and careful monitoring may be necessary to establish this causal relationship)
- A family history of similar or unexplained illness or death in a sibling
- A parent with symptoms similar to the child's medical problems or an illness history that itself is puzzling and unusual
- A suspected emotionally distant relationship between parents; the spouse often fails to visit the patient and has little contact with physicians even when the child is hospitalized with serious illness
- A parent who reports dramatic, negative events, such as house fires, burglaries, or car accidents, that affect him or her and their family while the child is undergoing treatment
- A parent who seems to have an insatiable need for adulation or who makes self-serving efforts for public acknowledgment of his or her abilities[50]

These indicators may or may not provide the need for further investigation but should be taken seriously until such time the allegations have been proven invalid.

Investigative Guidelines

☑ Consult with all possible experts, including psychologists.

☑ Exhaust every possible explanation in the cause of the child's illness or death.

☑ Find out who had exclusive control over the child when the symptoms of the illness began or at the time of the child's death.

☑ Find out if there is a history of abusive conduct toward the child.

☑ Find out if the nature of the child's illness or injury allows medical professionals to express an opinion that the child's illness or death was neither accidental nor the result of a natural cause or disease.

☑ In cases of hospitalization, use covert video surveillance to monitor the suspect. Some cases have been solved in this fashion.

☑ Determine whether the caretaker had any medical training or a history of seeking medical treatment needlessly. Munchausen syndrome by proxy is often a multigenerational condition.

Sudden Infant Death Syndrome

Sudden infant death syndrome (SIDS) is the diagnosis given for the sudden death of an infant one month to one year of age that remains unexplained after a complete investigation, which includes an autopsy, an examination of the death scene, and a review of the victim's medical and family history. SIDS is a recognized medical disorder. Infants who succumb to the syndrome appear healthy before the incident, even to a physician. At this time, there is no strong evidence to suggest that SIDS can be stopped because the first and only symptom is death. SIDS appears to occur after an infant has been put down for sleep. Victims may have been down for sleep for as little as 10 minutes. Studies show that there are no apparent signs of a struggle or suffering. Although SIDS is associated with an infant's sleep time and often occurs in the crib, the event may occur anywhere the infant is sleeping. SIDS events have occurred in infant seats, car seats, strollers, and in the parents' bed.

SIDS is not a positive finding; rather, it is a diagnosis made when there is no other medical explanation for the abrupt death of an apparently healthy infant. When a baby dies from shaking, intracranial injuries, peritonitis (inflammation of the peritoneum, the membrane that lines the abdominal cavity), apparent suffocation, or any other identifiable cause, SIDS is not even considered a possibility. SIDS rarely occurs in infants older than age seven months and almost never is an appropriate diagnosis for a child older than 12 months.[51]

Research shows that SIDS can occur at anytime between one month of age and one year of age; however, 91 percent of SIDS deaths occur before the age of six months, with the highest concentration occurring between two months and four months of age. The syndrome affects all races and socioeconomic groups. Environmental, behavioral, and physical influences may put some infants at greater risk for SIDS, and conversely, many SIDS victims meet no specific risk factors. Some general risk factors have, however, been identified. These include:

- Mother younger than 20 years of age
- Late or no prenatal care
- Premature infants
- Low birth weight infants
- Drug and alcohol use during pregnancy
- Smoking (mothers who smoke during and after pregnancy triple the risk of SIDS in their infants)[52]

SIDS cases must be approached with great sensitivity. However, before SIDS can be determined to be the cause of death, investigators must ensure that every other possible medical explanation has been explored and that there is no evidence of any other natural or accidental cause for the child's death.

An investigator's suspicions should be aroused when multiple alleged SIDS deaths have occurred under the custody of the same caretaker. Statistically, the occurrence of two or three alleged SIDS deaths in the care of the same person strongly suggests that some degree of child abuse was involved. Whenever there is evidence that the child who has died was abused or that other children in the family have been abused, SIDS is not an appropriate finding.

Even when there is no affirmative medical finding of the cause of death, prosecution may still be possible. In some cases, experts can explain what occurs when a child is suffocated and can render a medical opinion that suffocation is one of the ways that someone could cause the child's death without leaving obvious medical signs.

Sexual Abuse of Children

The abuse of children can take many forms. In addition to possible physical danger posed by an abusive caregiver or parent, a child can also be traumatized by being sexually abused. Consider the 1995 case when an 11-year-old testified that she was molested during sexual orgies supposedly staged by a Pentecostal preacher in Wenatchee, Washington. The child also testified that her foster father, who happened to be Detective Bob Perez, lead police investigator in the case, also physically abused her. Prosecutors charged 28 persons in the case, charging that they forced 50 children to have sex with each other and with adults in two sex rings. Nineteen people either pleaded guilty or were convicted in the case; only one person was acquitted. In yet another case, the Boy Scouts have dismissed more than 1,800 scoutmasters suspected of molesting children between 1971 and 1991; some of those dismissed may have moved to other troops to continue their abuse.[53]

In recent years, the problem of child sexual abuse has generated increased attention and is becoming more openly discussed than ever before. Child abuse can take a number of insidious forms. An example is the case of Catholic Priest John J. Geoghan, who was a key figure in the Roman Catholic sex abuse cases that rocked the Boston Archdiocese in the late 1990s and early 2000s. Geoghan's case eventually led to the resignation of Boston's archbishop, Cardinal Bernard Francis Law, on December 13, 2002.

Over a 30-year career in six parishes, Geoghan was accused of sexual abuse involving more than 130 children. Charges were brought in Cambridge, Massachusetts, concerning accusations of a molestation that took place in 1991. Geoghan was defrocked in 1998. In January 2002, he was found guilty of indecent assault and **battery** for grabbing the buttocks of a 10-year-old boy in a swimming pool at the Waltham Boys and Girls Club. In 1991, Geoghan was sentenced to 9 to 10 years in prison.

|Fig. 13.8| △

Former Catholic Priest John Geoghan with his attorney at trial.

JOHN BLANDING / AP Images

Numerous civil lawsuits resulted from Geoghan's actions because lawyers argued that the archdiocese had transferred Geoghan from parish to parish despite warnings of his behavior. On August 23, 2003, while in protective custody at the Souza-Baranowski Correctional Center in Shirley, Massachusetts, Geoghan was trapped in his cell, strangled, and stomped to death by another inmate, Joseph Druce.

Statistics also point out that child sexual abuse is a growing problem. Although it is difficult to estimate the incidence of child sexual abuse, stories of abuse such as those discussed above illustrate the seriousness of the problem. In one study by Diana Russell, women in the San Francisco area were surveyed, and Russell found that 38 percent had experienced intrafamilial or extrafamilial sexual abuse by the time they reached age 18 years.[54] A more recent survey of Minnesota students in grades 6, 9, and 12 revealed that about 2 percent of the boys and 7 percent of the girls had experienced incest, while 4 percent of males and 13 percent of females had experienced extrafamilial sexual abuse. Although the percentage of abused girls is smaller than that found by Russell, research by Glenn Wolfner and Richard Gelles indicates that up to one in five girls suffers sexual abuse.[55]

Although these results are alarming, it is probable that they still underestimate the true incidence of child sexual abuse. It is difficult to get people to respond to questions about child sexual abuse, and many victims either are too young to understand their abuse or have repressed their memory of such incidents. Of course, children may be inhibited because parents are reluctant to admit that abuse occurred. In one study, 57 percent of children referred to a clinic because they had sexually transmitted diseases claimed not to have been molested despite irrefutable evidence.[56]

As with the previous categories of sexual criminal activity, much misunderstanding exists regarding the sexual abuse of children. This category of offense includes:

- **Exploitation.** The use of children for illegal activities such as prostitution and pornography
- **Incest.** Sexual relations between children and their parents
- **Child sexual abuse.** The sexual molestation of children, as well as seduction and statutory rape

Case in Point

>>Jerry Sandusky and the Penn State Sex Abuse Scandal

In 2011 Penn State became embroiled in a sex abuse scandal that focused on former Pennsylvania State University football assistant coach Jerry Sandusky, who was alleged to have either sexually assaulted or had inappropriate contact with at least eight underage boys on or near university property. After an extensive grand jury investigation, Sandusky was indicted on 42 counts of child molestation dating from 1994 to 2009, even though the abuse may date as far back as the 1970s. Sandusky denied the allegations.

According to the investigation, a number of high-level school officials were charged with perjury, suspended, or dismissed for having covered up the incidents or by failing to properly notify authorities. In the wake of the scandal, head football coach Joe Paterno was fired and University president Graham Spanier was forced to resign.

Sandusky was an assistant coach under Head Coach Joe Paterno for the Penn State football team for 31

seasons from 1969 to 1999. For 23 of those years, he was the team's defensive coordinator. In 1977, Sandusky founded The Second Mile, a charity formed to help troubled young boys, in State College, Pennsylvania. In 1998, the University Police, State College Police, Centre County District Attorney, Pennsylvania Department of Public Welfare, and a child protection agency investigated him for sexual abuse of a child but no charges were filed. Sandusky was considered for spearheading a football program at Penn State Altoona in 1998–1999, but the idea was scrapped and he retired in 1999. After his retirement as Penn State's defensive coordinator, he remained as a coach emeritus with an office in, and access to, Penn State's football facilities.

The investigation was initiated in the spring of 2008, after the mother of a boy (identified in court papers as "Victim 1"), then a freshman at Central Mountain High School in Clinton County, Pennsylvania, reported that the boy had been sexually abused by Sandusky. Sandusky had allegedly been having a relationship involving "inappropriate touching" with "Victim 1" since 2005 or 2006, when the boy was 11 or 12. Sandusky had met the boy through the Second Mile program before retiring from the program in 2010. Sandusky was also volunteering as an assistant high school football coach at Central at

(continued)

Case in Point *(continued)*

the time of the alleged actions. The investigation included testimony from various persons at Penn State and The Second Mile. Pennsylvania Attorney General Linda Kelly characterized the grand jury investigation as an "uncooperative atmosphere" with regard to some of the Penn State officials.

In December 2010, Assistant Coach Mike McQueary appeared before the grand jury regarding the case involving Victim 1. He testified that, on March 1, 2002, at 9:30 P.M., he entered the locker room at the Lasch Football Building at Penn State and heard what he believed to be the sounds of sexual activity coming from the shower. He stated that he looked in the shower and "saw a naked boy (Victim 2), whose age he estimated to be ten years old, with his hands up against the wall, being subjected to anal intercourse by Sandusky who was naked at the time. The next

|Fig. 13.9| ▲

Jerry Sandusky, former Penn State Defensive Coordinator, became the subject of serious allegations of child rape and molestation in early 2011

Pat Little / Reuters

day, McQueary reported the incident to Joe Paterno, who informed Athletic Director Tim Curley and Gary Schultz, senior vice president for finance and business, who oversaw the Penn State police department at the time. Ultimately, the only action taken by Curley and Schultz was to order Sandusky not to bring any children from Second Mile to the football building—an action that was approved by University President Graham Spanier.

In their testimony before the grand jury, Paterno, Curley, and Schultz rejected the version of the incident presented by Mike McQueary. Paterno testified that he was only told about Sandusky "fondling or doing something of a sexual nature" to the victim. Curley and Schultz both denied having been told about alleged anal intercourse. Curley denied that McQueary reported anything of sexual nature whatsoever, and described the conduct as merely "horsing around." Graham Spanier likewise testified that he was only apprised of an incident involving Jerry Sandusky and a younger child "horsing around in the shower."

Despite Penn State banning Sandusky from bringing boys onto the main campus in 2002, he was allowed to operate a summer camp through his Sandusky Associates company from 2002 to 2008 at Penn State's Behrend satellite campus near Erie, where he had daily contact with boys from fourth grade to high school.

The Pennsylvania statewide investigating grand jury identified a total of eight boys singled out for sexual advances or assaults by Sandusky from 1994 to 2009, after six more victims were identified: Five alleged victims testified that they met Sandusky through The Second Mile; each also stated that they showered with him on the campus. According to the witnesses, the showers included physical contact ranging from hugs and wrestling to, in one case, Sandusky placing the boy's hand on his erect penis. On December 7, 2011, Sandusky was arrested and on June 22, 2012, he was found guilty on 45 of the 48 charges. He was sentenced on October 9, 2012 to 30 to 60 years in prison.

Thematic question

The investigation into sexual allegations in the Sandusky case presented a number of investigative challenges including the fact that Sandusky was a well-known figure in the Penn State Football program, that the allegations dated back over a decade, and that the investigation received considerable media scrutiny and public interest. How does a professional investigator balance these variables while maintaining objectivity in his or her investigation?

Source: Pennsylvania Attorney General's Office. (2012). Available at http://www.attorneygeneral.gov/press.aspx?id=6270; http://www.attorneygeneral.gov/press.aspx?id=6277 (retrieved on May 3, 2012).

The Preliminary Investigation

In the early phase of the investigation, the investigator must collect as much information about the charge as possible. This is typically done by interviews with people who are most closely associated with the child. Assuming that such persons are not suspects in the case, they could provide the investigator with information regarding any abnormalities in a child's physical appearance as well as unusual behaviors and actions by the child. In the event that the person being questioned becomes a suspect, investigators should be careful to avoid accusations or passing judgment. In addition, if the subject develops into a suspect during the interview, the officer must remember to afford the subject all of his or her due process rights under the Fourth, Fifth, and Fourteenth Amendments.

The Forensic Interview

For the most part, the child abuse investigation begins with information provided by the child victim. Obtaining this information is a vitally delicate task that normally requires a forensic interview of the child to determine whether he or she has been abused. In the case of a criminal investigation, the forensic interview can be conducted by a law enforcement officer or a member of child welfare or CPS, provided they are properly trained to do so. As such, child abuse investigations typically represent a collaborative effort between law enforcement and social service professionals.

In addition to yielding the information needed to make a determination about whether abuse or neglect has occurred, forensic interviewing provides evidence that will stand up in court if the investigation leads to criminal prosecution. Properly conducted forensic interviews are legally sound in part because they ensure the interviewer's objectivity; use nonleading, nonsuggestive techniques; and emphasize careful documentation of the interview. Generally, the forensic interview is used only during the assessment portion of a child abuse investigation and involves only the children who are the subject of the investigation.[57]

Although of vital importance in investigations in which it is likely substantiation will lead to criminal prosecution, such as cases of physical, sexual, or emotional abuse, forensic interviews occur in virtually all child abuse investigations. When responding to reports of neglect, at the point when investigators begin exploring the allegations with a child, they should approach this as a forensic interview opposed to a casual conversation.

Why Are Forensic Interviews Needed?

The reason forensic interviews are needed is because most perpetrators deny the abuse and most acts of maltreatment are not witnessed; the victim's statement is critical evidence in child abuse cases. Yet developmental issues, such as children's varying abilities to recall events and use language, as well as the trauma they may have experienced, complicate efforts to obtain information about the abuse. The forensic interview is designed to overcome these obstacles.[58]

The goal of the forensic interview is to obtain a statement from a child in an objective, developmentally sensitive, and legally defensible manner.[59] To ensure facts are gathered in a way that will stand up in court, forensic interviews are carefully controlled. For example:

- The interviewer's statements and body language must be neutral.
- Alternative explanations for a child's statements are thoroughly explored.
- The results of the interview are documented in such a way that they can bear judicial scrutiny.

In many jurisdictions, the backgrounds and professions of the persons who conduct forensic interviews vary from community to community and from investigation to investigation. Sometimes these interviews are conducted only by child welfare workers or law enforcement investigators in the field; sometimes another secondary forensic interview is conducted by a therapist or other specially trained professional in a controlled, child-friendly environment.[60]

The Initial Interview

In most jurisdictions, state child welfare investigators conduct the initial forensic interview because state laws often require that after a report is received that a child has been physically, emotionally,

|Fig. 13.10| △

Interviews with possible child abuse victims must be conducted with specially trained personnel.

Michael Lyman

or sexually abused, there must be an immediate face-to-face contact with the child. During this meeting, which must typically occur within 24 hours after the report is made, child welfare workers assess risk and determine whether steps need to be taken to ensure the child's immediate safety. When police investigators discover a possible child abuse case, he or she can contact state child welfare workers and then observe the interview.[61]

The location of the interview is an important consideration toward establishing the proper atmosphere for the child interview. Not only should the interview room specifically designed—comfortable, quiet, and free from distractions—but there should also be only one interviewer responsible for interviewing the child.

In joint investigations, such as those involving police investigators and child service workers, both may be present, but only one should be in the primary role. Moreover, to protect against outside influence, no person having a direct relationship with the child can be present, even for support. A trained victim advocate may accompany the child during the interview. The interview room needs to be equipped with nonintrusive video and audio equipment, and all interviews must be recorded. Such recordings document the interviewer's technique and capture the child's demeanor and statements.

The initial forensic interview can be influenced by a number of factors. These include the specific circumstances being investigated (e.g., the child may need to be referred for a medical examination, which is often accompanied by a secondary forensic interview); the investigating officer's proximity to and ability to access forensic interviewing resources, such as a local CAC; the protocols and procedures adopted by each agency; and the interviewer's skill and comfort level.

One of the objectives of forensic interviewing is to reduce the number of times children are interviewed. The concern is contamination of the child's memory of the incident(s) being investigated. Research and clinical experience indicate that the more times a child—especially a young child—is interviewed about alleged abuse, the less reliable and legally defensible that child's testimony may become.[62]

Lauren Flick, a psychologist who has conducted more than 3,000 child interviews, describes contamination this way:

If I am the first person to talk to a child about an event, that event is like a design on the bottom of a swimming pool filled with clear water—it is easy to read. But each conversation this child has with someone about the alleged abuse clouds the water. If he has talked with his principal, parents, a police officer, etc., it can be very hard or impossible to discern the design at the bottom of the pool.[63]

The Secondary Forensic Interview

More in-depth forensic interviews sometimes occur after the initial stages of an investigation. These are usually conducted by specially trained psychologists or professionals with graduate-level education in the areas relevant to this type of interviewing. Furthermore, these interviews usually take place at centers that facilitate the interview process—therapists and doctors sometimes have such facilities, as do most providers of child medical evaluations.[64]

CACs are also excellent resources for forensic interviewing. CACs offer comfortable rooms with children's furniture, toys, interviewing props, and other aids for observing and documenting interviews. Law enforcement and child welfare agencies are encouraged to work with CACs to avoid delays that can be detrimental to the overall success of the investigation.

Multidisciplinary Investigations

In most jurisdictions, forensic interviews can, and often are, multidisciplinary. This means that more than one agency participates in or observes the interview. The two agencies most commonly involved in multidisciplinary investigations are child welfare workers and law enforcement. Other participants can include representatives of mental health and the district attorney's office. Advocates of the multidisciplinary approach argue that they:

- Reduce the number of child interviews, thereby reducing stress on the child. Repeatedly asking a child to relive abuse amounts to revictimization.
- Improve evidence quality so that perpetrators can be held accountable for harming children and the public can be protected.[65]

Close collaboration and joint investigation of serious child physical and sexual abuse by child welfare workers and law enforcement is common.

Techniques of Forensic Interviewing

Because forensic interviews can play a pivotal role in investigations of sexual and emotional abuse of children, criminal investigators need to know how they are conducted. There are many ways to conduct the forensic interview, and there is no single model or method endorsed unanimously by experts in the field. Some of the many forensic interviewing models in use today include the child cognitive interview, stepwise interview, and narrative elaboration. Similar to many of the others in existence, these three interview types have been shown to be more effective in helping children recall information than standard interviewing techniques.

Despite the different styles of interviews, there are some basic elements common to most forensic interviews. These include phases such as introduction, rapport building, developmental assessment (including learning the child's names for different body parts), guidelines for the interview, competency assessment (during which, among other things, it is determined if the child knows the difference between lying and telling the truth), narrative description of the event or events under investigation, follow-up questions, clarification, and closure.[66]

Forensic interviews may also incorporate the use of aids and props, such as anatomically detailed dolls, anatomical diagrams, dollhouses, puppets, and so on. Despite the differences that exist in the approaches interviewers take, it is possible to get a general sense of what a forensic interview is like. To do this, the stepwise interview will be examined.

The Stepwise Interview

Developed by researcher John Yuille and his colleagues, the stepwise interview uses techniques to:

- Minimize any trauma the child may experience during the interview
- Maximize the amount and quality of the information obtained from the child while at the same time minimizing any contamination of that information
- Maintain the integrity of the investigative process for the agencies involved[67]

The steps in this method begin with the most open, least leading, least suggestive form of questioning and, if necessary, proceed to more specific and more leading questioning.[68] Basic questions fall into four categories and each carries different risks of influencing answers.

- *Open-ended questions.* These are invitations to provide information about an event or activity or prompts to elaborate on previously given information.
- *Specific questions.* These focus the inquiry or ask directly about a particular topic. These questions are often used to clarify information given by the interviewee.
- *Leading questions.* These are to be used with extreme caution. Such questions contain information that has not previously been mentioned by the interviewee.
- *Suggestive questions.* These are seldom used in forensic interviews. They are questions that imply or include an expected answer.[69]

Open-ended questioning is recommended for the forensic interview because any influence of the interviewer is reduced and the probability of the resulting information being accurate is increased. Specific questions and sometimes leading questions are necessary to clarify information given by the interviewee, but the interviewer should quickly return to open-ended questioning. Leading questions may be necessary at times, but remember that these are "high-risk questions" in the forensic setting. In all cases, suggestive questions must be avoided in the forensic interview.

The stepwise method begins with a rapport-building phase during which the interviewer puts the child at ease by asking questions about the child's interests. During this phase, the rules for the interview are discussed (e.g., "If you are unsure about an answer, please say so") and the child's level of development (e.g., linguistic, cognitive), body language, and affect are assessed. The child is commonly asked to recount two specific past experiences, such as a school outing. The interviewer uses these narratives as a basis for assessing the level of detail the child ordinarily conveys and as a way to teach the child to tell a story in a way that fits with the "rules" of the interview.

The interviewer then introduces the topic of concern with a general question such as, "Do you know why we are talking today?" The objective at this phase is to encourage the child to give an unprompted, free narrative account of the event under investigation. Younger children are less responsive to this kind of prompt. After the child has exhausted his or her free narrative, the interviewer moves to questioning.

This begins with open-ended questions and then, if necessary, the interviewer proceeds to use specific but nonleading questions, closed questions, and leading questions. As the interviewer descends in this hierarchy of questions, he or she can have less confidence in the accuracy of the child's responses, which make them less useful either for drawing a conclusion about abuse or as

Physical Evidence in Child Sexual Molestation Cases

☑ Camera or video equipment used for taking photographic images of the victim engaged in sexual acts with the offender.

☑ Notebooks, diaries, papers, or anything else linking the offender to the victim.

☑ Negatives or undeveloped film that depict the victim (or other juveniles).

☑ Magazines, books, or movies depicting juveniles in sexual situations.

☑ Newspapers, magazine clippings, or other publications listing phone numbers with other sexual interests that might tend to identify juveniles involved with the suspect.

☑ Evidence of occupancy, such as bills, letters, rent receipts, or other mail or correspondence showing that the suspect resides at a particular location or is in control of a particular location.

☑ Any items of physical evidence belonging to the victim or used by the subject in sexual acts.

forensic evidence. The interviewer ends the stepwise interview by thanking the child for participating, asking if the child has any questions, and explaining what will happen next.[70]

Children as Witnesses

One of the most compelling reasons children are such formidable victims is the fact that they may be considered incompetent witnesses in the courtroom. Indeed, many such cases rely heavily on testimony from child victims. If the incident really happened, the child can be irreparably scarred, but if it didn't, the accusation can ruin the life of the accused. Until about a decade ago, there was little discussion of the possibility of false allegations in child sexual abuse cases. In recent years, however, skepticism has grown, partly because of sophisticated studies showing that witnesses, especially younger ones, can be influenced by the biases of interviewers.

In 1989, the McMartin Preschool case involved nine children who accused staff members at a suburban Los Angeles day care center of wholesale sexual molestation. After what some newspapers called the longest criminal trial ever, charges against the school's founder, Virginia McMartin, and four teachers were dropped. The determination as to whether or not a child should be considered as a competent witness rests with the discretion of the courts. Experienced investigators suggest that children usually tell the truth to the best of their ability and that when they lie, it is to get out of trouble, not "into" trouble.

Factors considered by the trial judge were the child's age, intelligence, and sense of moral and legal responsibility. A child will be deemed competent to testify if he or she possesses the capacity to observe the events, recollect and communicate them, and understand questions and answer intelligently with an understanding of the duty to speak the truth.[71] In short, the child must understand that some form of punishment will result if the truth is not told. In the absence of clear physical evidence such as rectal or vaginal abrasions, it is difficult to distinguish false allegations from truthful ones. Typically, interviewers will have the child demonstrate the abuse incident with an anatomically correct doll. Some courts, however, have ruled out these dolls because they view them as suggestive.

David Raskin, a forensic psychologist at the University of Utah, devised a form of interview designed to show the quality of a child's story. Derived from experimental work done in Germany in the 1950s, the interview allows the child to begin the interview with a free narrative, holding off prompting as long as possible. A series of questions then follows and is succeeded by a validity assessment that looks for shifts of focus, reappearing elements, and digressions. Raskin asserts that when people anchor events in their memory, they are not told in a straightforward manner. Specifically, most people correct themselves, add elements momentarily forgotten, and redescribe the event. The technique is based on the premise that when someone is inventing a story, it is difficult for them to proceed in this fashion.

Characteristics of Child Victims[72]

- ☑ In the 8- to 16-year-old age group.
- ☑ Unsupervised.
- ☑ From unstable home environments.
- ☑ From low- or average-income families.
- ☑ Subject to abrupt changes in moods.
- ☑ Not necessarily delinquent.
- ☑ In possession of more money than normal, new toys, new clothes, and so on (gifts from the molester).
- ☑ Withdrawn from family and friends.

Child Molester Profiles

Child molesters represent the most common type of pedophile. The term *pedophile* is commonly used by medical treatment and law enforcement and psychology professionals alike and generally refers to one who engages in some form of child sexual exploitation. The specific images of the **child molester** conjured up by society vary greatly. Such images range from child molesters who coax or pressure their victims into sexual activity to the more violent child rapist who overpowers and threatens his or her victims and all variations in between. In reality, the child molester is not a crazed psychopath but more accurately is a product of his or her own emotional immaturity.

Herman Goldstein defines this offender as "a significantly older person who engages in any type of sexual activity with individuals legally defined as children."[73] The term *pedophile* is also associated with *child molester*, although the two terms may not portray the same type of person, that is, a pedophile, one whose sexual orientation is toward children, may harbor thoughts of sexual relations with children but may never act out such fantasies. Conversely, however, it might be a safe assumption to consider most child molesters as pedophiles, as their sexual desires are, indeed, manifested by sexual assault.

In most cases of abuse, only one child and one adult are involved, but cases involving several adults and several children have been reported as well. For example, a 54-year-old man who had previously won a community award for his work with youth was arrested for child molestation involving boys as young as 10 years old. The man would encourage and photograph sexual acts between the boys, such as mutual masturbation and oral and anal sex. He would then have sex with one of them.[74]

A study of 229 convicted child molesters revealed the following information. Nearly 25 percent of their victims were younger than six years of age. An additional 25 percent were ages 6 to 10 years old, and about 50 percent were 11 to 13 years old. Fondling of the child was the most common sexual behavior, followed by vaginal and oral–genital contact. Bribery was most often used to gain the participation of the victims.[75] Studies have shown that pedophiles have the highest recidivism rate of all sex offenders, approximately 25 percent.[76] Incidents of child molestation are believed to be one of the most underreported types of crime. This can be attributed to several phenomena, including embarrassment on the part of the child, fears of bearing the blame for the incident, a fear of being labeled after the incident is exposed, apprehension about the court process, concern that no one will believe the child victim, and fear of reprisal by the offender.

For investigative purposes, the child molester can be viewed as falling into two distinct typological categories: situational and preferential. The **situational molester** doesn't necessarily suffer from any specified psychological disorder but may commit such crimes because of one of several external factors. These include intoxication, drug abuse, mood or mental conditions, or other social conditions. In contrast, the **preferential molester** has sexual desires focusing on children and typically has a more identifiable psychological disorder.

Accordingly, studies of child molesters have revealed two psychological types: fixated and regressed.[77] The **fixated child molester** is one whose primary sexual orientation is toward children and whose sociosexual maturation develops as a result of unresolved conflicts in his or her development. With this offender, children have always been the focus of sexual interests, and sexual contacts with age mates have been situational but never preferred. The child molester will probably not be a stranger to the victim, that is, statistics have shown that such offenders are not only commonly known but are also frequently related to their victims. Examples are:

- A natural parent or other family member, including a stepfather, stepmother, or uncle
- A trusted adult, neighbor, boyfriend, or familiar person
- A remote acquaintance (e.g., coworker of one of the child's parents)

The **regressed child molester**, however, represents a clear (but possibly temporary) departure from a primary orientation toward age mates, as the child becomes a substitute for an adult partner. Unlike the fixated offender, regressed child molesters did not previously exhibit preferences for younger persons in their formative years. Rather, when adult relationships develop conflicts and become emotionally unfulfilling, sexual attraction to children emerges.

Case in Point

>>Warren Jeffs and the FLDS

Some may describe Warren Jeffs as a tall, gangly, and clean-cut looking man. But according to his followers, Jeffs was distinguished as a "Prophet" of the polygamous sect known as the Fundamentalist Latter Day Saints (FLDS). This group separated itself from mainstream Mormonism in 1890 after polygamy was banned. Estimated at approximately 10,000 followers, the FLDS has communities in Hildale, Utah, and Colorado City, Arizona.

After Jeffs' 92-year-old father died, his legacy was passed on to him. And, in 2002, Jeffs became the leader of the FLDS. While maintaining this position, Jeffs was the only person empowered to perform marriages between minor females and adult males within the FLDS community. Jeffs also assumed the authority to strip male followers of their wives, children, and property without forethought or question.

Jeffs was wanted for two counts of sexual assault on a minor. These alleged offenses took place in March of 2002, and on or between July 1 and December 31, 2002. Jeffs was also being sought for conspiracy to commit sexual conduct with a minor. This incident allegedly happened sometime between January and June of 2002. All of the alleged offenses took place in the vicinity of Colorado City, Arizona.

On June 9, 2005, a Mohave County grand jury charged Jeffs with sexual conduct with a minor and conspiracy to commit sexual conduct with a minor. A state arrest warrant was issued in Arizona on June 10, 2005. Additionally, a federal arrest warrant was issued in Arizona on June 27, 2005. Jeffs was charged with unlawful flight to avoid prosecution. On May 6, 2006, the FBI placed Warren Jeffs, a former accountant and private schoolteacher, on the "Ten Most Wanted Fugitives" list.

Jeffs probably had better days, but August 28, 2006, was not likely one of them. While he was riding in a 2007 red Cadillac Escalade, a Nevada Department of Public Safety trooper pulled over the car for a traffic stop. This occurred after the trooper noticed that valid license plates were not displayed on the vehicle. After questioning one of the occupants in the vehicle, it became apparent to the trooper that this individual resembled Warren Jeffs, an FBI

|Fig. 13.11| ▲

Warren Jeffs was the president of the Fundamentalist Church of Jesus Christ of Latter Day Saints and before he was arrested for child molestation charges in 2006 he was expanding his compounds in Colorado, Utah, and Texas.

GEORGE FREY / Newscom

"Ten Most Wanted Fugitive." The trooper contacted the FBI and agents responded to the scene. Jeffs was identified by the FBI and taken into custody.

Thematic question

Considering the close-knit nature of FLDS and Jeffs' authority over his followers, what are some investigative challenges that one might encounter in investigating child sexual abuse within the FDLS?

Source: FBI. (2012). *Famous cases*. Available at http://www.fbi.gov/stats-services/publications/ten-most-wanted-fugitives-60th-anniversary-1950-2010/famous_cases (retrieved on May 3, 2012).

Investigating the Molester

It is important for any investigator to understand, as fully as possible, the methods used by child sex offenders. When an investigator understands the molester's desires and intentions, he or she can more adequately seek out the proper evidence for prosecution. For example, investigations have shown that child molesters frequently collect pornography and child erotica. Such items aid the prosecution in establishing intent or motive of some offenders. Pornography fuels the desires

|Fig. 13.12| △

Child molesters fit no one stereotypical type. Here, Dean Arthur Schwartzmiller smiles with his attorney Melinda Hall in a San Jose, California, courtroom on January 29, 2007, as he was sentenced to 150 years to life for sexually abusing two 12-year-old boys.

Paul Sakuma / AP Images

that child molesters harbor for sexual contact with children.[78] Studies have also shown that child sexual assault is frequently a premeditated act, that is, offenders might only casually consider a particular course of action (fantasizing) without a specific plan or act, or they might take a more overt action in stalking and abducting their victim.

Premeditation and Intent

The circumstances of any given incident can show premeditation on the part of the molester. For example, in one such case, a man boarded a transit bus loaded with children. The offender was then seated next to a young girl approximately 10 years old, and during the bus ride, the man's arm came to rest on the child's inner thigh or upper leg. Subsequent investigation revealed that the same man was frequently among a group of children at the time a local school let out and had no business being there. Here he also used his "hand trick" as was used on the bus.[79]

As this case illustrates, premeditation may be demonstrated through comparing different situations with which the same suspect was involved and establishing a mode of operation. As indicated, investigators should remember that molesters frequent places where there are children in their target group. This will help establish the molester's intent and might also help establish probable cause to stop, detain, identify, and possibly arrest offenders.

In conclusion, both the medical and legal professions have made great strides in identifying nonaccidental trauma inflicted on children and the suspected sexual abuse of them. This progress accounts for what appears to be an increase in the number of identified child abuse homicides. Sadly, however, there will always be some children who die of abuse that is never discovered. Children deserve investigators' best efforts to turn over every stone in cases involving any suspicion of abuse of children.

The Pedophile/Child Molester

- ☑ Has access through family, enticement, or
- ☑ Lures the child, or tricks the child into sex acts; sometimes pressures the child into sexual activity
- ☑ Gives gifts or rewards to the child
- ☑ Cautions his or her victims against disclosure
- ☑ Frequently explains that the activity must be kept a "secret" between the offender and the child
- ☑ Gives the child attention, acceptance, recognition in exchange for sex
- ☑ Often targets children with disabilities who are loners
- ☑ May target the child of a single parent who may have no male figure in the immediate family
- ☑ May be a child rapist (forcible)
- ☑ Overpowers and controls the child much as do adult rapists
- ☑ Uses physical force or threats
- ☑ Is part of a small minority of sex offenders of children

Child Sexual Exploitation

The term *child sexual exploitation* is difficult to define, meaning different things to different people. For some it implies a financial or monetary element in the victimization. For some it means sexual victimization of a child perpetrated by someone other than a family member or legal guardian. According to Kenneth Lanning (2010), sexual exploitation of children refers to forms of victimization involving significant dynamics that go beyond an offender, a victim, and a sexual act. It includes victimization involving sex rings, child pornography, the use of information technology, sex tourism, and child prostitution.[80] One of the more disturbing and rapidly emerging concerns is the spread of child pornography and the use of the Internet as a delivery system for such activities.

Child Pornography on the Internet

Since the beginning of the twenty-first century, the use of the Internet to sell and view child pornography has been growing. The treatment of children as sexual objects, however, has existed through the ages, and so too has the production of erotic literature and drawings involving children.[81] However, pornography in the modern sense began with the invention of the camera in the early nineteenth century. Almost immediately, sexualized images involving children were produced, traded, and collected. Even so, child pornography remained a restricted activity through most of the twentieth century.

Images were usually locally produced, of poor quality, expensive, and difficult to obtain. In the 1960s, the relaxation of censorship standards led to an increase in the availability of child pornography, and, by 1977, some 250 child pornography magazines were circulating in the United States, many imported from Europe.[82] Despite concern about the extent of child pornography, law enforcement agencies had considerable success in stemming the trafficking of these traditional hardcopy forms. However, the advent of the Internet in the 1980s dramatically changed the scale and nature of the child pornography problem, and has required new approaches to criminal investigation.

Internet child pornography is different than most crimes local police departments investigate. For example, local citizens may access child pornography images that were produced and/or stored in another city or on another continent. What's more, they may produce or distribute images that are downloaded by people thousands of miles away. Complicating matters further, an investigation that begins in one police district will almost certainly cross jurisdictional boundaries. Therefore, most of the major investigations of Internet child pornography have involved cooperation among jurisdictions, often at an international level, hence the establishment of Internet child pornography task forces.

Within this broader scheme, however, criminal investigators with local police departments have a critical role to play. By concentrating on components of the problem that occur within their local jurisdictions, they may uncover evidence that initiates a wider investigation. On the other hand, they may receive information from other jurisdictions about offenders in their districts. Because of the increasing use of computers in society, most police departments are likely to encounter Internet child pornography crimes. Therefore, it is important that all police departments develop strategies for dealing with the problem.

Larger departments or districts may have their own dedicated Internet child pornography teams, but smaller ones do not, and the responsibility for day-to-day investigations will fall to general-duties officers. It would be a mistake to underestimate the importance of local police in detecting and preventing Internet child pornography offenses. For example, one study found that 56 percent of arrests for Internet child pornography crimes originated from nonspecialized law enforcement agencies.[83]

Defining Internet Child Pornography

The idea of protecting children from sexual exploitation is relatively recent. As late as the 1880s in the United States, the age of consent for girls was just 10 years.[84] As recent as 1977, only two states had legislation specifically outlawing the use of children in obscene material. The first federal law concerning child pornography was passed in 1978, and the first laws that specifically referred to computers and child pornography were passed in 1988.[85] Since that time, there has been a steady tightening of child pornography laws.

Today, under federal law (18 U.S.C. §2256), child pornography is defined as "any visual depiction, including any photograph, film, video, picture, or computer or computer-generated image or picture, whether made or produced by electronic, mechanical, or other means, of sexually explicit conduct, where:

- The production of the visual depiction involves the use of a minor engaging in sexually explicit conduct; or
- The visual depiction is a digital image, computer image, or computer-generated image that is, or is indistinguishable from, that of a minor engaging in sexually explicit conduct; or
- The visual depiction has been created, adapted, or modified to appear that an identifiable minor is engaging in sexually explicit conduct."[86]

To further summarize the current federal legal situation in the United States, a child is defined as any person under the age of 18. Legislation has attempted to broaden the law to include computer-generated images (virtual images that do not involve real children) and people over eighteen who appear to be minors. However, the court overturned both of these provisions. As a result, Congress has made a number of amendments to tighten federal law in these areas.

From a legal standpoint, a different and harsher standard is applied to images involving children than to images involving adults. Pornography involving a child does not have to involve obscene behavior, but may include sexually explicit conduct that is lascivious or suggestive. For example, in *United States* v. *Knox (1993)*, a man was convicted for possessing videos in which the camera focused on the clothed genital region of young girls.[87] Possession of (not just production and trading of) child pornography is an offense. In the case of the Internet, images do not have to be saved for an offense to have occurred—they simply need to have been accessed.

Most states have followed the federal lead with specific legislation, allowing state police to join federal agencies in the fight against child pornography. However, the exact nature of the legislation varies considerably among states. There is also a wide variation in international laws covering child pornography, and this can have significant implications for law enforcement.

Components of the Problem

The problem of Internet child pornography can be divided into three components—the production, distribution, and downloading of images. In some cases, the same people are involved in each stage. However, some producers and/or distributors of child pornography are motivated solely by financial gain and are not themselves sexually attracted to children.

Production Production involves the creation of pornographic images. Collectors place a premium on new child pornography material. However, many images circulating on the Internet may be decades old, taken from earlier magazines and films. Images may be produced professionally, and, in these cases, often document the abuse of children in third-world countries. However, more commonly, amateurs make records of their own sexual abuse exploits, particularly now that electronic recording devices such as digital cameras and web cams permit individuals to create high-quality, homemade images. With the advent of multimedia messaging (MMR) mobile phones, clandestine photography of children in public areas is becoming an increasing problem.

Distribution Distribution is the uploading and dissemination of pornographic images. These images may be stored on servers located almost anywhere in the world. Distribution may involve sophisticated pedophile rings or organized crime groups that operate for profit, but in many cases, is carried out by individual amateurs who seek no financial reward. Child pornography may be uploaded to the Internet on websites or exchanged via e-mail, instant messages, newsgroups, bulletin boards, chat rooms, and peer-to-peer (P2P) networks.[88] Efforts by law enforcement agencies and Internet Service Providers (ISPs) to stop the dissemination of child pornography on the Internet have led to changes in offenders' methods.

Child pornography websites are often shut down as soon as they are discovered, and openly trading in pornography via e-mail or chat rooms is risky because of the possibility of becoming ensnared in a police sting operation (e.g., undercover police entering chat rooms posing as pedophiles or as minor children). Increasingly, those distributing child pornography are employing more sophisticated security measures to elude detection and are being driven to hidden levels of the Internet.

Downloading Downloading is the function of accessing child pornography via the Internet. The images do not need to be saved to the computer's hard drive or to a removable disk to constitute downloading. In some cases a person may receive spam advertising child pornography, a pop-up link may appear in unrelated websites, or he may inadvertently go to a child pornography website (e.g., by mistyping a key word). In most cases, however, users must actively seek out pornographic websites or subscribe to a group dedicated to child pornography. In fact, it has been argued that genuine child pornography is relatively rare in open areas of the Internet, and, increasingly, those seeking to find images need good computer skills and inside knowledge of where to look.[89] Most child pornography is downloaded via newsgroups and chat rooms. Access to websites and online pedophile groups may be closed and require paying a fee or using a password.

Pedophilia

The basis of sexual misconduct with children, whether it is sexual assault, molestation, or Internet pornography, is **pedophilia**, which is sexual attraction to children. A surprising number of people share this preference, and some are more willing than others to make physical overtures toward satisfying their desires. Surprisingly, there have been groups formed to promote sex with children. Such groups produce manuals and literature to support their perspective and have actually approached legislatures to restructure or eliminate laws governing "age of consent."

One such group, Paedophilia (British spelling), asserts that its members possess a natural sexual attraction toward children and that the attraction is as natural as the attraction of a man to a woman. Indeed, this group even suggests that for some, the sexual attraction to children is as natural as certain people's orientation toward homosexuality or heterosexuality and may therefore be impossible to change. Groups sharing similar goals and desires are the following:

- The René Guyon Society
- The North American Man/Boy Love Association
- The Pedophile Information Exchange
- The Child Sensuality Circle
- The Pedo-Alert Network
- Lewis Carroll Collectors Guide

All of these groups advocate adult–child sex and the changing of laws that make it a crime.[90] In any case, it is clear that a subculture exists regarding this problem and that a great deal of misunderstanding also exists about how best to deal with the situation. In addition to these organizations, yet another category of child sexual offender exists: the stereotypic child molester or child rapist. Unlike people associated with the above-mentioned organizations, this class of offender usually conducts deeds individually with the victim.

In any case, the investigation of sexual offenses involving children must be handled carefully through the use of technical investigative techniques and training. Additionally, investigators must have an in-depth understanding of the underground subculture of groups or individuals who exploit children sexually through incest, child pornography, prostitution, and molestation.

Summary Checklist

In this chapter, we examine child abuse and its many forms. Depending on the nature of the offense, investigators must consider specific indicators that a crime occurred and evidence to support a possible criminal charge.

The number of child abuse cases, of course, reflects only cases that come to the attention of the police. It is likely that many more cases exist. Forms of assault against children may include physical harm, sexual abuse, emotional abuse, and neglect and often include forms of pushing, shoving, slapping, and whipping.

See how well you are able to answer the following questions in your checklist.

1. **Identify and define the three main types of child maltreatment**.

   There is no single universally accepted definition of child maltreatment. However, there are three main types of child maltreatment which often co-occur:

   - Physical abuse may range in severity from minor bruising to death. The risk of physical abuse decreases as the child gets older. It occurs disproportionately among economically disadvantaged families. Income also affects the seriousness of abuse.

   - Sexual abuse may involve varying degrees of coercion and violence. Children ages 7 to 12 are at highest risk. Girls appears significantly more likely to be sexually abused, but it is possible that boys are simply less likely to report their victimization.

   - Neglect ranges from the failure to provide food, clothing, or shelter to the failure to provide medical care, supervision, or schooling. Exposing a child to dangerous conditions or hazards may also be considered neglect. The mean age of victims of neglect is six years old and risk generally declines with age. Boys and girls are at equal risk of neglect.

2. **Explain the scope of the child abuse problem**.

   The National Child Abuse and Neglect Data System, maintained by the U.S. Department of Health and Human Services, is a voluntary national database providing information on the incidence of child abuse and neglect. Data are provided by state child protective agencies.

   - In 2010, an estimated 3.3 million referrals involved the alleged maltreatment of approximately 5.9 million children. Of the nearly 1.8 million reports that required an investigation, 436,321 were substantiated.

   - Over 75 percent of child victims suffered neglect, over 15 percent suffered physical abuse, and less than 10 percent suffered sexual abuse.

   - Every day, at least four children in the United States die from maltreatment. The majority are under four years of age.

3. **Explain who reports child abuse and what the laws say regarding mandatory child abuse reporting**.

   According to the U.S. Department of Health and Human Services, approximately three-fifths of reports of alleged child abuse and neglect were made by professionals, while the rest were made by nonprofessionals.

   - The three largest percentages of report sources were from professionals such as teachers, law enforcement and legal personnel, and social services staff.

   - Anonymous sources, parents, other relatives, and friends and neighbors accounted for nearly all of the nonprofessional reporters.

   Mandatory child abuse reporting laws vary across states but most specify the following:

   - The categories of people required to report suspected abuse or neglect.

   - The conditions under which a professional must make a report.

   - Immunity from legal liability for reporters and penalties for the failure to report suspected abuse.

   - Timelines within which people must make a report.

   - Agencies responsible for receiving and investigating reports.

4. **Explain battered child syndrome and how it should be handled**.

   Battered child syndrome is defined as the collection of injuries sustained by a child as a result of repeated mistreatment or beating.

   - If the child's injuries indicate intentional trauma or appear to be more severe than could reasonably be expected from an accident, battered child syndrome should be suspected.

   - In such cases, the investigator must conduct a full investigation, including:

     - Interviewing possible witnesses about other injuries the child may have suffered

     - Obtaining the caretaker's explanation for those injuries

     - Assessing the conclusions of medical personnel who may have seen the victim before

5. Define shaken baby syndrome and identify the signs.

Shaken baby syndrome (SBS) is a form of child abuse that occurs when an abuser violently shakes an infant or small child, creating a whiplash-type motion that causes acceleration–deceleration injuries.

- SBS affects between 1,200 and 1,600 children in the United States each year.
- Most child victims are younger than 18 months.
- Classic medical symptoms associated with SBS include:

  - Retinal hemorrhaging
  - Subdural or subarachnoid hematomas
  - Absence of other external signs of abuse (not always)

- Retinal hemorrhaging is generally conclusive evidence of SBS in the absence of a good explanation, such as a severe auto accident or a fall from several stories onto a hard surface.
- The shaking necessary to cause death or severe intracranial injuries is never an unintentional or nonabusive action.

6. What do you know about the problem of Munchausen Syndrome by Proxy and how to detect it?

Munchausen syndrome is a psychological disorder in which a patient fabricates symptoms of disease or injury in order to undergo medical tests, hospitalization, or even medical or surgical treatment.

In cases of Munchausen syndrome by proxy, parents or caretakers with Munchausen syndrome attempt to bring medical attention to themselves by inducing illness in their children.

Key indications of Munchausen syndrome include:

- A child with one or more medical problems that do not respond to treatment or that follow an unusual course that is persistent, puzzling, and unexplained
- Physical or laboratory findings that are highly unusual, discrepant with history, or physically or clinically impossible
- A parent who appears to be medically knowledgeable or fascinated with medical details and hospital gossip, appears to enjoy the hospital environment, and expresses interest in the details of other patients' problems
- A highly attentive parent who is reluctant to leave the child's side and who him- or herself seems to require constant attention
- A parent who appears to be unusually calm in the face of serious difficulties in the child's medical course while being highly supportive and encouraging of the physician, or a parent who is angry;

devalues staff; and demands further intervention, more procedures, second opinions, and transfers to other, more sophisticated, facilities

- The suspected parent may work in the health care field him- or herself or profess interest in a health-related job
- The signs and symptoms of a child's illness do not occur in the parent's absence
- A family history of similar or unexplained illness or death in a sibling
- A parent with symptoms similar to the child's medical problems or an illness history that itself is puzzling and unusual
- A suspected emotionally distant relationship between parents; the spouse often fails to visit the patient and has little contact with physicians even when the child is hospitalized with serious illness
- A parent who reports dramatic, negative events, such as house fires, burglaries, or car accidents, that affect him or her and their family while the child is undergoing treatment
- A parent who seems to have an insatiable need for adulation or who makes self-serving efforts for public acknowledgment of his or her abilities

7. Identify the types of child sexual abuse.

The category of child sexual abuse includes:

- Exploitation: the use of children for illegal activities such as prostitution and pornography
- Incest: sexual relations between children and their parents
- Child sexual abuse: the sexual molestation of children, as well as seduction and statutory rape

8. Describe the profile of the child molester.

Child molesters are the most common type of pedophiles.

- The term *pedophile* is commonly used by medical treatment and law enforcement and psychology professionals alike and generally refers to one who engages in some form of child sexual exploitation.
- The term *pedophile* is also associated with child molesters.

For investigative purposes, the child molester can be viewed as falling into two distinct typological categories:

- Situational molesters may commit such crimes because of external factors such as intoxication, drug abuse, mood or mental conditions, or other social conditions.
- Preferential molesters have sexual desires focusing on children and typically have more identifiable psychological disorders.

Studies of child molesters have revealed two psychological types:

- A fixated child molester is one whose primary sexual orientation is toward children.

- A regressed child molester represents a departure from a primary orientation toward age mates because the child becomes a substitute for an adult partner.

Key Terms

abandoned children
acquaintance molestation
acute maltreatment
acute neglect
battered child
battered child syndrome
battery
child abuse
child molestation
child molester

Child Protective Services (CPS)
chronic maltreatment
child sexual abuse
circumstantial evidence
direct evidence
exploitation
fixated child molester
incest
Munchausen syndrome by proxy
neglect

pedophilia
physical abuse
preferential molester
premeditation
regressed child molester
shaken baby syndrome (SBS)
situational molester
sudden infant death
    syndrome (SIDS)
tolerance

Discussion Questions

1. Discuss the three types of child maltreatment and how they differ.
2. How have society's views of child maltreatment changed over the years?
3. Describe some of the physical indications of child abuse.
4. Define battered child syndrome and explain how officers can recognize abuse.
5. Describe the "typical" child molester and how the actual offender differs from the stereotypical offender.
6. Explain the importance of the forensic interview.
7. List and explain the various "syndromes" of child abuse.
8. Discuss the steps that investigators should follow when investigating suspected child abuse.

Notes

1. U.S. DEPARTMENT OF HEALTH AND HUMAN SERVICES, ADMINISTRATION ON CHILDREN, YOUTH, AND FAMILIES. (2008). *Child Maltreatment 2006*. Washington, DC: U.S. Government Printing Office.
2. BARNETT, O., C. MILLER-PERRIN, AND R. PERRIN. (2005). *Family violence across the lifespan: An introduction,* 2nd ed. Thousand Oaks, CA: Sage.
3. IBID.
4. LANNING, K. (2010). Child molesters: A behavioral analysis. *Center for missing and exploited children*, 5th ed. Washington, DC: U.S. Department of Justice, Office of Juvenile Justice and Delinquency Prevention.
5. IBID.
6. IBID.
7. IBID.
8. IBID.
9. DEDEL, K. (March 2010). *Child abuse and neglect in the home,* guide No. 55. Center of Problem Oriented Policing. U.S. Department of Justice.
10. LANNING. (2010). Child molesters.
11. DEDEL, K. (2010). *Child Abuse and Neglect in the Home.*
12. LANNING. (2010). Child molesters.
13. U.S. DEPARTMENT OF HEALTH AND HUMAN SERVICES. (2010). *Child Maltreatment 2010*. Available at http://www.acf.hhs.gov/programs/cb/pubs/cm10/index.htm

14. LANNING. (2010). Child molesters.

15. U.S. DEPARTMENT OF HEALTH AND HUMAN SERVICES. (2010). *Child maltreatment 2010.*

16. IBID.

17. BESHAROV (1990); Martin and Besharov (1991); Broadhurst and Knoeller (1979); American Prosecutors Research Institute (2004). Available at http://www.nsvrc.org/organizations/243

18. DEDEL, K. (2010). *Child abuse and neglect in the home.*

19. IBID.

20. BARNETT, MILLER-PERRIN, AND PERRIN. (2005). *Family violence across the lifespan;* AMERICAN PROSECUTORS RESEARCH INSTITUTE, NATIONAL CENTER FOR PROSECUTION OF CHILD ABUSE. (2004). *Investigation and prosecution of child abuse,* 3rd ed. Thousand Oaks, CA: Sage.

21. BARNETT, MILLER-PERRIN, AND PERRIN. (2005). *Family violence across the lifespan.*

22. SMALLBONE, S., W.L. MARSHALL, AND R. WORTLEY. (2008). *Preventing child sexual abuse: Evidence, policy and practice.* Portland, OR: Williams Publishing.

23. IBID.

24. SMALLBONE, MARSHALL, AND WORTLEY. (2008). *Preventing child sexual abuse;* DEDEL. (2010). *Child abuse and neglect in the home.*

25. WALSH, B. (August 2005). *Investigating child fatalities.* Washington, DC: United States Department of Justice, Office of Justice Programs, Office of Juvenile Justice and Delinquency Prevention.

26. BONNER, B. L., S. M. CROW, AND M. B. LOUGE. (2002). Fatal child neglect. In Dubowitz H (Ed.), *Neglected children.* Thousand Oaks, CA: Sage Publications, pp.156–173.

27. IBID.

28. BRIERE, J., L. BERLINER, J. A. BULKLEY, ET. AL. (Eds). (1998). *The APSAC handbook on child maltreatment,* 2nd ed. Thousand Oaks, CA: Sage Publications.

29. WALSH. (2005). *Investigating child fatalities.*

30. IBID.

31. KOCHANEK, K. D. AND B. L. SMITH. (2002). Deaths: Preliminary data for 2002. *National Vital Statistics Reports* 52(13):27; NATIONAL CLEARINGHOUSE ON CHILD ABUSE AND NEGLECT INFORMATION (NCCANI). (August 2003). *Child abuse and neglect fatalities: Statistics and interventions. Fact sheet.* Washington, DC: U.S. Department of Health and Human Services, Administration for Children and Families, NCCANI.

32. PENCE, D. AND C. WILSON. (1994). *Team investigation of child sexual abuse.* Thousand Oaks, CA: Sage Publications.

33. WALSH. (2005). *Investigating child fatalities*

34. PENCE AND WILSON. (1994). *Team investigation of child sexual abuse.*

35. WALSH. (2005). *Investigating child fatalities.*

36. IBID.

37. ZULAWSKI, D.E. AND D. E. WICKLANDER. (1993). *Practical aspects of interview and interrogation.* Boca Raton, FL: CRC Press.

38. IBID.

39. WALSH. (2005). *Investigating child fatalities.*

40. REECE, R. M. (Ed.). (1994). *Child abuse: Medical diagnosis and management.* Malvern, PA: Lea and Febiger.

41. IBID.

42. COOK, N. AND M. HERMANN. (1996). *Criminal defense checklists.* Deerfield, IL: CBC.

43. IBID.

44. WALSH. (2005). *Investigating child fatalities.*

45. U.S. OFFICE OF JUVENILE JUSTICE AND DELINQUENCY PREVENTION. (2002). *Battered child syndrome: Investigating physical abuse and homicide.* U.S. Department of Justice office of Justice Programs.

46. GEBERTH, V. (1990). *Practical homicide investigation,* 2nd ed. New York: Elsevier.

47. NATIONAL CENTER FOR INJURY PREVENTION AND CONTROL. (2006). *Child maltreatment: Fact sheet.* Centers for Disease Control and Prevention (CDC). Available at http://www.cdc.gov/ncipc/factsheets/cmfacts.htm

48. AMERICAN ACADEMY OF PEDIATRICS: COMMITTEE ON CHILD ABUSE AND NEGLECT. (2001). Shaken baby syndrome: Rotational cranial injuries. Technical report. *Pediatrics* 108(1):206–210. Available at http://pediatrics.aappublications.org/cgi/content/full/108/1/206

49. ELDER W., I. C. COLETSOS, AND H. J. BURSZTAJN. (2010). In F. J Domino (Ed.). *Factitious disorder/Munchhausen syndrome. The 5-minute clinical consult,* 18th ed. Philadelphia: Wolters Kluwer/Lippincott.

50. VENNEMANN B., M. G. PERDEKAMP, AND W. WEINMANN, ET. AL. (2006). A case of Munchausen syndrome by proxy with subsequent suicide of the mother. *Forensic Science International* 158(2–3):195–199.

51. KROUS, H. F., ET. AL. (2004). Sudden infant death syndrome and unclassified sudden infant deaths: A definitional and diagnostic approach. Pediatrics: Official Journal of the American Academy of Pediatrics. DOI: 10.1542/peds.114.1.234, pp. 114–234.

52. PROTECTIVE AND FAMILY SERVICES, State of Texas. (September 23, 2012). Available at http://www.dfps.state.tx.us/Child_Care/Information_for_Providers/sbs_sids.asp

53. GEISSINGER, S. (1993). Boy Scouts dismissed 1,800 suspected molesters from 1971 to 1991. *Boston Globe*, October 15:3.

54. RUSSELL, D. (1983). The incidence and prevalence of intrafamilial and extrafamilial sexual abuse of female children. *Child Abuse and Neglect* 7:133–146.

55. WOLFNER, G. AND R. GELLES. (1993). A profile of violence toward children: A national study. *Child abuse and neglect* 17:144–146.

56. LAWSON, L. AND M. CHIFFEN. (1992). False negatives in sexual abuse disclosure interviews. *Journal of interpersonal violence* 7(4):532–542.

57. SORENSON, E., B. L. BOTTOMS, AND A. PERONA. (1997). *Handbook on intake and forensic interviewing in the children's advocacy center setting.* Washington, DC: Office of Juvenile Justice and Delinquency Prevention.

58. SAYWITZ, K. J. AND G. S. GOODMAN. (1996). Interviewing children in and out of court. In J. Briere, L. Berliner, J. A. Bulkley, et al. (Eds.), *The APSAC handbook on child maltreatment,* 2nd ed. Thousand Oaks, CA: Sage Publications, pp. 297–317.

59. IBID.

60. CRONCH, L. E., ET. AL. (2006). *Forensic interviewing in child abuse cases: Current techniques and future directions.* Faculty Publications: Department of Psychology. University of Nebraska-Lincoln, April 1, 2006.

61. SORENSON, E., B. L. BOTTOMS, AND A. PERONA. (1997). *Handbook on intake and forensic interviewing in the children's advocacy center setting.* Washington, DC: Office of Juvenile Justice and Delinquency Prevention.

62. SAYWITZ AND GOODMAN. (1996). Interviewing children in and out of court.

63. FLICK, J. AND J. CAYE. (2001). *Introduction to child sexual abuse (curriculum).* Chapel Hill, NC: UNC-CH School of Social Work.

64. CRONCH, ET. AL. (2006). *Forensic interviewing in child abuse cases.*

65. AMERICAN PROFESSIONAL SOCIETY ON THE ABUSE OF CHILDREN. (2012). *Investigative interviewing in cases of alleged child abuse,* 3rd ed. See Chapter 20 by Saywitz, Lyon & Goodman on Interviewing Children. Available at http://www.apsac.org/practice-guidelines; CORDISCO STEELE, L. AND C.N. CARNES. (2002). *Child centered forensic interviewing.* International Society for Prevention of Child Abuse and Neglect. Available at http://www.ispcan.org/TCBYAUTHOR.htm

66. CORDISCO STEELE AND CARNES. (2002). *Child centered forensic interviewing.*

67. YUILLE, J. C., R. HUNTER, R. JOFFE, AND J. ZAPARNIUK. (1993). *Interviewing children in sexual abuse cases.* In G. Goodman and B. Bottoms (Eds.), *Understanding and improving children's testimony: Clinical, developmental and legal implications.* New York: Guilford Press.

68. GRAY, J. (Ed.). (1994). Improving investigations: Strategies for professionals. *Virginia Child Protection Newsletter* 44 (Winter):8–12.

69. FALLER, K. C. (1993). *Child sexual abuse: Intervention and treatment issues.* Washington, DC: US DHHS Administration for Children and Families. Available at http://nccanch.acf.hhs.gov/pubs/usermanuals/sexabuse/index.cfm; FINKELHOR, D. (1994).Current information on the scope and nature of child sexual abuse. *The Future of Children* 4(2, summer/fall). Available at http://www.futureofchildren.org/information2826/information_show.htm?doc_id=74226

70. YUILLE, HUNTER, JOFFE, AND ZAPARNIUK. (1993). Interviewing children in sexual abuse cases. FLICK, J. AND J. CAYE. (2001). *Introduction to child sexual abuse (curriculum);* SATTLER, J. M. (1998). *Clinical and forensic interviewing of children and families.* San Diego, CA: Jerome M. Sattler Publishing, Inc.

71. KLOTTER, J. (1990). *Criminal law,* 3rd ed. Cincinnati, OH: Anderson.

72. LANNING. (2010). Child molesters.

73. GOLDSTEIN, H. (1977). *Policing a free society.* Cambridge, MA: Ballinger.

74. BURGESS, A. W., C. R. HARTMAN, AND M. P. MCCAUSLAND. (1984). Response pattern in children and adolescents exploited through sex rings and pornography. *American Journal of Psychiatry* 141(5):656–662.

75. ERICKSON, W. D., N. H. WALBEK, AND R. K. SEELY. (1988). Behavior patterns of child molesters.*Archives of Sexual Behavior* 17(1):77–86.

76. IBID.

77. GROTH, A. N. AND J. BIRNBAUM (1981). *Men who rape: The psychology of the offender.* New York: Plenum Press.

78. GOLDSTEIN. (1977). *Policing a free society.*

79. IBID.

80. LANNING. (2010). Child molesters.

81. WORTLEY, R. AND S. SMALLBONE. (2006). *Child pornography on the Internet.* Washington, DC: U.S. Department of Justice, Center for Problem Oriented Policing, May, p. 1

82. IBID.; CREWDSON, J. (1998). *By silence betrayed: Sexual abuse of children in America.* Boston: Little Brown.

83. WORTLEY AND SMALLBONE. (2006). *Child pornography on the Internet;* WOLAK, J., K. MITCHELL, AND D. FINKELHOR (2003). Escaping or connecting? Characteristics of youth who form close online relationships. *Journal of Adolescence* 26:105–119.

84. JENKINS, P. (2001). *Beyond tolerance: Child pornography on the Internet.* New York: New York University Press.

85. ADLER, A. (2001). The perverse law of child pornography. *Columbia law review* 101(2):209–273; GRAHAM, W., JR. (2000). Uncovering and eliminating child pornography rings on the Internet: Issues regarding and avenues facilitating law enforcement's access to 'Wonderland'. *The Law Review of Michigan State University-Detroit College of Law* 2:457–484; GRASZ, L. AND P. PFALTZGRAFF. (1998). Child pornography and child nudity: Why and how states may constitutionally regulate the production, possession, and distribution of nude visual depictions of children. *Temple Law Review* 71:609–636.

86. CORNELL UNIVERSITY LAW SCHOOL. Located at http://www.law.cornell.edu/uscode/text/18/2256 (retrieved at April 19, 2012).

87. *United States* v. *Knox,* 32 F.3d 733 (3d Cir. 1994), cert denied, 513 U.S. 1109 (1995); JENKINS. (2001). *Beyond tolerance.*

88. WORTLEY, R. AND S. SMALLBONE. (2006). *Child Pornography on the Internet.* Center for Problem Oriented Policing. U.S. Department of Justice, May, p. 17

89. WORTLEY AND SMALLBONE. (2006). *Child pornography on the Internet;* FORDE, P. AND A. PATTERSON (1998). *Paedophile Internet activity.* Trends & Issues in Crime and Criminal Justice, No. 97. Canberra: Australian Institute of Criminology.

90. GOLDSTEIN. (1977). *Policing a free society,* p. 1.

This chapter will enable you to:

1. Summarize the trends and elements of burglary.

2. Describe the types of burglaries and types of burglars.

3. Describe how burglary investigations are conducted.

4. Summarize the trends and types of larceny–theft.

5. Describe how larceny–theft investigations are conducted.

6. Describe the different types of fraud and how fraud investigations are conducted.

7. Describe the crime of motor vehicle theft and how motor vehicle theft investigations are conducted.

© picsfive / Fotolia

Theft-Related Offenses

Introduction

 *In the preceding chapters we considered violent crime and various crimes against persons. This chapter addresses crimes against property and the extent such crimes present problems to society. Such crimes represent considerable cost and inconvenience to the victim. Residual costs include those associated with the functions of the police, courts, and corrections in handling violators as well as soaring costs for insurance companies.*

The statistics measuring property crime are instructive. For example, in 2010, the FBI reported that there were an estimated 9,082,887 property crime offenses in the United States.[1] While this seems like an unusually large figure, the five-year trend, comparing 2010 data with that of 2006, showed a 9.3 percent drop. Specifically, in 2010 burglary accounted for 23.8 percent, motor vehicle theft for 8.1 percent, and larceny–theft for 68.1 percent. Property crimes in 2010 resulted in losses estimated at 15.7 billion dollars.[2]

Burglary

Of the many property crimes, the crime of **burglary** is one of the most pervasive. Burglary is generally considered a covert crime in which the criminal works during the nighttime, outside the presence of witnesses. The burglar has often been portrayed in the media as a cunning masked person who is quick to elude police. In actuality, burglars are represented by virtually every creed, gender, and color and may indeed be skillful in their techniques, but they may also be bungling amateurs. In fact, it is estimated that opportunists commit most burglaries. Burglary is considered a **property crime**. The crime differs from robbery because burglars are more concerned with financial gain and less prepared for a violent altercation with the victim. Their goal is to steal as much valuable property as possible and sell what they steal (usually to a fence, who has connections to dispose of the property before police can discover it).

The Uniform Crime Reports (UCR) program uses three classifications of burglary: forcible entry, unlawful entry or no force used, and attempted forcible entry. In most jurisdictions, force need not be used for a crime to be classified as burglary. Unlocked doors and open windows are invitations to burglars, and the crime of burglary consists not so much of a forcible entry as it does of the intent of the offender to trespass and steal.

Many people fear nighttime burglary of their residence. They imagine themselves asleep in bed when a stranger breaks into their home, resulting in a violent confrontation. Although such scenarios do occur, daytime burglaries are more common. Many families now have two or more breadwinners, and because children are in school during the day, some homes—and even entire neighborhoods—remain unoccupied during daylight hours. This shift in patterns of social activity has led to growing burglary threats against residences during the daytime.

Trends

As with other categories of crime, trends in burglary are typically measured by the use of crime statistics. According to the FBI, in 2010, there were an estimated 2,159,878 burglaries. This number represents a decrease of 2.0 percent from 2009. Of the estimated number of property crimes

|Fig. 14.1| △

Burglary: Percent change.

From Federal Bureau of Investigation (2008). Crime in the United States—2007.

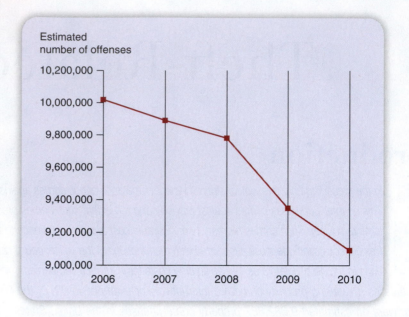

committed in 2010, burglary accounted for 23.8 percent.[3] Of those, over 60 percent involved forcible entry, 33 percent were unlawful entries (without force), and the remainder, approximately 6 percent, were forcible entry "attempts." The 2010 statistics also show that burglary cost its victims almost $5 billion in lost property.[4] Overall, the average dollar loss for each burglary offense was $2,119. Finally, burglaries of residential properties accounted for about 74 percent of all burglary offenses.[5]

Burglary Trends	
Year	**Number of Offenses**
2010	2,034,268
2009	2,068,376
Percent change	−1.6

Source: Federal Bureau of Investigation. (2011). *Crime in the United States—2010.*

Burglary versus Robbery

A distinction should be made between the terms *burglary* and *robbery* because they are commonly confused. Burglary is considered a property crime in which the thief seeks to avoid direct contact with people during commission of the crime. In addition, locations of burglaries are usually unoccupied homes or businesses where no witnesses are present. The crime of robbery is quite different. Here, the robber chooses to confront his or her victim at a location where witnesses are present. Robbery is therefore classified as a crime against persons. In this chapter, we examine burglary.

Why Criminals Burglarize

Burglary is an appealing alternative to the criminal because it offers a quick opportunity to acquire money or other valuables on short notice. Drug addicts have typically been associated with burglaries because they need a constant source of cash with which to purchase drugs. Some burglars are violent in nature, but experience has shown that they usually try to avoid confrontations during the commission of their act. In fact, many actually flee the area when confronted.

Inside lights remaining off at night indicating no one is home

Newspapers collecting on driveway or yard indicating that owners are away

Shrubs are not trimmed

Area around the home is not properly lighted

House keys located around the home

Windows or doors left unlocked

No vehicles located in the driveway or in front of the home indicating that owners are away

|Fig. 14.2| ◬

How a house can be an attractive target to a burglar. Research shows that the average burglar spends no more than five minutes tying to break into a house.

Elements of Burglary

Although the elements of the crime are defined by each state's criminal code, many differences exist regarding these laws. Some commonalities, however, are also present and are generally reflected in the elements of the crime.

Burglary is a crime against the dwelling that is violated. Accordingly, no violence need be directed toward any occupants. As a rule, after the burglar is inside the structure, no additional felony need be committed for the legal elements of the crime to be met. Exceptions are when the person believes that the structure he or she is entering is open to the general public. Decisions as to the validity of this claim are typically left up to the jury.

How a Thief Works

Although many jurisdictions report an increase in daytime burglaries, some occur at night, typically between 7 P.M. and 12 P.M. It is during those hours that a burglar becomes most inconspicuous on the street. In selecting a target, the burglar will look for certain things to indicate that a structure is vacant. These include:

- Newspapers collecting in the front of the residence, indicating that no one has been home for a while
- Empty garage left open
- House with too many lights on or just one light left on

When a daytime burglary occurs, it is usually during the time that most people are working. To approach the residence, a more innovative burglar may pose as a salesperson, insurance agent, public utility worker, or other "legitimate" person. This permits him or her to verify that no one is home. After it is determined that the residence is vacant, either a quick, forceful entry can be made into the house, or the burglar can look for a tree or large bush that might cloak a window, which he or she can then use to enter the house unnoticed by neighbors.

Types of Burglaries

Burglaries can be divided into two general categories: **residential burglary** and **commercial burglary**. Residential burglars may focus on apartments or houses and usually work the higher-income areas of town. In both cases, the experienced burglar will be familiar with preventive

measures used by residents. Such measures are sometimes easily defeated through knowledge of how they work. For example, an apartment dweller was careful in placing a steel rod in the track of the sliding glass door leading to the patio area before he left town. The burglar, however, simply removed the six screws securing the "nonmovable" piece of glass next to the sliding door, slid the pane of glass to the side, and entered the apartment. After the burglar is inside the structure, money is most typically sought, but other valuables might be taken as well.

Warehouses, stores, taverns, and restaurants are all common targets of commercial burglaries. Occasionally, employees of companies will be implicated in such thefts because they have direct knowledge of the types of merchandise in stock and locations of cash.

Residential Burglaries

To many, burglary is a difficult problem because solving the crime is demanding and it is one in which the police role more or less involves documenting the crime and reassuring the victims. Although burglaries have declined in recent years, police strategies such as *Neighborhood Watch* and target-hardening have had limited success in reducing these crimes. However, some quite specific, highly focused burglary prevention efforts show promise.[6]

Single-family detached houses are often attractive targets—with greater rewards—and more difficult to secure because they have multiple access points. Indeed, burglars are less likely to be seen entering larger houses that offer greater privacy. In general, greater accessibility to such houses presents opportunities to offenders.

In contrast to residents of other types of housing, private homeowners may use their own initiative to protect their property—and often have both the resources and incentive to do so. Residents of single-family houses do not depend on a landlord, who may have little financial incentive to secure a property. Most police offense reports include a premise code to help police distinguish single-family houses from other types of residences.[7]

Although burglaries of multifamily homes are the most numerous, some studies demonstrate that single-family houses are at higher risk. National burglary averages tend to mask the prevalence of burglaries of single-family houses in suburban areas, where such housing is more common. The proportion of burglaries of single-family houses will vary from one jurisdiction to another, based on the jurisdiction's housing types, overall burglary rates, neighborhood homogeneity—especially economic homogeneity, proximity to offenders, and other factors.[8]

TIMES WHEN BURGLARIES OCCUR Burglary does not typically reflect large seasonal variations, although in the United States, burglary rates are the highest in August, and the lowest in February. Seasonal variations reflect local factors, including the weather and how it affects occupancy, particularly of vacation homes.[9] In warm climates and seasons, residents may leave windows and doors open, providing easy access, while storm windows or double-pane glass to protect against harsh weather provides a deterrent to burglary. The length of the days, the availability of activities that take families away from home, and the temperature may all have some effect on burglary.[10]

Exactly when a burglary has occurred is often difficult for victims or police to determine. Usually, victims suggest a time range during which the offense occurred. Some researchers have divided burglary times into four distinct categories: morning (7 A.M. to 11 A.M.), afternoon (12 P.M. to 5 P.M.), evening (5 P.M. to 10 P.M.), and night (10 P.M. to 7 A.M.). This scheme naturally reflects residents' presence at various times as well as offender patterns.[11] Some research suggests that burglars most often strike on weekdays, from 10 A.M. to 11 A.M. and from 1 P.M. to 3 P.M.—times when even routinely occupied houses may be empty.[12]

In many cases, determining the times when burglaries occur helps in developing crime prevention strategies and in identifying potential suspects. For example, burglaries by juveniles during school hours may suggest truancy problems. After-school burglaries may be related to the availability of alternative activities.[13]

TARGET SELECTION Burglars select targets based on a number of key factors, including the following:

- Familiarity with the target, and convenience of the location
- Occupancy
- Visibility or surveillability
- Accessibility
- Vulnerability or security
- Potential rewards[14]

These elements interact. Visibility and accessibility are more important than vulnerability or security, which a burglar typically cannot assess from afar unless the resident has left the house visibly open.

> *Familiarity with the target, and convenience of the location*. Offenders tend to commit crimes relatively close to where they live, although older, more professional burglars tend to be more mobile and travel farther. Burglars often target houses on routes from home to work, or on other routine travel routes.[15] This tendency makes the following houses more vulnerable to burglary:
>
> *Houses near a ready pool of offenders*. These include houses near large youth populations, drug addicts, shopping centers, sports arenas, transit stations, and urban high-crime areas.[16]
>
> *Houses near major thoroughfares*. Heavy vehicle traffic that brings outsiders into an area may contribute to burglaries. Burglars become familiar with potential targets, and it is more difficult for residents to recognize strangers. Houses close to pedestrian paths are also more vulnerable to burglary.[17]
>
> *Houses on the outskirts of neighborhoods*. Like houses near major thoroughfares, those on the outskirts of neighborhoods have greater exposure to strangers. Strangers are more likely to be noticed by residents of houses well within neighborhood confines, where less traffic makes their presence stand out.[18] Such houses include those on dead-end streets and cul-de-sacs—locations with few outlets.
>
> *Houses previously burglarized*. Such houses have a much higher risk of being burglarized than those never burglarized, partly because the factors that make them vulnerable once, such as occupancy or location, are difficult to change. Compared with nonburglarized houses, those previously targeted are up to four times more likely to be burglarized; any subsequent burglary is most likely to occur within six weeks of the initial crime.[19]

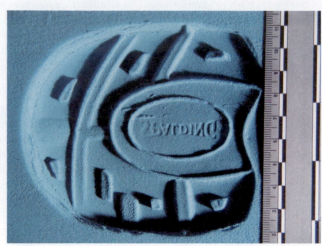

|Fig. 14.4| ▲

A. Heel of a suspect's shoe that was seized as evidence. B. Comparison imprint of the suspect's shoe heel found at the scene of the burglary; the matching shoe was seized in the investigation.

Mike Himmel / Missouri State Highway Patrol Crime Laboratory

There are a variety of reasons suggested for re-victimization: some houses offer cues of a good payoff or easy access; burglars return to houses for property left behind during the initial burglary; or burglars tell others about desirable houses. Burglars may also return to a target months later, to steal property the owners have presumably replaced through insurance proceeds. Numerous studies show that re-victimization is most concentrated in lower-income areas, where burglaries are the most numerous.[20]

Houses near burglarized houses Such houses face an increased risk of burglary after the neighbor is burglarized. Offenders may return to the area of a successful burglary and, if the previous target has been hardened, select another house, or they may seek similar property in a nearby house.

OCCUPANCY Most burglars do not target occupied houses, taking great care to avoid them. Some studies suggest burglars routinely ring doorbells to confirm residents' absence. How long residents are away from home is a strong predictor of the risk of burglary, which explains why single-parent, one-person, and younger-occupant homes are more vulnerable.[21]

The following houses are at higher risk of burglary:

• Houses vacant for extended periods. Vacation or weekend homes, and those of residents away on vacation, are particularly at risk of burglary and re-victimization.

• Signs of vacancy—such as open garage doors or accumulated mail—may indicate that no one is home.

• Houses routinely vacant during the day. Houses that appear occupied—with the lights on, a vehicle in the driveway, visible activity, or audible noises from within—are less likely to be burglarized. Even houses near occupied houses generally have a lower risk of burglary.

• Houses of new residents. Neighborhoods with higher mobility—those with shorter-term residents—tend to have higher burglary rates, presumably because residents do not have well-established social networks.

• Houses without dogs. A dog's presence is a close substitute for human occupancy, and most burglars avoid houses with dogs. Small dogs may bark and attract attention, and large dogs may pose a physical threat, as well. On average, burglarized houses are less likely to have dogs than are nonburglarized houses, suggesting that dog ownership is a substantial deterrent.[22]

STOLEN PROPERTY Burglars are most likely to steal cash and goods they can easily carry and sell, including jewelry, weapons, televisions, stereo equipment, and computers. They need transportation to move larger items, such as electronic equipment, while they often make off with cash and jewelry on foot.[23]

Few burglars keep the goods they steal. According to research, they typically disposed of stolen property within 24 hours, usually after stashing it in a semipublic location. They thus minimized their risk by moving goods only short distances. They appeared to have few concerns about being arrested for selling stolen property, reporting they safely sold goods to strangers and pawnbrokers.[24]

Burglars tend to dispose of stolen goods through local pawnshops, taxi drivers, and small-store owners. Few burglars use professional fences. Pawnshops—often outlets for stolen goods—have come under increasing scrutiny and regulation in many communities. Some burglars sell stolen goods on the street, occasionally trading them for drugs. Burglars commonly sell stolen goods in bars and gas stations; in bars, they usually sell the goods to staff, rather than customers. In many cases, burglars get little return for the goods.[25]

ENTRY METHODS In about two-thirds of reported U.S. burglaries (including commercial ones), the offenders force entry. Unsecured windows and doors (including sliding glass doors) are common entry points. Burglars typically use simple tools such as screwdrivers or crowbars to pry open weak locks, windows and doors, or they may simply break a window or kick in a door.[26]

In about one-third of burglaries, the offenders do not force entry; they enter through unlocked or open windows and doors, especially basement windows and exterior and interior garage doors. There is no consensus about the most common entry point—it depends on the house's architecture and physical location on its lot.

Retail Burglaries

Retail burglaries present an ongoing problem for many communities. Research shows that stores lose as much to burglars as they do to shoplifters. These losses impact the viability of businesses and, as a result, the communities around them. Although much research has been conducted on burglary in general, little of it has specifically focused on retail burglaries—break-ins at stores to steal cash or goods.[27] However, the research that has been done points to a number of effective responses to the problem.

|Fig. 14.5| ▲

(Left) Tire track evidence documented and preserved at a burglary scene. (Right) Tire matching tire impressions from the scene. Investigators must remember to photograph all tread on the suspect tire to capture the section of tread that touched the ground.

Mike Himmel / Missouri State Highway Patrol Crime Laboratory

Retail burglaries include shops in downtown areas, strip malls, covered malls, and retail parks. They also include stand-alone superstores, neighborhood stores, and rural stores, as well as restaurants, beauty parlors, and off-track betting establishments. The problem of retail burglaries should be distinguished from those of (1) other retail thefts and (2) other commercial burglaries.[28] These problems, which should be addressed separately, include:

- robberies of retail establishments
- shoplifting
- stockroom thefts by employees
- thefts by delivery personnel
- insurance frauds involving false burglary reports made by store owners
- burglaries of banks (considered a separate problem due to banks' much greater security)
- burglaries of other commercial spaces such as offices, manufacturing premises, transport facilities, construction sites, and cargo-handling facilities
- false burglar alarms.[29]

Compared with residential burglaries, commercial burglaries—especially retail burglaries—have been the subject of few studies. In part, this is due to the much larger number of residential burglaries, but it is also generally believed that commercial burglaries have less serious consequences for victims and for the community at large. However, growing recognition of the important part small businesses play in urban regeneration has heightened concern about crimes that might reduce their viability. In turn, this has led to more research on crimes against businesses (including retailers).[30] As a result, there is more known about retail burglaries, though a comprehensive understanding is still unclear. The following are what the research shows:[31]

- Even though there are considerably fewer retail burglaries than residential burglaries, the risk of retail burglary per number of premises is very high. For example, one survey found that 24 percent of retail establishments were burglarized compared with just 4 percent of residences. This is because stores tend to be empty at night; may, if big, offer many entry points to burglars; and may contain a lot of goods (and, sometimes, cash).
- Most retail and residential burglars are young men who commit a variety of predatory crimes. Interviews reveal that their main motivation is economic, though some burglars also claim to enjoy the excitement. They do not do much planning, but show some care in selecting "safer" targets. They claim to be little deterred by physical security, but try to avoid being seen. Many have drug or alcohol habits.
- A small number of retail burglars are highly prolific, accounting for many burglaries. Some retail burglars are also more sophisticated in their planning and methods. They work in small gangs and generally rely on disabling the alarm, which allows them more undisturbed time on the premises. They target high-value goods and the safe, which they may remove entirely.
- Most retail burglaries occur at night or on weekends, when stores are closed (while most residential burglaries occur on weekday afternoons, when residents are not likely to be home).
- Retail burglars generally enter the premises through doors or windows. They force door locks, break through doors or side panels, or force/break windows. The use of vehicles to break through doors or windows (ram raiding) is much less common.
- Substantial variations in burglary risks exist among stores, depending on the location, premises, goods sold, and security.
- As with some residences, some stores suffer substantial repeat victimization. This is due to their location or security, the attractiveness of their goods, and the fact that, once successful, burglars may strike the same premises again. National data for Britain show that 2 percent of retail premises experienced a quarter of the retail burglaries in 1993. A repeat burglary can occur soon after the initial one—usually within a month.
- The average financial loss due to burglary is about 20 percent greater for stores than for residences. Perhaps for this reason, a larger proportion of retail burglaries (about 95 percent) are reported to the police than domestic burglaries. Comparatively, in the United Kingdom, a national survey of retailers revealed that stores lose as much to burglary as to shoplifting, and only rarely recover stolen goods.
- Burglary, especially repeat burglary, can have serious consequences for stores. They can become insolvent, and owners are sometimes forced to lay off staff, increase prices, or close the stores. Staff can suffer psychological effects similar to those suffered by people whose homes

have been burgled. They report feeling that their personal space has been invaded, and they worry that the offenders might return when they are on the premises.

- Unless burglars are caught in the act, they are very difficult to detect. The clearance rate for burglaries as a whole (figures for retail burglaries are not available) is the lowest for the eight UCR index crimes.

ATM Burglaries

In February 1998, six people in Orlando, Florida, were charged in connection with three ATM (automated teller machine) thefts after a predawn gun battle with police. The suspects were thought to be connected with a Yugoslav–Albanian–Croatian crime ring that targets ATM machines nationwide. In another February 1998 case, three people in Los Angeles were charged with burglarizing seven bank ATMs. In one case, one suspect disabled the alarms in the machines and then destroyed the surveillance tapes while the other two served as lookouts.

Burglaries of ATMs are one new form of burglary that is on the increase. The ability of banks to provide increased security measures, along with the proliferation of small, freestanding ATMs, has become a concern for criminal investigators. In 1997, there were more than 200 ATM burglaries (and attempted burglaries) compared with 70 in 1992. This compares with a reduction of bank robberies, down 13 percent during 1997.[32] Of course, the use of ATMs is also up considerably in recent years. In 1997, there were 11 billion ATM transactions compared with 4 billion in 1985. The amount stolen from ATMs ranges from $15,000 to $250,000, so the "take" for a successful burglar can be fairly substantial.[33]

Types of Burglars

Criminals who commit property crimes can be categorized into one of two groups: amateurs or professionals. Although both pose a problem to society, each group has special characteristics.

THE AMATEUR BURGLAR The amateur burglar might travel a broad geographical area in search of the best opportunities for stealing. Many such persons resort to more personal contact with victims, such as purse snatching, muggings, or even robbery. The amateur thief is sometimes armed and can pose a serious threat to communities in which he or she operates.

Juveniles pose another type of amateur thief. Most juveniles are opportunists who search for homes and businesses with unlocked doors or open windows. It is also characteristic of juveniles to resort to needless destruction of property during the commission of their crimes. In one case, three juveniles entered a residence to steal some liquor, but while they were there, they carved their initials in a grand piano, broke record albums in half, and spray-painted obscenities on the walls. Juvenile burglars sometimes go to the kitchen and consume food from the cabinets or refrigerator during the commission of the crime. In these cases, fingerprints may be lifted from the walls, cabinets, and so on for later use in identifying a possible suspect.

THE PROFESSIONAL BURGLAR The professional thief represents a unique criminal type. Such a person takes a great deal of time in planning a crime to avoid detection and net the greatest

---

Elements of Burglary

Burglary is committed when a person:

- ☑ Knowingly breaks or
- ☑ Remains in
- ☑ A building or structure belonging to another
- ☑ For the purpose of committing a crime therein

cache of property possible. The "pro" commonly relies on the expert use of tools for entry into otherwise secure structures. He or she might also consider making a bogus burglary call to another part of town to occupy the local police, thus giving him or her more freedom in his work. Pros typically drive trucks or vans, which conceal and transport their tools. Fake company names may even be painted on the sides of vehicles to deter suspicion by neighbors.

The Preliminary Investigation

The patrol division is usually the first to respond to a burglary call. The first thing officers should do is determine whether a crime is currently in progress. If so, an ample number of officers should be dispatched to prevent the escape of the suspect(s). Officers approaching the burglary location should do so quietly without warning emergency lights or siren. En route, officers should also be on the lookout for persons fleeing the scene. It is also important for each officer to know exactly which fellow officers are responding to the call. As a rule, the first officer to receive the call will assume responsibility for placement of assisting officers.

After arriving, great care should be taken not to slam car doors, to turn down police radios, and to avoid the jangling of keys while approaching the residence. In addition, officers should approach the residence on both the front and back sides in the event that the suspect attempts to flee.

Indications of Burglary

At the scene, certain reliable indicators that a burglary has been (or is being) committed can be observed (e.g., open doors or windows). Sometimes a burglar who makes his or her entrance through a window will remove the glass. This makes it difficult for the officer to detect a break-in with only a superficial glance. So when checking glass, the officer should look for a reflection with the use of a flashlight. Sometimes burglaries can be detected by spotting debris on the floor from shelves or counters. Also, debris can be found around desks and cabinets. Other indicators include vehicles parked near the suspect location for no apparent reason or trucks parked close enough to a building to permit access to a roof or to conceal a window or door. In the case of a building burglary, a burglar alarm is another indicator of possible entry. Although wind, stormy conditions, or

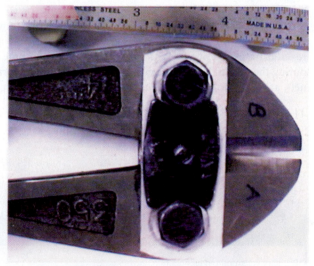

|Fig. 14.6| ▲

Bolt cutters are considered a pinching type of tool and have interactive blades that oppose each other.

malfunctions can set off some alarms, the responding officer should not assume anything. Every alarm situation should be responded to as though it were a burglary in progress.

Yet another sign of a burglary in progress is a person serving as a lookout. Lookouts may be on, in, or near buildings or sitting in cars. Burglars have been known to use such tactics as parking a car a few feet down the street, raising the car's hood, using citizens-band walkie-talkies, or just blowing the horn as a signal that police are approaching.

Approach with Caution!

Officers should enter the structure with weapons drawn, using their flashlights for illumination rather than room lights. This is done as a precaution to avoid the forming of silhouettes. In addition, officers should hold flashlights to their sides while flashing them sporadically to avoid making targets of themselves. After the location has been secured, or "flushed" for suspects, certain aspects of the scene should be documented, such as:

- Document the time of the call.
- Record details about the type of structure.
- Record and document the method of entry and exit used by the suspect.
- Determine the whereabouts of the owner.
- Log all items of property taken and their original locations.
- Discuss with neighbors whether they noticed anything suspicious.

If no suspects are located in the structure, investigators should follow the preliminary investigation steps outlined in Chapter 3. If suspects are thought to be inside the burglary location, entry should not be considered until sufficient backup has arrived and each officer knows the exact location of other officers at the time of entry.

Physical Evidence

Experience has shown that most burglars are convicted on circumstantial evidence. Therefore, any physical evidence located at the burglary crime scene is critical to the case. In addition to forensic evidence such as broken glass, tool marks, and fingerprints at the burglary crime scene, other evidence should also be sought by the investigator. In the case of safe burglaries, safe insulation can be used to link the suspect to the crime scene.

|Fig. 14.7| △

(Left) A copper wire that was cut by a pair of bolt cutters. Notice how the cut is peaked (arrows) and not flat. (Right)A micrograph of the copper wires. The bolt cutters in Figure 14.6 were identified as cutting this copper wire.

Investigative Techniques in Burglary Cases

- ☑ Determine the point of entry.
- ☑ Check to see if a window or door was forced open.
- ☑ What type of tool was used?
- ☑ Are there tool marks?
- ☑ Is there evidence of lock picks?
- ☑ Look for footprints, tire tracks, and so on.
- ☑ Look for other trace evidence such as cigarette butts, fibers, hair, and pieces of broken tools.
- ☑ Sketch the scene.
- ☑ Interview victims and witnesses.
- ☑ Make a list of property taken (include serial numbers).
- ☑ Make a list of all persons on the crime scene.

|Fig. 14.8| △

Burglary tools.

Courtesy of Mike Himmel

Possession of Burglary Tools

Possession of **burglary tools** is considered a separate felony offense by most jurisdictions. If circumstances surrounding the confiscation of the tools indicate that they were intended for use in a burglary, possession of them is usually sufficient for a conviction, even though a burglary has not yet been committed.

Many legitimate uses, of course, can be found for the tools and materials. The investigating officer should therefore determine if possession of the tools is legitimate and if there is any criminal "intent" present that would support criminal charges. Burglary tools can consist of numerous items.

Tracing Stolen Property

After a successful burglary has occurred, the thief will probably seek to get rid of the stolen property as soon as possible. To this end, a **fence** is used. The fence is a person who buys and sells stolen property with criminal intent.

The Fence

Fencing operations can range from professional to highly unorganized. For example, a nonprofessional fence might simply take a trunk full of stolen property in his or her vehicle to a location such as a factory parking lot, where workers on break can come for "good deals." A professional fence may operate from an otherwise legitimate business such as a pawnshop or used-furniture store. People operating in this fashion don't necessarily consider themselves criminals but yet seldom question the lawful ownership of property they receive. From this fixed location, the fence purchases property on a random basis from thieves in the area. This arrangement tends to foster a degree of dependency between the thief and the fence, each needing the services of the other.

Proving the Receipt of Stolen Property

Establishing proof of a fencing operation is a grueling and time-consuming task. However, a fence is most vulnerable during the possession and storage of stolen property. Although many arrests result from lengthy investigations, many are made when suspected stolen property is identified. This is sometimes necessary when there is a risk of losing the property and confiscation is required. As a first rule of thumb, the property in question must be identified as stolen, a task that is more difficult than it may first seem. For instance, many suspected thieves are in possession of property that bears no identification numbers. Without some type of identification number, positive identification is extremely difficult.

In addition, many companies fail to maintain adequate inventory control. Poorly kept records also make it difficult to trace property even when identification numbers are present. Another category of untraceable goods is **fungible goods**, items such as tools, liquor, and clothing that are indistinguishable from others like them. In the absence of some type of identifying numbers, such items are virtually untraceable. To convict a thief for a property offense in this category, investigators must prove that the suspect received stolen property. Laws addressing stolen property also include possession, concealment, and sale of stolen property. Because evidence in this category is sometimes difficult to obtain, investigators might have to rely on circumstantial evidence for prosecution.

One method of showing possession of stolen property is to locate the property on the premises of the suspect. This finding, however, may not be sufficient to prove "criminal intent." It is helpful to show that the stolen goods are in close proximity with personal goods owned by the suspect. This will avoid the defense that the stolen goods were in the possession of someone else living at the same residence.

Circumstantial Evidence

Other than the evidence discussed previously, investigators might need to rely on circumstantial evidence to prove receipt of stolen property. Such evidence is described as follows:

- Did the suspect pay for the merchandise with a check or cash?
- Was the property purchased for considerably lower than the normal retail price?
- Does the suspect have a receipt for the property?
- Were the stolen items isolated from other items in storage?
- Is there property from several different thefts present at the location?

After property has been retrieved, a determination should be made as to how it got there. The owner of the property should examine it and make a positive identification. In many cases, a secondhand store or pawnshop owner can make a positive identification of a fence.

Larceny–Theft

In 2002, 25-year-old Ted Roberts and 22-year-old Tiffany Fowler were arrested in Orlando, Florida, and charged with stealing moon rocks from the Johnson Space Center in Houston, Texas. Roberts had been working as a student intern at the center, and Fowler was a Space Center employee. Officials realized that the lunar samples, along with a number of meteorites, were missing when they discovered that a 600-pound safe had disappeared from the Houston facility. They had been alerted to the loss by messages placed on a Web site run by a mineralogy club in Antwerp, Belgium, offering "priceless Moon rocks collected by Apollo astronauts" for sale for up to $5,000 per gram. Roberts and Fowler were arrested by federal agents pretending to be potential buyers for the moon rocks.

Probably the most commonly committed crime of personal gain is larceny–theft. It is defined as the unlawful taking, carrying, leading, or riding away of property from the possession of another.

Larceny–theft is one of the eight Index crimes according to the UCR. Generally, the two terms are considered synonymous. In some states, criminal law recognizes simple larceny (e.g., shoplifting) and grand larceny (e.g., auto theft). In most cases, what distinguishes one form of larceny from another is the dollar amount of the items stolen. Often, when anything stolen is valued under $200, the charge is simple larceny, while stolen property valued in excess of that figure is grand larceny. As a rule, thefts of any amount are considered larceny. The following offenses are examples of larceny:

- Pocket picking
- Breaking into coin machines
- Purse snatching
- Shoplifting
- Stealing bicycles
- Stealing motor vehicles
- Stealing valuables left in unattended buildings
- Stealing motor vehicle accessories

Larceny–Theft Offenses

There are many types of larceny–theft offenses, and their rate of occurrence is considerable. A lack of witnesses or other "concrete" evidence makes larceny a difficult crime to solve. Although there are many different types of larceny–theft offenses, in this book we attempt to discuss only a few of the most problematic. Before the investigator can determine whether a crime has been committed, he or she must understand the legal elements.

Larceny–Theft Trend	
Year	**Number of Offenses**
2009	5,950,908
2010	5,801,900
Percent change	−2.5

Source: Federal Bureau of Investigation. (2011). *Crime in the United States—2010.*

In larceny–theft investigations, the state must show that there was a "taking," at least for a brief time, and that the defendant had control over the property "of another." The taking must be deliberate and with the intent to steal.

The UCR defines larceny–theft as the unlawful taking, carrying, leading, or riding away of property from the possession or constructive possession of another. It includes crimes such as shoplifting, pocket picking, purse snatching, thefts from motor vehicles, thefts of motor vehicle parts and accessories, and bicycle thefts, in which no use of force, violence, or fraud occurs. In the

Elements of Larceny–Theft

A person commits the crime of larceny–theft if he or she:

☑ Takes and carries away

☑ The personal property

☑ Of another

☑ Without consent and with the intent to steal

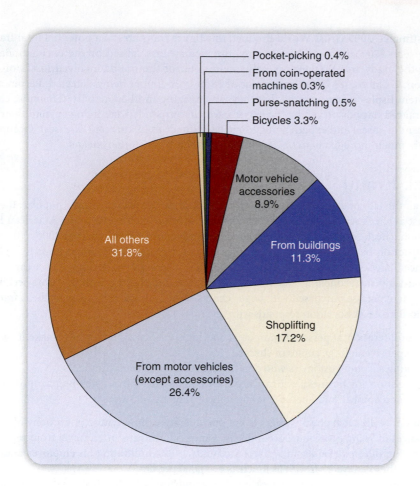

Pocket-picking 0.4%
From coin-operated machines 0.3%
Purse-snatching 0.5%
Bicycles 3.3%
Motor vehicle accessories 8.9%
From buildings 11.3%
All others 31.8%
Shoplifting 17.2%
From motor vehicles (except accessories) 26.4%

|Fig. 14.9| △

Larceny-theft percent pistribution — 2010.

Crime in the United States, 2010

UCR program, this crime category does not include embezzlement, confidence games, forgery, or worthless checks. Motor vehicle theft is also excluded from this category inasmuch as it is a separate Crime Index offense.

Trends

According to the FBI, in 2010, there were an estimated 6,185,867 larceny–thefts nationwide.[34] The number of estimated larceny–thefts dropped 6.6 percent from the 2006 estimate. The rate of estimated larceny–thefts in 2010 was 2,003.5 per 100,000 inhabitants. Statistics also show that larceny–thefts accounted for an estimated 68.1 percent of property crimes in 2010. The average value of property taken during larceny–thefts was $988 per offense. The overall loss to victims was over $6.1 billion. An estimated 26 percent (26.4) of larceny–thefts were thefts from motor vehicles.[35]

Forgery and Fraud

Theft crimes in the form of forgery or fraud accounted for 54 percent of the 28,012 white-collar felony dispositions in 1993. In addition, fraud constituted 38 percent, and embezzlement made up 8 percent of white-collar dispositions. Fraud cases may be enigmatic in nature. For example, in 1992, physician Cecil Jacobson (the sperm doctor) was convicted of secretly fathering the children of as many as 75 of his patients through artificial insemination. In this case, the federal jury ruled that he wrongfully used his sperm instead of that of anonymous donors to impregnate patients after promising to use donors who resembled their husbands and that he used hormone injections to trick women into thinking they were pregnant and then told them they'd miscarried, ensuring that they would return.

The financial impact of fraud to organizations is considerable. For example, according to the Association of Certified Fraud Examiners (ACFE) *Report to the Nations on Occupational Fraud & Abuse*, the typical organization loses 5 percent of its annual revenue to fraud. Applied to the estimated 2009 Gross World Product, this figure translates to a potential total fraud loss of more than $2.9 trillion.[36] Additionally, the median loss caused by the occupational fraud cases in the study was $160,000. Nearly one-quarter of the frauds involved losses of at least $1 million.[37] The frauds lasted an average of 18 months before being detected. Perpetrators of fraud often display warning signs that they are engaging in illicit activity. The most common behavioral red flags displayed by the perpetrators in our study were living beyond their means (43 percent of cases) and experiencing financial difficulties (36 percent of cases). Occupational frauds are much more likely to be detected by tip than by any other means.[38]

Check Fraud

Despite all the talk of electronic banking, one low-tech device is increasingly popular: the checkbook. Just as check writing has boomed, so has check fraud. According to the American Bankers Association, check fraud is a growing concern, costing banks $12.2 billion in 2006.[39] In addition to its impact on banks is its effect on consumers. For example, check fraud leads to higher fees for bounced checks, and when a person is a victim of check fraud, dealing with it can impose a severe hardship in reconciling and closing an account and dealing with creditors seeking payment for merchandise purchased with bogus checks. Why is there an increase in check fraud? The American Bankers Association responds with several reasons:

- The proliferation of personal computers and high-quality copiers, which make it easier and less expensive to forge copies of checks
- Checking account customers who don't safeguard their account numbers
- Competition for business, which discourages some banks from stepping up procedures to detect and combat fraud because it might inconvenience customers

Criminals realize that check forgery is not only lucrative, but because it is a nonviolent crime, their chances of being prosecuted are unlikely. Bands of criminals often travel from region to region targeting different banks and payroll accounts. After infiltrating an employer and forging documents, they can walk off with as much as $300,000 per day.

Forgery of a victim's personal check involves acquiring both the check and a form of identification of the victim. He or she must then be able to forge the victim's name on the instrument

A Closer Look

Nigerian Letter or "419" Fraud

Nigerian letter frauds combine the threat of impersonation fraud with a variation of an advance fee scheme in which a letter mailed from Nigeria offers the recipient the "opportunity" to share in a percentage of millions of dollars that the author—a self-proclaimed government official—is trying to transfer illegally out of Nigeria. The recipient is encouraged to send information to the author, such as blank letterhead stationery, bank name and account numbers, and other identifying information using a fax number provided in the letter. Some of these letters have also been received via e-mail through the Internet. The scheme relies on convincing a willing victim, who has demonstrated a "propensity for larceny" by responding to the invitation, to send money to the author of the letter in Nigeria in several installments of increasing amounts for a variety of reasons.

Payment of taxes, bribes to government officials, and legal fees are often described in great detail with the promise that all expenses will be reimbursed as soon as the funds are spirited out of Nigeria. In actuality, the millions of dollars do not exist, and the victim eventually ends up with nothing but loss. Once the victim stops sending money, the perpetrators have been known to use the personal information and checks that they received to impersonate the victim, draining bank accounts and credit card balances. While such an invitation impresses most law-abiding citizens as a laughable hoax, millions of dollars in losses are caused by these schemes annually. Some victims have been lured to Nigeria, where they have been imprisoned against their will along with losing large sums of money. The Nigerian government is not sympathetic to victims of these schemes, since the victim actually conspires to remove funds from Nigeria in a manner that is contrary to Nigerian law. The schemes themselves violate section 419 of the Nigerian criminal code, hence the label "419 fraud."

successfully to the point that it closely resembles the original. In addition to the signature, amounts of checks can sometimes be altered to represent larger amounts. This can be accomplished in several ways. For example, the amount $10 can be altered to read $100 simply by adding a zero onto the designated amount and then altering the written portion of the instrument. Forgery of government checks is another growing problem in many parts of the country. Many such checks, such as welfare and unemployment payments, are mailed in groups at regular intervals and are sometimes stolen directly from mailboxes.

Banking institutions often consider the government check as legitimate because of its "official" appearance. Therefore, its legitimacy often goes unquestioned. Once passed, the forged government check may go undetected for months before the crime is discovered. Another method of forgery includes the use of fictitious checks drawn on a nonexistent firm or person. These schemes, called **check kiting**, are commonly encountered by law enforcement authorities. Kiting consists of drawing cash on accounts made up of uncollected funds. By using two different banking institutions, the kiter may use funds from one bank to cover checks drawn on another. Each time the bank pays out funds against the account balance, the kiter has been successful in cheating the bank out of its own funds.

Banks are responding with new methods designed to stop bank fraud. For example, in 1995, the Texas Banking Association began experimenting with a new program in which a thumbprint is required from nonaccount holders who wish to cash checks. The thumbprints are kept on file only until the check clears. Pilot programs in Nevada and Arizona have resulted in a 40 to 80 percent reduction in check fraud losses.[40] Other services, such as the Duplex/BEI Check Fraud Prevention Program, aid banks in identifying patterns of criminal behavior to single out suspicious checks before they lose money. For example, a criminal opens an account with a small amount of money and waits a few months to deposit a fraudulent check for $80,000. He or she then withdraws the money after two business days, knowing that the bank is required to make the money available promptly. By the time the bank finds out that a check is counterfeit, a criminal is already gone with the money.

Investigating Check Forgery

One problem presenting itself in forgery cases is when the victim desires only restitution from the suspect and is unwilling to follow through with prosecution. The posture of the victim must therefore be determined early by the investigating law enforcement agency; otherwise, the police simply become a collection agency for the victim, and much valuable time is lost. To deal with this problem, many law enforcement agencies ask the forgery victims to sign a written agreement in which they agree to prosecute. Failure to sign the agreement would result in future claims of forgery being declined for investigation by the police. Witnesses in a check fraud case may include employees who both accepted and deposited a forged instrument.

A logical first step of the forgery investigation is to interview the person who was the recipient of the bad check: the acceptor. This is probably the most important source of investigative leads. After all, the acceptor is a witness to the crime, and he or she alone can describe the actual circumstances surrounding the crime. The investigator should consider asking the acceptor the following questions:

- What remarks did the suspect make during passing of the check?
- Was the check written or signed in the presence of the acceptor?
- What credentials, if any, were offered as identification?
- What was the suspect's description? (This should include his or her physical appearance, dress, and mannerisms.)
- Was the customer a repeat customer or known to the acceptor?
- What type of transportation was used to and from the institution?

Responses to these inquiries, along with the investigator's personal evaluation of the competency of the acceptor, may help identify the suspect. The depositor is the next player who should be interviewed. This is the actual person whose account was used to draw funds from. The depositor should be asked to examine the forged check for anything that might be observed from it. If the signature on the check is not that of the depositor, a statement to that effect should be made to the investigator. Next, the investigator should inquire as to whether another party was allowed to use the depositor's account.

An affidavit should then be acquired from the depositor along with standards of the depositor's handwriting as it appears on his or her checks. The depositor should be asked how the suspect may have acquired the stolen checks. In the event that the depositor claims that checks were stolen during a burglary, the offense report should be pulled and reviewed. It is in the investigator's interest at this point to identify a possible discrepancy between the statement of the depositor and information from an offense report. Finally, the instrument itself must be secured as evidence and a receipt for it should be issued to the victim.

Embezzlement

Embezzlement is a low-profile crime that typically consists of employees of organizations stealing large amounts of money over a long period of time. Embezzlement is also extremely difficult to detect. Those who are successful in the embezzling of funds can cause extensive fiscal damage to victim organizations, frequently resulting in their financial ruin.

The crime of embezzlement is increasing at 15 percent per year and has an estimated annual cost of $4 billion.[41] The number of people arrested for embezzlement, however, has increased 40 percent since 1985, indicating that more employees are willing to steal from their employers, more employers are willing to report instances of embezzlement, or law enforcement officials are more willing to prosecute people involved with the crime of embezzlement.

Embezzlement is usually defined under individual state statutes dealing with grand theft. Generally speaking, however, it can be described as a fraudulent appropriation of property by a person to whom that property has been entrusted. Although the elements of the crime may vary, some common elements can be generalized:

- A trusting relationship exists between the suspect and the victim.
- The perpetrator had lawful possession of the pilfered belongings at some time during the relationship.
- The property was stolen or converted to a form of possession that was contrary to the trust relationship.
- There was criminal intent to deprive the lawful owner of the property, either temporarily or permanently.

The element of trust is critical in establishing the crime of embezzlement. For example, a bank teller has the lawful right to handle a bank's cash. Secretly taking quantities of that cash for his or her own personal use, however, is a form of possession that is contrary to the trust relationship with the bank.

Investigating Embezzlement

A primary element of the crime of embezzlement is the element of trust. So, to investigate this type of crime, the investigator must show that the suspect first accepted the property in the scope of employment and then misappropriated it for his or her own use. Intent is relatively easy to

Crime Prevention Key: Avoiding Becoming a Victim of Check Fraud

- ☑ Don't give your checking account number or the numbers at the bottom of your checks to people you don't know, including people who say they are from your bank. They have no business requesting such information.
- ☑ Reveal checking account information only to businesses you know are reputable.
- ☑ Guard your checkbook. Report lost or stolen checks immediately.
- ☑ Properly store or dispose of canceled checks.
- ☑ Report any inquiries or suspicious behavior to your banker, who will take steps to protect your account and to notify authorities.
- ☑ Do not leave your ATM receipt at the ATM because these receipts contain your account information. Dispose of it safely and securely.

demonstrate in these cases, however, because it usually requires some form of concealment or secrecy, such as altering business records. The investigation of embezzlement allegations is a tenacious and time-consuming task because paper trails are sometimes difficult to follow. Yet the investigator must be able to explain fully to a prosecutor, judge, and jury how the crime was committed and offer convincing evidence to support the findings of the case. This task can be especially perplexing when dealing with a company whose record-keeping practices are already haphazard.

Because many embezzlement cases require a degree of accounting expertise, investigators lacking such expertise may become frustrated, and the successful outcome of the case may then be jeopardized. The most common way of overcoming this obstacle is for the investigator to solicit the victim's help in providing technical support during the investigation. Company executives and consultants outside the company are generally willing and able to explain specific accounting processes. Embezzlers usually prefer to steal cash because it is both difficult to trace and easy to conceal. Investigators may, however, find this to be an advantage. For example, if an employee is found to be spending significantly large amounts of cash, he or she might also be hard-pressed to explain the origin of the money.

To seek a complaint, the investigator must put together a complete investigative file on the suspect and all circumstances surrounding the violation. The file should contain the following:

- A complete investigative report that identifies specific funds that were taken without authorization
- Methods used for the pilfering
- Photocopies of all checks and related documents pertaining to the theft(s)
- A statement of determination outlining the economic and psychological impact of the crime on its victim

Categories of Embezzlement

Many different types of embezzlement exist. These vary depending on the degree of trust that exists between the suspect and victim, but they typically fall into one of several categories discussed below.

THEFT OF CURRENCY The most common form of embezzlement is the theft of cash from a trusted party. Although a serious crime, such thefts are usually for modest amounts of money that may not be considered all that financially damaging to the victim company. Theft schemes most commonly used include:

- Taking cash from the register and then entering a negative of the same amount so that the cash drawer balance agrees with the register tape balance. In the event that the register tape contains many (sometimes hundreds of) entries, the negative balance may be difficult to detect.
- Corporate executives working for lucrative companies that make "cash loans" and fail to pay them back.
- Failing to ring up a sale and taking the cash from the cash drawer for the same amount.
- Sales clerks charging more than the amount on the receipt and pocketing the difference, hoping customers won't notice the difference.

MANIPULATION OF ACCOUNTS Embezzlement cases in which accounts are manipulated typically involve employees of an accounting department. For example, a typical case would be an accountant who makes payments to a fictitious company for services never rendered or goods never received and then endorses the check for payment. A scheme such as this may result in insurmountable losses for the victim company. Another way to embezzle from records is to manipulate payroll accounts. Typically, this type of case involves entering a bogus employee on the records or failing to remove a former employee from the records. In either case, the suspect intercepts the payroll check, endorses it with the name of the person who is on the records, and cashes it.

RETAIL THEFT As indicated, one of the hallmarks of embezzlement is the stealing of merchandise by a company's employees, or **pilferage**. This form of crime is also extremely difficult to detect, and it is difficult to determine the value of goods taken by employees over a period. One estimate is that pilferage accounted for 30 to 75 percent of all shrinkage and amounts to losses of

$5 to $10 billion annually. According to McCaghy, several different methods are commonly used to steal from employers:[42]

- Factory workers zip up completed garments and take them home.
- Cashiers ring up lower prices on single-item purchases and pocket the difference. Many work with accomplices.
- Clerks do not tag sale merchandise and then sell it at its original price, pocketing the difference.
- Receiving clerks obtain duplicate keys to storage facilities and return after hours to steal.
- Truck drivers make fictitious purchases of fuel and repairs and split the difference with truck-stop owners.
- Some employees simply hide items in garbage pails or incinerators or under trash heaps until they can be retrieved.

Another form of inventory theft is when an inventory clerk writes a receipt for "damaged" goods that are shipped to an accomplice's residence. The goods can then be sold for cash. Because the merchandise was never returned to the manufacturer, the company will probably not detect a problem. The receipt indicating "returned goods" indicates that the goods were damaged; therefore, they will not be included in the victim company's inventory. Many companies consider this type of loss as shrinkage, that is, an unexplained loss.

In a 1983 study of theft in the workplace, John Clark and Richard Hollinger found that 35 percent of employees reported involvement in pilferage.[43] The study indicates that most theft is a result of factors relating to the workplace, such as job dissatisfaction and a general feeling of worker exploitation by employees.

Advance Fee Schemes

An advance fee scheme occurs when the victim pays money to someone in anticipation of receiving something of greater value—such as a loan, contract, investment, or gift—and then receives little or nothing in return.

The variety of advance fee schemes is limited only by the imagination of the con artists who offer them. They may involve the sale of products or services, the offering of investments, lottery winnings, "found money," or many other "opportunities." Clever con artists will offer to find financing arrangements for their clients who pay a "finder's fee" in advance. They require their clients to sign contracts in which they agree to pay the fee when they are introduced to the financing source. Victims often learn that they are ineligible for financing only after they have paid the "finder" according to the contract.[44] Such agreements may be legal unless it can be shown that the "finder" never had the intention or the ability to provide financing for the victims.

Credit Card Fraud

In September 1996, 36-year-old Nigerian-born Olushina Adekanbi was arrested on credit card fraud charges. What made this case unusual was the fact that Adekanbi, who also went by more than two dozen aliases, had earned the nickname "King of New York" because he ran the largest credit card fraud ring in the United States. The ring was wanted for obtaining at least $650,000 in goods and cash advances, as well as gaining illegal access to credit lines worth an estimated $8 million.[45]

Credit card fraud is a growing problem in the twenty-first century. The worldwide traffic in counterfeit cards costs issuers of plastic $1.6 billion a year in false charges.[46] Although credit cards were designed to provide consumers with convenience and increased purchasing power, the criminal has also identified ways to profit from this financial medium. Records from credit card transactions have provided law enforcement with a twofold benefit: the apprehension of the fraudulent credit card user and accurate records that often point to other crimes.

Millions of credit cards issued by both international and local banking institutions are negotiable instruments that can be used fraudulently to obtain goods and services. All credit cards have one thing in common: they can be used to obtain something of value simply by presenting the card. Therefore, the security of the card is of utmost importance. Many credit card companies go to great lengths to offer cardholders some type of security or "insurance" against unlawful use of the card.

OBTAINING CREDIT CARDS Credit cards are acquired by criminals through a variety of methods, including burglaries, robberies, mailbox thefts, and falsified applications to issuing companies. In addition, pickpockets and muggers may seek credit cards as readily as they seek cash. Waiters and retail clerks have been known to retain credit cards that are forgotten by customers. Such cards are sometimes sold to professional **plastic workers** who have experience in dealing with stolen credit cards.

USING STOLEN CREDIT CARDS Credit card thieves must act quickly to overcome protection systems offered by companies. Techniques used are designed to upset and confuse sales clerks while not attracting attention to the thief. The thief will typically stroll through a store as if he or she is shopping but is actually evaluating sales personnel. After he or she identifies a salesclerk who he or she feels is easily manipulatable, that person is selected as the target. It is the intent of the thief to manipulate the clerk so that he or she fails to follow the prescribed security measures established by the store.

The floor limit is one primary loophole that is easily exploitable. The conscientious plastic worker is careful to purchase items that are under the designated limit, typically $50 to $100. In the event that the thief is using a "hot" card, he or she must be careful that the clerk doesn't check the **hot list** or cancellation bulletin. Because these lists are so lengthy, clerks frequently fail to check them. This procedure is sometimes overlooked when the thief carefully plans his or her purchase at closing time when employees are rushed to balance their registers and go home.

INVESTIGATING CREDIT CARD THEFT Police officers investigating lost or stolen credit cards should consult the credit card company for assistance because many companies employ professional investigators who can offer valuable help in the investigation. Certain types of information are necessary during the credit card investigation that can be acquired with the assistance of the card company's investigator. Such information includes:

- The victim store's name and address
- The names of the store manager and clerk who were victimized (the clerk may be an excellent witness if he or she observed the signing of the card slip)
- The name of the legitimate cardholder and his or her address and telephone number
- The facts and circumstances surrounding the theft or loss of the card
- A detailed description of the item(s) purchased and the amount of the sale

After being identified, the plastic worker will be charged with each purchase as a separate offense, each of which must be supported by documentation and evidence. Investigations should always include how the credit card was obtained in the first place. Depending on the circumstances, this can constitute a separate offense. For example, the card could have been purchased from a pickpocket. The investigator should learn how, when, and where the card was acquired from its lawful owner.

Decisions to prosecute are usually left up to the office of the prosecutor who functions in the jurisdiction of the victimized merchant. In the event the case does go to court, the lawful owner of the card and experts from the credit card company can testify on behalf of the state.

Shoplifting

Shoplifting is a widespread property crime. Shops contain new goods, temptingly displayed. Self-service sales methods, now so common, provide ample opportunity for shoppers to handle goods (many of which are prepackaged) and conceal them in clothing or bags. People seem to have fewer inhibitions about stealing from shops than from private individuals. They know they have little chance of getting caught, and, if caught, they can often produce plausible excuses such as forgetting to pay.

The stock control in shops is so deficient that few retailers know how many goods they lose to shoplifters, or even to their own staff. So long as theft and damage of goods, known in the retail industry as shrinkage, does not rise above 2 to 3 percent of goods sold, retailers may pay little attention to shoplifting.[47] Indeed, they have certain incentives to do so: Stolen goods may be taken as tax write-offs; detection and prosecution of shoplifters takes time and energy; mistaken apprehensions can result in lawsuits; and the store could acquire a reputation for crime if it continually reports shoplifting. This means retailers may be unwilling to take official action against shoplifters, especially those who claim it is their first offense, show fear or remorse, and/or agree to pay for the items stolen.

|Fig. 14.10| △

The offense of shoplifting represents a significant percentage of larceny–theft crimes. Here a shoplifter conceals stolen merchandise.

Courtesy of Mike Himmel

In addition, some retailers believe that the police can do little about the problem and may be unwilling to get involved. Others see the role of the police as simply to take charge of thieves whom store detectives or security staff have caught, and to decide on their subsequent handling. When particularly blatant shoplifting occurs, or when "professional" shoplifters are thought to be operating, merchants may call upon the police to take some kind of preventive action, usually in the form of increased presence or patrols.[48] This may be of little deterrent value, since shoplifting takes place inside the store, away from police view.

In many cases, the most logical preventive measure is to persuade storeowners and managers to improve their security. This is difficult, because many retailers believe that the police should protect them from dishonest people, people who should be caught and punished. As mentioned, others are content to ignore the problem until it seriously affects profits. Whatever the reasons, the police often have an uphill task convincing retailers that their sales practices and lack of security may be contributing to the problem.

Faced with these attitudes, police are tempted to wash their hands of shoplifting and let the shops bear the consequences. But there are many reasons why this may be shortsighted, including the following:

- Shoplifting is often regarded as an entry crime, from which juveniles graduate to more serious offenses.
- Shoplifting can be said to fuel the drug trade, because it provides the income some addicts need to buy drugs.
- For stores in deprived neighborhoods, shoplifting can seriously erode profits and result in store closures. This can depress employment prospects and further erode the amenities in such neighborhoods.
- Shoplifting can consume a large proportion of police resources in processing offenders whom store security staff have detained. Indeed, the main police role in regard to this offense is to channel shoplifters caught by private security into the criminal justice system. In this regard, the police are at the mercy of merchants who may avoid changing their business practices in

favor of simply relying on security staff and police to handle shoplifters. Unfortunately, there is little hard evidence that this results in reduced shoplifting by those arrested or by others who learn about the arrests.[49]

According to the *Economic Crime Digest*, shoplifting is the form of theft that occurs most frequently in business and accounts for some of the greatest losses: an estimated $16 billion a year. The FBI reports that shoplifting acts number some 1 million yearly and have increased 30 percent since 1985. Because shoplifting is a kind of larceny–theft, it has basically the same elements of larceny–theft as discussed earlier.

Modern retail stores market their wares by allowing potential customers to examine them while on display. Computers may be tinkered with, clothes may be tried on, and television sets may be adjusted to demonstrate the clarity of the picture and the function of other features. The list goes on. Because stores often provide carts for the transportation of goods that the customer may wish to purchase, the courts have held that they have a lawful right to possess those goods for limited purposes. Concealment of goods by customers, however, is not allowed by businesses or the courts. Accordingly, the merchandise is offered for sale, and if a customer chooses not to purchase the merchandise, it must be returned to the display shelves in good condition.

Generally speaking, the shoplifter can be characterized as either professional or amateur. Whereas a professional shoplifter will steal goods for resale or bartering, an amateur steals merchandise for his or her own use. Records show that the majority of shoplifters fall into the amateur category. The professional shoplifter, however, represents a much greater problem for investigators. The professional often works in groups of three or four and often victimizes several shopping areas at a time. They are commonly trained on what items to steal, how to conceal them (e.g., wearing special clothing to help them conceal merchandise), and where to take the merchandise for resale after the theft. Investigations have revealed women who appear to be pregnant but who are wearing a specially made receptacle for small items. In another case, a heavy-set woman had been stealing small television sets by concealing them in a prerigged harness that was located between her legs.

A classic study of shoplifting was conducted by Mary Owen Cameron, who found that about 10 percent of all shoplifters were professionals who derived the majority of their income from shoplifting.[50] Sometimes called *boosters* or *heels*, professional shoplifters resell stolen merchandise to pawnshops or fences at usually one-half to one-fourth the original price. According to Cameron's study, most shoplifters are amateur pilferers, called **snitches**. Snitches are usually respectable persons who do not perceive themselves as thieves yet are systematic shoplifters who steal merchandise for their own use rather than for resale.

Investigating Shoplifting

One problem with shoplifting is that many customers who observe theft are reluctant to report it to managers or security personnel. Many store employees themselves don't want to get involved with apprehending a suspected shoplifter. In fact, an experiment by Hartmann and his associates found that customers observed only 28 percent of staged shoplifting acts that were designed to get their attention.[51] In addition, only 28 percent of people who said they had observed an incident reported it to store employees. Another study by Blankenburg showed that less than 10 percent of shoplifting was detected by store employees and that customers seemed unwilling to report even severe cases.[52] Even in stores with an announced policy of full reporting and prosecution, only 70 percent of the shoplifting detected by employees was actually reported to managers, and only 5 percent was prosecuted.

Shoplifting cases can be investigated in one of two ways: reactive or proactive. A reactive investigation will include interviews of witnesses, collection of physical evidence, and conducting of other follow-up functions. A proactive case will probably be handled by in-house security personnel and will focus on the shoplifter who is caught in the act. In the case of proactive investigation, investigators should follow several rules of thumb:

- Be sure that probable cause exists before restraining a suspect.
- Observe the person concealing store merchandise that has not been paid for, not simply concealing "something" that cannot be positively identified as store merchandise.
- Keep the person under observation.
- Before arresting the person, always ask first for a receipt.

Remember, if the person has not yet walked beyond the last pay station, an arrest may not be lawful or appropriate, but confronting the person may still result in reclaiming of the merchandise. Most shoplifting cases are handled through local police and sheriff's departments and are prosecuted locally as well. When a store is involved with cases such as these, store policy should be considered as well as the opinions of the local prosecuting attorney.

THE GROWING PROBLEM OF RETAIL THEFT Addressing retail theft has both direct and indirect costs for retailers.[53] According to a 2009 survey of 25 major U.S. retailers, over 1 million offenders were apprehended for retail theft at those retailers alone, a nearly 17 percent increase from the previous year. Over $111 million worth of stolen goods was recovered.[54] But with research indicating that a shoplifter is apprehended only once in 48 times, the total loss to the retail industry is easily in the billions, without accounting for the cost of surveillance measures, security staff, and other preventive and responsive measures.

Retail theft costs the industry more than $37 billion in 2005, up from $31 billion in 2003. Retail theft becomes especially problematic during the holiday season, when overcrowded stores make shoplifting more difficult to detect and fraudulent returns easier to conceal. In 2006, it was estimated that retailers expected to lose $3.5 billion due to just fraudulent returns after December's busy holiday season.

Retailers are particularly concerned about gangs that have established supply chains that make organized theft, known as "boosting," too profitable to give up without a fight. For example, a single **booster** operating as part of the gang can steal up to $200,000 worth of merchandise in a weekend. In August 2006, for example, in Ocala, Florida, Beall's cameras caught a gang of exotic dancers that stole approximately $170 worth of goods from the Bradenton store. Apparel from other retailers filled the women's rented SUV. Two of the three women, who worked for an exotic dancing and escort service called Black Xtasy, admitted that they were traveling the state to steal. The suspected leader of the gang had retail theft warrants against her in two other Florida counties.

In another case, Walgreens' Divisional Coordinator for Organized Retail Crime, Jerry Biggs, stated that one group shoplifted from 24 of the drugstores in seven hours. In a videotaped interview with police, shoplifter Jesus Hernandez said he could easily boost $10,000 worth of merchandise in four hours. Fernandez specialized in stealing diabetic test strip packages, which sell for up to $100.

During a typical boosting, one or more gang members distract store clerks while one or two others lift merchandise. Some members stand outside the store doors, ready to signal if police or security officials are coming. Still others are in parking lots ready with getaway cars. The gangs are often armed with knives, guns, and even brass knuckles for fighting off store security personnel.

The thieves typically seem to stay one step ahead of security devices. Even locked glass display cases can be cracked. For example, in 2006, 14 Target stores in California, Illinois, and Colorado were hit by thieves who broke open locked cases, filled carts with iPods, and pushed the carts out the doors. Professional shoplifters usually carry shopping bags lined with foil and duct tape to block the electric current that detects security tags. Some thieves remove security tags and hide merchandise under larger packages.

Some security analysts have suggested that antitheft systems seem to only work against people who don't know how to thwart them. Security personnel for retail stores must be cautious in making apprehensions. This is because retail companies must balance the importance of capturing thieves with possibly upsetting and frustrating paying customers.

Returns are one area where retailers have cracked down in recent years. Although some still give cash for a return without a receipt, many major retailers require receipts. In addition, many retailers use electronic receipts that track purchases made with a credit card or check. These receipts nearly eliminate the ability to use counterfeit receipts or to return stolen goods. They also use display devices that make it difficult to slide all the items on a hanging rack into a bag but that are not too difficult for legitimate customers to use.

The prosecution of retail crime is complicated in part because much of the merchandise stolen doesn't come with serial numbers. That makes it difficult for investigators to identify the merchandise as stolen. Unless merchandise is made under a retailer's private label and the store has alerted police of the theft, police who stop the driver of a car full of stolen items may have difficulty making an arrest and in many cases will not even seize merchandise as evidence.

In recent years, retail theft has become more organized. Businesses such as supermarkets, department stores, drugstores, electronics stores, and mass merchandisers are frequently the targets for such theft rings. Thieves work closely with fences who act on numerous levels to quickly turn over their stolen merchandise and place layers of people between each stolen merchandise transfer.

In short, the criminal world has recognized that retail theft is a much more profitable crime than burglary, with much less penalty. For example, although larceny overall was down 4.5 percent from 2000 to 2004, shoplifting increased nearly 12 percent, according to the 2005 *UCR* published by the FBI.[55]

Identity Theft

In 2000, golfer Tiger Woods discovered that his identity had been stolen and that credit cards taken out in his name had been used to steal $17,000 worth of merchandise, including a 70-inch TV, stereos, and a used luxury car. In 2001, the thief, 30-year-old Anthony Lemar Taylor, who looks nothing like Woods, was convicted of falsely obtaining a driver's license using the name Eldrick T. Woods (Tiger's given name), Wood's Social Security number, and his birth date. Because Taylor already had 20 previous convictions of all kinds on his record, he was sentenced to 200 years in prison under California's three strikes law. Like Woods, most victims of identity theft do not even know that their identities have been stolen until they receive bills for merchandise they haven't purchased.

Identity theft is a special kind of larceny which involves obtaining credit, merchandise, or services by fraudulent personal representation. According to a recent Federal Trade Commission (FTC) survey, identity theft directly impacts as many as 10 million victims annually, although most do not report the crime.

A report published in 2011 by Javelin Strategy & Research, titled *Identity Fraud Survey Report*, disclosed that the number of identity fraud victims in the United States rose 12 percent to 11.1 million adults in 2009, the highest level since the survey began in 2003.[56] The number of identity fraud victims increased 22 percent in 2008 to 9.9 million adults. However, the total annual fraud amount jumped just 7 percent to $48 billion. Women were 26 percent more likely to be victims of identity fraud than men in 2008. "Lost or stolen wallets, checkbooks and credit and debit cards" made up 43 percent of all ID theft incidents in which the "method of access" was known.[57]

According to the Federal Trade Commission, 8.3 million American adults, or 3.7 percent of all American adults, were victims of identity theft in 2005.[58] The latest report from the FTC showed that ID theft increased by 21 percent in 2008.[59] However, credit card fraud, the crime which is most closely associated with the crime of ID theft, has been declining as a percentage of all ID theft. In 2002, 41 percent of all ID theft complaints involved a credit card. That percentage has dropped to 21 percent in 2008.[60]

Identity theft can happen in a variety of ways, and there are a variety of sources from which identity thieves can obtain personal information. Such sources are credit card numbers, Social Security number, driver's license number, bank account information, and medical records. Once this information has been obtained, thieves put it to fraudulent use, generally for monetary gain. They may also use such information to get a job or medical treatment under someone else's name.

Identity theft in the United States has grown rapidly in recent years, due in large part to ever-improving technology. Computers and other electronic devices are now the preferred method of storing data and personal information, and the Internet has become a major means of communication and commerce. While beneficial to society, these new ways to exchange information have given criminals an entirely new way to obtain that information—which isn't to say that use of technology is the only means by which identity theft is committed. Thieves can get the information they want in many other ways, from picking through a victim's trash to paying someone else for the data. The resourcefulness of thieves is unsurprising, given that personal information has become a valuable commodity for criminals, both in this country and elsewhere in the world.

The value of personal information is due in part to it being a gateway to other criminal acts. Fraud (credit card, bank computer, and Internet) is closely associated with identity theft, as the information a thief gains can lead to substantial profit. This profit can then be used to fund other types of criminal activity—for example, drug trafficking and terrorism.

Since criminals have much to gain from identity theft, and since rapid improvement in technology has allowed them to commit their crimes with greater ease, identity theft is a problem that will likely grow and evolve in years to come, necessitating knowledgeable and resourceful law enforcement personnel to keep it in check.

Identity theft has become a major problem in the United States. The target of identity theft is information that will enable the thief to assume another's identity for a criminal purpose. In the past few years, personal information has become one of the commodities most sought after by criminals in this country and elsewhere. Because it is usually part of a larger criminal enterprise, the theft of personal information is one of the most serious of all crimes. On May 31, 2001, the *Washington Post* reported:

> Some law enforcement officials and regulators say identity theft has become one of their most pressing problems. The federal Office of the Comptroller of the Currency recently estimated that there are half a million victims of identity theft per year in the United States. The Justice Department told Congress last week that Internet fraud, including identity theft, is one of the nation's fastest-growing white-collar crimes. And James G. Huse, Jr., the Social Security Administration's inspector general, testified that the misuse of Social Security numbers in fraudulent activity is "a national crisis."[61]

Identity theft became a federal crime in 1998 with the passage of the Identity Theft and Assumption Deterrence Act. The law makes it a crime whenever anyone "knowingly transfers or uses, without lawful authority, a means of identification of another person with the intent to commit, or to aid or abet, any unlawful activity that constitutes a violation of federal law, or that constitutes a felony under any applicable state or local law."[62]

Although identity theft is in itself a criminal act under both federal and most state laws, the theft is almost always a stepping-stone to the commission of other crimes. Typical crimes associated with identity theft include credit card fraud, bank fraud, computer fraud, Internet fraud, fraudulent obtaining of loans, and other schemes designed to enable the perpetrator to profit from the original theft. Often, there are several types of fraud involved in, or resulting from, the initial identity theft. Furthermore, funds obtained illegally as a result of the identity theft and its resultant frauds may be used to finance other types of criminal enterprises, including drug trafficking and other major forms of criminal activity.

The escalation of identity theft in the United States is due in large part to the technology revolution, which has brought the country into the so-called information age. The vastly expanded use of computers to store personal data and the growing use of the Internet have provided criminals with new incentives and new means to steal and misuse personal information. As the use of technology to store and transmit information increases, so too will identity theft. Consequently, identity theft will likely become an even greater problem in the future.

FINANCIAL LOSSES Accurately defining the financial losses of the vast number of crimes committed by means of identity theft is not possible at this time. Many identity theft crimes are not reported to police, and there is no single source of information on this issue. The U.S. Secret Service, the U.S. Postal Inspection Service, and the FBI are among the principal federal enforcement agencies that share jurisdiction for investigation of these crimes. This does not include the thousands of reports and investigations that are handled by state and local authorities. It is fair to say, however, that the cumulative financial losses from identity theft and the various crimes that feed from it are staggering.

Financial loss statistics generated by investigations handled by the U.S. Secret Service's financial crimes division in fiscal year 2000 reveal total actual losses in closed identity theft cases totaled $248.1 million. However, the potential losses from identity theft cases discovered during the same period are estimated at nearly $1.5 billion. Furthermore, it is calculated that the average actual loss in each closed identity theft case in fiscal year 2000 was $46,119. These figures graphically illustrate the magnitude of the problem caused by identity theft in the United States today.

PERSONAL COSTS Perhaps even more tragic than the monetary loss is the personal cost of identity theft. Because identity theft by definition involves the fraudulent obtaining of funds in the name of someone else, the victim of identity theft may sustain not only great financial loss but also severe damage to his or her credit standing, personal reputation, and other vital aspects of the victim's personal life. For example, the victim may suffer garnishments, attachments, civil lawsuits, and other traumatic consequences stemming from the identity theft. In some cases, the victim may be forced into bankruptcy, further damaging his or her reputation and credit. In other instances, the victim may become subject to criminal prosecution because of crimes committed by the perpetrator of the identity theft in the victim's name.

Even if the victim ultimately clears his or her credit records and avoids other personal and financial consequences of identity theft, the physical and mental toll on the victim can be significant. Typically, a victim of identity theft will spend months or years trying to clear his or her credit records. Many hours of difficult and stressful effort are often necessary because the merchants and institutions that have been defrauded in the victim's name are not easily persuaded that the victim is innocent of any wrongdoing. The frustration and distress engendered by this heavy burden often take a significant toll on the mental well-being and physical health of the victim. And, worst of all perhaps, the victim's efforts to clear him- or herself may be unsuccessful, leaving the victim under a cloud for the rest of his or her life.

Virtually anyone may become the victim of identity theft. Contrary to popular misconception, personal information is not stolen just from the affluent. Persons of even modest means may become victims of identity theft. In the majority of cases, all that is required is good credit, which is what identity thieves use to steal thousands upon thousands of dollars in the name of the victim.

No particular age group is immune from identity theft. FTC data indicate that although 6.2 percent of individuals reporting identity theft to the FTC during the period from November 1999 to March 2001 were age 65 years or older, the average age of victims was 42 years, and the most commonly reported age was 33 years. Younger Americans may be victimized at a higher rate because they are more likely to use the Internet, which is the primary tool in many identity theft crimes. However, elderly Americans are highly vulnerable to other types of identity theft schemes, particularly the various telephone scams used by perpetrators to acquire personal information.[63] Elderly people have always been targeted by perpetrators of fraud and will no doubt continue to be frequent victims.

The victims of identity theft may be residents of almost any geographical area. The FTC reports that between November 1999 and March 2001, complaints of identity theft were received from all 50 states and the District of Columbia. According to the same data, the greatest number of complaints came from California, New York, Texas, and Florida. The highest concentration of complaints per 100,000 people reportedly came from the District of Columbia, Nevada, Arizona, California, and Maryland. The FTC also reports that the cities with the largest number of complaints were New York City, Chicago, Los Angeles, Houston, and Miami, in that order. However, one should not conclude from this that identity theft is confined to any particular city, state, or region. The problem is national in scope, and not even the residents of the smallest locality of the least populous states are safe from it.

The Role of the Federal Trade Commission

The FTC is the federal government's principal consumer protection agency, with broad jurisdiction extending over nearly the entire economy, including business and consumer transactions on the telephone, and the Internet. The FTC's mandate is to prohibit unfair or deceptive acts or practices and to promote vigorous competition in the marketplace. The FTC Act authorizes the commission to halt deception in several ways, including through civil actions filed by its own attorneys in federal district courts. Of particular importance in the realm of identity theft is the fact that the act also gives the FTC jurisdiction over cross-border consumer transactions. Many identity theft enterprises operate outside the borders of the United States.

Of particular importance here are the provisions of the federal Identity Theft and Assumption Deterrence Act of 1998 (18 U.S.C. §1028), which gives the FTC a substantial role in the campaign against identity theft. Under the Act, the FTC is empowered to act as a nationwide clearinghouse for information related to identity theft crimes. This is an important aspect of the effort to combat identity theft because in the past, one of the major factors that hampered detection, investigation, and prosecution of these cases was the lack of any central source of information about identity theft. Identity theft is widespread, and a single identity theft ring may operate over great distances and in many states. Consequently, the availability of a central database is essential to enable law enforcement agencies to identify organized or widespread identity theft operations and facilitate cooperation between appropriate federal and state agencies. Special agents from the federal enforcement branches previously mentioned work closely with the FTC in this regard.

In accordance with the mandate of the Identity Theft and Assumption Deterrence Act of 1998, the FTC has established a number of central resources to provide information to law enforcement agencies about identity theft crimes. The FTC also provides guidance to victims of identity theft to help them defend themselves against the effects of this crime.

Types of Identity Theft and Identity Theft Operations

We have already examined some of the national resources available for combating identity theft and alluded to the types of crimes that are committed as part of identity theft. In this section, we will take a closer look at the various types of identity theft schemes and the nature and modus operandi of the identity theft perpetrators.

Those who commit identity theft are generally after personal and confidential information that can be used for monetary gain. There are so many methods by which identity thieves may acquire personal information that it is impossible to catalog them all here. However, the following methods are commonly used:

- Stealing wallets and purses containing personal identification, credit cards, and bank cards.
- Stealing mail, including mail containing bank and credit card statements, preapproved credit card offers, telephone calling cards, and tax information.
- Completion of a false change-of-address form to divert the victim's mail to another location.
- Searching trash for personal data (a practice known as dumpster diving) found on such discarded documents as so-called preapproved credit card applications or credit card slips discarded by the victim. To thwart an identity thief who may pick through your trash to capture your personal information, tear or shred your charge receipts, copies of credit applications, insurance forms, bank checks and statements, expired charge cards, and credit offers you get in the mail.
- Obtaining credit reports, often by posing as a landlord, employer, or other person or entity that might have a legitimate need for and right to credit information.
- Obtaining personal information at the workplace or through employers of the victim.
- Discovering personal information during physical entries into the victim's home. Such entries may be unlawful, as in burglary, or initially lawful, as when friends, service personnel, or others are invited to enter the home.
- Obtaining personal information from the Internet. This may be information stolen by hackers or freely provided by the victim in the course of making purchases or other contacts. Many victims respond to unsolicited e-mail (spam) that requests personal information.
- Purchasing information from inside sources such as store employees, who may for a price provide identity thieves with information taken from applications for goods, services, or credit. At least one instance has been reported of an employee of a credit bureau collaborating with identity thieves to provide personal information from credit bureau records.
- Pretexting, in which a thief telephones the victim or contacts the victim via the Internet and requests that the victim provide personal information. For example, the thief may claim to be from a survey firm and ask for personal data. Another scheme is for the thief to claim that the victim has won a prize or been selected for some special honor or privilege that requires that the victim provide personal information. Still another means of theft is for the perpetrator to call the victim and pretend to have found something that the victim has lost and then demand that the victim provide personal information in order to obtain the return of the lost item.
- Shoulder surfing, a practice whereby the thief positions him- or herself near a victim to obtain personal information by overhearing the victim or seeing the victim's actions. For example, the thief may stand near a pay telephone in a public place and listen as the victim gives telephone credit card number information or other personal information in the course of making a call. Similarly, thieves may loiter near an ATM and visually observe the victim keying in password numbers on the machine.
- Skimming, which is the electronic lifting of the data encoded on a valid credit or ATM card and transferring that data to a counterfeit card. There are many variations of this practice. For example, an identity thief may recruit an employee of a retail store, restaurant, or other retail establishment. The employee is provided with a handheld electronic device that can read data from a person's credit card when the consumer presents it to the employee. The collusive employee then surreptitiously "swipes" the credit card through the handheld "reading" device, which records the electronic data from the card. The employee then returns the device to the thief, and the thief extracts the recorded data from the device.
- Identity thieves may also purchase personal information about potential victims from persons or entities that routinely collect such information. In some instances, these entities may be legitimate, but many times they are criminal enterprises formed for the specific purpose of selling information to thieves.

Classic Case of Organized Identity Theft for Financial Gain

Jane Sprayberry handed over her driver's license to an American Express customer service representative who had asked for it in order to replace Jane's lost credit card. True to the Amex promise, she received the replacement card without delay. The only trouble was that the recipient was not the real Jane Sprayberry. The driver's license had her name on it, but the photograph was not of her. In no time, the imposter ran up a big bill on high-priced jewelry, clothing, and appliances. Just a week before, Jane's husband's bank account had been emptied and his credit card cloned. A coincidence? Not at all. A ring of fraudsters in Detroit had gotten jobs at large businesses and had collected reams of personal information: personnel records, credit records, old rental-car agreements. Those offenders who were eventually caught had bags and books full of such records—records they had used over several years. They had run up an average of $18,000 in credit card charges per victim. And they had sold identities on the street for around $25 each. It took the real Jane Sprayberry and her husband more than six months to clean up the mess.

Source: Newman, G. (2004). *Identity Theft*. U.S. Department of Justice: Office of Community Oriented Policing Services, p. 16

How Stolen Information Is Used

There are literally hundreds of ways in which identity thieves may use the information they have stolen. The following are just a few examples:

- After they have a victim's credit card number, thieves may call the victim's credit card issuer and, pretending to be the victim, ask that the mailing address on the account be changed. The thieves then run up high charges on the credit card and because credit card statements are no longer being sent to the victim's real address, the victim might be unaware of what is happening for weeks or even months.
- These same thieves who have obtained a victim's credit card information may also request that the credit card company send them credit card "checks," which are written for cash just as are bank checks. Again, the charges are unknown to the victim because the credit card statements are no longer coming to the victim's address.
- Having obtained personal information such as the victim's name, date of birth, Social Security number, and so on, the thieves open new credit card accounts in the victim's name and run up charges until the victim becomes aware of the fraud. Similarly, credit accounts may be opened at stores using the victim's identity.
- The thieves open bank accounts in the victim's name and write bad checks on the account.
- The thieves obtain loans, such as real estate, auto, or personal loans, using the victim's identity.
- The thieves counterfeit checks or debit cards and drain the victim's bank accounts of funds.
- The thieves establish services such as utility, telephone, or cell phone service in the victim's name.
- The thieves make long-distance calls using stolen credit card numbers.
- The thieves may obtain other goods and privileges by using the victim's identity and information, either in person, by telephone, or via the Internet.[64]

These are only a few of the numerous schemes that an identity thief may use to obtain money, goods, or services at the expense of the unwitting victim.

Often a web of conspirators ties these individual criminal acts together. Investigation of one individual involved in identity theft therefore often leads to others working together, often in elaborate plots. The following actual case prosecuted in the western district of Washington State illustrates this point:

Between January 27, 1999, and April 14, 2000, a woman and other persons conspired to execute a scheme to defraud several commercial businesses in western Washington and elsewhere, including financial institutions, investment companies, credit card companies, merchant banks, and merchants, and to obtain money and merchandise from these businesses by means of false and fraudulent pretenses.

The conspirators assumed the identities of third persons and fraudulently utilized the Social Security account numbers and names of these persons. The conspirators then created false identity documents such as state identification cards, driver's licenses, and immigration cards. Using the identities and names of these third persons, the conspirators obtained credit cards and opened banking and investment accounts at numerous locations.

The conspirators also prepared fraudulent and counterfeit checks using the account names and numbers for actual bank accounts. The perpetrators then deposited the counterfeit checks into accounts opened by them, using one of their assumed identities. Shortly thereafter, they would withdraw the funds fraudulently credited to their accounts at the time they deposited the counterfeit checks. Over an eight-month period, counterfeit checks totaling over $1 million were deposited at various banks and investment firms.

In addition, the conspirators purchased legitimate cashier's checks with fraudulently obtained monies and then altered the checks to reflect much higher values than the amounts purchased. Over five months, these transactions accounted for more than $350,000.

The scheme also included telefaxed "letters of authorization" using other identities authorizing wire transfer of funds to co-conspirators, altered credit cards, and related offenses.

Such involved criminal conspiracies begin with, and are perpetuated by, identity theft. The result of all of these schemes may be that bill collectors begin to pursue the victim, the victim's credit standing is ruined, and legal procedures may be instituted to collect the fraudulent debts from the victim. Identity thieves may even file for bankruptcy in the victim's name to avoid paying debts incurred while using the victim's personal information or for other reasons, such as to avoid eviction from the house or apartment they have obtained by using the victim's identity.

The Investigative Response

The investigation and prosecution of identity theft cases is dependent on the combined efforts of local, state, and federal agencies, as well as the knowledge and experience of individual investigators. Therefore, one of the most important steps in fighting identity theft is for police personnel to understand what identity theft is, who commits it, and the ways in which it is committed. Police department personnel must also understand how local, state, and federal efforts combine in an effective investigation, and they must be aware of the resources at those levels that are available during such an investigation.

The investigation and prosecution of the case would not have been possible without the coordination of resources among different agencies. Due to its complicated nature, identity theft often requires such cooperation. A case of identity theft in one jurisdiction may have an impact on an investigation in another part of the country. Therefore, effective communication among agencies is an integral part of investigation.

Reports of Identity Theft

In the past, police have been slow to respond to reports of identity theft. In some cases, local police departments refused to take complaints about identity theft because the crime was not well understood, a state statute was lacking, or the department could not identify the venue in which the theft occurred or the perpetrator was operating. This attitude by local police often creates great frustration among victims and generated considerable ill will among these victims toward the departments concerned.

Today, identity theft has been identified as a major crime problem in the United States, and most states now have statutes making it a specific crime. A relative wealth of information and assistance currently exists to deal with identity theft. These and other factors combined make it essential for police departments to respond properly to identity theft complaints, initiate investigations, and prosecute violators where possible. In addition, departments have an obligation to assist the victims through counseling, advice, and referral when reasonable and appropriate. A proper investigative response to identity theft will include the following:

1. ***Develop a standardized procedure for taking identity theft reports.*** Complaints should be taken by the police department in detail and in a manner consistent with the severity of the crime. Aspects of the online reporting form used by the FTC may be useful as a guide to local law enforcement agencies in their efforts to gather all pertinent information about the crime. Victims should not be brushed off or arbitrarily referred to other agencies as a standard course of action. Thus, departments should not merely refer victims to prosecutors' offices or to private attorneys for civil actions. It is the department's obligation to take the complaint and act on it.

2. ***Initiate criminal investigations of identity theft reports.*** Police should initiate investigation of identity theft reports. Again, identity theft is as much a crime as any other offense and should be treated as such. Unless and until it develops that the complaint is unfounded or for some other reason the department cannot proceed further, identity theft should be aggressively and fully investigated.

3. ***Prosecute violators.*** Identity thieves should be prosecuted. Identity theft is not just a prank; it is a serious crime and should be prosecuted to the fullest extent of the law. Unfortunately, the maximum penalties for these types of crimes in some states are not sufficient to garner the attention of prosecutors, whose caseloads may already be overloaded with other criminal activity. In these states, a long-term effort by local police and prosecutors needs to address this through calls for harsher criminal penalties for identity theft.

4. ***Cooperate with other agencies.*** Investigations of multi-jurisdictional identity theft schemes may involve a number of agencies. Each police department should cooperate fully with any agency participating in an identity theft case. If it proves impossible to prosecute the identity thief in the department's own jurisdiction, full cooperation should be given to departments in other jurisdictions where there is a greater likelihood of successfully prosecuting the perpetrators.

5. ***Assist victims by providing the victims with helpful information.*** Victims of identity theft are often unaware of the proper steps to take to minimize the damage suffered because of the identity theft and protect themselves against further victimization. Each police department should provide every identity theft complainant with information as to the steps that the victim should take. Much of that information is available through counselors at the FTC. To summarize this and other information, police officers responding to victims of identity theft and taking crime reports on these matters should keep the following instructions in mind to deal most effectively with these crime victims:

   - Contact the fraud departments of each of the three credit reporting agencies. Give the agency full details of the theft, including a case number as provided by local police, and request that a fraud alert be placed in your file.
   - Request a copy of your credit report, review the report for errors or fraudulent entries, submit any changes necessary, and get a new copy at a later date to ensure that changes or problems have been corrected.
   - Contact all credit card companies where you have an account and notify them of the fraud. Close existing accounts and open new accounts with new personal identification numbers (PINs) and passwords.
   - Contact banks and financial institutions. To be safe, close accounts and open new accounts with new PINs and passwords. Major check verification companies should also be contacted and asked to notify retailers not to accept your stolen or misappropriated checks. The bank may be able and willing to do this for you. ATM cards that may have been compromised should be canceled and new ones obtained with new PINs and passwords.
   - If there is reason to believe that investment or brokerage accounts have been tampered with or otherwise compromised, contact the broker or investment account manager as well as the Securities and Exchange Commission.
   - If unauthorized new accounts have been opened through utility or telephone companies or if the victim's own service is being used to make unauthorized calls, contact the utility or service provider immediately. If the companies do not cooperate, contact the state's public utility commission, the Federal Communications Commission (FCC), or both.

- If there is reason to believe that the Social Security number is being misused, this should be reported to the Social Security Administration's fraud hotline. In addition, it is wise to contact the Social Security Administration to verify the accuracy of the earnings reported under the victim's Social Security number. Request a copy of your Social Security statement.

- If a driver's license or driver's license number is involved in the identity theft, contact the jurisdiction's department of motor vehicles. The same is true if a non driver's identity card is involved. If the driver's license number is the same as the victim's Social Security number, a different number should be substituted.

- If someone has filed bankruptcy in the victim's name, the victim should contact the U.S. Bankruptcy Trustee in the region where the bankruptcy was filed.

- In some instances, the perpetrator of the identity theft may have committed a crime in the victim's name. When this becomes known, the appropriate agencies should be contacted for information as to how the victim's name may be cleared. The procedures for this vary widely among jurisdictions, and it may be necessary for the victim to hire an attorney to accomplish the name-clearing process.

- The victim should contact other police departments where the victim resides or where the identity theft may have taken place. The victim should obtain a copy of the police report regarding the theft from each department to whom the theft has been reported. This is essential because even if the police do not apprehend the perpetrators, the police report may assist the victim in dealing with creditors during efforts to avoid financial liability for fraudulent actions and to repair the damage done to the victim's credit. The fact that a victim has reported and personally attested to the truth of the allegations in a written police report helps other agencies verify the credibility of the victim and take measures on his or her behalf.

- The victim should contact the FTC via telephone or mail to report the identity theft.[65]

- Because the types of identity theft schemes are so varied, other agencies or entities may need to be contacted. If any agency or entity not otherwise discussed above is involved in some manner, it should be contacted immediately. For example, the Internal Revenue Service (IRS) should be notified if tax issues may be involved.

Many of the reports and requests discussed above may be made initially by telephone. However, all such requests should be followed up in writing because telephone reports are often insufficient to preserve the victim's legal rights, and written reports may be necessary to obtain the cooperation of the entity being contacted.

The telephone numbers, addresses, Web sites, and other appropriate data necessary to enable the victims to contact these various agencies should be kept on file in the police department and made available to them. These addresses, telephone numbers, Web sites, and related information can be found in several current guides for identity theft victims, such as the FTC publication *ID Theft—When Bad Things Happen to Your Good Name*. Police departments should consider maintaining a supply of copies of this or similar publications and distributing them to identity theft complainants for their information and assistance.

It is important that local police departments take a proactive role in the education of the public regarding identity theft and the means of preventing it. Even though no person in the information age can completely control the dissemination of his or her personal information, there are specific steps that everyone can take to minimize exposure to identity theft. Crime prevention units and community policing officers should take advantage of their roles within the community by providing citizens with information they can use to protect themselves against identity theft. There is considerable literature available, both in printed form and on the Internet, about preventive measures. Officers should be aware of these sources and provide them to citizens whenever possible.[66]

Motor Vehicle Theft

Carlos Ponce was one of the longtime leaders of an auto theft ring that operated throughout South Florida and sold stolen cars around the country. Ponce, also known as El Rey de los Carros (King of the Cars), ran an interstate auto theft ring that stole luxury cars in South Florida. The ring renumbered the cars using the **vehicle identification number (VIN)** identities of other identical "clone" vehicles and then shipped the vehicles to out-of-state buyers using fraudulent Florida titles. The ring was responsible for stealing hundreds of vehicles, worth an estimated $8 million, from South Florida and using an illicit pipeline—maintained in part from inside a federal prison—to ship the vehicles as far away as Massachusetts and California. In 2006, a Miami-Dade Police investigation known as Operation Road Runner arrested Ponce and 10 of his associates.[67] The Ponce operation illustrates the level of sophistication and organization of some automobile theft operations and reminds us that there are considerable profits for criminals involved in automobile theft.

Since the turn of the century, the advent of the automobile has either directly or indirectly changed the lives of all people. Its impact has inspired both positive and negative uses. Indeed, it has not only enhanced private lives, business, and public service organizations but has also offered criminals innovative ways of transportation to and from their crimes. The value and utility of the motor vehicle have, therefore, become deeply ingrained in today's society.

According to the UCR, the crime of motor vehicle theft includes trains, airplanes, bulldozers, most farm and construction machinery, ships, boats, and spacecraft. Vehicles that are temporarily taken by individuals who have lawful access to them are not thefts. Consequently, spouses who jointly own all property may drive the family car, even though one spouse may think of the vehicle as his or her exclusive personal property. Because most insurance companies require police reports before they will reimburse car owners for their losses, most occurrences of motor vehicle theft are reported to law enforcement agencies. Some of these reports, however, may be false. People who have damaged their own vehicles in solitary crashes or who have been unable to sell them may try to force insurance companies to "buy" them through reports of theft. Motor vehicle theft can turn violent, as in cases of carjacking—a crime in which offenders usually force the car's occupants into the street before stealing the vehicle.

According to the FBI, auto theft is an estimated $7 billion business and continues to grow despite a declining theft rate across the United States. For record-keeping purposes, the UCR defines a motor vehicle as a self-propelled vehicle that runs on the ground and not on rails. This definition includes automobiles, motorcycles, bicycles, trucks, motor scooters, buses, and snowmobiles.

|Fig. 14.11| △

A car thief breaching the steering column of a vehicle.

Michael Lyman

Motor vehicles that are taken temporarily by persons having legal access to them are not considered motor vehicle theft.

Trends

In 2010, the FBI reported that there were an estimated 737,142 motor vehicle thefts. This figure represents a rate of 238.8 motor vehicle thefts per 100,000 inhabitants. The estimated number of motor vehicle thefts declined 7.4 percent when compared with data from 2009 and 38.5 percent when compared with 2006. Financially, in the United States more than $4.5 billion was lost to motor vehicle thefts in 2010. The average dollar loss per stolen vehicle was $6,152. Finally, approximately 73 percent (72.9) of all motor vehicles reported stolen in 2010 were automobiles.[68]

Motor vehicle thefts are common throughout the United States and as a rule require a police report before insurance companies will act on claims. Both police and insurance investigators know that sometimes motor vehicle theft reports are false. Such cases involve persons who attempt to defraud the insurance company or dispose of a vehicle after using it to commit a crime while trying to claim insurance money for it.

Auto theft is big business. Investigations have shown that some large organized groups of car thieves fill orders for contract buyers. Some cars are stolen for shipment out of the country, typically to Mexico. Juveniles often steal cars as a lark or on a dare to joyride. Some thieves intend to keep the car for themselves, but others sell the stolen car to an associate after disguising the vehicle with new paint, plates, and wheels. Stolen vehicles may even be used in other crimes, such as armed robbery or drive-by shootings. Stolen cars are often involved in hit-and-run accidents with injuries, leaving the owners to explain their alibis and prove that they didn't cause the incident and then file a false auto theft report to cover it up.

Motor Vehicle Theft Trend		
Year	Number of Offenses	Rate per 100,000 Inhabitants
2006	1,192,809	2,206.8
2007	1,095,769	2,177.8
Percent change	−8.1	−8.8

Source: Federal Bureau of Investigation—2008 (*Crime in the United States, 2009*).

Experienced car thieves can steal an automobile in less than a minute. Many crude thieves simply smash the driver's-side window. A majority of stolen cars are taken for the value of their parts. Some of the most frequently stolen types of cars have remained constant over the years, suggesting that they are being stolen for parts. According to insurance companies, a $20,000 stolen vehicle can be stripped and sold into $30,000 worth of parts inventory to unscrupulous scrap and auto-body shops. Stolen cars, vans, trucks, and motorcycles cause economic hardship for victims and increase insurance premiums for law-abiding citizens.

Motor vehicles are stolen from a variety of sources, including shopping malls, streets, driveways, parking lots, garages, and car dealerships. Auto theft seems to occur with greater frequency where large groups of cars are parked together for extended periods, such as at airports, shopping centers, colleges, sporting events, fairgrounds, movie complexes, and large apartment complexes.

Motor vehicle thieves target a wide range of popular passenger vehicles, often seeking valuable parts from older model year vehicles for sale on the black market. Their preferred targets for theft vary from one year to the next, but many models remain a constant. For example, the Toyota Camry, Honda Accord, and Ford Taurus are particularly attractive targets, along with sport utility vehicles (SUVs), pickup trucks, and mini-vans, according to a recent study by the National Insurance Crime Bureau (NICB), a not-for-profit insurance organization committed to combating vehicle theft and insurance fraud.

The NICB reported that the 1995 Honda Civic was the most stolen vehicle in 2007, the same as in 2006. Theft of older vehicles has remained constant for the past several years. Eight of the vehicles on the top 10 list shown below are 10 or more model years old. These vehicles have been consistent top sellers for many years, and some of their parts are interchangeable. Thieves dismantle them for their components.[69]

2010 National Top 10 Vehicles Stolen By Vehicle Name/Model		
Rank	Vehicle	Most Frequent Vehicle Year Stolen
1	Honda Accord	1994
2	Honda Civic	1995
3	Toyota Camry	1991
4	Chevrolet Pickup (Full Size)	1999
5	Ford F150 Series/Pickup	1997
6	Dodge Ram	2004
7	Dodge Caravan	2000
8	Acura Integra	1994
9	Ford Explorer	2002
10	Ford Taurus	1999

The Top 10 Metro Areas With Highest Auto Theft Rates In 2010

1. Modesto, California
2. Bakersfield-Delano, California
3. Spokane, Washington
4. Vallejo-Fairfield, California
5. Sacramento/Arden-Arcade/Roseville, California
6. Stockton, California
7. Visalia-Porterville, California
8. San Francisco/Oakland/Fremont, California
9. Yakima, Washington

Source: *National Insurance Crime Bureau* (2012)

Vehicles are typically taken for their parts, which are no longer manufactured and are too difficult or expensive to obtain. Individual car components in high demand are "tuners" or "street racers," which are often stolen for illegal export to Central and South America or Europe.

To help protect their vehicles, experts recommend that motorists always remove the keys from the ignition and vehicle, lock the doors, close the windows, hide valuable items, park in well-lit areas, and use a combination of antitheft devices. Motorists driving theft-prone vehicles need to take additional steps such as installing a visible deterrent such as a steering wheel lock, an alarm, a starter or fuel disabler, and a tracking device.

Historically, many vehicles have been stolen to remove major parts and sell them to salvage yards or repair shops. Today, another criminal goal has captured the attention of law enforcement authorities: vehicles that are stolen and stripped for valuable accessories, such as seats, expensive radios, custom wheels, and tires.

Motivations for Motor Vehicle Theft

Let us now take a closer look at the reasons for auto theft: joyriding, theft for resale, transportation for other crimes, and stripping and chop-shop operations. Understanding these explanations helps investigators identify motivations for the crime, providing clues on how to anticipate the instances of this crime as well as how to prevent such activity.

JOYRIDING For years, **joyriding** has ranked as the premier criminal motivation for motor vehicle theft, committed primarily by juvenile offenders. Since the mid-1970s, however, the average age of the auto theft criminal has risen steadily. While typically in the company of friends, the juvenile auto thief steals a car for enjoyment for short periods. When the ride is over, the vehicle is sometimes stripped of certain "resalable" items, such as cellular telephones, radio equipment, and so on. Tracing personal effects left in a vehicle is difficult because frequently the identification numbers of the items have not been recorded by the victim.

THEFT FOR RESALE Hard-core criminals have found motor vehicle theft for resale to be highly profitable, with minimal risk. Many methods are used to dispose of stolen vehicles. For example, many of these vehicles are transported to foreign countries for resale. Although this involves elaborate transportation schemes, after the vehicle makes it into the hands of the foreign car buyer, its chances of being recovered are minimal. Included in this category are luxury cars and heavy equipment, both of which frequently bring much higher illicit prices than the vehicle is actually worth.

TRANSPORTATION FOR OTHER CRIMES In addition to the profit motive, automobiles have been stolen for use in the commission of other crimes. Here, the vehicle may be used either as transportation to and from various crimes or used in the crime itself. This helps insulate the criminal from detection by not having to use his or her own vehicle in the perpetration of the crime. The availability of potential target vehicles and the opportunity to steal them typically dictate which type of vehicle is chosen. One of the greatest problems in investigating stolen vehicles is the ability of the law enforcement officer to "read" a vehicle properly as one that has been stolen. These identification techniques are discussed in the following sections.

STRIPPING AND CHOP-SHOP OPERATIONS The high profitability of stolen motor vehicles has created a secondary market of sorts for auto thieves. This market's commodity is the parts of certain stolen autos. The terms **chop-shop** and **stripping operations** refer to locations where stolen vehicles are disposed of. In a typical stripping operation, a stolen vehicle is taken to a location, typically a private garage in an unpopulated residential area of town. Such garages are usually rented by people using fictitious names to avoid detection by authorities.

The strip location can sometimes be spotted as buildings with covered windows in areas of frequent deliveries. In addition, people who are seen loading large items into vans in residential garages would be worthy of further investigation. In contrast, chop-shop operations vary in size and represent a growing business in which market entry is fairly easy. Anyone with a truck, garage, backyard, or a piece of secluded land can get into the business.

Although similar to strip locations, chop shops usually involve larger garages and deal in larger quantities of goods. They are sometimes large enough to house both the stolen vehicle and the **tin truck** (the auto parts transport vehicle) inside the building, where detection is much more difficult. Another difference between strip and chop-shop locations is that chop shops usually remove any identifying numbers from the remains of vehicles left behind after the valued parts have been removed. The unused parts are typically dumped in lakes or ponds or areas outside the location of the chop shop. Many salvage yards readily accept parts from auto thieves. Such parts are easily made part of the existing inventory.

Once inside the garage, the stolen vehicle is disassembled. It is here where the prime body parts are removed. These include bumpers, front-end assemblies, trunk lids, and doors. Interior parts, tires, and radios are also of great value to the thief.

Chop-shop operators use torches, power saws, or other tools to disassemble stolen vehicles. After thieves have stripped the stolen vehicle, the parts are transported in tin trucks, from which the parts are sold to repair shops and salvage yards that use them to repair damaged vehicles. After an auto has been stripped, the remaining parts are abandoned. Such vehicles are then typically driven or even pushed to a location away from the strip location.

Investigating officers should always remember that victims might be able to recall certain characteristic marks on their stolen vehicle. These markings, which include cigarette burns in the seat and dents on fenders, might be identifiable if they are shown to the victim.

The Preliminary Investigation

The investigation of a stolen auto typically begins with a report by the victim to the police. As a rule, it is the task of the patrol officer to respond to such complaints and determine the facts and circumstances surrounding the alleged theft. These inquiries should include:

- Where was the vehicle last seen?
- Who was the last person to use the vehicle?
- Were the keys left in the ignition?

Motor Vehicle Fraud—Some of the Most Common Schemes

Owner Give-Ups—The vehicle owner lies about the theft of his vehicle and then orchestrates its destruction to collect insurance money. He claims his vehicle was stolen, but then it is found burned or heavily damaged in a secluded area, submerged in a lake, or in extreme cases, buried underground.

30-Day Specials—Owners whose vehicles need extensive repairs oftentimes perpetrate the "30-day special" scam. They will report the vehicle stolen and hide it for 30 days—just long enough for the insurance company to settle the claim. Once the claim is paid, the vehicle is often found abandoned.

Export Fraud—After securing a bank loan for a new vehicle, an owner obtains an insurance policy for it. The owner reports the vehicle stolen to a U.S. law enforcement agency, but in reality it was illegally shipped overseas to be sold on the black market. The owner then collects on the insurance policy, as well as any illegal profits earned through overseas conspirators who sell the vehicle.

Phantom Vehicles—An individual creates a phony title or registration to secure insurance on a nonexistent vehicle. The insured then reports the vehicle stolen before filing a fraudulent insurance claim. Oftentimes antique or luxury vehicles are used in this scheme, since these valuable vehicles produce larger insurance settlements.

Source: National Crime Information Bureau (2012)

- Was the vehicle left unlocked?
- Is the victim in arrears on payments?
- Are others allowed to drive the vehicle?
- Was the vehicle equipped with special equipment, such as special wheels, fog lights, or special sound system?

Answers to these questions allow the officer to determine if a crime has been committed or if another situation is at hand, such as a civil dispute (divorce) or vehicle repossession by a bank or finance company. Other explanations for the disappearance of a vehicle might also exist. For example, the driver might have been intoxicated and may have been involved in a hit-and-run accident. The motor vehicle theft claim might be an effort to cover up the details and avoid suspicion.

True ownership of the vehicle must also be determined early in the investigation. This can be accomplished simply by requesting certain specific information from the victim, such as the title of the vehicle or a copy of the vehicle's insurance policy. Special characteristics of the vehicle should also be noted in the theft report. Details such as cigarette burns on the vehicle's seats, scratches or dents, rusted areas of the vehicle, decals or stickers, and so on will all distinguish the stolen vehicle from others like it on the street.

The Investigative Traffic Stop

Traffic stops are another way that motor vehicle theft investigations are commonly initiated. Again, the patrol officer is one of the primary players in this early stage of the investigation. After a motor vehicle has been observed as being in violation of the law, officers have legal authority to stop it. In most cases, law enforcement officers will focus their attention on the motor vehicle's license plates. These typically only provide officers with the information they are seeking regarding the registrant of the vehicle. In this situation, such limited information from the license plates includes the fact that the license plates are not stolen and that the owner's name and address match the registration.

It is here, however, that the motor vehicle thief may slip past the watchful eye of the patrol officer. Indeed, the officer making the stop should take time to record and check the validity of the VIN. In almost all cases, this will reveal whether or not the vehicle is properly registered or even stolen. Police officers must therefore have sufficient knowledge about the construction of the VIN to avoid common errors in recording and identifying it.

Professional motor vehicle thieves have practiced several methods of theft. Although complex to the inexperienced thief, these methods are commonly used in organized theft rings. Theft methods most commonly used include altering the VIN; **tagging**, or altering title documents; modifying body parts of a stolen vehicle; and dismantling the vehicle for sale or exchange of parts.

The Vehicle Identification Number

The VIN is as unique to a motor vehicle as a fingerprint is to a human being. It has no resemblance to other numbers commonly dealt with in criminal investigation, such as one's Social Security number or date of birth. Instead, it is assigned to the vehicle by the manufacturer at the time of production and is designed to distinguish each vehicle from all others. The primary purpose of the VIN is for identification and registration.

|Fig. 14.12| ▲

A typical vehicle identification number located on the dashboard of a vehicle.

Courtesy of Mike Himmel

|Fig. 14.13| ▲

A vehicle identification number located on the doorjamb of a vehicle.

Courtesy of Mike Himmel

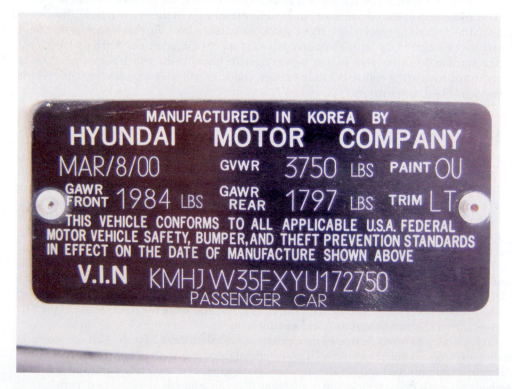

HISTORY OF THE VIN Before 1968, VIN locations varied from manufacturer to manufacturer depending on the make of the vehicle. Since then, however, all American-made automobiles are assembled with the VIN plate visible through the windshield on the driver's side of the automobile. It can also be found on a federal safety certification label located on the driver's door or the driver's doorpost.

Exceptions to typical VIN locations are those of certain luxury automobiles that have their VINs affixed to the left-side windshield post. Any alteration of the VIN should be grounds for a more complete inspection of the vehicle. Before 1981, manufacturers' VIN numbering systems varied. In fact, manufacturers used slightly different systems of VIN numbering. Since then, however, the standard 17-character VIN was adopted, requiring all vehicles manufactured in the United States to have the standardized VIN.

HOW THE VIN WORKS The VIN consists of a combination of letters and numbers. To the average car owner, these combinations would mean very little, but to the criminal investigator, they are invaluable in identifying a stolen motor vehicle. To understand the VIN better, let's look closer at the function of each digit of the 17 numbers. For illustration sake, we consider the following VIN:

1J3CJ45A0CR335521

The numbers and letters represent the following information:

1	Nation of origin
J	Name of the manufacturer (e.g., General Motors, Honda)
3	Specific make of the vehicle (e.g., Buick)
C	Type of restraint system
J45	Car line series and body type
A	Engine description
0	Check digit
C	Model year
R	Assembly plant location
3 3 5 5 2 1	Sequential production numbers

With the exception of the check digit, one can easily see the function of each of these characters. The ninth character is called the check digit. It may be a number or a letter; however, it is derived mathematically from the other characters in the VIN to reveal coding and recording errors. Beginning in 1968, U.S. automobile manufacturers have placed a portion of the VIN on other areas of the vehicle, such as the engine and the transmission.

THE ALTERED VIN Because many vehicles are stolen for the sole purpose of resale, many methods are used by the thief to disguise the true identity of the car. In fact, all outward appearances would indicate that the vehicle is legitimate, so after the VIN alteration has been accomplished, the stolen vehicle can then be sold to an unsuspecting customer.

Disguising the Stolen Vehicle

One common way of disguising a vehicle is to change the VIN and alter the documents that coincide with the VIN (i.e., tagging). Other ways that a vehicle's true identity can be altered include the salvage switch, a modified VIN, or a bogus VIN.

THE SALVAGE SWITCH METHOD The **salvage switch** involves the thief purchasing a wrecked vehicle that is unrepairable strictly for its certificate of title and for the VIN. The purchase can be made from an individual or an insurance company, but it is typically made from a wrecking or salvage yard. The vehicle must have both a VIN plate and documents to support ownership of the vehicle. Next, the thief steals a similar type of vehicle, removes its VIN tag, and replaces it with the salvaged vehicle's VIN. Any other numbers are either altered or removed from the vehicle. It is then sold either to an innocent buyer or to a person who may well suspect the validity of the transaction but participates anyway because of a favorable price.

THE MODIFIED VIN TECHNIQUE Another method of disguising a stolen vehicle is to replace the original VIN with a phony one. This can be done in several ways. One way is to use a simple label maker, which can easily be purchased at hardware stores. The VIN is then stamped on a label. Next, it is spray painted with flat black paint and placed over the original VIN. Other identifying numbers on the vehicle are either removed or altered. Vehicles tagged in this fashion should be fairly easily detected by observant investigators through observing the size, texture, and the size of the numbers of the tag. Another way that thieves have attempted to alter VINs is to remove the original VIN, alter it, and replace it on the vehicle. Again, this method is usually detected by the trained investigator but may appear legitimate to the untrained eye.

THE BOGUS VIN Still another method is to construct a completely bogus VIN that closely resembles the original. Many criminals will attempt to steal blank VIN tags, which are then stamped with numbers and placed on vehicles. This is where the ninth digit of the VIN, the check digit, is beneficial in determining the authenticity of the tag.

Since 1970, American-made vehicles have also displayed a federal safety certification label on the driver's door or the driver's doorpost. This label also displays the VIN for the vehicle and should match the VIN tag on the vehicle's dash. To dispose of the vehicle after it has been tagged, the auto thief adopts several methods. For example, in the salvage operation, the title will typically be placed in the fictitious name before sale. In instances in which the VIN has been altered or manufactured by the thief, phony title documents can then be prepared to match the bogus VIN. In other cases, title documents may not even exist, only the registration of the vehicle. In such cases, buyers who might suspect that the car is of suspicious origin might continue with the transaction because of a low sale price. Such sales are typically conducted in cash at the thief's request.

The Rip-Off

Typically, vehicles are stolen because of carelessness on the part of the owner—drivers who leave their keys in an unattended car or motorists who leave their cars running while they enter an establishment for a short period. Vehicle thieves commonly watch these locations to wait for the most opportune time to make their steal.

When the keys are not left in the ignition, many thieves have traditionally resorted to entry techniques ranging from the classic "smash-and-grab" technique to unobtrusive use of a screwdriver and flat iron. Today, entry into vehicles is becoming more innovative. One such innovation includes the use of porcelain chips broken from spark plugs. This technique involves attaching the chips to a wire, string, or other handle and simply hitting them against the vehicle glass for quick entry. This method reduces the time, noise, and chances of detection but may leave microscopic fragments of glass on the intruder's clothing.[70] These fragments are excellent evidence and hopefully can be located shortly after the theft by seizing the suspect's clothing for examination.

Another technique commonly used by thieves is to observe, or "case," a parking lot where cars are parked while people are at work. In this case, the thief has several hours' leeway from the time the vehicle is stolen to the time the theft is discovered. Thus, the vehicle may be transported far from the theft location by the time the theft is discovered.

Many motorists invest in antitheft devices in their vehicles. Although many of these devices have proven to be effective, thieves have learned methods of defeating them in many cases. The level of expertise in disabling an antitheft device depends on several variables, including the thieves' degree of mechanical experience, the quality and effectiveness of the device, and the location of the vehicle when stolen.

Tools of the Trade

Vehicles are obtained by many different means by professional thieves. For example, tow trucks are often used to transport a vehicle desired by the vehicle thief. Other common methods are the use of public parking facilities, such as mall parking lots and car rental lots. In these instances, all vehicles are prime targets, especially if they are left with the keys in the ignition. Entry into a

|Fig. 14.14|

The vehicle safety inspection (A) and vehicle registration (B) stickers also provide identifying numbers and investigative leads.

Courtesy of Mike Himmel

vehicle can be accomplished using several tools. Professional thieves become proficient in the use of these tools and use them in a manner in which little, if any, damage is done to the exterior of the vehicle, which could easily be noticed.

Many tools that thieves commonly use also have a legitimate function, which is, however, put to a sinister use by the criminal. When means are devised to counter or deter motor vehicle thefts, criminals inevitably devise methods with which to defeat these means.

Motor Vehicle Theft: Tools of the Trade

☑ *Slim jim.* This is a thin, easily obtainable piece of metal or aluminum that is notched at both ends. This tool enables easy entry by the thief, who slides the tool in the small crevice between the door and the door frame. After the lock is manipulated, the door is easily opened.

☑ *Slide hammer.* This tool is also referred to as a dent puller or slam puller. After the thief removes the lock cap of the ignition, the slam puller is inserted by screwing the tip into the keyway. Force is then applied to the slide mechanism, away from the steering column, and the lock is removed. The vehicle can then be started by inserting a screwdriver that is twisted just like a car key.

☑ *Ignition extractor.* The lock cap is removed upon getting into the vehicle. The extractor is attached and turned to remove the lock. The vehicle can then easily be started with a screwdriver.

☑ *Force tool.* The force tool is placed over the lock and tapped after removal of the lock cap. The ratchet is turned, thus destroying the locking mechanism.

☑ *Key cutter, codebook, and blank keys.* These tools enable entry into a single-key vehicle and are widely used. A door lock is pulled, and the code number from that lock can be obtained and a new key made. This gives the thief a new key that he or she can use at a time of his choosing.

Carjacking

Carjacking is defined by the U.S. Department of Justice as "completed or attempted robbery of a motor vehicle by a stranger to the victim."[71] Carjackings occur most frequently in urban areas.

The U.S. Bureau of Justice Statistics estimates that in about half of all carjacking attempts, the attacker succeeds in stealing the victim's car. It's estimated that, between 1987 and 1992, about 35,000 carjacking attempts took place per year; and between 1992 and 1996, about 49,000 attempts took place per year.[72]

A carjacking typically consists of a single gunman placing a pistol to the head of an unsuspecting driver at locations such as stoplights, garages, fast food restaurants, gas stations, and parking lots. Another common technique is the so-called bump and run, in which the thief stages a minor

|Fig. 14.15|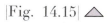

Carjacking is also a form of robbery and is one method used by criminals to acquire a desired vehicle.

Jack Star / Getty Images

rear-end collision. When the driver exits his or her vehicle to inspect the damage, one thief holds up the occupant(s) while, often, another person drives their vehicle.

The Anti-Car Theft Act, enacted in 1992, made armed auto theft ("carjacking") a federal offense. In 1994, the passage of the Violent Crime Control and Law Enforcement Act made carjacking resulting in death a federal crime punishable by death.[73]

According to the Bureau of Justice Statistics, an average of about 49,000 completed or attempted nonfatal carjackings took place each year in the United States between 1992 and 1996. In about half of those incidents, the offender was successful in taking the victim's vehicle. In addition, about 27 homicides by strangers each year involve automobile theft. Some of these may have been carjackings. Other statistics about carjackings include about seven of 10 completed carjackings involve firearms, most carjackings do not result in injury to the victims, and a majority of carjackings are committed at night.[74]

Motor Vehicle Fraud

The problem of motor vehicle fraud is also growing nationwide. For example, the **National Auto Theft Bureau (NATB)** estimates that 15 percent of all vehicles reported stolen were fraudulent claims. The person who commits motor vehicle fraud does so with a clear profit motive and usually attempts to collect payment through her or his insurance company. The problem is compounded by the notion that many people have the attitude that fraud is only an insurance problem and doesn't really hurt anyone. Some believe that after paying insurance premiums for years, they are entitled to get a return on their money. Indeed, many expenses are ultimately incurred in the detection, apprehension, prosecution, and incarceration of offenders.

Methods of Fraud

Although many methods of motor vehicle fraud exist, the most common is to alter the vehicle's identity by changing the VIN plate and reregistering the car. A second common method is the *owner give-up*. This term applies when the owner conspires with a third party, typically for a fee, to have the vehicle disposed of so that the owner can collect the insurance money. Reasons for motor vehicle fraud include:

- Desire for immediate cash
- End of costly repair bills
- Avoidance of the hassle of selling
- Breaking of the car lease

Red Flags to Indicate Motor Vehicle Fraud[75]

- ☑ Late-model vehicles are involved.
- ☑ There is a close relationship between the date of coverage and the date of the claim.
- ☑ The insured furnished the address and phone number of a bar, hotel, or motel as a place to be contacted by the claims adjuster.
- ☑ The insurance premium was paid in cash.
- ☑ The insured is unable to produce the title or proof of ownership.
- ☑ The vehicle has no lien noted, and the insured has no apparent means to have made a cash purchase.
- ☑ The previous owner cannot be located or is unknown to the claimant.
- ☑ The vehicle is reported stolen and is recovered a short time later, burned.
- ☑ The insured is unable to provide a sales invoice.

Many theft reports also include nonexistent vehicle contents such as camera equipment, furs, and golf clubs. Here, the greedy thief attempts to "sweeten the pot" and increase her or his criminal profits.

The National Insurance Crime Bureau

The NICB is a nonprofit private crime prevention agency underwritten by more than 600 property-casualty insurance companies.[76] The Chicago-based organization was established to aid law enforcement and insurance investigators in investigations and prosecutions of vehicle crimes such as vehicle theft, vehicle arson, and vehicle fraud. The NICB maintains district offices throughout the United States, Mexico, and Canada and publishes an annual manual for the identification of stolen automobiles. In addition, the NICB's role is to implement policies for the prevention of vehicle theft. To aid the investigator, the NICB publishes passenger identification manuals that interpret characters in the vehicle's VIN.

Case in Point

>>Possession of Burglary Tools

Ronald is standing in an alley behind a store late at night. A police car arrives, and the officers see Ronald. The officers also see a crowbar, a false key, a lock pick, and a force screw near the area where Ronald is standing. In addition, Ronald has no reasonable explanation for standing in the alley. Under these circumstances, Ronald has probably committed the crime of possession of burglary tools. Although many burglary tools can be purchased in hardware stores, investigators must show that the "intent" was present for the suspect to use them in a burglary. For example, the "reputation" or criminal history of the suspect can offer some evidence to show criminal intent to commit the crime.

Burglary tools may include:

- Explosives
- Slim jims
- Any instrument designed for cutting, burning, or opening containers, such as torches and welders
- Portable key cutters
- Key blanks
- Pry bars
- Bolt cutters
- Chemicals
- Tension wrenches
- Lock picks

Summary Checklist

In this chapter, we consider the ways that information about crimes is documented by criminal investigators. A properly documented case is one that is more likely to succeed in court. See how well you are able to answer the following questions in your checklist.

1. What is the difference between burglary and robbery?

Burglary and robbery are commonly confused.

- Burglary
  - A property crime in which the thief seeks to avoid direct contact with people during the commission of the crime
  - Locations of burglaries are usually unoccupied homes or businesses where no witnesses are present
- Robbery
  - A crime against persons where the robber chooses to confront a victim at a location where witnesses are present

2. What are the elements of burglary?

The elements of burglary are defined by the criminal codes of each state, so there are many differences regarding these laws. However, there are some commonalities that are generally reflected in the elements of the crime:

- Burglary is a crime against the dwelling targeted
- No violence is directed toward any of the occupants
- As a rule, after the burglar enters the structure, no additional felony must be committed for the legal elements of the crime to be met (there may be exceptions if the person believes the structure he or she enters is open to the general public)

3. What are the two main types of burglaries?

Burglaries can be divided into two categories: residential and commercial.

- Residential burglars may focus on apartment houses and usually work in the higher-income areas of the town.
- Warehouses, stores, taverns, and restaurants are all common targets of commercial burglaries.

4. Explain the steps in the preliminary investigation of burglary.

The patrol division usually is the first to respond to a burglary call.

- The first thing they should do is determine whether a crime is currently in progress.
- Officers approaching the location should do so quietly (no warning lights, siren, etc.).
- En route, officers should be on the lookout for persons entering the scene.
- After arriving, officers should take care to be quiet and should approach the structure from both the front and back in the event that the suspect attempts to flee.

Most burglars are convicted on circumstantial evidence so physical evidence at the crime scene is critical to the case.

- Forensic evidence may include broken glass, tool marks, and fingerprints at the burglary crime scene.
- Possession of burglary tools is considered a separate felony offense by most jurisdictions.

Preliminary investigative steps include:

- Determine the point of entry.
- Check to see if a window or door was forced open.
- What type of tool was used?
- Are there tool marks?
- Is there evidence of lock picks?
- Look for footprints, tire tracks, and so on.
- Look for other trace evidence (cigarette butts, fibers, hair, pieces of broken tools, etc.)

- Sketch the scene.
- Interview victims and witnesses.
- Make a list of property taken (include serial numbers).
- Make a list of all persons on the crime scene.

5. Identify methods to trace stolen property.

After a successful burglary has occurred, the thief will probably seek to get rid of the stolen property as soon as possible, often using a fence.

- A fence is a person who buys and sells stolen property with criminal intent.
- Fencing operations range from professional to highly unorganized.

Establishing proof of a fencing operation is difficult and time-consuming.

- First, the property in question must be identified as stolen.
- To convict a thief for a property offense in this category, investigators must prove that the suspect received stolen property.
- Investigators might need to rely on circumstantial evidence to prove receipt of stolen property.
  - Did the suspect pay for the merchandise with a check or cash?
  - Was the property purchased for considerably lower than the normal retail price?
  - Does the suspect have a receipt for the property?
  - Were the stolen items isolated from other items in storage?
  - Is there property from several different thefts present at the location?

6. What are the elements of the crime of embezzlement?

Embezzlement is usually defined under individual state statutes dealing with grand theft. It is basically a fraudulent appropriation of property by a person to whom that property has been entrusted. Although the elements of the crime may vary, some common elements can be generalized.

- A trusting relationship exists between the suspect and the victim.
- The perpetrator had lawful possession of the pilfered belongings at some time during the relationship.
- The property was stolen or converted to a form of possession that was contrary to the trust relationship.
- There was criminal intent to deprive the lawful owner of the property, either temporarily or permanently.

7. What are the main categories of embezzlement?

There are many different types of embezzlement. They vary depending on the degree of trust existing between the suspect and the victim. Categories of embezzlement include:

- Theft of currency
  - The most common type of embezzlement
  - Theft of cash from a trusted party
- Manipulation of accounts
  - Typically involves employees of an accounting department
- Retail theft/pilferage
  - The theft of merchandise by company employees

8. What is the extent of the problem of identity theft?

Identity theft is a special kind of larceny that involves obtaining credit, merchandise, or services by fraudulent personal representation. It became a federal crime in 1998 with the passage of the Identity Theft and Assumption Deterrence Act.

- Identity theft is almost always a stepping-stone to the commission of other crimes—credit card fraud, bank fraud, computer fraud, Internet fraud, etc.
- The illegally obtained funds may be used to finance other types of criminal enterprises, including drug trafficking
- Identity theft has escalated in the United States due in large part to the technological revolution
- Losses related to identity theft include:
  - Financial losses
  - Personal costs—damage to the victim's credit standings, personal reputation, etc.

9. Explain the crime of motor vehicle theft and how the crime is investigated.

The FBI defines motor vehicle theft as the stealing of automobiles, trucks, buses, motorcycles, motor scooters, snowmobiles, etc. According to the FBI, auto theft is an estimated $7 billion business that is continuing to grow.

- Motor vehicles are stolen from a variety of locations, including shopping malls, streets, driveways, parking lots, garages, and car dealerships.
- Motivations for auto theft include:
  - Joyriding
  - Theft for resale
  - Transportation for other crimes
  - Stripping and chop-shop operations

The investigation of a stolen auto typically begins with a report by the victim to the police. In general, it is the patrol officer's task to respond to these complaints. Inquiries should include:

- Where was the vehicle last seen?
- Who was the last person to use the vehicle?
- Were the keys left in the ignition?
- Was the vehicle left unlocked?
- Is the victim in arrears on payments?
- Are others allowed to drive the vehicle?
- Was the vehicle equipped with special equipment, such as special wheels, fog lights, or a special sound system?

Key Terms

booster	embezzlement	identity theft
burglary	fence	joyriding
burglary tools	forgery	larceny–theft
carjacking	fraud	National Auto Theft Bureau (NATB)
check kiting	fungible goods	National Insurance Crime Bureau (NICB)
chop shop	heel	
commercial burglary	hot list	pilferage

property crime

plastic workers

residential burglary

retail burglary

salvage switch

shoplifting

snitches

stripping operations

tagging

tin truck

vehicle identification number (VIN)

Discussion Questions

1. Discuss the distinction between robbery and burglary.

2. Describe the two types of burglaries and explain how targets are selected.

3. Explain the different types of burglars.

4. What physical evidence should be considered in investigating a burglary?

5. What role does a fence play in the crime of burglary?

6. What is check fraud and how is it investigated?

7. What are the categories of embezzlement, and how are they best investigated?

8. Explain some of the ways criminals obtain credit cards and some of the methods most commonly used by criminals to avoid detection when using stolen credit cards.

9. Discuss the ways that stolen information is used by criminals.

10. Describe some of the motivations for motor vehicle theft.

11. What is an investigative traffic stop and how does it contribute to motor vehicle investigations?

12. Explain the VIN and its role in criminal investigation of motor vehicle theft.

Notes

1. FEDERAL BUREAU OF INVESTIGATION. (2011). *Crime in the United States—2010*. Washington, DC: United States Department of Justice. Availableat http://www.fbi.gov/about-us/cjis/ucr/crime-in-the-u.s/2010/crime-in-the-u.s.-2010/property-crime

2. IBID.

3. FEDERAL BUREAU OF INVESTIGATION. (2011). *Crime in the United States—2010*. Available at http://www.fbi.gov/about-us/cjis/ucr/crime-in-the-u.s/2010/crime-in-the-u.s.-2010/property-crime/burglarymain

4. IBID.

5. IBID.

6. SKOGAN, W. AND G. ANTUNES. (1998). Information, apprehension and deterrence: Exploring the limits of police productivity. In D. Bayley (Ed.), *What works inpolicing*. New York: Oxford University Press.

7. HOPE, T. (1999). Property guardianship in the suburbs. In K. Painter and N. Tilley (Eds.), *Surveillance of public space: An evaluation of CCTV, street lighting and crime prevention*. Monsey, NY: Criminal Justice Press.

8. MIETHE, T. AND R. MCCORKLE. (1998). Residential and nonresidential burglary. In T. Miethe and R. McCorkle (Eds.), *Crime profiles: The anatomy of dangerous persons, places and situations*. Los Angeles: Roxbury Publishing Co.

9. WRIGHT, R. AND S. DECKER. (1994). *Burglars on the job: Street life and residential break-ins*. Boston: Northeastern University Press.

10. IBID.

11. FEDERAL BUREAU OF INVESTIGATION. (2009). *Crime in the United States—2008*. Washington, DC: U.S. Department of Justice, Federal Bureau of Investigation.

12. RENGERT, G. AND J. WASILCHICK. (2000). *Suburban burglary: A tale of two suburbs*, 2nd ed. Springfield, Ill.: Charles C. Thomas.

13. CROMWELL, P., J. OLSON, AND D. AVARY. (1999). Decision strategies of residential burglars. In P. Cromwell (Ed.), *Intheir own words: Criminals on crime*, 2nd ed. LosAngeles: Roxbury Publishing Co.

14. BEAVON, D., P. BRANTINGHAM, AND P. BRANTINGHAM. (1994). The influence of street Networks on the patterning of property offenses. In R. Clarke (Ed.), *Crime preventionstudies*, Vol. 2. Monsey, NY: Criminal Justice Press.

15. POYNER, B. AND B. WEBB. (1993). What works in crime prevention: Anverview of evaluations.*Crime prevention studies*, Vol. 1. Monsey, NY: Criminal Justice Press.

16. BRANTINGHAM, P. AND P. BRANTINGHAM. (1984). Burglary mobility and crime prevention planning. Boston: Kluwer-NijhoffPublishing, From Coping with Burglary, p. 77–95.

17. PEASE, K. (1992). Preventing burglary on a British public housing estate. In R. Clarke (Ed.), *Situational crime prevention: Successful case studies*. New York: Harrow and Heston.
18. POLVI, N., T. LOOMAN, C. HUMPHRIES, AND K. PEASE. (1990). Repeat break-and-entervictimization: Time course and crime prevention opportunity. *Journal of Police Science and Administration* 17(1):8–11.
19. IBID.
20. CROMWELL, OLSON, AND AVARY. (1999). Decision strategies of residential burglars
21. RENGERT AND WASILCHICK. (2000). *Suburban burglary*.
22. MIETHE AND MCCORKLE. (1998). Residential and nonresidential burglary.
23. WRIGHT AND DECKER. (1994). *Burglars on the job*.
24. TITUS, R. (1999). Declining residential burglary rates in the USA. *Security Journal* 12(4):59–63.
25. RENGERT AND WASILCHICK. (2000). *Suburban burglary*; CROMWELL. OLSON, AND AVARY. (1999). Decision strategies of residential burglars.
26. RENGERT AND WASILCHICK. (2000). *Suburban burglary*.
27. FELSON, M. AND R. CLARKE. (1997). *Business and crime prevention*. Monsey, NY: Criminal Justice Press.
28. SPELMAN, W. (1990). *Repeat offender programs for law enforcement*. Washington, DC: Police Executive Research Forum; RENGERT AND WASILCHICK. (2000). *Suburban burglary*.
29. IBID.
30. POYNER AND WEBB. (1993). What works in crime prevention.
31. RENGERT AND WASILCHICK. (2000). *Suburban burglary*; CROMWELL, OLSON, AND AVARY. (1999). Decision strategies of residential burglars.
32. LOWRY, T. (1998). Cash machines provide new target for burglars. *USA Today*, March 16, p. 1B.
33. IBID.
34. FEDERAL BUREAU OF INVESTIGATION. (2011). *Crime in the United States—2010*.
35. IBID.
36. ASSOCIATION OF CERTIFIED FRAUD EXAMINERS. (2012). *Report to the Nations on Occupational Fraud & Abuse: 2012 Global Fraud Study*. Available at http://www.acfe.com/cost-of-fraud. aspx?gclid=ClrQtsam-68CFYTsKgod0TU4FA# (retrieved on May 12, 2012).
37. IBID.
38. IBID.
39. AMERICAN BANKERS' ASSOCIATION. (2007). Banker's association deposit account fraud survey report. Available at http://www.aba.com/Press+Room/112707Deposit+FraudSurvey.htm
40. DUGAS, C. (1995). Check fraud costs banks, consumers. *USA Today*, November 14, p.4B.
41. BENNETT, W. AND K. HESS.(2001). *Criminal investigation*, 6th ed. Belmont, CA: Wadsworth.
42. MCCAGHY, C. (1976). *Deviant behavior*. New York: Macmillan, pp.348–349.
43. CLARK, J. AND R. HOLLINGER. (1983). Theft in the workplace. *Crime and Justice*, October:117–118.

44. FEDERAL BUREAU OF INVESTIGATION. (2011).*Crime in the United States—2010*.Availableat http://www.fbi.gov/scams-safety/fraud
45. GREENWALD, J. (1996). Credit where none is due. *Time*, February 19, p. 50.
46. IBID.
47. CLARKE, R. V. (September 2003).*Shoplifting*. U.S. Department of Justice.Office of Community Oriented Policing Services.
48. IBID.
49. IBID.
50. CAMERON, M. O. (1983).The scourge of shoplifting. *Criminal Justice Ethics*, Winter–Spring:3–15.
51. HARTMANN, D., D. GELFAND, B. PAGE, AND P. WALKER. (1972). Rates of bystander observation and reporting of contrived shoplifting incidents. *Criminology* 10:248.
52. BLANKENBURG, E. (1976). The selectivity of legal sanctions: An empirical investigation of shoplifting. *Law and Society Review* 11:109–129.
53. GOLD, E. AND J. LANG. (January2012). Diverting shoplifters: A research and planning guide. Washington, DC: Office of Community Oriented Policing Services.
54. IBID.
55. O'DONNELL, J. (2006). Stores protect turf from gangs of thieves. *USA Today*, November 17, pp.1B–2B; FEDERAL BUREAU OF INVESTIGATION. (2008). *Crime in the United States—2007*. Washington, DC: U.S. Department of Justice, Federal Bureau of Investigation.
56. JAVELIN STRATEGY AND RESEARCH. (2011). The 2010 identity fraud survey report. Available athttps://www.javelinstrategy.com/news/831/92/Javelin-Study-Finds-Identity-Fraud-Reached-New-High-in-2009-but-Consumers-are-Fighting-Back/d,pressRoomDetail (retrieved on May 12, 2012).
57. IBID.
58. FEDERAL TRADE COMMISSION. (2009). Protecting America's consumers. Available at http://www.ftc.gov/opa/2003/09/idtheft.shtm
59. IBID.
60. IBID.
61. ROBERT O'HARROW. (2001). Identity thieves thrive in information age. *Washington Post*, May 31, p.1. Available at http://www.washingtonpost.com
62. FEDERAL BUREAU OF INVESTIGATION. (2008). *Crime in the United States—2007*.
63. FEDERAL TRADE COMMISSION REPORT. *Identity theft complaint data, figures and trends on identity theft*, November 1999 – March 2001, p. 3.
64. NEWMAN, G. (June 2004). *Identity Theft*. Washington, DC: U.S. Department of Justice. Office of Community Oriented Policing Services.
65. These items are all listed in the FTC publication *ID Theft—When bad things happen to your good name: Federal Trade Commission* (August 2000).
66. FTC ONLINE PUBLICATIONS. (2001). *Pretexting: Your personal information revealed*. Available at http://www.ftc.gov/bep/conline/pubs/credit/pretext.htm

67. STATE OF FLORIDA ATTORNEY GENERAL. (August 14, 2006). Available at http://www.myfloridalegal.com

68. FEDERAL BUREAU OF INVESTIGATION. (2011). *Crime in the United States—2010*. Available at http://www.fbi.gov/about-us/cjis/ucr/crime-in-the-u.s/2010/crime-in-the-u.s.-2010/property-crime/mvtheftmain

69. NATIONAL INSURANCE CRIME BUREAU. Available at http://www.iii.org/media/hottopics/insurance/test4/

70. FERGUSON, B. E. (1990). Porcelain chips: An auto theft innovation. *Law and Order*, September:154–155.

71. KLAUS, P. (March 1999). *Carjacking in the United States, 1992–1996, Special Report*. Washington, DC: U.S. Department of Justice, Bureau of Justice Statistics.

72. KLAUS. (1999). *Carjackings in the United States*.

73. IBID.

74. IBID.

75. IBID.

76. NATIONAL INSURANCE CRIME BUREAU. Available at https://www.nicb.org/about-nicb/our_story (retrieved on September 23, 2012).

Mark Ide

This chapter will enable you to:

1. Summarize the trends and elements of arson.

2. Summarize the motivations and characteristics of arsonists.

3. Describe how arson investigations are conducted.

4. Describe the investigation of bombings and bomb threats.

5. Summarize the acts and types of terrorism.

6. Describe counterterrorism efforts.

Arson, Bombings, and Terrorism

Introduction

Beginning on December 29, 2011, a series of car fires were set in Los Angeles. Most of the fires occurred over New Year's weekend. While no persons were injured as a result of the fires, it was considered the worst case of arson reported in 20 years in Los Angeles.

Vehicles that were set on fire were often parked in carports or next to apartment buildings. On January 2, 2012, a sheriff deputy stopped a van because it matched a description by witnesses of a vehicle seen at the time of the fires. Arrested was a 24-year-old suspect, Harry Burkhart. Burkhart was wanted in Germany on suspicion of burning down his own home. He was charged with 28 counts of arson of property and nine counts of arson of an inhabited structure in connection with the Los Angeles fires. Investigators learned that Burkhart was "motivated by rage against Americans" and sought to terrorize as many people as possible when he torched dozens of cars, homes, and garages late at night, when most residents were sleeping, to inflict maximum fear and damage.[1]

Perhaps one of the oldest known crimes is the act of arson. It creates a severe threat to human life and costs society billions of dollars per year. Although arson can be defined as the malicious or fraudulent burning of property, it can also be considered a crime against both persons and property. Furthermore, it receives little media attention and is difficult to investigate because evidence is difficult to locate and criminal intent is difficult to prove. Unlike other "sensational" media events such as murder cases and drug raids, arson is generally considered a low-priority crime even by law enforcement agencies. Several explanations can be cited for this:

- *Arson is a time-consuming and difficult crime to investigate.*
- *There is much misunderstanding about the motives behind the crime of arson.*
- *Few arson cases lead to arrests, and fewer than 20 percent of arrests result in convictions.*
- *Arson used to be classified as a property crime rather than a crime of violence, as it is today.*

Arson: A Brief Overview

As Sherlock Holmes pointed out, many types of investigations are susceptible to prejudgment, but few as often as fire scene investigations. Fires, by their very nature, destroy the evidence of their origin and progress as they grow. Investigations are compromised, and often scenes are further compromised by the activities of the fire service, whose primary responsibilities are to save lives and protect property against further damage. Complicating things further, fire scenes typically involve all manner of public entities: emergency medical, law enforcement, and fire services. Public utilities such as gas and electric companies may be involved. Passers-by, owners, tenants, customers, delivery agents all may have important information.

Members of the media and curious onlookers attracted to large fire scenes can also complicate investigations, as they make security a necessity. It has often been said, "A fire investigation is like a picture puzzle. Everyone involved with it has some of the pieces, but no one has the whole picture. It is up to the investigator to gather enough of these pieces together to solve the puzzle."[2]

Problems facing arson investigators today represent nothing new. Since Roman times, civil authorities have recognized the threat that fire represents, not only to the well-being of citizens, but also, and perhaps more importantly, to the welfare and security of the community as a whole. In the days of wooden walls and roofs and straw-covered floors, any fire could ravage an entire city. So, it was in the interest of all concerned to thoroughly investigate fires and establish how they began. Accordingly, civil authorities attempted to control the fire risk by assessing penalties if an accidental fire was allowed to get out of control. Dangerous practices, such as leaving cooking fires unguarded, were identified and controlled.

William the Conqueror issued an edict that cooking fires be damped or covered after a particular time of evening so that unattended fires could not flare up. This policy of *couvre feu* (cover the fire) gave rise to the "curfew" of today.[3] If authorities could determine the fire was deliberately set, the perpetrator could be identified and punished. Some of the oldest English common laws regarded arson to be the crime of burning the house or dwelling of another. The crime of arson was considered to be such a danger that it was punishable by death.[4]

The same rationale applies today. Fires of accidental cause need to be identified, so that dangerous practices, such as filling kerosene room heaters with gasoline, can be eliminated by public education, or so that defective or dangerous products, such as instant-on televisions or room heaters with no overheating or tip-over protection, can be taken off the market or modified so they no longer pose a significant fire risk. Fires of incendiary, or deliberate, cause must be detected, so that the fire setter can be intercepted before doing more harm and punished as necessary.

Arson Offenses

The Uniform Crime Reporting (UCR) program defines arson as any willful or malicious burning or attempt to burn, with or without intent to defraud, a dwelling house, public building, motor vehicle or aircraft, personal property of another, and so on.[5] Only fires determined through investigation to have been willfully or maliciously set are classified as arsons. Fires of suspicious or unknown origins are excluded from this category.

Trends

Statistics showing the instances of arson are revealing. For example, in 2011, the FBI reported that during 2010, law enforcement agencies reported 56,825 arsons.[6] Of those, arsons involving structures (e.g., residential, storage, public) accounted for 45.5 percent of the total number of arson offenses; mobile property was involved in 26 percent of arsons, and other types of property (such as crops, timber, fences) accounted for over 28 percent of arsons. Breaking these numbers down, the average dollar loss due to arson was $17,612 but arsons of industrial/manufacturing structures resulted in the highest average dollar losses, an average of $133,717 per arson. In spite of these numbers, arson offenses for 2010 decreased 7.6 percent when compared with arson data reported in 2009.[7]

Arson Trends, 2009–2010			
	Structure	Mobile	Other
2009	23,713	15,009	14,647
2010	22,470	12,680	13,931

Source: Federal Bureau of Investigation. (2011). *Crime in the United States—2010.* Washington, DC: U.S. Government Printing Office.

National statistics show that "when measured on a cost per incident basis, arson is the most expensive crime committed." The high cost and widespread misunderstanding associated with the crime of arson can be attributed to several factors, which include:

- A lack of public education concerning the problem of arson
- A reluctance on the part of prosecutors to file arson cases that rely on circumstantial evidence
- Quick payments on fire losses by insurance companies
- A lack of adequate training for investigators

Many arson crime scenes are not recognized or treated as such, and much evidence is destroyed. Despite the fact that many of the preceding considerations are no longer considered as great a problem as they used to be, arson still accounts for substantial losses to victims. For example, property losses alone are estimated at $5 billion annually.[8]

Because valuable evidence is sometimes destroyed during a blaze, it is often difficult to determine that arson was committed. Other complicating factors include the fact that there are few, if any, witnesses to the crime; physical evidence is difficult to locate; and if the crime is executed properly, it is difficult to determine the fire's point of origin. Finally, often the victim of the fire ends up being the perpetrator of the crime. For these reasons, arson investigation is one of the more difficult crimes to solve.

Elements of Arson

As with all crimes, the elements must be established before a criminal charge can be levied against the suspect. As with most other crimes, the elements of arson differ from one state to another, but some commonalties do exist.

LEGAL CATEGORIES Arson is also legally characterized by two distinct categories: aggravated arson and simple arson. **Aggravated arson** is the deliberate burning of property while creating an imminent danger to human life or risking great bodily harm. **Simple arson**, a lesser offense, is the burning of property that does not result in such a risk to human life. In addition to aggravated and simple arson, most states have recognized that attempted arson is also punishable under law.

The severity of the crime of arson can be seen in the case of Dr. Deborah Green. On the windy night of October 24, 1995, a raging fire demolished the Green home, a $400,000, six-bedroom home in Prairie Village, Kansas. Accelerants were poured in several areas of the house and fed the flames. Dr. Green escaped the fire through her back bedroom door on the first floor. One of her daughters, 10-year-old Kate, survived by climbing through her second-floor bedroom window onto the garage

|Fig. 15.1| ▲

Dr. Deborah Green on trial in Johnson County District Court on Wednesday, January 31, 1996, during a hearing in Olathe, Kansas. The videotape was of her interview immediately after the fatal fire that killed two of her children.

Dave Kaup / AP Wide World Photos

roof and jumping. The fire took the lives of 6-year-old Kelly Green and 13-year-old Tim Farrar. Green's husband, Dr. Michael Farrar, was not home when the fire broke out.

The investigation also included a closer look at a fire about 16 months earlier that damaged the family's previous home and the mysterious illness of the children's father, Dr. Michael Farrar, weeks before the October fire. Dr. Farrar was hospitalized again after the fire with apparent poisoning. The investigation revealed that Green had set the fire. As the investigation continued, evidence also showed that on at least three occasions, Green had poisoned her husband, Michael Farrar, with ricin, a derivative of castor beans.

Dr. Deborah Green was charged with aggravated arson and two counts of first-degree murder in the deaths of the children. Green was also charged with two counts of attempted first-degree murder of her husband and surviving daughter. She was held on $3 million bond.

The Deborah Green case demonstrates how arson can be a means to commit a crime or a means to cover one up. Despite the many underlying issues in the Deborah Green case, it is clear that investigators must have knowledge and resources to properly investigate this serious and violent criminal act to bring the perpetrators to justice.

The Police and Fire Alliance

After a fire has been determined to have a suspicious origin, investigators from the local fire and police departments, as well as the victim's insurance company, become involved with the case. Problems and confusion sometimes unfold if investigators from these agencies fail to understand differences in their roles. The traditional role of the fire department is to investigate every fire for cause and origin. Accordingly, 80 percent of the fire protection in the United States is provided by volunteer fire departments.[9] To this end, firefighters are usually trained in the suppression of fire rather than its investigation.

When a suspicious fire is discovered, however, it is generally while it is being extinguished. So what, then, is the role of the firefighter? As a rule, it is threefold: (1) to extinguish the fire, (2) to investigate the origin of the fire, and (3) to "detect" the possibility of arson but not to investigate arson. Few fire departments have the legal authority to investigate arson fires, although their assistance in such an investigation is not disputed.

When the fire investigation becomes a question of who committed the crime, the matter then becomes a law enforcement concern. This is critical because after it has been determined that law enforcement should take over the investigation, fire investigators should yield the crime scene to the arson investigators and respond to them in an adjunct role. Acceptance of this principle minimizes confusion and duplication of efforts at the crime scene.

The police investigator has a statutory role in investigating arson because it is a violation of state or federal law. The principal goal of the police investigation in an arson case is to identify the perpetrator(s) of the crime and to identify and secure sufficient evidence to prosecute and convict.

Finally, the role of the insurance investigator is to make a determination as to whether or not the insurance company owes payment for the fire loss. The insurance investigator is not a law enforcement officer. His or her authority to investigate is specified in the insured's contract. This contract refers to many of the provisions of the 1943 New York Standard Policy, which sets forth conditions subscribed to by the insured in the event of a loss.[10] In kind, most insurance companies state that coverage is void if the company's investigation proves arson or fraud.

Arson Investigative Techniques

The act of arson has been described as a stealthy, cowardly crime that, by its very nature, leaves very little direct evidence as to the identity of the arsonist. Many arsonists, however, fail to cover their tracks adequately and may therefore leave some type of evidence behind. For example, in many commercial arsons, the suspect leaves a **paper trail** that investigators can follow. This includes financial records, inflated insurance coverage, little or no inventory, and excessive debts. In an ideal situation, the arsonist will either be convicted, through the use of well-documented motives and opportunity, or might be willing to cooperate with authorities in identifying accomplices, motives, and prior victims.

The Preliminary Investigation of Arson

The preliminary investigation of arson begins basically like many other crimes, with a thorough examination of the crime scene. Arson does not have an immediate corpus delicti. It is, therefore, the responsibility of the investigator to prove that a specific fire did occur and that it was ignited deliberately. To accomplish this, both direct and circumstantial evidence can be used to show that the fire was ignited. Such evidence, however, may not reveal the opportunity or motive of the fire setter. As with most crimes, the motive is important, but the key responsibility of the arson investigator is to connect the suspect with the crime scene regardless of the motive.

IDENTIFY THE POINT OF ORIGIN The first step in an arson investigation is to determine the fire's **point of origin**. This may be the most critical phase of the investigation because it includes the ruling out of natural or accidental causes. The materials used in the setting of the fire, along with the type of material being burned, may show a distinct burn pattern. Hence, it is important to identify the point at which the fire originated because it is here that most of the physical evidence can be located indicating a fire of incendiary nature. The fire's point of origin may be determined in several ways. The questioning of witnesses could reveal the necessary information. In addition, an inspection of the ruins at the fire scene might reveal valuable evidence.

FINDING ACCELERANTS IN ARSON INVESTIGATIONS Arson investigators can prove that a fire was set intentionally by finding an accelerant at the scene of a fire. An accelerant is a chemical fuel that causes a fire to burn hotter, spread more quickly than usual, or be unusually difficult to extinguish. The presence of an accelerant in fire debris can be used as evidence of arson.[11]

The most commonly used accelerants are gasoline, kerosene, turpentine, and diesel fuel. These are all organic compounds containing mixtures of hydrocarbon molecules. As accelerants evaporate, the hydrocarbons more into the air above the fire debris, which is called the "headspace."[12]

Various techniques exist to detect accelerants at a fire scene. These range from an experienced fire investigator or a specially trained "sniffer" dog using its sense of smell to detect the characteristic odor of various accelerants in the surrounding air to more complex laboratory methods.

One of the most advanced techniques for detecting accelerants in fire debris is called *headspace gas chromatography*. Gas chromatography involves separating mixtures of gases into their individual components based on the different boiling points of their hydrocarbons. Each gas in the mixture can then be identified because each one produces a distinct chemical fingerprint called a *chromatogram*.[13]

In headspace gas chromatography, solid debris taken from the suspected point of origin of the fire is placed in an airtight vial to prevent any accelerants from evaporating. The vial is then heated, releasing the accelerant's hydrocarbons into the trapped headspace above the debris. A needle is inserted through the cap of the vial to remove a sample of the hydrocarbons and inject them into an instrument called a *gas chromatogram* for separation and analysis.[14]

If an accelerant is used to start a fire, a small amount will likely still be present in the charred debris. Identification of the accelerant can serve as physical evidence to support a charge of arson.

OBSERVE THE SPAN OF THE FIRE Determining the time **span of the fire** is also of paramount importance. Although the majority of evidence collection is conducted at the crime scene, much can be learned simply by observing the fire. Specifically, physical characteristics of the fire, such as smoke, direction, flames, and distance of travel, are important. Immediately after the fire is extinguished, samples of debris should be collected that might have been the material used for starting the fire. When the rubble is being cleaned up, investigators should be present to observe any additional evidence that might be uncovered.

Elements of Arson

A person knowingly damages a building or property of another by

☑ Starting a fire or explosion, or
☑ Procuring or causing such property to be burned

PHOTOGRAPH THE SCENE Complete photographs of the structure should be taken to help preserve the crime scene for the courtroom. This makes a "record" of the condition of the scene at the time the fire was extinguished. When taking photos, the investigator should focus on the location of rags, large amounts of paper, cans, or empty receptacles that might have been used in setting the fire.

IDENTIFY PLANTS OR TRAILERS Finally, identifying the areas of **plants** (preparations used to set the fire) and **trailers** (materials used to spread the fire) can reveal important clues to the investigator.

- *Plants.* Preparations used to set the fire. These include newspapers, rags, and other flammable waste material.
- *Trailers.* Materials used in spreading the fire. These include gunpowder; rags soaked in flammable liquid; and flammable liquids such as gasoline, kerosene, and alcohol.

Some arsonists prefer to use delayed timing devices to allow a time lag between the setting up of the arson and the fire's outbreak. To this end, mechanical devices and chemicals are commonly used. Such devices may well be intact when probing the crime scene for evidence.

QUESTION WITNESSES Witnesses also play an important role in determining causes of the fire and possible suspects. Questions to be asked of the witnesses include:

- Who are you and why were you present at the fire?
- What attracted your attention to the fire?

The witnesses' observations of the intensity, color, and direction of the fire may also prove to be of great value. Certainly, the observations of witnesses should only be viewed as information to give the investigator a lead as to where to begin looking for evidence. The actual point of origin, of course, must be determined by a thorough examination of the premises.

OBSERVE ALLIGATORING The term **alligatoring** refers to the pattern of crevices formed by the burning of a wooden structure. Resembling the skin of an alligator, this pattern reveals a minimum amount of charring, with alligatoring in large segments, when a fire is extinguished rapidly. As the fire continues to burn, the alligatoring will become smaller, with charring becoming deeper.

In a fire crime scene, liquids tend to flow downward and pool around fixed objects such as furniture. Their trails, however, are relatively easy to trace and provide the investigator with good evidence. An accelerant such as gasoline, kerosene, or alcohol can be traced from the point it was spilled to the lowest point of flow. At times, unburned amounts of these liquids may be found at low points, where the heat was not intense enough for ignition.

OTHER CLUES Many things may indicate that a fire of suspicious origin was arson. In one example, many fires were set at the scene, but evidence showed that each was set independently, with no proof of spontaneous combustion. Other clues include:

- *Flames.* The color of the flame is noteworthy in the early phases of a fire. For instance, a blue-orange flame represents burning alcohol. Certainly, if this material is not normally stored on the premises, one could assume that it was used as the accelerant in the fire. Information as to the description of the fire can be gained from witnesses who arrived on the scene before investigators.
- *Smoke.* As indicated earlier, smoke can also be of value in determining what substance was used to start a fire. If smoke can be observed at the beginning of a fire, before spreading to other parts of a structure, its color should be noted. For example, black smoke indicates that the material is made with a petroleum base. White smoke, conversely, indicates that vegetable matter is burning, such as straw or hay. If the structure is completely engulfed in flames, it will be difficult to make determinations as to what materials are being burned.
- *Size of the fire.* Depending on certain factors, such as the time element of the fire, the size of the fire might give investigators information to determine an act of arson. For example, structures that are engulfed in flames in a short period might indicate arson. Fire investigators recognize that fires of "natural" origin burn in a definable pattern. Therefore, fires burning quickly or in a direction that is not logical will indicate that an accelerant has been used. Factors to aid the investigator in determining the "normal" course or pattern for a fire should consider such variables as ventilation and contents of the structure.

- *Odors.* Distinguishable odors can be emitted from certain types of fires that might indicate a specific fire starter, such as kerosene, gasoline, and alcohol. These materials ensure that a fire will erupt, and arsonists expect any evidence of these accelerants to be destroyed in the fire. Investigators should, therefore, try to detect any odors by using their own **olfactory senses**.

Motivations of the Arsonist

As a defense attorney once said, "It is not a crime to have a motive." Indeed, when an investigator is successful in the collection of evidence to show the insured's participation in the crime, along with evidence of a motive showing arson as a reasonable alternative for the arsonist, a prosecutable case may have been developed. After it has been determined that the fire was of incendiary origin, possible motives must be examined to help identify the suspect. Motives for arson include profit, revenge, vandalism, crime concealment, and pyromania.

ARSON FOR PROFIT This category represents an estimated 50 percent of all fire-related property damage in the United States and the corresponding increase in the number of arsons reported to officials in recent years.[15] The typical arson-for-profit criminal is a businessperson who sets fire to his or her business or hires a professional arsonist to do the task. Traditionally, this category of arson has posed relatively low risk and high profit for the criminal and has virtually become a business in and of itself.

Economic gain from this type of arson may be either direct or indirect. For example, a home or business owner will see a direct financial gain when the insurance company pays the claim. In comparison, an employee in a warehouse who starts a fire and readily extinguishes it might benefit from a raise or promotion for his or her quick and "responsible" response and effort in saving the business. As indicated earlier, insurance fraud is a common motive for arson, perhaps one of the most frequent. A common method of insurance-related fraud is the purchasing of old, run-down buildings in inner-city areas. Over a period of several months, shrewd businesspersons then sell and resell the property. Each of these transactions raises the value of the property, at least on paper. The properties are then insured for the highest possible dollar amount. Sometimes the target of the arsonist is not the building itself but what it contains. A computer dealer, for example, might remove any valuable computers and software from his or her business and leave behind computers and software that are outdated or in which he or she has invested too much money. After the fire destroys the building, the arsonist simply claims the insurance coverage that covered the burned stock and realizes a "market" return on the stock.

Not all arson-for-profit crimes focus on businesses or are perpetuated by people in big business. Indeed, high car payments or excessive mechanical difficulties with an automobile may compel the ordinary citizen to commit automobile arson to collect on the insurance. This type of criminal activity has resulted in an estimated 1,500 automobile arsons each year.[16]

Arson for profit can take many forms, so in all circumstances, the conditions surrounding suspicious fires must be investigated thoroughly for possible motives. These motives should include the possibility that arson was used to cover up another crime, such as homicide or burglary.

Types of Evidence in Arson Cases

- ☑ *Evidence of incendiary origin.* The basic type of evidence in this category are physical evidence (e.g., laboratory analysis of fire debris), expert observation of burn patterns and fire characteristics, and negative corpus evidence (e.g., elimination of accidental causes).

- ☑ *Evidence of motive.* In fraud cases, evidence of motive may involve a complex analysis of financial and property records. Here, a distinction can be made between evidence of a general hostility (e.g., a previous argument) and specific hostility (e.g., threats to burn). In addition, the motive can be important in cases involving a pyromaniac and vandalism, which are frequently irrational acts.

- ☑ *Evidence linking a suspect to the commission of arson.* Direct linkage, such as eyewitness testimony or a confession, is clearly preferable to circumstantial linkage, which simply reflects opportunity.

ARSON FOR REVENGE A high percentage of arsons are attributed to revenge, jealousy, and spite. People committing such acts are usually adults who target both individuals and property. Offenders include jilted lovers in personal relationships, disgruntled employees, feuding neighbors, persons who were cheated in business and personal transactions, and persons motivated by racial prejudice. From an investigative standpoint, after revenge has been identified as a possible motive in a fire, the list of suspects can be narrowed greatly. From here, care should be exercised in interview and interrogation techniques to extract sufficient and pertinent information.

ARSON FOR VANDALISM Not much planning or preparation is required for a fire designated as vandalism. In addition, readily available materials are commonly used by arsonists. As discussed later, about 95 percent of the arsons for vandalism are caused by juveniles, owing in large part to peer pressure. Statistics show that most violators in this category are youths from lower socioeconomic groups who choose to commit the crime in the morning or early afternoon.

Motives in this category differ from case to case but include vandalism and revenge. Typically, however, the motive is profit. Indeed, people who have been unable to contract a professional arsonist have been known to hire juveniles to commit such acts. Certainly, a juvenile fire starter will work for much less than a professional "torch."

Children of many ages have experimented with fire out of curiosity. Some, according to theorists, are abused children and set fires as a call for help. Juvenile fire-setter programs have sprung up across the country to identify these problem children and to deal with their underlying problems.

ARSON FOR CRIME CONCEALMENT It is common for some criminals to try to cover up their crimes through the use of a fire. Murders, burglaries, and other crimes have been concealed through the use of this method. Fire investigators must consider this as an alternative motive for all fires.

PYROMANIA A pyromaniac is a person who is a compulsive fire starter. This person is motivated by several aspects of the fire-setting experience. For example, some experts claim that pyromaniacs gain sexual stimulation by starting and viewing fires. In addition, excitation is achieved by the crowds that gather and the emergency vehicles that converge on the scene. Pyromaniacs are impulsive fire setters; their acts are seldom planned. Investigators can only examine the routes or paths that the fires seem to establish. Investigations have revealed that pyromaniacs may have a sordid past, which includes being abused as a child, bedwetting, and cruelty to animals.

Serial Fire Setters

Serial criminals of any type pose great concerns for communities and law enforcement officials alike. A serial arsonist can be defined as one who sets fires repeatedly. This criminal, however, is at somewhat of an advantage because expertise in fire investigations is not as common as in other crimes. The FBI's National Center for the Analysis of Violent Crime (NCAVC) has conducted

Evidence of Planning or Pre-knowledge

- ☑ Removing items of value from the crime scene before a fire.
- ☑ Before the fire, making off-the-cuff remarks or jokes about burning the structure.
- ☑ Increasing insurance coverage or obtaining coverage for the first time before the fire.
- ☑ Making unusual changes in business practices just before the fire (e.g., closing earlier or later, having different people lock up).
- ☑ Taking obvious actions designed to avoid suspicion, such as booking for banquets that the insured has no intention of carrying out, filing for bankruptcy, and so on.

Firedogs That Sniff out Arsonists

In 2012, a fire-tracking dog named "Blaze," who is owned by the Alabama Forestry Commission's arson investigation team, gained notoriety for his ability to lead investigators right to the front door of arsonists. In 2011, Blaze helped track an arson suspect in connection with a series of woods fires in Baldwin County, Alabama. Once Blaze picked up on the scent, he led investigators to a subdivision where he passed several doors before he jumped on the front door of the suspect. The suspect was arrested and other witnesses soon came forward.

Statistics show that most woods arsonists live within a few miles of where they set fires and usually walk into the area where they set the fire. Once the dog picks up on the trail, it usually leads investigators to the home of the fire starter. This is because people often leave evidence of a crime behind and human scent is just as unique as a fingerprint.

The State of Alabama is one of only a few states that have adopted firedogs as part of their arson investigation teams. Private foundations and businesses such as State Farm Insurance usually fund such dogs. Since 1993, State Farm Insurance has sponsored a program that trains 10 dogs each year—exclusively Labradors. Dogs are trained twice a year for four weeks.

Other states such as West Virginia and Virginia were the first states to use firedogs, starting in the mid-1990s. Virginia uses two bloodhounds, Lacy and Summer. Lacy has been responsible for over 30 convictions over a period of seven years and Summer has 12 convictions to her credit.

Because arson cases are so difficult to prosecute, if a prosecutor has physical or forensic evidence in an arson case, their chances of being successful in court are greatly enhanced.

Sources: *Fire and Arson Scene Evidence: A Guide for Public Safety Personnel.* (June 2000). *Research report.* U.S. Department of Justice Technical Working Group on Fire and Arson; Rodney, M. (2012). Dogs showing they can help sniff out arsonists. *USA Today.* April 5, p. 3A.

research in this area and has concluded that compulsive fire setting can be classified as mass, spree, and serial.

- A *mass arsonist* sets three or more fires at the same location.
- A *spree arsonist* sets fires at three or more separate locations, with no cooling-off period between them.
- The *serial arsonist* sets three or more separate fires with a definite cooling-off period between them. This period may last for days, weeks, or months.

Profiling the Fire Starter

After identifying a possible motive, the investigator may wonder to what extent the fire starter shows a propensity for violence. Surprisingly, David Berkowitz, the "Son of Sam" mass murderer who terrorized New York in 1976 by killing five people and wounding seven others, reported to the police that he was personally responsible for setting more than 2,000 fires from 1974 to 1977.[17] Police reports also showed that Berkowitz set these fires in cars, dumpsters, brush, and vacant and unoccupied stores. In addition, police seized notepads bearing handprinted notes by Berkowitz that gave details on 1,411 fires for the years of 1974, 1975, and 1977, including the dates and times of the fires, the streets, the type of weather, and the fire department code, indicating the type of responding apparatus and property burned. The following questions are therefore raised:

- Does Berkowitz typify the fire starter?
- Are arsonists homicidal?
- Do they keep meticulous diaries of their fires?

According to James in his article "Psychological Motives for Arson," gender, age, education, intellectual level, and economic status do not in any way limit the possibility that a person will engage in arson.[18] On the other hand, from a study of large samples, it does appear that, statistically, persons of certain ages and with certain characteristics are more apt to set fires than are others.

The Role of the Insurance Industry

Because of the severe financial strain arson has placed on the insurance industry, insurance companies are becoming more involved with investigations involving arson. Insurance carriers are usually more than willing to assist local law enforcement and fire officials during the course of an investigation. In fact, independent information offered by an insurance company might prove to be highly valuable in discovering motives and suspects for a crime. Indeed, the crime of arson is one that permits the investigator to work hand in hand with the "victim." In addition, many insurance carriers might even offer financial assistance to fire investigators. This may come in the form of providing heavy machinery for aid in processing the crime scene or by bringing in experts in arson investigations to aid local investigators in the investigation.

Insurance company assistance may come in many other forms, such as providing local investigators with financial audits and income tax returns; such information may not be readily available to local investigators. To protect insurance companies from civil recourse in disclosing some of the information discussed previously, many states have passed laws granting limited civil immunity to insurance companies that assist local arson investigators during the course of an ongoing investigation. This contributes to an increased flow of information from insurance companies to local investigators, which increases the chance of an eventual prosecution of the arsonist and subsequent relief from civil claims liability for the insurance company.

Problems in Arson Investigation

- ☑ Locating witnesses
- ☑ Locating and preserving physical evidence
- ☑ Determining whether the victim is also the suspect
- ☑ Coordinating the investigation among police, fire, and insurance agents
- ☑ Determining if the fire was arson or had some other cause

Characteristics of the Fire Setter[19]

- ☑ *Age.* Typically around age 17 years
- ☑ *Gender.* Usually male
- ☑ *Race.* Predominantly white
- ☑ *Intelligence.* Research indicates that fire setters are often mentally deficient
- ☑ *Academic performance.* Most have a history of poor academic performance
- ☑ *Rearing environment.* Most appear to come from unstable home environments within lower socioeconomic groups
- ☑ *Social relationships.* Typically experience difficulties in relationships
- ☑ *Sexual disturbance.* Usually associated with sexual perversion; fire setting tends to serve as a sexual substitute
- ☑ *Motive.* Revenge most typically the underlying motive

|Fig. 15.2| △

An arson investigator
examining the scene
to determine the ori-
gin of the fire.

James Shaffer / PhotoEdit Inc.

Prosecution of Arson Cases

There is an old adage, "Without the **fire triangle**—heat, fuel, and oxygen—there can be no fire."
Similarly, the successful prosecution of an arson case must include a triangle consisting of police
detectives, fire investigators, and a prosecutor. Sadly, in many parts of the United States, prosecution of arson crimes may never occur. Some reasons include:

1. There is no one qualified or trained to conduct the investigation.
2. The time required for a thorough arson investigation by police or fire authorities is not
   available.
3. Prosecuting attorneys are reluctant to file and pursue prosecution. This is the most prevalent
   reason because arson cases are difficult to prosecute.

Prosecution of an arson case is time consuming and requires expertise. Courts have ruled that
circumstantial evidence, the most common type of evidence in an arson case, has the same probative value as direct evidence, but it is up to the prosecution to weave the web of circumstantiality.[20]
Many prosecutors find this an intimidating and unrewarding task.

A good arson investigator begins with the notion that he or she must collect sufficient circumstantial evidence to convince a jury that the suspect committed the crime. Statistics reveal that
most successful arson prosecutors rely on circumstantial evidence.

Proving the arson case "beyond a reasonable doubt" through the use of circumstantial evidence
is difficult but not impossible. Prosecutors are frequently reluctant to proceed with charges in an
arson case because evidence is fragmented and circumstantial. A trained investigator, however,
knows what evidence to look for and is aware of the amount of evidence sufficient to remove reasonable doubt from the minds of prospective jurors.

Bombing Incidents

Even though this section addresses bomb investigations, a brief opening discussion about terrorism is prudent because a number of terrorist organizations in the twenty-first century have used
bombs in various forms. The World Trade Center and Pentagon terrorist attacks of September 11,
2001, marked a dramatic escalation in a trend toward more destructive terrorist attacks that began
in the 1980s. Until the September 11 attack, the October 23, 1983, truck bombings of U.S. and
French military barracks in Beirut, Lebanon, which claimed a total of 295 lives, stood as the most

Evidence for Arson Prosecution

☑ *Evidence of participation.* This might be the disabling of a fire alarm or rearranging combustibles at a fire's location.

☑ *Exclusive access.* If firefighters are required to use force to gain entrance into a structure, the arsonist would have difficulty doing the same to set the fire. This indicates the complicity of the business owner in locking up the structure.

☑ *Motive.* Establishment of a motive is one critical element in showing jurors a suspect's criminal intent.

☑ *False statements.* A convincing element in an arson prosecution is the "victim's" false statements to the investigators.

deadly act of terrorism. The attacks of September 11 produced casualty figures more than 10 times higher than those of the 1983 barracks attacks.

The September 11 attack also reflected a trend toward more indiscriminate targeting among international terrorists. The vast majority of the more than 3,000 victims of the attack were civilians. In addition, the attack represented the first known case of suicide attacks carried out by international terrorists in the United States. The September 11 attack also marked the first successful act of international terrorism in the United States since the vehicle bombing of the World Trade Center in February 1993.

Today, the most serious international terrorist threat to U.S. interests stems from Sunni Islamic extremists, such as Osama bin Laden and individuals affiliated with his Al-Qaeda organization. Al-Qaeda leaders, including Osama bin Laden, were harbored in Afghanistan since 1996 by the extremist Islamic regime of the Taliban. Despite recent military setbacks suffered by the Taliban and the death of Al-Qaeda leader Osama bin Laden in May 2011, Al-Qaeda is still considered a capable terrorist network. The network's willingness and capability to inflict large-scale violence and destruction against U.S. persons and interests—as it demonstrated with the September 11 attack, the bombing of the U.S.S. *Cole* in October 2000, and the bombings of two U.S. embassies in east Africa in August 1998, among other plots—make it a clear and imminent threat to the United States and pose a number of unique challenges for criminal investigators.

Individuals who have been investigated for possible terrorist links include Richard Reid and Zacarias Moussaoui. Let's now consider investigative leads as well as evidence developed against these terrorist suspects to illustrate.

On December 22, 2001, Richard C. Reid was arrested after a flight attendant on American Airlines Flight 63 observed him attempting apparently to ignite an improvised explosive in his sneakers while on board a Paris–Miami flight. Aided by passengers, attendants overpowered and subdued Reid, and the flight was diverted to Logan International Airport in Boston. Evidence strongly suggests that Reid, who was traveling on a valid British passport, was affiliated with the Al-Qaeda network. Reid was indicted on nine counts, including placing an explosive device on an aircraft and attempted murder. The FBI investigation has determined that the explosives in Reid's shoes, if detonated in certain areas of the passenger cabin, could have blown a hole in the fuselage of the aircraft.

Investigators also learned that Reid and another subject, Zacarias Moussaoui, were known associates. Moussaoui came to the attention of the FBI while taking flight-training classes in Minnesota in August 2001. Moussaoui paid more than $8,000 in cash for flight simulator lessons on a 747-400, which far exceeded his training level as a pilot. Moussaoui showed unusual interest in the instructor's comment that airplane cabin doors could not be opened during flight. In addition, his flight instructor was concerned that Moussaoui expressed interest only in learning how to take off and not how to land the 747-400. In preparation for high-fidelity simulator training, he expressed strong interest in "piloting" a simulated flight from London's Heathrow Airport to John F. Kennedy Airport in New York. When the instructor took his concerns to the FBI, Moussaoui was interviewed by Special Agents from the FBI and the U.S. Immigration and Naturalization Service (INS). He was determined to be an INS overstay and was detained by the INS on August 16, 2001.

ASSOCIATED PRESS

After his detention, Moussaoui refused to allow a search to be conducted of his possessions, including a laptop computer and a computer disc. Attempts were made to obtain authority to conduct a search of this computer. However, because of the lack of probable cause and lack of predication, neither a criminal nor intelligence search could be conducted. After the September 11 attack, a criminal search of the computer was conducted. Nothing was located that connected Moussaoui with the events of September 11; however, information about crop dusting was located on the computer. As a result, crop-dusting operations in the United States were grounded briefly on two occasions in September 2001. On December 11, 2001, the U.S. District Court for the Eastern District of Virginia indicted Moussaoui on six counts of conspiracy for his role in the events of September 11, 2001.

What Is a Bomb?

Bombs can be constructed to look like almost anything and can be placed or delivered in any number of ways. Bombs are often made out of common household items regularly found in the kitchen, garage, or under the sink. The easiest bomb to construct is the pipe bomb, which is often packed with screws and nails that act as projectiles, similar to a hand grenade. These are materials that the bomber relies on, partly to help conceal his or her identity. Because they are usually homemade,

---

A Closer Look

Arson and Trace Evidence

In California in early 1989, a pipe bomb that had been placed on a vehicle exploded, killing the driver. An investigation by the ATF; the

Rialto, California, Police Department; and the San Bernardino Sheriff's Department ensued. Evidence recovered at the scene was forwarded to the ATF laboratory for examination. Intact powder particles found at the end caps of the bomb enabled chemists to identify the type and brand of powder used. A subsequent search of the suspect's residence uncovered a can of smokeless powder identical to the powder identified. Additional evidence recovered during the search linked the suspect to the bombing, for which he was arrested and tried on state murder charges.

Sources: Harnett, D. M. (April 1990). Bombing and arson investigations enhanced by advances in ATF labs. *Police Chief*, pp. 20, 24, 26, 28; James, J. (March 1965). Psychological motives for arson. *Popular Government*.

these bombs are limited in their design only by the imagination of the bomber. So when searching for a bomb, the investigator should simply look for anything that appears unusual.

Statistics show that the use of bombs by drug traffickers is becoming more common. In 1990, the ATF reported an increase of 1,000 percent between 1987 and 1989. These included 126 bombings across the country.

In addition to drug traffickers, in 1990, the ATF showed an increase in mail bombs. The mail bomber attempts to gain from violence and intimidation what he or she fails to attain peacefully. Such devices are typically sent by "hate" or special-interest groups representing a particular lifestyle or belief or protesting certain laws. During 1990, for example, mail bombs killed a federal judge and a city alderman.

Bombings by Teens

A disturbing trend across the nation is the growing number of teenagers who have been linked with bombing incidents. Many techniques of how to construct a bomb cheaply have been learned through the Internet. Experts theorize that well-publicized bombing incidents such as the Oklahoma City bombing and the Unabomber saga have stimulated interest among teenagers in bomb making.[21] It is unclear whether teen bombers are really interested in hurting anyone or are just intrigued by their ability to manufacture a bomb. How-to information is also readily available in bomb-making manuals such as the *Anarchist's Cookbook* and the *Poor Man's James Bond*. These manuals have also been found online.

The Internet has given teens a way to communicate with like-minded youths who may also be curious about bomb building. In 1996, a Montgomery County, Maryland, neighbor who suspected that illegal drugs were being shipped to teenagers at a vacant house tipped off the police, who found bomb-making ingredients and plans for making a bomb. In a better-known case, Harvey "Buddy" Waldron, a Washington State football player, was killed in an explosion in Pullman, Washington, in 1993 when he and a teammate assembled an 8-inch pipe bomb, wired to a clock, that they had planned to detonate in a wheat field. To combat the spread of bombings, in 1996, the state of Georgia enacted the first comprehensive antibomb law, which includes penalties for both teens and adults.

Investigating Bomb Threats

Bomb threats are delivered in a variety of ways, but most are telephoned in to the target. Occasionally, these calls are through a third party. Sometimes a threat is communicated through writing and recording. There are two general explanations as to why bombers communicate a bomb threat:

1. The caller has definite knowledge or believes that an explosive or incendiary bomb has been or will be placed, and he or she wants to minimize personal injury or property damage. The caller may be the person who placed the device or someone who has become aware of such information.
2. The caller wants to create an atmosphere of anxiety and panic that will, in turn, result in a disruption of normal activities at the facility where the device is supposedly placed.

Whatever the reason, there will certainly be a reaction to it. Through proper planning, however, the wide variety of uncontrollable reactions can be minimized. The bomb threat caller is the best source of information about a bomb. When a bomb threat is called in, the following steps should be implemented:

- Keep the caller on the line as long as possible.
- Ask him or her to repeat the message and record every word spoken by the person.
- Ask the caller the location of the bomb and the time of detonation of the device.
- Inform the caller that the building is occupied and the detonation of a bomb could kill or injure innocent people.
- Pay particular attention to background noise such as motors running, music playing, or any other noise that may give a clue as to the location of the caller.
- Listen closely to the voice (male or female), voice quality (calm or excited), accents, and speech impediments.
- Interview the person who received the call for the preceding information.

WRITTEN BOMB THREATS When a written threat is received, all materials should be saved, including envelopes and containers. Remember that paper is an excellent preservative of latent fingerprints. In addition, handwriting, typewriting, and postal markings can provide good investigative leads. Therefore, after the message has been recognized as a bomb threat, further handling of the material should be minimized, and it should be stored in a safe place.

BOOBY TRAPS The use of bombs and **booby traps** has also become of particular concern to drug enforcement officials over the years. Many drug manufacturers have learned the skills of protecting their marijuana plots or chemical laboratories with such devices. The booby trap provides low-cost protection to the illegal drug operation and is designed to serve any of the following three purposes:

1. To warn the suspect of any intruders by the sound of explosive devices
2. To deny any intruder or police access to the inhabited area by injuring or killing them
3. To slow down police pursuit in a raid situation by injuring or killing officers

If explosives are located, officers should never attempt to dismantle or defuse them unless they have received technical training in bomb disposal. Instead, they should be sufficiently trained to identify such devices so that they can be avoided and properly trained personnel can be notified.

Explosive booby traps are activated by numerous methods, including remote control, manual control, or activation by the victim (usually, a trip wire or hidden pressure plates installed in the ground). Booby traps can be placed either outside or inside the suspect's residence, and their design is limited only by the imagination of the criminal. For example, one exterior trap is called the *mouse trap* because it literally uses a mouse trap that is used as a firing pin for a shotgun shell that is also attached to the trap. The trap can be affixed to trees or fence posts and can either maim or

|Fig. 15.3| △

Rescue personnel convergeon the scene of the 1995 bombing of the Murrah Federal Building.

Pat Sullivan / AP Wide World Photos

kill the intruder. An example of an indoor trap is the magazine bomb. This device consists of a magazine that has had a portion of the inner pages removed to conceal a hidden mouse trap. When the magazine is opened, the trap detonates a blasting cap.

SAFETY PRECAUTIONS In raid or search situations in which explosive devices are expected to be encountered, investigators should be accompanied by an explosives expert. This person can be used to inform officers of what type of device is at hand and how best to proceed safely with the raid. Other precautions include the following:

- Only one officer at a time should approach the suspected booby trap.
- When trip wires are located, both ends of the wire should be checked (some devices use more than one trip wire).
- Wires that appear to be electric should not be cut.
- Be aware of fuses or obvious means of detonation (e.g., mercury fuses).
- No containers should be opened without a thorough examination.

No single strategy exists to adequately safeguard officers from all hazards posed by booby traps and explosives. Each case is different and should be evaluated individually, with consideration given to the number of possible suspects (and their backgrounds) and the location of the raid. In any case, keen observation and prudent judgment are still the best investigative precautions.

Bomb Search Techniques

The following room search technique is based on the use of a two-person searching team. There are many minor variations possible in searching a room. The following contains only the basic techniques. When the two-person search team enters the room to be searched, they should first move to various parts of the room and stand quietly with their eyes closed and listen for a clockwork device. Frequently, a clockwork mechanism can be quickly detected without use of special equipment. Even if no clockwork mechanism is detected, the team is now aware of the background noise level within the room itself.

Background noise or transferred sound is always disturbing during a building search. If a ticking sound is heard but cannot be located, one might become unnerved. However, the ticking sound may come from an unbalanced air conditioner fan several floors away or from a dripping sink down the hall.

Sound transfers through air-conditioning ducts, along water pipes, and through walls. One of the most difficult buildings to search is one that has steam or hot water heat. This type of building constantly thumps, cracks, chatters, and ticks because of the movement of the steam or hot water through the pipes and the expansion and contraction of the pipes. Background noise may also include outside traffic sounds, rain, and wind.

The lead investigator of the room-searching team should look around the room and determine how the room is to be divided for searching and to what height the first searching sweep should extend. The first searching sweep should cover all items resting on the floor up to the selected height.

The room should be divided into two virtually equal parts. This equal division should be based on the number and type of objects in the room to be searched and not on the size of the room. An imaginary line is then drawn between two objects in the room (e.g., the edge of the window on the north wall and the floor lamp on the south wall).

Case in Point

>>Understanding Fire Behavior

In one ATF (Alcohol, Tobacco, and Firearms) case, two eyewitnesses saw the two owners exiting the building while splashing liquid. One of the witnesses mentioned this to one of the firefighters during the fire, who suggested that she tell her story to one of the detectives. As sometimes happens, the witness chose not to bother and left the scene. Fortunately, when the detectives went to reinterview the witnesses in the case, both of them were able to remember that they saw two men setting the fire. Therefore, it pays to reinterview witnesses.

Sources: Moenssens A. A., J. E. Starrs, C. E. Henderson, and F. E Inbau. (1995). *Scientific evidence in civil and criminal cases.* Westbury, NY: The Foundation Press, pp.16–417.

FIRST ROOM-SEARCHING SWEEP Look at the furniture or objects in the room and determine the average height of the majority of items resting on the floor. In an average room, this height usually includes table or desktops and chair backs. The first searching height usually covers the items in the room up to hip height.

After the room has been divided and a searching height has been selected, both people should go to one end of the room division line and start from a back-to-back position. This is the starting point, and the same point will be used on each successive searching sweep. Each person now starts searching his or her way around the room, working toward the other person, checking all items resting on the floor around the wall area of the room.

When the two people meet, they will have completed a wall sweep. They should then work together and check all items in the middle of the room up to the selected hip height, including the floor under the rugs. This first searching sweep should also include items that may be mounted on or in the walls, such as air-conditioning ducts, baseboard heaters, and built-in wall cupboards, if these fixtures are below hip height. The first searching sweep usually consumes the most time and effort. During all the searching sweeps, an electronic or medical stethoscope is used on walls, furniture items, and floors.

SECOND ROOM-SEARCHING SWEEP The lead investigator again looks at the furniture or objects in the room and determines the height of the second searching sweep. This height is usually from the hip to the chin or the top of the head. The two persons return to the starting point and

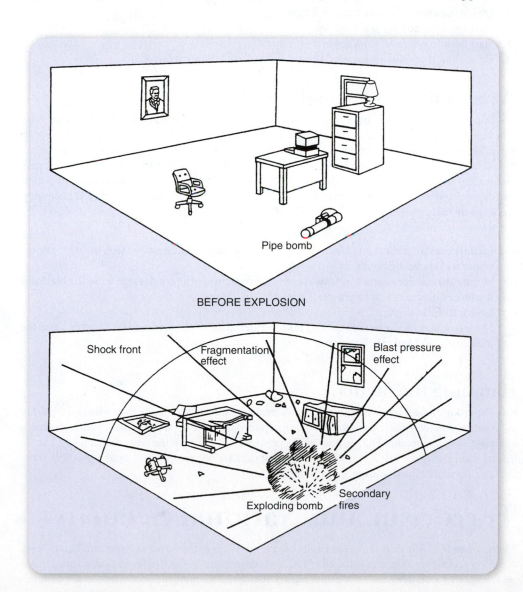

BEFORE EXPLOSION

Shock front | Fragmentation effect | Blast pressure effect

Exploding bomb | Secondary fires

|Fig. 15.4| ▲

Graphic representation of fragmentation, blast pressure, and secondary forces produced by an explosion.

repeat the searching technique at the second selected searching height. This sweep usually covers pictures hanging on the walls, built-in bookcases, and tall table lamps.

THIRD ROOM-SEARCHING SWEEP When the second searching sweep is completed, the lead investigator again determines the next searching height, usually from the chin or the top of the head up to the ceiling. The third sweep is then made. This sweep usually covers high-mounted air-conditioning ducts and hanging light fixtures.

FOURTH ROOM-SEARCHING SWEEP If the room has a false or suspended ceiling, the fourth sweep involves investigation of this area. Flush or ceiling-mounted light fixtures, air-conditioning or ventilation ducts, sound or speaker systems, electrical wiring, and structural frame members should all be checked. Have a sign or marker indicating "Search Completed" posted conspicuously in the area. Place a piece of colored cellophane tape across the door and doorjamb approximately two feet above floor level if the use of signs is not practical.

The room-searching technique can be expanded. The same basic technique can be applied to search any enclosed area. Encourage the use of common sense or logic in searching. For example, if a guest speaker at a convention has been threatened, common sense would indicate searching the speaker's platform and microphones first, but always return to the searching technique. Do not rely on random or spot checking of only logical target areas because the bomber may not be a logical person.

In conclusion, the following steps should be taken when searching a room:

1. Divide the area and select a search height.
2. Start from the bottom and work up.
3. Start back to back and work toward each other.
4. Go around the walls and proceed toward the center of the room.

When a Bomb Is Found

It is important to stress that personnel involved in a search be instructed that their only mission is to search for and report suspicious objects. Under no circumstances should officers attempt to move, jar, or touch a suspicious object or anything attached to it. The actual removal of the bomb should be left to professional bomb disposal personnel. After the suspected bomb has been located, the location and description of the object should be reported to the supervisor or command center. Fire department and rescue personnel should also be notified and placed on standby. If necessary, sandbags or mattresses (never metal shields) should be placed around the suspicious object. Do not attempt to cover the object. Instead, you should:

- Identify the danger area and block it off with a "clear zone" of at least 300 feet, including floors below and above the object.
- Be sure that all doors and windows are open to minimize primary damage from the blast and secondary damage from fragmentation.
- Evacuate the building.
- Not permit reentry into the building until the device has been removed or disarmed and the building is declared safe for reentry.

Handling the Media

It is important that all inquiries from the news media be directed to one person who is designated as spokesperson. All other persons should be instructed not to discuss the situation with outsiders, especially the news media. The purpose of this provision is to furnish the news media with accurate information and to see that additional bomb threat calls are not precipitated by irresponsible statements from uninformed sources.

Terrorism and National Security

Never before in U.S. history have Americans been more aware of the threat of terrorism. Today, it is a common occurrence to hear of yet another incident occurring in the United States that is linked in one way or another with terrorism. The Times Square attempted bombing incident is one such example.

On May 1, 2010, a dark blue 1993 Nissan Pathfinder sport utility vehicle with dark tinted windows entered Times Square, New York, at approximately 6:28 P.M. It parked on a tourist-crowded block at the eastern corner of 1 Astor Plaza, near the entrance to the Minskoff Theatre. About two minutes later, a T-shirt vendor noticed smoke drifting from the vehicle, which was parked, with its emergency flashers on. The vendor alerted a nearby NYPD police officer, who then approached the vehicle to investigate and observed smoke coming from vents near the backseat, unidentified canisters, and the smell of gunpowder. The officer immediately called for backup, a bomb disposal team, and the New York City Fire Department.

An area stretching from 43rd Street to 49th Street on Seventh Avenue and 45th Street from Seventh Avenue to Eighth Avenue was quickly evacuated of all vehicles and foot traffic, and the area was barricaded. Several buildings near the vehicle, including the New York Marriott Marquis hotel, in front of which the Pathfinder was parked, were also evacuated. The vehicle was set ablaze, but did not detonate.

Upon arrival, the bomb disposal team used a remote-controlled robotic device to break out a window of the vehicle and explore its contents. Inside, they found in the rear of the vehicle two alarm clocks with batteries that apparently were fashioned as triggering devices, connected by electrical wires to two full five-gallon cans of gasoline, sandwiching 40+ consumer-grade M-88 firecrackers inside a 20-ounce metal container (wrapped in duct tape, with its end removed), gunpowder, three 20-gallon propane tanks, and a green metal gun locker "pressure cooker" holding eight bags with approximately 250 pounds (113 kg) of urea-based fertilizer and 120 M-88s. A bomb disposal expert with information on the contents indicated that the design of the device was more consistent with that of an incendiary device than that of a traditional bomb. The improvised explosive device's ignition source failed to set it off as intended.

On May 3, 2010, federal agents arrested Faisal Shahzad, a 30-year-old Pakistani-born resident of Bridgeport, Connecticut, who had become a U.S. citizen in April 2009. He had boarded Emirates Flight 202 to Dubai at John F. Kennedy International Airport, but was arrested before the plane taxied from the gate. He admitted his role in the attempted bombing and said that he had trained at a Pakistani terrorist training camp.

According to the *New York Times*, Shahzad implicated himself and gave information to authorities after his arrest. Seven or eight people were arrested by Pakistani officials in connection with the plot.

The Times Square bombing attempt is another of many such attempts by would-be terrorists on American soil. As of the preparation of this text, it is not yet known to what extent Shahzad's attempt was at the behest of any specific larger criminal organization.

Most acts of terrorism have three basic elements: the perpetrator, the victim, and the audience affected (or the target). Although the perpetrator often is difficult to identify, the victim of the attack is usually the most noticeable. The issue of terrorism is clouded because it is commonly viewed as a form of low-intensity, unconventional aggression on the lower end of the warfare spectrum. In this unrealistic view, terrorism is an act of war rather than a criminal activity, which gives it a purpose and some sense of dignity. However, most people recognize that embassy bombings, political hostage taking, and aircraft hijackings are criminal terrorist acts. Accordingly, they understand that such acts are designed to shock and stun and are outside the warfare conventions.

Terrorism Defined

Whether domestic or international, terrorism is pervasive throughout the world and remains one of the most complex and difficult issues facing law enforcement in the twenty-first century. There is no single, universally accepted definition of the word *terrorism*. It is defined in a number of ways by a number of organizations. Simply stated, terrorism is policy intended to intimidate or cause terror.[22] The Federal Foreign Relations Authorization Act defines *terrorism* in terms of four primary elements. The act says that terrorism is:

1. Premeditated
2. Politically motivated
3. Violent
4. Committed against noncombatant targets.[23]

Some definitions also include acts of unlawful violence or unconventional warfare, but at present, there is no internationally agreed-upon definition of terrorism.[24] A person who practices terrorism is generally referred to as a *terrorist*. Acts of terrorism are criminal acts, according to UN Security Council Resolution 1373 and the domestic jurisprudence of almost all nations.

Regardless of the origin of its definition, the word *terrorism* is politically and emotionally charged,[25] and this greatly compounds the difficulty of providing a precise definition. A 1988 study by the U.S. Army found that more than 100 definitions of the word *terrorism* have been used.[26] The concept of terrorism is itself controversial because it is often used by states to delegitimize political or foreign opponents and potentially legitimize the state's own use of terror against them.

The history of terrorist organizations suggests that they do not practice terrorism only for its political effectiveness; individual terrorists are also motivated by a desire for social solidarity with other members.[27]

Terrorism has been practiced by a broad array of political organizations for furthering their objectives. It has been practiced by right- and left-wing political parties, nationalistic groups, religious groups, revolutionaries, and ruling governments.[28]

Acts of terrorism can be carried out by individuals, groups, or states. According to some definitions, clandestine or semi-clandestine state actors may also carry out terrorist acts outside the framework of a state of war. However, the most common image of terrorism is that it is carried out by small and secretive cells that are highly motivated to serve a particular cause, and many of the most deadly operations in recent times, such as the September 11 attacks, the London underground bombing, and the 2002 Bali bombing, were planned and carried out by close cliques composed of friends, family members, and other strong social networks.

These groups benefited from the free flow of information and efficient telecommunications to succeed where others had failed.[29] Over the years, many people have attempted to come up with a terrorist profile to attempt to explain these individuals' actions through their psychology and social circumstances. Others, such as Roderick Hindery, have sought to discern profiles in the propaganda tactics used by terrorists. Some security organizations designate these groups as violent nonstate actors.[30]

Recent research and investigations into terrorist operations have shown that terrorists look, dress, and behave like "normal" people until they execute the assigned mission. Therefore, terrorist profiling based on personality or physical or sociological traits does not appear to be particularly useful. The physical and behavioral description of a terrorist could describe almost any average person.[31]

The Federal Code of Regulations defines terrorism as "the unlawful use of force and violence against persons or property to intimidate or coerce a government, the civilian population, or any segment thereof, in furtherance of social or political objectives" (28 CFR, Section 0.85). In comparison, the Federal Bureau of Investigation website FBI.gov (2010) offers a more compartmentalized definition addressing both domestic and international terrorism:

> Domestic terrorism: the unlawful use, or threatened use of force by a group or individual, based and operating entirely within the United States without foreign direction, committed against persons or property to intimidate or coerce a government, the civilian population, or any segment thereof, in furtherance of social or political objectives.
>
> International terrorism: violent acts or acts that are a danger to human life that are a violation of the criminal law of the United States or any state or that would be a criminal violation if committed within the jurisdiction of the United States or any state. These acts appear to be intended to intimidate or coerce a civilian population, influence the policy of a government by intimidation or coercion, or affect the conduct of government by assassination or kidnapping. International terrorist acts occur outside the United States or transcend national boundaries in terms of the means by which they are to be accomplished, the persons they appear intended to coerce or intimidate or the locale in which the perpetrators operate or seek asylum.

The literature of terrorism has been closely associated with the word *guerilla*, which can be defined as "little war" (Friedlander 1982). Georges-Abeyie (1983) distinguishes the two by suggesting that terrorist groups have a more urban focus, usually attack innocent civilians and property, and operate in small groups or bands of three to five persons.

Identifying the Terrorists

The political and social circumstances that lead to the creation of terrorist groups vary widely around the world. Persons who carry out such acts vary in age, race, and cultural background. In 1986, the President's Task Force on Combating Terrorism (PTFCT) reported that an estimated 60 percent of the Third World population are under 20 years of age and half are 15 years or younger. This being the case, a volatile mixture of youthful aspirations coupled with economic and political frustrations tends to create a pool of possible terrorists in those countries. Today's terrorists have a deep-seated belief in the justice of their causes. They are tough and cunning and have little regard for their lives or the lives of others. Terrorists' weaponry often comes from the illegal international arms market and could originate with legitimate arms vendors, which are, to a great extent, unregulated. Through their expansive organizational structure, many terrorists have the ability to acquire timely information on potential targets and the security precautions for these targets. If governmental pressures become more effective against them, terrorists will simply focus on easier targets.

Terrorists can be a part of a large organization or can act with only a few persons who share similar beliefs. Examples of large terrorist organizations are the Palestine Liberation Front (PLF), which has an estimated 300 members operating among three factions. The Abu Nidal Organization (ANO) boasts a membership of 500 and has an international theater of operation. Many terrorist organizations have memberships in the thousands. In his book *Terrorism and Homeland Security*, Jonathan White points out that most terrorist groups have a membership of fewer than 50 people; under a command element, which usually consists of a few people, the group is divided according to specific tasks.[32] For example, intelligence sections are responsible for accessing targets, support sections provide the means to carry out the assault, and tactical sections actually carry out the terrorist act. Organizationally and operationally, these groups are structured much like other organized crime groups.

Criteria Describing Terrorists

Official definitions determine counterterrorism policy and are often developed to serve it. Most government definitions outline the following key criteria to describe terrorism: target, objective, motive, perpetrator, and legitimacy or legality of the act. Terrorism variables typically include the following:

VIOLENCE According to Walter Laqueur of the Center for Strategic and International Studies, "The only general characteristic of terrorism generally agreed upon is that terrorism involves violence and the threat of violence." However, the criterion of violence alone does not produce a useful definition because it includes many acts not usually considered terrorism such as war, riot, organized crime, and even a simple assault. Property destruction that does not endanger life is not usually considered a violent crime, but some have described property destruction by the Earth Liberation Front and Animal Liberation Front as violence and terrorism.

PSYCHOLOGICAL IMPACT AND FEAR This means that the attack was carried out in such a way as to maximize the severity and length of the psychological impact. Each act of terrorism is a "performance" devised to have an impact on many large audiences. Terrorists also attack national symbols to show power and to attempt to shake the foundation of the country or society to which they are opposed. This may negatively affect a government while increasing the prestige of the given terrorist organization or the ideology behind a terrorist act.[33]

PERPETRATED FOR A POLITICAL GOAL Something that many acts of terrorism have in common is a political purpose. Terrorism is a political tactic, such as letter writing or protesting, which is used by activists when they believe that no other means will effect the kind of change they desire. The change is desired so badly that failure to achieve change is seen as a worse outcome than the deaths of civilians. This is often where the inter-relationship between terrorism and religion occurs. When a political struggle is integrated into the framework of a religious or "cosmic" struggle, such as over the control of an ancestral homeland or holy site such as Israel and Jerusalem, failing in the political goal (nationalism) becomes equated with spiritual failure, which, for the highly committed, is worse than their own death or the deaths of innocent civilians.[34]

One definition that combines the key elements was developed at the George C. Marshall Center for European Security Studies by Carsten Bockstette:

> Terrorism is defined as political violence in an asymmetrical conflict that is designed to induce terror and psychic fear (sometimes indiscriminate) through the violent victimization and destruction of noncombatant targets (sometimes iconic symbols). Such acts are meant to send a message from an illicit clandestine organization. The purpose of terrorism is to exploit the media in order to achieve maximum attainable publicity as an amplifying force multiplier in order to influence the targeted audience(s) in order to reach short- and midterm political goals and/or desired long-term end states.[35]

DELIBERATE TARGETING OF NONCOMBATANTS It is commonly held that the distinctive nature of terrorism lies in its intentional and specific selection of civilians as direct targets. Specifically, the criminal intent is shown when babies, children, mothers, and elderly people are murdered or injured and put in harm's way. Much of the time, the victims of terrorism are targeted not because they are threats but because they are specific "symbols, tools, animals or corrupt beings" that tie into a specific view of the world that the terrorists possess. Their suffering accomplishes the terrorists' goals of instilling fear, getting their message out to an audience, or otherwise satisfying the demands of their often radical religious and political agendas.[36]

DISGUISE Some terrorists pretend to be noncombatants, hide among such noncombatants, fight from vantage points in the midst of noncombatants, and (when they can) strive to mislead and provoke the government soldiers into attacking other people so that the government will be blamed.[37]

UNLAWFULNESS OR ILLEGITIMACY Some official (notably government) definitions of terrorism add a criterion of illegitimacy or unlawfulness to distinguish between actions authorized by a government (and thus "lawful") and those of other actors, including individuals and small groups.[38] Using this criterion, actions that would otherwise qualify as terrorism would not be considered terrorism if they were government sanctioned.

For example, firebombing a city, which is designed to affect civilian support for a cause, would not be considered terrorism if it were authorized by a government. This criterion is inherently problematic and is not universally accepted because it denies the existence of state terrorism; the same act may or may not be classed as terrorism, depending on whether its sponsorship is traced to a "legitimate" government; "legitimacy" and "lawfulness" are subjective, depending on the perspective of one government or another; and it diverges from the historically accepted meaning and origin of the term.[39] For these reasons, this criterion is not universally accepted; most dictionary definitions of the term do not include this criterion.

Forms of Terrorism

Jonathan White suggests that five distinct forms of terrorism can be considered: criminal terrorism, ideological terrorism, nationalistic terrorism, state-sponsored terrorism, and revolutionary terrorism.[40]

Criminal terrorism involves the use of terror for profit or psychological gain. Criminal terrorism fails to merit the same attention as does nationalistic violence. Criminal terrorists seem to lack the political sophistication and support of other types of terrorists. Thus, the control of criminal terrorist activity typically becomes a law enforcement matter.

Ideological terrorism is normally an effort to change the current political power. It has been argued that ideological terrorism involves a revolution, but this is not always the case. For example, some governments employ the use of death squads, whose actions might appear to be part of a repressive government, but this could be an extension of revolutionary terrorism.

Nationalistic terrorism is characterized by activity that supports the interests of an ethnic or nationalistic group, regardless of its political ideology. Nationalistic terrorists often align with either Western or Eastern ideologies. This could be viewed in terms of superpower support (food, supplies, weapons, etc.) for nationalistic interests. In other words, we could say that the West tends to supply our terrorists, while the East tends to supply theirs. Stated differently, the goals of democracy are opposed to those of Marxist socialism.[41]

State-sponsored terrorism occurs when governmental regimes use or threaten to use violence in international relations outside established diplomatic protocol. The term became somewhat popular during the Reagan administration in describing low-level violence used against U.S. diplomatic and military installations. This form of terrorism is typified by such events as the 1979 takeover of the U.S. embassy in Teheran and the bombings aimed against U.S. military personnel in the Middle East. Countries that support such activities are known as terrorist states. Iran, Syria, Afghanistan, Chile, Argentina, El Salvador, and Libya are among the most notorious state sponsors of terrorism.

States (countries) sponsor terrorism for many different reasons. One is to achieve foreign policy objectives that could not otherwise be achieved through political or military means. Sometimes states sponsor terrorism to create or expand their power and influence among ideological movements. Other state-sponsored incidents attempt to stifle domestic opposition through assassination of dissidents abroad. These types of terrorists are easy for a state to disavow. The use of state-sponsored terrorism represents a low-risk, low-budget method of conducting foreign policy. State-supported terrorists can benefit by receiving government assistance in arms or explosives, communications, travel documents, and safe havens for training operatives. Their actions are frequently difficult to trace, so the governments involved can maintain respectability and legitimacy in the international community while secretly financing and supporting terrorist activities to achieve their goals.

Revolutionary terrorism involves persons whose guerrilla-like tactics invoke fear in those holding political power and their supporters. The goal is to overthrow the current power base and replace it with political leaders who share the terrorists' views. Common tactics used by revolutionary terrorists are kidnappings, bombings, and assassinations, all of which are skillfully designed to force the existing government to respond with repressive measures. The terrorist then uses media coverage to attempt to expose the government as being inhumane and in need of being overthrown. Examples of revolutionary terrorism are Mao Tse-tung's takeover of China from Chiang Kai-shek and Fidel Castro's successful takeover of the Cuban government from the Batista regime during the late 1950s.

Recent Terrorist Threats

Attempted terrorist incidents continue and highlight the need for increased use of investigative techniques. For example, the investigation of Najibullah Zazi demonstrates how intelligence and law enforcement investigative tools were used to collect valuable intelligence on a subject's network. Zazi was arrested in September 2009 and on February 22, 2010, pled guilty to terrorism charges related to his plans to attack the New York City subway system.

Also in September of 2009, Michael C. Finton was arrested in Illinois and Hosam Smadi in Texas for unrelated bomb plots. Investigators used online undercover agents and confidential informants who monitored the activities of these violent extremist subjects up to the time of their arrests.

U.S. citizen David Headley was arrested in October 2009 in Chicago for planning terrorist attacks against a Danish newspaper and two of its employees. During the course of this investigation, investigators collected intelligence that uncovered Headley's role in the 2008 attacks in Mumbai, India, and connected him to a separate plot to kill an individual in Denmark. On January 14, 2010, an indictment was filed against Headley relating to his conspiring with others to plan and execute attacks in both Denmark and India, and in March 2010, he pled guilty on all counts.

In yet another case, during January 2010, Umar Farouk Abdulmutallab was charged in a six-count criminal indictment for his alleged role in the attempted Christmas Day bombing of Northwest Airlines flight 253 from Amsterdam to Detroit. Within days of the Christmas Day attack, the FBI established a Yemen fusion cell to coordinate intelligence and counterterrorism assets in response to threat by Al-Qaeda in the Arabian Peninsula to the United States and its interests overseas. The FBI gained important intelligence from the interrogation of Abdulmutallab.

Finally, in May 2010, Faisal Shahzad attempted to detonate a car bomb in Times Square, an attack for which Tehrik-e-Taliban in Pakistan claimed responsibility. Forensics and technical investigators developed important evidence in this investigation. The intelligence gained from this investigation was considered highly significant.

International Terrorism

In 2001, Islamic terrorist Osama bin Laden demonstrated to the world how terrorists can successfully strike American targets on U.S. soil when members of its organization attacked the World Trade Center and the Pentagon using commandeered airliners. As a result of these terrorist acts, approximately 3,000 people lost their lives. Earlier, in 1998, bin Laden's agents struck American embassies in Nairobi, Kenya, and Dares Salaam, Tanzania, killing 257 people, including 12 Americans. In 2003, another coordinated attack by Islamic extremists on a residential compound for foreigners in Riyadh, Saudi Arabia, killed 34 people, including eight Americans, and wounded many more.

Many believe that the wars in Afghanistan and Iraq, as well as a coordinated international effort against Al-Qaeda (discussed later in this chapter), may have substantially weakened that organization's ability to carry out future strikes outside the Middle East.[42] Experts in international terrorism, however, point out that *jihadism*, or the Islamic Holy War movement, survives independent of any one organization and appears to be gaining strength around the world. Jihadist principles continue to serve as the organizing rationale for extremist groups in much of the Muslim world. As such, Islamic fundamentalism continues to pose an ongoing global threat.

ISLAMIC TERRORISM Islamic terrorism has its roots in **Islamism** (Islam+ism; Arabic: al-'islamiyya), a set of ideologies holding that Islam is not only a religion but also a political system and that modern Muslims must return to their roots of their religion and unite politically.

Islamism is a controversial term, and definitions of it sometimes vary. Leading Islamist thinkers emphasized the enforcement of sharia (Islamic law); of pan-Islamic political unity; and of the elimination of non-Muslim, particularly Western, military, economic, political, social, or cultural influences in the Muslim world, which they believe to be incompatible with Islam.[43]

Some observers suggest Islamism's tenets are less strict and can be defined as a form of identity politics or "support for [Muslim] identity, authenticity, broader regionalism, revivalism, [and] revitalization of the community."[44] Others define *Islamism* as "an Islamic militant, anti-democratic movement, bearing a holistic vision of Islam whose final aim is the restoration of the caliphate."[45]

Many of those described as "Islamists" oppose the use of the term, maintaining that they are simply Muslims and that their political beliefs and goals are an expression of Islamic religious belief.[46] Similarly, some scholars instead favor the term *activist Islam* or *political Islam*.[47]

It is important to distinguish between Islamists and Islamist terrorists:

> While ignoring the overwhelming majority of Islamists who have little or nothing to do with terror and making them virtually irrelevant and stigmatized in Western political discourse.... To ignore the complexity of political Islam and tar all Islamists with the same brush of terrorism guarantees bin Laden's success.[48]

International Crisis Group warns that the tendency of "policy-makers...to lump all forms of Islamism together, brand them as radical and treat them as hostile...is fundamentally misconceived."[49] Furthermore, the International Crisis Group states:

> ...the issues and grievances which have been grist to the mill of Sunni jihadism across the Muslim world have not been resolved or even appreciably attenuated since 2001, but, on the contrary, aggravated and intensified. The failure to address the Palestinian question and, above all, the decision to make war on Iraq and the even more extraordinary mishandling of the post-war situation there have unquestionably motivated and encouraged jihadi activism across the Muslim world. Unsophisticated Western understanding and rhetoric that tends to discredit all forms of political Islamism, coupled with the lumping together of the internal, irredentist and global jihadis....[50]

AL-QAEDA Al-Qaeda (also spelled al-Qaida and sometimes al-Qa'ida; Arabic translation: "the base") is perhaps the most widely known Islamist group. It was founded sometime between August 1988 and late 1989 or early 1990,[51] and it operates as a network composed of both a multinational arm and a fundamentalist Sunni movement.[52]

Al-Qaeda has attacked civilian and military targets in various countries, the most notable being the infamous September 11 attacks in 2001. These actions were followed by the U.S. government's launching the "war on terrorism." As of 2009, Al-Qaeda is believed to have between 200 and 300 members.[53]

Al-Qaeda's characteristic techniques include suicide attacks and simultaneous bombings of different targets.[54] Activities ascribed to it may involve members of the movement, who have taken a pledge of loyalty to Osama bin Laden or the much more numerous "Al-Qaeda–linked" individuals who have undergone training in one of its camps in Afghanistan or Sudan but not taken any pledge.[55]

Al-Qaeda's objectives include the end of foreign influence in Muslim countries and the creation of a new Islamic caliphate. Reported beliefs include that a Christian–Jewish alliance is conspiring to destroy Islam and that the killing of bystanders and civilians is Islamically justified in jihad.[56]

The management philosophy of Al-Qaeda has been described as "centralization of decision and decentralization of execution."[57] After the September 11 attacks and the beginning of the war on terrorism, it is thought that Al-Qaeda's leadership has become "geographically isolated," leading to the "emergence of decentralized leadership" of regional groups using the Al-Qaeda "brand name."[58]

Domestic Terrorism

The term *domestic terrorism* was used commonly throughout the 1960s and 1970s. In a broad, general sense, acts of domestic terrorism in the United States are considered to be rare, but this has not always been the case. For example, according to the FBI, between 1980 and 2000, 250 of the 335 incidents confirmed as or suspected to be terrorist acts in the United States were carried out by American citizens.[59]

The statutory definition of *domestic terrorism* in the United States has changed many times over the years; also, it can be argued that acts of domestic terrorism have been occurring since long before any legal definition was set forth.

According to a memo produced by the FBI's Terrorist Research and Analytical Center in 1994, domestic terrorism was defined as "the unlawful use of force or violence, committed by a group(s) of two or more individuals, against persons or property to intimidate or coerce a government, the civilian population, or any segment thereof, in furtherance of political or social objectives."[60] Under current U.S. law, set forth in the USA PATRIOT Act, acts of domestic terrorism are those that:

1. "Involve acts dangerous to human life that are a violation of the criminal laws of the United States or of any State;
2. Appear to be intended—(a) to intimidate or coerce a civilian population; (b) to influence the policy of a government by intimidation or coercion; or (c) to affect the conduct of a government by mass destruction, assassination, or kidnapping; and
3. Occur primarily within the territorial jurisdiction of the United States."[61]

Examples abound of domestic terrorism. One of the most memorable is the 1995 bombing of the federal Murrah building in Oklahoma City. In that case, a powerful truck bomb exploded outside the Federal building in downtown Oklahoma City. In that event, 168 people died, and hundreds more were wounded. The perpetrator, 29-year-old Timothy McVeigh, was found guilty of 11 criminal counts, including conspiracy to first-degree murder. As a result, McVeigh was sentenced to death and was executed by lethal injection at the United States penitentiary in Terre Haute, Indiana in 2001.

One year after the Oklahoma City bombing, 38-year-old Eric Robert Rudolph detonated a makeshift bomb during the 1996 Olympics in which one person died and 111 were injured. This explosion, known as the Atlanta's Centennial Park bombing, resulted from Rudolph's antiabortion and antigay visions of America's future. After eluding police for years, Rudolph was captured, prosecuted, and sentenced to life imprisonment without the possibility of parole.

Today, the domestic terrorism movement continues to remain active, and several recent domestic terrorism incidents demonstrate the scope of the threat. For example,

- In March 2010, nine members of the Michigan-based Hutaree Militia were indicted for their alleged involvement in a plot to kill law enforcement officers.
- In January 2011, a pipe bomb was discovered at a Martin Luther King Day parade in Spokane, Washington, and a subject has been arrested by the FBI's JTTF.
- In February 2011, three subjects were arrested on weapons and firearms charges in relation to alleged domestic terrorist activity in Fairbanks, Alaska.[67]

Domestic Terrorism Organizations in the United States

☑ *The Ku Klux Klan (KKK).* From Reconstruction at the end of the Civil War to the end of the civil rights movement, the KKK used threats, violence, arson, and murder to further its white supremacist, antisemitic, anti-Catholic agenda.

☑ *The Weathermen.* The Weathermen was a U.S. radical left organization active from 1969 to 1975. Its members referred to themselves as a "revolutionary organization of communist women and men." Their goal was the revolutionary overthrow of the U.S. government. Toward this end, and to change U.S. policy in Vietnam, they bombed a number of police and military targets. The group collapsed shortly after the U.S. withdrawal from Vietnam in 1975.

☑ *The Jewish Defense League (JDL).* The JDL was founded in 1969 by Rabbi Meir Kahane in New York City, with its declared purpose the protection of Jews from harassment and anti-Semitism.[62] FBI statistics show that from 1980 to 1985, 15 terrorist attacks were attempted in the United States by members of the JDL.[63] The FBI's Mary Doran described the JDL in 2004 Congressional testimony as "a proscribed terrorist group."[64] The National Consortium for the Study of Terror and Responses to Terrorism states that during the JDL's first two decades of activity, it was an "active terrorist organization."[65] Kahane later founded the far-right Israeli political party Kach. The group's present-day website condemns all forms of terrorism.[66]

☑ *The Symbionese Liberation Army (SLA).* The SLA was an American self-styled, radical-left "urban guerrilla warfare group" that considered itself a revolutionary vanguard army. The group committed bank robberies, two murders, and other acts of violence between 1973 and 1975. Among the SLA's most notorious acts was the kidnapping and brainwashing of newspaper heiress Patty Hearst.

☑ *Army of God (AOG).* The AOG is a loose network of individuals and groups connected by ideological affinity and the determination to use violence to end the legal practice of abortion in the United States. Its affiliates consist of right-wing Christian militants who have committed violent acts against abortion providers. Acts of antiabortion violence increased in the mid-1990s, culminating in a series of bombings by Eric Rudolph, whose targets included two abortion clinics, a gay and lesbian nightclub, and the 1996 Olympics in Atlanta. Letters Rudolph sent to newspapers claiming responsibility in the name of the AOG focused attention on the issue of right-wing extremism.

☑ *Animal Liberation Front (ALF).* The ALF is a name used internationally by animal liberation activists who engage in direct action tactics on behalf of animals. This includes removing animals from laboratories and fur farms and sabotaging facilities involved in animal testing and other animal-based industries. According to ALF statements, any act that furthers the cause of animal liberation, in which all reasonable precautions are taken not to endanger life, may be claimed as an ALF action. The group is listed by the U.S. Department of Homeland Security as a domestic terrorist organization.

☑ *Earth Liberation Front (ELF).* The ELF is a group associated with environmental extremism and advocates direct action against alleged high polluters. Several fire bombings of SUV dealerships have been attributed to the ELF.

☑ *Black Liberation Army (BLA).* A splinter group made up of the more radical members of the Black Panther Party, the BLA sought to overthrow the U.S. government in the name of racial separatism and Marxist ideals. The Fraternal Order of Police blames the BLA for the murders of 13 police officers. According to a Justice Department report on BLA activity, the BLA was suspected of involvement in more than 60 incidents of violence between 1970 and 1981.

Tactics to Destabilize Terrorist Organizations

The most visible and immediately effective tactic of U.S. terrorist financing strategy has been designating and blocking the accounts of terrorists and those associated with financing terrorist activity. Publicly designating terrorists, terrorist supporters, and facilitators and blocking their ability to receive and move funds through the world's financial system have been and area crucial component in the fight against terrorism. On September 24, 2001, President Bush issued Executive Order 13244, blocking property and prohibiting transactions with persons who commit, threaten to commit, or support terrorism.[68]

The Department of the Treasury's Office of Enforcement, in conjunction with the Treasury's Office of International Affairs and the Office of Foreign Assets Control, has helped lead U.S. efforts to identify and block the assets of terrorist-related individuals and entities within the United States and worldwide. Currently, 250 individuals and entities are publicly designated as terrorists or terrorist supporters by the United States, and since September 11, 2001, more than $113 million in assets of terrorists has been frozen around the world.[69] Beyond simply freezing assets, these U.S. and international actions to publicly identify terrorists and their supporters advance global interests in terrorist financing and combating terrorism by:

- Shutting down the pipeline by which designated parties moved money and operated financially in the mainstream financial sectors
- Informing third parties who may be unwittingly financing terrorist activity of their association with supporters of terrorism
- Providing leverage over those parties not designated who might otherwise be willing to finance terrorist activity
- Exposing terrorist financing "money trails" that may generate leads to previously unknown terrorist cells and financiers
- Forcing terrorists to use alternative and potentially more costly informal means of financing their activities
- Supporting diplomatic effort to strengthen other countries' capacities to combat terrorist financing through the adoption and implementation of legislation that allows states to comply with their obligations under U.N. Security Council Resolutions 1390 and 1373

Currently, more than 165 countries and jurisdictions have blocking orders in force. Alternative financial mechanisms to combat terrorist financing conducted through these mechanisms include the following measures:

- *Protecting charities from terrorist abuse.* Under the authority of Executive Order 13224, the United States has designated 12 charitable organizations as having ties to Al-Qaeda or other terrorist groups.
  The Financial Action Task Force (FATF) Special Recommendation VIII on Terrorist Financing commits all member nations to ensure that nonprofit organizations cannot be misused by financiers of terrorism.
- *Regulating hawalas.* Informal value transfer systems. Terrorists have also used hawalas and other informal value transfer systems as a means of terrorist financing. The word **hawala** (meaning "trust") refers to a fast and cost-effective method for the worldwide remittance of money or value, particularly for persons who may be outside the reach of the traditional financial sector. In some nations, hawalas are illegal; in others, they are active but unregulated. It is, therefore, difficult to accurately measure the total volume of financial activity associated with the system; however, it is estimated that, at a minimum, tens of billions of dollars flow through hawalas and other informal value transfer systems on an annual basis.
- *Combating bulk cash smuggling.* Bulk cash smuggling has proven to be yet another means of financing adopted by terrorists and their financiers. Customs has executed 650 bulk cash seizures totaling $21 million, including $12.9 million with Middle East connections. Pursuing bulk cash smuggling from a domestic perspective, however, is not enough; disruption of this tactic requires a global approach.
- *Investigating trade-based terrorist financing.* With respect to trade-based financial systems, authorized enforcement agencies continue to investigate the use of licit and illicit international trade commodities (e.g., diamonds, gold, honey, and cigarettes, as well as narcotics) to fund terrorism. The U.S. Customs Service has developed a state-of-the-art database system to identify anomalous trade patterns for imports and exports to and from the United States. In the past, Customs has demonstrated this system to other nations, including Colombia, with excellent results.
- *Investigating terrorist cyberfund-raising activities.* Terrorist groups now exploit the Internet to recruit supporters and raise terrorist funds. Developing a strategy to counter such cyberfund-raising activities is a responsibility that the Treasury Department assumed in its 2002 Anti-Money Laundering Strategy.

U.S. Efforts in Combating Terrorism

In addition to the international impetus placed on combating terrorism, the United States has enacted numerous laws, strategies, and programs designed to protect Americans from international terrorism. However, laws designed to limit terrorist actions have not yet shown to be totally effective. The Federal Terrorist Firearms Detection Act of 1988 is an example. Designed to prevent the development of plastic firearms by requiring handguns to contain at least 3.7 oz of detectable metal, it applies only to weapons manufactured within U.S. borders. In 1996, the Antiterrorism and Effective Death Penalty Act became law. Included in its provisions are the following:

- It bans fund-raising and financial support within the United States for international terrorist organizations.
- It provides $1 billion for enhanced terrorism fighting measures by federal and state authorities.
- It allows foreign terrorism suspects to be deported or to be kept out of the United States without the disclosure of classified evidence against them.
- It permits a death sentence to be imposed on anyone committing an international terrorist act in the United States in which a death occurs.
- It makes a federal crime to use the United States as a base for planning terrorist acts overseas.
- It orders identifying chemical markers known as taggits to be added to plastic explosives during manufacture.
- It orders the feasibility study on marketing other explosives (with the exception of gunpowder).[70]

After the September 11 attacks on the World Trade Center and the Pentagon, Congress enacted the USA PATRIOT Act. The act created a number of new crime categories, such as terrorist attacks against mass transportation and harboring or concealing terrorists. Those crimes were set forth in title VIII of the act titled "Strengthening the Criminal Laws Against Terrorism."

Case in Point

>>The Case Against the Unabomber

Ted Kaczynski, a math professor-turned-hermit, was charged with four of the 16 bombings linked to the Unabomber. After his arrest in 1996, he initially pleaded innocent of the charges and was remanded to the Sacramento, California, jail. After his arrest, Kaczynski's Montana cabin was searched by federal agents, who found, among other things, a bomb (which they exploded safely), the original antitechnology manuscript, and his secret identification number. Under law, the prosecution must also provide the defense with any evidence it has that might show that the accused is innocent. Here is what prosecutors filed in federal court:

- Investigators found a deposit credited to Kaczynski's account at Western Federal Savings in Helena, Montana, on December 11, 1985, the same day that he was alleged to have planted his first fatal bomb 900 miles away in Sacramento. But the deposit slip was actually dated December 9.

- The ATF determined that a bomb placed at the University of Utah in October 1981 was a hoax. What prosecutors failed to say was that the FBI and postal inspectors disagreed. Also, in a letter to the *New York Times*, the Unabomber described that bomb as a botched operation.

- Crime scene investigators found in excess of 20 latent fingerprints, some of which were identified and some which were not, and none of which were Kaczynski's fingerprints. But the Unabomber's letter boasted about using gloves to avoid leaving fingerprints.

- In earlier affidavits, FBI analysts had pointed to scores of similarities between Kaczynski's writings and the Unabomber's manifesto and letters, including similarly misspelled words. But in a later filing, prosecutors suggested that defense attorneys talk to a political science professor at Brigham Young University concerning his work on the Unabomber case.

In January 1998, Kaczynski admitted to the FBI that he was in fact the Unabomber and agreed to a plea bargain, pleading guilty to two counts of murder in exchange for a life sentence without the possibility of parole.

Summary Checklist

In this chapter, we consider the ways that information about crimes is documented by the criminal investigator. A properly documented case is one that is more likely to succeed in court. See how well you are able to answer the following questions in your checklist.

1. **What do you know about the crime of arson and the alliance between police and fire departments?**

   The UCR defines arson as any willful or malicious burning or attempt to burn, with or without intent to defraud, a dwelling house, public building, motor vehicle or aircraft, personal property of another, etc.

   - Only fires that have been determined, through investigation, to have been willfully or maliciously set are classified as arsons.
   - Fires of suspicious or unknown origins are excluded from this category.

   Arson is legally characterized by two distinct categories: aggravated arson and simple arson.

   - Aggravated arson is the deliberate burning of property while creating an imminent danger to human life or risking great bodily harm.
   - Simple arson is the burning of property that does not result in such a risk to human life.

   After a fire has been determined to have a suspicious origin, investigators from the local fire and police departments (as well as the victim's insurance company) will become involved with the case.

   The role of the fire department is:

   - To extinguish the fire
   - To investigate the origins of the fire
   - To "detect" the possibility of arson, but not investigate it

   When the investigation becomes a question of who committed the crime, it becomes a concern for the police.

   - After it has been determined that law enforcement should take over the investigation, fire investigators should yield the crime scene to the arson investigators.
   - Police have a statutory role in investigating the arson because it is a violation of state or federal law.

2. **What are the investigative steps of an arson investigation?**

   It is the investigator's responsibility to prove that a specific fire did occur and that it was ignited deliberately. The arson investigation involves several steps:

   - The first step is to identify the fire's point of origin.
     - This may be the most critical phase of the investigation because it includes the ruling out of natural or accidental causes.
     - Point of origin may be determined in several ways, including questioning of witnesses and an inspection of the fire scene.
   - Search for accelerants:
     - The presence of accelerants may show that a fire was set intentionally and can be used as evidence of arson.
     - Accelerants are chemical fuels that cause a fire to burn hotter, spread more quickly than usual, or be unusually difficult to extinguish.
     - Commonly used accelerants include gasoline, kerosene, turpentine, and diesel fuel.
   - Observe the span of the fire:
     - Physical characteristics of the fire, such as smoke, direction, flames, and distance of travel, are important.
   - Take complete photographs of the structure to help preserve the crime scene for the courtroom.
   - Identify the areas of plants and trailers:
     - Plants—preparations used to set the fire, such as newspapers, rags, or other flammable waste material
     - Trailers—materials used to spread the fire, such as gunpowder, flammable liquids, and rags soaked in flammable liquids
   - Question witnesses
   - Observe "alligatoring"—the pattern of crevices formed by the burning of a wooden structure.
   - Look for other clues, such as the color of the flames and smoke, the size of the fire, and distinguishable odors.

3. Explain the motivations of arsonists.

After it has been determined that the fire was of incendiary origin, possible motives must be examined to help identify the suspect.

- Profit—this is the motive for about 50 percent of fire-related property damage in the United States.
- Revenge—usually involves adults targeting individuals and property out of revenge, jealousy, and spite.
- Vandalism—about 95 percent of vandalism arsons are caused by juveniles.
- Crime concealment—committed by offenders who are attempting to cover up another crime through the use of a fire.
- Pyromania—compulsive fire starting

4. Describe the methods to prosecute an arson case.

The evidence needed to prosecute an arson case is included in the old adage, "Without the fire triangle—heat, fuel, and oxygen—there can be no fire."Similarly, the successful prosecution of arson must include a triangle consisting of police detectives, fire investigators, and a prosecutor.

Evidence needed for arson prosecution includes:

- Evidence of participation: This might be the disabling of a fire alarm or rearranging combustibles at a fire's location.
- Exclusive access: If firefighters are required to use force to gain entrance into a structure, the arsonist would have difficulty doing the same to set the fire. This indicates the complicity of the business owner in locking up the structure.
- Motive: Establishment of a motive is one critical element in showing jurors a suspect's criminal intent.
- False statements: A convincing element in an arson prosecution is false statements by the "victim" to the investigators.

5. What factors are involved in investigating bombing incidents?

Bomb threats are delivered in a variety of ways, but most are telephoned in to the target. When a bomb threat is called in, the following steps should be implemented:

- Keep the caller on the line as long as possible.
- Ask him or her to repeat the message and record every word spoken by the person.
- Ask the caller the location of the bomb and the time of detonation of the device.
- Inform the caller that the building is occupied and the detonation of a bomb could kill or injure innocent people.

- Pay particular attention to background noise such as motors running, music playing, or any other noise that may give a clue as to the location of the caller.
- Listen closely to the voice (male or female), voice quality (calm or excited), accents, and speech impediments.
- Interview the person who received the call for the preceding information.

After the suspected bomb is located, the following procedures should be followed:

- Report the location and description of the object to the supervisor or command center.
- Fire department and rescue personnel should also be notified and placed on standby.
- Identify the danger area and block it off with a "clear zone" of at least 300 feet, including floors below and above the object.
- Be sure that all doors and windows are open to minimize primary damage from the blast and secondary damage from fragmentation.
- Evacuate the building.
- Do not permit reentry into the building until the device has been removed or disarmed and the building is declared safe for reentry.

6. List the four elements that define terrorism.

Terrorism is policy intended to intimidate or cause terror. The Federal Foreign Relations Authorization Act defines terrorism in terms of four primary elements. The act says that terrorism is:

- Premeditated
- Politically motivated
- Violent
- Committed against noncombatant targets

7. Distinguish between domestic and international terrorism.

No one definition of terrorism (international or domestic) has been universally accepted. The FBI has a definition that addresses both domestic and international terrorism:

- Domestic terrorism is the unlawful use or threatened use of force by a group or individual, based and operating entirely within the United States without foreign direction, committed against persons or property to intimidate or coerce a government, the civilian population, or any segment thereof, in furtherance of social or political objectives.
- International terrorism involves violent acts or acts that are a danger to human life that are a violation of the criminal law of the United States or any state or that would be a criminal violation if committed within the

jurisdiction of the United States or any state. These acts appear to be intended to intimidate or coerce a civilian population, influence the policy of a government by intimidation or coercion, or affect the conduct of government by assassination or kidnapping.

International terrorist acts occur outside the United States or transcend national boundaries in terms of the means by which they are to be accomplished, the persons they intend to coerce or intimidate, or the locale in which the perpetrators operate or seek asylum.

Key Terms

accelerant	hawala	pyromania
aggravated arson	international terrorism	simple arson
alligatoring	Islamism	span of the fire
arson	olfactory senses	terrorism
booby traps	paper trail	trailers
domestic terrorism	plants	
fire triangle	point of origin	

Discussion Questions

1. Discuss the reasons why arson is considered a low-priority crime.

2. Discuss the relationship between fire and police departments and the insurance companies that represent victims of arson.

3. Discuss the main things to remember in the preliminary investigation of suspected arson.

4. What significance does a fire's point of origin have regarding the investigation of a suspected arson fire?

5. What are the primary motives for arson?

6. Explain the three sides of the fire triangle.

7. What types of evidence are necessary in the successful prosecution of an arson case?

8. What are the general explanations as to why bombers communicate a bomb threat?

9. Discuss the searching sweep methods that should be used when attempting to locate a bomb or booby trap.

10. Explain the procedures to follow in the event that an explosive device is discovered.

11. Explain the main elements of terrorism and distinguish between domestic and international terrorism.

12. What are the five distinct forms of terrorism?

13. Discuss some of the U.S. and international actions taken to destabilize terrorist organizations.

Notes

1. WELCH, W. AND B. JANSEN. (2012). Arrest made in Los Angles car fires. *USA Today*, January 3, p. 3A.

2. FIRE AND ARSON SCENE EVIDENCE: A GUIDE FOR PUBLIC SAFETY PERSONNEL. (June 2000). *Research report*. Washington, DC: U.S. Department of Justice, National Institute of Justice. U.S. Government Printing Office.

3. IBID.

4. IBID.

5. FEDERAL BUREAU OF INVESTIGATION. (2011). *Crime in the United States—2010*. Washington, DC: U.S. Government Printing Office.

6. IBID.

7. IBID.

8. WOODFORK, W. G. (1990). Not just a fire department problem. *Police Chief* 57 (December):28.

9. O'CONNER, J. J. (1987). *Practical fire and arson investigation*. New York: Elsevier.

10. GOODNIGHT, K. M. (1990). Arson for profit: The insurance investigation. *Police Chief* 57 (December):53.

11. SAFERSTEIN, R. (1998). *Criminalistics. An introduction to forensic science*. Upper Saddle River, NJ: Prentice Hall, p. 265.

12. WHITE, P. (Ed.). (1998). *Crime scene to court: The essentials of forensic science.* Glasgow, UK: The Royal Society of Chemistry, pp. 133–138.

13. MOENSSENS, A. A., J. E. STARRS, C. E. HENDERSON, AND F. E INBAU. (1995). *Scientific evidence in civil and criminal cases.* Westbury, NY: The Foundation Press, pp. 416–417.

14. IBID.

15. O'CONNER. (1987). *Practical fire and arson investigation.*

16. IBID.

17. RIDER, A. O. (1980). The firesetter: A psychological profile. *FBI Law Enforcement Bulletin* 49 (June–August):9.

18. JAMES, J. (1965). Psychological motives for arson. *Popular Government*, March:24.

19. RIDER. (1980). The firesetter.

20. HART. (1990). The arson equation: Arson + Circumstantial evidence. National Emergency Training Center, 1990.

21. FRANKEL, B. AND G. FIELDS. New teen fad: Building bombs. *USA Today*, June 5, 1996.

22. OXFORD ENGLISH DICTIONARY, 2nd ed. (1989). Second general definition of terrorism: "A policy intended to strike with terror those against whom it is adopted; the employment of methods of intimidation; the fact of terrorizing or condition of being terrorized."

23. Foreign Relations Authorization Act, US Code, Title 22, Section 2656 f (d)(2).

24. ANGUS, M. (2002). *The right of self-defence under international law: The response to the terrorist attacks of 11 September.* Australian Law and Bills Digest Group, Parliament of Australia, February 12; THALIF D. (2005). *Politics: UN member states struggle to define terrorism.* Inter Press Service, July 25.

25. HOFFMAN, B. (1998). *Inside terrorism.* Columbia University Press, p.32. See review in *The New York Times*.

26. RECORD, J. *Bounding the global war on terrorism.* Available at http://www.carlisle.army.mil/ (retrieved on September 23, 2012).

27. ABRAHMS, M. (2008). *What terrorists really want: Terrorist motives and counterterrorism strategy. International Security* 32(4):86–89. Available at http://maxabrahms.com/pdfs/DC_250-1846.pdf.

28. TERRORISM. Encyclopedia Britannica. Available at http://www.britannica.com/eb/article-9071797 (retrieved on September 23, 2012).

29. SAGEMAN, M. (2004). *Social networks and the jihad.* Philadelphia: University of Pennsylvania Press, pp.166–167.

30. WILLIAMS, P. (2008). Violent non-state actors and national and international security. Available at https://docs.google.com/viewer?a=v&q=cache:nP2P4pbAsoIJ:centreforforeignpolicystudies.dal.ca/pdf/msc2009/Wood_Crime_11Jun09.ppt+&hl=en&gl=us&pid=bl&srcid=ADGEESh8UBV_FTOL5-N6AXc7Qitmf8b5Ywr8W7-iNCSrN25nd6MrIFPjfByQSqpOXoQKPG0JBgvrjGunY81-0nGudRa4QewU0eDecgQEgUTDtBhGwZp-Jcimlrgt8EPNWIkv3DUx8giY&sig=AHIEtbSq2Wuw-En6XX8y0eHs8PGIS0Bq1Pw (retrieved on September 23, 2012.

31. LIBRARY OF CONGRESS. (1999). *The sociology and psychology of terrorism:* A report prepared under an interagency agreement by the Federal Research Division, Library of Congress. Library of Congress Federal Research Division, Washington, DC, September, 1999.

32. WHITE, J. (2012). *Terrorism and homeland security*, 7th ed. Wadsworth Publishing.

33. JUERGENSMEYER, M. (2000). *Terror in the mind of God.* Berkeley, CA: University of California Press, pp. 125–135.

34. IBID.

35. BOCKSTETTE, C. (2008). *Jihadist terrorist use of strategic communication management techniques.* George C. Marshall center occasional paper series, No. 20. Available at http://www.marshallcenter.org/mcpublicweb/MCDocs/files/College/F_ResearchProgram/occPapers/occ-paper_20-en.pdf.

36. JUERGENSMEYER. (2000). *Terror in the mind of God*, pp.127–128.

37. BOCKSTETTE. (2008). *Jihadist terrorist use of strategic communication management techniques.*

38. FEDERAL BUREAU OF INVESTIGATION. (1999). *Terrorism in the United States 1999.* Counterterrorism threat assessment and warning unit counterterrorism division. Available at http://www.fbi.gov/publications/terror/terror99.pdf (retrieved on September 22, 2012).

39. UNITED NATIONS. (2009). *UN Reform.* Available at http://web.archive.org/web/20070427012107/http://www.un.org/unifeed/script.asp?scriptId=73. The second part of the report, titled "Freedom from fear backs the definition of terrorism—an issue so divisive agreement on it has long eluded the world community" defines *terrorism* as any action "intended to cause death or serious bodily harm to civilians or non-combatants with the purpose of intimidating a population or compelling a government or an international organization to do or abstain from doing any act."

40. WHITE. (2012). *Terrorism and homeland security.*

41. IBID.

42. STEVENS, P. (2005). All nostalgia is futile at the beginning of history. *Financial Times*, May 27, p. 13.

43. EIKMEIER, D. C. (2007). Qutbism: An ideology of Islamic-fascism. *Parameters*(Spring):85–98.

44. FULLER, G. E. (2003). *The future of political Islam.* New York: Palgrave MacMillan, p. 21

45. Footnotes of *9/11 commission report*, MEHDI MOZAFFARI. (2002). Bin Laden and Islamist terrorism. *Militant Tidsskrift*, 131(March):1.

46. KRAMER, M. (2003). Coming to terms, fundamentalists or Islamists? *Middle East Quarterly*(Spring):65–77.

47. INTERNATIONAL CRISIS GROUP. (2005). *Understanding Islamism.* Available at http://merln.ndu.edu/archive/icg/Islamism2Mar05.pdf; STANLEY, T. (2005). *Definition: Islamism, Islamist, Islamiste, Islamicist, perspectives on world history and current events.* Available at http://www.pwhce.org/islamism.html.

48. FULLER. (2003). *The future of political Islam.*

49. *Understanding Islamism Middle East/North Africa.* Report No. 37, March 2, 2005.

50. IBID.

51. UNITED STATES DISTRICT COURT, Southern District of New York, February 6, 2001. Testimony of Jamal Ahmad Al-Fadl. *United States* v. *Usama bin Laden* et al., defendants. James Martin Center for Nonproliferation Studies. Available at http://cns.miis.edu/pubs/reports/binladen.htm.

52. GUNARATNA. (2002). pp. 95–96. "Al Qaeda's global network, as we know it today, was created while it was based in

Khartoum, from December 1991 till May 1996. To coordinate its overt and covert operations as Al Qaeda's ambitions and resources increased, it developed a de-centralised, regional structure....As a global multinational, Al Qaeda makes its constituent nationalities and ethnic groups, of which there are several dozen, responsible for a particular geographic region. Although its modus operandi is cellular, familial relationships play a key role."

53. NOAH, T. (2009). The terrorists-are-dumb theory: Don't mistake these guys for criminal masterminds. *Slate*, February 25. Available at http://www.slate.com/id/2211994/.

54. WRIGHT, L. (2006). *The looming tower: Al-Qaeda and the road to 9/11*. New York: Knopf.

55. IBID.

56. FU'ADHUSAYN, A. Z. (2005). The second generation of al-Qa'ida, part 14. *Al-Quds al-Arabi*, July 13.

57. AL-HAMMADI, K. (2005). The inside story of al-Qa'ida, part 4. *Al-Quds al-Arabi*, March 22.

58. FEISER, J. (2004). Evolution of the al-Qaeda brand name. *Asia Times On-line*. Available at http://www.atimes.com/atimes/Middle_East/FH13Ak05.html.

59. COUNCIL ON FOREIGN RELATIONS. *Militant extremists in the United States*. Available at http://www.cfr.org/publication/9236/ (retrieved on September 23, 2012).

60. PRESLEY, S. M. (1996). *Rise of domestic terrorism and its relation to United States Armed Forces*. Available at http://www.fas.org/irp/eprint/presley.htm.

61. Available at http://frwebgate.access.gpo.gov/cgi-bin/getdoc.cgi?dbname=107_cong_public_laws&docid=f:publ056.107.pdf.

62. ANTI-DEFAMATION LEAGUE. (2009). *Backgrounder: The Jewish Defense League*. Available at http://www.adl.org/extremism/jdl_chron.asp.

63. BOHN, M. K. (2004). *The achillelauro hijacking: Lessons in the politics and prejudice of terrorism*. Washington, DC: Brassey, p.67.

64. FEDERAL BUREAU OF INVESTIGATION. *Congressional testimony: Special Agent Mary Deborah (Debbie) Doran before the 9/11/2001 Commission*, June 16, 2004. Available at http://www.fbi.gov/congress/congress04/doran061604.htm.

65. NATIONAL CONSORTIUM FOR THE STUDY OF TERROR AND RESPONSES TO TERRORISM. (2007). Terrorist *Organization profile: Jewish Defense League (JDL)*. Available at http://www.start.umd.edu/start/data/tops/terrorist_organization_profile.asp?id=183.

66. COUNCIL ON FOREIGN RELATIONS. *Militant extremists in the United States*.

67. FEDERAL BUREAU OF INVESTIGATION. *Comments from Mark Giuliano, Assistant Director Counter Terrorism Division*, April 14, 2011. Available at http://www.fbi.gov/news/speeches/the-post-9-11-fbi-the-bureaus-response-to-evolving-threats (retrieved on June 1, 2011).

68. INTERNATIONAL MONETARY FUND. (2003). *Enhancing contributions to combating money laundering: Policy paper*. Available at http://www.imf.org/external/np/ml/2001/eng/042601.htm.

69. U.S. TREASURY DEPARTMENT. (2003). *High intensity money laundering and related financial crimes areas (HIFCAs) designations*. Available at http://www.ustreas.gov/fincen/hifcadesignations.html.

70. *National Strategy for Combating Terrorism*. (September 2006). United Department of State.

PART 6 | **Vice and Profit-Related Crime**

Chapter **16** | Special Investigations: Drug Trafficking and Gangs
Chapter **17** | Special Investigations: White-Collar, Corporate, and Computer-Related Crimes

CHAPTER **16**

Alain Dex / Science Source / Photo Researchers

This chapter will enable you to:

1. Summarize the U.S. gang problem.

2. Describe the activities of drug-trafficking organizations.

3. Identify the types of dangerous drugs and the operations of drug-selling organizations.

4. Summarize the structure of drug laws.

5. Describe how drug investigations are conducted.

Special Investigations: Drug Trafficking and Gangs

Introduction

Transnational criminal organizations operating in the United States produce, import, or distribute illicit drugs throughout the nation, posing an ongoing hazard to public health and safety as well as persistent and violent threats to law enforcement. Drug-trafficking organizations use parcel services, tunnels, aircraft, trains, boats, vehicles with hidden compartments, and other conveyances to traffic drugs into and throughout the nation, particularly along the Southwest and Northern borders.

Once in the United States, drug traffickers increasingly use criminal gangs to control the retail distribution of drugs, particularly in major and midsize cities. In addition to traditional drugs, communities are now faced with new synthetic drugs, such as those commonly sold as "bath salts" and synthetic cannabinoids sold as "Spice" or "K2." Ultimately, criminal organizations employ complex methods to conceal their illicit profits.

In this chapter we will discuss drugs, drug trafficking and manufacture, and the organizations that are responsible for their distribution. We will also consider how criminal investigators can conduct investigations into these groups and their violations.

Today's Illicit Drug Problem

Most of the cocaine, heroin, and MDMA (ecstasy) and much of the methamphetamine consumed in the United States is smuggled into the United States by international criminal organizations from source countries in Latin America, Asia, and (for MDMA) Europe. Cocaine consumption in the United States, the world's most important and largest market, has declined somewhat since its peak in the late 1980s but has remained relatively stable for most of the past decade. Cocaine is produced in the South American Andean countries of Colombia, Peru, and Bolivia; Colombia is the source of an estimated 90 percent of the cocaine supply in the U.S. market (U.S. Department of State, 2000; United Nations, 2000).

Fueled by high-purity, low-cost heroin introduced into the U.S. market by Southeast Asian and Colombian traffickers, heroin use in the United States increased significantly in the early to mid-1990s and has leveled off in recent years. The purity of heroin currently available in the United States is higher than ever. Southwest Asia's "Golden Crescent" (Afghanistan, Iran, and Pakistan) and Southeast Asia's "Golden Triangle" (Myanmar, Laos, and Thailand) are the world's major sources of heroin for the international market, but Colombia is the largest source of supply for the U.S. heroin market (Mexico is the second largest). Colombia and Mexico account for about 75 percent of the U.S. heroin market, with heroin from Southeast Asia making up most of the remainder.

The use of synthetic drugs in the United States, many of which come from abroad, has increased over the past few decades. Beginning in the 1990s, there has been a dramatic surge in the worldwide production and consumption of synthetic drugs—particularly amphetamine-type stimulants, including methamphetamine and ecstasy. The majority of methamphetamine available in the U.S. market is produced by Mexican traffickers operating in the United States or in Mexico; the U.S. Drug Enforcement Administration (DEA) estimates that Mexican trafficking groups control 70 to 90 percent of the U.S. methamphetamine supply. There has been a significant increase in methamphetamine production in Southeast Asia in recent years. Although little has found its way to the U.S. market from Southeast Asia, increasing quantities of "Thai tabs" have been seized in the western United States.

Most of the ecstasy in the U.S. market is produced in the Netherlands. Amsterdam, Brussels, Frankfurt, and Paris are major European hubs for transshipping ecstasy to foreign markets, including the United States. U.S. law enforcement reporting indicates that the Dominican Republic, Suriname, and Curaçao are used as transshipment points for U.S.-bound ecstasy from Europe and that Mexican and South American traffickers are becoming involved in the ecstasy trade.

Marijuana remains the most widely used and readily available illicit drug in the United States. Most of the marijuana consumed in the United States is from domestic sources, including both outdoor and indoor cannabis cultivation in every state, but a significant share of the U.S. market is met by marijuana grown in Mexico, with lesser amounts coming from Jamaica, Colombia, and Canada. Very little of the cannabis grown in other major producing countries—including Morocco, Lebanon, Afghanistan, Thailand, and Cambodia—comes to the United States.

International drug-trafficking organizations have extensive networks of suppliers as well as front companies and businesses to facilitate narcotics smuggling and laundering of illicit proceeds. Colombian and Mexican trafficking organizations dominate the drug trade in the Western Hemisphere. Colombia supplies most of the cocaine and contributes the largest share of heroin to the U.S. market, and Mexico is the major avenue for cocaine trafficking into the United States as well as a major supplier of heroin, marijuana, and methamphetamine. In the Asian source regions, heroin production is dominated by large trafficking organizations, but the trafficking networks smuggling heroin from Asia are more diffuse. Asian heroin shipments typically change hands among criminal organizations as the drug is smuggled to markets in the United States and elsewhere.

The evolution of the international drug trade in the past decade has included greater involvement by a growing number of players and more worldwide trafficking of synthetic drugs. Criminal organizations whose principal activities focus more on traditional contraband smuggling, racketeering enterprises, and fraud schemes have become increasingly involved in international drug trafficking. Although they generally are not narcotics producers themselves, many organized crime groups—including those from Russia, China, Italy, and Albania—have cultivated and expanded ties to drug-trafficking organizations to obtain cocaine, heroin, and synthetic drugs for their own distribution markets and trafficking networks. Traffickers from many countries are increasingly eschewing traditional preferences for criminal partnerships with single ethnic groups and collaborating in the purchase, transportation, and distribution of illegal drugs.

Taking advantage of more open borders and modern telecommunications technology, international drug-trafficking organizations are sophisticated and flexible in their operations. They adapt quickly to law enforcement pressures by finding new methods for smuggling drugs, new transshipment routes, and new mechanisms to launder money. In many of the major cocaine-and-heroin-producing and -transit countries, drug traffickers have acquired significant power and wealth through the use of violence, intimidation, and payoffs of corrupt officials.

Distribution of Illegal Drugs

Drug sales networks differ somewhat from one case to another. For example, trafficking not only differs from rural to urban areas but also depends on the type of drug and the techniques of the group distributing it. Most large urban areas have sections of town that are known as drug distribution areas. These areas, sometimes called **copping areas**, are typically well known to drug users. Often these areas are nothing more than street corners or public parks where small amounts of drugs are sold. Here it is common for many different drug sales to take place in a short period of time. Buyers go to the copping area, pay cash for the drugs, and leave—all in a matter of seconds. Investigations have shown that dealers operating in copping areas often sell to known customers and strangers alike. As a rule, dealers in copping areas will employ lookouts and steerers, who watch for both police and potential customers. Once dealers are tipped off about the presence of police in the area, they can dispose of their drugs before being caught in possession of them.

A Closer Look

The Homegrown Marijuana Business

Domestic growers of marijuana cultivate the plant for the flowering tops, which produce high concentrations of the mind-altering substance THC. Accordingly, the high THC concentration in the plant is sought by marijuana consumers. Marijuana was first regulated in 1937 with the passage of the Marijuana Tax Act. Today, although some states have chosen to decriminalize the drug, it is still basically illegal to one extent or another. The effects of marijuana are somewhat difficult to articulate because different users are affected in different ways. Frequently, the effects of marijuana depend on the user's experience and expectations as well as on the activity of the drug itself. In low doses, restlessness and a sense of well-being are experienced. This is followed by a feeling of relaxation and sometimes hunger pangs, especially for sweets. High doses may result in image distortion, a loss of personal identity, and possible hallucinations.

Marijuana "Grow Houses"

As of 2006, marijuana cultivators have increasingly begun to conceal their growing operation by making use of "grow houses." The grow house has proven to be a predominantly suburban phenomenon. For example, in December 2006, the DEA reported that more than 10,000 plants were seized in a four-bedroom house in Derry, New Hampshire. In California, such operations have grown considerably.

Growers have been known to pay as much as $750,000 in new subdivisions and typically obtain 100 percent financing and put no money down. Interiors are then gutted to make use of every available square foot for growing apparatuses and for the plants themselves. Irrigation systems with timing devices are also commonly installed and operated using water tanks, pumps, generators, and power packs. To avoid suspicion resulting from large power usage, growers have been known to bypass an electric company's utility meter and create their own circuit boxes. Grow houses are typically unoccupied.

As a rule, criminal investigators need a search warrant for entry into a grow house. Seizure of equipment, plants, and establishment of residency, however, can provide the basis for an arrest and prosecution under applicable state or federal law.

Neighborhood bars, truck stops, or homes in affluent areas of town are sometimes fixed locations for drug dealing. Studies into the habits of dealers and users have revealed that middle-class buyers will often make their purchases away from the typical urban copping area to avoid getting arrested. In some cases, drug deals are arranged by telephone and a drop-off location is chosen. **Crack houses** are yet another example of a fixed location for drug dealing. Such locations emerged during the mid-1980s and are often abandoned buildings or apartments in public housing projects located near copping areas. In the crack house are the necessary paraphernalia for taking cocaine. This equipment includes needles and syringes for injecting as well as pipes and heat sources for smoking **crack**. The Detroit Police Department identified two types of crack houses: (1) a "buy-and-get-high party" house, where drugs are consumed on the premises in conjunction with illicit sex acts, and (2) a "hole in the wall" house, where buyers would literally put cash into a hole in the wall at the front door of a house and receive crack cocaine from an unidentified seller on the other side.

Gangs and the Drug Trade

It is almost impossible to have a discussion about drugs without also discussing the gangs who create, transport, and sell them. Stereotypically, we tend to think of organized crime when we consider the nation's drug problem but to a great extent gangs and organized crime share many of the same attributes.

A subtle distinction between gangs and organized crime can be made with regard to the size of the groups and the length of time they have been in existence. In a general sense, a gang is a group of people who, through the organization, formation, and establishment of an assemblage, share a common identity. In current usage, *gang* typically denotes a criminal organization or a criminal affiliation. In early usage, the word *gang* referred to a group of workmen. The word *gang* often carries a negative connotation; however, within a gang that defines itself in opposition to mainstream norms, members may adopt the phrase as a statement of identity or defiance.

The term **gangster** (or *mobster*) refers to a criminal who is a member of a crime organization, such as a gang. The terms are widely used in reference to members of gangs associated with American prohibition and the American offshoot of the Italian Mafia, such as the Chicago Outfit or the Five Families.

Understanding the Extent of Gangs

Recent research shows that gangs are expanding, evolving, and posing an increasing threat to U.S. communities nationwide. Many gangs are sophisticated criminal networks with members who are violent, distribute wholesale quantities of drugs, and develop and maintain close working relationships with members and associates of transnational criminal/drug-trafficking organizations.

Additionally, gangs are becoming more violent while engaging in less typical and lower-risk crime, such as prostitution and white-collar crime. Gangs are more adaptable, organized, sophisticated, and opportunistic, exploiting new and advanced technology as a means to recruit, communicate discretely, target their rivals, and perpetuate their criminal activity.

In 2012, the National Gang Threat Assessment Center reported that there are approximately 1.4 million active street, prison, and outlaw motorcycle gang (OMG) gang members comprising more than 33,000 gangs in the United States.[1] Gang membership increased most significantly in the Northeast and Southeast regions, although the West and Great Lakes regions boast the highest number of gang members. Neighborhood-based gangs, hybrid gang members, and national-level gangs such as the Sureños are rapidly expanding in many jurisdictions. Many communities are also experiencing an increase in ethnic-based gangs such as African, Asian, Caribbean, and Eurasian gangs. Furthermore, the following attributes have been observed about gangs:

- Gangs are responsible for an average of 48 percent of violent crime in most jurisdictions and up to 90 percent in several others, according to the National Gang Intelligence Center (NGIC) analysis. Major cities and suburban areas experience the most gang-related violence. Local neighborhood-based gangs and drug crews continue to pose the most significant criminal threat in most communities. Aggressive recruitment of juveniles and immigrants, alliances and conflict between gangs, the release of incarcerated gang members from prison, advancements in technology and communication, and Mexican drug gang involvement in drug distribution have resulted in gang expansion and violence in a number of jurisdictions.[2]

- Gangs are increasingly engaging in nontraditional gang-related crime, such as alien smuggling, human trafficking, and prostitution. Gangs are also engaging in white-collar crime such as counterfeiting, identity theft, and mortgage fraud, primarily due to the high profitability and much lower visibility and risk of detection and punishment than drug and weapons trafficking.

- U.S.-based gangs have established strong working relationships with Central American and Mexican drug gangs to perpetrate illicit cross-border activity, as well as with some organized crime groups in some regions of the United States. U.S.-based gangs and Mexican groups are establishing wide-reaching drug networks; assisting in the smuggling of drugs, weapons, and illegal immigrants along the Southwest Border; and serving as enforcers for Mexican trafficking interests on the U.S. side of the border.

- Many gang members continue to engage in gang activity while incarcerated. Family members play pivotal roles in assisting or facilitating gang activities and recruitment during a gang members' incarceration. Gang members in some correctional facilities are adopting radical religious views while incarcerated.

- Gangs encourage members, associates, and relatives to obtain law enforcement, judiciary, or legal employment in order to gather information on rival gangs and law enforcement operations. Gang infiltration of the military continues to pose a significant criminal threat, as members of

|Fig. 16.1| △

Juvenile Chain Gangs such as this in Phoenix are often breeding grounds for juvenile gangs once inmates are released from custody. Here, after removing weeds and brush in the desert heat, inmates walk back to a van that will take them to the Maricopa County Jail.

UPPA / Photoshot

at least 53 gangs have been identified on both domestic and international military installations. Gang members who learn advanced weaponry and combat techniques in the military are at risk of employing these skills on the street when they return to their communities.[3]

- Gang members are acquiring high-powered, military-style weapons and equipment, which poses a significant threat because of the potential to engage in lethal encounters with law enforcement officers and civilians. Typically firearms are acquired through illegal purchases, straw purchases via surrogates or middlemen, and thefts from individuals, vehicles, residences, and commercial establishments. Gang members also target military and law enforcement officials, facilities, and vehicles to obtain weapons, ammunition, body armor, police gear, badges, uniforms, and official identification.

- Gangs on Indian Reservations often emulate national-level gangs and adopt names and identifiers from nationally recognized urban gangs. Gang members on some Indian Reservations are associating with gang members in the community to commit crime.

- Gangs are becoming increasingly adaptable and sophisticated, employing new and advanced technology to facilitate criminal activity discreetly, enhance their criminal operations, and connect with other gang members, criminal organizations, and potential recruits nationwide and even worldwide.[4]

GANG-RELATED TRENDS Gang membership continues to expand throughout communities nationwide, as gangs evolve, adapt to new threats, and form new associations. Consequently, gang-related crime and violence is increasing as gangs employ violence and intimidation to control their territory and illicit operations. Many gangs have advanced beyond their traditional role as local retail drug distributors in large cities to become more organized, adaptable, and influential in large-scale drug trafficking.

Gang members are migrating from urban areas to suburban and rural communities to recruit new members, expand their drug distribution territories, form new alliances, and collaborate with rival gangs and criminal organizations for profit and influence. Local neighborhood, hybrid, and female gang membership is on the rise in many communities.[5] Prison gang members, who exert control over many street gang members, often engage in crime and violence upon their return to the community. Gang members returning to the community from prison have an adverse and lasting impact on neighborhoods, which may experience notable increases in crime, violence, and drug trafficking.

Street gangs are involved in a host of violent criminal activities, including assault, drug trafficking, extortion, firearms offenses, home invasion robberies, homicide, intimidation, shootings, and weapons trafficking. Recent statistics indicate that gang control over drug distribution and disputes over drug territory have increased, which may be responsible for the increase in violence in many areas. Conflict between gangs, gang migration into rival gang territory, and the release of incarcerated gang members back into the community have also resulted in an increase in gang-related crime and violence in many jurisdictions

GANG MEMBERSHIP AND EXPANSION Of the approximately 1.4 million active street gangs, outlaw motorcycle gangs and prison gang members, comprising more than 33,000 gangs, are active within all 50 states, the District of Columbia, and Puerto Rico. According to the U.S. Department of Justice, this represents a 40 percent increase from an estimated 1 million gang members in 2009. This increase in gang membership is attributed primarily to better reporting, more aggressive recruitment efforts by gangs, the formation of new gangs, new opportunities for drug trafficking, and collaboration with rival gangs and drug-trafficking organizations.

The increase in gang membership is often attributed to a number of factors including the gangster rap culture, the facilitation of communication and recruitment through the Internet and social media, the proliferation of generational gang members, and a shortage of resources to combat gangs.[6]

Neighborhood-based gangs continue to pose the greatest threat in most law enforcement jurisdictions nationwide. According to recent research, since 2009, gang membership increased most significantly in the Northeast and Southeast regions, although the West and North Central regions—particularly Arizona, California, and Illinois—report the highest number of gang members.[7]

Sureño gangs, including **Mara Salvatrucha** (also known as the MS-13), 18th Street, and Florencia 13, are expanding faster than other national-level gangs, both in membership and geographically. In fact, 20 states plus the District of Columbia report an increase of Sureño

|Fig. 16.2| △

Major Cities Reporting Gang-Related Drug Activity in 2010.
Source: National Gang Intelligence Center, 2012.

migration into their region between 2008 and 2011.[8] California has experienced a substantial migration of Sureño gangs into northern California and neighboring states, such as Arizona, Nevada, and Oregon.

There has also been a significant increase in OMGs in a number of jurisdictions, with approximately 44,000 members nationwide comprising approximately 3,000 gangs. The most significant increase in OMGs has been seen in Alaska, Arizona, Colorado, Connecticut, Delaware, Florida, Georgia, Iowa, Missouri, Montana, Oregon, Pennsylvania, South Carolina, Tennessee, Utah, and Virginia. This increases the potential for gang-related turf wars with other local OMGs.

Gang	Definition
Street	Street gangs are criminal organizations formed on the street operating throughout the United States.
Prison	Prison gangs are criminal organizations that originated within the penal system and operate within correctional facilities throughout the United States, although released members may be operating on the street. Prison gangs are also self-perpetuating criminal entities that can continue their criminal operations outside the confines of the penal system.
Outlaw Motorcycle Gangs	OMGs are organizations whose members use their motorcycle clubs as conduits for criminal enterprises. Although some law enforcement agencies regard only One Percenters as OMGs, for the purpose of this book the term covers all OMG criminal organizations, including OMG support and puppet clubs.
One Percenter OMGs	ATF defines *One Percenters* as any group of motorcyclists who have voluntarily made a commitment to band together to abide by their organization's rules enforced by violence and who engage in activities that bring them and their club into repeated and serious conflict with society and the law. The group must be an ongoing organization, association of three (3) or more persons which have a common interest and/or activity characterized by the commission of or involvement in a pattern of criminal or delinquent conduct. ATF estimates there are approximately 300 One Percenter OMGs in the United States.
Neighborhood/Local	Neighborhood or local street gangs are confined to specific neighborhoods and jurisdictions and often imitate larger, more powerful national gangs. The primary purpose for many neighborhood gangs is drug distribution and sales.

Source: Emerging Trends. (2012). *National Gang Threat Assessment—2011*. Washington, DC: National Gang Intelligence Center.

Gang Identifiers

Gangs often establish distinctive, characteristic identifiers, including graffiti tag colors, hand signals, clothing, jewelry, hairstyles, fingernails, slogans, and signs (e.g., the swastika, the noose, the cross, five-and six-pointed stars, crowns, and tridents).[9] Flags (e.g., the Confederate flag), secret greetings, slurs, code words, and other group-specific symbols associated with the gang's common beliefs, rituals, and mythologies are used to define and differentiate themselves from rival groups and gangs.[10] As an alternative language, hand signals, symbols, and slurs in speech, graffiti, print, music, or other media communicate specific informational cues used to threaten, disparage, taunt, harass, intimidate, alarm, influence, or exact specific responses including obedience, submission, fear, or terror.[11]

One study focused on terrorism and symbols states, "…Symbolism is important because it plays a part in impelling the terrorist to act and then in defining the targets of their actions."[12] Displaying a gang sign, such as the noose, as a symbolic act can be construed as:

> …a threat to commit violence communicated with the intent to terrorize another, to cause evacuation of a building, or to cause serious public inconvenience, in reckless disregard of the risk of causing such terror or inconvenience…an offense against property

or involving danger to another person that may include but is not limited to recklessly endangering another person, harassment, stalking, ethnic intimidation, and criminal mischief.[13]

INCREASING GANG SOPHISTICATION Recent experience with the investigation of gangs shows that gang members are becoming more sophisticated in their structure and operations and are learning to avoid scrutiny by the police and work around laws focusing on gang enforcement. Recent research shows that gangs in numerous cities have changed or stopped traditional or stereotypical gang signs and symbols by no longer displaying their colors, tattoos, or hand signs. Other gangs are forming **hybrid gangs** to avoid police attention and make it more difficult for police to identify and monitor them. Furthermore, many gangs are engaging in more sophisticated criminal schemes, including white-collar and cyber crime, targeting and infiltrating sensitive systems to gain access to sensitive areas or information, and targeting and monitoring law enforcement.

EXPANSION OF ETHNIC-BASED AND NONTRADITIONAL GANGS Law enforcement officials in jurisdictions nationwide report an expansion of African, Asian, Eurasian, Caribbean, and Middle Eastern gangs, according to NGIC reporting. Many communities are also experiencing increases in hybrid and nontraditional gangs.

Asian Gangs Asian gangs, historically limited to regions with large Asian populations, are expanding throughout communities nationwide. Although often considered street gangs, Asian gangs operate similar to Asian criminal enterprises with a more structured organization and hierarchy. They are not tur foriented like most African American and Hispanic street gangs and typically maintain a low profile to avoid law enforcement scrutiny. Asian gang members are known to prey on their own race and often develop a relationship with their victims before victimizing them. Police have limited knowledge of Asian gangs and often have difficulty penetrating these gangs because of language barriers and gang distrust of non-Asians.[14] As of the writing of this book, Asian gangs are involved in a number of criminal activities that include violent crime, drug and human trafficking, and white-collar crime. The recent increase in Asian gang membership is also thought to be due to the recruitment of non-Asian members into the gang in order to compete better with other street gangs for territory and control of illicit markets.

EAST AFRICAN GANGS

Somali Gangs Somali gang presence has increased in several cities throughout the United States. Somali gangs are most prevalent in the Minneapolis-St. Paul, Minnesota; San Diego, California; and Seattle, Washington, areas, primarily as a result of proximity to the Mexican and Canadian

|Fig. 16.3|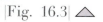

Members of Mexican security forces stand guard over 105 tons of processed and packaged Mexican-grown marijuana seized in March 2010. The marijuana was wrapped in 10,000 packages. This single seizure demonstrates the capabilities and high stakes of the Mexican drug-trafficking industry.

Xinhua / Photoshot

borders, according to ICE, NGIC, and law enforcement reporting. Somali gang activity has also been reported in other cities throughout the United States such as Nashville, Tennessee; Clarkston, Georgia; Columbus, Ohio; East Brunswick, New Jersey; and Tucson, Arizona. Unlike most traditional street gangs, Somali gangs tend to align and adopt gang names based on clan or tribe, although a few have joined well-established national gangs such as the Crips and Bloods.

Somalian gangs are involved in drug and weapons trafficking, human trafficking, credit card fraud, prostitution, and violent crime. Homicides involving Somali victims are often the result of clan feuds between gang members. Sex trafficking of females across jurisdictional and state borders for the purpose of prostitution is also a growing trend among Somalian gangs.

CARIBBEAN GANGS Although largely confined to the East Coast, Caribbean gangs, such as Dominican, Haitian, and Jamaican gangs, are expanding in a number of communities throughout the United States.

Dominican Gangs The Trinitarios, the most rapidly expanding Caribbean gang and the largest Dominican gang, are a violent prison gang with members operating on the street. The Trinitarios are involved in homicide, violent assaults, robbery, theft, home invasions, and street-level drug distribution. Although predominate in New York and New Jersey, the Trinitarios have expanded to communities throughout the eastern United States, including Georgia, Massachusetts, Pennsylvania, and Rhode Island. Dominicans Don't Play (DDP), the second largest Dominican gang based in Bronx, New York, are known for their violent machete attacks and drug-trafficking activities in Florida, Michigan, New Jersey, New York, and Pennsylvania. An increase in the Dominican population in several eastern U.S. jurisdictions has resulted in the expansion and migration of Dominican gangs such as the Trinitarios.

Haitian Gangs Haitian gangs, such as the Florida-based Zoe Pound, have proliferated in many states primarily along the East Coast in recent years, according to NGIC reporting. These gangs are present in Connecticut, Florida, Georgia, Indiana, Maryland, Massachusetts, New Jersey, New York, North Carolina, South Carolina, and Texas. An example is the Zoe Pound gang, a street gang founded in Miami, Florida, by Haitian immigrants in the United States.

The gang is involved in drug trafficking, robbery, and related violent crime. According to the FBI, in February 2010, 22 suspected Zoe Pound members in Chicago, Illinois, were charged with the possession of, and conspiracy to traffic, powder and crack cocaine from Illinois to Florida.[15]

Jamaican Gangs Traditional Jamaican gangs operating in the United States are generally unsophisticated and lack a significant hierarchical structure, unlike gangs in Jamaica.[16] Many active Jamaican gangs operating in the United States maintain ties to larger criminal organizations and gangs in Jamaica, such as the Shower Posse or the Spangler Posse. Jamaican gang members in the United States engage in drug and weapons trafficking.[17]

PRISON GANGS Prison gang-related crime and violence in the nation's corrections system poses a significant threat to facility employees and a growing threat in many communities. Once incarcerated, most street gang members join an established prison gang to ensure their protection. Estimates are that there are approximately 230,000 gang members incarcerated in federal and state prisons nationwide. Their large numbers and dominant presence allows prison gangs to employ bribery, intimidation, and violence to exert influence and control over many correctional facilities. Violent disputes over control of drug territory and enforcement of drug debts frequently occur among incarcerated gang members.

Incarcerated gang members often rely on family, friends, corrupt lawyers, and corrections personnel to transmit their messages to gang members on the street. Incarcerated gang members exploit attorney–client privileges, which include unmonitored visiting and legal mail, to pass coded or concealed communications.

Smuggled cell phones are an ongoing problem for prison administrators in correctional facilities throughout the country. Smuggled cell phones and smart phones afford incarcerated gang members more influence and control over street gangs through unrestricted access and unmonitored conversations via voice calling, Internet access, text messaging, e-mail, and social networking websites.[18] Instances of violence directed by inmates using mobile devices are also a growing concern for corrections officials. Incarcerated gang members communicate covertly with illegal cell phones to plan or direct criminal activities such as drug distribution, assault, and murder.[19]

GANG INFILTRATION OF CORRECTIONS AND LAW ENFORCEMENT Gang infiltration of law enforcement, government, and correctional agencies poses a significant security threat due to the access criminals have to sensitive information pertaining to investigations or protected persons. Gang members serving in law enforcement agencies and correctional facilities may compromise security and criminal investigations and operations while acquiring knowledge and training in police tactics and weapons. Corrupt law enforcement officers and correctional staff have assisted gang members in committing crimes and have impeded investigations.

- A Crip gang member applied for a law enforcement position in Oklahoma.
- OMGs engage in routine and systematic exploitation and infiltration of law enforcement and government infrastructures to protect and perpetrate their criminal activities. OMGs regularly solicit information of intelligence value from government or law enforcement employees.
- In November 2010, a parole worker in New York was suspended for relaying confidential information to a Bloods gang member in Albany.[20]
- In July 2010, a Riverside County, California, detention center sheriff deputy was convicted of assisting her incarcerated Mexican Mafia (EME) boyfriend with murdering two witnesses in her boyfriend's case.[21]
- In April 2010, a former Berwyn, Illinois, police officer pleaded guilty to charges of conspiracy to commit racketeering and to obstruct justice for his part in assisting an OMG member in targeting and burglarizing rival businesses.[22]

NONTRADITIONAL GANGS

Hybrid Gangs The expansion of hybrid gangs—nontraditional gangs with multiple affiliations—is a continued phenomenon in many jurisdictions nationwide. Because of their multiple affiliations, ethnicities, migratory nature, and nebulous structure, hybrid gangs are difficult to track, identify, and target as they are transient and continuously evolving. Furthermore, these multiethnic, mixed-gender gangs pose a unique challenge to law enforcement because they are adopting national symbols and gang members often crossover from gang to gang. Hybrid gangs are of particular concern to law enforcement because members often escalate their criminal activity in order to gain attention and respect.

Hybrid gangs, which are present in at least 25 states, are fluid in size and structure, yet tend to adopt similar characteristics of larger urban gangs, including their own identifiers, rules, and recruiting methods.[23] Like most street gangs, hybrid gang members commit a multitude of street and violent crime. Hybrid gangs have now evolved from neighborhood crews that formed to expand drug trafficking, or from an absence of, or loyalty to, nationally recognized gangs in their areas.

Juggalos The U.S. Department of Justice reported in 2011 that the Juggalos, a loosely organized hybrid gang, is rapidly expanding into many U.S. communities. Although recognized as a gang in only four states, many Juggalos subsets exhibit gang-like behavior and engage in criminal activity and violence. Law enforcement officials in at least 21 states have identified criminal Juggalos subsets.[24]

Most crimes committed by Juggalos are sporadic, disorganized, individualistic, and often involve simple assault, personal drug use and possession, petty theft, and vandalism. However, according to recent research, a small number of Juggalos are forming more organized subsets and engaging in more gang-like criminal activity, such as felony assaults, thefts, robberies, and drug sales. Social networking websites are a popular conveyance for Juggalos subculture to communicate and expand.[25]

GANGS AND ALIEN SMUGGLING, HUMAN TRAFFICKING, AND PROSTITUTION
Gang involvement in alien smuggling, human trafficking, and prostitution is increasing primarily due to their higher profitability and lower risks of detection and punishment than that of drug and weapons trafficking. Over the past year, federal, state, and local law enforcement officials in at least 35 states and U.S. territories have reported that gangs in their jurisdictions are involved in alien smuggling, human trafficking, or prostitution.

Alien Smuggling Many street gangs are becoming involved in alien smuggling as a source of revenue. According to U.S. law enforcement officials, tremendous incentive exists for gangs to diversify their criminal enterprises to include alien smuggling, which can be more lucrative and less risky than the illicit drug trade. Over the past two years numerous federal, state, and local law enforcement agencies nationwide have reported gang involvement in incidents of alien smuggling. In some instances, gang members were among those being smuggled across the border into the United States following deportation. In other cases, gang members facilitated the movement of migrants across the U.S.-Mexico border

Human Trafficking Human trafficking is another source of revenue for some gangs. Victims—typically women and children—are often forced, coerced, or led with fraudulent pretense into prostitution and forced labor. The Bloods, MS-13, Sureños, and Somali gangs have been reportedly involved in human trafficking.[26]

Prostitution Prostitution is also a major source of income for many gangs. Gang members often operate as pimps, luring or forcing at-risk, young females into prostitution and controlling them through violence and psychological abuse. Asian gangs, Bloods, Crips, Gangster Disciples, MS-13, Sureños, Vice Lords, and members of OMGs are involved in prostitution operations, according to FBI, NGIC, and multiple law enforcement reporting.[27]

Gangs and Drug-Trafficking Organizations Many gangs in the United States have established strong working relationships with Central America and Mexico-based drug gangs to cause the smuggling of drugs across the U.S.-Mexico and U.S.-Canada borders. Mexican drug gangs now control most of the cocaine, heroin, methamphetamine, and marijuana trafficked into the United States from Mexico and regularly employ deadly force to protect their drug shipments in Mexico and while crossing the U.S.–Mexico border.

Mexican Drug-Trafficking Organizations Mexican drug-trafficking organizations are among the most prominent drug gangs primarily because of their control over the production of most drugs consumed in the United States. They are known to regularly collaborate with U.S.-based street and prison gang members and occasionally work with select OMG and White Supremacist groups, purely for financial gain. The prospect of financial gain is resulting in the suspension of traditional racial and ideological division among U.S. prison gangs, providing Mexican drug gangs the means to further expand their control over drug trafficking in the United States.[28] Hispanic and African American street gangs are also expanding their influence over drug distribution in rural and suburban areas and acquire drugs directly from Mexican drug gangs in Mexico or along the Southwest border.[29]

U.S.-Based Gangs with Ties to Mexican Drug Gangs	
Arizona New Mexican	Mara Salvatrucha
Mafia	(MS-13)
Aryan Brotherhood	Mexican Mafia
Avenues	Mongols
Bandidos	Norteños
Barrio Azteca	Satins Disciples
Barrio Westside	Sureños
Black Guerilla Family	Tango Blast
Bloods	Texas Mexican Mafia
California Mexican	(Mexikanemi)
Mafia (Eme)	Texas Syndicate
Crips	Tri-City Bombers
Hardtimes 13	Vagos
Happytown Pomona	Vatos Locos
Hells Angels	Westside Nogalitas
Hermanos de	Wetback Power
Pistoleros Latinos	Wonder Boys
(HPL)	18th Street Gang
La NuestraFamilia	
Latin Kings	
Lennox 13	

Source: FBI, 2012

|Fig. 16.4| △

Nicaraguan police hand over Saul Antonio Turcios Angel (front) who is regarded as boss of the criminal gang MS-13 or Mara Salvatrucha. Angel, 29, is considered by Interpol as being "highly dangerous" and is know to have been active in drug-trafficking activities in the United States.

Xinhua / Photoshot

Mexican drug gangs have been known to contract with street and prison gangs along the Southwest border to enforce and secure smuggling operations in Mexico and the United States, particularly in California and Texas border communities.[30] Gang members who are U.S. citizens are valuable to Mexican traffickers, as they can generally cross the U.S.-Mexico border with less law enforcement scrutiny and are therefore less likely to have illicit drug loads interdicted.[31] Mexican drug-trafficking gangs use street and prison gang members in Mexico, Texas, and California to protect smuggling routes, collect debts, transport illicit goods, including drugs and weapons, and execute rival traffickers.[32]

Many of these crimes are committed in exchange for money and drugs, and as a result, street and prison gangs in the United States have gained greater control over drug distribution in rural and suburban areas. Gang members, including Barrio Azteca, MS-13, and Sureños, have been intercepted driving with weapons and currency toward Mexico from such states as California, Colorado, Georgia, and Texas.

Gangs' increased collaboration with Mexican traffickers has altered the dynamics of the drug trade at the wholesale level. U.S. gangs, which traditionally served as the primary organized retail or mid-level distributor of drugs in most major U.S. cities, are now purchasing drugs directly from the cartels, thereby eliminating the mid-level wholesale dealer. Furthermore, advanced technology, such as wireless Internet and Voice over Internet Protocol capabilities, has made the recruitment, collaboration, and coordination of criminal activity more efficient and lucrative, and allows direct contact between the gangs and drug traffickers.[33] To increase their control over drug trafficking in smaller markets, street gangs have acquired large wholesale quantities of drugs at lower prices directly from drug traffickers in Mexico and along the U.S.-Southwest border.[34]

Like most criminal organizations in the early stages of establishing their control of a market share in prohibited substances, Mexican syndicates still cling to the excessive use of violence as a means of control. As of late 2011, Mexican drug traffickers had been documented forging alliances with U.S. drug gangs such as prison gangs and outlaw motorcycle gangs to expand their operations in the United States. The use of such U.S. gangs has made it difficult for police to identify the managers of Mexican drug operations. Of the many drug cartels operating in Mexico, the most prominent are the Gulf, Sinaloa, Juárez, and Tijuana cartels.

The Southwest Border   As of the preparation of this book the U.S.-Southwest border region represents a continuing criminal threat to the United States. The rugged, rural, and porous area along the nearly 2,000 miles of contiguous U.S.-Mexican territory invites widespread criminal activity, including drug and arms trafficking, alien smuggling, human trafficking, extortion, kidnapping, and public corruption. U.S.-based gangs, Mexican drug gangs, and other criminal organizations in both the United States and Mexico are taking advantage of this fluid region and make enormous profit by establishing wide-reaching drug networks; assisting in the smuggling of drugs, arms, and illegal immigrants; and serving as enforcers for MDTO interests on the U.S. side of the border.

Mexican Drug-Trafficking Gang Aliances And Rivals, 2011		
Cartel	**Aligned With**	**Rivals**
The Sinaloa Cartel (aka Guzman-Loera Organization or Pacific Cartel)	Hermanos de Pistoleros Latinos New Mexico Syndicate Los Carnales Latin Kings Mexican Mafia (California) Sureños MS-13 Arizona Mexican Mafia (Old & New) Wet Back Power Sinaloa Cowboys West Texas Tangos Los Negros Valencia Cartel (Considered a branch of the Sinaloa Cartel) Sonora Cartel (Considered a branch of the Sinaloa Cartel) Colima Cartel (Considered a branch of the Sinaloa Cartel) Border Brothers (California) Border Brothers (Arizona)	Los Zetas Cardenas-Guillen Cartel (Gulf) Tijuana Cartel Beltran-Leyva Cartel Juarez Cartel
La Familia Michoacana Cartel (Formerly part of Los Zetas under the authority of the Gulf Cartel)	Sinaloa Cartel Cardenas-Guillen Cartel (Gulf) Sureños MS-13 West Texas Tangos	Los Zetas Cardenas-Guillen Cartel (Gulf Cartel) The Beltran-Leyva Cartel Vincente Carrillo-Fuentes Cartel (Juarez Cartel)
Los Zetas	Vincente Carrillo-Fuentes Cartel (Juarez) Beltran-Leyva Cartel Barrio Azteca Hermanos de Pistoleros Latinos Mexikanemi Texas Syndicate MS-13	Arellano-Felix Cartel (Tijuana) Cartel de la Sierra (Sierra Cartel) Sinaloa Cartel La Familia Michoacana Cartel Cardenas-Guillen Cartel (Gulf)
Cardenas-Guillen Cartel (Gulf Cartel)	Sinaloa Cartel La Familia Michoacana Cartel Hermanos de Pistoleros Latinos Partido Revolutionary Mexicano Raza Unida Texas Chicano Brotherhood	Los Zetas La Familia Michoacana Cartel The Sinaloa Cartel
Vincente Carrillo-Fuentes Cartel (Juarez Cartel)	Los Zetas Hermanos de Pistoleros Latinos Barrio Azteca New Mexico Syndicate Los Carnales	The Sinaloa Cartel La Familia Michoacana Cartel
The Beltran-Leyva Cartel (expected to soon be taken over by the Sierra Cartel)	Los Zetas	Los Zetas La Familia Michoacana Cartel
Arellano-Felix Cartel (Tijuana Cartel)	Mexican Mafia (California) Sureños Arizona Mexican Mafia (Old & New) Border Brothers (California)	Los Zetas The Sinaloa Cartel

Source: *National Gang Threat Assessment—2011.*

|Fig. 16.5| △

A Mara 18 gang member being assisted by other gang members following a prison riot in Guatemala between the Mara 18 and the MS-13 gangs for prison superiority. The Mara 18 gang is another active drug-trafficking gang with ties throughout the United States.

WpN / Photoshot

Violence in Mexico—particularly in its northern border states—has escalated with over 34,000 murders committed in Mexico over the past four years. While intensified scrutiny from Mexican law enforcement has forced significant disruptions in several dangerous Mexican drug gangs, such disruptions have also served to disrupt the balance of power among these organizations. This has prompted drug cartel rivalries to employ more aggressive tactics as they attempt to assert control over the Southwest border region and its highly lucrative drug-trafficking corridors. Although the majority of the violence from feuding drug cartels occurs in Mexico, Mexican drug cartel activity has fueled crime in the U.S.-Southwest border region, where easy access to weapons, a high demand for drugs, ample opportunity for law enforcement corruption, and a large Hispanic population ripe for recruitment and exploitation exist.

Hispanic prison gangs along the Southwest border region are strengthening their ties with Mexican drug gangs to acquire wholesale quantities of drugs, according to NDIC reporting. In exchange for a consistent drug supply, U.S.-based gangs smuggle and distribute drugs, collect drug proceeds, launder money, smuggle weapons, commit kidnappings, and serve as lookouts and enforcers on behalf of the Mexican drug gangs. These gangs subsequently profit from increased drug circulation in the United States, while U.S.-based gangs have access to a consistent drug supply, which expands their influence, power, and ability to recruit.

THE SCOPE OF DRUG TRAFFICKING ON THE SOUTHWEST BORDER To better understand the impact of Mexico and the illicit drug industry, it is important to understand Mexico's influence on the United States. It could be said that no other country in the world has a greater impact on the drug situation in the United States than does Mexico. The influence of Mexico on the U.S. drug trade is truly unmatched: the result of a shared border; Mexico's strategic location between drug-producing and drug-consuming countries; a long history of cross-border smuggling; and the existence of diversified, poly-drug, profit-minded drug gangs. Each of the four major drugs of abuse—marijuana, cocaine, heroin, and methamphetamine—is either produced in, or transshipped through, Mexico before reaching the United States. The vast majority of bulk currency interdicted within the United States is derived from drug-trafficking activities.

It is estimated that approximately 18 to 39 billion dollars annually is moved from the interior of the U.S. to the Southwest border on behalf of Mexican and Colombian drug organizations. Thus, billions of U.S. dollars are sent back to Mexico annually. From the Mexican perspective, the flow of vast sums of money engenders corruption. The strategic consequence of the continuous seeping of illicit proceeds into the Mexican economy discourages the long-term growth of—indeed even the incentive to sustain—legitimate businesses and institutions.

Heroin Mexico is an opium poppy–cultivating/heroin-producing country. While Mexico accounts for only about 6 percent of the world's opium poppy cultivation and heroin production, it is a major supplier of heroin to abusers in the United States, particularly in regions west of the

Case in Point

>>The Zetas and the Gulf Cartel

The *Gulf cartel* is a Mexican drug cartel based in Matamoros. The Zetas, a criminal group in Mexico, have created their own niche among drug enforcer gangs in that they operate "as a private army under the orders of Cárdenas' Gulf cartel, the first time a drug lord has had his own paramilitary." Most reports indicate that the Zetas were created by a group of 30 lieutenants and sub-lieutenants who deserted from the Mexican military's Special Air Mobile Force Group (Grupo Aeromovil de Fuerzas Especiales, GAFES) to the Gulf cartel in the late 1990s. As such, the Zetas were able to carry out more complex operations and use more sophisticated weaponry.

The Zetas were instrumental in the Gulf cartel's domination of the drug trade in Nuevo Laredo and have fought to maintain the cartel's influence in that city following the 2003 arrest of its leader, Osiel Cárdenas. Press reports have charged that these soldiers-turned-cartel-enforcers were trained in the United States; however, the Washington Office on Latin America was unable to confirm this claim. Estimates on the number of Zetas range from 31 up to 200. Reports indicate that although the Zetas initially comprised members of special forces, they now include federal, state, and local law enforcement personnel as well as civilians. In September 2005, testimony to the Mexican Congress by then Defense Secretary Clemente Vega indicated that the Zetas had also hired at least 30 former Guatemalan special forces (*Kaibiles*) to train new recruits because "the number of former Mexican special forces men in their ranks had shrunk from 50 to no more than a dozen, and they were finding it hard to entice more members of the Mexican military to join."

The Zetas act as assassins for the Gulf cartel. They also traffic arms, kidnap, and collect payments for the cartel on its drug routes. Mexican law enforcement officials report that the Zetas have become an increasingly sophisticated, three-tiered organization with leaders and middlemen who coordinate contracts with petty criminals to carry out street work. The Zetas have maintained the territory of the Gulf cartel in the northern cities of Matamoros and Nuevo Laredo. In addition, they are believed to control trafficking routes along the eastern half of the U.S.-Mexico border. Thus, the Zetas now have a presence in southern Mexico, where the Gulf cartel is

|Fig. 16.6| △

Here, Mexican military members guard Daniel Elizondo Rameriz aka "el locl," the alleged leader of the drug cartel Los Zetas during his presentation to the media on May 21, 2012. The Zetas are thought to be the most violent of the competing Mexican drug cartels.

|Fig. 16.7| △

Photo of the Mexican Sinaloa Cartel's leader Martin Beltran Coronel, aka "Aguila" following his arrest on May 13, 2011.

(continued)

Case in Point (continued)

disputing territory previously controlled by the Juárez and Sinaloa cartels. A recent federal investigation found that the Zetas also engage in kidnapping, drug dealing, and money laundering.

In July 2006, local police in the southern state of Tabasco unknowingly arrested Mateo Díaz López, believed to be a leader of the Zetas. The arrest prompted an assault on the police station, killing four people, including two police officers. However, the assault did not succeed in liberating Díaz López, who was subsequently transferred to a prison in Guadalajara. The Zetas also trained the Michoacán-based La Familia enforcer gang, which has carried out numerous executions in that state. The Familia maintains close ties to the Zetas but is a smaller entity.

Sources: Mexican Drug Cartels. (October 16, 2007). *Congressional Research Service.* Washington, DC: U.S. Government Printing Office; *National Gang Threat Assessment—2011.*

Mississippi River. It is alarming to note that Mexican black tar and brown heroin has appeared increasingly in eastern-U.S. drug markets over the past several years.

Marijuana Mexico is the number one foreign supplier of marijuana abused in the United States. In fact, according to a 2008 interagency report, marijuana is the top revenue generator for Mexican drug-trafficking organizations—a cash crop that finances corruption and the carnage of violence year after year. The profits derived from marijuana trafficking—an industry with minimal overhead costs, controlled entirely by the traffickers—are used not only to finance other drug enterprises by Mexico's poly-drug cartels, but also to pay recurring "business" expenses, purchase weapons, and bribe corrupt officials.

Methamphetamine Mexico is also the number one foreign supplier of methamphetamine to the United States. Although the Mexican government has made enormous strides in controlling—even banning—the importation of methamphetamine precursor chemicals such as ephedrine, pseudo-ephedrine, and phenyl acetic acid, Mexican methamphetamine-producing and -trafficking organizations are proving to be extremely resourceful in circumventing the strict regulatory measures put in place by the Calderon administration. As with heroin, there is considerable financial incentive for the Mexican drug organizations to sustain a trade they control from manufacture to distribution and, in fact, Mexican authorities seized more methamphetamine labs in 2009—210—than in the previous five years combined.

Cocaine Mexico's importance in the cocaine trade cannot be overstated. Since the 1980s, Mexico has served as a primary transportation corridor for cocaine destined for the United States. While Mexico is not a coca-producing country and therefore cannot control the trade from beginning to end, traffickers in Mexico have managed nonetheless to exert increasing control over the trade in exchange for shouldering the greater risk inherent in transporting the cocaine and ensuring its distribution in the United States. In recent years, Mexican trafficking organizations have extended their reach deep into South America to augment—or personally facilitate—cooperation with Colombian sources of supply, or to develop relationships with alternate sources of supply in other cocaine-producing countries, particularly Peru. Demonstrating an even further reach into global cocaine markets, Mexican drug traffickers have evolved into intermediate sources of supply for cocaine in Europe, Australia, Asia, and the Middle East.

As of the preparation of this book, an estimated 93 percent of the cocaine leaving South America for the United States moves through Mexico. In 2009, more cocaine—about 60 percent of the 90 percent, according to interagency estimates—stopped first in a Central American country, before onward shipment to Mexico, than at any time since the interagency began tracking cocaine movement. This trend suggests that the Mexico's drug enforcement initiatives, particularly those related to port security and the tracking of suspicious aircraft, are showing some promise on how the cartels do business, requiring them to take the extra—and ostensibly more costly and vulnerable—step of arranging multistage transportation systems.

Changes in cocaine movement patterns are not the only measurable trend. Beginning in January of 2007—immediately after the Calderon government was installed—the price per gram of cocaine in the United States began to rise, with a correlative drop in cocaine purity.

VIOLENCE IN MEXICO: STATISTICS AND CAUSES While it may seem counterintuitive, the extraordinary level of violence in Mexico is another signpost of successful law-and-order campaigns by military gangs and law enforcement officials in Mexico. The violence in Mexico can be organized into three broad categories: intra-cartel violence that occurs among and between members of the same criminal syndicate, inter-cartel violence that occurs between rival groups, and cartel-versus-government violence. It is important to note that intra- and inter-cartel violence have always been associated with the Mexican drug trade.

The drug trade in Mexico has been rife with violence for decades, though the level and the severity of violence we are seeing today is unprecedented. Without minimizing the severity of the problems we are confronted with today, it is nonetheless critical to understand the background of the "culture of violence" associated with Mexican drug-trafficking organizations and the cyclical nature of the "violence epidemics" with which Mexico is periodically beset. One does not have to go very far back in history to recall the cross-border killing spree engaged in by Los Zetas operatives in the Laredo-Nuevo Laredo area during 2004–2005. But one thing must remain clear in any discussion of violence in Mexico, or violence practiced by Mexican traffickers operating in the United States: drug gangs are inherently violent, and nowhere is this more true than in Mexico, where Wild West–style shootouts between the criminals and the cops, and/or elements of opposing trafficking groups arefar too common. Between 2007 and 2010, there have been over 22,000 drug-related murders in Mexico, as reported by the Mexican Attorney General's Office.

We cringe at news stories detailing the arrest of a "pozolero" (stew-maker), a killer who disposes of his victims' body parts in barrels of acid, or the discovery of a mass grave containing the remains of countless victims decomposing under a layer of lime. But these and other gruesome tactics are not new. What is both new and disturbing are the sustained efforts of Mexican drug traffickers to use violence as a tool to undermine public support for the government's counter-drug efforts. Traffickers have made a concerted effort to send a public message through their bloody campaign of violence. They now often resort to leaving the beheaded and mutilated bodies of their tortured victims out for public display with the intent of intimidating government officials and the public alike.

Particularly worrisome are those tactics intended to intimidate police and public officials, and law-abiding citizens. The intimidation of public and police officials through violence or the threat of violence has a more insidious side. Not all corruption is a clear-cut, money-for-cooperation, negotiation: the intimidation of officials, threats against their lives or their families' lives, is a much more widespread and effective tactic, and likely accounts for a plurality of corrupt law enforcement officials in Mexico.

Murder is not solely a coercive strategy on the part of the cartels. The murders are acts of desperation. Operational successes by the military and law enforcement, and massive reforms being undertaken by the judiciary, have provided the catalyst for much of the violence. The deployment of tens of thousands of military troops—mobilized specifically to confront drug organizations in "hot spots" throughout the country—along with concerted law enforcement operations targeting specific cartel members or specific import/export hubs, has disrupted supply routes both into and out of Mexico, and has shattered alliances. Entry ports for large maritime shipments of cocaine from South America, previously wholly controlled by the cartels through corruption, intimidation, and force, are instead patrolled and inspected by vetted members of Mexico's armed forces. The lucrative transportation corridors within Mexico and into the United States, once incontestably held by cartel "gatekeepers" and "plaza bosses," are now riddled with military checkpoints and monitored by Mexican law enforcement.

Disrupted supply routes translate to intense competition between the drug-trafficking organizations who control still-viable routes and those who want to control them. These stressors are further compounded by shifting alliances, long-standing feuds, and record-breaking seizures by the GOM. Challenging the status quo and holding the traffickers accountable demonstrate the resolve of President Calderon's government. Successfully transforming the situation from one that represents a serious threat to the national security of both Mexico and the United States to a problem that can effectively be dealt with as a traditional criminal justice problem will require considerably more work, particularly with regard to institutional reform and anticorruption efforts. Fortunately, President Calderon has already committed to these reforms, both in rhetoric and in action.

SPILLOVER VIOLENCE Excessive violence by the cartels is a national security problem for Mexico, and—as our close neighbor and political ally—presents high stakes for the United States. In the past year, U.S. intelligence and law enforcement agencies have worked diligently to reach

|Fig. 16.8|

Geographical locations occupied by major Mexican drug cartels. Source: National Gang Intelligence Center, 2012.

a consensus view on "spillover" violence and on U.S. vulnerability to the Mexican cartels' violent tactics. These discussions required the interagency to define "spillover" in practical terms. As agreed to by the interagency community, spillover violence entails deliberate, planned attacks by the cartels on U.S. assets, including civilian, military, or law enforcement officials; innocent U.S. citizens; and physical institutions such as government buildings, consulates, and businesses. This definition does not include trafficker on trafficker violence, whether perpetrated in Mexico or the United States.

Spillover violence is a complicated issue. It is crucial, in order to address the problem with the appropriate programs, resources, and operations, that we understand the difference between the intentional targeting of innocent civilians in the United States, or official U.S. government interests in Mexico or the United States, and actions that are characteristic of violent drug culture, such as the killing of an individual who owes a drug debt to the organization. Certain isolated incidents in the United States, such as the torture by a Mexican trafficker of a Dominican drug customer in Atlanta, are frightening, but do not represent a dramatic departure from the violence that has always been associated with the drug trade.

Much of the risk of spillover violence is posed by younger-generation traffickers whose approach to the drug trade is less rational and profit-minded than that of their "elders," or by multinational street and prison gangs working in concert with Mexican cartels as enforcers and street-level drug distributors. As the GOM has continuously and successfully disrupted the cartels' command and control structure through operations against their leaders, less-experienced "junior" cartel members are inhabiting roles formerly held by traffickers of long standing who, while violent, tended to be more deliberate and cautious in their actions. In Ciudad Juarez, where three individuals associated with the U.S. consulate were killed in March, the Barrio Azteca (BA) street gang is the best known of several gangs being used as enforcers by La Linea, gatekeepers for the Juarez Cartel. The BA has been linked to drug trafficking, prostitution, extortion, assaults, murder, and the retail sale of drugs obtained by Mexican drug-trafficking organizations. Elsewhere in Mexico, the link between street gangs and the Mexican cartels is more fluid and tenuous, with gang members typically filling retail drug sales roles rather than providing enforcement.

GANGS AND THE FUTURE Street, prison, and motorcycle gang membership and criminal activity continue to flourish in U.S. communities where gangs identify opportunities to control street-level drug sales, and other profitable crimes. Gangs will not only continue to defend their territory from rival gangs, but will also increasingly seek to diversify both their membership and their criminal activities in recognition of potential financial gain. New alliances between rival gangs will likely form as gangs suspend their former racial ideologies in pursuit of mutual profit. Gangs will continue to evolve and adapt to current conditions and law enforcement tactics, diversify their criminal activity, and employ new strategies and technology to enhance their criminal operations while facilitating lower-risk and more profitable schemes, such as white-collar crime.

The expansion of communications networks, especially in wireless communications and the Internet, will allow gang members to form associations and alliances with other gangs and criminal organizations—both domestically and internationally—and enable gang members to better facilitate criminal activity and enhance their criminal operations discreetly without the physical interfacing once necessary to conduct these activities.

Changes in immigrant populations, which are susceptible to victimization and recruitment by gangs, may have the most profound effect on street gang membership. Continued drug trafficking–related violence along the U.S.-Southwest border could trigger increased migration of Mexicans and Central Americans into the United States and, as such, provide a greater pool of victims, recruits, and criminal opportunities for street gangs as they seek to profit from the illegal drug trade, alien smuggling, and weapons trafficking. Likewise, increased gang recruitment of youths among the immigrant population may result in an increase in gang membership and gang-related violence in a number of regions.

Street gang activity and violence may also increase as more dangerous gang members are released early from prison and reestablish their roles armed with new knowledge and improved techniques. Prison gang members, already an ideal target audience for radicalization, may expand their associations with foreign gang members or radical criminal organizations, both inside correctional institutions and in the community upon their release.

Gang members armed with high-powered weapons and knowledge and expertise acquired from employment in law enforcement, corrections, or the military may pose an increasing nationwide threat, as they employ these tactics and weapons against law enforcement officials, rival gang members, and civilians.

Globalization, sociopolitical change, technological advances, and immigration will result either in greater gang expansion and gang-related crime or displace gang members as they search for criminal opportunities elsewhere. Stagnant or poor economic conditions in the United States, including budget cuts in law enforcement, may undercut gang dismantlement efforts and encourage gang expansion as police agencies redirect their resources and disband gang units and taskforces, as reported by a large number of law enforcement agencies.

Drug-Related Offenses

Without question, the common denominator between gangs and organized crime groups across the globe is illegal drugs. Over the years, the scope of the drug problem has expanded to the point where an estimated two of every three crimes committed are a result of some type of substance abuse. Drugs such as marijuana, cocaine, heroin, PCP (phencyclidine), LSD (lysergic acid diethylamide), methamphetamine, and **designer drugs** are representative of the most popular substances of abuse in the United States and, consequently, account for much of the nation's crime.

Because of the widespread nature of the problem in both the political and social arenas, policy makers are at a crossroads as to what to do about it. Drug crimes, for example, are generated from two general areas: drug users (both addicts and recreational users) and drug sellers (independent and organized factions). Therefore, the supply-and-demand argument is debated as police

|Fig. 16.9| △

Photo of a criminal investigator with the Kansas City, Missouri, Police Gang Squad "field testing" suspected cocaine. If the tested substance turns blue, it indicates it is cocaine. The field test is typically used to provide probable cause for arrest or search until additional evidence can be identified.

© Mikael Karlsson / Alamy

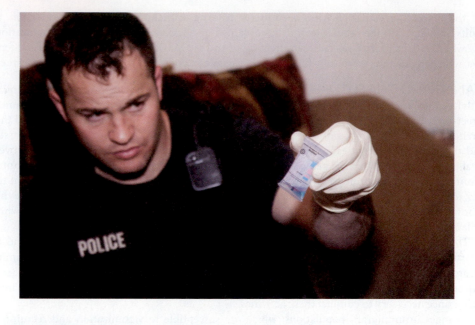

continue to concentrate on the arrest of dealers or users. In either case, police authorities are duty bound to enforce existing drug control laws vigorously on both local and national levels. Although much media attention has been given to drug control in recent years, law enforcement's drug control mission has been well underway since early in the twentieth century. It was during that period that one of the first major drug laws was passed by Congress: the 1914 Harrison Narcotic Act.[35]

Enforcement of this act required federal agents to arrest and interrogate suspects, search and seize contraband, and infiltrate criminal organizations through undercover techniques. Such duties represent only a few investigative responsibilities in this complex area. Many techniques have evolved since then, some more traditional and some controversial. In this chapter, we examine the many areas of concern for criminal investigators in investigating drug offenses.

The General Structure of Drug Laws

As with all criminal violations, drug investigators must familiarize themselves with the law in order to make prosecutable cases. Laws governing illicit drugs appear in virtually all levels of government. Accordingly, drug penalties under different levels of government will also vary from one jurisdiction to another. Generally, criminal law considers several categories of illegal behavior regarding drug abuse:

- **Possession.** Possession usually manifests itself in one of two ways: actual physical custody of the drugs or constructive possession. The latter requires the subject to have knowledge of the presence of the substance and the power and intent to control use of the drug.
- **Distribution.** The charge of drug distribution is of a more serious nature than possession and is most commonly imposed for any exchange of illegal drugs between two or more persons. Exchanges also include drug sales, passing drugs to another, or delivering an illicit drug whether or not for sale or profit.
- **Manufacturing.** Criminal charges can also be assessed for producing illicit drugs. Drugs such as LSD, methamphetamine, fentanyl, and PCP are more typically products of illicit drug labs. Most criminal laws also include as manufacturing the growing of cannabis (marijuana) or conversion of one drug to another, such as cocaine to crack. As drug distribution networks become larger and more sophisticated, more powerful laws may be needed for successful prosecution. Laws such as the **RICO Act,** the Continuing Criminal Enterprise (CCE) Act, and conspiracy statutes better enable prosecutors to attack the management figures of drug-dealing organizations.

The 1970 Controlled Substances Act

The **CSA** has been the legal foundation of the federal government's battle against illicit drug abuse since its implementation in 1970. This comprehensive law includes numerous laws dealing with the manufacture, distribution, and possession of dangerous drugs. The CSA basically took all drugs considered dangerous under existing federal law and placed them into one of five schedules. The placement of a drug under any particular category was based on its medical use, potential for abuse, and safety or propensity for **dependence.** Under this act, drugs can be added, removed, or rescheduled at the initiation of the Department of Health and Human Services, by the DEA, or by the petition of any interested person (i.e., a drug manufacturer, medical association, pharmacy association, public interest group, state or local agency, or individual citizen).

The point of concern in changing a drug's status is whether it has a potential for abuse. If a drug does not have a potential for abuse, it cannot be controlled. Unfortunately, the term *potential for abuse* is not clearly defined under the CSA and therefore has many different interpretations. Generally, however, the following items have determined whether or not a drug has a potential for abuse:

- There is evidence that people are taking the drug(s) containing such a substance in amounts sufficient to create a hazard to their health or to the safety of other people or the community.
- There is sufficient diversion of the drug(s) from legitimate drug channels.
- People are taking the drug(s) containing such a substance on their own initiative rather than on the basis of medical advice from a practitioner licensed by law to administer such drugs in the course of his or her professional practice.
- The drug(s) containing such a substance are new drugs so related in their action to the drug(s) already listed as having potential for abuse.

Tools and Techniques in Drug Investigations

Because of ongoing public concern about drug abuse and violent crime, drug investigations have become a mainstay in many law enforcement agencies. Goals of drug investigation are to:

- Identify and locate known or suspected drug sellers.
- Understand the different types of drugs available on the street, their prices, and packaging methods.
- Identify locations of frequent drug abuse activity.
- Collect evidence on those involved in drug trafficking.
- Reduce the availability of drugs through the aggressive apprehension of drug users and sellers.

The planning and initiation phase of a drug case involves several steps that usually begin with the receipt and verification of information. In this early phase, investigators learn of suspected criminal activity through various sources of information. Great discretion is required here because not every source of information is reliable. Information sources include:

- Other law enforcement agencies (e.g., police departments, sheriff's departments, federal agencies)
- Other units within the police department (e.g., prostitution and vice divisions, the patrol division)
- "Unofficial" information from other officers within the department
- Other criminal justice agencies (e.g., probation and parole, the courts)
- Information provided by good citizens

Confidential Informants

Planning drug investigations through the use of informant information is one of the most common avenues in which drug cases are initiated. Ironically, such information may prove to be extremely valuable or extremely worthless, and investigators must determine its reliability early in the investigation so that costly time is not wasted. After information is received, the investigator must make an effort, independent of the initial source, to verify it. This is generally accomplished by one of three basic methods: surveillance, the development of an informant, and the use of specific sources outside the investigator's agency.

Case Planning

Drug cases frequently net suspects from all walks of society, from the old to the young, the very rich to the very poor, the meek to the violent. Over the years, thousands of drug cases have endured the scrutiny of many a prosecutor, defense attorney, and court of law. Therefore, investigative methods have been somewhat refined over the years, thus dictating that drug enforcement is not an area for trial-and-error tactics. Drug arrests and raids also typically draw media attention, and investigative methods and techniques might fall under close scrutiny. The drug case might also ultimately use sophisticated federal laws such as conspiracy, the RICO Act, and the CCE Act. Implementation of these laws may not be apparent early in the investigation because drug investigations typically gain momentum over time. Accordingly, investigators should plan their cases carefully and thoroughly in anticipation of the use of these laws.

The target of the investigation usually determines the level of involvement of the law enforcement agency. One important planning element is the extent of violations being committed by the target individual. The investigator should establish:

- Whether the person is a drug user or drug dealer
- If he or she is a dealer, whether the level is wholesale or retail
- Any other crimes that the target person is responsible for or involved in (e.g., assault, robbery, murder)
- Whether the target can be used to reach others in the drug organization

Other considerations are also determined by the level of involvement of the target individual. One of the most critical is the arrest strategy to be used. This consideration examines the use of a particular type of drug buy (buy-bust or buy-walk). This determination rests on whether or not the suspect is being considered for later use as an informant. Departmental factors also play a significant role in drug case planning. Obviously, some law enforcement agencies have more resources than others, but certain critical factors should be considered. Investigative resources to consider are:

- *Personnel.* Drug investigations require a sizable commitment of human resources, particularly sworn personnel. Multiple officers are required during **undercover** operations, raids, and surveillance operations.
- *Money.* As with many police operations, money is always an issue. Drug investigations, however, require large amounts of cash for drug transactions between undercover agents and suspects, as well as for overtime, investigative expenses, and equipment.
- *Equipment.* Drug investigations are becoming increasingly more technical with the introduction of high-technology equipment. Most equipment of this nature is typically used for surveillance operations, but investigators must be aware of what type of equipment is available and which is best suited for the agency's mission.

The resources cited earlier represent only a few of the most critical. Others include legal assistance, which should be a required ingredient in any drug investigation. Drug laws are becoming more complex in nature, thereby increasing the opportunities for investigators to make "technical" mistakes during their investigations. If there is any legal question in the mind of the investigator, he or she should always consult a knowledgeable prosecutor for advice before proceeding.

The list of potential informational resources is limited only by the investigator's imagination. The investigator should always keep in mind that information on just about everyone is available somewhere.

The Investigation of Illicit Drug Laboratories

The investigation of illicit drug laboratories usually begins with a base of criminal intelligence information. Such information can be acquired through many sources, including other law enforcement agencies or criminal informants. Other than the preceding sources of information, the drug laboratory can be discovered by other means. For example, an abundance of a drug such

Drug Schedules Under the Controlled Substance Act

Schedule I

The drug or other substance has a high potential for abuse. The drug or other substance has no currently accepted medical use in treatment in the United States. There is a lack of accepted safety for use of the drug under medical supervision.

Examples: Heroin, LSD, marijuana, peyote, methaqualone

Schedule II

The drug or other substance has a high potential for abuse. The drug or other substance has a currently accepted medical use in treatment in the United States or a currently accepted medical use with severe restrictions. Abuse of the drug or other substance may lead to severe psychological or physical dependence.

Examples: Amphetamines, some morphine derivatives, cocaine, PCP

Schedule III

The drug or other substance has a potential for abuse less than the drugs or other substances in Schedules I and II. The drug or other substance has a currently accepted medical use in treatment in the United States. Abuse of the drug or other substance may lead to moderate or low physical dependence or high **psychological dependence.**

Examples: Some barbiturates, some opium derivatives, glutethimide

Schedule IV

The drug or other substance has a low potential for abuse relative to the drugs or other substances in Schedule III. The drug or other substance has a currently accepted medical use in treatment in the United States. Abuse of the drug or other substance may lead to limited physical dependence or psychological dependence relative to the drugs or other substances in Schedule III.

Examples: Chloral hydrate, tranquilizers, some stimulants and depressants

Schedule V

The drug or other substance has a low potential for abuse relative to the drugs or other substances in Schedule IV. The drug or other substance has a currently accepted medical use in treatment in the United States. Abuse of the drug or other substance may lead to limited physical dependence or psychological dependence relative to the drugs or other substances in Schedule IV.

Examples: Some extracts of opium, some extracts of morphine, some derivatives of codeine.

Since passing of the CSA, most states have adopted state versions of the law, which typically include a localized model of the five federal schedules. This allows prosecutors to file charges under either federal or state criminal justice systems, depending on the type of crime committed and the desired result of the criminal prosecution.

|Fig. 16.10| △

Diversion of prescription drugs pose a serious dangerous drug source. Here, a sheriff's deputy and a DEA diversion investigator are auditing a California pharmacy.

London Entertainment / Splash / Newscom

as methamphetamine or PCP that is selling at an unusually low price might indicate a laboratory nearby. When officers suspect an illicit drug lab, the following investigative steps should be considered:

- Check with the local utility companies to see if unusually large amounts of electricity are being used.
- Verify who is receiving mail at the suspect residence by checking with U.S. postal officials in the area.
- Conduct a criminal background investigation on each suspect.
- Survey the suspect location for evidence of exhaust fans used for ventilation.
- Be aware of any unusual odors in the area indicating the presence of a lab.
- Acquire a court order for the telephone tolls of the suspect's phone to reveal associates.

After the preliminary information has been acquired and verified, a second phase of the investigation should be conducted. This phase is designed to give information to the investigator of much greater depth to prepare for possible search warrants, undercover surveillance, or raids. The investigator should:

- Determine the number of inhabitants of the lab.
- Learn the identity of the inhabitants.
- Learn if any weapons are present at the lab location.
- Determine if any security measures have been taken by the suspects (e.g., use of guard dogs, booby traps).
- Attempt to determine the stage of the cooking process. (Is there any finished product available to seize?)
- Determine what chemicals are being used in the drug lab. These may serve as precursors, solvents, or reagents in the synthesis process. In addition, chemicals may be corrosive or even explosive in nature. For example, methamphetamine and PCP laboratories require large amounts of ether, which is extremely unstable and poses an imminent danger to anyone present on the scene.

Becoming a DEA Diversion Investigator

A Diversion Investigator (DI) is a specialist responsible for addressing the problem of controlled pharmaceutical and regulated chemical diversion from their legitimate channels in which they are manufactured, distributed, and dispensed. DIs aid pharmaceutical and chemical industries in complying with the CSA and other pertinent acts, as well as international treaties and conventions. DIs investigate and uncover suspected sources of diversion and take appropriate criminal, civil, or administrative actions. To accomplish this mission, a wide range of work activities is used. One activity, for example, is the scheduled investigation of registered handlers of controlled substances. These investigations serve to deter diversion through evaluation of the registrants' record-keeping procedures, security safeguards, and general compliance with the CSA and implementing regulations. Legitimate handlers of controlled substances who are subject to investigation are drug manufacturers, distributors, importers and exporters, and narcotic treatment programs. Recently, there has been a push to investigate the diversion of controlled substances via the Internet. The rapidly changing environment and the increased diversion of controlled substances using the Internet have created the need for programs to target these sources of diversion.

Frequently, DIs are involved in investigations aimed at serious violators of controlled substance laws and regulations. These registrant violators have a documented or suspected history of drug and chemical diversion to illicit markets. DIs collect and analyze information developed during their investigations and consult with supervisory personnel to determine if criminal prosecution is warranted. DIs also work closely with DEA special agents and state and local law enforcement officers to provide assistance in making undercover purchases and executing search warrants. DIs work closely with attorneys for the DEA, the U.S. Attorneys Office, and state and local prosecutors. DIs are frequently required to testify about the results of their investigations in criminal trials, grand jury proceedings, and administrative hearings.

The job of a DEA DI involves maintaining contact with all levels of the drug and chemical registrant population. DIs often answer questions from registrants concerning their responsibilities under the CSA.

(continued)

A Closer Look... (continued)

Qualifications

- *General.* Candidates must be U.S. citizens and possess a valid driver's license.

- *Physical.* Candidates are required to obtain a medical examination to determine their physical and mental fitness and must be free of any impairment that would interfere with normal work performance. Distant vision should be 20/40 (uncorrected or corrected with glasses or contact lenses). Near vision should be 20/25 and must be sufficient to read Jaeger Type #2 at 14 inches (glasses or contact lenses permitted). Depth perception and the ability to distinguish shades of color (color plate test) are essential. Candidates must be able to hear conversational voices at a distance of 20 feet with both ears. The use of a hearing aid is permissible.

- *Education.* Candidates must have a bachelor's degree (any major) and meet one of the following Superior Academic Achievement Provisions: a grade-point average (GPA) of "B" (2.95 or higher) for all completed undergraduate courses or a GPA of "B+" (3.5 or higher) for all courses in the major field of study or rank in the upper third of class in the college, university, or major subdivision.

- *Experience.* One year of specialized experience equivalent to the next lowest grade level or an equivalent combination of education and experience is required.

- *Special skills.* In addition to the minimal qualifications, credit may be given to individuals who possess one or more of the following special skills: investigative experience, proficiency in a foreign language, accounting experience or degree, chemistry experience or degree, pharmacology or pharmacist experience or degree, computer skills or experience, military service, or law enforcement experience or degree.

Reverse Drug Sting Operations

The reverse sting narcotic sale is one in which undercover investigators, posing as dealers, sell large quantities of narcotics to known traffickers (also see Chapter 7 on undercover operations and surveillance). These types of operations have proven successful in penetrating otherwise untouchable drug markets. The same reverse sting techniques can also be used against drug consumers on the street.

Street-level reverse sting operations can be used whenever any type of controlled substance is being sold in a high-traffic environment. However, police agencies have found it particularly effective in dealing with rock cocaine sales. Rock cocaine, or crack, has become the drug of choice and a serious crime problem on the streets of many American towns and cities.

PLANNING THE REVERSE STING The "rock reverse" is almost always set up on the street in an area generally occupied by large numbers of street dealers or directly in front of a known crack house.

The operation is dangerous for undercover officers and takedown officers, so it is important that personnel be selected carefully for this assignment. All weapons that may be used in the operation should be thoroughly inspected, and officers should wear soft body armor, as they should during all assignments.

Reverse sting operations are manpower intensive. The reverse sting operation discussed here requires between 20 and 25 officers to be conducted safely and efficiently. Although this is a considerable expenditure in manpower, the operation can be justified based on the large number of arrests that can be made and the positive impact this has on the community. Additionally, considerable amounts of property and assets may be forfeited to the jurisdiction as a result of these operations.

MANPOWER CONSIDERATIONS Three undercover investigators should be designated to perform the principal street sales assignments. Each officer should be dressed in a manner characteristic of the local dealers. Primary undercover officer "A" is responsible for making the drug sale while undercover officers "B" and "C" position themselves within 200 feet of officer "A" on each side. Vehicle assignments are as follows:

- *Vehicle 1* is the principal vehicle used to accommodate officers making the arrest. Ideally, this vehicle should be an inconspicuous panel or step van without rear or side windows and with double folding side doors. Five officers should be assigned to this vehicle, three of whom should be uniformed and the remaining two wearing reflective raid jackets. Three of these officers should be designated to use weapons during the arrest, and the other two should be assigned to searching and handcuffing the arrestees.

- *Vehicles 2 and 3* are designated as blockade cars. These cars should be unmarked, inconspicuous sedans or other vehicles with two undercover officers assigned to each. Parked about 100 feet on each side of the van, these vehicles are pulled up to a position to block the suspect's vehicle at the time of the arrest or takedown.
- *Vehicle 4* should be a surveillance van with audio/video and night vision capabilities. The surveillance van is stationary and is placed undercover within 100 feet of the primary undercover officer (A).
- *Vehicles 5 and 6* are marked units with two uniformed officers in each. These vehicles are assigned locations just outside the takedown area and are meant to provide additional coverage if the suspects flee the area.

In addition to these assignments, a prisoner transportation van should be stationed just outside the operations area to ensure expeditious handling of arrestees.

CONDUCTING THE STING The primary takedown vehicle must be in close proximity to the primary undercover officer because rapid response is essential in making the arrest. There must also be an appropriate place to locate the surveillance van so it will be inconspicuous and provide for good audiovisual coverage. In some cases, officers may choose to conduct surveillance from a building location directly opposite the takedown area rather than use a van.

After the operational area has been identified, diagrams of the neighborhood should be developed. These diagrams should include all relevant buildings and features and identify the positions of all police vehicles and personnel to be deployed in the operational area. The diagram should be used during the personnel briefings to walk through the entire operation. If feasible, it is preferred that the entire operation be practiced in a nonpublic area just before being used in the target area.

The reverse sting requires that a quantity of crack cocaine be packaged for sale. A court order may be required for use of this or other contraband from police property control. Preferably, the crack that is used in the sale should be laboratory tested.

Each cocaine rock should be sealed in clear plastic tape, a plastic bag, balloon, or other means. The method for sealing the rock should correspond with the method popularly used in a given area. The plastic bag or other method also allows the cocaine to be marked and discourages suspects from attempting to swallow the evidence.

Before sealing the crack, a piece may also be broken off from each rock and stored as evidence, a measure that helps in prosecuting buyers who manage to swallow or otherwise dispose of the evidence during their arrest. It should be noted that if the suspect swallows the cocaine, he or she should be immediately transported to an emergency medical facility. A potentially lethal overdose can thus be avoided.

Approximately 20 minutes before the operation begins, marked police vehicles with uniformed officers should be sent into the target area to disperse any actual drug dealers. While in the area, these officers should also make contact with the citizens and request that they and their children stay out of the operational area. Most citizens will comply, particularly in view of the fact that their neighborhood may have been overrun by the drug dealers for some time.

The primary undercover officer is responsible for selling the rocks while the two other undercover officers direct potential customers to him or her and provide backup protection. If the operation lasts for an extended period of time, these three officers should rotate assignments.

The primary undercover officer should be positioned directly opposite the takedown van so that takedown officers will be in position almost immediately after their exit from the vehicle. The primary undercover officer should also be wired with a body transmitter so that the transaction can be recorded verbatim. The transmitter also serves as a backup safety device so problems that may develop can be overheard by the officer in the surveillance van.

The undercover officer who is responsible for the sale has the major responsibility for ensuring that an "entrapment" situation is not created by what he or she says or does. The guidelines for the operation developed with the local prosecutor must be specific in terms of the types of language and actions that can be used to establish contact and a dialogue with potential buyers.

Typical guidelines for reverse sting operations instruct undercover officers to stand alongside the street in the target area and act in a manner generally characteristic of local street dealers. Officers are told to ask (after first being approached by a suspect) general questions such as, "What do you want?" or "What are you looking for?" After the customer states that he or she is looking for crack, the officer is free to negotiate a price and conclude the sale.

Through the careful development of an acceptable dialogue between the undercover officer and customer, the danger of entrapment is virtually eliminated. Predisposition of the suspect to commit the crime can easily be shown through audio and video recordings of the incident. The suspect can be seen on videotape slowly driving into an area frequented by crack cocaine dealers. The suspect can be heard asking the undercover detective for cocaine. Predisposition can also generally be established by prior arrest records for drug offenses or by the presence of drug paraphernalia that may be found in the suspect's vehicle.

It should also be noted that in most cases, it is necessary that the suspect actually take possession of the cocaine before he or she can be arrested and charged with possession. Examining the cocaine before purchase does not normally constitute possession.

Case in Point

>>When a Sting Operation Goes Bad: Operation Fast and Furious

Imagine a sting operation called *Operation Fast and Furious* run by federal agents whereby weapons were sold by U.S. agents to known Mexican traffickers for the purpose of tracking those same weapons and arresting all parties involved in the purchase. The problem is, once U.S. agents sold the weapons, they weren't tracked. Instead, the weapons ended up in the arsenals of Mexican traffickers and at one point even used to murder a U.S. agent. This is not hypothetical—it actually happened.

Operation Fast and Furious was a sting operation run by the U.S. Bureau of Alcohol, Tobacco, Firearms and Explosives (ATF) Phoenix Field Division between 2009 and 2010. Fast and Furious was an offshoot of another operation—Project Gunrunner, a Southwest border strategy

first implemented back in 2006 to stem the flow of illegal firearms trafficking into Mexico. The goal of the operation was to allow otherwise-suspected "straw purchasers" of firearms to complete the weapon's purchase and travel back to Mexico. Doing so would ostensibly allow U.S. agents to build a bigger case against Mexican cartels suspected of being the ultimate buyer.

Operation Fast and Furious started in the fall of 2009 and ended in late 2010 shortly after the death of Brian Terry, a U.S. Border Patrol agent, and has since become the subject of controversy and a U.S. Congressional investigation.

Brian Terry was a U.S. Border Patrol agent who, on December 14, 2010, was killed in a gunfight near Rio Rico, Arizona, while trying to apprehend a group of armed suspects. Two weapons found at the crime scene were traced to a Glendale, Arizona, gun store that had cooperated with ATF officials in "Fast and Furious." ATF field agents monitoring the U.S.–Mexicoborder had intended to apprehend gun smugglers attempting to cross over into Mexico with large numbers of guns, but were told by their superiors to stand down and let the smugglers pass.

|Fig. 16.11| △

U.S. attorney general testifying before the House Judiciary Committee during an oversight hearing on Operation Fast and Furious on December 8, 2011.

Photoshot

(continued)

Case in Point (continued)

During Fast and Furious, the ATF facilitated the sale of at least 2,000 guns, being fully aware that most of them would be smuggled into Mexico. By June 2011, the guns had been linked to an estimated 179 crime scenes in Mexico. This was done using "e Trace," ATF's electronic tracing program. By August 2011, 21 additional guns were recovered from violent crime scenes in Mexico. Of the 2,000 guns intentionally released by ATF agents, only 600 are reported as recovered by officials. The remaining 1,400 guns were not recovered.

On November 8, 2011, Attorney General Eric Holder openly stated in Congressional testimony that the operation was "flawed in its concept and flawed in its execution," and he furthermore stated that his office mischaracterized the program in previous letters sent to Congress. Holder remarked that his staff had not kept him informed about the program, and denied any personal wrongdoing. The ATF defended the program by stating that allowing guns to "walk" was done in the past in a controlled manner that involved surveillance and the eventual seizure of the weapons before they disappeared.

Numerous other accounts of Fast and Furious guns have surfaced. For example, on February 15, 2011, U.S. Immigration and Customs Enforcement agent Jaime Zapata was shot to death by Mexican drug cartel members in northern Mexico. Federal investigators traced the gun used to kill Zapata to a Dallas-area man, but there have still been reports connecting the shooting to the Phoenix-based Operation Fast and Furious. In another case, a gun used by drug cartel criminals to shoot at a Mexican military helicopter, forcing it to land, was found to have been one allowed into Mexico by the ATF. In yet another case, two AK-47s sold as part of Operation Fast and Furious and recovered by Mexican police were determined to have been used by members of the Sinaloa Cartel in the high-profile kidnapping of attorney Mario González Rodríguez.

Evidence has surfaced that in April 2011, 40 of the weapons from the operation were found by Mexican police at a home owned by Torres Marrufo in Ciudad Juarez. Marrufo is thought to be the top enforcer for the Sinaloa Cartel, which U.S. intelligence officials consider to be the most powerful drug-trafficking organization in the world.

Problems with Operation Fast and Furious, as reported by the National Rifle Association Institute for Legislative Action, included:

- "…the ATF knowingly allowed as many as 2,500 firearms to be sold illegally to known or suspected straw purchasers. One of those purchasers accounted for over 700 illegal guns."
- "…the ATF ordered its agents working the program not to arrest illegal gun buyers or to interdict thousands of guns that were allowed to 'walk' into criminal hands."
- "…Senior ATF officials in Washington were regularly briefed on the operation and approved of the tactics employed."
- "…the ATF agents who opposed the operation and who raised **objections** were told to 'get with the program' and threatened with job retaliation if they continued their opposition."

On October 3, 2011, CBS News reported that internal Department of Justice e-mails showed that U.S. Attorney General Eric Holder had been sent briefings about "Fast and Furious" as far back as July 2010. This contradicted his testimony to Congress from May 3. In spite of this, Holder was subsequently cleared of any wrongdoing in the Fast and Furious operation.

Thematic questions

We must accept that drug trafficking and violence by sophisticated criminals such as the Mexican drug traffickers must be countered by innovative investigative techniques by U.S. agents. But considering the potential dangers of undercover "sting" operations, such as those associated with Operation Fast and Furious, are such investigative initiatives worth the risk? If so then how can problems such as those seen in Operation Fast and Furious be minimized? Finally, is it even possible, or should it be possible, to conduct such operations without political interference?

Sources: Ahlers, M. (July 11, 2011). Feds expand gun sales reporting requirements in four border states. *CNN U.S.* Available at http://articles.cnn.com/2011-07-11/us/rifle.sales.reporting_1_gun-dealers-gun-sales-atf?_s=PM:US; Attkisson, S. (October 2011). ATF fast and furious: New documents show attorney general Eric Holder was briefed in July 2010. *CBS News Investigates*. Available at http://www.nraila.org/Legislation/Read.aspx?ID=6927; National Rifle Association Institute for Legislative Action (June 17, 2011). Available at http://www.nraila.org/Legislation/Read.aspx?ID=6927.

Some agencies use prearranged signals between the undercover officer and the takedown team to initiate the arrest when the transaction is complete. A discrete signal, such as scratching one's face or another movement, is most useful if a body transmitter is not used by the undercover officer. If the transmitter is used in conjunction with visual surveillance, however, the officer conducting the surveillance should order the takedown. This latter approach is preferable for two reasons:

1. Police officers involved in undercover drug sales have been robbed of their drugs at gunpoint.
2. Some drug buyers, particularly those who have been arrested in stings on prior occasions, can readily detect commonly used police signals.

As soon as the takedown command is given, the officers from the van should exit the vehicle, announce that they are police, and establish a good field of fire that will not jeopardize the undercover officer or other police personnel. Speed in making the takedown is essential. It is far more likely that control and compliance of suspects can be established if officers deploy rapidly and thwart any attempts of the suspect to flee or otherwise react.

As officers exit the van for the takedown, the blocking vehicles should move into positions that will reduce the likelihood of an attempted escape. Officers in the blocking vehicles can also serve as backup for those in the van.

After all suspects are in custody, a prisoner van can be summoned, and other personnel can drive the suspect's vehicle to the impoundment area.

Extraordinary Drug Enforcement Techniques

The scourge of illicit drugs across the United States in the past two decades has resulted in vigorous enforcement of many drug control laws. Along with such aggressive enforcement of traditional drug laws (i.e., distribution, possession, and manufacturing of drugs) comes a wave of nontraditional drug control techniques. The use of nontraditional drug control measures has resulted from criminals who, through expensive attorneys, vast experience in drug trafficking, and common sense, have learned to avoid detection. Since the late 1980s, such control tactics have resulted in convictions of drug dealers, raids, curfews, random searches, and the forfeiture of property. Such measures have not only become increasingly more popular with the police and the general public but they also have enjoyed broad support from the courts. Proponents of unconventional enforcement techniques argue that such measures are necessary to combat the violence and social degradation that accompany drug abuse. Conversely, some civil libertarians claim that such techniques only tend to erode basic rights such as the safeguard against unreasonable search and seizure. Let's now take a look at a couple of the most commonly used nontraditional drug enforcement techniques.

Drug Courier Profiling

Since 1985, the DEA has used a tactic that has since been called a **drug courier profile** (known as Operation Pipeline). Basically, it involves agents observing suspected drug traffickers and developing a pattern of behavior typical of those who use commercial airlines or public highways for drug trafficking. The profiling technique originated with law enforcement officers stationed at airports looking for people paying for plane tickets with cash, using aliases, boarding long flights without checking luggage, and staying briefly in distant cities known to be drug-source cities.

Because these actions can also be innocent, the practice has drawn criticism from civil libertarians. They claim that profiling is a shortcut to establishing the level of suspicion required by the Constitution before the police can interfere with a person's liberty. Most lower courts have responded by upholding the practice because of earlier Supreme Court decisions that permit the use of a "totality of the circumstances" approach to brief detentions by police.

In a precedent-setting decision by the Supreme Court, the technique of drug courier profiling was upheld. The drug decision, *United States* v. *Sokolow* (1989), was written by Judge William H. Rehnquist, and it overruled an earlier decision by the U.S. Court of Appeals in California. In the earlier decision, the court ruled that a brief detention by drug agents of a passenger at Honolulu International Airport was unconstitutional. In his opinion, Chief Judge Rehnquist described evidence available to the agents in what he called "a typical attempt to smuggle drugs through one of the nation's airports." Rehnquist added that "any one of these factors is not by itself proof of any illegal conduct and is quite consistent with innocent travel. But we think taken together they amount to reasonable suspicion."

The agents detained the man long enough to let a trained dog sniff his luggage, and then they found several pounds of cocaine in his shoulder bag. When they stopped him, the agents knew little about him except that he had paid $2,100 for tickets from a roll of $20 bills, had just made a round-trip flight from Honolulu to Miami, stayed in Miami less than 48 hours with no checked luggage, looked nervous, and had used a name that did not match the name under which his

|Fig. 16.12| △

Major domestic drug smuggling corridors targeted by Drug Courier Profiling
(a Domestic Highway Enforcement initiative).

telephone number was listed. The man, Andrew Sokolow, was eventually convicted on federal drug charges. The issue was whether the factors matching Sokolow to a drug courier profile were sufficient to justify his stop and subsequent search without a warrant. The Court held that the stop was within the law.

In the Supreme Court's opinion, certain facts of the *Sokolow* case were pointed out, including Sokolow's attire of a black jumpsuit with gold jewelry and the roll of $20 bills appearing to contain a total of $4,000. Chief Justice Rehnquist also remarked, "while the trip from Honolulu to Miami, standing alone, is not a cause of any sort of suspicion, there was more: Surely few residents of Honolulu travel from that city for 20 hours to spend only 48 hours in Miami during the month of July." Airport detentions have now expanded to the highways, where the DEA's Operation Pipeline identifies vehicles and their occupants who seem to "fit" a certain set of criteria common to those who transport drugs or drug money across the country. Although practices such as drug courier profiling remain controversial, there seems to be growing support in the law enforcement community, the public sector, and the courts for innovative drug control stratagems such as these.

Asset Forfeiture

Because of the increasingly high profits of the drug trade, the practice of asset forfeiture has become an essential tool in drug control. Generally, the theory behind asset forfeiture is to take the profit out of illicit drug sales by seizing money or property that was either used to facilitate a drug crime or acquired with illicit drug revenues. Today, in addition to federal forfeiture laws, most state laws also provide for seizure of assets in drug cases. Although federal seizure laws have been used effectively since the late 1960s, the locus for forfeiture on the federal level is now the 1984

Basic Principles of Drug Courier Profile Use

1. *Drug courier profiles may be used only as a basis for further investigation. Such profiles do not, standing alone, justify an arrest.*

   This principle has been made clear by the courts. Any attempt to arrest a drug courier based solely on the use of the courier profile will almost certainly result in all evidence being suppressed and the criminal charge being dismissed. In addition, the officers and agencies involved may face a very real threat of civil liability as a result of their actions.[36]

2. *The factors that make up the elements of a drug courier profile may, however, under certain circumstances justify an "investigative stop."*

   United States v. *Sokolow* and other court decisions have held that it is not the drug courier profile in itself but the facts and circumstances known to the officers at the time they decide to make an investigative stop that determine whether or not the stop was valid. If, under the totality of the circumstances, the officer's suspicion was reasonable, the stop is valid. The fact that the behavioral characteristics of the suspect that aroused the officer's suspicion happened to appear on a "profile" is irrelevant. It is the circumstances that determine a reasonable suspicion, not the existence or absence of a formal "profile."

   Therefore, the profile can be used only as a starting point: *All* of the circumstances of the case must be considered, not just the items appearing in the profile.

   Even though the profile may certainly be used, it must not be applied in a mechanical, unthinking manner. The officer must consider the profile items in connection with the particular circumstances existing at the time and place. However, the officer may evaluate the circumstances in light of his or her own experience. Conduct seemingly innocent may, when viewed as a whole, reasonably appear suspicious to an officer who is familiar with the practices of drug smugglers and the methods used by them to avoid detection.[37]

3. *The officer must be able to articulate the factors that led him or her to form a reasonable suspicion of the person stopped.*

   Unless the involved officer can successfully explain to the court the factors that justified the stop, the stop will be held invalid, and any subsequent arrest, search, or seizure will likely be invalidated, too. It doesn't do any good to say to the court, "I just had a feeling that something was wrong." The officer must be able to list and explain the specific and particular observations that led him or her to conclude that the person in question might be a drug courier. The ability of the officer to state and explain his or her decision in clear, concrete terms can and often does make the difference between winning and losing a case of this type. Therefore:

4. *Know not only what factors are included in the profile but also why they are included.*

   Because the unthinking, mechanical use of a profile has been disapproved by the courts, the officer must be able to demonstrate to the court that the use of the profile was made intelligently and with an understanding of the meaning of the profile factors.[38]

5. *When possible, try to identify for the court factors in addition to those listed in the profile that contributed to the overall decision to detain the suspect.*

   This helps demonstrate to the court that the use of the profile was not mechanical and unthinking.

6. *Limit detention of the suspect to the minimum necessary to obtain further information.*

   Even if the initial detention is valid, if you hold the suspect for too long or otherwise exceed the balance of "reasonable" detention, the case may be thrown out by the courts. If the initial detention produces additional grounds for suspicion, the detention may be extended, but after a reasonable time, the officers must make the decision to arrest or release the suspect. This is particularly sensitive when the suspect has been removed to a private room for questioning.

7. *If the suspect has not yet been arrested, obtain either a valid consent or a search warrant before searching the suspect's luggage or automobile.*

   Because of the limitations imposed by *Terry* v. *Ohio*, do not permit a complete search of person, luggage, or automobile of the detained suspect unless an arrest has been made or probable cause for such a search has arisen. It will be necessary to have either the suspect's consent or a warrant before anything more than the *Terry* "frisk" can be conducted. Therefore, if the valid consent to search the suspect's luggage or automobile cannot be obtained and there is not yet probable cause for an arrest or a complete search, get a search warrant before searching luggage or vehicles. If the foregoing principles are observed, the use of drug courier profiles will be both proper and effective.

Comprehensive Crime Control Act (CCCA), which provides a revised civil provision for asset forfeiture. A unique aspect of this act is that it specifically recognizes the important role played by local and state law enforcement in drug control. Therefore, included in the act is a provision that enables federal and local law enforcement agencies to work together in facilitating the seizure of property. This can be accomplished on the federal level even though a federal agency was not involved directly in the investigation. The following types of property may be seized under federal forfeiture laws:

- All controlled substances
- Raw materials and equipment used to manufacture controlled substances
- Property used as a container for controlled substances
- Vehicles, boats, and aircraft to transport materials used in violation of the CSA
- All money, negotiable instruments, securities, or other things of value exchanged for controlled substances and all proceeds traceable to such an exchange
- Real property and any improvements thereon used or intended to be used to commit or facilitate a violation of the CSA

Under the 1984 act, the attorney general or a designee can make an "equitable" transfer of the forfeited property so as to reflect the contribution of the state or local agency that participated in any of the facts that led to the seizure of the property. Under these circumstances, all agencies—federal, state, and local—benefit.

Source: Available at http://www.streetgangs.com/crips/.

Summary Checklist

In this chapter, we consider the ways information about crimes is documented by criminal investigators. A properly documented case is one that is more likely to succeed in court. See how well you are able to answer the following questions in your checklist.

1. **Describe the process of distribution of illegal drugs.**

   Drug sales networks differ depending on the type of area (rural or urban), the type of drug, and the techniques of the group distributing the drug.

   - Most large urban areas have copping areas—sections of town known as drug distribution areas—that are well known to drug users.
   - Neighborhood bars, truck stops, or homes in affluent areas of town are sometimes fixed locations for drug dealing.
   - Crack houses, often abandoned buildings or apartments in public housing projects located near copping areas, are also fixed locations for drug dealing.

2. **Explain the extent that gangs exist in the United States and nearby countries.**

   Gangs appear to be expanding, evolving, and posing an increasing threat to U.S. communities.

   - Many are sophisticated criminal networks with members who are violent, distribute wholesale quantities of drugs, and develop and maintain close working relationships with members and associates of transnational criminal/drug-trafficking organizations.
   - Gangs are becoming more violent and are engaging in less-typical and lower-risk crime.
   - Gangs are more adaptable, organized, sophisticated, and opportunistic.

   In 2012 there were approximately 1.4 million active street, prison, and outlaw motorcycle gang members comprising over 33,000 gangs in the United States.

   - Gang membership has increased most significantly in the Northeast and Southeast regions.
   - Neighborhood-based gangs, hybrid gang members, and national-level gangs are expanding rapidly in many jurisdictions.
   - Ethnic-based gangs are increasing in many communities.
   - Gangs are responsible for an average of 48 percent of violent crime in most jurisdictions and up to 90 percent in several others.

3. **What are the different types of gangs in the United States?**

   There are a number of different types of gangs. These include:

   - Street gangs—criminal organizations formed on the street operating throughout the United States

- Prison gangs—criminal organizations that originated within the penal system and operate within correctional facilities throughout the United States. Released members may be operating on the street
- Outlaw motorcycle gangs (OMGs)—organizations whose members use their motorcycle clubs as conduits for criminal enterprises
- One Percenter OMGs—any group of motorcyclists who have voluntarily made a commitment to band together to abide by their organization's rules enforced by violence and who engage in activities that bring them and their club into repeated and serious conflict with society and the law
- Neighborhood/local gangs—street gangs that are confined to specific neighborhoods and jurisdictions. They often imitate larger, more powerful gangs.

4. Outline the various businesses conducted by members of organized crime in the United States.

Gangs are involved in a variety of businesses. Some of the activities in which gang involvement is increasing include:

- Alien smuggling
- Human trafficking
- Prostitution
- Drug trafficking

5. Explain the general structure of drug laws.

Laws governing illicit drugs appear in virtually all levels of government. Drug penalties under different levels of government vary from one jurisdiction to another. Generally, criminal law considers several categories of illegal behavior regarding drug abuse:

- Possession: This can involve actual physical custody of the drug or constructive possession
- Distribution: This is a more serious charge than possession and is most commonly imposed for any exchange of illegal drugs between two or more persons
- Manufacturing: The production of illicit drugs

The 1970 Controlled Substances Act (CSA) has been the legal foundation of the federal government's battle against illicit drug abuse since its implementation. It includes numerous laws dealing with the manufacture, distribution, and possession of dangerous drugs. The CSA basically took all drugs considered dangerous under existing federal law and placed them into one of five schedules, or categories, based on the drug's medical use, potential for abuse, and safety or propensity for dependence.

6. What are the main goals of drug investigations?

The main goals of drug investigation are to:

- Identify and locate known or suspected drug sellers
- Understand the different types of drugs available on the street, their prices, and packaging methods
- Identify locations of frequent drug abuse activity
- Collect evidence on those involved in drug trafficking
- Reduce the availability of drugs through the aggressive apprehension of drug users and seller

7. What is a reverse drug sting?

A reverse drug sting operation is one in which undercover investigators, posing as dealers, sell large quantities of narcotics to known traffickers.

- These have been successful in penetrating otherwise untouchable drug markets.
- This operation can also be used against drug consumers on the street.
- Reverse stings are particularly effective in dealing with sales of rock cocaine ("crack").

8. Identify some special or extraordinary techniques in drug enforcement.

Drug courier profiling (Operation Pipeline) has been used by the DEA since 1985.

- It involves agents observing suspected drug traffickers and developing a pattern of behavior typical of those who use commercial airlines or public highways for drug trafficking.
- It has drawn criticism from civil libertarians because some of the profiled behavior patterns can also be innocent.
- The U.S. Supreme Court upheld the technique of drug courier profiling in *United States* v. *Sokolow* (1989).

Asset forfeiture has become an essential tool in drug control because of the increasingly high profits of the drug trade.

- The theory behind asset forfeiture is to take the profit out of illicit drug sales by seizing money or property that was either used to facilitate a drug crime or acquired with illicit drug revenues.
- The 1984 Comprehensive Crime Control Act (CCCA) provides civil provisions for asset forfeiture.
- Most state laws also provide for the seizure of assets in drug cases.

Key Terms

asset forfeiture

confidential informant

copping areas

crack

crack house

CSA

dependence

designer drugs

diversion

drug courier profile

gang

gangster

hybrid gangs

Mara Salvatrucha

neighborhood gang

objection

One Percenter OMG

outlaw motorcycle gangs (OMG)

prison gang

psychological dependence

reverse drug sting operation

RICO Act

street gang

undercover

Discussion Questions

1. Explain some of the gang-related trends in the United States today.

2. List and define the various types of gangs that exist in the United States today.

3. Discuss the infiltration of gangs into law enforcement, government, and correctional agencies and explain why it is such a significant threat.

4. What are some of the illegal activities in which gangs are becoming increasingly involved today?

5. What is the general structure of drug laws in the United States and what is the Controlled Substances Act?

6. List and discuss the five drug schedules or categories under the Controlled Substances Act.

7. What are the main sources of information through which the police learn about suspected criminal activity?

8. Discuss the process for the investigation of illicit drug laboratories.

9. Explain the reverse drug sting operation.

10. What is drug courier profiling?

Notes

1. EMERGING TRENDS. (2012). *National gang threat assessment—2011*. Washington, DC: National Gang Intelligence Center.

2. IBID.

3. IBID.

4. IBID.

5. IBID.

6. FBI REPORTS AND PUBLICATIONS. (2012). *National Gang Threat Assessment*. Available at FBI.gov.

7. EMERGING TRENDS. (2012). *National gang threat assessment—2011*.

8. IBID.

9. DINGLEY, J. AND M. KIRK-SMITH. (2002). Symbolism and sacrifice in terrorism. *Small Wars & Insurgencies* 13(1):102–128.

10. SCHAFER, J. R. (2003). The seven-stage hate model. *FBI Law Enforcement Bulletin*. Washington, DC: United States Department of Justice, Federal Bureau of Investigation.

11. IBID.

12. IBID.

13. U.S. LEGAL DEFINITIONS. Available at http://definitions.uslegal.com/t/terroristic-threat (retrieved on September 24, 2012).

14. OPEN SOURCE NEWS ARTICLE. Tips for dealing with Asian gangs. *Police One*, May 21, 2009. Available at www.Policeone.com.

15. FBI INDIANAPOLIS DIVISION. Twenty-two charged federally in evansville drug trafficking case. *Press Release*, February 4, 2010. Available at http://indianapolis.fbi.gov/dojpressrel/pressrel10/ip020410.htm.

16. OPEN SOURCE NEWS ARTICLE. Hybrid gangs responsible for rise in North Las Vegas crime.13 *action news Las Vegas*, July 25, 2010, p. 13. Available at http://www.ktnv.com/Global/story.asp.

17. NAGIA QUICK GUIDE TO GANGS. (April 2010). National Alliance of Gang Investigators Association.

18. OPEN SOURCE NEWS ARTICLE. (June 11, 2010). N. J. Inmate's ordered killing shows danger of cell phones in prison. Available at http://www.nj.com/news/index.ssf/2010/06/nj_state_prison_inmate_is_char.html; ONLINE NEWS ARTICLE. (June 12, 2010). Prosecutor: Trenton prison inmate Anthony Kidd used cell phone to order murder of girlfriend Kendra Degrasse. Available at http://www.trentonian.com/articles/2010/06/11/news/doc4c11432d64621687151693.txt.

19. OPEN SOURCE NEWS ARTICLE. (September 13, 2010). Prisoner ordered hit outside of prison with smuggle cell phone. Available at http://newsone.com/nation/associatedpress4/prisoner-ordered-hit-outside-of-prison-with-smuggled-cell-phone/.

20. OPEN SOURCE NEWS ARTICLE. Parole worker leaked information to gang member. *Fox News New York*, November 1, 2010. Available at www.myfoxny.com.

21. OPEN SOURCE NEWS ARTICLE. Former deputy headed for prison. *PE.com*, July 30, 2010. Available at www.pe.com.

22. OPEN SOURCE NEWS ARTICLE. Ex-Cop, James Formato, pleads guilty in mob case. *CBS news Chicago*, April 25, 2010. Available at www.thechicagosyndicate.com/2010/04/ex-cop-james-formato-pleads-guilty-in.html.

23. NAGIA QUICK GUIDE TO GANGS. (April 2010).

24. OPEN SOURCE NEWS ARTICLE. Man charged with shooting couple on Maple Valley trail. *The Seattle Times*, January 3, 2011. Available at http://seattletimes.nwsource.com/html/theblotter/2013837934_man_charged_with_xx_in_connect.html.

25. OPEN SOURCE NEWS ARTICLE. Teen gets probation in attacks on homeless. *Gazette-Times*, January 22, 2010. Available at http://www.gazettetime.com/news/local/article_3b43539a-07ab-11df-b6ae-001cc4c03286.html.

26. U.S. IMMIGRATION CUSTOMS ENFORCEMENT (ICE); 8 arrested as ICE dismantles alien smuggling ring linked to Notorious local street gang. *News Release*, October 14, 2009. Available at www.ice.gov/news/releases/0910/091014losangeles.htm.

27. OPEN NEWS SOURCE ARTICLE. Report links street gangs to child prostitution. *KPBS news*, November 23, 2010. Available at www.kpbs.org/news/2010/nov/09/report-links-street-gangs-child-prostitution.

28. OPEN SOURCE NEWS ARTICLE, JOHNSON, K. Drug cartels unite rival gangs to work for common bad. *USA Today*, March 16, 2010. Available at www.usatoday.com.

29. USDOJ. (February 2010). *National drug threat assessment 2010*. National Drug Intelligence Center.

30. IBID.

31. OPEN SOURCE NEWS ARTICLE. U.S. Mexico drug gangs form Alliances. *Washington Times*, March 26, 2010. Available at www.washingtimes.com.

32. JOHNSON. Drug cartels unite rival gangs to work for common bad.

33. OPEN SOURCE NEWS ARTICLE. U.S. Mexico drug gangs form Alliances

34. USDOJ. *National drug threat assessment 2010*; OPEN SOURCE NEWS ARTICLE. U.S. Mexico drug gangs form Alliances.

35. LYMAN, M. AND G. POTTER. (2002). *Drugs in society: Causes, concepts and control*, 4th ed. Cincinnati, OH: Anderson.

36. IBID.

37. IBID.

38. IBID.

Kheng Ho Toh / Cutcaster Images

This chapter will enable you to:

1. Describe white-collar and corporate crime.

2. Summarize the crime of money laundering.

3. Identify the different types of computer crime.

4. Describe how computer crime investigations are conducted.

5. Know what evidence to look for in the investigation of computer crimes.

Special Investigations: White-Collar, Corporate, and Computer-Related Crimes

Introduction

 *In the 1930s, criminologist Edwin Sutherland first coined the phrase white-collar crime to describe the criminal activities of the rich and powerful. He defined white-collar crime as "a crime committed by a person of respectability and high social status in the course of his occupation." Historically, law enforcement has paid little attention to the phenomenon of white-collar crime. In the past, even when a conviction did occur, offenders would typically get off with little more than a small fine and admonition by the court. Let's now consider the impact of white-collar crime by looking at the Martin Frankel embezzlement case.*

Neighbors knew there was something strange going on in 44-year-old Martin Frankel's sprawling stone mansion well before firefighters found piles of documents burning in two fireplaces and the rest of the 12-room house ransacked and empty. There had been an all-day, late-night parade of limousines and leased Mercedes; armed guards, surveillance cameras, and spotlights; and the suicide of a young New York woman, who was found hanging in a nearby house leased by Frankel. Then there was Frankel himself, a reclusive man who bought one, then another, $3 million estate on a secluded cul-de-sac in Greenwich, Connecticut's, backcountry neighborhood, paying cash for both.

In May 1999, Frankel vanished along with hundreds of millions of dollars in insurance company money. He left behind a smoldering to-do list that included "launder money" and astrological charts asking, "Will I go to prison?" Among receipts found in the mansion was one for $10 million paid to a Los Angeles diamond broker.

The Frankel case was complicated, to say the least. Upon his disappearance, police investigators began sorting out the clues that suggested billions of dollars in fraud. Those clues led to places such as the Vatican, a dozen Bible Belt insurance companies, and even past and present Justice Department officials.

Federal investigators uncovered an unlicensed brokerage operation on Frankel's Greenwich estates that siphoned investment money from a dozen insurance companies in Mississippi, Oklahoma, Tennessee, Missouri, and Arkansas. The companies were placed in state receivership because they could not account for the millions of dollars invested with Frankel's Liberty National Securities Inc., a firm not licensed by the Securities and Exchange Commission (SEC). Frankel systematically drained these assets through various financial accounts and transferred them into accounts outside the United States under his control. State regulators claimed that at least $218 million was missing; another estimate was as high as $915 million. Also missing was as much as $1.98 billion from the St. Francis of Assisi Foundation, a charitable organization that Frankel established in the Virgin Islands.

The scale of Frankel's operation was apparent by 1997, when Greenwich police went to interview him about the hanging of a 22-year-old woman living in a home Frankel rented for $15,000 a month. The interview took place in an office-type room with numerous computer monitors displaying information from various financial markets. The death was ruled a suicide, and the police went away. But when police returned one month later to investigate a fire, they found 80 computers, computer servers, and a sophisticated fiber-optic network tied to securities information services. It was a well-thought-out con.

But Frankel had even bigger plans. He established the Assisi Foundation in August 1998 and recruited the help of prominent people, including Thomas Bolan, a New York lawyer, and two priests, the Reverend Peter Jacobs and Monsignor Emilio Colagiovanni. But the operation began to crumble when Mississippi and Tennessee regulators became concerned about the money flow from local insurance companies to Frankel's unlicensed investment firm. After initial inquiries were made, Frankel's Greenwich neighbors saw moving vans at his mansion.[1]

The Frankel case was closed with his arrest on September 6, 1999, at a luxury hotel in Hamburg, Germany. Frankel's arrest stemmed from an anonymous tip.[2]

Defining White-Collar Crime

According to the Bureau of Journal Statistics (BJS), white-collar crime is not an official crime category, but it represents a unique area of criminality that differs from other categories of criminality, such as violence and property crime. *White-collar crime* is a somewhat generic term meaning different things to different people. Although white-collar offenses are less visible than crimes such as burglary and robbery, their overall economic impact may be considerably greater. The appropriate definition of white-collar crime has long been a matter of dispute among criminal justice practitioners. A particular point of contention is whether it is defined by the nature of the offense or by the status, profession, or skills of the offender.

In an effort to understand this criminal phenomenon better, the *Dictionary of Criminal Justice Data Terminology* offers the following definition of white-collar crime: "non-violent crime for financial gain committed by means of deception by persons whose occupational status is entrepreneurial, professional or semi-professional, and utilizing their special occupational skills and opportunities." Simply put, white-collar crime could be explained as "nonviolent crime committed for financial gain and accomplished by means of deception."[3] Some of the most notable white-collar crimes are insider trading, money laundering, confidence games, and computer crime.

Corporate Crime

Corporate crime is a form of white-collar crime whereby trusted executives working within a company mishandle funds or otherwise betray the trust of customers or other consumers. Motivations for corporate crime include gaining or increasing power or realizing personal wealth through mishandling funds. Corporate crime may also affect a small number of persons or millions depending on the extent of the actions of the players involved.

The twenty-first century has not been immune to corporate scandals. One of the best-known corporate scandals is the Enron scandal of 2001. Before its bankruptcy in 2001, Enron, the Houston-based Enron Creditors Recovery Corporation (formerly Enron Corporation; former NYSE ticker symbol ENE) employed approximately 22,000 people and was one of the world's leading electricity, natural gas, pulp and paper, and communications companies, with claimed revenues of nearly $101 billion in 2000.[4] *Fortune* named Enron "America's Most Innovative Company" for six consecutive years. At the end of 2001, it was revealed that Enron's reported financial condition was sustained substantially by institutionalized, systematic, and creatively planned accounting fraud, known as the "Enron scandal." Enron has since become a popular symbol of willful corporate fraud and corruption. The scandal was also considered a landmark case in the field of business fraud and brought into question the accounting practices of many corporations throughout the United States.[5]

Enron filed for bankruptcy protection in the Southern District of New York in late 2001. It emerged from bankruptcy in November 2004 after one of the biggest and most complex bankruptcy cases in U.S. history. On September 7, 2006, Enron sold Prisma Energy International, Inc., its last remaining business, to Ashmore Energy International, Ltd. After the scandal, lawsuits against Enron's directors were notable because the directors settled the suits by paying very significant sums of money personally. The scandal also caused the dissolution of the Arthur Andersen accounting firm, affecting the wider business world.[6]

After a series of revelations involving irregular accounting procedures bordering on fraud perpetrated throughout the 1990s involving Enron and its accounting firm Arthur Andersen, Enron stood on the verge of undergoing the largest bankruptcy in history by mid-November 2001 (the largest Chapter 11 bankruptcy until that of the investment bank Lehman Brothers on September 15, 2008). A white knight rescue attempt by a similar, smaller energy company, Dynegy, was not viable.[7]

As the scandal unraveled, Enron shares dropped from more than $90 to just pennies. Enron had been considered a *blue chip* stock, so this was an unprecedented and disastrous event in the financial world. Enron's plunge occurred after it was revealed that much of its profits and revenue were the result of deals with special purpose entities (limited partnerships that it controlled). The result was that many of Enron's debts and the losses it suffered were not reported in its financial statements.

Enron filed for bankruptcy on December 2, 2001. In addition, the scandal caused the dissolution of Arthur Andersen, which was one of the world's top accounting firms at the time. The firm was found guilty of obstruction of justice in 2002 for destroying documents related to the Enron audit and was forced to stop auditing public companies. Although the U.S. Supreme Court threw out the conviction in 2005, the damage to the Andersen name has prevented it from returning as a viable business.[8] Enron also withdrew a naming rights deal with the Houston Astros Major League Baseball club to have its name associated with its new stadium, which was formerly known as Enron Field (now known as Minute Maide Park).

Enron had created offshore entities, units that may be used for planning and avoidance of taxes, increasing the profitability of a business. This provided ownership and management with full freedom of currency movement and the anonymity that allowed the company to hide losses. These entities made Enron look more profitable than it actually was and created a dangerous spiral in which each quarter, corporate officers would have to perform more and more contorted financial deception to create the illusion of billions in profits while the company was actually losing money.[9] This practice drove up the company's stock price to new levels, at which point the executives began to work on insider information and trade millions of dollars worth of Enron stock. The executives and insiders at Enron knew about the offshore accounts that were hiding losses for the company; however, the investors knew nothing of this. Chief Financial Officer Andrew Fastow led the team that created the off-books companies, and he manipulated the deals to provide himself, his family, and his friends with hundreds of millions of dollars in guaranteed revenue at the expense of the corporation for which he worked and its stockholders.[10]

Other corruption cases have also gained national prominence. For example, Adelphia Communications Corporation, named after the Greek word "brothers," was the fifth largest cable company in the United States before filing for bankruptcy in 2002 as a result of internal corruption. Adelphia was founded in 1952 in the town of Coudersport, Pennsylvania, by John Rigas, which remained the company's headquarters until it was moved to Greenwood Village, Colorado, shortly after filing for bankruptcy. The majority of Adelphia's revenue-generating assets were officially acquired by Time Warner Cable and Comcast on July 31, 2006. LFC, an Internet-based real estate marketing firm, auctioned off the remaining Adelphia real estate assets.[11]

As a result of this acquisition, Adelphia no longer exists as a cable provider. Adelphia's long-distance telephone business, with 110,000 customers in 27 states (telephone and long-distance services), was sold to Pioneer Telephone for about $1.2 million. Had the 110,000 telephone customers been shut off versus being sold to Pioneer Telephone, those customers would have more than likely left Adelphia cable and high-speed Internet services. The potential financial damage to the creditors of Adelphia was more than $150 million dollars. Although the purchase price by Pioneer Telephone was relatively small ($1.2 million), the transaction was very significant.[12]

Upon divesting its cable assets, Adelphia retained a skeleton crew of 275 employees to handle its remaining bankruptcy issues. It still exists as a corporate entity, continuing largely to settle ongoing financial obligations and litigation claims, as well as to consummate settlements with the SEC and the U.S. attorney.

Another case revolved around Metabolife International, Inc., an American corporation based in San Diego, California, that manufactures dietary supplements. Metabolife's best-selling product, an ephedra-based supplement called Metabolife 356, once generated hundreds of millions of dollars in annual sales. However, Metabolife 356 and other ephedra-containing supplements were linked to thousands of serious adverse events, including deaths. These deaths caused the U.S. Food and Drug Administration (FDA) to ban the sale of ephedra-containing dietary supplements in 2004.

Subsequently, Metabolife's founder was convicted of lying to the FDA and concealing evidence of ephedra's dangers, and the company and its owner were both convicted of income tax evasion. A congressional investigation found that Metabolife had received thousands of reports of serious adverse events, many occurring in young and otherwise healthy people, and that Metabolife concealed the reports and acted with "indifference to the health of consumers."

In 2005, former Tyco International chairman and chief executive Dennis Kozlowski and former chief financial officer Mark H. Swartz were accused of the theft of more than $150 million from the company. During their trial in March 2004, they contended the board of directors authorized it as compensation.[13]

During jury deliberations, juror Ruth Jordan, while passing through the courtroom, appeared to make an "okay" sign with her fingers to the defense table. She later denied she had intended that gesture, but the incident received much publicity (including a caricature in the *Wall Street Journal*), and the juror received threats after her name became public. Judge Michael Obus declared a mistrial on April 2, 2004.

On June 17, 2005, after a retrial, Kozlowski and Swartz were convicted on all but one of the more than 30 counts against them. The verdicts carried potential jail terms of up to 25 years in state prison. Kozlowski himself was sentenced to no less than eight years and four months and no more than 25 years in prison. Then in December 2007, New Hampshire Federal District Court Judge Paul Barbadoro approved a class action settlement whereby Tyco agreed to pay $75 million to a class of defrauded shareholders.[14]

Confidence Games

As with corporate crime, so-called **confidence games** are crimes that betray the trust of the victim. For decades, criminals have practiced the art of getting something for nothing by stealing from a trusting person. When reading the following con-artist scams, it might be difficult to believe that intelligent people could actually fall victim to such manipulation. Indeed, they do. Let's examine some of the more common con games.

The Pigeon Drop

Probably the most practiced confidence game of all time, the **pigeon drop** comes in many varieties. In this scam, a lot of losers pay a few winners. Although these scams are conducted in different ways, most seem to follow the basic pattern. Here's how it works: Con man 1 finds a wallet, purse, attaché case, or even a paper bag apparently filled with money. An unsuspecting victim standing nearby witnesses the discovery. At that time, con man 2 appears and claims that he is entitled to a share of the loot just as much as the other.

It should occur to the victim at this point that he or she should share in the proceeds. An argument then breaks out about whether they should divide the money immediately or check it out to see if it is stolen. Con man 1 says his "boss" has police "connections" and can check. A quick phone call is then made by con man 1 who then says that the money was probably dropped by some drug dealer or big-time gambler and that they should divide it between them.

The boss offers to hold the money until all three can produce a substantial amount of their own money to show that they are acting in good faith and can be trusted to keep the secret. Con man 2, apparently determined not to be cut out of the deal, produces a large sum of money on the spot to prove his reliability. Con man 1 and the victim then hurry off to get their part of the money. When the victim returns and hands over his share, it is the last he or she sees of the cons, the money, or the boss.

The key to the success of this scam is the powerful acting between the cons—in particular, the bickering between the two men that makes the victim feel that he or she will be left out unless they abide by the conditions of the agreement. The reliability of the boss is the convincer (sometimes this character portrays a police detective). The amount of money in question is always so great that the victim wants to believe.

The Bank Examiner Scheme

In this scam, con artists pose as FBI agents, bank examiners, police officers, detectives, or bank officials. The victim is then contacted by them pretending to need help in conducting an investigation. The con asks the victim to verify his or her present balance, which is, say, $5,000. After doing so, the victim is advised that the bank's records reflect a lesser amount (e.g., $3,000), and it is suggested that someone might be tampering with the account.

Con man 1 instructs the victim to meet him at the bank, and con man 2 remains in the neighborhood and observes the victim leaving. After arriving at the bank, con man 1 meets the victim and accompanies him or her to the teller, where the money is withdrawn. During this process, the victim is told that one of the tellers might be the thief and not to act nervous. After the withdrawal, con man 1 advises the victim just to hang onto the money until the bank contacts him or her.

Later that day, con man 2 goes to the home of the victim and explains that a sting operation will occur to apprehend the suspect teller and that the victim should now give the money to con man 2 so that he can redeposit it at the "suspect" teller's window. Con man 2 then uses the victim's phone to call "the bank" and speak with con man 1. The victim is then allowed to speak to con man 1, who reassures the victim that the money will be kept safe. As a valued bank customer and upstanding citizen, the victim complies, and the money and the cons are never seen again.

The Pyramid "Get Rich Quick" Scheme

"Earn thousands the easy way. A small investment could earn you $100,000 in less than a year!" Among the oldest con games, pyramid rackets have been used to swindle millions of dollars annually, using everything from dollar bills to chain letters to more sophisticated schemes that sell franchises to unsuspecting persons who then must sell more franchises to more victims, and so on.

Theoretically, a **pyramid scheme** can continue indefinitely, but it actually "bubbles" and soon collapses because of the sheer numbers involved. A typical operation swept California during the 1970s. In the scheme, two players paid an entry fee of $1,000 apiece. Half this amount, $500, went to the top of the pyramid, while the remaining $500 from each of the two new players went to the player who recruited them. So the first player got his or her money back and then waited to move up another rung on the pyramid as each of the two new players recruited two more players so that they could also recover their initial $1,000 investment. As each step of the pyramid was mounted, the initial player moved from rung 16, to rung 8, to rung 4, to rung 2, and finally to rung 1. After reaching the top rung, the player received the money that accumulated at the top for him or her: $16,000.

Although it may seem fairly easy for new players to induce two new players to the scheme, the numbers become astronomical. Essentially, each player on rung 16 creates two entirely new pyramids, and the progression gets bigger and bigger. For example, there are 16 players on the bottom rung, and it takes 32 new players to get them to advance to the next rung. Each of these 32 players must now recruit two new players, bringing the total number to 64. Those 64 must now recruit two new players, each totaling 128 people. The total then jumps to 256, at which time the original 16 players have reached the top of the pyramid. However, for the players on the next rung, 512 players are needed for them to advance to the next rung. For the next group, the required number is 1,024, and so on. The California pyramid scam finally died out as cons were unable to attract enough gullible people to keep it alive.

Travel Scams

"Dear Consumer: You have just won a free vacation for five days and four nights in the Bahamas. Just call this 800 number for details." Postcards with messages such as this are becoming more common throughout the United States. The way this scam works is that when the victim calls the number, she is told that she will receive a package in the mail detailing the vacation offer. The operator then asks the victim for her credit card number, telling her that a small service charge will be made to her account if she accepts the vacation offer. The victim is assured, however, that she will have a review period to decide if she wants the package before her account is billed for the service charge. The company is slow in sending the vacation package materials, and when it does arrive, the review period, according to the company, has already expired. The company then quickly bills the victim's credit card for hundreds of dollars for its "service fee."

Home Repair Scams

The home repair scam begins with a worker who goes door to door offering repair services for a modest fee. Services include driveway repair and roof repair. **Scammers** accept money for repair jobs that they never finish or fail to honor warranties on home improvement projects. One such scam is the asphalt scam. Here, the worker offers to use the remaining asphalt from one job to repave a second driveway. More often than not, the worker either starts the job and then claims it will cost hundreds or thousands of dollars more to complete, or he will just lay black paint instead of asphalt on the driveway and leave town with the victim's money.

Elderly people are prime targets for such scams because many of them own their own homes, and many of those are older homes. Many such homes actually are in need of repairs, and the crafty con artist looks for this. The criminal will generally ask for a large down payment before he or she begins the work, and there have been cases in which the worker will accompany the victim to the bank to withdraw the money. The con will sometimes use the obituaries to seek out elderly persons living alone. The con then claims to be a building or health inspector who is there to check out the furnace. Once in the basement, the con either causes damage or claims that a health or safety threat exists. Then they demand money from the victim for either repairs or reassembly.

Contest Cons

Contest cons usually begin by sending a computerized "personal" letter to the victim stating that he or she has just won a new car, a diamond necklace, a food processor, and so on. All the victim needs to do to collect the prize is visit a time-share resort. If the victim does so, however, he or she will be subjected to high-pressure sales tactics to buy one of the units. Then when prizes are given, they are usually cheap imitations of the real thing. Letters of this sort may appear urgent and may represent companies with names that resemble official organizations.

The Magazine Subscription Scam

The magazine subscription scam begins with a phone call asking the victim if he or she would like to receive five magazines for two years at no cost. The offer is that all the victim has to pay is a nominal fee, say $1.75 per week, as a service charge. The caller will then request the victim's credit card number. Victims may find that they are charged several hundred dollars of fees that are unwarranted. The scammers are so slick that consumers are unaware that they have purchased magazines until they receive the bill. Some salespeople avoid identifying themselves as magazine subscription salespeople or with the name of their company. Others encourage consumers to make purchases without giving the total costs or ask the consumer for a credit card number for "verification" purposes and then use the number to charge for unwanted subscriptions.

Because crime scenes are virtually nonexistent in cases involving fraud and confidence games, investigators should focus on learning as much as possible about the victim and those who are responsible for the crime. In addition, records and documents should be identified and examined for possible clues as to the identities of the perpetrators. Investigative efforts to identify suspects in the case are often stymied by the victim's inability to remember details about the swindler(s).

Check and Credit Card Fraud

This section will discuss fraud involving (1) all types of checks and (2) plastic cards, including debit, charge, credit, and "smart" cards. Each can involve a different payment method. While there are some obvious differences between check and card fraud, the limitations and opportunities for fraud and its prevention and control by local police are similar enough to warrant addressing them together. Furthermore, some cards (e.g., debit cards) are used and processed in a similar way to checks, and electronic checks are processed in a similar way to cards, so that the traditional distinction between cards and checks is fast eroding.

In 2000, Visa International estimated that the yearly cost of fraud worldwide was about 0.05 cent per every dollar spent. This small amount works out to an estimated $1 billion in the United States. Since 1995, the amount of fraud losses on payment cards has consistently risen in the United States; the losses from online credit card fraud alone were estimated to reach $3.2 billion in 2007.

Apart from the obvious financial loss caused by check and card fraud, it is a serious crime that affects multiple victims and significantly contributes to other types of crime. At the most basic level, fraud is easy to commit, and the chances of apprehension and punishment are minimal. Thus check and credit card fraud is an ideal entry-level crime from which people may graduate to more serious offenses.

When a credit card is lost or stolen, it can be used until the owner notifies the issuer that the card is missing. Most issuers have free 24-hour telephone numbers to encourage prompt reporting. Still, it is possible for a thief to make unauthorized purchases on a card until it is canceled. Without

Fueling The Flames of Fraud

Crimes that either feed off check and card fraud or facilitate its commission include the following:

☑ *Drug trafficking.* Addicts forge checks or fraudulently use credit cards (often bought cheaply as "second string" cards—that is, stolen or counterfeit cards that have already been used). So the fraud fuels the drug trade.

☑ *Identity theft.* There is increasing evidence to suggest that obtaining or accessing credit card accounts is the main motive for identity theft, a crime that causes victims very serious economic harm (ranging from $5,000 to $20,000 per victim) and psychological harm. Sophisticated technology has made the counterfeiting of checks and plastic cards much more difficult over the last decade. Although there is no definitive research available, it is likely that, as counterfeiting has become increasingly difficult, offenders have turned to the next best thing: stealing cardholders' identity, and using legitimate cards. Thus identity theft has become a serious crime; the U.S. Congress has passed a special bill to deal with it.

☑ *Mail fraud.* Offenders intercept checks, credit cards, or bankcards in the mail, or do not forward mail that card issuers or banks send to a customer's old address.

☑ *Burglaries, robberies, and thefts from cars.* Offenders may commit these crimes specifically to get plastic cards, or they may get them as a by-product of the crime.

☑ *Pick pocketing.* Pickpocket may be attracted to shopping malls and other crowded shopping venues where people use checks and cards.

☑ *Fencing.* In areas where offenders commit check and card fraud to buy high-priced goods, a fencing operation may arise to facilitate conversion of the goods into cash.

☑ *Extortion.* Customer databases that include credit card and other personal information are very valuable to businesses. They have therefore become targets in their own right, and hackers sometimes steal them and hold them for ransom.

☑ *Organized crime.* Counterfeiting and marketing cards require considerable organization, for both production and distribution. International organized crime rings working out of East Asia tend to be involved in such operations.

☑ *Local gang-related crime.* Small gangs may feed the needs of addicts and the poor by using second-string cards to buy food and other items at supermarkets. The locals may protect these gangs, because they provide a "service" to the community.

☑ *Cons and scams.* The Internet now carries a wide range of cons and scams offenders use to get credit card and other personal information from unknowing victims. People can easily create false websites and storefronts, as little skill is required to do so. Furthermore, many websites offer information on setting up such websites and on running scams.

☑ *Financial crimes against the elderly.* The elderly are prime targets of cons and scams, including check and credit card fraud.

☑ *Shoplifting.* Committing check and card fraud is simply another way of "lifting" products from retailers. Using a credit card fraudulently at checkout is much less risky (because the authentication methods are so cursory). This type of theft from retail stores is probably much greater than regular shoplifting, or it may be used in concert with shoplifting.

☑ *Car theft.* Car rental companies are prime targets for credit card fraud. Offenders may sell fraudulently rented cars in the stolen vehicles market.

other security measures, a thief could potentially purchase thousands of dollars in merchandise or services before the cardholder or the card issuer realize that the card is in the wrong hands.

The only common security measure on all cards is a signature panel, but signatures are relatively easy to forge. Some merchants will demand to see a picture ID, such as a driver's license, to verify the identity of the purchaser, and some credit cards include the holder's picture on the card itself. However, the cardholder has a right to refuse to show additional verification, and asking for such verification is usually a violation of the merchant's agreement with the credit card companies. Self-serve payment systems (gas stations, kiosks, etc.) are common targets for stolen cards, as there is no way to verify the cardholder's identity.

A common countermeasure is to require the user to key in some identifying information, such as the user's ZIP or postal code. This method may deter casual theft of a card found alone, but if the cardholder's wallet is stolen, it may be trivial for the thief to deduce the information by looking at other items in the wallet. For instance, a U.S. driver license commonly has the holder's home address and ZIP code printed on it. Visa Inc. offers merchants lower rates on transactions if the customer provides a zip code.

Card issuers have several countermeasures, including sophisticated software that can, prior to an authorized transaction, estimate the probability of fraud. For example, a large transaction occurring a great distance from the cardholder's home might seem suspicious. The merchant may be instructed to call the card issuer for verification, or to decline the transaction, or even to hold the card and refuse to return it to the customer. The customer must contact the issuer and prove who they are to get their card back (if it is not fraud and they are actually buying a product).

Money Laundering

Whether money has been derived through activities such as drug trafficking or corporate crime, the mere existence of large amounts of cash poses problems for those who possess it. This is because if the money is discovered, the government will seize the cash and those possessing it will be arrested and prosecuted. As such, criminals constantly search for methods to hide their financial rewards and make them appear to be legitimate. This process is known as *money laundering*. Investigations have revealed that such laundering activities commonly use the services of many Fortune 500 companies. To many, money laundering is a criminal activity undertaken only by drug traffickers and terrorists but it in fact extends to all segments of society. Consider, for example, the 2011 money laundering conviction of U.S. Representative Tom DeLay.

On October 3, 2005, a Travis County, Texas, grand jury indicted U.S. representative Tom DeLay on a felony conspiracy charge to move $190,000 in corporate donations to Republican candidates

|Fig. 17.1| △

Former U.S. representative Tom DeLay was convicted of money laundering in 2011.

WpN / Photoshot

in the Texas State Legislature in 2002. On October 20, 2005, DeLay turned himself in to the Harris County Sheriff Office. The day after, a warrant was issued for his arrest. He was released after posting a $10,000 bond. On November 24, 2010, a jury in Austin, Texas, found DeLay guilty of money laundering and conspiracy to commit money laundering. On January 10, 2011, DeLay was sentenced to three years in prison and 10 years' probation.

The History of Money Laundering

The practice of money laundering began in Switzerland during the 1930s as concerned Europeans began funneling their capital beyond the clutches of Hitler's Third Reich. In time, Switzerland's infamous numbered accounts became an enormously profitable business. Today, Swiss bank secrecy laws have been relaxed because of numerous criminal cases involving money laundering. Criminals are therefore seeking other financial havens in which to deposit their ill-gotten gains. The flooding of entire regions with drug money is one of the more sinister and surreptitious types of drug-related crime. The term **flooding**, tracked by the regional Federal Reserve Banks, seems to describe this phenomenon with great precision.

In 1985, another scandal surfaced involving the prestigious First National Bank of Boston. In this case, federal prosecutors charged that the bank was making unreported cash shipments of $1.2 million. It would receive $529,000 in small bills and send $690,000 in bills of $100 or more. The bank was fined $500,000 for violating federal reporting requirements under the **Bank Secrecy Act (BSA)**. In 1991, a New York State grand jury indicted the London-based Bank of Credit and Commerce International (BCCI) and its two principal officers for fraud, bribery, money laundering, and grand larceny after a two-year investigation. BCCI had looted depositors out of more than $5 billion, which was called "the largest bank fraud in history." In this case, bank officials knowingly made billions of dollars in loans to confederates who had no intention of repayment.

Examples of Money Laundering

One look at the daily news is proof that the crimes dealing with or motivated by money make up the majority of criminal activity in the nation. Tax evasion, public corruption, health care fraud, money laundering, and drug trafficking are all examples of the types of crimes that revolve around money. In these cases, a financial investigation often becomes the key to a conviction.

Money laundering investigations focus where the underlying conduct is a violation of the income tax laws or violations of the federal Bank Secrecy Act. Money laundering is the means by which criminals evade paying taxes on illegal income by concealing the source and the amount of profit. Essentially, money laundering is tax evasion in progress.

We should remember that when no other crimes could be pinned to Al Capone, a conviction was obtained for tax evasion. As the astonished Capone left the courthouse, he said, "This is preposterous. You can't tax illegal income!" But the fact is, under federal law, income from whatever source derived (legal or illegal) is taxable income. Had the money laundering statutes been on the books in the 1930s, Capone would also have been charged with money laundering. However, since October 1986, with the passage of the Money Laundering Control Act, organized crime members and many others have been charged and convicted of both tax evasion and money laundering. Consider these recent cases of money laundering:

- On February 29, 2012, in Amarillo, Texas, Amy Fernandez was sentenced to 12 months in prison and ordered to pay a money judgment of $99,950 for structuring financial transactions to avoid the reporting requirements. Fernandez admitted that she purchased cashier's checks from four separate financial institutions each day during the week of February 22, 2010, through February 26, 2010. In order to avoid federal reporting requirements, Fernandez purchased these cashier's checks in either $3,000 or $2,950 amounts, for a combined total of $59,550. Fernandez tendered cash that she removed from large, gallon-sized plastic bags that she carried in her purse. During one transaction, she stated that she had to make certain that she stayed under the $3,000 threshold.[15]
- On April 12, 2012, Joseph P. Loomis, of Holmen, Wisconsin, was sentenced to 240 months in prison. Loomis was the leader of a drug organization that distributed between 15 and 50 kilograms of cocaine in the La Crosse, Wisconsin, area from approximately April 2006

to September 2008. He also distributed large quantities of marijuana from 2006 through the spring of 2011. Loomis maintained stash houses and used other persons to pick up, package, store, and distribute drugs. He also used another individual to collect drug debts. Loomis laundered drug proceeds by using a Netspend stored value card. He deposited large sums of cash onto the card and then used the card to purchase items.[16]

- On April 26, 2012, in Charlotte, North Carolina, Eric Mark Giles was sentenced to 196 months in prison for drug, money laundering, and firearm charges. Giles, a student at the University of North Carolina (UNC), led a large marijuana distribution organization, which generated drug proceeds in excess of $1 million in a two-and-a-half-year time period. Giles was primarily responsible for the shipment of high-grade marijuana from Santa Cruz, California, to distributors based in the UNC Charlotte area. The group used bank accounts to launder their drug proceeds by making large cash deposits in branches in North Carolina and corresponding cash withdrawals in California. The co-conspirators kept their individual transactions under $10,000 in an effort to avoid Federal Currency Transaction Reporting (CTR) requirements.[17]

These cases illustrate that when criminals have a large amount of illegal income, they have to do something with it in order to hide it from the IRS. They attempt to "launder" it to make it appear as if it was from a legitimate source, allowing them to spend it or invest it in assets without having to worry about the IRS and tax consequences.

One of the ways to launder illegal proceeds is to move the money out of the United States and then bring it back in a clean form, often disguised as loan proceeds. Another method is to channel or co-mingle the money through various business activities to give the appearance that the money was derived from a legal source.

Combating the Money Laundering Problem

It's ironic that the very institutions that could do the most to stop money laundering seem to have the least incentive to do so. For example, whereas the basic fee for recycling money of a suspicious origin averages 4 percent, the rate for drug cash and other "hot" money may range from 7 to 10 percent. Perhaps one could inquire why the investment of drug money in legitimate businesses should be cause for concern. Considered very narrowly, the influx of large amounts of cash has provided some short-term financial benefits for Latin American debtor nations as well as domestic beneficiaries of illegal drug money.

It cannot be overemphasized, however, that this flood of money is not only a consequence of the drug problem but is also a major problem in its own right. For example, the money that enters the local economy is a primary cause of inflation. Even the banks that stand to gain from accommodating drug traffickers ultimately bear the costs of any losses that drug-related transactions generate. Part of the problem the United States has regarding money laundering activities is that U.S. drug users are primarily consumers rather than producers of drugs. Additionally, the United States is used as a repository for large amounts of drug proceeds.

Most drug profits are funneled to upper echelon members of drug cartels rather than the low-level producers and growers. Therefore, it is because of the tremendous profits of drug trafficking organizations that new members are constantly being lured into this illicit business. Unfortunately, profits are also so large that any losses, owing to forfeitures by the government, can usually be easily absorbed through future illicit dealings, making it unlikely that drug organizations will actually be put out of business.

Presumably, dealers consider that the risk of imprisonment or loss of assets is a mere risk of conducting business. Therefore, if we assume that the motivation behind the illicit drug trade is profit, we should conclude that government action against such a lucrative class of crime must include an attack against the proceeds of that criminal act. The success enjoyed by drug traffickers poses somewhat of a dilemma for them: how to reduce the likelihood of detection and subsequent asset seizure by law enforcement officials. This is accomplished by a criminal technique known as money laundering in which illegal cash proceeds are made to appear legitimate or the sources of illegal proceeds are disguised. As money laundering laws become increasingly more effective against the leaders of drug organizations, the risk of detection of such leaders is more likely.

The money laundering process can take many forms, including (1) simply merging illicit money with a legitimate cash source, which usually uses a business that generates large amounts of cash, and (2) using sophisticated international money laundering techniques (discussed next). The goal of the financial investigation is to reduce the rewards achieved through drug trafficking and therefore immobilize drug trafficking organizations.

Techniques of Money Laundering

On April 20, 2009, in Denver, Colorado, Edgar Diaz-Calderon was sentenced to prison for conspiracy to launder money and possession with intent to distribute cocaine. The investigation, which resulted in 53 arrests and the seizure of over $1 million in cash, showed that Diaz-Calderon was associated with organized gang activity that involved the distribution of more than 150 kilograms of cocaine in the Metro Denver area between 2005 and 2006. Using trusted runners and couriers, the cocaine was purchased in Mexico and transported to Denver. The cash proceeds of the illegal sales were then returned to Mexico to sustain the importation–distribution business cycle.[18] The Diaz–Calderon case is typical of money laundering efforts by drug traffickers and demonstrates how much money can go undetected if not properly investigated.

The amount of money earned by drug trafficking organizations and laundered through money laundering schemes is staggering. For example, a 2005 Drug Enforcement Administration (DEA) study determined that during 2003 and 2004, there were excess U.S. dollars present in Mexico that could not be accounted for from legitimate sources totaling at least $9.2 billion and $10.2 billion, respectively. It is estimated that the four major drugs that are smuggled into the United States from Mexico (methamphetamine, heroin, cocaine, and marijuana) generate as much as $22 billion per year for the sources of supply.[19]

Syndicates earn huge profits on the illegal goods and services they sell to the public and through their extortionary relations with the business world. Much of this profit is in the form of cash, and virtually all of it must be converted to legitimate forms before it can be invested or spent. Drug traffickers and other racketeers who accumulate large cash inventories face serious risks of confiscation and punishment if considerable unexplained hoards of cash are discovered. For these criminals to enjoy the fruits of their illegal enterprises, they must first convert those cash proceeds to a medium that is both easier than cash to use in everyday commerce and that avoids pointing, even indirectly, to the illegal activity that produced it.

Money laundering conceals the source of the illegal money and gives that money a legitimate history and paper trail. Despite extensive media saturation on the topic, our knowledge of the money laundering problem remains limited. Estimates of how much money is laundered are virtually impossible to make with any precision. The President's Commission on Organized Crime estimated that billions of dollars in illegal drug profits are laundered in the United States each year. The Commission further asserted that between $5 billion and $15 billion of those drug profits are laundered through international financial channels.[20]

Illegal drug transactions are usually cash transactions, commonly using large amounts of currency to pay off the various actors in each drug deal and to purchase sophisticated equipment. It is important for the trafficker to legitimize his or her cash proceeds in a fashion that permits the trafficker to spend it wherever and whenever he or she desires without attracting suspicion. Obviously, the trafficker could choose to store the cash in a strongbox or wall safe, but such methods would not be plausible for the trafficker who generates hundreds of thousands or even millions of dollars in illegal cash each year. To combat this technique, the Treasury Department implemented the CTR, requiring banks to report cash transactions of $10,000 or more. In 1989, the U.S. government processed an estimated 7,000,000 CTRs compared with an estimated 100,000 ten years earlier. Traffickers quickly circumvented this requirement by developing such activities as corrupting bank employees.

The many different techniques for laundering illicit proceeds are limited only by a trafficker's imagination and cunningness. An entire "wash cycle"—to transform small denominations of currency to businesses, money market deposits, or real estate—may take as little as 48 hours.

The method chosen by any given trafficker will no doubt reflect his or her own situation and any unique circumstances involved. Money laundering techniques illustrate the ingenuity of the drug trafficker in hiding millions (and even billions) of dollars of illicitly gained revenues. Money laundering techniques include bank methods, smurfing, currency exchanges, double invoicing, and acquisition of financial institutions.

A Closer Look

Layering: A One-Man Smurfing Operation

A single suspect laundered more than $700,000 worth of drug proceeds for a money laundering group associated with Colombian narcotics traffickers. The suspect wired funds to bank accounts in Panama, Barbados, and Honduras. As part of the suspect's money laundering scheme, between November 1998 and June 2000, he made structured cash purchases of money orders totaling more than $600,000 without ever causing a Currency Transaction Report to be filed. On more than 50 occasions, the defendant made multiple small purchases of postal money orders at various post office locations, as many as 11 on a single day, keeping them below the $3,000 recordkeeping threshold. The suspect completed the money orders in his name, the name of his company, and the names of relatives and friends and then deposited the money orders into his company's business bank account. The suspect also exchanged more than $500,000 worth of what he understood was drug money for checks from various business accomplices, including numerous carpet dealers. This activity was determined to have been an intentional avoidance of federal reporting requirements.

Source: Office of National Drug Control Policy. (2008). *2007 money laundering strategy*.

BANK METHODS The most common method for laundering money is called *bank methods*. In this basic technique, the traffickers take their cash to a bank and conduct several transactions that usually involve trading currency of small denominations for larger ones. This is done for obvious portability purposes. It is also common for cash to be exchanged for Treasury bills, bank drafts, letters of credit, traveler's checks, or other monetary instruments.

During the early 1980s in Miami (considered the hub of the cocaine banking business in the United States), large daily shipments of currency would arrive and be deposited in numerous accounts, but they would then be disbursed immediately through the writing of checks payable to true or nominee names. Ultimately, these funds were deposited in other domestic accounts in the same or different banks or wire transferred to offshore bank accounts in foreign countries with strict bank secrecy laws.

Ironically, there is no requirement to report these transactions because the BSA's reporting requirements don't pertain to interbank transfers. Therefore, the biggest problem posed to the traffickers is the initial depositing of the currency into the banks. After funds are deposited, a trafficker can communicate with the bank through a fax machine or personal computer and literally route funds all over the world without ever coming face to face or even speaking with a banker. One method of conducting mass deposits, called **smurfing**, first appeared during the mid-1980s and is discussed next.

SMURFING A trafficker provides several individuals, or "smurfs," with cash from drug sales. Each smurf goes to different banks and purchases cashier's checks in denominations of less than $10,000, thus bypassing the reporting requirement. The smurfs then turn the checks over to a second person, who facilitates their subsequent deposit into domestic banks or transports them physically to banks in Panama or Colombia. In some instances, the monetary instruments are premarked "for deposit only," making them nonnegotiable to the courier.

CURRENCY EXCHANGES Traffickers may also use either money exchanges or brokerage houses for facilitating movement of their money. Foreign currency exchanges are frequently set up as storefronts that deal regularly in large cash transactions. In using the exchange, the trafficker can avoid using traditional banking institutions and therefore avoid risky reporting requirements. Banks traditionally deal with exchange companies and customarily don't question large transactions from them. The currency exchange business can also move money in other ways for the trafficker. In particular, money sent to other jurisdictions in payment for foreign drug shipments is common. Using a dummy corporation, a trafficker will sometimes contact

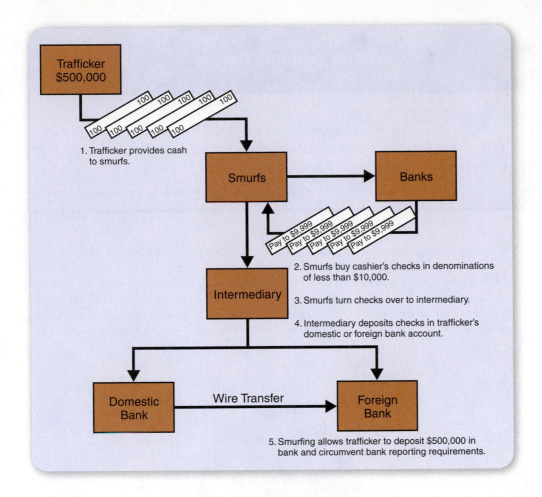

|Fig. 17.2| △

The smurfing process

his or her lawyer and request that the lawyer accept a huge deposit into the lawyer's foreign account. The lawyer will then wire the money directly into the dummy account, where it remains unsuspected.

DOUBLE INVOICING Double invoicing is yet another popular method of hiding illicit financial gains. In this technique, a company orders merchandise from a foreign subsidiary at an inflated price. The difference between the inflated price and the actual price is deposited by the subsidiary in a special offshore account. Occasionally, the same technique is used in reverse: The company sells merchandise at an artificially low price, and the difference between the two prices is deposited in a secret foreign bank account maintained by the company.

ACQUISITION OF FINANCIAL INSTITUTIONS This fifth money laundering method, possibly the most difficult to detect, simply involves acquiring a domestic or international financial institution. By controlling an entire institution, traffickers can go far beyond the immediate aim of concealing illicit earnings. They effectively take over part of the local banking system and divert it to their own needs. Such operations, which have been identified in South Florida and southern California, enable traffickers to manipulate correspondent banking relations, make overnight deposits, arrange Eurodollar loans, and take advantage of the abuse list (customers exempted from cash-reporting requirements).

These techniques represent only a few of the ways that traffickers hide their illicit revenues from drug sales. It is generally thought that traffickers, regardless of their national origin, make regular use of these techniques. The fact that so many different and unique mechanisms exist for money laundering makes investigation of these crimes difficult and presents many unique challenges to investigators. One great aid to law enforcement attempts was the passing of the Money Laundering Control Act of 1986, which gave investigators more latitude in investigating this type of criminal activity and in uncovering these myriad techniques.

The Smurfing Process

1. The trafficker provides cash to smurfs.
2. The smurfs buy cashier's checks in denominations under $10,000.
3. The smurfs turn the checks over to an intermediary.
4. The intermediary deposits checks in trafficker's domestic or foreign bank account.

Smurfing allows trafficker to deposit $500,000 in bank and circumvent bank reporting requirements.

Although investigations of money laundering are routinely performed by such agencies as the Federal Bureau of Investigation (FBI), DEA, and the Internal Revenue Service (IRS), a recently established investigative unit housed under the Department of the Treasury called the Financial Crimes Enforcement Network (FinCEN) also conducts such investigations. FinCEN, established in 1990, is a multiagency support unit that analyzes intelligence information that develops suspects in money laundering schemes. In addition to providing assistance to federal agencies, FinCEN also

|Fig. 17.3| ▲

Typical cycle of money laundering through the use of money orders.

From Office of National Drug Control Policy. (2008). *2007 money laundering strategy.*

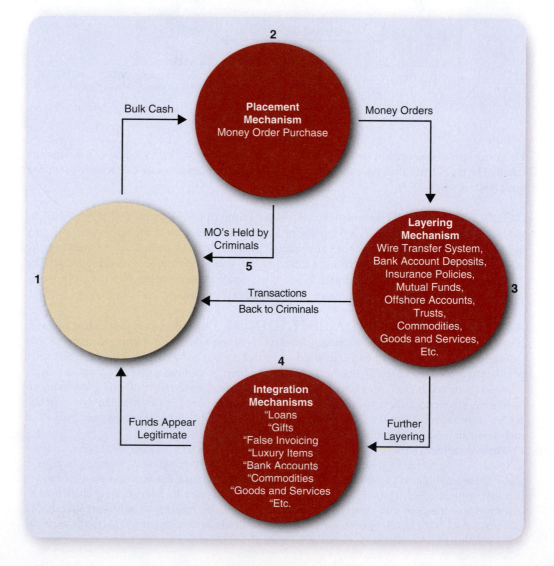

offers services to state and local police organizations investigating financial crimes, especially those associated with violations of the Bank Secrecy Act and the Money Laundering Control Act.

Money Laundering Using Money Orders

Money orders have proven to be a versatile vehicle for money laundering. Their use has been seen in crimes including narcotics trafficking, firearms trafficking, and depositing illicit proceeds from alien smuggling and corporate fraud.

In the legitimate world, money orders are used by approximately 30 million people annually to conduct business such as paying bills and sending money to families in foreign countries. It is estimated that more than 830 million money orders in excess of $100 billion are issued annually. The money order industry is small and easier to assess for criminals. Eighty percent of all money orders are issued by the U.S. Postal Service (USPS), Western Union, and Traveler's Express/MoneyGram. The remaining 20 percent are issued by smaller, regional companies scattered throughout the United States.

The greatest volume of money order activity is currently seen in New York/New Jersey, Los Angeles, El Paso, Dallas, Miami, Boston, and San Francisco. The extent that money orders are used is seen in national statistics. For example, the OCDETF has consistently reported that approximately 20 percent of its newly initiated money laundering investigations contains a money order component.[21] Law enforcement has documented a steady stream of money order use by launderers moving bulk cash from narcotics transactions to Mexico and other regions of Latin America. The process of money laundering using money orders is seen in Figure 17.3.

Computer Crime

A decade or so ago, if a college student used a camera to spy on his gay roommate and passed the pictures around, hardly anyone would have made a fuss—least of all the criminal justice system. It might have been passed off as a youthful prank. The perpetrator would probably not have been arrested and prosecuted, much less convicted and sentenced to jail. But in 2010, just such a case set off a firestorm focusing national attention on cyber-bullying faced by gay and lesbian teens.

Tyler Clementi was an eighteen-year-old student at Rutgers University in Piscataway, New Jersey, who jumped to his death from the George Washington Bridge on September 22, 2010. Without Clementi's knowledge, on September 19 his roommate, Dharun Ravi, and a fellow student, Molly

|Fig. 17.4| ▲

On March 16, 2012, Dharun Ravi, a former Rutgers University student, was tried and convicted on 15 counts of crimes relating to the suicide death of Tyler Clementi, who was secretly videoed by Ravi while having a gay sexual encounter.

Photoshot

Wei, used a webcam on Ravi's computer and a computer in Wei's dorm room to view Clementi kissing another man. On September 21, the day prior to the suicide, Ravi notified friends and followers on Twitter to watch via his webcam a second encounter between Clementi and his friend.

Ravi and Wei were indicted for their roles in the webcam incidents, though they were not charged with involvement in the suicide itself. Wei accepted a plea agreement on May 6, 2011, allowing her to avoid prosecution. On March 16, 2012, Ravi was found guilty of 15 counts involving crimes of invasion of privacy, attempted invasion of privacy, bias intimidation, tampering with evidence, and witness tampering. He was given a sentence including a 30-day jail term.

The death of Tyler Clementi followed another computer-related "cyber-bullying" case involving Megan Meier. Meier was a thirteen-year-old from Dardenne Prairie, Missouri. Soon after opening an account on MySpace, Meier received a message from Lori Drew, who had assumed a false identity of a 16-year-old boy, Josh Evans.[22] Meier and Josh became online friends but never met in person or spoke. Meier thought he was attractive and began to exchange messages with the fabricated Josh Evans. She was described by family as having had her "spirits lifted."[23]

On October 15, 2006, the tone of the messages changed, with Drew saying (via the account), "I don't know if I want to be friends with you anymore because I've heard that you are not very nice to your friends."[24] Similar messages were sent; some of Megan's messages were shared with others; and bulletins were posted about her. After telling her mother, Tina Meier, about the increasing number of hurtful messages, the two got into an argument over the vulgar language Meier used in response to the messages and the fact that she did not log off when her mother told her to.[25]

After the argument, Meier ran upstairs to her room. According to Meier's father, Ronald Meier, and a neighbor who had discussed the hoax with Drew, the last message sent by the Evans account read: "Everybody in O'Fallon knows how you are. You are a bad person and everybody hates you. Have a shitty rest of your life. The world would be a better place without you."[26] Meier responded with a message reading: "You're the kind of boy a girl would kill herself over." The last few correspondences were made via AOL Messenger instead of MySpace. She was found 20 minutes later, hanging by the neck in a closet. Despite attempts to revive her, she was pronounced dead the next day.

Both the Tyler Clementi and Megan Meier cases are sobering reminders that modern-day computer crime is not limited to criminals with a profit motive. Rather, they are evidence that cyber criminals out for revenge or other motives are keenly aware of potential victims who are young and impressionable. Worse yet, such criminals are often able to hide behind false identities while prowling the Internet and avoiding detection by the police.

With the personal computer now in many households and mainframe computers acting as the epicenter of almost all Fortune 500 companies, the problem of computer crime, or **cybercrime**, is now a mainstream social problem. According to one definition, cybercrime is "the destruction, theft or unauthorized use, modification, or copying of information, programs, services, equipment or communication networks."[27]

Some of the fastest-growing crimes in the country now are those labeled as cybercrimes, or crimes that take place over the Internet. Disturbingly, the Internet has become a popular hunting ground for child predators of all ages. It allows them to hide their identities and assume the roles of virtually anyone they choose. As a result, such criminals hide in chat rooms and sign up for popular social networking sites where children and teens socialize. Pretending to be teenagers, predators talk kids and teens into meeting with them, where they have been known to rape, molest, and sometimes murder them.

Perhaps one of the most frightening statistics about all of this is that in 100 percent of the cases, the victims met up willingly with their attacker, thinking they were meeting someone entirely different. The problem of Internet predators has become so great that many police departments have established dedicated units to investigate such crimes. In this capacity, undercover police also monitor chat rooms and try to attract predators by pretending to be teenage girls or other types of persons that might attract predators; they are then arrested. Investigators also discover Internet predators by acting on tips from parents or teens who have encountered or who believe they have come across an online predator.

For obvious reasons, cybercrime has had a relatively short history. Although electronic crime has been somewhat of a problem for the past three decades, it wasn't until the 1970s that a new term entered the public lexicon—**hacker**. Early hackers began using school computers for a number of misdeeds—the least of which was altering grades. By the end of the decade, modems (devices linking computers to telephone lines) and computerized bulletin board services emerged.

Although the first generation of hackers during the 1980s seemed more mischievous than criminal, their emergence was the predecessor for a far more insidious type of computer crime. Many large corporate computers are now "hacked" not as a prank but as a target of large-scale theft. Indeed, computers have provided opportunistic criminals with a new genre in which to ply their crimes, and many of today's criminals are quite computer literate. One early example of cyber-crime involved the planting of an unauthorized program known as a Trojan horse, which automatically transferred money to an illegal account whenever a legal transaction was made. To many thieves and hackers, this was akin to striking pure gold.

Computer criminals today have posed as financial advisers or licensed brokers on the Internet and solicited investments in fictitious mutual funds.[28] In some cases, they have attempted to extort money from their victims. In one of the biggest cases of **cyber-extortion**, a computer hacker stole credit card numbers from an online music retailer, CD Universe, and released thousands of them on a website when the company refused to pay $100,000 ransom. In January 2000, the *New York Times* reported that the hacker claimed to have taken the numbers of 300,000 CD Universe customers. The hacker turned out to be a 19-year-old from Russia going by the name of Maxim.[29]

Defining Computer Crime

As indicated, many different types of crimes are committed through illegal use of the computer. Computer crime, however, is not well understood in the criminal justice community partially because of its newness on the criminal frontier and the level of competency required for many such offenses. Other factors also contribute to confusion about the crime, such as media sensationalizing of events involving computers. Because of this, a consensus of the definition of computer crime is difficult to obtain.

According to the National Institute of Justice (NIJ), state and federal criminal codes contain more than 50 different definitions of computer crime, each somewhat different from the other. For the sake of simplicity, let's define computer crimes as violations of criminal law that require a knowledge of computers for their perpetration.

Internal computer crimes are alterations to computer programs that result in the performance of unauthorized functions within a computer program. Such crimes have been around for years and have acquired names such as Trojan horses, logic bombs, and trap doors to indicate different programming techniques designed to carry out the unauthorized functions.

The Nature of the Crime

Computer crime is difficult, if not impossible, to detect. According to the FBI, it is believed to cost private and public businesses anywhere from $40 to $100 billion yearly. The gradual evolution of occupations in this field has created new opportunities for criminals, who benefit as computer programmers, operators, tape librarians, and electronic engineers. Here, criminality is removed from the street and resides in the privacy of the homes of computer criminals, many of which have raised flooring, lowered ceilings, flashing lights, and air-conditioning motors. Hence, methods of crime have changed. A new computer jargon has now developed that has identified automated criminal methods such as data diddling, Trojan horses, logic bombs, salami techniques, superzapping, scavenging, data leakage, and asynchronous attacks.

Targets or victims of computer crime have also taken on a nontypical effigy. For example, electronic transactions and money, as well as paper and plastic money (credit cards), are typical targets for automated loss. Financial transactions are typically conducted over telephone lines where money is debited and credited inside computers. In essence, the computer has become the vault for the business community. Physical assets such as warehouse inventories and materials leaving factories are also tracked through the use of computers.

The timing of computer crimes also differs greatly from traditional crimes. From a traditional standpoint, most crimes are measured in minutes, hours, or even days. In contrast, some computer crimes are measured in milliseconds (as little as 0.003 of a second).

Another atypical dimension to computer crime is that geographical constraints do not hinder the computer criminal, as with many other types of crime. A telephone with an attached computer terminal (modem) in one country can easily be used to engage in a crime in a different nation. All of these factors and more should be considered in dealing with the problem of computer crimes.

The extent that computer crime can result in violent crime is seen in the "Craigslist killer" case. In 2009, the Craigslist website came under intense scrutiny and criticism after Phillip Markoff, a 23-year-old Boston University medical student, was arrested as a suspect in the death of Julissa Brisman of New York City. Brisman advertised her erotic massage services on Craigslist. Phillip Markoff quickly became known in the popular media as the "Craigslist killer." Craigslist is a centralized network of online communities, featuring free online classified advertisements. It has sections for jobs, housing, personal ads, for sale ads, services, community, gigs, résumés, and discussion forums.

The investigation revealed that Markoff had not been sexually assaulting his victims but instead robbing them to pay off gambling debts and was keeping his victims' underwear as souvenirs of his crimes. Brisman is the only reported death in the alleged crime spree.

Craigslist defended the site, insisting that the murder is not the direct result of the erotic services ads and that without that section, those types of services would propagate all over the site in other sections. They argue that the erotic section was a good way to contain adult rated ads in one, avoidable place.[30]

Markoff's wasn't the only case that caused concern. After investigating for months, in the spring of 2009, Connecticut Police filed harassment and computer crimes charges against 38-year-old Jonathan Medina, a former CVS pharmacist who stole a woman's personal information from the pharmacy computer and posted it online in a fake Craigslist erotic services posting. The victim stated that the morning after visiting the pharmacy, she started receiving numerous phone calls from men looking for a "good time."

On May 13, 2009, Craigslist closed the "Erotic services" section of its site, replacing it with an "adult services" section where the postings would be reviewed by Craigslist employees.[31] The Craigslist cases are examples of how criminals can target victims by using legitimate computer networking businesses that offer dating or other personal services.

Computer Crime Investigations

Computer crime investigations are dynamic in nature. Therefore, their detection and investigation differ in several respects from that of other more traditional crimes. These differences include:

- Physical evidence in computer crimes is different from that in traditional crimes.
- The volume of evidence encountered in computer crimes can be burdensome.
- Offenders can commit their crimes with ease.
- Offenders can destroy evidence with ease.

Such investigations require a greater amount of technical expertise by investigators and prosecutors. Despite the contrasts cited earlier, certain approaches of the computer crime investigation remain consistent. For example, such investigations generally require a considerable investment of time, sometimes taking from one month to a full year in duration. This is due, in part, to the fact that identification and analysis of data are necessary to organize information for complicated search warrants. In addition, the investigation of computer crime requires interaction between investigators and victims. Victims, because of their knowledge of computer systems, can aid the investigator in providing technical expertise.

Another commonality in computer crime investigations is that they are largely investigative in nature (i.e., standard investigative procedures can be used), using an estimated 90 percent traditional police work and 10 percent technical skill.[32]

Yet another distinguishing attribute of computer crime investigations is that they are typically proactive in nature. Proactive initiatives include the monitoring of electronic bulletin boards and regular contact with local schools and businesses to help prevent and detect possible crimes with computers.

Classification of Computer Crimes

Because computers have been used in almost all types of crimes, their classification extends beyond the simple category of white-collar crime. Computer crimes involve the use of both computer hardware and software. **Hardware** is generally considered the physical computer itself and any peripherals associated with it, such as printers, telephone modems, and external disk drives. **Software**, conversely, refers to the media on which information is stored (e.g., computer tapes and floppy disks).

During the mid-1970s, the federal government attempted to amend the U.S. Criminal Code to make crimes of unauthorized acts in, around, and with the use of computers. In 1986, President Reagan authorized another law, outlawing the illegal use of computers: the Electronic Communications Privacy Act. This law basically prohibits eavesdropping on electronic mail, conversations on cellular phones, video conference calls, and computer-to-computer transactions.

In recent years, four main categories of computer crime have been identified:

1. The introduction of fraudulent records or data into a computer system
2. Unauthorized use of computer-related facilities
3. The alteration or destruction of information or files
4. The stealing, whether by electronic means or otherwise, of money, financial instruments, property, services, or valuable data

Computer crime has also been classified by the types of information loss, including modification, destruction, disclosure, and use or denial of use. These violations may involve changing information, prohibiting access to information, and removing or copying it wrongfully.

Typical Forms of Computer Crimes

Many computer crimes take the form of traditional crimes. They may, however, also concern special crimes in which the computer is the primary tool of the criminal of such crimes. These crimes have been labeled according to their criminal function and include computer hacking, scanning, masquerading, false data entry, Trojan horses, and computer viruses.

COMPUTER HACKING In its most favorable use, the term *computer hacker* signifies a compulsive computer programmer who explores, tests, and pushes the computer to its limits, regardless of its consequences. In reality, hacking may involve the destruction of valuable data, resulting in massive costs. According to a report issued by the NIJ, the typical computer hacker is a juvenile possessing a home computer with a telephone modem who uses electronic bulletin boards for a variety of illegal purposes. Such criminals may become involved in crimes such as credit card fraud and using unauthorized numbers to arrange mail-order purchases to vacant homes where the delivery can be intercepted and kept.

SCANNING Scanning is the process of presenting sequentially changing information to an automated system to identify those items receiving a positive response. The method is typically used to identify telephone numbers that access computers, user identifications, passwords that facilitate access to computers, and credit card numbers that are used illegally for purchasing merchandise or services through telemarketing. Many computer systems can deter scanners by limiting the number of access attempts and therefore create a long delay designed to discourage the scanning process.

MASQUERADING Masquerading is the most common activity of computer system intruders. It is also one of the most difficult to prove after the case goes to trial. It is the process of one person assuming the identity of an authorized computer user by acquiring items, knowledge, or characteristics. For one to have physical access to a computer terminal or system, many such systems require that the user enter a specified identifier such as a security code or password. Anyone possessing the correct security code or password can masquerade as another person.

An example of a clever masquerade occurred when a young man posed as a magazine writer and called a telephone company, indicating that he was writing an article on the computer system used by the phone company. The conversation revealed a detailed briefing on all of the computer facilities and applications systems. As a result, the perpetrator was able to steal more than $1 million worth of telephone equipment from the company.

Evidence showing the act of masquerading is difficult to obtain. When an intrusion occurs, the investigator must obtain evidence identifying the masquerader at a terminal as performing the acts producing the events in the computer. This task is especially difficult when network-weaving connections through several switched telephone systems interfere with tracing devices (e.g., pen registers and dialed number recorders).

FALSE DATA ENTRY (DATA DIDDLING) The false data entry type of computer crime is usually the simplest, safest, and most commonly used method. It involves changing data before or during their input to computers. Generally, anybody associated with or having access to the process of recording, encoding, examining, checking, converting, updating, or transforming data that ultimately are entered in a computer can change these data.

A typical example of a false data entry, or **data diddling**, is the case of a timekeeping clerk who filled out data forms of hours worked by 300 employees in a railroad company department. He noticed that all data on the forms entered into the timekeeping and payroll system on the computer included both the name and employee number of each worker. However, the computer used only employee numbers for processing. He also noticed that outside the computer, all manual processing and control were based only on employee names because nobody identified people by their numbers.

He took advantage of this situation by filling out forms for overtime hours worked, using the names of employees who frequently worked overtime, but entering his own employee number. The scheme was successful for years until detected by an auditor examining W-2s, who noticed the clerk's unusually high annual income. A subsequent examination of the timekeeping computer files and data forms, and a discussion with the clerk's supervisor revealed the source of the income.

TROJAN HORSES The **Trojan horse** method is the secret placement or alteration of computer instructions so that the computer will tell a second computer how to perform illegal functions. It is unique in that it usually also allows the victim computer to perform most or all of the functions for its originally intended purposes. The Trojan horse program is also the primary method used for inserting instructions for other abusive acts, such as logic bombs, salami attacks, and viruses.

In 1981, one Trojan horse technique, the electronic letter bomb attack, received considerable news media attention because its use would have made most computers with terminal-to-terminal communication vulnerable to compromise. The attack method consisted of sending messages to other terminals with embedded control characters ending with the send-line or the block-mode control command. When the messages reach the intelligent terminals, the send-line or block-mode control command is sensed, and the entire message is sent back to the computer for execution of the embedded control character commands as though they came from the victim at the receiving terminal with all of his or her computer access authority.

Many local police computers are linked with state and national crime information networks. The Trojan horse technique can be prevented in two ways. First, send-line or block-mode types of commands can be removed from all terminals allowed access to the computer. Next, a logic filter can be placed in the computer to prevent all control character commands from being sent in terminal-to-terminal messages. Trojan horses can be detected by comparing a copy of the operational program under suspicion with a master or other copy known to be free of unauthorized changes. The suspect program can be tested with a wide range of data that might expose the purpose of the Trojan horse.

COMPUTER VIRUSES A **computer virus** is a set of computer instructions that reproduces itself in computer programs when they are executed within unauthorized programs. The program may be inserted through a special program designed for that purpose or through use of a Trojan horse—hidden instructions inserted into a computer program that the victim uses. Then the virus multiplies itself into other programs when they are executed, creating new viruses. Such programs can lie dormant in computer systems for weeks or even months and may infect entire computer networks, rendering them useless. Although the first three cases of computer viruses were reported in November 1987, hundreds of subsequent cases have since appeared in various academic and research cultures. Some cases have emerged as a result of disgruntled employees of computer program manufacturers who have contaminated products during delivery to customers.

Investigators should first interview the victims to identify the nature of the suspected attack. They should then use the necessary tools (not resident system utilities) to examine the contents after a suspected event

SUPERZAPPING This superzapping technique stems from Superzapper, a macro or utility program used in most IBM mainframe computer centers as a systems tool. Most computer centers have a secure operating mode that requires a "break-glass-in-case-of-emergency" program that will bypass all controls to disclose any of the contents of the computer. Illegal use of the Superzapper program enables thieves, for example, to tinker with the program so that checks can be issued to their private accounts.

SALAMI TECHNIQUES The salami technique is an automated form of the Trojan horse method where small amounts of assets (i.e., money) are taken from specified accounts or sources

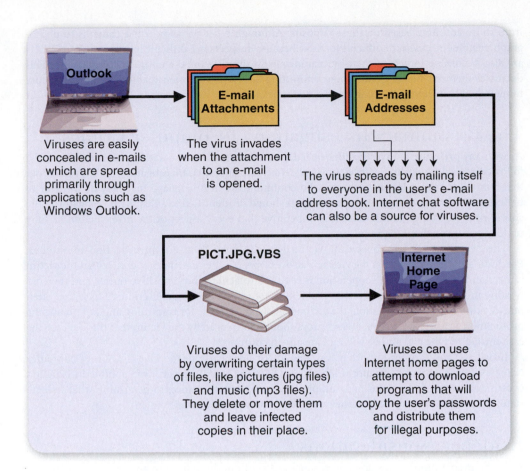

|Fig. 17.5| △

The anatomy of a computer virus.

and where the whole appears to be unaffected. In this way, over time, a substantial amount of money can be diverted to the thief's personal account while going undetected.

TRAP DOORS A trap door is a technique in which programmers insert debugging aids that break security codes in the computer and then insert an additional code of their own. This enables entry into the program for such purposes as false data entry.

LOGIC BOMBS A logic bomb is a set of instructions inserted in a computer program that looks for specific errors in a computer's normal functioning. After it has been identified, the logic bomb kicks into action and exploits the error identified. The end result is the victim computer reacting in certain ways that might result in crashing of the program.

ASYNCHRONOUS ATTACKS Many computer functions rely on the asynchronous functioning of a computer to complete certain functions, such as calling for the output of certain reports in a predesignated order. Frequently, many such functions are programmed into the computer at once. The asynchronous attack confuses the computer system, making it unable to differentiate one job from another.

COMPUTER PROGRAM PIRACY Piracy is the unauthorized copying and use of computer programs in violation of copyright and trade secret laws.

Automatic Teller Machine Frauds

Most states that have a computer crime statute include a provision for fraudulent use of automatic teller machines (ATMs). Typically, ATM fraud involves persons with legitimate bank accounts who made fraudulent deposits (e.g., depositing empty envelopes) and then withdrawing money from those accounts based on those deposits. Although most banks now use cameras to photograph customers, cases are difficult to make because suspects are difficult to locate. (Note: ATMs are also becoming targets of theft by criminals who simply steal the entire ATM machine. This decreases their risk of being shot while committing the crime and often enables them to steal more money than in other types of commercial robberies.)

The Preliminary Investigation of Computer Crimes

As with any preliminary investigation, each department's standard operating procedure should be followed regarding dealing with victims, evidence, and suspects. Investigators should remember that computer crimes involve persons who communicate in a language that may be difficult to understand. Because of this, a computer expert should be identified to assist the investigator in the course of the investigation. Indeed, it is imperative that every aspect of the investigation be fully understood throughout the inquiry.

The degree of cooperation by the victim will also vary from one investigation to another. Precluding the possibility that the victim is also a suspect in the case, it is imperative that the victim understands that maximum cooperation is required to achieve both positive results and to avoid wasting much valuable time. Another problem encountered in computer crime cases is that often midway through the investigation, the victim will decide to settle for restitution and not pursue the prosecution further. Therefore, investigators should be assured by the victim that they will see the case through to the end and be willing to testify in court.

Jurisdiction is another important variable to consider early in the investigation of computer crimes. Often, a suspect computer will have been used in facilitating a crime in another jurisdiction because of complex computer networking. It is necessary, therefore, to determine what federal, state, or local laws might apply to the type of computer crime committed.

Evidence Considerations

As in the preparation of any case for criminal prosecution, the collection and preservation of evidence are critical elements. Experience has shown that the most typical defense ploy in a computer crime case is to attack the admissibility of evidence seized. Such attacks often result in the suppression of evidence that might otherwise easily incriminate the suspect.

OBTAINING COMPUTER CRIME EVIDENCE It is fairly easy to obtain documents in computer crime cases because such documents are easily identified by noncomputer experts. These include computer manuals, program documentation, logs, data and program input forms, and computer-printed forms. Ascertaining whether they are complete, originals, or copies can be determined by document custodians.

Requesting specific program documentation may require assistance and knowledge of computer concepts to determine the extent and types of documentation required. In addition, taking possession of other computer media may be more complicated. Magnetic tapes and diskettes, for example, are usually labeled externally. Additionally, a large tape or disk file may reside on more than one reel or cartridge. In this case, assistance may be needed to check the contents of a tape or disk by using a comparable computer. The search for information inside a computer is usually highly complex and probably requires the aid of an expert. Preparing a search warrant for this task also requires expert advice. In both cases, expert advice can come from the following sources:

- Systems analysts
- Programmers who wrote the programs
- Staff who prepared the data in computer-readable form
- Tape librarians
- Electronic maintenance engineers who maintain the hardware

Advice and help from such people aid the investigator in his or her role in the investigation. When the case goes to court, the same people can offer expert testimony to establish the integrity and reliability of the evidence seized.

EXAMINING EVIDENCE FOR CRIMINAL CONTENT Computers can maintain an extremely large amount of information in a small amount of space. A floppy disk is small enough

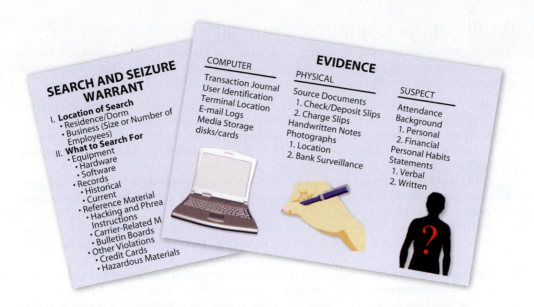

|Fig. 17.6| △

Computer evidence

From National Institute of Justice. (2004).
Research in Brief: *Computer Crime.*
Washington, DC: U.S. Government Printing
Office.

to fit inside a pocket and can easily be hidden in books or taped to the bottom of a keyboard. The contents of a "flash drive" can hold more than enough information to make a case by providing direct evidence or direction to evidence.

If there is printer activity, this information can require a great deal of time to sort through. It is important not to blindly push this potential evidence aside; doing so may very well cost a case. Buried deep inside the amount of paper could be the secret bank account number where the suspects have hidden their assets or their list of past, present, and future victims for rape and murder.[33]

PRESERVING COMPUTER CRIME EVIDENCE Determining if the evidence can be collected and preserved for future analysis is not as easy as it sounds. Investigators must check their warrants constantly for what they can and cannot seize. If something is found that is needed but is not covered in a search warrant, the wording must be amended before seizure of that item can proceed. Seizing materials not included in a search warrant could cost an investigator the success of an entire investigation.

Some types of computer evidence require special care and attention. Because of this, storage areas must be controlled, and special care must be given to protect the evidence from physical damage. Certain care measures are required for the most common types of computer evidence:

- *Magnetic tape and disks.* These must be handled with care. This type of evidence is also easily destroyed by exposure to magnetic fields such as stereo speakers and printers.
- *Printed computer listings.* No restrictions on storage are required for paper printouts of computerized data except that they should not be stored in direct sunlight. This practice will reduce the chance of fading.
- *Computer.* All types of computers are sensitive—be careful. Even when a computer is turned off, disruption by moving it may occur. If there is a hard drive, it should be "parked" before being moved to avoid destroying information contained on the disk.
- *Additional computer hardware.* Investigators should document the configuration of a computer, what add-on equipment is involved, and how it should be disconnected. This equipment may include telephone modems, autodialers, and printers.

Investigators must also remember that the owners of computer-related evidence may have special problems when the evidence is removed from their possession. Such material may be necessary for continuing their legitimate business or other activities. One manner of dealing with this situation is to arrange for copying the material. After this is accomplished, the copy, not the original, is returned to the rightful owner.

Profile of the Computer Criminal

Computer crimes suspects can sometimes be identified on the basis of characteristics of known computer criminals who have been interviewed in computer abuse studies. Research shows that organizations are more vulnerable to people with the following described characteristics:

- *Age.* Most perpetrators are young and were educated in colleges and universities where computer attacks are common and sometimes condoned as "educational activity."
- *Skills and knowledge.* Most suspects are among the most skilled and higher-performing technologists. This is seen, in particular, in organizations in which a worker is overqualified for the work he or she is doing.
- *Positions of trust.* In most cases, perpetrators perform their acts while working at their jobs. Investigators should anticipate that vulnerabilities identified will usually result in the most qualified person taking advantage of them.
- *Assistance.* Perpetrators in many types of computer crime have been known to need assistance. This is because computer crimes require more knowledge and access than one person usually possesses.
- *Differential association.* Frequently, people working together may encourage each other to engage in unauthorized acts that escalate into serious crimes.
- *Robin Hood syndrome.* Most computer crime perpetrators interviewed in the study differentiated between harming people and organizations, the latter of which was easily condoned. In addition, they rationalized that they were only harming a computer and not causing any loss to people or organizations.

Interviewing the Computer Crime Suspect

To investigate computer crime, investigators should have a thorough understanding of the damage that a suspect can do in the computing facility. For example, if an employee believes that he or she is a suspect, the employee may have the means to go into the computer system and destroy valuable evidence, even after the crime has been committed. In addition, logic bombs could be inserted into the computer to render the system dysfunctional. In all cases, suspects should be restricted from access to the computer system after becoming a suspect except under strictly supervised conditions.

In addition, a criminal background check should be performed on both the suspect and victim. This is particularly important in computer crime cases because most employers fail to do this. Many suspects voluntarily talk with investigators because they may believe that their actions might be unethical or immoral but not criminal in nature.

Case in Point

>>A Ponzi Scheme[34]

The Ponzi scheme struck again, this time by a French businessman seeking fame and fortune in the United States. What made this case a little different, though, was the fact that the victims of the scam fought back—and to a certain extent succeeded—in getting back their hard-earned money.

What Is a Ponzi Scheme?

What are Ponzi schemes? They're an illegal investment named after Charles Ponzi, an Italian immigrant who settled in Boston and scammed thousands of victims in New England and others in a postage stamp speculation investment during the 1920s. According to the SEC, Ponzi said he made large profits by taking advantage of fluctuations in differences between U.S. and foreign currencies used to buy and sell international mail stamps. He raised millions of dollars from investors after claiming he could produce a 40 percent investment return within 90 days, far higher than the average 5 percent interest banks offered at the time for savings accounts.

As money poured in, Ponzi used funds from new customers to pay those who invested earlier. He ultimately took in an estimated $15 million, but the investment stream dried up as the government stopped paying cash for surrendered stamps shortly after Ponzi began his infamous scheme. He was never able to pay more than a fraction of the promised returns. Investors, hearing rumors that Ponzi had gone bankrupt, sought to get their

(continued)

Case in Point *(continued)*

money back. The redemption demands caused the scam to collapse.

The scams are also known as pyramid schemes, based on a geometric shape of a system in which money from large numbers of new investors at the base is funneled upward to small numbers who invested earlier. Typically, pyramid scheme investors are offered too-good-to-be-true returns for simply investing your money and convincing others to do the same. The schemes ultimately grow too large and promoters can attract enough new investors to pay all the earlier ones. The scam then collapses.

Modern Example of a Ponzi Scheme

One of history's greatest Ponzi schemes was perpetrated by Bernard Madoff and uncovered in 2008. The Madoff investment scandal occurred after the discovery that former NASDAQ chairman Bernard Madoff's asset management business was actually a giant Ponzi scheme that generated an estimated $50 billion. Alerted by his sons, federal authorities arrested Madoff on December 11, 2008. On March 12, 2009, Madoff pled guilty to 11 felonies and admitted to operating the largest investor fraud ever committed by an individual. According to a federal criminal complaint, client statements showing $65 billion in stock holdings were fictitious, and no stocks were ever purchased since the scheme began in the 1980s.[35]

Madoff's sales pitch was an investment strategy consisting of purchasing blue-chip stocks and then taking options contracts on them, which is sometimes called a split-strike conversion or a collar.[36]

> Typically, a position will consist of the ownership of 30–35 S&P 100 stocks, most correlated to that index, the sale of out-of-the-money "calls" on the index and the purchase of out-of-the-money "puts" on the index. The sale of the "calls" is designed to increase the rate of return, while allowing upward movement of the stock portfolio to the strike price of the "calls." The "puts," funded in large part by the sales of the "calls," limit the portfolio's downside.[37]

Rather than offer high returns to all comers, Madoff offered modest but steady returns to an exclusive clientele. The investment method was marketed as "too complicated for outsiders to understand." He was secretive about the firm's business and kept his financial statements closely guarded.[38] Madoff "worked the so-called 'Jewish circuit' of well-heeled Jews he met at country clubs on

|Fig. 17.7| ▲

In March 2009, Bernie Madoff (center) pleaded guilty to 11 federal felonies and admitted turning his wealth management business into a Ponzi scheme whereby thousands of investors were defrauded of billions of dollars.

© Everett Collection Inc / Alamy

Long Island and in Palm Beach." The *New York Times* reported that Madoff courted many prominent Jewish executives and organizations; according to the Associated Press, they "trusted [Madoff] because he is Jewish."[39] One of the most prominent promoters was J. Ezra Merkin, whose fund Ascot Partners steered $1.8 billion toward Madoff's firm. A scheme that targets members of a particular religious or ethnic community is a type of affinity

(continued)

Case in Point *(continued)*

fraud, and a *Newsweek* article identified Madoff's scheme as "an affinity Ponzi."[40]

The scheme began to unravel in December 2008 as the stock market continued to plunge. Subsequently, as the general market downturn accelerated, investors tried to withdraw $7 billion from the firm, and in the weeks before his arrest, Madoff struggled to keep the scheme afloat. To pay off those investors, Madoff needed new money from other investors.[41]

On December 10, 2008, he suggested to his sons, Mark and Andrew, that the firm pay out several million dollars in bonuses two months ahead of schedule, from $200 million in assets that the firm still had.[42] According to the complaint, Mark and Andrew, reportedly unaware of the firm's pending insolvency, confronted their father, asking him how the firm could pay bonuses to employees if it could not pay investors. Madoff then admitted that he was "finished" and that the asset management arm of the firm was in fact a Ponzi scheme. Mark and Andrew then reported him to the authorities.

Summary Checklist

In this chapter, we consider the ways information about crimes is documented by criminal investigators. A properly documented case is one that is more likely to succeed in court. See how well you are able to answer the following questions in your checklist.

1. Explain the definition of white-collar crime.

- Edwin Sutherland originally defined white-collar crime as "a crime committed by a person of respectability and high social status in the course of his occupation."

- Today, according to the Bureau of Justice Statistics, white-collar crime is not an official crime category, but it represents a unique area of criminality that differs from other categories of criminality, such as violence and property crime.

- *White-collar crime* is a generic term that means different things to different people—the appropriate definition has long been a matter of dispute among criminal justice practitioners.

- One modern definition of white-collar crime is as follows:"non-violent crime for financial gain committed by means of deception by persons whose occupational status is entrepreneurial, professional, or semi-professional, and utilizing their special occupational skills and opportunities."

- Some of the most notable white-collar crimes are insider trading, money laundering, confidence games, and computer crime.

2. Do you understand the concept of corporate crime?

- Corporate crime is a form of white-collar crime whereby trusted executives working within a company mishandle funds or otherwise betray the trust of customers or other consumers

- Motivations include gaining or increasing power or realizing personal wealth through mishandling funds.

- Corporate crime may affect a small number of people or millions of people.

3. Describe how confidence games work.

Confidence games are crimes that betray the trust of the victim.

- The pigeon drop, probably the most practiced confidence game of all time, is a scam whereby a lot of losers pay a few winners.

- The bank examiner scam involves con artists who pose as FBI agents, bank examiners, police officers, detectives, or bank officials and who contact a victim and pretend to need help in conducting an investigation.

- A pyramid scheme involves selling franchises to unsuspecting persons who must then sell more franchises to more victims, and so on. These schemes ultimately grow too large and collapse when the promoters can no longer attract enough new victims to keep the scheme alive.

- Other confidence games include:

  - Travel scams

  - Home repair scams

  - Contest cons

  - Magazine subscription scams

4. Explain what money laundering is and how it is conducted.

Money laundering is the process of making illegally obtained funds appear legitimate. It is the means by which criminals evade paying taxes on illegal income, by concealing the source and amount of profit. Essentially it is tax evasion in progress.

There are a number of money laundering techniques:

- Bank methods are the most common method for laundering money. In this technique, traffickers take their cash to a bank and conduct several transactions that usually involve trading currency of small denominations for larger ones, or for Treasury bills, bank drafts, letters of credit, traveler's checks, or other monetary instruments.

- Smurfing involves a trafficker providing several individuals ("smurfs") with cash from drug sales. Each smurf goes to different banks and purchases cashier's checks in denominations of less than $10,000 (thus avoiding federal reporting requirements). The checks are turned over to a second person who facilitates their deposit into domestic or overseas banks.

- Currency exchanges—traffickers may use foreign currency exchanges or brokerage houses to facilitate movement of money.

- Double invoicing—a company orders merchandise from a foreign subsidiary at an inflated price. The subsidiary deposits the difference between the inflated and actual price in a special offshore account.

- Acquisition of financial institutions—traffickers acquire a domestic or international financial institution. By controlling an entire institution, traffickers can go far beyond the immediate aim of concealing illicit earnings. They effectively take over part of the local banking system and divert it to their own needs.

5. **Describe what cybercrime is, and some of the forms of computer crime**.

Cybercrime is "the destruction, theft or unauthorized use, modification, or copying of information, programs, services, equipment or communication networks."

Four main categories of computer crime have been identified:

- The introduction of fraudulent records or data into a computer system
- Unauthorized use of computer-related facilities
- The alteration or destruction of information or files
- The stealing of money, financial instruments, property, services, or valuable data

Many computer crimes take the form of traditional crimes but they may also involve special crimes in which the computer is the primary tool of the criminal.

- Computer hacking may involve the destruction of valuable data, resulting in massive costs.

- Scanning is the process of sequentially changing information to an automated system to identify those items receiving a positive response. It is typically used to identify telephone numbers that access computers, user identifications, passwords that facilitate access to computers, and credit cards that are used illegally for purchasing merchandise or services through telemarketing.

- Masquerading is the process of one person assuming the identity of an authorized computer user by acquiring items, knowledge, or characteristics.

- False data entry (data diddling) involves changing data before or during their input to computers.

- Trojan horse method is the secret placement or alteration of computer instructions so that the computer will tell a second computer how to perform illegal functions.

- Computer viruses are sets of computer instructions that reproduce themselves in computer programs when they are executed within unauthorized programs.

- Superzapping stems from the Superzapper, a macro or utility program used in most IBM mainframes as a systems tool.

- Salami techniques are an automated form of the Trojan horse method where small amounts of assets are taken from specified accounts or sources and where the whole appears to be unaffected.

- Trap door is a technique in which programmers insert debugging aids that break security codes in the computer and then insert an additional code of their own to enable entry into the program for such purposes as false data entry.

- A logic bomb is a set of instructions inserted into a computer program that looks for specific errors in a computer's normal functioning and then exploits the identified error.

- Asynchronous attacks confuse the computer system, making it unable to differentiate one job from another.

- Computer program piracy is the unauthorized copying and use of computer programs in violation of copyright and trade secret laws.

- Automatic teller machine (ATM) fraud involves persons with legitimate bank accounts making fraudulent deposits and then withdrawing money from those accounts based on those deposits.

Key Terms

bank examiner scheme	data diddling	salami technique
Bank Secrecy Act (BSA)	double invoicing	scammers
computer crime	flooding	scanning
computer hacking	hacker	smurfing
computer virus	hardware	software
confidence game	logic bomb	superzapping
corporate crime	masquerading	trap doors
currency exchange	money laundering	Trojan horse
cybercrime	pigeon drop	white-collar crime
cyber-extortion	pyramid scheme	

Discussion Questions

1. Define white-collar and corporate crime.
2. What is meant by the term *confidence game*?
3. Explain the details of the pigeon drop scam and why it is used so widely.
4. Explain some of the other types of confidence games used by con artists.
5. Explain check and credit card fraud and some of the common counter measures.
6. Explain money laundering and list and discuss the most common techniques used by traffickers to launder illicitly gained currency.
7. Define computer crime and explain how computer crimes differ from traditional crimes.
8. List and discuss the typical forms of computer crimes.
9. Discuss the steps that investigators should consider during the preliminary investigation phase of the computer crime investigation.
10. List and discuss the primary types of computer crime evidence and how they should be collected and preserved.
11. Explain the profile of a computer criminal.

Notes

1. BAYLES, F. (1999). Man, millions vanish in Greenwich, Conn. *USA Today*, June 29, p. 4A.
2. BLOCK, S. (1999). Fugitive goes from high life to prison cell. *USA Today*, September 7, p. 3A.
3. U.S. BUREAU OF JUSTICE STATISTICS. (1986). The impact of white collar crime in America. *Research in Brief*. Washington, DC: U.S. Department of Justice, National Institute of Justice.
4. MACLEAN, B. and P. ELKIND. (2003). *Smartest guys in the room: The amazing rise and scandalous fall of Enron: Penguin Press*, September.
5. HEALY, P. and K. PALEPU. (2003). The fall of Enron. *Journal of Economics Perspectives* 17(2):3.
6. IBID.
7. NORRIS, F. (2001). Enron taps all its credit lines to buy back $3.3 billion of debt. *The New York Times*, October 27.
8. OPPEL, R. JR. and A. BERENSON. (2001). Enron's chief executive quits after only six months in job. (Jeffrey Skilling). *The New York Times*, August 15.
9. BERENSON, A. (2001). S.E.C. opens investigation into Enron; a company fails to explain dealings. *The New York Times*, November 1.
10. GILPIN, K. (2001). Enron reports $1 billion in charges and a loss. *The New York Times*, October 17; HEALY AND PALEPU. (2003). The fall of Enron.
11. IBID.
12. HEALY and PALEPU. (2003). The fall of Enron.
13. TYCO INTERNATIONAL SECURITIES CLASS ACTION SETTLEMENT WEBSITE. Available at http://www.settlementboard.com/top-settlements/class-action-settlements/class-action-settlements-tyco-international/ (retrieved on September 24, 2012).

14. SHORN, D. (2007). Dennis kozlowski: Prisoner 05A4820. *CBS news 60 minutes*, July 29. Available at http://www.cbsnews.com/stories/2007/03/22/60minutes/main2596123.shtml.

15. INTERNAL REVENUE SERVICE WEB SITE. (2012). Available at http://www.irs.gov/compliance/enforcement/article/0,,id=246537,00.html (retrieved on May 28, 2012).

16. IBID.

17. IBID.

18. INTERNAL REVENUE SERVICE. Available at http://www.irs.gov/uac/Compliance-&-Enforcement (retrieved on September 24, 2012).

19. DRUG ENFORCEMENT ADMINISTRATION. (n.d.). *Money laundering*. Available at http://www.usdoj.gov/dea/programs/money.htm.

20. PRESIDENT'S COMMISSION ON ORGANIZED CRIME. (1984). *The impact*. Washington, DC: U.S. Government Printing Office.

21. U.S. MONEY LAUNDERING THREAT ASSESSMENT. (2008). *2007 national money laundering strategy*. Washington, DC: U.S. Government Printing Office.

22. WOODARD, T. Prosecutor to review MySpace suicide. *Fox2News, St. Louis*. Available at http://newsgroups.derkeiler.com/Archive/Alt/alt.true-crime/2007-11/msg01446.html (retrieved on September 24, 2012).

23. POKIN, S. (2007). "MySpace" hoax ends with suicide of Dardenne Prairie teen. *St. Louis Post-Dispatch*, November 11.

24. PARENTS SAY FAKE ONLINE "FRIEND" LED TO GIRL'S SUICIDE. (2007). *CNN*, November 17. Available at http://www.cnn.com/2007/US/11/17/internet.suicide.ap/index.html.

25. ANONYMOUS. (2008). Annal of crime: The friend game. *The New Yorker*, January 21.

26. TAYLOR, B. (2007). Lawyer: Mother unaware of cruel messages. *Associated Press*, December 5.

27. PERRY, R. (1986). *Computer crime*. New York: Franklin Watts.

28. ROSNOFF, S. M., ET AL. (1998). *Profit without honor*. Upper Saddle River, NJ: Prentice Hall.

29. HACKER'S RANSOM. (2000). *USA Today*, January 11, p. 3A.

30. JORDAN AND SAMANTHA, CO-OWNERS OF OYSTERS & CHOCOLATE EROTIC. (2009). Craigslist to pull erotic services ads. *Examiner*, May 14. Available at http://www.examiner.com/x-2092-Sex-Scandal-Examiners~y2009m5d14-Craigslist-to-pull-erotic-services-ads.

31. STONE, B. (2009). Craigslist to remove category for erotic services. *The New York Times*, May 13. Available at http://www.nytimes.com/2009/05/14/technology/companies/14craigslist.html.

32. NATIONAL INSTITUTE OF JUSTICE. (1989). *Research in Brief*. Washington, DC: U.S. Department of Justice, National Institute of Justice, June.

33. CLARK, F. and K. DILIBERTO. (1996). *Investigating computer crime*. Boca Raton, FL: CRC Press.

34. FEDERAL BUREAU OF INVESTIGATION. (2000). Available at http://www.fbi.gov.

35. REID, T. (2008). Wall Street legend Bernard Madoff arrested over $50 billion Ponzi scheme. *Times Online*, December 12. Available at http://www.timesonline.co.uk/tol/news/world/us_and_americas/article5331997.ece.

36. MOYER, L. (2008). Could SEC have stopped Madoff scam in 1992? *Forbes*, December 23. Available at http://www.forbes.com/business/2008/12/23/madoff-fraud-sec-biz-wall-cx_lm_1223madoff.html.

37. See: Available at http://www.reuters.com/article/topNews/idUSTRE52A5JK20090311?pageNumber=2&virtualBrandChannel=0&sp=true

38. BIGGS, B. (2009). The affinity Ponzi scheme. *Newsweek*, January 3. Available at http://www.newsweek.com/id/177679.

39. ASSOCIATED PRESS. (2009). Tough task ahead to find Madoff money, co-schemers, *Daily News*, March 13. Available at http://www.google.com/hostednews/ap/article/ALeqM5hnkPe640MG8WMCAvAwv5GqtqxsOAD96T6K8G0.

40. BIGGS. (2009). The affinity Ponzi scheme.

41. IBID.

42. CARUSO, D. (2009). A trusted man, $50B, a "giant Ponzi scheme." *Associated Press*. Available at http://seattletimes.nwsource.com/html/businesstechnology/2008508111_invest13.html.

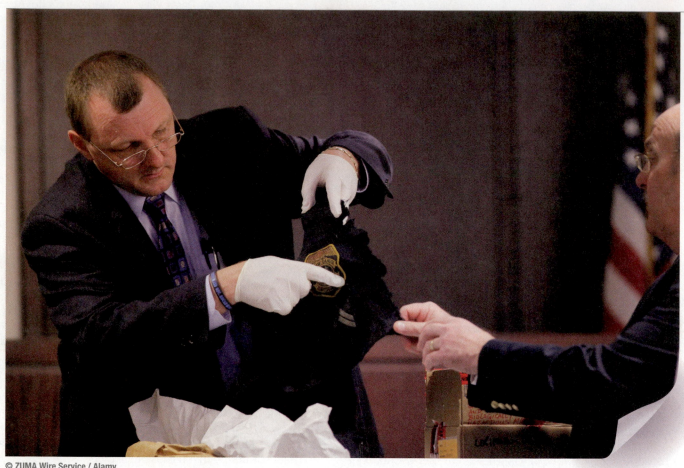

© ZUMA Wire Service / Alamy

This chapter will enable you to:

1. Learn the role of pretrial procedures in prosecution of the defendant.

2. Understand how the criminal trial process operates.

3. Evaluate the differences between direct and cross-examination.

4. Learn how investigators prepare for court.

5. Understand the techniques most commonly used by defense attorneys to discredit an investigator's testimony.

6. Learn the importance of good courtroom demeanor when testifying in court.

Preparation for Court

Introduction

Not all criminal cases go to trial. In fact, most are settled outside the courtroom through the plea-bargaining process. For cases that make it to the trial stage, however, it is imperative that the evidence be well organized and that the investigator, who is essentially the "star witness," be prepared to give skilled courtroom testimony in the case. As we have discussed throughout the book, the admissibility of evidence in court is the compelling reason for investigators to follow closely the correct procedures in evidence collection. After investigators are satisfied that the evidence has been collected appropriately, the question of how best to present the evidence to the judge and jurors is addressed. For such a critical task, the role of the investigator in the courtroom is not always understood by all investigators. After all, police officers spend most of their time on the street and not in the courtroom. In this chapter, we examine several critical aspects of the courtroom process and how this important criminal justice function interacts with the duties of the criminal investigator.

Types of Witnesses and Testimony

In the theater of courtroom testimony, there are a number of different types of witnesses who may contribute to providing the jury information about the nature of the incident. In addition to the investigator's testimony, fact and expert witnesses may also testify.

A fact witness has personal knowledge of events pertaining to a case and can only testify to things he personally has observed. For example, "Fred told me he was mad at his boss." "I saw Fred reach for something in his glove compartment."[1] He may not, however, offer opinions such as, "Based on Fred's behavioral profile and history of violence, he is likely to seek revenge for even small slights."[2] Opinions can only be stated by an expert witness retained either by the prosecution or defense or appointed by the court to make statements about aspects of the case.

Experts are permitted to offer opinions that may assist the judge or jury in understanding specialized technical knowledge that, otherwise, would be beyond the expertise of those sitting on the jury (e.g., typically, the role of credentialed specialists in forensic-related fields, such as a medical examiner, crime lab expert, firearms specialist, or forensic psychologist). Although experts usually are allowed more leeway in testimony than fact witnesses, courts carefully evaluate the content of their testimony for admissibility.

Police officers may find that their testimonies sometimes straddle the domains of fact and expert witness. For example, an officer may be queried about what he did and what the defendant did (like a fact witness) and then be asked to state an opinion (like an expert witness). Or, he may state an opinion that the opposing attorney challenges, and the judge must decide whether or not to admit it in the record.

Preparing for Trial

The importance of proper trial preparation cannot be overemphasized. In some instances, officers are overly casual about their prospective trial appearances. This often results in their appearing unprepared in court to testify effectively. The following principles should be understood and observed by officers in efforts to adequately prepare for court presentation.

First, officers should cooperate fully with prosecutors in the preparation of trial testimony and other evidence. Requests from the prosecutor's office should be complied with in all respects, when possible. If for some reason, a request cannot be fulfilled, the prosecutor's office should be made aware of the problem and alternate mutually agreed upon plans. Sometimes poor relations between the prosecutor's office and the police department cause a lack of communication or cooperation between these agencies. Such problems benefit no one but the criminals being brought to trial. Police agency managers must make it clear to all police officers that full and willing cooperation with prosecutors is expected by the department. Political feuds, "turf wars," personality conflicts, and the like cannot be tolerated. If a problem arises, it should be resolved quickly and without regard to who was right and who was wrong, and steps should be taken by the department to minimize the possibility of the same problem arising again in the future.

One of the typical areas of conflict between prosecutors and police revolves around the issue of when a case presented by the police will be brought to trial by the prosecutor's office. When the prosecutor declines to prosecute or a pretrial plea bargain is arranged that appears to be excessively favorable to the defendant, it is sometimes difficult for police officers who have labored on the case to understand why the matter is not being carried forward to trial. Police resentment toward the prosecutor's office is frequently the result. Officers must understand that the prosecutor's job is a difficult one and that sometimes hard decisions have to be made, decisions that may be unpopular with the police and others. For example, the heavy workload burdening the average prosecutor's office and the lack of adequate manpower to deal with that workload sometimes limit the number of cases that can be brought to trial. The result may be plea bargains or a decision not to go to trial on minor cases or on cases that appear to the prosecutor to be weak or to have technical problems that may make a successful trial result doubtful. The prosecutors are in the best position to judge the strength of the case and the probability of conviction, and officers should be sufficiently well-versed in the rules of evidence and the realities of the criminal justice system to accept the prosecutor's decision without resentment or recrimination. Blaming the prosecutor for the shortcomings of the judicial process is counterproductive and should be avoided.

This is not to say that all prosecutors are blameless when difficult working relationships develop between their office and the police. Prosecutors often share in the problem by not providing appropriate and timely feedback to police personnel on case progress and decisions, failing to brief officers adequately before trial, failing to work cooperatively with officers responsible for the evidence control aspects of criminal cases, and related matters. When poor prosecutor–police relations exist, there is generally sufficient blame to go around. The larger point to be made is that the police and the office of the prosecutor must come to understand that they are on the same team and each must take the steps necessary to maximize their collective efforts. Several steps can be taken to accomplish this.

For example, whenever possible, a **pretrial conference** should be held between the prosecutor and all officers testifying in a given case. Often this is difficult because of the busy schedules of both police and prosecutors, but it should be done in all cases when feasible and without fail in cases involving serious crimes or in those in which the testimony may be complicated.[3]

Regardless of the normal procedure, in any case in which police officers involved believe that a conference with prosecutors is needed, a request for such a conference should be made. If, after such a request, the prosecutor's office refuses or fails to hold the conference, this fact should be noted in the appropriate departmental records for the protection of the department and the officers concerned.

Officers should provide prosecutors with all information relevant to the case. No detail should be considered too minor because many cases turn upon minute factual or legal points, the significance of which may become apparent only in the full context of the trial. In particular, officers should disclose the following:

1. *Information beneficial to the defendant (disclosure of exculpatory evidence).* The prosecution's job is to convict the guilty, not the innocent. It is therefore the ethical as well as the legal obligation of every officer to disclose to the prosecution any information that may tend

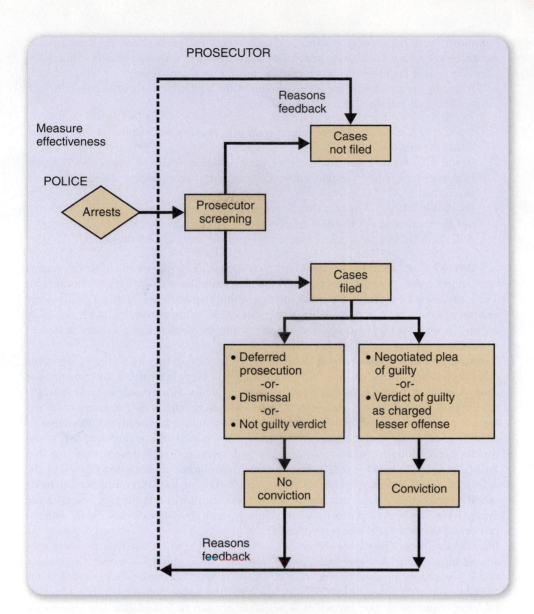

|Fig. 18.1| △

Diagram of the relationship between police and prosecutors.

to establish the innocence of the defendant as well as guilt. From the purely legal standpoint, failure to disclose exculpatory matters may lead to a wrongful conviction, a mistrial, a reversal on appeal, or other unfavorable results.

2. ***Disclosure of exculpatory information or other flaws in the case.*** Full disclosure should be made by police to the prosecutor's office of any problems that may be associated with the evidence in the case. This is a frequent source of dissatisfaction with prosecutors, who may sometimes believe they have been misled into bringing a case to trial when some defect in the case, known to the police but unknown to the prosecutors, makes conviction unlikely. For example, if an officer knows or suspects that a search was or may have been unlawful or an arrest invalid, the problem should be disclosed to the prosecutor, either in the written report, during the pretrial conference, or by other means. This is not an easy thing for an officer to do, especially if the defect is due to some error on the part of the officer. But candor is vital, however painful or embarrassing it may be. In many instances, the prosecutor who is aware of such a problem may be able to deal with it effectively at the trial, avoiding adverse consequences from the defect. By contrast, when such a defect surfaces unexpectedly during the trial, the prosecutor is often powerless to save the situation, with resulting embarrassment for all concerned. Advance disclosure, however painful, greatly minimizes the potential ill effects of flaws in any case.

3. *Familiarity with the rules of evidence.* Officers should be familiar with the basic rules of evidence applicable to the court in which the trial is to be held. Although dealing with evidentiary questions at the trial is the province of the prosecutor and such questions will ultimately be decided by the trial judge, an understanding of the applicable rules of admissibility will assist police in several ways, including the following:

- It will enable officers to identify and discuss with prosecutors possible flaws in the case before the trial date.
- It will help officers prepare and give their testimony because fundamental errors (e.g., testifying in a forum that will render the testimony as inadmissible hearsay) can be avoided.
- It will help officers to understand the reasons behind a prosecutor's strategy in the trial of a given case and will also help them to accept the decision without resentment when a prosecutor decides not to take a case to trial because of evidentiary problems.

Before the trial date, the officers should review carefully all reports and other documents relevant to the case to ensure that they are completely familiar with all of the pertinent facts. The more complex the case, the more important this step becomes. Nothing destroys the chances of a conviction more quickly than a police officer on the witness stand who is visibly unfamiliar with the facts and whose testimony is thus incomplete and generally lacking in credibility to the jury.

4. *Notes and reports in the courtroom.* In many instances, officers may wish to carry reports or other documents into the courtroom for reference while they are testifying. In some types of cases, particularly traffic cases, this is routine in many courts. However, in any case in which the use by police officers of notes, reports, or other items to refresh their memory is not automatic or routine in that particular court, the officer should discuss with the prosecutor in advance of the court date the necessity for and the desirability of carrying such aids to the witness stand. Although rules of evidence vary in different courts, in general, anything that the officer uses while on the witness stand to refresh his or her memory may be seen by the defense attorneys and may be used by them to cross-examine the officer or otherwise to attack the prosecution's case. Thus, the decision to take such items into the courtroom for use during testimony is not a matter to be taken lightly, and it should be discussed fully with the prosecutor before the trial whenever possible.

5. *Physical evidence.* Procedures for getting evidence and related materials to court vary among jurisdictions. In some cases, the prosecutor's office may take custody of evidence that is planned for introduction in court in a pending trial and make arrangements for its availability at trial. In other instances, it falls upon the police department to ensure that evidence requested by the prosecutor is available in court in accordance with established schedules provided by the prosecutor. Whatever the arrangement, the police should provide any assistance requested by, or necessary to, the prosecution to ensure that all of the **physical evidence** pertinent to the case will be available at the time of trial. This includes, for example, transporting exhibits to the courtroom and ensuring the availability of any supporting documentation (e.g., chain-of-evidence receipts) that may be needed. Laboratory certificates or other forensic reports that may be required in connection with the case should also be ready for presentation.

6. *Witnesses.* Failure of witnesses to appear at trial is a recurrent problem and one that often results in dismissal of criminal charges against defendants or failure of the prosecution's case. Officers should provide prosecutors with assistance as needed in ensuring that witnesses will be present and ready to testify on the day of the trial. The extent of this assistance should depend on local practice and any requests that may be made by the prosecutor's office in a specific case. In some jurisdictions, for example, victim and witness advocates are available to assist in this effort. Ideally, the prosecutor's office might fulfill most or all of these functions, but caseloads and lack of manpower often make it impossible for the prosecutor to interview witnesses adequately in advance of the trial. In addition, the police officer has usually dealt personally with the witnesses during the investigative stage of the case and may therefore be the person best able to work with the witnesses in the trial phase and to make certain they are ready, willing, and able to testify as planned. Therefore, unless

local practice or a specific request dictates otherwise, officers should be prepared to ensure that witnesses:

- Have been informed of the date, time, and place of trial
- Have transportation to the place of trial
- Have been adequately informed of what is expected of them during testimony
- Have been advised to respond truthfully to questions posed to them on the stand
- Have been advised to state facts and not to offer personal opinions or conjecture while on the stand unless requested to do so by the prosecutor
- Have been briefed on any other matters that will enable the witness to testify in a timely and effective manner[4]

Police officers should also ascertain whether the witnesses have any questions regarding the trial, whether regarding legal matters or other aspects of the witnesses' appearance in court. Questions that the officer cannot readily and fully answer should be referred to the prosecutor for clarification and the clarification transmitted to the witness.

7. ***Communication with defense attorneys.*** Defense attorneys frequently attempt to interview police officers about a case in the hope of developing information that will enable them to achieve a favorable result for their clients. There should be no communication between officers and defense attorneys regarding pending criminal cases without the express approval of the prosecutor's office.[5]

8. ***Testifying for the defendant.*** On some occasions, the defense attorney may summon a police officer as a witness on the defendant's behalf. This places the police officer in an extremely awkward position. The generally accepted practice is that officers shall not testify for a defendant in any criminal case without being legally summoned to appear, prior knowledge of the agency chief executive, and written authorization of the prosecutor's office. However, regardless of department policy or any other factor, if the officer is subpoenaed by the defense and the subpoena is not quashed, the officer is obligated to appear and testify. Any officer receiving such a subpoena should immediately notify the officer's supervisor (or other designated department official) and the prosecutor's office.

Going to Court

Before actually attending the criminal court proceeding, officers should ready themselves for the situation. One of the first steps is for the officer to prepare him- or herself psychologically by strengthening his or her feelings of confidence and self-assurance. Officers should also realize that as witnesses, they are also on display, as they are when on duty. It is a simple fact that the general public expects more stringent behavior from a law enforcement officer than from an average citizen. As a result, the following steps should be followed before entering a courtroom:

- ***Know which courtroom you'll be testifying in.*** If you are unfamiliar with the particular courthouse or courtroom, check it out before the trial so you will know your way around.
- ***Do not discuss anything about the case in public or where your conversation might be overheard.*** Anyone could be a juror or defense witness.
- ***Treat people with respect, as if they were the judge or a juror.*** Your professionalism, politeness, and courtesy will be noted and remembered, especially by those who see you in court in an official capacity.
- ***Do not discuss your personal life, official business, biases, prejudices, likes and dislikes, or controversial subjects in public, for the same reasons as listed above.*** You might impress a judge, juror, or witness the wrong way.
- ***Be punctual.*** Judges and attorneys have little patience with officers appearing in court late, so be on time. Know when you will be expected to testify.
- ***Dress appropriately.*** Look businesslike and official. If in uniform, it should be neat, clean, and complete. If not in uniform, a sport coat and slacks are as appropriate as a business suit.
- ***Avoid contact with the defense counsel and any defense witnesses before the trial.*** Assume that they will try to get you to say something about the case to their advantage.

These suggestions, in addition to the pretrial conference, will prepare an officer well for the courtroom experience. Above all, however, officers are expected to tell the truth.

The Investigator As a Witness

The **testimony** given by the investigator is a crucial part of any criminal trial. An experienced and knowledgeable witness can make the job of the prosecutor and subsequent conviction of the defendant much easier. Conversely, a witness who is disorganized, unkempt, and unclear in thought can inadvertently sabotage even the best of criminal cases.

Preparing for Court

The best way for investigators to prepare for trial is not to wait for one or two days before trial to get organized but to keep the rules of evidence in mind from the beginning of the investigation through its closure (months or even years, in some cases). In addition, the investigator should be sure to meet with the prosecutor sometime before trial for the pretrial conference. The officer should check all personal reports and notes pertaining to the case and be sure that he or she has sufficient information to respond to the anticipated "who, what, when, where, why, and how" questions.

Reviewing Evidence and Reports

Before the trial, the investigator should go back over his or her list of evidence and be sure that all is accounted for and easily identifiable. The chain of custody should also be reexamined to be sure that all necessary persons who were involved with the evidence will be available if needed to testify in court. The investigator should also consider how the evidence will be transported to court and who will maintain possession of it after the court proceeding is underway. In the case of drug or forensic evidence, it is likely that the police chemist will already have custody and transport it to court. The investigator, however, might be required to locate and transport other items in evidence, such as written statements, cassettes or videotapes of transactions and statements, or photographs. All such evidence should be closely reviewed by the officer before the trial.

Because the investigator may not testify solely from notes and reports, they should be reviewed before the trial. Although lawful and appropriate to do so, the defense attorney may inquire of the officer on the witness stand whether this was done before trial and may even attempt to take custody of the report to place into evidence under the "past recollection recorded" exception to the hearsay rule. If the defense attorney gains access to the official report of the investigator, the report will be used to attack the **credibility** of the investigator. One typical defense ploy is to attack the credibility of the officer by highlighting any inconsistencies between the testimony given by the officer and what is reflected in the official report. Most attorneys can identify an inconsistency in just about anything but inconsistencies typically focus on facts testified to that differ from the report or a seemingly important fact in the report that the witness failed to mention in his or her testimony.

In the event that this occurs, it is usually a better idea to acknowledge the discrepancy and not become defensive about it. The prosecutor can then decide whether or not to "clean up" the problem through additional questioning if it appears to be of any consequence to the prosecution's strategy.

Investigator's Courtroom Checklist[6]

- ☑ Elements of offense
- ☑ Probable cause for arrest
- ☑ Defendant's story
- ☑ Confession of suspect
- ☑ Prior statements and testimony of witnesses
- ☑ Reliability of witnesses
- ☑ Warrants and affidavits
- ☑ Physical evidence
- ☑ Exhibits, sketches, and diagrams

Credibility as a Witness

Other than the technique cited earlier, defense attorneys use other means to attack an officer's credibility. This is usually accomplished through attempting to demonstrate the officer's bias or that he or she is lying. Bias can be raised in many different circumstances. For example, the defense attorney can try to convince the jury that the officer is just trying to protect his or her conviction record by embellishing his or her answers to make the suspect look more guilty, thus resulting in a conviction.

In addition, racial bias can sometimes be argued if the defendant is a minority and has a different ethnic background from that of the officer. In this case, the officer must testify only to the facts of the case that indicate guilt of the defendant, not on stereotypic perceptions of the defendant's racial or ethnic group. Credibility can also be attacked on the basis of the officer's reputation for truthfulness. This is most typically used against undercover officers, who are required to work proactively and assume a false identity (e.g., a cover story and an assumed name). It is common for the attorney to have the officer affirm that he or she was required to "lie" while working undercover and then turn around and try to convince the jury that the officer is a liar by nature. If successful, the defense can argue that the investigator's testimony is not credible.

Appearance in Court

If for any reason it appears that the officer will be late in appearing for a court date or will be unable to appear at the specified time, he or she must notify the court as soon as possible. The notification should include the officer's name, the defendant's name, the court in which the appearance is scheduled (including the name of the presiding judge, if known), and the reason for the absence or tardiness. When absence or tardiness occurs, the matter should be reviewed by the officer's supervisor or other designated department official. If the reasons are inadequate, the matter may be referred for disciplinary action.

Some fail to appreciate the importance of the officer's physical appearance and personal conduct while the officer is testifying in court. In reality, these matters are of the greatest possible significance and literally can make or break a case. In this regard, there are several matters that officers should know when appearing in court.

Officers should dress appropriately when testifying in court. The International Association of Chiefs of Police (IACP) states that officers' personal appearance in court should "conform to the highest professional police standards." Uniformed personnel should wear the departmental uniform approved for such appearances; detectives and other plainclothes personnel should conform to their departmental dress standards for courtroom testimony.[7] Whether the officer is in uniform or in civilian dress, the clothing should be neat and clean, the shoes should be shined, and similar matters should be attended to. This is not just a matter of departmental pride; psychological studies reveal that jurors frequently give less credibility to the testimony of

|Fig. 18.3|

A prosecutor examining a criminal investigator.

Courtesy of Mike Himmel

witnesses who are dressed sloppily. This is why exceptional care is taken by defense attorneys in dressing their clients (particularly in high-profile cases) in the most appropriate clothing. If the officer is in civilian clothes, conservative dress is normally appropriate. Extreme styles of clothing may prove distracting to the jurors, causing them to pay less attention to the substance of the officer's testimony and even in some cases arousing hostility toward the officer. Although the investigator may wear faded blue jeans when on duty, it is important for him or her to dress more formally for court. Some disagreement exists in this area because some think that the witness's choice of clothing should coincide with the atmosphere of the community. Others believe that a uniformed officer should wear plain clothes in court to avoid the authoritarian appearance depicted by the uniform.

The foregoing are general rules only; departmental guidelines regarding courtroom attire should be followed at all times. This includes specific courtroom regulations regarding the carrying of firearms in the courtroom.

Courtroom Demeanor

The investigator should also remember that a certain amount of theatrics plays a role in a trial. Both the judge and jury will be watching the investigator's **demeanor** closely as well as listening to what he or she has to say. First impressions can make a difference. Juries expect a certain type of person as a police witness. They expect that an organized, intelligent, serious, no-nonsense kind of person will be representing the government. There are times, however, when witnesses may reveal a sense of humor, and the jury can be impressed. Such displays of humor in the courtroom should not be directed toward anyone in particular and should be made with caution so as not to offend any member of the jury.

Testifying in Court

Many law enforcement officers cite testifying in court as one of the most stressful aspects of their job, perceiving it as an adversarial system where defense attorneys may skewer them during aggressive cross-examination. While many patrol officers will testify only a few times in their careers, for others, such as traffic cops and criminal investigators, court testimony constitutes a regular part of their work routine. As witnesses, law enforcement officers must ensure that the facts they present communicate the complete story and that their delivery of those facts makes their testimony clear and credible.[8]

The manner in which an officer testifies may be as important as the content of the testimony. An officer's conduct on the stand often determines the degree of credibility that will be given to the officer's statements by the jury. Thus, the demeanor of the officer on the stand may be critical to the outcome of the case. Officers should remember that a trial is an adversarial proceeding and that defense attorneys will not hesitate to take advantage of any shortcomings displayed by the officer while on the witness stand. Therefore, officers must keep several principles in mind while testifying in court, including the following:

1. ***Confine the testimony to known facts.*** Officers should normally restrict their statements to those that are personally known by them to be the truth. If the officer is making a statement based on information or belief only, that should be made clear in the testimony. Defense attorneys are skilled at finding discrepancies in an officer's testimony and using those discrepancies to the detriment of the officer and the prosecution's case.

2. ***Avoid expressing opinions or conclusions except when they are specifically authorized by the rules of evidence.*** Police officers normally testify as **lay witnesses**, meaning that they should state only facts and not express opinions or engage in conjecture or speculation. In some specific instances, lay witnesses are permitted to express opinions, and this applies to police officers as well as to any other witness. However, officers should not offer opinions or conclusions on **direct examination** unless an opinion or conclusion has been specifically solicited by the prosecutor. Officers should avoid expressing opinions during **cross-examination** by the defense attorney; when the defense attempts to get an officer to express an opinion, it is usually with the intent of using that opinion to embarrass the officer and discredit the officer's testimony. If the defense attorney on cross-examination asks the officer to express an opinion, the officer should delay answering to allow the prosecution an opportunity to object.

3. ***Do not volunteer information.*** Officers should respond only to the question asked. They should not volunteer information over and above the minimum required to answer the question posed. There are two reasons for this.

    First, if the officer is testifying on direct examination, the prosecutor is intentionally attempting to place specific facts before the jury in a predetermined order. If the officer volunteers information that has not been requested, this may disrupt the prosecution's presentation of the case.[9] It may also provide the defense with an unexpected windfall that the defense can exploit to the benefit of the defendant and the detriment of the prosecution.

    Secondly, if the officer is testifying on cross-examination, the defense attorney may be deliberately attempting to manipulate the officer to volunteer something that the defense can use to discredit the officer, the prosecution's case, or both. Defense attorneys are skilled in this technique. Therefore, on cross-examination, the officer should respond only to the question asked to avoid giving the defense an opening that may prove fatal to the prosecution.

4. ***Speak calmly and audibly in a natural voice.*** Always speak in a calm tone of voice. Keep the voice at its normal pitch; do not attempt to alter the natural voice because this causes stress and will be sensed by the jury.

    Speak in a tone of voice that is clearly audible to the jurors. Officers must remember that it is the jury that will decide the case, and jurors will not be persuaded by testimony they cannot hear. Studies indicate that when jurors have difficulty hearing or understanding the witnesses' testimony, their attention span becomes limited, they lose interest in the witness, and the witness's evidence is therefore wasted. This does not mean that the witness should shout when on the witness stand, but particularly in courtrooms where microphones are not used, testifying officers should make certain that they speak at a level that will make their words audible to the jury without requiring the jurors to strain to hear what is being said.

5. ***Use plain, easily understood terms.*** The officer must testify in plain, easily understood language. If the jury does not understand the words being used, the testimony will be unpersuasive. Officers should avoid using police terminology or slang; such terms confuse many jurors and may convey an adverse impression of the witness. This is a common error among police officers inexperienced in courtroom testimony, and it should be avoided.

    If technical terms are used, they should be explained in a straightforward manner, without any hint of condescension. Jurors, like anyone else, do not like to be patronized or talked down to.

6. ***Maintain self-control.*** During the stress of a courtroom appearance, it is often difficult for a witness to retain his or her composure. This is particularly true when a defense attorney is deliberately attempting to goad the witness, which is an all-too-common tactic. However, keeping one's self-control is vital on the witness stand, whatever the provocation.

    There is an old saying that "he who loses his temper loses the battle." This applies in the courtroom, too. The witness who loses his or her temper on the witness stand makes the defense attorney's whole day. Studies indicate that when any witness becomes visibly angry or otherwise loses composure, the jurors tend to lose respect for that witness and thereafter give that witness's testimony less weight. This is particularly true for police witnesses. Jurors apparently feel that a police officer who cannot retain self-control is not a credible witness—or a good police officer.

One aspect of retaining self-control is remaining courteous on the stand. It is only human to feel the need to make a sharp or sarcastic retort to some insulting question or comment by the defense attorney, but to do so plays into the defense's hands. Courteous replies to discourteous questions enhance a police officer's status with the jury and defeat the defense attorney's goal of discrediting the officer.

The ability to maintain self-control and a courteous manner in difficult situations is an important tool for a police officer in any situation. It is the mark of a true law enforcement professional, and this is so regardless of whether the officer is in the courtroom or on the street. If the officer behaves in a professional manner on the witness stand, the prosecution's case is materially enhanced, and the chances of a conviction are increased accordingly.

Tell the Truth

One would think that this conversation is unnecessary considering the cornerstone for professional police work and criminal investigation is the search for truth. The history of criminal investigation, prosecutions, and trials shows, however, that in some cases lies are told under oath and in many cases certain unscrupulous officers "spin" the truth in order to secure a conviction.

What Is Lying?

In her book *Lying: Moral Choice in Public and Private Life*, Sissela Bok defines a lie as any intentionally deceptive stated message.[10] According to Bok, lies are statements that are communicated either verbally or in writing. Lying is a subset of the larger category of deception, and deception is undertaken when one intends to dupe others by communicating messages meant to mislead and meant to make the recipients believe what the agent (the person performing or committing the act) either knows or believes to be untrue.

Deception encompasses not only spoken and written statements but also any conduct that conveys a message to the listener. Deceptive conduct can range from verbal statements or writings to physical expressions such as a shoulder shrug, eye movement, or silence—any intentional action that conveys a message.

Historically, not all intentionally deceptive conduct in social interactions has been considered improper. Indeed, as early as the Middle Ages, Saint Thomas Aquinas classified deceptive conduct as helpful, joking, or malicious. Aquinas argued that lying helpfully and lying in jest may be acceptable forms of conduct, whereas telling malicious lies, lies told deliberately to harm someone, was a mortal sin.[11]

Acknowledging that some deceptive conduct is acceptable helps to define deceptive misconduct. For example, the classic dilemma, argued about for centuries, is what to do if a murderer approaches you and asks the location of his intended victim. If you tell the truth, the murderer will kill the victim. If you lie, the intended victim will have the opportunity to escape. Although this hypothetical dilemma forces you to choose between insufficient options with no other choices, it is illustrative of Aquinas's argument. Lying to a murderer to protect a potential victim is helpful, and it may be both morally and ethically the proper thing to do because it is the lesser of evils under the circumstances.[12]

Cautions Regarding the *Brady* Decision

One of the areas where investigators have been known to deceive and be untruthful is the disclosure of the investigative file to the prosecution as identified under the *Brady* decision. Depending on the nature of the evidence that is not properly disclosed, failure to do so can deprive the defense of a viable defense. The professional investigator is not in the business of securing a conviction. Rather, the "true north" for the professional investigator is to make the truth known and allow the court and trial process to take their course.

Truthfulness and the 1963 *Brady* decision have become hot topics in law enforcement circles. Although years went by without much concern with the *Brady* decision, recent U.S. Supreme Court decisions have enforced *Brady* to include evidence maintained in a police officer's personnel files. Under *Brady*, evidence affecting the credibility of the police officer as a witness may be exculpatory evidence and should be given to the defense during discovery. Indeed, evidence that the officer has had in his personnel file a sustained finding of untruthfulness is clearly exculpatory to the defense.

As a reminder, in 1963 the Supreme Court ruled in *Brady* v. *Maryland* that the defense has the right to examine all evidence that may be of an exculpatory nature. This landmark case stands for the proposition that the prosecution will not only release evidence that the defendant might be guilty of a crime but also release all evidence that might show that the defendant is innocent as well. Today many police executives have recognized the importance of officer credibility and have established a "No Lies" proclamation. As simple as No Lies sounds, it is far more complex and difficult to manage.

Lies are not a fixed target; rather, deception exists on a continuum, from what is commonly called social lies or little white lies to egregious misconduct that warrants dismissal or even prosecution. The true challenge is in dealing with deceptive conduct that lies somewhere in the middle of the continuum—not so far on one end of the continuum for termination and not far enough toward the other end of the continuum to be justifiable or excusable.

Safeguarding Against Lying

Professional law enforcement administrators have responded to these judicial decisions by imposing strict rules and, on the surface, "No Lies" seems to be a prudent idea. This black-and-white rule certainly appears to be one upon which everyone can agree. To achieve a goal of maintaining the officer's and the department's credibility, ruling out all lies is the simplest solution and the most straightforward to enforce. But are police administrators really prepared to enforce the rule as it is communicated in the No Lies policy?

There is a premise in management circles that rules should be explained and tools provided so employees can achieve the vision set out for them. No Lies, however, does not express the true concern of police administrators. Rather, the concern is with improper, intentional, deceptive conduct that affects an officer's credibility, whether that deceptive conduct consists of lying, making material omissions, or engaging in other unacceptable deliberate actions.

Not only should there be a policy defining improper, intentional, deceptive misconduct but there should also be a clear definition of deceptive conduct that is accepted by an agency. In police work, deceptive conduct in some areas is not only condoned but also encouraged or even required. The key to developing a policy is an understanding of the difference between deceptive conduct and deceptive misconduct.

Pitfalls When Testifying in Court

As stated earlier in this book, the investigator makes an arrest, his or her role in the case is not over. The next phase of the investigation now begins. Indeed, the investigator must now turn over the case file materials to the prosecutor and get prepared for testifying in court. For many, being sworn in and testifying under oath is a stressful situation. While this, to an extent is a true statement, investigators can overcome the stress of testifying by not only knowing the case facts and circumstances but also by knowing what "curveballs" the defense will throw.

For example, when testifying, investigators should be aware of questions involving distance and time. If estimates must be made, the investigator must make sure that everyone understands that the testimony is an estimate. Another tactic is when defense attorneys ask if you are willing to swear to your version of the events. After all, investigators are sworn to tell the truth when they take the stand, so they should not be afraid of saying so.

Opposing counsel may also ask if you have spoken to the prosecutor, the witnesses, or other officers. If you have, admit it freely as this sort of preparation before trial is expected in each case. If you are asked if you talked with the prosecutor about your testimony, admit that you met with him or her, talked about the case, and were instructed to tell the truth.

Under cross-examination, investigators might even be asked why they don't like the defendant. A proper response would be to state that you feel sorry for any man in trouble, but you must tell the truth, and if the defendant is guilty, he should be convicted.

Also beware of questions asking you if another witness was telling the truth or lying. You can only tell the truth based upon your observations. You have no way of knowing what another person observed, especially when you did not hear that person testify. Another tactic is the simple question, "Why are you here today?" Investigators would remember that they are not in court to volunteer information in order to convict. Investigators are not advocates; rather, they are unbiased witnesses. The investigator's presence in the courtroom is in response to being served with a subpoena issued by the court clerk.

The Role of the Expert Witness

Prosecutors may locate an officer with extensive experience in a given area and qualify him or her as an **expert witness**. This often strengthens the prosecution's case and paves the way for testimony by other witnesses. When an officer is designated by the court as an expert, conclusions may be drawn, and the officer may give his or her personal opinion as to the facts and circumstances

A Closer Look

How Reliable Is Eyewitness Testimony?

One August night in Altoona, Iowa, the local McDonald's was filled with customers when a man with a gun in his pocket walked in, looking for cash. He slipped a note to the night manager, who led him to the office, opened the safe, pulled out money, and gave it to him. Before the police arrived, the gunman fled through a rear door, commandeered a car from a drive-through lane, ordered the driver out at gunpoint, and sped away.

Initial descriptions were contradictory, the defense lawyer would later argue, but with the help of McDonald's employees, the artist rendered a composite drawing, which led to a photographic lineup and eventually the arrest of Terry Eugene Schultz. Several eyewitnesses said Schultz was the gunman, and he was convicted and sentenced to 25 years in prison—based solely on eyewitness testimony. Powerful, indeed, but no physical evidence tied Schultz to the crime, and his girlfriend insisted that he'd been with her at the time. So, how accurate are eyewitness identifications?

Some experts say "not very." Now there's mounting evidence through DNA science that innocent people have been convicted as the result of faulty identifications. DNA evidence has already freed scores

of convicts, and more could be in line if recommendations proposed in September 1999 by the National Commission on the Future of DNA Evidence become a reality. It's difficult to estimate just how many cases of mistaken identity occur, but in 2007, the Innocence Project concluded that over 75 percent of the more than 192 wrongful convictions in the United States involved mistaken identification.

Increasingly, courts are allowing experts to tell juries that eyewitness identifications are sometimes more convincing than they are reliable and that juries should be especially wary when certain problematic factors exist. Mistakes are more likely, for example, when the witness and suspect are of different races, especially when the witness is white and the suspect is black. We also now know that extreme stress, especially when violence or the threat of violence exists, interferes with recall.

Another problem that researchers found is that viewing a composite drawing or lineup can change witnesses' memories of an event. That is, a witness viewing a photo array may pick out a photo that resembles the culprit but isn't. But from that point, the photo becomes part of the witness's memory of the culprit. It is difficult, if not impossible, to quantify the overall reliability of stranger-to-stranger identifications, say experts. In some cases, experts estimate that the chance of faulty identification is as high as 20 percent.

As for Terry Schultz, his case—the McDonald's robbery in 1998—became the vehicle for the Iowa Supreme Court to reverse its own precedent. Citing the wealth of new research on memory, the court reversed his conviction and said that Schultz should be allowed to present such evidence at retrial. However, at retrial, even with new expert testimony, the defense would have to overcome several eyewitnesses' testimony. Schultz, who had already spent two years in prison, didn't want to risk spending more time in jail. He pleaded guilty to lesser charges and received a probated sentence.

surrounding the case. The expert witness is one whose knowledge exceeds the knowledge of anyone with a moderate education or experience in the field. Qualifications for the expert witness to establish when on the witness stand include the following:

- Name
- Occupation (and how long)
- Department (and how long)
- Specialized experience (e.g., drug enforcement and how long)
- Officer's training
- Number of training course hours
- Number of similar investigations in which the officer has participated
- Number of arrests made in this type of investigation
- Past experience as an expert witness (and how many court appearances)

At the end of the questioning, the judge will excuse the witness. Officers must remember that the eyes of the jury are still watching and making judgments; therefore, when exiting, witnesses should refrain from staring, smiling, or showing any emotion toward anyone in the courtroom.

Summary Checklist

In this chapter, we consider the ways information about crimes is documented by criminal investigators. A properly documented case is one that is more likely to succeed in court. See how well you are able to answer the following questions in your checklist.

1. **Describe the types of witnesses and what they may testify in a courtroom.**

   There are a number of different types of witnesses who may provide information about the nature of an incident:

   - **Fact witness:** Has personal knowledge of events pertaining to a case and can only testify to things he or she personally saw
   - **Expert witness:** Is permitted to offer opinions that may assist the judge or jury in understanding specialized technical knowledge that would otherwise be beyond their expertise
   - **Police officer:** Straddles the domains of fact and expert witnesses. May be asked about what he and/or the defendant did (like a fact witness) and then be asked to state an opinion (like an expert witness)

2. **What steps are needed to prepare for an upcoming trial?**

   For cases that make it to the trial stage, it is imperative that the evidence be well organized and that the investigator be prepared to give skilled courtroom testimony in the case.

   - Officers should cooperate fully with prosecutors in the preparation of trial testimony and other evidence.

   - A pretrial conference should be held between the prosecutor and all officers testifying in a given case.
   - Officers should provide prosecutors with all information relevant to the case and no detail should be considered too minor. Information to be disclosed should include:

     - Information beneficial to the defendant (disclosure of exculpatory evidence)
     - Information revealing flaws in the prosecution's case

   - Officers should be familiar with the rules of evidence.

   When preparing for court, one of the first steps is for officers to prepare themselves for the situation, including being prepared psychologically by strengthening feelings of confidence and self-assurance. The following steps are important before trial:

   - Know which courtroom you will be testifying in.
   - Do not discuss anything about the case in public or your conversation might be overheard.
   - Treat people with respect, as if they were the judge or a juror.
   - Do not discuss your personal life, official business, biases, prejudices, likes and dislikes, or controversial subjects in public.
   - Be punctual.
   - Dress appropriately.
   - Avoid contact with the defense counsel and any defense witnesses before the trial.

3. **How should one properly testify on the witness stand?**

Investigators must keep several principles in mind while testifying in court, including:

- Confine the testimony to known facts.
- Avoid expressing opinions or conclusions except when they are specifically authorized by the rules of evidence.
- Do not volunteer information.
- Speak calmly and audibly in a natural voice.
- Use plain, easily understood terms.
- Maintain self-control.

4. **Identify some of the possible pitfall that may arise when testifying in court.**

It is important for officers testifying in court to not only know the case facts and circumstances, but also to know what "curveballs" the defense may throw.

- Be aware of questions involving distance and time and, if estimates must be made, make certain that everyone understands that the testimony is an estimate.
- If asked by opposing counsel if you have spoken to the prosecutor, witness, or other officers, admit this freely if true.
- If asked why you do not like the defendant, respond that you feel sorry for anyone in trouble but are required to tell the truth, and if the defendant is guilty, he or she should be convicted.
- If asked whether another witness was truthful, be aware that you can only tell the truth based on your own observations and have no way of knowing what another person observed.
- If asked, "Why are you here," the proper response is that you are in the courtroom in response to being served with a subpoena issued by the court clerk.

Key Terms

credibility	direct examination	lying
cross-examination	expert witness	physical evidence
deception	fact witness	pretrial conference
demeanor	lay witness	testimony

Discussion Questions

1. What are the different types of witnesses and what types of testimony may each type provide in court?

2. What key principles should be understood and observed by officers to adequately prepare for court presentation?

3. What is a pretrial conference and why should it be held?

4. Explain the distinction between direct examination and cross-examination.

5. In what ways can a defense attorney attack an officer's credibility in court?

6. What is meant by courtroom demeanor and how can the officer leave the best positive impression?

7. Explain the *Brady* decision and how it may affect police officers.

Notes

1. MILLER, L. (2006). On the spot: Testifying in court for the law enforcement officer. *FBI Law Enforcement Bulletin* 75(October):1–7.
2. IBID.
3. INTERNATIONAL ASSOCIATION OF CHIEFS OF POLICE. (1998). *Court appearance*. Alexandria, VA: Model Policy Center.
4. IBID.
5. IBID.
6. WOOLNER, A. (1999). Courts eye the problems of eyewitness identifications. *USA Today*, September 29, p.15A.
7. INTERNATIONAL ASSOCIATION OF CHIEFS OF POLICE. (1996). *Testifying in court*. Alexandria, VA: Model Policy Center.
8. MILLER. (2006). *On the Spot*.
9. IBID.
10. SISSELA, B. (1999). *Lying: Moral choice in public and private life*. New York: Pantheon Books, 1978; Vintage paperback editions.
11. NOBLE, J. (2003). Police officer truthfulness and the Brady decision. *Police Chief Magazine*, May 12.
12. IBID.

Appendix A

COLLECTION AND PRESERVATION OF PHYSICAL EVIDENCE

The impact that a single piece of evidence can have in court is considerable. In maximizing the effectiveness of this evidence, correct collection and preservation techniques must be used by the investigator. By following the suggestions presented below, the investigator diminishes the possibility that his or her evidence will become contaminated or damaged, thus elevating its importance to the investigation.

Collection and Preservation

It is important that each item submitted as evidence be sealed with tamperproof evidence tape, dated, initialed, and labeled as to its contents and its association with the victim or suspect. Evidence stained with bodily fluids (e.g., blood, semen) must be air dried before packaging and submission to the laboratory. All items should be packaged and sealed separately in breathable, nonplastic (e.g., paper), loose-fitting containers. Packages should not be tightly bound; the criminalists must return items to containers, which must be resealed after examinations.

Serology/DNA Analysis

Bodily fluid stains are valuable evidence that can be used to associate a suspect with the crime or to eliminate him or her from consideration. For instance, the presence of seminal stains is confirmation that a sexual act has occurred.

Tips for Packaging Evidence in the Proper Manner

1. Always submit a completed laboratory analysis request with each case. Use more than one if necessary.
2. Latent evidence submission envelopes should be used only with 10-print cards or latent-print cards. Other types of packaging should be used for nonprint evidence.
3. Do not package weapons with items of clothing or drug paraphernalia. (Firearms will probably be checked immediately to make certain that they are unloaded.)
4. Always package urine separately from blood. Leave expansion room in urine containers; they will be stored in a freezer.
5. Always package tubes of blood separately from clothing. Clothing will be stored in a freezer; whole blood is placed in a refrigerator.
6. Sexual assault kits should never be packaged with clothing. The kits contain whole blood and should be stored in a refrigerator.
7. Whole blood should always be packaged separately from drug-related items.
8. Never package items for prints with items for serology, trace, firearms identification, and so on.
9. Do not submit open liquor containers to the lab. All containers should be capped and sealed.
10. Evidence stained with bodily fluids (e.g., blood, semen) must be air dried before packaging and submission to the laboratory.
11. Do not submit syringes with uncapped needles or knives or razor blades without protective coverings.
12. Do not submit wet or moist marijuana in plastic bags to the lab; air dry it before submitting.
13. Do not submit drug paraphernalia or miscellaneous items that do not need to be analyzed.

BLOOD When materials stained with blood are to be sent to the laboratory:

- Air dry the stained material on a piece of clean paper placed in a ventilated area. Place the dried material in a paper bag; label it with your initials, the date, and an exhibit number; and seal the bag.
- Any debris that falls from the material onto the paper during the drying process should also be placed in a metal pillbox, labeled, and sealed. If you must fold the material, protect the stained area with a piece of paper.
- Wrap each bloodstained item separately after drying. Do not package items when they are still moist. Allow them to dry thoroughly. Package items from the victim(s) and suspect(s) into separate containers.
- Collect in a purple-capped Vacutainer a comparison blood standard from each person directly involved in the incident. Freeze or refrigerate dried specimens until ready for transport to the laboratory.

When items stained with blood cannot be sent to the laboratory:

- Always scrape dried blood from an object if possible. Using a clean knife or razor blade, scrape the dried blood into a paper fold and place in an envelope.
- If scraping is not possible, moisten a cotton swab with just enough water to make the tip damp. Do not saturate the swab completely with water. Rub the stained area with the swab to pick up the blood. Keep the blood as concentrated as possible on the tip of the swab. Air dry the swab and place it in an envelope or small paper bag.
- Large fabric items with bloodstains may be processed by cutting out the stained area and sending the cutting to the laboratory. Written notes, photographs, or both detailing the location and condition of the stain should be taken before the cutting(s) is removed. Place the cutting(s) in an envelope or paper bag.
- When a puddle of blood is available, soak up the moist blood with cotton swabs. Air dry the swabs before placing them in an envelope or small paper bag.
- Label all containers with your initials, the date, and the exhibit number and then seal them.
- If scrapings were taken, package and preserve the razor blade used.
- Collect a comparison blood standard from each person directly involved in the incident.
- Freeze or refrigerate dried specimens until ready for transport to the laboratory.

Comparison Standard for Blood Obtain the standard by having a medical examiner or other qualified person collect at least 5 cubic centimeters of blood from the victim and all suspects. Use purple-capped Vacutainer tubes for the collection of whole blood. Label each tube with the donor's name, the physician's name, and other relevant information. Refrigerate the tubes until ready for transport to the laboratory. Do not freeze whole-blood samples.

SEMEN Air dry the stained material on a piece of clean paper placed in a ventilated area. Condoms to be submitted should be frozen as soon as possible after collection. Stained areas on large items or items that cannot be sent to the laboratory may be cut out and submitted. Place the dried material in a paper bag, label it with your initials, the date, and an exhibit number and then seal the bag. If you must fold the material, protect the stained area with a piece of paper. Wrap each stained item separately.

Do not package items when they are still moist; allow them to dry thoroughly. Obtain a victim sexual assault kit and a suspect sexual assault kit (one per suspect) and follow the instructions provided with the kits. Label the kits with your initials, the date, and the exhibit number and then seal them. Refrigerate kits until ready for transport to the laboratory. Freeze or refrigerate dried specimens until ready for transport to the laboratory. Sexual assault kits can be obtained from your local crime laboratory.

SALIVA Air dry the stained material on a piece of clean paper placed in a ventilated area. Place the dried material in a paper bag; label it with your initials, the date, and an exhibit number; and seal the bag. If you must fold the material, protect the stained area with a piece of paper. Wrap each stained area separately. Do not package items when they are still moist; allow them to dry thoroughly. Collect a comparison standard. Freeze or refrigerate dried specimens until ready for transport to the laboratory.

Comparison Standard for Saliva Obtain saliva samples from the victim and suspect, waiting 30 minutes if a person has eaten or been smoking. Have the person spit on a piece of clean cotton cloth about 1 square inch in size. Outline stain areas with a pencil, air dry them, and place the samples in separate envelopes. Freeze or refrigerate dried specimens until ready for transport to the laboratory. Obtain a comparison blood standard as described in the preceding section.

Accelerants and Explosives

Evidence in bomb and arson cases is difficult to find because of its small size, because of the presence of a large amount of debris, and because potentially useful evidence is often washed away when a fire is extinguished. For this reason, great care must be used in the collection and preservation of such evidence.

ARSON DEBRIS Porous substances absorb liquid accelerants readily and therefore make good debris for laboratory testing. Consider carpeting, carpet padding, wood, and clothing or cloth products when collecting debris. Collect fire debris in unused metal paint cans or plastic bags approved for fire debris (e.g., nylon or Kapak bags). Submit liquids in their original containers if they can be sealed properly.

EXPLOSIVE DEBRIS Collect any items that may have been part of the explosive device. Collect items that were impacted directly by fragments of the explosive device. If explosive residues are found on these items, the type of explosive used may be determined. Package the items in plastic bags or metal containers.

EXPLOSIVE SUBSTANCES AND DEVICES Any undetonated explosive device must be deactivated before it is submitted to the laboratory. If the device is to be processed for latent fingerprints, package and label it accordingly.

Fingerprints

Generally, latent fingerprints on nonporous materials deteriorate rapidly upon prolonged exposure to high temperature and humidity; consequently, items should be processed or forwarded to a laboratory as soon as possible. With the assistance of the Automated Fingerprint Identification System (AFIS), we are now able to search the entire fingerprint file; we do not need a suspect. A thorough file search can be made only if correct processing procedures are followed to obtain the best latent print evidence.

ON ABSORBENT MATERIALS Place paper or other absorbent material in a plastic bag or cellophane protector. Do not handle the material with your fingers. Do not attempt to develop latent fingerprints on absorbent surfaces yourself. Label the bag or protector with your initials, the date, and an exhibit number. Collect a comparison standard.

ON HARD SURFACES Dust plastic cards, metal plates, glass bottles, or other hard-surfaced objects for latent fingerprints. Remove developed prints with lifting tape and place the tape on a 3" × 5" card that contrasts in color with the dusting powder used. Mark the card with your initials, the date, and an exhibit number; place it in an envelope; and seal the envelope.

ON SOFT SURFACES Carefully remove putty, caulking compound, or other soft material bearing visible fingerprint impressions. Leave as much excess material surrounding the fingerprint as possible. Glue the mass of material to a stiff section of cardboard that is marked with your initials, the date, and an exhibit number. Tape a protective cover over the specimen. A paper cup or baby food jar is useful for this purpose. Do not touch or otherwise distort the fingerprint. Collect a comparison standard.

Comparison Standard for Fingerprints Collect and identify fingerprints of suspects and other persons under investigation who may have touched an object. Place fingerprint records in a stiff envelope to protect them from being bent. Seal the envelope and label it with your initials, the date, and an exhibit number.

INKED PRINTS Enclose all inked prints for comparison and designate either on the print or in a cover letter whether prints are for elimination or are of the suspect. If latent prints are reported as palm prints, palm prints should also be submitted to the laboratory.

PACKING OF EVIDENCE Use ingenuity to construct special containers to protect latent print-bearing surfaces. Never place cotton or cloth next to latent impressions. Any amount of paper or cardboard specimens may be placed in one wrapper. Hard-surfaced latent print-bearing objects should never come in contact with another surface (e.g., paper sacks, plastic bags).

IDENTIFICATION There is no set requirement of latent print size for a positive identification, and there is no specific number of characteristics required to effect an identification. As a general rule, if the investigator develops an area that appears to have several ridges, regardless of the size of the area, it should be lifted, marked, and submitted to the laboratory.

Firearms and Ammunition

Firearms leave unique markings on bullets and cartridge cases as well as detectable residues on shooters' hands.

GUNSHOT RESIDUE KITS The discharge of a firearm can deposit gunshot residues on any object in close proximity to the firearm and sometimes at a considerable distance downrange. Gunshot residue kits may be used to test the residue levels deposited on hands. Crime labs are usually capable of analyzing two different types of gunshot residue kits:

1. An A.A. kit consists of five cotton swabs with a bottle of dilute nitric acid and is analyzed using an atomic absorption spectrophotometer.
2. A SEM/EDX kit consists of two adhesive-coated aluminum stubs and is analyzed using a scanning electron microscope equipped with an x-ray dispersive detector.

Each kit contains specific instructions for its use as well as a request for certain information in regard to the shooting incident. Be sure to include the type of weapon, ammunition, and time interval until collection of the kit. Kits must be used as soon as possible after a shooting incident and before hands are cleaned or processed in any other way. An A.A. kit should not be used if the time interval until the collection of the kit exceeds six hours for an active person.

When shooting distance information is requested, submit the victim's clothing with the bullet hole along with the firearm and ammunition used. If the clothing is bloody, air dry it completely and package it in a paper bag. If the victim was not clothed over the area of the wound, take close-up photographs of the wound and remember to include a scale in the photographs. Gunshot residue kits can be obtained from the crime laboratory.

HANDGUNS AND SHOULDER ARMS Never insert anything into the barrel of a firearm. All firearms should be unloaded before submission to the laboratory. Process the firearm for fingerprints if necessary. Take notes describing the position of any expended cartridge cases or live cartridges in the cylinder of the revolver. If pertinent to an investigation, make notes on a safety's position, hammer position, and so on. Remove the cartridge magazine from any semiautomatic firearm and process the exterior for fingerprints if necessary. Cartridge magazines can be placed in separate containers and submitted along with the firearms in a larger container. Attach an identification tag to the firearm that describes the item, serial number, case number, chain of custody, and other pertinent details.

Handguns should be submitted in plastic bags, paper bags, or boxes. If handguns are to be processed for fingerprints or serology, do not submit them in plastic bags. Shoulder arms are generally larger items and cannot always be submitted in containers.

SERIAL NUMBER RESTORATION If a firearm's serial number has been obliterated, make an identifying mark on it for future identification. The obliterated area can be restored in the laboratory using one of several methods.

EXPENDED BULLETS, CARTRIDGE CASES, AND SHOTGUN SHELLS After recovering an expended ammunition component, it should be placed in a sturdy, unbreakable container such as a small box or metal canister. Bullets that are removed at an autopsy should be washed in warm running water (if not for trace or serology examinations), wrapped in tissue or similar material, and put in an appropriate container.

Do not scratch the sides or bearing surface of a bullet when it is being removed from an object. The base or nose of a bullet can be scribed for identification purposes. Do not scratch or scribe the head stamp area or primer of a cartridge case or shotgun shell. If a casing or shotgun shell must be marked for identification, do so on or near the open mouth area.

Expended ammunition components should be separated and packaged in separate containers. The component's location, case number, and related information can be labeled on the outside of the container. Each container should be sealed with tamperproof evidence tape before submission to the laboratory.

Food and Drug Specimens

Because food and drug specimens exhibit a wide variety of identifiable characteristics, they may corroborate other evidence or link a suspect with a crime scene. When handling this evidence, it is important to prevent contamination among the specimens or from other sources. Do not package too much evidence into a container because doing so could cause a break in the container, with a loss of integrity of the evidence. Also, do not completely cover the evidence container with evidence tape because doing so could prevent the container from being adequately sealed later.

LIQUIDS Try to collect a minimum of 4 ounces of a specimen using a leakproof container. Seal the container with adhesive tape and label it with your initials, the date, and an exhibit number. If the container used is glass or has a glass stopper, mark it as fragile. Collect a comparison standard of the same brand and concentration, especially when tampering of medical, food, or other commercial products is suspected. Submit unknown and comparison liquid samples to the laboratory.

PLANT MATERIAL Without heating, dry the sample thoroughly in a secure area by spreading it on clean paper for at least 24 hours. After the sample has dried, place it in a pillbox, vial, or other container and secure it with adhesive tape. Do not mix samples. Package each sample separately to avoid mixing during mailing. Label the outside of the container with your initials, the date, and an exhibit number. Collect a comparison standard. If wet plant material is collected in evidence containers (especially plastic bags), it will mold and degrade to the point where positive test results may not be obtained. These molds are also hazardous to your health.

When numerous plants, bales, or bundles of plant material are seized, submit to the laboratory only representative samples of plant material from these items. Photograph the entire number of original evidence items with a ruler as scale and weigh them. In a large drug seizure, do not submit the entire amount of evidence to the laboratory. A lab will not have sufficient evidence locker space for all drug seizures. Also, small amounts of drugs submitted to a laboratory allow for quicker testing.

POWDERS AND SOLIDS Place powders and solids in a container such as a pillbox, plastic vial, or pharmacy fold. Seal the container and label it with your initials, the date, and an exhibit number. Refrigerate samples as needed. Do not add preservatives to solid food samples. Collect a comparison standard.

TABLETS AND CAPSULES Place tablets and capsules in a container such as a pillbox or plastic vial. Seal the container and label it with your initials, the date, and an exhibit number. Collect a comparison standard.

Comparison Standard for Liquids, Powders, Solids, Plant Material, Tablets, and Capsules Collect comparison standards for food, liquids, plant material, tablets, and capsules (in cases such as unattended deaths and suspected poisonings). When collecting standards, search the refrigerator, cupboards, and storage places for similar material, particularly that is labeled. Do not remove these samples from their original containers; seal them in clean (sterile, if possible) second containers. Refrigerate samples as necessary to retard further growth of microorganisms and deterioration. Expedite their delivery to a forensic laboratory.

Comparison standards for drugs should be collected in the manner described above. When collecting standards, collect any containers displaying prescription labels. Do not remove pills, capsules, powders, or liquids from their original containers; seal them in clean second containers and label them. Never mix specimens regardless of the proximity to the scene or their similarity in appearance.

Glass

All glass except small fragments might contain latent fingerprints and should be handled accordingly. When glass fragments might be present on clothing, shoes, tools, or other objects, the articles should be submitted to the laboratory as soon as possible.

LARGE FRAGMENTS Dust large fragments for latent fingerprints and submit the prints. Protect thin protruding edges of fragments against damage by embedding them in modeling clay, putty, or a similar substance. Avoid chipping the fragments. Use tweezers or similar tools to collect glass. Exercise care in protecting the edges and avoid scratching the surface. Place adhesive tape on each piece for identification. Place your initials and the date on the tape.

Wrap each piece separately in cotton; place it in a sturdy box with a tight-fitting lid; and seal and label each package with your initials, the date, and an exhibit number. Package questioned pieces of glass separately from known pieces. If you are submitting glass for the purpose of determining the direction of a bullet's impact or for other fracture analysis, mark surfaces with tape indicating whether the glass was found outside or inside the building. Similarly, mark glass taken from a window frame to indicate which side was facing out. Collect a comparison standard.

SMALL FRAGMENTS Examine articles of clothing and shoes for the presence of small glass fragments. Use tweezers or similar tools to collect glass. Use care in protecting the edges and avoid scratching the surface. Wrap each article of clothing containing fragments separately in clean paper or plastic bags. Package any questioned pieces of glass separately from known pieces. Seal each bag and label each bag with your initials, the date, and specimen information.

Place shoes and other solid objects in separate containers such as shoeboxes. Tape each object to the bottom of containers to prevent rattling. Do not pack articles containing microscopic fragments in cotton or other soft protective materials. Seal each package completely, making sure that there are no holes through which glass fragments might be lost. Place loose glass fragments in pillboxes or plastic or glass vials and seal them tightly. Place cotton in the container to prevent rattling and chipping during transit. Do not use envelopes as containers. Label everything with your initials, the date, and specimen information. Collect a comparison standard.

Comparison Standard for Glass Always collect glass standards from an area as near as possible to the point of impact. Collect samples that are at least the size of a quarter and wrap each comparison sample according to appropriate procedures.

Hairs and Fibers

In crimes involving physical contact, particles are often transferred among the victim, suspect, and weapon or other objects. Hairs and fibers are among the most common evidentiary items and can be extremely valuable to an investigation. When submitting hair and fiber evidence, be specific as to their source and association to the victim or suspect. Good evidence containers are a paper fold, pillbox, or tape lift. Each container used should be enclosed within an outside envelope.

COLLECTION OF UNKNOWNS If hairs or fibers are observed, remove them from the surface with clean tweezers. On suitable surfaces, a tape lift using wide transparent adhesive tape is an excellent procedure.

COLLECTION OF KNOWNS Of the various hair regions on the human body, only head hair and pubic hair are considered suitable for comparison purposes.

Head Hair Standards Pull 40 to 50 hairs from all over the head, taking approximately 10 hairs each from the top front, top back, back of head, right side, and left side.

Pubic Hair Standards Pull approximately 25 hairs representative of the pubic region. Hair standards should be packaged in paper folds and enclosed in an outer envelope.

Impressions

Impressions made by footwear, tires, and tools can easily be destroyed during a preliminary crime scene search. To prevent inadvertent loss of such evidence, one of the earliest concerns of any crime scene investigation should be the security of the scene and the collection and preservation of impressions. Impressions should be photographed properly before attempting lifts or casting.

FOOTWEAR AND TIRE IMPRESSIONS Photograph each impression with a ruled scale next to it. Photograph the impression from directly above (use of a tripod is highly recommended). Photographs should be taken while a detached flash is held low and to the side of the impression. Each impression should be flashed from four different sides. Black-and-white film gives the best quality photographs for comparison purposes. Photographs of impressions for comparisons should be blown up to a 1:1 scale before submission to the laboratory.

After photographing an impression, a lift may be attempted if a residue impression is on a hard surface that cannot be submitted to the laboratory. Adhesive lifters, gelatin lifters, or electrostatic lifting techniques may be used. Residue impressions are delicate in nature and can easily be destroyed by improper handling.

Casting techniques should be practiced before crime scene utilization. Dental stone or die stone casting material is recommended for the casting of three-dimensional impressions. (The use of plaster of Paris for casting of impressions is discouraged.)

Approximately 12 ounces of water should be added to and mixed with 2 pounds of dental stone or die stone. This amount is generally sufficient to prepare casting material for a footwear impression. A 1-gallon plastic Ziploc bag containing premeasured casting material is ideal for the mixing and casting process. A 12-ounce beverage container can be used for measuring the water. Additional casting material will need to be mixed for larger impressions such as tire impressions. Prepare the dental or die stone materials into a pancake batter—like consistency in a plastic Ziploc bag.

Pour the solution off the side of the impression, not directly onto or into it. Allow the casting material to flow into the impression. A tongue depressor can be used gently to help the casting material flow over the entire impression. When the dental or die stone has set, place your initials, date, and case-identifying information into the back of the cast.

When submitting a cast to the laboratory, place it in a sturdy box or similar container with sufficient cushioning material (e.g., Styrofoam peanuts or scrap newspaper). If more than one cast is submitted, put each cast in its own box or container. Do not remove the dirt or debris adhering to a cast, footwear, or tire. Each container should be sealed with tamperproof evidence tape before submission to the laboratory.

TOOL MARKS Do not insert a suspect tool into a tool mark. Whenever possible, preserve tool marks as you find them and submit the intact object bearing the questioned tool marks to the laboratory. If it is not possible to submit the object, remove the portion or section of the object bearing the tool mark. Before a portion or section of a large item is removed, photograph the entire item with the inclusion of a ruled scale. Also take close-up photographs of the questioned tool marks with the inclusion of a ruled scale for reference.

If an item cannot be submitted, a Mikrosil or silicon typecast of the tool mark(s) should be made and submitted to the laboratory for comparison. Tools, casts of tool marks, and so on should be submitted individually in separate containers. Information pertinent to an investigation should be labeled on the outside of the containers. Each container should be sealed with tamperproof evidence tape before submission to the laboratory.

Paint

Paint evidence can be in the form of liquid, chips, or smears. A dried paint specimen should be collected in a paper fold, placed in an outer envelope, and marked clearly as to its source. Any questioned paint specimen should also have a known paint standard submitted. Package specimens separately for comparison purposes.

LIQUID PAINTS Specimens of liquid paint should be submitted in original containers whenever possible.

Questioned Documents

Questioned documents contain a wide variety of identifiable characteristics that can be used to corroborate other evidence and associate a suspect with a crime. Similarly, these can be used by a laboratory to clear a suspect of a crime in certain instances.

CHARRED DOCUMENTS A thin but strong section of cardboard can be inserted gently under charred debris. Thick, firm cotton batting is then placed on a flat surface, with the charred paper deposited onto the batting. Place it in a crushproof container; label it with your initials, the date, and an exhibit number; and seal it. Mark the container "Fragile" in a conspicuous spot.

CRUMPLED DOCUMENTS Do not unfold a crumpled document; rather, enclose it in a crushproof container. Label it with your initials, the date, and an exhibit number and then seal it. Mark the container "Fragile" in a conspicuous spot.

INTACT DOCUMENTS Whenever possible, submit the original document rather than a photograph, photocopy, or other type of copy. Handle the document carefully; preserve latent fingerprints using tweezers or gloves as necessary. When identification is necessary, mark in a noncritical area of the document. Use a medium different from that used on the document (e.g., use pencil when the document is in ink). Do not use staples or pins on documents and do not fold documents. Place them in a protective covering such as an envelope or cover with plastic. Seal and label them with your initials, the date, and an exhibit number. Collect a comparison standard.

Comparison Standard for Questioned Documents Standards for questioned documents are not the questioned documents themselves but facsimiles or replicas of handwriting, typewriter print, or ink visible on questioned document(s) that might have been made by the maker(s) of the original document.

ADEQUATE EXEMPLARS Remember that unlike fingerprints, handwriting and hand printing will change over a period of time and can easily be disguised. Each of us has a normal range of variation in our writing. To make a proper comparison, the examiner must determine the range of variation in each suspect's writing. It is impossible to say whether this range will be shown in 6, 16, or 60 samples. Handwriting (cursive) cannot be compared with hand printing. Age, gender, and writing hand cannot be determined conclusively. About the best that we can do in these areas is to make an educated guess.

Don't use a single sheet of paper or a single-page exemplar. To get an adequate sample of writing or printing from a person, it is much better to use several, perhaps 20 or 30, single pieces of paper as your exemplar. Using paper that is about the same size and texture as the document in question is suggested. Always try to duplicate the conditions under which the questioned items were prepared.

Guidelines for Obtaining Known Handwriting Exemplars The following guidelines may be used to obtain known handwriting or hand printing exemplars from a person:

* Reproduce the original conditions as nearly as possible with respect to text speed, slant, size of paper, size of writing, type of writing instrument, and so on.
* Obtain samples from dictation until it is believed that normal writing has been produced. (The number of samples necessary cannot be determined in advance.)
* Do not allow the writer to see either the original document in question or a photograph thereof.
* Remove each sample from the sight of the writer as soon as it is completed.
* Do not give instructions in spelling, punctuation, or arrangement.
* Use the same writing media, such as type and size of paper, writing instruments, and printed forms such as checks or notes.
* Obtain the full text of the questioned writing in word-for-word order at least once, if possible. Signatures and less extensive writing should be prepared several times, each time on a different piece of paper. In hand-printing cases, both uppercase (capital) and lowercase samples should be obtained.
* In forgery cases, the laboratory should also be furnished with genuine signatures of the person whose name has been forged.

- Obtain samples of supplementary writings such as sketches, drawings, and manner of addressing an envelope.
- Have the writer sign and date each page.
- Witness each sample with date and initials (or name).
- Consider furnishing undictated specimens to supplement the dictated specimens.
- Obtain and submit original documents when possible.
- Familiarize yourself with all aspects of the questioned document involved in a case. Furnish copies of the documents to assist other officers when they are requested to obtain known writing.

TYPEWRITER EXAMPLES Collect specimens of typewriting from the typewriter believed to have been used and submit them to a document analyst. When obtaining these examples, use the typewriter in the condition in which it is found (i.e., the same ribbon). Type the text of the questioned material three times, once through carbon paper with the ribbon adjustment set on "stencil." On each specimen, record the brand name, model number, and serial number of the typewriter that was used.

Place specimens in a plastic or reinforced envelope. Do not fold them. Label them with your initials, the date, and an exhibit number. Film-type ribbon cartridges and correction tapes should also be collected and submitted for examination.

INK EXAMPLES Collect samples of unquestioned documents that contain the type of ink used in the questioned document. If you are unsure whether the ink on the standard is the same as that on the questioned document, submit samples of all available inks that might have been used. If samples of fluid ink are available, place the bottles containing the ink in a suitable container that is labeled with your initials, the date, and an exhibit number. Label the container as fragile and submit it to the laboratory.

INDENTED WRITINGS Loose papers and writing pads should be collected for possible writing and typing impression restoration.

Soil

The success of soil comparisons depends mainly on the quality of the samples collected. Soils located on the sides of suspect shoes are most suitable for soil comparisons. Consider the nature of the crime scene. Is it conducive to the transfer of soil onto a shoe (e.g., a paved parking lot compared with an open field)? Soil standards from the scene should consist of an area approximately 6 inches square by 1/4 inch deep. Plastic bags or metal cans are good containers for soil samples.

Toxicology

BLOOD ALCOHOL DETERMINATIONS Whole blood is the best body fluid for alcohol testing; urine is not a reliable specimen for accurate determination of a blood alcohol level. Blood should be collected in a sterile gray stopper blood collection tube that contains the additives sodium fluoride (NaF) and potassium oxalate (KOx). These additives are required to preserve a blood sample for alcohol testing. A new sterile needle must be used as well as a nonalcoholic skin cleanser. The needle cover or wrapper bearing the word "sterile" as well as the package from the skin cleanser should be preserved. These are needed in court to prove that legal collection requirements were followed. Do not preserve the needle itself.

After the blood is collected, mix the blood and the additives in the tube by gently inverting the tube at least 15 to 20 times. This prevents the blood from clotting. Mark the tube with the person's name and any other pertinent case information. One tube of blood (5 to 10 milliliters) is sufficient for alcohol testing. Do not freeze the blood sample. Protect the blood from extreme heat. Do not store the blood sample in a hot car during the summer.

TOLUENE OR SOLVENT ABUSE AND GLUE SNIFFING When glue sniffing or other solvent abuse is suspected, collect a blood sample as described above for alcohol testing. Toluene and other solvents cannot be detected reliably in urine samples.

DRUG TESTING Urine is the specimen of choice for drug testing. Many more positive test results are found in urine than in blood. Drug tests on their own will not establish impairment at the time of arrest because different drugs take differing amounts of time to be excreted in the urine. The officer's observations relating to the person's degree of impairment is very important in establishing intoxication.

Urine collection must be observed to prevent the person from adulterating the sample. An officer of the same gender as the person should accompany the person into the bathroom stall and actually observe the urine flowing into the cup. At least 50 milliliters of urine should be collected if possible. If the person cannot provide sufficient urine, have the person drink some water and wait 15 minutes to try again. After the urine is collected, the sample should be marked with the person's name and sealed. The specimen cup should then be placed in a leakproof plastic bag. If the urine sample cannot be delivered to the laboratory within 24 hours of collection, the urine must be refrigerated. This is a legal requirement. For long-term storage (more than one day), the urine sample should be frozen.

Blood can also be tested for drugs. However, drugs do not remain in the bloodstream for long periods of time. Some drugs may be detectable in blood only for a couple of hours or less. Also, drugs have much lower concentrations in blood than in urine. For these reasons, urine is the preferred specimen for drug testing. If blood is submitted to the laboratory for drug testing, it should be collected in the same manner as for alcohol testing. At least two tubes of blood (20 milliliters) should be collected if a drug test is requested. When submitting evidence for drug testing, indicate which drugs are suspected.

CARBON MONOXIDE If carbon monoxide poisoning is suspected, collect a blood sample in the same manner as for alcohol testing.

SAFETY CONSIDERATIONS Assume that all samples are infected with something. Wash your hands after handling blood tubes or urine samples. Package all samples in a way that will contain leakage. Notify the laboratory if you believe that a suspect is infected with any disease.

Miscellaneous

Items such as cigarette butts, tobacco, jewelry, magnetic tape recordings, and writing instruments can all serve as evidence to connect a suspect to a crime. Each item, either through its use or basic structure, can provide a unique, identifiable characteristic. For instance, tape recordings of anonymous voices received as part of a threat before a bombing or extortion may be identified with known voices of a suspect through voiceprint analysis, provided that care is exercised during the recording of questions and known voices.

Cigarette Butts and Tobacco.

Pick up the cigarette butt on a piece of paper or with tweezers and place in a pillbox. Do not handle the cigarette butt directly with your hands. Mark a label with your initials, the date, and an exhibit number as well as where the object was found. Place the label on the container and seal it. Empty tobacco material from pipes or clothes pockets into a pillbox. Mark and seal it as above.

Comparison Standard for Cigarette Butts and Tobacco No comparison standard of the cigarette material need be collected. If serological testing is desired, however, saliva standards should be collected from both victims and suspects.

JEWELRY Handle with tweezers or cloth gloves. Dust for fingerprints and place in a suitable crushproof container. If the composition of precious metals such as gold, silver, or platinum must be determined to prove a common origin, send appropriate metal samples for comparison purposes. Label each sample container by writing on it in ink your initials, the date, and an exhibit number. Collect a comparison standard.

Comparison Standard for Jewelry When possible, submit comparison samples of jewelry along with any questioned samples. The origin of some stolen jewelry may be traced to a particular jewelry store by analyzing the adhesive used to glue a precious stone to its setting. Known samples of the adhesive used by the jeweler should be submitted for comparison with questioned samples. Place samples in crushproof containers and seal them.

SMALL OBJECTS At each crime scene, search for small objects such as burned matches, fragments of glass, broken fingernails, and cigarette butts. Follow known procedures for each item. If you do not have specific directions for an item of evidence, place it in a crushproof container without touching it directly with your fingers. Seal and identify the container by writing on it in ink your initials, the date, and an exhibit number. Collect a comparison standard whenever possible.

Comparison Standard for Small Objects Comparison samples of small objects or items found in the possession of a suspect or in his or her belongings should be submitted so that a comparison with items found at the crime scene can be made. Package and identify comparison samples.

WRITING INSTRUMENTS Handle these with tweezers or cloth gloves, being careful not to smudge fingerprints. Dust for and collect fingerprints. Look for and submit instruments bearing teeth marks. Place the instrument in a suitable crushproof container and identify the container by writing on it in ink your initials, the date, and an exhibit number. Collect a comparison standard.

Collect any writing instruments found in the possession of a suspect or in his or her belongings in the manner described above. Package and identify comparison samples as described above.

Appendix B

CASES

Arenson v. Jackson, 97 Misc. 606, 162 N.Y.S. (1916)

Arizona v. Evans, 514 U.S. 1 (1995)

Arizona v. Gant, 556 U.S. 332 (2009)

Arizona v. Hicks, 480 U.S. 321 (1987)

Barnett v. State, 104 Ohio St. 298, 135 N.E. (1922)

Berger v. New York, 388 U.S. 41 (1967)

Berkemer v. McCarty, 486 U.S. 420 (1984)

Brady v. Maryland, 373 U.S. 83 (1963)

Brigham City v. Stuart, 547 U.S. 398 (2006)

Brinegar v. United States, 338 U.S. 160, 69 S.Ct. (1949)

Brown v. Mississippi, 297 U.S. 278 (1936)

Bumper v. North Carolina, 391 U.S. 543 (1968)

California v. Acevedo, 500 U.S. 565 (1991)

California v. Hodari, 499 U.S. 62 (1991)

California v. Prysock, 451 U.S. 1301 (1981)

Carroll v. United States, 267 U.S. 132 (1925)

Chambers v. Maroney, 399 U.S. 42 (1970)

Cheadle v. Barwell, 95 Mont. 299 (1933)

Chimel v. California, 395 U.S. 752 (1969)

Coolidge v. New Hampshire, 403 U.S. 443 (1971)

County of Riverside v. McLaughlin, 500 U.S. 413 (1991)

Cupp v. Murphy, 412 U.S. 291 93 S.Ct. 200 (1973)

Daubert v. Merrell Dow Pharmaceuticals, 509 U.S. 579 (1993)

Davis v. United States, 512 U.S. 452 (1994)

Department of Justice v. Landano, 508 U.S. 165 (1993)

Draper v. United States, 358 U.S. 307, 79 S.Ct. (1959)

Edwards v. Arizona, 451 U.S. 477 (1981)

Escobedo v. Illinois, 378 U.S. 478 (1964)

Florida v. Bostick, 501 U.S. 429 (1991)

Florida v. Jimeno, 499 U.S. 934 (1991)

Florida v. Royer, 460 U.S. 491 (1983)

Foster v. California, 394 U.S. 440 (1969)

Frye v. United States, 54 App. D.C. 46, 293 (1923)

Gilbert v. California, 388 U.S. 263 (1967)

Graham v. Connor, 490 U.S. 396 (1989)

Harris v. United States, 390 U.S. 234 (1968)

Hayes v. Florida, 470 U.S. 811 (1985)

Horton v. California, 496 U.S. 128 (1990)

Illinois v. Gates

Illinois v. Rodriguez, 497 U.S. 177 (1990)

Illinois v. Wardlow, [98-1036] 183 Ill. 2nd 306, 701 N.E. 2d 484 (2000)

Katz v. United States, 389 U.S. 347 (1967)

Ker v. California, 374 U.S. 23 (1963)

Kirby v. Illinois, 406 U.S. 682, 688-89 (1972)

Kyllo v. U.S. 533 U.S. 27 (2001)

Landsdown v. Commonwealth, 226 Va. 204, 308 S.E.2d 106 (1983)

Lee v. Florida, 392 U.S. 378 (1968)

Lee v. U.S. 343 U.S. 747 (1952)

Lopez v. U.S. 373 U.S. 427 (1963)

Mallory v. United States, 354 U.S. 449 (1957)

Manson v. Brathwaite, 432 U.S. 98 (1977)

Mapp v. Ohio, 367 U.S. 643 (1961)

Maryland v. Buie, 494 U.S. 325 (1990)

Massachusetts v. Sheppard, 468 U.S. 981 (1984)

McNabb v. United States, 318 U.S. 332 (1943)

Michigan v. Chesternut, 486 U.S. 567 (1988)

Michigan v. Tyler, 436 U.S. 499 (1978)

Mincey v. Arizona, 437 U.S. 385 (1978)

Minnesota v. Murphy, 405 U.S. 420, 104 S. Ct. (1984)

Minnick v. Mississippi, 498 U.S. 146 (1990)

Miranda v. Arizona, 384 U.S. 436 (1966)

Muehler v. Mena, 544 U.S. 93 (2005)

Naler v. State, 148 So. 880, 25 (1933)

Neil v. Biggers, 409 U.S. 188 (1972)

New York v. Belton, 453 U.S. 454 (1981)

New York v. Quarles, 467 U.S. 649 (1984)

Nix v. Williams, 467 U.S. 431 (1984)

Oliver v. United States, 466 U.S. 170 (1984)

Olmstead v. United States, 277 U.S. 438 (1928)

Oregon v. Bradshaw, 462 U.S. 1039 (1983)

Oregon v. Elstad, 470 U.S. 298 (1985)

Payton v. New York, 455 U.S. 573 (1980)

People v. Deutsch, 96 C.D.O.S. 2827 (1996)

People v. Forts, 18 N.C. [2nd] 31 (1933)

People v. Lawrence, 481 P.2d 212 (1971)

People v. Mccann, 76 Ill. App. 3rd 184, 186, 394 N.E.2d 1055, 1056 (2d Dist. 1979)

Reno v. ACLU, 117 S. Ct. 2329 (1997)

Rhode Island v. Innis, 446 U.S. 291 (1980)

Schneckloth v. Bustamonte, 412 U.S. 218 (1973)

Simmons v. United States, 390 U.S. 377 (1968)

Stansbury v. California, 114 S. Ct. 1526, 1529 128 L.Ed2d 293 (1994)

Stansbury v. California, 511 U.S. 318 (1994)

State v. Bohner, 210 Wis. 651, 246 N.W. 314 (1933)

Stovall v. Denno, 388 U.S. 293 (1967)

Tennessee v. Garner, 471 U.S. 1 (1985)

Terry v. Ohio, 392 U.S. 1 (1968)

Texas v. Brown, 460 U.S. 730 (1983)

United States v. Ash Jr., 413 U.S. 300 (1973)

United Stastes. v. Ask, 413 U.S. 300 (1973)

United States v. Dunn, 480 U.S. 294 (1987)

United States v. Grubbs, 377 F.3d 1072 (2004).

United States v. Henry, 259 F.2d 725 7th Cir. (1958)

United States v. Jones, 565 US, 132 S.Ct. 945 (2012)

United States v. Karo, 468 U.S. 705 (1984)

United States v. Knox, 977 F.2d 815, 818–19 (1993)

United States v. Knox, 32 F.3d 733 (3d Cir. 1994), cert denied, 513 U.S. 1109 (1995)

United States v. Leon, 468, U.S. 897 (1984)

United States v. Lewis, 547 F.2d 1030, 1035 (8th Cir. 1976)

United States v. Lott, 870 F.2d 778 (1st Cir. 1989)

United States v. Mendenhall, 446 U.S. 544 (1980)

United States v. Montoya de Hernandez, 473 U.S. 531, 105 S. Ct. 3304 (1985)

United States v. *Puerta,* 982 F.2d 1297, 1300 (9th Cir. 1992)

United States v. *Ross,* 456 U.S. 798 (1982)

United States v. *Scott,* 436 U.S. 128 (1978)

United States v. *Sokolow,* 109 S. Ct. 1581 (1989)

United States v. *Usama bin Laden* et al., 397 F.Supp.2d 465 2005 WL 287404 (2001)

United States v. *Wade,* 388 U.S. 218 (1967)

United States v. *White,* 401 U.S. 745 (1971)

Warden v. *Hayden,* 387 U.S. 294 (1967)

Wayne v. *United States,* 318 F.2d 205, 212; 115 U.S. App. D.C. 234, 241 (D.C. Cir. 1963)

Weeks v. *United States,* 232 U.S. 383 (1914)

Wilson v. *Arkansas,* 514 U.S. 927 (1995)

Wong Sun v. *United States,* 371 U.S. 471 (1963)

Wyoming v. *Houghton,* 526 U.S. 295 (1999)

Yarborough v. *Alvarado,* U.S. Supreme Court No. 02-1684 (2004)

Glossary

A

Abandoned children. When claims over one's offspring are relinquished with the intent of never again resuming or reasserting them.

Absolute judgment. When eyewitnesses compare each photograph or person in a lineup only with their memory of what the offender looked like.

Abduction. The process of proposing a likely explanation for an event that must then be tested.

Accelerant. Any substance that can bond, mix, or disturb another substance and cause an increase in the speed of a natural, or artificial, chemical process, typically used in context with arson.

Accidental death. The death of a person that is unintentional and unforseen

Accusatory. To assert one's involvement or role in an event.

Acquaintance stalking. When a stalker and victim know each other casually.

Acquaintance molestation. The sexual abuse of children by persons known to them other than family.

Acute maltreatment. When a child's death is directly related to injuries suffered as a result of a specific incident or abuse or act of negligence.

Acute neglect. A term commonly associated with child abuse when a perpetrator is responsible to provide care for a victim who is unable to care for himself or herself, but fails to provide adequate care.

Admission. A self-incriminating statement made by a suspect that falls short of an acknowledgment of guilt.

Affidavit. A legal document that presents facts that the officer believes constitute probable cause to justify the issuance of a warrant.

AFIS system. The automated fingerprint identification system.

Aggravated arson. The deliberate burning of property while creating an imminent danger tohuman life or risking great bodily harm.

Aggravated assault. A personal crime associated with a high probability of death; serious, permanent disfigurement; permanent or protracted loss or impairment of the function of any body member or organ; or other severe bodily harm.

Alcoholic robber. A criminal robber whose judgment is impaired by the consumption of alcohol.

Alligatoring. The pattern of crevices formed by the burning of a wooden structure.

Amber Alert. A system that quickly posts information about child abductions.

Amido black protein. A liquid substance used in to stain for total *protein* on transferred membrane blots. It is typically used in criminal investigations to detect *blood* present with latent *fingerprints*.

Analysis. A scientific examination.

Anger rapist. A general category including the anger-retaliatory rapist and the anger excitation rapist

Anger-excitation rapist. A category of rapist who has a strong propensity toward sadism and is prone to severely injure or even murder his victim.

Anger-retaliatory rapist. A person who vents his anger and frustration toward the opposite sex by punishing them.

Anticipatory search warrant. A search warrant issued before the evidence is actually known to exist but is anticipated to exist.

Arrest. The act of a police officer taking a person into custody after making a determination that he or she has violated a law.

Arson. The malicious or fraudulent burning of property.

Assault. To intentionally put someone in fear of immediate battery or to threaten someone while having the apparent ability to carry out that threat.

Asset forfeiture. *Confiscation*, by the *state*, of *assets* which are either (a) the alleged proceeds of crime or (b) the alleged instrumentalities of crime, and more recently, alleged terrorism.

Associative evidence. Evidence that links a suspect with a crime.

Autoerotic death. Death induced by solo sexual activity in which the participant incorporates the use of self-induced bondage and a ligature to reduce the flow of oxygen while attempting to achieve orgasm through masturbation.

B

Ballistics. The science of tracking the path of a bullet.

Bank examiner scheme – A criminal scheme when con artists pose as FBI agents, bank examiners, police officers, detectives, or bank officials. The victim is then contacted by them pretending to need help in conducting an investigation.

Bank robbery. The unlawful taking of money or other assets from a bank through the use of face-to-face contact between suspect and victims.

Bank Secrecy Act (BSA). A federal law passed in 1970 to require reporting of large-scale case transactions.

Baseline technique. Crime scene measuring technique in which a line is drawn between two known points.

Battered child syndrome. A clinical term referring to the collection of injuries sustained by a child as a result of repeated mistreatment or beating.

Battered children. Children who suffer from physical abuse.

Battery. An intentional nonconsensual bodily contact that a reasonable person would consider harmful.

Bertillon system. An early criminal identification or classification system based on the idea that certain aspects of the human body, such as skeletal size, ear shape, and eye color, remained the same after a person had reached full physical maturity. This system used a combination of photographs with standardized physical measurements.

Best evidence rule. A legal doctrine of evidence that says that no evidence will be admissible in court if it is secondary in nature.

Beyond a reasonable doubt. The standard of proof in a criminal case in which the deciders of fact are entirely satisfied that the defendant is guilty as charged.

Bill of Rights. A constitutional doctrine granting individual freedoms.

Binding material. Material used to incapacitate a victim during the course of a robbery.

Biohazardous material. Substances that pose a threat to the health of living organisms, primarily that of humans. This includes medical waste or samples of a *microorganism*, *virus* or *toxin* (from a biological source) that can impact human health.

Bobbies. The name of London Metropolitan Police Department officers; they were named this after the department's founder, Home Secretary Sir Robert Peel.

Body-packing. Associated with a *mule* or *courier* who *smuggles* something with them (as opposed to sending by mail, etc.) across a national border, including bringing in to and out of an international plane, especially a small amount, transported for a *smuggling organization*.

Booby traps. Deadly and dangerous devices used to warn the suspect of any intruders by the sound of explosive devices.

Bookmaking. A type of gambling that usually involves taking bets on sporting events.

Boosters. Professional shoplifters who resell stolen merchandise to pawn shops or fences at usually one-half to one-fourth the original price.

Bow Street Runners. A group of English crime fighters formed by Henry Fielding during the eighteenth century.

Burden of proof. The duty to establish the validity or factuality of the charge against a person.

Burglary. A covert crime in which the criminal works during the nighttime, outside the presence of witnesses.

Burglary tools. Any instrument designed for unlawfully entering a structure.

Burned. A term used in undercover operations when an undercover agent is identified by a criminal suspect.

Bootlegging. Smuggling or manufacturing untaxed alcohol or cigarettes.

Buy-bust. When an undercover agent makes a purchase of illicit narcotics and the suspect is immediately arrested.

Buy-walk. When an undercover agent makes a purchase of illicit narcotics and the suspect is allowed to leave for the purposes of continuing the investigation.

C

CSI effect. Any of several ways in which the exaggerated portrayal of *forensic science* on crime television shows such as *CSI: Crime Scene Investigation* influences public perception.

Carjacking. When an armed robber forces the driver of an automobile out of the vehicle before stealing it.

Carnal knowledge. A specific sex act such as contact between a *penis* and *vagina*, Some laws elaborating on this to include even slight penile penetration of female *sex organs*. The term sometimes includes a set of sex acts that include *sodomy* and/or *oral sex*, while some statutes specifically exclude such acts.

Carroll Doctrine. A legal principle that enables officers to search an automobile without a search warrant provided that they have probable cause to believe it contains contraband and that the vehicle is mobile.

Case linkage. Also called "linking analysis" refers to the process of determining whetheror not there are discrete connections between two more previously unrelatedcases through crime scene analysis

Chain of custody. Documentation of all who handle evidence in a criminal case.

Check kiting. Drawing cash on accounts made up of uncollected funds.

Child abduction. The unauthorized removal of a *minor* (a child under the age of *legal adulthood*) from the *custody* of the child's *natural parents* or *legally appointed guardians*.

Child abuse. The physical, sexual, or emotional abuse of children.

Child molestation. Another term for child molestation

Child molester. One who engages in some form of child sexual exploitation.

Child Protection Act of 2003. Legislation that created Amber Alerts

Child Protective Services (CPS). The name of a *governmental agency* in many *states* of the *United States* that responds to reports of *child abuse* or neglect.

Child sexual abuse. The unwanted sexual physical contact of an underage child

Chop shop. A secret location where auto thieves dismantle stolen vehicles for the purpose of selling the parts.

Chronic maltreatment. Occurs when a child's death is directly related to injuries caused by maltreatment or neglect occurring over an extended period.

Circumstantial evidence. Evidence that tends to incriminate a person without offering positive proof.

Closed files. Intelligence files that are maintained apart from criminal investigation files to prevent unauthorized inspection of data.

Code Adam. An internationally recognized "missing child" safety program in the United States (and Canada) originally created by Walmart retail stores in 1994.

Coerced-compliant confessions. The use of fear tactics that include direct threats, intimidation or actual physical abuse.

Coerced internalization. When highly suggestible and confused suspects who actually begin to believe that they are guilty of the crime they didn't commit.

Coercion. The use or threat of illegal physical means to induce a suspect to make an admission or confession.

Cognitive interview. A method of interviewing in which *eyewitnesses* and victims report what they remember from a *crime scene*.

Cold case. A crime or an accident that has not yet been solved to the full and is not the subject of a recent *criminal investigation*, but for which new information could emerge from new witness testimony, reexamined archives, retained material evidence, as well as fresh activities of the suspect.

Collation. The process of comparing texts carefully to clarify or give meaning to information.

Commercial burglary. Burglaries of bussinesses and other commercialestablishments

Commercial robbery. Robbery of stores and businesses located close to major thorough fares such as main streets, highways, and interstates.

Commodity flow analysis. charting the logical flow of such commodities as drugs, money, and illegal arms shipments.

Composite. A freehand drawing of a suspected criminal.

Computer crime. A violation of criminal law that requires some knowledge of computers for perpetration.

Computer errors exception – an exception to the exclusionary rule that holds that a vehicle stop based on an arrest warrant stored improperly is still lawful.

Computer hacking. a compulsive computer programmer who explores, tests, and pushes the computer to its limits, regardless of its consequences.

Computer virus. A set of illegal computer instructions designed to ruin computer hardware or software while reproducing itself in the computer program when it is executed.

Confession. Direct acknowledgment by the suspect of his or her guilt in the commission of a specific crime or as an integral part of a specific crime.

Confidence game. The criminal practice of gaining the confidence of a would-be victim for the sole purpose of swindling money from them.

Confidential informant. A person who provides privileged information about a person or organization to an agency. The term is usually used within the law enforcement world, where they are officially known as confidential or criminal informants (CI), and can often refer pejoratively to the supply of information without the consent of the other parties with the intent of malicious, personal, or financial gain.

Consent search. When police gain permission to search without a warrant.

Conspiracy. An agreement between two or more persons to commit a criminal act, accompanied by the commission of at least one overt act in furtherance of the crime.

Constable. A term given to peace officers during the early formation of policing in England.

Contact wound. A gunshot wound incurred while the muzzle of the firearm is in direct contact with the body at the moment of discharge.

Contamination of evidence. The act of adversely affecting evidence by allowing it to be tampered with or by not protecting the chain of custody.

Convenience store robbery. The armed robbery of a convenience store.

Cooperating witness. a person whose relationship with the government is concealed until testimony at trial is required and who contributes substantial operational assistance to the resolution of a case through active participation in an investigation

Coordinate method. Measuring an object from two fixed points of reference.

Copping areas. Areas known for open-air drug trafficking.

Corporate crime. a form of white-collar crime whereby trusted executives working within a company mishandle funds or otherwise betray the trust of customers or other consumers.

Corpus delicti evidence. Evidence that establishes that a crime has been committed.

Corroboration. supportive evidence that tends to prove that a crime was committed.

Cover story. A fictitious story contrived by an undercover investigator to explain his or her presence as a drug buyer to criminal suspects.

Covert information collection. A clandestine process of data collection on criminal acts that have not yet occurred but for which the investigator must prepare.

Crack. A freebase form of cocaine.

Crack house. abandoned buildings or apartments in public housing projects located near copping areas.

Credibility. One's ability to be believed.

Crime. Any act prohibited under criminal law that is punishable by a fine, imprisonment, or death.

Crime scene. The location where the crime took place.

Crime scene evidence. Physical, trace, biological, or other evidence located at the scene of a crime.

Crime scene report. A police report designed to document the facts and circumstances of a suspected crime along with associated evidence.

Crime Scene Sketch a scale drawing that locates evidence in relation to other factors.

Crime scene walk-through. The investigative act of investigators walking through a scene of crime for the purpose to give investigators perspective in relation to the crime.

Crime stoppers. A program separate from the *emergency telephone number* system that allows a member of the *community* to provide *anonymous* information about *criminal* activity.

Criminal intelligence. Documented information regarding past, present, or future criminal activity.

Criminal investigative analysis. identifying psychological and social characteristics surrounding the crime as well as the manner in which it was committed

Cross-examination. A legal line of questioning in a criminal trial designed to weaken or discredit any testimony given during direct examination.

Cross-projection method. Used in indoor crime scenes, it is basically a top-down view of the crime scene where the walls of the room have been "folded" down to reveal locations of bullet holes, blood-spatter evidence, and so on.

CSA. Controlled Substances Act of 1970.

Currency exchange – A brokerage house for facilitating movement of illicit money

Curtilage the area surrounding buildings and houses

Custodial interrogations. A process of questioning a suspect when his or her liberty has been restricted to a degree that is associated with arrest.

Custodial parent. Terms which are used to describe the legal and practical relationship between a *parent* and his or her child, such as the right of the parent to make decisions for the child, and the parent's duty to care for the child.

Cybercrime. The destruction, theft or unauthorized use, modification, or copying of information, programs, services, equipment, or communication networks.

Cyber-extortion. When a computer criminal extorts money from a victim.

Cyberstalking. Preying on a victim through his or her computer.

D

Data diddling. False data entry.

Date rape. Rape that occurs when the victim and offender are acquainted before the crime is committed.

Date rape drug. Another term for the drug Rohypnol.

Daubert standard. A rule of evidence regarding the admissibility of *expert witnesses' testimony* during U.S. federal legal proceedings.

Deadly force. Actions of police officers that result in the killing of a person.

Deception. when one intends to dupe others by communicating messages meant to mislead and meant to make the recipients believe what the agent (the person performing or committing the act) either knows or believes to be untrue.

Decomposition. The process by which organic substances are broken down into simpler forms of matter.

Deductive reasoning. The ability to draw conclusions based on critical thinking.

Deep cover. Working undercover for extended periods of time.

Demeanor. One's persona and how one is perceived.

Demonstrative evidence. Evidence used to clarify an issue rather than to prove something.

Deoxyribonucleic acid. DNA, the genetic material used in criminal investigations.

Dependence. The degree of an illegal and addicting drug's legal use.

Designer drugs. A class of illicit drugs that are specifically designed to emulate controlled substances.

Detention. Something less than an arrest but more than a consensual encounter.

Digital imaging. Generally referring to photographs taken with a digital camera and stored on digital media.

Digital recorder. An electronic device that can digitally record audio or video.

Direct examination. A courtroom procedure whereby a witness is asked what he or she knows about an alleged offense and asked to give a brief explanation as to how he or she personally observed or knew about the incident.

Direct evidence. Evidence that is directly experienced. Usually the experience is by sight or hearing, though it may come through any sense, including touch or pain.

Dissemination. The phase of the intelligence process whereby information is shared with other law enforcement agencies.

Diversion. The trafficking of pharmaceutical drugs to the street from normal, legal channels.

DNA analysis. A scientific process among the newest and most sophisticated of techniques used to test for genetic disorders, which involves direct examination of the *DNA molecule* itself.

DNA technology. The science of identifying the genetic facsimile, or "blueprint," of any particular organism in every cell within each human body.

Domestic terrorism. the unlawful use, or threatened use of force by a group or individual,based and operating entirely within the United States without foreigndirection, committed against persons or property to intimidate or coercea government, the civilian population, or any segment thereof, infurtherance of social or political objectives.

Domestic violence. A pattern of abusive behaviors by one partner against another in an *intimate relationship* such as marriage, dating, family, or cohabitation.

Double invoicing. a company orders merchandise from a foreign subsidiary at an inflated price

Drug addict robber. robber robs to support his or her drug habit

Drug courier profile. The practice of observing suspected drug traffickers to develop a pattern of behavior that would constitute legal cause for a stop and search by police.

Drowning A form of death that occurs when liquid enters the breathing passages, preventing air from getting to the lungs.

Drug Enforcement Administration (DEA). Established in 1973, the DEA is the only federal investigative body whose sole duty it is to enforce federal drug laws in the United States.

Due process. The essential elements of fairness under the law, ensuring that no person is deprived of life, liberty, or property without notice of charges, assistance from legal counsel, a hearing, and a chance to confront one's accusers.

Duress. The imposition of restrictions on physical behavior such as prolonged interrogation and deprivation of water, food, or sleep.

Dust print. A visible fingerprint

Dying declaration. A statement given by a dying person that implicates the killer. The legal requirements of a dying declaration are that the victim must be rational and competent and must ultimately die of the wounds.

E

Electronic evidence. Information and data of investigative value that is stored in or transmitted by an electronic device.

Electronic surveillance. The monitoring of the *behavior*, activities, or other changing information, usually of people for the purpose of influencing, managing, directing, or protecting.

Elements of a crime. The legal characteristics of a crime.

Elimination samples. Evidence used to eliminate persons as suspects.

Embezzlement. A low-profile crime consisting of employees who steal large amounts of money over long periods of time.

Entrapment. When an undercover officer convinces a criminal suspect to commit a crime he or she was not predisposed to commit.

Event flow analysis. A process whereby events are documented, they are connected by arrows to indicate the direction of the sequence.

Evidence. A statement, object, or other item bearing on or establishing the point in question in a court of law.

Exclusionary rule. The legal rule that excludes evidence that has been determined to have been obtained illegally.

Exemplars. Samples, as of a suspect's handwriting.

Exigent circumstances. Circumstances whereby a search may be legally conducted without a warrant.

Expert systems. A process of using artificial intelligence by computers to make inferences based on available information and to draw conclusions or make recommendations to the systems operators.

Expert witness. A witness whose knowledge exceeds the knowledge of anyone with a moderate education or experience in the field.

Exploitation. Commonly used in context with sexual exploitation, which is the use of sexual material that focuses on a particular person who is an unwilling contributor.

F

False confession. An admission of *guilt* in a crime in which the confessor is not responsible for the crime.

Face sheet. An "at-a-glance" summary of the investigation.

Facial composite. A graphical representation of an *eyewitness*'s memory of a face, as recorded by a composite artist.

Fact witness – A witness who has personal knowledge of events pertaining to a case and can only testify to things he personally has observed.

Family abduction. An abduction related to a domestic or custody dispute.

Federal Bureau of Investigation. Established in 1924, the primary federal investigative bureau within the U.S. Department of Justice.

Field interview card method of documenting information on the street

Federal Kidnapping Act. Following the historic *Lindbergh kidnapping* (the abduction and murder of *Charles Lindbergh*'s toddler son), the *U.S. Congress* adopted a federal kidnapping statute—popularly known as the Federal Kidnapping Act.

Felony. A category of crime that is of a more serious nature than a misdemeanor, usually punishable by more than one year in prison up to the death penalty.

Fence. A person who buys and sells stolen property with criminal intent.

Field interview. Interviewing technique used when patrol officers happen on people or circumstances that appear suspicious but when there is not sufficient cause for arrest.

Field notes. An investigator's most personal and readily available record of the crime scene search.

Field operations. The wide array of police patrol duties.

Fingerprints. The anatomical sense, is a mark made by the pattern of ridges on the pad of a human finger.

Finished sketches. A completed crime scene sketch drawn to scale.

Fire triangle. What a fire needs to burn: heat, fuel, and oxygen.

First degree murder. A form of homicide that includes premeditation and preplanning

Fixated child molester. One whose primary sexual orientation is toward children and whose sociosexual maturation develops as a result of unresolved conflicts in his or her development.

Fixed surveillance. Observing from a stationary location.

Flash description. An emergency radio broadcast generally made by the first officer to reach a crime scene, to other officers in the area, in which descriptions of the suspect and his or her vehicle are communicated.

Fleeing-felon rule. A legal doctrine, no longer in effect, allowing police officers to shoot suspected felons.

Flipping. A term used to describe an arrested person who chooses to work for the government in the capacity as an informant.

Flooding. Over saturating entire regions with drug money is one of the more sinister and surreptitious types of drug-related crime.

Flowcharting. An informational tracking system that demonstrates a chain of events or activities over a period of time.

Follow-up investigation. A continuing phase of the investigation in which information that is learned in the preliminary investigation is added to or built on.

Forcible rape. A type of *sexual assault* usually involving *sexual intercourse*, which is initiated by one or more persons against another person without that person's *consent*.

Forensic anthropology. The application of the science of *physical anthropology* and human *osteology* in a legal setting, most often in criminal cases where the victim's remains are in the advanced stages of *decomposition*.

Forensic autopsy. A postmortem examination, necropsy (particularly as to nonhuman bodies), autopsia cadaverum, or obduction—is a highly specialized surgical procedure that consists of a thorough *examination* of a *corpse* to determine the cause and manner of *death* and to evaluate any *disease* or *injury* that may be present.

Forensic chemistry. The *application* of *chemistry* to law enforcement to reveal what chemical changes occurred during an incident, and so help reconstruct the sequence of events.

Forensic dentistry. Scientific examination of dental records.

Forensic entomology. The *scientific* study of *insects*, a branch of *arthropodology*, which in turn is a branch of *biology* commonly used in criminal investigation to determine time of death.

Forensic pathology. A branch of *pathology* concerned with determining the *cause of death* by examination of a corpse.

Forensic photography. Referred to as forensic imaging or crime scene photography, is the art of producing an accurate reproduction of a *crime scene* or an *accident* scene using *photography* for the benefit of a court or to aid in an investigation.

Forgery. Fraudulent theft by using the false signature of another

Forward-looking infrared. A surveillance technology that measures radiant energy in the radiant heat portion and displays readings as thermographs.

Fraud. Theft by deceit

Fruit of the poisonous tree. A legal metaphor in the United States used to describe evidence that is obtained illegally.

Frye test. A legal standard used to determine the admissibility of scientific evidence.

Fugitive Felon Act. Also referred to as the Fugitive Felon Act (18 U.S.C. § 1073). Unlawful Flight to Avoid Prosecution is a *U.S. federal law*. Though drawn as a penal statute, and therefore permitting prosecution by the federal government for its violation, the primary purpose of the Fugitive Felon Act is to permit the federal government to assist in the location and apprehension of fugitives from state justice.

Fungible goods. Items such as tools, liquor, and clothing that are indistinguishable from others like them.

G

Gambling. The wagering of money or other valuables on the outcome of a game or event.

Gang. a group of people who, through the organization, formation, and establishment of an assemblage, share a common identity.

Gang rape. When a group of people participate in the rape of a single victim.

Gangster. A slang term for a gang member

Geographic profiling. A criminal investigative methodology that analyzes the locations of a connected series of crimes to determine the most probable area of offender residence.

Global Navigation Satellite System (GNSS). A system of satellites that provides autonomous geo-spatial positioning with global coverage. It allows small *electronic* receivers to determine their location (*longitude*, *latitude*, and *altitude*) to within a few metres using *time signals* transmitted along a *line-of-sight* by radio from *satellites*.

Good faith exception. A *legal doctrine* providing an exemption to the *exclusionary rule*.

GPS. Global Positioning Satellite.

Gunshot residue (GSR). Burnt and unburnt particles from the *explosive primer*, the *propellant*, as well as components from the *bullet*, the *cartridge* case, and the *firearm* used.

H

Hacker. A computer programmer who explores, tests, and pushes the computer to its limits, regardless of the consequences.

Hardware. The physical computer and any peripherals associated with it, such as printers, telephone modems, and external disk drives.

Hawala. An *informal value transfer system* based on the performance and honor of a huge network of money brokers, which are primarily located in the *Middle East*, *North Africa*, the *Horn of Africa*, and *South Asia*.

Herschel, William. A pioneer in the mid-nineteenth century in the use of fingerprinting for purposes of identification.

Holdup. The *crime* of taking or attempting to take something of value by force or threat of force or by putting the victim in fear.

Home invasion. The act of illegally entering a private and occupied *dwelling* with violent intent for the purpose of committing a crime against the occupants such as robbery, assault, rape, murder, or *kidnapping*.

Homicide. The unlawful killing of one human being by another.

Homicide Investigation Tracking System (HITS) – A system developed out of a research project funded by the National Institute of Justice (NIJ) initially designed to record information on homicides in Washington State between 1981 and 1986

Hoover, J. Edgar. Director of the FBI for almost 50 years.

Hot list. A cancellation bulletin for stolen credit cards.

Hybrid gangs. Criminal gangs whose members' composition is that of more than one racial or ethnic group.

I

Identity theft. A form of stealing someone's *identity* in which someone pretends to be someone else by assuming that person's identity, typically in order to access resources or obtain credit and other benefits in that person's name.

Identi-kit. A computer-generated composite of a suspected criminal.

Incest. Sexual relations between children and their parents.

Indirect evidence. evidence that tends to incriminate a person without offering conclusive proof.

Inductive reasoning. Also known as induction, is a kind of *reasoning* that constructs or evaluates general *propositions* that are derived from specific examples.

Inevitable discovery doctrine. A legal doctrine stating that illegally seized evidence is admissible in court provided that eventually it would have been discovered anyway.

Infiltration. An attempt to penetrate a group or organization in a covert manner.

Informant. Anyone who provides information of an investigative nature to law enforcement authorities.

Inside team. A surveillance team responsible for briefing officers concerning their actions if a crime occurs.

Initial page an "at-a-glance" summary of the investigation.

Integrated Automated Fingerprint Identification System (IAFIS). A national *automated fingerprint identification* and criminal history system maintained by the *Federal Bureau of Investigation* (FBI). IAFIS provides automated *fingerprint* search capabilities, latent searching capability, electronic image storage, and electronic exchange of fingerprints and responses.

Intelligence gathering. The covert process of gathering information on criminal activity.

International Child Abduction Remedies Act. A *U.S. federal law*. H.R. 3971, April 29, 1988, was assigned Public law 100-300 in 42 U.S.C. 11601. ICARA establishes procedures to implement the *Hague Convention on the Civil Aspects of International Child Abduction* done at The Hague on October 25, 1980, and for other purposes.

International terrorism. Violent acts or acts that are a danger to human life that are a violation of the criminal law of the United States or any state or that would be a criminal violation if committed within the jurisdiction of the United States or any state.

Interrogation. The systematic questioning of a person suspected of involvement in a crime for the purpose of obtaining a confession.

Interview. A relatively formal conversation conducted for the purpose of obtaining information.

Intimate or former intimate stalking. When a stalker and victim were married or divorced, current or former lovers, serious or casual sexual partners, or former sexual partners.

Investigative psychology. A new field that attempts to describe the actions of offenders and to develop an understanding of crime.

Involuntary manslaughter. The unlawful killing of a human being without *malice aforethought*, either express or implied.

Islamism. A set of ideologies holding that Islam is not only a religion but also a political system and that modern Muslims must return to their roots of their religion and unite politically.

J

Jacob Wetterling Crimes Against Children and Sexually Violent Offender Registration Act. A *U.S. law* that requires states to implement a *sex offender* and crimes against children *registry*. It was enacted as part of the *Federal Violent Crime Control and Law Enforcement Act of 1994*.

Jailhouse snitch. A criminal informant who is incarcerated and willing to provide information to police in exchange for favors.

Joyriding. When a juvenile auto thief steals a car for enjoyment for short periods of time.

L

Labeling. Classifying a missing child case.

Larceny-theft. The unlawful taking, carrying, leading, or riding away of property from the possession of another.

Latent evidence. Evidence that is not readily visible to the naked eye.

Latent fingerprints. Fingerprints that are nonvisible unless developed through a fingerprint-lifting process.

Latent prints impressions produced by the ridged skin on human fingers, palms, and soles of the feet.

Lay witness. Witnesses who are not expert witnesses

Lineup. The police practice of allowing witnesses or victims to view several suspects for identification purposes.

Link analysis. A charting technique designed to show relationships between individuals and organizations using a graphic visual design.

Lividity. A bloodstain on the body of a deceased person.

Loansharking. Usurious loans made to people for exorbitant interest rates, whose payment is enforced by the use of violence.

Locard exchange principle. Holds that the perpetrator of a crime will bring something into the crime scene and leave with something from it, and that both can be used as *forensic evidence*.

Logic bomb. a set of instructions inserted in a computer program that looks for specific errors in a computer's normal functioning.

London Metropolitan Police England's first paid, full-time police force, consisting of about 1,000 uniformed officers

Lying. Not telling the truth

M

Major case squads. Multi-jurisdictional or metro crime investigative teams, drawing from the most talented investigative personnel from all jurisdictions.

Manslaughter. The deliberate killing of another person, characterized by either voluntary or involuntary classifications.

Markers. Items placed in crime scene photos that call attention to specific objects or enable the viewer of the photo to get a sense of the size of the object or the distance between objects.

Masquerading. The process of one person assuming the identity of an authorized computer user by acquiring the victim's items, knowledge, or characteristics.

Mara Salvatrucha. A relatively new violent Salvadoran gang that continues to spread despite law enforcement efforts; also known as MS-13.

Mass murder. The commission of four or more murders in a single incident within a short span of time.

Maximization. The exaggeration of evidence available, telling the person that the interrogator knows he or she is guilty or stressing the consequences of the crime.

Megan's Law. An informal name for laws in the *United States* requiring *law enforcement* authorities to make information available to the public regarding registered *sex offenders*, which was created in response to the *murder of Megan Kanka*.

Medical examiner. Public official who makes official determinations of the cause and time of death in wrongful death cases.

Merchandise robbery – a robbery that involves the forcible taking of goods from a store.

Method of operation (MO). The behavior of the criminal during the commission of the crime.

Microtremors. Tiny frequency modulations in the human voice

Minimization. A term used when law enforcement is required to limit their monitoring of criminal suspects.

***Miranda* warning.** The legal guidelines to protect the rights of the accused were defined further by the Supreme Court in such cases as *Miranda*.

Misdemeanor. A less serious crime than a felony, usually punishable by less than one year in the county jail, a fine, or both. (MCAA).

Missing Children Act of 1982. Legislation that allowed the entry of missing children into the National Crime Information Center (NCIC) even though the noncustodial parent would not be charged with a crime

Missing Children's Assistance Act (MCAA). Legislation that created a national clearinghouse for missing children and authorizing research to determine the extent of the problem within this country.

MO. The method of operation used by a criminal to commit a crime.

Mobile surveillance. Observing a criminal suspect from a moving vehicle.

Money laundering. A process whereby illegally earned cash is made to appear legitimate or the sources of the cash are disguised.

Motion. A written request (also called a petition) or an oral request made to the court anytime before, during, or after court proceedings.

Motivation. Reasons why someone does something.

Mugging. A strong arm robbery.

Multilateration. A *navigation* technique based on the measurement of the difference in distance to two or more stations at known locations that broadcast signals at known times.

Munchausen syndrome by proxy. A clinical term referring to when a parent or caretaker attempts to bring medical attention to him- or herself by inducing illness in his or her children.

Murder. The purposeful, premeditated, and unlawful taking of human life by another person.

Mutual assault. When both people involved in an altercation committed assault

N

NATB. National Auto Theft Crime Bureau.

National Insurance Crime Bureau (NICB). a not-for-profit insurance organization committed to combating vehicle theft and insurance fraud.

Natural death. A death that is primarily attributed to natural agents: usually an illness or an internal malfunction of the body.

NCAVC. National Center for the Analysis of Violent Crime.

NCIC. National Crime Information Center.

NCMEC. National Center for Missing and Exploited Children.

Neglect. A passive form of *abuse* in which a perpetrator is responsible to provide care for a victim who is unable to care for himself or herself, but fails to provide adequate care.

Neighborhood canvass. A door-to-door search of the area of a crime to identify witnesses.

Neighborhood gang. A criminal gang that claims a particular geographical area or neighborhood

Neighborhood Watch. A program whereby merchants and residents are encouraged to take a more proactive role in detecting and reporting activity that might be criminal in nature.

NISMART. National Incidence Studies for Missing, Abducted, Runaway and Thrownaway Children.

Nonaccusatory An interview in which the subject being interviewed is not addressed as the accuser

Noncustodial parent. A parent who does not have legal custody of his or her child.

Nonfamily abduction. When a child is removed from his or her family through force or trickery.

O

Objection. A protest to the judge regarding the "form" of the question being asked of the witness.

Olfactory Senses. Pertaining to smell. A distinguishable odor may indicate a specific type of crime.

One Percenter OMG. A term that refers to outlaw motorcycle gangs whose members consider membership a lifestyle that is supported by criminal activity.

Olfactory senses. The ability to smell distinguishable odors emitted from certain types of fires that might indicate a specific fire starter, such as kerosene, gasoline, and alcohol

Open-field search. A term that refers to the open fields doctrine was first articulated by the *U.S. Supreme Court* in *Hester v. United States* which stated that "the special protection accorded by the Fourth Amendment to the people in their 'persons, houses, papers, and effects,' is not extended to the open fields."

Open files. Criminal information developed for the purpose of eventually making an arrest and gaining a conviction in a court of law.

Opportunistic robber. A robber who steals to obtain small amounts of money when he or she identifies what seems to be a vulnerable target

Outlaw motorcycle gangs (OMG). Criminal gangs commonly affiliated with motorcycles

Outside team. The arrest team in a surveillance.

Overt information collection. A method of collecting information involving personal interaction with individuals, many of whom are witnesses to crimes, victims of crimes, or the suspects themselves.

P

Paper trail. Evidence in an arson case that shows motive. This includes financial records, inflated insurance coverage, little or no inventory, and excessive debts.

Parental Kidnapping Prevention Act. A law that establishes national standards for the assertion of *child custody jurisdiction*.

Pat-down search. A search of a person's outer clothing wherein a person runs his or her hands along the outer garments to detect any concealed *weapons* or *contraband*.

Patent fingerprint. A latent fingerprint

Pedophilia. The basis of sexual misconduct with children.

Peel, Sir Robert. The founder of the London Metropolitan Police Department during the early nineteenth century.

Personality profile. A means of identifying the type of person responsible for a particular crime. This is accomplished by identifying the psychological and social characteristics surrounding the crime as well as the manner in which it was committed.

Photo lineup. The use of photographs that are shown to a victim or witness in the identification process.

Physical abuse. A term referring to the physical assault or other harmful physical contact between a subject and a underaged child

Physical evidence. Any type of evidence having shape, size, or dimension.

Physical surveillance. The act of law enforcement officers visually observing a suspect or location.

Prison gang. criminal organizations that originated within the penal system and operate within correctional facilities throughout the United States

Professional robber. A robber who has a long-term commitment to crime as a source of livelihood, planning and organizing crimes before committing them, and pursuing money to support a particular lifestyle

Psychological profiling. A behavioral and investigative tool that is intended to help *investigators* to accurately predict and profile the characteristics of unknown criminal subjects or offenders.

Pigeon drop. A commonly used confidence game.

Pilferage. The stealing of merchandise.

Pinkerton, Allan. The founder of the Pinkerton National Detective Agency in 1850.

Pinkerton National Detective Agency. Founded by Allan Pinkerton in 1850, this was one of the first criminal investigation bodies to exist in the United States.

Plain-view doctrine. A legal doctrine whereby police officers have the opportunity to confiscate evidence, without a warrant, based on what they find in plain view and open to public inspection.

Plants. Preparations used to set an arson fire.

Plastic fingerprint. A fingerprint impression left when a person presses against a plastic material such as putty, wax, or tar.

Plastic workers. White-collar criminals who have experience in dealing with stolen credit cards.

Point of origin. The location on an arson scene where the fire originated.

Polygraph. A mechanical device designed to aid investigators in obtaining information.

Polymerase chain reaction (PCR). A process in which DNA strips can be rapidly reproduced for scientific analysis.

Postmortem lividity. A purplish coloration of the skin of a deceased person.

Power-assertive rapist. A rapist who attempts to demonstrate his manhood to the victim through sexual assault.

Power-reassurance rapist. A rapist who has the primary motivation of power over his victim

Preferential molester. A child molester who has sexual desires focusing on children and typically has a more identifiable psychological disorder.

Preliminary investigation. A term referring to the early stages of crime scene processing, usually conducted by the first officer on the crime scene.

Premeditation. Planning beforehand that shows intent to commit a criminal act.

Pretrial conference. A meeting between the prosecutor and the investigator at which the prosecution strategy to a criminal case is discussed.

Preventive response. Prevention through deterrence that sometimes achieved by arresting the criminal and by aggressive prosecution.

Prima facie evidence. Evidence established by law that proves a fact in dispute.

Primary physical aggressor. If the police have sufficient reason to believe that a person, within the preceding four hours, committed an active domestic violence or spousal battery, the officer is required to arrest a person. This person is known as the primary physical aggressor.

Private eye. A private investigator.

Proactive patrol. An effective police patrol tool to prevent burglary as well as many other crimes.

Proactive response. An investigative approach to crime solving in which criminal activity is investigated before it occurs.

Probable cause. The minimum amount of information necessary to cause a reasonable person to believe that a crime has been or is being committed by a particular person.

Profile. A method used to identify an offender's motivations.

Prohibition. Lasting from 1920 to 1933, the period in which the manufacture, sale, and consumption of alcoholic beverages was outlawed in the United States.

Proof. The end or net result of the evidence collection process.

Property crime. A type of crime whereby the criminal is more concerned with financial gain and less prepared for a violent altercation with the victim.

Protection orders. A legal document that orders one person to stay away from another.

Psychological dependence. Feeling that a drug is necessary to one's well-being.

Public safety exception. A Supreme Court ruling that found that police officers who are reasonably concerned for public safety may question persons who are in custody and who have not been read the Miranda warning

Pyramid scheme. A commonly used confidence game.

Pyromaniac. A person with a psychological disorder in which sexual gratification is obtained through the setting of fires.

Q

Questioned documents. Documents that are suspected of being associate with criminal activity.

R

Rape. Unlawful sexual intercourse, achieved through force and without consent.

Rape kit. A set of items used by medical personnel for gathering and preserving physical evidence following an allegation of *sexual assault*, which can be used in *rape investigation*.

Reactive response. An approach to crime solving that addresses crimes that have already occurred, such as murder, robbery, and burglary.

Reasonable grounds. Grounds for an arrest that usually depend on the facts and circumstances surrounding the specific case.

Reasonable deadly force. The use of deadly force by a law enforcement officer that is consistent with the constitutional standard of "objectively reasonable" as identified under *Graham v. Conner* (1989).

Regressed child molester. A child molester who views the victim as a substitute for an adult partner.

Relative judgment. When eyewitnesses compare lineup photographs or members with each other rather than with their memory of the offender.

Relevancy test. Permits, in a court of law, the admission of relevant evidence that is helpful to the trier of fact.

Relevant evidence. Evidence that is considered logical or rational.

Residential burglary. The burglary of one's residence

Residential robbery. Robbery when an armed intruder breaks into a home and holds the residents at gun- or knifepoint.

Resistance. Physical or psychological unwillingness to comply.

Restraining order. A form of legal *injunction* that requires a party to do, or to refrain from doing, certain acts.

Retail burglary. Theft of a place of business generally occurring when the business is unoccupied

Reverse drug sting operation. An undercover police operation whereby the police pose as criminals, such as drug dealers or prostitutes, for the purpose of arresting persons who offer to pay for services offered by the undercover officer.

RICO Act. The 1970 Racketeering Influenced and Corrupt Organizations Act.

Rigor mortis. The process of stiffening or contraction of the muscles of a deceased person after the vital functions cease.

RISS projects. Programs of the federal Regional Information Sharing System.

Robbery. Face-to-face taking of property from the victim by the offender.

Rogues' gallery. A compilation of descriptions, methods of operation, hiding places, and the names of associates of known criminals in the 1850s.

Rough sketch. The initial crime scene sketch drawn by officers on the crime scene.

Runaway or lost child. A category of missing children that is the most commonly encountered by law enforcement.

S

Salami technique. An automated form of the Trojan horse method where small amounts of assets (i.e., money) are taken from specified accounts or sources and where the whole appears to be unaffected.

Salvage switch. When a car thief purchases a wrecked vehicle that is unrepairable, strictly for its certificate of title and for the vehicle identification number.

Scammers. Criminals who defraud; for example, attempt to obtain prescriptions for controlled drugs.

Scanning. A procedure used in computer crime whereby the criminal presents sequentially changing information to an automated system to identify those items receiving a positive response.

Scene-conscious. When the crime scene investigator becomes aware of the crime scene situation and is prepared to take certain immediate actions.

School robbery. Instances of petty extortion or "shakedowns" of students and teachers in public schools.

Scope of the search. An officer's authority to search incident to an arrest.

Scotland Yard. One of the first criminal investigative bodies originally formed in England in the mid-nineteenth century.

Search and seizure. A legal procedure used in many *civil law* and *common law* legal systems whereby *police* or other authorities and their agents, who suspect that a *crime* has been committed, do a search of a person's property and confiscate any relevant evidence to the crime.

Search warrant. A legal document enabling a police officer to search.

Search warrant return. An itemized inventory of all property and material seized by officers at the location of the search.

Second degree murder. A form of homicide there the suspect intended unsuccessfully to kill their victim

Seed money. Money required to initiate an undercover drug transaction.

Self-defense. To protect oneself from harm.

Sensational murder. A series or group of murders that arouse the interest of the general public.

Serial murder. A sequence of murders in which there is a time break between victims of two days to several months.

Serology. The scientific analysis of blood.

Sequential lineup. A police lineup method whereby people or photographs are presented to a witness one at a time.

Sexual assault. An *assault* of a sexual nature on another person, or any sexual act committed without consent.

Sexual battery. A criminal *offense* involving unlawful physical contact, distinct from *assault* which is the apprehension, not fear, of such contact.

Shaken baby syndrome. A medical term for murder of infants who are violently shaken.

Shoplifting. A common form of theft involving the taking of goods from retail stores.

Show-up. A type of lineup where only one suspect is shown to the victim or witness.

Simple arson. The burning of property that does not result in such a risk to human life.

Simple assault. Threats by one person to cause bodily harm or death to another or purposely inflicting bodily harm on another.

Simultaneous lineup. A lineup procedure whereby the eyewitness views all the people or photos at the same time.

Situational molester. Child molester who commits such crimes because of one of several external factors. These include intoxication, drug abuse, mood or mental conditions, or other social conditions.

Smash-and-grab robbery. A type of robbery whereby the robbers approach a car, break the window, and hold up the driver at gunpoint.

Smurfing. When money launderers go to different banks and purchase cashier's checks in denominations of less than $10,000 for the purpose of bypassing the reporting requirement.

Snitches. Amateur pilferers who are usually respectable persons who do not perceive of themselves as thieves yet are systematic shoplifters who steal merchandise for their own use rather than for resale.

Software. The medium on which information is stored, such as computer tapes and floppy disks.

Solvability factors. Those factors or evidence known to the criminal investigator that provide guidance to the investigation regarding what occurred or who was responsible.

Span of the fire. Physical characteristics of an arson fire such as smoke, direction, flames, and distance of travel.

Spree. Numerous acts occurring in a short span of time.

Stakeout. Another term for stationary or fixed surveillance.

Stalking. A term commonly used to refer to unwanted or obsessive *attention* by an individual or group toward another person.

Stationary surveillance. Another term for fixed surveillance or stakeout.

Statutory rape. A term that refers to *sexual activities* in which one person is below the age required to legally consent to the behavior.

Stickup. An alternate term for robbery

Stranger stalking. When the stalker and victim do not know each other.

Strategic intelligence. Information that provides the investigator with information as to the capabilities and intentions of target subjects.

Street gang. Criminal organizations formed on the street operating throughout the United States.

Street robbery. Robbery committed on public streets and alleyways.

Stripping operation. A criminal endeavor in which stolen vehicles are disposed of.

Stop and frisk. When an officer stops and searches a person for weapons.

Strong-arm robbery. A face-to-face robbery of a victim whereby no weapon is used.

Sudden infant death syndrome (SIDS). A diagnosis made when there is no other medical explanation for the abrupt death of an apparently healthy infant.

Suicide. The deliberate taking of one's own life.

Superzapping. A macro or utility program used in most IBM mainframe computer centers as a systems tool that enables thieves to tinker with the program so that checks can be issued to their private accounts.

Support officer. A surveillance officer, sometimes called an intelligence, cover, or tactical officer, who works in plainclothes and who works with the undercover unit but not in an undercover capacity.

Surveillance. Surreptitious observation.

T

Tactical intelligence. Information that furnishes the police agency with specifics about individuals, organizations, and different types of criminal activity.

Tagging. A process of altering title documents for stolen automobiles.

Tattooing. A term referring to the deposit of gunpowder on the skin of a shooting victim who was shot at close range.

Terrorism. Actions or policy intended to intimidate or cause terror

Terry stop. A brief detention of a person by police.

Testimonial evidence. Evidence based on statements provided by suspects, witnesses, or victims of a crime.

Testimony. A statement made in response to a question or a series of questions.

Texas Rangers. One of the earliest law enforcement and criminal investigative units; formed in Texas before Texas became a state.

Thermal imaging. Technology that is used to identify heat sources that might reveal criminal activity.

Thief catchers. People recruited from the riffraff of the streets to aid law enforcement officials in locating criminals during the European Industrial Revolution.

Think-aloud interviewing. An interview technique used to describe a specific type of activity in which subjects are explicitly instructed to "think aloud" as they answer the survey questions.

Tin truck. A truck used to transport parts of a stolen vehicle.

Tolerance. A physical condition that develops when a person needs increasing doses of a drug to experience its initial effects.

Totality of the circumstances. A term of art that refers to an officer's understanding of all available facts and information relating to a particular incident or crime.

Toxicology. A branch of *biology*, *chemistry*, and *medicine* concerned with the study of the adverse effects of *chemicals* on living organisms.

Trace evidence. A minute or even microscopic fragment of matter such as hair or fiber that is not immediately detectable by the naked eye.

Trailers. Materials used in spreading an arson fire.

Transfer of evidence theory. The theory that whenever two objects meet, some evidence, however microscopic, may remain to demonstrate that the encounter did occur.

Trap doors. A technique in which programmers insert debugging aids that break security codes in the computer and then insert an additional code of their own.

Triangulation the process of finding one's position on a given plane when two visual landmarks are known.

Triangulation method. A bird's-eye view of the crime scene using fixed objects from which to measure.

Triggering condition. An anticipated future event giving rise to a probable cause to search.

Trojan horse. A criminal computer program that automatically transfers money to an illegal account whenever a legal transaction is made.

U

Undercover. A form of criminal investigation utilizing operatives who do not appear to be law enforcement

Undercover officer. When a police officer poses as a criminal to gain evidence for criminal prosecution.

Undercover operations. *Disguising* one's own identity or using an assumed identity for the purposes of gaining the trust of an individual or organization to learn secret information or to gain the trust of targeted individuals in order to gain information or evidence.

Uniform Child Custody Jurisdiction Act (UCCJA). Legislation which made the practice of moving to another state for the purpose of changing custody illegal.

V

Vehicle identification number (VIN). A 17-digit number assigned to each vehicle by the manufacturer at the time of production designed to distinguish each vehicle from all others.

Vehicle robbery. A robbery of persons driving vehicles that include delivery vehicles, taxicabs, and buses, while the people involved make easy targets for the robber because they frequently work alone and in sparsely populated areas of town

VI-CAP. Violent Criminal Apprehension Program; operated by the FBI.

Vice. Generally associated with organized crime, vice crimes supply illegal goods and services.

Victimless crime. Most typically, a vice crime in which all parties of the criminal act are willing participants.

Visible fingerprints. A type of fingerprint left at a crime scene that results from being adulterated with some foreign matter, such as blood, flour, or oil.

Voice stress analyzer (VSA). Technology that records *psychophysiological* stress responses that are present in human voice, when a person suffers *psychological stress* in response to a stimulus (question) and where the consequences may be dire for the subject being "tested."

Voluntary manslaughter. The killing of a human being in which the offender had no prior intent to kill and acted during "the heat of passion," under circumstances that would cause a reasonable person to become emotionally or mentally disturbed.

W

White-collar crime. A nonviolent crime committed for financial gain and accomplished by means of deception.

WITSEC Program. The federal witness security program operated by the U.S. Marshals Service.

Z

Zone search method. A searching technique; also known as the quadrant method.

Index